T0137181

Lecture Notes in Computer Science 12171

More information about this series at http://www.springer.com/series/7410

Daniele Micciancio · Thomas Ristenpart (Eds.)

Advances in Cryptology – CRYPTO 2020

40th Annual International Cryptology Conference, CRYPTO 2020
Santa Barbara, CA, USA, August 17–21, 2020
Proceedings, Part II

 Springer

Editors
Daniele Micciancio (iD)
UC San Diego
La Jolla, CA, USA

Thomas Ristenpart (iD)
Cornell Tech
New York, NY, USA

ISSN 0302-9743   ISSN 1611-3349   (electronic)
Lecture Notes in Computer Science
ISBN 978-3-030-56879-5   ISBN 978-3-030-56880-1   (eBook)
https://doi.org/10.1007/978-3-030-56880-1

LNCS Sublibrary: SL4 – Security and Cryptology

This Springer imprint is published by the registered company Springer Nature Switzerland AG
The registered company address is: Gewerbestrasse 11, 6330 Cham, Switzerland

Preface

The 40th International Cryptology Conference (Crypto 2020), sponsored by the International Association of Cryptologic Research (IACR), was exceptional in many ways. The COVID-19 pandemic meant that for the first time in the conference's 40-year history, Crypto was not held at the University of California, Santa Barbara. Safety mandated that we shift to an online-only virtual conference.

Crypto 2020 received 371 submissions. Review occurred during what, for many countries, was the height thus far of pandemic spread and lockdowns. We thank the 54 person Program Committee (PC) and the 286 external reviewers for their efforts to ensure that, in the face of challenging work environments, illness, and death, we nevertheless were able to perform a standard double-blind review process in which papers received multiple independent reviews, authors were allowed a rebuttal, and papers were subsequently further reviewed and discussed. The two program chairs were not allowed to submit a paper, and PC members were limited to two submissions each. The PC ultimately selected 85 papers for acceptance, a record number for Crypto.

The PC selected four papers to receive recognition via awards, via a voting-based process that took into account conflicts of interest (including for the program chairs). Three papers were selected to receive a Best Paper award and were invited to the Journal of Cryptology: "Improved Differential-Linear Attacks with Applications to ARX Ciphers" by Christof Beierle, Gregor Leander, and Yosuke Todo; "Breaking the Decisional Diffie-Hellman Problem for Class Group Actions using Genus Theory" by Wouter Castryck, Jana Sotáková, and Frederik Vercauteren; and "Chosen Ciphertext Security from Injective Trapdoor Functions" by Susan Hohenberger, Venkata Koppula, and Brent Waters. One paper was selected to receive the Best Paper by Early Career Researchers award: "Handling Adaptive Compromise for Practical Encryption Schemes" by Joseph Jaeger and Nirvan Tyagi.

In addition to the regular program, Crypto 2020 included the IACR Distinguished Lecture by Silvio Micali on "Our Models and Us" and an invited talk by Seny Kamara on "Crypto for the People". Crypto 2020 carried forward the long-standing tradition of having a rump session, this year organized in a virtual format by Antigoni Polychroniadou, Bertram Poettering, and Martijn Stam.

The chairs would also like to thank the many people whose hard work helped ensure Crypto 2020 was a success:

- Leonid Reyzin (Boston University) – Crypto 2020 general chair.
- Sophia Yakoubov for helping with general chair duties, and Muthuramakrishnan Venkitasubramaniam, Tal Rabin, and Fabrice Benhamouda for providing valuable advice to the general chair.
- Carmit Hazay (Bar Ilan University) – Crypto 2020 workshop chair.
- Antigoni Polychroniadou, Bertram Poettering, and Martijn Stam – Crypto 2020 rump session chairs.

- Chris Peikert for his role in overseeing reviews and the Best Paper by Early Career Researchers award selection for which the program chairs were conflicted.
- Kevin McCurley and Christian Cachin for their critical assistance in setting up and managing a (new for Crypto) paper submission and review system.
- Kevin McCurley, Kay McKelly, and members of the IACR's emergency pandemic team for their work in designing and running the virtual format.
- Whitney Morris and Eriko Macdonald from UCSB event services for their help navigating the COVID-19 shutdown logistics.
- Anna Kramer and her colleagues at Springer.

July 2020

Daniele Micciancio
Thomas Ristenpart

Organization

General Chair

Leonid Reyzin   Boston University, USA

Program Committee Chairs

Daniele Micciancio   UC San Diego, USA
Thomas Ristenpart   Cornell Tech, USA

Program Committee

Adi Akavia   University of Haifa, Israel
Martin Albrecht   Royal Holloway, University of London, UK
Roberto Avanzi   ARM, Germany
Lejla Batina   Radboud University, The Netherlands
Jeremiah Blocki   Purdue University, USA
David Cash   University of Chicago, USA
Melissa Chase   Microsoft Research, USA
Hao Chen   Microsoft Research, USA
Ilaria Chillotti   KU Leuven, Zama, Belgium
Henry Corrigan-Gibbs   EPFL, Switzerland, and MIT CSAIL, USA
Craig Costello   Microsoft Research, USA
Joan Daemen   Radboud University, The Netherlands
Thomas Eisenbarth   University of Lübeck, Germany
Pooya Farshim   University of York, UK
Sanjam Garg   UC Berkeley, USA
Daniel Genkin   University of Michigan, USA
Steven Goldfeder   Cornell Tech, USA
Shay Gueron   University of Haifa, Israel, and AWS, USA
Felix Günther   ETH Zurich, Switzerland
Tetsu Iwata   Nagoya University, Japan
Tibor Jager   Bergische Universitaet, Germany
Antoine Joux   CISPA – Helmholtz Center for Information Security,
                                  Germany
Jonathan Katz   George Mason Univeristy, USA
Eike Kiltz   Ruhr University Bochum, Germany
Elena Kirshanova   I.Kant Baltic Federal University, Russia
Venkata Koppula   Weizmann Institute of Science, Isarel
Anna Lysyanskaya   Brown University, USA
Vadim Lyubashevsky   IBM Research Zurich, Switzerland
Mohammad Mahmoody   University of Virginia, USA

Giulio Malavolta	Carnegie Mellon University and UC Berkeley, USA
Florian Mendel	Infineon Technologies, Germany
María Naya-Plasencia	Inria, France
Adam O'Neill	University of Massachusetts, USA
Olya Ohrimenko	The University of Melbourne, Australia
Claudio Orlandi	Aarhus University, Denmark
Elisabeth Oswald	University of Klagenfurt, Austria
Chris Peikert	University of Michigan, USA
Bertram Poettering	IBM Research Zurich, Switzerland
Antigoni Polychroniadou	JP Morgan AI Research, USA
Ananth Raghunathan	Google, USA
Mariana Raykova	Google, USA
Christian Rechberger	TU Graz, Austria
Alon Rosen	IDC, Israel
Mike Rosulek	Oregon State University, USA
Alessandra Scafuro	NC State University, USA
Dominique Schroeder	Florida Atlantic University, USA
Thomas Shrimpton	University of Florida, USA
Fang Song	Texas A&M University, USA
Marc Stevens	CWI Amsterdam, The Netherlands
Dominique Unruh	University of Tartu, Estonia
Michael Walter	IST, Austria
David Wu	University of Virginia, USA

Additional Reviewers

Masayuki Abe	Fabrice Benhamouda
Shweta Agrawal	Sebastian Berndt
Shashank Agrawal	Ward Beullens
Shweta Agrawal	Ritam Bhaumik
Gorjan Alagic	Nina Bindel
Navid Alamati	Alex Block
Greg Alpar	Xavier Bonnetain
Joel Alwen	Charlotte Bonte
Elena Andreeva	Carl Bootland
Gilad Asharov	Jonathan Bootle
Thomas Attema	Raphael Bost
Saikrishna Badrinarayanan	Christina Boura
Shi Bai	Elette Boyle
Foteini Baldimtsi	Zvika Brakerski
Marshall Ball	Benedikt Bünz
James Bartusek	Matteo Campanelli
Carsten Baum	Anne Canteaut
Asli Bay	André Chailloux
Mihir Bellare	Suvradip Chakraborty

Yilei Chen
Jie Chen
Nai-Hui Chia
Arka Rai Choudhuri
Kai-Min Chung
Michele Ciampi
Carlos Cid
Michael Clear
Ran Cohen
Kelong Cong
Aisling Connolly
Sandro Coretti
Daniele Cozzo
Tingting Cui
Benjamin Curtis
Jan Czajkowski
Dana Dachman-Soled
Alex Davidson
Leo De Castro
Luca De Feo
Thomas Debris
Jean Paul Degabriele
Cyprien Delpech de Saint Guilhem
Patrick Derbez
Apoorvaa Deshpande
Benjamin Diamond
Christoph Dobraunig
Nico Doettling
Benjamin Dowling
Yfke Dulek
Stefan Dziembowski
Christoph Egger
Maria Eichlseder
Daniel Escudero
Saba Eskandarian
Serge Fehr
Rex Fernando
Dario Fiore
Ben Fisch
Wieland Fischer
Nils Fleischhacker
Daniele Friolo
Georg Fuchsbauer
Tommaso Gagliardoni
Juan Garay
Romain Gay

Nicholas Genise
Rosario Gennaro
Marios Georgiou
Riddhi Ghosal
Satrajit Ghosh
Esha Ghosh
Koustabh Ghosh
Irene Giacomelli
Andras Gilyen
S. Dov Gordon
Rishab Goyal
Lorenzo Grassi
Matthew Green
Hannes Gross
Aldo Gunsing
Tim Güneysu
Mohammad Hajiabadi
Shai Halevi
Koki Hamada
Dominik Hartmann
Eduard Hauck
Carmit Hazay
Alexander Helm
Lukas Helminger
Julia Hesse
Dennis Hofheinz
Alex Hoover
Akinori Hosoyamada
Kathrin Hövelmanns
Andreas Hülsing
Ilia Iliashenko
Gorka Irazoqui
Joseph Jaeger
Eli Jaffe
Abhishek Jain
Aayush Jain
Samuel Jaques
Stanislaw Jarecki
Zhengfeng Ji
Zhengzhong Jin
Saqib Kakvi
Daniel Kales
Chethan Kamath
Akinori Kawachi
Mahimna Kelkar
Hamidreza Khoshakhlagh

Contents – Part II

Lattice-Based and Post-quantum Cryptography

Multi-party computation

Public Key Cryptanalysis

A Polynomial-Time Algorithm for Solving the Hidden Subset Sum Problem

Jean-Sébastien Coron$^{(\boxtimes)}$ and Agnese Gini$^{(\boxtimes)}$

University of Luxembourg, Esch-sur-Alzette, Luxembourg
jean-sebastien.coron@uni.lu, agnese.gini@uni.lu

Abstract. At Crypto '99, Nguyen and Stern described a lattice based algorithm for solving the hidden subset sum problem, a variant of the classical subset sum problem where the n weights are also hidden. While the Nguyen-Stern algorithm works quite well in practice for moderate values of n, we argue that its complexity is actually exponential in n; namely in the final step one must recover a very short basis of a n-dimensional lattice, which takes exponential-time in n, as one must apply BKZ reduction with increasingly large block-sizes.

In this paper, we describe a variant of the Nguyen-Stern algorithm that works in polynomial-time. The first step is the same orthogonal lattice attack with LLL as in the original algorithm. In the second step, instead of applying BKZ, we use a multivariate technique that recovers the short lattice vectors and finally the hidden secrets in polynomial time. Our algorithm works quite well in practice, as we can reach $n \simeq 250$ in a few hours on a single PC.

1 Introduction

The hidden subset-sum problem. At Crypto '99, Nguyen and Stern described a lattice based algorithm for solving the hidden subset sum problem [NS99], with an application to the cryptanalysis of a fast generator of random pairs $(x, g^x \pmod{p})$ from Boyko et al. from Eurocrypt '98 [BPV98]. The hidden subset sum problem is a variant of the classical subset sum problem where the n weights α_i are also hidden.

Definition 1 (Hidden Subset Sum Problem). *Let M be an integer, and let $\alpha_1, \ldots, \alpha_n$ be random integers in $\mathbb{Z}_M$. Let $\mathbf{x}_1, \ldots, \mathbf{x}_n \in \mathbb{Z}^m$ be random vectors with components in $\{0, 1\}$. Let $\mathbf{h} = (h_1, \ldots, h_m) \in \mathbb{Z}^m$ satisfying:*

$$\mathbf{h} = \alpha_1 \mathbf{x}_1 + \alpha_2 \mathbf{x}_2 + \cdots + \alpha_n \mathbf{x}_n \pmod{M} \tag{1}$$

Given M and $\mathbf{h}$, recover the vector $\boldsymbol{\alpha} = (\alpha_1, \ldots, \alpha_n)$ and the vectors $\mathbf{x}_i$'s, up to a permutation of the α_i's and $\mathbf{x}_i$'s.

Recall that the classical subset sum problem with known weights α_i's can be solved in polynomial time by a lattice based algorithm [LO85], when the density $d = n/\log M$ is $\mathcal{O}(1/n)$. Provided a shortest vector oracle, the classical subset

© International Association for Cryptologic Research 2020
D. Micciancio and T. Ristenpart (Eds.): CRYPTO 2020, LNCS 12171, pp. 3–31, 2020.
https://doi.org/10.1007/978-3-030-56880-1_1

sum problem can be solved when the density d is less than $\simeq 0.94$. The algorithm is based on finding a shortest vector in a lattice built from $h, \alpha_1, \ldots, \alpha_n, M$; see [CJL+92]. For the hidden subset sum problem, the attack is clearly not applicable since the weights α_i's are hidden.

The Nguyen-Stern algorithm. For solving the hidden subset-sum problem, the Nguyen-Stern algorithm relies on the technique of the orthogonal lattice. This technique was introduced by Nguyen and Stern at Crypto '97 for breaking the Qu-Vanstone cryptosystem [NS97], and it has numerous applications in cryptanalysis, for example cryptanalysis of the Ajtai-Dwork cryptosystem [NS98b], cryptanalysis of the Béguin-Quisquater server-aided RSA protocol [NS98a], fault attacks against RSA-CRT signatures [CNT10, BNNT11], attacks against discrete-log based signature schemes [NSS04], and cryptanalysis of various homomorphic encryption schemes [vDGHV10, LT15, FLLT15] and multilinear maps [CLT13, CP19, CN19].

The orthogonal lattice attack against the hidden subset sum problem is based on the following technique [NS99]. If a vector $\mathbf{u}$ is orthogonal modulo M to the public vector of samples $\mathbf{h}$, then from (1) we must have:

$$\langle \mathbf{u}, \mathbf{h} \rangle \equiv \alpha_1 \langle \mathbf{u}, \mathbf{x_1} \rangle + \cdots + \alpha_n \langle \mathbf{u}, \mathbf{x_n} \rangle \equiv 0 \pmod{M}$$

This implies that the vector $\mathbf{p_u} = (\langle \mathbf{u}, \mathbf{x_1} \rangle, \ldots, \langle \mathbf{u}, \mathbf{x_n} \rangle)$ is orthogonal to the hidden vector $\boldsymbol{\alpha} = (\alpha_1, \ldots, \alpha_n)$ modulo M. Now, if the vector $\mathbf{u}$ is short enough, the vector $\mathbf{p_u}$ will be short (since the vectors $\mathbf{x}_i$ have components in $\{0, 1\}$ only), and if $\mathbf{p_u}$ is shorter than the shortest vector orthogonal to $\boldsymbol{\alpha}$ modulo M, we must have $\mathbf{p_u} = 0$, and therefore the vector $\mathbf{u}$ will be orthogonal in $\mathbb{Z}$ to all vectors $\mathbf{x}_i$. The orthogonal lattice attack consists in generating with LLL many short vectors $\mathbf{u}$ orthogonal to $\mathbf{h}$; this reveals the lattice of vectors orthogonal to the $\mathbf{x}_i$'s, and eventually the lattice $\mathcal{L}_{\mathbf{x}}$ generated by the vectors $\mathbf{x}_i$'s. In a second step, by finding sufficiently short vectors in the lattice $\mathcal{L}_{\mathbf{x}}$, one can recover the original vectors $\mathbf{x}_i$'s, and eventually the hidden weight $\boldsymbol{\alpha}$ by solving a linear system.

Complexity of the Nguyen-Stern algorithm. While the Nguyen-Stern algorithm works quite well in practice for moderate values of n, we argue that its complexity is actually exponential in the number of weights n. Namely in the first step we only recover a basis of the lattice $\mathcal{L}_{\mathbf{x}}$ generated by the binary vectors $\mathbf{x}_i$, but not necessarily the original vectors $\mathbf{x}_i$'s, because the basis vectors that we recover can be much larger than the $\mathbf{x}_i$'s. In order to recover the $\mathbf{x}_i$'s, in a second step one must therefore compute a very short basis of the n-dimensional lattice $\mathcal{L}_{\mathbf{x}}$, and in principle this takes exponential-time in n, as one must apply BKZ reduction [Sch87] with increasingly large block-sizes. In their practical experiments, the authors of [NS99] were able to solve the hidden subset sum problem up to $n = 90$; for the second step, they used a BKZ implementation from the NTL library [Sho] with block-size $\beta = 20$. In our implementation of their algorithm, with more computing power and thanks to the BKZ 2.0 [CN11] implementation from [fpl16], we can reach $n = 170$ with block-size $\beta = 30$, but we face an exponential barrier beyond this value.

Our contributions. Our first contribution is to provide a more detailed analysis of both steps of the Nguyen-Stern algorithm. For the first step (orthogonal lattice attack with LLL), we first adapt the analysis of [NS99] to provide a rigorous condition under which the hidden lattice $\mathcal{L}_\mathbf{x}$ can be recovered. In particular, we derive a rigorous lower bound for the bitsize of the modulus M; we show that the knapsack density $d = n/\log M$ must be $\mathcal{O}(1/(n\log n))$, and heuristically $\mathcal{O}(1/n)$, as for the classical subset-sum problem.

We also provide a heuristic analysis of the second step of Nguyen-Stern. More precisely, we provide a simple model for the minimal BKZ block-size β that can recover the secret vectors $\mathbf{x}_i$, based on the gap between the shortest vectors and the other vectors of the lattice. While relatively simplistic, our model seems to accurately predict the minimal block-size β required for BKZ reduction in the second step. We show that under our model the BKZ block-size must grow almost linearly with the dimension n; therefore the complexity of the second step is exponential in n. We also provide a slightly simpler approach for recovering the hidden vectors $\mathbf{x}_i$ from the shortest lattice vectors. Eventually we argue that the asymptotic complexity of the full Nguyen-Stern algorithm is $2^{\Omega(n/\log n)}$.

Our main contribution is then to describe a variant of the Nguyen-Stern algorithm for solving the hidden subset sum problem that works in polynomial-time. The first step is still the same orthogonal lattice attack with LLL. In the second step, instead of applying BKZ, we use a multivariate technique that recovers the short lattice vectors and finally the hidden secrets in polynomial time, using $m \simeq n^2/2$ samples instead of $m = 2n$ as in [NS99]. Our new second step can be of independent interest, as its shows how to recover binary vectors in a lattice of high-dimensional vectors. Asymptotically the heuristic complexity of our full algorithm is $\mathcal{O}(n^9)$. We show that our algorithm performs quite well in practice, as we can reach $n \simeq 250$ in a few hours on a single PC.

Cryptographic applications. As an application, the authors of [NS99] showed how to break the fast generator of random pairs $(x, g^x \pmod p)$ from Boyko, Peinado and Venkatesan from Eurocrypt '98. Such generator can be used to speed-up the generation of discrete-log based algorithms with fixed base g, such as Schnorr identification, and Schnorr, ElGamal and DSS signatures. We show that in practice our polynomial-time algorithm enables to break the Boyko et al. generator for values of n that are beyond reach for the original Nguyen-Stern attack; however, we need more samples from the generator, namely $m \simeq n^2/2$ samples instead of $m = 2n$.

Source code. We provide in

https://pastebin.com/ZFk1qjfP

the source code of the Nguyen-Stern attack and our new attack in SageMath [Sag19], using the L^2 [NS09] implementation from [fpl16].

2   Background on Lattices

Lattices and bases. In this section we recall the main definitions and properties of lattices used throughout this paper; we refer to the full version of this paper [CG20] for more details. Let $\mathbf{b}_1, \ldots, \mathbf{b}_d \in \mathbb{Z}^m$ be linearly independent vectors. The *lattice* generated by the basis $\mathbf{b}_1, \ldots, \mathbf{b}_d$ is the set

$$\mathcal{L}(\mathbf{b}_1, \ldots, \mathbf{b}_d) = \left\{ \sum_{i=1}^d a_i \mathbf{b}_i \mid a_1, \ldots, a_d \in \mathbb{Z} \right\}.$$

We say that a matrix $\mathbf{B}$ is a *base matrix* for the lattice generated by its rows $\mathbf{b}_1, \ldots, \mathbf{b}_d$. Two basis $\mathbf{B}, \mathbf{B}'$ generate the same lattice if and only if there exists an unimodular matrix $\mathbf{U} \in \mathrm{GL}(\mathbb{Z}, d)$ such that $\mathbf{UB} = \mathbf{B}'$. Given any basis $\mathbf{B}$ we can consider its Gram-determinant $d(\mathbf{B}) = \sqrt{\det(\mathbf{BB^\mathsf{T}})}$; this number is invariant under base change. The *determinant* of a lattice $\mathcal{L}$ is the Gram-determinant of any of its basis $\mathbf{B}$, namely $\det(\mathcal{L}) = d(\mathbf{B})$.

The *dimension* $\dim(\mathcal{L})$, or *rank*, of a lattice is the dimension as vector space of $E_\mathcal{L} := \mathrm{Span}_\mathbb{R}(\mathcal{L})$, namely the cardinality of its bases. We say that a lattice is *full rank* if it has maximal dimension. We say that $\mathcal{M} \subseteq \mathcal{L}$ is a *sublattice* of a lattice $\mathcal{L}$ if it is a lattice contained in $\mathcal{L}$, further we say that $\mathcal{L}$ is a *superlattice* of $\mathcal{M}$. If $\dim(\mathcal{M}) = \dim(\mathcal{L})$, we say that $\mathcal{M}$ is a full-rank sublattice of $\mathcal{L}$, and we must have $\det(\mathcal{L}) \leq \det(\mathcal{M})$.

Orthogonal lattice. Consider the Euclidean norm $\|\cdot\|$ and the standard scalar product $\langle \cdot, \cdot \rangle$ of $\mathbb{R}^m$. The *orthogonal lattice* of a lattice $\mathcal{L} \subseteq \mathbb{Z}^m$ is

$$\mathcal{L}^\perp := \{\mathbf{v} \in \mathbb{Z}^m \mid \forall \mathbf{b} \in \mathcal{L}, \ \langle \mathbf{v}, \mathbf{b} \rangle = 0\} = E_\mathcal{L}^\perp \cap \mathbb{Z}^m$$

We define the *completion* of a lattice $\mathcal{L}$ as the lattice $\bar{\mathcal{L}} = E_\mathcal{L} \cap \mathbb{Z}^m = (\mathcal{L}^\perp)^\perp$. Clearly, $\mathcal{L}$ is a full rank sublattice of $\bar{\mathcal{L}}$. We say that a lattice is *complete* if it coincides with its completion, i.e. $\bar{\mathcal{L}} = \mathcal{L}$. One can prove that $\dim \mathcal{L} + \dim \mathcal{L}^\perp = m$ and $\det(\mathcal{L}^\perp) = \det(\bar{\mathcal{L}}) \leq \det(\mathcal{L})$; we recall the proofs in the full version of this paper [CG20]. By Hadamard's inequality, we have $\det(\mathcal{L}) \leq \prod_{i=1}^d \|\mathbf{b}_i\|$ for any basis $\mathbf{b}_1, \ldots, \mathbf{b}_d$ of a lattice $\mathcal{L}$; this implies that $\det(\mathcal{L}^\perp) \leq \prod_{i=1}^d \|\mathbf{b}_i\|$ for any basis $\mathbf{b}_1, \ldots, \mathbf{b}_d$ of $\mathcal{L}$.

Lattice minima. The *first minimum* $\lambda_1(\mathcal{L})$ of a lattice $\mathcal{L}$ is the minimum of the norm of its non-zero vectors. Lattice points whose norm is $\lambda_1(\mathcal{L})$ are called *shortest vectors*. The *Hermite constant* γ_d, in dimension d, is the supremum of

$\lambda_1(\mathcal{L})^2/\det(\mathcal{L})^{\frac{2}{d}}$ over all the lattices of rank d. Using Minkowski convex body theorem, one can prove that for each $d \in \mathbb{N}^+$, $0 \le \gamma_d \le d/4 + 1$.

More generally, for each $1 \le i \le \dim \mathcal{L}$, the i-th minimum $\lambda_i(\mathcal{L})$ of a lattice $\mathcal{L}$ is the minimum of the $\max_j \{\|\mathbf{v}_j\|\}$ among all sets $\{\mathbf{v}_j\}_{j \le i}$ of i linearly independent lattice points. Minkowski's Second Theorem states that for each $1 \le i \le d$

$$\left(\prod_{j=1}^{i} \lambda_i(\mathcal{L})\right)^{\frac{1}{i}} \le \sqrt{\gamma_d}\,\det(\mathcal{L})^{\frac{1}{d}}.$$

Lattice reduction. LLL-reduced bases have many good properties. In particular the first vector $\mathbf{b}_1$ of an LLL-reduced basis is not much longer than the shortest vector of the lattice.

Lemma 1 (LLL-reduced basis). Let $\mathbf{b}_1, \dots, \mathbf{b}_d$ an LLL-reduced basis of a lattice $\mathcal{L}$. Then $\|\mathbf{b}_1\| \le 2^{\frac{d-1}{2}} \lambda_1(\mathcal{L})$, and $\|\mathbf{b}_j\| \le 2^{\frac{d-1}{2}} \lambda_i(\mathcal{L})$ for each $1 \le j \le i \le d$.

The LLL algorithm [LLL82] outputs an LLL-reduced basis of a rank-d lattice in $\mathbb{Z}^m$ in time $\mathcal{O}(d^5 m \log^3 B)$, from a basis of vectors of norm less than B. This was further improved by Nguyen and Stehlé in [NS09] with a variant based on proven floating point arithmetic, called L^2, with complexity $\mathcal{O}(d^4 m(d + \log B) \log B)$ without fast arithmetic. In this paper, when we apply LLL, we always mean the L^2 variant. We denote by log the logarithm in base 2.

Heuristics. For a "random lattice" we expect $\lambda_1(\mathcal{L}) \approx \sqrt{d}\det(\mathcal{L})^{\frac{1}{d}}$ by the *Gaussian Heuristic* and all lattice minima to be approximately the same. Omitting the $\sqrt{d}$ factor, for a lattice $\mathcal{L}$ generated by a set of d "random" vectors in $\mathbb{Z}^m$ for $d < m$, we expect the lattice $\mathcal{L}$ to be of rank d, and the short vectors of $\mathcal{L}^\perp$ to have norm approximately $(\det \mathcal{L}^\perp)^{1/(m-d)} \simeq (\det \mathcal{L})^{1/(m-d)} \simeq (\prod_{i=1}^{d} \|\mathbf{b}_i\|)^{1/(m-d)}$.

3 The Nguyen-Stern Algorithm

In this section we recall the Nguyen-Stern algorithm for solving the hidden subset sum problem. We explain why the algorithm has complexity exponential in n and provide the result of practical experiments. Then in Sect. 4 we will describe our polynomial-time algorithm.

Recall that in the hidden subset sum problem, given a modulus M and $\mathbf{h} = (h_1, \dots, h_m) \in \mathbb{Z}^m$ satisfying

$$\mathbf{h} = \alpha_1 \mathbf{x}_1 + \alpha_2 \mathbf{x}_2 + \cdots + \alpha_n \mathbf{x}_n \pmod{M} \tag{2}$$

we must recover the vector $\boldsymbol{\alpha} = (\alpha_1, \dots, \alpha_n) \in \mathbb{Z}_M^n$ and the vectors $\mathbf{x}_i \in \{0, 1\}^m$. The Nguyen-Stern algorithm proceeds in 2 steps:

1. From the samples $\mathbf{h}$, determine the lattice $\bar{\mathcal{L}}_{\mathbf{x}}$, where $\mathcal{L}_{\mathbf{x}}$ is the lattice generated by the $\mathbf{x}_i$'s.
2. From $\bar{\mathcal{L}}_{\mathbf{x}}$, recover the hidden vectors $\mathbf{x}_i$'s. From $\mathbf{h}$, the $\mathbf{x}_i$'s and M, recover the weights α_i.

3.1 First Step: Orthogonal Lattice Attack

The orthogonal lattice attack. The goal of the orthogonal lattice attack is to recover the hidden lattice $\bar{\mathcal{L}}_{\mathbf{x}}$, where $\mathcal{L}_{\mathbf{x}} \subset \mathbb{Z}^m$ is the lattice generated by the n vectors $\mathbf{x}_i$. Let $\mathcal{L}_0$ be the lattice of vectors orthogonal to $\mathbf{h}$ modulo M:

$$\mathcal{L}_0 := \Lambda_M^{\perp}(\mathbf{h}) = \{\mathbf{u} \in \mathbb{Z}^m \mid \langle \mathbf{u}, \mathbf{h} \rangle \equiv 0 \pmod{M}\}$$

Following [NS99], the main observation is that if $\langle \mathbf{u}, \mathbf{h} \rangle \equiv 0 \pmod{M}$, then from (2) we obtain:

$$\langle \mathbf{u}, \mathbf{h} \rangle \equiv \alpha_1 \langle \mathbf{u}, \mathbf{x}_1 \rangle + \cdots + \alpha_n \langle \mathbf{u}, \mathbf{x}_n \rangle \equiv 0 \pmod{M}$$

and therefore the vector $\mathbf{p_u} = (\langle \mathbf{u}, \mathbf{x}_1 \rangle, \ldots, \langle \mathbf{u}, \mathbf{x}_n \rangle)$ is orthogonal to the vector $\boldsymbol{\alpha} = (\alpha_1, \ldots, \alpha_n)$ modulo M. Now, if the vector $\mathbf{u}$ is short enough, the vector $\mathbf{p_u}$ will be short (since the vectors $\mathbf{x}_i$ have components in $\{0, 1\}$ only), and if $\mathbf{p_u}$ is shorter than the shortest vector orthogonal to $\boldsymbol{\alpha}$ modulo M, then we must have $\mathbf{p_u} = 0$ and therefore $\mathbf{u} \in \mathcal{L}_{\mathbf{x}}^{\perp}$.

   Therefore, the orthogonal lattice attack consists in first computing an LLL-reduced basis of the lattice $\mathcal{L}_0$. The first $m - n$ short vectors $\mathbf{u}_1, \ldots, \mathbf{u}_{m-n}$ will give us a generating set of the lattice $\mathcal{L}_{\mathbf{x}}^{\perp}$. Then one can compute a basis of the lattice $\bar{\mathcal{L}}_{\mathbf{x}} = (\mathcal{L}_{\mathbf{x}}^{\perp})^{\perp}$. This gives the following algorithm, which is the first step of the Nguyen-Stern algorithm; we explain the main steps in more details below.

Algorithm 1. Orthogonal lattice attack [NS99]

Input: $\mathbf{h}, M, n, m$.
Output: A basis of $\bar{\mathcal{L}}_{\mathbf{x}}$.
 1: Compute an LLL-reduced basis $\mathbf{u}_1, \ldots, \mathbf{u}_m$ of $\mathcal{L}_0$.
 2: Extract a generating set of $\mathbf{u}_1, \ldots, \mathbf{u}_{m-n}$ of $\mathcal{L}_{\mathbf{x}}^{\perp}$.
 3: Compute a basis $(\mathbf{c}_1, \ldots, \mathbf{c}_n)$ of $\bar{\mathcal{L}}_{\mathbf{x}} = (\mathcal{L}_{\mathbf{x}}^{\perp})^{\perp}$.
 4: **return** $(\mathbf{c}_1, \ldots, \mathbf{c}_n)$

Constructing a basis of $\mathcal{L}_0$. We first explain how to construct a basis of $\mathcal{L}_0$. If the modulus M is prime we can assume $h_1 \neq 0$, up to permutation of the coordinates; indeed the case $\mathbf{h} = \mathbf{0}$ is trivial. More generally, we assume $\gcd(h_1, M) = 1$. We write $\mathbf{u} = [u_1, \mathbf{u}']$ where $\mathbf{u}' \in \mathbb{Z}^{m-1}$. Similarly we write $\mathbf{h} = [h_1, \mathbf{h}']$ where $\mathbf{h}' \in \mathbb{Z}^{m-1}$. Since h_1 is invertible modulo M, we get:

$$\mathbf{u} \in \mathcal{L}_0 \iff u_1 \cdot h_1 + \langle \mathbf{u}', \mathbf{h}' \rangle \equiv 0 \pmod{M}$$
$$\iff u_1 + \langle \mathbf{u}', \mathbf{h}' \rangle \cdot h_1^{-1} \equiv 0 \pmod{M}$$

Therefore, a basis of $\mathcal{L}_0$ is given by the $m \times m$ matrix of row vectors:

$$\mathcal{L}_0 = \begin{bmatrix} M & \\ -\mathbf{h}' \cdot h_1^{-1}[M] & \mathbf{I}_{m-1} \end{bmatrix}$$

To compute a reduced basis $\mathbf{u}_1, \ldots, \mathbf{u}_m$ of the lattice $\mathcal{L}_0$ we use the L^2 algorithm. The complexity is then $\mathcal{O}(m^5(m + \log M) \log M)$ without fast arithmetic. We show in Sect. 3.2 below that for a sufficiently large modulus M, the first $m - n$ vectors $\mathbf{u}_1, \ldots, \mathbf{u}_{m-n}$ must form a generating set of $\mathcal{L}_{\mathbf{x}}^{\perp}$.

Computing a basis of $\bar{\mathcal{L}}_{\mathbf{x}} = (\mathcal{L}_{\mathbf{x}}^{\perp})^{\perp}$. From the vectors $\mathbf{u}_1, \ldots, \mathbf{u}_{m-n}$ forming a generating set of the lattice $\mathcal{L}_{\mathbf{x}}^{\perp}$, we can compute its orthogonal $\bar{\mathcal{L}}_{\mathbf{x}} = (\mathcal{L}_{\mathbf{x}}^{\perp})^{\perp}$ using the LLL-based algorithm from [NS97]. Given a lattice $\mathcal{L}$, the algorithm from [NS97] produces an LLL-reduced basis of $\mathcal{L}^{\perp}$ in polynomial time; we refer to the full version of this paper [CG20] for a detailed description of the algorithm. Therefore we obtain an LLL-reduced basis of $\bar{\mathcal{L}}_{\mathbf{x}} = (\mathcal{L}_{\mathbf{x}}^{\perp})^{\perp}$ in polynomial-time.

3.2   Rigorous Analysis of Step 1

We now provide a rigorous analysis of the orthogonal lattice attack above. More precisely, we show that for a large enough modulus M, the orthogonal lattice attack recovers a basis of $\bar{\mathcal{L}}_{\mathbf{x}}$ in polynomial time, for a significant fraction of the weight α_i's.

Theorem 1. *Let $m > n$. Assume that the lattice $\mathcal{L}_{\mathbf{x}}$ has rank n. With probability at least $1/2$ over the choice of $\boldsymbol{\alpha}$, Algorithm 1 recovers a basis of $\bar{\mathcal{L}}_{\mathbf{x}}$ in polynomial time, assuming that M is a prime integer of bitsize at least $2mn \log m$. For $m = 2n$, the density is $d = n/\log M = \mathcal{O}(1/(n \log n))$.*

The proof is based on the following two lemmas. We denote by $\Lambda_M^{\perp}(\boldsymbol{\alpha})$ the lattice of vectors orthogonal to $\boldsymbol{\alpha} = (\alpha_1, \ldots, \alpha_n)$ modulo M.

Lemma 2. *Assume that the lattice $\mathcal{L}_{\mathbf{x}}$ has rank n. Algorithm 1 computes a basis of the lattice $\bar{\mathcal{L}}_{\mathbf{x}}$ in polynomial time under the condition $m > n$ and*

$$\sqrt{mn} \cdot 2^{\frac{m}{2}} \cdot \lambda_{m-n}\left(\mathcal{L}_{\mathbf{x}}^{\perp}\right) < \lambda_1\left(\Lambda_M^{\perp}(\boldsymbol{\alpha})\right). \tag{3}$$

Proof. As observed previously, for any $\mathbf{u} \in \mathcal{L}_0$, the vector

$$\mathbf{p_u} = (\langle \mathbf{u}, \mathbf{x}_1 \rangle, \ldots, \langle \mathbf{u}, \mathbf{x}_n \rangle)$$

is orthogonal to the vector $\boldsymbol{\alpha}$ modulo M; therefore if $\mathbf{p_u}$ is shorter than the shortest non-zero vector orthogonal to $\boldsymbol{\alpha}$ modulo M, we must have $\mathbf{p_u} = 0$, and therefore $\mathbf{u} \in \mathcal{L}_{\mathbf{x}}^{\perp}$; this happens under the condition $\|\mathbf{p_u}\| < \lambda_1\left(\Lambda_M^{\perp}(\boldsymbol{\alpha})\right)$. Since $\|\mathbf{p_u}\| \leq \sqrt{mn}\|\mathbf{u}\|$, given any $\mathbf{u} \in \mathcal{L}_0$ we must have $\mathbf{u} \in \mathcal{L}_{\mathbf{x}}^{\perp}$ under the condition:

$$\sqrt{mn}\|\mathbf{u}\| < \lambda_1\left(\Lambda_M^{\perp}(\boldsymbol{\alpha})\right). \tag{4}$$

The lattice $\mathcal{L}_0$ is full rank of dimension m since it contains $M\mathbb{Z}^m$. Now, consider $\mathbf{u}_1, \ldots, \mathbf{u}_m$ an LLL-reduced basis of $\mathcal{L}_0$. From Lemma 1, for each $j \leq m - n$ we have

$$\|\mathbf{u}_j\| \leq 2^{\frac{m}{2}} \cdot \lambda_{m-n}(\mathcal{L}_0) \leq 2^{\frac{m}{2}} \cdot \lambda_{m-n}\left(\mathcal{L}_{\mathbf{x}}^{\perp}\right) \tag{5}$$

since $\mathcal{L}_\mathbf{x}^\perp$ is a sublattice of $\mathcal{L}_0$ of dimension $m - n$. Combining with (4), this implies that when

$$\sqrt{mn} \cdot 2^{\frac{m}{2}} \cdot \lambda_{m-n}\left(\mathcal{L}_\mathbf{x}^\perp\right) < \lambda_1\left(\Lambda_M^\perp(\boldsymbol{\alpha})\right)$$

the vectors $\mathbf{u}_1, \ldots, \mathbf{u}_{m-n}$ must belong to $\mathcal{L}_\mathbf{x}^\perp$. This means that $\langle \mathbf{u}_1, \ldots, \mathbf{u}_{m-n}\rangle$ is a full rank sublattice of $\mathcal{L}_\mathbf{x}^\perp$, and therefore $\langle \mathbf{u}_1, \ldots, \mathbf{u}_{m-n}\rangle^\perp = \bar{\mathcal{L}}_\mathbf{x}$. Finally, Algorithm 1 is polynomial-time, because both the LLL reduction step of $\mathcal{L}_0$ and the LLL-based orthogonal computation of $\mathcal{L}_\mathbf{x}^\perp$ are polynomial-time. □

The following Lemma is based on a counting argument; we provide the proof in the full version of this paper [CG20].

Lemma 3. *Let M be a prime. Then with probability at least $1/2$ over the choice of $\boldsymbol{\alpha}$, we have $\lambda_1(\Lambda_M^\perp(\boldsymbol{\alpha})) \geq M^{1/n}/4$.* □

Combining the two previous lemmas, we can prove Theorem 1.

Proof (of Theorem 1). In order to apply Lemma 2, we first derive an upper-bound on $\lambda_{m-n}\left(\mathcal{L}_\mathbf{x}^\perp\right)$. The lattice $\mathcal{L}_\mathbf{x}^\perp$ has dimension $m - n$ and by Minkowski's second theorem we have

$$\lambda_{m-n}\left(\mathcal{L}_\mathbf{x}^\perp\right) \leq \sqrt{\gamma_{m-n}}^{m-n} \det\left(\mathcal{L}_\mathbf{x}^\perp\right) \leq m^{m/2} \det\left(\mathcal{L}_\mathbf{x}^\perp\right). \tag{6}$$

From $\det \mathcal{L}_\mathbf{x}^\perp = \det \bar{\mathcal{L}}_\mathbf{x} \leq \det \mathcal{L}_\mathbf{x}$ and Hadamard's inequality with $\|\mathbf{x}_i\| \leq \sqrt{m}$, we obtain:

$$\det \mathcal{L}_\mathbf{x}^\perp \leq \det \mathcal{L}_\mathbf{x} \leq \prod_{i=1}^n \|\mathbf{x}_i\| \leq m^{n/2} \tag{7}$$

which gives the following upper-bound on $\lambda_{m-n}\left(\mathcal{L}_\mathbf{x}^\perp\right)$:

$$\lambda_{m-n}\left(\mathcal{L}_\mathbf{x}^\perp\right) \leq m^{m/2} m^{n/2} \leq m^m.$$

Thus, by Lemma 2, we can recover a basis of $\bar{\mathcal{L}}_\mathbf{x}$ when

$$\sqrt{mn} \cdot 2^{\frac{m}{2}} \cdot m^m < \lambda_1\left(\Lambda_M^\perp(\boldsymbol{\alpha})\right).$$

From Lemma 3, with probability at least $1/2$ over the choice of $\boldsymbol{\alpha}$ we can therefore recover the hidden lattice $\bar{\mathcal{L}}_\mathbf{x}$ if:

$$\sqrt{mn} \cdot 2^{\frac{m}{2}} \cdot m^m < M^{1/n}/4.$$

For $m > n \geq 4$, it suffices to have $\log M \geq 2mn \log m$. □

3.3   Heuristic Analysis of Step 1

In the previous section, we have shown that the orthogonal lattice attack provably recovers the hidden lattice $\bar{\mathcal{L}}_\mathbf{x}$ in polynomial time for a large enough modulus M, namely we can take $\log M = \mathcal{O}(n^2 \log n)$ when $m = 2n$. Below we show that heuristically we can take $\log M = \mathcal{O}(n^2)$, which gives a knapsack density $d = n/\log M = \mathcal{O}(1/n)$. We also give the concrete bitsize of M used in our experiments, and provide a heuristic complexity analysis.

Heuristic size of the modulus M. In order to derive a heuristic size for the modulus M, we use an approximation of the terms in the condition (3) from Lemma 2.

We start with the term $\lambda_{m-n}\left(\mathcal{L}_{\mathbf{x}}^{\perp}\right)$. For a "random lattice" we expect the lattice minima to be balanced, and therefore $\lambda_{m-n}\left(\mathcal{L}_{\mathbf{x}}^{\perp}\right)$ to be roughly equal to $\lambda_1\left(\mathcal{L}_{\mathbf{x}}^{\perp}\right)$. This means that instead of the rigorous inequality (6) from the proof of Theorem 1, we use the heuristic approximation:

$$\lambda_{m-n}\left(\mathcal{L}_{\mathbf{x}}^{\perp}\right) \simeq \sqrt{\gamma_{m-n}} \det(\mathcal{L}_{\mathbf{x}}^{\perp})^{\frac{1}{m-n}}.$$

Using (7), this gives:

$$\lambda_{m-n}\left(\mathcal{L}_{\mathbf{x}}^{\perp}\right) \lesssim \sqrt{\gamma_{m-n}} m^{\frac{n}{2(m-n)}}. \tag{8}$$

For the term $\lambda_1\left(\Lambda_M^{\perp}(\boldsymbol{\alpha})\right)$, using the Gaussian heuristic, we expect:

$$\lambda_1\left(\Lambda_M^{\perp}(\boldsymbol{\alpha})\right) \simeq \sqrt{\gamma_n} M^{\frac{1}{n}}.$$

Finally the $2^{m/2}$ factor in (3) corresponds to the LLL Hermite factor with $\delta = 3/4$; in practice we will use $\delta = 0.99$, and we denote by $2^{\iota m}$ the corresponding LLL Hermite factor. Hence from (3) we obtain the heuristic condition:

$$\sqrt{mn} \cdot 2^{\iota \cdot m} \cdot \sqrt{\gamma_{m-n}} \cdot m^{\frac{n}{2(m-n)}} < \sqrt{\gamma_n} M^{1/n}.$$

This gives the condition:

$$2^{\iota \cdot m} \sqrt{\gamma_{m-n} \cdot n} \cdot m^{\frac{m}{2(m-n)}} < \sqrt{\gamma_n} M^{1/n}$$

which gives:

$$\log M > \iota \cdot m \cdot n + \frac{n}{2} \log(n \cdot \gamma_{m-n}/\gamma_n) + \frac{mn}{2(m-n)} \log m. \tag{9}$$

If we consider $m = n + k$ for some constant k, we can take $\log M = \mathcal{O}(n^2 \log n)$. If $m > c \cdot n$ for some constant $c > 1$, we can take $\log M = \mathcal{O}(m \cdot n)$. In particular, for $m = 2n$ we obtain the condition:

$$\log M > 2\iota \cdot n^2 + \frac{3n}{2} \log n + n \tag{10}$$

which gives $\log M = \mathcal{O}(n^2)$ and a knapsack density $d = n/\log M = \mathcal{O}(1/n)$. In practice for our experiments we use $m = 2n$ and $\log M \simeq 2\iota n^2 + n \log n$ with $\iota = 0.035$. Finally, we note that smaller values of M could be achieved by using BKZ reduction of $\mathcal{L}_0$ instead of LLL.

Heuristic complexity. Recall that for a rank-d lattice in $\mathbb{Z}^m$, the complexity of computing an LLL-reduced basis with the L^2 algorithm is $\mathcal{O}(d^4 m(d + \log B) \log B)$ without fast integer arithmetic, for vectors of Euclidean norm less than B. At Step 1 we must apply LLL-reduction twice.

The first LLL is applied to the rank-m lattice $\mathcal{L}_0 \in \mathbb{Z}^m$. Therefore the complexity of the first LLL is $\mathcal{O}(m^5(m + \log M) \log M)$. If $m = n + k$ for some constant k, the heuristic complexity is therefore $\mathcal{O}(n^9 \log^2 n)$. If $m > c \cdot n$ for some constant c, the heuristic complexity is $\mathcal{O}(m^7 \cdot n^2)$.

The second LLL is applied to compute the orthogonal of $\mathcal{L}(\mathbf{U})$ where $\mathbf{U}$ is the matrix basis of the vectors $\mathbf{u}_1, \ldots, \mathbf{u}_{m-n} \in \mathbb{Z}^m$. From (5) and (8), we can heuristically assume $\|\mathbf{U}\| \leq 2^{m/2} \cdot \sqrt{m} \cdot m^{\frac{n}{2(m-n)}}$. For $m = n+k$ for some constant k, this gives $\log \|\mathbf{U}\| = \mathcal{O}(n \log n)$, while for $m > c \cdot n$ for some constant $c > 1$, we obtain $\log \|\mathbf{U}\| = \mathcal{O}(m)$. The heuristic complexity of computing the orthogonal of $\mathbf{U}$ is $\mathcal{O}(m^5(m + (m/n) \log \|\mathbf{U}\|)^2)$ (see the full version of this paper [CG20]). For $m = n + k$, the complexity is therefore $\mathcal{O}(n^7 \log^2 n)$, while for $m > c \cdot n$, the complexity is $\mathcal{O}(m^9/n^2)$.

We summarize the complexities of the two LLL operations in Table 1; we see that the complexities are optimal for $m = c \cdot n$ for some constant $c > 1$, so for simplicity we take $m = 2n$. In that case the heuristic complexity of the first step is $\mathcal{O}(n^9)$, and the density is $d = n/\log M = \mathcal{O}(1/n)$, as in the classical subset-sum problem.

Table 1. Modulus size and time complexity of Algorithm 1 as a function of the parameter m.

m	$\log M$	LLL $\mathcal{L}_0$	LLL $(\mathcal{L}_{\mathbf{x}}^{\perp})^{\perp}$
$\gg n$	$\mathcal{O}(n \cdot m)$	$\mathcal{O}(m^7 \cdot n^2)$	$\mathcal{O}(m^9/n^2)$
n^2	$\mathcal{O}(n^3)$	$\mathcal{O}(n^{16})$	$\mathcal{O}(n^{16})$
$2n$	$\mathcal{O}(n^2)$	$\mathcal{O}(n^9)$	$\mathcal{O}(n^7)$
$n + 1$	$\mathcal{O}(n^2 \log n)$	$\mathcal{O}(n^9 \log^2 n)$	$\mathcal{O}(n^7 \log^2 n)$

3.4   Second Step of the Nguyen-Stern Attack

From the first step we have obtained an LLL-reduced basis $(\mathbf{c}_1, \ldots, \mathbf{c}_n)$ of the completed lattice $\bar{\mathcal{L}}_{\mathbf{x}} \subset \mathbb{Z}^m$. However this does not necessarily reveal the vectors $\mathbf{x}_i$. Namely, because of the LLL approximation factor, the recovered basis vectors $(\mathbf{c}_1, \ldots, \mathbf{c}_n)$ can be much larger than the original vectors $\mathbf{x}_i$, which are among the shortest vectors in $\mathcal{L}_{\mathbf{x}}$. Therefore, to recover the original vectors $\mathbf{x}_i$, one must apply BKZ instead of LLL, in order to obtain a better approximation factor; eventually from $\mathbf{h}$, the $\mathbf{x}_i$'s and M, one can recover the weights α_i by solving a linear system; this is the second step of the Nguyen-Stern algorithm.

The authors of [NS99] did not provide a time complexity analysis of their algorithm. In the following, we provide a heuristic analysis of the second step of the Nguyen-Stern algorithm, based on a model of the gap between the shortest vectors of $\mathcal{L}_{\mathbf{x}}$ (the vectors $\mathbf{x}_i$), and the "generic" short vectors of $\mathcal{L}_{\mathbf{x}}$. While relatively simplistic, our model seems to accurately predict the minimal blocksize β required for BKZ reduction; we provide the result of practical experiments in the next section. Under this model the BKZ block-size β must increase almost linearly with n; the complexity of the attack is therefore exponential in n. In our analysis below, for simplicity we heuristically assume that the lattice $\mathcal{L}_{\mathbf{x}}$ is complete, i.e. $\bar{\mathcal{L}}_{\mathbf{x}} = \mathcal{L}_{\mathbf{x}}$.

Short vectors in $\mathcal{L}_{\mathbf{x}}$. The average norm of the original binary vectors $\mathbf{x}_i \in \mathbb{Z}^m$ is roughly $\sqrt{m/2}$. If we take the difference between some $\mathbf{x}_i$ and $\mathbf{x}_j$, the components remain in $\{-1, 0, 1\}$, and the average norm is also roughly $\sqrt{m/2}$. Therefore, we can assume that the vectors $\mathbf{x}_i$ and $\mathbf{x}_i - \mathbf{x}_j$ for $i \neq j$ are the shortest vectors of the lattice $\mathcal{L}_{\mathbf{x}}$.

We can construct "generic" short vectors in $\mathcal{L}_{\mathbf{x}}$ by taking a linear combination with $\{0, 1\}$ coefficients of vectors of the form $\mathbf{x}_i - \mathbf{x}_j$. For $\mathbf{x}_i - \mathbf{x}_j$, the variance of each component is $1/2$. If we take a linear combination of $n/4$ such differences (so that roughly half of the coefficients with respect to the vectors $\mathbf{x}_i$ are 0), the variance for each component will be $n/4 \cdot 1/2 = n/8$, and for m components the norm of the resulting vector will be about $\sqrt{nm/8}$. Therefore heuristically the gap between these generic vectors and the shortest vectors is:

$$\frac{\sqrt{nm/8}}{\sqrt{m/2}} = \frac{\sqrt{n}}{2}.$$

Running time with BKZ. To recover the shortest vectors, the BKZ approximation factor $2^{\iota \cdot n}$ should be less than the above gap, which gives the condition:

$$2^{\iota \cdot n} \leq \frac{\sqrt{n}}{2} \tag{11}$$

which gives $\iota \leq (\log(n/4))/(2n)$. Achieving an Hermite factor of $2^{\iota n}$ heuristically requires at least $2^{\Omega(1/\iota)}$ time, by using BKZ reduction with block-size $\beta = \omega(1/\iota)$ [HPS11]. Therefore the running time of the Nguyen-Stern algorithm is $2^{\Omega(n/\log n)}$, with BKZ block-size $\beta = \omega(n/\log n)$ in the second step.

Recovering the vectors $\mathbf{x}_i$. It remains to show how to recover the vectors $\mathbf{x}_i$. Namely as explained above the binary vectors $\mathbf{x}_i$ are not the only short vectors in $\mathcal{L}_{\mathbf{x}}$; the vectors $\mathbf{x}_i - \mathbf{x}_j$ are roughly equally short. The approach from [NS99] is as follows. Since the short vectors in $\mathcal{L}_{\mathbf{x}}$ probably have components in $\{-1, 0, 1\}$, the authors suggest to transform the lattice $\mathcal{L}_{\mathbf{x}}$ into a new one $\mathcal{L}'_{\mathbf{x}} = 2\mathcal{L}_{\mathbf{x}} + \mathbf{e}\mathbb{Z}$, where $\mathbf{e} = (1, \dots, 1)$. Namely in that case a vector $\mathbf{v} \in \mathcal{L}_{\mathbf{x}}$ with components in $\{-1, 0, 1\}$ will give a vector $2\mathbf{v} \in \mathcal{L}'_{\mathbf{x}}$ with components in $\{-2, 0, 2\}$, whereas a vector $\mathbf{x} \in \mathcal{L}_{\mathbf{x}}$ with components in $\{0, 1\}$ will give a vector $2\mathbf{x} - \mathbf{e} \in \mathcal{L}'_{\mathbf{x}}$ with components in $\{-1, 1\}$, hence shorter. This should enable to recover the secret vectors $\mathbf{x}_i$ as the shortest vectors in $\mathcal{L}'_{\mathbf{x}}$.

Below we describe a slightly simpler approach in which we stay in the lattice $\mathcal{L}_{\mathbf{x}}$. First, we explain why for large enough values of m, we are unlikely to obtain vectors in $\{0, \pm 1\}$ as combination of more that two $\mathbf{x}_i$'s. Namely if we take a linear combination of the form $\mathbf{x}_i - \mathbf{x}_j + \mathbf{x}_k$, each component will be in $\{-1, 0, 1\}$ with probability 7/8; therefore for m components the probability will be $(7/8)^m$. There are at most n^3 such triples to consider, so we want $n^3 \cdot (7/8)^m < \varepsilon$, which gives the condition $m \geq 16 \log n - 6 \log \varepsilon$. With $m = 2n$ and $\varepsilon = 2^{-4}$, this condition is satisfied for $n \geq 60$; for smaller values of n, one should take $m = \max(2n, 16 \log n + 24)$.

Hence after BKZ reduction with a large enough block-size β as above, we expect that each of the basis vectors $(\mathbf{c}_1, \ldots, \mathbf{c}_n)$ is either equal to $\pm \mathbf{x}_i$, or equal to a combination of the form $\mathbf{x}_i - \mathbf{x}_j$ for $i \neq j$. Conversely, this implies that all rows of the transition matrix between $(\mathbf{c}_1, \ldots, \mathbf{c}_n)$ and $(\mathbf{x}_1, \ldots, \mathbf{x}_n)$ must have Hamming weight at most 4. Therefore while staying in the lattice $\mathcal{L}_{\mathbf{x}}$ we can recover each of the original binary vectors $\mathbf{x}_i$ from the basis vectors $(\mathbf{c}_1, \ldots, \mathbf{c}_n)$, by exhaustive search with $\mathcal{O}(n^4)$ tests. In the full version of this paper [CG20] we describe a greedy algorithm that recovers the original binary vectors $\mathbf{x}_i$ relatively efficiently.

Recovering the weights α_i. Finally, from the samples $\mathbf{h}$, the vectors $\mathbf{x}_i$'s and the modulus M, recovering the weights α_i is straightforward as this amounts to solving a linear system:

$$\mathbf{h} = \alpha_1 \mathbf{x}_1 + \alpha_2 \mathbf{x}_2 + \cdots + \alpha_n \mathbf{x}_n \pmod{M}$$

Letting $\mathbf{X}'$ be the $n \times n$ matrix with the first n components of the column vectors $\mathbf{x}_i$ and letting $\mathbf{h}'$ be the vector with the first n components of $\mathbf{h}$, we have $\mathbf{h}' = \mathbf{X}' \cdot \boldsymbol{\alpha}$ where $\boldsymbol{\alpha} = (\alpha_1, \ldots, \alpha_n) \pmod{M}$. Assuming that $\mathbf{X}'$ is invertible modulo M, we get $\boldsymbol{\alpha} = \mathbf{X}'^{-1} \mathbf{h}' \pmod{M}$.

3.5 Practical Experiments

Running times. We provide in Table 2 the result of practical experiments. The first step is the orthogonal lattice attack with two applications of LLL. For the second step, we receive as input from Step 1 an LLL-reduced basis of the lattice $\mathcal{L}_{\mathbf{x}}$. We see in Table 2 that for $n = 70$ this is sufficient to recover the hidden vectors $\mathbf{x}_i$. Otherwise, we apply BKZ with block-size $\beta = 10, 20, 30, \ldots$ until we recover the vectors $\mathbf{x}_i$. We see that the two LLLs from Step 1 run in reasonable time up to $n = 250$, while for Step 2 the running time of BKZ grows exponentially, so we could not run Step 2 for $n > 170$. We provide the source code of our SageMath implementation in https://pastebin.com/ZFk1qjfP, based on the L^2 [NS09] and BKZ 2.0 [CN11] implementations from [fpl16].

Hermite factors. Recall that from our heuristic model from Sect. 3.4 the target Hermite factor for the second step of the Nguyen-Stern algorithm is $\gamma = \sqrt{n}/2$, which can be written $\gamma = a^n$ with $a = (n/4)^{1/(2n)}$. We provide in Table 2 above the corresponding target Hermite factors as a function of n.

In order to predict the Hermite factor achievable by BKZ as a function of the block-size β, we have run some experiments on a different lattice, independent

Table 2. Running time of the [NS99] attack, under a 3,2 GHz Intel Core i5 processor.

			Step 1			Step 2		
n	m	$\log M$	LLL $\mathcal{L}_0$	LLL $\mathcal{L}_x^{\perp}$	Hermite	Reduction		Total
70	140	772	3 s	1 s	1.021^n	LLL	ε	6 s
90	180	1151	10 s	4 s	1.017^n	BKZ-10	1 s	18 s
110	220	1592	28 s	12 s	1.015^n	BKZ-10	3 s	50 s
130	260	2095	81 s	24 s	1.013^n	BKZ-20	10 s	127 s
150	300	2659	159 s	44 s	1.012^n	BKZ-30	4 min	8 min
170	340	3282	6 min	115 s	1.011^n	BKZ-30	438 min	447 min
190	380	3965	13 min	3 min	1.010^n	–	–	–
220	440	5099	63 min	29 min	1.009^n	–	–	–
250	500	6366	119 min	56 min	1.008^n	–	–	–

from our model of Sect. 3.4. For this we have considered the lattice $\mathcal{L} \in \mathbb{Z}^n$ of row vectors:

$$\mathcal{L} = \begin{bmatrix} p & & & & \\ c_1 & 1 & & & \\ c_2 & & 1 & & \\ \vdots & & & \ddots & \\ c_{n-1} & \cdots & & & 1 \end{bmatrix}$$

for some prime p, with random c_i's modulo p. Since $\det \mathcal{L} = p$, by applying LLL or BKZ we expect to obtain vectors of norm $2^{\iota n} (\det L)^{1/n} = 2^{\iota n} \cdot p^{1/n}$, where $2^{\iota n}$ is the Hermite factor. We summarize our results in Table 3 below. Values up to $\beta = 40$ are from our experiments with the lattice $\mathcal{L}$ above, while for $\beta \geq 85$ the values are reproduced from [CN11], based on a simulation approach.

Table 3. Experimental and simulated Hermite factors for LLL ($\beta = 2$) and for BKZ with block-size β.

Block-size β	2	10	20	30	40	85	106	133
Hermite factor	1.020^n	1.015^n	1.014^n	1.013^n	1.012^n	1.010^n	1.009^n	1.008^n

In summary, the minimal BKZ block-sizes β required experimentally in Table 2 to apply Step 2 of Nguyen-Stern, seem coherent with the target Hermite factors from our model, and the experimental Hermite factors from Table 3. For example, for $n = 70$, this explains why an LLL-reduced basis is sufficient, because the target Hermite factor is 1.021^n, while LLL can achieve 1.020^n. From Table 3, BKZ-10 can achieve 1.015^n, so in Table 2 it was able to break the instances $n = 90$ and $n = 110$, but not $n = 130$ which has target Hermite factor 1.013^n. However we see that BKZ-20 and BKZ-30 worked better than expected; for example BKZ-30 could break the instance $n = 170$ with target Hermite factor 1.011^n, while in principle from Table 3 it can only achieve 1.013^n. So it could be that our model from Sect. 3.4 underestimates the target Hermite factor. Nevertheless, we believe that our model and the above experiments confirm that the complexity of the Nguyen-Stern algorithm is indeed exponential in n.

4 Our Polynomial-Time Algorithm for Solving the Hidden Subset-Sum Problem

Recall that the Nguyen-Stern attack is divided in the two following steps.

1. From the samples $\mathbf{h}$, determine the lattice $\bar{\mathcal{L}}_{\mathbf{x}}$, where $\mathcal{L}_{\mathbf{x}}$ is the lattice generated by the $\mathbf{x}_i$'s.
2. From $\bar{\mathcal{L}}_{\mathbf{x}}$, recover the hidden vectors $\mathbf{x}_i$'s. From $\mathbf{h}$, the $\mathbf{x}_i$'s and M, recover the weights α_i.

In the previous section we have argued that the complexity of the second step of the Nguyen-Stern attack is exponential in n. In this section we describe an alternative second step with polynomial-time complexity. However, our second step requires more samples than in [NS99], namely we need $m \simeq n^2/2$ samples instead of $m = 2n$. This means that in the first step we must produce a basis of the rank-n lattice $\bar{\mathcal{L}}_{\mathbf{x}} \subset \mathbb{Z}^m$, with the much higher vector dimension $m \simeq n^2/2$ instead of $m = 2n$.

For this, the naive method would be to apply directly Algorithm 1 from Sect. 3.1 to the vector $\mathbf{h}$ of dimension $m \simeq n^2/2$. But for $n \simeq 200$ one would need to apply LLL on a $m \times m$ matrix with $m \simeq n^2/2 \simeq 20\,000$, which is not practical; moreover the bitsize of the modulus M would need to be much larger due to the Hermite factor of LLL in such large dimension (see Table 1). Therefore, we first explain how to modify Step 1 in order to efficiently generate a lattice basis of $\bar{\mathcal{L}}_{\mathbf{x}} \subset \mathbb{Z}^m$ for large m. Our technique is as follows: instead of applying LLL on a square matrix of dimension $n^2/2$, we apply LLL in parallel on $n/2$ square matrices of dimension $2n$, which is much faster. Eventually we show in Sect. 5 that a single application of LLL is sufficient.

4.1 First Step: Obtaining a Basis of $\bar{\mathcal{L}}_{\mathbf{x}}$ for $m \gg n$

In this section, we show how to adapt the first step, namely the orthogonal lattice attack from [NS99] recalled in Sect. 3.1, to the case $m \gg n$. More precisely, we show how to generate a basis of n vectors of $\bar{\mathcal{L}}_{\mathbf{x}} \subset \mathbb{Z}^m$ for $m \simeq n^2/2$, while applying LLL on matrices of dimension $t = 2n$ only. As illustrated in Fig. 1, this is relatively straightforward: we apply Algorithm 1 from Sect. 3.1 on $2n$ components of the vector $\mathbf{h} \in \mathbb{Z}^m$ at a time, and each time we recover roughly the projection of a lattice basis of $\bar{\mathcal{L}}_{\mathbf{x}}$ on those $2n$ components; eventually we recombine those projections to obtain a full lattice basis of $\bar{\mathcal{L}}_{\mathbf{x}}$.

More precisely, writing $\mathbf{h} = [\mathbf{h}_0, \ldots, \mathbf{h}_d]$ where $m = (d+1) \cdot n$ and $\mathbf{h}_i \in \mathbb{Z}^n$, we apply Algorithm 1 on each of the d sub-vectors of the form $(\mathbf{h}_0, \mathbf{h}_i) \in \mathbb{Z}^{2n}$ for $1 \le i \le d$. For each $1 \le i \le d$ this gives us $\mathbf{C}_0^{(i)} \| \mathbf{C}_i \in \mathbb{Z}^{n \times 2n}$, the completion

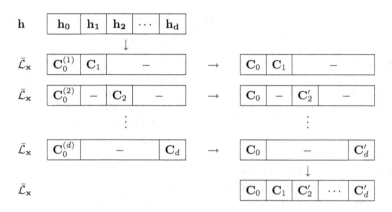

Fig. 1. Computation of a lattice basis of $\bar{\mathcal{L}}_{\mathbf{x}}$.

of the projection of a lattice basis of $\mathcal{L}_{\mathbf{x}}$. To recover the m components of the basis, we simply need to ensure that the projected bases $\mathbf{C}_0^{(i)} \| \mathbf{C}_i \in \mathbb{Z}^{n \times 2n}$ always start with the same matrix $\mathbf{C}_0$ on the first n components; see Fig. 1 for an illustration. This gives Algorithm 2 below. We denote Algorithm 1 from Sect. 3.1 by OrthoLat.

Algorithm 2. Orthogonal lattice attack with $m = d \cdot n$ samples

---
Input: $\mathbf{h} \in \mathbb{Z}^m, M, n, m = d \cdot n$.
Output: A base matrix of $\bar{\mathcal{L}}_{\mathbf{x}}$.
  1: Write $\mathbf{h} = [\mathbf{h}_0, \ldots, \mathbf{h}_d]$ where $\mathbf{h}_i \in \mathbb{Z}^n$ for all $0 \le i \le d$.
  2: **for** $i \leftarrow 1$ to d **do**
  3:     $\mathbf{y}_i \leftarrow [\mathbf{h}_0, \mathbf{h}_i]$
  4:     $\mathbf{C}_0^{(i)} \| \mathbf{C}_i \leftarrow \mathsf{OrthoLat}(\mathbf{y}_i, M, n, 2n)$
  5:     $\mathbf{Q}_i \leftarrow \mathbf{C}_0^{(1)} \cdot (\mathbf{C}_0^{(i)})^{-1}$
  6:     $\mathbf{C}_i' \leftarrow \mathbf{Q}_i \cdot \mathbf{C}_i$
  7: **end for**
  8: **return** $[\mathbf{C}_0, \mathbf{C}_1, \mathbf{C}_2', \cdots, \mathbf{C}_d']$

    A minor difficulty is that in principle, when applying OrthoLat (Algorithm 1) to a subset $\mathbf{y}_i \in \mathbb{Z}^{2n}$ of the sample $\mathbf{h} \in \mathbb{Z}^m$, we actually recover the completion of the projection of $\mathcal{L}_{\mathbf{x}}$ over the corresponding coordinates, rather than the projection of the completion $\bar{\mathcal{L}}_{\mathbf{x}}$ of $\mathcal{L}_{\mathbf{x}}$. More precisely, denote by π a generic projection on some coordinates of a lattice $\mathcal{L}_{\mathbf{x}}$. It is always true that $\pi(\mathcal{L}_{\mathbf{x}}) \subseteq \pi(\bar{\mathcal{L}}_{\mathbf{x}}) \subseteq \overline{\pi(\mathcal{L}_{\mathbf{x}})}$. Thus applying Algorithm 1 with a certain projection π we recover the completion $\overline{\pi(\mathcal{L}_{\mathbf{x}})}$. Assuming that the projection $\pi(\mathcal{L}_{\mathbf{x}})$ is complete, we obtain $\pi(\mathcal{L}_{\mathbf{x}}) = \overline{\pi(\mathcal{L}_{\mathbf{x}})} = \pi(\bar{\mathcal{L}}_{\mathbf{x}})$. Therefore, to simplify the analysis of Algorithm 2, we assume that the projection over the first n coordinates has rank n, and that the projection over the first $2n$ coordinates is complete. This implies that the transition matrices $\mathbf{Q}_i \leftarrow \mathbf{C}_0^{(1)} \cdot (\mathbf{C}_0^{(i)})^{-1}$ for $2 \leq i \leq d$ must be integral; in our practical experiments this was always the case.

Theorem 2. *Let $m = d \cdot n$ for $d \in \mathbb{N}$ and $d > 1$. Assume that the projection of the lattice $\mathcal{L}_{\mathbf{x}} \in \mathbb{Z}^m$ over the first n components has rank n, and that the projection of $\mathcal{L}_{\mathbf{x}}$ over the first $2n$ coordinates is complete. With probability at least $1/2$ over the choice of $\boldsymbol{\alpha}$, Algorithm 2 recovers a basis of $\bar{\mathcal{L}}_{\mathbf{x}}$ in polynomial time, assuming that M is a prime of bitsize at least $4n^2(\log n + 1)$.*

Proof. From Theorem 1, we recover for each $1 \leq i \leq d$ a basis $\mathbf{C}_0^{(i)} \| \mathbf{C}_i$ corresponding to the completed projection of $\mathcal{L}_{\mathbf{x}}$ to the first n coordinates and the $i + 1$-th subset of n coordinates, with probability at least $1/2$ over the choice of $\boldsymbol{\alpha}$. Let us denote by $\mathbf{X}$ the base matrix whose rows are the vectors $\mathbf{x}_i$'s. By assumption the vectors $\mathbf{x}_i$ are linear independent, the first $n \times n$ minor $\mathbf{X}_0$ is invertible and the matrices $\mathbf{C}_0^{(i)}$ for $i = 1, \ldots, d$ must generate a superlattice of $\mathbf{X}_0$. In particular, there exists an invertible integral matrix $\mathbf{Q}_i$ such that $\mathbf{Q}_i \cdot \mathbf{C}_0^{(i)} = \mathbf{C}_0^{(1)}$ for each $i = 1, \ldots, d$. So, applying $\mathbf{Q}_i = \mathbf{C}_0^{(1)}(\mathbf{C}_0^{(i)})^{-1}$ to $\mathbf{C}_i$ we find $\mathbf{C}_i'$, which contains the $i + 1$-th subset of n coordinates of the vectors in a basis having $\mathbf{C}_0 := \mathbf{C}_0^{(1)}$ as projection on the first n coordinates. This implies that $[\mathbf{C}_0, \mathbf{C}_1, \mathbf{C}_2', \cdots \mathbf{C}_d']$ is a basis of $\bar{\mathcal{L}}_{\mathbf{x}}$. $\qquad\square$

Heuristic analysis. For the size of the modulus M, since we are working with lattices in $\mathbb{Z}^{2n}$, we can take the same modulus size as in the heuristic analysis of Step 1 from Sect. 3.3, namely

$$\log M \simeq 2\iota n^2 + n \log n$$

with $\iota = 0.035$. The time complexity of Algorithm 2 is dominated by the cost of applying OrthoLat (Algorithm 1) to each $\mathbf{y}_i$, which is heuristically $\mathcal{O}(n^9)$ from Sect. 3.3. Therefore, the heuristic complexity of Algorithm 2 is $d \cdot \mathcal{O}(n^9) = \mathcal{O}(m \cdot n^8)$. In particular, for $m \simeq n^2/2$, the heuristic complexity of Algorithm 2 is $\mathcal{O}(n^{10})$, instead of $\mathcal{O}(n^{16})$ with the naive method (see Table 1). In Sect. 5 we will describe an improved algorithm with complexity $\mathcal{O}(n^9)$.

4.2   Second Step: Recovering the Hidden Vectors $\mathbf{x}_i$'s

By the first step we recover a basis $\mathbf{C} = (\mathbf{c}_1, \ldots, \mathbf{c}_n)$ of the hidden lattice $\bar{\mathcal{L}}_{\mathbf{x}} \in \mathbb{Z}^m$. The goal of the second step is then to recover the original vectors $\mathbf{x}_1, \ldots, \mathbf{x}_n \in \bar{\mathcal{L}}_{\mathbf{x}}$, namely to solve the following problem:

Problem 1. *Let $\mathbf{X} \leftarrow \{0, 1\}^{n \times m}$. Given $\mathbf{C} \in \mathbb{Z}^{n \times m}$ such that $\mathbf{WC} = \mathbf{X}$ for some $\mathbf{W} \in \mathbb{Z}^{n \times n} \cap \mathrm{GL}(\mathbb{Q}, n)$, recover $\mathbf{W}$ and $\mathbf{X}$.*

We show that for $m \simeq n^2/2$ the above problem can be solved in heuristic polynomial time, using a multivariate approach. Namely we reduce the problem to solving a system of multivariate quadratic equations and we provide an appropriate algorithm to solve it.

Heuristically we expect the solution to be unique up to permutations of the rows when $m \gg n$. Indeed for large enough m we expect the vectors $\mathbf{x}_i$ to be the unique vectors in $\bar{\mathcal{L}}_{\mathbf{x}}$ with binary coefficients. More precisely, consider a vector $\mathbf{v} = \mathbf{x}_i + \mathbf{x}_j$ or $\mathbf{v} = \mathbf{x}_i - \mathbf{x}_j$ for $i \neq j$. The probability that all components of $\mathbf{v}$ are in $\{0,1\}$ is $(3/4)^m$, so for $n^2/2$ possible choices of i,j the probability is at most $n^2 \cdot (3/4)^m$, which for $m \simeq n^2/2$ is a negligible function of n. Therefore we can consider the equivalent problem:

Problem 2. *Given* $\mathbf{C} \in \mathbb{Z}^{n \times m}$ *of rank* n, *suppose there exist exactly* n *vectors* $\mathbf{w}_i \in \mathbb{Z}^n$ *such that* $\mathbf{w}_i \cdot \mathbf{C} = \mathbf{x}_i \in \{0,1\}^m$ *for* $i = 1, \ldots, n$, *and assume that the vectors* $\mathbf{w}_i$ *are linearly independent. Find* $\mathbf{w}_1, \ldots, \mathbf{w}_n$.

We denote by $\tilde{\mathbf{c}}_1, \ldots, \tilde{\mathbf{c}}_m$ the column vectors of $\mathbf{C}$, which gives:

$$
\begin{bmatrix} \mathbf{w}_1 \\ \vdots \\ \mathbf{w}_n \end{bmatrix}
\begin{bmatrix} \tilde{\mathbf{c}}_1 & \cdots & \tilde{\mathbf{c}}_m \end{bmatrix}
=
\begin{bmatrix} \mathbf{x}_1 \\ \vdots \\ \mathbf{x}_n \end{bmatrix}
$$

Multivariate approach. The crucial observation is that since all components of the vectors $\mathbf{x}_i$ are binary, they must all satisfy the quadratic equation $y^2 - y = 0$. Therefore for each $i = 1, \ldots, n$ we have:

$$
\begin{aligned}
\mathbf{w}_i \cdot \mathbf{C} \in \{0,1\}^m &\iff \forall j \in [1,m], \ (\mathbf{w}_i \cdot \tilde{\mathbf{c}}_j)^2 - \mathbf{w}_i \cdot \tilde{\mathbf{c}}_j = 0 \\
&\iff \forall j \in [1,m], \ (\mathbf{w}_i \cdot \tilde{\mathbf{c}}_j)(\mathbf{w}_i \cdot \tilde{\mathbf{c}}_j)^{\mathsf{T}} - \mathbf{w}_i \cdot \tilde{\mathbf{c}}_j = 0 \\
&\iff \forall j \in [1,m], \ \mathbf{w}_i \cdot (\tilde{\mathbf{c}}_j \cdot \tilde{\mathbf{c}}_j^{\mathsf{T}}) \cdot \mathbf{w}_i^{\mathsf{T}} - \mathbf{w}_i \cdot \tilde{\mathbf{c}}_j = 0
\end{aligned}
$$

Given the known column vectors $\tilde{\mathbf{c}}_1, \ldots, \tilde{\mathbf{c}}_m$, the vectors $\mathbf{w}_1, \ldots, \mathbf{w}_n$ and $\mathbf{0}$ are therefore solutions of the quadratic polynomial multivariate system

$$
\begin{cases}
\mathbf{w} \cdot \tilde{\mathbf{c}}_1 \tilde{\mathbf{c}}_1^{\mathsf{T}} \cdot \mathbf{w}^{\mathsf{T}} - \mathbf{w} \cdot \tilde{\mathbf{c}}_1 = 0 \\
\quad \vdots \\
\mathbf{w} \cdot \tilde{\mathbf{c}}_m \tilde{\mathbf{c}}_m^{\mathsf{T}} \cdot \mathbf{w}^{\mathsf{T}} - \mathbf{w} \cdot \tilde{\mathbf{c}}_m = 0
\end{cases}
\tag{12}
$$

In the following we provide a heuristic polynomial-time algorithm to solve this quadratic multivariate system, via linearization and computation of eigenspaces. More precisely, as in the XL algorithm [CKPS00] we first linearize (12); then we prove that the $\mathbf{w}_i$'s are eigenvectors of some submatrices of the kernel matrix, and we provide a method to recover them in polynomial time. We observe that such approach is deeply related to Gröbner basis techniques for zero dimensional ideals. Namely, the system (12) of polynomial equations defines an ideal J. If the homogeneous degree 2 parts of such polynomials generate the space of monomials of degree 2, a Gröbner basis of J can be obtained via linear transformations, and the $\mathbf{x}_i$'s recovered in polynomial time. We refer to [CLO05] for the Gröbner basis perspective. For this approach the minimal condition is clearly $m = (n^2 + n)/2$.

Linearization. Since $(\tilde{\mathbf{c}}_j)_i = \mathbf{C}_{ij}$, for all $1 \leq j \leq m$, we can write:

$$\mathbf{y} \cdot \tilde{\mathbf{c}}_j \tilde{\mathbf{c}}_j^\mathsf{T} \cdot \mathbf{y}^\mathsf{T} = \sum_{i=1}^n \sum_{k=1}^n y_i y_k \mathbf{C}_{ij} \mathbf{C}_{kj} = \sum_{i=1}^n \sum_{k=i}^n y_i y_k (2 - \delta_{i,k}) \mathbf{C}_{ij} \mathbf{C}_{kj}$$

with $\delta_{i,k} = 1$ if $i = k$ and 0 otherwise. In the above equation the coefficient of the degree 2 monomial $y_i y_k$ for $1 \leq i \leq k \leq n$ is $(2 - \delta_{i,k}) \mathbf{C}_{ij} \mathbf{C}_{kj}$. Thus, we consider the corresponding vectors of coefficients for $1 \leq j \leq m$:

$$\mathbf{r}_j = ((2 - \delta_{i,k}) \mathbf{C}_{ij} \mathbf{C}_{kj})_{1 \leq i \leq k \leq n} \in \mathbb{Z}^{\frac{n^2+n}{2}}. \tag{13}$$

We set $\mathbf{R} \in \mathbb{Z}^{\frac{n^2+n}{2} \times m}$ to be the matrix whose columns are the $\mathbf{r}_j$'s and

$$\mathbf{E} = \left[\begin{array}{c} \mathbf{R} \\ \hline -\mathbf{C} \end{array} \right] \in \mathbb{Z}^{\frac{n^2+3n}{2} \times m};$$

we obtain that (12) is equivalent to

$$\begin{cases} [\, \mathbf{z} \mid \mathbf{y} \,] \cdot \mathbf{E} = 0 \\ \mathbf{z} = (y_i y_k)_{1 \leq i \leq k \leq n} \in \mathbb{Z}^{\frac{n^2+n}{2}} \end{cases} \tag{14}$$

For $m > (n^2 + n)/2$ we expect the matrix $\mathbf{R}$ to be of rank $(n^2 + n)/2$. In that case we must have $\mathrm{rank}\,\mathbf{E} \geq (n^2 + n)/2$, and so $\dim \ker \mathbf{E} \leq n$. On the other hand, consider the set of vectors

$$\mathcal{W} = \{((w_i w_k)_{1 \leq i \leq k \leq n}, \mathbf{w}) \in \mathbb{Z}^{\frac{n^2+3n}{2}} \mid \mathbf{w} \in \{\mathbf{w}_1, \dots, \mathbf{w}_n\}\}.$$

Since by assumption the vectors $\mathbf{w}_i$'s are linearly independent, $\mathrm{Span}(\mathcal{W})$ is a subspace of dimension n of $\ker \mathbf{E}$. This implies that $\dim \ker \mathbf{E} = n$, and that a basis of $\ker \mathbf{E}$ is given by the set $\mathcal{W}$. In the following, we show how to recover $\mathcal{W}$, from which we recover the matrix $\mathbf{W}$ and eventually the n vectors $\mathbf{x}_i$.

Kernel computation. Since the set of n vectors in $\mathcal{W}$ form a basis of $\ker \mathbf{E}$, the first step is to compute a basis of $\ker \mathbf{E}$ over $\mathbb{Q}$ from the known matrix $\mathbf{E} \in \mathbb{Z}^{\frac{n^2+3n}{2} \times m}$. However this does not immediately reveal $\mathcal{W}$ since the n vectors of $\mathcal{W}$ form a privileged basis of $\ker \mathbf{E}$; namely the vectors in $\mathcal{W}$ have the following structure:

$$((w_i w_k)_{1 \leq i \leq k \leq n}, w_1, \dots w_n) \in \mathbb{Z}^{\frac{n^2+3n}{2}}.$$

To recover the vectors in $\mathcal{W}$ we proceed as follows. Note that the last n components in the vectors in $\mathcal{W}$ correspond to the linear part in the quadratic equations of (12). Therefore we consider the base matrix $\mathbf{K} \in \mathbb{Q}^{n \times \frac{n^2+3n}{2}}$ of $\ker \mathbf{E}$ such that the matrix corresponding to the linear part is the identity matrix:

$$\mathbf{K} = \left[\, \mathbf{M} \mid \mathbf{I}_n \,\right] \tag{15}$$

where $\mathbf{M} \in \mathbb{Q}^{n \times \frac{n^2+n}{2}}$. A vector $\mathbf{v} = (v_1, \ldots, v_n) \in \mathbb{Z}^n$ is then a solution of (14) if and only if $\mathbf{v} \cdot \mathbf{K} \in \mathcal{W}$, which gives:

$$\mathbf{v} \cdot \mathbf{M} = (v_i v_k)_{1 \le i \le k \le n}.$$

By duplicating some columns of the matrix $\mathbf{M}$, we can obtain a matrix $\mathbf{M}' \in \mathbb{Z}^{n^2 \times n}$ such that:

$$\mathbf{v} \cdot \mathbf{M}' = (v_i v_k)_{1 \le i \le n, 1 \le k \le n}.$$

We write $\mathbf{M}' = [\mathbf{M}_1, \ldots, \mathbf{M}_n]$ where $\mathbf{M}_i \in \mathbb{Z}^{n \times n}$. This gives:

$$\mathbf{v} \cdot \mathbf{M}_i = v_i \cdot \mathbf{v}$$

for all $1 \le i \le n$.

This means that the eigenvalues of each $\mathbf{M}_i$ are exactly all the possible i-th coordinates of the target vectors $\mathbf{w}_1, \ldots, \mathbf{w}_n$. Therefore the vectors $\mathbf{w}_j$'s are the intersections of the left eigenspaces corresponding to their coordinates.

Eigenspace computation. Consider for example the first coordinates $w_{j,1}$ of the vectors $\mathbf{w}_j$. From the previous equation, we have:

$$\mathbf{w}_j \cdot \mathbf{M}_1 = w_{j,1} \cdot \mathbf{w}_j.$$

Therefore the vectors $\mathbf{w}_j$ are the eigenvectors of the matrix $\mathbf{M}_1$, and their first coordinates $w_{j,1}$ are the eigenvalues. Assume that those n eigenvalues are distinct; in that case we can immediately compute the n corresponding eigenvectors $\mathbf{w}_j$ and solve the problem. More generally, we can recover the vectors $\mathbf{w}_j$ that belong to a dimension 1 eigenspace of $\mathbf{M}_1$; namely in that case $\mathbf{w}_j$ is the unique vector of its eigenspace such that $\mathbf{w}_j \cdot \mathbf{C} \in \{0,1\}^m$, and we recover the corresponding $\mathbf{x}_j = \mathbf{w}_j \cdot \mathbf{C}$.

Our approach is therefore as follows. We first compute the eigenspaces $E_1, \ldots, E_s$ of $\mathbf{M}_1$. For every $1 \le k \le s$, if $\dim E_k = 1$ then we can compute the corresponding target vector, as explained above. Otherwise, we compute $\mathbf{M}_{2,k}$ the restriction map of $\mathbf{M}_2$ at E_k and we check the dimensions of its eigenspaces. As we find eigenspaces of dimension 1 we compute more target vectors, otherwise we compute the restrictions of $\mathbf{M}_3$ at the new eigenspaces and so on. We iterate this process until we find all the solutions; see Algorithm 3 below.

In order to better analyze this procedure, we observe that we essentially construct a tree of subspaces of $\mathbb{Q}^n$, performing a breadth-first search algorithm. The root corresponds to the entire space, and each node at depth i is a son of a node E at depth $i-1$ if and only if it represents a non-trivial intersection of E with one of the eigenspaces of $\mathbf{M}_i$. Since these non-trivial intersections are exactly the eigenspaces of the restriction of $\mathbf{M}_i$ to E, our algorithm does not compute unnecessary intersections. Moreover, we know that when the dimension of the node is 1 all its successors represent the same space; hence that branch of the algorithm can be closed; see Fig. 2 for an illustration.

Algorithm 3. Multivariate attack

Input: $\mathbf{C} \in \mathbb{Z}^{n \times m}$ a basis of $\bar{\mathcal{L}}_\mathbf{x}$.

Output: $\mathbf{x}_1, \ldots, \mathbf{x}_n \in \{0,1\}^m$, such that $\mathbf{w}_i \cdot \mathbf{C} = \mathbf{x}_i$ for $i = 1, \ldots, n$.

1: Let $\mathbf{r}_j = ((2 - \delta_{i,k})\mathbf{C}_{ij}\mathbf{C}_{kj})_{1 \le i \le k \le n} \in \mathbb{Z}^{\frac{n^2+n}{2}}$ for $1 \le j \le m$.

2: $\mathbf{E} = \begin{bmatrix} \mathbf{r}_1 \cdots \mathbf{r}_m \\ -\mathbf{C} \end{bmatrix} \in \mathbb{Z}^{\frac{n^2+3n}{2} \times m}$

3: $\mathbf{K} \leftarrow$ Ker $\mathbf{E}$ with $\mathbf{K} = \begin{bmatrix} \mathbf{M} & | & \mathbf{I}_n \end{bmatrix} \in \mathbb{Q}^{n \times \frac{n^2+3n}{2}}$

4: Write $\mathbf{M} = [\tilde{\mathbf{m}}_{ik}]_{1 \le i \le k \le n}$ where $\tilde{\mathbf{m}}_{ik} \in \mathbb{Q}^n$.

5: Let $\mathbf{M}_i \in \mathbb{Q}^{n \times n}$ with $\mathbf{M}_i = [\tilde{\mathbf{m}}_{ik}]_{1 \le k \le n}$, using $\tilde{\mathbf{m}}_{ik} := \tilde{\mathbf{m}}_{ki}$ for $i > k$.

6: $L \leftarrow [\mathbf{I}_n]$

7: **for** $i \leftarrow 1$ to n **do**

8:     $L_2 \leftarrow []$

9:     **for all** $\mathbf{V} \in L$ **do**

10:        **if** rank $\mathbf{V} = 1$ **then**

11:           Append a generator $\mathbf{v}$ of $\mathbf{V}$ to L_2.

12:        **else**

13:           Compute $\mathbf{A}$ such that $\mathbf{V} \cdot \mathbf{M}_i = \mathbf{A} \cdot \mathbf{V}$.

14:           Append all eigenspaces $\mathbf{U}$ of $\mathbf{A}$ to L_2.

15:        **end if**

16:     **end for**

17:     $L \leftarrow L_2$

18: **end for**

19: $X \leftarrow []$

20: **for all** $\mathbf{v} \in L$ **do**

21:     Find $c \ne 0$ such that $\mathbf{x} = c \cdot \mathbf{v} \cdot \mathbf{C} \in \{0,1\}^m$, and append $\mathbf{x}$ to X.

22: **end for**

23: **return** X

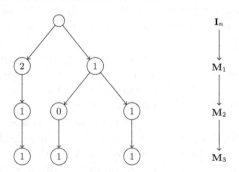

Fig. 2. Example of the tree we obtain for $\mathbf{w}_1 = (2,1,1), \mathbf{w}_2 = (1,0,1), \mathbf{w}_3 = (1,1,1)$. The matrix $\mathbf{M}_1$ has an eigenspace of dimension 1 $E_{1,2}$ and one of dimension 2 $E_{1,1}$. At the first iteration we obtain therefore $\mathbf{w}_1$. Then we compute the restriction of $\mathbf{M}_2$ to $E_{1,1}$; this has two distinct eigenvalues 0 and 1, which enables to recover the eigenvectors $\mathbf{w}_2$ and $\mathbf{w}_3$. All the nodes at depth 2 represent dimension one spaces, hence the algorithm terminates.

Analysis and reduction modulo p. Our algorithm is heuristic as we must assume that the matrix $\mathbf{R} \in \mathbb{Z}^{\frac{n^2+n}{2} \times m}$ has rank $(n^2 + n)/2$. In our experiments we took $m = (n^2 + 4n)/2$ and this hypothesis was always satisfied. The running time of the algorithm is dominated by the cost of computing the kernel of a matrix $\mathbf{E}$ of dimension $\frac{n^2+3n}{2} \times m$. For $m = (n^2 + 4n)/2$, this requires $\mathcal{O}(n^6)$ arithmetic operations. Thus we have shown:

Lemma 4. *Let $\mathbf{C} \in \mathbb{Z}^{n \times m}$ be an instance of Problem 2 and $\mathbf{R} \in \mathbb{Z}^{\frac{n^2+n}{2} \times m}$ the matrix whose columns are the $\mathbf{r}_i$ constructed as in (13). If $\mathbf{R}$ has rank $\frac{n^2+n}{2}$, then the vectors $\mathbf{x}_i$ can be recovered in $\mathcal{O}(n^6)$ arithmetic operations.*

In practice it is more efficient to work modulo a prime p instead of over $\mathbb{Q}$. Namely Problem 1 is defined over the integers, so we can consider its reduction modulo a prime p:

$$\overline{\mathbf{W}}\mathbf{C} = \overline{\mathbf{X}} \pmod p$$

and since $\overline{\mathbf{X}}$ has coefficients in $\{0,1\}$ we obtain a system which is exactly the reduction of (12) modulo p. In particular, we can compute $\mathbf{K} = \ker \mathbf{E}$ modulo p instead of over $\mathbb{Q}$, and also compute the eigenspaces modulo p. Setting $\overline{\mathbf{R}} = \mathbf{R} \bmod p$, if $\overline{\mathbf{R}}$ has rank $\frac{n^2+n}{2}$, then $\mathbf{X}$ can be recovered by $\mathcal{O}(n^6 \cdot \log^2 p)$ bit operations.

Note that we cannot take $p = 2$ as in that case any vector $\mathbf{w}_i$ would be a solution of $\mathbf{w}_i \cdot \mathbf{C} = \mathbf{x}_i \pmod 2$, since $\mathbf{x}_i \in \{0,1\}^m$. In practice we took $p = 3$ and $m = (n^2 + 4n)/2$, which was sufficient to recover the original vectors $\mathbf{x}_1, \ldots, \mathbf{x}_n$. In that case, the heuristic time complexity is $\mathcal{O}(n^6)$, while the space complexity is $\mathcal{O}(n^4)$. We provide the results of practical experiments in Sect. 7, and the source code in https://pastebin.com/ZFk1qjfP.

5   Improvement of the Algorithm First Step

The first step of our new attack is the same as in [NS99], except that we need to produce $m - n$ orthogonal vectors in $\mathcal{L}_{\mathbf{x}}^{\perp}$ from $m = n(n+4)/2$ samples, instead of only $m = 2n$ samples in the original Nguyen-Stern attack. Therefore, we need to produce $n(n + 2)/2$ orthogonal vectors in $\mathcal{L}_{\mathbf{x}}^{\perp}$, instead of only n. In Sect. 4.1, this required $m/n \simeq n/2$ parallel applications of LLL to compute those $m - n$ vectors in $\mathcal{L}_{\mathbf{x}}^{\perp}$, and similarly $n/2$ parallel applications of LLL to compute the orthogonal $\bar{\mathcal{L}}_{\mathbf{x}} = (\mathcal{L}_{\mathbf{x}}^{\perp})^{\perp} \in \mathbb{Z}^m$. Overall the heuristic time complexity was $\mathcal{O}(n^{10})$.

In this section, we show that only a single application of LLL (with the same dimension) is required to produce the $m - n$ orthogonal vectors in $\mathcal{L}_{\mathbf{x}}^{\perp}$. Namely we show that once the first n orthogonal vectors have been produced, we can very quickly generate the remaining $m - 2n$ other vectors, by size-reducing the original basis vectors with respect to an LLL-reduced submatrix. Similarly a single application of LLL is required to recover a basis of $\bar{\mathcal{L}}_{\mathbf{x}}$. Eventually the heuristic time complexity of the first step is $\mathcal{O}(n^9)$, as in the original Nguyen-Stern algorithm. This implies that the heuristic complexity of our full algorithm for solving the hidden subset sum problem is also $\mathcal{O}(n^9)$.

5.1 Closest Vector Problem

Size reduction with respect to an LLL-reduced sub-matrix essentially amounts to solving the approximate closest vector problem (CVP) in the corresponding lattice.

Definition 2 (Approximate closest vector problem). *Fix* $\gamma > 1$. *Given a basis for a lattice* $\mathcal{L} \subset \mathbb{Z}^d$ *and a vector* $\mathbf{t} \in \mathbb{R}^d$, *compute* $\mathbf{v} \in \mathcal{L}$ *such that* $\|\mathbf{t} - \mathbf{v}\| \leq \gamma \|\mathbf{t} - \mathbf{u}\|$ *for all* $\mathbf{u} \in \mathcal{L}$.

To solve approximate-CVP, Babai's nearest plane method [Bab86] inductively finds a lattice vector close to a vector $\mathbf{t}$, based on a Gram-Schmidt basis. Alternatively, Babai's rounding technique has a worse approximation factor γ but is easier to implement in practice.

Algorithm 4. Babai's rounding method

Input: a basis $\mathbf{b}_1, \ldots, \mathbf{b}_d$ of a lattice $\mathcal{L} \subset \mathbb{Z}^d$. A vector $\mathbf{t} \in \mathbb{Z}^d$.
Output: a vector $\mathbf{v} \in \mathcal{L}$.
  1: Write $\mathbf{t} = \sum_{i=1}^{d} u_i \mathbf{b}_i$ with $u_i \in \mathbb{R}$.
  2: **return** $\mathbf{v} = \sum_{i=1}^{d} \lfloor u_i \rceil \mathbf{b}_i$

Theorem 3 (Babai's rounding [Bab86]). *Let* $\mathbf{b}_1, \ldots, \mathbf{b}_d$ *be an LLL-reduced basis (with respect to the Euclidean norm and with factor* $\delta = 3/4$) *for a lattice* $\mathcal{L} \subset \mathbb{R}^d$. *Then the output* $\mathbf{v}$ *of the Babai rounding method on input* $\mathbf{t} \in \mathbb{R}^d$ *satisfies* $\|\mathbf{t} - \mathbf{v}\| \leq (1 + 2d(9/2)^{d/2})\|\mathbf{t} - \mathbf{u}\|$ *for all* $\mathbf{u} \in \mathcal{L}$.

5.2 Generating Orthogonal Vectors in $\mathcal{L}_{\mathbf{x}}^{\perp}$

We start with the computation of the orthogonal vectors in $\mathcal{L}_{\mathbf{x}}^{\perp}$. Consider the large $m \times m$ matrix of vectors orthogonal to $h_1, \ldots, h_m$ modulo M corresponding to the lattice $\mathcal{L}_0$. Our improved technique is based on the fact that once LLL has been applied to the small upper-left $(2n) \times (2n)$ sub-matrix of vectors orthogonal to $(h_1, \ldots, h_{2n})$ modulo M, we do not need to apply LLL anymore to get more orthogonal vectors; namely it suffices to size-reduce the other rows with respect to these $2n$ already LLL-reduced vectors. After size-reduction we obtain short vectors in $\mathcal{L}_0$, and as previously if these vectors are short enough, they are guaranteed to belong to the orthogonal lattice $\mathcal{L}_{\mathbf{x}}^{\perp}$; see Fig. 3 for an illustration. Such size-reduction is much faster than repeatedly applying LLL as in Sect. 4.1. We describe the corresponding algorithm below.

Fig. 3. In the initial basis matrix the components of the first column are big. Then by applying LLL on the $2n \times 2n$ submatrix the corresponding components become small; this already gives n orthogonal vectors in $\mathcal{L}_{\mathbf{x}}^{\perp}$. Then by size-reducing the remaining $m - 2n$ rows, one obtains small components on the $2n$ columns, and therefore $m - 2n$ additional orthogonal vectors. In total we obtain $m - n$ orthogonal vectors.

Algorithm 5. Fast generation of orthogonal vectors

Input: $\mathbf{h} \in \mathbb{Z}^m$, M, n, m.
Output: A generating set of $\mathcal{L}_{\mathbf{x}}^{\perp} \subset \mathbb{Z}^m$.
1: Let $\mathbf{B} \in \mathbb{Z}^{m \times m}$ be a basis of row vectors of the lattice $\mathcal{L}_0$ of vectors orthogonal to $\mathbf{h}$ modulo M, in lower triangular form.
2: Apply LLL to the upper-left $(2n) \times (2n)$ submatrix of $\mathbf{B}$.
3: Let $\mathbf{a}_1, \ldots, \mathbf{a}_{2n} \in \mathbb{Z}^{2n}$ be the $2n$ vectors of the LLL-reduced basis.
4: **for** $i = 2n + 1$ to m **do**
5:     Let $\mathbf{t}_i = [-h_i h_1^{-1}[M] \ 0 \ \cdots \ 0] \in \mathbb{Z}^{2n}$.
6:     Apply Babai's rounding to $\mathbf{t}_i$, with respect to $(\mathbf{a}_1, \ldots, \mathbf{a}_{2n})$. Let $\mathbf{v} \in \mathbb{Z}^{2n}$ be the resulting vector.
7:     Let $\mathbf{a}_i' = [(\mathbf{t}_i - \mathbf{v}) \ 0 \ 1 \ 0] \in \mathbb{Z}^m$ where the 1 component is at index i.
8: **end for**
9: For $1 \le i \le n$, extend the vectors $\mathbf{a}_i$ to $\mathbf{a}_i' \in \mathbb{Z}^m$, padding with zeros.
10: Output the n vectors $\mathbf{a}_i'$ for $1 \le i \le n$, and the $m - 2n$ vectors $\mathbf{a}_i'$ for $2n + 1 \le i \le m$.

The following Lemma shows that under certain conditions on the lattice $\mathcal{L}_{\mathbf{x}}^{\perp}$, Algorithm 5 outputs a generating set of $m - n$ vectors of $\mathcal{L}_{\mathbf{x}}^{\perp}$. More specifically, we have to assume that the lattice $\mathcal{L}_{\mathbf{x}}^{\perp}$ contains short vectors of the form $[\mathbf{c}_i \ 0 \ \ldots \ 1 \ \ldots \ 0]$ with $\mathbf{c}_i \in \mathbb{Z}^{2n}$; this assumption seems to be always verified in practice. We provide the proof in the full version of this paper [CG20].

Lemma 5. *Assume that the lattice $\mathcal{L}_{\mathbf{x}}^{\perp}$ contains n linearly independent vectors of the form $\mathbf{c}_i' = [\mathbf{c}_i \ 0 \cdots \ 0] \in \mathbb{Z}^m$ for $1 \le i \le n$ with $\mathbf{c}_i \in \mathbb{Z}^{2n}$ and $\|\mathbf{c}_i\| \le B$, and $m - 2n$ vectors of the form $\mathbf{c}_i' = [\mathbf{c}_i \ 0 \ \ldots \ 1 \ \ldots \ 0] \in \mathbb{Z}^m$ where the 1 component is at index i, for $2n + 1 \le i \le m$ with $\mathbf{c}_i \in \mathbb{Z}^{2n}$ and $\|\mathbf{c}_i\| \le B$. Then if $(\gamma B + 1)\sqrt{mn} \le \lambda_1 \left(\Lambda_M^{\perp}(\boldsymbol{\alpha}) \right)$ where $\gamma = 1 + 4n(9/2)^n$, Algorithm 5 returns a set of $m - n$ linearly independent vectors in $\mathcal{L}_{\mathbf{x}}^{\perp}$, namely n vectors $\mathbf{a}_i' \in \mathcal{L}_{\mathbf{x}}^{\perp}$ for $1 \le i \le n$, and $m - 2n$ vectors $\mathbf{a}_i' \in \mathcal{L}_{\mathbf{x}}^{\perp}$ for $2n + 1 \le i \le m$.*

Complexity analysis. Since the approximation factor γ for CVP is similar to the LLL Hermite factor, we use the same modulus size as previously, namely $\log M \simeq 2\iota n^2 + n \cdot \log n$ with $\iota = 0.035$. As in Sect. 3.3 the complexity of the first LLL reduction with L^2 is $\mathcal{O}(n^5 \log^2 M) = \mathcal{O}(n^9)$.

We now consider the size-reductions with Babai's rounding. To apply Babai's rounding we must first invert a $2n \times 2n$ matrix with $\log M$ bits of precision; this has to be done only once, and takes $\mathcal{O}(n^3 \log^2 M) = \mathcal{O}(n^7)$ time. Then for each Babai's rounding we need one vector matrix multiplication, with precision $\log M$ bits. Since the vector has actually a single non-zero component, the complexity is $\mathcal{O}(n \log^2 M) = \mathcal{O}(n^5)$. With $m = \mathcal{O}(n^2)$, the total complexity of size-reduction is therefore $\mathcal{O}(n^7)$. In the full version of this paper [CG20], we describe a further improvement of the size-reduction step, with complexity $\mathcal{O}(n^{20/3})$ instead of $\mathcal{O}(n^7)$.

Overall the heuristic complexity of Algorithm 5 for computing a generating set of $\mathcal{L}_\mathbf{x}^\perp$ is therefore $\mathcal{O}(n^9)$, instead of $\mathcal{O}(n^{10})$ in Sect. 4.1.

5.3   Computing the Orthogonal of $\mathcal{L}_\mathbf{x}^\perp$

As in the original [NS99] attack, once we have computed a generating set of the rank $m - n$ lattice $\mathcal{L}_\mathbf{x}^\perp \subset \mathbb{Z}^m$, we need to compute its orthogonal, with $m = n(n+4)/2$ instead of $m = 2n$. As previously, this will not take significantly more time, because of the structure of the generating set of vectors in $\mathcal{L}_\mathbf{x}^\perp$. Namely as illustrated in Fig. 4, the matrix defining the $m - n$ orthogonal vectors in $\mathcal{L}_\mathbf{x}^\perp$ is already almost in Hermite Normal Form (after the first $2n$ components), and therefore once the first $2n$ components of a basis of n vectors of $\bar{\mathcal{L}}_\mathbf{x} = (\mathcal{L}_\mathbf{x}^\perp)^\perp$ have been computed (with LLL), computing the remaining $m - 2n$ components is straightforward.

More precisely, from Algorithm 5, we obtain a matrix $\mathbf{A} \in \mathbb{Z}^{(m-n)\times m}$ of row vectors generating $\mathcal{L}_\mathbf{x}^\perp$, of the form:

$$\mathbf{A} = \begin{bmatrix} \mathbf{U} & \\ \mathbf{V} & \mathbf{I}_{m-2n} \end{bmatrix}$$

$$\mathcal{L}_\mathbf{x}^\perp :$$

Fig. 4. Structure of the generating set of $\mathcal{L}_\mathbf{x}^\perp$.

where $\mathbf{U} \in \mathbb{Z}^{n \times 2n}$ and $\mathbf{V} \in \mathbb{Z}^{(m-2n) \times 2n}$. As in Sect. 3.1, using the LLL-based algorithm from [NS97], we first compute a matrix basis $\mathbf{P} \in \mathbb{Z}^{2n \times n}$ of column vectors orthogonal to the rows of $\mathbf{U}$, that is $\mathbf{U} \cdot \mathbf{P} = 0$. We then compute the matrix:

$$\mathbf{C} = \begin{bmatrix} \mathbf{P} \\ -\mathbf{VP} \end{bmatrix} \in \mathbb{Z}^{m \times n}$$

and we obtain $\mathbf{A} \cdot \mathbf{C} = 0$ as required. Therefore the matrix $\mathbf{C}$ of column vectors is a basis of $\bar{\mathcal{L}}_{\mathbf{x}} = (\mathcal{L}_{\mathbf{x}}^{\perp})^{\perp}$.

6 Cryptographic Applications

In [NS99], the authors showed how to break the fast generator of random pairs $(x, g^x \pmod{p})$ from Boyko et al. [BPV98], using their algorithm for solving the hidden subset-sum problem. Such generator can be used to speed-up the generation of discrete-log based algorithms with fixed base g, such as Schnorr identification, and Schnorr, ElGamal and DSS signatures. The generator of random pairs $(x, g^x \pmod{p})$ works as follows. We consider a prime number p and $g \in \mathbb{Z}_p^*$ of order M.

Preprocessing Step: Take $\alpha_1, \ldots, \alpha_n \leftarrow \mathbb{Z}_M$ and compute $\beta_j = g^{\alpha_j}$ for each $j \in [1, n]$ and store (α_j, β_j).

Pair Generation: To generate a pair $(g, g^x \bmod p)$, randomly generate a subset $S \subseteq [1, n]$ such that $|S| = \kappa$; compute $b = \sum_{j \in S} \alpha_j \bmod M$, if $b = 0$ restart, otherwise compute $B = \prod_{j \in S} \beta_j \bmod p$. Return (b, B).

In [NS99] the authors described a very nice passive attack against the generator used in Schnorr's signatures, based on a variant of the hidden subset-sum problem, called the affine hidden subset-sum problem; the attack is also applicable to ElGamal and DSS signatures. Under this variant, there is an additional secret s, and given $\mathbf{h}, \mathbf{e} \in \mathbb{Z}^m$ one must recover s, the $\mathbf{x}_i$'s and the α_i's such that:

$$\mathbf{h} + s\mathbf{e} = \alpha_1 \mathbf{x}_1 + \alpha_2 \mathbf{x}_2 + \cdots + \alpha_n \mathbf{x}_n \pmod{M}$$

Namely consider the Schnorr's signature scheme. Let q be a prime dividing $p-1$, let $g \in \mathbb{Z}_p$ be a q-th root of unity, and $y = g^{-s} \bmod p$ be the public key. The signer must generate a pair $(k, g^k \bmod p)$ and compute the hash $e = H(\mathsf{mes}, x)$ of the message mes; it then computes $y = k + se \bmod q$; the signature is the pair (y, e). We see that the signatures (y_i, e_i) give us an instance of the affine hidden subset-sum problem above, with $\mathbf{h} = (y_i)$, $\mathbf{e} = (-e_i)$ and $M = q$.

In the full version of this paper [CG20], we recall how to solve the affine hidden subset-sum problem using a variant of the Nguyen-Stern algorithm (in exponential time), and then using our multivariate algorithm (in polynomial time).

7   Implementation Results

We provide in Table 4 the result of practical experiments with our new algorithm; we provide the source code in https://pastebin.com/ZFk1qjfP, based on the L^2 implementation from [fpl16]. We see that for the first step, the most time consuming part is the first application of LLL to the $(2n) \times (2n)$ submatrix of $\mathcal{L}_0$; this first step produces the first n orthogonal vectors. The subsequent size-reduction (SR) produces the remaining $m - n \simeq n^2/2$ orthogonal vectors, and is much faster; for these size-reductions, we apply the technique described in Sect. 5, with the improvement described in the full version of this paper [CG20], with parameter $k = 4$. Finally, the running time of the second LLL to compute the orthogonal of $\mathcal{L}_{\mathbf{x}}^{\perp}$ has running time comparable to the first LLL. As explained previously we use the modulus bitsize $\log M \simeq 2\iota n^2 + n \cdot \log n$ with $\iota = 0.035$.

Table 4. Running time of our new algorithm, for various values of n, under a 3,2 GHz Intel Core i5 processor. We provide the source code and the complete timings in https://pastebin.com/ZFk1qjfP.

n	m	$\log M$	LLL $\mathcal{L}_0$	SR	LLL $\mathcal{L}_{\mathbf{x}}^{\perp}$	Kernel mod 3	Eigenspaces	Total
			Step 1			Step 2		
70	2590	772	3 s	3 s	1 s	8 s	7 s	24 s
90	4230	1151	10 s	8 s	5 s	23 s	17 s	66 s
110	6270	1592	32 s	18 s	11 s	52 s	37 s	153 s
130	8710	2095	87 s	40 s	26 s	112 s	71 s	6 min
150	11550	2659	3 min	70 s	48 s	3 min	122 s	12 min
170	14790	3282	7 min	125 s	81 s	5 min	3 min	20 min
190	18430	3965	23 min	3 min	3 min	9 min	5 min	46 min
220	24640	5099	54 min	7 min	34 min	18 min	8 min	124 min
250	31750	6366	119 min	12 min	65 min	30 min	15 min	245 min

In the second step, we receive as input from Step 1 an LLL-reduced basis of the lattice $\bar{\mathcal{L}}_{\mathbf{x}}$. As described in Algorithm 3 (Step 2), one must first generate a big matrix $\mathbf{E}$ of dimension roughly $n^2/2 \times n^2/2$, on which we compute the kernel $\mathbf{K} = \ker \mathbf{E}$; as explained in Sect. 4.2, this can be done modulo 3. As illustrated in Table 4, computing the kernel is the most time consuming part of Step 2. The computation of the eigenspaces (also modulo 3) to recover the original vectors $\mathbf{x}_i$ is faster.

Comparison with Nguyen-Stern. We compare the two algorithms in Table 5. We see that our polynomial time algorithm enables to solve the hidden subset-sum problem for values of n that are beyond reach for the original Nguyen-Stern attack. Namely our algorithm has heuristic complexity $\mathcal{O}(n^9)$, while the Nguyen-Stern algorithm has heuristic complexity $2^{\Omega(n/\log n)}$. However, we need more samples, namely $m \simeq n^2/2$ samples instead of $m = 2n$.

Table 5. Timing comparison between the Nguyen-Stern algorithm and our algorithm, for various values of n, where m is the number of samples from the generator.

		90	110	130	150	170	190	220	250
n									
Nguyen-Stern	m	180	220	260	300	340			
attack [NS99]	time	18 s	50 s	127 s	8 min	447 min	–	–	–
Our attack	m	4230	6270	8710	11550	14790	18430	24640	31750
	time	66 s	153 s	6 min	12 min	20 min	46 min	124 min	245 min

Reducing the number of samples. In the full version of this paper [CG20] we show how to slightly reduce the number of samples m required for our attack, with two different methods; in both cases the attack remains heuristically polynomial time under the condition $m = n^2/2 - \mathcal{O}(n \log n)$. We provide the results of practical experiments in Table 6, showing that in practice the running time grows relatively quickly for only a moderate decrease in the number of samples m.

Table 6. Running time of our new algorithm for $n = 190$, for smaller values of m, for the two methods described in the full version of this paper [CG20].

		Method 1		Method 2	
n	m	Eigenspaces	Total	Eigenspaces	Total
190	17 670	13 min	43 min	2 min	39 min
190	17 480	18 min	57 min	4 min	55 min
190	17 290	29 min	71 min	5 min	50 min
190	17 100	68 min	99 min	8 min	54 min
190	16 910	182 min	217 min	15 min	66 min
190	16 720	–	–	32 min	80 min
190	16 530	–	–	72 min	116 min

References

[Bab86] Babai, L.: On Lovász' lattice reduction and the nearest lattice point problem. Combinatorica **6**(1), 1–13 (1986)

[BNNT11] Brier, É., Naccache, D., Nguyen, P.Q., Tibouchi, M.: Modulus fault attacks against RSA-CRT signatures. In: Preneel, B., Takagi, T. (eds.) CHES 2011. LNCS, vol. 6917, pp. 192–206. Springer, Heidelberg (2011). https://doi.org/10.1007/978-3-642-23951-9_13

[BPV98] Boyko, V., Peinado, M., Venkatesan, R.: Speeding up discrete log and factoring based schemes via precomputations. In: Nyberg, K. (ed.) EUROCRYPT 1998. LNCS, vol. 1403, pp. 221–235. Springer, Heidelberg (1998). https://doi.org/10.1007/BFb0054129

[CG20] Coron, J.-S., Gini, A.: A polynomial-time algorithm for solving the hidden subset sum problem. Full version of this paper. Cryptology ePrint Archive, Report 2020/461 (2020). https://eprint.iacr.org/2020/461

[CJL+92]   Coster, M.J., Joux, A., LaMacchia, B.A., Odlyzko, A.M., Schnorr, C.-P., Stern, J.: Improved low-density subset sum algorithms. Comput. Complex. **2**, 111–128 (1992)

[CKPS00]   Courtois, N., Klimov, A., Patarin, J., Shamir, A.: Efficient algorithms for solving overdefined systems of multivariate polynomial equations. In: Preneel, B. (ed.) EUROCRYPT 2000. LNCS, vol. 1807, pp. 392–407. Springer, Heidelberg (2000). https://doi.org/10.1007/3-540-45539-6_27

[CLO05]   Cox, D.A., Little, J., Oshea, D.: Using Algebraic Geometry. Springer, New York (2005). https://doi.org/10.1007/b138611

[CLT13]   Coron, J.-S., Lepoint, T., Tibouchi, M.: Practical multilinear maps over the integers. In: Canetti, R., Garay, J.A. (eds.) CRYPTO 2013, Part I. LNCS, vol. 8042, pp. 476–493. Springer, Heidelberg (2013). https://doi.org/10.1007/978-3-642-40041-4_26

[CN11]   Chen, Y., Nguyen, P.Q.: BKZ 2.0: better lattice security estimates. In: Lee, D.H., Wang, X. (eds.) ASIACRYPT 2011. LNCS, vol. 7073, pp. 1–20. Springer, Heidelberg (2011). https://doi.org/10.1007/978-3-642-25385-0_1

[CN19]   Coron, J.-S., Notarnicola, L.: Cryptanalysis of CLT13 multilinear maps with independent slots. In: Galbraith, S.D., Moriai, S. (eds.) ASIACRYPT 2019, Part II. LNCS, vol. 11922, pp. 356–385. Springer, Cham (2019). https://doi.org/10.1007/978-3-030-34621-8_13

[CNT10]   Coron, J.-S., Naccache, D., Tibouchi, M.: Fault attacks against EMV signatures. In: Pieprzyk, J. (ed.) CT-RSA 2010. LNCS, vol. 5985, pp. 208–220. Springer, Heidelberg (2010). https://doi.org/10.1007/978-3-642-11925-5_15

[CP19]   Coron, J.-S., Pereira, H.V.L.: On Kilian's randomization of multilinear map encodings. In: Galbraith, S.D., Moriai, S. (eds.) ASIACRYPT 2019, Part II. LNCS, vol. 11922, pp. 325–355. Springer, Cham (2019). https://doi.org/10.1007/978-3-030-34621-8_12

[FLLT15]   Fouque, P.-A., Lee, M.S., Lepoint, T., Tibouchi, M.: Cryptanalysis of the Co-ACD assumption. In: Gennaro, R., Robshaw, M. (eds.) CRYPTO 2015, Part I. LNCS, vol. 9215, pp. 561–580. Springer, Heidelberg (2015). https://doi.org/10.1007/978-3-662-47989-6_27

[fpl16]   The FPLLL development team. FPLLL, a lattice reduction library (2016). https://github.com/fplll/fplll

[HPS11]   Hanrot, G., Pujol, X., Stehlé, D.: Analyzing blockwise lattice algorithms using dynamical systems. In: Rogaway, P. (ed.) CRYPTO 2011. LNCS, vol. 6841, pp. 447–464. Springer, Heidelberg (2011). https://doi.org/10.1007/978-3-642-22792-9_25

[LLL82]   Lenstra, A.K., Lenstra, H.W., Lovasz, L.: Factoring polynomials with rational coefficients. Math. Ann. **261**, 515–534 (1982). https://doi.org/10.1007/BF01457454

[LO85]   Lagarias, J.C., Odlyzko, A.M.: Solving low-density subset sum problems. J. ACM **32**(1), 229–246 (1985)

[LT15]   Lepoint, T., Tibouchi, M.: Cryptanalysis of a (somewhat) additively homomorphic encryption scheme used in PIR. In: Brenner, M., Christin, N., Johnson, B., Rohloff, K. (eds.) FC 2015. LNCS, vol. 8976, pp. 184–193. Springer, Heidelberg (2015). https://doi.org/10.1007/978-3-662-48051-9_14

[NS97]   Nguyen, P., Stern, J.: Merkle-Hellman revisited: a cryptanalysis of the Qu-Vanstone cryptosystem based on group factorizations. In: Kaliski, B.S. (ed.) CRYPTO 1997. LNCS, vol. 1294, pp. 198–212. Springer, Heidelberg (1997). https://doi.org/10.1007/BFb0052236

[NS98a] Nguyen, P., Stern, J.: The Béguin-Quisquater server-aided RSA protocol from Crypto '95 is not secure. In: Ohta, K., Pei, D. (eds.) ASIACRYPT 1998. LNCS, vol. 1514, pp. 372–379. Springer, Heidelberg (1998). https://doi.org/10.1007/3-540-49649-1_29

[NS98b] Nguyen, P., Stern, J.: Cryptanalysis of the Ajtai-Dwork cryptosystem. In: Krawczyk, H. (ed.) CRYPTO 1998. LNCS, vol. 1462, pp. 223–242. Springer, Heidelberg (1998). https://doi.org/10.1007/BFb0055731

[NS99]   Nguyen, P., Stern, J.: The hardness of the hidden subset sum problem and its cryptographic implications. In: Wiener, M. (ed.) CRYPTO 1999. LNCS, vol. 1666, pp. 31–46. Springer, Heidelberg (1999). https://doi.org/10.1007/3-540-48405-1_3

[NS09]   Nguyen, P.Q., Stehlé, D.: An LLL algorithm with quadratic complexity. SIAM J. Comput. 39(3), 874–903 (2009)

[NSS04] Naccache, D., Smart, N.P., Stern, J.: Projective coordinates leak. In: Cachin, C., Camenisch, J.L. (eds.) EUROCRYPT 2004. LNCS, vol. 3027, pp. 257–267. Springer, Heidelberg (2004). https://doi.org/10.1007/978-3-540-24676-3_16

[Sag19] The Sage Developers. Sagemath, the Sage Mathematics Software System (Version 8.9) (2019). https://www.sagemath.org

[Sch87] Schnorr, C.-P.: A hierarchy of polynomial time lattice basis reduction algorithms. Theor. Comput. Sci. 53, 201–224 (1987)

[Sho]   Shoup, V.: Number theory C++ library (NTL) version 3.6. http://www.shoup.net/ntl/

[vDGHV10] van Dijk, M., Gentry, C., Halevi, S., Vaikuntanathan, V.: Fully homomorphic encryption over the integers. In: Gilbert, H. (ed.) EUROCRYPT 2010. LNCS, vol. 6110, pp. 24–43. Springer, Heidelberg (2010). https://doi.org/10.1007/978-3-642-13190-5_2

Asymptotic Complexities of Discrete Logarithm Algorithms in Pairing-Relevant Finite Fields

Gabrielle De Micheli[(✉)], Pierrick Gaudry[(✉)], and Cécile Pierrot[(✉)]

Université de Lorraine, CNRS, Inria, LORIA, Nancy, France
gabrielle.de-micheli@inria.fr, Pierrick.Gaudry@loria.fr,
Cecile.Pierrot@inria.fr

Abstract. We study the discrete logarithm problem at the boundary case between small and medium characteristic finite fields, which is precisely the area where finite fields used in pairing-based cryptosystems live. In order to evaluate the security of pairing-based protocols, we thoroughly analyze the complexity of all the algorithms that coexist at this boundary case: the Quasi-Polynomial algorithms, the Number Field Sieve and its many variants, and the Function Field Sieve. We adapt the latter to the particular case where the extension degree is composite, and show how to lower the complexity by working in a shifted function field. All this study finally allows us to give precise values for the characteristic asymptotically achieving the highest security level for pairings. Surprisingly enough, there exist special characteristics that are as secure as general ones.

1 Introduction

The discrete logarithm problem (DLP) is one of the few hard problems at the foundation of today's public key cryptography. Widely deployed cryptosystems such as the Diffie-Hellman key exchange protocol or El Gamal's signature protocol base their security on the computational hardness of DLP. In the early 2000s, pairing-based cryptography also introduced new schemes whose security is related to the computation of discrete logarithms. Indeed, for primitives such as identity-based encryption schemes [8], identity-based signature schemes [11] or short signature schemes [9], the security relies on pairing-related assumptions that become false if the DLP is broken.

In 1994, Shor introduced a polynomial-time quantum algorithm to compute discrete logarithms. This implies that no scheme relying on the hardness of DLP would be secure in the presence of quantum computers. However, as of today, quantum computers capable of doing large scale computations are non-existent, even though impressive progress has been made in the recent years (see [2] for a recent 53-qubit machine). Still, pairing-based cryptography is at the heart of numerous security products that will continue to be brought to market in the upcoming years, and research on efficient primitives using them is very active, in particular in the zero-knowledge area with the applications of zk-SNARKs to smart contracts. Hence, evaluating the classical security of those schemes remains fundamental regardless of their post-quantum weakness.

© International Association for Cryptologic Research 2020
D. Micciancio and T. Ristenpart (Eds.): CRYPTO 2020, LNCS 12171, pp. 32–61, 2020.
https://doi.org/10.1007/978-3-030-56880-1_2

Concretely, the discrete logarithm problem is defined as follows: given a finite cyclic group G, a generator $g \in G$, and some element $h \in G$, find x such that $g^x = h$. In practice, the group G is chosen to be either the multiplicative group of a finite field $\mathbb{F}_{p^n}$ or the group of points on an elliptic curve $\mathcal{E}$ defined over a finite field. Pairing-based cryptography illustrates the need to consider both the discrete logarithm problems on finite fields and on elliptic curves. A cryptographic pairing is a bilinear and non-degenerate map $e : \mathbb{G}_1 \times \mathbb{G}_2 \to \mathbb{G}_T$ where $\mathbb{G}_1$ is a subgroup of $\mathcal{E}(\mathbb{F}_p)$, the group of points of an elliptic curve $\mathcal{E}$ defined over the prime field $\mathbb{F}_p$, $\mathbb{G}_2$ is another subgroup of $\mathcal{E}(\mathbb{F}_{p^n})$ where we consider an extension field and $\mathbb{G}_T$ is a multiplicative subgroup of that same finite field $\mathbb{F}_{p^n}$. To construct a secure protocol based on a pairing, one must assume that the DLPs in the groups $\mathbb{G}_1, \mathbb{G}_2, \mathbb{G}_T$ are hard.

Evaluating the security in $\mathbb{G}_1$ and $\mathbb{G}_2$ is straightforward, since very few attacks are known for DLP on elliptic curves. The most efficient known algorithm to solve the DLP in the elliptic curve setup is Pollard's rho algorithm which has an expected asymptotic running time equal to the square root of the size of the subgroup considered.

On the contrary, the hardness of the DLP over finite fields is much more complicated to determine. Indeed, there exist many competitive algorithms that solve DLP over finite fields and their complexities vary depending on the relation between the characteristic p and the extension degree n. When p is relatively small, quasi-polynomial time algorithms can be designed, but when p grows, the most efficient algorithms have complexity in $L_{p^n}(1/3, c)$, where the L_{p^n}-notation is defined as

$$L_{p^n}(\alpha, c) = \exp((c + o(1))(\log(p^n))^\alpha (\log \log p^n)^{1-\alpha}),$$

for $0 \leqslant \alpha \leqslant 1$ and some constant $c > 0$. We will avoid writing the constant c and simply write $L_{p^n}(\alpha)$ when the latter is not relevant.

To construct a secure protocol based on a pairing, one must first consider a group $\mathbb{G}_T$ in which quasi-polynomial time algorithms are not applicable. This implies, to the best of our knowledge, that the algorithms used to solve DLP on the finite field side have an $L_{p^n}(1/3)$ complexity. Moreover, we want the complexities of the algorithms that solve DLP on both sides to be comparable. Indeed, if the latter were completely unbalanced, an attacker could solve DLP on the easier side. A natural idea is then to equalize the complexity of DLP on both sides. This requires having $\sqrt{p} = L_{p^n}(1/3)$. Hence, the characteristic p is chosen of the form $p = L_{p^n}(1/3, c_p)$ for some constant $c_p > 0$.

Yet, when the characteristic p is of this form, many algorithms coexist rendering the estimation of the hardness of DLP all the more difficult. A recent approach, followed in [20] is to derive concrete parameters for a given security level, based on what the Number Field Sieve algorithm (NFS) would cost on these instances. Our approach complements this: we analyze the security of pairings in the asymptotic setup, thus giving insight for what would become the best compromise for higher and higher security levels.

More generally, finite fields split into three main categories. When $p = L_{p^n}(\alpha)$, we talk of large characteristic if $\alpha > 2/3$, medium characteristic if

$\alpha \in (1/3, 2/3)$, and small characteristic if $\alpha < 1/3$. The area we are interested in is thus the boundary case between small and medium characteristics.

For finite fields of medium characteristics, NFS and its variants remain as of today the most competitive algorithms to solve DLP. Originally introduced for factoring, the NFS algorithm was first adapted by Gordon in 1993 to the discrete logarithm context for prime fields [17]. A few years later, Schirokauer [40] extended it to finite fields with extension degrees $n > 1$. In [25], Joux, Lercier, Smart and Vercauteren finally showed that the NFS algorithm can be used for all finite fields. Since then, many variants of NFS have appeared, gradually improving on the complexity of NFS. The extension to the Multiple Number Field Sieve (MNFS) was originally invented for factorization [13] and was then adapted to the discrete logarithm setup [6,33]. The Tower Number Field Sieve (TNFS) [5] was introduced in 2015. When n is composite, this variant has been extended to exTNFS in [30,31]. The use of primes of a special form gives rise to another variant called the Special Number Field Sieve (SNFS) [27]. Most of these variants can be combined with each other, giving rise to MexTNFS and S(ex)TNFS.

In the case of small characteristic, Coppersmith [12] gave a first $L(1/3)$ algorithm in 1984. Introduced in 1994 by Adleman, the Function Field Sieve (FFS) [1] also tackles the DLP in finite fields with small characteristic. The algorithm follows a structure very similar to NFS, working with function fields rather than number fields. In 2006, Joux and Lercier [24] proposed a description of FFS which does not require the theory of function fields, and Joux further introduced in [21] a method, known as pinpointing, which lowers the complexity of the algorithm.

In 2013, after a first breakthrough complexity of $L_{p^n}(1/4 + o(1))$ by Joux [22], a heuristic quasi-polynomial time algorithm was designed [4] by Barbulescu, Gaudry, Joux and Thomé. Variants were explored in the following years [18,19, 26,28] with two different goals: making the algorithm more practical, and making it more amenable to a proven complexity. We mention two key ingredients. First, the so-called zig-zag descent allows to reduce the problem to proving that it is possible to rewrite the discrete logarithm of any degree-2 element in terms of the discrete logarithms of linear factors, at least if a nice representation of the finite field can be found. The second key idea is to replace a classical polynomial representation of the target finite field by a representation coming from torsion points of elliptic curves. This led to a proven complexity in 2019 by Kleinjung and Wesolowski [32]. To sum it up, the quasi-polynomial (QP) algorithms outperform all previous algorithms both theoretically and in practice in the small characteristic case.

The study of the complexities of all these algorithms at the boundary case requires a significant amount of work in order to evaluate which algorithm is applicable and which one performs best. Figure 1 gives the general picture, without any of the particular cases that can be encountered.

Contributions:

– **Thorough analysis of the complexity of FFS, NFS and its variants.**
  We first give a precise methodology for the computation of the complexity of

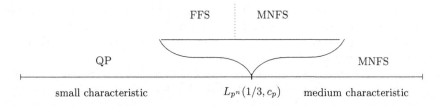

Fig. 1. Best algorithms for DLP in small, medium characteristics and at the boundary case $p = L_{p^n}(1/3, c_p)$.

NFS and its variants at the boundary case, which differs from the computations done in medium and large characteristics. We revisit some commonly accepted hypotheses and show that they should be considered with care. In addition, our analysis allowed us to notice some surprising facts. First of all, not all the variants of NFS maintain their $L_{p^n}(1/3)$ complexity at the boundary case. The variant STNFS, for example, has a much higher complexity in this area, and thus should not be used for a potential attack on pairings. For all composite extensions, the multiple variant of exTNFS is not better than exTNFS itself, and for some special characteristics, SNFS is also not faster than MNFS, as one could expect. We also distinguish and correct errors in past papers, both in previous methodologies or computations.

FFS still remains a competitor for small values of c_p. Our work then takes a closer look at its complexity, also fixing a mistake in the literature. Furthermore, in the case where the extension degree n is composite, we show how to lower the complexity of FFS by working in a *shifted* function field.

– **Crossover points between all the algorithms.** This complete analysis allows us to identify the best algorithm at the boundary case as a function of c_p and give precise crossover points for these complexities. When c_p is small enough, the FFS algorithm remains the most efficient algorithm outperforming NFS and all of its variants. When the extension degree n is prime, and the characteristic has no special form, the algorithm MNFS outperforms FFS when $c_p \geq 1.23$. When n is composite or p taken of a special form, variants such as exTNFS and SNFS give crossover points with lower values for c_p, given in this work.

Moreover, we compare the complexity of FFS and the complexity of the quasi-polynomial algorithms. Since the crossover point occurs when p grows slightly slower than $L_Q(1/3)$, we introduce a new definition in order to determine the exact crossover point between the two algorithms.

– **Security of pairings.** All the work mentioned above allows us to answer the following question: asymptotically what finite field $\mathbb{F}_{p^n}$ should be considered in order to achieve the highest level of security when constructing a pairing? To do so, we justify why equating the costs of the algorithms on both the elliptic curve side and the finite field side is correct and argue that in order for this assumption to make sense, the complete analysis given in this work was necessary. Finally, we give the optimal values of c_p for the various forms of p

and extension degree n, also taking into account the so-called ρ-value of the pairing construction. Surprising fact, we were also able to distinguish some special characteristics that are asymptotically as secure as characteristics of the same size but without any special form.

Asymptotic complexities versus practical estimates. The fact that STNFS is asymptotically no longer the best algorithm for optimally chosen pairing-friendly curves is not what could be expected from the study of [20], where fixed security levels up to 192 bits are considered. This could be interpreted as a hint that cryptanalysts have not yet reached some steady state when working at a 192-bit security level. To sum it up, evaluating the right parameters for relevant cryptographic sizes (e.g. pairings at 256-bit of security level) is still hard: estimates for lower sizes and asymptotic analysis do not match, and there is no large scale experiment using TNFS or variants to provide more insight.

Organization. In Sect. 2, we give a general description of FFS, NFS and its variants. In Sect. 3, we summarize the analysis of the complexity of FFS, and we recall the pinpointing technique. Moreover, we present our improvement for the complexity of FFS using a shifted function field. In Sect. 4, we explain our general methodology to compute the complexity of NFS and its variants at the boundary case studied in this paper. In Sect. 5, we recall the various polynomial selections that exist and are used in the various algorithms. In Sect. 6, we illustrate our methodology by detailing the complexity analyses of three variants and give results for all of them. In Sect. 7, we compute the exact crossover points between the complexities of all algorithms considered in this paper. Finally in Sect. 8, we consider the security of pairing-based protocols.

2   The General Setting of FFS, NFS and Its Variants

2.1   Overview of the Algorithms

We introduce a general description, which covers all the variants of NFS and FFS. Consider a ring R that is either $\mathbb{Z}$ in the most basic NFS, a number ring $\mathbb{Z}[\iota]/(h(\iota))$ in the case of Tower NFS, or $\mathbb{F}_p[\iota]$ in the case of FFS. This leads to the construction given in Fig. 2, where one selects V distinct irreducible polynomials $f_i(X)$ in $R[X]$ in such a way that there exist maps from $R[X]/(f_i(X))$ to the target finite field $\mathbb{F}_{p^n}$ that make the diagram commutative. For instance, in the simple case where $R = \mathbb{Z}$, this means that all the f_i's share a common irreducible factor of degree n modulo p.

Based on this construction, the discrete logarithm computation follows the same steps as any index calculus algorithm:

- Sieving: we collect relations built from polynomials $\phi \in R[X]$ of degree $t - 1$, and with bounded coefficients. If R is a ring of integers, we bound their norms, and if it is a ring of polynomials, we bound their degrees. A relation is obtained when two norms N_i and N_j of ϕ mapped to $R[X]/(f_i(X))$

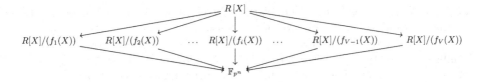

Fig. 2. General diagram for FFS, NFS and variants.

and $R[X]/(f_j(X))$ are B-smooth, for a smoothness bound B fixed during the complexity analysis. We recall that an integer (resp. a polynomial) is B-smooth if all its factors are lower than B (resp. of degree lower than B). Each relation is therefore given by a polynomial ϕ for which the diagram gives a linear equation between the (virtual) logarithms of ideals of small norms coming from two distinct number or function fields. We omit details about the notion of virtual logarithms and Schirokauer maps and refer readers to [39]. For FFS, similar technicalities can be dealt with.

- Linear algebra: The relations obtained in the previous step form a system of linear equations where the unknowns are logarithms of ideals. This system is sparse with at most $O(\log p^n)$ non-zero entries per row, and can be solved in quasi-quadratic time using the block Wiedemann algorithm [14].
- Individual logarithms: The previous step outputs the logarithms of ideals with norms smaller than the smoothness bound B used during sieving. The goal of the algorithm is to compute the discrete logarithm of an arbitrary element in the target field. The commonly used approach for this step proceeds in two sub-steps. First, the target is subject to a smoothing procedure. The latter is randomized until after being lifted in one of the fields it becomes smooth (for a smoothness bound much larger than the bound B). Second, a special-q descent method is applied to each factor obtained after smoothing which is larger than the bound B. This allows to recursively rewrite their logarithms in terms of logarithms of smaller ideals. This is done until all the factors are below B, so that their logarithms are known. This forms what is called a descent tree where the root is an ideal coming from the smoothing step, and the nodes are ideals that get smaller and smaller as they go deeper. The leaves are the ideals just above B. We refer to [16,25] for details.

2.2 Description of the Variants

Let us now describe the variants of NFS which we study in this paper, and see how they can be instantiated in our general setting.

Number Field Sieve. In this paper, we call NFS, the simplest variant, where the ring R is $\mathbb{Z}$, there are only $V = 2$ number fields, and the polynomials f_1 and f_2 are constructed without using any specific form for p or the possible compositeness of n.

Multiple Number Field Sieve. The variant **MNFS** uses V number fields, where V grows to infinity with the size of the finite field. From two polynomials f_1 and f_2 constructed as in NFS, the $V - 2$ other polynomials are built as linear combinations of f_1 and f_2: we set $f_i = \alpha_i f_1 + \beta_i f_2$, for $i \geq 3$, where the coefficients α_i, β_i are in $O(\sqrt{V})$. These polynomials have degree $\max(\deg(f_1), \deg(f_2))$ and their coefficients are of size $O(\sqrt{V} \max(\mathrm{coeff}(f_1), \mathrm{coeff}(f_2)))$.

There exist two variants of MNFS: an asymmetric one, coming from factoring [13], where the relations always involve the first number field, and a symmetric one [6], where a relation can involve any two number fields. The asymmetric variant is more natural when one of the polynomials has smaller degree or coefficients than the others. When all the polynomials have similar features, at first it could seem that the symmetric case is more advantageous, since the number of possible relations grows as V^2 instead of V. However, the search time is also increased, since for each candidate ϕ, we always have to test V norms for smoothness, while in the asymmetric setup when the first norm is not smooth we do not test the others. At the boundary case studied, we did not find any cases where the symmetric variant performed better. Hence, in the rest of the paper, when talking about MNFS, we refer to its asymmetric variant.

(Extended) Tower Number Field Sieve. The **TNFS** or **exTNFS** variants cover the cases where $R = \mathbb{Z}[\iota]/h(\iota)$, where h is a monic irreducible polynomial. In the TNFS case, the degree of h is taken to be exactly equal to n, while the exTNFS notation refers to the case where $n = \kappa\eta$ is composite and the degree of h is η. Both TNFS and exTNFS can use either two number fields or $V \gg 2$ number fields. In the latter case, the prefix letter M is added referring to the MNFS variant. Details about (M)(ex)TNFS and their variants are given in [5,30,31,38].

Special Number Field Sieve. The **SNFS** variant [27] applies when the characteristic p is the evaluation of a polynomial of small degree with constant coefficients, which is a feature of several pairing construction families. Thus, the algorithm differs from NFS in the choice of the polynomials f_1 and f_2. To date, there is no known way to combine this efficiently with the multiple variant of NFS. However, it can be applied in the (ex)TNFS setup, giving STNFS and SexTNFS.

Function Field Sieve. The FFS algorithm can be viewed in our general setting by choosing the polynomial ring $R = \mathbb{F}_p[\iota]$. The polynomials f_1 and f_2 are then bivariate, and therefore define plane curves. The algebraic structures replacing number fields are then function fields of these curves. FFS cannot be combined efficiently with a multiple variant. In fact, FFS itself is already quite similar to a special variant; this explains this difficulty to combine it with the multiple variant, and to design an even more special variant. The tower variant is relevant when n is composite, and it can be reduced to a change of base field. We discuss this further in Sect. 3.3.

In [24], Joux and Lercier proposed a slightly different setting. Although not faster than the classical FFS in small characteristic, it is much simpler, and furthermore, it gave rise to the pinpointing technique [21] which is highly relevant in our case where the characteristic is not so small. We recall their variant now, since this is the setting we will use in the rest of the paper. The algorithm starts by choosing two univariate polynomials $g_1, g_2 \in \mathbb{F}_p[x]$ of degrees n_1, n_2 respectively such that $n_1 n_2 \geq n$ and there exists a degree-n irreducible factor f of $x - g_2(g_1(x))$. Then, let us set $y = g_1(x)$. In the target finite field represented as $\mathbb{F}_p[x]/(f(x))$, we therefore also have the relation $x - g_2(y)$. The factor basis $\mathcal{F}$ is defined as the set of all univariate, irreducible, monic polynomials of degree D for some constant D, in x and y. As usual, the sieving phase computes multiplicative relations amongst elements of the factor basis, that become linear relations between discrete logarithms. We sieve over bivariate polynomials $T(x, y)$ of the form $T(x, y) = A(x)y + B(x)$, where A, B have degrees d_1, d_2 and A is monic. As an element of the finite field, this can be rewritten either as a univariate polynomial in x, namely $F_x(x) = T(x, g_1(x))$, or as a univariate polynomial in y, namely $F_y(y) = T(g_2(y), y)$. We get a relation if both $F_x(x)$ and $F_y(y)$ are D-smooth. Once enough relations are collected, the linear algebra and descent steps are performed.

Several improvements to FFS exist when the finite field is a Kummer extension. This is not addressed in this work, since the situation does not arise naturally in the pairing context, and can be easily avoided by pairing designers.

3   The FFS Algorithm at the Boundary Case

We consider a finite field of the form $\mathbb{F}_{p^n}$, where p is the characteristic and n the extension degree. From now on, we set $Q = p^n$. Since our analysis is asymptotic, any factor that is ultimately hidden in the $o(1)$ notation of the L_Q expression is ignored. Furthermore, inequalities between quantities should be understood asymptotically, and up to negligible factors.

3.1   Complexity Analysis of FFS

Our description of the complexity analysis of FFS is based on [35]. However, we slightly deviate from their notations as theirs lead to wrong complexities (see Appendix 4 of our longer version [15] of this article for details).

First, a parameter $\Delta \geq 1$ is chosen which controls the balance between the degrees of the defining polynomials g_1 and g_2. We select g_1 and g_2 of degree $\deg g_1 = n_1 = \lceil n\Delta \rceil$ and $\deg g_2 = n_2 = \lceil n/\Delta \rceil$. Since we use the pinpointing technique, which we recall in Sect. 3.2, we also enforce $g_1(x) = x^{n_1}$ or $g_2(y) = y^{n_2}$, depending on which side we want to pinpoint with.

For the analysis, the smoothness bound $D \geq 1$ is also fixed. Once c_p, Δ and D are fixed, we look at the complexity of the three steps of the algorithm. For the linear algebra, the cost $\mathcal{C}_{\text{linalg}}$ is quadratic in the size of the factor basis, and we get $\mathcal{C}_{\text{linalg}} = L_Q(1/3, 2c_p D)$. For the other steps, the complexity depends on bounds d_1 and d_2 on the degree of the polynomials A and B, used to find relations. Asymptotically, no improvement is achieved by taking $d_1 \neq d_2$. Therefore, we set the following notation: $d_{12} = d_1 = d_2$. However, the value d_{12} is not necessarily the same for the sieving and descent steps.

Analysis of the sieving step. Asymptotically, we have $\deg F_x = n_1$ and $\deg F_y = d_{12} n_2$. Note that in truth $\deg F_x = n_1 + d_{12}$ but d_{12} is a constant, hence can be ignored, since n_1 goes to infinity. From these values and the smoothness bound D, we apply Flajolet, Gourdon and Panario's theorem [34] and deduce the following smoothness probabilities P_{F_x} and P_{F_y}:

$$P_{F_x} = L_Q\left(\frac{1}{3}, \frac{-\sqrt{\Delta}}{3D\sqrt{c_p}}\right), \quad \text{and} \quad P_{F_y} = L_Q\left(\frac{1}{3}, \frac{-d_{12}}{3D\sqrt{c_p\Delta}}\right).$$

The number of (A, B) pairs to explore before having enough relations is then $P_{F_x}^{-1} P_{F_y}^{-1}$ times the size of the factor base, *i.e.*, p^D. This is feasible only if the degree d_{12} of A and B is large enough, and, recalling that A is monic, this leads to the following constraint: $p^{2d_{12}+1} \geq P_{F_x}^{-1} P_{F_y}^{-1} p^D$.

Furthermore, using the pinpointing technique allows to find relations faster than exploring them all. We simply state here that the cost per relation with pinpointing is $\min(P_{F_x}^{-1}, P_{F_y}^{-1}) + p^{-1} P_{F_x}^{-1} P_{F_y}^{-1}$. The total cost $\mathcal{C}_{\text{siev}}$ for constructing the whole set of relations is then this quantity multiplied by p^D and we get

$$\mathcal{C}_{\text{siev}} = p^{D-1} P_{F_x}^{-1} P_{F_y}^{-1} + p^D \min(P_{F_x}^{-1}, P_{F_y}^{-1}). \tag{1}$$

Analysis of the descent step. During the descent step, it can be shown that the bottleneck happens at the leaves of the descent tree, *i.e.*, when descending polynomials of degree $D + 1$, just above the smoothness bound. The smoothness probabilities P_{F_x} and P_{F_y} take the same form as for the sieving step, but the feasibility constraint and the cost are different. Since we only keep the (A, B) pairs for which the degree $D + 1$ polynomial to be descended divides the corresponding norm, we must subtract $D + 1$ degrees of freedom in the search space, which becomes $p^{2d_{12}-D}$. The descent step will therefore succeed under the following constraint: $p^{2d_{12}-D} \geq P_{F_x}^{-1} P_{F_y}^{-1}$. Indeed, the cost of descending one element is $P_{F_x}^{-1} P_{F_y}^{-1}$, as only one relation is enough. Finally, the number of nodes in a descent tree is polynomial, and the total cost $\mathcal{C}_{\text{desc}}$ of this step remains $\mathcal{C}_{\text{desc}} = P_{F_x}^{-1} P_{F_y}^{-1}$.

Overall complexity. To obtain the overall complexity for a given value of c_p, we proceed as follows: for each $\Delta \geq 1$ and $D \geq 1$, we look for the smallest value of $d_{12} \geq 1$ for which the feasibility constraint is satisfied for sieving and get the corresponding $\mathcal{C}_{\text{siev}}$; then we look for the smallest value of $d_{12} \geq 1$ such that the feasibility constraint is satisfied for the descent step and get the corresponding $\mathcal{C}_{\text{desc}}$. The maximum complexity amongst the three costs gives a complexity for these values of Δ and D. We then vary Δ and D and keep the lowest complexity. The result is shown on the left of Fig. 3, where the colors indicate which step is the bottleneck for each range of c_p values.

3.2 The Pinpointing Technique

In [21], Joux introduces a trick that allows to reduce the complexity of the sieving phase. We briefly recall the main idea in the particular case where we use

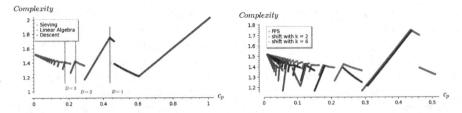

Fig. 3. On the left, the complexity of FFS at the boundary case and the dominant phase as a function of c_p, obtained after fixing the error in [35]. On the right, assuming n has appropriate factors, the lowered complexity of FFS for small values of c_p when considering shifts. In this plot, we consider $\kappa = 2, 6$. We only plot points of the curves $\mathcal{C}_2$ and $\mathcal{C}_6$ which are lower than the original FFS curve.

pinpointing on the x-side, and when $d_{12} = 1$. The polynomial g_1 is restricted to the particular form $g_1(x) = x^{n_1}$. For a pair of polynomials $A(x) = x + a$, $B(x) = bx + c$, the polynomial $F_x(x)$ becomes $F_x(x) = T(x, g_1(x)) = x^{n_1+1} + ax^{n_1} + bx + c$. One can then perform the change of variable $x \mapsto tx$ for t in $\mathbb{F}_p^*$, and, making the expression monic, one gets the following polynomial $G_t(x) = x^{n_1+1} + at^{-1}x^{n_1} + bt^{-n_1}x + ct^{-n_1-1}$. If $F_x(x)$ is D-smooth, so is $G_t(x)$, which corresponds to $F_x(x)$ with the (A, B)-pair given by $A(x) = x + at^{-1}$ and $B(x) = (bt^{-n_1}x + ct^{-n_1-1})$.

To evaluate $\mathcal{C}_{\text{siev}}$ using the pinpointing technique, we first need to consider the cost of finding the initial polynomial, *i.e.*, an (A, B)-pair such that $F_x(x)$ is D-smooth. Then, varying $t \in \mathbb{F}_p^*$ allows to produce $p - 1$ pairs which, by construction, are also smooth on the x-side. We then need to check for each of them if $F_y(y)$ is also smooth. The total cost is thus $P_{F_x}^{-1} + p$, and the number of relations obtained is pP_{F_y}. Finally the cost per relation is $P_{F_y}^{-1} + (pP_{F_x}P_{F_y})^{-1}$. By symmetry, the only difference when doing pinpointing on the y-side is the first term which is replaced by $P_{F_x}^{-1}$. Choosing the side that leads to the lowest complexity, and taking into account that we have to produce p^D relations leads to the overall complexity for the sieving step given in Eq. (1) above.

3.3   Improving the Complexity of FFS in the Composite Case

We are able to lower the complexity of FFS when the extension degree n is composite. This case often happens in pairings for efficiency reasons.

Let $n = \eta\kappa$. This means we can rewrite our target field as $\mathbb{F}_{p^n} = \mathbb{F}_{p^{\eta\kappa}} = \mathbb{F}_{p'^\eta}$, where $p' = p^\kappa$. Note that this would not work in the NFS context because p' is no longer a prime. From $p = L_Q(1/3, c_p)$, we obtain $p' = L_Q(1/3, \kappa c_p)$. Thus looking at the complexity of FFS in $\mathbb{F}_{p^n}$ for some $c_p = \alpha$ is equivalent to looking at the complexity of FFS in $\mathbb{F}_{p'^\eta}$ at some value $c_p' = \kappa\alpha$. This corresponds to a shift of the complexity by a factor of κ. More generally, assume n can be decomposed as a product of multiple factors. For each factor κ of n, one can consider the target field $\mathbb{F}_{p'^r}$, where $p' = p^\kappa$ and $r = n/\kappa$. This gives rise to a new complexity curve C_κ, shifted from the original one by a factor of κ. One can then consider the final curve $C = \min_{\kappa \geq 1} C_\kappa$, that assumes that n has many small factors. This lowers the complexity of FFS for small values of c_p as can be seen in Fig. 3. One of the most significant examples is when $c_p = (1/6) \times (2/81)^{1/3} = 0.049$. The FFS complexity is $L_Q(1/3, 1.486)$ in this case, while if n is a multiple of 6, we can use $p' = p^6$, so that we end up at the point where FFS has the lowest complexity, and we reach $L_Q(1/3, 1.165)$.

More generally, even when the characteristic is small, if $n = \eta\kappa$ is composite we can work with $\mathbb{F}_{p^\kappa}$ as a base field, and if p^κ has the appropriate size we can have a complexity that is lower than the $L_Q(1/3, (32/9)^{1/3})$ of the plain FFS in small characteristic. The optimal case is when $\kappa = (2/81)^{1/3} n^{1/3} (\log_p n)^{2/3}$. This strategy is very similar to the extended Tower NFS technique where we try to emulate the situation where the complexity of NFS is the best.

4   Tools for the Analysis of NFS and Its Variants

The main difficulty when evaluating the complexity of NFS is the amount of parameters that influence in a non-trivial way the running time or even the termination of the algorithm. In this section we explain our methodology to find the set of parameters leading to the fastest running time. We do not consider the space complexity. Indeed, in all the variants of NFS under study, the memory requirement is dominated by the space required to store the matrix of relations, which is equal (up to logarithmic factors) to the square root of the running time to find a kernel vector in this matrix.

4.1   General Methodology

Parameters and their constraints. As often done in an asymptotic complexity analysis, even if parameters are assumed to be integers, they are considered as real numbers. This is a meaningful modelling as long as the numbers tend to infinity since the rounding to the nearest integer will have a negligible effect. In some of the variants, however, some integer parameters remain bounded. This is the case for instance of the (r, k) parameters in MNFS-$\mathcal{A}$, detailed in Sect. 6. We call continuous parameters the former, and discrete parameters the latter.

The analysis will be repeated independently for all values of the discrete parameters, so that we now concentrate on how to optimize the continuous parameters for a given choice of discrete parameters. We call a set of parameters valid if the algorithm can be run and will finish with a high probability. Many parameters are naturally constrained within a range of possible values in $\mathbb{R}$. For instance, a smoothness bound must be positive. In addition, one must consider another general constraint to ensure the termination of the algorithm: the number of relations produced by the algorithm for a given choice of parameters must be larger than the size of the factor basis. We will refer to this constraint as the Main Constraint in the rest of the paper.

This inequality can be turned into an equality with the following argument (similarly as in Sect. 3, equality is up to asymptotically negligible factors). Assume a set of parameters gives a minimum running time, and for these parameters the number of relations is strictly larger than the size of the factor basis. Then, by reducing the bound on the coefficients of the polynomials ϕ used for sieving, one can reduce the cost of the sieving phase, while the costs of linear algebra and individual logarithm steps stay the same. Therefore, one can construct a new set of parameters with a smaller running time.

The costs of the three phases. Let $\mathcal{C}_{\text{siev}}, \mathcal{C}_{\text{linalg}}$ and $\mathcal{C}_{\text{desc}}$ be the costs of the three main phases of NFS. The overall cost of computing a discrete logarithm is then the sum of these three quantities. Up to a constant factor in the running time, the optimal cost can be deduced by minimizing the maximum of these three costs instead of their sum. Given the form of the formulas in terms of the parameters, this will be much easier to handle.

A natural question that arises is whether, at the optimum point, one cost "obviously" dominates the others or on the contrary is negligible. The two following statements were previously given without justification and we correct this issue here. First, the best running time is obtained for parameters where the linear algebra and the sieving steps take a similar time. We explain why there is no reason to believe this assumption is necessarily true. Secondly, the cost of the individual logarithm step is negligible. We justify this in this setting with a theoretical reason.

Equating the cost of sieving and linear algebra. In the most simple variant of NFS for solving the discrete logarithm in a prime field using two number fields, the best complexity is indeed obtained at a point where linear algebra and sieving have the same cost. However, we would like to emphasize that this is not the result of an "obvious" argument. Let us assume that the linear algebra is performed with an algorithm with complexity $O(N^\omega)$, where ω is a constant. The matrix being sparse, the only lower bound we have on ω is 1, while the best known methods [14] give $\omega = 2$. By re-analyzing the complexity of NFS for various values of ω, we observe that the optimal cost is obtained at a point where the linear algebra and the sieving have similar costs only when $\omega \geq 2$. Were there to be a faster algorithm for sparse linear algebra with a value of ω strictly less than 2, the complexity obtained with $\mathcal{C}_{\text{siev}} = \mathcal{C}_{\text{linalg}}$ would not be optimal. Therefore, any "obvious" argument for equating those costs should take into account that the current best exponent for sparse linear algebra is 2.

Negligible cost of individual logarithm step. As explained previously, the individual logarithm phase consists of two steps: a smoothing step and a descent by special-q. We refer to [16, Appendix A] where a summary of several variants is given, together with the corresponding complexities. The smoothing part is somewhat independent and has a complexity in $L_Q(1/3, 1.23)$, that is lower than all the other complexities. Note however that [16] does not cover the case where a discrete logarithm in an extension field is sought. The adaptation can be found in [6, Appendix A] and the complexity remains the same. For the special-q descent step, the analysis of [16] does not need to be adapted, since all the computations take place at the level of number fields. Using sieving with large degree polynomials, it is shown that all the operations except for the ones at the leaves of the descent trees take a negligible time $L_Q(1/3, o(1))$. Finally the operations executed at the leaves of the tree are very similar to the ones performed during sieving to find a single relation. Therefore they also take a negligible time compared to the entire sieving step that must collect an $L_Q(1/3)$ subexponential quantity of relations, while we only require a polynomial quantity for the descent. As a consequence, in the context of NFS and its variants, the individual logarithm phase takes a much smaller time than the sieving phase.

Overall strategy for optimizing the complexity. First we fix values for the discrete parameters. Since these values are bounded in our model, there are only finitely many choices. We then apply the following recursive strategy where all the local minima encountered are compared in the end and the smallest is returned. The strategy executes the following two steps. First, in the subvariety of valid parameters satisfying the Main Constraint, search for local minima of the cost assuming $\mathcal{C}_{\mathrm{siev}} = \mathcal{C}_{\mathrm{linalg}}$. Then, recurse on each plausible boundary of the subvariety of parameters.

In order for our analysis to remain as general as possible, we have also considered the case where the costs of sieving and linear algebra are not equal. We then look for local minima for $\mathcal{C}_{\mathrm{siev}}$ and see if this results in a lower complexity. We do not detail this case since this situation has not occurred in our analyses, but we insist on the necessity to perform these checks.

We emphasize that we have indeed to first look for minima in the interior of the space of valid parameters and then recurse on its boundaries. This is imposed by the technique we use to find local minima. Indeed, we assume that all the quantities considered are regular enough to use Lagrange multipliers. However, this technique cannot be used to find a minimum that would lie on a boundary. This is the case for example of STNFS as explained in Sect. 6.3.

In general, only few cases are to be considered. For instance, except for a few polynomial selection methods, there are no discrete parameters. Also, boundary cases are often non-plausible, for example, when the factor base bound tends to zero or infinity. Some cases are also equivalent to other variants of NFS, for instance when the number of number fields in MNFS goes to zero, the boundary case is the plain NFS.

Notations. In the analysis of NFS and its variants, parameters that grow to infinity with the size Q of the finite field must be chosen with the appropriate form to guarantee an overall $L_Q(1/3)$ complexity. We summarize in Table 1 the notations used for these parameters, along with their asymptotic expressions. For convenience, in order to have all the notations at the same place, we include parameters that will be introduced later in the paper.

Table 1. Notations and expressions for most of the quantities involved in the analysis of NFS and its variants.

Notation	Asympt. expression	Definition
General parameters		
p	$L_Q(1/3, c_p)$	Characteristic of finite field $\mathbb{F}_Q$, where $Q = p^n$
n	$\frac{1}{c_p}\left(\frac{\log Q}{\log\log Q}\right)^{2/3}$	Exponent of finite field $\mathbb{F}_Q$, where $Q = p^n$
B	$L_Q(1/3, c_B)$	Smoothness bound
t	$\frac{c_t}{c_p}\left(\frac{\log Q}{\log\log Q}\right)^{1/3}$	Degree of the sieving polynomials ϕ
A	$(\log Q)^{c_A c_p}$	Bound on coefficients of ϕ. Note $A^t = L_Q(1/3, c_A c_t)$
P	$L_Q(1/3, p_r)$	Probability that ϕ leads to a relation
MNFS parameters		
V	$L_Q(1/3, c_V)$	Number of number fields in MNFS
B'	$L_Q(1/3, c_{B'})$	Second smoothness bound for asymmetric MNFS
P_1	$L_Q(1/3, p_{r1})$	Probability of smoothness in the first number field
P_2	$L_Q(1/3, p_{r2})$	Probability of smoothness in any other number field
Other parameters		
d	$\delta\left(\frac{\log Q}{\log\log Q}\right)^{2/3}$	Degree of polynomial in the case of JLSV2
η	$c_\eta\left(\frac{\log Q}{\log\log Q}\right)^{1/3}$	Factor of n in the case of (ex)TNFS; $\deg h = \eta$
κ	$c_\kappa\left(\frac{\log Q}{\log\log Q}\right)^{1/3}$	Other factor of n in the case of (ex)TNFS; $c_\kappa = \frac{1}{c_p c_\eta}$

4.2 Smoothness Probability

During the sieving phase, we search for B-smooth norms. A key assumption in the analysis is that the probability of a norm being smooth is the same as that of a random integer of the same size. This allows us to apply the theorem by Canfield-Erdős-Pomerance [10]. We use the following specific version:

Corollary 1. *Let $(\alpha_1, \alpha_2, c_1, c_2)$ be four real numbers such that $1 > \alpha_1 > \alpha_2 > 0$ and $c_1, c_2 > 0$. Then the probability that a random positive integer below $L_Q(\alpha_1, c_1)$ splits into primes less than $L_Q(\alpha_2, c_2)$ is given by*

$$L_Q\left(\alpha_1 - \alpha_2, (\alpha_1 - \alpha_2)c_1 c_2^{-1}\right)^{-1}.$$

The norms are estimated based on their expressions as resultants. In the classical (non-tower) version of NFS, for a given candidate ϕ, the norm N_i in the i-th number field given by f_i takes the form $N_i = c\operatorname{Res}(f_i, \phi)$, where c is a constant coming from the leading coefficient of f_i that can be considered smooth (possibly by including its large prime factors in the factor basis).

The definition of the resultant as the determinant of the Sylvester matrix gives a bound that follows from Hadamard's inequality (see [7]):

$$|\operatorname{Res}(f_i, \phi)| \le (d+1)^{(t-1)/2} t^{d/2} ||f_i||_\infty^{(t-1)} ||\phi||_\infty^d,$$

where $d = \deg f$ and $t = 1 + \deg h$. Note that in our setting, d must be larger than n which is roughly in $(\log Q)^{2/3}$, while t is in $(\log Q)^{1/3}$, so that the factor $(d+1)^{(t-1)/2}$ will be negligible but the factor $t^{d/2}$ will not.

A note on Kalkbrener's corollary. Recent papers including [3,27,36,37] have mentioned a result from Kalkbrener [29] to upper bound the value of the combinatoric term that appears in the resultant. In [29], Theorem 2 counts the number of monomials in the matrix. However, two permutations can give the same monomial, and thus the number of permutations is not bounded by the number of monomials. We emphasize that this result cannot be used this way; this error leads to wrong (and underestimated) complexities. Indeed combinatorial terms cannot be neglected at the boundary case.

When analyzing tower variants (see [30, Lemma 1] and [38, Equation 5]), the ring R is $\mathbb{Z}[\iota]/h(\iota)$, and in all cases, the optimal value for the degree of $\phi(X)$ is 1 (i.e. $t = 2$, in the general setting). A polynomial ϕ is therefore of the form $\phi(X) = a(\iota) + b(\iota)X$, where a and b are univariate polynomials over $\mathbb{Z}$ of degree less than $\deg h$, with coefficients bounded in absolute value by A. Up to a constant factor which can be assumed to be smooth without loss of generality, the norm $N_i(\phi)$ in the field defined by $f_i(X)$ is then given by $\mathrm{Res}_\iota\left(\mathrm{Res}_X\left(a(\iota) + b(\iota)X, f_i(X)\right), h(\iota)\right)$, and this can be bounded in absolute value by

$$|N_i(\phi)| \leq A^{(\deg h)(\deg f_i)}||f_i||_\infty^{\deg h}||h||_\infty^{\deg f_i((\deg h)-1)} C(\deg h, \deg f_i),$$

the combinatorial contribution C being $C(x,y) = (x+1)^{(3y+1)x/2}(y+1)^{3x/2}$.

In the case of TNFS where n is prime, the degree of h is equal to n, thus both factors of the combinatorial contribution are non-negligible. On the other hand, when $n = \eta\kappa$ is composite with appropriate factor sizes, one can use exTNFS and take $\deg h = \eta$ and $\deg f \geq \kappa$, in such a way that only the first factor of C will contribute in a non-negligible way to the size of the norm.

4.3   Methodology for the Complexity Analysis of NFS

During sieving, we explore A^t candidates, for which a smoothness test is performed. A single smoothness test with ECM has a cost that is non-polynomial, but since it is sub-exponential in the smoothness bound, it will be in $L_Q(1/6)$ and therefore contribute only in the $o(1)$ in the final complexity. We therefore count it as a unit cost in our analysis. In the plain NFS, the cost of sieving is therefore A^t. In the asymmetric MNFS, we should in principle add the cost of testing the smoothness of the $V - 1$ remaining norms when the first one is smooth. With the notations of Table 1, the sieving cost is therefore $A^t(1+P_1V)$. In what follows, we will assume that $P_1V \ll 1$, i.e. $p_{r1}+c_V < 0$ and check at the end that this hypothesis is valid. As for the linear algebra, the cost is quadratic in the size of the factor basis. According to the prime number theorem, the number of prime ideals of norm bounded by B is proportional to B up to a logarithmic factor. In the asymmetric MNFS setting, the cost is $(B+VB')^2$, and in general, we balance the two terms and set $B = VB'$. Therefore, in the main case where we assume equality between sieving and linear algebra, for both the plain NFS and the asymmetric MNFS variant we get $A^t = B^2$.

The Main Constraint also requires to have as many relations as the size of the factor bases. This translates into the equation $A^t P = B$, where P is the probability of finding a relation, which is equal to $P_1 P_2 V$ in the MNFS case. Combining this with the first constraint simplifies to $BP = 1$, or, in terms of exponents in the L-notation:

$$p_r + c_B = 0, \tag{2}$$

where $p_r = p_{r_1} + p_{r_2} + c_V$ in the case of MNFS.

From the characteristics of the polynomials outputted by the polynomial selection, one can use the formulae of Sect. 4.2 to express p_r in terms of the parameters c_B, c_t, and also c_V in the MNFS case. Note that we use the equation $A^t = B^2$ to rewrite c_A as $c_A = 2c_B/c_t$.

It remains to find a minimum for the cost of the algorithm under the constraint given by Eq. (2). To do so, we use Lagrange multipliers. Let $c = p_r + c_B$ be the constraint seen as a function of the continuous parameters. The Lagrangian function is given by $\mathcal{L}(\text{parameters}, \lambda) = 2c_B + \lambda c$, where λ is an additional non-zero variable. At a local minimum for the cost, all the partial derivatives of $\mathcal{L}$ are zero, and this gives a system of equations with as many equations as indeterminates (not counting c_p which is seen as a fixed parameter). Since all the equations are polynomials, it is then possible to use Gröbner basis techniques to express the minimum complexity as a function of c_p.

More precisely, in the case of the asymmetric MNFS where the variables are c_B, c_t and c_V, the system of equations is

$$\begin{cases} \frac{\partial \mathcal{L}}{\partial c_B} = 2 + \lambda \frac{\partial c}{\partial c_B} = 0 \\ \frac{\partial \mathcal{L}}{\partial c_t} = \lambda \frac{\partial c}{\partial c_t} = 0 \\ \frac{\partial \mathcal{L}}{\partial c_V} = \lambda \frac{\partial c}{\partial c_V} = 0 \\ p_{r1} + p_{r2} + c_V + c_B = 0 \ , \end{cases}$$

where the first equation plays no role in the resolution, but ensures that λ is non-zero, thus allowing to remove the λ in the second and third equation. This becomes an even simpler system in the case of the plain NFS, where the parameter c_V is no longer present, thus leading to the system

$$\begin{cases} \frac{\partial c}{\partial c_t} = 0 \\ p_r + c_B = 0 \ . \end{cases}$$

In the case where the expressions depend on discrete parameters, we can keep them in the formulae (without computing partial derivatives with respect to them, which would not make sense) and compute a parametrized Gröbner basis. If this leads to a system for which the Gröbner basis computation is too hard, then we can instantiate some or all the discrete parameters and then solve the system for each choice.

The cases not covered by the above setting, including the cases where we do not assume equality between sieving and linear algebra are handled similarly.

5 Polynomial Selections

The asymptotic complexity of all the algorithms presented in Sect. 2 depends on the characteristics of the polynomials outputted by the polynomial selection method considered. We briefly summarize in this section the various existing polynomial selection methods. We distinguish the cases when n is composite and when p is of a special form, which leads to considering different algorithms. The parameters for all the polynomial selections we are going to consider are summarized in Table 2.

5.1 Polynomial Selections for NFS and MNFS

We first list the methods where no particular considerations are made on the extension degree n or the characteristic p.

JLSV0. This is the simplest polynomial method there exists. We consider a polynomial f_1 of degree n irreducible mod p such that the coefficients of f_1 are in $O(1)$. We construct $f_2 = f_1 + p$ and thus coefficients of f_2 are in $O(p)$ and the degree of f_2 is also n. Then trivially we have the condition that $f_2 | f_1 \mod p$ as required for the algorithms to work.

JLSV1. This method was introduced in [25] and we refer to the paper for details. We only note here that the degree of the polynomials outputted are the same as those of JLSV0. However, the size of coefficients are balanced as opposed to JLSV0. This difference does not affect the overall complexity of the algorithm.

JLSV2. This polynomial selection is presented in [25]. This method uses lattices to output the second polynomial, the idea being that in order to produce a polynomial with small coefficients, the latter are chosen to be the coefficients of a short vector in a reduced lattice basis.

GJL. The Generalized Joux-Lercier (GJL) method is an extension to the non-prime fields of the method presented in 2003 by Joux and Lercier in [23]. It was proposed by Barbulescu, Gaudry, Guillevic and Morain in [3, Paragraph 6.2], and uses lattice reduction to build polynomials with small coefficients.

Conjugation. In [3], the authors propose two new polynomial selection methods, one of which is Conjugation. It uses a continued fraction method like JLSV1 and the existence of some square roots in $\mathbb{F}_p$.

Algorithm $\mathcal{A}$. We recall in [15, Appendix B] Algorithm $\mathcal{A}$ as given in [37] and refer to [37] for more details about it. This algorithm also uses lattices to output the second polynomial and introduces two new parameters: d and r such that $r \geq \frac{n}{d} := k$. The parameters r and k are discrete in the complexity analysis. Note that the parameter d used in this polynomial selection is also discrete whereas the polynomial degree also denoted d used in JLSV2 and GJL is continuous.

5.2 Polynomial Selections for exTNFS and MexTNFS

We now look at polynomial selections with composite extension degree $n = \eta\kappa$. The most general algorithms are the algorithms $\mathcal{B}, \mathcal{C}$ and $\mathcal{D}$ presented in [36,38] that extend algorithm $\mathcal{A}$ to the composite case. Thus, the construction of the polynomials f_1 and f_2 follow very similar steps as the ones in algorithm $\mathcal{A}$. We merely point out the main differences with algorithm $\mathcal{A}$. These algorithms require the additional condition $\gcd(\eta, \kappa) = 1$. Similarly as for algorithm $\mathcal{A}$, they introduce two new parameters: d and r such that $r \geq \kappa/d := k$.

Algorithm $\mathcal{B}$. This algorithm is identical to algorithm $\mathcal{A}$ adapted to the composite setup where $n = \eta\kappa$. Note that if $\eta = 1$ and $\kappa = n$, we recover algorithm $\mathcal{A}$. For convenience, we recall it in [15, Appendix B].

Algorithms $\mathcal{C}$ and $\mathcal{D}$. The polynomial selection $\mathcal{C}$ is another extension of $\mathcal{A}$ to the setup of exTNFS. It introduces a new variable $\lambda \in [1, \eta]$ that plays a crucial role in controlling the size of the coefficients of f_2. However, in our case, when analysing the complexity of M(ex)TNFS-$\mathcal{C}$ one realizes that the lowest complexity is achieved when $\lambda = 1$ which brings us back to the analysis of $\mathcal{B}$. As for algorithm $\mathcal{D}$, this is a variant that allows to replace the condition $\gcd(\eta, \kappa) = 1$ by the weaker condition $\gcd(\eta, k) = 1$. Since the outputted polynomials share again the same properties as algorithm $\mathcal{B}$, the complexity analysis is identical. Therefore, we will not consider $\mathcal{C}$ or $\mathcal{D}$ in the rest of the paper.

5.3 Polynomial Selections for SNFS and STNFS

For SNFS and STNFS, the prime p is given as the evaluation of a polynomial P of some degree λ and with small coefficients. In particular, we can write $p = P(u)$, for $u \approx p^{1/\lambda}$. Note that the degree λ is a fixed parameter which does not depend on p. We summarize the construction of the polynomials f_1 and f_2 given in [27]. The first polynomial f_1 is defined as an irreducible polynomial over $\mathbb{F}_p$ of degree n and can be written as $f_1(X) = X^n + R(X) - u$, where R is a polynomial of small degree and coefficients taken in the set $\{-1, 0, 1\}$. The polynomial R does not depend on P so $||f_1||_\infty = u$, and from $p = P(u)$ we get $||f_1||_\infty = p^{1/\lambda}$. The polynomial f_2 is chosen to be $f_2(X) = P(f_1(X) + u)$. This implies $f_2(X)$ $\pmod{f_1(X)} = p$, and thus $f_2(X)$ is a multiple of $f_1(X)$ modulo p.

6 Complexity Analyses of (M)(ex)(T)NFS

Following the method explained in Sect. 4, we have computed the complexities of the algorithms presented in Sect. 2 with the polynomial selections given in Sect. 5. We report the norms and the complexities in Table 3. Since each norm has the form $L_Q(2/3, c)$, and each complexity has the form $L_Q(1/3, c)$, we only report the values of c. We illustrate our methodology by giving details of the computation of the complexity analysis of the best performing variants.

6.1 (M)NFS

In the case of (M)NFS, the best complexity is achieved by the MNFS variant using the polynomial selection $\mathcal{A}$ and when equating the cost of sieving and of

Table 2. Parameters of the polynomials f_1, f_2 outputted by various polynomial selection methods for (M)NFS in the first table, (M)exTNFS in the second table and S(T)NFS in the third table.

Polynomial	NFS				MNFS			
selection	$\deg f_1$	$\deg f_2$	$\|\|f_1\|\|_\infty$	$\|\|f_2\|\|_\infty$	$\deg f_1$	$\deg f_2$	$\|\|f_1\|\|_\infty$	$\|\|f_2\|\|_\infty$
JLSV0	n	n	$O(1)$	$O(p)$	$-$	$-$	$-$	$-$
JLSV1	n	n	$O(\sqrt{p})$	$O(\sqrt{p})$	n	n	$O(\sqrt{p})$	$O(\sqrt{V}\sqrt{p})$
JLSV2	n	$d > n$	$O(p^{n/(d+1)})$	$O(p^{n/(d+1)})$	n	$d > n$	$O(p^{n/(d+1)})$	$O(\sqrt{V}p^{n/(d+1)})$
GJL	$d+1 > n$	d	$O(1)$	$O(p^{n/(d+1)})$	$d+1 > n$	d	$O(1)$	$O(\sqrt{V}p^{n/(d+1)})$
Conjugation	$2n$	n	$O(\log p)$	$O(\sqrt{p})$	$2n$	n	$O(\log p)$	$O(\sqrt{V}\sqrt{p})$
$\mathcal{A}$	$d(r+1)$	dr	$O(\log p)$	$O(p^{n/d(r+1)})$	$d(r+1)$	dr	$O(\log p)$	$O(\sqrt{V}p^{n/d(r+1)})$

Polynomial	exTNFS				MexTNFS			
selection	$\deg f_1$	$\deg f_2$	$\|\|f_1\|\|_\infty$	$\|\|f_2\|\|_\infty$	$\deg f_1$	$\deg f_2$	$\|\|f_1\|\|_\infty$	$\|\|f_2\|\|_\infty$
JLSV2	κ	$d > \kappa$	$O(p^{\kappa/(d+1)})$	$O(p^{\kappa/(d+1)})$	κ	$d > \kappa$	$O(p^{\kappa/(d+1)})$	$O(\sqrt{V}p^{\kappa/(d+1)})$
$\mathcal{B}$	$d(r+1)$	dr	$O(\log p)$	$O(p^{k/(r+1)})$	$d(r+1)$	dr	$O(\log p)$	$O(\sqrt{V}p^{k/(r+1)})$

Polynomial selection	$\deg f_1$	$\deg f_2$	$\|\|f_1\|\|_\infty$	$\|\|f_2\|\|_\infty$
SNFS	n	$n\lambda$	$p^{1/\lambda}$	$O((\log n)^\lambda)$
STNFS	κ	$\kappa\lambda$	$p^{1/\lambda}$	$O\left((\log \kappa)^\lambda\right)$

linear algebra. The continuous parameters to consider in this case are B, A, t, V, and the discrete parameters are r and k.

The norms of the polynomials outputted by the polynomial selection $\mathcal{A}$ are bounded by $t^{d(r+1)/2}(d(r+1))^t(\log p)^t A^{d(r+1)}$ and $t^{dr/2}(dr)^t Q^{t/d(r+1)}\sqrt{V}^t A^{dr}$. Using Corollary 1, we compute the probabilities of smoothness for both norms. The constants in the L_Q notation for these probabilities are given by $p_{r1} = \frac{-1}{3c_B}\left(\frac{r+1}{6kc_p} + \frac{(r+1)c_A}{k}\right)$, and $p_{r2} = \frac{-1}{3(c_B - c_V)}\left(\frac{r}{6kc_p} + \frac{rc_A}{k} + \frac{kc_t}{r+1} + \frac{c_t c_V}{2c_p}\right)$. Using the condition $P = 1/B$ allows us to obtain a non-linear equation in the various parameters considered. In order to minimize $2c_B$ under this non-linear constraint, we use Lagangre multipliers and solve the system exhibited in Sect. 4 with Gröbner basis. This allows us to obtain an equation of degree 15 in c_B, degree 9 in c_p, and degrees 10 and 8 in r and k. The equation is given in [15, Appendix C]. Recall that r and k are discrete values. One can loop over the possible values of r, k and keep the values which give the smallest complexity. When $c_p \geq 1.5$, the optimal set of parameters is given by $(r, k) = (1, 1)$. When $1.2 \leq c_p \leq 1.4$, the values of (r, k) need to be increased to find a valid complexity. For $c_p \leq 1.1$, no values of (r, k) allow us to find a positive root for c_V, thus there is no valid complexity with this method.

The last step of our strategy consists in recursing on each plausible boundary of the subvariety of parameters. This case is already covered by the previous steps. Indeed, the only parameter where it makes sense to consider the boundary is V, and when the latter goes to zero, this means we are considering NFS again.

An attempt at lowering the complexity of MNFS. Some polynomial selections such as $\mathcal{A}$ and JLSV2 output two polynomials f_1 and f_2 where f_2 is taken to be the polynomial which coefficients are the coefficients of the shortest vector in an LLL-reduced lattice of some dimension D. The remaining $V - 2$ number fields are defined by polynomials which are linear combinations of f_1 and f_2. From the properties of LLL, we assume the vectors in the LLL-reduced basis have similar norms. Instead of building f_i as $\alpha_i f_1 + \beta_i f_2$ where $\alpha_i, \beta_i \approx \sqrt{V}$, one can take a linear combination of more short vectors, and thus have $f_i = \alpha_{i,1} f_1 + \alpha_{i,2} f_2 + \cdots + \alpha_{i,D} f_D$ and $\alpha_{i,j} \approx V^{1/2D}$. However, this does not affect the asymptotic complexity. When $c_p \to \infty$, the coefficient term becomes negligible. On the other hand, when c_p is small, the norms become smaller and this results in a slightly lower complexity. However the gain is very small, nearly negligible.

When looking at TNFS. We consider a linear polynomial g and a polynomial f of degree d where both polynomials have coefficients of size $O\left(p^{1/(d+1)}\right)$. This corresponds to the naive base-m polynomial selection. The TNFS setup requires a polynomial h of degree n with coefficients of size $O(1)$. As usual, to compute the complexity, we are interested in the size of the norms. This is given in Sect. 4.2 and when evaluating the term $C(n, d)$, which is not negligible due to the size of n as opposed to the large characteristic case presented in [5], we note that the overall complexity of TNFS at this boundary case is greater than the usual $L_Q(1/3)$. Indeed, we have

$$\log C(n, d) = \frac{\delta}{c_p} (\log Q)^{4/3} (\log\log Q)^{-1/3} + \frac{4}{3c_p} (\log Q)^{2/3} (\log\log Q)^{1/3}.$$

Since $(\log Q)^{4/3} (\log\log Q)^{-1/3} > (\log Q)^{2/3} (\log\log Q)^{1/3}$ for large enough value of Q, we have $C(n, d) > L_Q(2/3, x)$ for any constant $x > 0$. Thus this algorithm is not applicable in this case. Moreover, if we write $p = L_Q(\alpha, c)$, this argument is valid as soon as $\alpha \leq 2/3$.

6.2   (M)exTNFS

When the extension degree $n = \eta\kappa$ is composite, using the extended TNFS algorithm and its multiple field variant allows to lower the overall complexity.

Before starting the complexity analysis, we want to underline a main difference with other analyses seen previously. So far, the degree t of the sieving polynomials has always been taken to be a function of $\log Q$, i.e., we usually set $t = \frac{c_t}{c_p} \left(\frac{\log Q}{\log\log Q} \right)^{1/3}$. In the following analysis, the value of t is a discrete value. Indeed, if one chooses to analyze the complexity using t as a function of $\log Q$, we get the following value in the product of the norms: $Q^{(t-1)/(d(r+1))} = L_Q(1, kc_t c_\eta/(r + 1))$. This implies that the norms become too big to give a final complexity in $L_Q(1/3)$.

We now concentrate on the analysis of exTNFS, using Algorithm $\mathcal{B}$. Continuous parameters are B, A, η and the discrete values are r, k, t. For simplicity we report only the case $t = 2$. The product of the norms is given by

$$N_1 N_2 = A^{\eta d(2r+1)} p^{k\eta/(r+1)} C(\eta, dr) C(\eta, d(r+1)).$$

The two combinatorial terms are not negligible at this boundary case. The probability of getting relations is given by

$$P = L_Q \left(\frac{1}{3}, \frac{-1}{3c_B} \left(\frac{(2r+1)c_A}{k} + \frac{kc_\eta c_p}{r+1} + \frac{2r+1}{2kc_p} \right) \right),$$

and using the condition $P = 1/B$ allows us to obtain a non-linear equation in the various parameters considered. In order to minimize $2c_B$ under this non-linear constraint, we use Lagrange multipliers and solve the system exhibited in Sect. 4 with a Gröbner basis approach. This allows us to obtain an equation of degree 4 in c_B and r and degree 2 in c_p and k. The equation is given in [15, Appendix C]. Since r, k are discrete values, one can then loop through their possible values and pick the ones which give the smallest complexity.

A note on the JLSV2 polynomial selection. When considering the JLSV2 polynomial selection for exTNFS (same for MexTNFS), the norms are bounded by

$$|N_1| < A^{\eta\kappa} \|f\|_\infty^\eta C(\eta, \kappa) = A^{\eta\kappa} p^{\kappa\eta/(d+1)} C(\eta, \kappa),$$
$$|N_2| < A^{\eta d} \|g\|_\infty^\eta C(\eta, d) = A^{\eta d} p^{\kappa\eta/(d+1)} C(\eta, d).$$

The terms $C(\eta, \kappa)$ and $C(\eta, d)$ are not negligible in this case, and $C(\eta, \kappa) = L_Q(2/3, c_\eta c_\kappa/2)$. Similarly, we have $C(\eta, d) = L_Q(2/3, \delta c_\eta/2)$. By looking at the first term of N_2, that is $A^{\eta d}$, and the value of $C(\eta, d)$, one notes that the norm is minimized when $\eta = 1$. This means that n is not composite. Thus, no improvement to JLSV2 can be obtained by considering a composite n.

6.3 S(T)NFS

We give as an example the complexity analysis of SNFS and then explain why STNFS is not applicable at this boundary case.

SNFS. From the characteristics of the polynomials outputted by the polynomial selection used for SNFS given in Table 2, we compute the product of the norms which is given by $N_1 N_2 = n^{2t} \lambda^t t^{n(\lambda+1)} p^{1/\lambda} A^{n(\lambda+1)} (\log(n))^{\lambda t}$. The probability that both norms are smooth is given by $\mathcal{P} = L_Q \left(\frac{1}{3}, \frac{-1}{3c_B} \left(\frac{\lambda+1}{3c_p} + (\lambda+1)c_A + \frac{c_t}{\lambda} \right) \right)$. We consider the usual constraint given by the NFS analysis, $c_B + p = 0$. By deriving this constraint with respect to c_t and using a Gröbner basis approach, we obtain the following equation of c_B as a function of c_p:

$$81 c_B^4 c_p^2 \lambda^2 - 18 c_B^2 c_p \lambda^3 - 18 c_B^2 c_p \lambda^2 - 72 c_B c_p^2 \lambda^2 - 72 c_B c_p^2 \lambda + \lambda^4 + 2\lambda^3 + \lambda^2 = 0.$$

When $c_p \to \infty$, the complexity is given by $2c_B = (64(\lambda+1)/(9\lambda))^{1/3}$. When $\lambda = 1$, this value is equal to $(128/9)^{1/3}$. When $\lambda \geq 2$, the complexity becomes better than $(128/9)^{1/3}$. If λ is chosen to be a function of $\log Q$, for example if $\lambda = n$, then the norms become too big, and the resulting complexity is much higher. The complexity of SNFS for various values of λ is given in Fig. 4.

STNFS. We look at the composite case where $n = \eta\kappa$ and consider the exTNFS algorithm with the special variant. From Table 2, we have the following norms: $N_1 = A^n p^{\eta/\lambda} C(\eta, \kappa)$ and $N_2 = A^{n\lambda} (\log \kappa)^{n\lambda} C(\eta, \kappa\lambda)$.

First, the term $(\log \kappa)^{n\lambda}$ is negligible due to the size of κ and η. Among the remaining terms, for a fixed λ value, one can see that the size of the norms is minimized when $\eta = 1$, thus when n is not composite. Hence, applying the special variant to the exTNFS algorithm will not output any valid complexity. The STNFS algorithm can be used in medium characteristics as shown in [30]. In this case, the value of λ is chosen to be a function of $\log Q$, and allows to obtain a minimal value for the complexity where the value of η is not necessarily equal to 1. In particular, the product $n\lambda$ can be chosen such as to keep the norm in $L_Q(2/3)$ since n is not fixed as opposed to the boundary case.

Table 3. Norms and complexities for (M)(ex)(S)NFS algorithms.

Algorithm	N_1	N_2	Complexity $2c_B$		
			$c_p = 1$	$c_p = 5$	$c_p \to \infty$
NFS-JLSV0	$\frac{1}{6c_p} + \frac{c_t}{2} + c_A$	$\frac{1}{6c_p} + \frac{c_t}{2} + c_A$	2.54	2.45	$\left(\frac{128}{9}\right)^{1/3} \approx 2.4$
NFS-JLSV1	$\frac{1}{6c_p} + \frac{c_t}{2} + c_A$	$\frac{1}{6c_p} + \frac{c_t}{2} + c_A$	2.54	2.45	$\left(\frac{128}{9}\right)^{1/3} \approx 2.4$
NFS-JLSV2	$\frac{1}{6c_p} + \frac{c_t}{\delta c_p} + c_A$	$\frac{\delta}{6} + \frac{c_t}{\delta c_p} + \delta c_A c_p$	2.87	2.62	$\left(\frac{128}{9}\right)^{1/3} \approx 2.4$
NFS-A	$\frac{r+1}{6kc_p} + \frac{(r+1)c_A}{k}$	$\frac{r}{6kc_p} + \frac{rc_A}{k} + \frac{kc_t}{r+1}$	2.39	2.24	$\left(\frac{96}{9}\right)^{1/3} \approx 2.2$
MNFS-JLSV1	$\frac{1}{6c_p} + \frac{c_t}{2} + c_A$	$\frac{1}{6c_p} + \frac{c_t}{2} + c_A + \frac{c_t c_V}{2c_p}$	2.52	2.36	$\frac{2\sqrt[3]{7}+4\sqrt{3}}{3^{2/3}} \approx 2.31$
MNFS-JLSV2	$\frac{1}{6c_p} + \frac{c_t}{\delta c_p} + c_A$	$\frac{\delta}{6} + \frac{c_t}{\delta c_p} + \delta c_p c_A + \frac{c_t c_V}{2c_p}$	–	2.62	$\frac{2}{3}\sqrt[3]{23 + \frac{13\sqrt{13}}{2}} \approx 2.396$
MNFS-A	$\frac{r+1}{6kc_p} + \frac{(r+1)c_A}{k}$	$\frac{r}{6kc_p} + \frac{rc_A}{k} + \frac{kc_t}{r+1} + \frac{c_t c_V}{2c_p}$	–	2.22	$2\sqrt[3]{\frac{3}{5} + \frac{4\sqrt{\frac{2}{5}}}{5}} \approx 2.156$
exTNFS-B	$\frac{(r+1)c_A}{k} + \frac{r+1}{2kc_p}$	$\frac{rc_A}{k} + \frac{kc_\eta c_p}{r+1} + \frac{r}{2kc_p}$	2.23	1.89	$\left(\frac{48}{9}\right)^{1/3} \approx 1.747$
MexTNFS-B	$\frac{(r+1)c_A}{k} + \frac{r+1}{2kc_p}$	$\frac{rc_A}{k} + \frac{kc_\eta c_p}{r+1} + \frac{r}{2kc_p} + \frac{c_V c_\eta}{2}$	2.66	2.02	$2\sqrt[3]{\frac{3}{10} + \frac{2\sqrt{\frac{2}{3}}}{5}} \approx 1.71$
SNFS-λ	$\frac{1}{6c_p} + \frac{c_t}{\lambda} + c_A$	$\frac{\lambda}{6c_p} + \lambda c_A$	–	–	$\left(\frac{64(\lambda+1)}{9\lambda}\right)^{1/3}$
SNFS-2	$\frac{1}{6c_p} + \frac{c_t}{2} + c_A$	$\frac{2}{6c_p} + 2c_A$	2.39	2.24	$\left(\frac{192}{18}\right)^{1/3} \approx 2.20$
SNFS-56	$\frac{1}{6c_p} + \frac{c_t}{56} + c_A$	$\frac{56}{6c_p} + 56c_A$	4.27	2.63	$\left(\frac{3648}{504}\right)^{1/3} \approx 1.93$
STNFS	$c_A + \frac{c_\eta c_p}{\lambda} + \frac{c_\eta c_\kappa}{2}$	$\lambda c_A + \frac{c_\eta c_\kappa \lambda}{2}$	–	–	–

7 Crossover Points Between NFS, FFS and the Quasi-polynomial Algorithms

7.1 Quasi-polynomial Algorithms

After half a decade of both practical and theoretical improvements led by several teams and authors, the following result was finally proven in 2019:

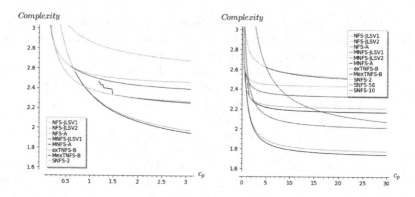

Fig. 4. Complexities of NFS and all its variants as a function of c_p.

Theorem 1 (Theorem 1.1. [32]). Given any prime number p and any positive integer n, the discrete logarithm problem in the group $\mathbb{F}_{p^n}^{\times}$ can be solved in expected time $C_{\text{QP}} = (pn)^{2\log_2(n)+O(1)}$.

This complexity is quasi-polynomial only when p is fixed or slowly grows with Q. When p is in the whereabouts of $L_Q(1/3)$ and n in $(\log Q)^{2/3}$, we obtain a complexity comparable to $L_Q(1/3)$. Therefore this algorithm must come into play in our study; we abbreviate it by QP, even if in our range of study its complexity is no longer quasi-polynomial.

7.2   Crossover Between FFS and QP

When $p = L_Q(1/3, c_p)$, the complexity of QP algorithms is a power of the term $\exp\left(\log(Q)^{1/3}(\log\log Q)^{5/3}\right)$ larger than any $L_Q(1/3)$ expression. The crossover point is therefore for a characteristic p growing slower than an $L_Q(1/3)$ expression. In this area, the complexity of FFS is $C_{\text{FFS}} = L_Q(1/3, (32/9)^{1/3})$ or $C_{\text{shifted FFS}} = L_Q(1/3, (128/81)^{1/3})$ if n is composite and has a factor of exactly the right size so that the shifted FFS yields an optimal complexity.

The crossover point is when the expression of C_{QP} takes the $L_Q(1/3)$ form. More precisely, this occurs when p has the following expression

$$p = \exp\left(\gamma_p(\log Q)^{1/3}(\log\log Q)^{-1/3}\right) =: M_Q(1/3, \gamma_p),$$

where we define the notation $M_Q(\alpha, \beta) = \exp\left(\beta(\log Q)^\alpha(\log\log Q)^{-\alpha}\right)$. This M_Q function fits as follows with the L_Q function: for any positive constants α, β, γ, and ε, when Q grows to infinity we have the following inequalities $L_Q(1/3 - \varepsilon, \beta) \ll M_Q(1/3, \gamma) \ll L_Q(1/3, \alpha)$.

Writing $Q = p^n$ with p of this form, the formula for the extension n becomes $n = \frac{1}{\gamma_p}(\log Q)^{2/3}(\log \log Q)^{1/3}$, so that the cost of the QP algorithm is

$$C_{QP} = L_Q\left(\frac{1}{3}, \frac{4\gamma_p}{3\log 2}\right).$$

Equating this cost with the complexity of FFS, we obtain the crossover point. If only the non-shifted FFS is available, for instance because n is prime, then the crossover is when $p = M_Q(1/3, (\frac{3}{2})^{1/3}\log 2)$. Otherwise, if n has a factor of an appropriate size for the shifted FFS, the crossover is at $p = M_Q(1/3, (\frac{2}{3})^{1/3}\log 2)$.

7.3   Crossover Between NFS and FFS

We compare the performance of FFS with the best variants of NFS. All complexities are expressed as $L_Q(1/3, c)$, where c is a function of c_p. Thus, it is enough to compare the values of c for each algorithm. Let c_{FFS} be this value in the case of FFS and c_{NFS} for NFS and all its variants.

We look for the value of c_p for which $c_{FFS} = c_{NFS}$, where the best variant of NFS depends on the considerations made on n and p. Indeed, when no special considerations are made on either n or p, the best algorithm among the variants of NFS is MNFS-$\mathcal{A}$ as seen in Sect. 6. When n is composite, the algorithm that performs best when c_p is small is (M)exTNFS-$\mathcal{B}$ depending on c_p. Finally, when p is taken to have a special form, the SNFS algorithm gives a complexity when c_p is small and MNFS does not. For each of these algorithms, we know c_{NFS} as a function of c_p. Moreover, when looking at the FFS algorithm, we note that the crossover value is located in the area where the linear algebra phase is the dominant and that in this area the value of D is 1. Thus $c_{FFS} = 2c_p$. Hence, we are able to compute exact values of these crossover points which we report in Table 4. The complexity of SNFS depends on the value of λ. We report in Table 4 the smallest value for c_p for the crossover point with FFS, which corresponds to $\lambda = 3$. Note also that for the range of c_p for which the NFS variants intersect FFS, the variant exTNFS performs similarly than MexTNFS, and thus we only report the crossover point with MexTNFS.

Table 4. Values of c_p for crossover points between FFS and variants of NFS, together with their relative complexities $L_Q(1/3, c)$.

	normal p	special p, $\lambda = 3$
n prime	$c_p = 1.23$, $c = 2.46$, MNFS-$\mathcal{A}$	$c_p = 1.17$, $c = 2.34$, SNFS-3
n composite	$c_p = 1.14$, $c = 2.28$, MexTNFS-$\mathcal{B}$	–

8   Considering Pairings

When constructing a pairing $e : \mathcal{E} \times \mathcal{E} \to \mathbb{F}_{p^n}$ for some elliptic curve $\mathcal{E}$ over the finite field $\mathbb{F}_p$, one must take into account the hardness of DLP in both a subgroup of $\mathcal{E}$ and in $\mathbb{F}_{p^n} = \mathbb{F}_Q$. A natural question arises.

Question *Asymptotically what finite field $\mathbb{F}_{p^n}$ should be considered in order to achieve the highest level of security when constructing a pairing?*

The goal is to find the optimal p and n that answers the above question. Note that pairings always come with a given parameter that indicates whether the prime-order subgroup of $\mathcal{E}$ is large. More precisely, this parameter ρ is defined as $\rho = \log p / \log r$ where r is the size of the relevant prime-order subgroup of $\mathcal{E}$ over $\mathbb{F}_p$. In all the known constructions, we have $\rho \in [1, 2]$.

8.1   Landing at $p = L_Q(1/3)$ is Not as Natural as It Seems

The fastest known algorithm to solve the DLP on elliptic curves is Pollard rho with a running-time of $O(\sqrt{r})$, which means $O(p^{1/2\rho})$. In order to optimize the security of the scheme that uses such a pairing, a naive and common approach is to balance the two asymptotic complexities, namely $p^{1/2\rho}$ and $L_Q(1/3)$. This would result in $p = L_Q(1/3)$. This equality is not as simple to justify. In the FFS algorithm, the cost of sieving and linear algebra are not taken to be equal, which is a common hypothesis made in the complexity analyses of NFS for example. Assuming this equality would potentially lead to worse complexities. For the same reason, equalizing the cost of the DLPs on the elliptic curve and on the finite field may miss other better options. Interestingly enough, we need the full comprehension of asymptotic complexities at this boundary case to understand why we consider finite fields of this size.

In order to avoid quasi-polynomial algorithms, it is clear that one must choose $p \geqslant M_Q(1/3, (2/3)^{1/3} \log 2)$. Since FFS and all the variants of NFS have a complexity in $L_Q(1/3, c)$, we then look for finite fields for which the algorithms give the largest c. We distinguish five different areas:

1. **Small characteristic when $p \geqslant M_Q(1/3, (2/3)^{1/3} \log 2)$.** FFS reaches a complexity with $c = (32/9)^{1/3} \approx 1.53$, or lower if n is composite.
2. **Boundary case studied in this article.** Various algorithms coexist. When considering the complexity of the optimal algorithms, c roughly varies from 1.16 to 2.46. Note that 2.46 is the best complexity reached at the crossover point between FFS and MNFS-$\mathcal{A}$ when nothing is known about p and n.
3. **Medium characteristic.** The best complexity in the general case is reached by MNFS-$\mathcal{A}$, giving $c \approx 2.15$.
4. **Boundary case between medium and large characteristics.** The lowest complexities in the general case are reached by MNFS-$\mathcal{A}$ or MTNFS. In all cases, $1.70 \leq c \leq 2.15$.
5. **Large characteristic.** The lowest complexity in the general case is reached again by MNFS-$\mathcal{A}$, giving here $c \approx 1.90$.

Thus, we see that the best choice is indeed $p = L_Q(1/3)$ so one can expect to reach the highest complexities for DLPs, in particular higher than $L_Q(1/3, 2.15)$.

8.2 Fine Tuning of c_p to Get the Highest Security

Let us now find c_p that optimizes the security. Let $\mathcal{C}_{\mathcal{E}}$ (resp. $\mathcal{C}_{\mathbb{F}_Q}$) be the cost of the discrete logarithm computation on the subgroup of the elliptic curve $\mathcal{E}$ (resp. the finite field $\mathbb{F}_Q$). On one hand, we have $\mathcal{C}_{\mathcal{E}} = p^{1/2\rho}$. This can be rewritten as $\mathcal{C}_{\mathcal{E}} = L_Q(1/3, c_p/2\rho)$. For ρ fixed, $\mathcal{C}_{\mathcal{E}}$ is an increasing function of c_p.

On the other hand, the best algorithm to compute discrete logarithms in a finite field depends on three parameters: the size of the characteristic p, the form of p and whether the extension degree n is composite.

General case. Assuming nothing about n and p, the best variant of NFS at this boundary case is MNFS-$\mathcal{A}$. Thus, we have

$$
\mathcal{C}_{\mathbb{F}_Q} = \begin{cases} L_Q\left(1/3, c_{\mathrm{FFS}}(c_p)\right), & \text{when } c_p \leq \sigma \\ L_Q\left(1/3, c_{\mathrm{MNFS\text{-}}\mathcal{A}}(c_p)\right), & \text{when } c_p \geq \sigma \end{cases}
$$

where $c_{\mathrm{algo}}(c_p)$ is the constant in the L_Q expression of the complexity of the algorithm "algo", and σ is the crossover value of c_p between FFS and MNFS-$\mathcal{A}$. We then want to find the value of c_p that maximizes $\min(\mathcal{C}_{\mathcal{E}}, \mathcal{C}_{\mathbb{F}_Q})$. Figure 5 shows how the relevant algorithms varies with respect to c_p. Note that the crossover point between $\mathcal{C}_{\mathcal{E}}$ and $\mathcal{C}_{\mathbb{F}_Q}$ is not with FFS: we just need to compare $\mathcal{C}_{\mathcal{E}}$ with the complexity of MNFS-$\mathcal{A}$. The latter being a decreasing function with respect to c_p, whereas $\mathcal{C}_{\mathcal{E}}$ is an increasing function, we conclude that the highest complexities are given at the crossover points between these curves.

For $\rho = 1$, the optimal choice is $p = L_Q(1/3, 4.45)$, which results in an asymptotic complexity in $L_Q(1/3, 2.23)$. For $\rho = 2$, the optimal choice is $p = L_Q(1/3, 8.77)$ resulting in a complexity in $L_Q(1/3, 2.19)$. Increasing ρ from 1 to 2 increases the optimal value of c_p, and thus the asymptotic complexity decreases.

If the extension degree n is composite. The best option as an adversary is to use MexTNFS-$\mathcal{B}$. Its complexity is a decreasing function below the complexity of MNFS-$\mathcal{A}$ (see [15, Appendix D]). Thus, the strategy remains the same. With $\rho = 1$ and $c_p = 3.81$ we obtain an asymptotic complexity in $L_Q(1/3, 1.93)$. With $\rho = 2$ and $c_p = 7.27$ we have a complexity in $L_Q(1/3, 1.82)$.

Special sparse characteristics can be used! When p is given by the evaluation of a polynomial of low degree λ, SNFS is applicable. Yet Fig. 4 shows that SNFS is not always a faster option than MNFS-$\mathcal{A}$. The behavior of SNFS with regards to MNFS-$\mathcal{A}$ depends on λ:

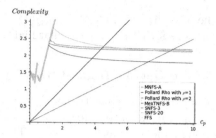

Fig. 5. Comparing the complexities of FFS, MNFS-$\mathcal{A}$ and Pollard rho for $\rho = 1$ and $\rho = 2$. I_1 and I_2 are the crossover points of $\mathcal{C}_\mathcal{E}$ and $\mathcal{C}_{\mathbb{F}_Q}$.

- If $\lambda = 2$ or $\lambda \geq 29$, then MNFS-$\mathcal{A}$ if faster than the related SNFS for all ρ.
- If $3 \leq \lambda \leq 16$, the related SNFS if faster than MNFS-$\mathcal{A}$ for all ρ.
- If $17 \leq \lambda \leq 28$, the best choice depends on ρ. For instance, if $\lambda = 20$ MNFS-$\mathcal{A}$ is faster if $\rho \leq 1.3$ but SNFS becomes faster if $1.3 \leq \rho$, see Fig. 6.

Surprisingly enough, this means that we can construct a pairing with a special sparse characteristic without asymptotically decreasing the security of the pairing. For instance, with $\lambda = 20$, $\rho = 1$, the best option is to take $c_p = 4.45$. This gives a complexity in $L_Q(1/3, 2.23)$, which is the one obtained with a normal p of the same size. But for $\lambda = 20$ and $\rho = 2$ the security gets weaker than in the normal case: taking $c_p = 8.51$ allows to decrease the complexity from $L_Q(1/3, 2.19)$ (for a normal p) to $L_Q(1/3, 2.13)$ (for this special p).

Combining special p and composite n. We saw in Sect. 6.3 that combining SNFS and exTNFS-$\mathcal{B}$ is not possible at this boundary case. Since MexTNFS-$\mathcal{B}$ is always lower than SNFS for the c_p considered, with both n composite and p special, the best option is to ignore the form of p, and apply MexTNFS-$\mathcal{B}$.

8.3   Conclusion

We studied all possible cases regarding p and n in order to extract the optimized values of c_p, leading to the highest asymptotic security of the related pairing. Table 5 summarizes these complexities depending on what is known about p and n. We give our results for the $\rho = 1$ particular case to get bounds on complexities. Indeed, decreasing ρ decreases the complexities as well, so the values in Table 5 are upperbounds on the asymptotic complexities of all currently known pairing constructions. Moreover, $\rho = 1$ is achieved with some well-known efficient pairing friendly curves such as MNT or BN curves. Yet we emphasize that these families are not asymptotic and, to the best of our knowledge, designing an efficient asymptotic family of pairings reaching $\rho = 1$ is still an open question.

The best asymptotic security is given by $\rho = 1$, n prime, and $p = L_Q(1/3, 4.45)$, with p either normal or the evaluation of a degree d polynomial, with $d \geq 29$ or $d = 2$. The asymptotic complexities of all relevant attacks are in $L_Q(1/3, 2.23)$.

Table 5. Optimal choices for pairing constructions, depending on the form of p and n. Each cell gives the value c_p determining p as $p = L_Q(1/3, c_p)$, together with $c_{\mathbf{algo}}$, which gives the best asymptotic complexity $L_Q(1/3, c_{\mathbf{algo}})$ reached by the algorithm **algo** for the related case.

	normal p	special p $\lambda = 20$	special p $\lambda = 3$
n prime	$c_p = 4.45$, $c_{\mathbf{MNFS\text{-}A}} = 2.23$	$c_p = 4.36$, $c_{\mathbf{SNFS\text{-}3}} = 2.18$	
n composite	$c_p = 3.81$, $c_{\mathbf{MexTNFS\text{-}B}} = 1.91$		

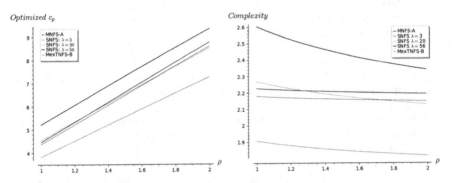

Fig. 6. Increasing ρ makes the security decrease. The first figure gives optimized values of c_p as a function of ρ, and the second figure shows the second constant in the complexities, as a function of ρ, depending on the algorithm.

References

1. Adleman, L.M.: The function field sieve. In: Adleman, L.M., Huang, M.-D. (eds.) ANTS 1994. LNCS, vol. 877, pp. 108–121. Springer, Heidelberg (1994). https://doi.org/10.1007/3-540-58691-1_48
2. Arute, F., Arya, K., Babbush, R., et al.: Quantum supremacy using a programmable superconducting processor. Nature **574**, 505–510 (2019)
3. Barbulescu, R., Gaudry, P., Guillevic, A., Morain, F.: Improving NFS for the discrete logarithm problem in non-prime finite fields. In: Oswald, E., Fischlin, M. (eds.) EUROCRYPT 2015, Part I. LNCS, vol. 9056, pp. 129–155. Springer, Heidelberg (2015). https://doi.org/10.1007/978-3-662-46800-5_6
4. Barbulescu, R., Gaudry, P., Joux, A., Thomé, E.: A heuristic quasi-polynomial algorithm for discrete logarithm in finite fields of small characteristic. In: Nguyen, P.Q., Oswald, E. (eds.) EUROCRYPT 2014. LNCS, vol. 8441, pp. 1–16. Springer, Heidelberg (2014). https://doi.org/10.1007/978-3-642-55220-5_1
5. Barbulescu, R., Gaudry, P., Kleinjung, T.: The tower number field sieve. In: Iwata, T., Cheon, J.H. (eds.) ASIACRYPT 2015, Part II. LNCS, vol. 9453, pp. 31–55. Springer, Heidelberg (2015). https://doi.org/10.1007/978-3-662-48800-3_2
6. Barbulescu, R., Pierrot, C.: The multiple number field sieve for medium and high characteristic finite fields. LMS J. Comput. Math. **17**, 230–246 (2014)
7. Bistritz, Y., Lifshitz, A.: Bounds for resultants of univariate and bivariate polynomials. Linear Algebra Appl. **432**, 1995–2005 (2010)

8. Boneh, D., Franklin, M.K.: Identity-based encryption from the Weil pairing. In: Kilian, J. (ed.) CRYPTO 2001. LNCS, vol. 2139, pp. 213–229. Springer, Heidelberg (2001). https://doi.org/10.1007/3-540-44647-8_13

9. Boneh, D., Lynn, B., Shacham, H.: Short signatures from the Weil pairing. In: Boyd, C. (ed.) ASIACRYPT 2001. LNCS, vol. 2248, pp. 514–532. Springer, Heidelberg (2001). https://doi.org/10.1007/3-540-45682-1_30

10. Canfield, E.R., Erdős, P., Pomerance, C.: On a problem of Oppenheim concerning "factorisatio numerorum". J. Number Theory 17, 1–28 (1983)

11. Choon, J.C., Hee Cheon, J.: An identity-based signature from gap Diffie-Hellman groups. In: Desmedt, Y.G. (ed.) PKC 2003. LNCS, vol. 2567, pp. 18–30. Springer, Heidelberg (2003). https://doi.org/10.1007/3-540-36288-6_2

12. Coppersmith, D.: Fast evaluation of logarithms in fields of characteristic two. IEEE Trans. Inf. Theory 30, 587–594 (1984)

13. Coppersmith, D.: Modifications to the number field sieve. J. Cryptol. 6(3), 169–180 (1993). https://doi.org/10.1007/BF00198464

14. Coppersmith, D.: Solving homogeneous linear equations over $GF(2)$ via block Wiedemann algorithm. Math. Comput. 62, 333–350 (1994)

15. De Micheli, G., Gaudry, P., Pierrot, C.: Asymptotic complexities of discrete logarithm algorithms in pairing-relevant finite fields. Cryptology ePrint Archive, Report 2020/329 (2020). https://eprint.iacr.org/2020/329

16. Fried, J., Gaudry, P., Heninger, N., Thomé, E.: A kilobit hidden SNFS discrete logarithm computation. In: Coron, J.-S., Nielsen, J.B. (eds.) EUROCRYPT 2017, Part I. LNCS, vol. 10210, pp. 202–231. Springer, Cham (2017). https://doi.org/10.1007/978-3-319-56620-7_8

17. Gordon, D.: Discrete logarithms in $GF(P)$ using the number field sieve. SIAM J. Discrete Math. 6, 124–138 (1993). https://doi.org/10.1137/0406010

18. Granger, R., Kleinjung, T., Zumbrägel, J.: Breaking '128-bit secure' supersingular binary curves - (or how to solve discrete logarithms in $\mathbb{F}_{2^{4 \cdot 1223}}$ and $\mathbb{F}_{2^{12 \cdot 367}}$). In: Garay, J.A., Gennaro, R. (eds.) CRYPTO 2014, Part II. LNCS, vol. 8617, pp. 126–145. Springer, Heidelberg (2014). https://doi.org/10.1007/978-3-662-44381-1_8

19. Granger, R., Kleinjung, T., Zumbrägel, J.: Indiscreet logarithms in finite fields of small characteristic. Adv. Math. Commun. 12, 263–286 (2018)

20. Guillevic, A.: A short-list of pairing-friendly curves resistant to special TNFS at the 128-bit security level. In: Kiayias, A., Kohlweiss, M., Wallden, P., Zikas, V. (eds.) PKC 2020, Part II. LNCS, vol. 12111, pp. 535–564. Springer, Cham (2020). https://doi.org/10.1007/978-3-030-45388-6_19

21. Joux, A.: Faster index calculus for the medium prime case application to 1175-bit and 1425-bit finite fields. In: Johansson, T., Nguyen, P.Q. (eds.) EUROCRYPT 2013. LNCS, vol. 7881, pp. 177–193. Springer, Heidelberg (2013). https://doi.org/10.1007/978-3-642-38348-9_11

22. Joux, A.: A new index calculus algorithm with complexity $L(1/4 + o(1))$ in small characteristic. In: Lange, T., Lauter, K., Lisoněk, P. (eds.) SAC 2013. LNCS, vol. 8282, pp. 355–379. Springer, Heidelberg (2014). https://doi.org/10.1007/978-3-662-43414-7_18

23. Joux, A., Lercier, R.: Improvements to the general number field sieve for discrete logarithms in prime fields. A comparison with the Gaussian integer method. Math. Comput. 72, 953–967 (2003)

24. Joux, A., Lercier, R.: The function field sieve in the medium prime case. In: Vaudenay, S. (ed.) EUROCRYPT 2006. LNCS, vol. 4004, pp. 254–270. Springer, Heidelberg (2006). https://doi.org/10.1007/11761679_16

25. Joux, A., Lercier, R., Smart, N., Vercauteren, F.: The number field sieve in the medium prime case. In: Dwork, C. (ed.) CRYPTO 2006. LNCS, vol. 4117, pp. 326–344. Springer, Heidelberg (2006). https://doi.org/10.1007/11818175_19

26. Joux, A., Pierrot, C.: Improving the polynomial time precomputation of Frobenius representation discrete logarithm algorithms - simplified setting for small characteristic finite fields. In: Sarkar, P., Iwata, T. (eds.) ASIACRYPT 2014, Part I. LNCS, vol. 8873, pp. 378–397. Springer, Heidelberg (2014). https://doi.org/10.1007/978-3-662-45611-8_20

27. Joux, A., Pierrot, C.: The special number field sieve in $\mathbb{F}_{p^n}$ - application to pairing-friendly constructions. In: Cao, Z., Zhang, F. (eds.) Pairing 2013. LNCS, vol. 8365, pp. 45–61. Springer, Cham (2014). https://doi.org/10.1007/978-3-319-04873-4_3

28. Joux, A., Pierrot, C.: Algorithmic aspects of elliptic bases in finite field discrete logarithm algorithms. Cryptology ePrint Archive, Report 2019/782 (2019). https://eprint.iacr.org/2019/782

29. Kalkbrener, M.: An upper bound on the number of monomials in determinants of sparse matrices with symbolic entries. Mathematica Pannonica **8**, 73–82 (1997)

30. Kim, T., Barbulescu, R.: Extended tower number field sieve: a new complexity for the medium prime case. In: Robshaw, M., Katz, J. (eds.) CRYPTO 2016, Part I. LNCS, vol. 9814, pp. 543–571. Springer, Heidelberg (2016). https://doi.org/10.1007/978-3-662-53018-4_20

31. Kim, T., Jeong, J.: Extended tower number field sieve with application to finite fields of arbitrary composite extension degree. In: Fehr, S. (ed.) PKC 2017, Part I. LNCS, vol. 10174, pp. 388–408. Springer, Heidelberg (2017). https://doi.org/10.1007/978-3-662-54365-8_16

32. Kleinjung, T., Wesolowski, B.: Discrete logarithms in quasi-polynomial time in finite fields of fixed characteristic. Cryptology ePrint Archive, Report 2019/751 (2019). https://eprint.iacr.org/2019/751

33. Matyukhin, D.V.: On asymptotic complexity of computing discrete logarithms over $GF(p)$. Discrete Math. Appl. **13**, 27–50 (2003)

34. Panario, D., Gourdon, X., Flajolet, P.: An analytic approach to smooth polynomials over finite fields. In: Buhler, J.P. (ed.) ANTS 1998, III. LNCS, vol. 1423, pp. 226–236. Springer, Heidelberg (1998). https://doi.org/10.1007/BFb0054865

35. Sarkar, P., Singh, S.: Fine tuning the function field sieve algorithm for the medium prime case. IEEE Trans. Inf. Theory **62**, 2233–2253 (2016)

36. Sarkar, P., Singh, S.: A general polynomial selection method and new asymptotic complexities for the tower number field sieve algorithm. In: Cheon, J.H., Takagi, T. (eds.) ASIACRYPT 2016, Part I. LNCS, vol. 10031, pp. 37–62. Springer, Heidelberg (2016). https://doi.org/10.1007/978-3-662-53887-6_2

37. Sarkar, P., Singh, S.: New complexity trade-offs for the (multiple) number field sieve algorithm in non-prime fields. In: Fischlin, M., Coron, J.-S. (eds.) EUROCRYPT 2016, Part I. LNCS, vol. 9665, pp. 429–458. Springer, Heidelberg (2016). https://doi.org/10.1007/978-3-662-49890-3_17

38. Sarkar, P., Singh, S.: A unified polynomial selection method for the (tower) number field sieve algorithm. Adv. Math. Commun. **13**, 435–455 (2019)

39. Schirokauer, O.: Virtual logarithms. J. Algorithms **57**, 140–147 (2005)

40. Schirokauer, O.: Using number fields to compute logarithms in finite fields. Math. Comput. **69**, 1267–1283 (2000)

Comparing the Difficulty of Factorization and Discrete Logarithm: A 240-Digit Experiment

Fabrice Boudot[1]([⊠]), Pierrick Gaudry[2]([⊠]), Aurore Guillevic[2]([⊠])(iD),
Nadia Heninger[3]([⊠]), Emmanuel Thomé[2]([⊠]), and Paul Zimmermann[2]([⊠])(iD)

[1] Université de Limoges, XLIM, UMR 7252, F-87000 Limoges, France
`Fabrice.Boudot@orange.fr`
[2] Université de Lorraine, CNRS, Inria, LORIA, F-54000 Nancy, France
`Pierrick.Gaudry@loria.fr,`
`{Aurore.Guillevic,Emmanuel.Thome,Paul.Zimmermann}@inria.fr`
[3] University of California, San Diego, USA
`nadiah@cs.ucsd.edu`

In memory of Peter L. Montgomery.

Abstract. We report on two new records: the factorization of RSA-240, a 795-bit number, and a discrete logarithm computation over a 795-bit prime field. Previous records were the factorization of RSA-768 in 2009 and a 768-bit discrete logarithm computation in 2016. Our two computations at the 795-bit level were done using the same hardware and software, and show that computing a discrete logarithm is not much harder than a factorization of the same size. Moreover, thanks to algorithmic variants and well-chosen parameters, our computations were significantly less expensive than anticipated based on previous records.

The last page of this paper also reports on the factorization of RSA-250.

1 Introduction

The Diffie-Hellman protocol over finite fields and the RSA cryptosystem were the first practical building blocks of public-key cryptography. Since then, several other cryptographic primitives have entered the landscape, and a significant amount of research has been put into the development, standardization, cryptanalysis, and optimization of implementations for a large number of cryptographic primitives. Yet the prevalence of RSA and finite field Diffie-Hellman is still a fact: between November 11, 2019 and December 11, 2019, the ICSI Certificate Notary [21] observed that 90% of the TLS certificates used RSA signatures, and 7% of the TLS connections used RSA for key exchange. This holds despite the much longer key sizes required by these primitives compared to elliptic curves: based on the asymptotic formulas for the best known cryptanalysis algorithms, the required key size for RSA or finite field Diffie-Hellman is roughly estimated to grow as a cubic

© International Association for Cryptologic Research 2020
D. Micciancio and T. Ristenpart (Eds.): CRYPTO 2020, LNCS 12171, pp. 62–91, 2020.
https://doi.org/10.1007/978-3-030-56880-1_3

function of the security parameter, while the required key size for elliptic curve cryptosystems grows only as a linear function of the security parameter.[1]

Over the last few years, the threat posed by quantum computers has been used as a justification to postpone the impending replacement of RSA and finite field Diffie-Hellman by alternatives such as elliptic curve cryptography [33], resulting in implementation choices that seem paradoxical from the perspective of classical cryptanalysis.

Key sizes for RSA and finite field Diffie-Hellman have become unwieldy. To meet a 128-bit security strength, it is widely accepted that both schemes require a key size of approximately 3072 bits (see e.g., the 2018 ECRYPT-CS Recommendations). While it is easy to deal with such key sizes in environments where computing power is plentiful (laptop and desktop computers, or cell phones), a surprising amount of public key cryptography in use employs weak key strengths. There are two main factors contributing to the use of weak key sizes in practice. First, implementations may use weak key sizes to ensure backward compatibility. For example, a crucial component in the FREAK and Logjam attacks was the widespread support for weakened "export-grade" cipher suites using 512-bit keys [1]; the Java JDK versions 5–8 originally supported Diffie-Hellman and DSA primes of at most 1024 bits by default. Second, in embedded environments, or when very little computational power is allotted to public-key cryptographic operations, small key sizes are not rare. As an example, in 2018, an off-the-shelf managed network switch purchased by the authors shipped with a default RSA ssh host key of 768 bits (despite a $2,000 USD list price), a key size that has been broken since 2009 in the academic world.

The main goal of this article is to assess the difficulty of the mathematical problems that underpin the security of RSA and finite field Diffie-Hellman and DSA, namely integer factorization (IF) and discrete logarithm (DL). We are interested both in the feasibility of cryptanalysis of these problems as well as in their relative difficulty. Our targets are RSA-240, from the RSA Factoring Challenge, and DLP-240, denoting the challenge of computing discrete logarithms modulo $p = $ RSA-240 $+ 49204$, which is the smallest safe prime above RSA-240 (i.e., $(p-1)/2$ is also prime). Both previous records were 768-bit keys, with results dating back to 2009 [27] and 2016 [29]. The total cost of our computation is about 1000 core-years for RSA-240, and 3200 core-years for DLP-240. Here and throughout this article, the core-years we mention are relative to the computing platform that we used most, namely Intel Xeon Gold 6130 CPUs with 16 physical cores (32 hyperthreaded cores) running at 2.10 GHz. A core-year is the use of one of these physical cores for a duration of one year. As in the previous records, our computations used the Number Field Sieve algorithm (NFS for short), which has variants both for integer factoring and finite field discrete logarithms.

Improvements in cryptanalysis records are to be expected. In this article, our contribution is not limited to reaching new milestones (and reminding people to

---

[1] A security parameter ϵ asserts that cryptanalysis requires 2^ϵ operations; assuming Moore's law, the security parameter could be seen as growing linearly with time.

get rid of outdated keys). Rather, it is interesting to report on *how* we reached them:

- We developed a testing framework that enabled us to precisely select, among a wide variety with complex interactions, parameters that influence the running time of NFS. We were able to accurately predict important measures such as the matrix size.
- Some folklore ideas that have been known for some time in the NFS community played a very important role in our computation. In particular the *composite special-q* used in relation collection for DLP-240 proved extremely beneficial, and so did *batch smoothness detection*, which we used both for RSA-240 and DLP-240. This is the first time that this latter technique has been used in a factoring record for general numbers (it was used in [28], in a very specific context). These techniques, together with our careful parameter selection, contributed to a significantly faster computation than extrapolation from the running times of previous records would have suggested. Even on similar hardware, our relation collection effort for the 795-bit DLP computation took 25% less time than the reported relation collection effort of the previous 768-bit DLP record.
- Furthermore, we computed two records of the same size, RSA-240 and DLP-240, at the same time and using hardware of the same generation. This is completely new and gives a crucial data point for the assessment of the relative difficulty of IF and DL. While it is commonly believed that DL is much harder than IF, we show that the hardness ratio is roughly a factor of 3 for the current 800-bit range for safe primes, much less than previously thought.
- Last but not least, our computations were performed with the open-source software Cado-NFS [36]. Reproducing our results is possible: we have set up a companion code repository at https://gitlab.inria.fr/cado-nfs/records that holds the required information to reproduce them.

We complement the present work with another record computation, the factoring of RSA-250, for which we used parameters similar to RSA-240. Details for this additional record are given at the end of the paper.

This article is organized as follows. We give a brief introduction to key aspects of NFS in Sect. 2. In Sects. 3 to 7 we detail the main steps of NFS, how we chose parameters, and how our computations proceeded, both for factoring and discrete logarithm. Section 8 gives further details on the simulation mechanism that we used in order to predict the running time. Section 9 concludes with a comparison with recent computational records, and a discussion on the relative hardness of the discrete logarithm and factoring problems.

2   Background on the Number Field Sieve

The Number Field Sieve (NFS) is an algorithmic framework that can tackle either of the two following problems:

- Integer factorization (IF): given a composite integer N, find a non-trivial factorization of N.
- Discrete logarithm in finite fields (DL): given a prime-order finite field[2] $\mathbb{F}_p$ and a subgroup G of prime order ℓ within $\mathbb{F}_p^*$, compute a non-trivial homomorphism from G to $\mathbb{Z}/\ell\mathbb{Z}$. By combining information of this kind for various ℓ, given $g, y \in \mathbb{F}_p^*$, one can compute x such that $g^x = y$.

When the need arises, the algorithms for the two problems above are denoted NFS and NFS-DL, respectively. Most often the acronym NFS is used for both cases. Furthermore, in the few cases in this paper where we work with the prime factors of N, we call them p and q. Of course, p here shall not be confused with the prime p of the DLP case. The context allows to avoid the confusion.

NFS is described in the book [30]. So-called "special" variants of NFS exist as well, and were historically the first to be developed. These variants apply when the number N or p has a particular form. Large computations in these special cases were reported in [2,17,28]. In this work, we are concerned only with the general case (GNFS). The time and space complexity can be expressed as

$$L_N(1/3, (64/9)^{1/3})^{1+o(1)} = \exp\left((64/9)^{1/3}(\log N)^{1/3}(\log\log N)^{2/3}(1+o(1))\right)$$

for factoring. For discrete logarithms in a subgroup of $\mathbb{F}_p^*$, N is substituted by p in the above formula. In both cases, the presence of $(1 + o(1))$ in the exponent reveals a significant lack of accuracy in this complexity estimate, which easily swallows any speedup or slowdown that would be polynomial in $\log N$.

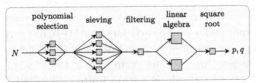

NFS for factoring: given an RSA modulus N, find p, q such that $N = pq$.

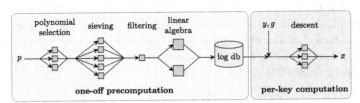

NFS for DLP: given $g^x \equiv y \bmod p$, find x.

Fig. 1. Main steps of NFS and NFS-DL.

The Number Field Sieve is made up of several independent steps, which are depicted in Fig. 1. The first step of NFS, called polynomial selection, determines

---

[2] Variants for non-prime finite fields also exist, but are not covered here.

a mathematical setup that is well suited to dealing with the input N (or p). That is, we are searching for two irreducible polynomials f_0 and f_1 in $\mathbb{Z}[x]$ that define two algebraic number fields $K_0 = \mathbb{Q}(\alpha_0)$ and $K_1 = \mathbb{Q}(\alpha_1)$ (with $f_i(\alpha_i) = 0$), subject to some compatibility condition. The resulting maps are depicted in the diagram in Fig. 2.

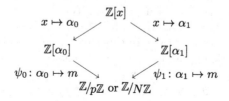

$$\begin{array}{ccc} & \mathbb{Z}[x] & \\ x \mapsto \alpha_0 \swarrow & & \searrow x \mapsto \alpha_1 \\ \mathbb{Z}[\alpha_0] & & \mathbb{Z}[\alpha_1] \\ \psi_0 : \alpha_0 \mapsto m \searrow & & \swarrow \psi_1 : \alpha_1 \mapsto m \\ & \mathbb{Z}/p\mathbb{Z} \text{ or } \mathbb{Z}/N\mathbb{Z} & \end{array}$$

Fig. 2. The mathematical setup of NFS.

To be compatible, f_0 and f_1 should have a common root m modulo p (or, likewise, modulo N), used in the maps ψ_0 and ψ_1 in Fig. 2. This condition is difficult to ensure modulo a composite integer N, and most efficient constructions are limited to choosing f_0 as a linear polynomial, so that $\mathbb{Z}[\alpha_0]$ is a subring of $\mathbb{Q}$. This leads to commonly used terminology that distinguishes between the "rational side" (f_0) and the "algebraic side" (f_1). When dealing with IF-related considerations, we also use this terminology. In contrast, for NFS-DL, other constructions exist that take advantage of the ability to find roots modulo p.

Based on the mathematical setup above, the most time-consuming phase of NFS consists of collecting relations. We search for elements $a - bx \in \mathbb{Z}[x]$, preferably with small coefficients, such that the two integers[3] $\mathrm{Res}(a - bx, f_0)$ and $\mathrm{Res}(a - bx, f_1)$ are *smooth*, i.e., factor into small prime numbers below some chosen *large prime bound*. This ensures that the ideals $(a - b\alpha_0)\mathcal{O}_{K_0}$ and $(a - b\alpha_1)\mathcal{O}_{K_1}$ both factor into ideals within finite sets called $\mathcal{F}_0$ and $\mathcal{F}_1$.[4]

The main mathematical obstacle to understanding NFS is that we cannot expect $a - b\alpha_i$ for $i \in \{0, 1\}$ to factor into elements of $\mathbb{Z}[\alpha_i]$. Only factorization into prime ideals, within the maximal orders $\mathcal{O}_{K_i}$, holds. As such, even given known ideal factorizations of the form $(a - b\alpha_i)\mathcal{O}_i = \prod_{\mathfrak{p} \in \mathcal{F}_i} \mathfrak{p}^{e_{\mathfrak{p},a,b}}$, it is impossible to use the diagram in Fig. 2 to write a relation of the following kind (in either $\mathbb{Z}/N\mathbb{Z}$ or $\mathbb{Z}/p\mathbb{Z}$, depending on the context):

$$\prod_{\mathfrak{p} \in \mathcal{F}_0} \psi_0(\mathfrak{p}^{e_{\mathfrak{p},a,b}}) \text{ "}\equiv\text{" } \prod_{\mathfrak{p} \in \mathcal{F}_1} \psi_1(\mathfrak{p}^{e_{\mathfrak{p},a,b}}). \tag{1}$$

---

[3] A common abuse of terminology is to use the term "norm" to denote $\mathrm{Res}(a - bx, f_i)$, while in fact the latter coincides with the norm of $a - b\alpha_i$ only when f_i is monic.

[4] The terms *smoothness bound* and *factor base* are fairly standard, but lead to ambiguous interpretations as we dive into the technical details of how relation collection is performed. Both are therefore avoided here, on purpose.

Indeed the maps ψ_i are defined on elements, not ideals. A prime ideal, or a factorization into prime ideals, does not uniquely identify an element of K_i, because of obstructions related to the unit group and the class group of the number field K_i. To make an equality similar to (1) work, additional data is needed, called quadratic characters in the context of factoring [10, §6] and Schirokauer maps in the discrete logarithm context [35]. With this additional information, relations that are functionally equivalent to Eq. (1) can be obtained. The general goal of NFS, once relations have been collected, is:

- in the IF context, to combine (multiply) many relations together so as to form an equality of squares in $\mathbb{Z}/N\mathbb{Z}$. To achieve this goal, it suffices to only keep track of the valuations $e_{\mathfrak{p},a,b}$ modulo 2. The right combination can be obtained by searching for a left nullspace element of a binary matrix;
- in the DL context, to view the multiplicative relations as additive relations involving unknown logarithms of the elements in $\mathcal{F}_0$ and $\mathcal{F}_1$, and to solve the corresponding linear system for these unknowns. These logarithms, and the linear system, are defined modulo ℓ, which is the order of the subgroup of $\mathbb{F}_p^*$ that we are working in. (If the system were homogeneous, solving it would require a right nullspace element of a matrix defined modulo ℓ.)

In both cases (factoring and discrete logarithm), we need a linear algebra calculation. The matrix rows are vectors of valuations, which are by construction very sparse. Note however that record-size computations with NFS typically collect billions of relations, which is a rather awkward data set to deal with. The linear algebra step therefore begins with a preprocessing step called *filtering*, which carries out some preliminary steps of Gaussian elimination with the aim of reducing the matrix size significantly while keeping it relatively sparse.

The linear algebra step that follows is the second most expensive computational step of NFS. Once the solution to the linear algebra problem has been found, the final task is to factor N given an equality of squares modulo N, or to compute arbitrary discrete logarithms based on a database of known logarithms derived from the solution of the linear system. This final result is obtained via some additional steps which, while nontrivial, are computationally insignificant compared to the rest of the computation.

NFS can be implemented in software. Our computation was carried out exclusively with the Cado-NFS implementation [36]. In Sects. 3 to 7, we examine the underlying algorithms as well as the computational specifics of the different steps of NFS.

3   Polynomial Selection

Polynomial selection can be done using a variety of algorithms, both in the factoring context [3,25,26,32] or in the discrete logarithm context, which allows additional constructions such as [22]. Not all choices of polynomials (f_0, f_1) that permit the structure in the diagram in Fig. 2 perform equally well. Hence, it is useful to try many different pairs (f_0, f_1) until a good one is found. The main optimization criteria are meant to ensure that on the one hand $\text{Res}(a - bx, f_0)$ and $\text{Res}(a - bx, f_1)$ are somewhat small, and on the other hand they are likely to have many small prime factors.

As detailed in [25], the most important task in polynomial selection is to quickly discard the less promising pairs, and efficiently rank the promising ones with a sequence of estimators, from coarse-grained estimators to finer-grained ones. Finally, a small-scale sieving test can be run in order to select the polynomial pair to use for the rest of the computation among the final set of candidates.

We followed exactly this approach, using the Murphy-E value from [32] as well as the modified estimator E' suggested in [14] as estimators. We performed sample sieving for a few dozen of the best candidates. Cado-NFS can do this easily with the `random-sample` option.

3.1   Computational Data

RSA-240. We used Kleinjung's algorithm [25, 26], with improvements from [3], and searched for a polynomial pair with $\deg f_0 = 1$ and $\deg f_1 = 6$. We forced the leading coefficient $f_{1,6}$ of f_1 to be divisible by 110880, to ensure higher divisibility by $2, 3, 5, 7, 11$. The parameter P used (see [26]) was $P = 2 \cdot 10^7$ and we searched up to $f_{1,6} = 2 \cdot 10^{12}$.

The cost of the search was about 76 core-years. It was distributed over many computer clusters, and took only 12 days of calendar time. We kept 40 polynomial pairs: the top 20 with the best Murphy-E values, and the top 20 with the modified E' value [14]. After some sample sieving, two clear winners emerged, and distinguishing between both was actually quite hard. In the end we chose the one optimized for the classical Murphy-E value, with $|\text{Res}(f_0, f_1)| = 120N$:

$$f_1 = 10853204947200\,x^6 - 221175588842299117590564542609977016567191860$$
$$- 4763683724115259920\,x^5 + 15957125533693354304961257950831466688523\,x$$
$$- 63817444612798679419616701670\,x^4 + 1792005735336657213102106407380 61170\,x^2$$
$$+ 974448934853864807690675067037\,x^3$$
$$f_0 = 17780390513045005995253\,x - 105487753732969860223795041295860517380$$

For each polynomial $f_i(x)$, we denote by $F_i(x, y) = y^{\deg f_i} f_i(x/y)$ the corresponding homogeneous bivariate polynomial.

DLP-240. As in [29], we used the Joux-Lercier selection algorithm [22], searching for a pair (f_0, f_1) with f_1 of degree d with small coefficients, and f_0 of degree $d - 1$ with coefficients of order $p^{1/d}$. As in [29], we used $d = 4$ which is optimal for this size, with coefficients of f_1 bounded by 150 in absolute value, compared to 165 in [29].

The cost of the search was about 152 core-years, and only about 18 days of calendar time. We kept the 100 best pairs according to their Murphy-E value, and chose the winning polynomial pair based on the results of sample sieving.

As in the RSA-240 case, the very best handful of polynomials provided almost identical yields. We ended up using the following pair, with $|\mathrm{Res}(f_0, f_1)| = 540p$:

$$f_1 = 39x^4 + 126x^3 + x^2 + 62x + 120$$

$$
\begin{aligned}
f_0 =\ & 2865121727006754119869668463943599248745765364087863680 56x^3 \\
& + 2490882030071576613647511598243973551658188860381725553 9890x^2 \\
& - 1876369756001301656440395392832712103558040945994485465 2737x \\
& - 2366104088270002562501908382208241229978789945957854322 02599
\end{aligned}
$$

Note that although there is a clear correlation between the efficiency of a polynomial pair and its Murphy-E value, the ranking is definitely not perfect [14]; in particular, the top scoring polynomial pair according to Murphy-E finds 10% fewer relations than the above one.

4   Relation Collection

The relation collection uses a technique called *lattice sieving* [34]. Lattice sieving borrows from the terminology of *special-q sieving* [15]. We call special-q ideals a large set of ideals of one of the two number fields[5]. For each such special-q, the search for relations is done among the pairs (a, b) such that the prime ideals dividing q appear in the factorization[6] of $(a - b\alpha_0)\mathcal{O}_{K_0}$ (or $(a - b\alpha_1)\mathcal{O}_{K_1}$). These (a, b) pairs form a lattice $\mathcal{L}_q$ in $\mathbb{Z}^2$, which depends on q. Let $(\boldsymbol{u}, \boldsymbol{v})$ be a Gauss-reduced basis of $\mathcal{L}_q$. To enumerate small points in $\mathcal{L}_q$, we consider small linear combinations of the form $(a, b) = i\boldsymbol{u} + j\boldsymbol{v}$. In order to search for good pairs (a, b) in $\mathcal{L}_q$, we use the change of basis given by $(\boldsymbol{u}, \boldsymbol{v})$, and instead search for good pairs (i, j) such that both $\mathrm{Res}(a - bx, f_0)$ and $\mathrm{Res}(a - bx, f_1)$ are smooth.

The set of explored pairs (i, j) is called the *sieve area*, which we commonly denote by $\mathcal{A}$. For performance it is best to have $\mathcal{A}$ of the form $[-I/2, I/2) \times [0, J)$ for some integers I and J, and I a power of two. This implies that as we consider multiple special-qs, the sieved rectangles drawn in Fig. 3(a) (whose intersections with $\mathbb{Z}^2$ most often have very few common points, since divisibility conditions are distinct) lead us to implicitly consider (a, b) pairs that generally have small norm, but are not constrained to some area that has been defined a priori. In fact, various strategies can be used to make small adjustments to the sieve area depending on q in order to limit the spread of the zones reached in Fig. 3(a).

Relation collection finds pairs (a, b) (or, equivalently, pairs (i, j)) such that two smoothness conditions hold simultaneously (see §2). We thus have two sides to consider. In the description below, we use $\mathcal{F}$ to denote either $\mathcal{F}_0$ or $\mathcal{F}_1$, as

---

[5] It is possible to mix special-q ideals from both number fields, as done in [17], or even hybrid special-q involving contributions from both sides.

[6] By factorization, we implicitly mean "numerator of the factorization". Furthermore we factor ideals such as $(a - b\alpha)\mathcal{O}_K$, yet the maximal order $\mathcal{O}_K$ is generally too expensive to compute. It turns out that if $\mathrm{Res}(a - bx, f)$ is smooth and fully factored, then it is easy to do. How to deal with these technicalities is well known, and not discussed here (see [12, chapters 4 and 6]).

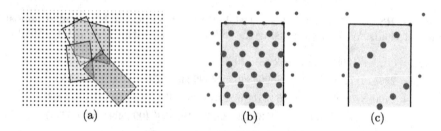

Fig. 3. (a): Examples of (i,j) rectangles for various lattices $\mathcal{L}_q$ within the (a,b) plane. (b): Sieving for a prime p in the (i,j) rectangle. (c): Sieved locations can be quite far apart, and accessing them naively can incur a significant memory access penalty.

the same processing can be applied to both sides. Likewise, we use f and α to denote either f_0 and α_0, or f_1 and α_1.

One of the efficient ways to find the good pairs (i,j) is to use a *sieving* procedure. Let $\mathfrak{p}$ be a moderate-size prime ideal in $\mathcal{F}$, subject to limits on $|\mathrm{Norm}\,\mathfrak{p}|$ that will be detailed later. Identify the locations (i,j) such that $\mathfrak{p} \mid (a - b\alpha)$. These locations again form a lattice in the (i,j) coordinate space, as seen in Figs. 3(b)–(c) and hence implicitly a sub-lattice of $\mathcal{L}_q$. Record the corresponding contribution in an array cell indexed by (i,j). Repeat this process for many (not necessarily all) prime ideals in $\mathcal{F}$, and keep the array cells whose recorded contribution is closest to the value $|\mathrm{Res}(a - bx, f)|$: those are the most promising, i.e., the most likely to be smooth on the side being sieved. Proceed similarly for the other side, and check the few remaining (a,b) pairs for smoothness. Note that as $\mathfrak{p}$ varies, the set of locations where $\mathfrak{p}$ divides $(a - b\alpha)$ becomes sparser (see Fig. 3(c)), and dedicated techniques must be used to avoid large memory access penalties.

An alternative approach is to identify the good pairs (i,j) with product trees, using "batch smoothness detection" as explained in [6]. Among a given set of norms, determine their smooth part by computing their gcd with the product of the norms of all elements of $\mathcal{F}$ at once. This is efficient because it can be done while taking advantage of asymptotically fast algorithms for multiplying integers. This approach was used profitably for the previous 768-bit DLP record [29].

Among the mind-boggling number of parameters that influence the sieving procedure, the most important choices are the following.

- The large prime bound that determines the set $\mathcal{F}$. These bounds (one on each side) define the "quality" of the relations we are looking for. Cado-NFS uses the notation lpb for these bounds.
- The q-range and the size of the sieve area $\#\mathcal{A}$. This controls how many special-qs we consider, and how much work is done for each. The amount of work can also vary depending on the norm of q. The ratio between the norms of the smallest and largest special-q is important to examine: a large ratio increases the likelihood that the same relations are obtained from several different special-q (called *duplicates*), and causes diminishing returns. Enlarging the sieve area increases the yield per special-q, but also with diminishing returns

for the larger area, and costs extra memory. In order to collect the expected number of relations, it is necessary to tune these parameters.

- The size of the prime ideals $\mathfrak{p} \in \mathcal{F}$ being sieved for, and more generally *how* (and *if*) these ideals are sieved. Cado-NFS uses the notation `lim` for this upper bound, and we refer to it as the *sieving (upper) bound*. As a rule of thumb, we should sieve with prime ideals that are no larger than the size of the sieve area, so that *sieving* actually makes sense. The inner details of the lattice sieving implementation also define how sieving is performed, e.g., how we transition between algorithms in different situations like those depicted in Figs. 3(b) and 3(c), along with more subtle distinctions. This has a significant impact on the amount of memory that is necessary for sieving.

  When sieving is replaced by batch smoothness detection, we also use the notation `lim` to denote the maximum size of primes that are detected with product trees.

- Which criteria are used to decide that (a, b) are "promising" after sieving, and the further processing that is applied to them. Typically, sieving identifies a smooth part of $\mathrm{Res}(a - b\alpha, f)$, and a remaining unfactored part (cofactor). Based on the cofactor size, one must decide whether it makes sense to seek its complete factorization into elements of $\mathcal{F}$. In this case Cado-NFS uses the Bouvier-Imbert mixed representation [9]. Any prime ideal that appears in this "cofactorization" is called a large prime. By construction, large primes are between the sieving bound and the large prime bound.

4.1   Details of Our Relation Search

One of the key new techniques we adopt in our experiments is how we organize the relation search. The picture is quite different in the two cases. For IF, this phase is the most costly, and can therefore be optimized more or less independently of the others. On the other hand for DL, the linear algebra becomes the bottleneck by a large margin if the parameters of the relation search are chosen without considering the size of the matrix they produce.

The first component that we adjust is the family of special-qs that we consider. In the DL case, a good strategy to help the filtering and have a smaller matrix is to try to limit the number of large ideals involved in each relation as much as possible. The approach taken in [29] was to have special-qs that stay small, and therefore to increase the sieve area $\#\mathcal{A}$, which comes at a cost. We instead chose to use *composite special-qs* (special-q ideals with composite norm), reviving an idea that was originally proposed in [24] in the factoring case to give estimates for factoring RSA-1024. This idea was extended in [7, Sect. 4.4] to the discrete logarithm case, but to our knowledge it was never used in any practical computation. We pick composite special-qs that are larger than the large prime bound, but whose prime factors are small, and do not negatively influence the filtering. Because there are many of them, this no longer requires a large sieve area, so that we can tune it according to other tradeoffs.

In the context of IF, we chose the special-qs more classically, some of them below `lim`, and some of them between `lim` and `lpb`.

Another important idea is to adapt the relation search strategy depending on the type of special-q we are dealing with and on the quality of the relations that are sought. A graphical representation of these strategies is given in Fig. 4.

In the DL case, we want to limit as much as possible the size of the matrix and the cost of the linear algebra. To this end, we used small sieving bounds, and allowed only two large primes on each side, with rather small large prime bounds. These choices have additional advantages: a very small number of (i, j) candidates survive the sieving on the f_0-side (the side leading to the largest norms), so that following [29], we skipped sieving on the f_1-side entirely and used factorization trees to handle the survivors, thus saving time and memory by about a factor of 2 compared to sieving on both sides.

In the IF case, the same idea can also be used, at least to some extent. The first option would be to have large prime bounds and allowed number of large primes that follow the trend of previous factorization records. Then the number of survivors of sieving on one side is so large that it is not possible to use factorization trees on the other side, and we have to sieve on both sides. The other option is to reduce the number of large primes on the algebraic side (the more difficult side), so that after sieving on this side there are fewer survivors and we can use factorization trees. Of course, the number of relations per special-q will be reduced, but on the other hand the cost of finding them is reduced by about a factor of 2. In our RSA-240 computation, we found that neither option appeared to be definitively optimal, and after numerous simulations, we chose to apply the traditional strategy for the small qs (below the sieving bound lim) and the new strategy for the larger ones.

4.2 Distribution and Parallelization

For large computations such as the ones reported in this article, the relation collection step is a formidable computing effort, and it is also embarrassingly parallel: as computations for different special-qs are independent, a large number of jobs can run simultaneously, and need no inter-process communication. A large amount of computing power must be harnessed in order to complete this task in a reasonable amount of time. To this end, several aspects are crucially important.

Distribution. First, the *distribution* of the work is seemingly straightforward. We may divide the interval $[q_{min}, q_{max})$ into sub-intervals of any size we see fit, and have independent jobs process special-qs whose norm lie in these sub-intervals. This approach, however, needs to be refined if we use multiple computing facilities with inconsistent software (no common job scheduler, for instance), inconsistent hardware, and intermittent availability, possibly resulting in jobs frequently failing to complete. On several of the computing platforms we had access to, we used so-called *best-effort* jobs, that can be killed anytime by other users' jobs. This approach means that it is necessary to keep track of all "work units" that have been assigned at any given point in time, and reliably collect all results from clients. For the computations reported in this article, the machinery

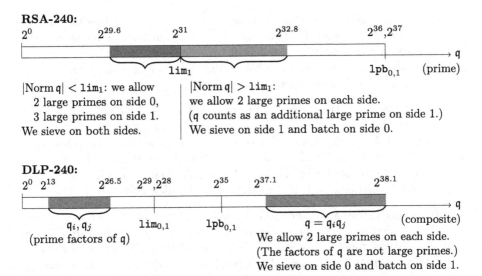

Fig. 4. Position of special-q ranges with respect to the sieving bounds lim and the large prime bounds lpb (values not to scale). For RSA-240, there are 2 distinct sub-ranges with different kinds of relations that are sought, with different strategies. For DLP-240, the special-q range is well beyond the large prime bound, thanks to the use of composite special-qs.

implemented in Cado-NFS was sufficient. It consists of a standalone server where each work unit follows a state machine with the following states: AVAILABLE (a fresh work unit submitted for processing), ASSIGNED (when a client has asked for work), OK (result successfully uploaded to server), ERROR (result failed a sanity check on server, or client error), and CANCELED (work unit timed out, presumably because the client went offline). Work units that reach states ERROR or CANCELED are resubmitted up to a few times, to guard against potential infinite loops caused by software bugs. This approach was sufficient to deal with most computation mishaps, and the few remaining "holes" were filled manually.

Parallelization. The second crucial aspect is parallelism. The lattice sieving algorithm that we use in relation collection is not, in itself, easy to parallelize. Furthermore, it is a memory-intensive computation that is quite demanding in terms of both required memory and memory throughput. In the most extreme case, having many CPU cores is of little help if the memory throughput is the limiting factor. The following (simplified) strategy was used to run the lattice sieving program at the whole machine level.

– Given the program parameters, determine the amount of memory m that is needed to process one special-q. On a machine with v virtual cores and memory M, determine the maximal number s of sub-processes and the number of

threads t per sub-process such that $sm \leq M$, $st = v$, and t is a meaningful subdivision of the machine. This strategy of maximizing s is meant to take advantage of coarse-grained parallelism.
- Each of the s sub-processes is bound to a given set of t (virtual) cores of the machine, and handles one special-$\mathfrak{q}$ at a time.

For each special-$\mathfrak{q}$, sub-processes function as follows. First divide the set of $\mathfrak{p} \in \mathcal{F}$ for which we sieve (that is, whose norm is less than $\mathtt{lim}$) into many *slices* based on several criteria (bounded slice size, constant value for $\lfloor \log |\mathrm{Norm}\,\mathfrak{p}| \rceil$, same number of conjugate ideals of $\mathfrak{p}$). The largest sieved prime ideals in $\mathcal{F}_0$ have somewhat rare hits (as in Fig. 3(c)). We handle them with so-called "bucket sieving", which proceeds in two phases that are parallelized differently:

- "fill buckets": slices are processed in parallel, and "updates" are precomputed and appended to several lists, one for each "region" of the sieve area. These lists are called "buckets". A region is typically 64kB in size. In order to avoid costly concurrent writes, several independent sets of buckets can be written to by threads working on different slices.
- "apply buckets": regions are processed in parallel. This entails reading the information from "fill buckets", that is, the updates stored in the different lists. Together with this second phase of the computation, we do everything that is easy to do at the region level: sieve small prime ideals, compute $\log |\mathrm{Res}(a - bx, f_0)|$, and determine whether the remaining cofactor is worth further examination.

A rough approximation of the memory required by the above procedure is as follows, with $\#\mathcal{A}$ denoting the size of the sieve area, and bounds 2^I and $\mathtt{lim}$ being the two ends of the bucket-sieved range, as represented in Fig. 5.

$$\text{memory required} \approx \#\mathcal{A} \times \sum_{\substack{\mathfrak{p} \in \mathcal{F}_0 \\ \mathfrak{p} \text{ bucket-sieved}}} \frac{1}{|\mathrm{Norm}\,\mathfrak{p}|}.$$

$$\approx \#\mathcal{A} \times \left(\log \log \mathtt{lim} - \log \log 2^I \right).$$

The formula above shows that if bucket sieving is used as described above for prime ideals around 2^I, which is not very large, the number of updates to store before applying them becomes a burden. To alleviate this, and deal with (comparatively) low-memory hardware, Cado-NFS can be instructed to do the "fill buckets" step above in several stages. Medium-size prime ideals (below a bound called $\mathtt{bkthresh1}$, mentioned in Fig. 5) are actually considered for only up to 256 buckets at a time. Updates for prime ideals above $\mathtt{bkthresh1}$, on the other hand, are handled in two passes. This leads to:

$$\text{memory required} \approx \#\mathcal{A} \times (\log \log \mathtt{lim} - \log \log \mathtt{bkthresh1})$$
$$+ \frac{\#\mathcal{A}}{256} \left(\log \log \mathtt{bkthresh1} - \log \log 2^I \right).$$

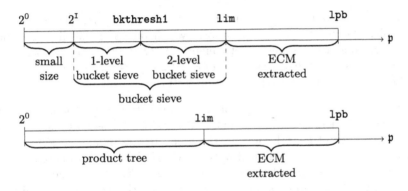

Fig. 5. Bucket sieve and product-tree sieve.

Interaction with batch smoothness detection. If the algorithms inspired by [6] are used, the impact on distribution and parallelization must be considered. The cost analysis assumes that the product of the primes to be extracted has roughly the same size as the product of *survivors* to be tested. Only then can we claim a quasi-linear asymptotic complexity. In this context, a survivor is an (a, b) pair for which the sieving done on one side reveals a smooth or promising enough norm so that the norm on the other side will enter the batch smoothness detection. The situation depends on the number of survivors per special-q.

In the DLP-240 case, the sieving parameters are chosen to reduce the size of the matrix. This has the consequence that the desired relations that are "high quality" relations are rare, so that the number of survivors per special-q is small (about 7000 per special-q, for $\#\mathcal{A} = 2^{31}$). In this setting, it makes sense to accumulate all the survivors corresponding to all the special-q of a work unit in memory, and handle them at the end. There are so few survivors that the cost of the batch smoothness detection remains small. This strategy deviates from the asymptotic analysis but works well enough, and does not interfere with the distribution techniques used by Cado-NFS.

In the RSA-240 case, the situation is quite different. The number of survivors per special-q is high, so that the relative cost of the batch smoothness detection is non-negligible. It is therefore important to accumulate the correct number of survivors before starting to build the product trees. In our setting, this corresponds to between 100 and 200 special-qs, depending on their size. In order to keep the implementation robust to these variations and to a non-predefined work unit size, we had the sieving software print the survivors to files. A new file is started after a given number of survivors have been printed. This way, the processing can be handled asynchronously by other independent jobs. Again with simplicity and robustness in mind, we preferred to have the production and the processing of the survivors running on the same node, so as to avoid network transfers. Therefore the survivor files were stored on a local disk (or even on a RAM-disk for disk-less nodes). The next question is how to share the resources on a single node, taking into account the fact that the top level of the product tree involves large integer multiplications, which do not parallelize efficiently, and yet consume a large amount of memory. After running some experiments, we found that nodes with at least 4 GB of RAM per physical core could smoothly and efficiently accommodate the following setting:

- One main job does the sieving on one side and continuously produces survivor files, each of them containing about 16M survivors. It uses as many threads as the number of logical cores on the node. In the parallelization strategy mentioned on page 12, only half of the RAM is considered available.
- About half a dozen parallel jobs wait for survivor files to be ready, and then run the batch smoothness detection followed by the final steps required to write relations. Each of these jobs has an upper limit of (for example) 8 threads. The parallelization allows us to treat product trees and ECM curves in parallel, but each multiplication is single-threaded.

We rely on the task scheduler of the operating system to take care of the competing jobs: in our setting the total number of threads that could in principle be used is larger than the number of logical cores. But since the jobs that process the survivors are restricted to just one thread when performing a long multiplication, it is important that the sieving makes full use of the cores during these potentially long periods of time.

4.3 Choosing Parameters

There are so many parameters controlling the relation collection, each of which can be tuned and that interact in complex ways, that it is tempting to choose them according to previous work and educated guesses based on what is known to be efficient for smaller sizes where many full experiments can be done. However, techniques like batch smooth detection might only be relevant for large enough sizes. We attempted as much as possible to be rigorous in our parameter selection, and for this we developed dedicated tools on top of Cado-NFS to analyze a given set of parameters. First, we carried out sample sieving over a wide q-range to deduce the projected yield, with duplicate relations removed on the fly. Second, we developed a simulator that could infer the corresponding matrix size with good accuracy, given some of the sample relations generated above. Both tools are detailed in §8.

Equipped with these tools, there was still a wide range of parameters to explore. We give some general ideas about how we narrowed our focus to a subset of the parameter ranges. This is different for the case of DL and IF.

For RSA-240, we first looked for appropriate parameters in the classical setting where we sieve on both sides and can then allow as many large primes on each side as we wish. It quickly became clear that a sieving bound of 2^{31} was perhaps not optimal but close to it. Since 2^{31} is also the current implementation limit of Cado-NFS, this settled the question. Then the sieve area $\mathcal{A}$ has to be at least around this size, so that sieving is amortized. The range of special-qs is then taken around the sieving bound. We can use the following rules to choose good large prime bounds. When doubling the large prime bounds, the number of required relations roughly doubles. Therefore the number of (unique) relations per special-q should more than double to compensate for this increased need. When this stops to be the case, we are around the optimal value for the large prime bounds. These considerations gave us a first set of parameters. We estimated that we were not too far from the optimal. Then we explored around it using our tools, also adding the possibility of having a different choice of parameters to allow batch smoothness detection for the large special-q.

In the DLP-240 case, the choices of the sieving and large prime bounds were dictated by constraints on the size of the resulting matrix. The general idea we used for this is that when the relations include at most 2 large primes on each side, the matrix size after filtering depends mostly on the sieving bound, which bounds the number of dense columns in the matrix that will be hard to eliminate during the filtering. Keeping the large prime bound small was also important to reduce the number of survivors that enter the batch smoothness detection. We used another empirical rule that helped us look for appropriate parameters. In the case of composite special-q where the number of duplicate relations could quickly increase, keeping a q-range whose upper bound is twice the lower bound is a safe way to ensure that the duplicate rate stays under control. In order to have enough qs in the range, the consequence of this was then to have them beyond the large prime bound, which might look surprising at first. Our simulation tools were crucial to validate these unusual choices before running the large-scale computation.

4.4   Computational Data

RSA-240. The relation collection for RSA-240 was carried out with large prime bounds of 36 bits on side 0 (the "rational side": f_0 is the linear polynomial) and 37 bits on side 1 (the "algebraic side": f_1 has degree 6). We used two parameter sets, both with sieve area size $\#\mathcal{A} = 2^{32}$. We considered special-qs on side 1.

For special-qs whose norm is within 0.8G–2.1G, we sieved on both sides, with sieving bounds $\lim_0 = 1.8G$ and $\lim_1 = 2.1G$. We permitted cofactors no larger than 72 bits on side 0 and 111 bits on side 1, which allowed for up to two 36-bit large primes on side 0 and three 37-bit large primes on side 1.

For special-qs whose norm is within 2.1G–7.4G, we sieved only on side 1 using $\lim_1 = 2.1G$ as above, and used "batch smoothness detection" on side 0, as done in [29] (albeit the other way around). We allowed one fewer large prime than above on side 1, which accounts for the contribution of the special-q (see Fig. 4). The "classical sieving" took 280 core-years, while "sieving + batch smoothness detection" took 514 core-years, for a total of 794 core-years.

DLP-240. For DLP-240, we allowed large primes of up to 35 bits on both sides. We used composite special-qs on side 0, within 150G–300G, and prime factors between $p_{\min} = 8192$ and $p_{\max} = 10^8$ (see also Fig. 4). Since $p_{\max} < 150G$ and $p_{\min}^3 > 300G$ this forced special-qs with two factors. We had 3.67G of these.

The sieve area size was $\#\mathcal{A} = 2^{31}$. We sieved on side 0 only, with a sieving bound of 2^{29}. We used batch smoothness detection on side 1 to detect ideals of norm below 2^{28}. Up to two 35-bit large primes were allowed on each side. This relation collection task took a total of 2400 core-years.

5 Filtering

Prior to entering the linear algebra phase, the preprocessing step called *filtering* is mostly hampered by the size of the data set that it is dealing with. Overall this phase takes negligible time, but it needs a significant amount of core memory, and the quality of the filtering matters. As filtering proceeds, the number of rows of the matrix decreases, and its density (number of non-zero elements per row) increases slightly. Filtering can be stopped at any point, which we choose to minimize the cost of the linear algebra computation that follows.

Filtering starts with "singleton" and "clique" removal [11]. This reduces the *excess* (difference between the number of relations and the number of ideals appearing in them) to almost zero. Then follows another step, called *merge* in Cado-NFS, which does some preliminary steps of Gaussian elimination to reduce the matrix size, while increasing its density as little as possible.

Section 8 describes simulations that were performed before the real filtering, to estimate the final matrix size. Filtering was done on a dual-socket, 56-core Intel Xeon E7-4850 machine with 1.5 TB of main memory. The *merge* step was performed with the parallel algorithm from [8].

RSA-240. For special-qs in 0.8G–7.4G, we collected a total of 8.9G relations which gave 6.0G unique relations. See Table 1 for exact figures. After singleton removal (note that the initial excess was negative, with 6.3G ideals), we had 2.6G relations on 2.4G ideals. After "clique removal", 1.2G relations remained, with an excess of 160 relations. The *merge* step took about 110 min of wall-clock time, plus 40 min of I/O time. It produced a 282M-dimensional matrix with 200 non-zero elements per row on average. We forgot to include around 4M free relations, which would have decreased the matrix size by 0.1%.

DLP-240. For special-qs in 150G–300G, we collected a total of 3.8G relations, which gave 2.4G unique relations. After singleton removal, we had 1.3G relations on 1.0G ideals, and therefore had an enormous excess of around 30%. After "clique removal", 150M relations remained, with an excess of 3 more relations than ideals, so we reduced the matrix size by a factor of almost 9. The *merge* step took less than 20 min, plus 8 min of I/O. It produced a 36M-dimensional matrix, with an average of 253 non-zero elements per row. We generated several other matrices, with target density ranging from 200 to 275, but the overall expected time for linear algebra did not vary much between these matrices.

6   Linear Algebra

We used the block Wiedemann algorithm [13] for linear algebra. In the short
description below, we let M be the sparse matrix that defines the linear system,
and $\#M$ denotes its number of rows and columns. We choose two integers m
and n called *blocking factors*. We also choose x and y, which are blocks of m
and n vectors. The main ingredient in the block Wiedemann algorithm is the
sequence of $m \times n$ matrices $(x^T M^i y)_{i \geq 0}$. We look at these matrices column-wise,
and form *several* sequences, n in the DLP case, and $n/64$ in the factoring case,
since for the latter it is worthwhile to handle 64 columns at a time because the
base field is $\mathbb{F}_2$. The algorithm proceeds as follows.

- The *Krylov* step computes the sequences. For each of the n sequences, this
  involves $(1/m + 1/n) \cdot \#M$ matrix-times-vector operations. In the factoring
  case, the basic operation is the multiplication of M by a *block* of 64 binary
  vectors, in a single-instruction, multiple-data manner. Note that sequences
  can be computed independently.
- The *Lingen* step computes a matrix linear generator [5,18,37].
- The *Mksol* step "makes the solution" from the previously computed data.
  This requires $1/n \cdot \#M$ matrix-times-vector operations [23, §7].

6.1   Main Aspects of the Block Wiedemann Steps

In order to make good use of a computer cluster for the block Wiedemann
algorithm, several aspects must be considered. These are intended to serve as a
guide to the choice of blocking factors m and n, along with other implementation
choices. To simplify the exposition, we assume below that the ratio m/n is
constant. It is fairly typical to have $m = 2n$.

First, the matrix-times-vector operation often *must* be done on several
machines in parallel, as the matrix itself does not fit in RAM. Furthermore,
vectors that must be kept around also have a significant memory footprint. This
opens up a wealth of MPI-level and thread-level parallelization opportunities,
which are supported by the Cado-NFS software. Two optimization criteria matter: the time per iteration, and the aggregated time over all nodes considered.
Since the computation pattern is very regular, it is easy to obtain projected
timings from a small number of matrix-times-vector iterations. Note that the
scaling is not perfect here: while having a larger number of nodes participating
in matrix-times-vector operation usually decreases the time per operation, the
decrease is not linear, since it is impeded by the communication cost.

Since no communication is needed between sequences in the Krylov step,
it is tempting to increase the parameter n in order to use more coarse-grained
parallelism. If n increases (together with m, since we assumed constant m/n), the
aggregate Krylov time over all nodes does not change, but the time to completion
does. In other words, the scaling is perfect. On the other hand, large blocking
factors impact the complexity of the Lingen step. It is therefore important to
predict the time and memory usage of the Lingen step.

The input data of the Lingen step consists of $(m + n)\#M$ elements of the base field (either $\mathbb{F}_p$ or $\mathbb{F}_2$). The space complexity of the quasi-linear algorithms described in [5,18,37] is linear in the input size, with an effectively computable ratio. Their main operations are multiplications and middle products of matrices with large polynomial entries [20]. This calls for FFT transform caching: for example, in order to multiply two $n \times n$ matrices, one can compute transforms for $2n^2$ entries, compute n^3 pointwise products and accumulate them to n^2 transforms, which are finally converted back to entries of the resulting product. However this technique must be used with care. As described above, it needs memory for $3n^2$ transforms. With no change in the running time, mindful scheduling of the allocation and deallocation of transforms leads to only $n^2 + n + 1$ transforms that are needed in memory, and it is fairly clear that it is possible to trade a leaner memory footprint with a moderately larger run time.

Another property of the Lingen step is that its most expensive operations (multiplications and middle products of matrices with large polynomial entries) parallelize well over many nodes and cores. This aspect was key to the success of the block Wiedemann computation in the reported computations.

The Mksol step represents only a fraction of the computational cost of the Krylov step. It is also straightforward to distribute, provided that some intermediate checkpoints are saved in the Krylov step. In order to allow K-way distribution of the Mksol step, it is sufficient to store checkpoints every $\#M/(nK)$ iterations during the Krylov step, for a total storage cost of $Kn \cdot \#M$ base field elements, typically stored on disk.

6.2   Choosing Parameters

In line with the observations above, we used the following roadmap in order to find appropriate parameters for linear algebra.

- Run sample timings of the matrix-times-vector iterations with a variety of possible choices that the implementation offers: number of nodes participating in iterations, number of threads per node, and binding of threads to CPU cores. While it is possible to identify sensible choices via some rules of thumb, the experience varies significantly with the hardware. We chose to pursue a simple-minded exploratory approach over an overly complex automated approach, whose benefit was unclear to us.
- Estimate the running time of the Lingen step with a simulated run. All internal steps of the algorithm used for the computation of the linear generator are well-identified tasks. Their individual cost is often tiny, but they must be repeated a large number of times. For example, for DLP-240 this involved 2^{18} repeated multiplications of polynomials of degree 1.1×10^6 over $\mathbb{F}_p$. Obtaining a reasonable estimate of the timings is therefore fairly straightforward, although it is made somewhat more complex by including multithreading, parallelism at the node level, and memory constraints.
- Estimate timings for the Mksol step, using techniques similar to the Krylov step. The wall-clock time also depends on the number of checkpoints that are saved during the Krylov step, as it governs the distribution of the work.

- The collected data gives expected wall-clock time and aggregated CPU time for the different steps as functions of the parameter choices. Then the only remaining step was to choose an optimum. Ultimately, the optimal choice very much depends on criteria visible only to an end user, or that are platform-specific. For example we had to take into account fixed compute budgets on one of the clusters that we used, as well as limits on the number of different jobs that can run simultaneously.

6.3   Checkpoints

Checkpoints have a number of uses in the computation. They allowed us to parallelize the Mksol step, to recover from failures, and in addition, they allow offline verification of the computation. All of the checks described in [16] are implemented in Cado-NFS. This helped us diagnose problems with the intermediary data that were caused by transient storage array failures.

As it turned out, there were mishaps during the linear algebra computation, because some data files were affected by transient errors from the storage servers, which thus affected the resulting computations on them. The ability to verify the data offline more than saved our day.

6.4   Computational Data

RSA-240. We ran the block Wiedemann algorithm with parameters $m = 512$, $n = 256$. The Krylov step used *best-effort* jobs, using $n/64 = 4$ sequences, 8 nodes per sequence, with two Intel Xeon Gold 6130 processors on each node and 64 virtual cores per node. The nodes were connected with Intel Omni-Path hardware. The cost per matrix-times-vector product was 1.3 s, roughly 30% of which was spent in communications. This cost 69 core-years in total, and the computation took 37 days of wall-clock time. Despite the best-effort mode, we were able to use the (otherwise busy) cluster more than 66% of the time. The Lingen step was run on 16 similar nodes, and took 13 h (0.8 core-year). The Mksol step was divided into 34 independent 8-node jobs, and took 13 core-years.

DLP-240. We ran the block Wiedemann algorithm with parameters $m = 48$, $n = 16$. The Krylov step used 4 nodes per sequence, with two Intel Xeon Platinum 8168 processors (96 virtual cores per node). The nodes were connected with Mellanox EDR hardware. The cost per matrix-times-vector product was about 2.4 s, roughly 35% of which was spent on communication. We used $16 \times 4 = 64$ nodes almost full time for 100 days, for an aggregated cost of 700 core-years. The Lingen step was run on 36 nodes, and took 62 h (12 core-years). The Mksol step was divided into 70 independent 8-node jobs running simultaneously, and was completed in slightly more than one day (70 core-years). Note that these timings were obtained on slightly different hardware than used elsewhere in this document. Table 1 reports our measurements with respect to the Xeon Gold 6130 processors that we used as a reference, leading to a slightly smaller aggregate cost (close to 650 core-years).

7 Final Steps: Square Root and Descent

In the factoring context, from the combination found by linear algebra we have a congruence of the form $x^2 \equiv y^2 \mod N$, but we only know x^2, not x. By computing two square roots we can write the potential factorization $(x - y)(x + y) \equiv 0 \mod N$. This square root computation can be done with Montgomery's square root algorithm [31], but a simple approach based on p-adic lifting also works and has quasi-linear complexity [38].

In the discrete logarithm context, the output of linear algebra consists of a large database of known logarithms. To answer a query for the logarithm of an arbitrary element, the *descent* procedure needs to search for relations that establish the link between the queried element and the known logarithms. This requires a specially adapted version of the relation collection software.

RSA-240. The final computations for RSA-240 were performed on the same hardware that was used for the filtering step (§5). After reading the 1.2G relations that survived the clique removal, and taking the quadratic characters into account, we obtained 21 dependencies in a little more than one hour.

For the square root step, we used the direct (lifting) approach described in [38]. Each dependency had about 588M relations. On the rational side, we simply multiplied the corresponding $F_0(a, b)$ values, which gave an integer of about 11 GB; we then computed its square root using the Gnu MP library [19], and reduced it modulo N. As usual, we were eager to get the factors as soon as possible. This square root step therefore prompted some development effort to have a program with a high degree of parallelism. The rational square roots of the first four dependencies were obtained on November 22 in the end of the afternoon; each one took less than two hours of wall-clock time, with a peak memory of 116 GB. The first algebraic square root was computed in 17 h wall-clock time, and finished at 02:38 am on November 24. Further code improvements reduced the wall-clock time to only 5 h. We were a bit lucky, since this first square root led to the factors of RSA-240.

DLP-240. The individual logarithm step (called "descent" for short) is dominated by the first *smoothing* step, after which subsequent descent trees must be built. We followed a practical strategy similar to the one described in [17], but since there is no rational side, sieving is not available during the smoothing step. Therefore, for a target element z, we tried many randomizations $z' = z^e$ for random exponents e, each of them being lifted to the f_1-side, LLL-reduced to get a small representative modulo the prime ideal above p used in the diagram of Fig. 2, and then tested for smoothness with a chain of ECMs. In fact, we handled a pool of candidates simultaneously, keeping only the most promising ones along the chain of ECM they go through. This strategy, which has been implemented in Cado-NFS, can be viewed as a practical version of the admissibility strategy described in [4, Chapter 4], which yields the best known complexity for this step. The chain of ECMs that we used is tuned to be able to extract with a high probability all prime factors up to 75 bits. But of course, many non-promising candidates are discarded early in the chain. We enter the descent step when we find a candidate which is 100-bit smooth.

The descent step itself consists of rewriting all prime ideals of unknown logarithm in terms of ideals of smaller norms, so that we can ultimately deduce the discrete logarithms from the ones that were computed after the linear algebra phase. As predicted by the theory, these descent trees take a short amount of time compared to the smoothing. Although this last step can be handled automatically by the general Cado-NFS machinery, we used some custom (and less robust) tools written to avoid lengthy I/O, and to reduce the wall clock time because, then again, we were eager to get the result.

No effort was made to optimize the CPU-time of this step which took a few thousand core-hours, mostly taken by the smoothing phase that was run on thousands of cores in parallel. (This resulted in us finding several smooth elements, while only one was necessary).

8   NFS Simulation

The goal of an NFS simulation is, given a set of parameters, to predict the running times of the main phases of the algorithm together with relevant data like the size of the matrix. In this section, we give some details about the tools that we developed and used before running the computations.

We assume that we are given the number N to factor (or the prime p, in the DLP case), together with a pair of polynomials, maybe not the final optimal choice, but reasonably close to the best we expect to find. We also have a set of NFS parameters that we want to test.

The general idea is to let the sieving program run for a few special-qs and use the resulting relations as models, to produce at very high speed *fake* relations corresponding to the full range of special-q. Then the filtering programs are applied to these relations, in order to produce a fake matrix. By timing a few matrix-times-vector operations, we can also estimate the linear algebra cost.

Sampling relations. For a set of special-qs evenly sampled in the target special-q range, we run the sieving program with the target parameters and keep the corresponding relations for future use. The relations that would be found as duplicates in the real filtering step are removed. These can be detected quickly as follows: for each prime ideal in the factorization of the relation that belongs to the special-q range and is less than the current special-q, we analyze whether the relation would have been found when sieving for this smaller special-q. In Cado-NFS, this online duplicate removal option has almost no impact on the sieving time and is almost perfect.

Producing fake relations. Let I be a special-q ideal for which we want to produce fake relations. We start by looking at a set S_I of special-qs of about the same size that were sieved during the sampling phase. The number of fake relations

Table 1. Comparison of 795-bit factoring and computing 795-bit prime field discrete logarithm. "$x \times y$ nodes" means that x independent jobs, each using y nodes simultaneously, were run, either in parallel (most often) or sequentially (at times). All timings are scaled to physical cores of Intel Xeon Gold 6130 processors.

	RSA-240	DLP-240
polynomial selection	76 core-years	152 core-years
$\deg f_0, \deg f_1$	1,6	3,4
relation collection		
large prime bounds	$\mathrm{lpb}_0 = 2^{36}$, $\mathrm{lpb}_1 = 2^{37}$	$\mathrm{lpb}_0 = \mathrm{lpb}_1 = 2^{35}$
type of special-qs	prime (side 1)	composite ($\mathfrak{q}_1\mathfrak{q}_2$, side 0)
method	a: lattice sieving for f_0 and f_1,	lattice sieving for f_0
	$\lvert \mathrm{Norm}\, \mathfrak{q} \rvert \in [0.8\mathrm{G}, 2.1\mathrm{G}]$	and factorization tree for f_1
	b: lattice sieving for f_1 and	$\lvert \mathrm{Norm}\, \mathfrak{q} \rvert \in [150\mathrm{G}, 300\mathrm{G}]$
	factorization tree for f_0,	
	$\lvert \mathrm{Norm}\, \mathfrak{q} \rvert \in [2.1\mathrm{G}, 7.4\mathrm{G}]$	
sieving bounds	a: $\mathrm{lim}_0 = 1.8\mathrm{G}$, $\mathrm{lim}_1 = 2.1\mathrm{G}$	$\mathrm{lim}_0 \approx 540M$
	b: $\mathrm{lim}_1 = 2.1\mathrm{G}$	
product tree bound	b: $\mathrm{lim}_0 = 2^{31}$	$\mathrm{lim}_1 = 2^{28}$
# large primes per side	a: $(2,3)$, b: $(2,2)$	$(2,2)$
sieve area $\mathcal{A}$	2^{32}	2^{31}
raw relations	8 936 812 502	3 824 340 698
unique relations	6 011 911 051	2 380 725 637
total time	794 core-years	2400 core-years
filtering		
after singleton removal	2 603 459 110 × 2 383 461 671	1 304 822 186 × 1 000 258 769
after clique removal	1 175 353 278 × 1 175 353 118	149 898 095 × 149 898 092
after merge	282M rows, density 200	36M rows, density 253
linear algebra		
blocking factors	$m = 512$, $n = 256$	$m = 48$, $n = 16$
Krylov	4 × 8 nodes, 69 core-years	16 × 4 nodes, 544 core-years
Lingen	16 nodes, 0.8 core-years	36 nodes, 12 core-years
Mksol	34 × 8 nodes, 13 core-years	70 × 8 nodes, 69 core-years
total time	83 core-years	625 core-years

that will be produced for I is chosen by picking a random element I' in S_I and taking as many relations as for I'. Then, for each relation to be produced, we pick a random relation R among all the relations of all the special-qs in S_I and modify it: replace the special-q by I, and replace each of the other ideals by another one picked randomly among the ideals of norm $\pm 20\%$ of the original norm on the same side. We therefore keep the general statistical properties of the relations (distribution of the number of large primes on each side, weight of the columns taking into account the special-qs, etc.).

Emulating the filtering. The filtering step can be run as if the relations were genuine. The only difference is that the duplicate removal must be skipped, since our relation set is based on a sample in which duplicate relations have been removed. This produces a matrix whose characteristics resemble the ones of the true matrix, and which can be used to anticipate the cost of linear algebra.

A mini-filter approach. The simulation technique we have sketched takes a tiny fraction of the total time of the real computation. However, in terms of disk and memory space, it has the same requirements and this might be prohibitive when exploring many different parameters. We propose a strategy to faithfully simulate the whole computation with all the data being reduced by a *shrink factor*, denoted σ. Typical values will be between 10 and 100 depending on the size of the experiment that has to be simulated and the expected precision.

For each special-q, the number of fake relations we produce is divided by σ. If this number is close to or smaller than 1, this is done in a probabilistic way; for instance if we have to produce 0.2 relations for the current special-q, then we produce one relation with probability 0.2 and zero otherwise. This reduces the number of relations (rows of the matrix before filtering) by a factor σ, as expected. In order to also reduce the number of columns, we divide the index of each ideal in the relation by σ, keeping each side independent of the other one. This simultaneous shrinking of rows and columns has the following properties:

- The average weight per row and per column is preserved (not divided by σ);
- More generally the row- and column-weight distributions are preserved;
- The effects of the special-qs are preserved: the average weight of the columns corresponding to special-qs will be increased by the average number of relations per special-q of that size;
- The variations of the weight distribution of the columns that depend on their size and on whether they are above or below the sieving bound are preserved.

The filtering step can then be applied to these shrunk fake relations. The final matrix is expected to be σ times smaller than the true matrix. Of course, this matrix cannot be used to directly estimate the running time of the linear algebra step: it needs to be expanded again. But often, already being able to compare the size of the matrices can help discard some bad parameter choices before only a few of the most promising ones can be simulated again, perhaps with a smaller value of σ or no shrink at all.

This very simple and easy-to-implement technique produces good results as long as the shrink factor σ is not too large. In our still very partial experiments, if the final shrunk matrix has at least a few tens of thousands of rows and columns, then the result is meaningful.

Estimates for RSA-240 and DLP-240. For DLP-240, we used such a set of fake relations in August 2018, i.e., at the very start of the relation collection. The set contained 2244M unique relations. After singleton and clique removal we obtained a matrix of size 144M, and after merge we obtained a matrix of size 37.1M with average density 200.

The closest run with real relations was carried out in the end of February 2019, with 2298M unique relations, giving a matrix of size 159M after singleton and clique removal, and a matrix of size about 40.7M with average density 200 after merge. In comparison, our actual computation collected a few more relations, and would have led to a matrix with 38.9M rows if we had stopped the filtering at density 200, while we ultimately chose to use the matrix with density 250 instead, which had 36.2M rows. Hence our technique allowed us to obtain an early precise estimate—with error below 10%—for the final matrix size.

For RSA-240 we also used the *mini-filter* approach, with a *shrink factor* of 100. In December 2018 we started with a matrix of size 66M, which gave a matrix of size 15.7M after singleton and clique removal, and a matrix of size 3.3M after merge. This is within 17% of the size of the real matrix we obtained in mid-2019, taking into account the shrink factor of 100.

Prospects for more precise simulations. Our simulation machinery is still experimental, but allowed us to be sure beforehand that we would be able to run the linear algebra with our available resources. This was especially relevant for DLP-240, where the sieving parameters are chosen with the aim of reducing the size of the matrix.

A more systematic study is needed to validate this simulator and improve its precision. In particular, we expect better results from taking a more sophisticated strategy for building fake relations based on a sample of real ones. Also, with the shrink factor, a better handling of the columns corresponding to small very dense ideals would probably help, with if possible a different algorithm for discrete logarithm and integer factorization.

9   Conclusion

It is natural to ask how our computational records compare to previous ones, and how much of our achievement can be attributed to hardware progress. A comparison with RSA-768, which was factored 10 years before the present work, would have very limited meaning. Instead, we prefer to compare to the DLP-768 record from 2017. Extrapolations based on the $L(1/3, c)$ formula suggest that DLP-240 is about 2.25 times harder than DLP-768. The article [29] reports that the DLP-768 computation required 5300 (physical) core-years on Intel Xeon E5-2660 processors, and further details indicate that the relation collection time was about 4000 core-years. We ran the Cado-NFS relation collection code with our parameters on exactly identical processors that we happened to have available. The outcome is that on these processors, we would have been able to complete the DLP-240 relation collection in only about 3100 core-years. So our parameter choice allowed us to do more work in less time.

The timeline of previous records is misleading: RSA-768 was factored in 2009, and DLP-768 was solved in 2016. Furthermore, the latter required more resources than the former (a raw ratio of core-years gives a factor of 3.5, but this would be amplified significantly if we used identical hardware). This contributes to the idea that for similar size problems, finite field discrete logarithm is much harder than integer factoring. Our experiments show that this difference is not as striking as commonly thought. Based on the data in Table 1, the ratio is only 3.3 with identical hardware: 3177 versus 953 core-years. Furthermore, this ratio only holds if we consider the DLP modulo "safe primes", which leads to more difficult linear algebra. In the so-called "DSA-like" situation where we seek discrete logarithms in a small subgroup of $\mathbb{F}_p^*$, the linear algebra becomes easier, which leads to trade-offs between relation collection and linear algebra: the ratio is likely to drop, perhaps close to or maybe even below a factor of two.

Another reason that finite field discrete logarithm is considered to be much harder than integer factoring is that the linear algebra step is believed to be a major bottleneck. It is true to some extent: in our computation, as well as in previous ones, the balance in aggregated CPU time is shifted towards less expensive linear algebra, because more infrastructure (in particular, interconnect and storage) is required for linear algebra than for sieving. However, it is important to notice that with adequate parameter choices, large sparse linear systems occurring in NFS computations *can* be handled, and at this point we are not facing a technology barrier.

Acknowledgements. We thank Gérald Monard and the support team of the EXPLOR computing center for their help, the engineers of the Grid'5000 platform, and Joshua Fried, Luke Valenta, and Rafi Rubin for sysadmin help at the University of Pennsylvania.

Funding. This work was possible thanks to a 32M-hour allocation on the Juwels super-computer from the PRACE research infrastructure. Experiments presented in this paper were carried out using the Grid'5000 testbed, supported by a scientific interest group hosted by Inria and including CNRS, RENATER and several Universities as well as other organizations (see https://www.grid5000.fr). This work was supported by the French "Ministère de l'Enseignement Supérieur et de la Recherche", by the "Conseil Régional de Lorraine", by the European Union, through the "Cyber-Entreprises" project, and by the US National Science Foundation under grant no. 1651344. High Performance Computing resources were partially provided by the EXPLOR centre hosted by the University de Lorraine. Computations carried out at the University of Pennsylvania were performed on Cisco UCS servers donated by Cisco.

References

1. Adrian, D., et al.: Imperfect forward secrecy: How Diffie-Hellman fails in practice. Commun. ACM **62**(1), 106–114 (2018). https://doi.org/10.1145/3292035
2. Aoki, K., Franke, J., Kleinjung, T., Lenstra, A.K., Osvik, D.A.: A kilobit special Number Field Sieve factorization. In: Kurosawa, K. (ed.) ASIACRYPT 2007. LNCS, vol. 4833, pp. 1–12. Springer, Heidelberg (2007). https://doi.org/10.1007/978-3-540-76900-2_1

3. Bai, S., Bouvier, C., Kruppa, A., Zimmermann, P.: Better polynomials for GNFS. Math. Comput. **85**(298), 861–873 (2016). https://doi.org/10.1090/mcom3048
4. Barbulescu, R.: Algorithmes de logarithmes discrets dans les corps finis. thèse de doctorat, Université de Lorraine, France (2013). https://tel.archives-ouvertes.fr/tel-00925228
5. Beckerman, B., Labahn, G.: A uniform approach for the fast computation of matrix-type Padé approximants. SIAM J. Matrix Anal. Appl. **15**(3), 804–823 (1994). https://doi.org/10.1137/S0895479892230031
6. Bernstein, D.J.: How to find small factors of integers (2002). http://cr.yp.to/papers.html#sf
7. Boudot, F.: On improving integer factorization and discrete logarithm computation using partial triangulation. Cryptology ePrint Archive, Report 2017/758 (2017). https://eprint.iacr.org/2017/758
8. Bouillaguet, C., Zimmermann, P.: Parallel structured Gaussian elimination for the Number Field Sieve (2019). https://hal.inria.fr/hal-02098114, preprint
9. Bouvier, C., Imbert, L.: Faster cofactorization with ECM using mixed representations. In: Kiayias, A., Kohlweiss, M., Wallden, P., Zikas, V. (eds.) PKC 2020, Part II. LNCS, vol. 12111, pp. 483–504. Springer, Cham (2020). https://doi.org/10.1007/978-3-030-45388-6_17
10. Buhler, J.P., Lenstra, H.W., Pomerance, C.: Factoring integers with the Number Field Sieve. In: Lenstra, Lenstra, Jr. [30], pp. 50–94. https://doi.org/10.1007/BFb0091534
11. Cavallar, S.: Strategies in filtering in the Number Field Sieve. In: Bosma, W. (ed.) ANTS 2000. LNCS, vol. 1838, pp. 209–231. Springer, Heidelberg (2000). https://doi.org/10.1007/10722028_11
12. Cohen, H.: A course in computational algebraic number theory. In: Axler, S., Ribet, K. (eds.) Graduate Texts in Mathematics, vol. 138. Springer, Heidelberg (1993). https://doi.org/10.1007/978-3-662-02945-9
13. Coppersmith, D.: Solving linear equations over GF(2) via block Wiedemann algorithm. Math. Comput. **62**(205), 333–350 (1994). https://doi.org/10.1090/S0025-5718-1994-1192970-7
14. David, N., Zimmermann, P.: A new ranking function for polynomial selection in the Number Field Sieve. Contemporary Mathematics (to appear) (2019). https://hal.inria.fr/hal-02151093
15. Davis, J.A., Holdridge, D.B.: Factorization using the quadratic sieve algorithm. In: Chaum, D. (ed.) CRYPTO'83, pp. 103–113. Plenum Press, New York (1983)
16. Dumas, J., Kaltofen, E., Thomé, E., Villard, G.: Linear time interactive certificates for the minimal polynomial and the determinant of a sparse matrix. In: Abramov, S.A., Zima, E.V., Gao, X. (eds.) ISSAC 2016, pp. 199–206. ACM (2016). https://doi.org/10.1145/2930889.2930908
17. Fried, J., Gaudry, P., Heninger, N., Thomé, E.: A kilobit hidden SNFS discrete logarithm computation. In: Coron, J.-S., Nielsen, J.B. (eds.) EUROCRYPT 2017, Part I. LNCS, vol. 10210, pp. 202–231. Springer, Cham (2017). https://doi.org/10.1007/978-3-319-56620-7_8
18. Giorgi, P., Lebreton, R.: Online order basis algorithm and its impact on the block Wiedemann algorithm. In: Nabeshima, K., Nagasaka, K., Winkler, F., Szántó, Á. (eds.) ISSAC 2014, pp. 202–209. ACM (2014). https://doi.org/10.1145/2608628.2608647
19. Granlund, T.: the GMP development team: GNU MP: The GNU Multiple Precision Arithmetic Library, version 6.1.2 (2016). http://gmplib.org/

20. Hanrot, G., Quercia, M., Zimmermann, P.: The middle product algorithm I. AAECC **14**(6), 415–438 (2004). https://doi.org/10.1007/s00200-003-0144-2
21. ICSI certificate notary (2019). https://notary.icsi.berkeley.edu/
22. Joux, A., Lercier, R.: Improvements to the general Number Field Sieve for discrete logarithms in prime fields: a comparison with the Gaussian integer method. Math. Comput. **72**(242), 953–967 (2003). https://doi.org/10.1090/S0025-5718-02-01482-5
23. Kaltofen, E.: Analysis of Coppersmith's block Wiedemann algorithm for the parallel solution of sparse linear systems. Math. Comput. **64**(210), 777–806 (1995). https://doi.org/10.1090/S0025-5718-1995-1270621-1
24. Kleinjung, T.: Cofactorisation strategies for the Number Field Sieve and an estimate for the sieving step for factoring 1024-bit integers. In: Proceedings of SHARCS 2006 (2006). http://www.hyperelliptic.org/tanja/SHARCS/slides06.html
25. Kleinjung, T.: On polynomial selection for the general Number Field Sieve. Math. Comput. **75**(256), 2037–2047 (2006). https://doi.org/10.1090/S0025-5718-06-01870-9
26. Kleinjung, T.: Polynomial selection. Slides presented at the CADO workshop on integer factorization (2008). http://cado.gforge.inria.fr/workshop/abstracts.html
27. Kleinjung, T., et al.: Factorization of a 768-bit RSA modulus. In: Rabin, T. (ed.) CRYPTO 2010. LNCS, vol. 6223, pp. 333–350. Springer, Heidelberg (2010). https://doi.org/10.1007/978-3-642-14623-7_18
28. Kleinjung, T., Bos, J.W., Lenstra, A.K.: Mersenne factorization factory. In: Sarkar, P., Iwata, T. (eds.) ASIACRYPT 2014. LNCS, vol. 8873, pp. 358–377. Springer, Heidelberg (2014). https://doi.org/10.1007/978-3-662-45611-8_19
29. Kleinjung, T., Diem, C., Lenstra, A.K., Priplata, C., Stahlke, C.: Computation of a 768-bit prime field discrete logarithm. In: Coron, J.-S., Nielsen, J.B. (eds.) EUROCRYPT 2017. LNCS, vol. 10210, pp. 185–201. Springer, Cham (2017). https://doi.org/10.1007/978-3-319-56620-7_7
30. Lenstra, A.K., Lenstra Jr., H.W. (eds.): The Development of the Number Field Sieve. LNM, vol. 1554. Springer, Heidelberg (1993). https://doi.org/10.1007/BFb0091534
31. Montgomery, P.L.: Square roots of products of algebraic numbers. In: Gautschi, W. (ed.) Mathematics of Computation 1943–1993: a Half-Century of Computational Mathematics. Proceedings Symposium Applied Mathematics, vol. 48, p. 567–571. American Mathematical Soc. Providence (1994). Complemented by two later unpublished drafts in 1995 and 1997
32. Murphy, B.A.: Polynomial selection for the Number Field Sieve integer factorisation algorithm. Ph.D. thesis, Australian National University (1999). http://maths-people.anu.edu.au/~brent/pd/Murphy-thesis.pdf
33. National Security Agency: Commercial national security algorithm suite (2015). https://apps.nsa.gov/iaarchive/programs/iad-initiatives/cnsa-suite.cfm
34. Pollard, J.M.: The lattice sieve. In: Lenstra, A.K., Lenstra, H.W. (eds.) The development of the Number Field Sieve. LNM, vol. 1554, pp. 43–49. Springer, Heidelberg (1993). https://doi.org/10.1007/BFb0091538
35. Schirokauer, O.: Discrete logarithms and local units. Philos. Trans. Roy. Soc. London Ser. A **345**(1676), 409–423 (1993). https://doi.org/10.1098/rsta.1993.0139
36. The CADO-NFS Development Team: CADO-NFS, an implementation of the Number Field Sieve algorithm (2019). http://cado-nfs.gforge.inria.fr/. Development version

37. Thomé, E.: Subquadratic computation of vector generating polynomials and improvement of the block Wiedemann algorithm. J. Symb. Comput. **33**(5), 757–775 (2002). https://doi.org/10.1006/jsco.2002.0533
38. Thomé, E.: Square root algorithms for the Number Field Sieve. In: Özbudak, F., Rodríguez-Henríquez, F. (eds.) WAIFI 2012. LNCS, vol. 7369, pp. 208–224. Springer, Cham (2012). https://doi.org/10.1007/978-3-642-31662-3_15

A   Challenge Results

To prove that we have computed discrete logarithms modulo $p = $ RSA-240 + 49204, we consider the integer y whose hexadecimal expansion corresponds to the ASCII encoding of the sentence "The magic words are still Squeamish Ossifrage" (without newline, and with big-endian convention, i.e., $y = $ 0x54...65). In $\mathbb{F}_p^*$, the discrete logarithm of y to base $g = 5$ is

$$\log_5 y = \text{92603135928144195363094955331732855502961099191437611616167294}$$
$$\text{20475898744562365366788100548099072093487548258752802923264}$$
$$\text{47367244150096121629264809207598195062213366889859186681269}$$
$$\text{28982506005127728321426751244111412371767375547225045851716}$$

With respect to RSA-240, the factors are given by RSA-240 $= p \times q$, with

$$\text{RSA-240} = \text{12462036678171878406583504460810659043482037465167880575481}\text{8}$$
$$\text{78888328966680118821085503603957027250874750986476843845862}\text{1}$$
$$\text{05486553797025393057189121768431828636284694840530161441643}\text{0}$$
$$\text{46806687569941524699318570418303051254959437137215902923609}\text{9,}$$
$$p = \text{5094359522858399145550510235808437141326483820241114731866}\text{60}$$
$$\text{29652182120646974670062031644347887383760625372049619334517,}$$
$$q = \text{2446242088383181505678131390240028966538209257893140145204}\text{1}$$
$$\text{22133655847709517815525821889773503059066904130204590807144}\text{7.}$$

B   RSA-250 Details

We selected the following polynomial pair, with $\text{Res}(f_0, f_1) = 48 \times$ RSA-250:

$f_1 = 86130508464000\,x^6 - 8158351307642904883773378143837698412296111200\text{0}$
$\quad - 66689953322631501408\,x^5 - 1721614429538740120011760034829385792019395\,x$
$\quad - 52733221034966333966198\,x^4 - 3113627253613202265126907420550648326\,x^2$
$\quad + 4626212456402143713674452346587\text{9}\,x^3$

$f_0 = 18511296881863829288191\text{3}\,x - 3256571715934047438664355774734330386901$

We used the following important parameters: $\text{lim}_{0,1} = 2^{31}$, $\text{lpb}_0 = 2^{36}$, $\text{lpb}_1 = 2^{37}$. We used lattice sieving for f_0 and f_1 when $|\text{Norm}\,q| \in [1G, 4G]$ with 2 large primes for f_0 and 3 large primes for f_1, and lattice sieving for f_1 and factorization tree for f_0 when $|\text{Norm}\,\mathfrak{q}| \in [4G, 12G]$, with 2 large primes for both f_0 and f_1. The sieve area was 2^{33}.

Sieving gave a total of 8 745 268 073 raw relations, of which 6.1G were unique (70.1%). After the singleton removal, there were 2.7G relations remaining on 2.6G ideals. After clique removal, there were 1.8G relations remaining, with an excess of 160. The merge step produced a matrix of about 405M rows, with average density 252 (about 100G non-zero elements). We computed 64 dependencies with the block Wiedemann algorithm, with parameters $m = 1024$ and $n = 512$. For each dependency, the square root step took about 2.3 h on the rational side (on a dual-socket, 56-core Intel Xeon E7-4850), and 10.5 h on the algebraic side.

We obtained the factorization RSA-250 $= p \times q$, with

RSA-250 $=$ 21403246502407449612644230728393335630086147151447550177975492
0881418023447140136643345519095804679610992851872470914587687396
2619215573630474547705208051190564931066876915900197594056934574
522305893259766974716817380693648946998715784949759374979937,

$p =$ 64135289477071580278790190170577389084825014742943447208116859632
02453234463023862359875266834770873766192558569463979885336 7,

$q =$ 33372027594978156556226010605355114227940760344767554666784520987
023841729210037080257448673296881877565718986258036932062711

Using the same reference (Intel Xeon Gold 6130 at 2.10 GHz) as elsewhere in this paper, the total computation time for RSA-250 was roughly 2700 core-years, including 2450 core-years for the sieving step and 250 core-years for the linear algebra step.

Complete details of the RSA-240, DLP-240, and RSA-250 computations can be found in https://gitlab.inria.fr/cado-nfs/records.

Breaking the Decisional Diffie-Hellman Problem for Class Group Actions Using Genus Theory

Wouter Castryck[1(✉)], Jana Sotáková[2], and Frederik Vercauteren[1(✉)]

[1] imec-COSIC, KU Leuven, Leuven, Belgium
wouter.castryck@esat.kuleuven.be, frederik.vercauteren@kuleuven.be
[2] QuSoft/University of Amsterdam, Amsterdam, The Netherlands
j.s.sotakova@uva.nl

Abstract. In this paper, we use genus theory to analyze the hardness of the decisional Diffie–Hellman problem (DDH) for ideal class groups of imaginary quadratic orders, acting on sets of elliptic curves through isogenies; such actions are used in the Couveignes–Rostovtsev–Stolbunov protocol and in CSIDH. Concretely, genus theory equips every imaginary quadratic order $\mathcal{O}$ with a set of assigned characters $\chi : \mathrm{cl}(\mathcal{O}) \to \{\pm 1\}$, and for each such character and every secret ideal class $[\mathfrak{a}]$ connecting two public elliptic curves E and $E' = [\mathfrak{a}] \star E$, we show how to compute $\chi([\mathfrak{a}])$ given only E and E', i.e. without knowledge of $[\mathfrak{a}]$. In practice, this breaks DDH as soon as the class number is even, which is true for a density 1 subset of all imaginary quadratic orders. For instance, our attack works very efficiently for all supersingular elliptic curves over $\mathbb{F}_p$ with $p \equiv 1 \bmod 4$. Our method relies on computing Tate pairings and walking down isogeny volcanoes.

Keywords: Decisional Diffie-Hellman · Isogeny-based cryptography · Class group action · CSIDH

1 Introduction

"The Decision Diffie–Hellman assumption (DDH) is a gold mine", Dan Boneh wrote in his 1998 overview paper [3]. This statement still holds true (maybe even more so), since DDH is fundamental to prove security of many widely used protocols such as Diffie–Hellman key agreement [16], El Gamal encryption [18], but can also be used to construct pseudo-random functions [24], and more advanced functionalities such as circular-secure encryption [4] and UC-secure oblivious transfer [25].

This work was supported in part by the Research Council KU Leuven grants C14/18/067 and STG/17/019, and by CyberSecurity Research Flanders with reference number VR20192203. JS was supported by the Dutch Research Council (NWO) through Gravitation-grant Quantum Software Consortium - 024.003.037. Date of this document: 13th July 2020.

D. Micciancio and T. Ristenpart (Eds.): CRYPTO 2020, LNCS 12171, pp. 92–120, 2020.
https://doi.org/10.1007/978-3-030-56880-1_4

Let $(G, \cdot)$ be a finite cyclic group with generator g, then the DDH problem states that it is hard to distinguish the distributions (g^a, g^b, g^{ab}) and (g^a, g^b, g^r) where a, b, r are chosen randomly in $[1, \#G]$. Due to its very definition as a distinguishing problem, DDH can be used quite naturally as a building block for provably secure constructions, i.e. IND-CPA or IND-CCA encryption [12]. In practice, the group G is typically chosen as a cyclic prime order subgroup of the multiplicative group $\mathbb{F}_p^*$ of a finite prime field or of an elliptic curve group $E(\mathbb{F}_p)$. Although Diffie and Hellman [16] originally worked in the full multiplicative group $\mathbb{F}_p^*$, it is easy to see that DDH is not secure in this case since the Legendre symbol easily distinguishes both distributions. An equivalent interpretation is that the Legendre symbol provides an efficiently computable character, mapping $\mathbb{F}_p^*$ onto the group $\{\pm 1\}$, which acts as a distinguisher.

The classical hardness of DDH is well understood and clear recommendations [13] to attain certain security levels have been agreed upon by the cryptographic community. In the quantum setting however, DDH is easy as shown by Shor [28], who devised an algorithm to solve the discrete logarithm problem (DLP) in any group in polynomial time and space. The DLP asks, given a tuple (g, g^a), to recover the exponent a. Solving DLP efficiently implies solving DDH efficiently.

Class group actions. Shor's algorithm relies on the fact that the group operation in G can be efficiently computed, i.e. group elements can be represented such that they can be composed efficiently. To devise a post-quantum secure alternative for group-based DDH one could try to represent the group G by an object with much less inherent structure, e.g. a set X. Such a representation can be obtained from a group action, which is a map $\star : G \times X \to X : (g, E) \mapsto g \star E$ compatible with the group operation, i.e. $(g \cdot h) \star E = g \star (h \star E)$. If the group action is free and transitive, i.e. for every $E, E' \in X$ there exists exactly one $g \in G$ such that $E' = g \star E$, then X is called a principal homogeneous space for G. Note that for every fixed base point $E \in X$ we thus obtain a representation of the group G by mapping g to $g \star E$.

As first observed by Couveignes [10] and later independently by Rostovtsev and Stolbunov [26], generalizing the Diffie–Hellman key agreement to group actions is immediate: Alice and Bob agree on a base point $E \in X$, each choose a secret element a and b in G, and exchange $a \star E$ and $b \star E$. Since G is commutative and $\star$ a group action, both can compute the common element $(a \cdot b) \star E$. Recovering $a \in G$ from $a \star E$ is called the vectorization problem (generalizing DLP), and recovering $(a \cdot b) \star E$ from $a \star E$ and $b \star E$ is called parallelization (generalizing CDH). When both problems are hard, Couveignes called X a hard homogeneous space for G. Couveignes, Rostovtsev and Stolbunov (CRS) and more recently CSIDH [8] by Castryck, Lange, Martindale, Panny and Renes instantiated this framework as follows: G is the class group $\mathrm{cl}(\mathcal{O})$ of an order $\mathcal{O}$ in an imaginary quadratic field, and $X = \mathcal{Ell}_p(\mathcal{O}, t)$ is the set of elliptic curves over a finite prime field $\mathbb{F}_p$ with $\mathbb{F}_p$-rational endomorphism ring $\mathcal{O}$ and trace of Frobenius t. Whereas CRS restricted to ordinary elliptic curves, CSIDH uses supersingular elliptic curves and is several orders of magnitude faster than CRS.

Using the above group action can be seen as a trade-off: the lack of a natural operation on the set X itself makes the construction possibly post-quantum secure, but also limits its flexibility, i.e. it is not possible to simply translate any DLP-based protocol into an equivalent one using group actions. Furthermore, since X is supposed to "hide" G, it is unknown whether the group structure of G itself has any influence on the hardness of the underlying group action problems. In this paper, we show that it does.

Contributions. The decisional Diffie-Hellman problem (sometimes called decisional parallelization) for class group actions asks to distinguish between the distributions $([\mathfrak{a}] \star E, [\mathfrak{b}] \star E, ([\mathfrak{a}] \cdot [\mathfrak{b}]) \star E)$ and $([\mathfrak{a}] \star E, [\mathfrak{b}] \star E, [\mathfrak{r}] \star E)$ with $[\mathfrak{a}], [\mathfrak{b}], [\mathfrak{r}]$ random elements in $\mathrm{cl}(\mathcal{O})$. A natural attack strategy would be to try to exploit the group structure of $\mathrm{cl}(\mathcal{O})$, as was done for DDH in $\mathbb{F}_p^*$ using the Legendre symbol. We immediately run into two problems:

1. In general, very little is known about the concrete structure of $\mathrm{cl}(\mathcal{O})$ as an abelian group. For instance, computing the order of $\mathrm{cl}(\mathcal{O})$ is already a highly non-trivial task [1,19]. A notable exception is the structure of the 2-torsion subgroup of $\mathrm{cl}(\mathcal{O})$: genus theory [11, I.§3 & II.§7] provides a very explicit description of $\mathrm{cl}(\mathcal{O})[2] \simeq \mathrm{cl}(\mathcal{O})/\mathrm{cl}(\mathcal{O})^2$ by defining a set of characters $\chi_i : \mathrm{cl}(\mathcal{O}) \to \{\pm 1\}$ and recovering $\mathrm{cl}(\mathcal{O})^2$ as the intersection of the kernels of the χ_i. The characters χ_i correspond to the prime factors m_i of the discriminant $\Delta_{\mathcal{O}}$ (with the prime 2 requiring special treatment) and can be computed in time polynomial in the size of m_i. Note that each of these characters χ_i (if non-trivial) can be used to break DDH in $\mathrm{cl}(\mathcal{O})$ itself; however we are not trying to solve DDH in $\mathrm{cl}(\mathcal{O})$, but DDH for class group *actions*.
2. Given the structure of $\mathrm{cl}(\mathcal{O})[2]$ through genus theory, it is unclear how the characters χ_i can be computed directly on elements in X, i.e. given an element $[\mathfrak{a}] \star E$ for some unknown $[\mathfrak{a}] \in \mathrm{cl}(\mathcal{O})$, we need to compute $\chi_i([\mathfrak{a}])$ (without computing $[\mathfrak{a}]$ first, since vectorization is assumed hard).

The main contribution of this paper is an algorithm to compute the characters χ_i directly on the set $X = \mathcal{E}\ell\ell_p(\mathcal{O}, t)$ in time exponential in the size of m_i. Since we only need to compute one such χ_i efficiently to break DDH, we conclude that DDH for class group actions is insecure when $\mathrm{cl}(\mathcal{O})[2]$ is non-trivial and the discriminant $\Delta_{\mathcal{O}}$ is divisible by a small enough prime factor. Since $\mathrm{cl}(\mathcal{O})[2]$ is only trivial when $\Delta_{\mathcal{O}} = -q$ or $\Delta_{\mathcal{O}} = -4q$ with $q \equiv 3 \bmod 4$ prime, and since almost all integers contain polynomially small prime factors (this follows, at least heuristically, from Mertens' third theorem; see [32, III.§6] for more precise statements), we expect that our attack works in polynomial time (in $\log p$) for a subset of density 1 of all imaginary quadratic orders.

In the special case of supersingular elliptic curves over $\mathbb{F}_p$, our attack does not apply for primes $p \equiv 3 \pmod 4$. However, for $p \equiv 1 \pmod 4$, we have $\mathcal{O} = \mathbb{Z}[\sqrt{-p}]$ and $\Delta_{\mathcal{O}} = -4p$. Genus theory defines a non-trivial character δ associated with the prime divisor 2 of $\Delta_{\mathcal{O}}$. We derive a very simple formula to compute $\delta([\mathfrak{a}])$ that uses only the Weierstrass equations of E and $E' = [\mathfrak{a}] \star E$.

In this case, our attack is particularly efficient and we can break DDH using a few exponentiations in $\mathbb{F}_p$.

High level overview of the attack. To explain the main underlying ideas, we detail the thought process we followed to derive the attack in a simple (yet very general) setting. Fixing a base curve E, the class group action $\star$ gives us a representation of $\mathrm{cl}(\mathcal{O})$ on the set $X = \mathcal{E}\ell\ell_p(\mathcal{O}, t)$ by mapping a class $[\mathfrak{a}]$ to $E' = [\mathfrak{a}] \star E$. For every odd prime divisor m of the discriminant $\Delta_\mathcal{O}$, genus theory provides a character

$$\chi : \mathrm{cl}(\mathcal{O}) \to \{\pm 1\} : [\mathfrak{a}] \mapsto \left(\frac{\mathrm{N}(\mathfrak{a})}{m} \right),$$

where $\left(\frac{\cdot}{\cdot} \right)$ denotes the Legendre symbol and the representative $\mathfrak{a}$ of the class $[\mathfrak{a}]$ is chosen such that its norm $\mathrm{N}(\mathfrak{a})$ is coprime to m. The goal is to compute $\chi([\mathfrak{a}])$ given only the pair (E, E').

Let $\varphi : E \to E'$ denote the isogeny corresponding to $\mathfrak{a}$, then $\mathrm{N}(\mathfrak{a}) = \deg(\varphi)$, so to compute χ, it suffices to determine $\deg(\varphi) \bmod m$, up to non-zero squares in $\mathbb{Z}/(m)$. The starting idea is the following: assume we know a tuple $(P, Q) \in E^2$ with $P \in E[m]$ and the corresponding tuple $(\varphi(P), \varphi(Q)) \in E'^2$, computing $\deg(\varphi) \bmod m$ is easy thanks to the compatibility of the reduced m-Tate pairing T_m

$$T_m(\varphi(P), \varphi(Q)) = T_m(P, Q)^{\deg(\varphi)}.$$

If the pairing is non-trivial, both sides will be primitive m-th roots of unity, so computing discrete logs gives $\deg(\varphi) \bmod m$.

The difficulty is of course, that in practice we are not given such corresponding tuples (P, Q) and $(\varphi(P), \varphi(Q))$, so we need to find a workaround. The only information we really have about φ is that it is an $\mathbb{F}_p$-rational isogeny of degree coprime to m. Under the assumption that $E(\mathbb{F}_p)$ has a *unique* subgroup of order m, this implies that $E'(\mathbb{F}_p)$ similarly has such a unique subgroup, and furthermore, $\varphi(E(\mathbb{F}_p)[m]) = E'(\mathbb{F}_p)[m]$. If we let P be a generator of $E(\mathbb{F}_p)[m]$ and P' a generator of $E'(\mathbb{F}_p)[m]$, then we know there exists some $k \in [1, m-1]$ such that $\varphi(P) = kP'$. Note however, that if we assume we know a point Q and its image $\varphi(Q)$ (but not the image of P under φ), we do not learn anything since the values $T_m(kP', \varphi(Q)) = T_m(P', \varphi(Q))^k$ run through the whole of μ_m for $k = 1, \ldots, m-1$ and we do not know k.

The main insight now is that we do not need to recover $\deg(\varphi)$ exactly but only up to squares, so if we could recover $k^2 \deg(\varphi)$ then it is clear we can still compute $\chi([\mathfrak{a}])$. This hints at a possible solution as long as Q is somehow derived from P and that the *same* unknown scalar k can be used to compensate for the difference not only between $\varphi(P)$ and P', but also between $\varphi(Q)$ and Q'. Indeed, computing $T_m(P', Q')$ would then recover the correct value up to a square in the exponent, namely $T_m(P, Q)^{\deg(\varphi)k^2}$. The simplest choice clearly is to take $Q = P$ and $Q' = P'$, and if there is no $\mathbb{F}_p$-rational m^2-torsion, we can show that the self-pairings $T_m(P, P)$ and $T_m(P', P')$ are non-trivial. This feature is specific to the

Tate pairing, and resorting to the Weil pairing would fail. Denote with $\mathrm{val}_m(N)$ the m-adic valuation of N, i.e. the maximum power v such that $m^v \mid N$, then $\mathrm{val}_m(\#E(\mathbb{F}_p)) = 1$ is equivalent to the existence of a unique rational subgroup of order m and the non-existence of rational m^2-torsion.

In the more general case of $v = \mathrm{val}_m(\#E(\mathbb{F}_p)) > 1$, we first walk down to the floor of the m-isogeny volcano reaching a curve E_0 with $E_0(\mathbb{F}_q)[m^\infty] = \mathbb{Z}/(m^v)$, and then choose points P and P' of order m and corresponding points Q and Q' of order m^v satisfying $m^{v-1}Q = P$ and $m^{v-1}Q' = P'$. Note that also in this case, the same unknown scalar k will compensate for both differences.

To sum up, we use the Tate pairing of certain points to obtain information on $\deg \varphi$ (up to squares $\mathrm{mod}\, m$). By genus theory, we see that we are actually computing the assigned characters of $\mathrm{cl}(\mathcal{O})$ directly from curves in $\mathscr{Ell}_p(\mathcal{O}, t)$. Whenever the characters are non-trivial, their multiplicative property allows us to break DDH in $\mathscr{Ell}_p(\mathcal{O}, t)$.

Paper organization. In Sect. 2 we recall the necessary background on isogenies and isogeny volcanoes, class group actions, genus theory and the Tate pairing. In Sect. 3 we derive an algorithm to compute the assigned characters in the case of ordinary elliptic curves, whereas in Sect. 4 we deal with supersingular curves. In Sect. 5 we analyze the impact on the DDH problem for class group actions, report on our implementation of the attack, and propose countermeasures. Finally, Sect. 6 concludes the paper and provides avenues for further research.

2 Background

2.1 Isogenies

Let $E, E'/\mathbb{F}_q$ be elliptic curves. An *isogeny* $\varphi : E \to E'$ is a non-constant morphism such that $\varphi(\mathbf{0}_E) = \mathbf{0}_{E'}$, where $\mathbf{0}$ denotes the point at infinity. Equivalently, an isogeny is a surjective group homomorphism of elliptic curves, which is also an algebraic morphism. An *endomorphism* of E is either the zero map or an isogeny from E to itself, and the set of endomorphisms forms a ring $\mathrm{End}(E)$ under addition and composition. We write $\mathrm{End}_{\mathbb{F}_q}(E)$ to denote the subring of endomorphisms defined over $\mathbb{F}_q$. Two important examples of endomorphisms are: the multiplication-by-n map $[n] : E \to E, P \mapsto [n]P$ (often simply denoted by n) and the q-power Frobenius endomorphism $\pi_q : E \to E : (x, y) \mapsto (x^q, y^q)$. If q is clear from the context, we will simply write π. In $\mathrm{End}(E)$, the Frobenius endomorphism satisfies $\pi^2 - t\pi + q = 0$ where $t = \mathrm{tr}\,\pi$ is called the *trace of Frobenius* and satisfies $|t| \le 2\sqrt{q}$. Alternatively, the trace of Frobenius is characterized by $\#E(\mathbb{F}_q) = q + 1 - t$. If $\gcd(t, q) = 1$, the curve is called ordinary, otherwise it is called supersingular. Unless $|t| = 2\sqrt{q}$, which can only happen for supersingular elliptic curves over even degree extension fields, we have that $\mathcal{O} = \mathrm{End}_{\mathbb{F}_q}(E)$ is an order in the imaginary quadratic field $K = \mathbb{Q}(\pi) = \mathbb{Q}(\sqrt{t^2 - 4q})$. Since $\mathcal{O}$ always contains $\mathbb{Z}[\pi]$ as a suborder, its discriminant $\Delta_{\mathcal{O}}$ satisfies $\Delta_{\mathbb{Z}[\pi]} = t^2 - 4q = c^2 \Delta_{\mathcal{O}}$ for some non-zero $c \in \mathbb{Z}$.

The degree of an isogeny φ is just its degree as a morphism, which equals the size of the kernel $\ker(\varphi)$ (we say φ is a *separable* isogeny), except possibly if $\mathrm{char}(\mathbb{F}_q)\,|\,\deg(\varphi)$, where it may happen that the kernel is smaller (we say φ is an *inseparable* isogeny). Separable isogenies can always be reconstructed from their kernel. When the kernel $\ker(\varphi)$ is invariant under Frobenius (as a set), the corresponding isogeny φ is $\mathbb{F}_q$-rational. Note that we do not necessarily have $\ker(\varphi) \subset E(\mathbb{F}_q)$, but only that φ can be given by $\mathbb{F}_q$-rational maps. The kernel of the multiplication by n map is denoted as $E[n]$, and we set $E[n^\infty] = \cup_{k\in\mathbb{N}_{>0}} E[n^k]$.

For a prime $m \nmid \mathrm{char}\,\mathbb{F}_q$, isogenies of degree m are called *m-isogenies* and their kernel $\ker\varphi \subset E[m]$ is always a cyclic subgroup of $E[m]$. It is therefore natural that the m-isogenies of an elliptic curve E depend on the structure of $E(\mathbb{F}_q)[m^\infty]$. Moreover, for any isogeny $\varphi : E \to E'$, there is a *dual isogeny* $\hat{\varphi} : E' \to E$ satisfying $\varphi \circ \hat{\varphi} = [\deg\varphi]$ and $\hat{\varphi} \circ \varphi = [\deg\varphi]$. The dual isogeny $\hat{\varphi}$ has the same degree as φ.

2.2 Volcanoes

By Tate's theorem [31], two elliptic curves over $\mathbb{F}_q$ are isogenous (over $\mathbb{F}_q$) if and only if they have the same number of $\mathbb{F}_q$-rational points, which is equivalent to having the same trace of Frobenius. Let $\mathcal{E}\ell\ell_q(t)$ be the set of $\mathbb{F}_q$-isomorphism classes of elliptic curves over $\mathbb{F}_q$ with trace of Frobenius t, and assume that $\mathcal{E}\ell\ell_q(t)$ is non-empty.

For a prime number $m \nmid q$, we define the *m-isogeny graph* $G_{q,m}(t)$ as follows: the set of vertices is $\mathcal{E}\ell\ell_q(t)$ and the edges are m-isogenies. Away from elliptic curves with extra automorphisms (i.e., away from the curves with j-invariant 0 or 1728), this graph can be made undirected by identifying dual isogenies.

An *m-volcano* is a connected undirected graph with vertices partitioned into levels $V_0, \dots, V_h$ such that

- the subgraph V_h (the *crater*) is a regular connected graph of degree ≤ 2,
- for all $0 \leq i < h$, every vertex in level V_i is connected to exactly one vertex in V_{i+1},
- for all $i > 0$, every vertex in V_i has degree $m + 1$.

Note that this implies that all the vertices on level V_0 (*the floor*) have degree 1. We call h the *height* of the volcano (some authors swap V_h and V_0 and call h the *depth*). The crater V_h is also sometimes called the surface of the volcano. An example of a volcano can be seen in Fig. 1.

Theorem 1. *Let $G_{q,m}(t)$ be as above, and assume that $\gcd(t,q) = 1$, so that we are in the ordinary case. Take any connected component V of $G_{q,m}(t)$ that does not contain curves with j-invariant 0 or 1728. Then V is a volcano, say of height h, and*

1. the elliptic curves on level i all have the same endomorphism ring $\mathcal{O}_i$, with discriminant $\Delta_{\mathcal{O}_i} = m^{2(h-i)}\Delta_{\mathcal{O}_h}$,

2. the endomorphism ring $\mathcal{O}_h$ of the elliptic curves on the crater V_h is locally maximal at m; equivalently, if m is odd then $m^2 \nmid \Delta_{\mathcal{O}_h}$, while if $m = 2$ and $4 \mid \Delta_{\mathcal{O}_h}$ then $\Delta_{\mathcal{O}_h}/4 \equiv 2, 3 \bmod 4$,

3. the endomorphism ring $\mathcal{O}_0$ of the elliptic curves on the floor V_0 satisfies $\mathrm{val}_m(\Delta_{\mathcal{O}_0}) = \mathrm{val}_m(t^2 - 4q)$.

In particular, if m is odd then $h = \lfloor \mathrm{val}_m(t^2 - 4q)/2 \rfloor$, while if $m = 2$ then h may be 1 less than this value.

Proof. This follows from Proposition 23 in [21] (note that the name volcano was introduced only later by [17]).

An analogous volcano structure for supersingular curves over $\mathbb{F}_p$ was given in [15], but will not be needed in our discussion of supersingular curves in Sect. 4.

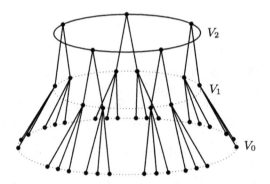

Fig. 1. A 3-volcano of height $h = 2$, together with its levels. This corresponds to the case where the prime 3 splits in $\mathcal{O}_h$, into two degree 3 prime ideals whose ideal-classes (which are each other's inverses) have order 5.

Suppose $E \in V_i$ and $E' \in V_j$. We say that an m-isogeny $\varphi : E \to E'$ is *ascending (descending, horizontal)* if $j = i+1$ ($j = i-1$, $j = i$). On the volcano, this corresponds to the crater being on top, the floor on the bottom, while the horizontal steps are permitted along the crater only.

Remark 2. If $j = 0$ or $j = 1728$ do appear in V, then the theorem remains "sufficiently valid" for our purposes; the only difference is that $G_{q,m}(t)$ may become directed: there may exist descending isogenies from the crater V_h to level V_{h-1} which need to be considered with multiplicity, while the dual ascending isogeny still accounts for multiplicity 1. We will ignore this issue in what follows: the endomorphism rings of the curves with j-invariant 0 or 1728 have trivial class groups, so this remark only affects suborders of (certain) number fields having class number 1. Such suborders are usually not considered in isogeny-based cryptography, although they make an appearance in the recent OSIDH protocol due to Colò and Kohel [9].

2.3 Diffie–Hellman for Class Group Actions

Let $\mathcal{O}$ be an order in an imaginary quadratic number field and let $t \in \mathbb{Z}$. To each prime power $q = p^n$ we associate the set

$$\mathcal{E}\ell\ell_q(\mathcal{O}, t) = \{\,\text{elliptic curves } E/\mathbb{F}_q \mid \text{End}_{\mathbb{F}_q}(E) \cong \mathcal{O} \text{ and } \text{tr}\,\pi_q = t\,\}/\cong_{\mathbb{F}_q}.$$

If this set is non-empty, then the ideal-class group $\text{cl}(\mathcal{O})$ acts freely on $\mathcal{E}\ell\ell_q(\mathcal{O}, t)$: for any invertible ideal $\mathfrak{a} \subset \text{End}_{\mathbb{F}_q}(E)$ of norm coprime with p (every ideal class contains such ideals), we set $E[\mathfrak{a}] = \cap_{\alpha \in \mathfrak{a}} \ker \alpha$ and define

$$[\mathfrak{a}] \star E = E/E[\mathfrak{a}].$$

In other words, we let $[\mathfrak{a}] \star E$ be the (unique) codomain of a separable $\mathbb{F}_q$-rational isogeny φ with domain E and kernel $E[\mathfrak{a}]$.

The action is usually transitive but exceptionally there may be two orbits; this happens if and only if the discriminant $\Delta_{\mathcal{O}}$ is a quadratic non-residue modulo p (which is a very rare event, and not possible in the case of ordinary elliptic curves because $t^2 - 4q = c^2 \Delta_{\mathcal{O}}$ for some c). For a proof of the above claims, see [34] and the erratum pointed out in [27, Thm. 4.5].

Remark 3. The set $\mathcal{E}\ell\ell_q(t)$ is not the same as $\mathcal{E}\ell\ell_q(\mathcal{O}, t)$. One should think of the sets $\mathcal{E}\ell\ell_q(\mathcal{O}, t)$ for the various orders $\mathcal{O}$ as horizontal slices of $\mathcal{E}\ell\ell_q(t)$. Indeed, in Theorem 1, we saw that the curves on the same level of an m-volcano have the same endomorphism ring $\mathcal{O}$.

When $\#\text{cl}(\mathcal{O})$ is large, the set $\mathcal{E}\ell\ell_q(\mathcal{O}, t)$ is conjectured to be a hard homogeneous space in the sense of Couveignes [10], who was the first to propose its use for Diffie–Hellman style key exchange; we refer to [8,14] for recent advances in making this construction efficient. Couveignes' proposal was rediscovered by Rostovtsev and Stolbunov [26], and elaborated in greater detail in Stolbunov's PhD thesis, which contains the first appearance of the decisional Diffie–Hellman problem for group actions [29, Prob. 2.2].

Definition 4 (DDH-CGA). *Let $\mathbb{F}_q, t, \mathcal{O}$ be as above and let $E \in \mathcal{E}\ell\ell_q(\mathcal{O}, t)$. The decisional Diffie–Hellman problem is to distinguish with non-negligible advantage between the distributions $([\mathfrak{a}] \star E, [\mathfrak{b}] \star E, [\mathfrak{ab}] \star E)$ and $([\mathfrak{a}] \star E, [\mathfrak{b}] \star E, [\mathfrak{c}] \star E)$ where $[\mathfrak{a}], [\mathfrak{b}], [\mathfrak{c}]$ are chosen at random from $\text{cl}(\mathcal{O})$.*

Stolbunov writes: "As far as we are concerned, the most efficient approach is to solve the corresponding $\mathcal{CL}$ group action inverse problem ($\mathcal{CL}$-GAIP)." In our terminology, this reads that in order to break DDH-CGA, one needs to obtain $[\mathfrak{a}]$ from $[\mathfrak{a}] \star E$. This paper clearly disproves this statement.

2.4 Genus Theory

Genus theory studies which natural numbers arise as norms of ideals in a given ideal class of an imaginary quadratic order $\mathcal{O}$. It shows that this question is governed by the coset of $\mathrm{cl}(\mathcal{O})^2$, the subgroup of squares inside $\mathrm{cl}(\mathcal{O})$, to which the ideal class belongs. The details are as follows; this section summarizes parts of [11, I.§3 & II.§7].

Let $\Delta_{\mathcal{O}} \equiv 0, 1 \bmod 4$ be the discriminant of $\mathcal{O}$, say with distinct odd prime factors $m_1 < m_2 < \ldots < m_r$. If $\Delta_{\mathcal{O}} \equiv 1 \bmod 4$ then we call

$$\chi_i : (\mathbb{Z}/\Delta_{\mathcal{O}})^* \to \{\pm 1\} : a \mapsto \left(\frac{a}{m_i}\right) \qquad \text{(for } i = 1, \ldots, r)$$

the *assigned characters* of $\mathcal{O}$. If $\Delta_{\mathcal{O}} = -4n \equiv 0 \bmod 4$, then we extend this list with δ if $n \equiv 1, 4, 5 \bmod 8$, with ϵ if $n \equiv 6 \bmod 8$, with $\delta\epsilon$ if $n \equiv 2 \bmod 8$, and with both δ and ϵ if $n \equiv 0 \bmod 8$. Here

$$\delta : a \mapsto (-1)^{(a-1)/2} \qquad \text{and} \qquad \epsilon : a \mapsto (-1)^{(a^2-1)/8}.$$

If $n \equiv 3, 7 \bmod 8$ then the list is not extended.

Let $\mu \in \{r, r+1, r+2\}$ denote the total number of assigned characters and consider the map $\Psi : (\mathbb{Z}/\Delta_{\mathcal{O}})^* \to \{\pm 1\}^\mu$ having these assigned characters as its components. Then Ψ is surjective and its kernel H consists precisely of those integers that are coprime with (and that are considered modulo) $\Delta_{\mathcal{O}}$ and arise as norms of non-zero principal ideals of $\mathcal{O}$. This leads to a chain of maps

$$\Phi : \mathrm{cl}(\mathcal{O}) \longrightarrow \frac{(\mathbb{Z}/\Delta_{\mathcal{O}})^*}{H} \xrightarrow{\cong} \{\pm 1\}^\mu,$$

where the first map sends an ideal class $[\mathfrak{a}]$ to the norm of $\mathfrak{a}$ (it is always possible to choose a representant of norm coprime with $\Delta_{\mathcal{O}}$) and the second map is induced by Ψ. Basically, genus theory tells us that $\ker \Phi = \mathrm{cl}(\mathcal{O})^2$, the subgroup of squares in $\mathrm{cl}(\mathcal{O})$; the cosets of $\mathrm{cl}(\mathcal{O})^2$ inside $\mathrm{cl}(\mathcal{O})$ are called *genera*, with $\mathrm{cl}(\mathcal{O})^2$ itself being referred to as the *principal genus*.

Remark 5. By abuse of notation, we can and will also view $\chi_1, \chi_2, \ldots, \chi_r, \delta, \epsilon$ as morphisms $\mathrm{cl}(\mathcal{O}) \to \{\pm 1\}$, obtained by composing Φ with projection on the corresponding coordinate.

It can be shown that the image of Φ is a subgroup of $\{\pm 1\}^\mu$ having index 2, so that the cardinality of $\mathrm{cl}(\mathcal{O})/\mathrm{cl}(\mathcal{O})^2 \cong \mathrm{cl}(\mathcal{O})[2]$ equals $2^{\mu-1}$. More precisely, if we write $\Delta_{\mathcal{O}} = -2^a b$ with $b = m_1^{e_1} m_2^{e_2} \cdots m_r^{e_r}$, then this is accounted for by the character

$$\chi_1^{e_1} \cdot \chi_2^{e_2} \cdots \chi_r^{e_r} \cdot \delta^{\frac{b+1}{2} \bmod 2} \cdot \epsilon^{a \bmod 2}, \tag{1}$$

which is non-trivial when viewed on $(\mathbb{Z}/\Delta_{\mathcal{O}})^*$, but becomes trivial when viewed on $\mathrm{cl}(\mathcal{O})$. For example, if $\Delta_{\mathcal{O}}$ is squarefree and congruent to 1 mod 4, then the image of Φ consists of those tuples in $\{\pm 1\}^r$ whose coordinates multiply to 1.

Our main goal is to break DDH in $\mathcal{E}\ell\ell_q(\mathcal{O}, t)$. To do this, we will compute the coordinate components of the map Φ, i.e. upon input of two elliptic curves $E, E' \in \mathcal{E}\ell\ell_q(\mathcal{O}, t)$ that are connected by a secret ideal class $[\mathfrak{a}] \in \mathrm{cl}(\mathcal{O})$, for each assigned character χ we will describe how to compute $\chi(E, E') := \chi([\mathfrak{a}])$. This is done in the next sections.

Example 6. In Sect. 4, we will study supersingular elliptic curves defined over $\mathbb{F}_p$ with $p \equiv 1 \bmod 4$. Here $\mathcal{O} = \mathbb{Z}[\sqrt{-p}]$ has discriminant $-4p$, thus there are two assigned characters: δ and the Legendre character χ associated with p. But (1) tells us that $\chi([\mathfrak{a}]) = \delta([\mathfrak{a}])$ and also that χ and δ are necessarily non-trivial characters of $\mathrm{cl}(\mathcal{O})$. So it suffices to compute $\delta([\mathfrak{a}])$, which as we will see can be done very efficiently.

2.5 The Tate Pairing

We briefly recall the main properties of the (reduced) *Tate pairing* T_m, which is defined as

$$T_m : E(\mathbb{F}_{q^k})[m] \times E(\mathbb{F}_{q^k})/mE(\mathbb{F}_{q^k}) \to \mu_m : (P, Q) \mapsto f_{m,P}(D)^{(q^k-1)/m}.$$

Here k is the embedding degree, i.e. the smallest extension degree k such that $\mu_m \subset \mathbb{F}_{q^k}^*$; the function $f_{m,P}$ a so-called Miller function, i.e. an $\mathbb{F}_{q^k}$-rational function with divisor $(f_{m,P}) = m(P) - m(\mathbf{0})$; D an $\mathbb{F}_{q^k}$-rational divisor equivalent to $(Q) - (\mathbf{0})$ coprime to the support of $(f_{m,P})$. If the Miller function $f_{m,P}$ is normalized, and $Q \neq P$, then the pairing can be simply computed as $T_m(P, Q) = f_{m,P}(Q)^{(q^k-1)/m}$.

The reduced Tate pairing T_m has the following properties:

1. Bilinearity: $T_m(P, Q_1 + Q_2) = T_m(P, Q_1)T_m(P, Q_2)$ and $T_m(P_1 + P_2, Q) = T_m(P_1, Q)T_m(P_2, Q)$.
2. Non-degeneracy: for all $P \in E(\mathbb{F}_{q^k})[m]$ with $P \neq \mathbf{0}$, there exists a point $Q \in E(\mathbb{F}_{q^k})/mE(\mathbb{F}_{q^k})$ such that $T_m(P, Q) \neq 1$. Similarly, for all $Q \in E(\mathbb{F}_{q^k})$ with $Q \notin mE(\mathbb{F}_{q^k})$, there exists a $P \in E(\mathbb{F}_{q^k})[m]$ with $T_m(P, Q) \neq 1$.
3. Compatibility: let φ be an $\mathbb{F}_q$-rational isogeny, then

$$T_m(\varphi(P), \varphi(Q)) = T_m(P, Q)^{\deg(\varphi)}.$$

4. Galois invariance: let $\sigma \in \mathrm{Gal}(\overline{\mathbb{F}}_q/\mathbb{F}_q)$ then $T_m(\sigma(P), \sigma(Q)) = \sigma(T_m(P, Q))$.

3 Computing the Characters for Ordinary Curves

Let $E/\mathbb{F}_q$ be an ordinary elliptic curve with endomorphism ring $\mathcal{O}$ and let m be a prime divisor of $\Delta_\mathcal{O}$. Note that $m \nmid q$, since otherwise $m \mid \Delta_\mathcal{O} \mid t^2 - 4q$ would imply that $\gcd(t, q) \neq 1$, contradicting that E is ordinary. By extending the base field if needed, we can assume without loss of generality that $\mathrm{val}_m(\#E(\mathbb{F}_q)) \geq 1$. The approach described in the introduction corresponds to $\mathrm{val}_m(\#E(\mathbb{F}_q)) = 1$, which implies that $E(\mathbb{F}_q)[m^\infty] \cong \mathbb{Z}/(m)$. The idea was to recover the character from the self-pairings $T_m(P, P)$ and $T_m(P', P')$, with P (resp. P') any non-zero $\mathbb{F}_q$-rational m-torsion point on E (resp. E').

In general we have $E(\mathbb{F}_q)[m^\infty] \cong \mathbb{Z}/(m^r) \times \mathbb{Z}/(m^s)$ for integers $1 \le r \ge s \ge 0$. The next theorem shows that by walking all the way down to the floor of the m-isogeny volcano, we always end up on a curve $E_0/\mathbb{F}_q$ with $E_0(\mathbb{F}_q)[m^\infty] \cong \mathbb{Z}/(m^v)$, where $v = \mathrm{val}_m(\#E(\mathbb{F}_q))$.

Theorem 7. *Consider an m-isogeny volcano of ordinary elliptic curves over a finite field $\mathbb{F}_q$, and let N be their (common) number of $\mathbb{F}_q$-rational points. Assume $v = \mathrm{val}_m(N) \ge 1$ and let h denote the height of the volcano.*

- *If v is odd and E is a curve on level $0 \le i \le h$, or if v is even and E is a curve on level $0 \le i \le v/2$, then*

$$E(\mathbb{F}_q)[m^\infty] \cong \frac{\mathbb{Z}}{(m^{v-i})} \times \frac{\mathbb{Z}}{(m^i)}.$$

- *If v is even and E is a curve on level $v/2 \le i \le h$, then*

$$E(\mathbb{F}_q)[m^\infty] \cong \frac{\mathbb{Z}}{(m^{v/2})} \times \frac{\mathbb{Z}}{(m^{v/2})}.$$

(Note that the latter range may be empty, i.e. one may have $h < v/2$.)

Proof. See [22, Cor. 1] for $m = 2$ and [23, Thm. 3] for m odd. □

Note that it is easy to verify whether a given curve $E/\mathbb{F}_q$ is located on the floor of its volcano. Indeed, for λ random points $P \in E(\mathbb{F}_q)$ one simply tests whether $(N/m)P = 0$. As soon as one point fails the test, we know that E is on the floor. If all points pass the test, we are on the floor with probability $1/m^\lambda$. Given such a verification method, a few random walks allow one to find a shortest path down to the floor, see e.g. the algorithm FINDSHORTESTPATHTOFLOOR in [30]. Note that this is considerably easier than navigating the volcano in a fully controlled way, see again [30] and the references therein.[1]

Once we are on E_0, the natural generalization of the case $v = 1$ is to compute the m-Tate pairing $T_m(P, Q)$ with $\mathrm{ord}(P) = m$ and $\mathrm{ord}(Q) = m^v$ satisfying $m^{v-1}Q = P$. The following theorem applied to $n = 1$ shows that the m-Tate pairing is non-trivial and, for a fixed P, independent of the choice of Q. (Note that we indeed have $m \mid q - 1$ because $m \mid t^2 - 4q = (q-1)^2 - 2(q+1)N + N^2$, where $N = \#E_0(\mathbb{F}_q)$.)

Theorem 8. *Let $E_0/\mathbb{F}_q$ be an ordinary elliptic curve and let m be a prime number. Assume that $m^n | (q - 1)$ for $n \ge 1$ and that*

$$E_0(\mathbb{F}_q)[m^\infty] \cong \frac{\mathbb{Z}}{(m^v)}$$

---

[1] In the context of this paper, it is worth highlighting the work of Ionica and Joux [20] on this topic, who use the Tate pairing as an auxiliary tool for travelling through the volcano.

for some $v \geq n$. Then for any P, Q with $\mathrm{ord}(P) = m^n$ and $\mathrm{ord}(Q) = m^v$, the reduced Tate pairing $T_{m^n}(P, Q)$ is a primitive m^n-th root of unity. Furthermore, for a fixed P, the pairing $T_{m^n}(P, \cdot)$ is constant for all Q with $\mathrm{ord}(Q) = m^v$ and $m^{v-n}Q = P$.

Proof. Assume that $T_{m^n}(P, Q)$ is not a primitive m^n-th root of unity, then $T_{m^n}(P, Q) \in \mu_{m^{n-1}}$, and in particular

$$1 = T_{m^n}(P, Q)^{m^{n-1}} = T_{m^n}(m^{n-1}P, Q).$$

Since P has order m^n, the point $m^{n-1}P$ is not the identity element $\mathbf{0}$. Further, since Q generates $E_0(\mathbb{F}_q)[m^\infty]$, we conclude that $T_{m^n}(m^{n-1}P, \cdot)$ is degenerate on the whole of $E_0(\mathbb{F}_q)/m^n E_0(\mathbb{F}_q)$, which contradicts the non-degeneracy of the Tate pairing. Thus we conclude that $T_{m^n}(P, Q)$ is a primitive m^n-th root of unity. The solutions to $m^{v-n}X = P$ are given by $Q + R$ with $\mathrm{ord}(R)|m^{v-n}$. But then $R \in m^n E_0(\mathbb{F}_q)$ and so $T_{m^n}(P, R) = 1$, which shows that $T_{m^n}(P, Q)$ is independent of the choice of Q. $\qquad\square$

3.1   Computing the Characters χ_i

Let χ be one of the characters χ_i associated with an odd prime divisor $m = m_i$ of $\Delta_\mathcal{O}$. As before, we let $\varphi : E \to E'$ denote the isogeny corresponding to $\mathfrak{a}$ of degree $\deg(\varphi) = \mathrm{N}(\mathfrak{a})$. Recall that the goal is to compute $\chi([\mathfrak{a}]) = \left(\frac{\mathrm{N}(\mathfrak{a})}{m} \right)$.

Since $\mathrm{End}(E) = \mathrm{End}(E')$, by Theorem 1, the curves E and E' are on the same level of their respective m-isogeny volcanoes. By taking the same number of steps down from E and E' to the floor on these volcanoes, we end up with two respective elliptic curves E_0, E_0' in $\mathcal{Ell}_q(\mathcal{O}_0, t)$, where $\mathcal{O}_0 \subset \mathcal{O}$ is a suborder having discriminant $\Delta_{\mathcal{O}_0} = m^{2s} \Delta_\mathcal{O}$, with s the number of steps taken to reach the floor.

Since both curves E_0 and E_0' are now on the floor, we can choose non-trivial points $P \in E_0[m](\mathbb{F}_q)$ and $P' \in E_0'[m](\mathbb{F}_q)$, and corresponding points Q, Q' of order exactly m^v satisfying $m^{v-1}Q = P$ and $m^{v-1}Q' = P'$. We know that the class group $\mathrm{cl}(\mathcal{O}_0)$ acts transitively on $\mathcal{Ell}_q(\mathcal{O}_0, t)$, see Sect. 2.3, so there exists an invertible ideal $\mathfrak{b} \subset \mathcal{O}_0$ such that

$$E_0' = [\mathfrak{b}] \star E_0,$$

where by [11, Cor. 7.17] it can be assumed that $\mathrm{N}(\mathfrak{b})$ is coprime with $\Delta_{\mathcal{O}_0}$, hence coprime with m. Let $\varphi_0 : E_0 \to E_0'$ denote the corresponding degree $\mathrm{N}(\mathfrak{b})$ isogeny. Then there exists a $k \in \{1, \ldots, m-1\}$ with $k\varphi_0(P) = P'$. Clearly, the point $k\varphi_0(Q)$ also has order m^v and satisfies $m^{v-1}X = P'$. From Theorem 8 and the compatibility of the Tate pairing, it then follows:

$$T_m(P', Q') = T_m(k\varphi_0(P), k\varphi_0(Q)) = T_m(P, Q)^{k^2 \deg(\varphi_0)},$$

and thus

$$\left(\frac{\mathrm{N}(\mathfrak{b})}{m} \right) = \left(\frac{\deg(\varphi_0)}{m} \right) = \left(\frac{\log_{T_m(P,Q)} T_m(P', Q')}{m} \right).$$

We now show that this in fact equals $\chi([\mathfrak{a}])$. Indeed, since $N(\mathfrak{b})$ is coprime with $\Delta_{\mathcal{O}_0}$, from [11, Prop. 7.20] we see that the ideal $\mathfrak{b}\mathcal{O} \subset \mathcal{O}$ is invertible and again has norm $N(\mathfrak{b})$. From the second paragraph of the proof of [30, Lem. 6] we see that $E' = [\mathfrak{b}\mathcal{O}] \star E$, and because the action of $cl(\mathcal{O})$ on $\mathcal{E}ll_q(\mathcal{O}, t)$ is free we conclude that $[\mathfrak{b}\mathcal{O}] = [\mathfrak{a}]$. Summing up, we can compute

$$\chi([\mathfrak{a}]) = \chi([\mathfrak{b}\mathcal{O}]) = \left(\frac{N(\mathfrak{b}\mathcal{O})}{m}\right) = \left(\frac{N(\mathfrak{b})}{m}\right) = \left(\frac{\log_{T_m(P,Q)} T_m(P', Q')}{m}\right).$$

Note that, in particular, this outcome is independent of the choice of the walks to the floor of the isogeny volcano.

Remark 9. In the appendix we provide an alternative (but more complex) proof that shows it is not needed to walk all the way down to the floor. However, since the height of the volcano is about $\frac{1}{2}\operatorname{val}_m(t^2 - 4q)$ (see Theorem 1), the volcanoes cannot be very high (in the worst case a logarithmic number of levels), so walking to the floor of the volcano is efficient. Furthermore, for odd m, the probability of the volcano being height zero is roughly $1 - 1/m$.

3.2   Computing the Characters δ, $\delta\epsilon$ and ϵ

For $\Delta_{\mathcal{O}} = -4n$, genus theory (Sect. 2.4) may give extra characters δ, ϵ or $\delta\epsilon$ depending on $n \bmod 8$. Recall that these characters are defined as

$$\delta : [\mathfrak{a}] \mapsto (-1)^{(N(\mathfrak{a})-1)/2} \quad \text{and} \quad \epsilon : [\mathfrak{a}] \mapsto (-1)^{(N(\mathfrak{a})^2-1)/8},$$

where the ideal $\mathfrak{a}$ is chosen to have odd norm. Determining the value of δ is easily seen to be equivalent to computing $N(\mathfrak{a}) \bmod 4$. In case both δ and ϵ exist (i.e. when $n \equiv 0 \bmod 8$), determining both character values is equivalent to computing $N(\mathfrak{a}) \bmod 8$.

For $m = 2$, the previous approach using Theorem 8 with $n = 1$ remains valid, but does not result in sufficient information since it only determines $N(\mathfrak{a}) \bmod 2$, which is known beforehand since the norm is odd. The solution is to use a 4-pairing (i.e. $n = 2$) to derive δ and an 8-pairing (i.e. $n = 3$) in the case both δ and ϵ exist.

Character δ. Recall that the character δ exists when $n \equiv 0, 1, 4, 5 \bmod 8$. By taking a field extension if needed, we can assume without loss of generality that $v = \operatorname{val}_2(\#E(\mathbb{F}_q)) \geq 2$ and that $4 \mid (q - 1)$. As before, by walking down the volcano we reach a curve E_0 on the floor (and similarly E_0') satisfying $E_0(\mathbb{F}_q)[2^\infty] = \mathbb{Z}/(2^v)$. We can now apply Theorem 8 for $m = 2$ and $n = 2$, and if $\mathfrak{b}$ is an ideal connecting E_0 and E_0', we can compute the exact value

$$N(\mathfrak{b}) \bmod 4 = \log_{T_4(P,Q)} T_4(P', Q') \tag{2}$$

for appropriately chosen points $P, Q \in E_0(\mathbb{F}_q)[2^\infty]$ and $P', Q' \in E_0'(\mathbb{F}_q)[2^\infty]$. Indeed, recall that the points P' and Q' are only determined by P and Q up to a scalar $k \in (\mathbb{Z}/(4))^*$, i.e. $k \equiv 1, 3 \bmod 4$, and so $k^2 \equiv 1 \bmod 4$.

A similar reasoning as before then shows that $[\mathfrak{b}\mathcal{O}] = [\mathfrak{a}]$, where we can assume $N(\mathfrak{b}\mathcal{O}) = N(\mathfrak{b})$, so we find that

$$\delta([\mathfrak{a}]) = \delta([\mathfrak{b}\mathcal{O}]) = (-1)^{(N(\mathfrak{b}\mathcal{O})-1)/2} = (-1)^{(\log_{T_4(P,Q)} T_4(P',Q')-1)/2},$$

or, equivalently, we find that $N(\mathfrak{a}) \bmod 4$ equals (2).

Characters $\delta\epsilon$ and ϵ. Recall that the character $\delta\epsilon$ exists when $n \equiv 0, 2 \bmod 8$ and the character ϵ exists when $n \equiv 0, 6 \bmod 8$. Again, by taking a field extension if needed, we can assume without loss of generality that $v = \mathrm{val}_2(\#E(\mathbb{F}_q)) \geq 3$ and that $8 \mid (q-1)$. Notice that, if δ and ϵ do not exist simultaneously, then we are necessarily on the surface of the 2-volcano, hence it takes at least one step to go to curves E_0 and E_0' on the floor. During this step the discriminant becomes multiplied by a factor of 4. Hence, on the floor, we are certain that both characters exist.

Now applying Theorem 8 for $m = 2$ and $n = 3$, and using the fact that for $k \equiv 1, 3, 5, 7 \bmod 8$ we have $k^2 \equiv 1 \bmod 8$, we know that the norm of an ideal $\mathfrak{b}$ connecting E_0 and E_0' satisfies

$$N(\mathfrak{b}) \bmod 8 = \log_{T_8(P,Q)} T_8(P', Q'), \tag{3}$$

for appropriately chosen points $P, Q \in E_0(\mathbb{F}_q)[2^\infty]$ and $P', Q' \in E_0'(\mathbb{F}_q)[2^\infty]$. The same reasoning as before then shows that $[\mathfrak{b}\mathcal{O}] = [\mathfrak{a}]$, where we can assume $N(\mathfrak{b}\mathcal{O}) = N(\mathfrak{b})$, hence we find

$$\epsilon([\mathfrak{a}]) = \epsilon([\mathfrak{b}\mathcal{O}]) = (-1)^{(N(\mathfrak{b}\mathcal{O})^2-1)/8} = (-1)^{((\log_{T_8(P,Q)} T_8(P',Q'))^2-1)/8},$$

and similarly for $\delta\epsilon$. We stress that, in general, we cannot conclude that $N(\mathfrak{a}) \bmod 8$ equals (3). E.g., if $n \equiv 6 \bmod 8$, in the presence of ϵ but in the absence of δ, an ideal class containing ideals having norm 1 mod 8 will also contain ideals having norm 7 mod 8. It is during the first step down the volcano that both congruence classes become separated.

4   Computing the Characters for Supersingular Curves

We now turn our attention to supersingular elliptic curves over prime fields $\mathbb{F}_p$ with $p > 3$. Recall that any such curve $E/\mathbb{F}_p$ has exactly $p+1$ rational points and its Frobenius satisfies $\pi^2 + p = 0$, therefore $\mathcal{O} = \mathrm{End}_{\mathbb{F}_p}(E)$ has discriminant

$$\Delta_{\mathcal{O}} = \begin{cases} -4p & \text{if } p \equiv 1 \bmod 4, \\ -p \text{ or } -4p & \text{if } p \equiv 3 \bmod 4. \end{cases}$$

From genus theory, we see that $\mathrm{cl}(\mathcal{O})$ has non-trivial 2-torsion only in the former case. So we will restrict our attention to $p \equiv 1 \bmod 4$, in which case $\mathcal{O} = \mathbb{Z}[\sqrt{-p}]$. There are two assigned characters: the Legendre character associated with p, and δ. From the character relation (1) (see also Example 6), we see that these coincide on $\mathrm{cl}(\mathcal{O})$, therefore it suffices to compute δ. Unfortunately, due to the peculiar behaviour of supersingular elliptic curves over $\mathbb{F}_{p^2}$, we cannot apply our strategy of "extending the base field and going down the volcano".

Instead, we can compute δ directly on the input curves, i.e. not involving vertical isogenies. This is handled by the following theorem, which can be used to compute δ in many ordinary cases, too. The proof is entirely self-contained, although its flavour is similar to that of Sect. 3.

Theorem 10. *Let $q \equiv 1 \bmod 4$ be a prime power and let $E, E'/\mathbb{F}_q$ be elliptic curves with endomorphism ring $\mathcal{O}$ and trace of Frobenius $t \equiv 0 \bmod 4$, connected by an ideal class $[\mathfrak{a}] \in \mathrm{cl}(\mathcal{O})$. Then δ is an assigned character of $\mathcal{O}$, and if we write*

$$E : y^2 = x^3 + ax^2 + bx \quad resp. \quad E' : y^2 = x^3 + a'x^2 + b'x \qquad (4)$$

then $\delta([\mathfrak{a}]) = (b'/b)^{(q-1)/4}$.

Proof. As $t \equiv 0 \bmod 4$, we have $\#E(\mathbb{F}_q) = \#E'(\mathbb{F}_q) = q + 1 - t \equiv 2 \bmod 4$, and therefore both curves contain a unique rational point of order 2. When positioned at $(0,0)$, we indeed obtain models of the form (4). We point out that $b^{(q-1)/4}$ does not depend on the specific choice of such a model: it is easy to check that the only freedom left is scaling a by u^2 and b by u^4 for some $u \in \mathbb{F}_q^*$. Of course, the same remark applies to $b'^{(q-1)/4}$.

On E, the points (x_0, y_0) doubling to $P = (0,0)$ satisfy the condition

$$\frac{3x_0^2 + 2ax_0 + b}{2y_0} = \frac{y_0}{x_0},$$

which can be rewritten as $x_0(x_0^2 - b) = 0$. Therefore these points are

$$\left(\sqrt{b}, \pm\sqrt{b(a + 2\sqrt{b})} \right) \quad \text{and} \quad \left(-\sqrt{b}, \pm\sqrt{b(a - 2\sqrt{b})} \right), \qquad (5)$$

from which we see that b is a non-square. Indeed, if we would have $\sqrt{b} \in \mathbb{F}_q$, then one of $a \pm 2\sqrt{b}$ would be a square in $\mathbb{F}_q$ because their product $a^2 - 4b$ is not (since there is only one $\mathbb{F}_q$-rational point of order 2). This would imply the existence of an $\mathbb{F}_q$-rational point of order 4, contradicting $\#E(\mathbb{F}_q) \equiv 2 \bmod 4$. The same reasoning shows that b' is a non-square.

Choose a representative $\mathfrak{a}$ of $[\mathfrak{a}]$ having odd norm coprime to q. It suffices to prove that

$$(-b')^{(q-1)/4} = \left((-b)^{(q-1)/4} \right)^{\mathrm{N}(\mathfrak{a})} \qquad (6)$$

(the reason for including the minus signs, which cancel out, will become apparent soon). Indeed, both sides are primitive 4th roots of unity, whose ratio is either 1 or -1 depending on whether $\mathrm{N}(\mathfrak{a}) \equiv 1 \bmod 4$ or $\mathrm{N}(\mathfrak{a}) \equiv 3 \bmod 4$, as wanted.

Let $\varphi : E \to E'$ denote the isogeny corresponding to $\mathfrak{a}$, where we note that $\varphi(P) = P'$ because φ is defined over $\mathbb{F}_q$. From (5), using that b is a non-square, we see that we can characterize $-b$ as $x(Q) \cdot x(\pi_q(Q))$, where Q denotes any of the four halves of P. Similarly, $-b'$ equals $x(Q') \cdot x(\pi_q(Q'))$, with Q' any of the four halves of $P' = (0,0) \in E'$. In particular, since $\varphi(Q)$ is a half of $\varphi(P) = P'$, we have $-b' = x(\varphi(Q)) \cdot x(\pi_q(\varphi(Q)))$.

Remark 11. Observe that x is the normalized Miller function $f_{2,P}$, hence

$$(-b)^{(q-1)/4} = (x(Q) \cdot x(\pi_q(Q)))^{(q-1)/4} = \left(f_{2,P}(Q)^{1+q}\right)^{(q-1)/4} = f_{2,P}(Q)^{\frac{q^2-1}{4}},$$

and similarly for $(-b')^{(q-1)/4}$, so proving (6) amounts to proving a compatibility rule for a non-fully reduced 2-Tate pairing.

Denote by $\pm K_1, \pm K_2, \ldots, \pm K_{(N(\mathfrak{a})-1)/2}$ the non-trivial points in $\ker \varphi$, say with x-coordinates $x_1, x_2, \ldots, x_{(N(\mathfrak{a})-1)/2} \in \overline{\mathbb{F}}_q$. Besides P itself, the points mapping to P' are $P \pm K_1, P \pm K_2, \ldots, P \pm K_{(N(\mathfrak{a})-1)/2}$, and an easy calculation shows that the x-coordinates of these points are $b/x_1, b/x_2, \ldots, b/x_{(N(\mathfrak{a})-1)/2}$. This implies that the function

$$x \left(\prod_{i=1}^{(N(\mathfrak{a})-1)/2} \frac{x - \frac{b}{x_i}}{x - x_i} \right)^2$$

viewed on E has the same divisor as $x \circ \varphi$, therefore both functions are proportional. To determine the constant involved, we can assume that our curve E' is obtained through an application of Vélu's formulae [33], composed with a translation along the x-axis that positions P' at $(0,0)$. We then see that the leading coefficient of the numerator of $x \circ \varphi$ equals $N(\mathfrak{a}) - 3(N(\mathfrak{a}) - 1) + 2(N(\mathfrak{a}) - 1) = 1$. So the involved constant is just 1, i.e. equality holds.

We then compute

$$-b' = x(\varphi(Q)) \cdot x(\pi_q(\varphi(Q)))$$
$$= (x \circ \varphi)(Q) \cdot (x \circ \varphi)(\pi_q(Q))$$
$$= -b \left(\prod_{i=1}^{(N(\mathfrak{a})-1)/2} \frac{(\sqrt{b} - \frac{b}{x_i})(-\sqrt{b} - \frac{b}{x_i})}{(\sqrt{b} - x_i)(-\sqrt{b} - x_i)} \right)^2$$
$$= \frac{(-b)^{N(\mathfrak{a})}}{\left(\prod_{i=1}^{(N(\mathfrak{a})-1)/2} x_i \right)^4},$$

and (6) follows by raising both sides to the power $(q - 1)/4$. □

5   Impact on DDH and Countermeasures

5.1   Impact on Decisional Diffie–Hellman for Class Group Actions

It is clear that any non-trivial character χ (or δ, ϵ, $\delta\epsilon$) can be used to determine whether a sample $(E^{(1)} = [\mathfrak{a}] \star E, E^{(2)} = [\mathfrak{b}] \star E, E^{(3)})$ is a true Diffie-Hellman sample, i.e. whether $E^{(3)} = [\mathfrak{a} \cdot \mathfrak{b}] \star E$ or not. For instance, one could compute $\chi([\mathfrak{a}])$ in two different ways, namely as $\chi(E, E^{(1)})$ and compare with $\chi(E^{(2)}, E^{(3)})$. Similarly, one could compute $\chi([\mathfrak{b}])$ in two ways, as $\chi(E, E^{(2)})$ as well as $\chi(E^{(1)}, E^{(3)})$. If the sample is not a true Diffie–Hellman sample this will be detected with probability $1/2$. In many cases we have more than one character available, so if we assume that $s < \mu$ linearly independent characters are computable (see below for the complexity of a single character), this probability increases to $1 - 1/2^s$.

Supersingular curves. For supersingular curves over $\mathbb{F}_p$ with $p \equiv 1 \bmod 4$, the character δ exists and is always non-trivial (see Example 6). As shown in Sect. 4, computing this character requires computing a 2-torsion point, one inversion and one exponentiation in $\mathbb{F}_p$, so in this case, DDH can be broken in time $O(\log p \cdot M_p)$ with M_p the cost of a multiplication in $\mathbb{F}_p$.

Ordinary curves. For ordinary curves, we will order the characters (if they exist) according to their complexity: δ, ϵ, $\delta\epsilon$, χ_{m_i} for $i = 1, \ldots, r$. From genus theory, it follows that at most one of the μ characters is trivial (since $\#\mathrm{cl}(\mathcal{O})[2] = 2^{\mu-1}$), so if the easiest to compute character is trivial, we immediately conclude that the second easiest to compute character is non-trivial. To determine the complexity, assume that m is an odd prime divisor of $\Delta_\mathcal{O}$. To be able to apply our attack, we first need to find the smallest extension $\mathbb{F}_{q^k}$ such that $\mathrm{val}_m(\#E(\mathbb{F}_{q^k})) \geq 1$. Since $m \mid \Delta_\mathcal{O} \mid t^2 - 4q$, we conclude that the matrix of Frobenius on $E[m]$ is of the form

$$\begin{pmatrix} \lambda & 1 \\ 0 & \lambda \end{pmatrix} \quad \text{or} \quad \begin{pmatrix} \lambda & 0 \\ 0 & \lambda \end{pmatrix},$$

with $\lambda^2 \equiv q \bmod m$. In both cases, for $k = \mathrm{ord}(\lambda) \in \mathbb{Z}/(m)^*$, we conclude that $\mathrm{val}_m(\#E(\mathbb{F}_{q^k})) \geq 1$. Furthermore, since the determinant of the k-th power equals $q^k \equiv \lambda^{2k} \equiv 1 \bmod m$, we conclude that $\mu_m \subset \mathbb{F}_{q^k}$ and thus the m-Tate pairing is defined over $\mathbb{F}_{q^k}$. We see that in the worst case, we have $k = m - 1$. Computing the m-Tate pairing requires $O(\log m \cdot M_{q^k})$ which is $O(m^{1+\varepsilon} \cdot M_q)$ assuming fast polynomial arithmetic and using $k < m$. The cost of walking down the volcano [30] over $\mathbb{F}_{q^k}$ in the worst case is given by $O(h \cdot (m^{3+\varepsilon} \cdot \log q) \cdot M_q)$ assuming fast polynomial arithmetic (and $k < m-1$), with h a bound on the height of the volcano. Once we reached the floor of the volcano, we need to solve the equation $m^{v-1}Q = P$, with P an m-torsion point, and $v = \mathrm{val}_m(\#E(\mathbb{F}_{q^k}))$. This can be computed deterministically using division polynomials, or probabilistically as follows: first generate a point Q_1 of order m^v, and compute $P_1 = m^{v-1}Q_1$. Since we are on the floor, $E(\mathbb{F}_q)[m]$ is cyclic, so there exists a k with $P = kP_1$. Then $Q = kQ_1$ is a solution. This randomized approach can be done in expected time $O(m^{3+\varepsilon} \cdot \log q \cdot M_q)$.

As remarked before, we note that in the majority of cases (probability roughly $1 - 1/m$), the height of the m-volcano is zero and the complexity of the attack is solely determined by the computation of the Tate pairing.

Computing the exact coset modulo $cl(\mathcal{O})^2$. Genus theory shows that $cl(\mathcal{O})^2$ equals the intersection of the kernels of the assigned characters. Thanks to the class group relation (1), we are allowed to omit one character. If all remaining characters have a manageable complexity then, given two elliptic curves E and $[\mathfrak{a}] \star E$, this allows to determine completely the coset of $cl(\mathcal{O})^2$ inside $cl(\mathcal{O})$ to which the connecting ideal class $[\mathfrak{a}]$ belongs. In general, we can determine which coset of $C \supset cl(\mathcal{O})^2$ contains $[\mathfrak{a}]$, where C denotes the intersection of the kernels of the characters whose computation is feasible.

As an application, one can reduce the vectorization problem for $cl(\mathcal{O})$ to that for C. Indeed, one simply chooses an ideal class $[\mathfrak{b}]$ belonging to the same coset as $[\mathfrak{a}]$, so that $[\mathfrak{a} \cdot \mathfrak{b}] \in C$, and one considers the vectorization problem associated with E and $[\mathfrak{a} \cdot \mathfrak{b}] \star E = [\mathfrak{b}] \star ([\mathfrak{a}] \star E)$. After finding $[\mathfrak{a} \cdot \mathfrak{b}]$, one recovers $[\mathfrak{a}]$ as $[\mathfrak{b}]^{-1} \cdot [\mathfrak{a} \cdot \mathfrak{b}]$. In the optimal case where $C = cl(\mathcal{O})^2$, this reduces the group size by a factor $2^{\mu-1}$.

5.2 Implementation Results

We implemented our attack in the Magma computer algebra system [5] and the code is given in Appendix B. The main functions are ComputeEvenCharacters, ComputeOddCharacter and ComputeSupersingularDelta. We also use a very simple randomized method to walk to the floor of the volcano in the function ToFloor. A more efficient approach can be found in [30].

To illustrate the code, we apply it to an example found in [14, Section 4]. In particular, let

$$p = 7 \left(\prod_{\substack{2 \leq \ell \leq 380 \\ \ell \text{ prime}}} \ell \right) - 1$$

and consider the elliptic curve $E : y^2 = x^3 + Ax^2 + x$ with

$$A = 10861338504649280383859950140772947007703646408372831934324660566888732797778932142488253565145603672591944602210571423767689240032829444439469242521864171 \quad ,$$

then $\text{End}(E)$ is the maximal order and E lies on the surface of a volcano of height 2. By construction, the curve has $\mathbb{F}_p$-rational subgroups of order ℓ with $\ell \in [3, 5, 7, 11, 13, 17, 103, 523, 821, 947, 1723]$. The discriminant is of the form $-4n$ with $n \equiv 2 \mod 8$, so we will be able to compute the character $\delta\epsilon$.

The code first computes a random isogeny of degree 523 (easy to compute since it is rational), to obtain the "challenge" $E' = [\mathfrak{a}] \star E$. After going to a degree 2 extension, it then descends the volcano to the floor, and on the floor, it computes both δ as well as ϵ, from which it derives that $\delta\epsilon(E, E') = 1$, which is consistent with the fact that $\delta\epsilon([\mathfrak{a}]) = \delta\epsilon(523) = 1$.

5.3 Countermeasures

Since the attack crucially relies on the existence of 2-torsion in $\text{cl}(\mathcal{O})$, the simplest countermeasure is to restrict to a setting where $\text{cl}(\mathcal{O})[2]$ is trivial, e.g. supersingular elliptic curves over $\mathbb{F}_p$ with $p \equiv 3 \bmod 4$. This corresponds precisely to the CSIDH setting [8], so our attack does not impact CSIDH.

Another standard approach is to work with co-factors: since all characters become trivial on $\text{cl}(\mathcal{O})^2$ we can simply restrict to elements which are squares, i.e. in the Diffie-Hellman protocol one would sample $[\mathfrak{a}]^2$ and $[\mathfrak{b}]^2$.

Warning. We advise to be much more cautious than simply squaring. Genus theory gives the structure of $\text{cl}(\mathcal{O})[2]$, but one can also derive the structure of the 2-Sylow subgroup $\text{cl}(\mathcal{O})[2^\infty]$ using an algorithm going back to Gauss and analyzed in detail by Bosma and Stevenhagen [6]. Although our attack is currently not refined enough to also exploit this extra information, we expect that a generalization of our attack will be able to do so. As such, instead of simply squaring, we advise to use as co-factor an upper bound on the exponent of the 2-Sylow subgroup.

6 Conclusion

We showed how the characters defined by genus theory for the class group $\text{cl}(\mathcal{O})$ can be computed from the group action of $\text{cl}(\mathcal{O})$ on $\mathcal{Ell}_q(\mathcal{O}, t)$, knowing only the equations of two elliptic curves E and $E' = [\mathfrak{a}] \star E$, for an unknown ideal class $[\mathfrak{a}]$. For a character χ associated to the prime divisor $m \mid \Delta_{\mathcal{O}}$, the complexity is exponential in the size of m, and it is thus efficiently computable only for smallish m. However, since only one such character is required to break DDH for class group actions, we conclude that for a subset of density 1 of ordinary curves, and for all supersingular curves over $\mathbb{F}_p$ with $p \equiv 1 \bmod 4$, DDH (without appropriate countermeasures) is broken. Note that CSIDH [8] is not affected, since it relies on supersingular elliptic curves over $\mathbb{F}_p$ with $p \equiv 3 \bmod 4$.

The main, quite surprising, insight of this paper is that the structure of the class group $\text{cl}(\mathcal{O})$ does actually matter, and cannot be assumed to be fully hidden when represented as $\mathcal{Ell}_q(\mathcal{O}, t)$ under the class group action $\star$. Philosophically, one might argue that this is inherently caused by the fact that the structure of $\text{cl}(\mathcal{O})[2]$ is easily computable. As such, it is imperative to analyze the following two cases which also give partial information about the class group $\text{cl}(\mathcal{O})$:

- As already mentioned in Sect. 5.3, the algorithm described by Bosma and Stevenhagen [6] determines the structure of the 2-Sylow group $\text{cl}(\mathcal{O})[2^\infty]$. Can our attack be extended to take this extra information into account?
- The class number formula expressing the class number of a suborder $\mathcal{O}$ in terms of the class number of the maximal order $\mathcal{O}_K$ and the conductor c

$$h(\mathcal{O}) = \frac{h(\mathcal{O}_K)c}{[\mathcal{O}_K^* : \mathcal{O}^*]} \prod_{p \mid c} \left(1 - \left(\frac{\Delta_{\mathcal{O}_K}}{p} \right) \frac{1}{p} \right),$$

can be used to derive certain prime factors of $h(\mathcal{O})$ without knowing $h(\mathcal{O}_K)$. For instance, in the case of CSIDH with $p \equiv 3 \bmod 8$ where $\mathcal{O} = \mathbb{Z}[\sqrt{-p}]$, the above formula implies that $h(\mathcal{O})$ is divisible by 3. Can an attack be devised where such factors are exploited?

Finally, we note that in most settings the exact structure of $\mathrm{cl}(\mathcal{O})$ is unknown, so the usual approach of restricting to a large prime order subgroup does not apply. As a precaution, we therefore advise to work with supersingular curves $E/\mathbb{F}_p$ with $p \equiv 3 \bmod 4$, such that $\mathrm{End}(E) = \mathcal{O}_K$, i.e. restrict to curves on the surface as was done in the recent CSURF construction [7].

Acknowledgements. The authors would like to thank Alex Bartel, Steven Galbraith and the anonymous referees for useful feedback on an earlier version of the paper.

A   Not Walking to the Floor

As explained in Sect. 3, our approach to computing $\chi(E, E')$ is to take an arbitrary walk to the floor of the respective m-isogeny volcanoes of E and E'. In fact, one can stop walking down as soon as one reaches a level where the m^∞-torsion is sufficiently unbalanced. We illustrate this by means of the following modification of Theorem 8 (for $n = 1$), which is likely to admit further generalizations.

Theorem 12. *Let $E/\mathbb{F}_q$ be an ordinary elliptic curve and let m be a prime divisor of $q-1$. Assume that E is not located on the crater of its m-volcano and that*

$$E(\mathbb{F}_q)[m^\infty] \cong \frac{\mathbb{Z}}{(m^r)} \times \frac{\mathbb{Z}}{(m^s)}$$

for some $r > s + 1$. Let $P \in E(\mathbb{F}_q)[m] \setminus \{0\}$ be such that there exists a point $Q \in E(\mathbb{F}_q)$ for which $m^{r-1}Q = P$. Then the reduced Tate pairing

$$T_m(P, \cdot) : E(\mathbb{F}_q)/mE(\mathbb{F}_q) \to \mu_m : X \mapsto T_m(P, X) \tag{7}$$

is trivial if and only if X belongs to $E[m^s]$ mod $mE(\mathbb{F}_q)$. In particular, $T_m(P,Q)$ is a primitive m-th root of unity which, for a fixed P, does not depend on the choice of Q.

Proof. The assumption $m \mid (q-1)$ implies that $\mu_m \subset \mathbb{F}_q$. As explained in [2, IX.7.1], the kernel of $T_m(P, \cdot)$ is a codimension 1 subspace of $E(\mathbb{F}_q)/mE(\mathbb{F}_q)$, when viewed as a vector space over $\mathbb{F}_m$. Therefore it suffices to prove that $T_m(P, \cdot)$ is trivial on $E[m^s]$ mod $mE(\mathbb{F}_q)$, because the latter space indeed has codimension 1. More precisely, it has dimension 0 if $s = 0$ and dimension 1 if $s \geq 1$.

Now, since we are not on the crater, we know from Theorem 7 that there exists an elliptic curve $E'/\mathbb{F}_q$ and an $\mathbb{F}_q$-rational m-isogeny $\varphi : E' \to E$ such that $E'(\mathbb{F}_q)[m^\infty] \cong \mathbb{Z}/(m^{r-1}) \times \mathbb{Z}/(m^{s+1})$. We note:

- $E[m^s] \subset \varphi(E'[m^{s+1}]) \subset \varphi(E'(\mathbb{F}_q))$, hence each $X \in E[m^s]$ can be written as $\varphi(X')$ for some $X' \in E'(\mathbb{F}_q)$.

– The kernel of the dual isogeny $\hat{\varphi} : E \to E'$ equals $\langle P \rangle$, as otherwise E' would admit $\mathbb{F}_q$-rational m^r-torsion. Therefore P is the image of a point $P' \in E'[m] \subset E'(\mathbb{F}_q)$.

We conclude that

$$T_m(P, X) = T_m(\varphi(P'), \varphi(X')) = T_m(P', X')^{\deg(\varphi)} = T_m(P', X')^m = 1,$$

as wanted.   □

B   Magma Code

```
1  // Returns factors with multiplicity up to bound B
2
3  function SimpleTrialDivision(a, B)
4    facs := TrialDivision(a, B);
5    if (#facs gt 0 and facs[#facs][1] gt B) then
6      // removing last factor if too large
7      Remove(~facs, #facs);
8    end if;
9    return facs;
10 end function;
11
12 // The next four functions allow us to walk to the floor
13 // They also return the distance to the floor
14
15 function OnFloor(E, m, numpts)
16   v := Valuation(numpts, m);
17   onfloor := false;
18   for i in [1..80] do
19     if m^(v-1)*(numpts div m^v)*Random(E) ne E ! 0 then
20       onfloor := true;
21       break i;
22     end if;
23   end for;
24   return onfloor;
25 end function;
26
27 // Random point of order m whose Weil pairing with Q is
28 // non-trivial assumes m-torsion is fully rational
29
30 function FindIndependentOrdermPoint(E, Q, m)
31   Fq := BaseField(E);
32   R<X> := PolynomialRing(Fq);
33   coeffs := Eltseq(E);
34   defpol := X^3 + coeffs[2]*X^2 + coeffs[4]*X + coeffs[5];
35   xcoords := [rt[1] : rt in Roots(DivisionPolynomial(E,m))];
36   repeat
37     x := Random(xcoords);
38     y := Sqrt(Evaluate(defpol,x));
39     P := E ! [x,y,1];
40   until WeilPairing(P,Q,m) ne 1;
```

```
41    return P;
42  end function;
43
44  // Random point of order m
45
46  function FindOrdermPoint(E, m)
47    Fq := BaseField(E);
48    R<X> := PolynomialRing(Fq);
49    coeffs := Eltseq(E);
50    defpol := X^3 + coeffs[2]*X^2 + coeffs[4]*X + coeffs[5];
51    xcoords := [rt[1] : rt in Roots(DivisionPolynomial(E,m))];
52    x := Random(xcoords);
53    y := Sqrt(Evaluate(defpol,x));
54    return E ! [x,y,1];
55  end function;
56
57  // Walking to the floor of the volcano
58  // Returns height and distance to the floor
59  // Assumes existence of point of order m
60
61  function ToFloor(E, m, numpts)
62    Fq := BaseField(E);
63    q := #Fq;
64    t := q + 1 - numpts;
65    disc_frob := t^2 - 4*q;
66    h := Floor(Valuation(disc_frob,m)/2); // height of the volcano
67    if m eq 2 and (disc_frob div 4^h) mod 4 in {2,3} then
68        h -:= 1;
69    end if;
70    if OnFloor(E, m, numpts) then
71      return E, h, 0;
72    else
73      R<X> := PolynomialRing(Fq);
74      repeat
75        pathtofloor := 0;
76        Efloor := E;
77        Q := FindOrdermPoint(Efloor, m);
78        repeat
79          P := FindIndependentOrdermPoint(Efloor, Q, m);
80          if m eq 2 then
81            Efloor, phi := IsogenyFromKernel(Efloor, X - P[1]);
82          else
83            Efloor, phi := IsogenyFromKernel(Efloor, &*[X - (i*P)
          [1] : i in [1..(m-1) div 2]]);
84          end if;
85          Q := phi(Q);
86          pathtofloor +:= 1;
87        until pathtofloor gt h or OnFloor(Efloor, m, numpts);
88      until pathtofloor le h; // otherwise we passed through
        surface
89      return Efloor, h, pathtofloor;
90    end if;
91  end function;
92
```

```
 93  // Computes minimal extension such that m-torsion is rational
 94  // Returns extension degree and number of points over extension
 95
 96  function MinimalExtensionmTorsion(m, p, numpts)
 97    t := p+1-numpts;
 98    Ts := [t, t^2 - 2*p];
 99    Ns := [numpts, p^2 + 1 - Ts[2]];
100    for i := 3 to m-1 do
101      Append(~Ts, t*Ts[i-1] - p*Ts[i-2]);
102    end for;
103    for d in Divisors(m-1) do
104      if (Valuation(p^d + 1 - Ts[d], m) ge 1) then
105        return d, p^d + 1 - Ts[d];
106      end if;
107    end for;
108    return 0, 0;
109  end function;
110
111  // Listing available characters smaller than bound B
112  // Odd primes m appearing in t^2 - 4*p to an even power,
113  // or for which we need to go to a large extension to see
114  // some m-torsion are currently ignored.
115
116  function ListCharacters(E, B, numpts)
117
118    p := #BaseField(E);
119    t := p+1-numpts;
120    disc_frob := t^2 - 4*p;
121
122    factors := SimpleTrialDivision(disc_frob, B);
123
124    even_chars := [];
125    odd_chars := [];
126    for fac in factors do
127      if fac[1] ne 2 then
128        if IsOdd(fac[2]) then // prime definitely divides Delta_0
129          m := fac[1];
130          if (MinimalExtensionmTorsion(m, p, numpts) lt 50)
131          then odd_chars cat:= [m];
132          end if;
133        end if;
134      else
135        ext, numpts_ext := MinimalExtensionmTorsion(2, p, numpts);
136        q := p^ext;
137        Fq := GF(p, ext);
138        E_ext := BaseChange(E, Fq);
139        _, h, pathtofloor := ToFloor(E_ext, 2, numpts_ext);
140        real_disc := disc_frob div 4^pathtofloor; // locally
          around 2, but enough
141        if IsEven(real_disc) then
142          if (-real_disc div 4) mod 4 le 1 then
143            even_chars := ["delta"];
144          end if;
145          case (-real_disc div 4) mod 8:
```

```
146            when 0, 6: Append(~even_chars, "epsilon");
147            when 2: Append(~even_chars, "delta*epsilon");
148          end case;
149        end if;
150      end if;
151    end for;
152
153    return even_chars, odd_chars;
154 end function;
155
156 // This function computes characters associated to odd prime
157
158 function ComputeOddCharacter(m, E, Eisog, numpts)
159
160    print "Computing character associated with odd prime m =", m;
161
162    p := #BaseField(E);
163    t := p+1-numpts;
164
165    ext, numpts_ext := MinimalExtensionmTorsion(m, p, numpts);
166    v := Valuation(numpts_ext, m);
167    q := p^ext;
168    print "    (constructing field Fq of degree", ext,"over Fp)";
169    Fq := GF(p, ext);
170
171    Tm := [];
172    if v eq 1 then
173      print "    Base case using self-pairing";
174      for ell_curve in [E, Eisog] do
175        ell_ext := BaseChange(ell_curve, Fq);
176        repeat
177          P := (numpts_ext div m)*Random(ell_ext);
178        until P ne ell_ext ! 0;
179        Tm cat:= [TatePairing(P,P,m)^((q-1) div m)];
180      end for;
181    else
182      for ell_curve in [E, Eisog] do
183        ell_ext := BaseChange(ell_curve, Fq);
184      print " Walking to floor...";
185        Efloor, h := ToFloor(ell_ext, m, numpts_ext);
186      print " Heigth of volcano is ", h;
187        repeat
188          P := (numpts_ext div m)*Random(Efloor);
189        until P ne Efloor ! 0;
190        repeat
191          Q := (numpts_ext div m^v)*Random(Efloor);
192        until m^(v-1)*Q eq P;
193        Tm cat:= [TatePairing(P,Q,m)^((q - 1) div m)];
194      end for;
195    end if;
196
197    // Computing discrete log naively
198
199    for expo in [1..m-1] do
```

```
200     if Tm[2] eq Tm[1]^expo then
201       return LegendreSymbol(expo, m);
202     end if;
203   end for;
204
205   return 0;
206
207 end function;
208
209 // This procedure computes characters associated to prime 2
210
211 function ComputeEvenCharacters(even_chars, E, Eisog, numpts)
212
213   print "Computing characters associated with m = 2:";
214
215   p := #BaseField(E);
216   t := p+1-numpts;
217   S<X> := PolynomialRing(Integers());
218
219   ext := 0;
220   repeat
221     ext +:= 1;
222     numpts_ext := Resultant(1 - X^ext, X^2 - t*X + p);
223     v := Valuation(numpts_ext, 2);
224     q := p^ext;
225   until q mod 8 eq 1 and v ge 3; // v ge 2 would have sufficed
          for delta
226   q := p^ext;
227   print "    Constructing field Fq of degree", ext,"over Fp";
228   Fq := GF(p, ext);
229
230   T8 := [];
231
232   for ell_curve in [E, Eisog] do
233     ell_ext := BaseChange(ell_curve, Fq);
234   print "     Walking to floor...";
235     Efloor, h := ToFloor(ell_ext, 2, numpts_ext);
236   print "     Heigth of volcano is ", h;
237     repeat
238       P := (numpts_ext div 2^3)*Random(Efloor);
239     until 4*P ne Efloor ! 0;
240     repeat
241       Q := (numpts_ext div 2^v)*Random(Efloor);
242     until 2^(v-3)*Q eq P;
243     T8 cat:= [TatePairing(P,Q,8)^((q-1) div 8)];
244   end for;
245
246   for e in [1,3,5,7] do
247     if T8[2] eq T8[1]^e then
248       expo := e;
249     end if;
250   end for;
251
252   delta := (-1)^((expo - 1) div 2);
```

```
253    epsilon := (-1)^((expo^2 - 1) div 8);
254    result := [];
255    for char in even_chars do
256      case char:
257        when "delta": Append(~result, delta);
258        when "epsilon": Append(~result, epsilon);
259        when "delta*epsilon": Append(~result, delta*epsilon);
260      end case;
261    end for;
262
263    return result;
264  end function;
265
266  // Computes character delta for supersingular curve
267  // over F_p with p = 1 mod 4
268
269  function ComputeSuperingularDelta(E, Eisog)
270
271    Fpx<x> := PolynomialRing(BaseField(E));
272    Ew := WeierstrassModel(E);
273    Eisogw := WeierstrassModel(Eisog);
274    a := Coefficients(Ew)[4];
275    r := Roots(x^3 + Fpx ! Reverse(Coefficients(Ew)), BaseField(E))
          [1][1];
276    aiso := Coefficients(Eisogw)[4];
277    riso := Roots(x^3 + Fpx ! Reverse(Coefficients(Eisogw)),
          BaseField(E))[1][1];
278
279    char := ((aiso + 3*riso^2)/(a + 3*r^2))^((#BaseField(E) - 1)
          div 4);
280    if (char ne 1) then char := -1; end if;
281
282    return char;
283
284  end function;
285
286  // Computes even character given degree ell
287
288  function ComputeEvenChar(cha, ell)
289    case cha:
290      when "delta": return (-1)^((ell-1) div 2);
291      when "epsilon": return (-1)^((ell^2-1) div 8);
292      when "delta*epsilon": return (-1)^( ((ell-1) div 2) + ((ell
          ^2-1) div 8));
293    end case;
294    return 0;
295  end function;
296
297  // Defining Kieffer-de Feo-Smith example
298
299  p := 12037340738208845034383383978222801137092029451270 1979\
300  23071397735408251586669938291587857560356890516069961904754\
301  171956588530344066457839297755929645858769;
302  A := 10861338504649280383859950140772947007703646408372 83193\
```

```
303  4324660566888732797778932142488253565145603672591944602210570\
304  14237676892400328294444394692425218641710;
305  ell := 5230;
306  N := 12037340738208845034383383978222801137092029451270197920\
307  30713977354082515866700854811380300884617909382018741716527700\
308  13441440432682982199470261884715988380600;
309  Fp := GF(p);
310  R<x> := PolynomialRing(Fp);
311  E := EllipticCurve([0, Fp ! A, 0, 1, 0]);
312
313  // constructing isogeneous curve
314
315  repeat
316    P := (N div ell)*Random(E);
317  until (P ne E ! 0);
318  Eisog := IsogenyFromKernel(E, &*[x - (i*P)[1] : i in [1..Floor(
         ell/2)]]);
319  even_chars, odd_chars := ListCharacters(E, 1000, N);  // bound
         1000 on character
320
321  if #even_chars ne 0 then
322    r_even := ComputeEvenCharacters(even_chars, E, Eisog, N);
323    ind := 0;
324    for char in even_chars do
325      ind := ind+1;
326    print "Computed char ", char, " = ", r_even[ind], "vs ", char,
         " = ", ComputeEvenChar(char, ell);
327    end for;
328  end if;
329
330  for m in odd_chars do
331    char_m := ComputeOddCharacter(m, E, Eisog, N);
332    print "Computed char = ", char_m, "vs Leg(ell, m) = ",
         LegendreSymbol(ell, m);
333  end for;
```

References

1. Beullens, W., Kleinjung, T., Vercauteren, F.: CSI-FiSh: efficient isogeny based signatures through class group computations. In: Galbraith, S.D., Moriai, S. (eds.) ASIACRYPT 2019, Part I. LNCS, vol. 11921, pp. 227–247. Springer, Cham (2019). https://doi.org/10.1007/978-3-030-34578-5_9

2. Blake, I.F., Seroussi, G., Smart, N.P. (eds.): Advances in Elliptic Curve Cryptography. London Mathematical Society Lecture Note Series, vol. 317. Cambridge University Press, Cambridge (2005)

3. Boneh, D.: The decision Diffie-Hellman problem. In: Buhler, J.P. (ed.) ANTS-III, 1998. LNCS, vol. 1423, pp. 48–63. Springer, Heidelberg (1998). https://doi.org/10.1007/BFb0054851. https://crypto.stanford.edu/~dabo/pubs/papers/DDH.pdf

4. Boneh, D., Halevi, S., Hamburg, M., Ostrovsky, R.: Circular-secure encryption from decision Diffie-Hellman. In: Wagner, D. (ed.) CRYPTO 2008. LNCS, vol. 5157, pp. 108–125. Springer, Heidelberg (2008). https://doi.org/10.1007/978-3-540-85174-5_7

5. Bosma, W., Cannon, J., Playoust, C.: The Magma algebra system I: the user language. J. Symbolic Comput. **24**(3–4), 235–265 (1997). Computational algebra and number theory (London, 1993)

6. Bosma, W., Stevenhagen, P.: On the computation of quadratic 2-class groups. J. de Théorie des Nombres de Bordeaux **8**(2), 283–313 (1996)

7. Castryck, W., Decru, T.: CSIDH on the surface. In: Ding, J., Tillich, J.-P. (eds.) PQCrypto 2020. LNCS, vol. 12100, pp. 111–129. Springer, Cham (2020). https://doi.org/10.1007/978-3-030-44223-1_7. https://ia.cr/2019/1404

8. Castryck, W., Lange, T., Martindale, C., Panny, L., Renes, J.: CSIDH: an efficient post-quantum commutative group action. In: Peyrin, T., Galbraith, S. (eds.) ASIACRYPT 2018, Part III. LNCS, vol. 11274, pp. 395–427. Springer, Cham (2018). https://doi.org/10.1007/978-3-030-03332-3_15. https://ia.cr/2018/383

9. Colò, L., Kohel, D.: Orienting supersingular isogeny graphs (2019). http://nutmic2019.imj-prg.fr/confpapers/OrientIsogGraph.pdf

10. Couveignes, J.-M.: Hard homogeneous spaces. IACR Cryptology ePrint Archive 2006/291 (1997). https://ia.cr/2006/291

11. Cox, D.A.: Primes of the Form $x^2 + ny^2$: Fermat, Class Field Theory, and Complex Multiplication. Pure and Applied Mathematics, 2nd edn. Wiley, Hoboken (2013)

12. Cramer, R., Shoup, V.: A practical public key cryptosystem provably secure against adaptive chosen ciphertext attack. In: Krawczyk, H. (ed.) CRYPTO 1998. LNCS, vol. 1462, pp. 13–25. Springer, Heidelberg (1998). https://doi.org/10.1007/BFb0055717. https://ia.cr/1998/006

13. ECRYPT - CSA. Algorithms, key size and protocols report (2018). https://www.ecrypt.eu.org/csa/documents/D5.4-FinalAlgKeySizeProt.pdf

14. De Feo, L., Kieffer, J., Smith, B.: Towards practical key exchange from ordinary isogeny graphs. In: Peyrin, T., Galbraith, S. (eds.) ASIACRYPT 2018, Part III. LNCS, vol. 11274, pp. 365–394. Springer, Cham (2018). https://doi.org/10.1007/978-3-030-03332-3_14. https://ia.cr/2018/485

15. Delfs, C., Galbraith, S.D.: Computing isogenies between supersingular elliptic curves over $\mathbb{F}_p$. Des. Codes Crypt. **78**(2), 425–440 (2016). https://arxiv.org/abs/1310.7789

16. Diffie, W., Hellman, M.E.: New directions in cryptography. IEEE Trans. Inf. Theory **22**(6), 644–654 (1976)

17. Fouquet, M., Morain, F.: Isogeny volcanoes and the SEA algorithm. In: Fieker, C., Kohel, D.R. (eds.) ANTS-V, 2002. LNCS, vol. 2369, pp. 276–291. Springer, Heidelberg (2002). https://doi.org/10.1007/3-540-45455-1_23

18. El Gamal, T.: A public key cryptosystem and a signature scheme based on discrete logarithms. In: Blakley, G.R., Chaum, D. (eds.) CRYPTO 1984. LNCS, vol. 196, pp. 10–18. Springer, Heidelberg (1985). https://doi.org/10.1007/3-540-39568-7_2

19. Hafner, J.L., McCurley, K.S.: A rigorous subexponential algorithm for computation of class groups. J. Am. Math. Soc. **2**, 837–850 (1989)

20. Ionica, S., Joux, A.: Pairing the volcano. Math. Comput. **82**(281), 581–603 (2013). https://arxiv.org/abs/1110.3602

21. Kohel, D.R.: Endomorphism rings of elliptic curves over finite fields. Ph.D thesis (1996)

22. Miret, J., Moreno, R., Sadornil, D., Tena-Ayuso, J., Valls, M.: An algorithm to compute volcanoes of 2-isogenies of elliptic curves over finite fields. Appl. Math. Comput. **176**(2), 739–750 (2006)

23. Miret, J., Sadornil, D., Tena-Ayuso, J., Tomàs, R., Valls, M.: Volcanoes of ℓ-isogenies of elliptic curves over finite fields: the case $\ell = 3$. Publ. Mat. **51**, 165–180 (2007)

24. Naor, M., Reingold, O.: Number-theoretic constructions of efficient pseudo-random functions. In: FOCS, pp. 458–467. IEEE Computer Society (1997)
25. Peikert, C., Vaikuntanathan, V., Waters, B.: A framework for efficient and composable oblivious transfer. In: Wagner, D. (ed.) CRYPTO 2008. LNCS, vol. 5157, pp. 554–571. Springer, Heidelberg (2008). https://doi.org/10.1007/978-3-540-85174-5_31. https://ia.cr/2007/348
26. Rostovtsev, A., Stolbunov, A.: Public-key cryptosystem based on isogenies. IACR Cryptology ePrint Archive 2006:145 (2006)
27. Schoof, R.: Nonsingular plane cubic curves over finite fields. J. Combin. Theory Ser. A **46**(2), 183–211 (1987)
28. Shor, P.W.: Polynomial-time algorithms for prime factorization and discrete logarithms on a quantum computer. SIAM J. Comput. **26**(5), 1484–1509 (1997). https://arxiv.org/abs/quant-ph/9508027
29. Stolbunov, A.: Cryptographic schemes based on isogenies. Ph.D thesis (2012)
30. Sutherland, A.V.: Isogeny volcanoes. In: ANTS-X. Open Book Series, vol. 1, pp. 507–530. MSP (2013). https://arxiv.org/abs/1208.5370
31. Tate, J.: Endomorphisms of abelian varieties over finite fields. Invent. Math. **2**(2), 134–144 (1966). https://doi.org/10.1007/BF01404549
32. Tenenbaum, G.: Introduction to Analytic and Probabilistic Number Theory. Graduate Studies in Mathematics, vol. 163, 3rd edn. American Mathematical Society, Providence (2015). Translated from the 2008 French edition by Patrick D. F. Ion
33. Vélu, J.: Isogénies entre courbes elliptiques. C. R. Acad. Sci. Paris Sér. A-B **273**, A238–A241 (1971)
34. Waterhouse, W.C.: Abelian varieties over finite fields. Ann. Sci. École Norm. Sup. **2**, 521–560 (1969)

A Classification of Computational Assumptions in the Algebraic Group Model

Balthazar Bauer[1], Georg Fuchsbauer[2(✉)], and Julian Loss[3(✉)]

[1] Inria, ENS, CNRS, PSL, Paris, France
balthazar.bauer@ens.fr
[2] TU Wien, Vienna, Austria
georg.fuchsbauer@tuwien.ac.at
[3] University of Maryland, College Park, USA
jloss@umiacs.umd.edu

Abstract. We give a taxonomy of computational assumptions in the algebraic group model (AGM). We first analyze Boyen's Uber assumption family for bilinear groups and then extend it in several ways to cover assumptions as diverse as Gap Diffie-Hellman and LRSW. We show that in the AGM every member of these families is implied by the q-discrete logarithm (DL) assumption, for some q that depends on the degrees of the polynomials defining the Uber assumption.

Using the meta-reduction technique, we then separate $(q+1)$-DL from q-DL, which yields a classification of all members of the extended Uber-assumption families. We finally show that there are strong assumptions, such as one-more DL, that provably fall outside our classification, by proving that they cannot be reduced from q-DL even in the AGM.

Keywords: Algebraic group model · Uber assumption · Pairing-based cryptography

1 Introduction

A central paradigm for assessing the security of a cryptographic scheme or hardness assumption is to analyze it within an *idealized model of computation*. A line of work initiated by the seminal work of Nechaev [Nec94] introduced the *generic group model* (GGM) [Sho97, Mau05], in which all algorithms and adversaries are treated as generic algorithms, i.e., algorithms that do not exploit any particular structure of a group and hence can be run in *any* group. Because for many groups used in cryptography (in particular, groups defined over some elliptic curves), the best known algorithms are in fact generic, the GGM has for many years served as the canonical tool to establish confidence in new cryptographic hardness assumptions. Moreover, when cryptographic schemes have been too difficult to analyze in the standard model, they have also directly been proven secure in the GGM (for example LRSW signatures [LRSW99, CL04]).

Following the approach first used in [ABM15], a more recent work by Fuchsbauer, Kiltz, and Loss [FKL18] introduces the *algebraic group model*, in which all algorithms are assumed to be algebraic [PV05]. An *algebraic algorithm* generalizes the notion of a generic algorithm in that all of its output group elements must

© International Association for Cryptologic Research 2020
D. Micciancio and T. Ristenpart (Eds.): CRYPTO 2020, LNCS 12171, pp. 121–151, 2020.
https://doi.org/10.1007/978-3-030-56880-1_5

still be computed by generic operations; however, the algorithm can freely access the structure of the group and obtain more information than what would be possible by purely generic means. This places the AGM between the GGM and the standard model. In contrast to the GGM, one cannot give information-theoretic lower bounds in the AGM; instead, one analyzes the security of a scheme by giving security reductions from computational hardness assumptions.

Because of its generality and because it provides a powerful framework that simplifies the security analyses of complex systems, the AGM has readily been adopted, in particular in the context of SNARK systems [FKL18,MBKM19, Lip19,GWC19]. It has also recently been used to analyze blind (Schnorr) signatures [FPS20], which are notoriously difficult to prove secure in the standard or random oracle model. Another recent work by Agrikola, Hofheinz and Kastner [AHK20] furthermore shows that the AGM constitutes a plausible model, which is instantiable under falsifiable assumptions in the standard model.

Since its inception, many proofs in the AGM have followed a similar structure, which often consists of a series of tedious case distinctions. A natural question is whether it is possible to unify a large body of relevant hardness assumptions under a general 'Uber' assumption. This would avoid having to prove a reduction to a more well-studied hardness assumption for each of them in the AGM separately. In this work, we present a very rich framework of such Uber assumptions, which contain, as special cases, reductions between hardness assumptions in the AGM from prior work [FKL18,Los19]. We also show that there exists a natural hierarchy among Uber assumptions of different strengths. Together, our results give an almost complete classification in the AGM of common hardness assumptions over (bilinear) groups of prime order.

1.1   Boyen's Uber Assumption Framework

The starting point of our generalizations is the Uber assumption framework by Boyen [Boy08], which serves as an umbrella assumption in the bilinear GGM. Consider a bilinear group $\mathcal{G} = (\mathbb{G}_1, \mathbb{G}_2, \mathbb{G}_T, e, p)$, where $\mathbb{G}_i$ is a group of prime order p and $e\colon \mathbb{G}_1 \times \mathbb{G}_2 \to \mathbb{G}_T$ is a (non-degenerate) bilinear map, and let g_1, g_2 and g_T be generators of $\mathbb{G}_1, \mathbb{G}_2$ and $\mathbb{G}_T$, respectively. Boyen's framework captures assumptions that are parametrized by polynomials $R_1, \ldots, R_r, S_1, \ldots, S_s, T_1, \ldots, T_t$ and F in a set of formal variables $X_1, \ldots, X_m$ as follows. The challenger picks a vector of randomly chosen points $\vec{x} = (x_1, \ldots, x_m) \in \mathbb{Z}_p^m$ and gives the adversary a list of group elements

$$\left(g_1^{R_1(\vec{x})}, \ldots, g_1^{R_r(\vec{x})}, g_2^{S_1(\vec{x})}, \ldots, g_2^{S_s(\vec{x})}, g_T^{T_1(\vec{x})}, \ldots, g_T^{T_t(\vec{x})}\right).$$

The adversary is considered successful it is able to compute $g_T^{F(\vec{x})}$. Note that for this *not* to be trivially computable, F must be independent from $\vec{R}, \vec{S}$ and $\vec{T}$. That is, it must not be a linear combination of elements from $\vec{T}$ and (pairwise products of) elements of $\vec{R}$ and $\vec{S}$; otherwise, $g_T^{F(x)}$ could be computed from the given group elements via group operations and the bilinear map.

Boyen gives lower bounds for this family of assumptions following the common proof paradigm within the GGM. He also extends the idea of this first Uber assumption [BBG05] with a fixed target polynomial F to an adaptive version called *flexible Uber Assumption*, in which the adversary can choose the target polynomial F itself (as long as it satisfies the same notion of independence from $\vec{R}$, $\vec{S}$ and $\vec{T}$ that makes computing $g_T^{F(\vec{x})}$ non-trivial). Finally, Boyen proposes an extension of his bounds to assumptions in which the elements of $(\vec{R}, \vec{S}, \vec{T})$ and F may be *rational fractions*, that is, fractions of polynomials. We start with considering a straightforward generalization of Boyen's framework where the solution the adversary must find can also be in one of the source groups, that is, of the form $g_1^{F_1(\vec{x})}$ or $g_2^{F_2(\vec{x})}$, as long as they satisfy some non-triviality conditions (Definition 5). We next discuss the details of our adaptation of (our generalization of) Boyen's framework to the AGM.

1.2 An Uber-Assumption Framework for the AGM

The main challenge in analyzing Boyen's framework in the AGM setting is that we can no longer prove lower bounds as in the GGM. The next best thing would be to reduce the Uber assumption to a well-established assumption such as the discrete logarithm (DLog) assumption. Due to the general nature of the Uber assumption, this turns out to be impossible; in particular, our negative result (see below) establishes that *algebraic reductions in the AGM* can only reduce DLog to Uber assumptions that are defined by *linear polynomials*.

Indeed, as for Boyen's [Boy08] proofs in the GGM, the degrees of the involved polynomials are expected to appear in our reductions. In our first theorem in Sect. 3 we show that in the AGM any Uber assumption is implied by a parametrized variant of the discrete logarithm problem: in the q-DLog problem the adversary, on top of the instance g^z, is also given $g^{z^2}, \ldots, g^{z^q}$ and must compute z. We prove that if the maximum total degree of the challenge polynomials in $(\vec{R}, \vec{S}, \vec{T})$ of an Uber assumption is at most q, then it is implied by the hardness of the q-DLog problem. This establishes that under q-DLog, anything that is not trivially computable from a given instance (represented by $(\vec{R}, \vec{S}, \vec{T})$) is infeasible to compute. We prove this by generalizing a technique first used by Fuchsbauer et al. [FKL18] to prove soundness of Groth's SNARK [Gro16] under the q-DLog assumption in the AGM.

Proof idea. To convey our main idea, consider a simple instance of the Uber assumption parametrized by polynomials $R_1, \ldots, R_r, F_1$ and let $\vec{S} = \vec{T} = \emptyset$. That is, the adversary is given group elements $\mathbf{U}_1 = g_1^{R_1(\vec{x})}, \ldots, \mathbf{U}_r = g_1^{R_r(\vec{x})}$ for a random $\vec{x}$ and must compute $\mathbf{U}' = g_1^{F_1(\vec{x})}$. For this problem to be non-trivial, F_1 must be linearly independent of $R_1, \ldots, R_r$, that is, for all $\vec{a} \in \mathbb{Z}_p^r$ we have $R'(\vec{X}) \neq \sum_i a_i R_i(\vec{X})$.

Since the adversary is assumed to be algebraic (see Definition 2), it computes its output $\mathbf{U}'$ from its inputs $\mathbf{U}_1, \ldots, \mathbf{U}_r$ by generic group operations, that is, for some vector $\vec{\mu}$ we have $\mathbf{U}' = \prod_i \mathbf{U}_i^{\mu_i}$. In the AGM, the adversary is assumed to output this vector $\vec{\mu}$. Taking the logarithm of the previous equation yields

$$R'(\vec{x}) = \sum_{i=1}^{r} \mu_i R_i(\vec{x}). \tag{1}$$

Since R' is independent from $\vec{R}$, the polynomial $P(\vec{X}) := R'(\vec{X}) - \sum_i \mu_i R_i(\vec{X})$ is non-zero. On the other hand, (1) yields $P(\vec{x}) = 0$ for a successful adversary.

The adversary has thus (implicitly) found a non-zero polynomial P, which has the secret $\vec{x}$ among its roots. Now, in order to use this to solve a q-DLog instance $(g_1, g_1^z, \ldots, g_1^{z^q})$, we embed a randomized version of z into every coordinate of $\vec{x}$. In particular, for random vectors $\vec{y}$ and $\vec{v}$, we implicitly let $x_i := y_i z + v_i \bmod p$. By leveraging linearity, the reduction can compute the group elements $\mathbf{U}_i = g_1^{R_i(\vec{x})}$, etc, from its DLog instance.

If $P(\vec{X})$ is non-zero then $Q(Z) := P(y_1 Z + v_1, \ldots, y_m Z + v_m)$ is non-zero with overwhelming probability: the values v_i guarantee that the values y_i are perfectly hidden from the adversary and, as we show (Lemma 1), the leading coefficient of Q is a non-zero polynomial evaluated at $y_1, \ldots, y_m$, values that are independent of the adversary's behavior. Schwartz-Zippel thus bounds the probability that the leading coefficient of Q is zero, and thus, that $Q \equiv 0$. Since $Q(z) = P(\vec{x}) = 0$, we can factor the univariate polynomial Q and find the DLog solution z, which is among its roots.

Extensions. We next extend our approach to a flexible (i.e., adaptive) version of the static Uber assumption, where the adversary can adaptively choose the polynomials (Sect. 4) as well as a generalization from polynomials to rational fractions (Sect. 5). We combine the flexible framework with the rational fraction framework in Sect. 6. After these generalizations, our framework covers assumptions such as strong Diffie-Hellman [BB08], where the adversary must compute a rational fraction of its own choice in the exponent.

In a next step (Sect. 7), we extend our framework to also cover gap-type assumptions such as Gap Diffie-Hellman (GDH) [OP01], which was recently proven equivalent to the DLog assumption in the AGM by Loss [Los19]. GDH states that the CDH assumption remains true even when the DDH assumption no longer holds. Informally, the idea of the proof given in [Los19] (first presented in [FKL18] for a restricted version of GDH) is to argue that the DDH oracle given to an algebraic adversary is useless, unless the adversary succeeds in breaking CDH during an oracle query. The reduction simulates the DDH oracle by always returning false. We generalize this to a broader class of assumptions, using a different simulation strategy, which avoids a security loss.

We also present (Sect. 8) an extension of our (adaptive) framework that allows to capture assumptions as strong as the LRSW assumption [LRSW99], which forms the basis of the Camenisch-Lysyanskaya signature scheme [CL04]. The LRSW assumption falls outside (even the adaptive version of) Boyen's Uber framework, since the adversary need not output the polynomial it is computing in the exponent.

The LRSW and GDH assumptions were previously studied in the AGM in the works of [FKL18,Los19], who gave very technical proofs spanning multiple pages of case distinctions. By comparison, our Uber Framework offers a more general and much simpler proof for both of these assumptions. Finally, we are able to prove all these results using *tight reductions*. This, in particular, improves upon the non-tight reduction of DLog to LRSW in [FKL18].

1.3 Classifying Assumptions in Our Framework

Finally, we prove two separation results that show the following:

Separating $(q + 1)$-DLog from q-DLog. This shows that with respect to currently known (i.e., algebraic) reduction techniques, the Uber assumption, for increasing degrees of the polynomials, defines a natural hierarchy of assumptions in the AGM. More concretely, the q-lowest class within the established hierarchy consists of all assumptions that are covered by a specific instantiation of the Uber assumption which can be reduced from the q-DLog problem. Our separation result (Theorem 7) shows that there is no algebraic reduction from the q-DLog problem to the $(q + 1)$-DLog problem in the AGM. This implies that assumptions within different classes are separated with respect to algebraic reductions. Interestingly, we are even able to show our separation for reductions that can rewind and choose the random coins of the solver for the $(q + 1)$-DLog problem freely.

Separating OMDL from q-DLog. Our second result (Theorem 8) shows a separation result between the one-more-DLog problem (OMDL) (where the adversary has to solve q DLog instances and is given an oracle that computes discrete logarithms, which it can access $q - 1$ times) and the q-DLog problem (for any q) in the AGM. Our result strengthens a previous result by Bresson, Monnerat, and Vergnaud [BMV08], who showed a separation between the discrete logarithm problem (i.e, where $q = 1$) and the 2-one-more-DLog problem with respect to *black-box reductions*. By comparison, our result holds even in the AGM, where reductions are inherently non-black-box, as the AGM implicitly assumes an efficient extractor algorithm that extracts algebraic coefficients from the algebraic adversary. As the extractor is non-black-box (since it depends on the algebraic adversary), neither is any reduction that non-trivially leverages the AGM.

Our result clearly establishes the limits of our framework, as it excludes the OMDL family of assumptions. Unlike our first separation, this one comes with the caveat that it only applies to reductions that are "black-box in the AGM", meaning that they simply obtain the algebraic coefficients via the extractor, but cannot rewind the adversary or choose its random coins.

1.4 Related Work

A long line of research has considered frameworks to capture general classes of assumptions. We give an overview of the most closely related works. The first Uber assumptions were introduced by Boyen et al. [BBG05, Boy08]. Others later gave alternative concepts to classify assumptions within cyclic groups. The works of Chase et al. [CM14, CMM16] study assumptions in bilinear groups of *composite* order, which are not considered in the original Uber framework. They show that several q-type assumptions are implied by (static) "subgroup-hiding" assumptions. This gives evidence that this type of assumption, which is specific to composite-order groups, is particularly strong.

More recently, Ghadafi and Groth [GG17] studied a broader class of assumptions in which the adversary must compute a group element from $\mathbb{G}_T$. Like our work, their framework applies to prime-order groups and extends to the case where the exponents can be described by rational fractions, and they also separate classes of assumptions from each other. However, their framework only deals with non-interactive assumptions, which do not cover the adaptive type of assumptions we study in our flexible variants (in fact, the authors mention extending their work to interactive assumptions as an open problem [GG17]). Their work does not cover assumptions such as GDH or LRSW, which we view as particularly interesting (and challenging) to classify. Indeed, our framework appears to be the first in this line of work that offers a classification comprising this type of assumptions.

A key difference is that Ghadafi and Groth's results are in the standard model whereas we work in the AGM. While this yields stronger results for reductions, their separations are weaker (in addition to separating less broad types of Uber assumptions), as they are with respect to generic reductions, whereas ours hold against algebraic reductions that can assume that the *adversary is algebraic*. Furthermore, their work considers *black-box reductions* that treat the underlying solver as an (imperfect) oracle, while we show the non-existence of reductions in the AGM, which are, by definition, non-black-box (see above). A final difference to the work of [GG17] lies in the tightness of all our reductions, whereas non of theirs are tight.

At CT-RSA'19 Mizuide, Takayasu, and Takagi [MTT19] studied static (i.e., non-flexible) variants and generalizations of the Diffie-Hellman problem in prime-order groups (also with extensions to the bilinear setting) by extending proofs from [FKL18] in the obvious manner. Most of their results are special cases of our Uber assumption framework. Concretely, when restricting the degrees of all input polynomials to 1 in our static Uber Assumption, our non-triviality condition implies all corresponding theorems in their paper (except the ones relating to Matrix assumptions, which are outside the scope of this work). By our separation of q-DLog for different q, our results for higher degrees do not follow from theirs by currently known techniques. Finally, they do not cover the flexible (adaptive) variants nor oracle-enhanced- and hidden-polynomial-type assumptions (such as GDH and LRSW).

A further distinction that sets our work apart from these prior works is our formulation of the aforementioned 'hidden-type' assumptions, where we allow the adversary to solve the problem with respect to a group generator *of its own choice* instead of the one provided by the game. A recent work [BMZ19] shows that even in the GGM, allowing randomly chosen generators results in unexpected complications when proving lower bounds. Similarly, giving the adversary this additional freedom makes proving (and formalizing) our results more challenging. We also give this freedom to the reductions that we study (and prove impossible) in our separation results.

2 Algebraic Algorithms and Preliminaries

ALGORITHMS. We denote by $s \xleftarrow{\$} S$ the uniform sampling of the variable s from the (finite) set S. All our algorithms are probabilistic (unless stated otherwise) and written in uppercase letters A, B. To indicate that algorithm A runs on some inputs $(x_1, \ldots, x_n)$ and returns y, we write $y \xleftarrow{\$} \mathsf{A}(x_1, \ldots, x_n)$. If A has access to an algorithm B (via oracle access) during its execution, we write $y \xleftarrow{\$} \mathsf{A}^{\mathsf{B}}(x_1, \ldots, x_n)$.

POLYNOMIALS AND RATIONAL FRACTIONS. We denote polynomials by uppercase letters P, Q and specify them by a list of their coefficients. If m is an integer, we denote by $\mathbb{Z}_p[X_1, \ldots, X_m]$ the set of m-variate polynomials with coefficients in $\mathbb{Z}_p$ and by $\mathbb{Z}_p(X_1, \ldots, X_m)$ the set of rational fractions in m variables with coefficients in $\mathbb{Z}_p$. We define the *total degree* of a polynomial $P(X_1, \ldots, X_n) = \sum_{\vec{i} \in \mathbb{N}^m} \lambda_{i_1, \ldots, i_m} \prod_{j=1}^m X_j^{i_j} \in \mathbb{Z}_p[X_1, \ldots, X_m]$ as $\max_{\vec{i} \in \mathbb{N}^m \,:\, \lambda_{i_1, \ldots, i_m} \not\equiv_p 0} \{\sum_{j=1}^m i_j\}$.

For the degree of rational fractions we will use the "French" definition [AW98]: for $(P, Q) \in \mathbb{Z}_p[X_1, \ldots, X_m] \times (\mathbb{Z}_p[X_1, \ldots, X_m] \setminus \{0\})$ we define

$$\deg \frac{P}{Q} := \deg P - \deg Q.$$

This definition has the following properties: The degree does not depend on the choice of the representative; it generalizes the definition for polynomials; and the following holds: $\deg(F_1 \cdot F_2) = \deg F_1 + \deg F_2$, and $\deg(F_1 + F_2) \leq \max\{\deg F_1, \deg F_2\}$.

We state the following technical lemma, which we will use in our reductions and prove in the full version.

Lemma 1. *Let P be a non-zero multivariate polynomial in $\mathbb{Z}_p[X_1, \ldots, X_m]$ of total degree d. Define $Q(Z) \in (\mathbb{Z}_p[Y_1, \ldots, Y_m, V_1, \ldots, V_m])[Z]$ as $Q(Z) := P(Y_1 Z + V_1, \ldots, Y_m Z + V_m)$. Then the coefficient of maximal degree of Q is a polynomial in $\mathbb{Z}_p[Y_1, \ldots, Y_m]$ of degree d.*

We will use the following version of the Schwartz-Zippel lemma [DL77]:

Lemma 2. *Let $P \in \mathbb{Z}_p[X_1, \ldots, X_m]$ be a non-zero polynomial of total degree d. Let $r_1, \ldots, r_m$ be selected at random independently and uniformly from $\mathbb{Z}_p^*$. Then $\Pr\left[P(r_1, \ldots, r_m) \equiv_p 0\right] \leq \frac{d}{p-1}$.*

BILINEAR GROUPS. We next state the definition of a *bilinear group*.

Definition 1 (Bilinear group). *A bilinear group (description) is a tuple $\mathcal{G} = (\mathbb{G}_1, \mathbb{G}_2, \mathbb{G}_T, e, \phi, \psi, p)$ such that*

- *$\mathbb{G}_i$ is a cyclic group of prime order p, for $i \in \{1, 2, T\}$;*
- *e is a non-degenerate bilinear map $e : \mathbb{G}_1 \times \mathbb{G}_2 \to \mathbb{G}_T$, that is, for all $a, b \in \mathbb{Z}_p$ and all generators g_1 of $\mathbb{G}_1$ and g_2 of $\mathbb{G}_2$ we have that $g_T := e(g_1, g_2)$ generates $\mathbb{G}_T$ and $e(g_1^a, g_2^b) = e(g_1, g_2)^{ab} = g_T^{ab}$;*
- *ϕ is an isomorphism $\phi : \mathbb{G}_1 \to \mathbb{G}_2$, and ψ is an isomorphism $\psi : \mathbb{G}_2 \to \mathbb{G}_1$.*

All group operations and the bilinear map e must be efficiently computable. $\mathcal{G}$ is of Type 1 if the maps ϕ and ψ are efficiently computable; $\mathcal{G}$ is of Type 2 if there is no efficiently computable map ϕ; and $\mathcal{G}$ is of Type 3 if there are no efficiently computable maps ϕ and ψ. We require that there exist an efficient algorithm GenSamp *that returns generators g_1 of $\mathbb{G}_1$ and g_2 of $\mathbb{G}_2$, so that g_2 is uniformly random, and (for Types 1 and 2) $g_1 = \psi(g_2)$ or (Type 3) g_1 is also uniformly random. By* GenSamp$_i$ *we denote a restricted version that only returns g_i.*

In the following, we fix a bilinear group $\mathcal{G} = (\mathbb{G}_1, \mathbb{G}_2, \mathbb{G}_T, e, \phi, \psi, p)$.

(ALGEBRAIC) SECURITY GAMES. We use a variant of (code-based) *security games* [BR04]. In game $\mathbf{G}_{\mathcal{G}}$ (defined relative to $\mathcal{G}$), an adversary A interacts with a challenger that answers oracle queries issued by A. The game has a main procedure and (possibly zero) oracle procedures which describe how oracle queries are answered. We denote the output of a game $\mathbf{G}_{\mathcal{G}}$ between a challenger and an adversary A by $\mathbf{G}_{\mathcal{G}}^{\mathsf{A}}$. A is said to *win* if $\mathbf{G}_{\mathcal{G}}^{\mathsf{A}} = 1$. We define the *advantage* of A in $\mathbf{G}_{\mathcal{G}}$ as $\mathbf{Adv}_{\mathcal{G},\mathsf{A}}^{\mathbf{G}} := \Pr\left[\mathbf{G}_{\mathcal{G}}^{\mathsf{A}} = 1\right]$ and the running time of $\mathbf{G}_{\mathcal{G}}^{\mathsf{A}}$ as $\mathbf{Time}_{\mathcal{G},\mathsf{A}}^{\mathbf{G}}$. In this work, we are primarily concerned with *algebraic security games* $\mathbf{G}_{\mathcal{G}}$, in which we syntactically distinguish between elements of groups $\mathbb{G}_1, \mathbb{G}_2$ and $\mathbb{G}_T$ (written in bold, uppercase letters, e.g., $\mathbf{Z}$) and all other elements, which must not depend on any group elements.

We next define algebraic algorithms. Intuitively, the only way for an algebraic algorithm to output a new group element $\mathbf{Z}$ is to derive it via group operations from known group elements.

Definition 2 (Algebraic algorithm for bilinear groups). *An algorithm* $\mathsf{A}_{\mathsf{alg}}$ *executed in an algebraic game* $\mathbf{G}_{\mathcal{G}}$ *is called* algebraic *if for all group elements $\mathbf{Z} \in \mathbb{G}$ (where $\mathbb{G} \in \{\mathbb{G}_1, \mathbb{G}_2, \mathbb{G}_T\}$) that* $\mathsf{A}_{\mathsf{alg}}$ *outputs, it additionally provides a representation in terms of received group elements in $\mathbb{G}$ and those from groups from which there is an efficient mapping to $\mathbb{G}$; in particular: if $\mathbf{U}_0, \ldots, \mathbf{U}_\ell \in \mathbb{G}_1$, $\mathbf{V}_0, \ldots, \mathbf{V}_m \in \mathbb{G}_2$ and $\mathbf{W}_0, \ldots, \mathbf{W}_t \in \mathbb{G}_T$ are the group elements received so far then* $\mathsf{A}_{\mathsf{alg}}$ *provides vectors $\vec{\mu}, \vec{\nu}, \vec{\zeta}, \vec{\eta}, \vec{\delta}$ and matrices $A = (\alpha_{i,j}), B = (\beta_{i,j}), \Gamma = (\gamma_{i,j})$ such that*

- $\mathbf{Z} \in \mathbb{G}_1$ *(Type 1 and 2):* $\mathbf{Z} = \prod_i \mathbf{U}_i^{\mu_i} \cdot \prod_i \psi(\mathbf{V}_i)^{\nu_i}$
  (Type 3): $\mathbf{Z} = \prod_i \mathbf{U}_i^{\mu_i}$
- $\mathbf{Z} \in \mathbb{G}_2$ *(Type 1):* $\mathbf{Z} = \prod_i \phi(\mathbf{U}_i)^{\zeta_i} \cdot \prod_i \mathbf{V}_i^{\eta_i}$
  (Type 2 and 3): $\mathbf{Z} = \prod_i \mathbf{V}_i^{\eta_i}$
- $\mathbf{Z} \in \mathbb{G}_T$: $\mathbf{Z} = \prod_i \prod_j e\left(\mathbf{U}_i, \mathbf{V}_j\right)^{\alpha_{i,j}} \cdot \prod_i \prod_j e\left(\mathbf{U}_i, \phi(\mathbf{U}_j)\right)^{\beta_{i,j}}$
  $$\cdot \prod_i \prod_j e\left(\psi(\mathbf{V}_i), \mathbf{V}_j\right)^{\gamma_{i,j}} \cdot \prod_i \mathbf{W}_i^{\delta_i},$$
  where $\beta_{i,j} = 0$ for Type 2 and $\beta_{i,j} = \gamma_{i,j} = 0$ for Type 3.

We remark that oracle access to an algorithm B in the AGM includes any (usually non-black-box) access to B that is needed to extract the algebraic coefficients. Thus, our notion of black-box access in the AGM mainly rules out techniques such as rewinding B or running it on non-uniform random coins.

2.1   Generic Security Games and Algorithms

Generic algorithms A_{gen} are only allowed to use generic properties of a group. Informally, an algorithm is generic if it works regardless of what group it is run in. This is usually modeled by giving an algorithm indirect access to group elements via abstract handles. It is straight-forward to translate all of our algebraic games into games that are syntactically compatible with generic algorithms accessing group elements only via abstract handles. We measure the running times of generic algorithms as queries to an oracle that implements the abstract group operation, i.e., every query accounts for one step of the algorithm. We highlight this difference by denoting the running time of a generic algorithm with the letter o rather than t. We say that winning algebraic game $\mathbf{G}_{\mathcal{G}}$ is (ε, o)-*hard in the generic group model* if for every generic algorithm A_{gen} it holds that

$$\mathbf{Time}^{\mathbf{G}}_{\mathcal{G}, \mathsf{A}_{gen}} \leq o \implies \mathbf{Adv}^{\mathbf{G}}_{\mathcal{G}, \mathsf{A}_{gen}} \leq \varepsilon.$$

As all of our reductions run the adversary only once and without rewinding, the overhead in the running time of our reductions is *additive* only. We make the reasonable assumption that, compared to the running time of the adversary, this is typically small, and therefore ignore the losses in the running times for this work in order to keep notational overhead low.

We assume that a generic algorithm A_{gen} provides the representation of $\mathbf{Z}$ relative to all previously received group elements, for all group elements $\mathbf{Z}$ that it outputs. This assumption is w.l.o.g. since a generic algorithm can only obtain new group elements by querying two known group elements to the generic group oracle; hence a reduction can always extract a valid representation of a group element output by a generic algorithm. This way, every generic algorithm is also an algebraic algorithm.

Furthermore, if B_{gen} is a generic oracle algorithm and A_{alg} is an algebraic algorithm, then $\mathsf{B}_{alg} := \mathsf{B}_{gen}^{\mathsf{A}_{alg}}$ is also an algebraic algorithm. We refer to [Mau05] for more on generic algorithms.

SECURITY REDUCTIONS. All our security reductions are (bilinear) generic algorithms, which allows us to compose all of our reductions with hardness bounds in the (bilinear) generic group model (see next paragraph). Let $\mathbf{G}_{\mathcal{G}}, \mathbf{H}_{\mathcal{G}}$ be security games. We say that algorithm R_{gen} is a *generic* $(\Delta_{\varepsilon}^{(\cdot)}, \Delta_{\varepsilon}^{(+)}, \Delta_{o}^{(\cdot)}, \Delta_{o}^{(+)})$-*reduction from* $\mathbf{H}_{\mathcal{G}}$ *to* $\mathbf{G}_{\mathcal{G}}$ if R_{gen} is generic and if for every algebraic algorithm A_{alg}, algorithm B_{alg} defined as $\mathsf{B}_{alg} := \mathsf{R}_{gen}^{\mathsf{A}_{alg}}$ satisfies

$$\mathbf{Adv}^{\mathbf{H}}_{\mathcal{G}, \mathsf{B}_{alg}} \geq \frac{1}{\Delta_{\varepsilon}^{(\cdot)}} \cdot \left(\mathbf{Adv}^{\mathbf{G}}_{\mathcal{G}, \mathsf{A}_{alg}} - \Delta_{\varepsilon}^{(+)} \right),$$

$$\mathbf{Time}^{\mathbf{H}}_{\mathcal{G}, \mathsf{B}_{alg}} \leq \Delta_{o}^{(\cdot)} \cdot \left(\mathbf{Time}^{\mathbf{G}}_{\mathcal{G}, \mathsf{A}_{alg}} + \Delta_{o}^{(+)} \right).$$

Furthermore, for simplicity of notation, we will make the convention of referring to $\left(1, \Delta_{\varepsilon}, 1, \Delta_{o}\right)$-reductions as $(\Delta_{\varepsilon}, \Delta_{o})$-reductions.

$q\text{-}\mathbf{dlog}_{\mathcal{G}_i}^{\mathsf{A}}$	$(q_1, q_2)\text{-}\mathbf{dlog}_{\mathcal{G}}^{\mathsf{A}}$
01 $g \xleftarrow{\$} \mathsf{GenSamp}_i$	01 $(g_1, g_2) \xleftarrow{\$} \mathsf{GenSamp}$
02 $z \xleftarrow{\$} \mathbb{Z}_p^*$	02 $z \xleftarrow{\$} \mathbb{Z}_p^*$
03 $z^* \xleftarrow{\$} \mathsf{A}\big(g, g^z, g^{z^2}, \dots, g^{z^q}\big)$	03 $z^* \xleftarrow{\$} \mathsf{A}\big(g_1, g_1^z, g_1^{z^2}, \dots, g_1^{z^{q_1}}, g_2, g_2^z, \dots, g_2^{z^{q_2}}\big)$
04 Return $(z^* = z)$	04 Return $(z^* = z)$

Fig. 1. q-discrete logarithm game $q\text{-}\mathbf{dlog}_{\mathcal{G}_i}$ (left) and (q_1, q_2)-discrete logarithm game $(q_1, q_2)\text{-}\mathbf{dlog}_{\mathcal{G}}$ (right) relative to group $\mathcal{G}_i, i \in \{1, 2\}$ and $\mathcal{G}$, resp., and adversary A.

COMPOSING INFORMATION-THEORETIC LOWER BOUNDS WITH REDUCTIONS IN THE AGM. The following lemma from [Los19] explains how statements in the AGM compose with bounds from the GGM.

Lemma 3. Let $\mathbf{G}_{\mathcal{G}}$ and $\mathbf{H}_{\mathcal{G}}$ be algebraic security games and let $\mathsf{R}_{\mathsf{gen}}$ be a generic $\big(\Delta_\varepsilon^{(\cdot)}, \Delta_\varepsilon^{(+)}, \Delta_o^{(\cdot)}, \Delta_o^{(+)}\big)$-reduction from $\mathbf{H}_{\mathcal{G}}$ to $\mathbf{G}_{\mathcal{G}}$. If $\mathbf{H}_{\mathcal{G}}$ is (ε, o)-secure in the GGM, then $\mathbf{G}_{\mathcal{G}}$ is (ε', o')-secure in the GGM where

$$\varepsilon' = \varepsilon \cdot \Delta_\varepsilon^{(\cdot)} + \Delta_\varepsilon^{(+)}, \quad o' = o/\Delta_o^{(\cdot)} - \Delta_o^{(+)}.$$

THE q-DISCRETE LOGARITHM ASSUMPTION AND VARIANTS. For this work, we consider two generalizations of the DLog assumption, which are parametrized (i.e., "q-type") variants of the DLog assumption. We describe them via the algebraic security games $q\text{-}\mathbf{dlog}_{\mathcal{G}_i}$ and $(q_1, q_2)\text{-}\mathbf{dlog}_{\mathcal{G}}$ in Fig. 1.

The following Lemma, which follows similarly to the generic security of q-SDH in [BB08], is proved (asymptotically) in [Lip12]. For completeness, we give a concrete proof in the full version.

Lemma 4. Let $o, q_1, q_2 \in \mathbb{N}$, let $q := \max\{q_1, q_2\}$. Then q-DLog and (q_1, q_2)-DLog are $\big(\frac{(o+q+1)^2 q}{p-1}, o\big)$-secure in the bilinear generic group model.

We remark that all though our composition results are stated in the bilinear GGM, it is straight forward to translate them to the standard GGM if the associated hardness assumption is stated over a pairing-free group. This is true, because in those cases, our reductions will also be pairing-free and hence are standard generic algorithms themselves.

3   The Uber-Assumption Family

Boyen [Boy08] extended the Uber-assumption framework he initially introduced with Boneh and Goh [BBG05]. We start with defining notions of independence for polynomials and rational fractions (of which polynomials are a special case):

Definition 3. Let $\vec{R} \in \mathbb{Z}_p(X_1, \dots, X_m)^r$ and $W \in \mathbb{Z}_p(X_1, \dots, X_m)$. We say that W is linearly dependent on $\vec{R}$ if there exist coefficients $(a_i)_{i=1}^r \in \mathbb{Z}_p^r$ such that $W = \sum_{i=1}^r a_i R_i$. We say that W is (linearly) independent from $\vec{R}$ if it is not linearly dependent on $\vec{R}$.

$(\vec{R}, \vec{S}, \vec{F}, R', S', F')$-über$_{\mathcal{G}}^{\mathsf{A}_{\mathsf{alg}}}$

01 $(g_1, g_2) \xleftarrow{\$} \mathsf{GenSamp}$; $g_T \leftarrow e(g_1, g_2)$

02 $\vec{x} = (x_1, \ldots, x_m) \xleftarrow{\$} \mathbb{Z}_p^m$

03 $\vec{\mathbf{U}} := (g_1^{R_1(\vec{x})}, \ldots, g_1^{R_r(\vec{x})})$

04 $\vec{\mathbf{V}} := (g_2^{S_1(\vec{x})}, \ldots, g_2^{S_s(\vec{x})})$

05 $\vec{\mathbf{W}} := (g_T^{F_1(\vec{x})}, \ldots, g_T^{F_f(\vec{x})})$

06 $(\mathbf{U}', \mathbf{V}', \mathbf{W}') \xleftarrow{\$} \mathsf{A}_{\mathsf{alg}}(\vec{\mathbf{U}}, \vec{\mathbf{V}}, \vec{\mathbf{W}})$

07 Return $\left((\mathbf{U}', \mathbf{V}', \mathbf{W}') = (g_1^{R'(\vec{x})}, g_2^{S'(\vec{x})}, g_T^{F'(\vec{x})})\right)$

Fig. 2. Algebraic game for the Uber assumption relative to bilinear group $\mathcal{G}$ and adversary $\mathsf{A}_{\mathsf{alg}}$, parametrized by (vectors of) or polynomials $\vec{R}, \vec{S}, \vec{F}, R', S'$ and F'

Definition 4 ([Boy08])**.** *Let* $\vec{R}$, $\vec{S}$, $\vec{F}$ *and* W *be vectors of rational fractions from* $\mathbb{Z}_p(X_1, \ldots, X_m)$ *of length* r, s, f *and* 1*, respectively. We say that* W *is ("bilinearly") dependent on* $(\vec{R}, \vec{S}, \vec{F})$ *if there exist coefficients* $\{a_{i,j}\}$, $\{b_{i,j}\}$, $\{c_{i,j}\}$ *and* $\{d_k\}$ *in* $\mathbb{Z}_p$ *such that*

$$W = \sum_{i=1}^{r} \sum_{j=1}^{s} a_{i,j} R_i S_j + \sum_{i=1}^{r} \sum_{j=1}^{r} b_{i,j} R_i R_j + \sum_{i=1}^{s} \sum_{j=1}^{s} c_{i,j} S_i S_j + \sum_{k=1}^{f} d_k F_k.$$

We call the dependency of Type 2 *if* $b_{i,j} = 0$ *for all* i, j *and of* Type 3 *if* $b_{i,j} = c_{i,j} = 0$ *for all* i, j*. Else, it is of* Type 1*. We say that* W *is (Type-τ) independent from* $(\vec{R}, \vec{S}, \vec{F})$ *if it is not (Type-τ) dependent on* $(\vec{R}, \vec{S}, \vec{F})$*. (Thus, W can be Type-3 independent but Type-2 dependent.)*

Consider the Uber-assumption game in Fig. 2, which is parametrized by vectors of polynomials $\vec{R}$, $\vec{S}$ and $\vec{F}$ and polynomials R', S' and F'. For a random vector $\vec{x}$, the adversary receives the evaluation of the (vectors of) polynomials in the exponents of the generators g_1, g_2 and g_T; its goal is to find the evaluation of the polynomials R', S' and F' at $\vec{x}$ in the exponents. Note that we do not explicitly give the generators to the adversary. This is without loss of generality because we can always set $R_1 = S_1 = F_1 \equiv 1$.

It is easily seen that the game can be efficiently solved if one of the following conditions hold (where we distinguish the different types of bilinear groups and interpret all polynomials over $\mathbb{Z}_p$):

(Type 1) If R' is dependent on $\vec{R}$ and $\vec{S}$, and S' is dependent on $\vec{R}$ and $\vec{S}$, and F' is Type-1 dependent (Definition 4) on $(\vec{R}, \vec{S}, \vec{F})$.

(Type 2) If R' is dependent on $\vec{R}$ and $\vec{S}$, S' is dependent on $\vec{S}$, and F' is Type-2 dependent (Definition 4) on $(\vec{R}, \vec{S}, \vec{F})$.

(Type 3) If R' is dependent on $\vec{R}$, S' is dependent on $\vec{S}$, and F' is Type-3 dependent (Definition 4) on $(\vec{R}, \vec{S}, \vec{F})$.

For example, in Type-2 groups, if $R' = \sum_i a_i' R_i + \sum_i b_i' S_i$ and $S' = 1$, and $F' = \sum_i \sum_j a_{i,j} R_i S_j + \sum_i \sum_j c_{i,j} S_i S_j$, then from a challenge $(\vec{\mathbf{U}}, \vec{\mathbf{V}}, \vec{\mathbf{W}})$, one can easily compute a solution $\mathbf{U}' := \prod_i \mathbf{U}_i^{a_i'} \cdot \psi(\prod_i \mathbf{V}_i^{b_i'})$, $\mathbf{V}' := g_2$, $\mathbf{W}' := \prod_i \prod_j e(\mathbf{U}_i, \mathbf{V}_j)^{a_{i,j}} \cdot \prod_i \prod_j e(\psi(\mathbf{V}_i), \mathbf{V}_j)^{b_{i,j}}$.

In our main theorem, we show that whenever the game in Fig. 2 cannot be trivially won, then for groups of Type $\tau \in \{1, 2\}$, it can be reduced from q-**dlog**$_{\mathcal{G}_2}$, and for Type-3 groups, it can be reduced from (q_1, q_2)-**dlog**$_{\mathcal{G}}$ (for appropriate values of q, q_1, q_2). To state the theorem for all types of groups, we first define the following non-triviality condition (which again we state for the more general case of rational fractions):

Definition 5 (Non-triviality). *Let* $\vec{R} \in \mathbb{Z}_p(X_1, \ldots, X_m)^r$, $\vec{S} \in \mathbb{Z}_p(X_1, \ldots, X_m)^s$, $\vec{F} \in \mathbb{Z}_p(X_1, \ldots, X_m)^f$, $R', S', F' \in \mathbb{Z}_p(X_1, \ldots, X_m)$. *We say that the tuple* $(\vec{R}, \vec{S}, \vec{F}, R', S', F')$ *is* non-trivial *for groups of type* τ, *for* $\tau \in \{1, 2, 3\}$, *if:*

- R' *is linearly independent from* $\vec{R}$ *and* $\vec{S}$ *in case* $\tau \in \{1, 2\}$,
  R' *is linearly independent from* $\vec{R}$ *in case* $\tau = 3$; $(\tau.1)$
- **or** S' *is linearly independent from* $\vec{R}$ *and* $\vec{S}$ *in case* $\tau = 1$,
  S' *is linearly independent from* $\vec{S}$ *in case* $\tau \in \{2, 3\}$; $(\tau.2)$
- **or** F' *is Type-*τ *"bilinearly" independent (Definition 4) from* $(\vec{R}, \vec{S}, \vec{F})$. $(\tau.T)$

We have argued above that if the tuple $(\vec{R}, \vec{S}, \vec{F}, R', S', F')$ is trivial then the $(\vec{R}, \vec{S}, \vec{F}, R', S', F')$-**über** problem is trivial to solve, even with a generic algorithm. In Theorem 1 we now show that if the tuple is *non-trivial* then the corresponding Uber assumption holds for algebraic algorithms, as long as a type of q-DLog assumption holds (whose type depends on the type of bilinear group).

The (additive) security loss of the reduction depends on the degrees of the polynomials involved (as well as the group type and its order). E.g., in Type-3 groups, if R' is independent of $\vec{R}$ then the probability that the reduction fails is the maximum degree of R' and the components of $\vec{R}$, divided by the order of $\mathcal{G}$. In Type-1 and Type-2 groups, due to the homomorphism ψ, the loss depends on the maximum degree of R', $\vec{R}$ and $\vec{S}$. Similar bounds hold when S' is independent of $\vec{S}$ (and $\vec{R}$ for Type 1); and slightly more involved ones for the independence of F'. If several of R', S' and F' are independent then the reduction chooses the strategy that minimizes the security loss.

Definition 6 (Degree of non-trivial tuple of polynomials). *Let* $(\vec{R}, \vec{S}, \vec{F}, R', S', F')$ *be a non-trivial tuple of polynomials in* $\mathbb{Z}_p[X_1, \ldots, X_m]$. *Define* $d_{\vec{R}} := \max\{\deg R_i\}_{1 \le i \le r}$, $d_{\vec{S}} := \max\{\deg S_i\}_{1 \le i \le s}$, $d_{\vec{F}} := \max\{\deg F_i\}_{1 \le i \le f}$. *We define the type-*$\tau$ *degree* d_τ *of* $(\vec{R}, \vec{S}, \vec{F}, R', S', F')$ *as follows:*

- *If* $(\tau.1)$ *holds, let* $d_{\tau.1} := \max\{\deg R', d_{\vec{R}}, d_{\vec{S}}\}$ *in case* $\tau \in \{1, 2\}$ *and*
  $d_{\tau.1} := \max\{\deg R', d_{\vec{R}}\}$ *in case* $\tau = 3$.
- *If* $(\tau.2)$ *holds, let* $d_{\tau.2} := \max\{\deg S', d_{\vec{R}}, d_{\vec{S}}\}$ *in case* $\tau = 1$ *and*
  $d_{\tau.2} := \max\{\deg S', d_{\vec{S}}\}$ *in case* $\tau \in \{2, 3\}$.
- *If* $(\tau.T)$ *holds, let* $d_{\tau.T} := \max\{\deg F', 2 d_{\vec{R}}, 2 d_{\vec{S}}, d_{\vec{F}}\}$ *when* $\tau = 1$,
  $d_{\tau.T} := \max\{\deg F', d_{\vec{R}} + d_{\vec{S}}, 2 d_{\vec{S}}, d_{\vec{F}}\}$ *in case* $\tau = 2$ *and*
  $d_{\tau.T} := \max\{\deg F', d_{\vec{R}} + d_{\vec{S}}, d_{\vec{F}}\}$ *in case* $\tau = 3$.

If (τ, i) does not hold, we set $d_{\tau,i} := \infty$ and define $d_\tau := \min\{d_{\tau.1}, d_{\tau.2}, d_{\tau.T}\}$. (By non-triviality, $d_\tau < \infty$.)

Theorem 1 (DLog implies Uber in the AGM). *Let $\mathcal{G}$ be of type $\tau \in \{1, 2, 3\}$ and $(\vec{R}, \vec{S}, \vec{F}, R', S', F') \in (\mathbb{Z}_p[X_1, \ldots, X_m])^{r+s+f+3}$ be a tuple of polynomials that is non-trivial for type τ and define $d_{\vec{R}} := \max\{\deg R_i\}$, $d_{\vec{S}} := \max\{\deg S_i\}$, $d_{\vec{F}} := \max\{\deg F_i\}$. Let q, q_1, q_2 be such that $q \geq \max\{d_{\vec{R}}, d_{\vec{S}}, d_{\vec{F}}/2\}$ as well as $q_1 \geq d_{\vec{R}}, q_2 \geq d_{\vec{S}}$ and $q_1 + q_2 \geq d_{\vec{F}}$. If*

(Type 1) *q-$\mathbf{dlog}_{\mathcal{G}_1}$ or q-$\mathbf{dlog}_{\mathcal{G}_2}$ is (ε, t)-secure in the AGM,*
(Type 2) *q-$\mathbf{dlog}_{\mathcal{G}_2}$ is (ε, t)-secure in the AGM,*
(Type 3) *(q_1, q_2)-$\mathbf{dlog}_{\mathcal{G}}$ is (ε, t)-secure in the AGM,*

then $(\vec{R}, \vec{S}, \vec{F}, R', S', F')$-$\mathbf{über}_{\mathcal{G}}$ is (ε', t')-secure in the AGM with

$$\varepsilon' \leq \varepsilon + \tfrac{d_\tau}{p-1} \text{ and } t' \leq t + o_1,$$

where d_τ is the maximal degree of $(\vec{R}, \vec{S}, \vec{F}, R', S', F')$, as defined in Definition 6, $o_1 := o_0 + 2 + (2\lfloor \log_2(p) \rfloor)((d_{\vec{R}}+1)r + (d_{\vec{S}}+1)s + (d_{\vec{F}}+1)f + d_\tau) + rd_{\vec{R}} + sd_{\vec{S}} + fd_{\vec{F}}$ with $o_0 := d_{\vec{R}} + d_{\vec{F}} + 2$ for Types 1 and 2, and $o_0 := d_{\vec{F}} + 1$ for in Type 3.

Proof. We give a detailed proof for Type-2 bilinear groups and then explain how to adapt it to Types 1 and 3. For $u \in \mathbb{Z}_p$ and $i \in \{1, 2, T\}$ we let $[u]_i$ denote g_i^u.

Let $\mathsf{A}_{\mathsf{alg}}$ be an algebraic algorithm against $\mathbf{über}_{\mathcal{G}}$ that wins with advantage ε in time t. We construct a generic reduction with oracle access to $\mathsf{A}_{\mathsf{alg}}$, which yields an algebraic adversary $\mathsf{B}_{\mathsf{alg}}$ against q-$\mathbf{dlog}_{\mathcal{G}_2}$. There are three (non-exclusive) reasons for $(\vec{R}, \vec{S}, \vec{F}, R', S', F')$ being non-trivial, which correspond to conditions (2.1), (2.2) and (2.T) in Definition 5. Each condition enables a different type of reduction, of which $\mathsf{B}_{\mathsf{alg}}$ runs the one that minimizes d_2 from Definition 6.

We start with Case (2.1), that is, R' is linearly independent from $\vec{R}$ and $\vec{S}$.

Adversary $\mathsf{B}_{\mathsf{alg}}(g_2, \mathbf{Z}_1, \ldots, \mathbf{Z}_q)$: On input a problem instance of game q-$\mathbf{dlog}_{\mathcal{G}_2}$ with $\mathbf{Z}_i = [z^i]_2$, $\mathsf{B}_{\mathsf{alg}}$ simulates $\mathbf{über}_{\mathcal{G}}$ for $\mathsf{A}_{\mathsf{alg}}$. It defines $g_1 \leftarrow \psi(g_2)$ and $g_T \leftarrow e(g_1, g_2)$. Then, it picks random values $\vec{y} \xleftarrow{\$} (\mathbb{Z}_p^*)^m$ and $\vec{v} \xleftarrow{\$} \mathbb{Z}_p^m$, implicitly sets $x_i := y_i z + v_i \mod p$ and computes $\mathbf{U} := [\vec{R}(x_1, \ldots, x_m)]_1$, $\mathbf{V} := [\vec{S}(x_1, \ldots, x_m)]_2$, $\mathbf{W} := [\vec{F}(x_1, \ldots, x_m)]_T$ from its q-DLog instance, the isomorphism $\psi \colon \mathbb{G}_2 \to \mathbb{G}_1$ and the pairing $e \colon \mathbb{G}_1 \times \mathbb{G}_2 \to \mathbb{G}_T$. It can do so efficiently since the total degrees of the polynomials in $\vec{R}, \vec{S}$ and $\vec{F}$ are bounded by q, q and $2q$ respectively.[1]

Next, $\mathsf{B}_{\mathsf{alg}}$ runs $(\mathbf{U}', \mathbf{V}', \mathbf{W}') \xleftarrow{\$} \mathsf{A}_{\mathsf{alg}}(\mathbf{U}, \mathbf{V}, \mathbf{W})$. Since $\mathsf{A}_{\mathsf{alg}}$ is algebraic, it also returns vectors and matrices $\vec{\mu}, \vec{\nu}, \vec{\zeta}, \vec{\delta}, A = (\alpha_{i,j})_{i,j}, \Gamma = (\gamma_{i,j})_{i,j}$ such that

$$\mathbf{U}' = \prod_i \mathbf{U}_i^{\mu_i} \cdot \prod_i \psi(\mathbf{V}_i)^{\nu_i} \tag{2a}$$

---

[1] E.g., $\mathsf{B}_{\mathsf{alg}}$ can compute $[x_1^q]_1 = [(y_1 z + v_1)^q]_1$ as $\prod_i \psi(\mathbf{Z}_i)^{\binom{q}{i} y_1^i v_1^{q-i}}$ and $[x_1^{2q}]_T$ as $e\big(\prod_i \psi(\mathbf{Z}_i)^{\binom{q}{i} y_1^i v_1^{q-i}}, \prod_i \mathbf{Z}_i^{\binom{q}{i} y_1^i v_1^{q-i}}\big)$ and similarly for terms in more variables.

$$\mathbf{V}' = \textstyle\prod_i \mathbf{V}_i^{\eta_i} \tag{2b}$$

$$\mathbf{W}' = \textstyle\prod_i \prod_j e(\mathbf{U}_i, \mathbf{V}_j)^{\alpha_{i,j}} \cdot \prod_i \prod_j e(\psi(\mathbf{V}_i), \mathbf{V}_j)^{\gamma_{i,j}} \cdot \prod_i \mathbf{W}_i^{\delta_i}. \tag{2c}$$

$\mathsf{B}_{\mathsf{alg}}$ then computes the following multivariate polynomial, which corresponds to the exponents of (2a):

$$P_1(\vec{X}) = R'(\vec{X}) - \textstyle\sum_{i=1}^{r} \mu_i R_i(\vec{X}) - \sum_{i=1}^{s} \nu_i S_i(\vec{X}), \tag{3}$$

which is non-zero because in Case (2.1) R' is independent from $\vec{R}$ and $\vec{S}$. From P_1, it defines the univariate polynomial

$$Q_1(Z) := P_1(y_1 Z + v_1, \ldots, y_m Z + v_m). \tag{4}$$

If Q_1 is the zero polynomial then $\mathsf{B}_{\mathsf{alg}}$ aborts. $\hspace{3cm} (*)$
Else, it factors Q_1 to obtain its roots $z_1, \ldots$ (of which there are at most $\max\{\deg R', d_{\vec{R}}, d_{\vec{S}}\}$; we analyse the degree of Q_1 below). If for one of them we have $g_2^{z_i} = \mathbf{Z}$, then $\mathsf{B}_{\mathsf{alg}}$ returns z_i.

We analyze $\mathsf{B}_{\mathsf{alg}}$'s success probability. First note that $\mathsf{B}_{\mathsf{alg}}$ perfectly simulates game $\mathbf{\ddot{u}ber}_{\mathcal{G}}$, as the values x_i are uniformly distributed in $\mathbb{Z}_p$ and $\vec{\mathbf{U}}$, $\vec{\mathbf{V}}$ and $\vec{\mathbf{W}}$ are correctly computed.

Moreover, if $\mathsf{B}_{\mathsf{alg}}$ does not abort in $(*)$ and $\mathsf{A}_{\mathsf{alg}}$ wins game $\mathbf{\ddot{u}ber}_{\mathcal{G}}$, then $\mathbf{U}' = [R'(\vec{x})]_1$. On the other hand,

$$\mathbf{U}' = \textstyle\prod_i \mathbf{U}_i^{\mu_i} \cdot \psi(\prod_i \mathbf{V}_i^{\nu_i}) = \left[\sum_i \mu_i R_i(\vec{x}) + \sum_i \nu_i S_i(\vec{x}) \right]_1.$$

Together, this means that $P_1(\vec{x}) \equiv_p 0$ and since $x_i \equiv_p y_i z + v_i$, moreover $Q_1(z) \equiv_p 0$. By factoring Q_1, reduction $\mathsf{B}_{\mathsf{alg}}$ finds thus the solution z.

It remains to bound the probability that $\mathsf{B}_{\mathsf{alg}}$ aborts in $(*)$, that is, the event that $0 \equiv Q_1(Z) = P_1(y_1 Z + v_1, \ldots, y_m Z + v_m)$. Interpreting Q_1 as an element from $(\mathbb{Z}_p[Y_1, \ldots, Y_m, V_1, \ldots, V_m])[Z]$, Lemma 1 yields that its maximal coefficient is a polynomial $Q_1^{\max}$ in $Y_1, \ldots, Y_m$ whose degree is the same as the maximal (total) degree d of P_1. From $P_1 \not\equiv 0$ and $P_1(\vec{x}) = 0$, we have $d > 0$.

We note that the values $y_1 z, \ldots, y_m z$ are completely hidden from $\mathsf{A}_{\mathsf{alg}}$ because they are "one-time-padded" with $v_1, \ldots, v_m$, respectively. This means that the values $(\vec{\mu}, \vec{\nu})$ returned by $\mathsf{A}_{\mathsf{alg}}$ are independent from $\vec{y}$. Since $\vec{y}$ is moreover independent from R', $\vec{R}$ and $\vec{S}$, it is also independent from P_1, Q_1 and $Q_1^{\max}$. The probability that $Q_1 \equiv 0$ is thus upper-bounded by the probability that its maximal coefficient $Q_1^{\max}(\vec{y}) \equiv_p 0$ when evaluated at the random point $\vec{y}$. By the Schwartz-Zippel lemma, the probability that $Q_1(Z) \equiv 0$ is thus upper-bounded by $\frac{d}{p-1}$. The degree d of Q_1 (and thus of $Q^{\max}$) is upper-bounded by the total degrees of P_1, which is $\max\{d'_R, d_{\vec{R}}, d_{\vec{S}}\} = d_{2.1}$ in Definition 6. $\mathsf{B}_{\mathsf{alg}}$ thus aborts in line $(*)$ with probability at most $\frac{d_{2.1}}{p-1}$.

Case (2.2), that is, S' is linearly independent from $\vec{S}$, follows completely analogously, but with $d = d_{2.2} = \max\{d_{S'}, d_{\vec{S}}\}$.

Case (2.T), when F' is type-2-independent of $\vec{R}$, $\vec{S}$ and $\vec{F}$, is also analogous; we highlight the necessary changes: From $\mathsf{A_{alg}}$'s representation $(A = (\alpha_{i,j}), \Gamma = (\gamma_{i,j}), \vec{\delta}) \in \mathbb{Z}_p^{r \times s} \times \mathbb{Z}_p^{s \times s} \times \mathbb{Z}_p^{f}$ for $\mathbf{W}'$ (see (2c)), that is,

$$
\begin{aligned}
\mathbf{W}' &= \prod_i \prod_j e(\mathbf{U}_i, \mathbf{V}_j)^{\alpha_{i,j}} \cdot \prod_i \prod_j e(\psi(\mathbf{V}_i), \mathbf{V}_j)^{\gamma_{i,j}} \cdot \prod_i \mathbf{W}_i^{\delta_i} \\
&= \left[\sum_i \sum_j \alpha_{i,j} R_i(\vec{x}) S_j(\vec{x}) + \sum_i \sum_j \gamma_{i,j} S_i(\vec{x}) S_j(\vec{x}) + \sum_i \delta_i F_i(\vec{x}) \right]_T. \quad (5)
\end{aligned}
$$

Analogously to (3) we define

$$
\begin{aligned}
P_T(\vec{X}) := F'(\vec{X}) &- \sum_{i=1}^{r} \sum_{j=1}^{s} \alpha_{i,j} R_i(\vec{X}) S_j(\vec{X}) \\
&- \sum_{i=1}^{s} \sum_{j=1}^{s} \gamma_{i,j} S_i(\vec{X}) S_j(\vec{X}) - \sum_{i=1}^{f} \delta_i F_i(\vec{X}), \quad (6)
\end{aligned}
$$

which is of degree at most $d_{2.T} := \max\{\deg F', d_{\vec{R}} + d_{\vec{S}}, 2 \cdot d_{\vec{S}}, d_{\vec{F}}\}$. Polynomial P_T is non-zero by Type-2-independence of F' (Definition 4). The reduction also computes $Q_T(Z) := P_T(y_1 Z + v_1, \ldots, y_m Z + v_m)$.

If $\mathsf{A_{alg}}$ wins then $\mathbf{W}' = [F'(\vec{x})]_T$, which together with (5) implies that $P_T(\vec{x}) \equiv_p 0$ and thus $Q_T(z) \equiv_p 0$. Reduction $\mathsf{B_{alg}}$ can find z by factoring Q_T; unless $Q_T(Z) \equiv 0$, which by an analysis analogous to the one for case (2.1) happens with probability $\frac{d_{2.T}}{p-1}$. (We detail the reduction for the case where $\mathbf{W}'$ is independent in the proof of Theorem 3, which proves a more general statement.)

Theorem 1 for Type-2 groups now follows because $\mathbf{Adv}_{\mathcal{G}_2, \mathsf{B_{alg}}}^{q\text{-dlog}} \geq \mathbf{Adv}_{\mathcal{G}, \mathsf{A_{alg}}}^{\text{über}} -$ $\Pr[\mathsf{B_{alg}} \text{ aborts}]$ and $\mathsf{B_{alg}}$ follows the type of reduction that minimizes its abort probability to $\min\left\{\frac{d_{2.1}}{p-1}, \frac{d_{2.2}}{p-1}, \frac{d_{2.T}}{p-1}\right\} = \frac{d_2}{p-1}$.

Groups of Type 1 and 3. The reduction for bilinear groups of Type 1 to $q\text{-dlog}_{\mathcal{G}_2}$ is almost the same proof. The only change is that for Case (1.T) the polynomial P_T in (6) has an extra term $-\sum_{i=1}^{r} \sum_{j=1}^{r} \beta_{i,j} R_i(\vec{X}) R_j(\vec{X})$, because of the representation of $\mathbf{W}'$ in Type-1 groups (see Definition 2); the degree of P_T is then bounded by $\max\{\deg F', 2 d_{\vec{R}}, 2 d_{\vec{S}}, d_{\vec{F}}\}$. Analogously for Case (1.2), S' can now depend on $\vec{S}$ as well as $\vec{R}$. The reduction for Type-1 groups to $q\text{-dlog}_{\mathcal{G}_1}$ is completely symmetric by swapping the roles of $\mathbb{G}_1$ and $\mathbb{G}_2$ and replacing ψ by ϕ.

The reduction for Type-3 groups relies on the $(q_1, q_2)\text{-dlog}_{\mathcal{G}}$ assumption, as it requires $\{[z_i]_1\}_{i=1}^{q_1}$ and $\{[z_i]_2\}_{i=1}^{q_2}$ to simulate $\{[R_i(\vec{x})]_1\}_{i=1}^{r}$ and $\{[S_i(\vec{x})]_2\}_{i=1}^{s}$ without using any homomorphism ϕ or ψ. Apart from this, the proof is again analogous. (We treat the Type-3 case in detail in the proof of Theorem 3.) In the full version we detail the analysis of the running times of these reductions. $\square$

Using Lemmas 3 and 4 we obtain the following corollary to Theorem 1:

Corollary 1. *Let $\mathcal{G}$ be of type τ and $(\vec{R}, \vec{S}, \vec{F}, R', S', F')$ be non-trivial for τ of maximal degree d_τ. Then $(\vec{R}, \vec{S}, \vec{F}, R', S', F')\text{-über}_{\mathcal{G}}$ is $\left(\frac{(o+o_1+1+q)^2 q}{p-1} + \frac{d_\tau}{p-1}, o\right)$-secure in the generic bilinear group model.*

Comparison to previous GGM results. Boneh, Boyen and Goh [BBG05, Theorem A.2] claim that the decisional Uber assumption for the particular case

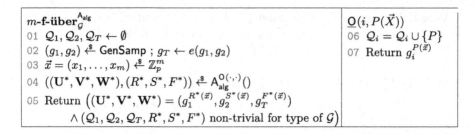

Fig. 3. Algebraic game for the flexible Uber assumption

$r = s$ and $f = 0$ is $\left(\frac{(o+2r+2)^2 q}{2p}, o\right)$-secure in the generic group model, and with the same reasoning, one can obtain the more general bound $\left(\frac{(o+r+s+f+2)^2 q}{2p}, o\right)$. Note that the loss in their bound is only linear in the maximum degree while ours *cubic*. Our looser bound is a result of our reduction, whereas Boneh, Boyen and Goh prove their bound directly in the GGM.[2]

4   The Flexible Uber Assumption

Boyen [Boy08] generalizes the Uber assumption framework to *flexible* assumptions, where the adversary can define the target polynomials (R', S' and F' in Fig. 2) itself, conditioned on the solution not being trivially computable from the instance, for *non-triviality* as in Definition 5. In Sect. 6 we consider this kind of flexible Uber assumption in our generalization to rational fractions and thereby cover assumptions like q-strong Diffie-Hellman [BB08].

For polynomials, we generalize this further by allowing the adversary to also (adaptively) choose the polynomials that constitute the challenge. The adversary is provided with an oracle that takes input a value $i \in \{1, 2, T\}$ and a polynomial $P(\vec{X})$ of the adversary's choice, and returns $g_i^{P(\vec{x})}$, where $\vec{x}$ is the secret value chosen during the game. The adversary then wins if it returns polynomials (R^*, S^*, F^*), which are independent from its queries, and $\left(g_1^{R^*(\vec{x})}, g_2^{S^*(\vec{x})}, g_T^{F^*(\vec{x})}\right)$. The game for this flexible Uber assumption is specified in Fig. 3.

Theorem 2. *Let $m \geq 1$, let $\mathcal{G}$ be a bilinear-group of type $\tau \in \{1, 2, 3\}$ and consider an adversary $\mathsf{A}_{\mathsf{alg}}$ in game m-**f-über**$_{\mathcal{G}}$. Let $d'_1, d'_2, d'_T, d_1^*, d_2^*, d_T^*$ be such that $\mathsf{A}_{\mathsf{alg}}$'s queries $(i, P(\vec{X}))$ satisfy $\deg P \leq d'_i$ and its output values R^*, S^*, F^* satisfy $\deg R^* \leq d_1^*$, $\deg S^* \leq d_2^*$, $\deg F^* \leq d_T^*$. Let q, q_1, q_2 be such that $q \geq \max\{d'_1, d'_2, d'_T/2\}$ as well as $q_1 \geq d'_1$, $q_2 \geq d'_2$ and $q_1 + q_2 \geq d'_T$. If*

(Type 1) q-**dlog**$_{\mathcal{G}_1}$ *or* q-**dlog**$_{\mathcal{G}_2}$ *is (ε, t)-secure in the AGM,*
(Type 2) q-**dlog**$_{\mathcal{G}_2}$ *is (ε, t)-secure in the AGM,*
(Type 3) (q_1, q_2)-**dlog**$_{\mathcal{G}}$ *is (ε, t)-secure in the AGM,*

---

[2] We did not consider the bound claimed in [Boy08, Theorem 1], because it is an incorrect copy of the one in [BBG05].

$(\vec{R}, \vec{S}, \vec{F}, R', S', F')$-**rüber**$_{\mathcal{G}}^{\mathsf{A_{alg}}}$ $// R_i = \hat{R}_i/\check{R}_i$, for $\hat{R}_i, \check{R}_i \in \mathbb{Z}_p[\vec{X}]$, etc

01   $(g_1, g_2) \stackrel{\$}{\leftarrow} \mathsf{GenSamp}$; $g_T \leftarrow e(g_1, g_2)$

02   $\vec{x} = (x_1, \ldots, x_m) \stackrel{\$}{\leftarrow} \mathbb{Z}_p^m$

03   If for some i: $\check{R}_i(\vec{x}) \equiv_p 0$ or $\check{S}_i(\vec{x}) \equiv_p 0$ or $\check{F}_i(\vec{x}) \equiv_p 0$ then return 1

04   If $\check{R}'(\vec{x}) \equiv_p 0$ or $\check{S}'(\vec{x}) \equiv_p 0$ or $\check{F}'(\vec{x}) \equiv_p 0$ then return 1

05   $\vec{\mathbf{U}} := (g_1^{R_1(\vec{x})}, \ldots, g_1^{R_r(\vec{x})})$; $\vec{\mathbf{V}} := (g_2^{S_1(\vec{x})}, \ldots, g_2^{S_s(\vec{x})})$; $\vec{\mathbf{W}} := (g_T^{F_1(\vec{x})}, \ldots, g_T^{F_f(\vec{x})})$

06   $(\mathbf{U}', \mathbf{V}', \mathbf{W}') \stackrel{\$}{\leftarrow} \mathsf{A_{alg}}(\vec{\mathbf{U}}, \vec{\mathbf{V}}, \vec{\mathbf{W}})$

07   Return $\left((\mathbf{U}', \mathbf{V}', \mathbf{W}') = (g_1^{R'(\vec{x})}, g_2^{S'(\vec{x})}, g_T^{F'(\vec{x})})\right)$

Fig. 4. Algebraic game for the Uber assumption relative to bilinear group $\mathcal{G}$ and adversary $\mathsf{A_{alg}}$, parametrized by (vectors of) rational fractions $\vec{R}, \vec{S}, \vec{F}, R', S'$ and F'

then m-**f-über**$_{\mathcal{G}}$ *is* (ε', t')-*secure in the AGM with*

$$\varepsilon' \leq \varepsilon + \frac{d_\tau}{p-1} \text{ and } t' \approx t,$$

where d_τ *is as in Definition 6 after the following replacements:* $d_{\vec{R}} \leftarrow d_1'$, $d_{\vec{S}} \leftarrow d_2'$, $d_{\vec{F}} \leftarrow d_F'$, $\deg R' \leftarrow d_1^*$, $\deg S' \leftarrow d_2^*$ *and* $\deg F' \leftarrow d_T^*$.

Proof (sketch). Inspecting the proof of Theorem 1, note that the values $[R_i(\vec{x})]_1$, $[S_i(\vec{x})]_2$ and $[F_i(\vec{x})]_T$ need not be known in advance and can be computed by the reduction at any point, as long as the degrees of R_i and S_i are bounded by q and those of F_i by $2q$. The adversary could thus specify the polynomials via oracle calls and the reduction can compute $\mathbf{U}_i$, $\mathbf{V}_i$ and $\mathbf{F}_i$ on the fly.

Likewise, the polynomials P_1, P_2 and P_T (and their univariate counterparts which the reduction factors) are only defined after $\mathsf{A_{alg}}$ stops; therefore, R', S' and F', from which they are defined, need only be known then. The proof of Theorem 1 is thus adapted to prove Theorem 2 in a very straightforward way. $\square$

5   The Uber Assumption for Rational Fractions

Reconsider the Uber assumption in Fig. 2, but now let $\vec{R}, \vec{S}, \vec{F}, R', S'$ and F' be *rational fractions* over $\mathbb{Z}_p$ rather than polynomials. We will show that even this generalization of the Uber assumption is implied by q-DLog assumptions. We start with introducing some notation. We view a rational fraction as defined by two polynomials, its numerator and its denominator, and assume that the fraction is reduced. For a rational fraction $R \in \mathbb{Z}_p(X_1, \ldots, X_m)$, we denote its numerator by $\hat{R}$ and its denominator by $\check{R}$. That is $\hat{R}, \check{R} \in \mathbb{Z}_p[X_1, \ldots, X_m]$ are such that $R = \hat{R}/\check{R}$. As rational fractions are not defined everywhere, we modify the game from Fig. 2 so the adversary wins should the experiment choose an input $\vec{x}$ for which one of the rational fractions is not defined. The rational-fraction uber game is given in Fig. 4.

For a vector of rational fractions $\vec{R} \in \mathbb{Z}_p(X_1, \ldots, X_m)^r$, we define its *common denominator* $\mathrm{Den}(\vec{R})$ as a least common multiple of the denominators of the components of $\vec{R}$. In particular, fix an algorithm LCM that given a set of polynomials returns a least common multiple of them. Then we define:

$$\text{Den}(\vec{R}) = \text{Den}(\hat{R}_1/\check{R}_1, \ldots, \hat{R}_r/\check{R}_r) := \text{LCM}\{\check{R}_1, \ldots, \check{R}_r\}.$$

We let $\check{d}_{\vec{R}}$ denote the degree of $\text{Den}(\vec{R})$ and $d_{\vec{R}}$ denote the maximal degree of the elements of $\vec{R}$, that is $d_{\vec{R}} := \max\{\deg(R_1), \ldots, \deg(R_r)\}$. Note that this integer could be negative and is lower bounded by $-\check{d}_{\vec{R}}$. The security loss in Theorem 3 depends on the type of the bilinear group, the reason for the tuple $(\vec{R}, \vec{S}, \vec{F}, R', S', F')$ being non-trivial, as well as the degrees of the numerators and denominators of the involved rational fractions. We summarize this in the following technical definition.

Definition 7 (Degree of non-trivial tuple of rational fractions). *Let* $(\vec{R}, \vec{S}, \vec{F}, R', S', F')$ *be a non-trivial tuple whose elements are rational fractions in* $\mathbb{Z}_p(X_1, \ldots, X_m)$. *Let* $d_{\text{den}} := \check{d}_{\vec{R}\|\vec{S}\|\vec{F}\|R'\|S'\|F'}$. *We define the type-$\tau$ degree* d_τ *of* $(\vec{R}, \vec{S}, \vec{F}, R', S', F')$ *as follows, distinguishing the kinds of non-triviality defined in Definition 5.*

(Type 1)   – *If (1.1) holds, let* $d_{1.1} := d_{\text{den}} + \check{d}_{R'} + \check{d}_{\vec{R}\|\vec{S}} + \max\{d_{R'}, d_{\vec{R}}, d_{\vec{S}}\}$
    – *if (1.2) holds, let* $d_{1.2} := d_{\text{den}} + \check{d}_{S'} + \check{d}_{\vec{R}\|\vec{S}} + \max\{d_{S'}, d_{\vec{R}}, d_{\vec{S}}\}$
    – *if (1.T) holds,* $d_{1.T} := d_{\text{den}} + \check{d}_{F'} + \check{d}_{\vec{R}\|\vec{S}\|\vec{F}} + \check{d}_{\vec{R}\|\vec{S}} + \max\{d_{F'}, 2d_{\vec{S}}, 2d_{\vec{R}}, d_{\vec{F}}\}$
(Type 2)   – *If (2.1) holds, let* $d_{2.1} := d_{\text{den}} + \check{d}_{R'} + \check{d}_{\vec{R}\|\vec{S}} + \max\{d_{R'}, d_{\vec{R}}, d_{\vec{S}}\}$
    – *if (2.2) holds, let* $d_{2.2} := d_{\text{den}} + \check{d}_{S'} + \check{d}_{\vec{S}} + \max\{d_{S'}, d_{\vec{S}}\}$
    – *if (2.T) holds,* $d_{2.T} := d_{\text{den}} + \check{d}_{F'} + \check{d}_{\vec{R}\|\vec{S}\|\vec{F}} + \check{d}_{\vec{S}} + \max\{d_{F'}, 2d_{\vec{S}}, d_{\vec{R}} + d_{\vec{S}}, d_{\vec{F}}\}$
(Type 3)   – *If (3.1) holds, let* $d_{3.1} := d_{\text{den}} + \check{d}_{R'} + \check{d}_{\vec{R}} + \max\{d_{R'}, d_{\vec{R}}\}$
    – *if (3.2) holds, let* $d_{3.2} := d_{\text{den}} + \check{d}_{S'} + \check{d}_{\vec{S}} + \max\{d_{S'}, d_{\vec{S}}\}$
    – *if (3.T) holds,* $d_{3.T} := d_{\text{den}} + \check{d}_{F'} + \check{d}_{\vec{R}\|\vec{F}} + \check{d}_{\vec{S}} + \max\{d_{F'}, d_{\vec{R}} + d_{\vec{S}}, d_{\vec{F}}\}$

If (τ, i) *does not hold, set* $d_{\tau,i} := \infty$. *Define* $d_\tau := \min\{d_{\tau.1}, d_{\tau.2}, d_{\tau.T}\}$.

Theorem 3 (DLog implies Uber for rational fractions in the AGM). *Let* $\mathcal{G}$ *be a bilinear group of type* $\tau \in \{1, 2, 3\}$ *and let* $(\vec{R}, \vec{S}, \vec{F}, R', S', F') \in (\mathbb{Z}_p (X_1, \ldots, X_m))^{r+s+f+3}$ *be a tuple that is non-trivial for type* τ *(Definition 5). Let* q, q_1 *and* q_2 *be such that* $q \geq \check{d}_{\vec{R}\|\vec{S}\|\vec{F}} + \max\{d_{\vec{R}}, d_{\vec{S}}, d_{\vec{F}}/2\}$ *and* $q_1 \geq \check{d}_{\vec{R}\|\vec{F}} + d_{\vec{R}}$ *and* $q_2 \geq \check{d}_{\vec{S}} + d_{\vec{S}}$ *and* $q_1 + q_2 \geq \check{d}_{\vec{R}\|\vec{F}} + \check{d}_{\vec{S}} + d_{\vec{F}}$. *If*

(Type 1) q-**dlog**$_{\mathcal{G}_1}$ *or* q-**dlog**$_{\mathcal{G}_2}$ *is* (ε, t)-*secure in the AGM,*
(Type 2) q-**dlog**$_{\mathcal{G}_2}$ *is* (ε, t)-*secure in the AGM,*
(Type 3) (q_1, q_2)-**dlog**$_{\mathcal{G}}$ *is* (ε, t)-*secure in the AGM,*

then $(\vec{R}, \vec{S}, \vec{F}, R', S', F')$-**rüber**$_{\mathcal{G}}$, *as defined in Fig. 4, is* (ε', t')-*secure in the AGM with*

$$\varepsilon' \leq \varepsilon + \frac{d_\tau}{p-1} \text{ and } t' \approx t,$$

where d_τ *is the maximal degree of* $(\vec{R}, \vec{S}, \vec{F}, R', S', F')$, *as defined in Definition 7.*

$(\vec{R}, \vec{S}, \vec{F})$-**f-rüber**$_{\mathcal{G}}^{A_{alg}}$

01 $(g_1, g_2) \xleftarrow{\$} \mathsf{GenSamp}$; $g_T \leftarrow e(g_1, g_2)$
02 $\vec{x} = (x_1, \ldots, x_m) \xleftarrow{\$} \mathbb{Z}_p^m$
03 If for some i: $\check{R}_i(\vec{x}) \equiv_p 0$ or $\check{S}_i(\vec{x}) \equiv_p 0$ or $\check{F}_i(\vec{x}) \equiv_p 0$ then return 1
04 $\vec{\mathbf{U}} := (g_1^{R_1(\vec{x})}, \ldots, g_1^{R_r(\vec{x})})$; $\vec{\mathbf{V}} := (g_2^{S_1(\vec{x})}, \ldots, g_2^{S_s(\vec{x})})$; $\vec{\mathbf{W}} := (g_T^{F_1(\vec{x})}, \ldots, g_T^{F_f(\vec{x})})$
05 $((\mathbf{U}^*, \mathbf{V}^*, \mathbf{W}^*), (R^*, S^*, F^*)) \xleftarrow{\$} A_{alg}(\vec{\mathbf{U}}, \vec{\mathbf{V}}, \vec{\mathbf{W}})$
06 Return $\big((\mathbf{U}^*, \mathbf{V}^*, \mathbf{W}^*) = (g_1^{R^*(\vec{x})}, g_2^{S^*(\vec{x})}, g_T^{F^*(\vec{x})})$
$\wedge \ (\vec{R}, \vec{S}, \vec{F}, R^*, S^*, F^*)$ non-trivial for type of $\mathcal{G}\big)$

Fig. 5. Algebraic game for the flexible-targets Uber assumption

The proof extends the ideas used to prove Theorem 1 by employing a technique from [BB08]. Consider a group of Type 1 or 2. The reduction computes $D := \mathrm{Den}(\vec{R}\|\vec{S}\|\vec{F})$, a least common multiple of the denominators of the instance. Given a q-DLog instance $g_2, g_2^z, g_2^{z^2}, \ldots$, it first implicitly sets $x_i := y_i z + v_i \bmod p$, then it checks whether any denominator evaluates to zero at $\vec{x}$ (this entails the additive loss d_{den}). Then it computes a new random generator $h_2 := g_2^{D(y_1 z + v_1, \ldots, y_m z + v_m)}$ and $h_1 := \psi(h_2)$. For rational fractions $S_i = \hat{S}_i / \check{S}_i$, it then uses h_1, h_2 to compute the Uber challenge elements $h_2^{S_i(\vec{x})}$ as $g_2^{\overline{S}(\vec{x})}$ for the *polynomial* $\overline{S}(\vec{X}) := (\hat{S}_i \cdot D/\check{S}_i)(\vec{X})$, and likewise for R_i and F_i. This explains the lower bound on q in the theorem statement. When the adversary returns a group element $h_i^{R'(\vec{x})}$ so that R' is non-trivial, then from the algebraic representations of this element we can define a polynomial (which with overwhelming probability is non-zero) that vanishes at z. The difference here is that we expand by the denominator of R' in order to obtain a polynomial. The degree of this polynomial is bounded by the values in Definition 7, which also bound the failure probability of the reduction. In Type-3 groups, the reduction can set $h_1 := g_1^{\mathrm{Den}(\vec{R}\|\vec{F})(\vec{x})}$ and $h_1 := g_2^{\mathrm{Den}(\vec{S})(\vec{x})}$, which leads to better bounds. We detail this case in our proof of Theorem 3, which can be found in the full version due to space constraints.

6 The Uber Assumption for Rational Fractions and Flexible Targets

For rational fractions, we can also define a flexible generalization, where the adversary can choose the target polynomials R', S' and F' in Fig. 2 itself, conditioned on the tuple $(\vec{R}, \vec{S}, \vec{F}, R', S', F')$ being non-trivial. The game is specified in Fig. 5. This extension covers assumptions such as the q-strong DH assumption by Boneh and Boyen [BB08], which they proved secure in the generic group model. A q-SDH adversary is given $(g_i, g_i^z, g_i^{z^2}, \ldots, g_i^{z^q})$ for $i = 1, 2$ and must compute $(g_1^{(z+c)^{-1}}, c)$ for any $c \in \mathbb{Z}_p \setminus \{-z\}$ of its choice. This is an instance of the flexible game in Fig. 5 when setting $m = 1$, $r = s = q + 1$, $f = 0$ and $R_i(X) = S_i(X) = X^{i-1}$, and the adversary returns $R^*(X) = 1/(X + c)$, $S^*(X) = F^*(X) = 0$.

Theorem 4 (DLog implies flexible-target Uber for rational fractions in the AGM). *Let $\mathcal{G}$ be a bilinear group of type $\tau \in \{1, 2, 3\}$ and let $(\vec{R}, \vec{S}, \vec{F}) \in (\mathbb{Z}_p(X_1, \ldots, X_m))^{r+s+f}$ be a tuple of rational fractions.*

*Consider an adversary $\mathsf{A}_{\mathrm{alg}}$ in game $(\vec{R}, \vec{S}, \vec{F})$-**f-rüber** (Fig. 5) and let $d_1^*, d_2^*, d_T^*, \check{d}_1^*, \check{d}_2^*, \check{d}_T^*$ be such that $\mathsf{A}_{\mathrm{alg}}$'s outputs R^*, S^*, F^* satisfy $\deg R^* \leq d_1^*$, $\deg S^* \leq d_2^*$, $\deg F^* \leq d_T^*$, $\deg \check{R}^* \leq \check{d}_1^*$, $\deg \check{S}^* \leq \check{d}_2^*$ and $\deg \check{F}^* \leq \check{d}_T^*$.*

Let q, q_1 and q_2 be such that $q \geq \check{d}_{\vec{R}\|\vec{S}\|\vec{F}} + \max\{d_{\vec{R}}, d_{\vec{S}}, d_{\vec{F}}/2\}$ and let $q_1 \geq \check{d}_{\vec{R}\|\vec{F}} + d_{\vec{R}}$ and $q_2 \geq \check{d}_{\vec{S}} + d_{\vec{S}}$ and $q_1 + q_2 \geq \check{d}_{\vec{R}\|\vec{F}} + \check{d}_{\vec{S}} + d_{\vec{F}}$, where $\check{d}_{\vec{R}} = \check{d}_{(\hat{R}_1/\check{R}_1, \ldots, \hat{R}_r/\check{R}_r)} = \deg \mathrm{LCM}\{\check{R}_1, \ldots, \check{R}_r\}$. If

(Type 1) q-**dlog** $_{\mathcal{G}_1}$ *or* q-**dlog** $_{\mathcal{G}_2}$ *is (ε, t)-secure in the AGM,*
(Type 2) q-**dlog** $_{\mathcal{G}_2}$ *is (ε, t)-secure in the AGM,*
(Type 3) (q_1, q_2)-**dlog** $_{\mathcal{G}}$ *is (ε, t)-secure in the AGM,*

*then $(\vec{R}, \vec{S}, \vec{F})$-**f-rüber** $_{\mathcal{G}}$ is (ε', t')-secure in the AGM with*

$$\varepsilon' \leq \varepsilon + \tfrac{d_\tau}{p-1} \text{ and } t' \approx t,$$

where d_τ is defined as in Definition 7, except for defining $d_{\mathrm{den}} := \check{d}_{\vec{R}\|\vec{S}\|\vec{F}}$ and replacing $(\check{d}_{R'}, \check{d}_{S'}, \check{d}_{F'}, d_{R'}, d_{S'}, d_{F'})$ by $(\check{d}_1^*, \check{d}_2^*, \check{d}_T^*, d_1^*, d_2^*, d_T^*)$.

Proof (sketch). Much in the way the proof of Theorem 1 is adapted to Theorem 2, Theorem 4 is proved similarly to Theorem 3. Since P_1, P_2 and P_T are only defined once the adversary returns its rational fractions R^*, S^*, F^*, they need not be known in advance. (Note that, unlike for polynomials (Theorem 2), the instance $(\vec{R}, \vec{S}, \vec{F})$ does have to be fixed, as the reduction uses it to set up the generators h_1 and h_2.) A difference to Theorem 4 is the value d_{den} in the security loss, which is now smaller since the experiment need not check the denominators of the target fractions. □

7   Uber Assumptions with Decisional Oracles

In this section we show that we can provide the adversary, essentially *for free*, with an oracle that checks whether the logarithms of given group elements satisfy any polynomial relation. In more detail, the adversary is given access to an oracle that takes as input a polynomial $P \in \mathbb{Z}_p[X_1, \ldots, X_n]$ and group elements $\mathbf{Y}_1, \ldots, \mathbf{Y}_n$ (from any group $\mathbb{G}_1, \mathbb{G}_2$ or $\mathbb{G}_T$) and checks whether $P(\log \mathbf{Y}_1, \ldots, \log \mathbf{Y}_n) \equiv_p 0$. Decisional oracles can be added to any type of Uber assumption; for concreteness, we extend the most general variant from the previous section. The game **f-drüber** ("d" for decisional oracles) is defined in Fig. 6. This extension covers assumptions such as Gap Diffie-Hellman (DH) [OP01], where the adversary must solve a DH instance while being given an oracle that checks whether a triple $(\mathbf{Y}_1, \mathbf{Y}_2, \mathbf{Y}_3)$ is a DH tuple, i.e., $\mathbf{Y}_1^{\log \mathbf{Y}_2} = \mathbf{Y}_3$. This oracle is a special case of the one in Fig. 6, when called with $P(X_1, X_2, X_3) := X_1 X_2 - X_3$.

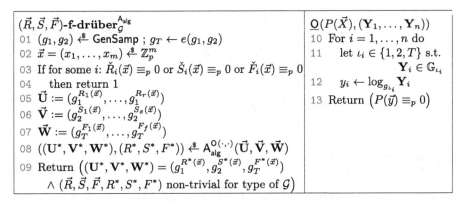

Fig. 6. Algebraic game for the flexible-targets Uber assumption with decisional oracles

Theorem 5 (DLog implies flexible-target Uber for rational fractions with decisional oracles in the AGM). *The statement of Theorem 4 holds when* **f-rüber** *is replaced by* **f-drüber**.

Proof (sketch). The reduction $\mathsf{B}_{\mathsf{alg}}$ from $(\vec{R}, \vec{S}, \vec{F})$-**f-drüber** to q-DLog (or (q_1, q_2)-DLog) works as for Theorem 4 (as detailed in the proof of Theorem 3), except that $\mathsf{B}_{\mathsf{alg}}$ must also answer $\mathsf{A}_{\mathsf{alg}}$'s oracle queries, which we describe in the following for Type-3 groups.

As for Theorem 4, $\mathsf{B}_{\mathsf{alg}}$, on input $(\vec{\mathbf{Y}}, \vec{\mathbf{Z}})$ with $\mathbf{Y}_i = [z^i]_1$ and $\mathbf{Z}_i = [z^i]_2$, for $0 \leq i \leq q$, computes LCMs of denominators $D := \mathrm{Den}(\vec{R}\|\vec{S}\|\vec{F})$, $D_1 := \mathrm{Den}(\vec{R}\|\vec{F})$ and $D_2 := \mathrm{Den}(\vec{S})$. It picks $\vec{y} \xleftarrow{\$} (\mathbb{Z}_p^*)^m$ and $\vec{v} \xleftarrow{\$} \mathbb{Z}_p^m$, implicitly sets $x_i := y_i z + v_i \bmod p$ and checks if $D(\vec{x}) \equiv_p 0$. If so, the reduction derives the corresponding univariate polynomial and finds z. Otherwise it computes $h_1 := [D_1(\vec{x})]_1$, $h_2 := [D_2(\vec{x})]_2$ (note that $D_1(\vec{x})$ and $D_2(\vec{x})$ are non-zero), $\mathbf{U}_i = [(D_1 \cdot R_i)(\vec{x})]_1$, $\mathbf{V}_i = [(D_2 \cdot S_i(\vec{x})]_2$ and $\mathbf{W}_i = [(D_1 \cdot D_2 \cdot F_i)(\vec{x})]_T$.

Consider a query $\mathsf{O}(P, (\mathbf{Y}_1, \ldots, \mathbf{Y}_n))$ for some n and $P \in \mathbb{Z}_p[X_1, \ldots, X_n]$, and $\mathbf{Y}_i \in \mathbb{G}_{\iota_i}$ for $\iota_i \in \{1, 2, T\}$. Since $\mathsf{A}_{\mathsf{alg}}$ is algebraic, it provides representations of the group elements $\mathbf{Y}_i$ with respect to its input $(\vec{\mathbf{U}}, \vec{\mathbf{V}}, \vec{\mathbf{W}})$; in particular, for each $\mathbf{Y}_i$, depending on the group, it provides $\vec{\mu}_i$ or $\vec{\eta}_i$ or $(A_i, \vec{\delta}_i)$ such that:

$$(\mathbf{Y}_i \in \mathbb{G}_1)\ \ \mathbf{Y}_i = \prod_{j=1}^r \mathbf{U}_j^{\mu_{i,j}} = \left[\sum_{j=1}^r \mu_{i,j}(D_1 \cdot R_j)(\vec{x})\right]_1 =: [Q_i(z)]_1$$

$$(\mathbf{Y}_i \in \mathbb{G}_2)\ \ \mathbf{Y}_i = \prod_{j=1}^s \mathbf{V}_j^{\eta_{i,j}} = \left[\sum_{j=1}^s \eta_{i,j}(D_2 \cdot S_j)(\vec{x})\right]_2 =: [Q_i(z)]_2$$

$$(\mathbf{Y}_i \in \mathbb{G}_T)\ \ \mathbf{Y}_i = \prod_{j=1}^r \prod_{k=1}^s e(\mathbf{U}_j, \mathbf{V}_k)^{\alpha_{i,j,k}} \cdot \prod_{j=1}^f \mathbf{W}_j^{\delta_{i,j}}$$
$$= \left[\sum_{j=1}^r \sum_{k=1}^s \alpha_{i,j,k}(D_1 \cdot R_j)(\vec{x})(D_2 \cdot S_j)(\vec{x}) + \sum_{j=1}^f \delta_{i,j}(D_1 \cdot D_2 \cdot F_j)(\vec{x})\right]_T$$
$$=: [Q_i(z)]_T,$$

where $D_1 \cdot R_j$, $D_2 \cdot S_j$ and $D_1 \cdot D_2 \cdot F_j$ are multivariate polynomials (not rational fractions) and Q_i is the polynomial defined by replacing X_i by $y_i Z + v_i$. Let $D_i'(Z)$ be defined from $D_i(\vec{X})$ analogously. Then we have $\log_{g_{\iota_i}} \mathbf{Y}_i = Q_i(z)$ and furthermore $\log_{h_{\iota_i}} \mathbf{Y}_i = Q_i(z)/D_{\iota_i}(z)$, where $D_T := D_1 \cdot D_2$.

To answer the oracle query, $\mathsf{B_{alg}}$ must therefore determine whether the function $P(Q_1/D_{i_1}, \ldots, Q_n/D_{i_n})$ vanishes at z. Since $D_1(z), D_2(z) \not\equiv_p 0$, this is the case precisely when $\overline{P} := D_1^d \cdot D_2^d \cdot P(Q_1/D_{i_1}, \ldots, Q_n/D_{i_n})$ vanishes at z, where d is the maximal degree of P. Note that $\overline{P}$ is a polynomial. The reduction distinguishes 3 cases:

1. $\overline{P} \equiv 0$: in this case, the oracle replies 1.
2. $\overline{P} \not\equiv 0$: in this case, $\mathsf{B_{alg}}$ factorizes $\overline{P}$ to find its roots $z_1, \ldots$, checks whether $\mathbf{Z}_1 = g^{z_i}$ for some i. If this is the case, it stops and returns the solution z_i to its (q_1, q_2)-DLog instance.
3. Else, the oracle replies 0.

Correctness of the simulation is immediate, since the correct oracle reply is 1 if and only if $\overline{P}(z) \equiv_p 0$. $\qquad\qquad\qquad\qquad\qquad\qquad\qquad\qquad\qquad\qquad\qquad\quad\square$

8 The Flexible Gegenuber Assumption

In this section, we show how to extend the Uber framework even further, by letting the adversary generate its own generators (for the outputs), yielding the *GeGenUber* assumption. Consider the $\overline{\text{LRSW}}$ assumption [LRSW99] in Type-1 bilinear groups: given $(X = g^x, Y = g^y)$ (which can be viewed as a signature verification key [CL04]) and an oracle, which on input (a message) $m \in \mathbb{Z}_p$ returns (a signature) $(g^a, g^{ay}, g^{a(x+mxy)})$ for a random $a \xleftarrow{\$} \mathbb{Z}_p$, it is infeasible to return (a signature on a fresh message) $((g^{a^*}, g^{a^*y}, g^{a^*(x+m^*xy)}, m^*))$ for any a^* and m^* different from the queried values. Since the adversary need not return the value a^*, this cannot be cast into the Uber framework. Associating the a-values chosen by the signing oracle to formal variables, in the Uber framework $\vec{X}$ would correspond to $(X, Y, A_1, \ldots, A_\ell)$ and signing queries to the polynomials A_i, A_iY and $A_iX + m_iA_iXY$. Now the adversary can choose a fresh generator $g^* := g^{a^*}$ and must return $((g^*)^{R_i^*(\vec{X})})_{i=1}^3$ for $R_1^* \equiv 1, R_2^* = Y$ and $R_3^* = X + m^*XY$ for some $m^* \in \mathbb{Z}_p^*r$ of its choice.

Our last generalization now extends the flexible Uber assumption from Sect. 4 by letting the adversary generate its own generators $\mathbf{U}, \mathbf{V}$ and $\mathbf{W}$ of $\mathbb{G}_1, \mathbb{G}_2$ and $\mathbb{G}_T$, resp., and return polynomials R^*, S^* and F^*, as well as $(\mathbf{U}^{R^*(\vec{x})}, \mathbf{V}^{S^*(\vec{x})}, \mathbf{W}^{F^*(\vec{x})})$. The game m-**gegenüber** is defined in Fig. 7. However, this additional freedom for the adversary induces a necessary change in the definition of non-triviality, as illustrated by the following simple (univariate) example: after the challenger chooses $x \xleftarrow{\$} \mathbb{Z}_p$, the adversary makes queries $R_1 := X$ and $R_2 := X^3$ and receives $\mathbf{U}_1$ and $\mathbf{U}_2$. For all Uber assumptions so far, the polynomial $R^* := X^2$ would be considered non-trivial. However, in game **gegenüber** the adversary could return $\mathbf{U} := \mathbf{U}_1 = g^x$ and $\mathbf{U}^* := \mathbf{U}_2 = g^{x^3} = \mathbf{U}^{R^*(x)}$.

Whereas until now the target polynomial R^* was not allowed to be a linear combination of the queried polynomials $P_1, \ldots, P_\ell$ (or of products of such polynomials, depending on the group types), for the Gegenuber assumption we also need to exclude fractions of such linear combinations (such as X^3/X in the example above) to thwart trivial attacks.

For a family E of polynomials, we denote by $\mathrm{Span}(E)$ all linear combinations of elements of E, which we extend to fractions as

$$\mathrm{FrSp}(E) := \{\hat{P}/\check{P} \mid (\hat{P}, \check{P}) \in \mathrm{Span}(E) \times (\mathrm{Span}(E) \setminus \{0\})\}.$$

Moreover, by $E_1 * E_2$ we denote the set $\{P_1 \cdot P_2 \mid (P_1, P_2) \in E_1 \times E_2\}$.

Definition 8 (Non-triviality for Gegenuber assumption). *Let $\mathcal{Q}_1, \mathcal{Q}_2$ and $\mathcal{Q}_T$ be sets of polynomials and let R^*, S^* and F^* be polynomials. We say that $(\mathcal{Q}_1, \mathcal{Q}_2, \mathcal{Q}_T, R^*, S^*, F^*)$ is* gegenuber-non-trivial *for groups of type τ, if the following holds:*

- $R^* \notin \mathrm{FrSp}(\mathcal{Q}_1 \cup \mathcal{Q}_2)$ *for* $\tau \in \{1,2\}$ *and* $R^* \notin \mathrm{FrSp}(\mathcal{Q}_1)$ *for* $\tau = 3$,   (τ.1)
- **or** $S^* \notin \mathrm{FrSp}(\mathcal{Q}_1 \cup \mathcal{Q}_2)$ *for* $\tau = 1$ *and* $S^* \notin \mathrm{FrSp}(\mathcal{Q}_2)$ *for* $\tau \in \{2,3\}$,   (τ.2)
- **or** $F^* \notin \mathrm{FrSp}(\mathcal{Q}_T \cup (\mathcal{Q}_1 \cup \mathcal{Q}_2) * (\mathcal{Q}_1 \cup \mathcal{Q}_2))$ *for* $\tau = 1$ (1.T)
  $F^* \notin \mathrm{FrSp}(\mathcal{Q}_T \cup (\mathcal{Q}_1 \cup \mathcal{Q}_2) * \mathcal{Q}_2)$ *for* $\tau = 2$ (2.T)
  $F^* \notin \mathrm{FrSp}(\mathcal{Q}_T \cup (\mathcal{Q}_1 * \mathcal{Q}_2))$ *for* $\tau = 3$.   (3.T)

Definition 9 (Degree of non-triviality for Gegenuber assumption). *Let $(\mathcal{Q}_1, \mathcal{Q}_2, \mathcal{Q}_T, R^*, S^*, F^*)$ be a non-trivial tuple of polynomials in $\mathbb{Z}_p[X_1, \ldots, X_m]$. For $i \in \{1, 2, T\}$ define $d'_i := \max\{\deg P\}_{P \in \mathcal{Q}_i}$. We define the type-$\tau$ degree d_τ of $(\mathcal{Q}_1, \mathcal{Q}_2, \mathcal{Q}_T, R^*, S^*, F^*)$ as follows:*

- *If (τ.1) holds, let* $d_{\tau.1} := \max\{1, \deg R^*\} \cdot \max\{d'_1, d'_2\}$ *in case* $\tau \in \{1,2\}$ *and*
  $d_{\tau.1} := \max\{1, \deg R^*\} \cdot d'_1$ *in case* $\tau = 3$.
- *If (τ.2) holds, let* $d_{\tau.2} := \max\{1, \deg S^*\} \cdot \max\{d'_1, d'_2\}$ *in case* $\tau = 1$ *and*
  $d_{\tau.2} := \max\{1, \deg S^*\} \cdot d'_2$ *in case* $\tau \in \{2,3\}$.
- *If (τ.T) holds, let* $d_{\tau.T} := \max\{1, \deg F^*\} \cdot \max\{2\,d'_1, 2\,d'_2, d'_T\}$ *for* $\tau = 1$
  $d_{\tau.T} := \max\{1, \deg F^*\} \cdot \max\{d'_1 + d'_2, 2\,d'_2, d'_T\}$ *for* $\tau = 2$,
  $d_{\tau.T} := \max\{1, \deg F^*\} \cdot \max\{d'_1 + d'_2, d'_T\}$ *for* $\tau = 3$.

If (τ, i) does not hold, set $d_{\tau,i} := \infty$. Define $d_\tau := \min\{d_{\tau.1}, d_{\tau.2}, d_{\tau.T}\}$.

Note that for all Uber variants, the adversary only outputs one element per group $\mathbb{G}_i$, which is without loss of generality, as a vector of group elements would be non-trivial if at least one component is non-trivial. We defined the Gegenuber assumption analogously, so one might wonder how this covers LRSW, where the adversary must output group elements corresponding to two polynomials Y and $X + m^*XY$. The reason is that LRSW holds even if the adversary only has to output the latter polynomial: In the GGM this follows from LRSW being an instance of Gegenuber, Theorem 6 (see below for both) and Lemmas 3 and 4.

To show that LRSW is gegenuber-non-trivial, consider the set of queries an adversary can make, namely:

$$\mathcal{Q} := \big\{1, X, Y, \{A_i, A_iY, A_iX + m_iA_iXY\}_{i=1}^{\ell}\big\}.$$

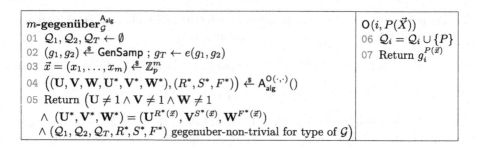

Fig. 7. Algebraic game for the flexible Gegenuber assumption

To prove that the stronger variant of LRSW satisfies non-triviality as defined in Definition 8, we show that for $0 \neq m^* \notin \{m_1, \ldots, m_\ell\}$: $R^* := X + m^* XY \notin$ FrSp($\mathcal{Q}$). For the sake of contradiction, assume that for some $\check{P}, \hat{P} \in$ Span($\mathcal{Q}$), $\check{P} \not\equiv 0$:

$$(X + m^* XY)\check{P} = \hat{P}. \tag{7}$$

Since $\hat{P} \in$ Span($\mathcal{Q}$), its total degree in X and Y is at most 2, which implies that $\check{P}$ must be of degree 0 in X and Y. We can thus write $\check{P}$ as $\eta + \sum_{j=1}^\ell \alpha_j A_j$ for some η and $\vec{\alpha}$. Since X is a factor of the left-hand side of (7), $\hat{P}$ cannot have terms without X and must therefore be of the form $\hat{P} = \xi X + \sum_{j=1}^\ell \mu_j A_j (X + m_j XY)$ for some ξ and $\vec{\mu}$. Equation (7) becomes thus

$$(X + m^* XY)\left(\eta + \sum_{j=1}^\ell \alpha_j A_j\right) = \xi X + \sum_{j=1}^\ell \mu_j A_j (X + m_j XY).$$

By equating coefficients, we get: $\eta = \xi$ (from coeff. X) and $m^* \eta \equiv_p 0$ (from XY) and for all $j \in [1, \ell]$: $\alpha_j = \mu_j$ (from $A_j X$) and $\alpha_j m^* \equiv_p \mu_j m_j$ (from $A_j XY$). Since $m^* \neq 0$, we have $\eta = \xi = 0$. Furthermore, if $\alpha_j \neq 0$ for some j, then $m_j = m^*$, meaning it was not a valid solution. If $\alpha_j = 0$ for all j then $\check{P} \equiv 0$, which shows such $\hat{P}$ and $\check{P}$ do not exist and thus $X + m^* XY \notin$ FrSp($\mathcal{Q}$).

Theorem 6. *Let $m \geq 1$, let $\mathcal{G}$ be a bilinear group of type $\tau \in \{1, 2, 3\}$ and let $\mathsf{A}_{\mathsf{alg}}$ be an adversary in game m-**gegenüber**$_\mathcal{G}$. Let $d_1', d_2', d_T', d_1^*, d_2^*, d_T^*$ be such that $\mathsf{A}_{\mathsf{alg}}$'s queries $(i, P(\vec{X}))$ satisfy $\deg P \leq d_i'$ and its output satisfies $\deg R^* \leq d_1^*$, $\deg S^* \leq d_2^*$, $\deg F^* \leq d_T^*$. Let q, q_1, q_2 be such that $q \geq \max\{d_1', d_2', d_T'/2\}$, as well as $q_1 \geq d_1'$, $q_2 \geq d_2'$ and $q_1 + q_2 \geq d_T'$. If*

*(Type 1) q-**dlog**$_{\mathcal{G}_1}$ or q-**dlog**$_{\mathcal{G}_2}$ is (ε, t)-secure in the AGM,*
*(Type 2) q-**dlog**$_{\mathcal{G}_2}$ is (ε, t)-secure in the AGM,*
*(Type 3) (q_1, q_2)-**dlog**$_\mathcal{G}$ is (ε, t)-secure in the AGM,*

*then **gegenüber**$_\mathcal{G}$ is (ε', t')-secure in the AGM with*

$$\varepsilon' \leq \varepsilon + \frac{d_\tau}{p-1} \text{ and } t' \approx t,$$

with d_τ from Definition 9 after replacing $\deg R^*$, $\deg S^*$ and $\deg F^*$ by d_1^*, d_2^* and d_T^*, respectively.

The proof can be found in the full version. It is an adaptation of the one for the flexible uberassumption, which adapts the proof of Theorem 1.

In the proof of Theorem 6, the adversary also outputs a new generator $\mathbf{U}$, whose algebraic representation yields a polynomial $Q \in \mathrm{Span}(\mathcal{Q}_1 \cup \mathcal{Q}_2)$ so that $\mathbf{U} = [Q(\vec{x})]_1$. For a valid solution $\mathbf{U}^*$, we thus have $\mathbf{U}^* = [R^*(\vec{x}) \cdot Q(\vec{x})]_1$. On the other hand, the representation of $\mathbf{U}^*$ yields $\mathbf{U}^* = [Q^*(\vec{x})]_1$ for some $Q^* \in \mathrm{Span}(\mathcal{Q}_1 \cup \mathcal{Q}_2)$. We thus have that $P_1(\vec{X}) := R^*(\vec{X}) \cdot Q(\vec{X}) - Q^*(\vec{X})$ vanishes at $\vec{x}$. By non-triviality, $R^* \notin \mathrm{FrSp}(\mathcal{Q}_1 \cup \mathcal{Q}_2)$, which implies $P_1 \not\equiv 0$, so the reduction can find the roots of $P_1(y_1 Z + x_1, \ldots, y_n Z + x_n)$ and solve q-DLog.

9   Separation of $(q+1)$-DL from q-DL

Now that we have shown that every Uber assumption falls into a (minimal) class of assumptions that are equivalent to q-DLog, we show that these classes can be separated according to their parameter q. We prove that, assuming that q-DLog is hard, there does not exist an algebraic reduction from q-DLog to $(q + 1)$-DLog. In particular, we show that if there exists a reduction $\mathsf{R}_{\mathsf{alg}}$ that has access to a $(q + 1)$-DLog (algebraic) adversary $\mathsf{A}_{\mathsf{alg}}$ and can solve q-DLog, then there exists a meta-reduction that uses $\mathsf{R}_{\mathsf{alg}}$ to break q-DLog. In the following, we use the notation $\mathsf{R}_{\mathsf{alg}}(\mathsf{A}_{\mathsf{alg}})$ to denote that $\mathsf{R}_{\mathsf{alg}}$ has complete access to $\mathsf{A}_{\mathsf{alg}}$'s internal state. In particular, $\mathsf{R}_{\mathsf{alg}}$ is allowed to rewind $\mathsf{A}_{\mathsf{alg}}$ to any point of an execution and run $\mathsf{A}_{\mathsf{alg}}$ on any choice of random coins as many times as it wants.

Theorem 7. *Let $\mathcal{G}_i$ be a group of prime order p. There exists an algorithm M such that the following holds. Let $\mathsf{R}_{\mathsf{alg}}$ be an algebraic algorithm s.t. for every algorithm $\mathsf{A}_{\mathsf{alg}}$ that (t, ϵ)-breaks $(q + 1)$-$\mathbf{dlog}_{\mathcal{G}_i}$, $\mathsf{B} = \mathsf{R}_{\mathsf{alg}}(\mathsf{A}_{\mathsf{alg}})$ is an algorithm that (t', ϵ')-breaks q-$\mathbf{dlog}_{\mathcal{G}_i}$. If $t \geq 2\,(2q + 1)\lceil \log_2 p \rceil$ then $\mathsf{M}^{\mathsf{R}_{\mathsf{alg}}}(t', \epsilon')$-breaks q-$\mathbf{dlog}_{\mathcal{G}_i}$.*

We start with a proof overview. Consider a reduction $\mathsf{R}_{\mathsf{alg}}$, which on input a q-DLog instance $(g, g^x, \ldots, g^{x^q})$ can run an algebraic adversary $\mathsf{A}_{\mathsf{alg}}$ multiple times on $(q+1)$-DLog instances $(\mathbf{Z}, \mathbf{Z}^y, \ldots, \mathbf{Z}^{y^{q+1}})$; that is, $\mathsf{R}_{\mathsf{alg}}$ can choose a new generator $\mathbf{Z}$ and a new problem solution y. Since $\mathsf{R}_{\mathsf{alg}}$ is algebraic, it outputs a representation of the group elements composing its $(q+1)$-DLog instance in terms of the received q-DLog instance. We distinguish two cases: if (a) y is independent from x then the representation reveals y, which means that a meta-reduction M can simulate a successful $\mathsf{A}_{\mathsf{alg}}$ to $\mathsf{R}_{\mathsf{alg}}$, and the latter must thus find x. On the other hand, if (b) y depends on x, then this yields a non-trivial equation in x, which the meta-reduction can solve and thereby (without needing to simulate $\mathsf{A}_{\mathsf{alg}}$) solve the q-DLog instance. To simplify the probability analysis, we let M simulate $\mathsf{A}_{\mathsf{alg}}$ even when $\mathsf{R}_{\mathsf{alg}}$ behaves as in the second case (as it can compute y from x). To correctly argue about the probability distributions, we ensure that any malformed instance provided by the algebraic reduction $\mathsf{R}_{\mathsf{alg}}$ is detected. We will use the following lemma in the proof of Theorem 7:

Lemma 5. *Let $q \geq 1$, let $F \in \mathbb{Z}_p(X)$ and let $0 \not\equiv P \in \mathbb{Z}_p[X]$ be of degree at most q. If $F^{q+1} \cdot P$ is a polynomial and of degree at most q, then F is constant.*

Proof. Let $\hat{F}, \check{F} \in \mathbb{Z}_p[X]$ be coprime such that $F = \hat{F}/\check{F}$. Then $\hat{F}^{q+1}$ and $\check{F}^{q+1}$ are coprime as well. From this and the premise that $\hat{F}^{q+1} \cdot P/\check{F}^{q+1}$ is a polynomial, we get that $\check{F}^{q+1}$ divides P, and thus $(q+1) \cdot \deg \check{F} \leq \deg P$. Since the latter is at most q, we have $\deg \check{F} = 0$.

Furthermore, we assumed that $q \geq \deg(F^{q+1} \cdot P) = (q+1) \cdot \deg \hat{F} + \deg P$, and thus $\deg \hat{F} = 0$. Together, this means F is constant. $\qquad\square$

Proof (of Theorem 7). Let $\mathsf{R}_{\mathsf{alg}}$ be an algebraic algorithm s.t. for every algorithm $\mathsf{A}_{\mathsf{alg}}$ that (t, ϵ)-breaks $(q+1)$-**dlog**$_{\mathcal{G}_i}$, $\mathsf{B} = \mathsf{R}_{\mathsf{alg}}(\mathsf{A}_{\mathsf{alg}})$ is an algorithm that (t', ϵ')-breaks q-**dlog**$_{\mathcal{G}_i}$. In the following, we describe a meta-reduction M s.t. $\mathsf{M}^{\mathsf{R}_{\mathsf{alg}}}$ (t', ϵ')-breaks q-**dlog**$_{\mathcal{G}_i}$.

$\mathsf{M}(g, \mathbf{X}_1, \ldots, \mathbf{X}_q)$: Run $\mathsf{R}_{\mathsf{alg}}$ on the received q-DLog instance $(g, g^x, \ldots, g^{x^q})$. Whenever $\mathsf{R}_{\mathsf{alg}}$ runs adversary $\mathsf{A}_{\mathsf{alg}}$ on $(q+1)$-DLog input $(\mathbf{Z}_0, \mathbf{Z}_1, \ldots, \mathbf{Z}_{q+1})$, do the following. Let $\vec{z}_i = (z_{i,0}, \ldots, z_{i,q})$ for $0 \leq i \leq q+1$ be the representation vectors for $\mathbf{Z}_0, \ldots, \mathbf{Z}_{q+1}$ provided by $\mathsf{R}_{\mathsf{alg}}$; that is, $\mathbf{Z}_i = \prod_{j=0}^{q}(g^{x^j})^{z_{i,j}}$. If $\mathbf{Z}_0 = 1$ then return $\bot$. $\hfill(*)$
Else define

$$P_i(X) := \sum_{j=0}^{q} z_{i,j} X^j \quad \text{for } 0 \leq i \leq q+1 \quad \text{and} \tag{8}$$

$$Q_i := P_{i+1} P_0 - P_i P_1 \quad \text{for } 0 \leq i \leq q. \tag{9}$$

M now distinguishes two cases:

(a) $Q_i \equiv 0$ for all $i \in [0, q]$: Then (as we argue below) $P_1/P_0 \equiv c$, that is, a constant polynomial. M returns c as $\mathsf{A}_{\mathsf{alg}}$'s output.

(b) For some $k \in [0, q]$: $Q_k \not\equiv 0$: Compute the roots $x_1, \ldots$ of Q_k and check if for some j: $g^{x_j} = \mathbf{X}_1$. If not, then return $\bot$ as $\mathsf{A}_{\mathsf{alg}}$'s output. $\hfill(**)$
Else let $y := P_1(x_j)/P_0(x_j) \bmod p$. ($1 \neq \mathbf{Z}_0 = g^{P_0(x_j)}$, thus $P_0(x_j) \not\equiv_p 0$.)
If for some $i \in [1, q+1]$: $\mathbf{Z}_i \neq \mathbf{Z}_0^{y^i}$, return $\bot$ as $\mathsf{A}_{\mathsf{alg}}$'s output. $\hfill(***)$
Else return y.

Correctness of simulation. We now argue that M always correctly simulates an adversary $\mathsf{A}_{\mathsf{alg}}$ that solves $(q+1)$-DLog if it received a correct instance, and returns $\bot$ otherwise. Consider the case where $\mathsf{R}_{\mathsf{alg}}$ provides a valid $(q+1)$-DLog instance, that is $\mathbf{Z}_0 \neq 1$ and

$$\exists y \in \mathbb{Z}_p^* \, \forall i \in [1, q+1] : \mathbf{Z}_i = \mathbf{Z}_0^{y^i}. \tag{10}$$

By (8), we have $\mathbf{Z}_i = g^{P_i(x)}$ for all i. Since $\mathbf{Z}_0 \neq 1$, M does not stop in line $(*)$ and $P_0(x) \not\equiv_p 0$. Moreover, from (10) we have $y \equiv_p P_1(x)/P_0(x)$ and

$$P_{i+1}(x) \equiv_p P_1(x)/P_0(x) \cdot P_i(x), \tag{11}$$

in other words, $Q_i(x) \equiv_p 0$ for all $i \in [0, q]$.

In case (a), $Q_i \equiv 0$, and thus, letting $F := P_1/P_0$, we have (by Definition (9)) $P_{i+1} = F \cdot P_i$ for all i, and by induction:

$$\forall i \in [0, q+1] : P_i = F^i \cdot P_0,$$

and in particular $P_{q+1} = F^{q+1} \cdot P_0$. Since P_{q+1} and P_0 are polynomials of degree at most q, by Lemma 5 we get $F \equiv c$ for $c \in \mathbb{Z}_p$. The meta-reduction M thus returns $c \equiv_p F(x) \equiv_p P_1(x)/P_0(x) \equiv_p y$.

In case (b), since $Q_k \not\equiv 0$ but, by (11), $Q_k(x) \equiv_p 0$, the meta-reduction finds x and M does not stop in line (∗∗) and neither in line (∗∗∗), since $y \equiv_p P_1(x)/P_0(x)$.

Now consider the case that $\mathsf{R_{alg}}$ sends a malformed instance: if $\mathbf{Z}_0$ is not a generator then $\mathsf{A_{alg}}$ returns $\bot$ in line (∗). Assume $\mathbf{Z}_0$ is a generator (and thus $P_0(x) \not\equiv_p 0$), but (10) is not satisfied. Using the algebraic representations of $\mathbf{Z}_0, \ldots, \mathbf{Z}_{q+1}$, this is equivalent to

$$\forall y \in \mathbb{Z}_p^* \ \exists k \in [1, q+1] : P_k(x) \not\equiv_p y^k P_0(x). \tag{12}$$

We first show that the meta-reduction M goes to case (b): Indeed, if $Q_i \equiv 0$ for all $i \in [0, q]$, then $P_{i+1}(x) \equiv_p P_1(x)/P_0(x) \cdot P_i(x)$ for all i and, by induction, $P_i(x) \equiv_p (P_1(x)/P_0(x))^i \cdot P_0(x)$, which, setting $y := P_1(x)/P_0(x) \bmod p$, contradicts (12).

Let $k \in [0, q]$ be such that $Q_k \not\equiv 0$. If x is not among the roots of Q_k, then M returns $\bot$ in line (∗∗). Otherwise, it sets $y := P_1(x)/P_0(x) \bmod p$. If for some $i \in [1, q+1]$: $P_i(x) \not\equiv_p y^i P_0(x)$ then M returns $\bot$ in line (∗∗∗). If not then this contradicts (12). Therefore, the simulation will return $\bot$ on invalid inputs.

For the simulation of $\mathsf{A_{alg}}$ the meta-reduction needs to compute at most $2q + 1$ exponentiations, each of which require at most $2\lceil \log_2 p \rceil$ group operations using square and multiply. The simulation of $\mathsf{A_{alg}}$ is thus perfect and takes at most t steps. The meta-reduction M succeeds in winning $q\text{-}\mathbf{dlog}_{\mathcal{G}_i}$ whenever $\mathsf{B} = \mathsf{R_{alg}}(\mathsf{A_{alg}})$ wins $q\text{-}\mathbf{dlog}_{\mathcal{G}_i}$. Therefore, we obtain

$$\Pr\left[q\text{-}\mathbf{dlog}_{\mathcal{G}_i}^{\mathsf{M}} = 1\right] = \Pr\left[q\text{-}\mathbf{dlog}_{\mathcal{G}_i}^{\mathsf{B}} = 1\right] \geq \varepsilon'.$$

Moreover, the running time of M is that of B, i.e., t'. This completes the proof. □

A similar result can be shown for $(q_1, q_2)\text{-}\mathbf{dlog}_{\mathcal{G}}$, that is, $(q_1, q_2)\text{-}\mathbf{dlog}_{\mathcal{G}}$ is not implied by $(q_1', q_2')\text{-}\mathbf{dlog}_{\mathcal{G}}$ if $q_1' > q_1$ or $q_2' > q_2$.

10 Separation of 2-One-More DL from q-DL

We conclude with showing that "one-more"-discrete logarithm (OMDL) assumptions fall outside of our q-DLog taxonomy. While it is known that there is no black-box reduction from DLog to OMDL [BMV08], we show that there is no algebraic reduction either, even one for algebraic adversaries.

To obtain the strongest possible impossibility result, we show that for no $q \in \mathbb{N}$, there exists an algebraic reduction from q-DLog (a stronger assumption than DLog) to 2-OMDL (the weakest variant of OMDL assumptions), unless q-DLog is easy. The game for 2-OMDL is depicted in Fig. 8. The proof uses the same high-level idea as for Theorem 8. If the representation of the group elements the reduction gives to the adversary is independent of its own q-DLog challenge, then the meta-reduction can directly simulate the adversary. Else, they depend on the q-DLog challenge in a way that allows the meta-reduction to derive a

$\textbf{2-omdl}_{\mathcal{G}_i}^{\mathsf{A}_{\mathsf{alg}}}$	$\underline{\mathrm{O}(\mathbf{Z})}$
00 $Q \leftarrow 0$	05 if $Q = 0$ then
01 $g \xleftarrow{\$} \mathsf{GenSamp}_i$	06 $\quad Q \leftarrow 1$
02 $y_1, y_2 \xleftarrow{\$} \mathbb{Z}_p^*$	07 $\quad$ Return $\log_g \mathbf{Z}$
03 $(y_1^*, y_2^*) \xleftarrow{\$} \mathsf{A}_{\mathsf{alg}}^{\mathrm{O}(\cdot)}\left(g, g^{y_1}, g^{y_2}\right)$	08 Return $\perp$
04 Return $((y_1^*, y_2^*) = (y_1, y_2))$	

Fig. 8. Game for 2-one-more discrete logarithm 2-**omdl**$_{\mathcal{G}_i}$ relative to bilinear group $\mathcal{G}_i, i \in \{1, 2\}$ and adversary $\mathsf{A}_{\mathsf{alg}}$

q-DLog solution. Compared to the previous section, we now restrict the algebraic reduction to only have black-box access (according to our notion of black-box) to the adversary. This is because a reduction that can choose the random coins of the adversary in a non-uniform (adaptive) way can make the simulation of the adversary by our meta-reduction fail.

We need to define the adversary's behavior, that is, its oracle call, beforehand; in particular, it must not depend on the type of representations obtained from the reduction, which makes the proof more complicated and restricts the simulation to adversaries that can fail with negligible probability. The adversary, after receiving a 2-OMDL challenge $(\mathbf{Y}_0, \mathbf{Y}_1, \mathbf{Y}_2)$, makes a query $(\mathbf{Y}_1^{r_1} \mathbf{Y}_2^{r_2})$ for random r_1, r_2 to its DLog oracle and then returns the 2-OMDL solution $(\log_{\mathbf{Y}_0} \mathbf{Y}_1, \log_{\mathbf{Y}_0} \mathbf{Y}_2)$. We now show how the meta-reduction simulates this adversary.

Since the reduction is algebraic, it provides with its 2-OMDL instance representations $\vec{z}_i = (z_{i,0}, \ldots, z_{i,q})$ in terms of its q-DLog challenge $(g, g^x, \ldots, g^{x^q})$, such that $\log_g \mathbf{Y}_i \equiv_p \sum_{j=0}^q z_{i,j} x^j$. From the reply y to the adversary's single oracle query, we get the following equation: $0 = \log_g(\mathbf{Y}_1^{r_1} \mathbf{Y}_2^{r_2}) - \log_g \mathbf{Y}_0^y \equiv_p \sum_{j=0}^q \left(r_1 z_{1,j} + r_2 z_{2,j} - y z_{0,j}\right) x^j$.

The q-DLog challenge x is thus the root of the polynomial with coefficients $a_j := (r_1 z_{1,j} + r_2 z_{2,j} - y z_{0,j}) \bmod p$, and the meta-reduction can find x if one of these coefficients is non-zero. Using x, it can then compute $\log_g \mathbf{Y}_i$ for all i from the representations and from that the OMDL solution $(\log_{\mathbf{Y}_0} \mathbf{Y}_1, \log_{\mathbf{Y}_0} \mathbf{Y}_2)$.

If, on the other hand, $a_j = 0$ for some j then by plugging in the definition of y, we get another polynomial which vanishes at x. We then show that, due to the randomizers r_1 and r_2, with overwhelming probability, the coefficients of this polynomial are non-zero – unless for some c_1, c_2 we have $\vec{z}_1 = c_1 \vec{z}_0$ and $\vec{z}_2 = c_2 \vec{z}_0$. But in this case (c_1, c_2) is the solution to the 2-OMDL instance and the meta-reduction can therefore finish the simulation of the adversary.

The proof of the following can be found in the full version.

Theorem 8. *Let $\mathcal{G}_i$ be a group of prime order p. There exists an algorithm M such that the following holds: Let $\mathsf{R}_{\mathsf{alg}}$ be an algebraic reduction s.t. for every algorithm $\mathsf{A}_{\mathsf{alg}}$ that (t, ϵ)-breaks 2-**omdl**$_{\mathcal{G}_i}$, $\mathsf{B} = \mathsf{R}_{\mathsf{alg}}^{\mathsf{A}_{\mathsf{alg}}}$ is an algorithm that (t', ϵ')-breaks q-**dlog**$_{\mathcal{G}_i}$. If $t \geq (6 + 2q)\lceil \log_2 p \rceil + 1$ and $\epsilon \leq 1 - 1/p$ then $\mathsf{M}^{\mathsf{R}_{\mathsf{alg}}}$ (t', ϵ')-breaks q-**dlog**$_{\mathcal{G}_i}$.*

Acknowledgements. This work is funded in part by the MSR–Inria Joint Centre. The second author is supported by the Vienna Science and Technology Fund (WWTF) through project VRG18-002. Parts of this work were done while he was visiting the Simons Institute for the Theory of Computing.

References

[ABM15] Abdalla, M., Benhamouda, F., MacKenzie, P.: Security of the J-PAKE password-authenticated key exchange protocol. In: 2015 IEEE Symposium on Security and Privacy, pp. 571–587. IEEE Press (2015)

[AHK20] Agrikola, T., Hofheinz, D., Kastner, J.: On instantiating the algebraic group model from falsifiable assumptions. In: Canteaut, A., Ishai, Y. (eds.) EUROCRYPT 2020, Part II. LNCS, vol. 12106, pp. 96–126. Springer, Cham (2020). https://doi.org/10.1007/978-3-030-45724-2_4

[AW98] Deschamps, C., Warusfel, A., Moulin, F.: Mathématiques 1ère année: Cours et exercices corrigés. Editions Dunod (1998)

[BB08] Boneh, D., Boyen, X.: Short signatures without random oracles and the SDH assumption in bilinear groups. J. Cryptol. **21**(2), 149–177 (2008). https://doi.org/10.1007/s00145-007-9005-7

[BBG05] Boneh, D., Boyen, X., Goh, E.-J.: Hierarchical identity based encryption with constant size ciphertext. In: Cramer, R. (ed.) EUROCRYPT 2005. LNCS, vol. 3494, pp. 440–456. Springer, Heidelberg (2005). https://doi.org/10.1007/11426639_26

[BMV08] Bresson, E., Monnerat, J., Vergnaud, D.: Separation results on the "one-more" computational problems. In: Malkin, T. (ed.) CT-RSA 2008. LNCS, vol. 4964, pp. 71–87. Springer, Heidelberg (2008). https://doi.org/10.1007/978-3-540-79263-5_5

[BMZ19] Bartusek, J., Ma, F., Zhandry, M.: The distinction between fixed and random generators in group-based assumptions. In: Boldyreva, A., Micciancio, D. (eds.) CRYPTO 2019, Part II. LNCS, vol. 11693, pp. 801–830. Springer, Cham (2019). https://doi.org/10.1007/978-3-030-26951-7_27

[Boy08] Boyen, X.: The uber-assumption family (invited talk). In: Galbraith, S.D., Paterson, K.G. (eds.) Pairing 2008. LNCS, vol. 5209, pp. 39–56. Springer, Heidelberg (2008). https://doi.org/10.1007/978-3-540-85538-5_3

[BR04] Bellare, M., Rogaway, P.: Code-based game-playing proofs and the security of triple encryption. Cryptology ePrint Archive, Report 2004/331 (2004). http://eprint.iacr.org/2004/331

[CL04] Camenisch, J., Lysyanskaya, A.: Signature schemes and anonymous credentials from bilinear maps. In: Franklin, M. (ed.) CRYPTO 2004. LNCS, vol. 3152, pp. 56–72. Springer, Heidelberg (2004). https://doi.org/10.1007/978-3-540-28628-8_4

[CM14] Chase, M., Meiklejohn, S.: Déjà Q: using dual systems to revisit q-type assumptions. In: Nguyen, P.Q., Oswald, E. (eds.) EUROCRYPT 2014. LNCS, vol. 8441, pp. 622–639. Springer, Heidelberg (2014). https://doi.org/10.1007/978-3-642-55220-5_34

[CMM16] Chase, M., Maller, M., Meiklejohn, S.: Déjà Q all over again: tighter and broader reductions of q-type assumptions. In: Cheon, J.H., Takagi, T. (eds.) ASIACRYPT 2016, Part II. LNCS, vol. 10032, pp. 655–681. Springer, Heidelberg (2016). https://doi.org/10.1007/978-3-662-53890-6_22

[DL77] DeMillo, R.A., Lipton, R.J.: A probabilistic remark on algebraic program testing. Technical report, Georgia Inst of Tech Atlanta School of Information and Computer Science (1977)

[FKL18] Fuchsbauer, G., Kiltz, E., Loss, J.: The algebraic group model and its applications. In: Shacham, H., Boldyreva, A. (eds.) CRYPTO 2018, Part II. LNCS, vol. 10992, pp. 33–62. Springer, Cham (2018). https://doi.org/10.1007/978-3-319-96881-0_2

[FPS20] Fuchsbauer, G., Plouviez, A., Seurin, Y.: Blind Schnorr signatures and signed ElGamal encryption in the algebraic group model. In: Canteaut, A., Ishai, Y. (eds.) EUROCRYPT 2020, Part II. LNCS, vol. 12106, pp. 63–95. Springer, Cham (2020). https://doi.org/10.1007/978-3-030-45724-2_3

[GG17] Ghadafi, E., Groth, J.: Towards a classification of non-interactive computational assumptions in cyclic groups. In: Takagi, T., Peyrin, T. (eds.) ASIACRYPT 2017, Part II. LNCS, vol. 10625, pp. 66–96. Springer, Cham (2017). https://doi.org/10.1007/978-3-319-70697-9_3

[Gro16] Groth, J.: On the size of pairing-based non-interactive arguments. In: Fischlin, M., Coron, J.-S. (eds.) EUROCRYPT 2016, Part II. LNCS, vol. 9666, pp. 305–326. Springer, Heidelberg (2016). https://doi.org/10.1007/978-3-662-49896-5_11

[GWC19] Gabizon, A., Williamson, Z.J., Ciobotaru, O.: PLONK: Permutations over Lagrange-bases for oecumenical noninteractive arguments of knowledge. Cryptology ePrint Archive, Report 2019/953 (2019). https://eprint.iacr.org/2019/953

[Lip12] Lipmaa, H.: Progression-free sets and sublinear pairing-based non-interactive zero-knowledge arguments. In: Cramer, R. (ed.) TCC 2012. LNCS, vol. 7194, pp. 169–189. Springer, Heidelberg (2012). https://doi.org/10.1007/978-3-642-28914-9_10

[Lip19] Lipmaa, H.: Simulation-extractable SNARKs revisited. ePrint Cryptogoly Archive, Report 2019/612 (2019)

[Los19] Loss, J.: New techniques for the modular analysis of digital signature schemes. Ph.D thesis, Ruhr University Bochum, Germany (2019)

[LRSW99] Lysyanskaya, A., Rivest, R.L., Sahai, A., Wolf, S.: Pseudonym systems. In: Heys, H., Adams, C. (eds.) SAC 1999. LNCS, vol. 1758, pp. 184–199. Springer, Heidelberg (2000). https://doi.org/10.1007/3-540-46513-8_14

[Mau05] Maurer, U.: Abstract models of computation in cryptography (invited paper). In: Smart, N.P. (ed.) Cryptography and Coding 2005. LNCS, vol. 3796, pp. 1–12. Springer, Heidelberg (2005). https://doi.org/10.1007/11586821_1

[MBKM19] Maller, M., Bowe, S., Kohlweiss, M., Meiklejohn, S.: Sonic: zero-knowledge SNARKs from linear-size universal and updatable structured reference strings. In: Cavallaro, L., Kinder, J., Wang, X., Katz, J. (eds.) ACM CCS 2019, pp. 2111–2128. ACM (2019)

[MTT19] Mizuide, T., Takayasu, A., Takagi, T.: Tight reductions for Diffie-Hellman variants in the algebraic group model. In: Matsui, M. (ed.) CT-RSA 2019. LNCS, vol. 11405, pp. 169–188. Springer, Cham (2019). https://doi.org/10.1007/978-3-030-12612-4_9

[Nec94] Nechaev, V.I.: Complexity of a determinate algorithm for the discrete logarithm. Math. Notes **55**(2), 165–172 (1994). https://doi.org/10.1007/BF02113297

[OP01] Okamoto, T., Pointcheval, D.: The gap-problems: a new class of problems for the security of cryptographic schemes. In: Kim, K. (ed.) PKC 2001. LNCS, vol. 1992, pp. 104–118. Springer, Heidelberg (2001). https://doi.org/10.1007/3-540-44586-2_8

[PV05] Paillier, P., Vergnaud, D.: Discrete-log-based signatures may not be equivalent to discrete log. In: Roy, B. (ed.) ASIACRYPT 2005. LNCS, vol. 3788, pp. 1–20. Springer, Heidelberg (2005). https://doi.org/10.1007/11593447_1

[Sho97] Shoup, V.: Lower bounds for discrete logarithms and related problems. In: Fumy, W. (ed.) EUROCRYPT 1997. LNCS, vol. 1233, pp. 256–266. Springer, Heidelberg (1997). https://doi.org/10.1007/3-540-69053-0_18

Lattice Algorithms and Cryptanalysis

Fast Reduction of Algebraic Lattices over Cyclotomic Fields

Paul Kirchner[1][(✉)], Thomas Espitau[1,2][(✉)], and Pierre-Alain Fouque[1][(✉)]

[1] Rennes Univ., IRISA/CNRS France, Rennes, France
{paul.kirchner,pierre-alain.fouque}@irisa.fr, t.espitau@gmail.com
[2] NTT Corp. Secure Plateform Laboratories, Rennes, France

Abstract. We describe two very efficient polynomial-time algorithms for reducing module lattices defined over arbitrary cyclotomic fields that solve the γ-Hermite Module-SVP problem. They both exploit the structure of tower fields and the second one also uses the symplectic geometry existing in these fields. We conjecture that a rank-2 module over a cyclotomic field of degree n with B-bit coefficients can be heuristically reduced within approximation factor $2^{\widetilde{O}(n)}$ in time $\widetilde{O}(n^2 B)$. In the symplectic algorithm, if the condition number C of the input matrix is large enough, this complexity shrinks to $\widetilde{O}(n^{\log_2 3}C)$. In cryptography, matrices are well-conditioned and we can take $C = B$, but in the worst case, C can be as large as nB. This last result is particularly striking as for some matrices, we can go below the $n^2 B$ swaps lower bound given by the analysis of LLL based on the potential. These algorithms are parallel and we provide a full implementation. We apply them on multilinear cryptographic concrete parameters by reducing matrices of dimension 4096 with 6675-bit integers in 4 days. Finally, we give a quasicubic time for the Gentry-Szydlo algorithm and run it in dimension 1024. It requires efficient ideal multiplications which need fast lattice reductions.

1 Introduction

Lenstra, Lenstra, and Lovász introduced in 1984 the LLL-algorithm to reduce lattice basis over the euclidean ring $\mathbf{Z}$ [27] in polynomial time. Nowadays, it is of utmost importance to extend it to non-euclidean rings. Indeed, most lattice-based cryptosystems proposed at the NIST Post-Quantum competition base their security on the *assumed* hardness of reducing structured lattices, a.k.a. ideal or module lattices [25,29]. More specifically, they relies on the average-case/hard-case problems, learning with errors (LWE) [39] and short integer solution (SIS) [1] problems, which have been proved to be as hard as solving worst-case instances of lattice problems, such as finding a god basis. Furthermore, these ideal or module lattices are usually defined over the integer rings $\mathcal{O}_{\mathbf{K}}$ of a power of two cyclotomic number fields $\mathbf{K}$ for efficiency and storage considerations. These structured lattices represent apparently easier instances than random lattice instances, but they also enjoy worst-case / average-case reductions. Module lattices are closer to random lattices than ideal lattices and allow

© International Association for Cryptologic Research 2020
D. Micciancio and T. Ristenpart (Eds.): CRYPTO 2020, LNCS 12171, pp. 155–185, 2020.
https://doi.org/10.1007/978-3-030-56880-1_6

better efficiency/security tradeoff. Currently, it is widely believed that there is no weakness in using structured lattices compared to random lattices.

An n-dimensional lattice is a discrete subgroup of $\mathbf{R}^n$ and reducing a lattice consists of finding a basis with short and nearly orthogonal vectors. Reducing lattices of high dimensions is a notoriously hard problem and we do not know how to solve it efficiently. Many hard problems have been defined on lattices and even finding a shortest non-zero vector is difficult. The LLL algorithm allows solving approximate versions of these two problems, Short Independent Vectors Problem (SIVP) and Shortest Vector Problem (SVP) within an exponential factor in the lattice dimension. In [27], Lenstra et al. show how to reduce lattices of dimension n by using a reduction algorithm for 2-dimensional lattices. For 2-dimensional euclidean lattice, Lagrange algorithm outputs optimal basis: the two output vectors achieve the minima of the lattice, smallest elements in independent directions. LLL outputs a basis of (relatively) good quality in polynomial time and the first vector of the basis lies within an exponential factor approximation of a shortest non-zero vector. Yet, the approximation factor is very large, exponential in the dimension. Many algorithms such as BKZ [41] or other reductions (HKZ [20], slide [12]) have been proposed to improve the approximation factor of the basis. In another direction, some papers have improved the running time analysis of LLL: starting from the quadratic LLL algorithm of Nguyen and Stehlé [36] in $O(n^3(n+B)B \cdot M(n))$, where $M(k)$ is the complexity of multiplying k-bit integers, using a nice numerical analysis for floating-point arithmetic (the algorithm is quadratic in B the number of bits of the input matrix), to the quasi-linear complexity, $O(n^{5+\epsilon}B + n^{\omega+1+\epsilon}B^{1+\epsilon})$, where $\epsilon > 0$ and ω is the exponent for matrix multiplication of [37] and more recently the $O(n^{4+\epsilon}B^{1+\epsilon})$ algorithm of Neumaier and Stehlé [35]. The two last algorithms do not only improve the analysis, they also make significant changes and are recursive algorithms. While [37] consider various precisions at each step of the algorithm, the way how we choose the sublattices to recurse also changes the behavior of the algorithm: for example [35] has a strategy close to BKZ passes. Since the analysis follows BKZ analysis [16], the upper bound is only given for the first vector and not all vectors. The main consequence is that we have a bound relative to the volume of the lattice and not the shortest vector.

In cryptography, we often need to reduce lattices of dimension several thousand with thousand of bits. Such lattices arise in Coppersmith cryptanalysis [8], in FHE or multilinear map. To reduce them, we absolutely need an LLL implementation linear in the bitlength B and with the smallest exponent in the dimension. For FHE and multilinear map, the approximation factor is not the most important parameter and some FHE parameters have been set by using the LLL complexity.

Reduction and cryptanalysis over number fields. The first generalization of LLL for number fields has been proposed by Napias [33]. She described such an algorithm for norm-Euclidean rings or orders. It works for cyclotomic rings up to $n = 8$. This algorithm has been extended by Kim and Lee in [21] for biquadratic fields if their rings of integers are norm-Euclidean; meaning that it is a Euclidean domain for the algebraic norm.

For other number fields, the natural solution is the following. A 2-rank module is defined by a 2-by-2 matrix with coefficients in $\mathcal{O}_{\mathbf{K}}$. Each coefficient in $\mathcal{O}_{\mathbf{K}}$ can be transformed to a n-by-n matrix over $\mathbf{Z}$ representing the multiplication by α in $\mathcal{O}_{\mathbf{K}}$. Therefore, the module can also be defined by a $(2n)$-dimensional matrix over $\mathbf{Z}$. Once we get a lattice over $\mathbf{Z}$, one can apply the LLL algorithm which will output a 2^{2n}-approximation of a shortest non-zero vector in polynomial time in n. The multiplication by n in the dimension rules out every practical computation for cryptographic instances. The problem with this approach is that it forgets completely the geometry of the underlying number fields. Our approach consists in reducing the matrix M directly over $\mathcal{O}_{\mathbf{K}}$. In [26], Lee et al. show a reduction between the computation of d-dimensional modules and the apparently simpler task of reducing rank-2 modules in general number fields. It is well-known by cryptanalysts that the 2-dimensional case already captures the inherent difficulty since it is the basic case in NTRU key recovery. By restricting to cyclotomic fields rather than general number fields as it is proposed in [26], we avoid one important problem: generally speaking, modules are not defined by basis but by pseudo-basis which makes things harder. Moreover, the use of cyclotomic fields always enables us to simplify some steps. In the reduction step, we have to find an element in $\mathcal{O}_{\mathbf{K}}$ close to an element in $\mathbf{K}$. Lee et al. propose a technique to circumvent this problem, while it is known that by using Cramer et al. result in cyclotomic fields [9], one can solve it efficiently.

The lattice reduction of NTRU shares some interesting connections with the reduction of lattice defined over cyclotomic fields. First of all, Gama et al. in [11] propose a new lattice reduction algorithm for NTRU lattice, called symplectic reduction. They observe that it is possible to speed up by a factor 2 the computation by using symmetries in the NTRU basis as the second half of the basis can be obtained for free from the first part. Let J_{2n} be a 2-by-2 matrix:

$$J_{2n} = \begin{pmatrix} 0 & \mathrm{Id}_n \\ -\mathrm{Id}_n & 0 \end{pmatrix}.$$

This is a skew-symmetric matrix of determinant 1 such that $J_{2n}^2 = -\mathrm{Id}_{2n}$. A $(2n)$-by-$(2n)$ matrix M is symplectic if $M^t J_{2n} M = J_{2n}$, i.e. the matrix M keep invariant the quadratic form J_{2n}. The NTRU public key is a symplectic matrix. In [11], they show that there exist transformations to reduce a basis that keeps the symplecticity of the matrix over $\mathbf{Z}$. The speed-up factor comes from the fact that some computations can be avoided as the Gram-Schmidt vectors satisfy the relations: $b_{2n+1-i}^* = \frac{1}{\|b_i^*\|} b_i^* J_{2n}$. This symmetry is present in all cyclotomic fields we considered and at each recursion level. Secondly, Albrecht et al. [2] show how one can exploit subfields to solve overstretched versions of the NTRU cryptosystems used in FHE schemes. In [38], Pornin et Prest improve the runtime of NTRU-based cryptosystems key generation by using a recursive algorithm in subfields. It is a generalization of the Extended Euclidean Algorithm to towers of cyclotomic fields and is a one-dimensional case of the lattice reduction problem.

Our contributions. In this work, we present two algorithms and conjecture their complexity. To assess these conjectures, we give a first rough analysis with more detailed information in [23]. We stress here that our aim is not to provide a full analysis of the running time in a floating-point computational model but to give evidence for the asymptotic behavior of our algorithms. To achieve these complexities, it is crucial to consider the precision used at each level of the recursion as when we descend in the recursion tree, the number of bits of the elements increases. The analysis follows the principle of the BKZ analysis by Hanrot et al. [16] which explains why we solve the γ-Hermite Module-SVP problem. Furthermore, we are interested in reducing matrices frequently encountered by cryptanalysts and not in worst-case instances. It is neither a worst-case analysis nor an average case, but these complexities are important to estimate the runtime on cryptographic instances. Besides, they conform rather well with our experiments and the size of the instances we have reduced. Finally, our implementation is in gp and is parallelized. If one is interested in the hidden constants in the big-O notation, it is worth implementing it in a low-level language.

Claim 1 (Informal). *Over a cyclotomic field of degree n and sufficiently smooth conductor, one can reduce a rank-2 module represented as a 2-by-2 matrix M whose number of bits in the input coefficients is uniformly bounded by $B > n$, in time $\widetilde{O}(n^2 B)$ heuristically. The first column of the reduced matrix has its coefficients uniformly bounded by*

$$2^{\widetilde{O}(n)}(\operatorname{vol} M)^{\frac{1}{2n}}.$$

The second algorithm fully exploits the symplectic structure of these lattices. It is polynomial in the *condition number* of the input matrix, with a dimensional factor below the classical bound in n^2. As the condition number is expected to be large, the second term component is negligible in most cases.

Claim 2 (Informal). *For cyclotomic fields with power of prime q conductor n, with the smoothness condition $q = O(\log n)$, we give a faster and heuristic symplectic lattice reduction algorithm with approximation factor $2^{\widetilde{O}(n)}$ in time:*

$$\widetilde{O}\left(n^{2+\frac{\log(1/2+1/2q)}{\log q}}C\right) + n^{O(\log\log n)}$$

where C is a bound on the condition number of the input matrix. For a power of two cyclotomic fields and large enough C, this complexity is a polynomial $\widetilde{O}(n^{\log_2(3)}C)$.

Practical impacts in cryptography. Our reduction algorithms run in polynomial time and only achieve an exponential approximation factor. They can not be used per se to reevaluate the security parameters of NIST candidates, as their security estimates are based on better algorithms such as theDBKZ [31]. However, using the symplectic structure, one can halve the complexity of this algorithm[1].

---

[1] The approximation factor loss appearing with this technique is *not* increasing the approximation factor of the whole DBKZ routine, as it acts only as a polynomial control of the bitsize of the elements and to transform generating families of lattices to bases without degrading the size of the vectors.

We test our algorithms on a large instance coming from multilinear map candidates based on ideal lattices [3] where $q \approx 2^{6675}$ and $N = 2^{16}$. It can be solved over the smaller field $n = 2^{11}$ in 13 core-days. If we compare this computation with the previous large computation with fplll [44], Albrecht *et al.* were able to compute with $n = 2^8$, $q \approx 2^{240}$ in 120 h. As the complexity of their code is about $n^4 \log(q)^2$ one can estimate an improvement factor of 4 million.

We improve the running time of the Gentry-Szydlo algorithm [14] using better ideal arithmetic. Instead of the classical **Z**-basis representation, we represent ideals with a small family of generators over the order of a subfield of **K**. The product of two ideals is the family of all products of generators. To make this work we need to sample a bit more than $[\mathbf{L} : \mathbf{K}]$ random elements in the product so that with overwhelming probability the ideal generated by these elements is the product ideal itself. As this increases the size of the family, we need fast lattice reductions to reduce the family as this operation is called many times. The overall complexity is $\widetilde{O}(n^3)$, while previous implementation runs in $O(n^6)$. The algorithm run in dimension 1024 in 103 h.

High-level description of the algorithms. The two algorithms leverage on the recursive strategy of Novocin et al. [37] to change the precisions at each level, of Albrecht et al. [2,38] to descend recursively in smaller subfields using the relative norm functions, and the approach of Villard to make the algorithm parallel. The symplectic algorithm deeply extends the work of Gama et al. [11] by mixing it with the recursion strategy. Our theorems are stated for 2-dimensional lattices, but the algorithms run for lattices of dimension d. The reason is that even though we begin with a 2-by-2 matrix, after one recursion step, if the relative extension degree is 2, we get a 4-by-4 matrix. Consequently, we have to deal with more general dimensions. A more general theorem is claimed in [23]. Figure 1 is a flowchart of the different subroutines used in the algorithms.

A module over **K** of rank d can be defined by a d-dimensional matrix M with coefficients in $\mathcal{O}_{\mathbf{K}}$. If $M \in (\mathcal{O}_{\mathbf{K}})^{d \times d}$ reducing M means finding a unimodular matrix $U \in (\mathcal{O}_{\mathbf{K}})^{d \times d}$ such that MU has short and nearly orthogonal vectors in $(\mathcal{O}_{\mathbf{K}})^d$. Unimodular matrices in $(\mathcal{O}_{\mathbf{K}})^{d \times d}$ form a multiplicative group whose determinants are units in $\mathcal{O}_{\mathbf{K}}$. It turns out that in such ring, the number of units is usually much higher than in **Z** where we only have ± 1. One can define orthogonality of vectors using a positive quadratic form as a generalization of the usual scalar product on $\mathbf{R}^d$, with vectors over **C**. There is two natural representations of elements for $\alpha = \sum_i a_i \zeta^i \in \mathcal{O}_{\mathbf{K}}$ with $a_i \in \mathbf{Z}$. The most simple one is the representation by coefficients $(a_0, \ldots, a_{n-1})$. The second representation is better in theory and is more convenient since it allows efficient computations: multiplication and addition can be achieved coefficient-wise. It sends α to all its conjugates: the evaluations at all nth primitive roots of unity $(\exp(2i\pi k/n)$ with $\gcd(k, n) = 1)$ of the polynomial $\alpha(X) = a_0 + a_1 X + \ldots + a_{n-1} X^{n-1}$. Finally, it is possible to define a geometric norm on the representation by evaluations, a.k.a. embeddings, by extending the norm over **C** to vectors. This norm induces a distance between elements of $\mathcal{O}_{\mathbf{K}}$.

As said in [26], the major challenges for reducing algebraic lattices is that the algebraic norm and embedding norm does not always coincide for algebraic lattices, contrary to the Euclidean case. Some operations in LLL require to work with the algebraic norm, when the volume of the lattice is involved, while when we have to take care of the size, we rely on a geometric norm, and unfortunately the algebraic norm is not a geometric norm.

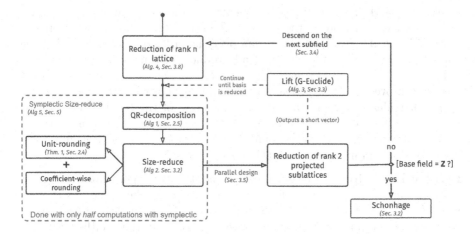

Fig. 1. Flowchart of the overall toplevel of the reduction algorithm.

Reduction of rank-n. This algorithm described in Sect. 3.8 is the main function of the algorithm and its goal is to reduce a lattice of rank $d = n$ at the beginning. It is a recursive function that at the leaves of the recursion tree (2-dimensional lattice over $\mathbf{Z}$) calls Schönhage algorithm. The idea is to progressively change the basis making its profile flatter step-by-step during ρ iterations. The value ρ hence controls the overall complexity. In dimension d for a precision p, ρ is in $O(d^2 \log p)$. The precision is estimated by the size of the ratio between the largest and smallest embeddings of the Gram-Schmidt at each of the ρ iterations. The best value for ρ is estimated via a dynamical system analysis, sharing similarities with the one of [16]. Interestingly, the complexity equation reminds the heat equation in physics, whose diffusion characteristic time is quadratic in the space diameter.

A single iteration is organized in the same way as in (classical) LLL pass on the whole basis: first, the Gram-Schmidt orthogonalization process is called, followed by a reduction in size of the Gram-Schmidt values. We call the first stage QR-decomposition as most modern LLL versions implement this algorithm. The size-reduction algorithm allows us to keep the manipulated matrices well-conditioned. The whole LLL process aimed at making the basis well-conditioned, i.e. making the ratio between the largest and smallest Gram-Schmidt vector as low as possible. The idea of LLL consists of pushing the weight of the heaviest Gram-Schmidt to the lightest ones using Lagrange reduction step of 2-dimensional lattices.

Then, the main loop of LLL is applied on the whole basis by splitting the base in 2-dimensional sublattices. This loop is orchestrated with odd-even steps à la Villard [45] depending on the parity of the iteration. Instead of reducing the vectors (b_i, b_{i+1}) for $i = 1$ to $n-1$ in LLL which is inherently a sequential process, Villard proposed to reduce vectors (b_{2i+1}, b_{2i+2}) for $i = 0$ to $n/2 - 1$ in odd passes and (b_{2i}, b_{2i+1}) for $i = 1$ to $n/2 - 1$ in even passes. Consequently, at each pass all 2-dimensional sublattices $\{(b_{2i+1}, b_{2i+2})\}_i$ or $\{(b_{2i}, b_{2i+1})\}_i$ can be reduced in parallel. According to some condition on consecutive Gram-Schmidt norms (similar to Lovász condition), we recurse on smaller sublattices by first calling the **Descend** algorithm and then the **Reduce** Algorithm in smaller dimension. Once we go back, we lift the unimodular matrix to the above subfield and apply it on the basis matrix. At the end of this algorithm, all unimodular matrices that have been computed during the ρ steps are multiplied together to obtain the global unimodular transformation.

The main parameter is how we define a *Lovász condition* for algebraic lattices. It is crucial to control the approximation factor of our algorithms and the slope of the profile is named α, the approximation factor will be in $2^{\alpha d}$. As previously mentioned, the goal is to transfer the weight of the first vector to the second one. Each iteration transforms consecutive Gram-Schmidt norms $R_{i,i}$ and $R_{i+1,i+1}$ to their average. The caveat of our algorithms is that the approximation factor will be higher than the one of LLL because when we lift the solution, the vectors will be a little larger. We are however able to keep it exponential in $\tilde{O}(n)$. As it depends on the number of subfields, this parameter will be different in the standard and symplectic algorithms. Indeed, in the symplectic algorithm, we cannot take any subfields and they have to be denser. Therefore, we recurse more and the approximation factor becomes higher.

QR-decomposition. This algorithm is described in Sect. 2.4 and computes the Gram-Schmidt decomposition. Since it uses purely algebraic operations, it is easy to adapt it for algebraic lattices once the hermitian product and norm are defined.

Size-reduce. This algorithm is given in Sect. 3.2 and its goal is to reduce the size of the vectors. When the field is **Q** in the classical LLL, we just round the coefficients to the nearest integer. Rounding in cyclotomic fields is not as easy as in **Z** as the $\mathcal{O}_\mathbf{K}$ lattice is less orthogonal. The idea is that we have to solve an approx-CVP instance in the $\mathcal{O}_\mathbf{K}$-lattice. In theory, we need to compute a unit close to $R_{i,i}$ as in [9] which is easy since the unit-log lattice is nearly orthogonal in the cyclotomic case. In practice, it is not needed and as it is reported in [38], it works well without it. This operation will not change the algebraic norm of the elements, but make the embedding coefficients all of the same sizes, so that it helps to make the matrix well-conditioned and avoid a blow-up in the precision. It is also very important in the **Lift** algorithm for controlling the size of the elements.

Reduction of rank-2 projected sublattices. The reduction of rank-2 projected sublattices first extracts 2 column vectors

$$\begin{pmatrix} R_{i,i} & R_{i+1,i} \\ 0 & R_{i+1,i+1} \end{pmatrix}.$$

and according to Lovász condition $\mathcal{N}_{\mathbf{K}_h/\mathbf{Q}}(R_{i,i}) \leqslant 2^{2(1+\varepsilon)\alpha n_h^2}\mathcal{N}_{\mathbf{K}_h/\mathbf{Q}}(R_{i+1,i+1})$, it continues the descent. The recursion to smaller subfields is composed of the Descend and **Ascend** algorithm explained in Sect. 3.4 and is mainly depacking/packing values. Once the recursion terminates, it calls back the Lift algorithm.

Lift and Generalized Euclidean Algorithm. This algorithm is described in Sect. 3.7. This operation requires to be careful otherwise the size of the lifted vectors will explode. The reduction at the bottom of the tree will return a short vector in the module. We need to complete this vector so that they both generate the same rank-2 module as the one given at the level of the recursion. The idea is to use a generalization of the extended Euclidean (**G-Euclide** algorithm in cyclotomic fields since we know that the determinant of the unimodal transformation has a determinant equal to 1. In the end, we size-reduce the basis to make vectors of the same size with balanced coefficients. We show that the operation works if we start with two elements a and b in a subfield $\mathbf{K}_h$ so that their absolute norms $\mathcal{N}_{\mathbf{K}_h/\mathbf{Q}}(a)$ and $\mathcal{N}_{\mathbf{K}_h/\mathbf{Q}}(b)$ in $\mathbf{Z}$ are coprime.

The lift operation can fail in some instances as when we lift small elements, they do not always generate the whole rank-2 module. We work around this problem by lifting many small elements. In practice, this heuristic always works.

Symplectic Algorithm. The algorithm is the same as the standard algorithm but it changes the size-reduction which is presented in Sect. 4. It uses operations that maintain the symplecticity of the matrix. We used the symplectic reduction [11] at each step of the recursion. To do this, we need to show that it is possible to define the symplectic geometry in all subfields when we descend the tower field.

Comparison with other works. More recently some independent line of research started to tackle the problem of reduction of algebraic lattices [26,32]. These papers give polynomial time reduction from γ-module-SVP (or γ-Hermite-SVP) in arbitrary rank to the same problem in small rank for all number fields. In particular in [26], for rank-2 modules, they present a γ-SVP heuristic algorithm with approximation factor is $2^{(\log d)^{O(1)}}$ in cyclotomic rings with quantum polynomial time given a CVP oracle that only depends on K in dimension more than d^2. Consequently, an implementation would rely on an actual oracle for the latter problem with running time 2^{d^2}.

Organization of the paper. The next section is devoted to a succinct presentation of the mathematical objects required in the presentation of our framework. In Sect. 3 we introduce an algorithm which reduces rank-2 modules. Then, in Sect. 4, we explain how to leverage a natural symplectic structure to obtain an even faster reduction. We give implementation details in Sect. 5 and some cryptographic applications in Sect. 6.

2 Background

2.1 Computational Model and Notations

We use the word-RAM model with unit cost and logarithmic size register (see for instance [30, Section 2.2]). An integer $n \in \mathbf{Z}$ is said *log-smooth* if all its prime factors are bounded by $\log(n)$. For a field $\mathbf{K}$, let us denote by $\mathbf{K}^{d \times d}$ the space of square matrices of size d over $\mathbf{K}$, $\mathrm{GL}_d(\mathbf{K})$ its group of invertibles. Denote classically the elementary matrices by $T_{i,j}(\lambda)$ and $D_i(\lambda)$ for respectively the transvection (or shear mapping) and the dilatation of parameter λ. We extend the definition of the product for any pair of matrices (A, B): for every matrix C with compatible size with A and B, we set: $(A, B) \cdot C = (AC, BC)$. We will denote the L_2 norm of a vector $x = (x_1, \dots x_d)$ by $\|x\| = \sqrt{\sum_i x_i^2}$ and the Frobenius norm of matrices by $\|A\|_2 = \sqrt{\sum_i \sum_j |A_{i,j}|^2}$ for a matrix $A = (A_{i,j})$. The condition number $\kappa(A) = \|A\|_2 \|A^{-1}\|_2$, where A is a real or complex matrix and the norm used here is the spectral norm. We adopt the following conventions for submatrix extraction: for any matrix $A = (A_{i,j}) \in \mathbf{K}^{d \times d}$ and $1 \leqslant i < j \leqslant d, 1 \leqslant k < \ell \leqslant d$, define the submatrix $A[i : j, k : \ell] = (A_{u,v})_{i \leqslant u \leqslant j, k \leqslant v \leqslant \ell}$, while A_u refers to the u-th column of A.

2.2 Cyclotomic Fields and Modules over $\mathbf{Z}[\zeta_f]$

Background on Algebraic number theory can be found in Neukirch's book [34]. Let $\Phi_f \in \mathbf{Z}[X]$ be the f-th cyclotomic polynomial, the unique monic polynomial whose roots $\zeta_f^k = \exp(2ik\pi/f)$ with $\gcd(k, f) = 1$ are the f-th primitive roots of the unity. Therefore it can be written as $\Phi_f = \prod_{k \in \mathbf{Z}_f^\times}(X - \zeta_f^k)$ and the cyclotomic field $\mathbf{Q}(\zeta_f)$ is obtained by adjoining a primitive root ζ_f to the rational numbers. As such, $\mathbf{Q}(\zeta_f)$ is isomorphic to the field $\mathbf{Q}[X]/(\Phi_f)$. Its degree over $\mathbf{Q}$ is $\deg(\Phi_f) = \varphi(f)$, the Euler totient of f. In this specific class of number fields, the ring of integers is precisely $\mathbf{Z}[X]/(\Phi_f) \cong \mathbf{Z}[\zeta_f]$ (see [34, Prop. 10.2]).

Canonical Hermitian structure. Let $\mathcal{M}$ be a free module of rank d over the cyclotomic ring of integers $\mathbf{Z}[\zeta_f]$. It is isomorphic to $\bigoplus_{i=1}^d \alpha_i \mathbf{Z}[\zeta_f]$, for some linearly independent vectors $\alpha_i = (\alpha_i^{(1)}, \dots, \alpha_i^{(d)}) \in \mathbf{Q}(\zeta_f)^d$. The Hermitian structure of $\mathbf{Q}(\zeta_f)^d$ lifts to $\mathcal{M}$ as defined by $\langle \alpha_i \, | \, \alpha_j \rangle = \sum_{t=1}^d \mathrm{tr}_{\mathbf{Q}(\zeta_f)/\mathbf{Q}}\left(\alpha_i^{(t)} \overline{\alpha_j^{(t)}}\right)$ on the basis elements and extended by (bi)linearity. We denote by $\|\cdot\|$ the corresponding norm. We use the same notation to denote the associated induced norm on endomorphisms (or associated matrices) over the vector space $\mathbf{Q}(\zeta_f)^d$.

Relative structure of the ring of integers in a tower. Let $\mathbf{K} \subseteq \mathbf{L}$ be a *cyclotomic* subfield of $\mathbf{L}$ of index n. Then $\mathcal{O}_\mathbf{K}$ is a subring of $\mathcal{O}_\mathbf{L}$, so that $\mathcal{O}_\mathbf{L}$ is a free module over $\mathcal{O}_\mathbf{K}$[2]. Henceforth, the module $\mathcal{M}$ can itself be viewed as a free module over $\mathcal{O}_\mathbf{K}$ of rank dn. Indeed, consider $(\xi_1, \dots, \xi_n)$ a basis of $\mathcal{O}_\mathbf{K}$ over $\mathcal{O}_\mathbf{L}$

---

[2] In whole generality, it is not necessarily free, but imposing both fields to be cyclotomics is sufficient to imply this property.

and $(v_1, \ldots, v_d)$ a basis of $\mathcal{M}$ over $\mathcal{O}_{\mathbf{K}}$. For any $1 \leqslant i \leqslant d$, each coefficient of the vector v_i decomposes uniquely in the basis (ξ_j). Grouping the corresponding coefficients yields a decomposition $v_i = v_i^{(1)} \xi_1 + \cdots + v_i^{(n)} \xi_n$, where $v_i^{(j)} \in \mathcal{O}_{\mathbf{L}}^{dn}$. The family $\left(v_i^{(j)} \xi_j \right)_{1 \leqslant i \leqslant d, 1 \leqslant j \leqslant n}$ is a basis of $\mathcal{M}$ viewed as $\mathcal{O}_{\mathbf{K}}$-module.

2.3 Unit Rounding in Cyclotomic Fields

The group of units of a number field is the group of invertible elements of its ring of integers. Giving the complete description of the units of a generic number field is a computationally hard problem in algorithmic number theory. However, in cyclotomic fields, it is possible to describe a subgroup of finite index of the unit group, called the *cyclotomic units*. This subgroup contains all the units that are products of elements of the form $\zeta_f^i - 1$ for any $1 \leqslant i \leqslant f$. As these units are dense, structured and explicit we can use them to round an element. The following theorem is a quasilinear variant of the result of [9, Theorem 6.3] which is proved in [23] and **Unit** is the corresponding algorithm.

Theorem 1. *Let* $\mathbf{K}$ *be the cyclotomic field of conductor* f. *There is a quasilinear time randomized algorithm that given any element in* $x \in (\mathbf{R} \otimes \mathbf{K})^\times$ *finds a unit* $u \in \mathcal{O}_{\mathbf{K}}^\times$ *such that for any field embedding* $\sigma : \mathbf{K} \to \mathbf{C}$ *we have*

$$\sigma\left(x u^{-1} \right) = 2^{O\left(\sqrt{f \log f} \right)} \mathcal{N}_{\mathbf{K}/\mathbf{Q}}(x)^{\frac{1}{\varphi(f)}}.$$

Remark 1. Since $\frac{f}{\varphi(f)} = \mathrm{O}(\log \log f)$ and $n = \varphi(f)$ the absolute degree of $\mathbf{K}$, the bound in Theorem 1 becomes $2^{O\left(\sqrt{n \log n \log \log n} \right)} \mathcal{N}_{\mathbf{K}/\mathbf{Q}}(x)^{\frac{1}{n}}$.

2.4 $\mathcal{O}_{\mathbf{K}}$-lattices

We now generalize the notion of Euclidean lattice to the higher-degree context. Recall that a Euclidean lattice is a finitely generated free $\mathbf{Z}$-module Λ endowed with a Euclidean structure on its real ambient space $\Lambda \otimes_{\mathbf{Z}} \mathbf{R}$. To extend this definition we replace the base-ring $\mathbf{Z}$ by the ring of integer $\mathcal{O}_{\mathbf{K}}$ of a number field $\mathbf{K}$. In the present context, we will keep the freeness condition of the module, even if this setting is slightly too restrictive in general number fields.

Definition 1 ($\mathcal{O}_{\mathbf{K}}$-lattice). *Let* $\mathbf{K}$ *be a cyclotomic field. An* $\mathcal{O}_{\mathbf{K}}$-*lattice—or algebraic lattice over* $\mathcal{O}_{\mathbf{K}}$ —*is a free* $\mathcal{O}_{\mathbf{K}}$-*module* Λ *endowed with a* $\mathbf{K} \otimes \mathbf{R}$-*linear positive definite self-adjoint form on the ambient vector space* $\Lambda \otimes_{\mathcal{O}_{\mathbf{K}}} \mathbf{R}$.

Orthogonalization process. Taking the basis $(m_1, \ldots, m_d)$ of $\mathcal{M}$, one can construct an orthogonal family $(m_1^*, \ldots, m_d^*)$ such that the flag of subspaces $(\oplus_{i=1}^k b_i \mathbf{K})_{1 \leqslant k \leqslant d}$ is preserved. This routine is exactly the same as for Euclidean lattices and is given in Algorithm 1, **Orthogonalize**. We present it here in its matrix form, which generalizes to $\mathrm{GL}_d(\mathbf{K} \otimes \mathbf{R})$ QR-decomposition in $\mathrm{GL}_d(\mathbf{R})$. The volume of $\mathcal{M}$ can be computed from the norms of the Gram-Schmidt stored in the matrix R as: $\mathrm{vol}\,(\mathcal{M}) = \mathcal{N}_{\mathbf{K}/\mathbf{Q}}\left(\prod_{i=1}^d R_{i,i} \right)$, while over $\mathbf{Z}$, it is $\prod_{i=1}^d R_{i,i}$.

Algorithm 1: QR-decomposition Algorithm

| **Input** | : Basis $M \in \mathcal{O}_{\mathbf{K}_h}^{d \times d}$ of an $\mathcal{O}_{\mathbf{K}_h}$−module $\mathcal{M}$ |
| **Output** | : R part of the QR-decomposition of M |

1 **for** $j = 1$ **to** d **do** $Q_j \leftarrow M_j - \sum_{i=1}^{j-1} \frac{\langle M_j \mid Q_i \rangle}{\langle Q_i \mid Q_i \rangle} Q_i$ **end for**

2 **return** $R = \left(\frac{\langle Q_i \mid M_j \rangle}{\|Q_i\|} \right)_{1 \leqslant i \leqslant j \leqslant d}$

---

3 Reduction of $\mathcal{O}_{\mathbf{K}}$-Modules in Cyclotomic Fields

We describe now our first reduction for lattices over cyclotomic fields. Let h be a non-negative integer, a tower of log-smooth conductor cyclotomic fields

$$\mathbf{K}_h^{\uparrow} = (\mathbf{Q} = \mathbf{K}_0 \subset \mathbf{K}_1 \subset \cdots \subset \mathbf{K}_h)$$

and $1 = n_0 < n_1 < \cdots < n_h$ their respective degrees over $\mathbf{Q}$. Then, we consider a free module $\mathcal{M}$ of rank d over the upper field $\mathbf{K}_h$, which is represented by a basis $(m_1, \ldots, m_d)$ given as the columns of a matrix $M \in \mathcal{O}_{\mathbf{K}_h}^{d \times d}$. We denote by $\langle a, b \rangle$ the $\mathcal{O}_{\mathbf{K}_h}$-module $a\mathcal{O}_{\mathbf{K}_h} \oplus b\mathcal{O}_{\mathbf{K}_h}$. The reduction algorithm returns a *unimodular transformation* such that the basis $M \cdot$ **Reduce**(M) has a small first vector.

3.1 Outer Iteration

To reduce the module $\mathcal{M}$ we adopt an iterative strategy to *progressively* modify the basis. For ρ steps, a reduction pass over the current basis is performed, with ρ being a parameter whose value is computed to optimize[3] the complexity of the whole algorithm while still ensuring the reduceness of the basis. As in the LLL algorithm a size-reduction operation is conducted to control the size of the coefficients of the basis and ensure that the running time of the reduction remains polynomial. Note that for number fields this subroutine is adapted to deal with units of $\mathcal{O}_{\mathbf{K}_h}$ when rounding. In a word, we make use of the numerous units of this field to shrink the discrepancy of the embeddings of the coefficients of the basis. This allows computation with less precision.

3.2 Unit-size-reduction for $\mathcal{O}_{\mathbf{K}_h}$-Modules

As indicated, in order to adapt the size-reduction process to the module setting, one needs to adjust the rounding function. When $\mathbf{K}_h = \mathbf{Q}$, the rounding boils down to finding the closest element in $\mathcal{O}_{\mathbf{K}} = \mathbf{Z}$, which is encompassed by the round function $\lceil \cdot \rfloor$. In the higher-dimensional context, we need to approximate any element of $\mathbf{K}_h$ by *a close element* of $\mathcal{O}_{\mathbf{K}_h}$.

Note that finding *the* closest integral element is not efficiently doable. The naive approach consists of reducing the problem to the resolution of the closest integer problem in the Euclidean lattice of rank n_h given by $\mathcal{O}_{\mathbf{K}_h}$ under the embedding.

---

[3] We defer the precise computation of this constant to [23].

Algorithm 2: Size-Reduce

Input	: R-factor of the QR-decomposition of $M \in \mathcal{O}_{\mathbf{K}_h}^{d \times d}$
Output	: A unimodular transformation U representing the size-reduced basis obtained from M.

1 $U \leftarrow \mathrm{Id}_{d,d}$
2 **for** $i = 1$ **to** d **do**
3 | $L \leftarrow D_i(\mathbf{Unit}(R_{i,i}))$// D_i is a dilation matrix
4 | $(U, R) \leftarrow (U, R) \cdot L^{-1}$
5 | **for** $j = i - 1$ **downto** 1 **do**
6 | | $\sum_{\ell=0}^{n-1} r_\ell X^\ell \leftarrow R_{i,j}/R_{j,j}$ // Extraction as a polynomial
7 | | $\mu \leftarrow \sum_{\ell=0}^{n-1} \lfloor r_\ell \rceil X^\ell$ // Approximate rounding of $R_{i,j}$ in $\mathcal{O}_{\mathbf{K}_h}$
8 | | $(U, R) \leftarrow (U, R) \cdot T_{i,j}(-\mu)$ // $T_{i,j}$ is a shear matrix
9 | **end for**
10 **end for**
11 **return** U

Nonetheless, finding a target vector *close enough* to the target suffices for our application. We simply define the rounding of an element $\alpha \in \mathbf{K}_h$ as the integral rounding on its coefficients when represented in the power base of $\mathbf{K}_h$.

We add here an important and necessary modification to the size-reduction algorithm: before the actual size-reduction occurred, we compute a unit u using Theorem 1 close to $R_{i,i}$. The vector M_i is then divided by u. While not changing the algebraic norms of the elements, this technicality forces the embeddings of the coefficients to be balanced and helps the reduced matrix to be well-conditioned. This avoids a blow-up of the precision required during the computation. This modified size-reduction is fully described in Algorithm 2, **Size-Reduce** (the two technical modifications to the usual size-reduction are encompassed at line 3 for the reconditioning using the unit rounding and at line 7 where the approximate rounding is performed coefficient-wise).

3.3   Step Reduction Subroutine

We now take a look at the step reduction pass, once the size-reduction has occurred. The LLL algorithm reduces to the treatment of rank-2 modules and more precisely to iteratively reduce *orthogonally projected* rank-2 modules. We use the same idea and the step reduction pass over the current basis is a sequence of reductions of projected rank 2 $\mathcal{O}_{\mathbf{K}_h}$–modules. However on the contrary to the LLL algorithm, we do not proceed progressively along the basis, but instead, reduce $\lfloor d/2 \rfloor$ independent rank 2 modules at each step. This design enables an efficient parallel implementation which reduces submodules simultaneously, in the same way that the classical LLL algorithm can be parallelized [17,45].

Formally, given the basis of $\mathcal{M}$ collected in the matrix M, let us decompose it as $M = QR$ with Q orthogonal and R upper triangular. For $1 \leqslant i \leqslant d - 1$, denote by r_i the vector $(R_{i,i}, R_{i+1,i} = 0)$, and r_i' the vector $(R_{i,i+1}, R_{i+1,i+1})$. The module $\mathcal{R}_i$ spanned by the vectors r_i and r_i' encodes exactly the projection of $\mathcal{M}_i = \langle m_{i-1}, m_i \rangle$ over the orthogonal space to the first $i - 1$ vectors $(m_1, \ldots, m_{i-1})$. In order to recursively call the reduction algorithm on $\mathcal{R}_i$ we need to *descend* it to the subfield $\mathbf{K}_{h-1}$ first. This means seeing this $\mathcal{O}_{\mathbf{K}_h}$-module of rank 2 as an $\mathcal{O}_{\mathbf{K}_{h-1}}$-module of rank $2[\mathbf{K}_h : \mathbf{K}_{h-1}]$.

3.4 Interlude: Descending to Cyclotomic Subfields

Remark now that since $\mathbf{K}_h$ is a cyclotomic extension of the cyclotomic field $\mathbf{K}_{h-1}$, there exists a root of unity ζ such that $\mathcal{O}_{\mathbf{K}_h} = \mathcal{O}_{\mathbf{K}_{h-1}} \oplus \zeta\mathcal{O}_{\mathbf{K}_{h-1}} \oplus \cdots \oplus \zeta^{q_h-1}\mathcal{O}_{\mathbf{K}_{h-1}}$, for $q_h = n_h/n_{h-1}$ being the relative degree of $\mathbf{K}_h$ over $\mathbf{K}_{h-1}$. As a consequence, the module $\mathcal{R}_i$ decomposes over $\mathcal{O}_{\mathbf{K}_{h-1}}$ as:

$$
\begin{aligned}
\mathcal{R}_i &= r_i \mathcal{O}_{\mathbf{K}_h} \oplus r'_{i+1} \mathcal{O}_{\mathbf{K}_h} \\
&= r_i \mathcal{O}_{\mathbf{K}_{h-1}} \oplus \zeta r_i \mathcal{O}_{\mathbf{K}_{h-1}} \oplus \cdots \oplus \zeta^{q_h-1} r_i \mathcal{O}_{\mathbf{K}_{h-1}} \oplus \\
&\quad\; r'_{i+1} \mathcal{O}_{\mathbf{K}_{h-1}} \oplus \zeta r'_{i+1} \mathcal{O}_{\mathbf{K}_{h-1}} \oplus \cdots \oplus \zeta^{q_h-1} r'_{i+1} \mathcal{O}_{\mathbf{K}_{h-1}},
\end{aligned}
$$

yielding a basis of $\mathcal{R}_i$ viewed as a free $\mathcal{O}_{\mathbf{K}_{h-1}}$-module of rank $2 \times q_h$. This module can then be recursively reduced, this time over a tower of height $h - 1$. This conversion from an $\mathcal{O}_{\mathbf{K}_h}$-module to an $\mathcal{O}_{\mathbf{K}_{h-1}}$- module is referred as the function **Descend**. Conversely, any vector $u \in \mathcal{O}_{\mathbf{K}_{h-1}}^{2q_h}$ can be seen with this decomposition as a vector of $\mathcal{O}_{\mathbf{K}_h}^2$ by grouping the coefficients as

$$
\left(\sum_{i=1}^{q_h} u[i]\zeta^i, \sum_{i=1}^{q_h} u[q_h + 1 + i]\zeta^i \right).
$$

We denote by **Ascend** this conversion.

3.5 Back on the Step Reduction

We start by reducing (with a recursive call after descending) all $\mathcal{O}_{\mathbf{K}_{h-1}}$-modules $\mathcal{R}_{2i} = \langle r_{2i-1}, r'_{2i} \rangle$ for $1 \leqslant i \leqslant \lfloor d/2 \rfloor$. By specification, each of these reductions allows to find a small element of the $\mathcal{O}_{\mathbf{K}_h}$-submodule $\mathcal{M}_{2i} = \langle m_{2i-1}, m_{2i} \rangle$ which is then *completed*[4] in a basis of $\mathcal{M}_{2i}$. But on the contrary to the classical LLL reduction, this sequence of pairwise independent reductions does not mix the elements m_{2i} and m_{2i+1}, in the sense that no reduction of the module projected from $\langle m_{2i}, m_{2i+1} \rangle$ is performed. To do so, we then perform the same sequence of pairwise reductions but with all indices shifted by 1: we reduce the planes $\langle r_{2i}, r'_{2i+1} \rangle$ for each $1 \leqslant i \leqslant \lfloor d/2 \rfloor$, as depicted in Fig. 2.

3.6 Reduction of the Leaves

As the recursive calls descend along the tower of number fields, the bottom of the recursion tree requires reducing $\mathcal{O}_{\mathbf{K}_0}(= \mathcal{O}_{\mathbf{Q}} = \mathbf{Z})$-modules, that is, Euclidean

---

[4] The precise definition of this completion and lifting is given in a dedicated paragraph.

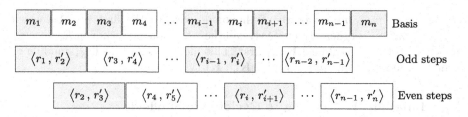

Fig. 2. Illustration of one pass of reduction (blocks of the shape $\langle a, b \rangle$ indicates a local reduction of the module spanned by a and b.).

lattices. As a consequence, the step reduction performs calls to a reduction oracle for plane Euclidean lattices. For the sake of efficiency we adapt Schönhage's algorithm [42] to reduce these lattices, which is faster than the traditional Gauss' reduction. This algorithm is an extension to the bidimensional case of the half-GCD algorithm, in the same way, that Gauss' algorithm can be seen as a bidimensional generalization of the classical GCD computation. The original algorithm of Schönhage only deals with the reduction of binary quadratic forms, but can be straightforwardly adapted to reduce rank 2 Euclidean lattices, and to return the corresponding unimodular transformation matrix. In all of the following, we denote by **Schonhage** this modified procedure.

3.7   The Lifting Phase

At this point, we recursively called the reduction procedure to reduce the descent of projected modules of rank 2 of the form $\mathcal{R}_i = \langle r_i, r'_{i+1} \rangle$, over $\mathbf{K}_{h-1}$. This yields a unimodular transformation $U' \in \mathcal{O}_{\mathbf{K}_{h-1}}^{2q_h \times 2q_h}$ where q_h is the relative degree of $\mathbf{K}_h$ over $\mathbf{K}_{h-1}$. We now need to find a reduced basis of this projected sublattice *over* $\mathcal{O}_{\mathbf{K}_h}$, so that we can apply the corresponding transformation on $m_i \mathcal{O}_{\mathbf{K}_h} \oplus m_{i+1} \mathcal{O}_{\mathbf{K}_h}$ (like in the classical LLL algorithm).

From U', we can find random short elements in the module (over $\mathbf{K}_{h-1}$) by computing a small linear combination of its first columns. By applying **Ascend** on one of them, we deduce some short $x = a \cdot m_i + b \cdot m_{i+1}$. But then to replace m_i by x in the current basis, we need to complete this vector into a basis (x, y) of $\mathcal{M}_i$ over $\mathcal{O}_{\mathbf{K}_h}$. Saying differently, we want to complete a vector of $\mathcal{O}_{\mathbf{K}_h}^2$ into a unimodular transformation. Indeed, suppose that such a vector y is found and denote by (v, u) its coordinates in the basis (m_i, m_{i+1}). By preservation of the volume we have:

$$\pm 1 = \det \begin{pmatrix} a & v \\ b & u \end{pmatrix} = au - bv.$$

Therefore, finding the element y to complete x reduces to solving the Bézout equation in the unknown u and v $au - bv = 1$ over the ring $\mathcal{O}_{\mathbf{K}_h}$. Since this ring is in general not Euclidean we can not apply directly the Euclidean algorithm to solve this equation using the extended GCD algorithm. However, we can use the algebraic structure of the tower $\mathbf{K}_h^\uparrow$ to recursively reduce the problem to the rational integers. This *generalized* Euclidean algorithm works as follows:

If $\mathbf{K}_h = \mathbf{Q}$: The problem is then an instance of extended GCD search, which can be solved efficiently by the binary-GCD algorithm.

If the tower $\mathbf{K}_h^\uparrow$ is not trivial: We make use of the structure of $\mathbf{K}_h^\uparrow$ and first *descend* the problem to the subfield $\mathbf{K}_{h-1}$ by applying the relative norm $\mathcal{N}_{\mathbf{K}_h/\mathbf{K}_{h-1}}$: then, by recursive call on $\mathcal{N}_{\mathbf{K}_h/\mathbf{K}_{h-1}}(a)$ and $\mathcal{N}_{\mathbf{K}_h/\mathbf{K}_{h-1}}(b)$, we find two algebraic integers μ and ν of $\mathcal{O}_{\mathbf{K}_{h-1}}$ fulfilling the equation:

$$\mu \mathcal{N}_{\mathbf{K}_h/\mathbf{K}_{h-1}}(a) - \nu \mathcal{N}_{\mathbf{K}_h/\mathbf{K}_{h-1}}(b) = 1. \tag{1}$$

But now remark that for any element $\alpha \in \mathcal{O}_{\mathbf{K}_h}$ we have, using the comatrix formula and the definition of the norm as a determinant that: $\mathcal{N}_{\mathbf{K}_h/\mathbf{K}_{h-1}}(\alpha) \in \alpha \mathcal{O}_{\mathbf{K}_h}$, so that $\alpha^{-1} \mathcal{N}_{\mathbf{K}_h/\mathbf{K}_{h-1}}(\alpha) \in \mathcal{O}_{\mathbf{K}_h}$. Then, from Eq. (1):

$$a \cdot \underbrace{\mu\, a^{-1} \mathcal{N}_{\mathbf{K}_h/\mathbf{K}_{h-1}}(a)}_{:=u \in \mathcal{O}_{\mathbf{K}_h}} - b \cdot \underbrace{\nu\, b^{-1} \mathcal{N}_{\mathbf{K}_h/\mathbf{K}_{h-1}}(b)}_{:=v \in \mathcal{O}_{\mathbf{K}_h}} = 1, \text{ as desired.}$$

Reduction of the size of solutions: The elements u, v found by the algorithm are not necessarily the smallest possible elements satisfying the Bézout equation. To avoid a blow-up in the size of the coefficients lifted, we do need to control the size of the solution at each step. Since the function **Size-Reduce** preserves the determinant by construction and reduces the norm of the coefficients, we can use it to reduce the bitsize of u, v to (roughly) the bitsize of a and b.

The translation of this method is given in Algorithm 3, **G-Euclide**. The number of bits needed to represent the relative norms does not depend on the subfield, and the size-reduction forces the output vector to have the same bitsize as the input one. This is the main idea of the *quasilinearity* of the **G-Euclide** algorithm. The algorithm needs $\mathcal{N}_{\mathbf{K}_h/\mathbf{Q}}(a)$ to be prime with $\mathcal{N}_{\mathbf{K}_h/\mathbf{Q}}(b)$. We assume that we can always find quickly such a, b with a short x. This will lead to Heuristic 1, and its validity is discussed in Sect. 5.4.

Remark 2. This algorithm is related to the one proposed in [38]. However, the claimed complexity of their algorithm is incorrect, as the size of the lifted solutions can not be controlled. This problem is resolved here by using the quasi-linear **Unit** rounding algorithm. More generally the unit rounding is in a LLL-type algorithm, at least theoretically, mandatory. In particular, a swap when the basis is not reduced with the definition in [21] may not lead to a reduction in potential so that the proof of [21, Theorem 3] is incorrect. We also point out that without a bound on the unit contributions, we have no polynomial bound on the number of bits used in their Algorithm 3. From a practical point of view, it does not seem to be a problem. If this is the case, our algorithm can be used every time we have a reasonable tower of number fields.

3.8 Wrapping-Up and Complexity

The lattice reduction algorithm is described in Algorithm 4. It is parametrized by two variables ε and α, which are related to the approximation factor of the

---

Algorithm 3: G-Euclide & Lift

---

1 **Function G-Euclide:**

    Input   : Tower of number fields $\mathbf{K}_h^\uparrow$, $a, b \in \mathbf{K}_h$ with coprime absolute norms $\mathcal{N}_{\mathbf{K}_h/\mathbf{Q}}(a)$ and $\mathcal{N}_{\mathbf{K}_h/\mathbf{Q}}(b)$.

    Output   : $u, v \in \mathbf{K}_h$, such that $au + bv = 1$

2   if $\mathbf{K}_h = \mathbf{Q}$ then return ExGcd(a, b)

3   $\mu, \nu \leftarrow$ G-Euclide$\left(\mathbf{K}_{h-1}^\uparrow, \mathcal{N}_{\mathbf{K}_h/\mathbf{K}_{h-1}}(a), \mathcal{N}_{\mathbf{K}_h/\mathbf{K}_{h-1}}(b)\right)$

4   $\mu', \nu' \leftarrow \mu\, a^{-1}\mathcal{N}_{\mathbf{K}_h/\mathbf{K}_{h-1}}(a), \nu\, b^{-1}\mathcal{N}_{\mathbf{K}_h/\mathbf{K}_{h-1}}(b)$

5   $W \leftarrow \begin{pmatrix} a & \nu' \\ b & \mu' \end{pmatrix}$

6   $V \leftarrow$ Size-Reduce(QR-decomposition(W))

7   **return** $W \cdot V[2]$

8 **Function Lift:**

    Input   : Tower of number fields $\mathbf{K}_h^\uparrow$, unimodular matrix $U' \in \mathcal{O}_{\mathbf{K}_{h-1}}^{2q_h}$

    Output   : Unimodular matrix $U \in \mathcal{O}_{\mathbf{K}_h}^{2 \times 2}$

9   $(a, b) \leftarrow$ Ascend$(\mathbf{K}_h, U[1])$

10   $(\mu, \nu) \leftarrow$ G-Euclide$\left(\mathbf{K}_{h-1}^\uparrow, a, b\right)$

11   $U \leftarrow \begin{pmatrix} a & \nu \\ b & \mu \end{pmatrix}$

12   **return** U

Algorithm 4: Reduce

    Input   : Tower of cyclotomic fields $\mathbf{K}_h^\uparrow$, Basis $M \in \mathcal{O}_{\mathbf{K}_h}^{d \times d}$ of the $\mathcal{O}_{\mathbf{K}_h}$−module $\mathcal{M}$

    Output   : A unimodular transformation $U \in \mathcal{O}_{\mathbf{K}_h}^{d \times d}$ representing a reduced basis of $\mathcal{M}$.

1 **if** $d = 2$ **and** $\mathbf{K}_h = \mathbf{Q}$ **then** **return** Schonhage(M)

2 **for** $i = 1$ **to** ρ **do**

3   $R \leftarrow$ QR-decomposition(M)

4   $U_i \leftarrow$ Size-Reduce(R)

5   $(M, R) \leftarrow (M, R) \cdot U_i$

6   **for** $j = 1 + (i \bmod 2)$ **to** d **by step of** 2 **do**

7   **if** $\mathcal{N}_{\mathbf{K}_h/\mathbf{Q}}(R_{j,j}) \leqslant 2^{2(1+\varepsilon)\alpha n_h^2}\mathcal{N}_{\mathbf{K}_h/\mathbf{Q}}(R_{j+1,j+1})$ **then**

8       $M' \leftarrow$ Descend$(\mathbf{K}_{h-1}^\uparrow, R[j : j+1, j : j+1])$

9       $U' \leftarrow$ Reduce$(\mathbf{K}_{h-1}^\uparrow, M')$

10       $(U_i, M) \leftarrow (U_i, M) \cdot$ Lift(U')

11   **end if**

12   **end for**

13 **end for**

14 **return** $\prod_{i=1}^{\rho} U_i$

---

reduction. The precise values of these constants depend on the conductor of the upper field. A more complete outline of the reduction is given in [23].

To express our complexity result, we introduce a mild heuristic, which claims that the size of the elements obtained after the **Lift** function is not too large.

Heuristic 1 (Size of lifting). *Denote by $R^{(i)}$ the R-part of the QR decomposition of the basis at the i-th step of the algorithm* **Reduce**. *For any $1 \leqslant i \leqslant \rho$ and any $1 \leqslant j \leqslant d$ where a call to* **Lift** *happened:*

$$\mathcal{N}_{\mathbf{K}_h/\mathbf{Q}}\left(R_{j,j}^{(i+1)}\right) \leqslant \min\left(2^{\alpha n_h^2}\sqrt{\mathcal{N}_{\mathbf{K}_h/\mathbf{Q}}\left(R_{j,j}^{(i)}R_{j+1,j+1}^{(i)}\right)}, \mathcal{N}_{\mathbf{K}_h/\mathbf{Q}}\left(R_{j,j}^{(i)}\right)\right).$$

A discussion on the validity of this heuristic is done in Sect. 5.4.

Claim 1. *Let f be a log-smooth integer. Under Heuristic 1, the complexity of Algorithm* **Reduce** *on rank 2-modules over $\mathbf{K} = \mathbf{Q}[x]/\Phi_f(x)$, represented as a matrix M whose number of bits in the input coefficients is uniformly bounded by $B > n$, is heuristically a $\widetilde{O}(n^2 B)$ with $n = \varphi(f)$. The first column of the reduced matrix has its coefficients uniformly bounded by $2^{\widetilde{O}(n)}(\text{vol } M)^{\frac{1}{2n}}$.*

A more technical analysis is given in [23] and we present here the basic steps. First, remark that the input matrix can always be reconditioned using **Unit** in time $\widetilde{O}(n^2 B)$ so that we might always suppose that its condition number is smaller than 2^B. We start by estimating the approximation factor of the reduction and deduce a bound in $O(d^2 \log p)$ on the number of rounds ρ required to achieve the reduction of the module $\mathcal{M}$, where p is the precision needed to handle the full computation. We then prove that the limiting factor for the precision has to be large enough to represent the shortest embedding of the norm of the Gram-Schmidt orthogonalization of the initial basis. After that, we devise a bound by looking at the sum of all the bit sizes used in the recursive calls and conclude on the complexity. The critical part of the proof is to use the potential to show that dividing the degrees by $\frac{d}{2}$ leads to a multiplication by a factor at most in $O(d^2)$ of the sum of all the precisions in the recursive calls, instead of the obvious $O(d^3 \log p)$. This discrepancy in the number of bits *actually needed* by the reduction compared with the obvious bound allows to reduce at sufficiently low precision to diminish the overall complexity.

4   Symplectic Reduction

Here we demonstrate how to generate additional structure which is compatible the tower of number fields and how to exploit it to speed-up the size-reduction procedure of our algorithm, at *every level* of the recursion. This additional structure is in substance a generalization of the so-called symplectic group to tower of fields, which gives additional symmetries to lattices. In a word, we design a size-reduction which is *compatible* with this symplectic group, in the sense that it allows to perform the computation with *only* the first part of the basis and get the rest of the reduction for free, using these symmetries.

This technique can be thought as an algebraic generalization of the work [11] of Gama, Howgrave-Graham and Nguyen on LLL-reduction for NTRU lattices. In particular, we demonstrate that such techniques can be used for all towers of number fields. Where [11] gains a factor 2 for the reduction of structured lattices over **Z**, we gain a factor 2 at each level of the recursive calls of the reduction, which combines into an overall polynomial factor improvement.

After introducing the symplectic group and Darboux bases, we show how to generalize these constructions to tower of fields. Then we show that this tower of symplectic groups is compatible with the descent we use to recurse (namely the descent of a symplectic lattice over a subfield has to remain symplectic). Eventually, we the show that we can replace the **size-reduce** sub-procedure by a tailored one for symplectic lattices.

4.1   On Symplectic Spaces and Symplectic Groups

We now briefly introduce the linear aspects of symplectic geometry and establish the parallel between the Euclidean and Symplectic spaces.

Definitions. A *symplectic space* is a finite dimensional vector space E endowed with an antisymmetric bilinear form $J : E \times E \to E$. We can define a natural orthogonality relation between vectors $x, y \in E$ as being $J(x, y) = 0$. The linear transformations of E letting the symplectic structure J invariant is a group, called the *J-symplectic group*(or symplectic group if the context makes J clear). This group plays a role similar to the *orthogonal group* for Euclidean spaces.

Darboux bases. Contrary to Euclidean spaces, a symplectic space does not possess an orthogonal basis, but instead a basis $e_1, \ldots, e_d, f_1, \ldots, f_d$, so that for any indices $i < j$ we have $J(e_i, e_j) = 0, J(f_i, f_j) = 0, J(e_i, f_j) = 0$ and $J(e_i, f_i) = -J(f_i, e_i) > 0$, called a Darboux base. It implies in particular that any symplectic space has even dimension. Recall that by Gram-Schmidt orthogonalization, we can transform any basis of a Euclidean space in an orthogonal basis. This construction can be adapted to the symplectic case, to construct a Darboux base iteratively.

Symplectic lattice, size reduction. Given a lattice Λ and a symplectic form J, we say that Λ is J-symplectic if the matrix representing Λ let invariant the form J (as a comparison, if J was an inner product form, a lattice Λ preserving J would be represented with an orthonormal basis).

As mentioned in Sect. 3.2, an important tool to reduce lattices is the *size-reduction* procedure, which can be viewed as a *discretization of the Gram-Schmidt orthogonalization*. It aims at reducing the bitsize and the condition number of the lattice basis. When dealing with symplectic lattices, we can also discretize the process to obtain a basis which can be seen as a *discretization of a Darboux basis*. Using this process instead of the classical size-reduction would retrieve the situation of [11].

As we generalized the lattice formalism to $\mathcal{O}_\mathbf{K}$-modules in number fields, we now generalize the notions of symplectic lattices to the algebraic context.

4.2 J-Symplectic Group and Compatibility with Extensions

In all the following, we fix an *arbitrary* tower of number fields

$$\mathbf{K}_h^\uparrow = (\mathbf{Q} = \mathbf{K}_0 \subset \mathbf{K}_1 \subset \cdots \subset \mathbf{K}_h).$$

For any $1 \leqslant i \leqslant h$ we denote by q_h the relative degree of $\mathbf{K}_h$ over $\mathbf{K}_{h-1}$. On any of these number fields, we can define a simple symplectic form, which derives from the determinant form.

Definition 2. *Let $\mathbf{K}$ be a field, and set J to be an antisymmetric bilinear form on $\mathbf{K}^2$. A matrix $M \in \mathbf{K}^{2\times 2}$ is said to be J-symplectic (or simply symplectic) if it lets the form J invariant, that is if $J \circ M = J$.*

Let us instantiate this definition in one of the fields of the tower $\mathbf{K}_h^\uparrow$ on the 2×2-determinant form. Let J_h be the antisymmetric bilinear form on $\mathbf{K}_h^2$ which is given as the determinant of 2×2 matrices in $\mathbf{K}_h$, i.e.

$$J_h\left(\begin{pmatrix} x_0 \\ x_1 \end{pmatrix}, \begin{pmatrix} y_0 \\ y_1 \end{pmatrix}\right) = x_0 y_1 - x_1 y_0.$$

Remark 3. In the presented case, M is J_h-symplectic iff $\det M = 1$. Hence, we can *always* scale a basis so that this condition is verified.

At this point we have introduced a symplectic structure on $\mathbf{K}_h$. But we want to have a symplectic structure at *every level* of the tower, so that we can use this structure at *every level* of the recursion when reducing a module. To do so, we need that the descent of a symplectic lattice over $\mathbf{K}_h$ is also a symplectic lattice over all of these subfields. Formally, this corresponds to finding a form compatible with the descent of a symplectic matrix to $\mathbf{K}_{h-1}$. Hence, we want to construct a form J_h' over $\mathbf{K}_{h-1}$, such that the following lemma is true.

Lemma 1. *Let M be a 2×2 matrix over $\mathbf{K}_h$ which is J_h-symplectic, then its descent $M' \in \mathbf{K}_{h-1}^{2q_h \times 2q_h}$ is J_h'-symplectic.*

To do so, we descend the form J_h to $\mathbf{K}_{h-1}$ by composition with a carefully constructed linear form $\mathbf{K}_h \to \mathbf{K}_{h-1}$. We then extend the definition of symplectism to $\mathbf{K}_{h-1}^{2q_h}$ by stating that a $2q_h \times 2q_h$ matrix M' is symplectic if it preserves the J_h' form, that is if $J_h' \circ M' = J_h'$.

But as the reduction is going, the current basis is subjected to transformations. In order to be able to continue to use the symmetries induced by the symplectism we need to ensure that the basis remains symplectic at *every moment* of the reduction. By induction, this boils down to show that every *elementary transformations* done by our algorithm **reduce** preserves the symplectic structure.

4.3 Module Transformations Compatible With J-Symplectism

We treat here the slightly simpler case of Kummer-like extensions, which is the case we implemented in our proof-of-concept, as it encompasses the cryptographic cases. The general case is covered in the full version of this paper [23].

Kummer-like extensions $K[X]/(X^{q_h} + a)$. We define R_{q_h} as the reverse diagonal of 1 in a square matrix of dimension q_h. We use the notation A^s as a shorthand for $R_{q_h} A^T R_{q_h}$, which corresponds to the reflection across the antidiagonal, that is exchanging the coefficients $A_{i,j}$ with A_{q_h+1-i,q_h+1-j}. We adapt here the work of Sawyer [40].

Suppose that the defining polynomial of $\mathbf{K}_h/\mathbf{K}_{h-1}$ is $X^{q_h} + a$. Recall that J_h is the 2×2-determinant form over $\mathbf{K}_h^2$. We can compose it by the linear form

$$
\left| \begin{array}{l} \mathbf{K}_h \cong \mathbf{K}_{h-1}[X]/(X^{q_h} + a) \longrightarrow \mathbf{K}_{h-1} \\ \qquad\qquad y \longmapsto \operatorname{tr}_{\mathbf{K}_h/\mathbf{K}_{h-1}}(\frac{Xy}{q_h a}) \end{array} \right. ,
$$

to obtain the matrix J_h', which becomes $J_h' = \begin{pmatrix} 0 & R_{q_h} \\ -R_{q_h} & 0 \end{pmatrix}$ in the power basis.

Lemma 2. *Fix a basis of the symplectic space where the matrix corresponding to J_h' is $\begin{pmatrix} 0 & R_{q_h} \\ -R_{q_h} & 0 \end{pmatrix}$. For any M a J_h'-symplectic matrix and its QR-decomposition, Q and R are both J_h'-symplectic.*

Proof. Direct from the explicit Iwasawa decomposition given by [40]. □

In the following, X^{-s} represents the matrix whose coefficients are the coefficients of X^{-1} exchanged over the antidiagonal.

Lemma 3 (Elementary J_h'-symplectic matrices).

- *For any $A \in GL(q_h, \mathbf{K}_h)$, $\begin{pmatrix} A & 0 \\ 0 & A^{-s} \end{pmatrix}$ is J_h'-symplectic.*

- *For any $A \in GL(2, \mathbf{K}_h)$ with $\det A = 1$ the block matrix $\begin{pmatrix} Id_{q_h-1} & 0 & 0 \\ 0 & A & 0 \\ 0 & 0 & Id_{q_h-1} \end{pmatrix}$ is J_h' symplectic.*

We now turn to the shape of triangular J_h' symplectic matrices.

Lemma 4. *Block triangular symplectic matrices are exactly the matrices of the form $\begin{pmatrix} A & AU \\ 0 & A^{-s} \end{pmatrix}$ where $U = U^s$.*

As we know the elementary operations that preserve the symplectism, we can use these transformations to effectively reduce a symplectic lattice.

Size-reduction of a J_h'-symplectic matrix. Consider M a J_h'-symplectic matrix, we want to *size-reduce* using the symmetries existing by symplecticity.

Let first take the R part of the QR-decomposition of M and make appear the factors A and U as in Lemma 4. Then, we can focus on the left-upper matrix A and size-reducing it into a matrix A'. All elementary operations performed are also symmetrically applied on A^s to obtain $(A')^s$. Eventually the size reduction is completed by dealing with the upper-right block, which is done by computing a global multiplication by

$$\begin{pmatrix} \mathrm{Id}_{q_h} & -\lfloor U \rceil \\ 0 & \mathrm{Id}_{q_h} \end{pmatrix}.$$

The corresponding algorithm is given in Algorithm 5. The recursive lattice reduction algorithm using the symplecticity is the same algorithm as Algorithm 4, where the size-reduction call of line 4 is replaced by **Symplectic-Size-Reduce**. The size reduction property on A' implies that both A' and A'^{-1} are small, and therefore it is easy to check that the same is true for the now reduced R' and of course for the corresponding size reduction of the matrix M itself.

Algorithm 5: Symplectic size reduce

Input	: R-factor of the QR decomposition of a J_h'-symplectic matrix $M \in \mathcal{O}_{\mathbf{K}_h}^{d \times d}$
Output	: A J_h'-symplectic unimodular transformation U representing the size-reduced basis obtained from M.

1 Set A, U such that $\begin{pmatrix} A & AU \\ 0 & A^{-s} \end{pmatrix} = R$

2 $V \leftarrow$ **Size-Reduce**(A)

3 **return** $\begin{pmatrix} V & -V\lfloor U \rceil \\ 0 & V^{-s} \end{pmatrix}$

This approach admits several algorithmic optimizations:

- Only the first half of the matrix R is actually needed to perform the computation since we can retrieve the other parts. Indeed, with the equation $QR = M$, R is upper triangular and it only depends on the first half of Q.
- We compute only the part above the antidiagonal of AU. This is actually enough to compute the part above the antidiagonal of $A^{-1}(AU)$, which is persymmetric.
- An interesting implication is that since we need to compute only half of the QR decomposition, we need (roughly) only half the precision.

Remark 4. To perform the fast size-reduction, we used the descended form J_h'. However, the **Reduce** algorithm will then call reduction of some rank 2 modules over $\mathbf{K}_{h-1}$. For the reduction of these modules, we will then use the form J_{h-1}, and its descent J_{h-1}' over the field $\mathbf{K}_{h-2}$ and so on.

4.4 Improved Complexity

We analyze the algorithm of Sect. 3 with the size-reduction of Sect. 4.3. By Lemma 3, we can use the transition matrix found after a reduction in the first half of the matrix to directly reduce the second half of the matrix. This means that in the symplectic reduction, we have recursive calls only for the first q_h steps of the tour at the toplevel of reduction. These are the only modifications to append to our algorithm. Remark that, during the entire algorithm, the R-part of the QR decomposition of the currently reduced basis remains symplectic.

To estimate the analysis we use an experimentally validated heuristic on the repartition of the potential during the reduction, which can be stated as follows:

Heuristic 2. *The half-potential $\Pi = \sum_{i=1}^{q_h}(q_h + 1 - i)\log \mathcal{N}_{\mathbf{L}/\mathbf{Q}}(R_{i,i})$ is, at the end of Reduce, always larger than the potential of an orthogonal matrix with the same volume.*

Remark 5. Heuristic 2 hinges on the fact that the sequence of $\mathcal{N}_{\mathbf{L}/\mathbf{Q}}(R_{i,i})$ is non-increasing, which is the case in practice for random lattices.

Claim 2. *Let f a power of $q = O(\log f)$ integer and $n = \varphi(f)$. Under Heuristic 1 and 2, the complexity for reducing a 2-dimensional matrix M over $\mathbf{L} = \mathbf{Q}[x]/\Phi_f(x)$ with condition number C is*

$$\tilde{O}\left(n^{2+\frac{\log(1/2+1/2q)}{\log q}}C\right) + n^{O(\log \log n)}.$$

Moreover, the first column of the reduced matrix has coefficients bounded by

$$2^{\tilde{O}(n)}\left|\mathcal{N}_{\mathbf{L}/\mathbf{Q}}(\det M)\right|^{\frac{1}{2n}}.$$

For $C = n^{\omega(1)}$ and $\varepsilon = \omega(1)$, we get a running time of $n^{2+\frac{\log(1/2+1/2q)}{\log q}+o(1)}C$.

Remark 6. This conjecture uses the condition number C instead of the classical bit length B of the matrix. In practice in cryptography, matrices are well-conditioned and we can take $C = B$. This is in particular the case of Coppersmith matrices. In the worst case, C can be as large as nB. Since the number of operations is smaller than $O(n^2 B)$, a single step of linear algebra is more costly than these operations. The condition number is a finer measure of the complexity in linear algebra [15,18] and we use Seysen algorithm [43] to compute the size-reduction more efficiently in [23].

5   Optimizations and Implementation

5.1   About the Implementation Used

The proof-of-concept program was written in the interpreted language Pari/gp [4]. It uses the native functions for multiplying field elements, which is not at all optimal, and even more so when we multiply matrices. Only the recursive calls were parallelized, and not the Gram-Schmidt orthogonalization nor the size reduction, which limits the speed-up we can achieve in this way. We used the Householder method for the QR decomposition. The symplectic optimization was used at each step and was not found to change the quality of the reduction. We now turn to two examples to showcase the efficiency of this program.

The algorithms given in Sect. 3 and Sect. 4 have been implemented and tested. Here, we give various optimizations and implementation choices, as well as an experimental assessment on the heuristics used in the complexity proofs.

5.2   On the Choice of the Base Case

Let $h > 0$ be a non-negative integer. The setting of the reduction is a tower of power-of-two cyclotomic fields $\mathbf{K}_h^\uparrow = (\mathbf{Q} = \mathbf{K}_0 \subset \mathbf{K}_1 \subset \cdots \subset \mathbf{K}_h = \mathbf{L})$.

Stopping the reduction before hitting Z. As stated before, the approximation factor increases quickly with the height of the tower. However, if we know how to perform a reduction over a number field above $\mathbf{Q}$, say $\mathbf{K}_1$ for instance, directly, then there is no need to reduce up to getting a $\mathbf{Z}$-module and we instead stop at this level. Actually, the largest the ring, the better the approximation factor becomes and the more efficient is the whole routine. It is well-known that it is possible to come up with a *direct* reduction algorithm for an algebraic lattice when the underlying ring of integer is *norm-Euclidean*, as first mentioned by Napias in [33]. The reduction algorithm over such a ring $\mathcal{O}_\mathbf{K}$ can be done exactly as for the classical LLL algorithm, by replacing the norm over $\mathbf{Q}$ by the algebraic norm over $\mathbf{K}$. Hence a natural choice would be $\mathbf{Z}[x]/(x^n + 1)$ with $n \leqslant 8$ as these rings are proved to be norm-Euclidean.

The ring $\mathbf{Z}[x]/(x^{16} + 1)$. However, it turns out that while $\mathbf{K} = \mathbf{Z}[x]/(x^{16} + 1)$ is not norm-Euclidean, we can still use this as our base case. As such, we need to slightly change the algorithm in case of failure of the standard algorithm. We denote by $\{x\}$, the fractional part of x. Given $a, b \in \mathbf{K}$ given by an embedding representation with complex numbers, we can compute $\sqrt{\{\mu\}}$ (computed coefficient-wise), with $\mu = a/b$. We can compute the *randomized* unit rounding of $\sqrt{\{\mu\}}$ using Theorem 1, which outputs a unit u such that $u^2\{\mu\}$ is rounded. We change the Lovász condition to

$$\mathcal{N}_{\mathbf{K}/\mathbf{Q}}(a - b(\lfloor \mu \rceil + \lfloor u\{\mu\} \rceil u^{-1})) < \mathcal{N}_{\mathbf{K}/\mathbf{Q}}(a)$$

which is now randomized and we restart up to a hundred times if it fails. This algorithm restarts on average 0.7 times and fails every 50000 times. On failure, one can, for example, use a more complicated approach; but as long as the number of bits is not gigantic, we can simply stop there since the other reductions around the two Gram-Schmidt norms will randomize everything and the algorithm can smoothly continue. The terms a, b tend to slowly accumulate a unit contribution when $n \geqslant 4$, and it is therefore needed to rebalance them using randomized rounding. For $n = 16$, this happens on average every 50 times.

Comparison between the base fields. We give in the Table 1 the properties of the various possible base cases between dimension 1 over $\mathbf{Q}$—that is $\mathbf{Q}$ itself— and 16, as described above.

Table 1. Lattice reduction with root factor α in dimension d over $\mathbf{Z}$ gives an element of Λ of norm around $\alpha^{d/2}\text{vol}\,(\Lambda)^{1/d}$. These numbers are given for random lattices.

Dimension	1	2	4	8	16
Root factor	1.031	1.036	1.037	1.049	1.11

Remark 7. We need the base case to be (relatively) fast in our implementation. To speed-up the reduction, even more, we followed the standard *divide-and-conquer* strategy: we first reduce the input matrix with half the precision, apply the transition matrix, and reduce the rest with about half the precision.

5.3 Decreasing the Approximation Factor

In several applications, it is interesting to decrease the approximation factor. To do so our technique is, at the lowest level of recursion, and when the precision is sufficiently low, to use a LLL-type algorithm. Each time the reduction is finished, we descend the matrix to a lower level where the approximation factor is lower. Since the basis is already reduced (over the upper field), it is in particular well-conditioned and the running-time of the this "over-reductions pass" is a fraction of the first reduction. In particular, in practice, we can recover the same approximation factor as the regular LLL algorithm (over $\mathbf{Z}$) for approximately the same cost as doing the reduction over the upper tower. Hence, for *practical applications*, we can consider that the defect of approximation factor induced by our algorithm to be inexistent compare to LLL.

Remark 8. This can be compared with some *experimental* strategies of the fplll [44] library where a first pass of reduction is performed at low precision and an over-pass is done right after to ensure the desired approximation factor.

5.4 Lifting a Reduction

One might expect that, as soon as the ideal generated by all the $\mathcal{N}_{\mathbf{L}/\mathbf{K}}(a_i)$ and $\mathcal{N}_{\mathbf{L}/\mathbf{K}}(b_i)$ is $\mathcal{O}_{\mathbf{K}}$, that for most of the small $x \in \mathcal{O}_{\mathbf{L}}$, we would have

$$\mathcal{N}_{\mathbf{L}/\mathbf{K}}(\langle a\,|\,x\rangle)\mathcal{O}_{\mathbf{K}} + \mathcal{N}_{\mathbf{L}/\mathbf{K}}(\langle b\,|\,x\rangle)\mathcal{O}_{\mathbf{K}} = \mathcal{O}_{\mathbf{K}}.$$

There is, however, a profusion of counterexamples to this and the algorithm often stumbles on them. This implies that the lift of a short vector can actually be quite large, depending on the norm of the ideal generated by the elements $\mathcal{N}_{\mathbf{L}/\mathbf{K}}(\langle a\,|\,x\rangle)$ and $\mathcal{N}_{\mathbf{L}/\mathbf{K}}(\langle b\,|\,x\rangle)$. A solution that practically works is to increase the number of short vectors we consider in the lifting phase: instead of lifting one vector, we lift multiple of them. As such, the lift step never causes problem when we are reducing a random lattice. In our experiments with random lattices, the average number of lifted vectors is around 1.5. To understand why the number of repetition is so low, we can model the coefficients of the lifted vector in the original basis as being random elements of $\mathcal{O_L}$[5]. As such, since we need our lifted vector to be primitive, we want its coefficients to be coprime. It is known[6] that the density of pairs of coprime algebraic integers is $1/\zeta_\mathbf{L}(2)$ where $\zeta_\mathbf{L}$ is the zeta function of the field $\mathbf{L}$. For fields in which the reduction is tractable, this value is indeed sufficiently big so that the number of required repetitions is very small.

When the lattice is not random, for example with a short planted element, it sometimes completely fails: at each round in the algorithm, the lift will return a long vector even if the recursive reduction found plenty of short ones. While this may not be a problem for some applications – finding a short vector in a NTRU lattice implies an ability to decrypt – it is an important one for others. Our proposed solution to this difficulty is to use a pseudo-basis instead of a basis. Indeed, it is a standard fact that the first element can be lifted into a unimodular pseudo-basis [7, Corollary 1.3.5]. From that result, we can control precisely the norm of the lifted pseudo-element. However, as pseudo-bases consist of vectors and ideals, the elementary operations on this representation require ideal arithmetic in $\mathcal{O_K}$. As such, we need to have a fast ideal arithmetic in these rings or the bottleneck of the reduction would become these operations. Getting faster arithmetic from the reduction process itself is however not straightforward.

6   Applications

6.1   Attacks on Multilinear Maps

In 2013, a construction for cryptographic multilinear maps was announced [13] by Garg, Gentry and Halevi with a heuristic security claim. An implementation of an optimization of the scheme was later published [3] by Albrecht et al.; however some of its uses, in particular involving an encoding of zero, were broken [19] by Hu and Jia. Subsequently, subfield attacks showed that the previous choice of parameters was unsafe [2,6,24], but these attacks were only asymptotical due to the extremely large dimension and length of the integers involved.

The improved scheme [3] gives encoding of the form $u_i = e_i/z \bmod q$ where $\|e_i\|$ is around $28eN^4\log(N)^{3/2}\sqrt{\pi\log(8N)}$ in the ring $\mathbf{Z}[x]/(x^N + 1)$ with N a power of two. The attack, attributed to Galbraith, consists in computing $u_1/u_2 = e_1/e_2$ and recovering short vectors in

$$\begin{pmatrix} q & u_1/u_2 \\ 0 & \mathrm{Id}_N \end{pmatrix}$$

which is manifestly solving a NTRU-like problem.

The present work revisits the results of the attacks presented in [24]: many instances can be broken even with a high approximation factor. A simple instance is with $N = 2^{16}$ and $q \approx 2^{6675}$, rated at the time at 56 bits of security [3, Table 1].

---

[5] For a distribution which cannot be quantified in closed form, however.
[6] As a generalization of the fact that the density of coprime integers is $1/\zeta(2)$.

We compute the norm of e_1/e_2 over $\mathbf{Z}[x]/(x^n+1)$ with $n = 2^{11}$ and solve the lattice problem over this smaller field. It took 13 core-days and 4 wall-time days to compute a solution. There are few running times of lattice reduction with high approximation factor on hard instances in the literature. It was reported in 2016 [2, Table 6] that the same problem with $n = 2^8$ and $q \approx 2^{240}$ takes 120 (single-threaded) hours with fplll [44]. As the complexity of their implementation is roughly proportional to $n^4 \log(q)^2$ we can estimate a running time of 40000 years, or 4000000 times slower than the algorithm presented in this work. This is the largest hard instance[7] of lattice reduction that we found in the literature.

6.2   Gentry-Szydlo Algorithm

The fast reduction procedure for cyclotomic ideals can be used to build a fast implementation of the Gentry-Szydlo algorithm [14]. This algorithm retrieves, in polynomial time, a generator of a principal ideal $f\mathcal{O}_\mathbf{K}$ given its relative norm $f\bar{f}$ in cyclotomic fields, or more generally in CM fields. This algorithm is a combination of algebraic manipulations of ideals in the field and lattice reduction.

On the Gentry-Szydlo algorithm. The Gentry-Szydlo algorithm [14] aims at solving the following problem, presented in its whole generality:

Problem 1 *(Principal ideal problem with known relative norm). Let $\mathbf{L}$ be a CM-field, of conjugation $x \mapsto \bar{x}$, and denote by $\mathbf{L}^+$ its maximal totally real subfield. Let $f \in \mathcal{O}_\mathbf{L}$ and set $\mathfrak{f} = f\mathcal{O}_\mathbf{L}$, the ideal spanned by this algebraic integer. Given the relative norm $\mathcal{N}_{\mathbf{L}/\mathbf{L}^+}(f) = f\bar{f}$ and a $\mathbf{Z}$-basis of the ideal $\mathfrak{f}$, retrieve the element f.*

It was proved by Lenstra and Silverberg that this problem can be solved in deterministic polynomial time [28]. Among the numerous applications of this algorithm, we shall highlight its use in cryptanalysis when some lattice-based scheme is leaking [2,10,14], for finding a generator of an ideal [5], and for solving geometric problems on ideals [13,22].

The idea of this process can be exposed as follows: from $\mathfrak{f}$ and $f\bar{f}$ we start by reducing the $\mathcal{O}_\mathbf{L}$-lattice $\frac{f\mathcal{O}_\mathbf{L}}{\sqrt{f\bar{f}}}$, of volume $\sqrt{|\Delta_\mathbf{L}|}$ and find an element of the shape fx where $x \in \mathcal{O}_\mathbf{L}$ and is small (say $\|x\| = 2^{\tilde{O}(n)}$). Now we have that:

$$\mathfrak{f} = \frac{f\bar{f}}{\overline{fx}} \cdot \bar{x}\mathcal{O}_\mathbf{L}.$$

As $x\bar{x} = \frac{fx\overline{fx}}{f\bar{f}}$, we have reduced the problem to the smaller instance $(\bar{x}\mathcal{O}_\mathbf{L}, x\bar{x})$.

For the sake of simplicity, we give here the outline of the remaining part of the algorithm for a cyclotomic field of conductor a power of two. The algorithm

---

[7] There are easy instances with a larger dimension, for example in [11]. They considered a NTRU instance with degree 317 and modulus 128, and reduced it in 519 s. The low modulus implies that we only have to reduce the middle dimension 90 matrix, which fplll [44] reduces in 0.2 s.

selects an integer e such that f^e mod r is known with a large r. Binary exponentiation with the above reduction computes a $x\mathcal{O}_{\mathbf{L}}$ with a short $x \in \mathcal{O}_{\mathbf{L}}$ and such that $f^e = Px$ with P known (and invertible) modulo r and q^k. Now we can deduce x mod r and since x is small, we know x.

The last step is to extract an e-th root modulo q^k. We choose q such that $q\mathcal{O}_{\mathbf{L}} = \mathfrak{q}\bar{\mathfrak{q}}$ which always exists in power of two cyclotomic fields since the group $(\mathbf{Z}/2n\mathbf{Z})^{\times}/\{-1,1\}$ is cyclic. Extracting e-th root modulo $\mathfrak{q}$ is easy, as e is smooth. There are $\gcd(e, q^{n/2} - 1)$ such roots, and we can choose q such that for each $p|e$ with p not a Fermat prime, $q^{n/2} \neq 1$ mod p. If we choose f mod $\mathfrak{q}$ as a root, then we know $\bar{f}$ mod $\bar{\mathfrak{q}}$, and we also know $f\bar{f}$ so we can deduce f mod $\bar{\mathfrak{q}}$. As a result, we know f mod q and Hensel lifting leads to f mod q^k. For k sufficiently large, we recover f.

We choose e to be the smallest multiple of $2n$, so that r, the product of primes p such that $2n|p-1|e$, is sufficiently large. One can show [22] that $\log e = O(\log n \log \log n)$ is enough and heuristically taking e as the product of n and a primorial reaches this bound.

Faster multiplication using lattice reduction. The bottleneck of the Gentry-Szydlo algorithm is to accelerate the ideal arithmetic. We represent ideals with a small family of elements over the order of a subfield $\mathcal{O}_{\mathbf{K}}$. One can represent the product of two ideals using the family of all products of generators. However, this leads to a blow-up in the size of the family. A reasonable approach is simply to sample a bit more than $[\mathbf{L}:\mathbf{K}]$ random elements in the product so that with overwhelming probability the ideal generated by these elements is the product ideal itself. It then suffices to reduce the corresponding module to go back to a representation with smaller generators.

An important piece is then the reduction of an ideal itself. Our practical approach is here to reduce a square matrix of dimension $[\mathbf{L}:\mathbf{K}]$, and every two rounds to add a new random element with a small Gram-Schmidt norm in the ideal at the last position. With these techniques, the overall complexity of the Gentry-Szydlo now becomes a $\tilde{O}(n^3)$.

In our experiment, we reduce up to 1.05^n (respectively 1.1^n) the first ideal to accelerate the powering with $n \leqslant 512$ (respectively $n = 1024$). The smallest e such that this approximation works at the end was chosen. The other reductions are done with an approximation factor of $2^{n/5}$ (respectively $2^{n/3}$) (Table 2).

Table 2. Implementation results

Dimension	e	Running time	Processor
256	15360	30 min	Intel i7-8650 (4 cores)
512	79872	4 h	Intel i7-8650 (4 cores)
1024	3194880	103 h	Intel E5-2650 (16 cores)

We emphasize that the implementation hardly used all cores: for example, the total running time over all cores in the last case was 354 h.

7 Conclusion

In this article, we presented two very efficient reduction algorithms for reducing lattices defined over the ring of integers of cyclotomic fields, which exploit the recursive structure of tower of their subfields. The first algorithm has a complexity close to the number of swaps $O(n^2 B)$ in LLL and the second one exploits the symplectic symmetries naturally present in such towers and goes even below this bound. One caveat of them is that their approximation factors are worse than the classical LLL approximation factor. However, such algorithms are nonetheless useful for various applications, such as breaking graded encoding schemes or manipulating ideals, as in the Gentry-Szydlo algorithm. We implemented all our algorithms and their observed performances are close to the complexities that we estimate under some assumptions. In particular, our implementation reduces to large base cases, that is all power of two cyclotomic fields of dimension $\leqslant 16$.

Our claims rely on some heuristics we introduce to justify their validity. It would be nice to provide a rigorous complexity analysis in a relevant computational model. It is possible to completely remove Heuristic 1 by using the pseudo-basis representation of modules over Dedekind rings. We also leave as future work the question of programming the algorithms in a more efficient language and to empirically compare our claimed complexities with the experimental ones.

Acknowledgment. We would like to thank Bill Allombert for his help in the parallelization of the program and Léo Ducas and Damien Stehlé for interesting discussions. Part of this work was done while the authors were visiting the Simons Institute for the Theory of Computing in February 2020. This work is supported by the European Union H2020 program under grant agreements ERC-669891 and PROMETHEUS PROJECT-780701.

References

1. Ajtai, M.: Generating hard instances of lattice problems (extended abstract). In: 28th STOC, pp. 99–108. ACM, May 1996
2. Albrecht, M., Bai, S., Ducas, L.: A subfield lattice attack on overstretched NTRU assumptions - cryptanalysis of some FHE and graded encoding schemes. In: Robshaw, M., Katz, J. (eds.) CRYPTO 2016, Part I. LNCS, vol. 9814, pp. 153–178. Springer, Heidelberg (2016). https://doi.org/10.1007/978-3-662-53018-4_6
3. Albrecht, M.R., Cocis, C., Laguillaumie, F., Langlois, A.: Implementing candidate graded encoding schemes from ideal lattices. In: Iwata, T., Cheon, J.H. (eds.) ASIACRYPT 2015, Part II. LNCS, vol. 9453, pp. 752–775. Springer, Heidelberg (2015). https://doi.org/10.1007/978-3-662-48800-3_31
4. Batut, C., Belabas, K., Bernardi, D., Cohen, H., Olivier, M.: PARI-GP (1998). ftp://megrez.math.u-bordeaux.fr/pub/pari
5. Biasse, J.-F., Espitau, T., Fouque, P.-A., Gélin, A., Kirchner, P.: Computing generator in cyclotomic integer rings - a subfield algorithm for the principal ideal problem in $L_{|\Delta_{\mathbb{K}}|}(\frac{1}{2})$ and application to the cryptanalysis of a FHE scheme. In: Coron, J.-S., Nielsen, J.B. (eds.) EUROCRYPT 2017, Part I. LNCS, vol. 10210, pp. 60–88. Springer, Cham (2017). https://doi.org/10.1007/978-3-319-56620-7_3

6. Cheon, J.H., Jeong, J., Lee, C.: An algorithm for NTRU-problems, cryptanalysis of the GGH multilinear map without an encoding of zero. In: ANTS (2016)
7. Cohen, H.: Advanced topics in Computational Number Theory, vol. 193. Springer, Heidelberg (2012)
8. Coppersmith, D.: Small solutions to polynomial equations, and low exponent RSA vulnerabilities. J. Cryptol. **10**(4), 233–260 (1997). https://doi.org/10.1007/s001459900030
9. Cramer, R., Ducas, L., Peikert, C., Regev, O.: Recovering short generators of principal ideals in cyclotomic rings. In: Fischlin, M., Coron, J.-S. (eds.) EUROCRYPT 2016, Part II. LNCS, vol. 9666, pp. 559–585. Springer, Heidelberg (2016). https://doi.org/10.1007/978-3-662-49896-5_20
10. Espitau, T., Fouque, P.-A., Gérard, B., Tibouchi, M.: Side-channel attacks on BLISS lattice-based signatures: exploiting branch tracing against strongSwan and electromagnetic emanations in microcontrollers. In: Thuraisingham, B.M., Evans, D., Malkin, T., Xu, D. (eds.) CCS 2017, pp. 1857–1874. ACM (2017)
11. Gama, N., Howgrave-Graham, N., Nguyen, P.Q.: Symplectic lattice reduction and NTRU. In: Vaudenay, S. (ed.) EUROCRYPT 2006. LNCS, vol. 4004, pp. 233–253. Springer, Heidelberg (2006). https://doi.org/10.1007/11761679_15
12. Gama, N., Nguyen, P.Q.: Finding short lattice vectors within Mordell's inequality. In: Ladner, R.E., Dwork, C. (eds.) 40th STOC, pp. 207–216. ACM (2008)
13. Garg, S., Gentry, C., Halevi, S.: Candidate multilinear maps from ideal lattices. In: Johansson, T., Nguyen, P.Q. (eds.) EUROCRYPT 2013. LNCS, vol. 7881, pp. 1–17. Springer, Heidelberg (2013). https://doi.org/10.1007/978-3-642-38348-9_1
14. Gentry, C., Szydlo, M.: Cryptanalysis of the revised NTRU signature scheme. In: Knudsen, L.R. (ed.) EUROCRYPT 2002. LNCS, vol. 2332, pp. 299–320. Springer, Heidelberg (2002). https://doi.org/10.1007/3-540-46035-7_20
15. Golub, G.H., Van Loan, C.F.: Matrix Computations, 3rd edn. The Johns Hopkins University Press, Baltimore (1996)
16. Hanrot, G., Pujol, X., Stehlé, D.: Analyzing blockwise lattice algorithms using dynamical systems. In: Rogaway, P. (ed.) CRYPTO 2011. LNCS, vol. 6841, pp. 447–464. Springer, Heidelberg (2011). https://doi.org/10.1007/978-3-642-22792-9_25
17. Heckler, C., Thiele, L.: Complexity analysis of a parallel lattice basis reduction algorithm. SIAM J. Comput. **27**(5), 1295–1302 (1998)
18. Higham, N.J.: Accuracy and Stability of Numerical Algorithms. SIAM, Philadelphia (2002)
19. Hu, Y., Jia, H.: Cryptanalysis of GGH map. In: Fischlin, M., Coron, J.-S. (eds.) EUROCRYPT 2016, Part I. LNCS, vol. 9665, pp. 537–565. Springer, Heidelberg (2016). https://doi.org/10.1007/978-3-662-49890-3_21
20. Kannan, R.: Improved algorithms for integer programming and related lattice problems. In: Johnson, D.S., et al. (eds.) Symposium on Theory of Computing, pp. 193–206. ACM (1983)
21. Kim, T., Lee, C.: Lattice reductions over Euclidean rings with applications to cryptanalysis. In: O'Neill, M. (ed.) IMACC 2017. LNCS, vol. 10655, pp. 371–391. Springer, Cham (2017). https://doi.org/10.1007/978-3-319-71045-7_19
22. Kirchner, P.: Algorithms on ideal over complex multiplication order. Cryptology ePrint Archive, Report 2016/220 (2016)
23. Kirchner, P., Espitau, T., Fouque, P.-A.: Algebraic and euclidean lattices: optimal lattice reduction and beyond. Cryptology ePrint Archive, Report 2019/1436 (2019)

24. Kirchner, P., Fouque, P.-A.: Revisiting lattice attacks on overstretched NTRU parameters. In: Coron, J.-S., Nielsen, J.B. (eds.) EUROCRYPT 2017, Part I. LNCS, vol. 10210, pp. 3–26. Springer, Cham (2017). https://doi.org/10.1007/978-3-319-56620-7_1

25. Langlois, A., Stehlé, D.: Worst-case to average-case reductions for module lattices. Des. Codes Crypt. **75**(3), 565–599 (2014). https://doi.org/10.1007/s10623-014-9938-4

26. Lee, C., Pellet-Mary, A., Stehlé, D., Wallet, A.: An LLL algorithm for module lattices. In: Galbraith, S.D., Moriai, S. (eds.) ASIACRYPT 2019, Part II. LNCS, vol. 11922, pp. 59–90. Springer, Cham (2019). https://doi.org/10.1007/978-3-030-34621-8_3

27. Lenstra, A.K., Lenstra, H.W.J., Lovász, L.: Factoring polynomials with rational coefficients. Math. Ann. **261**, 515–534 (1982)

28. Lenstra, H.W.J., Silverberg, A.: Testing isomorphism of lattices over CM-orders. SIAM J. Comput. **48**(4), 1300–1334 (2019)

29. Lyubashevsky, V., Peikert, C., Regev, O.: On ideal lattices and learning with errors over rings. In: Gilbert, H. (ed.) EUROCRYPT 2010. LNCS, vol. 6110, pp. 1–23. Springer, Heidelberg (2010). https://doi.org/10.1007/978-3-642-13190-5_1

30. Mehlhorn, K., Sanders, P.: Algorithms and Data Structures: The Basic Toolbox. Springer, Heidelberg (2008). https://doi.org/10.1007/978-3-540-77978-0

31. Micciancio, D., Walter, M.: Practical, predictable lattice basis reduction. In: Fischlin, M., Coron, J.-S. (eds.) EUROCRYPT 2016, Part I. LNCS, vol. 9665, pp. 820–849. Springer, Heidelberg (2016). https://doi.org/10.1007/978-3-662-49890-3_31

32. Mukherjee, T., Stephens-Davidowitz, N.: Lattice reduction for modules, or how to reduce Module-SVP to Module-SVP. Cryptology ePrint Archive, Report 2019/1142 (2019). Accepted to Crypto 2020

33. Napias, H.: A generalization of the LLL-algorithm over Euclidean rings or orders. J. théorie nombres Bordeaux **8**(2), 387–396 (1996)

34. Neukirch, J.: Algebraic Number Theory. Springer, Heidelberg (1988)

35. Neumaier, A., Stehlé, D.: Faster LLL-type reduction of lattice bases, In: International Symposium on Symbolic and Algebraic Computation, ISSAC, pp. 373–380. ACM (2016)

36. Nguên, P.Q., Stehlé, D.: Floating-point LLL revisited. In: Cramer, R. (ed.) EUROCRYPT 2005. LNCS, vol. 3494, pp. 215–233. Springer, Heidelberg (2005). https://doi.org/10.1007/11426639_13

37. Novocin, A., Stehlé, D., Villard, G.: An LLL-reduction algorithm with quasi-linear time complexity: extended abstract. In: Fortnow, L., Vadhan, S.P. (eds.) 43rd STOC, pp. 403–412. ACM Press, June 2011

38. Pornin, T., Prest, T.: More efficient algorithms for the NTRU key generation using the field norm. In: Lin, D., Sako, K. (eds.) PKC 2019, Part II. LNCS, vol. 11443, pp. 504–533. Springer, Cham (2019). https://doi.org/10.1007/978-3-030-17259-6_17

39. Regev, O.: On lattices, learning with errors, random linear codes, and cryptography. In: Gabow, H.N., Fagin, R. (eds.) 37th STOC, pp. 84–93. ACM Press (2005)

40. Sawyer, P.: Computing Iwasawa decomposition of classical Lie groups of noncompact type using QR-decomposition. Linear Algebra Appl. **493**, 573–579 (2016)

41. Schnorr, C., Euchner, M.: Lattice basis reduction: improved practical algorithms and solving subset sum problems. Math. Program. **66**, 181–199 (1994). https://doi.org/10.1007/BF01581144

42. Schönhage, A.: Fast reduction and composition of binary quadratic forms. In: International Symposium on Symbolic and Algebraic Computation, ISSAC 1991, pp. 128–133. ACM (1991)
43. Seysen, M.: Simultaneous reduction of a lattice basis its reciprocal basis. Combinatorica **13**(3), 363–376 (1993)
44. The FPLLL development team FPLLL, a lattice reduction library (2016). https://github.com/fplll/fplll
45. Villard, G.: Parallel lattice basis reduction. In: International Symposium on Symbolic and Algebraic Computation, ISSAC 1992, pp. 269–277. ACM (1992)

Faster Enumeration-Based Lattice Reduction: Root Hermite Factor $k^{1/(2k)}$ Time $k^{k/8+o(k)}$

Martin R. Albrecht[1]([✉]), Shi Bai[2]([✉]), Pierre-Alain Fouque[3]([✉]),
Paul Kirchner[3]([✉]), Damien Stehlé[4,5]([✉]), and Weiqiang Wen[3]([✉])

[1] Information Security Group, Royal Holloway, University of London,
Egham, England
martin.albrecht@royalholloway.ac.uk
[2] Department of Mathematical Sciences, Florida Atlantic University,
Boca Raton, USA
shih.bai@gmail.com, sbai@fau.edu
[3] Univ. Rennes, CNRS, IRISA, Rennes, France
pa.fouque@gmail.com, paul.kirchner@irisa.fr, weiqiang.a.wen@inria.fr
[4] Univ. Lyon, EnsL, UCBL, CNRS, Inria, LIP, 69342 Lyon Cedex 07, France
damien.stehle@gmail.com
[5] Institut Universitaire de France, Paris, France

Abstract. We give a lattice reduction algorithm that achieves root Hermite factor $k^{1/(2k)}$ in time $k^{k/8+o(k)}$ and polynomial memory. This improves on the previously best known enumeration-based algorithms which achieve the same quality, but in time $k^{k/(2e)+o(k)}$. A cost of $k^{k/8+o(k)}$ was previously mentioned as potentially achievable (Hanrot-Stehlé'10) or as a heuristic lower bound (Nguyen'10) for enumeration algorithms. We prove the complexity and quality of our algorithm under a heuristic assumption and provide empirical evidence from simulation and implementation experiments attesting to its performance for practical and cryptographic parameter sizes. Our work also suggests potential avenues for achieving costs below $k^{k/8+o(k)}$ for the same root Hermite factor, based on the geometry of SDBKZ-reduced bases.

1 Introduction

The cost of (strong) lattice reduction has received renewed attention in recent years due to its relevance in cryptography. Indeed, lattice-based constructions are presumed to achieve security against quantum adversaries and enable powerful functionalities such as computation on encrypted data. Concrete parameters for such schemes are derived from the difficulty of finding relatively short non-zero vectors in a lattice: the parameters are chosen based on extrapolations of the cost of the BKZ algorithm [SE94] and its variants [CN11, AWHT16, MW16].

This work was supported in part by EPSRC grants EP/S020330/1, EP/S0-2087X/1, by European Union Horizon 2020 Research and Innovation Program Grant 780701, by Innovate UK grant AQuaSec, by BPI-France in the context of the national project RISQ (P141580), and by NIST grants 60NANB18D216/60NANB18D217 as well as NATO SPS Project G5448. Part of this work was done while Martin Albrecht and Damien Stehlé were visiting the Simons Institute for the Theory of Computing.

© International Association for Cryptologic Research 2020
D. Micciancio and T. Ristenpart (Eds.): CRYPTO 2020, LNCS 12171, pp. 186–212, 2020.
https://doi.org/10.1007/978-3-030-56880-1_7

These algorithms make repeated calls to an oracle that solves the Shortest Vector Problem (SVP), i.e. that finds a shortest non-zero vector in any lattice. Concretely, BKZ with block size k finds relatively short vectors in lattices of dimensions $n \geq k$ using a k-dimensional SVP solver. The cost of this SVP solver is the dominating component of the cost of BKZ and its variants.

The SVP solver can be instantiated with enumeration-based algorithms, whose asymptotically most efficient variant is Kannan's algorithm [Kan83]. It has a worst-case complexity of $k^{k/(2\,e)+o(k)}$, where k is the dimension of the lattice under consideration [HS07]. This bound is sharp, up to the $o(k)$ term in the exponent [HS08]. If called on an n-dimensional lattice, then BKZ with block size k outputs a vector of norm $\approx \left(k^{1/(2k)}\right)^n \cdot \mathrm{Vol}(\mathcal{L})^{1/n}$ in time $\approx k^{k/(2\,e)}$, when n is sufficiently large compared to k. The $k^{1/(2k)}$ term is called the root Hermite factor and quantifies the strength of BKZ. The trade-off between root Hermite factor and running-time achieved by BKZ has remained the best known for enumeration-based SVP solvers since the seminal work of Schnorr and Euchner almost 30 years ago. (The analysis of Kannan's algorithm and hence BKZ was improved in [HS07], but not the algorithm itself.) Other algorithms, such as [GN08a, MW16, ALNS19], achieve the same asymptotic trade-off with milder conditions on n/k.

We note that while lattice reduction libraries, such as FPLLL [dt19a], the Progressive BKZ Library (PBKZ) [AWHT18] and NTL [Sho18], implement BKZ with an enumeration-based SVP solver, they do not rely on Kannan's algorithm: NTL implements enumeration with LLL preprocessing; FPLLL and PBKZ implement enumeration with stronger preprocessing (typically BKZ with a smaller block size) but not with sufficiently strong preprocessing to satisfy the conditions of [Kan83, HS07]. Hence, the running-times of these implementations is not established by the theorems in these works.

It has been suggested that the running-time achieved by BKZ for the same output quality might potentially be improved. In [HS10], it was argued that the same root Hermite factor would be achieved by BKZ in time $\approx k^{k/8}$ if the Gram–Schmidt norms of so-called HKZ-reduced bases were decreasing geometrically. In [Ngu10], the same quantity was suggested as a cost lower bound for enumeration-based lattice reduction algorithms. On this basis, several works have speculatively assumed this cost [ANS18, ACD+18]. However, so far, no lattice reduction algorithm achieving root Hermite factor $k^{1/(2k)}$ in time $\approx k^{k/8}$ was known.

Contributions. Our main contribution is an enumeration-based lattice reduction algorithm that runs in time $k^{k/8}$ and achieves root Hermite factor $k^{\frac{1}{2k}(1+o(1))}$, where k is a cost parameter akin to the "block size" of the BKZ algorithm (the notion of "block size" for our algorithm is less straightforward, see below). It uses polynomial memory and can be quantumly accelerated to time $k^{k/16}$ using [ANS18]. Our analysis relies on a strengthened version of the Gaussian Heuristic.

To estimate the cost of lattice reduction algorithms, the literature typically relies on concrete experiments and simulations that extrapolate them (see, e.g. [CN11, Che13, MW16, BSW18]). Indeed, the data given in [Che13] is very broadly appealed to. However, this data only covers up to block size of 250 (below cryptographically relevant block sizes) and no source code is available. As an intermediate contribution, we reproduce and extend the data in [Che13] using publicly available tools such as [dt19a, dt19b] (see Sect. 2.5). Using this extended dataset, we then argue that BKZ as implemented in public lattice reduction libraries has running-time closely matching $k^{k/(2\,e)}$ (Fig. 2). Our cost improvement hence required a different algorithm and not just an improved analysis of the state-of-the-art.

In Sect. 4 we propose a variant of our improved lattice reduction algorithm that works well in practice. We run simulations and conduct concrete experiments to verify its efficiency, while we leave as a future work to formally analyse it. The simulations suggest that it achieves root Hermite factors $\approx k^{\frac{1}{2k}}$ in time $k^{k/8}$, at least up to $k \approx 1,000$ (which covers cryptographic parameters). Our implementation of this algorithm beats FPLLL's SVP enumeration from dimension ≈ 100 onward. We consider the difference between these two variants as similar to the difference between Kannan's algorithm and what is routinely implemented in practice such as in FPLLL and PBKZ. We will refer to the former as the "asymptotic variant" and the latter as the "practical variant". Since our results rely on empirical evidence and simulations, we provide the source code used to produce our figures and the data being plotted as an attachment to the electronic version of the full version of this work.

Key idea. Our new algorithms decouple the preprocessing context from the enumeration context: they preprocess a projected sublattice of larger dimension than they aim to enumerate over (as a result, the notion of "block size" is less obvious than in prior works). More concretely, assume that the basis of the preprocessed projected sublattice is SDBKZ-reduced. Then, as shown in [MW16] under the Gaussian Heuristic, the first Gram–Schmidt norms $\|\boldsymbol{b}_i^*\|$ satisfy Schnorr's Geometric Series Assumption (GSA) [Sch03]: $\|\boldsymbol{b}_i^*\|/\|\boldsymbol{b}_{i+1}^*\| \approx r$ for some common r, for all i's corresponding to the start of the basis. On that "GSA part" of the lattice basis, the enumeration runs faster than on a typical preprocessed BKZ block of the same dimension. To achieve SDBKZ-reducedness at a low cost, our algorithms call themselves recursively.

As a side contribution, we show in the full version of this work that the bases output by BKZ do not satisfy the GSA (under the Gaussian Heuristic), contrarily to a common belief (see e.g. [YD17, ANS18, BSW18]). This is why we use SDBKZ in the asymptotic algorithm. Nevertheless, for handlable dimensions, BKZ seems to deviate only slightly from the GSA and as it is a little simpler to implement than SDBKZ, it seems to remain preferable in practice. This is why we use BKZ as preprocessing in the practical algorithm.

To illustrate the idea of our new algorithms, we consider a BKZ-reduced (resp. SDBKZ-reduced) basis with block size k, in a lattice of dimension $n = \lceil (1 + c) \cdot k \rfloor$ for various k and c. We choose $n \geq k$ to demonstrate the impact of the GSA region on the enumeration cost. We then estimate the enumeration cost (without pruning) for re-checking that the first basis vector is a shortest non-zero vector in the very first block of size k. For the implementation of this simulation, see simu_c_cost.py, attached to the electronic version of the full version of this work. We consider c for $c = 0$ to 1 with a step size of 0.01. For each c, we take k from $k = 100$ to 50,000 with a step size of 10. Then for each fixed c, we fit the coefficients a_0, a_1, a_2 of $a_0\, k \log k + a_1\, k + a_2$ over all k on the enumeration cost of the first block of size k. The result is plotted in Fig. 1. The x-axis denotes the value of c and the y-axis denotes the interpolated constant in front of the $k \log k$ term.

Let us make several remarks about Fig. 1. First, we stress that all leading constants in Fig. 1 are hypothetical (they do not correspond to efficient algorithms) as they assume an already (SD)BKZ-reduced basis with block size k, i.e. this ignores the preprocessing cost. With that in mind, for $c = 0$, the simulations show the interpolated constant for both BKZ and SDBKZ is close to $1/(2\,e)$, which corresponds to [HS07]. For $c = 1$, the interpolated constant is close to 1/8. This illustrates the impact of enumeration in the GSA region (corresponding to Theorem 1). As noted above, in the following section we will describe an algorithm that achieve the corresponding cost of $k^{k/8(1+o(1))}$. It is worth noting that for certain c around 0.3, the a_0 of the re-examination cost can be below 0.125. We stress that we do not know how to construct an algorithm that achieves a cost of $k^{a_0 \cdot k(1+o(1))}$ with $a_0 < 0.125$. However, our practical variant of the algorithm seems to achieve cost $k^{0.125 \cdot k}$ using the region corresponding to those $c \approx 0.3$.

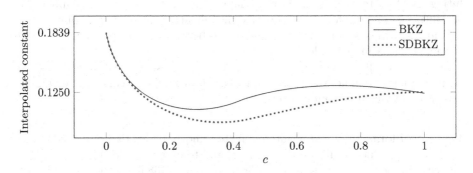

Fig. 1. Interpolated dominating constant a_0 on $k \log k$.

Discussion. At first sight, the endeavour in this work might appear pointless since lattice sieving algorithms asymptotically outperform lattice enumeration. Indeed, the fastest SVP solver currently known [BDGL16] has a cost of $2^{0.292\,n+o(n)}$, where n is the lattice dimension.[1] Furthermore, a sieving implementation [ADH+19] now dominates the Darmstadt SVP Challenge's Hall of Fame, indicating that the crossover between enumeration and sieving is well below

---

[1] When using this algorithm as the SVP subroutine in BKZ, we thus obtain a running time of $2^{0.292\,k+o(k)}$ for root Hermite factor $k^{1/(2k)}$.

cryptographic parameter sizes. However, the study of enumeration algorithms is still relevant to cryptography.

Sieving algorithms have a memory cost that grows exponentially with the lattice dimension n. For dimensions that are currently handlable, the space requirement remains moderate. The impact of this memory cost is unclear for cryptographically relevant dimensions. For instance, it has yet to be established how well sieving algorithms parallelise in non-uniform memory access architectures. Especially, the exponential memory requirement might present a serious obstacle in some scenarios. In contrast, the memory cost of enumeration grows as a small polynomial in the dimension.

Comparing sieving and enumeration for cryptographically relevant dimensions becomes even more complex in the context of quantum computations. Quantum computations asymptotically enable a quadratic speed-up for enumeration, and much less for sieving [Laa15, Sec. 14.2.10] even assuming free quantum-accessible RAM, which would a priori favour enumeration. However, deciding on how to compare parallelisable classical operations with strictly sequential Grover iterations is unclear and establishing the significant lower-order terms in the quantum costs of these algorithms is an ongoing research programme (see e.g. [AGPS19]).

Further, recent advances in sieving algorithms [LM18, Duc18, ADH+19] apply lessons learned from enumeration algorithms to the sieving context: while sieving algorithms are fairly oblivious to the Gram–Schmidt norms of the basis at hand, the cost of enumeration algorithms critically depend on their limited decrease. Current sieving strategies employ a simple form of enumeration (Babai's lifting [Bab86]) to exploit the lattice shape by sieving in a projected sublattice and lifting candidates for short vectors to the full lattice. Here, more sophisticated hybrid algorithms permitting flexible trade-offs between memory consumption and running time seem plausible.

Finally, as illustrated in Fig. 1, our work suggests potential avenues for designing faster enumeration algorithms based on further techniques relying on the graph of Gram–Schmidt norms.

Open problems. It would be interesting to remove the heuristics utilised in our analysis to produce a fully proved variant, and to extend the technique to other lattice reduction algorithms such as slide reduction [GN08a]. Further, establishing lower bounds on the root Hermite factor achievable in time $k^{k/8+o(k)}$ for a given dimension of the lattice is an interesting open problem suggested by this work.

2   Preliminaries

Matrices are denoted in bold uppercase and vectors are denoted in bold lowercase. By $B_{[i:j)}$ we refer to the submatrix spanned by the columns $b_i, \ldots, b_{j-1}$ of B. We let matrix indices start with index 0. We let $\pi_i(\cdot)$ denote the orthogonal projection onto the linear subspace $(b_0, \ldots, b_{i-1})^{\perp}$ (this depends on a matrix B that will always being clear from context). We let $v_n = \frac{\pi^{n/2}}{\Gamma(1+n/2)} \approx \frac{1}{\sqrt{n\pi}}\left(\frac{2\pi e}{n}\right)^{n/2}$

denote the volume of the n-dimensional unit ball. We let the logarithm to base 2 be denoted by log and the natural logarithm be denoted by ln.

Below, we may refer to the cost or enumeration parameter k of our algorithms as a "block size".

2.1 Lattices

Let $B \in \mathbb{Q}^{m \times n}$ be a full column rank matrix. The lattice $\mathcal{L}$ generated by B is $\mathcal{L}(B) = \{B \cdot x \mid x \in \mathbb{Z}^n\}$ and the matrix B is called a basis of $\mathcal{L}(B)$. As soon as $n \geq 2$, any given lattice $\mathcal{L}$ admits infinitely many bases, and full column rank matrices $B, B' \in \mathbb{Q}^{m \times n}$ span the same lattice if and only if there exists $U \in \mathbb{Z}^{n \times n}$ such that $B' = B' \cdot U$ and $|\det(U)| = 1$. The Euclidean norm of a shortest non-zero vector in $\mathcal{L}$ is denoted by $\lambda_1(\mathcal{L})$ and called the minimum of $\mathcal{L}$. The task of finding a shortest non-zero vector of $\mathcal{L}$ from an arbitrary basis of $\mathcal{L}$ is called the Shortest Vector Problem (SVP).

We let $B^* = (b_0^*, \ldots, b_{n-1}^*)$ denote the Gram–Schmidt orthogonalisation of B where $b_i^* = \pi_i(b_i)$. We write $\rho_{[a:b)}$ for the slope of the $\log \|b_i^*\|$'s with $i = a, \ldots, b - 1$, under a mean-squared linear interpolation. We let $\pi_i(B_{[i:j)})$ denote the local block $(\pi_i(b_i), \ldots, \pi_i(b_{j-1}))$ and let $\pi_i(\mathcal{L}_{[i:j)})$ denote the lattice generated by $\pi_i(B_{[i:j)})$. We will also write $\pi(\mathcal{L})$ if the index i and $\mathcal{L}$ are clear from the context. The volume of a lattice $\mathcal{L}$ with basis B is defined as $\mathrm{Vol}(\mathcal{L}) = \prod_{i<n} \|b_i^*\|$; it does not depend on the choice of basis of $\mathcal{L}$. Minkowski's convex body theorem states that $\lambda_1(\mathcal{L}) \leq 2 \cdot v_n^{-1/n} \cdot \mathrm{Vol}(\mathcal{L})^{1/n}$. We define the root Hermite factor of a basis B of a lattice $\mathcal{L}$ as $\mathrm{rhf}(B) = (\|b_0\|/\mathrm{Vol}(\mathcal{L})^{1/n})^{1/(n-1)}$. The normalization by the $(n-1)$-th root is justified by the fact that the lattice reduction algorithms we consider in this work achieve root Hermite factors that are bounded independently of the lattice dimension n. Given as input an arbitrary basis of $\mathcal{L}$, the task of finding a non-zero vector of $\mathcal{L}$ of norm $\leq \gamma \cdot \mathrm{Vol}(\mathcal{L})^{1/n}$ is called Hermite-SVP with parameter γ (γ-HSVP).

Lattice reduction algorithms and their analyses often rely on heuristic assumptions. Let $\mathcal{L}$ be an n-dimensional lattice and $\mathcal{S}$ a measurable set in the real span of $\mathcal{L}$. The *Gaussian Heuristic* states that the number of lattice points in $\mathcal{S}$ is $|\mathcal{L} \cap \mathcal{S}| \approx \mathrm{Vol}(\mathcal{S})/\mathrm{Vol}(\mathcal{L})$. If $\mathcal{S}$ is an n-ball of radius r, then the latter is $\approx v_n \cdot r^n / \mathrm{Vol}(\mathcal{L})$. By setting $v_n \cdot r^n \approx \mathrm{Vol}(\mathcal{L})$, we see that $\lambda_1(\mathcal{L})$ is close to $\mathrm{GH}(\mathcal{L}) := v_n^{-1/n} \cdot \mathrm{Vol}(\mathcal{L})^{1/n}$. Asymptotically, we have $\mathrm{GH}(\mathcal{L}) \approx \sqrt{\frac{n}{2\pi e}} \cdot \mathrm{Vol}(\mathcal{L})^{1/n}$.

2.2 Enumeration and Kannan's Algorithm

The Enum algorithm [Kan83,FP83] is an SVP solver. It takes as input a basis matrix B of a lattice $\mathcal{L}$ and consists in enumerating all $(x_i, \ldots, x_{n-1}) \in \mathbb{Z}^{n-i}$ such that $\|\pi_i(\sum_{j \geq i} x_j \cdot b_j)\| \leq A$ for every $i < n$, where A is an a priori upper bound on or estimate of $\lambda_1(\mathcal{L})$ (such as $\|b_1\|$ and $\mathrm{GH}(\mathcal{L})$, respectively). It may be viewed as a depth-first search of an optimal leaf in a tree indexed by tuples $(x_i, \ldots, x_{n-1})$, where the singletons x_{n-1} lie at the top and the full tuples $(x_0, \ldots, x_{n-1})$ are the leaves. The running-time of Enum is essentially the number of tree nodes (up to a small polynomial factor), and its space cost is polynomial. As argued in [HS07], the tree size can be estimated as $\max_{i<n}(v_i \cdot A^i / \prod_{j \geq n-i} \|b_j^*\|)$, under the Gaussian Heuristic. In [ANS18], it was showed that a quadratic speedup can be obtained quantumly using Montanaro's quantum backtracking algorithm (and the space cost remains polynomial). We will rely on the following (classical) cost bound, derived from [HS07, Subsection 4.1]. It is obtained by optimising the tree size $\max_{i<n}(v_i \cdot A^i / \prod_{j \geq n-i} \|b_j^*\|)$. We can replace A by twice the Gaussian Heuristic $\mathrm{GH}(\mathcal{L}) = v_n^{-1/n} \cdot \mathrm{Vol}(\mathcal{L})^{1/n}$, where $\mathrm{Vol}(\mathcal{L}) = \prod_{j<n} \|b_j^*\|$. By using the bounds $\|b_i^*\| \in c \cdot \delta^{-i} \cdot [1/2, 2]$, this optimisation problem boils down to maximising $\delta^{ni/2 - i^2/2}$ for $i < n$. The maximum is $\delta^{n^2/8}$ (for $i = n/2$). The other terms are absorbed in the $2^{O(n)}$ factor.

Theorem 1. *Let B be a basis matrix of an n-dimensional rational lattice $\mathcal{L}$. Assume that there exist $c > 0$ and $\delta > 1$ such that $\|b_i^*\| \in c \cdot \delta^{-i} \cdot [1/2, 2]$, for all $i < n$. Then, given B as input (with $A = 2 \cdot v_n^{-1/n} \cdot \mathrm{Vol}(\mathcal{L})^{1/n}$), the Enum algorithm returns a shortest non-zero vector of $\mathcal{L}$ within $\delta^{\frac{n^2}{8}} \cdot 2^{O(n)} \cdot \mathrm{poly}(\mathrm{size}(B))$ bit operations. Its space cost is $\mathrm{poly}(\mathrm{size}(B))$.*

Kannan's algorithm [Kan83] relies on recursive calls to Enum to improve the quality of the Gram–Schmidt orthogonalisation of B, so that calling Enum on the preprocessed B is less expensive. Its cost bound was lowered in [HS07] and that cost upper bound was later showed to be sharp in the worst case, up to lower-order terms [HS08].

Theorem 2. *Let B be a basis matrix of an n-dimensional rational lattice $\mathcal{L}$. Given B as input, Kannan's algorithm returns a shortest non-zero vector of $\mathcal{L}$ within $n^{\frac{n}{2e}(1+o(1))} \cdot \mathrm{poly}(\mathrm{size}(B))$ bit operations. Its space cost is $\mathrm{poly}(\mathrm{size}(B))$.*

In practice, enumeration is accelerated using two main techniques. The first one, inspired from Kannan's algorithm, consists in preprocessing the basis with a strong lattice reduction algorithm, such as BKZ (see next subsection). Note that BKZ uses an SVP solver in a lower dimension, so these algorithms can be viewed as calling themselves recursively, in an intertwined manner. The second one is tree pruning [SE94, GNR10]. The justifying observation is that some tree nodes are much more unlikely than others to have leaves in their subtrees, and are hence discarded. More concretely, one considers the strengthened conditioned $\|\pi_i(\sum_{j \geq i} x_j \cdot b_j)\| \leq t_i \cdot A$, for some pruning coefficients $t_i \in (0, 1)$. These coefficients can be used to extract a refined estimated enumeration cost as well as an estimated success probability (see, e.g. [Che13, Sec. 3.3]). By making the probability extremely small, the cost-over-probability ratio can be lowered and the probability can be boosted by re-randomising the basis and repeating the pruned enumeration. This strategy is called extreme pruning [GNR10].

2.3   Lattice Reduction

Given a basis matrix $B \in \mathbb{Q}^{m \times n}$ of a lattice $\mathcal{L}$, the LLL algorithm [LLJL82] outputs in polynomial time a basis C of $\mathcal{L}$ whose Gram–Schmidt norms cannot decrease too fast: $\|c_i^*\| \geq \|c_{i-1}^*\|/2$ for every $i < n$. In particular, we have $\mathbf{rhf}(C) \leq 2$. A lattice basis B is size-reduced if it satisfies $|\mu_{i,j}| \leq 1/2$ for $j < i < n$ where $\mu_{i,j} = \langle b_i, b_j^* \rangle / \langle b_j^*, b_j^* \rangle$. A lattice basis B is HKZ-reduced if it is size-reduced and satisfies $\|b_i^*\| = \lambda_1(\pi_i(\mathcal{L}_{[i:n]}))$, for all $i < n$. A basis B is BKZ-k reduced for block size $k \geq 2$ if it is size-reduced and further satisfies $\|b_i^*\| = \lambda_1(\pi_i(\mathcal{L}_{[i:\min(i+k,n)]}))$, for all $i < n$.

The Schnorr-Euchner BKZ algorithm [SE94] is the lattice reduction algorithm that is commonly used in practice, to obtain bases of better quality than those output by LLL (there exist algorithms that admit better analyses, such as [GN08a, MW16, ALNS19], but BKZ remains the best in terms of practical performance reported in the current literature). BKZ inputs a block size k and a basis matrix B of a lattice $\mathcal{L}$, and outputs a basis which is "close" to being BKZ-k reduced, up to algorithm parameters. The BKZ algorithm calls an SVP solver in dimensions $\leq k$ on projected sublattices of the working basis of an n-dimensional input lattice. A BKZ sweep consists in SVP solver calls for $\pi_i(\mathcal{L}_{[i:\min(i+k,n)]})$ for i from 0 to $n-2$. BKZ proceeds by repeating such sweeps, and typically a small number of sweeps suffices. At each execution of the SVP solver, if we have $\lambda_1(\pi_i(\mathcal{L}_{[i:\min(i+k,n)]})) < \delta \cdot \|b_i^*\|$ where $\delta < 1$ is a relaxing parameter that is close to 1, then BKZ updates the block $\pi_i(B_{[i:\min(i+k,n)]})$ by inserting the vector found by the SVP solver at index i. It then removes the created linear dependency, e.g. using a gcd computation (see, e.g. [GN08a]). Whether there was an insertion or not, BKZ finally calls LLL on the local block $\pi_i\left(B_{[i:\min(i+k,n)]}\right)$. The procedure terminates when no change occurs at all during a sweep or after certain termination condition is fulfilled. The higher k, the better the BKZ output quality, but the higher the cost: for large n, BKZ achieves root Hermite factor essentially $k^{1/(2k)}$ (see [HPS11]) using an SVP-solver in dimensions $\leq k$ a polynomially bounded number of times.

Schnorr [Sch03] introduced a heuristic on the shape of the Gram–Schmidt norms of BKZ-reduced bases, called the *Geometric Series Assumption* (GSA). The GSA asserts that the Gram–Schmidt norms $\{\|b_i^*\|\}_{i<n}$ of a BKZ-reduced basis behave as a geometric series, i.e., there exists $r > 1$ such that $\|b_i^*\|/\|b_{i+1}^*\| \approx r$ for all $i < n-1$. In this situation, the root Hermite factor is $\sqrt{r}$. It was experimentally observed [CN11] that the GSA is a good first approximation to the shape of the Gram–Schmidt norms of BKZ. However, as observed in [CN11] and studied in [YD17], the GSA does not provide an exact fit to the experiments of BKZ for the last k indices; similarly, as observed in [YD17] and studied in [BSW18], the GSA also does not fit for the very few first indices (the latter phenomenon seems to vanish for large k, as opposed to the former).

We will use the self-dual BKZ algorithm (SDBKZ) from [MW16]. SDBKZ proceeds similarly to BKZ, except that it intertwines forward and backward sweeps (for choosing the inputs to the SVP solver), whereas BKZ uses only forward sweeps. Further, it only invokes the SVP solver in dimension exactly k, so that a forward sweep consists in considering $\pi_i(\mathcal{L}_{[i:i+k)})$ for i from 0 to $n-k$ and a backward sweep consists in considering (the duals of) $\pi_i(\mathcal{L}_{[i:i+k)})$ for i from $n-k$ down to 0. We assume that the final sweep is a forward sweep. We use

SDBKZ in the theoretical analysis rather than BKZ because, under the Gaussian Heuristic and after polynomially many sweeps, the first $n - k$ Gram–Schmidt norms of the basis (almost) decrease geometrically, i.e. satisfy the GSA. This may not be necessary for our result to hold, but this simplifies the computations significantly. We adapt [MW16] by allowing SDBKZ to rely on a γ-HSVP solver $\mathcal{O}$ rather than on an exact SVP solver (which in particular is a $\sqrt{k}$-HSVP solver). We let SDBKZ$^{\mathcal{O}}$ denote the modified algorithm. The analysis of [MW16] can be readily adapted. We will rely on the following heuristic assumption, which extends the Gaussian Heuristic.

Heuristic 1. *Let $\mathcal{O}$ be a γ-HSVP solver in dimension k. During the SDBKZ$^{\mathcal{O}}$ execution, each call to $\mathcal{O}$ for a projected k-dimensional sublattice $\pi(\mathcal{L})$ of the input lattice $\mathcal{L}$ returns a vector of norm $\approx \gamma \cdot (\mathrm{Vol}(\pi(\mathcal{L})))^{\frac{1}{k}}$.*

The SDBKZ$^{\mathcal{O}}$ algorithm makes the Gram–Schmidt norms converge to a fix-point, very fast in terms of the number of HSVP calls [MW16, Subsection 4.2]. That fix-point is described in [MW16, Corollary 2]. Adapting these results leads to the following.

Theorem 3 (Under Heuristic 1). *Let $\mathcal{O}$ be a γ-HSVP solver in dimension k. Given as input a basis of an n-dimensional rational lattice $\mathcal{L}$, SDBKZ$^{\mathcal{O}}$ outputs a basis B of $\mathcal{L}$ such that, for all $i < n - k$, we have*

$$\|b_i^*\| \approx \gamma^{\frac{n-1-2i}{k-1}} \cdot (\mathrm{Vol}\,\mathcal{L})^{\frac{1}{n}}.$$

The number of calls to $\mathcal{O}$ is $\leq \mathrm{poly}(n)$ and the bit-size of the output basis is $\leq \mathrm{poly}(\mathrm{size}(B))$.

2.4   Simulating Lattice Reduction

To understand the behaviour of lattice reduction algorithms in practice, a useful approach is to conduct simulations. The underlying idea is to model the practical behaviour of the evolution of the Gram–Schmidt norms during the algorithm execution, without running a costly lattice reduction. Note that this requires only the Gram–Schmidt norms and not the full basis. Chen and Nguyen first provided a BKZ simulator [CN11] based on the Gaussian Heuristic and with an experiment-driven modification for the blocks at the end of the basis. It relies on the assumption that each SVP solver call in the projected blocks (except the ones at the end of the basis) finds a vector whose norm corresponds to the Gaussian Heuristic applied to that local block. The remaining Gram–Schmidt norms of the block are updated to keep the determinant of the block constant. (Note that in the original [CN11] simulator, these Gram–Schmidt norms are not updated to keep the determinant of the block constant, but are adjusted at the end of the sweep to keep the global determinant constant; our variant helps for taking enumeration costs into account.)

We extend this simulator in two ways: first, we adapt it to estimate the cost and not only the evolution of the Gram–Schmidt norms; second, we adapt it to other reduction algorithms, such as SDBKZ. To estimate the cost, we use the estimates of the full enumeration cost, or the estimated cost of an enumeration with (extreme) pruning. The full enumeration cost estimate is used in Sect. 3 to model our first algorithm for which we can heuristically analyse the quality/cost trade-off. The pruned enumeration cost estimate is used in Sect. 4, which aims to provide a more precise study for practical and cryptographic dimensions. To find the enumeration cost with pruning, we make use of FPyLLL's pruning module which numerically optimises pruning parameters for a time/success probability trade-off using a gradient descent.

In small block sizes, the enumeration cost is dominated by calls to LLL. In our code, we simply assume that one LLL call in dimension k costs the equivalent of visiting k^3 nodes. This is an oversimplification but avoids completely ignoring this polynomial factor. We will compare our concrete estimates with empirical evidence from timing experiments with the implementation in FPLLL, to measure the effect of this imprecision. This assumption enables us to bootstrap our cost estimates. BKZ in block size up to, say, 40 only requires LLL preprocessing, allowing us to estimate the cost of preprocessing with block size up to 40, which in turn enables us to estimate the cost (including preprocessing) for larger block sizes etc. To extend the simulation to SDBKZ, we simply run the simulation on the Gram–Schmidt norms of the dual basis $1/\|b_n^*\|, \ldots, 1/\|b_1^*\|$. Our simulation source code is available as simu.py, as an attachment to the electronic version of the full version of this work.

We give pseudocode for our costed simulation in Algorithm 1. For BKZ simulation, we call Algorithm 1 with $d = k$, $c = 0$ and with tail(x, y, z) simply outputting x. For our simulations we prepared Gram–Schmidt shapes for LLL-reduced lattices in increasing dimensions d on which we then estimate the cost of running the algorithm in question for increasingly heavy preprocessing parameters k', selecting the least expensive one. In our search, we initialise $c_2 = 2^3$ and then iteratively compute c_{j+1} given $c_2, \ldots, c_j$. When we instantiate Algorithm 1 we either manually pick some small t (Sect. 4) or pick $t = \infty$ (Sect. 3.3) which means to run the algorithm until no more changes are made to the basis.

2.5   State-of-the-Art Enumeration-Based SVP Solving in Practice

To the best of our knowledge, there is no extrapolated running-time for state-of-the-art lattice reduction implementations. Furthermore, the simulation data in [CN11, Che13] is only available up to a block size of 250. The purpose of this section is to fill this gap by providing extended simulations (and the source code used to produce them) and by reporting running times using the state-of-the-art FPyLLL [dt19b] and FPLLL [dt19a] libraries.

First, in Fig. 2 we reproduce the data from [Che13, Table 5.2] for the estimated cost of solving SVP up to dimension 250, using enumeration.

We then also computed the expected cost (expressed as the number of visited enumeration nodes) up to dimension 500 for Fig. 2, see `cost.py`, attached to the electronic copy of the full version of this work, and Algorithm 1. We note that the preprocessing strategy adopted in our code is to always run two sweeps of preprocessing but that preprocessing proceeds recursively, e.g. preprocessing block size 80 with block size 60 may trigger a preprocessing with block size 40, if previously we found that preprocessing to be most efficient for solving SVP-60, as outlined above. This approach matches that of the FPLLL/FPyLLL `strategizer` [dt17] which selects the default preprocessing and pruning strategies used in FPLLL/FPyLLL. Thus, the simulation approach resembles that of the actual implementation.

Algorithm 1: Costed simulation algorithm

Data: Gram–Schmidt profile $\ell_i = \log \|\boldsymbol{b}_i^*\|$ for $i = 0, \ldots, d-1$.
Data: Block size $k \geq 2$.
Data: Preprocessing block size $k' \geq 2$.
Data: Preprocessing sweep count t.
Data: Overshooting parameter $c \geq 0$.
Data: Configuration flags.
Data: Cost estimates c_j for solving (approx-)SVP in dimensions $j = 2, \ldots, k'$, including preprocessing cost estimates.
Result: Cost estimate for (approx-)SVP in dimension k.

1 if SDBKZ *flag is set in* flags then
2 | $(\ell_i)_i \leftarrow$ output of [CN11] style simulator for SDBKZ on $(\ell_i)_i$ for block size k' and $\leq t$ sweeps;
3 else
4 | $(\ell_i)_i \leftarrow$ output of [CN11] style simulator for BKZ on $(\ell_i)_i$ for block size k' and $\leq t$ sweeps;
5 end
   // account for early termination
6 $t \leftarrow$ number of preprocessing sweeps actually performed;
7 $C_p \leftarrow d^3$; // (estimated) cost of LLL
8 for $0 \leq i < d-1$ do
9 | $k^* \leftarrow \text{tail}(\min(k', d-i), c, d-i)$;
10 | $C_p \leftarrow C_p + t \cdot c_{k^*}$;
11 end
12 if *full enumeration cost flag is set in* flags then
13 | $C_e \leftarrow$ full enumeration cost for $\ell_0, \ldots, \ell_{k-1}$;
14 | $p_e \leftarrow 1$;
15 else
16 | $(t_i)_{i<k} \leftarrow$ optimised pruning coefficients for $(\ell_i)_{i<k}$ and preprocessing cost C_p;
17 | $C_e, p_e \leftarrow$ pruned enumeration cost and success probability, given $(t_i)_{i<k}$;
18 end
19 $C \leftarrow 1/p_e \cdot (C_p + C_e)$;
20 return C;

In Fig. 2, we also fitted the coefficients a_1, a_2 of $1/(2\,e)n \log n + a_1 \cdot n + a_2$ to dimensions n from 150 to 249.[2]

Furthermore, we plot the chosen preprocessing block sizes and success probability of a single enumeration (FPLLL uses extreme pruning) in Fig. 3. This highlights that, even in dimension 500, preprocessing is still well below the $n - o(n)$ required for Kannan's algorithm [Kan83, MW15].

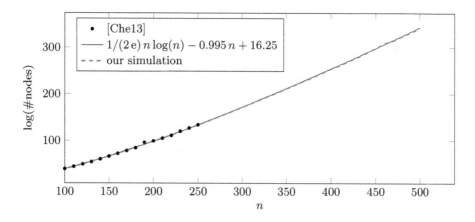

Fig. 2. Expected number of nodes visited during enumeration in dimension n.

Figure 4 plots the running-times of FPLLL in terms of enumeration nodes, timed using `call.py`, available as an attachment to the electronic version of the full version of this work. Concretely, running-time in seconds is first converted to CPU cycles by multiplying with the clock speed 2.6 GHz[3] and we then convert from cycles to nodes by assuming visiting a node takes about 64 clock cycles.[4] Fig. 4 illustrates that our simulation is reasonably accurate. We note that for running the timing experiments with FPLLL we relied on FPLLL's own (recursive call and pruning) strategies, not those produced by our simulator.

The largest computational results known for finding short vectors in unstructured lattices is the Darmstadt SVP Challenge [SG10]. This challenge asks contestants to find a vector at most 1.05 times larger than the Gaussian Heuristic. Thus, the challenge does not require to solve SVP exactly but the easier $(0.254\sqrt{n})$-HSVP problem. The strategy we used for SVP can be adapted to this problem as well, see `chal.py`, attached to the electronic version of the full

---

[2] Throughout this work, we fit curves to simulation data. For this, we use SciPy's `scipy.optimize.curve_fit` function [VGO+20] which implements a non-linear least-square fit. To prevent overfitting, we err on the side of fewer parameters and fit on a subset of the available data, using the remaining data to check the accuracy of the fit.

[3] CPU: Intel(R) Xeon(R) CPU E5-2690 v4 @ 2.60 GHz machine: "atomkohle".

[4] We note that [CN11] mentions 200 cycles per node, whereas [dt17]'s `set_mdc.py` reports 64 cycles per node on our test machine in dimension 55.

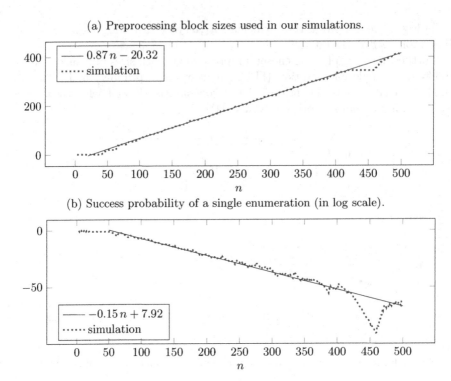

(a) Preprocessing block sizes used in our simulations.

(b) Success probability of a single enumeration (in log scale).

Fig. 3. Reduction strategies used for Fig. 2.

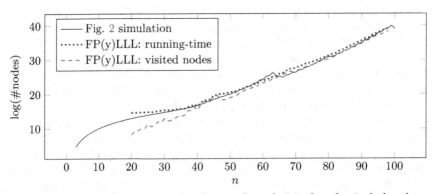

In our simulations, the estimate for the number of visited nodes includes the cost of LLL (expressed as a number of nodes), whereas actually "visited nodes" does not. The "running-time" (converted from seconds to a number of nodes), on the other hand, contains all operations as it literally is the cputime.

Fig. 4. Number of nodes visited during enumeration in dimension n.

version of document. To validate our simulation methodology against this data, we compare our estimates with various entries from the Hall of Fame for [SG10] and the literature in Fig. 5.

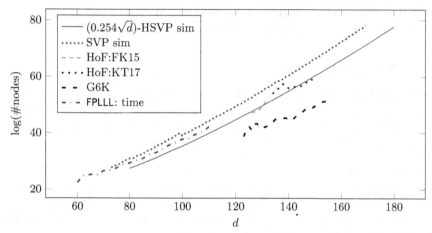

"HoF" stands for Hall of Fame [SG10]. Core hours are translated to #nodes by multiplying by $3600 \cdot 2 \cdot 10^7$, which assumes each core has a 2Ghz CPU and that one enumeration node costs 64 clock cycles to process. Except for G6K [ADH+19] which is a sieving implementation, all entries are for variants of lattice-point enumeration. We translate G6K timings to #nodes in the same way as for other timings, ignoring that it is not an enumeration implementation. In other words, #nodes is merely a unit of time here.

Fig. 5. Darmstadt SVP Challenge.

We conclude this section by interpreting our simulation results in the context of BKZ. The quality output by BKZ in practice has been studied in the literature [GN08b, Che13, AGVW17, YD17, BSW18]. Thus, our simulations imply that the running time of BKZ as implemented in [dt19a] achieves root Hermite factor $k^{1/(2k)}$ is bounded by $k^{k/(2e)+o(k)}$. Indeed, this bound is tight, i.e. BKZ does not achieve a lower running time. To see this, consider the sandpile model of BKZ's behaviour [HPS11]. It implies that even if we start with a GSA line, this line from index i onward deteriorates as we perform updates on indices $< i$. Furthermore, extreme pruning, which involves rerandomising local blocks, destroys the GSA shape. Thus, we can conclude that in practice BKZ

- achieves root Hermite factor $\approx \left(\frac{k}{2\pi e} \cdot (\pi k)^{\frac{1}{k}}\right)^{\frac{1}{2(k-1)}}$ [Che13]
- in time $\mathrm{poly}(d) \cdot 2^{1/(2e) \, k \log k - 0.995 \, k + 16.25} \approx \mathrm{poly}(d) \cdot 2^{1/(2e) \, k \log k - k + 16}$

where the unit of time is the number of nodes visited during enumeration. We note that a similar conclusion was already drawn in [APS15] and discussed in [ABD+16]. However, that conclusion was drawn for the unpublished implementation and limited data in [Che13].

3   Reaching Root Hermite Factor $k^{\frac{1}{2k}(1+o(1))}$ in Time $k^{\frac{k}{8}}$

This section contains our main contribution: a lattice reduction algorithm that achieves root Hermite factor $k^{\frac{1}{2k}(1+o(1))}$ in time $k^{\frac{k}{8}}$. We start by a quality running-time trade-off boosting theorem, based on SDBKZ. We then give and analyze the main algorithm, FastEnum, and finally propose a simulator for that algorithm.

3.1   A Boosting Theorem

We first show that SDBKZ allows to obtain a reduction from a γ'-HSVP solver in dimension n' to a γ-HSVP solver in dimension n achieving a larger root Hermite factor. This reduction is not polynomial-time, but we will later aim at making it no more costly than the cost of our γ-HSVP solver.

Theorem 4 (Under Heuristic 1). *Let $\mathcal{O}$ be a γ-HSVP solver in dimension n. Assume we are given as input a basis $\mathbf{B}$ of an n'-dimensional lattice $\mathcal{L}$, with $n' > n$. We first call $\mathrm{SDBKZ}^{\mathcal{O}}$ on $\mathbf{B}$: let $\mathbf{C}$ denote the output basis. Then we call the Enum algorithm on the sublattice basis made of the first $n' - n$ vectors of $\mathbf{C}$. This provides a γ'-HSVP solver in dimension n', with*

$$\gamma' \leq \sqrt{n' - n}\, \gamma^{\frac{n}{n-1}}.$$

The total cost is bounded by $\mathrm{poly}(n')$ calls to $\mathcal{O}$ and $\gamma^{\frac{(n'-n)^2}{4(n-1)}} \cdot 2^{O(n'-n)} \cdot \mathrm{poly}(\mathrm{size}(\mathbf{B}))$ bit operations.

Proof. By Theorem 3, we have $\|\mathbf{c}_i^*\| \in \gamma^{\frac{n'-1-2i}{n-1}} \cdot (\mathrm{Vol}(\mathcal{L}))^{\frac{1}{n'}} \cdot [1/2, 2]$, for all $i < n' - n$. Also, the number of calls to $\mathcal{O}$ is $\leq \mathrm{poly}(n')$ and the bit-size of $\mathbf{C}$ is $\leq \mathrm{poly}(\mathrm{size}(\mathbf{B}))$.

By Theorem 1 (with "$\delta = \gamma^{\frac{2}{n-1}}$"), the cost of the call to Enum is bounded as $\gamma^{\frac{(n'-n)^2}{4(n-1)}} \cdot 2^{O(n'-n)} \cdot \mathrm{poly}(\mathrm{size}(\mathbf{C}))$, which, by the above is $\leq \gamma^{\frac{(n'-n)^2}{4(n-1)}} \cdot 2^{O(n'-n)} \cdot \mathrm{poly}(\mathrm{size}(\mathbf{B}))$. Further, by Minkowski's theorem, the vector output by Enum has norm bounded from above by:

$$\sqrt{n' - n} \cdot \prod_{i=0}^{n'-n-1} \left(\gamma^{\frac{n'-1-2i}{n-1}} (\mathrm{Vol}(\mathcal{L}))^{\frac{1}{n'}} \right)^{\frac{1}{n'-n}} = \sqrt{n' - n} \cdot \gamma^{\frac{n}{n-1}} \cdot (\mathrm{Vol}(\mathcal{L}))^{\frac{1}{n'}}.$$

This completes the proof of the theorem. $\square$

Note that the result is not interesting if $n' - n$ is chosen too small, as such a choice results in an increased root Hermite factor. Also, if $n' - n$ is chosen too large, then the cost grows very fast. We consider the following instructive application of Theorem 4. By Theorem 2, Kannan's algorithm finds a shortest non-zero of $\mathcal{L}$ in time $n^{\frac{n}{2e}(1+o(1))} \cdot \mathrm{poly}(\mathrm{size}(\mathbf{B}))$, when given as input a basis $\mathbf{B}$ of an n-dimensional lattice $\mathcal{L}$. In particular, it solves γ-HSVP with $\gamma = \sqrt{n}$ and provides a root Hermite factor $\leq n^{\frac{1}{2n}}$. We want to achieve a similar root

Hermite factor, but for a lower cost. Now, for a cost parameter k, we would like to restrict the cost to $k^{\frac{k}{8}} \cdot \text{poly}(\text{size}(\mathbf{B}))$ (ideally, while still achieving root Hermite factor $k^{\frac{1}{2k}}$). We hence choose an integer $k_0 := \frac{e}{4}(1 + o(1))k$. This indeed provides a cost bounded as $k^{\frac{k}{8}} \cdot \text{poly}(\text{size}(\mathbf{B}))$, but this only solves γ_0-HSVP with $\gamma_0 = \Theta(\sqrt{k_0})$ in dimension k_0, i.e. only provides a root Hermite factor $\approx \sqrt{k_0}^{\frac{1}{k_0}} = k^{\frac{2}{ke}(1+o(1))} \approx k^{\frac{0.74}{k}}$, which is much more than $k^{\frac{1}{2k}}$. So far, we have not done anything but a change of variable. Now, let us see how Theorem 4 can help. We use it with $\mathcal{O}$ being Kannan's algorithm in dimension "$n = k_0$". We set "$n' = k_1$" with $k_1 = k_0 + \lceil \sqrt{k_0 k} \rceil$. This value is chosen so that the total cost bound of Theorem 4 remains $k^{\frac{k}{8}} \cdot \text{poly}(\text{size}(\mathbf{B}))$. The achieved root Hermite factor is $\leq k^{\frac{1}{k(e/4+\sqrt{e/4})}(1+o(1))} \approx k^{\frac{0.66}{k}}$. Overall, for a similar cost bound, we have decreased the achieved root Hermite factor.

3.2 The FastEnum Algorithm

We iterate the process above to obtain the FastEnum algorithm, described in Algorithm 2. For this reason, we define $k_0 = x_0 \cdot k$ with $x_0 = \frac{e}{4}(1 + o(1))$ and, for all $i \geq 1$:

$$ k_i = \lceil x_i \cdot k \rceil \quad \text{with} \quad x_i = x_{i-1} + \sqrt{\frac{x_{i-1}}{i}}. \tag{1} $$

We first study the sequence of x_i's.

Lemma 1. *We have* $i + 1 - \sqrt{i} < x_i < i + 1$ *for all* $i \geq 1$.

Proof. The upper bound can be readily proved using an induction based on (1). It may be numerically checked that the lower bound holds for $i \in \{1, 2, 3\}$. We show by induction to prove that $1 - \frac{x_i}{i} < \frac{1}{\sqrt{i}} - \frac{2}{i}$ for $i \geq 4$, which is a stronger statement. It may be numerically checked that the latter holds for $i = 4$. Now, assume it holds for some $i - 1 \geq 4$ and that we aim at proving it for i. We have

$$ 1 - \frac{x_i}{i} = \frac{1}{i}\left((i-1)\left(1 - \frac{x_{i-1}}{i-1}\right) + \left(1 - \sqrt{\frac{x_{i-1}}{i}}\right)\right) $$
$$ = \frac{1}{i}\left((i-1)\left(1 - \frac{x_{i-1}}{i-1}\right) + \sqrt{\frac{i-1}{i}}\left(1 - \sqrt{\frac{x_{i-1}}{i-1}}\right) + 1 - \sqrt{\frac{i-1}{i}}\right). $$

Now, note that $\sqrt{\frac{x_{i-1}}{i-1}} > 0.2$ (using our induction hypothesis). Using the bound $1 - \sqrt{t} < \frac{1}{2}(1 - t) + \frac{1}{4}(1 - t)^2$ which holds for all $t > 0.2$, we can bound $1 - \frac{x_i}{i}$ from above by:

$$ \frac{1}{i}\left((i-1)\left(1 - \frac{x_{i-1}}{i-1}\right) + 1 + \sqrt{\frac{i-1}{i}}\left(-1 + \frac{1}{2}\left(1 - \frac{x_{i-1}}{i-1}\right) + \frac{1}{4}\left(1 - \frac{x_{i-1}}{i-1}\right)^2\right)\right). $$

It now suffices to observe that the right hand side is smaller than $\frac{1}{\sqrt{i}} - \frac{2}{i}$, when $1 - \frac{x_{i-1}}{i-1}$ is replaced by $\frac{1}{\sqrt{i-1}} - \frac{2}{i-1}$. This may be checked with a computer algebra software. □

The FastEnum algorithm (Algorithm 2) consists in calling the process described in Theorem 4 several times, to improve the root Hermite factor while staying within a $k^{\frac{k}{8}}$ cost bound.

Algorithm 2: The FastEnum algorithm.

Data: A cost parameter k and a level $i \geq 0$.
Data: A basis matrix $\mathbf{B} \in \mathbb{Q}^{k_i \times k_i}$, with k_i defined as in (1).
Result: A short non-zero vector of $\mathcal{L}(\mathbf{B})$.

1   **if** $i = 0$ **then**
2 | $b \leftarrow$ output of Kannan's enumeration algorithm on $\mathbf{B}$;
3   **else**
4 | $C \leftarrow$ output of $\mathrm{SDBKZ}^{\mathcal{O}}$ on $\mathbf{B}$ with $\mathcal{O}$ being FastEnum for $i-1$;
5 | $b \leftarrow \mathrm{Enum}\left(C_{[0:k_i - k_{i-1})}\right)$ with k_{i-1} defined as in (1);
6   **end**
7   **return** b;

Theorem 5 (Under Heuristic 1). *Let $k \geq 4$ tending to infinity, and $i \leq 2^{o(k)}$.[5] The FastEnum algorithm with parameters k and i solves γ_i-HSVP in dimension k_i, with $\gamma_i \leq k^{\frac{i+1}{2}(1+o(1))}$. For $i \geq 1$, the corresponding root Hermite factor is below $k^{\frac{i+1}{2(i+1-\sqrt{i})k}(1+o(1))}$. Further, FastEnum runs in time $k^{\frac{k}{8}(1+o(1))+i\cdot O(1)} \cdot \mathrm{poly}(\mathrm{size}(\mathbf{B}))$.*

For constant values of i (as a function of k), the root Hermite factor is not quite $k^{\frac{1}{2k}(1+o(1))}$, but it is so for any choice of $i = \omega(1)$. For i satisfying both $i = \omega(1)$ and $i = o(k)$, FastEnum reaches a root Hermite factor $k^{\frac{1}{2k}(1+o(1))}$ in time $k^{\frac{k}{8}(1+o(1))} \cdot \mathrm{poly}(\mathrm{size}(\mathbf{B}))$.

Proof. For $\gamma_0 = \Theta(\sqrt{k})$ and, by Theorem 4, we have $\gamma_i \leq \sqrt{k_i - k_{i-1}} \cdot \gamma_{i-1}^{\frac{k_{i-1}}{k_{i-1}-1}}$ for all $i \geq 1$. Using the definition of the k_i's and the bounds of Lemma 1, we obtain, for $i \geq 1$:

$$\gamma_i \leq \left(1 + \frac{x_{i-1}}{i}k^2\right)^{1/4} \cdot \gamma_{i-1}^{\frac{k(i-\sqrt{i-1})+1}{k(i-\sqrt{i-1})-1}} \leq \sqrt{2k} \cdot \gamma_{i-1}^{1+\frac{2}{ki/2-1}}.$$

Using $k \geq 4$, we see that the latter is $\leq \sqrt{2k}\gamma_{i-1}^{1+\frac{8}{ki}}$. By unfolding the recursion, we get, for $i \geq 1$:

$$\gamma_i \leq \sqrt{2k}^{1+\sum_{j=0}^{i-1}\prod_{\ell=j}^{i-1}(1+\frac{8}{k(\ell+1)})} \cdot \gamma_0^{\prod_{\ell=0}^{i-1}(1+\frac{8}{k(\ell+1)})}.$$

Now, note that we have (using the bound $\sum_{\ell=0}^{i-1}\frac{1}{\ell+1} \leq \ln(i)+1$, and the inequalities $1+x \leq \exp(x) \leq 1+2x$ for $x \in [0,1]$)

$$\prod_{\ell=j}^{i-1}(1+\frac{8}{k(\ell+1)}) \leq \exp\left(\sum_{\ell=0}^{i-1}\frac{8}{k(\ell+1)}\right) \leq \exp\left(\frac{8}{k}(\ln(i)+1)\right) \leq 1+\frac{16}{k}(\ln(i)+1).$$

---

[5] We stress that in this theorem, all asymptotic notations are with respect to k only.

As $i \leq 2^{o(k)}$, the latter is $\leq 1 + o(1)$. Overall, this gives $\gamma_i \leq k^{\frac{i+1}{2}(1+o(1))}$. The claim on the root Hermite factor follows from the lower bound of Lemma 1.

We now consider the run-time of the algorithm, and in particular the term $\gamma_{i-1}^{\frac{(k_i-k_{i-1})^2}{4(k_{i-1}-1)}} \cdot 2^{O(k_i-k_{i-1})}$ from Theorem 4. Recall that by definition of the k_i's, we have $k_i - k_{i-1} \leq 1 + \sqrt{\frac{k_{i-1}k}{i}}$. Using the upper bound of Lemma 1, we obtain that $k_i - k_{i-1} \leq O(k)$, and hence that $2^{O(k_i-k_{i-1})} \leq 2^{O(k)}$. We also have

$$\gamma_{i-1}^{\frac{(k_i-k_{i-1})^2}{4(k_{i-1}-1)}} \leq k^{\frac{i}{2}(1+o(1))\frac{k_{i-1}k}{4i(k_{i-1}-1)}} \leq k^{\frac{k}{8}(1+o(1))}.$$

Further, the number of recursive calls is bounded as $\text{poly}(\prod_{j \leq i} k_j)$. By Lemma 1, this is $\leq k^{i \cdot O(1)}$. To complete the proof, it may be shown using standard techniques that all bases occurring during the algorithm have bit-sizes bounded as $\text{poly}(\text{size}(\mathbf{B}))$ (where the bound is independent from i). $\qquad\square$

3.3 Simulation of Asymptotic Behaviour

In this subsection, we instantiate the FastEnum algorithm as described in Algorithm 2 and confirm its asymptotic behaviour via simulations. Note that the FastEnum algorithm requires SDBKZ subroutines. To simulate this subroutine, we use the costed simulation of Algorithm 1 with flags: SDBKZ and full enumeration cost. We also omit the cost of LLL in the simulation as the enumeration cost dominates in the parameter range considered in this subsection.

To compare the simulation with the theorems, we consider two scenarios. In the first one, called "Theoretical" we numerically compute the k_i's, γ_i's and the slope of the Gram–Schmidt log-norms of the enumeration block (i.e. the first $k_i - k_{i-1}$ vectors) according to Theorem 5. Here the index i denotes the recursion level. Similarly, k_i and γ_i are defined in the same way as in (1) and Theorem 5, respectively. In the second one, called "Simulated" we still set the k_i's according to (1). However, at the i-th level, we first run an SDBKZ simulation on a lattice of dimension k_i, using the γ_{i-1}-HSVP (simulated) oracle from the previous level. Here, the Hermite factor γ_{i-1} is computed from the simulated basis at the $(i-1)$-th level. The initial γ_0 is computed from a simulated HKZ-reduced basis of dimension k_0. During the SDBKZ simulation, for each HSVP call, we assume that the same Hermite factor γ_{i-1} is achieved. We let the simulated SDBKZ run until no change occurs to the basis or if it has already achieved the theoretical root Hermite factor at the same level, as guided by the proof of Theorem 5. After the simulated SDBKZ preprocessing, we simulate an enumeration in the first block of dimension $k_i - k_{i-1}$. The enumeration cost is estimated using the full enumeration cost model (see Sect. 2.4), since here we are only interested in the asymptotic behaviour (we defer to Sect. 4 for the concrete behaviour). For a fixed cost parameter k, we consider $\lceil \ln k \rceil$ recursion levels $i = 0, \ldots, (\lceil \ln k \rceil - 1)$. For the implementation used for these experiments, we refer to `simu_asym.py` attached to the electronic version of the full version of this work. This simulation algorithm is an instantiation of Algorithm 1.

Using the simulator described above, we computed the achieved simulated root Hermite factors for various cost parameters k from 100 to 2,999. The results are plotted in Fig. 6. We also computed the theoretical root Hermite factors as established by Theorem 5. More precisely, we used the proof of Theorem 5 to update the root Hermite factors recursively, replacing the term $\sqrt{n'-n}$ of Theorem 4 by $v_{n'-n}^{-1/(n'-n)}$ (which corresponds to using the Gaussian Heuristic). It can be observed that the theoretical and simulated root Hermite factors agree closely.

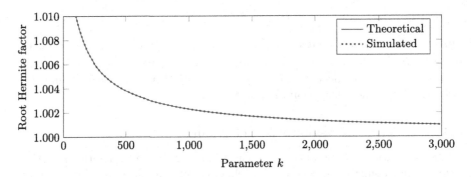

Fig. 6. Simulated and theoretical root Hermite factors for $k = 100$ to $2,999$ after $\ln k$ levels of recursion.

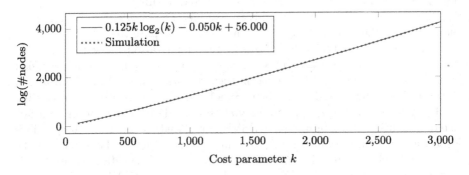

Fig. 7. Number of nodes in full enumeration visited during simulation, and a fit.

Figure 7 shows the number of nodes visited during the simulation from $k = 100$ to $2,999$, as well as a curve fit. As an example of the output, Fig. 8 plots the Gram–Schmidt log-norms of the (simulated) reduced basis for $k = 1,000$ right after 7 levels of recursion. Note that last Gram–Schmidt norms of the basis have the shape of those of an HKZ-reduced basis, since we use Kannan's algorithm at level 0. Also, the successive segments correspond to levels of recursion, their lengths decrease and their respective (negative) slopes decrease with the indices of the Gram–Schmidt norms.

Finally, we plot the Gram–Schmidt log-norms slope for $k = 1,000$ during the first 20 recursion levels. At level i, we compute the slope for the enumeration

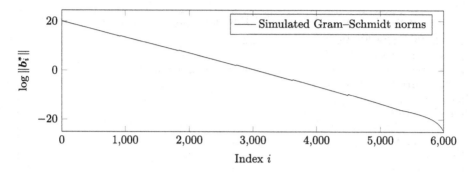

Fig. 8. Gram–Schmidt log-norms of simulated experiments with $k = 1,000$ after $7 \approx \ln k$ recursion levels.

region (i.e. the first block of size $k_i - k_{i-1}$). It can be observed that the simulated slope is indeed increasing (Fig. 9).

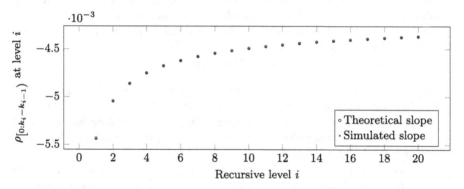

Fig. 9. Simulated and theoretical Gram–Schmidt log-norms slope of enumeration region, for $k = 1,000$ and during the first 20 iterations.

4 A Practical Variant

It can be observed that, in our analysis of Algorithm 2, the dimension of the lattice is relatively large. It is thus interesting to investigate algorithms that require smaller dimensions. In this subsection, we describe a practical strategy that works with dimensions $d = O(k)$ where the hidden constants are small. As mentioned in the introduction, practical implementations of lattice reduction algorithms often deviate from the asymptotically efficient variants, e.g. by applying much weaker preprocessing than required asymptotically. In this section, we use numerically optimised preprocessing and enumeration strategies to parameterise Algorithm 3, which we view as a practical variant of Algorithm 2, working with dimensions $d = \lceil (1 + c) \cdot k \rceil$ for some small constant $c \geq 0$. It differs from Algorithm 2 in two respects. First, it applies BKZ preprocessing instead of SDBKZ preprocessing. This is merely an artefact of the latter seemingly not providing an advantage in

---

Algorithm 3: Solving Approx-HSVP with preprocessing dimension larger than enumeration dimension.

Data: A basis matrix $B \in \mathbb{R}^{d \times d}$.
Data: Cost parameter $k \geq 2$ and an overshooting parameter $c > 0$.
Result: A short vector b.

1   $k^\star \leftarrow \text{tail}(k, c, d)$;
2   $k' \leftarrow \text{pre}(k^\star)$;
3   **if** $k' > 2$ **then**
4 | run Algorithm 4 on B with parameter k';
5   **else**
6 | run LLL on B;
7   **end**
8   $b \leftarrow \text{Enum}\left(B_{[0:k^\star)}\right)$;
9   **return** b;

---

the parameter ranges we considered. Second, the algorithm adapts the enumeration dimension based on the "space available" for preprocessing. This is to enforce that it stays within d dimensions, instead of requiring $\approx ik$ dimensions where i is the number of recursion levels.

We use the following functions in Algorithm 3:

- The function $\text{pre}(k)$ returns a preprocessing cost parameter for a given k.
- The function $\text{tail}(k, c, d)$ returns a new cost parameter $k^\star$ such that enumeration in dimension $k^\star$ after preprocessing with $\text{pre}(k^\star)$ in dimension d costs at most as much as enumeration in dimension k after preprocessing in dimension $\lceil (1 + c) \cdot k \rceil$. In particular, if $d \geq \lceil (1 + c) \cdot k \rceil$ then $k^\star = k$.
- Preprocessing (Step 4) calls Algorithm 4, perhaps restricted to a small number of while loops. Algorithm 4 is simply the BKZ algorithm where the SVP oracle is replaced by Algorithm 3.

We plot the output of our simulations for Algorithm 3 in Fig. 10. These simulations are instantiations of Algorithm 1 with $d > k$, $c > 0$ and $\text{tail}(x, y, z)$ matching those used in Algorithm 3. These were produced using `blck.py`, attached to the electronic version of the full version of this work. Our strategy finding strategy follows the same blueprint as described in Sect. 2.4. Through such simulation experiments we manually established that $c = 0.25$, four sweeps of preprocessing and using BKZ over SDBKZ seems to provide the best performance, which is why we report data on these choices.[6] We also fitted the coefficients a_0, a_1, a_2 of $a_0 \cdot k \log k + a_1 \cdot k + a_2$ to points from 100 to 249. Furthermore, we plot the data from Fig. 2 to provide a reference point for the performance of the new algorithm and also provide some data on the hypothetical performance of Algorithm 3 assuming the cost of all preprocessing costs is only as much as

---

[6] The choice $c = 0.25$ may be interpreted a posteriori as consistent with Fig. 1 where the minimum for BKZ is attained at $c \approx 0.30$. We note, however, that Fig. 1 considers BKZ-reduced bases for block size k, whereas here the algorithm encounters BKZ-reduced bases for block sizes $k' < k$.

Algorithm 4: BKZ with Algorithm 3 as Approx-HSVP oracle.

Data: A basis matrix $B \in \mathbb{R}^{d \times d}$.
Data: Cost parameter $k \geq 2$ and an overshooting parameter $c \geq 0$.
Result: A reduced basis of $L(B)$.

```
 1  B ← LLL(B);
 2  while change was made in previous iteration do
 3  |   for 0 ≤ κ < d − 1 do
 4  |   |   e ← min(d, κ + ⌈(1 + c) · k⌉);
 5  |   |   v ← output of Algorithm 3 on (π(B_{[κ:e]}), k, c);
 6  |   |   if ‖v‖ < ‖b*_κ‖ then
 7  |   |   |   insert v at index κ;
 8  |   |   |   call LLL to remove linear dependencies;
 9  |   |   |   record that a change was made;
10  |   |   end
11  |   end
12  end
13  return B;
```

LLL regardless of the choice of k'. This can be considered the best case scenario for Algorithm 3 and thus a rough lower bound on its running time.[7]

In Fig. 11 we give the preprocessing cost parameters and probabilities of success of a single enumeration selected by our optimisation. In particular, these figures suggest that the success probability per enumeration does not drop exponentially fast in Fig. 11b. This is consistent with the second order term in the time complexity which is closer to $1/2$ (corresponding to standard pruning) than 1 (corresponding to extreme pruning). Similarly, in contrast to Fig. 3a the preprocessing cost parameter (or "block size") k' in Fig. 11a does not seem to follow an affine function of k, i.e. it seems to grow faster for larger dimensions.

We also give experimental data comparing our implementation of Algorithm 3, impl.py, attached to the electronic version of the full version of document, with our simulations in Fig. 12. We note that our implementation of Algorithm 3 is faster than FPyLLL's SVP solver from dimension 82 onward. As in Sect. 2.5, we do not use the strategies produced by our simulation to run the implementation but rely on a variant of FPLLL's strategizer [dt17] to optimise these strategies.

Comparing Figs. 2 and 10 is meaningless without taking the obtained root Hermite factors into account. First, Algorithm 3 is not an SVP solver but an Approx-HSVP solver. Second, if $d < \lceil (1 + c) \cdot k \rceil$ then Algorithm 3 will reduce the enumeration dimension, further decreasing the quality of the output.

Since we are interested in running Algorithm 3 as a subroutine of Algorithm 4, we compare the latter against plain BKZ. For this comparison we consider the

---

[7] We note that this data only extends until $k = 323$. Computing pruning parameters requires increasing precision in increasing dimension and become more "brittle" the cheaper the preprocessing is compared to the enumeration cost. In other words, our simulation code simply crashed with a floating-point error in dimension 324. Since the trend is clear in the data already, we did not push it further using higher precision.

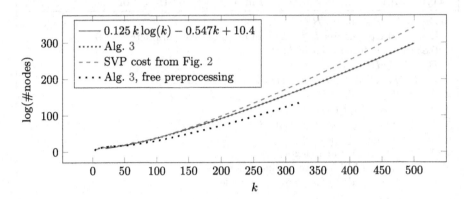

Fig. 10. Cost of one call to Algorithm 3 with enumeration dimension k, $c = 1/4$, $d = \lceil (1 + c) \cdot k \rceil$ and four preprocessing sweeps.

(a) Preprocessing cost parameters used in our simulations.

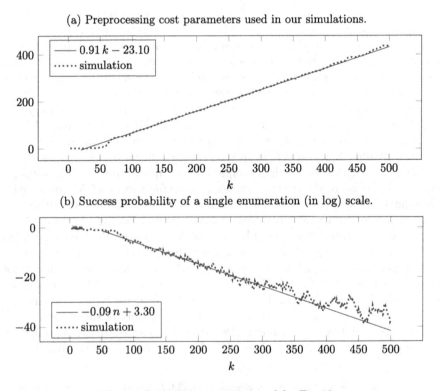

(b) Success probability of a single enumeration (in log) scale.

Fig. 11. Reduction strategies used for Fig. 10.

case $d = 2 \cdot k$, which corresponds to a typical setting encountered in cryptographic applications.

In Fig. 13, we plot the slope of the Gram–Schmidt log-norms as predicted by our simulations for BKZ on the one hand, and a self-dual variant of Algorithm 4. This variant first runs Algorithm 4 on the dual basis, followed by running Algorithm 4 on the original basis. Each run is capped at half the number of sweeps as used for BKZ. The rationale for this strategy is that it handles the quality degradation as the BKZ index i surpasses $d - \lceil (1+c) \cdot k \rceil$ where $k^{\star} < k$. As Fig. 13 illustrates, the obtained quality of the two algorithms is very close. Indeed our SD variant slightly outperforms BKZ, but we note that the ratio of the two is increasing, i.e. the quality advantage will invert as d increases.

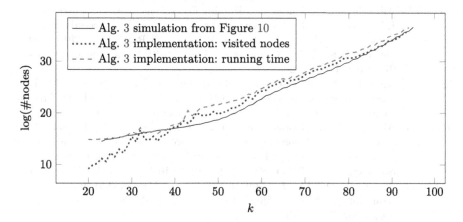

Fig. 12. Number of nodes visited during one Approx-HSVP call with enumeration dimension k, $c = 1/4$, $d = \lceil (1+c) \cdot k \rceil$ and four sweeps of preprocessing.

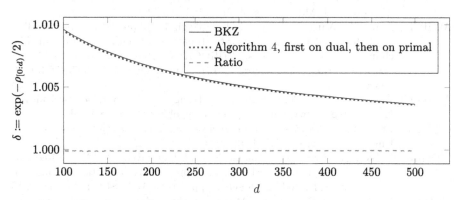

Four sweeps of Algorithm 4 on the dual, followed by four sweeps of Algorithm 4 on the primal lattice in dimension $d = 2 k$, using $c = 0.25$ and four preprocessing sweeps.

Fig. 13. Basis quality (BKZ vs SD-Algorithm 4)

Acknowledgments. The authors thank Léo Ducas, Elena Kirshanova and Michael Walter for helpful discussions. Shi Bai would like to acknowledge the use of the services provided by Research Computing at the Florida Atlantic University.

References

[ABD+16] Albrecht, M.R., et al.: Inaccurate security claims in NTRUprime, May 2016. https://groups.google.com/forum/#!topic/cryptanalytic-algorithms/BoSRL0uHIjM

[ACD+18] Albrecht, M.R., et al.: Estimate all the LWE, NTRU schemes!. In: Catalano, D., De Prisco, R. (eds.) SCN 2018. LNCS, vol. 11035, pp. 351–367. Springer, Cham (2018). https://doi.org/10.1007/978-3-319-98113-0_19

[ADH+19] Albrecht, M.R., Ducas, L., Herold, G., Kirshanova, E., Postlethwaite, E.W., Stevens, M.: The general sieve kernel and new records in lattice reduction. In: Ishai, Y., Rijmen, V. (eds.) EUROCRYPT 2019. LNCS, vol. 11477, pp. 717–746. Springer, Cham (2019). https://doi.org/10.1007/978-3-030-17656-3_25

[AGPS19] Albrecht, M.R., Gheorghiu, V., Postlethwaite, E.W., Schanck, J.M.: Estimating quantum speedups for lattice sieves. Cryptology ePrint Archive, Report 2019/1161 (2019). https://eprint.iacr.org/2019/1161

[AGVW17] Albrecht, M.R., Göpfert, F., Virdia, F., Wunderer, T.: Revisiting the expected cost of solving uSVP and applications to LWE. In: Takagi, T., Peyrin, T. (eds.) ASIACRYPT 2017. LNCS, vol. 10624, pp. 297–322. Springer, Cham (2017). https://doi.org/10.1007/978-3-319-70694-8_11

[ALNS19] Aggarwal, D., Li, J., Nguyen, P.Q., Stephens-Davidowitz, N.: Slide reduction, revisited - filling the gaps in SVP approximation. CoRR, abs/1908.03724 (2019)

[ANS18] Aono, Y., Nguyen, P.Q., Shen, Y.: Quantum lattice enumeration and tweaking discrete pruning. In: Peyrin, T., Galbraith, S. (eds.) ASIACRYPT 2018. LNCS, vol. 11272, pp. 405–434. Springer, Cham (2018). https://doi.org/10.1007/978-3-030-03326-2_14

[APS15] Albrecht, M.R., Player, R., Scott, S.: On the concrete hardness of learning with errors. J. Math. Cryptol. **9**(3), 169–203 (2015)

[AWHT16] Aono, Y., Wang, Y., Hayashi, T., Takagi, T.: Improved progressive BKZ algorithms and their precise cost estimation by sharp simulator. In: Fischlin, M., Coron, J.-S. (eds.) EUROCRYPT 2016. LNCS, vol. 9665, pp. 789–819. Springer, Heidelberg (2016). https://doi.org/10.1007/978-3-662-49890-3_30

[AWHT18] Aono, Y., Wang, Y., Hayashi, T., Takagi, T.: Progressive BKZ library (2018). http://www2.nict.go.jp/security/pbkzcode/index.html

[Bab86] Babai, L.: On Lovász' lattice reduction and the nearest lattice point problem. Combinatorica **6**(1), 1–13 (1986)

[BDGL16] Becker, A., Ducas, L., Gama, N. and Laarhoven, T.: New directions in nearest neighbor searching with applications to lattice sieving. In: Krauthgamer, R., (ed.) 27th SODA, pp. 10–24. ACM-SIAM, January 2016

[BSW18] Bai, S., Stehlé, D., Wen, W.: Measuring, simulating and exploiting the head concavity phenomenon in BKZ. In: Peyrin, T., Galbraith, S. (eds.) ASIACRYPT 2018. LNCS, vol. 11272, pp. 369–404. Springer, Cham (2018). https://doi.org/10.1007/978-3-030-03326-2_13

[Che13]   Chen, Y.: Réduction de réseau et sécurité concrète du chiffrement complètement homomorphe. Ph.D. thesis, Paris 7 (2013)

[CN11]   Chen, Y., Nguyen, P.Q.: BKZ 2.0: better lattice security estimates. In: Lee, D.H., Wang, X. (eds.) ASIACRYPT 2011. LNCS, vol. 7073, pp. 1–20. Springer, Heidelberg (2011). https://doi.org/10.1007/978-3-642-25385-0_1

[dt17]   The FPLLL development team. BKZ reduction strategy (preprocessing, pruning, etc.) (2017). https://github.com/fplll/strategizer

[dt19a]   The FPLLL development team. FPLLL, a lattice reduction library (2019). https://github.com/fplll/fplll

[dt19b]   The FPLLL development team. FPyLLL, a Python interface to fplll (2019). https://github.com/fplll/fpylll

[Duc18]   Ducas, L.: Shortest vector from lattice sieving: a few dimensions for free. In: Nielsen, J.B., Rijmen, V. (eds.) EUROCRYPT 2018. LNCS, vol. 10820, pp. 125–145. Springer, Cham (2018). https://doi.org/10.1007/978-3-319-78381-9_5

[FP83]   Fincke, U., Pohst, M.: A procedure for determining algebraic integers of given norm. In: van Hulzen, J.A. (ed.) EUROCAL 1983. LNCS, vol. 162, pp. 194–202. Springer, Heidelberg (1983). https://doi.org/10.1007/3-540-12868-9_103

[GN08a]   Gama, N., Nguyen, P.Q.: Finding short lattice vectors within Mordell's inequality. In: Ladner, R.E., Dwork, C. (eds.) 40th ACM STOC, pp. 207–216. ACM Press, May 2008

[GN08b]   Gama, N., Nguyen, P.Q.: Predicting lattice reduction. In: Smart, N. (ed.) EUROCRYPT 2008. LNCS, vol. 4965, pp. 31–51. Springer, Heidelberg (2008). https://doi.org/10.1007/978-3-540-78967-3_3

[GNR10]   Gama, N., Nguyen, P.Q., Regev, O.: Lattice enumeration using extreme pruning. In: Gilbert, H. (ed.) EUROCRYPT 2010. LNCS, vol. 6110, pp. 257–278. Springer, Heidelberg (2010). https://doi.org/10.1007/978-3-642-13190-5_13

[HPS11]   Hanrot, G., Pujol, X., Stehlé, D.: Analyzing blockwise lattice algorithms using dynamical systems. In: Rogaway, P. (ed.) CRYPTO 2011. LNCS, vol. 6841, pp. 447–464. Springer, Heidelberg (2011). https://doi.org/10.1007/978-3-642-22792-9_25

[HS07]   Hanrot, G., Stehlé, D.: Improved analysis of Kannan's shortest lattice vector algorithm. In: Menezes, A. (ed.) CRYPTO 2007. LNCS, vol. 4622, pp. 170–186. Springer, Heidelberg (2007). https://doi.org/10.1007/978-3-540-74143-5_10

[HS08]   Hanrot, G., Stehlé, D.: Worst-case Hermite-Korkine-Zolotarev reduced lattice bases. ArXiv, abs/0801.3331 (2008)

[HS10]   Hanrot, G., Stehlé, D.: A complete worst-case analysis of Kannan's shortest lattice vector algorithm Full version of [HS07, HS08] (2010). http://perso.ens-lyon.fr/damien.stehle/downloads/KANNAN_EXTENDED.pdf

[Kan83]   Kannan, R.: Improved algorithms for integer programming and related lattice problems. In: 15th ACM STOC, pp. 193–206. ACM Press, April 1983

[Laa15]   Laarhoven, T.: Search problems in cryptography. Ph.D. thesis, Eindhoven University of Technology (2015)

[LLJL82] Lenstra, A.K., Lenstra Jr., H.W., Lovász, L.: Factoring polynomials with rational coefficients. Math. Ann. **261**(12), 515–534 (1982)

[LM18]   Laarhoven, T., Mariano, A.: Progressive lattice sieving. In: Lange, T., Steinwandt, R. (eds.) PQCrypto 2018. LNCS, vol. 10786, pp. 292–311. Springer, Cham (2018). https://doi.org/10.1007/978-3-319-79063-3_14

[MW15]   Micciancio, D., Walter, M.: Fast lattice point enumeration with minimal overhead. In: Indyk, P. (ed.) 26th SODA, pp. 276–294. ACM-SIAM, January 2015

[MW16]   Micciancio, D., Walter, M.: Practical, predictable lattice basis reduction. In: Fischlin, M., Coron, J.-S. (eds.) EUROCRYPT 2016. LNCS, vol. 9665, pp. 820–849. Springer, Heidelberg (2016). https://doi.org/10.1007/978-3-662-49890-3_31

[Ngu10]   Nguyen, P.Q.: Hermite's constant and lattice algorithms. In: Nguyen, P., Vallée, B. (eds.) The LLL Algorithm. Information Security and Cryptography. Springer, Heidelberg (2010). https://doi.org/10.1007/978-3-642-02295-1_2

[Sch03]   Schnorr, C.P.: Lattice reduction by random sampling and birthday methods. In: Alt, H., Habib, M. (eds.) STACS 2003. LNCS, vol. 2607, pp. 145–156. Springer, Heidelberg (2003). https://doi.org/10.1007/3-540-36494-3_14

[SE94]   Schnorr, C.P., Euchner, M.: Lattice basis reduction: improved practical algorithms and solving subset sum problems. Math. Program. **66**, 181–199 (1994). https://doi.org/10.1007/BF01581144

[SG10]   Schneider, M., Gama, N.: Darmstadt SVP challenges (2010). https://www.latticechallenge.org/svp-challenge/index.php

[Sho18]   Shoup, V.: Number theory library 11.3.1 (NTL) for C++ (2018). http://www.shoup.net/ntl/

[VGO+20]   Virtanen, P., et al.: SciPy 1.0: fundamental algorithms for scientific computing in Python. Nat. Methods **17**(3), 261–272 (2020)

[YD17]   Yang, Y., Léo, D.: Second order statistical behavior of LLL and BKZ. In: Adams, C., Camenisch, J. (eds.) SAC 2017. LNCS, vol. 10719, pp. 3–22. Springer, Heidelberg (2017). https://doi.org/10.1007/978-3-319-72565-9_1

Lattice Reduction for Modules,
or How to Reduce ModuleSVP to ModuleSVP

Tamalika Mukherjee[1($\boxtimes$)] and Noah Stephens-Davidowitz[2($\boxtimes$)]

[1] Purdue University, West Lafayette, USA
tmukherj@purdue.edu
[2] Cornell University, Ithaca, USA
noahsd@gmail.com

Abstract. This is the extended abstract of [MS20]. See the full version at eprint:2019/1142.

We show how to generalize lattice reduction algorithms to module lattices. Specifically, we reduce γ-approximate ModuleSVP over module lattices with rank $k \geq 2$ to γ'-approximate ModuleSVP over module lattices with rank $2 \leq \beta \leq k$. To do so, we modify the celebrated slide-reduction algorithm of Gama and Nguyen to work with module filtrations, a high-dimensional generalization of the ($\mathbb{Z}$-)basis of a lattice.

The particular value of γ that we achieve depends on the underlying number field K, the order $R \subseteq \mathcal{O}_K$, and the embedding (as well as, of course, k and β). However, for reasonable choices of these parameters, the resulting value of γ is surprisingly close to the one achieved by "plain" lattice reduction algorithms, which require an arbitrary SVP oracle in the same dimension. In other words, we show that ModuleSVP oracles are nearly as useful as SVP oracles for solving higher-rank instances of approximate ModuleSVP.

Our result generalizes the recent independent result of Lee, Pellet-Mary, Stehlé, and Wallet, which works in the important special case when $\beta = 2$ and $R = \mathcal{O}_K$ is the ring of integers of K under the canonical embedding, while our reduction works. Indeed, at a high level our reduction can be thought of as a generalization of theirs in roughly the same way that block reduction generalizes LLL reduction.

In this extended abstract, we present a special case of the more general result to appear in the full version [MS20].

1 Introduction

A (rational) lattice $\mathcal{L} \subset \mathbb{Q}^d$ is the set of all integer linear combinations of finitely many generating vectors $\boldsymbol{y}_1, \ldots, \boldsymbol{y}_m \in \mathbb{Q}^d$,

$$\mathcal{L} := \{z_1 \boldsymbol{y}_1 + \cdots + z_m \boldsymbol{y}_m \ : \ z_i \in \mathbb{Z}\} \ .$$

T. Mukherjee—This work was done while being supported by The Center for Science of Information, an NSF Science and Technology Center, Cooperative Agreement # CCF 0939370.

N. Stephens-Davidowitz—Part of this work was supported by NSF-BSF grant number 1718161 and NSF CAREER Award number 1350619 via Vinod Vaikuntanathan. Part of this work was done while the author was at the Centre for Quantum Technologies at the National University of Singapore, Massachusetts Institute of Technology, and the Simons Institute in Berkeley.

D. Micciancio and T. Ristenpart (Eds.): CRYPTO 2020, LNCS 12171, pp. 213–242, 2020.
https://doi.org/10.1007/978-3-030-56880-1_8

For an approximation factor $\gamma \geq 1$, the γ-approximate Shortest Vector Problem (γ-SVP) asks us to find a non-zero vector $\boldsymbol{y} \in \mathcal{L}$ whose length is within a factor γ of the minimum possible.

Lattices have played a key role in computer science since Lenstra, Lenstra, and Lovász published their celebrated LLL algorithm, which solves γ-SVP for $\gamma = 2^{O(d)}$ in polynomial time [LLL82], essentially by reducing the problem to many instances of exact SVP in two dimensions. In spite of this very large approximation factor, the LLL algorithm has found innumerable applications [LLL82, Bab86, SE94, NV10, FS10].

Lattices have taken on an even larger role in recent years because of the growing importance of lattice-based cryptography [Ajt96, HPS98, GPV08, Reg09, Pei09, SSTX09, LPR10, Pei16]—that is, cryptography whose security relies on the hardness of γ-SVP (or a closely related problem) for some γ (typically, $\gamma = \mathrm{poly}(d)$). These schemes have several advantages, such as worst-case to average-case reductions, which show that some of these schemes are actually provably secure under the assumption that (the decision version of) γ'-SVP is hard in the worst case [Ajt96, MR07, Reg09, LPR10, LS15, PRS17]. They are also thought to be secure against quantum attackers, and for this reason, they are likely to be standardized by NIST (the United States' National Institute for Standards and Technology) for widespread use in the near future [NIS18].

However, one drawback of generic lattice-based constructions is their inefficiency (though, see [ABD+19]). Loosely speaking, this inefficiency arises from the fact that a lattice in dimension d typically requires about d^2 numbers to specify—at least d generating vectors, each with d coordinates. To get around this, cryptographers often use lattices with certain additional symmetries [HPS98, PR06, SSTX09, LPR10, SS11, LS12, DD12, LS15, PRS17], since such lattices can be described succinctly.

In particular, cryptographers typically use (variants of) *module lattices*. For a number field K of degree n (i.e., $K := \mathbb{Q}[x]/p(x)$ for an irreducible polynomial $p(x)$ of degree n) with an order $R \subseteq \mathcal{O}_K$ (i.e., a discrete full-rank subring, such as $\mathbb{Z}[x]/p(x)$ when $p \in \mathbb{Z}[x]$ is monic, or the ring of integers $\mathcal{O}_K$ of K), a module lattice over R is the set of all R-linear combinations of finitely many generating vectors $\boldsymbol{y}_1, \ldots, \boldsymbol{y}_m \in K^\ell$,

$$\mathcal{M} := \{r_1 \boldsymbol{y}_1 + \cdots + r_m \boldsymbol{y}_m \ : \ r_i \in R\} \ .$$

By embedding the number field K into $\mathbb{Q}^n$ (or by equipping K with an inner product, which is what we do in the sequel), we can view module lattices as (ℓn)-dimensional "plain" lattices. In particular, it makes sense to talk about the length of module elements. A key parameter is the *rank* k

of the module lattice, which is the dimension of its K-span. We typically think of n as large (i.e., $n \to \infty$) and k as a relatively small constant.[1]

We can then define (γ, k)-ModuleSVP over R as the restriction of γ-SVP to rank-k module lattices $\mathcal{M} \subset K^\ell$ over R (under some inner product). Clearly, (γ, k)-ModuleSVP is no harder than γ-SVP over lattices with rank kn. A key question is whether we can do (significantly) better. In other words, are there (significantly) faster algorithms for ModuleSVP than there are for SVP? Does the specialization to module lattices (which yields large efficiency benefits for cryptography) impact security?

Many cryptographic schemes rely on the assumption that no such algorithms exist. E.g., about half of the candidate encryption schemes still under consideration by NIST would be broken in practice if significantly faster algorithms were found for ModuleSVP [NIS18]. (Just one relies on "plain" lattices [ABD+19]). We would therefore like to understand the hardness of ModuleSVP as soon as possible.

Until recently, one might have conjectured that (γ, k)-ModuleSVP is essentially as hard as γ-SVP on rank kn lattices for all γ and k. However, a recent (growing) line of work has shown much faster algorithms for the $k = 1$ case [CGS14, CDPR16, CDW17, Duc17, DPW19, PHS19], in which case the problem is called IdealSVP. Most cryptographic schemes are not known to be broken by these algorithms (or even by an adversary with access to an oracle for exact IdealSVP). However, similar improvement for the case $k = 2$ would yield faster algorithms for both the Ring-LWE problem [SSTX09, LPR10] and the NTRU problem [HPS98], which would break most cryptographic schemes based on structured lattices. (We are intentionally ignoring many important details here for simplicity. See [Pei15, Duc17, DPW19, PHS19] for a more careful discussion.)

Therefore, (ignoring a number of important details) the security of many cryptographic schemes essentially relies on the assumption that (γ, k)-ModuleSVP for $k \geq 2$ is qualitatively different than γ-IdealSVP $= (\gamma, 1)$-ModuleSVP. More generally, this recent (surprising) line of work in the $k = 1$ case suggests that we need a better understanding of (γ, k)-ModuleSVP for all γ and k.

To that end, we observe that much of our understanding of γ-SVP comes from *basis reduction algorithms* [LLL82, SE94, GN08, MW16, ALNS19]. These algorithms allow us to reduce γ-SVP in a high dimension d to γ'-SVP in a lower dimension m (known as the block size) for some approximation factor

---

[1] Notice that module lattices correspond exactly to lattices that are closed under a certain set of linear transformations—the linear transformations corresponding to multiplication by elements of R.

γ depending on d, m, and γ'. Indeed, the LLL algorithm can be viewed as an example of such a reduction for the case $m = 2$. For the approximation factors relevant to cryptography, our fastest algorithms rely on basis reduction. In fact, these are more-or-less our only non-trivial algorithms for superconstant approximation factors. (See [ALNS19].)

In other words, to solve γ-SVP (or, for that matter, (γ, k)-ModuleSVP) for superconstant γ, the best known strategy works by reducing the problem to many instances of SVP with a smaller approximation factor over lower-dimensional "blocks." The current state of the art, due to [ALNS19] and building heavily on the work of Gama and Nguyen [GN08], achieves an approximation factor of

$$\gamma = \gamma' \cdot (\gamma' \sqrt{\beta n})^{\frac{2(k-\beta)}{\beta - 1/n}} \tag{1}$$

for block size $m := \beta n$ and dimension $d := kn$. (We have chosen this rather strange parameterization to more easily compare with our results for ModuleSVP.) For cryptanalysis, we typically must take $\beta = \Omega(k)$ and $\gamma' \leq \text{poly}(d)$ in order to achieve a final approximation factor γ that is polynomial in the dimension $d = kn$.

1.1   Our Results

Lattice reduction for Modules. Our primary contribution is the following reduction.

Theorem 1 (Informal, see the discussion below and the full version [MS20]). *For $2 \leq \beta < k$ with β dividing k, there is an efficient reduction from (γ, k)-ModuleSVP to (γ', β)-ModuleSVP, where*

$$\gamma = (\gamma')^2 n \cdot (\gamma' \sqrt{\beta n})^{\frac{2(k-\beta)}{\beta - 1}} .$$

The case $\beta = 2$ is of particular interest because of its relevance to cryptography. We note that, before this work was finished, Lee, Pellet-Mary, Stehlé, and Wallet published essentially the same reduction for this important special case [LPSW19]. (Formally, they only showed this for the canonical embedding for the ring of integers of a number field, but it is easy to see that this generalizes to arbitrary orders and a more general class of embeddings that we call "semi-canonical." They also showed a very interesting algorithm for $(\gamma, 2)$-ModuleSVP, which requires a CVP oracle over a lattice depending only on R. We refer the reader to [LPSW19] for the details.) For this $\beta = 2$ case, the reduction can be viewed as a generalization of the LLL algorithm. (In this extended abstract, we only present a special case of the $\beta = 2$ reduction. See [MS20] for the general reduction).

In the general case $\beta \geq 2$, we note the obvious resemblance between the approximation factor achieved by Theorem 1 and the approximation factor shown in Eq. (1). Indeed, our reduction can be viewed as a generalization of Gama and Nguyen's celebrated slide reduction [GN08] to the module case (see also [ALNS19]).[2] Therefore, we can interpret Theorem 1 as saying that "a ModuleSVP oracle is almost as good as a generic SVP oracle for basis reduction over module lattices."

Finally, notice that this informal version of Theorem 1 does not mention the number field K, the associated embedding, or the order $R \subseteq \mathcal{O}_K$. In fact, the reduction works for any nice enough number field K, *any* order $R \subseteq \mathcal{O}_K$, and a reasonably large class of embeddings that we call semicanonical. These are generalizations of the canonical embedding that might prove useful in other settings. (Formally, we consider semicanonical *inner products* on K. See Sects. 1.2 and 2.5.) Furthermore, the approximation factor that we achieve depends on certain geometric properties of the order and the embedding. (See the full version [MS20] for the precise statement.) The approximation factor shown in Theorem 1 is (a loose upper bound on) what we achieve for the canonical embedding of the ring of integers of a cyclotomic number field.

Two variants. As additional contributions, we note that our reduction can also be used to solve two variants of ModuleSVP.

The first variant is known as ModuleHSVP (where the H is in honor of Hermite). This problem asks us to find a non-zero vector that is short relative to the determinant of the module lattice $\mathcal{M}$, rather than relative to the shortest non-zero vector. I.e., (γ, k)-ModuleHSVP asks us to find a non-zero vector $\boldsymbol{x}$ in a rank-k module lattice $\mathcal{M}$ with $\|\boldsymbol{x}\| \leq \gamma \cdot \det(\mathcal{M})^{1/(kn)}$. For $\gamma \gtrsim \sqrt{kn}$, there is always a non-zero vector satisfying this inequality. (The minimal value of γ for which γ-HSVP is a total problem is called *Hermite's constant*, which explains the name.) In particular, $(\gamma\sqrt{kn}, k)$-ModuleHSVP trivially reduces to (γ, k)-ModuleSVP, but our reduction achieves a better approximation factor than what one would obtain by combining this trivial reduction with Theorem 1. (The same is true of many "plain" basis reduction algorithms [GN08, ALNS19].) This variant of SVP is enough for most cryptanalytic applications, so that this better approximation

---

[2] Indeed, if we take $n = 1$ and $\gamma' = 1$, then we recover the original slide reduction algorithm from [GN08]. Specializing further to $\beta = 2$ recovers LLL.

factor could prove to be quite useful in practice. (In particular, the analogous result for plain basis reduction algorithms is often used in cryptanalysis.)

Theorem 2 (Informal, see the full version [MS20]). *For* $2 \leq \beta < k$ *with* β *dividing* k, *there is an efficient reduction from* (γ_H, k)-*ModuleHSVP to* (γ', β)-*ModuleSVP, where*

$$\gamma_H := \gamma' \sqrt{n} \cdot (\gamma' \sqrt{\beta n})^{\frac{k-1}{\beta-1}} .$$

Again, the approximation factor shown in Theorem 2 is (a loose upper bound on) what we achieve for the canonical embedding of the ring of integers of a cyclotomic number field.

Our second variant has no analogue for plain lattices. We consider the (γ, k)-Dense Ideal Problem $((\gamma, k)$-DIP), in which the goal is to find a rank-one submodule $\mathcal{M}'$ (i.e., an ideal) such that $\det(\mathcal{M}')^{1/n}$ is within a factor γ of the minimum possible. This problem is in a sense more natural in our context. Indeed, Theorem 1 is perhaps best viewed as a consequence of Theorem 3. We again note the obvious similarity between Theorem 3 and Eq. (1). (There is an analogous result for what we might call "RankinDIP," in honor of Rankin's constants, which asks us to find an ideal whose determinant is small relative to $\det(\mathcal{M})^{1/(nk)}$, just like ModuleHSVP asks for a vector that is short relative to $\det(\mathcal{M})^{1/(kn)}$. For simplicity, we do not bother to make this formal.)

Theorem 3 (Informal, see the full version [MS20]). *For* $2 \leq \beta < k$ *with* β *dividing* k, *there is an efficient reduction from* (γ, k)-*DIP to* (γ', β)-*DIP, where*

$$\gamma := \gamma' \cdot (\gamma' \sqrt{\beta n})^{\frac{2(k-\beta)}{\beta-1}} .$$

Again, the resulting approximation factor depends on the geometry of the order R, and the above result corresponds to the case when $R = \mathcal{O}_K$ is the ring of integers of a number field K under the canonical embedding.

1.2   Our Techniques

From bases to filtrations. Lattice basis reduction algorithms take as input a ($\mathbb{Z}$-)basis $(\boldsymbol{b}_1, \ldots, \boldsymbol{b}_d)$ of a lattice $\mathcal{L} \subset \mathbb{Q}^d$ and they iteratively "shorten" the basis vectors using an oracle for SVP in $m < d$ dimensions. More specifically, let $\mathcal{L}_i$ be the lattice spanned by $\boldsymbol{b}_1, \ldots, \boldsymbol{b}_i$. Basis reduction algorithms work by finding short vectors in "blocks"—lattices of the form

$\mathcal{L}_{[i,j]} := \pi_{\mathcal{L}_{i-1}^{\perp}}(\mathcal{L}_j)$, where $\pi_{\mathcal{L}_i^{\perp}}$ represents projection onto the subspace orthogonal to $\mathcal{L}_i$. In the basis reduction literature, the $\mathcal{L}_i$ and $\mathcal{L}_{[i,j]}$ are typically not defined explicitly. Instead, corresponding bases for these lattices are defined.

To generalize this idea to module lattices, our first challenge is to find the appropriate analogue of a basis. Indeed, while lattices with rank d over $\mathbb{Z}$ have a $\mathbb{Z}$-basis consisting of d (linearly independent) lattice vectors, the analogous statement is typically not true for modules over more general orders R. In other words, our module lattice $\mathcal{M}$ of rank k will not always have an R-basis consisting of only k elements. (E.g., rank-one module lattices are ideals, and they have an R-basis consisting of a single element if and only if they are principal. More generally, all rank-k module lattices have an R-basis consisting of k vectors if and only if R is a principal ideal domain. Typically, the rings that interest us are *not* principal ideal domains.) This means that basis-reduction techniques do not really make sense over an R-basis.

So, instead of generalizing $\mathbb{Z}$-bases themselves, we work directly with the sublattices $\mathcal{L}_i$ and blocks $\mathcal{L}_{[i,j]}$. To that end, we define a *module filtration* $\mathcal{M}_1 \subset \mathcal{M}_2 \subset \cdots \subset \mathcal{M}_k = \mathcal{M}$ of $\mathcal{M}$ as a sequence of k (primitive) submodules with strictly increasing ranks (over K). Filtrations have the nice property that the projection $\mathcal{M}_{[i,j]} := \pi_{\mathcal{M}_{i-1}^{\perp}}(\mathcal{M}_j)$ of $\mathcal{M}_j$ orthogonal to $\mathcal{M}_i$ is itself a module lattice with rank $j - i + 1$. (We are being deliberately vague about what we mean by "projection" here. See Sects. 1.2 and 2.5.) They are well-behaved in other ways as well. For example, (for nice enough embeddings) the determinant of $\mathcal{M}$ is given by the product of the determinants of the rank-one projections $\widetilde{\mathcal{M}}_i := \pi_{\mathcal{M}_{i-1}}(\mathcal{M}_i)$, which is analogous to the fact that the determinant of a lattice is given by the product of the lengths of the Gram-Schmidt vectors $\widetilde{b}_i$ of any basis. These are the key properties that allow us to perform basis reduction using SVP oracle calls only on module lattices.[3]

From vectors to ideals (or sublattices). By working with filtrations, our reduction is most naturally viewed as a variant of basis reduction with the Gram-Schmidt vectors $\pi_{\mathcal{L}_{i-1}^{\perp}}(b_i)$ replaced by ideals $\pi_{\mathcal{M}_{i-1}^{\perp}}(\mathcal{M}_i)$, and lengths replaced by the determinant. This naturally gives rise to Theorem 3—a reduction from DIP to DIP.

---

[3] In [FS10, LPSW19], the authors work with *pseudobases*, which consist of vectors $b_1, \ldots, b_k \in K^k$ and ideals $\mathcal{I}_1, \ldots, \mathcal{I}_k \subset K$ such that $\mathcal{M} = \mathcal{I}_1 b_1 + \cdots + \mathcal{I}_k b_k$. These are quite similar to filtrations. E.g., a pseudobasis can be converted into the filtration given by $\mathcal{M}_i := \mathcal{I}_1 b_1 + \cdots + \mathcal{I}_i b_i$.

Indeed, this DIP-to-DIP reduction actually "never looks at the length of a vector." It only considers determinants of submodules. And, it can be viewed as a specialization to module lattices of a more general reduction from the problem of finding dense rank-n sublattices of a kn-dimensional lattice to the problem of finding dense rank-n sublattices in a βn-dimensional lattice (though we do not bother to show this formally).

From ideals back to vectors. In order to obtain our main result, we must convert this DIP-to-DIP reduction into a reduction from ModuleSVP to ModuleSVP. To do so, we use well-known relationships between the length of short non-zero vectors and the determinants of dense rank-one submodules. Specifically, we use (1) Minkowski's theorem, which states that any dense submodule must contain a short vector (which holds for all lattices, not just module lattices); and (2) the fact that the R-span of a short vector must be a relatively dense ideal, which has no analogue for lattices in general. (The latter property is a partial converse of Minkowski's theorem for ideals. The quantitative result depends on the geometry of the order R, which is the main reason that our approximation factors also depend on this geometry).

Therefore, a ModuleSVP oracle can be used to find a short vector, which must generate a dense ideal. And, we may use a DIP oracle to find a low-rank submodule that contains a short vector. This allows us to move freely between DIP and ModuleSVP (at the cost of a higher approximation factor), which yields our main result.

Projections. In order for our reduction to make sense, we need some kind of notion of "projection." In particular, we need to make sense of the "projection of a module lattice $\mathcal{M} \subset K^\ell$ orthogonal to some submodule lattice $\mathcal{M}' \subseteq \mathcal{M}$" (since this is necessary to define, e.g., $\mathcal{M}_{[i,j]}$). In what follows, we use the word *projection* to mean any $\mathbb{Q}$-linear map that equals its own square.

One way to define projection is by noting that our notion of length in K^ℓ comes from viewing $K^\ell = K \oplus \cdots \oplus K$ as an $n\ell$-dimensional $\mathbb{Q}$-vector space, and fixing some inner product $\langle \cdot, \cdot \rangle_\rho$ on K (which immediately yields an inner product on K^ℓ). Indeed, it does not make sense to talk about ModuleSVP without first fixing some notion of length in K^ℓ, and the most natural notion is given by $\|\boldsymbol{x}\|_\rho^2 := \langle \boldsymbol{x}, \boldsymbol{x} \rangle_\rho$. We can then define our projection as simply the standard orthogonal projection over any $\mathbb{Q}$ vector space. The projection map $\Pi_{\rho,W}$ onto a subspace $W \subseteq K^\ell$ is the unique $\mathbb{Q}$-linear map that leaves W unchanged and maps to zero all elements that are $\mathbb{Q}$-orthogonal to W.

This is of course the most natural notion of projection, and the projection Π_ρ has many nice properties (since it is just the standard notion of $\mathbb{Q}$-linear orthogonal projection). For example, Π_ρ is contracting (i.e., it cannot increase the length of a vector), and $\det(\mathcal{M}) = \det(V^\perp \cap \mathcal{M}) \cdot \det(\Pi_{\rho,V}(\mathcal{M}))$ (where length and the determinant are defined in terms of the inner product $\langle \cdot, \cdot \rangle_\rho$). However, the lattice $\Pi_{\rho,V}(\mathcal{M})$ might *not* be a module lattice. This is a serious issue because we wish to call our ModuleSVP oracle on this projection.

Another idea is to define a K-linear "inner product" $\langle \cdot, \cdot \rangle_K$ over K^ℓ, given by $\langle \boldsymbol{x}, \boldsymbol{y} \rangle_K := \sum_{i=1}^\ell x_i \overline{y_i}$, where $\overline{y_i}$ is the complex conjugate of y_i.[4] We can then define $(\mathcal{M}')^\perp := \{ \boldsymbol{x} \in K^\ell : \forall \boldsymbol{y} \in \mathcal{M}', \langle \boldsymbol{y}, \boldsymbol{x} \rangle_K = 0 \}$ and define the projection mapping $\Pi_K : K^\ell \to K^\ell$ to be the unique K-linear map that leaves $(M')^\perp$ fixed and sends all elements in $\mathcal{M}'$ to $\boldsymbol{0}$.

Since the map Π_K is K-linear (by definition), it maps the module lattice $\mathcal{M}$ to another module lattice $\Pi_K(\mathcal{M})$. So, it does not have the problem that Π_ρ had. However, Π_K might not interact nicely with $\langle \cdot, \cdot \rangle_\rho$. E.g., Π_K might increase the length of a vector (under the norm induced by Π_ρ), and we might *not* have $\det(\mathcal{M}) = \det(\mathcal{M}') \cdot \det(\Pi_K(\mathcal{M}))$. This is a big problem, since it means that, e.g., non-zero projections of short vectors in $\mathcal{M}$ "might not be found by a ModuleSVP oracle called on $\Pi_\rho(\mathcal{M})$." More generally, basis reduction algorithms rely heavily on both the contracting nature of projection and the identity $\det(\mathcal{M}) = \det(\mathcal{M}') \det(\Pi_\rho(\mathcal{M}))$.

In summary, Π_ρ is the "right" notion of orthogonal projection from a *geometric* perspective, since it behaves nicely in terms of geometric quantities like lengths and determinants. On the other hand, Π_K is the "right" notion of orthogonal projection from a *algebraic* perspective, since it preserves the module structure of lattices. Indeed, there is a sense in which Π_ρ is the *only* projection map that is "nice" geometrically, and Π_K algebraically.

We therefore restrict our attention to number fields K and inner products $\langle \cdot, \cdot \rangle_\rho$ for which $\Pi_\rho = \Pi_K$, so that a single projection has both the algebraic and geometric properties that we need. In particular, we take number fields K that are closed under complex conjugate (these are the totally real fields and CM fields) and inner products $\langle \cdot, \cdot \rangle_\rho$ that "respect

---

[4] Taking the complex conjugate is necessary to guarantee that $\langle \boldsymbol{x}, \boldsymbol{x} \rangle_K$ is non-zero (and totally positive) for $\boldsymbol{x} \neq \boldsymbol{0}$. Formally, this is not quite an inner product because the base field is neither $\mathbb{R}$ nor $\mathbb{C}$. But, it *is* a non-degenerate conjugate symmetric sesquilinear form, which makes the analogy useful.

field multiplication" in the sense that $\langle \alpha x, y \rangle_\rho = \langle x, \overline{\alpha} y \rangle_\rho$. Such *semi-canonical* inner products have a simple characterization in terms of (full-rank) linear maps $T : K \to \mathbb{Q}$:

$$\langle x, y \rangle_\rho := \sum_i T(x_i \overline{y_i}) .$$

(The *canonical* inner product is the important special case when $T := \mathrm{Tr}_{K/\mathbb{Q}}$ is the trace map.)

These same restrictions are also exactly what is needed to guarantee that the dual $\mathcal{M}^*$ of a module lattice is also a module lattice (which we also need for our reduction, for $k > 2$). See Sect. 2.5 for more details and other equivalent definitions.

1.3   Related Work

The most closely related work to this paper is the recent independent work of Lee, Pellet-Mary, Stehlé, and Wallet [LPSW19], which was published before this work was finished. [LPSW19] proved Theorem 1 in the important special case when $\beta = 2$ and $R = \mathcal{O}_K$ is the ring of integers of the number field K under the canonical embedding. Their reduction is essentially identical to ours, though they use a formally different notion of a reduced basis that seems not to generalize quite as nicely for larger β.[5] They also show a surprising algorithm for $(\gamma, 2)$-ModuleSVP (formally, a quantum polynomial-time reduction from this problem to the Closest Vector Problem over a lattice that depends only on K), which can be used to instantiate the $(\gamma, 2)$-ModuleSVP oracle.

For $\beta > 2$, our reductions are generalizations of the slide-reduction algorithm of Gama and Nguyen [GN08], and our work is largely inspired by theirs. Indeed, both our notion of a reduced filtration and our algorithm for constructing one are direct generalizations of the corresponding ideas in [GN08] from bases of $\mathbb{Z}$-lattices to filtrations of module lattices.

There are also other rather different notions of basis reduction for module lattices from prior work. For example, for certain Euclidean domains, Napias showed that the LLL algorithm (and Gauss's algorithm

---

[5] Specifically, in the notation introduced above, they work with the ratio of $\det(\pi_{\mathcal{M}_{i-1}^\perp}(\mathcal{M}_i))$ to $\det(\pi_{\mathcal{M}_i^\perp}(\mathcal{M}_{i+1}))$, while we work with the ratio of $\det(\pi_{\mathcal{M}_{i-1}^\perp}(\mathcal{M}_i))$ relative to the minimum possible for a rank-one submodule of $\pi_{\mathcal{M}_{i-1}^\perp}(\mathcal{M}_{i+1})$. The distinction is not particularly important for $\beta = 2$, but the analogous conditions for $\beta > 2$ are quite different. In particular, the most natural generalization of the first notion seems to only yield a solution to ModuleHSVP.

for rank-two lattices) generalizes quite nicely, with no need for an oracle [Nap96]. Follow-up work showed how to extend this to more Euclidean domains [GLM09,KL17]. However, it seems that algorithms of this type can only work in the Euclidean case [LPL18], and for the cryptographic applications that interest us most, the order R is typically not Euclidean—or even a principal ideal domain. (The algorithm of [LPSW19] for $(\gamma, 2)$-ModuleSVP is particularly surprising precisely because it seems to mimic Gauss's algorithm even though it works for non-Euclidean rings.) In another direction, Fieker and Stehlé showed how to efficiently convert an LLL-reduced $\mathbb{Z}$-basis for a module lattice into an LLL-reduced pseudobasis, which in our language is essentially a filtration that is reduced in a certain sense [FS10]. I.e., they show how to efficiently convert a relatively short $\mathbb{Z}$-basis into a relatively nice filtration.

2   Preliminaries

For $x \in \mathbb{C}$, we write $\bar{x}$ for the complex conjugate of x. For a $\mathbb{Q}$-subspace $V \subseteq \mathbb{Q}^d$ and a rational-valued inner product $\langle \cdot, \cdot \rangle_\rho$, we define the ρ-orthogonal projection onto V as the unique $\mathbb{Q}$-linear map $\Pi_{\rho,V} : \mathbb{Q}^d \to \mathbb{Q}^d$ that satisfies $\Pi_{\rho,V}(x) = x$ for $x \in V$ and $\Pi_{\rho,V}(x) = 0$ if $\langle y, x \rangle_\rho = 0$ for all $y \in V$. We write $\langle \cdot, \cdot \rangle_{\mathbb{Q}}$ for the standard inner product over $\mathbb{Q}^d$.

2.1   Lattices

A lattice $\mathcal{L} \subset \mathbb{R}^d$ is the $\mathbb{Z}$-span of finitely many vectors $y_1, \ldots, y_m \in \mathbb{Q}^d$ such that

$$\mathcal{L} := \{z_1 y_1 + \cdots + z_m y_m \ : \ z_i \in \mathbb{Z}\} \, ,$$

If $y_1, \ldots, y_m$ are $\mathbb{Q}$-linearly independent vectors, then we sometimes call this a $\mathbb{Z}$-basis, and we write $m := \mathrm{rank}_{\mathbb{Q}}(\mathcal{L})$. For any lattice $\mathcal{L} \subset \mathbb{Q}^d$ and sublattice $\mathcal{L}' \subseteq \mathcal{L}$, we say that $\mathcal{L}'$ is *primitive* if $\mathcal{L}' = \mathcal{L} \cap \mathrm{span}_{\mathbb{Q}}(\mathcal{L}')$. If $\mathcal{L}'$ is primitive and $W \subseteq \mathrm{span}_{\mathbb{Q}}(\mathcal{L}')$ is a $\mathbb{Q}$-subspace, then $W \cap \mathcal{L}'$ is also a primitive sublattice with $\mathrm{rank}_{\mathbb{Q}}(W \cap \mathcal{L}') = \dim_{\mathbb{Q}}(W)$.

The lattice determinant is $\det(\mathcal{L}) := \sqrt{\det(\mathbf{G})}$, where $\mathbf{G} \in \mathbb{Q}^{m \times m}$ is the Gram matrix $G_{i,j} := \langle \mathbf{b}_i, \mathbf{b}_j \rangle_{\mathbb{Q}}$ of $\mathbf{B} = (\mathbf{b}_1, \ldots, \mathbf{b}_m) \in \mathbb{Q}^{d \times m}$ for any $\mathbb{Z}$-basis $\mathbf{B}$ of $\mathcal{L}$ (the choice of basis does not matter). If $\mathcal{L}' \subset \mathcal{L}$ is primitive and $W \subset \mathbb{Q}^d$ is the subspace of all vectors that are $\mathbb{Q}$-orthogonal to $\mathcal{L}'$, then $\det(\mathcal{L}) = \det(\mathcal{L}') \det(\Pi_{\mathbb{Q},W}(\mathcal{L}))$.

We write $\lambda_1(\mathcal{L}) := \min_{\mathbf{y} \in \mathcal{L} \setminus \{\mathbf{0}\}} \langle \mathbf{y}, \mathbf{y} \rangle_{\mathbb{Q}}^{1/2}$ for the length of a shortest non-zero vector in $\mathcal{L}$.

The *dual lattice* $\mathcal{L}^*$ is the set of vectors in the span of $\mathcal{L}$ whose inner product with all lattice vectors is integral,

$$\mathcal{L}^* := \{ \mathbf{w} \in \mathrm{span}_{\mathbb{Q}}(\mathcal{L}) \ : \ \forall \mathbf{y} \in \mathcal{L}, \ \langle \mathbf{w}, \mathbf{y} \rangle_{\mathbb{Q}} \in \mathbb{Z} \} \ .$$

The dual has as a basis $\mathbf{B}\mathbf{G}^{-1}$ for any basis $\mathbf{B}$ of $\mathcal{L}$ with Gram matrix $\mathbf{G}$, and in particular, $(\mathcal{L}^*)^* = \mathcal{L}$ and $\det(\mathcal{L}^*) = 1/\det(\mathcal{L})$. We also have the identity $\Pi_{\mathbb{Q},W}(\mathcal{L})^* = W \cap \mathcal{L}^*$ for any subspace $W \subset \mathbb{Q}^n$, provided that $\Pi_{\mathbb{Q},W}(\mathcal{L})$ is a lattice. (Equivalently, this holds for any subspace W that is spanned by dual lattice vectors, or equivalently, a subspace W such that the subspace of vectors $\mathbb{Q}$-orthogonal to W is spanned by lattice vectors.)

For a positive integer k, Hermite's constant is

$$\delta_k := \sup \lambda_1(\mathcal{L})/\det(\mathcal{L})^{1/k} \ ,$$

where the supremum is over all lattices with rank k. Minkowski's celebrated theorem shows us that $\delta_k \leq \sqrt{2k/(\pi e)}$, and this is known to be tight up to a small constant factor.

2.2 Number Fields

A number field K is a finite degree algebraic field extension of the rational numbers $\mathbb{Q}$, i.e., $K \cong \mathbb{Q}[x]/p(x)$ for some irreducible polynomial $p(x) \in \mathbb{Q}[x]$. The degree $n = [K : \mathbb{Q}]$ of the number field is simply the degree of the polynomial p. In particular, a degree-n number field is isomorphic as a $\mathbb{Q}$-vector space to $\mathbb{Q}^n$. (To see this, notice that the elements $1, x, x^2, \ldots, x^{n-1} \in K$ form a $\mathbb{Q}$-basis for K.)

We associate a rational-valued inner product $\langle \cdot, \cdot \rangle_\rho : K \times K \rightarrow \mathbb{Q}$ with our number field K, which satisfies the usual three properties of symmetry, linearity in the first argument, and positive definiteness.

2.3 Orders, Ideals, and Module Lattices

For a number field K, the set of all algebraic integers in K, denoted by $\mathcal{O}_K \subset K$, forms a ring (under the usual addition and multiplication operations in K), called the ring of integers of K. (An algebraic integer is a root of a monic polynomial with coefficients in $\mathbb{Z}$.) The ring of integers $\mathcal{O}_K$ is a free $\mathbb{Z}$-module of rank $n = [K : \mathbb{Q}]$, i.e., it is the set of all $\mathbb{Z}$-linear combinations of some basis $B = \{b_1, \ldots, b_n\} \subset \mathcal{O}_K$.

An *order* of K is a subring $R \subseteq \mathcal{O}_K$ which is also a free $\mathbb{Z}$-module of rank n.

A (fractional) *ideal* $\mathcal{I}$ of R is the R-span of finitely many elements $y_1, \ldots, y_m \in K$,

$$\mathcal{I} := \{r_1 y_1 + \cdots + r_m y_m \ : \ r_i \in R\} \, .$$

More generally, a module lattice $\mathcal{M}$ over R is the R-span of finitely many vectors $\boldsymbol{y}_1, \ldots, \boldsymbol{y}_m \in K^\ell$

$$\mathcal{M} := \{r_1 \boldsymbol{y}_1 + \cdots + r_m \boldsymbol{y}_m \ : \ r_i \in R\} \, ,$$

The *rank* (over K) of a module lattice is the dimension (over K) of its span (over K), $\mathrm{rank}_K(\mathcal{M}) := \dim_K(\mathrm{span}_K(\mathcal{M}))$. We abuse language a bit and sometimes refer to rank-one module lattices as ideals, since rank-one module lattices are isomorphic to ideals (under an appropriate scaling of the inner product). We say that such an ideal is *principal* if it is the R-span of a single element $\boldsymbol{x} \in K^\ell$, and we say that $\boldsymbol{x}$ *generates* the ideal.

As the name suggests, module lattices are themselves lattices (when viewed as subsets of $\mathbb{Q}^{kn}$). To see this, it suffices to take a $\mathbb{Z}$-basis $r_1, \ldots, r_n$ of R and to observe that $\mathcal{M}$ is the $\mathbb{Z}$-span of $r_i \boldsymbol{y}_j$. In particular, if we fix some inner product $\langle \cdot, \cdot \rangle_\rho$ on K^ℓ, where this inner product is defined more rigorously in Subsect. 2.5, then we can define, e.g., $\det(\mathcal{M})$, $\lambda_1(\mathcal{M})$, $\mathcal{M}^*$, $\mathrm{rank}_\mathbb{Q}(\mathcal{M})$, primitive submodules, etc., in the natural way (see Subsect. 2.5).

Furthermore, we have $\mathrm{rank}_\mathbb{Q}(\mathcal{M}) = n \cdot \mathrm{rank}_K(\mathcal{M})$. To see this, it suffices to notice that for any $S \subseteq K^\ell$, $\dim_\mathbb{Q} \mathrm{span}_\mathbb{Q}(\{r\boldsymbol{y} \ : \ r \in R, \boldsymbol{y} \in S\}) = n \cdot \dim_K \mathrm{span}_K(S)$.

2.4   The Canonical Embedding and CM/TR Fields

The *canonical embedding* of a number field $K := \mathbb{Q}[x]/p(x)$ is an invertible $\mathbb{Q}$-linear map $\sigma : K \to \mathbb{C}^n$. Up to a reordering of the coordinates, it is the unique such map such that field multiplication between two elements $y = (y_1, \ldots, y_n) \in \sigma(K) \subset \mathbb{C}^n$ and $y' = (y'_1, \ldots, y'_n) \in \sigma(K) \subset \mathbb{C}^n$ is coordinate-wise, i.e., $\sigma(yy') = (y_1 y'_1, y_2 y'_2, \ldots, y_n y'_n)$. Equivalently, the embedding $\sigma(y)$ of y is $\sigma(y) = (\sigma_1(y), \ldots, \sigma_n(y)) \in \mathbb{C}^n$, where the σ_i are the

n distinct field embeddings of K into $\mathbb{C}$. Alternatively, if we view $y :=$ $y(x) \in \mathbb{Q}[x]/p(x)$ as a polynomial, then the σ_i correspond to polynomial evaluation at the n distinct roots in $\mathbb{C}$ of the defining polynomial p of K.

A number field K is totally real if all of its embeddings are real. It is totally imaginary if none of its embeddings lie in $\mathbb{R}$. In the sequel, we exclusively work over totally real fields or CM-fields. A number field K is a CM-field if it is a quadratic extension of K/F where the base field F is totally real but K is totally imaginary. We write "CM/TR field" to represent number fields that are either CM or totally real. One of the useful properties of CM/TR fields (and the one that we require) is that complex conjugation on $\mathbb{C}$ induces an automorphism on K which is independent of its embedding into $\mathbb{C}$. In other words, for every element $x \in K$, there exists an element $\overline{x} \in K$ such that every field embedding maps $\overline{x}$ to the complex conjugate of the embedding of x. This property allows us to define an "inner product" over K (see next Section).

The inner product induced by the canonical embedding is given by $\langle x, y \rangle_\sigma :=$ $\sum \sigma_i(x)\overline{\sigma_i(y)} \in \mathbb{Q}$ for any $x, y \in K$. We will not discuss the canonical embedding much explicitly in the sequel, but it is a very useful and important example.

2.5 Semicanonical Inner Products

For $\boldsymbol{w}, \boldsymbol{y} \in K^\ell$ for a CM/TR number field K, we define the "inner product" (conjugate symmetric form with $\langle \boldsymbol{w}, \boldsymbol{w} \rangle_K \neq 0$ for $\boldsymbol{w} \neq \boldsymbol{0}$) over K as $\langle \boldsymbol{w}, \boldsymbol{y} \rangle_K :=$ $\sum_{i=1}^k w_i \overline{y_i}$. We say that $\boldsymbol{w}$ and $\boldsymbol{y}$ are "K-orthogonal" if $\langle \boldsymbol{w}, \boldsymbol{y} \rangle_K = 0$. For a module lattice $\mathcal{M} \subset K^\ell$, we write

$$\mathcal{M}^\perp := \{ \boldsymbol{x} \in K^\ell \ : \ \forall \boldsymbol{y} \in \mathcal{M}, \ \langle \boldsymbol{y}, \boldsymbol{x} \rangle_K = 0 \}$$

for the set of vectors that are K-orthogonal to $\mathcal{M}$. This is a K-subspace of K^ℓ with dimension equal to $\ell - \mathrm{rank}_K(\mathcal{M})$.

In analogy with ρ-orthogonal projection, for a K-subspace $V \subseteq K^\ell$ we define the "K-orthogonal projection map onto V" $\Pi_{K,V} : K^\ell \to K^\ell$ as the unique K-linear map satisfying $\Pi_{K,V}(\boldsymbol{x}) = \boldsymbol{x}$ for $\boldsymbol{x} \in V$ and $\Pi_{K,V}(\boldsymbol{x}) = \boldsymbol{0}$ if $\langle \boldsymbol{y}, \boldsymbol{x} \rangle_K = 0$ for all $\boldsymbol{y} \in V$.

We now introduce the related notion of a semicanonical inner product, which is a generalization of the inner product induced by the canonical embedding, $\langle x, y \rangle_\sigma = \sum_i \sigma_i(x)\overline{\sigma_i(y)}$ described in the previous section. Semicanonical inner products share many of the nice geometric properties of $\langle \cdot, \cdot \rangle_\sigma$, as we will see below.

Definition 4 (Semicanonical inner product). *Given a rational-valued inner product $\langle \cdot, \cdot \rangle_\rho$ over a CM/TR number field K, we say that ρ is semicanonical if $\langle yz, w \rangle_\rho = \langle y, \overline{z}w \rangle_\rho$ for $w, y, z \in K$.*

It is easy to see that the inner product $\langle \cdot, \cdot \rangle_\sigma$ is semicanonical since for any $w, y, z \in K$, $\langle yz, w \rangle_\sigma = \sum_i \sigma_i(yz)\overline{\sigma_i(w)} = \sum_i \sigma_i(yz)\sigma_i(\overline{w}) = \sum_i \sigma_i(y)\sigma_i(z\overline{w}) = \sum_i \sigma_i(y)\overline{\sigma_i(\overline{z}w)} = \langle y, \overline{z}w \rangle_\sigma$.

For $\boldsymbol{w}, \boldsymbol{y} \in K^\ell$, we define $\langle \boldsymbol{w}, \boldsymbol{y} \rangle_\rho := \sum_{i=1}^{k} \langle w_i, y_i \rangle_\rho$. We also write $\|\boldsymbol{w}\|_\rho^2 := \langle \boldsymbol{w}, \boldsymbol{w} \rangle_\rho$.

Lemma 5. *Given a CM/TR number field K and inner product $\langle \cdot, \cdot \rangle_\rho$, the following statements are equivalent.*

1. *For $w, y \in K$, there exists a $\mathbb{Q}$-linear transformation $T : K \to \mathbb{Q}$ such that[6]*

$$\langle w, y \rangle_\rho = T(w\overline{y}) .$$

2. *ρ is semicanonical.*
3. *For $\boldsymbol{w}, \boldsymbol{y} \in K^\ell$, $\langle \boldsymbol{w}, \boldsymbol{y} \rangle_K = 0$ if and only if $\langle \alpha \boldsymbol{w}, \boldsymbol{y} \rangle_\rho = 0$ for all $\alpha \in K$.*
4. *For any $\boldsymbol{y} \in K^\ell$ and K-subspace $V \subseteq K^\ell$, we have*

$$\Pi_{K,V}(\boldsymbol{y}) = \Pi_{\rho,V}(\boldsymbol{y}) .$$

Proof (1 $\Leftrightarrow$ 2).
Assume that Condition 2 holds. Define the transformation $T : K \to \mathbb{Q}$ as,

$$T(z) := \langle z, 1 \rangle_\rho .$$

Since $\langle \cdot, \cdot \rangle_\rho$ is $\mathbb{Q}$-linear, we have that T is $\mathbb{Q}$-linear. For any $w, y \in K$, $\langle w, y \rangle_\rho = \langle w\overline{y}, 1 \rangle_\rho = T(w\overline{y})$.

Now, assume that Condition 1 holds, i.e. there exists a $\mathbb{Q}$-linear transformation $T : K \to \mathbb{Q}$ such that $\langle w, y \rangle_\rho = T(w\overline{y})$. For $w, y, z \in K$, we have

$$\langle yz, w \rangle_\rho = T(yz\overline{w}) = \langle y, \overline{z}w \rangle_\rho .$$

Therefore ρ is semicanonical.

(2 $\Leftrightarrow$ 3).
We will first assume Condition 2 and show that Condition 3 holds. Note that Condition 3 is a biconditional statement. We prove the forward direction first.

---

[6] For the special case of the canonical embedding $\langle \cdot, \cdot \rangle_\sigma$, T is the trace.

We need to show that for vectors $\boldsymbol{w}, \boldsymbol{y} \in K^\ell$ and $\alpha \in K$ satisfying $\langle \boldsymbol{w}, \boldsymbol{y} \rangle_K = \sum_{i=1}^{k} w_i \overline{y_i} = 0$, we have $\langle \alpha \boldsymbol{w}, \boldsymbol{y} \rangle_\rho = 0$. This follows directly from Condition 2,

$$\langle \alpha \boldsymbol{w}, \boldsymbol{y} \rangle_\rho = \sum_{i=1}^{k} \langle \alpha w_i, y_i \rangle_\rho = \sum_{i=1}^{k} \langle \alpha, \overline{w_i} y_i \rangle_\rho = \langle \alpha, \sum_{i=1}^{k} \overline{w_i} y_i \rangle_\rho = \langle \alpha, 0 \rangle_\rho = 0 \ .$$

Now we prove the backward direction for Condition 3, i.e. for vectors $\boldsymbol{w}, \boldsymbol{y} \in K^\ell$ such that for all $\alpha \in K$, $\langle \alpha \boldsymbol{w}, \boldsymbol{y} \rangle_\rho = 0$, we need to show that $\langle \boldsymbol{w}, \boldsymbol{y} \rangle_K = 0$. Based on our assumption and following the calculations above, we get

$$0 = \langle \alpha \boldsymbol{w}, \boldsymbol{y} \rangle_\rho = \langle \alpha, \sum_{i=1}^{k} \overline{w_i} y_i \rangle_\rho \ .$$

Since the above expression holds for all $\alpha \in K$, suppose that $\alpha = \sum_{i=1}^{k} \overline{w_i} y_i$, in which case, the above expression becomes $\langle \alpha, \alpha \rangle_\rho = 0$ which implies $\alpha = 0$, or in other words $\sum_{i=1}^{k} \overline{w_i} y_i = 0$.

Finally, we assume that Condition 3 holds and prove Condition 2. For $\alpha, w', y' \in K$, let $\boldsymbol{w} := (\alpha w', w', 0, \ldots, 0), \boldsymbol{y} := (y', -\overline{\alpha} y', 0, \ldots, 0)$. Observe that

$$\langle \boldsymbol{w}, \boldsymbol{y} \rangle_K = (\alpha w') \overline{y'} + (w')(-\overline{\alpha y'}) = 0 \ .$$

By Condition 3, this implies that $\langle \alpha \boldsymbol{w}, \boldsymbol{y} \rangle_\rho = \langle \alpha w', y' \rangle_\rho + \langle w', -\overline{\alpha} y' \rangle_\rho = 0$. In other words, $\langle \alpha w', y' \rangle_\rho = \langle w', \overline{\alpha} y' \rangle_\rho$. Therefore, ρ must be semicanonical.

$(3 \Leftrightarrow 4)$.

This follows immediately from the definitions of $\Pi_{K,V}$ and $\Pi_{\rho,V}$. In particular, both maps are $\mathbb{Q}$-linear (though $\Pi_{K,V}$ is also K-linear), which means that it suffices to show that they behave identically on some $\mathbb{Q}$-basis of K^ℓ. Indeed, by definition, both of them act as the identity map on V, and their kernels are respectively the subspace of K-orthogonal vectors to V and ρ-orthogonal vectors to V. Therefore, the two maps are the same if and only if the subspace of K-orthogonal vectors equals the subspace of ρ-orthogonal vectors. □

Corollary 6. *For a CM/TR field K, associated semicanonical inner product $\langle \cdot, \cdot \rangle_\rho$, order $R \subseteq \mathcal{O}_K$, module lattice $\mathcal{M} \subset K^\ell$ over R, and K-subspace $W \subseteq K^\ell$,*

1. If R is closed under conjugation then the dual denoted by $\mathcal{M}^*$ is also a module lattice, which satisfies $\det(\mathcal{M}^*) = 1/\det(\mathcal{M})$.

2. *For any primitive submodule $\mathcal{M}' \subset \mathcal{M}$ we have that*

$$\det(\mathcal{M}) = \det(\mathcal{M}') \det(\Pi_{K,(\mathcal{M}')^\perp}(\mathcal{M})) .$$

3. *For any $\boldsymbol{y} \in K^\ell$, $\|\Pi_{\rho,W}(\boldsymbol{y})\|_\rho \leq \|\boldsymbol{y}\|_\rho$.*
4. *If $\mathcal{M}$ has rank k, and $\mathcal{M}' := \Pi_{\rho,W}(\mathcal{M})$ is also a module lattice with rank k, then $\det(\mathcal{M}') \leq \det(\mathcal{M})$.*

Proof. To show Item 1, we need to show that for any $\boldsymbol{y} \in \mathcal{M}^*$ and $r \in R$, $r\boldsymbol{y} \in \mathcal{M}^*$. For any $\boldsymbol{w} \in \mathcal{M}$, by the semicanonical property, $\langle \boldsymbol{w}, r\boldsymbol{y} \rangle_\rho = \langle \overline{r}\boldsymbol{w}, \boldsymbol{y} \rangle_\rho$. Since R is closed under conjugation, $\overline{r} \in R$, and $\overline{r}\boldsymbol{w} \in \mathcal{M}$. Since $\boldsymbol{y} \in \mathcal{M}^*$ is a dual vector, $\langle \overline{r}\boldsymbol{w}, \boldsymbol{y} \rangle_\rho \in \mathbb{Z}$, which implies $\langle \boldsymbol{w}, r\boldsymbol{y} \rangle_\rho \in \mathbb{Z}$, i.e., $r\boldsymbol{y} \in \mathcal{M}^*$.

To show Item 2, recall from Sect. 2.1 that for a lattice $\mathcal{L} \subset \mathbb{Q}^d$ with primitive sublattice $\mathcal{L}' \subset \mathcal{L}$, we have the analogous fact: $\det(\mathcal{L}) = \det(\mathcal{L}') \det(\Pi_{\mathbb{Q},V}(\mathcal{L}))$, where V is the $\mathbb{Q}$-subspace of vectors that are $\mathbb{Q}$-orthogonal to $\mathcal{L}$. Since module lattices $\mathcal{M}$ under the inner product $\langle \cdot, \cdot \rangle_\rho$ are in fact lattices, it follows that $\det(\mathcal{M}) = \det(\mathcal{M}') \det(\Pi_{\rho,W}(\mathcal{M}))$. Finally, by Lemma 5, $\Pi_{\rho,W} = \Pi_{K,W}$, so that the identity holds for $\Pi_{K,W}$ as well.

Similarly, Items 3 and 4 follow from the corresponding facts about projections over $\mathbb{Q}$. $\qquad\square$

2.6   Some Geometric Quantities of Orders and Module Lattices

For an order R of a number field K of degree n with an inner product $\langle \cdot, \cdot \rangle_\rho$, we define

$$\alpha_R := \inf \frac{\lambda_1(\mathcal{I})}{\det(\mathcal{I})^{1/n}} ,$$

where the infimum is over all rank-one modules $\mathcal{I} \subset K^\ell$. (Notice that α_R depends heavily on the choice of inner product $\langle \cdot, \cdot \rangle_\rho$, so perhaps formally we should write $\alpha_{R,\rho}$. We write α_R instead for simplicity.)

For a module lattice $\mathcal{M}$, we define

$$\tau_1(\mathcal{M}) := \min_{\mathcal{I} \subset \mathcal{M}} \det(\mathcal{I})^{1/n} ,$$

where the infimum is over the rank-one submodules $\mathcal{I} \subset \mathcal{M}$ (i.e., ideals). This quantity can be viewed as a different way to generalize $\lambda_1(\mathcal{L})$ to module lattices over arbitrary orders. I.e., the rank-one "submodules" of a "module" $\mathcal{L}$ over $\mathbb{Z}$ are lattices spanned by a single vector, and the determinant of such a "submodule" is just the length of this vector. So, over $\mathbb{Z}$, $\tau_1 = \lambda_1$. For higher-dimensional orders R, the rank-one module lattices are n-dimensional lattices, which do not naturally correspond to a single vector. So, τ_1 and λ_1 are distinct quantities.

We define

$$\mu_{R,k} := \sup_{\mathcal{M}} \frac{\tau_1(\mathcal{M})}{\det(\mathcal{M})^{1/(kn)}} \, ,$$

where the supremum is over all rank-k module lattices $\mathcal{M} \subset K^{k'}$ (for any integer $k' \geq k$). (This can be thought of as the module analogue of either Rankin's constant or Hermite's constant.)

For a module lattice $\mathcal{M}$ of rank k, we have the simple inequality $\tau_1(\mathcal{M}) \leq \mu_{R,k} \det(\mathcal{M})^{1/(kn)}$, and the following relationship between τ_1 and λ_1, which is governed by α_R.

Lemma 7. *Given a number field K, order $R \subseteq \mathcal{O}_K$, a module lattice $\mathcal{M}$, and an inner product $\langle \cdot, \cdot \rangle_\rho$*

$$\frac{\lambda_1(\mathcal{M})}{\delta_n} \leq \tau_1(\mathcal{M}) \leq \frac{\lambda_1(\mathcal{M})}{\alpha_R} \, , \tag{2}$$

$$1 \leq \mu_{R,k} \leq \frac{\sqrt{kn}}{\alpha_R} \, . \tag{3}$$

Proof. Let $\mathcal{I} \subset \mathcal{M}$ be the ideal generated by a non-zero shortest vector in $\mathcal{M}$, so that $\lambda_1(\mathcal{I}) = \lambda_1(\mathcal{M})$. Then from the definition of α_R, we know

$$\det(\mathcal{I})^{1/n} \leq \frac{\lambda_1(\mathcal{I})}{\alpha_R} \, . \tag{4}$$

Since $\mathcal{I} \subset \mathcal{M}$, we also have that

$$\tau_1(\mathcal{M}) \leq \det(\mathcal{I})^{1/n} \, . \tag{5}$$

Combining Eqs. (4) and (5) yields the upper bound in (2).

Let $\mathcal{I}' \subset \mathcal{M}$ be an ideal satisfying $\det(\mathcal{I}')^{1/n} = \tau_1(\mathcal{M})$. Then by the definition of Hermite's constant, we have

$$\lambda_1(\mathcal{I}') \leq \delta_n \det(\mathcal{I}')^{1/n} = \delta_n \tau_1(\mathcal{M}) \, .$$

The lower bound in (2) follows by noting that $\lambda_1(\mathcal{M}) \leq \lambda_1(\mathcal{I}')$.

Observe that for rank k module lattices, Minkowski's theorem gives us $\lambda_1(\mathcal{M}) \leq \sqrt{kn} \det(\mathcal{M})^{1/(kn)}$. Combining this relation with the upper bound from (2) yields the upper bound in (3). The lower bound is witnessed by, e.g., $\mathcal{M} = R^k$, which satisfies $\tau_1(\mathcal{M}) = \det(R)^{1/n} = \det(\mathcal{M})^{1/(kn)}$. $\qquad\square$

We also have the following well-known property of the canonical embedding.

Lemma 8. *For any order $R \subseteq \mathcal{O}_K$ of any number field K under the inner product $\langle \cdot, \cdot \rangle_\sigma$ induced by the canonical embedding, we have*

$$\alpha_R = \frac{\sqrt{n}}{\det(R)^{1/n}} \ .$$

In particular, if $R := \mathcal{O}_K$ is the ring of integers of a cyclotomic number field K, then $\det(R)^{1/n} \leq \sqrt{n}$, so that $\alpha_R \geq 1$.

2.7 ModuleSVP and the Dense Ideal Problem

We now provide the formal definition of ModuleSVP, and its variant the Dense Ideal Problem.

Definition 9 (ModuleSVP). *For a number field K, order $R \subseteq \mathcal{O}_K$, rank $k \geq 1$, approximation factor $\gamma = \gamma(R, k) \geq 1$, and inner product $\langle \cdot, \cdot \rangle_\rho$, (γ, k)-ModuleSVP is defined as follows. The input is (a generating set for) a module lattice $\mathcal{M} \subset K^\ell$ with rank k. The goal is to output a module element $\boldsymbol{x} \in \mathcal{M}$ such that $0 < \|\boldsymbol{x}\|_\rho \leq \gamma \lambda_1(\mathcal{M})$.*

Definition 10 (The Dense Ideal Problem). *For a number field K, order $R \subseteq \mathcal{O}_K$, rank $k \geq 2$, approximation factor $\gamma = \gamma(R, k) \geq 1$, and inner product $\langle \cdot, \cdot \rangle_\rho$, the (γ, k)-Dense Ideal Problem, or (γ, k)-DIP, is the search problem defined as follows. The input is a (generating set for) module lattice $\mathcal{M} \subset K^\ell$ with rank k, and the goal is to find a submodule $\mathcal{M}' \subset \mathcal{M}$ with rank-one (i.e., an ideal lattice) such that $\det(\mathcal{M}')^{1/n} \leq \gamma \tau_1(\mathcal{M})$.*

Definition 11 (ModuleHSVP). *For a number field K, order $R \subseteq \mathcal{O}_K$, rank $k \geq 2$, approximation factor $\gamma = \gamma(R, k) \geq 1$, and inner product $\langle \cdot, \cdot \rangle_\rho$, (γ, k)-ModuleHSVP is defined as follows. The input is (a generating set for) a module lattice $\mathcal{M} \subset K^\ell$ with rank k. The goal is to output a module element $\boldsymbol{x} \in \mathcal{M}$ such that $0 < \|\boldsymbol{x}\|_\rho \leq \gamma \det(\mathcal{M})^{1/(kn)}$.*

Notice that a solution to the above problem is guaranteed to exist if $\gamma \geq \delta_{kn}$.

Theorem 12. *For a number field K, order $R \subseteq \mathcal{O}_K$, rank $\beta \geq 2$, approximation factor $\gamma' = \gamma'(R, \beta) \geq 1$, and an inner product $\langle \cdot, \cdot \rangle_\rho$, there exists a reduction from (γ, β)-DIP to (γ', β)-ModuleSVP where $\gamma := \frac{\gamma' \delta_n}{\alpha_R}$.*

Proof. The reduction takes as input a module lattice $\mathcal{M}$ of rank β, and uses the output from the (γ', β)-ModuleSVP oracle which is a non-zero vector $\boldsymbol{x} \in \mathcal{M}$ such that $0 < \|\boldsymbol{x}\|_\rho \leq \gamma'\lambda_1(\mathcal{M})$, to output a submodule $\mathcal{M}' \subset \mathcal{M}$ such that $\det(\mathcal{M}')^{1/n} \leq \gamma\tau_1(\mathcal{M})$.

Let $\mathcal{M}' := R\boldsymbol{x}$, i.e. $\mathcal{M}'$ is a principal ideal generated by $\boldsymbol{x}$. Note that $\lambda_1(\mathcal{M}') \leq \|\boldsymbol{x}\|_\rho \leq \gamma'\lambda_1(\mathcal{M})$. Then using Lemma 7, we have

$$\det(\mathcal{M}')^{1/n} \leq \frac{\lambda_1(\mathcal{M}')}{\alpha_R} \leq \frac{\gamma'\lambda_1(\mathcal{M})}{\alpha_R} \leq \frac{\gamma'}{\alpha_R} \cdot \delta_n \cdot \tau_1(\mathcal{M}) ,$$

as needed.   □

2.8   On Bit Representations

Throughout this work, we follow the convention (common in the literature on lattices) of avoiding discussion of the particular bit representation of elements in K. In practice, one can represent elements in K as polynomials with rational coefficients, and the inner product can be represented by specifying the pairwise inner products of basis elements (i.e., as a quadratic form). Since arithmetic operations may be performed efficiently with these representations, we are largely justified in ignoring such bit-level details.

In the full version [MS20], we discuss this a bit more, but see [GN08] for a more detailed discussion about the bit-level complexity of basis reduction, and [LPSW19] for a similar discussion in the context of module lattices specifically. We will need one fact that makes use of the bit-level representation.

Fact 13. *If the number field K, its inner product $\langle \cdot, \cdot \rangle_\rho$, and the order $R \subseteq \mathcal{O}_K$ are represented as described above, then for any integer $\ell \geq 1$ and any module lattice $\mathcal{M} \subset K^\ell$*

$$2^{-\mathrm{poly}(m,\ell)} \leq \det(\mathcal{M}) \leq 2^{\mathrm{poly}(m,\ell)} ,$$

where m is the bit length of this description together with the description of a generating set for $\mathcal{M}$.

3   Filtrations

For a module lattice $\mathcal{M} \subset K^\ell$ over an order $R \subseteq \mathcal{O}_K$ with rank k over a CM/TR field K, a *filtration* of $\mathcal{M}$ is a nested sequence $\mathcal{M}_1 \subset \mathcal{M}_2 \subset \cdots \subset \mathcal{M}_k = \mathcal{M}$ of module lattices over R such that

1. **Primitivity:** $\mathcal{M}_i = \mathcal{M} \cap \operatorname{span}_K(\mathcal{M}_i)$;
2. **Increasing ranks:** $\operatorname{rank}_K(\mathcal{M}_i) = i$; and
3. **Rank-one projections:** $\widetilde{\mathcal{M}}_i := \Pi_{K,\mathcal{M}_{i-1}^\perp}(\mathcal{M}_i)$ is a rank-one module lattice over R.

(In fact, primitivity together with the fact that $\mathcal{M}_i \subset \mathcal{M}_{i+1}$ is a strict containment already implies the other two conditions. E.g., this implies that $\operatorname{rank}_K(\mathcal{M}_i) < \operatorname{rank}_K(\mathcal{M}_{i+1})$, and since the ranks are positive integers with $\operatorname{rank}_K(\mathcal{M}_k) = k$, we must have $\operatorname{rank}_K(\mathcal{M}_i) = i$. Nevertheless, we find it helpful to state the other two conditions explicitly.) We also write $\mathcal{M}_{[i,j]} := \Pi_{K,\mathcal{M}_{i-1}^\perp}(\mathcal{M}_j)$, which we call a *block* of the filtration. We also adopt the convention that $\mathcal{M}_0 = \{\mathbf{0}\}$ is the zero module.

Filtrations for module lattices over R are analogues of bases for lattices over $\mathbb{Z}$. Specifically, the basis $\boldsymbol{b}_1, \ldots, \boldsymbol{b}_d \in \mathbb{Q}^d$ of a lattice naturally corresponds to the filtration given by $\mathcal{L}_i := \{z_1 \boldsymbol{b}_1 + \cdots + z_i \boldsymbol{b}_i : z_j \in \mathbb{Z}\}$. The $\widetilde{\mathcal{M}}_i$ defined above are the analogues of the Gram-Schmidt orthogonalization $\widetilde{\boldsymbol{b}}_1, \ldots, \widetilde{\boldsymbol{b}}_d$ of a lattice over $\mathbb{Q}$. We therefore call $\widetilde{\mathcal{M}}_i$ an *R-Gram-Schmidt orthogonalization*.

It is perhaps not immediately obvious that filtrations are nice to work with, or even that they always exist. So, we first note that they exist and can be found efficiently.

Fact 14. *For a CM/TR number field K, order $R \subseteq \mathcal{O}_K$, an inner product $\langle \cdot, \cdot \rangle_\rho$, and a module lattice $\mathcal{M} \subset K^\ell$ with rank k, there exists a filtration $\mathcal{M}_1 \subset \mathcal{M}_2 \subset \cdots \subset \mathcal{M}_k = \mathcal{M}$.*

Furthermore, R-generating sets for the $\mathcal{M}_i$ can be computed efficiently (given an R-generating set for $\mathcal{M}$), and if ρ is semicanonical, $\det(\mathcal{M}) = \det(\widetilde{\mathcal{M}}_1) \cdots \det(\widetilde{\mathcal{M}}_k)$.

Proof. Let $\boldsymbol{y}_1, \ldots, \boldsymbol{y}_m \in K^\ell$ be an R-generating set for $\mathcal{M}$, and suppose without loss of generality that $\boldsymbol{y}_1, \ldots, \boldsymbol{y}_k$ are linearly independent over K. We take $\mathcal{M}_i := \mathcal{M} \cap \operatorname{span}_K(\boldsymbol{y}_1, \ldots, \boldsymbol{y}_i)$. An R-generating set for $\mathcal{M}_i$ can be computed by finding a $\mathbb{Z}$-basis for $\mathcal{M}_i$ (as a lattice) and then noting that a $\mathbb{Z}$-basis is also an R-generating set.

The fact about the determinants follows from Item 2 in Corollary 6. $\qquad\square$

Finally, given a semi-canonical inner product $\langle \cdot, \cdot \rangle_\rho$ and R that is closed under conjugation, each filtration $\mathcal{M}_1 \subset \mathcal{M}_2 \subset \cdots \subset \mathcal{M}_k = \mathcal{M}$ of $\mathcal{M}$ induces a *dual filtration* given by $\Pi_{K,\mathcal{M}_{k-1}^\perp}(\mathcal{M})^* \subset \Pi_{K,\mathcal{M}_{k-2}^\perp}(\mathcal{M})^* \subset \cdots \subset \Pi_{K,\mathcal{M}_1^\perp}(\mathcal{M})^* \subset \mathcal{M}^*$, where $\Pi_{K,\mathcal{M}_i^\perp}(\mathcal{M})^*$ is a module lattice with rank $k - i$. Equivalently, the dual filtration is given by $\mathcal{M}^* \cap \mathcal{M}^{\perp}_{k-1} \subset (\mathcal{M}^* \cap \mathcal{M}^{\perp}_{k-2}) \subset \cdots \subset (\mathcal{M}^* \cap \mathcal{M}^{\perp}_1) \subset \mathcal{M}^*$. In particular, the R-Gram-Schmidt orthogonalization of the dual filtration is the dual of the reverse of the R-Gram-Schmidt orthogonalization of the original filtration, in analogy to the reversed dual basis $\mathbf{B}^{-s}$ that is commonly used in basis reduction. (See, e.g., [GN08, MW16].)

4   An LLL-style Algorithm for the Special Case of $\beta = 2$

Here, we present our reductions in the special case when $\beta = 2$ and when the number field is sufficiently nice. The results here are strictly generalized by and subsumed by those presented in the full version [MS20], and the proofs have many common features. (Our proofs are also essentially the same as those in [LPSW19].)

Recall that we denote blocks of the filtration $\mathcal{M}_1 \subset \cdots \subset \mathcal{M}_k = \mathcal{M}$ as $\mathcal{M}_{[i,j]} = \Pi_{K,\mathcal{M}^{\perp}_{i-1}}(\mathcal{M}_j)$, and rank-one projections as $\widetilde{\mathcal{M}}_i = \Pi_{K,\mathcal{M}^{\perp}_{i-1}}(\mathcal{M}_i)$.

Definition 15 (DIP reduction). *For a CM/TR number field K, an order $R \subseteq \mathcal{O}_K$, an inner product $\langle \cdot, \cdot \rangle_\rho$, and approximation factor $\gamma \geq 1$, a filtration $\mathcal{M}_1 \subset \mathcal{M}_2 \subset \cdots \subset \mathcal{M}_k = \mathcal{M}$ of a module $\mathcal{M}$ over R is γ-DIP-reduced if $\det(\mathcal{M}_1)^{1/n} \leq \gamma \cdot \tau_1(\mathcal{M})$.*

Definition 16 (γ-reduced filtration). *For a CM/TR number field K, an order $R \subseteq \mathcal{O}_K$, an inner product $\langle \cdot, \cdot \rangle_\rho$, and approximation factor $\gamma \geq 1$, a filtration $\mathcal{M}_1 \subset \mathcal{M}_2 \subset \cdots \subset \mathcal{M}_k$ of a module $\mathcal{M}$ over R is γ-reduced if $\mathcal{M}_{[i,i+1]}$ is γ-DIP-reduced for all $i \in [1, k-1]$.*

We now show a number of properties of γ-reduced filtrations that make them useful for solving ModuleSVP and its variants.

Lemma 17. *For a CM/TR number field K, an order $R \subseteq \mathcal{O}_K$, approximation factor $\gamma = \gamma(R, k) \geq 1$, a semicanonical inner product $\langle \cdot, \cdot \rangle_\rho$, and a γ-reduced filtration $\mathcal{M}_1 \subset \mathcal{M}_2 \subset \cdots \subset \mathcal{M}_k$, we have*

$$\det(\mathcal{M}_1)^{1/n} \leq (\gamma \mu_{R,2})^{2(i-1)} \det(\widetilde{\mathcal{M}}_i)^{1/n} ,$$

for all $1 \leq i \leq k$.

Proof. Since $\mathcal{M}_1 \subset \mathcal{M}_2 \subset \cdots \subset \mathcal{M}_k$ is γ-reduced,

$$\det(\widetilde{\mathcal{M}}_i)^{1/n} \leq \gamma \cdot \tau_1(\mathcal{M}_{[i,i+1]})$$
$$\leq \gamma \cdot \mu_{R,2} \cdot \det(\mathcal{M}_{[i,i+1]})^{1/(2n)}$$
$$= \gamma \cdot \mu_{R,2} \cdot \left(\det(\widetilde{\mathcal{M}}_i) \det(\widetilde{\mathcal{M}}_{i+1}) \right)^{1/(2n)} ,$$

where the last equality follows from Fact 14 (since ρ is semicanonical). Rearranging, we see that $\det(\widetilde{\mathcal{M}_i})^{1/n} \leq (\gamma\mu_{R,2})^2 \det(\widetilde{\mathcal{M}_{i+1}})^{1/n}$. By a simple induction argument, we see that $\det(\mathcal{M}_1)^{1/n} \leq (\gamma\mu_{R,2})^{2(i-1)} \det(\widetilde{\mathcal{M}_i})^{1/n}$. $\qquad\square$

Lemma 18. *For a CM/TR number field K, an order $R \subseteq \mathcal{O}_K$, an approximation factor $\gamma \geq 1$, and a semicanonical inner product $\langle\cdot,\cdot\rangle_\rho$, if a filtration $\mathcal{M}_1 \subset \mathcal{M}_2 \subset \cdots \subset \mathcal{M}_k$ is γ-reduced, then*

$$\det(\mathcal{M}_1)^{1/n} \leq \gamma \cdot (\gamma\mu_{R,2})^{2(k-2)} \cdot \tau_1(\mathcal{M}) , \quad and \tag{6}$$

$$\det(\mathcal{M}_1)^{1/n} \leq (\gamma\mu_{R,2})^{k-1} \cdot \det(\mathcal{M})^{1/(kn)} . \tag{7}$$

Proof. First, suppose that $\tau_1(\mathcal{M}_2) = \tau_1(\mathcal{M})$. Then, the result is immediate, from the fact that the filtration is γ-reduced, i.e., $\det(\mathcal{M}_1)^{1/n} \leq \tau_1(\mathcal{M}_2) = \tau_1(\mathcal{M})$.

Otherwise, let $i \in [2, k-1]$ be such that $\tau_1(\mathcal{M}_{i+1}) = \tau_1(\mathcal{M})$ but $\tau_1(\mathcal{M}_{i-1}) \neq \tau_1(\mathcal{M})$. Since $\mathcal{M}_k = \mathcal{M}$, there must exist such an i. In particular, there exists some rank-one module lattice $\mathcal{M}' \subset \mathcal{M}_{i+1}$ with $\mathcal{M}' \not\subset \mathcal{M}_{i-1}$ such that $\det(\mathcal{M}')^{1/n} = \tau_1(\mathcal{M})$. Since $\mathcal{M}_{i-1}$ is primitive, $\mathcal{M}' \not\subset \mathrm{span}_K \mathcal{M}_{i-1}$. Therefore, $\Pi_{K,\mathcal{M}_{i-1}^\perp}(\mathcal{M}') \subset \mathcal{M}_{[i,i+1]}$ is a non-zero rank-one module lattice. It follows that

$$\tau_1(\mathcal{M}_{[i,i+1]}) \leq \det(\Pi_{K,\mathcal{M}_{i-1}^\perp}(\mathcal{M}'))^{1/n} \leq \det(\mathcal{M}')^{1/n} = \tau_1(\mathcal{M}) ,$$

where the second inequality is Item 4 of Corollary 6. Then, since the filtration is γ-reduced,

$$\det(\widetilde{\mathcal{M}_i})^{1/n} \leq \gamma\tau_1(\mathcal{M}_{[i,i+1]}) \leq \gamma\tau_1(\mathcal{M}) .$$

By combining the expression above with Lemma 17, we have

$$\det(\mathcal{M}_1)^{1/n} \leq \gamma \cdot (\gamma\mu_{R,2})^{2(i-1)} \cdot \tau_1(\mathcal{M}) , \tag{8}$$

and recalling that $i \leq k-1$, we obtain Eq. (6).

Again, recall from Lemma 17 that $\det(\mathcal{M}_1)^{1/n} \leq (\gamma\mu_{R,2})^{2(i-1)} \det(\widetilde{\mathcal{M}_i})^{1/n}$. Taking the product of these inequalities for $1 \leq i \leq k$, we see that

$$\det(\mathcal{M}_1)^{k/n} \leq (\gamma\mu_{R,2})^{k(k-1)} \det(\mathcal{M})^{1/n} .$$

Raising both sides to the power $1/k$ yields Eq. (7). $\qquad\square$

Corollary 19. *For a CM/TR number field K, an order $R \subseteq \mathcal{O}_K$, an approximation factor $\gamma = \gamma(R, k) \geq 1$, and a semicanonical inner product $\langle \cdot, \cdot \rangle_\rho$, if a filtration $\mathcal{M}_1 \subset \mathcal{M}_2 \subset \cdots \subset \mathcal{M}_k$ is γ-reduced, then*

$$\lambda_1(\mathcal{M}_1) \leq \frac{\gamma \delta_n}{\alpha_R} \cdot (\gamma \mu_{R,2})^{2(k-2)} \cdot \lambda_1(\mathcal{M}) , \text{ and} \tag{9}$$

$$\lambda_1(\mathcal{M}_1) \leq \delta_n (\gamma \mu_{R,2})^{(k-1)} \cdot \det(\mathcal{M})^{1/(kn)} . \tag{10}$$

Proof. By combining Eq. (6) from Lemma 18 with Lemma 7, we have

$$\det(\mathcal{M}_1)^{1/n} \leq \gamma \cdot (\gamma \mu_{R,2})^{2(k-2)} \cdot \tau_1(\mathcal{M}) \leq \gamma \cdot (\gamma \mu_{R,2})^{2(k-2)} \cdot \frac{\lambda_1(\mathcal{M})}{\alpha_R} .$$

Using the definition of Hermite's constant δ_n with the above relation, we obtain Eq. (9):

$$\lambda_1(\mathcal{M}_1) \leq \delta_n \det(\mathcal{M}_1)^{1/n} \leq \delta_n \cdot \gamma (\gamma \mu_{R,2})^{2(k-2)} \cdot \frac{\lambda_1(\mathcal{M})}{\alpha_R} .$$

Equation (10) follows by directly applying the definition of Hermite's constant to Eq. (7) from Lemma 18. ☐

4.1   Finding γ-Reduced Filtrations

We are now ready to show how to find a γ-reduced filtration with access to a $(\gamma, 2)$-ModuleSVP oracle. The reduction is a natural analogue of the LLL algorithm, and essentially identical to the reduction in [LPSW19].

Definition 20 ($((\gamma, k)$-RFP). *For a CM/TR number field K, order $R \subseteq \mathcal{O}_K$, rank $k \geq 1$, approximation factor $\gamma = \gamma(R, k) \geq 1$, and inner product $\langle \cdot, \cdot \rangle_\rho$, the (γ, k)-Reduced Filtration Problem, or (γ, k)-RFP, is the search problem defined as follows. The input is (a generating set for) a module lattice $\mathcal{M} \subset K^\ell$ with rank k, and the goal is to find a γ-reduced filtration $\mathcal{M}_1 \subset \mathcal{M}_2 \subset \cdots \subset \mathcal{M}_k$.*

Theorem 21. *For any CM/TR number field K, order $R \subseteq \mathcal{O}_K$, rank $k \geq 2$, approximation factor $\gamma = \gamma(R, k) \geq 1$, semicanonical inner product $\langle \cdot, \cdot \rangle_\rho$, and constant $\varepsilon > 0$, there is an efficient reduction from $((1 + \varepsilon)\gamma, k)$-RFP to $(\gamma, 2)$-DIP.*

Proof. The idea is to use our $(\gamma, 2)$-DIP oracle to compute a $(1 + \varepsilon)\gamma$-reduced filtration just like the LLL algorithm computes a reduced basis. In particular, on input (a generating set for) a module lattice $\mathcal{M} \subset K^\ell$ with rank

k, the reduction first computes a filtration $\mathcal{M}_1 \subset \cdots \subset \mathcal{M}_k = \mathcal{M}$ of $\mathcal{M}$ (as in Fact 14). It then repeatedly updates this filtration in place as follows.

For each $\mathcal{M}_{[i,i+1]}$, the reduction calls the $(\gamma, 2)$-DIP oracle with $\mathcal{M}_{[i,i+1]}$ as input and receives as output some rank-one ideal $\widetilde{\mathcal{M}}_i' \subset \mathcal{M}_{[i,i+1]}$. We may assume without loss of generality that $\widetilde{\mathcal{M}}_i'$ is a primitive submodule of $\mathcal{M}_{[i,i+1]}$, i.e., that $\widetilde{\mathcal{M}}_i' = \mathcal{M}_{[i,i+1]} \cap \mathrm{span}_K(\widetilde{\mathcal{M}}_i')$. If $(1 + \varepsilon)^n \det(\widetilde{\mathcal{M}}_i') < \det(\widetilde{\mathcal{M}}_i)$ then the reduction sets $\mathcal{M}_i$ so that $\widetilde{\mathcal{M}}_i = \widetilde{\mathcal{M}}_i'$ and leaves $\mathcal{M}_j$ unchanged for $j \neq i$. (Formally, the reduction can do this by, e.g., picking any i-dimensional K-subspace W of $\mathrm{span}_K(\mathcal{M}_{i+1})$ such that $\Pi_{K, \mathcal{M}_{i-1}^{\perp}}(W) = \mathrm{span}_K(\widetilde{\mathcal{M}}_i')$ and $\mathcal{M}_{i-1} \subset W$ and setting $\mathcal{M}_i := W \cap \mathcal{M}$. As we noted in Sect. 2.1, $\mathcal{M}_i$ will then be a primitive submodule with rank i, and it follows from the conditions on W that $\mathcal{M}_{i-1} \subset \mathcal{M}_i \subset \mathcal{M}_{i+1}$ and $\widetilde{\mathcal{M}}_i = \widetilde{\mathcal{M}}_i'$.)

The reduction terminates and outputs the current filtration when none of these checks results in an update to the filtration, i.e., when for all i, $(1 + \varepsilon)^n \det(\widetilde{\mathcal{M}}_i') \geq \det(\widetilde{\mathcal{M}}_i)$.

We first observe that the output filtration is indeed $(1 + \varepsilon)\gamma$-reduced. To see this, notice that the reduction only terminates if the filtration satisfies

$$\det(\widetilde{\mathcal{M}}_i)^{1/n} \leq (1 + \varepsilon) \det(\widetilde{\mathcal{M}}_i')^{1/n} \leq (1 + \varepsilon)\gamma \cdot \tau_1(\mathcal{M}_{[i,i+1]}) ,$$

as needed.

It remains to show that the reduction terminates in polynomial time. Our proof is more-or-less identical to the celebrated proof in [LLL82] (and the proof in [LPSW19]). Consider the potential function

$$\Phi(\mathcal{M}_1, \ldots, \mathcal{M}_k) := \prod_{i=1}^{k} \det(\mathcal{M}_i) .$$

At the beginning of the reduction, $\log \Phi(\mathcal{M}_1, \ldots, \mathcal{M}_k)$ is bounded by a polynomial in the input size (since Φ is efficiently computable). And, by Fact 13, $-\log(\Phi(\mathcal{M}_1, \ldots, \mathcal{M}_k))$ is bounded by a polynomial in the input size throughout the reduction. Therefore, it suffices to show that the potential decreases by at least, say, a constant factor every time that the reduction updates the filtration.

Consider a step in the reduction in which it updates $\mathcal{M}_i$. Denote $\widehat{\mathcal{M}}_0$ as $\mathcal{M}_i$ before the update and $\widehat{\mathcal{M}}_1$ as $\mathcal{M}_i$ after the update. Then, since ρ

is semicanonical, by Item 2 of Corollary 6, we have

$$\det(\widehat{\mathcal{M}_1}) = \det(\mathcal{M}_{i-1})\det(\widetilde{\mathcal{M}_i'}) < \det(\mathcal{M}_{i-1})\frac{\det(\widetilde{\mathcal{M}_i})}{(1+\varepsilon)^n} = \frac{\det(\widehat{\mathcal{M}_0})}{(1+\varepsilon)^n} \ .$$

The other terms $\det(\mathcal{M}_j)$ for $i \neq j$ in the definition of Φ remain unchanged. Thus, the potential function decreases by a factor of at least $(1+\varepsilon)^n$ after each update, as needed. $\quad\square$

Finally, we derive the main results of this section as corollaries of Theorem 24.

Corollary 22. *For any CM/TR number field K, order $R \subseteq \mathcal{O}_K$, rank $k \geq 2$, approximation factor $\gamma' = \gamma'(R,k) \geq 1$, semicanonical inner product $\langle \cdot, \cdot \rangle_\rho$, and constant $\varepsilon > 0$, there exists an efficient reduction from (γ,k)-DIP to $(\gamma',2)$-DIP where*

$$\gamma := (1+\varepsilon)\gamma' \cdot ((1+\varepsilon)\gamma' \cdot \mu_{R,2})^{2(k-2)} \ .$$

Proof. The reduction takes as input a (generating set of a) module lattice $\mathcal{M}$ of rank k and runs the $((1+\varepsilon)\gamma',k)$-RFP procedure from Theorem 21, using the $(\gamma',2)$-DIP oracle, receiving as output some $((1+\varepsilon)\gamma')$-reduced filtration $\mathcal{M}_1 \subset \cdots \subset \mathcal{M}_k = \mathcal{M}$ of $\mathcal{M}$. Finally, the reduction outputs $\mathcal{M}_1$.

Clearly, the reduction runs in polynomial time. By Eq. (6) from Lemma 18, we must have

$$\det(\mathcal{M}_1)^{1/n} \leq (1+\varepsilon)\gamma' \cdot ((1+\varepsilon)\gamma' \cdot \mu_{R,2})^{2(k-2)}\tau_1(\mathcal{M}) = \gamma\tau_1(\mathcal{M}) \ ,$$

as needed. $\quad\square$

Corollary 23. *For any CM/TR number field K, order $R \subseteq \mathcal{O}_K$ closed under conjugation, rank $k \geq 2$, approximation factor $\gamma' = \gamma'(R,k) \geq 1$, semicanonical inner product $\langle \cdot, \cdot \rangle_\rho$, and constant $\varepsilon > 0$, there exists an efficient reduction from (γ_R,k)-RFP to $(\gamma',2)$-ModuleSVP where $\gamma_R := (1+\varepsilon)\frac{\gamma'\delta_n}{\alpha_R}$.*

Proof. The reduction takes as input a (generating set of a) module lattice $\mathcal{M}$ of rank k. It then runs the procedure from Theorem 21 with $\gamma := \gamma'\delta_n/\alpha_R$. Each time that this procedure requires a call to its $(\gamma,2)$-DIP procedure, it uses the procedure from Theorem 12 and its $(\gamma',2)$-ModuleSVP oracle to solve the $(\gamma,2)$-DIP instance.

Clearly, the reduction runs in polynomial time and outputs a γ_R-reduced filtration of $\mathcal{M}$, where $\gamma_R = (1+\varepsilon)\gamma = (1+\varepsilon)\frac{\gamma'\delta_n}{\alpha_R}$. $\quad\square$

Theorem 24 (Main Theorem). *For any CM/TR number field K, order $R \subseteq \mathcal{O}_K$, rank $k \geq 2$, approximation factor $\gamma = \gamma(R,k) \geq 1$, semicanonical inner product $\langle \cdot, \cdot \rangle_\rho$, and constant $\varepsilon > 0$, there is an efficient reduction from (γ, k)-ModuleSVP to $(\gamma', 2)$-ModuleSVP where*

$$\gamma := (1 + \varepsilon) \cdot \left(\frac{\gamma' \delta_n}{\alpha_R} \right)^2 \cdot \left((1 + \varepsilon)\gamma' \cdot \frac{\delta_n \mu_{R,2}}{\alpha_R} \right)^{2(k-2)} .$$

There is also an efficient reduction from (γ_H, k)-ModuleHSVP to $(\gamma', 2)$-ModuleSVP, where

$$\gamma_H := \gamma' \delta_n \cdot \left((1 + \varepsilon)\gamma' \cdot \frac{\delta_n \mu_{R,2}}{\alpha_R} \right)^{k-1} .$$

Proof. In fact, the reduction is the same for both ModuleSVP and ModuleHSVP. On input (a generating set for) a module lattice $\mathcal{M} \subset K^\ell$ with rank k, the reduction proceeds as follows. It obtains a γ_R-reduced filtration $\mathcal{M}_1 \subset \mathcal{M}_2 \subset \cdots \subset \mathcal{M}_k$ using its $(\gamma', 2)$-ModuleSVP oracle, where $\gamma_R := (1 + \varepsilon)\frac{\gamma' \delta_n}{\alpha_R}$ (by Corollary 23). It then calls its $(\gamma', 2)$-ModuleSVP on $\mathcal{M}_2$ which outputs a vector $\boldsymbol{x}$ such that $0 < \|\boldsymbol{x}\|_\rho \leq \gamma' \lambda_1(\mathcal{M}_2)$. It then simply outputs this vector.

Since $\mathcal{M}_1 \subset \mathcal{M}_2$, we have

$$0 < \|\boldsymbol{x}\|_\rho \leq \gamma' \lambda_1(\mathcal{M}_2) \leq \gamma' \lambda_1(\mathcal{M}_1) .$$

By Eq. (9) of Corollary 19,

$$
\begin{aligned}
\lambda_1(\mathcal{M}_1) &\leq \frac{\gamma_R \delta_n}{\alpha_R} \cdot (\gamma_R \mu_{R,2})^{2(k-2)} \cdot \lambda_1(\mathcal{M}) \\
&= \frac{(1+\varepsilon)\gamma' \delta_n^2}{\alpha_R^2} \cdot \left((1+\varepsilon)\frac{\gamma' \delta_n}{\alpha_R} \mu_{R,2} \right)^{2(k-2)} \cdot \lambda_1(\mathcal{M})
\end{aligned}
$$

Combining the above two expressions, we get

$$0 < \|\boldsymbol{x}\|_\rho \leq \frac{(1+\varepsilon)\gamma'^2 \delta_n^2}{\alpha_R^2} \cdot \left((1+\varepsilon)\frac{\gamma' \delta_n}{\alpha_R} \mu_{R,2} \right)^{2(k-2)} \cdot \lambda_1(\mathcal{M}) .$$

Therefore,

$$\gamma = (1 + \varepsilon) \cdot \left(\frac{\gamma' \delta_n}{\alpha_R} \right)^2 \cdot \left((1 + \varepsilon)\gamma' \cdot \frac{\delta_n \mu_{R,2}}{\alpha_R} \right)^{2(k-2)} ,$$

as needed.

Similarly, by Eq. (10) of Corollary 19,

$$\|\boldsymbol{x}\|_\rho \leq \gamma'\delta_n \cdot (\gamma_R\mu_{R,2})^{(k-1)} \cdot \det(\mathcal{M})^{1/(kn)}$$
$$= \gamma'\delta_n \cdot ((1+\varepsilon)\gamma'\delta_n\mu_{R,2}/\alpha_R)^{k-1} \cdot \det(\mathcal{M})^{1/(kn)} \,,$$

which gives the reduction from ModuleHSVP.   □

Acknowledgements. The authors thank Léo Ducas, Chris Peikert, and Alice Silverberg for very helpful discussions. We are also indebted to the anonymous Eurocrypt 2020 reviewers, who identified errors in an earlier version of this work, and the anonymous Crypto 2020 reviewers for their helpful comments.

References

[ABD+19] Alkim, E., et al.: FrodoKEM (2019). https://frodokem.org/

[Ajt96] Ajtai, M.: Generating hard instances of lattice problems. In: STOC (1996)

[ALNS19] Aggarwal, D., Li, J., Nguyen, P.Q., Stephens-Davidowitz, N.: Slide reduction, revisited–filling the gaps in SVP approximation (2019). https://arxiv.org/abs/1908.03724

[Bab86] Babai, L.: On Lovász' lattice reduction and the nearest lattice point problem. Combinatorica **6**(1), 1–13 (1986). https://doi.org/10.1007/BF02579403

[CDPR16] Cramer, R., Ducas, L., Peikert, C., Regev, O.: Recovering short generators of principal ideals in cyclotomic rings. In: Fischlin, M., Coron, J.-S. (eds.) EUROCRYPT 2016. LNCS, vol. 9666, pp. 559–585. Springer, Heidelberg (2016). https://doi.org/10.1007/978-3-662-49896-5_20

[CDW17] Cramer, R., Ducas, L., Wesolowski, B.: Short Stickelberger class relations and application to Ideal-SVP. In: Coron, J.-S., Nielsen, J.B. (eds.) EUROCRYPT 2017. LNCS, vol. 10210, pp. 324–348. Springer, Cham (2017). https://doi.org/10.1007/978-3-319-56620-7_12. https://eprint.iacr.org/2016/885.

[CGS14] Campbell, P., Groves, M., Shepherd, D.: Soliloquy: a cautionary tale. In: ETSI 2nd Quantum-Safe Crypto Workshop (2014)

[DD12] Ducas, L., Durmus, A.: Ring-LWE in polynomial rings. In: Fischlin, M., Buchmann, J., Manulis, M. (eds.) PKC 2012. LNCS, vol. 7293, pp. 34–51. Springer, Heidelberg (2012). https://doi.org/10.1007/978-3-642-30057-8_3

[DPW19] Ducas, L., Plançon, M., Wesolowski, B.: On the shortness of vectors to be found by the Ideal-SVP quantum algorithm. In: Boldyreva, A., Micciancio, D. (eds.) CRYPTO 2019. LNCS, vol. 11692, pp. 322–351. Springer, Cham (2019). https://doi.org/10.1007/978-3-030-26948-7_12

[Duc17] Ducas, L.: Advances on quantum cryptanalysis of ideal lattices. Nieuw Archief voor Wiskunde **18**(5), 184–189 (2017)

[FS10] Fieker, C., Stehlé, D.: Short bases of lattices over number fields. In: Hanrot, G., Morain, F., Thomé, E. (eds.) ANTS 2010. LNCS, vol. 6197, pp. 157–173. Springer, Heidelberg (2010). https://doi.org/10.1007/978-3-642-14518-6_15

[GLM09] Gan, Y.H., Ling, C., Mow, W.H.: Complex lattice reduction algorithm for low-complexity full-diversity MIMO detection. IEEE Trans. Signal Process. **57**(7), 2701–2710 (2009)

[GN08]   Gama, N., Nguyen, P.Q.: Finding short lattice vectors within Mordell's inequality. In: STOC (2008)

[GPV08] Gentry, C., Peikert, C., Vaikuntanathan, V.: Trapdoors for hard lattices and new cryptographic constructions. In: STOC (2008). https://eprint.iacr.org/2007/432

[HPS98] Hoffstein, J., Pipher, J., Silverman, J.H.: NTRU: a ring-based public key cryptosystem. In: Buhler, J.P. (ed.) ANTS 1998. LNCS, vol. 1423, pp. 267–288. Springer, Heidelberg (1998). https://doi.org/10.1007/BFb0054868

[KL17]   Kim, T., Lee, C.: Lattice reductions over Euclidean rings with applications to cryptanalysis. In: O'Neill, M. (ed.) IMACC 2017. LNCS, vol. 10655, pp. 371–391. Springer, Cham (2017). https://doi.org/10.1007/978-3-319-71045-7_19

[LLL82] Lenstra, A.K., Lenstra Jr., H.W., Lovász, L.: Factoring polynomials with rational coefficients. Math. Ann. **261**(4), 515–534 (1982)

[LPL18] Lyu, S., Porter, C., Ling, C.: Performance limits of lattice reduction over imaginary quadratic fields with applications to compute-and-forward. In: ITW (2018)

[LPR10] Lyubashevsky, V., Peikert, C., Regev, O.: On ideal lattices and learning with errors over rings. In: Gilbert, H. (ed.) EUROCRYPT 2010. LNCS, vol. 6110, pp. 1–23. Springer, Heidelberg (2010). https://doi.org/10.1007/978-3-642-13190-5_1

[LPSW19] Lee, C., Pellet-Mary, A., Stehlé, D., Wallet, A.: An LLL algorithm for module lattices. In: Galbraith, S.D., Moriai, S. (eds.) ASIACRYPT 2019. LNCS, vol. 11922, pp. 59–90. Springer, Cham (2019). https://doi.org/10.1007/978-3-030-34621-8_3. https://eprint.iacr.org/2019/1035.

[LS12]   Langlois, A., Stehlé, D.: Hardness of decision (R)LWE for any modulus (2012)

[LS15]   Langlois, A., Stehlé, D.: Worst-case to average-case reductions for module lattices. Des. Codes Crypt. **75**(3), 565–599 (2014). https://doi.org/10.1007/s10623-014-9938-4

[MR07]   Micciancio, D., Regev, O.: Worst-case to average-case reductions based on Gaussian measures. SIAM J. Comput. **37**(1), 267–302 (2007)

[MS20]   Mukherjee, T., Stephens-Davidowitz, N.: Lattice reduction for modules, or how to reduce ModuleSVP to ModuleSVP. In: CRYPTO (2020). https://eprint.iacr.org/2019/1142

[MW16]   Micciancio, D., Walter, M.: Practical, predictable lattice basis reduction. In: Fischlin, M., Coron, J.-S. (eds.) EUROCRYPT 2016. LNCS, vol. 9665, pp. 820–849. Springer, Heidelberg (2016). https://doi.org/10.1007/978-3-662-49890-3_31. http://eprint.iacr.org/2015/1123.

[Nap96] Napias, H.: A generalization of the LLL-algorithm over Euclidean rings or orders. Journal de Théorie des Nombres de Bordeaux **8**(2), 387–396 (1996)

[NIS18] Computer Security Division NIST: Post-quantum cryptography (2018). https://csrc.nist.gov/Projects/Post-Quantum-Cryptography

[NV10]   Nguyen, P.Q., Vallée, B. (eds.): The LLL Algorithm. Survey and Applications. Springer, Heidelberg (2010). https://doi.org/10.1007/978-3-642-02295-1

[Pei09] Peikert, C.: Public-key cryptosystems from the worst-case shortest vector problem. In: STOC (2009)

[Pei15] Peikert, C.: What does GCHQ's "cautionary tale" mean for lattice cryptography? (2015). https://web.eecs.umich.edu/~cpeikert/soliloquy.html

[Pei16] Peikert, C.: A decade of lattice cryptography. Found. Trends Theor. Comput. Sci. **10**(4), 283–424 (2016)

[PHS19] Pellet-Mary, A., Hanrot, G., Stehlé, D.: Approx-SVP in ideal lattices with pre-processing. In: Ishai, Y., Rijmen, V. (eds.) EUROCRYPT 2019. LNCS, vol. 11477, pp. 685–716. Springer, Cham (2019). https://doi.org/10.1007/978-3-030-17656-3_24

[PR06] Peikert, C., Rosen, A.: Efficient collision-resistant hashing from worst-case assumptions on cyclic lattices. In: Halevi, S., Rabin, T. (eds.) TCC 2006. LNCS, vol. 3876, pp. 145–166. Springer, Heidelberg (2006). https://doi.org/10.1007/11681878_8

[PRS17] Peikert, C., Regev, O., Stephens-Davidowitz, N.: Pseudorandomness of ring-LWE for any ring and modulus. In: STOC (2017). https://eprint.iacr.org/2017/258

[Reg09] Regev, O.: On lattices, learning with errors, random linear codes, and cryptography. J. ACM **56**(6), 1–40 (2009)

[SE94] Schnorr, C.-P., Euchner, M.: Lattice basis reduction: improved practical algorithms and solving subset sum problems. Math. Program. **66**, 181–199 (1994). https://doi.org/10.1007/BF01581144

[SS11] Stehlé, D., Steinfeld, R.: Making NTRU as secure as worst-case problems over ideal lattices. In: Paterson, K.G. (ed.) EUROCRYPT 2011. LNCS, vol. 6632, pp. 27–47. Springer, Heidelberg (2011). https://doi.org/10.1007/978-3-642-20465-4_4

[SSTX09] Stehlé, D., Steinfeld, R., Tanaka, K., Xagawa, K.: Efficient public key encryption based on ideal lattices. In: Matsui, M. (ed.) ASIACRYPT 2009. LNCS, vol. 5912, pp. 617–635. Springer, Heidelberg (2009). https://doi.org/10.1007/978-3-642-10366-7_36

Random Self-reducibility of Ideal-SVP via Arakelov Random Walks

Koen de Boer[1]($\boxtimes$), Léo Ducas[1]($\boxtimes$), Alice Pellet-Mary[2]($\boxtimes$),
and Benjamin Wesolowski[3,4]($\boxtimes$)

[1] Cryptology Group, CWI, Amsterdam, The Netherlands
{k.de.boer,ducas}@cwi.nl
[2] imec-COSIC, KU Leuven, Leuven, Belgium
alice.pelletmary@kuleuven.be
[3] Univ. Bordeaux, CNRS, Bordeaux INP, IMB, UMR 5251, 33400 Talence, France
[4] INRIA, IMB, UMR 5251, 33400 Talence, France
benjamin.wesolowski@math.u-bordeaux.fr

Abstract. Fixing a number field, the space of all ideal lattices, up to isometry, is naturally an abelian group, called the *Arakelov class group*. This fact, well known to number theorists, has so far not been explicitly used in the literature on lattice-based cryptography. Remarkably, the Arakelov class group is a combination of two groups that have already led to significant cryptanalytic advances: the class group and the unit torus.

In the present article, we show that the Arakelov class group has more to offer. We start with the development of a new versatile tool: we prove that, subject to the Riemann Hypothesis for Hecke L-functions, certain random walks on the Arakelov class group have a rapid mixing property. We then exploit this result to relate the average-case and the worst-case of the Shortest Vector Problem in ideal lattices. Our reduction appears particularly sharp: for Hermite-SVP in ideal lattices of certain cyclotomic number fields, it loses no more than a $\tilde{O}(\sqrt{n})$ factor on the Hermite approximation factor.

Furthermore, we suggest that this rapid-mixing theorem should find other applications in cryptography and in algorithmic number theory.

1 Introduction

The task of finding short vectors in Euclidean lattices (a.k.a. the approximate Shortest Vector Problem) is a hard problem playing a central role in complexity theory. It is presumed to be hard even for quantum algorithms, and thanks to the average-case to worst-case reductions of Ajtai [1] and Regev [40], it has become the theoretical foundation for many kinds of cryptographic schemes. Furthermore, these problems appear to have resisted the quantum-cryptanalytic efforts so far; the overlying cryptosystems are therefore deemed quantum-safe, and for this reason are currently being considered for standardization.

Instantiations of these problems over ideal lattices have attracted particular attention, as they allow very efficient implementations. The Ring-SIS [28,30,38] and Ring-LWE [29,43] problems were introduced, and shown to reduce to worst-case instances of Ideal-SVP (the specialization of approx-SVP to ideal lattices).

In this work, we propose to recast algebraic lattice problems in their natural mathematical abstraction. It is well known to number theorists (e.g. [41]) that

D. Micciancio and T. Ristenpart (Eds.): CRYPTO 2020, LNCS 12171, pp. 243–273, 2020.
https://doi.org/10.1007/978-3-030-56880-1_9

the space of all ideal lattices (up to isometry) in a given number field is naturally an abelian group, called the *Arakelov class group*. Yet, this notion has never appeared explicitly in the literature on lattice-based cryptography. The relevance of this perspective is already illustrated by some previous work which implicitly exploit Arakelov ideals [6,16] and even the Arakelov class group [26,39]. Beyond its direct result, our work aims at highlighting this powerful formalism for finer and more rigorous analysis of computational problems in ideal lattices.

1.1   Our Result

The first half of this work (Sect. 3) is dedicated to the development of a new versatile tool: we prove that, subject to the Riemann Hypothesis for Hecke *L*-functions, certain random walks on the Arakelov class group have a rapid mixing property. In the second half (Sect. 4), we exploit this result to relate the average-case and the worst-case of Ideal-SVP, due to the interpretation of the Arakelov class group as the space of all ideal lattices. Note that this reduction does not directly impact the security of existing schemes: apart from the historical Fully Homomorphic Encryption scheme of Gentry [17],[1] there exists no scheme based on the average-case version of Ideal-SVP. The value of our result lies in the introduction of a new tool, and an illustration of the cryptanalytic insights it offers.

A second virtue of our technique resides in the strong similarities it shares with a distant branch of cryptography: cryptography based on elliptic curves [22], or more generally on abelian varieties [23]. These works established that the discrete logarithm problem in a randomly chosen elliptic curve is as hard as in any other in the same isogeny class. The strategy consists in doing a random isogeny walk, to translate the discrete logarithm problem from a presumably hard curve to a uniformly random one. The core of this result is a proof that such walks are rapidly mixing within an isogeny graph (which is isomorphic to the Cayley graph of the class group of a quadratic number field). As long as the length of the random walk is polynomial, the reduction is efficient.

We proceed in a very similar way. The set of ideal lattices (up to isometry) of a given number field K can be identified with the elements of the Arakelov class group (also known as the degree zero part Pic_K^0 of the Picard Group). There are two ways to move within this group: given an ideal, one can obtain a new one by 'distorting' it, or by 'sparsifying' it. In both cases, finding a short vector in the target ideal also allows to find a short vector in the source ideal, up to a certain loss of shortness. This makes the length of the walk even more critical in our case than in the case of elliptic curves: it does not only affect the running time, but also the quality of the result.

Nevertheless, this approach leads to a surprisingly tight reduction. In the case of cyclotomic number fields of conductor $m = p^k$, under the Riemann Hypothesis for Hecke *L*-functions (which we abbreviate ERH for the Extended Riemann

---

[1] We here refer to the full fledge version of the scheme from Gentry's PhD Thesis, which differs from the scheme in [18], the latter having been broken already [6,10,11,16].

Hypothesis), and a mild assumption on the structure of the class groups, the loss of approximation factor is as small as $\tilde{O}(\sqrt{m})$. In other words:

Main Theorem (informal). *Let $m = p^k$ be a prime power. If there exists a polynomial-time algorithm for solving Hermite-SVP with approximation factor γ over random ideal lattices of $\mathbb{Q}(\zeta_m)$, then there also exists a polynomial time algorithm that solves Hermite-SVP in any ideal lattice with approximation factor $\gamma' = \gamma \cdot \sqrt{m} \cdot poly(\log m)$.*

In fact, this theorem generalizes to all number fields, but the loss in approximation factor needs to be expressed in more involved quantities. The precise statement is the object of Theorem 4.5.

Prerequisites. The authors are aware that the theory of Arakelov class groups, at the core of the present article, may not be familiar to all readers. Given space constraints, some definitions or concepts are introduced very briefly. We found Chapters I and VII of Neukirch's textbook [36] to be a good primer.

1.2 Overview

The Arakelov class group. Both the unit group [11] and the class group [12] have been shown to play a key role in the cryptanalysis of ideal lattice problems. In these works, these groups are exploited independently, in ways that nevertheless share strong similarities with each other. More recently, both groups have been used in combination for cryptanalytic purposes [26,39]. It therefore seems natural to turn to a unifying theory.

The Arakelov class group (denoted Pic_K^0) is a combination of the unit torus $T = \text{Log} K_\mathbb{R}^0 / \text{Log}(\mathcal{O}_K^*)$ and of the class group Cl_K. The exponent 0 here refers to elements of algebraic norm 1 (i.e., modulo renormalization), while the subscript $\mathbb{R}$ indicates that we are working in the topological completion of K. By 'a combination' we do not exactly mean that Pic_K^0 is a direct product; we mean that there is a short exact sequence

$$0 \longrightarrow T \longrightarrow \text{Pic}_K^0 \longrightarrow \text{Cl}_K \longrightarrow 0.$$

That is, T is (isomorphic to) a subgroup of Pic_K^0, and Cl_K is (isomorphic to) the quotient Pic_K^0 / T. The Arakelov class group is an abelian group which combines an uncountable (yet compact) part T and a finite part Cl_K; topologically, it should be thought of as $|\text{Cl}_K|$ many disconnected copies of the torus T.

A worst-case to average-case reduction for ideal-SVP. An important aspect of the Arakelov Class Group for the present work is that this group has a geometric interpretation: it can essentially be understood as the group of all ideal lattices up to K-linear isometries. Furthermore, being equipped with a metric, it naturally induces a notion of near-isometry. Such a notion gives a new handle to elucidate the question of the hardness of ideal-SVP: knowing a short vector in I, and a near-isometry from I to J, one can deduce a short vector of J up to a small loss induced by the distortion of the near-isometry. This suggests a strategy towards a worst-case to average-case reduction for ideal lattices, namely randomly distort a worst-case ideal to a random one.

However, there are two issues with this strategy: first near-isometry leaves one stuck in a fixed class of Cl_K; i.e., one is stuck in one of the potentially many separated copies of the torus that constitute the Arakelov class group. Second, even if $|\mathrm{Cl}_K| = 1$, the torus might be too large, and to reach the full torus from a given point, one may need near-isometry that are too distorted.

In the language of algebraic geometry, distortion of ideal lattices corresponds to the 'infinite places' of the field K, while we can also exploit the 'finite places', i.e., the prime ideals. Indeed, if $\mathfrak{a}$ is an integral ideal of small norm and $J = \mathfrak{a}I$, then J is a sublattice of I and a short vector of J is also a somewhat short vector of I, an idea already used in [12,39].

Random walk in the Arakelov class group. The questions of whether the above strategy for the self-reducibility of ideal-SVP works out, and with how much loss in the approximation factor therefore boils down to the following question:

How fast does a random walk in the Arakelov class group converges to the uniform distribution?

More specifically, this random walk has three parameters: a set $\mathcal{P}$ of finite places, i.e., a set of (small) prime ideals, a length N for the discrete walk on finite places, and finally a variance s for a continuous walk (e.g. a Gaussian) on infinite places. The loss in approximation factor will essentially be driven by $B^{N/n} \cdot \exp(s)$ where B is the maximal algebraic norm of the prime ideals in $\mathcal{P}$, and n the rank of the number field.

Because the Arakelov class group is abelian and compact, such a study is carried out by resorting to Fourier analysis: uniformity is demonstrated by showing that all the Fourier coefficients of the distribution resulting from the random walk tend to 0 except for the coefficient associated with the trivial character. For discrete walks, one considers the Hecke operator acting on distributions by making one additional random step, and shows that all its eigenvalues are significantly smaller than 1, except for the eigenvalue associated with the trivial character. This is merely an extension to compact groups of the spectral gap theorem applied to the Cayley graph of a finite abelian group, as done in [22].

Our study reveals that the eigenvalues are indeed sufficiently smaller than 1, but only for low-frequency characters. But this is not so surprising: these eigenvalues only account for the discrete part of the walk, using finite places, which leaves discrete distributions discrete, and therefore non-uniform over a continuous group. To reach uniformity we also need a continuous walk over the infinite places, and taking a Gaussian continuous walk effectively clears out the Fourier coefficients associated to high-frequency characters.

1.3 Related Work

Relation to recent cryptanalytic works. The general approach to this result was triggered by a heuristic observation made in [15], suggesting that the worst-case behavior of the quantum Ideal-SVP algorithm built out of [6,11,12,16] could be made not that far of the average-case behavior they studied experimentally. More specifically, we do achieve the hoped generalization of the class-group mixing theorem of [22,23] to Arakelov class groups; but we furthermore show that this result affects all algorithms, and not only the one they studied.

We also remark that recent works [26,39] were already implicitly relying on Arakelov theory. More specifically, the lattice given in Section 3.1 of [39] is precisely the lattice of Picard-class relations between the appropriate set of (degree 0) Arakelov Divisors. In fact, our theorem also implies upper bounds for the covering radius of the those relation lattices, at least for sufficiently large factor bases, and with more effort one may be able to eliminate Heuristic 4 from [39] or Heuristic 1 of [26].

Prior self-reduction via random walks. As already mentioned, our result shares strong similarities with a technique introduced by Jao, Miller and Venkatesan [22] to study the discrete logarithm problem on elliptic curves. Just as ideal lattices can be seen as elements of the Arakelov class group, elliptic curves in certain families are in bijective correspondence with elements of the class group of a quadratic imaginary number field. In [22], Jao et al. studied (discrete) random walks in class groups, and showed that they have a rapid mixing property. They deduced that from any elliptic curve, one can efficiently construct a random isogeny (a group homomorphism) to a uniformly random elliptic curve, allowing to transfer a worst case instance of the discrete logarithm problem to an average case instance. Instead of the finite class group, we studied random walks in the infinite Arakelov class group, which led us to consequences in lattice-base cryptography, an area seemingly unrelated to elliptic curve cryptography.

Prior self-reduction for ideal lattices. Our self-reducibility result is not the first of its kind: in 2010, Gentry already proposed a self-reduction for an ideal lattice problem [19], as part of his effort of basing Fully-Homomorphic Encryption on worst-case problems [17]. Our result differs in several point:

- Our reduction does not rely on a factoring oracle, and is therefore classically efficient; this was already advertised as an open problem in [19].
- The reduction of Gentry considers the Bounded Distance Decoding problem (BDD) in ideal lattices rather than a short vector problem. Note that this distinction is not significant with respect to quantum computers [40].
- The definition of average case distribution is significantly different, and we view the one of [19] as being somewhat ad-hoc. Given that the Arakelov class group captures exactly ideal lattices up to isometry, we consider the uniform distribution in the Arakelov class group as a much more natural and conceptually simpler choice.

– The loss on the approximation factor of our reduction is much more favorable than the one of Gentry [19]. For example, in the case of cyclotomic number fields with prime-power conductor, Gentry's reduction (on BDD) seems to loose a factor at least $\Theta(n^{4.5})$, while our reduction (on Hermite-SVP) only loses a factor $\tilde{O}(\sqrt{n})$ making a mild assumption on plus-part h^+ of the class number.

Other applications. Finally, we wish to emphasise that our rapid mixing theorem for Arakelov class groups appears to be a versatile new tool, which has already found applications beyond hardness proofs for ideal lattices.

One such application is the object of another work in progress. Namely, we note that many algorithms [4,5,8] rely on finding elements a in an ideal I such that aI^{-1} is easy to factor (e.g. prime, near-prime, or B-smooth). Such algorithms are analyzed only heuristically, by treating aI^{-1} as a uniformly sampled ideal, and applying know results on the density of prime or smooth ideals. Our theorem allows to adjust this strategy and make the reasoning rigorous. First, we show that if the Arakelov class of the ideal I is uniformly random, one can rigorously analyze the probability of aI^{-1} being prime or smooth. Then, our random-walk theorem allows to randomize I, while not affecting the usefulness of the recovered element a. However, due to space constraints and thematic distance, we chose to develop this application in another article.

As mentioned above, another potential application of random walk theorem may be the elimination of heuristics in cryptanalysis of ideal and module lattices [26,39].

2   Preliminaries

We denote by $\mathbb{N}, \mathbb{Z}, \mathbb{Q}, \mathbb{R}$ the natural numbers, the integers, the rationals and the real numbers respectively. All logarithms are in base e. For a rational number $p/q \in \mathbb{Q}$ with p and q coprime, we let size(p/q) refer to $\log|p| + \log|q|$. We extend this definition to vectors of rational numbers, by taking the sum of the sizes of all the coefficients.

2.1   Number Theory

Throughout this paper, we use a fixed number field K of rank $n \geq 3$ over $\mathbb{Q}$, having ring of integers $\mathcal{O}_K$, discriminant Δ, regulator R, class number h and group of roots of unity μ_K. Minkowski's theorem [34, pp. 261–264] states that there exists an absolute constant $c > 0$ such that $\log|\Delta| \geq c \cdot n$. The number field K has n field embeddings into $\mathbb{C}$, which are divided in $n_{\mathbb{R}}$ real embeddings and $n_{\mathbb{C}}$ conjugate pairs of complex embeddings, i.e., $n = n_{\mathbb{R}} + 2n_{\mathbb{C}}$. These embeddings combined yield the so-called Minkowski embedding $\Psi : K \to K_{\mathbb{R}} \subseteq \bigoplus_{\sigma:K \hookrightarrow \mathbb{C}} \mathbb{C}$, $\alpha \mapsto (\sigma(\alpha))_\sigma$, where

$$K_{\mathbb{R}} = \left\{ x \in \bigoplus_{\sigma:K \hookrightarrow \mathbb{C}} \mathbb{C} \;\middle|\; x_{\overline{\sigma}} = \overline{x_\sigma} \right\}.$$

Here, $\bar{\sigma}$ equals the conjugate embedding of σ whenever σ is a complex embedding and it is just σ itself whenever it is a real embedding. Note that we index the components of the vectors in $K_{\mathbb{R}}$ by the embeddings of K. Embeddings up to conjugation are called infinite places, denoted by ν. With any embedding σ we denote by ν_σ the associated place; and for any place we choose a fixed embedding σ_ν.

Composing the Minkowski embedding by the component-wise logarithm of the entries' absolute values yields the logarithmic embedding, denoted by Log.

$$\text{Log} : K^* \to \text{Log}\, K_{\mathbb{R}} \subseteq \bigoplus_{\sigma:K \hookrightarrow \mathbb{C}} \mathbb{R}, \ \alpha \mapsto (\log |\sigma(\alpha)|)_\sigma.$$

The multiplicative group of integral units $\mathcal{O}_K^*$ under the logarithmic embedding forms a lattice, namely the lattice $\Lambda_K = \text{Log}(\mathcal{O}_K^*) \subseteq \text{Log}\, K_{\mathbb{R}}$. This so-called logarithmic unit lattice has rank $\ell = n_{\mathbb{R}} + n_{\mathbb{C}} - 1$, is orthogonal to the all-one vector $(1)_\sigma$, and has covolume $\text{Vol}(\Lambda_K) = \sqrt{n} \cdot 2^{-n_{\mathbb{C}}/2} \cdot R$, where the $2^{-n_{\mathbb{C}}/2}$ factor is due to the specific embedding we use (see Lemma A.1 of the full version [7]). We denote by $H = \text{Span}(\Lambda_K)$ the hyperplane of dimension ℓ, which can also be defined as the subspace of $\text{Log}\, K_{\mathbb{R}}$ orthogonal to the all-one vector $(1)_\sigma$. We denote by $T = H/\Lambda_K$ the hypertorus defined by the logarithmic unit lattice Λ_K.

Fractional ideals of the number field K are denoted by $\mathfrak{a}, \mathfrak{b}, \ldots$, but the symbol $\mathfrak{p}$ is generally reserved for integral prime ideals of $\mathcal{O}_K$. The group of fractional ideals of K is denoted by $\mathcal{I}_K$. Principal ideals with generator $\alpha \in K^*$ are usually denoted by (α). For any integral ideal $\mathfrak{a}$, we define the norm $\mathcal{N}(\mathfrak{a})$ of $\mathfrak{a}$ to be the number $|\mathcal{O}_K/\mathfrak{a}|$; this norm then generalizes to fractional ideals and elements as well. The class-group of $\mathcal{O}_K$, denoted by $\text{Cl}(\mathcal{O}_K)$, is the quotient of the group $\mathcal{I}_K$ by the subgroup of principal ideals $\text{Princ}_K := \{(\alpha), \alpha \in K\}$. For any fractional ideal $\mathfrak{a}$, we denote the ideal class of $\mathfrak{a}$ in $\text{Cl}(\mathcal{O}_K)$ by $[\mathfrak{a}]$.

Extra attention is paid to the cyclotomic number fields $K = \mathbb{Q}(\zeta_m)$, for which we can prove sharper results due to their high structure. These results rely on the size of the class group $h_K^+ = |\text{Cl}(K^+)|$ of the maximum real subfield $K^+ = \mathbb{Q}(\zeta_m + \bar{\zeta}_m)$ of K, which is often conjectured to be rather small [9,32]. In this paper, we make the mild assumption that $h_K^+ \leq (\log n)^n$.

Extended Riemann Hypothesis. Almost all results in this paper rely heavily on the *Extended Riemann Hypothesis* (in the subsequent part of this paper abbreviated by ERH), which refers to the Riemann Hypothesis extended to Hecke L-functions (see [21, §5.7]). All statements that mention (ERH), such as Theorem 3.3, assume the Extended Riemann Hypothesis.

Prime Densities. In multiple parts of this paper, we need an estimate on the number of prime ideals with bounded norm. This is achieved in the following theorem, obtained from [2, Thm. 8.7.4].

Theorem 2.1 (ERH). *Let $\pi_K(x)$ be the number of prime integral ideals of K of norm $\leq x$. Then, assuming the Extended Riemann Hypothesis, there exists an* *absolute constant C (i.e., independent of K and x) such that*

$$|\pi_K(x) - \mathrm{li}(x)| \le C \cdot \sqrt{x}\,(n\log x + \log|\Delta|),$$

where $\mathrm{li}(x) = \int_2^x \frac{dt}{\ln t} \sim \frac{x}{\ln x}$.

Lemma 2.2 (Sampling of prime ideals, ERH). *Let a basis of $\mathcal{O}_K$ be known and let $\mathcal{P} = \{\mathfrak{p}\text{ prime ideal of }K \mid \mathcal{N}(\mathfrak{p}) \le B\}$ be the set of prime ideals of norm bounded by $B \ge \max((12\log\Delta + 8n + 28)^4, 3\cdot 10^{11})$. Then one can sample uniformly from $\mathcal{P}$ in expected time $O(n^3\log^2 B)$.*

Proof. The sampling algorithm goes as follows. Sample an integer uniformly in $[0, B]$ and check if it is a prime. If it is, factor the obtained prime p in $\mathcal{O}_K$ and list the different prime ideal factors $\{\mathfrak{p}_1, \ldots, \mathfrak{p}_k\}$ that have norm bounded by B. Choose one $\mathfrak{p}_i$ uniformly as random in $\{\mathfrak{p}_1, \ldots, \mathfrak{p}_k\}$ and output it with probability k/n. Otherwise, output 'failure'.

Let $\mathfrak{q} \in \mathcal{P}$ be arbitrary, and let $\mathcal{N}(\mathfrak{q}) = q^j$ with q prime. Then, the probability of sampling $\mathfrak{q}$ equals $\frac{1}{nB}$, namely $\frac{1}{n}$ times the probability of sampling q. Therefore, the probability of sampling successfully (i.e., no failure) equals $\frac{|\mathcal{P}|}{nB} \ge \frac{1}{2n\log B}$, since $|\mathcal{P}| \ge \frac{B}{2\log B}$, by Lemma A.3 of the full version [7].

The most costly part of the algorithm is the factorization of a prime $p \le B$ in $\mathcal{O}_K$. This can be performed using the Kummer-Dedekind algorithm, which essentially amounts to factoring a degree n polynomial modulo p. Using Shoup's algorithm [42] (which has complexity $O(n^2 + n\log p)$ [44, §4.1]) yields the complexity claim. $\square$

2.2   The Arakelov Class Group

The *Arakelov divisor group* is the group

$$\mathrm{Div}_K = \bigoplus_{\mathfrak{p}} \mathbb{Z} \times \bigoplus_{\nu} \mathbb{R}$$

where $\mathfrak{p}$ ranges over the set of all prime ideals of $\mathcal{O}_K$, and ν over the set of infinite primes (embeddings into the complex numbers up to possible conjugation). We write an arbitrary element in Div_K as

$$\mathbf{a} = \sum_{\mathfrak{p}} n_{\mathfrak{p}} \cdot (\!|\mathfrak{p}|\!) + \sum_{\nu} x_{\nu} \cdot (\!|\nu|\!),$$

with only finitely many non-zero $n_{\mathfrak{p}}$. We will consistently use the symbols $\mathbf{a}, \mathbf{b}, \mathbf{e}, \ldots$ for Arakelov divisors. Denoting $\mathrm{ord}_{\mathfrak{p}}$ for the valuation at the prime $\mathfrak{p}$, there is a canonical homomorphism

$$(\!|\cdot|\!) : K^* \to \mathrm{Div}_K, \quad \alpha \longmapsto \sum_{\mathfrak{p}} \mathrm{ord}_{\mathfrak{p}}(\alpha)(\!|\mathfrak{p}|\!) - \sum_{\nu} \log|\sigma_{\nu}(\alpha)| \cdot (\!|\nu|\!).$$

The divisors of the form $(\!|\alpha|\!)$ for $\alpha \in K^*$ are called *principal divisors*. Just as the ideal class group is the group of ideals quotiented by the group of principal ideals, the *Picard group* is the group of Arakelov divisors quotiented by the group of principal Arakelov divisors. In other words, the Picard group Pic_K is defined by the following exact sequence.

$$0 \to K^*/\mu_K \xrightarrow{(\!\cdot\!)} \mathrm{Div}_K \to \mathrm{Pic}_K \to 0.$$

For any Arakelov divisor $\mathbf{a} = \sum_{\mathfrak{p}} n_{\mathfrak{p}} \cdot (\!|\mathfrak{p}|\!) + \sum_{\nu} x_{\nu} \cdot (\!|\nu|\!)$, we denote its Arakelov class by $[\mathbf{a}]$; in the same fashion that $[\mathfrak{a}]$ denotes the ideal class of the ideal $\mathfrak{a}$.

Despite the Arakelov divisor and Picard group being interesting groups, for our purposes it is more useful to consider the *degree-zero* subgroups of these groups. The degree map is defined as follows:

$$\deg : \mathrm{Div}_K \to \mathbb{R}, \quad \sum_{\mathfrak{p}} n_{\mathfrak{p}} \cdot (\!|\mathfrak{p}|\!) + \sum_{\nu} x_{\nu} \cdot (\!|\nu|\!) \mapsto \sum_{\mathfrak{p}} n_{\mathfrak{p}} \cdot \log(\mathcal{N}(\mathfrak{p})) + \sum_{\nu \text{ real}} x_{\nu} + \sum_{\nu \text{ complex}} 2 \cdot x_{\nu}.$$

The degree map sends principal divisors $(\!|\alpha|\!)$ to zero; therefore, the degree map is properly defined on Pic_K, as well. We subsequently define the *degree-zero Arakelov divisor group* $\mathrm{Div}_K^0 = \{\mathbf{a} \in \mathrm{Div}_K \mid \deg(\mathbf{a}) = 0\}$ and the *Arakelov class group* $\mathrm{Pic}_K^0 = \{[\mathbf{a}] \in \mathrm{Pic}_K \mid \deg([\mathbf{a}]) = 0\}$.

Note that by 'forgetting' the infinite part of a (degree-zero) Arakelov divisor $\mathbf{a}$, one arrives at a fractional ideal. This projection

$$\mathrm{Div}_K^0 \to \mathcal{I}_K, \quad \sum_{\mathfrak{p}} n_{\mathfrak{p}} \cdot (\!|\mathfrak{p}|\!) + \sum_{\nu} x_{\nu} \cdot (\!|\nu|\!) \longmapsto \prod_{\mathfrak{p}} \mathfrak{p}^{n_{\mathfrak{p}}},$$

has the hyperplane $H \subseteq \mathrm{Log}\, K_{\mathbb{R}}$ as kernel under the inclusion $H \to \mathrm{Div}_K^0$, $(x_\sigma)_\sigma \mapsto \sum_{\nu} x_{\sigma_\nu} (\!|\nu|\!)$. This projection morphism $\mathrm{Div}_K^0 \to \mathcal{I}_K$ has the following section that we will use often in the subsequent part of this paper.

$$d^0 : \mathcal{I}_K \to \mathrm{Div}_K^0, \quad \mathfrak{a} \longmapsto \sum_{\mathfrak{p}} \mathrm{ord}_{\mathfrak{p}}(\mathfrak{a}) \cdot (\!|\mathfrak{p}|\!) - \frac{\log(\mathcal{N}(\mathfrak{a}))}{n} \sum_{\nu} (\!|\nu|\!)$$

The groups and their relations, that are treated above, fit nicely in the diagram of exact sequences given in Fig. 1, where the middle row sequence splits with the section d^0. It will be proven useful to show that the volume of the Arakelov class group roughly follows the square root of the field discriminant.

Lemma 2.3 (Volume of Pic_K^0). *We have* $\mathrm{Vol}(\mathrm{Pic}_K^0) = h\,\mathrm{Vol}(T) = hR\sqrt{n}2^{-n_C/2}$, *and*

$$\log \mathrm{Vol}(\mathrm{Pic}_K^0) \leq n \left(\frac{1}{2} \log(|\Delta|^{1/n}) + \log\log(|\Delta|^{1/n}) + 1 \right)$$

Proof. The volume of the Arakelov class group follows from the above exact sequence and the volume computation of T in Appendix A of the full version [7]. The bound on the logarithm is obtained by applying the class number formula

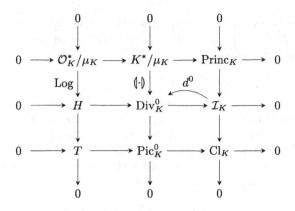

Fig. 1. A commutative diagram of exact sequences.

[37, VII.§5, Cor 5.11] and Louboutin's bound [27] on the residue of the Dedekind zeta function at $s = 1$:

$$\mathrm{Vol}(\mathrm{Pic}_K^0) = hR\sqrt{n}2^{-n_\mathbb{C}/2} = \frac{\rho\sqrt{|\Delta|}\omega_K\sqrt{n}}{2^{n_\mathbb{R}}(2\sqrt{2}\pi)^{n_\mathbb{C}}} \le \rho\sqrt{|\Delta|} \le \sqrt{|\Delta|}\left(\frac{e\log|\Delta|}{n}\right)^n,$$

where $\omega_K = |\mu_K|$ is the number of roots of unity in K. For the bound on the logarithm, use $n\log(e\log|\Delta|/n) = n\log\log(|\Delta|^{1/n}) + n$. □

We let $\mathcal{U}(\mathrm{Pic}_K^0) = \frac{1}{\mathrm{Vol}(\mathrm{Pic}_K^0)} \cdot \mathbf{1}_{\mathrm{Pic}_K^0}$ denote the uniform distribution over the Arakelov class group.

Fourier theory over the Arakelov class group. As the Arakelov class group Pic_K^0 is a compact abelian group, every function in[2] $L_2(\mathrm{Pic}_K^0) = \{f : \mathrm{Pic}_K^0 \to \mathbb{C} \mid \int_{\mathrm{Pic}_K^0} |f|^2 < \infty\}$ can be uniquely decomposed into a character sum

$$f = \sum_{\chi \in \widehat{\mathrm{Pic}_K^0}} a_\chi \cdot \chi,$$

with $a_\chi \in \mathbb{C}$. In the proof of Theorem 3.3, we will make use of Parseval's identity [13, Thm. 3.4.8] in the following form.

$$\int_{\mathrm{Pic}_K^0} |f|^2 = \|f\|_2^2 = \frac{1}{\mathrm{Vol}(\mathrm{Pic}_K^0)} \sum_{\chi \in \widehat{\mathrm{Pic}_K^0}} |a_\chi|^2 \tag{1}$$

---

[2] The measure on the Arakelov class group is unique up to scaling – it is the Haar measure. By fixing the volume of Pic_K^0 as in Lemma 2.3, we fix this scaling as well. We use then *this* particular scaling of the Haar measure for the integrals over the Arakelov class group.

2.3   Lattices

A lattice Λ is a discrete subgroup of a real vector space. In the following, we assume that this real vector space has dimension m and that the lattice is full-rank, i.e., span(Λ) equals the whole real space. A lattice can be represented by a basis $(b_1, \cdots, b_m)$ such that $\Lambda = \{\sum_i x_i b_i,\ x_i \in \mathbb{Z}\}$. Important notions in lattice theory are the volume $\mathrm{Vol}(\Lambda)$, which is essentially the volume of the hypertorus span$(\Lambda)/\Lambda$ (alternatively, $\mathrm{Vol}(\Lambda)$ is the absolute determinant of any basis of Λ); the first minimum $\lambda_1(\Lambda) = \min_{v \in \Lambda \setminus \{0\}} \|v\|$; and the last minimum $\lambda_m(\Lambda)$, which equals the minimal radius $r > 0$ such that $\{v \in L \mid \|v\| \leq r\}$ is of full rank m.

We will be interested into the following algorithmic problem over lattices.

Definition 2.4 (γ-Hermite-SVP). *Given as input a basis of a rank m lattice Λ, the problem γ-Hermite-SVP consists in computing a non-zero vector v in λ such that*
$$\|v\| \leq \gamma \cdot \mathrm{Vol}(\Lambda)^{1/m}.$$

For a rank-m lattice $\Lambda \subset \mathbb{R}^m$, we let Λ^* denote its dual, that is $\Lambda^* = \{x \in \mathbb{R}^m : \forall v \in \Lambda,\ \langle v, x \rangle \in \mathbb{Z}\}$.

2.4   Divisors and Ideal Lattices

It will be proven useful to view both ideals and Arakelov divisors as lattices in the real vector space $K_{\mathbb{R}}$, where $K_{\mathbb{R}}$ has its (Euclidean or maximum) norm inherited from the complex vector space it lives in. Explicitly, the Euclidean and maximum norm of $\alpha \in K$ are respectively defined by the rules $\|\alpha\|_2^2 = \sum_{\sigma} |\sigma(\alpha)|^2$ and $\|\alpha\|_{\infty} = \max_{\sigma} |\sigma(\alpha)|$, where σ ranges over all embeddings $K \to \mathbb{C}$. By default, $\|\alpha\|$ refers to the Euclidean norm $\|\alpha\|_2$.

For any ideal $\mathfrak{a}$ of K, we define the associated lattice $\mathcal{L}(\mathfrak{a})$ to be the image of $\mathfrak{a} \subseteq K$ under the Minkowski embedding Ψ, which is clearly a discrete subgroup of $K_{\mathbb{R}}$. In particular, $\mathcal{L}(\mathcal{O}_K)$ is a lattice and we will always assume throughout this article that we know a basis $(b_1, \cdots, b_n)$ of $\mathcal{L}(\mathcal{O}_K)$. For Arakelov divisors $\mathbf{a} = \sum_{\mathfrak{p}} n_{\mathfrak{p}} \cdot (\!|\mathfrak{p}|\!) + \sum_{\nu} x_{\nu} \cdot (\!|\nu|\!)$, the associated lattice is defined as follows.

$$\mathcal{L}(\mathbf{a}) = \left\{ (e^{x_{\nu_{\sigma}}} \cdot \sigma(\alpha))_{\sigma} \mid \alpha \in \prod \mathfrak{p}^{n_{\mathfrak{p}}} \right\} = \mathrm{diag}\left((e^{x_{\nu_{\sigma}}})_{\sigma} \right) \cdot \mathcal{L}\left(\prod \mathfrak{p}^{n_{\mathfrak{p}}} \right) \subseteq K_{\mathbb{R}},$$

where diag denotes a diagonal matrix. Note that we have

$$\mathrm{Vol}(\mathcal{L}(\mathfrak{a})) = \sqrt{|\Delta|}\, \mathcal{N}(\mathfrak{a}) \quad \text{and} \quad \mathrm{Vol}(\mathcal{L}(\mathbf{a})) = \sqrt{|\Delta|} \cdot \prod_{\sigma} e^{x_{\nu_{\sigma}}} \cdot \mathcal{N}(\prod_{\mathfrak{p}} \mathfrak{p}^{n_{\mathfrak{p}}}) = \sqrt{|\Delta|} \cdot e^{\deg(\mathbf{a})}$$

The associated lattice $\mathcal{L}(\mathbf{a})$ of a divisor is of a special shape, which we call *ideal lattices*, as in the following definition.

Definition 2.5 (Ideal lattices). *An ideal lattice is an $\mathcal{O}_K$-module $I \subseteq K_{\mathbb{R}}$ for which holds that there exists an invertible $x \in K_{\mathbb{R}}$ such that $xI = \mathcal{L}(\mathfrak{a})$ for some ideal $\mathfrak{a}$ of $\mathcal{O}_K$. We let IdLat_K denote the set of all ideal lattices.*

Note that the lattices $\mathcal{L}(\mathfrak{a})$ for $\mathfrak{a} \in \mathcal{I}_K$ are special cases of ideal lattices, which we will call *fractional ideal lattices*. Since the Minkowski embedding is injective, the map $\mathcal{L}(\cdot)$ provides a bijection between the set of fractional ideals and the set of fractional ideal lattices.

The set IdLat_K of ideal lattices forms a group; the product of two ideal lattices $I = x\,\mathcal{L}(\mathfrak{a})$ and $J = y\,\mathcal{L}(\mathfrak{b})$ is defined by the rule $I \cdot J = xy\,\mathcal{L}(\mathfrak{a}\mathfrak{b})$. It is clear that $\mathcal{L}(\mathcal{O}_K)$ is the unit ideal lattice and $x^{-1}\,\mathcal{L}(\mathfrak{a}^{-1})$ is the inverse ideal lattice of $x\,\mathcal{L}(\mathfrak{a})$. The map $\mathcal{L} : \mathrm{Div}_K^0 \rightarrow \mathrm{IdLat}_K, \mathfrak{a} \mapsto \mathcal{L}(\mathfrak{a})$ sends an Arakelov divisor to an ideal lattice. The image under this map is the following subgroup of IdLat_K.

$$\mathrm{IdLat}_K^0 = \{x\,\mathcal{L}(\mathfrak{a}) \mid \mathcal{N}(\mathfrak{a}) \prod_\sigma x_\sigma = 1 \text{ and } x_\sigma > 0 \text{ for all } \sigma\}.$$

Definition 2.6 (Isometry of ideal lattices). *For two ideal lattices $L, L' \in \mathrm{IdLat}_K^0$, we say that L and L' are K-isometric, denoted by $L \sim L'$, when there exists $(\xi_\sigma) \in K_{\mathbb{R}}$ with $|\xi_\sigma| = 1$ such that $(\xi_\sigma)_\sigma \cdot L = L'$.*

It is evident that being K-isometric is an equivalence relation on IdLat_K^0 that is compatible with the group operation. Denoting Iso_K for the subgroup $\{L \in \mathrm{IdLat}_K^0 \mid L \sim \mathcal{L}(\mathcal{O}_K)\} \subset \mathrm{IdLat}_K^0$, we have the following result.

Lemma 2.7 (Arakelov classes are ideal lattices up to isometries). *Denoting $P : \mathrm{IdLat}_K^0 \rightarrow \mathrm{Pic}_K^0$ for the map $x\,\mathcal{L}(\mathfrak{a}) \longmapsto \sum_{\mathfrak{p}} \mathrm{ord}_{\mathfrak{p}}(\mathfrak{a})[\mathfrak{p}] + \sum_\nu \log(x_{\sigma_\nu})[\nu]$ modulo principal divisors, we have the following exact sequence.*

$$0 \rightarrow \mathrm{Iso}_K \rightarrow \mathrm{IdLat}_K^0 \xrightarrow{P} \mathrm{Pic}_K^0 \rightarrow 0.$$

Proof. This is a well-known fact (e.g., [41]), but we give a proof for completeness. It suffices to show that P is a well-defined surjective homomorphism and its kernel is Iso_K. In order to be well-defined, P must satisfy $P(x\,\mathcal{L}(\mathfrak{a})) = P(x'\,\mathcal{L}(\mathfrak{a}'))$ whenever $x\,\mathcal{L}(\mathfrak{a}) = x'\,\mathcal{L}(\mathfrak{a}')$. Assuming the latter, we obtain $x^{-1}x'\,\mathcal{L}(\mathcal{O}_K) = \mathcal{L}((\mathfrak{a}')^{-1}\mathfrak{a}) = \mathcal{L}(\alpha\mathcal{O}_K)$, for some $\alpha \in K^*$, as the module is a free $\mathcal{O}_K$-module. This implies that $(x^{-1}x')_\sigma = \sigma(\eta\alpha)$ for all embeddings $\sigma : K \rightarrow \mathbb{C}$, for some unit $\eta \in \mathcal{O}_K^*$. Therefore, we have, $P(x\,\mathcal{L}(\mathfrak{a})) - P(x'\,\mathcal{L}(\mathfrak{a}')) = \sum_{\mathfrak{p}} \mathrm{ord}_{\mathfrak{p}}(\alpha)[\mathfrak{p}] + \sum_\nu \log((x_{\sigma_\nu})^{-1}x'_{\sigma_\nu})[\nu] = (\!|\eta\alpha|\!)$; i.e., their difference is a principal divisor, meaning that their image in Pic_K^0 is the same.

One can check that P is a homomorphism, and its surjectivity can be proven by constructing an ideal lattice in the pre-image of a representative divisor $\mathbf{a} = \sum_{\mathfrak{p}} n_{\mathfrak{p}}[\mathfrak{p}] + \sum_\nu x_\nu[\nu] \in \mathrm{Div}_K^0$ of an Arakelov class $[\mathbf{a}]$, e.g., $(e^{x_{\nu\sigma}})_\sigma \cdot \mathcal{L}(\prod_{\mathfrak{p}} \mathfrak{p}^{n_{\mathfrak{p}}})$.

We finish the proof by showing that the kernel of P indeed equals Iso_K. Suppose $x\,\mathcal{L}(\mathfrak{a}) \in \ker(P)$, i.e., $P(x\,\mathcal{L}(\mathfrak{a})) = \sum_{\mathfrak{p}} \mathrm{ord}_{\mathfrak{p}}(\mathfrak{a})[\mathfrak{p}] + \sum_\nu \log(x_{\sigma_\nu})[\nu] = (\!|\alpha|\!)$ is a principal divisor. This means that $\mathfrak{a} = \alpha\mathcal{O}_K$ and $x = (|\sigma(\alpha)|^{-1})_\sigma$, i.e., $x\,\mathcal{L}(\mathfrak{a}) = (|\sigma(\alpha)|^{-1})_\sigma\,\mathcal{L}(\alpha\mathcal{O}_K) = \left(\frac{\sigma(\alpha)}{|\sigma(\alpha)|}\right)_\sigma \cdot \mathcal{L}(\mathcal{O}_K)$, so $x\,\mathcal{L}(\mathfrak{a}) \sim \mathcal{L}(\mathcal{O}_K)$, implying $x\,\mathcal{L}(\mathfrak{a}) \in \mathrm{Iso}_K$. This shows that $\ker P \subseteq \mathrm{Iso}_K$. The reverse inclusion starts with the observation that $x\,\mathcal{L}(\mathfrak{a}) \sim \mathcal{L}(\mathcal{O}_K)$ directly implies that $\mathfrak{a} = \alpha\mathcal{O}_K$

is principal, by the fact that $x\,\mathcal{L}(\mathfrak{a})$ is a free $\mathcal{O}_K$-module. So, $(x_\sigma\sigma(\alpha))_\sigma\cdot\mathcal{L}(\mathcal{O}_K) = x\,\mathcal{L}(\alpha\mathcal{O}_K) = (\xi_\sigma)_\sigma \cdot \mathcal{L}(\mathcal{O}_K)$ for some $(\xi_\sigma)_\sigma \in K_\mathbb{R}$ with $|\xi_\sigma| = 1$. Therefore, $|x_\sigma\sigma(\eta\alpha)| = |\xi_\sigma| = 1$, i.e., $|x_\sigma| = |\sigma(\eta\alpha)|^{-1}$ for some unit $\eta \in \mathcal{O}_K^*$. From here one can directly conclude that $P(x\,\mathcal{L}(\mathfrak{a})) = P((|\sigma(\eta\alpha)|^{-1})_\sigma\,\mathcal{L}(\alpha\mathcal{O}_K)) = (\!(\eta\alpha)\!)$, a principal divisor. $\qquad\square$

Lemma 2.8. *For any ideal lattice L in* IdLat_K, *we have*

$$\lambda_n(L) \le \sqrt{n} \cdot \lambda_n(\mathcal{L}(\mathcal{O}_K)) \cdot \mathrm{Vol}(L)^{1/n}.$$

Moreover, it holds that $\lambda_n(\mathcal{L}(\mathcal{O}_K)) \le \sqrt{n} \cdot \sqrt{\Delta}$.

Proof. Write $L = x\,\mathcal{L}(\mathfrak{a})$ and choose a shortest element $x\alpha \in x\,\mathcal{L}(\mathbf{a})$. That means $\|x\alpha\| = \lambda_1(x\,\mathcal{L}(\mathbf{a}))$. Then $x\,\mathcal{L}(\mathbf{a}) \supset x\,\mathcal{L}(\alpha\mathcal{O}_K)$, and therefore

$$\lambda_n(x\,\mathcal{L}(\mathbf{a})) \le \lambda_n(x\,\mathcal{L}(\alpha\mathcal{O}_K)) \le \|x\alpha\|_\infty \lambda_n(\mathcal{L}(\mathcal{O}_K)) \le \|x\alpha\|_2 \lambda_n(\mathcal{L}(\mathcal{O}_K))$$
$$\le \lambda_1(x\,\mathcal{L}(\mathbf{a})) \cdot \lambda_n(\mathcal{L}(\mathcal{O}_K)) \le \sqrt{n} \cdot \lambda_n(\mathcal{L}(\mathcal{O}_K)) \cdot \mathrm{Vol}(x\,\mathcal{L}(\mathbf{a}))^{1/n}$$

where the last inequality is Minkowski's theorem. The bound on $\lambda_n(\mathcal{L}(\mathcal{O}_K))$ is proven using Minkowski's second theorem (in the infinity norm) and the fact that $\lambda_1^{(\infty)}(\mathcal{L}(\mathcal{O}_K)) \ge 1$. $\qquad\square$

2.5 The Gaussian Function and Smoothing Errors

Let n be a fixed positive integer. For any parameter $s > 0$, we consider the n-dimensional *Gaussian function*

$$\rho_s^{(n)} : \mathbb{R}^n \to \mathbb{C}, \, x \mapsto e^{-\frac{\pi\|x\|^2}{s^2}},$$

(where we drop the (n) whenever it is clear from the context), which is well known to satisfy the following basic properties.

Lemma 2.9. *For all $s > 0$, $n \in \mathbb{N}$ and $x, y \in \mathbb{R}^n$, we have* $\int_{z\in\mathbb{R}^n} \rho_s(z)dz = s^n$, $\mathcal{F}_{\mathbb{R}^n}\{\rho_s\} = \int_{y\in\mathbb{R}^n} \rho_s(y)e^{-2\pi i\langle y,\cdot\rangle}dy = s^n\rho_{1/s}$ *and* $\rho_s(x)^2 = \rho_{s/\sqrt{2}}(x)$.

The following two results (and the variations we discuss below) will play an important role and will be used several times in this paper: *Banaszczyk's bound*, originating from [3], and the *smoothing parameter*, as introduced by Micciancio and Regev [31]. They allow us to control

$$\rho_s(X) := \sum_{x\in X} \rho_s(x),$$

for certain discrete subsets $X \subseteq \mathbb{R}^m$. For ease of notation, we let

$$\beta_z^{(n)} := \left(\frac{2\pi ez^2}{n}\right)^{n/2} e^{-\pi z^2},$$

which decays super-exponentially in z (for fixed n). In particular, we have $\beta_t^{(n)} \le e^{-t^2}$ for all $t \ge \sqrt{n}$. The following formulation of Banaszczyk's lemma is obtained from [33, Equation (1.1)].

Lemma 2.10 (Banaszczyk's Bound). *Whenever* $r/s \geq \sqrt{\frac{n}{2\pi}}$,

$$\rho_s\big((\Lambda + t) \setminus B_r\big) \leq \beta_{r/s}^{(n)} \cdot \rho_s(\Lambda),$$

where $B_r = B_r(0) = \{x \in \mathbb{R}^n \mid \|x\|_2 < r\}$.

Definition 2.11 (Smoothing parameter). *Given an* $\varepsilon > 0$ *and a lattice* Λ, *the* smoothing parameter $\eta_\varepsilon(\Lambda)$ *is the smallest real number* $s > 0$ *such that* $\rho_{1/s}(\Lambda^*) \leq \varepsilon$. *Here,* Λ^* *is the dual lattice of* Λ.

Lemma 2.12 (Smoothing Error). *Let* $\Lambda \in \mathbb{R}^n$ *be a full rank lattice, and let* $s \geq \eta_\epsilon(\Lambda)$. *Then, for any* $t \in \mathbb{R}^n$,

$$(1 - \epsilon)\frac{s^n}{\det \Lambda} \leq \rho_s(\Lambda + t) \leq (1 + \epsilon)\frac{s^n}{\det \Lambda}. \tag{2}$$

We have the following two useful upper bounds for full-rank n-dimensional lattices Λ [31, Lemma 3.2 and 3.3]: $\eta_\epsilon(\Lambda) \leq \sqrt{\log(2n(1 + 1/\epsilon))} \cdot \lambda_n(\Lambda)$ for all $\epsilon > 0$ and $\eta_1(\Lambda) \leq \eta_{2^{-n}}(\Lambda) \leq \sqrt{n}/\lambda_1(\Lambda^*) \leq \sqrt{n} \cdot \lambda_n(\Lambda)$. The latter leads to the following corollary.

Corollary 2.13. *Let* L *be an ideal lattice in* IdLat_K. *Let* $t \in \mathbb{R}^n$ *be arbitrary and* $s \geq n \cdot \lambda_n(\mathcal{L}(\mathcal{O}_K)) \cdot \mathrm{Vol}(L)^{1/n}$. *Then it holds that*

$$\left| \frac{\rho_s(L - t) \cdot \mathrm{Vol}(L)}{s^n} - 1 \right| \leq 2^{-n}, \tag{3}$$

Proof. By the assumption on s and by Lemma 2.8, we have $s \geq n \cdot \lambda_n(\mathcal{L}(\mathcal{O}_K)) \cdot \mathrm{Vol}(L)^{1/n} \geq \sqrt{n} \cdot \lambda_n(L) \geq \eta_{2^{-n}}(\Lambda)$. The result follows then from Lemma 2.12. $\square$

2.6   Gaussian Distributions and Statistical Distance

Statistical distance. For two random variables X and Y, we let $\mathrm{SD}(X, Y)$ denote their statistical distance (or total variation distance). This distance is equal to half of the ℓ_1-distance between the two corresponding distributions. In particular, if X and Y live in a countable set S, then

$$\mathrm{SD}(X, Y) = \frac{1}{2} \cdot \sum_{s \in S} |\mathbb{P}(X = s) - \mathbb{P}(Y = s)|.$$

Continuous Gaussian distribution. For a real vector space H of dimension n, a parameter $s > 0$ and a center $c \in H$, we write $\mathcal{G}_{H,s,c}$ the continuous Gaussian distribution over H with density function $\rho_s(x - c)/s^n$ for all $x \in H$. When the center c is 0, we simplify the notation as $\mathcal{G}_{H,s}$.

Discrete Gaussian distributions. For any lattice $L \subset \mathbb{R}^n$, we define the discrete Gaussian distribution over L of standard deviation $s > 0$ and center $c \in \mathbb{R}^n$ by

$$\forall x \in L, \, \mathcal{G}_{L,s,c} = \frac{\rho_s(x - c)}{\rho_s(L - c)}.$$

When the center c is 0, we simplify the notation as $\mathcal{G}_{L,s}$.

Observe that we use almost the same notation for discrete Gaussian distributions and for continuous ones. What allows us to make a distinction between them are the indexes L or H (if the index is a lattice, then the distribution is discrete whereas if the index is a real vector space, then the distribution is continuous).

The following lemma states that one can sample from a distribution statistically close to a discrete Gaussian distribution over a lattice L (provided that the standard deviation s is large enough).

Proposition 2.14 (Theorem 4.1 of [20]). *There exists a probabilistic polynomial time algorithm that takes as input a basis $(b_1, \cdots, b_n)$ of a lattice $L \subset \mathbb{R}^n$, a parameter $s \geq \sqrt{n} \cdot \max_i \|b_i\|$ and a center $c \in \mathbb{R}^n$ and outputs a sample from a distribution $\widehat{\mathcal{G}}_{L,s,c}$ such that $SD(\mathcal{G}_{L,s,c}, \widehat{\mathcal{G}}_{L,s,c}) \leq 2^{-n}$.*

We will refer to the algorithm mentioned in Proposition 2.14 as Klein's algorithm [25]. We note that Theorem 4.1 of [20] states the result for a statistical distance negligible (i.e., of the form $n^{-\omega(1)}$), but the statement and the proof can be easily adapted to other statistical distances.

3   Random Walk Theorem for the Arakelov Class Group

In this section, we prove Theorem 3.3, on random walks in the Arakelov class group. Starting with a point in the hyperplane $H \subseteq \mathrm{Div}_K^0$, sampled according to a Gaussian distribution, we prove that multiplying this point sufficiently often by small random prime ideals yields a random divisor that is very close to uniformly distributed in the Arakelov class group (i.e., modulo principal divisors). The proof of Theorem 3.3 requires various techniques, extensively treated in Sects. 3.2 to 3.6, and summarised in the following.

Hecke operators. The most important tool for proving Theorem 3.3 is that of a Hecke operator, whose definition and properties are covered in Sect. 3.2. This specific kind of operator acts on the space of probability distributions on Pic_K^0, and has the virtue of having the characters of Pic_K^0 as eigenfunctions.

Eigenvalues of Hecke operators. The aim of the proof is showing that applying this Hecke operator repeatedly on an appropriate initial distribution yields the uniform distribution on Pic_K^0. The impact of consecutive applications of the Hecke operator can be studied by considering its eigenvalues of the eigenfunctions (which are the characters of Pic_K^0). Classical results from analytic number theory show that the eigenvalues of these characters are (in absolute value) sufficiently smaller than 1, whenever the so-called analytic conductor of the corresponding character is not too large. An exception is the unit character, which is fixed under each Hecke operation. This classical result and how to apply it in our specific setting is covered in Sect. 3.3.

The analytic conductor. The Hecke operator thus quickly 'damps out' all characters with small analytic conductor (except the unit character). In Sect. 3.4, we examine which quantities of a character of Pic_K^0 define the analytic conductor. It turns out that this analytic conductor is closely related to how the character acts on the hypertorus defined by the log unit lattice. The higher the frequency of this character on the hypertorus, the larger the analytic conductor. This frequency can be measured by the norm of the uniquely associated dual log unit lattice point of the character. In fact, we establish a bound on the analytic conductor of a character in terms of the norm of its associated dual lattice point.

Fourier analysis on the hypertorus. To summarize, low-frequency (non-trivial) characters on Pic_K^0 (i.e., with small analytic conductor) are quickly damped out by the action of the Hecke character, whereas for high-frequency characters we do not have good guarantees on the speed at which they damp out. To resolve this issue, we choose an initial distribution whose character decomposition has only a negligible portion of high-frequency oscillatory characters. An initial distribution that nicely satisfies this condition is the Gaussian distribution (on the hypertorus). To examine the exact amplitudes of the occurring characters of this Gaussian distribution, we need Fourier analysis on this hypertorus, as covered in Sect. 3.5.

Splitting up the character decomposition. In this last part of the proof, which is covered in Sect. 3.6, we write the Gaussian distribution into its character decomposition, where we separate the high-frequency characters, the low-frequency ones and the unit character. Applying the Hecke operator often enough damps out the low-frequency ones, and as the high-frequency characters were only negligibly present anyway, one is left with (almost only) the unit character. This corresponds to a uniform distribution.

3.1 Main Result

Definition 3.1 (Random Walk Distribution in Div_K^0). *We denote by* $\mathcal{W}_{\mathrm{Div}_K^0}(B, N, s)$ *the distribution on* Div_K^0 *that is obtained by the following random walk procedure.*

Sample $x \in H \subseteq \log K_{\mathbb{R}}$ *according to a centered Gaussian distribution with standard deviation* s. *Subsequently, sample* N *ideals* $\mathfrak{p}_j$ *uniformly from the set of all prime ideals with norm bounded by* B. *Finally, output* $x + \sum_{j=1}^N d^0(\mathfrak{p}_j)$, *where* $x \in \mathrm{Div}_K^0$ *is understood via the injection* $H \hookrightarrow \mathrm{Div}_K^0$.

Definition 3.2 (Random Walk Distribution in Pic_K^0). *By* $\mathcal{W}_{\mathrm{Pic}_K^0}(B, N, s)$, *we denote the distribution on the Arakelov class group obtained by sampling* **a** *from* $\mathcal{W}_{\mathrm{Div}_K^0}(B, N, s)$ *and taking the Arekalov class* $[\mathbf{a}] \in \mathrm{Pic}_K^0$.

Theorem 3.3 (Random Walks in the Arakelov Class Group, ERH).
Let $\varepsilon > 0$ *and* $s > 0$ *be any positive real numbers and let* $k \in \mathbb{N}_{>0}$ *be a positive integer. Putting* $s' = \min(\sqrt{2} \cdot s, 1/\eta_1(\Lambda_K^*))$, *there exists a bound* $B = \tilde{O}(n^{2k}[n^2(\log\log(1/\varepsilon))^2 + n^2(\log(1/s'))^2 + (\log \Delta_K)^2])$ *such that for any* $N \geq \frac{\frac{\ell}{2} \cdot \log(1/s') + \frac{1}{2}\log(\mathrm{Vol}(\mathrm{Pic}_K^0)) + \log(1/\varepsilon) + 1}{k \log n}$, *the random walk distribution* $\mathcal{W}_{\mathrm{Pic}_K^0}(B, N, s)$ *is* ε-*close to uniform in* $L_1(\mathrm{Pic}_K^0)$, *i.e.,*

$$\left\| \mathcal{W}_{\mathrm{Pic}_K^0}(B, N, s) - \mathcal{U}(\mathrm{Pic}_K^0) \right\|_1 \leq \varepsilon.$$

Below, we instantiate Theorem 3.3 with specific choices of ε and k that are tailored to give an optimal approximation factor in Sect. 4. As a consequence, the value of B in Corollary 3.4 is exponential in n. We note however that this value could be made as small as polynomial in n and $\log \Delta$, but at the cost of a slightly worse approximation factor for the reduction of Sect. 4.

The key difference between those two instantiations is how we deal with the smoothing parameter of the dual log-unit lattice, $\eta_1(\Lambda_K^*)$. In the general case, we rely on works of Dobrolowski and Kessler [14,24] to lower bound the first minimum of the primal log unit lattice. In the case of cyclotomics, we obtain a sharper bound by resorting to the analysis of dual cyclotomic unit lattice from Cramer et al. [11].

Corollary 3.4 (Application to General Number Fields, ERH).
Let $s > 1/\ell$, *there exists a bound* $B = \tilde{O}(\Delta^{1/\log n})$ *such that for*

$$N \geq \frac{(n - n_\mathbb{C})(\log n)^2}{\log(\Delta)} \left(1 + \frac{30 \log\log n}{\log n} \right) + \frac{n \log n}{\log \Delta} \left[\frac{1}{2} \log(\Delta^{1/n}) + \log\log(\Delta^{1/n}) \right]$$

holds that the random walk distribution $\mathcal{W}_{\mathrm{Pic}_K^0}(B, N, s)$ *satisfies*

$$SD\left(\mathcal{W}_{\mathrm{Pic}_K^0}(B, N, s), \mathcal{U}(\mathrm{Pic}_K^0) \right) \leq 2^{-n}.$$

Corollary 3.5 (Application to Prime-Power Cyclotomic Number Fields, ERH). *Let* $K = \mathbb{Q}(\zeta_{p^k})$ *be a prime-power cyclotomic number field and assume* $h_K^+ = \mathrm{Cl}(K^+) \leq (\log n)^n$. *For* $s = 1/\log^2(n)$, *there exists a bound* $B = \tilde{O}(n^{2+2\log n})$ *such that, for* $N \geq \frac{n}{2\log n}\left(1/2 + \frac{8\log(\log(n))}{\log n} \right)$, *the random walk distribution* $\mathcal{W}_{\mathrm{Pic}_K^0}(B, N, s)$ *satisfies*

$$SD\left(\mathcal{W}_{\mathrm{Pic}_K^0}(B, N, s), \mathcal{U}(\mathrm{Pic}_K^0) \right) \leq 2^{-n}.$$

The proof of these corollaries can be found in the full version [7].

3.2   Hecke Operators

A key tool to analyse random walks on Pic_K^0 are Hecke operators, which allow to transform a given distribution into a new distribution obtained by adding one random step.

Definition 3.6 (The Hecke operator). *Let $\mathcal{P}$ be a finite subset of prime ideals of the number field K, and let Pic_K^0 be the Arakelov class group. Then we define the* Hecke operator $H_\mathcal{P} : L^2(\mathrm{Pic}_K^0) \to L^2(\mathrm{Pic}_K^0)$ *by the following rule:*

$$H_\mathcal{P}(f)(x) := \frac{1}{|\mathcal{P}|} \sum_{\mathfrak{p} \in \mathcal{P}} f(x - [d^0(\mathfrak{p})])$$

Lemma 3.7 (Eigenfunctions of the Hecke operator). *The Hecke operator $H_\mathcal{P} : L^2(\mathrm{Pic}_K^0) \to L^2(\mathrm{Pic}_K^0)$ has the characters $\chi \in \widehat{\mathrm{Pic}_K^0}$ as eigenfunctions, with eigenvalues $\lambda_\chi = \frac{1}{|\mathcal{P}|} \sum_{\mathfrak{p} \in \mathcal{P}} \overline{\chi}([d^0(\mathfrak{p})])$, i.e.,*

$$H_\mathcal{P}(\chi) = \lambda_\chi \chi.$$

Proof. We have $H_\mathcal{P}(\chi)(x) = \frac{1}{|\mathcal{P}|} \sum_{\mathfrak{p} \in \mathcal{P}} \chi(x - [d^0(\mathfrak{p})]) = \frac{1}{|\mathcal{P}|} \sum_{\mathfrak{p} \in \mathcal{P}} \chi(x)\overline{\chi}([d^0(\mathfrak{p})])$. So $H_\mathcal{P}(\chi) = \lambda_\chi \chi$ with $\lambda_\chi = \frac{1}{|\mathcal{P}|} \sum_{\mathfrak{p} \in \mathcal{P}} \overline{\chi}([d^0(\mathfrak{p})])$.   □

Note that $H_\mathcal{P}(\mathbf{1}_{\mathrm{Pic}_K^0}) = \mathbf{1}_{\mathrm{Pic}_K^0}$, for the trivial character $\mathbf{1}_{\mathrm{Pic}_K^0}$, so $\lambda_{\mathbf{1}_{\mathrm{Pic}_K^0}} = 1$. For any other character χ it is evident from the above that $|\lambda_\chi| \leq 1$.

3.3   Bounds on Eigenvalues of Hecke Operators

Using results from analytic number theory, one can prove the following proposition.

Proposition 3.8 (Bound on the eigenvalues of the Hecke operator, ERH). *Let $\mathcal{P}$ be the set of all primes of K with norm bounded by $B \in \mathbb{N}$. Then the eigenvalue λ_χ of any non-constant eigenfunction $\chi \in \widehat{\mathrm{Pic}_K^0}$ of the Hecke operator satisfies*

$$\lambda_\chi = O\left(\frac{\log(B)\log(B^n \cdot \Delta \cdot \mathfrak{q}_\infty(\chi))}{B^{1/2}} \right),$$

where $\mathfrak{q}_\infty(\chi)$ is the infinite part of the analytic conductor of the character χ, as in Definition 3.11 (cf. [21, Eq. (5.6)]).

The proof of this proposition can be found in the full version [7].

3.4   The Analytic Conductor

In the bounds of Sect. 3.3, the infinite part of the analytic conductor $\mathfrak{q}_\infty(\chi)$ of a character $\chi : \mathrm{Pic}^0_K \to \mathbb{C}$ plays a large role. In this section, we show that this infinite part of the analytic conductor is closely related to the dual logarithmic unit lattice point $\ell^* \in \Lambda^*_K$ that is uniquely associated with the character $\chi|_T : T \to \mathbb{C}$.

The infinite part of the analytic conductor can be defined using the so-called *local parameters* of the character $\chi \in \widehat{\mathrm{Pic}^0_K}$. To define these, we need $F^0 = \{(a_\nu)_\nu \in \bigoplus_{\nu \text{ infinite}} K_\nu \mid \prod_\nu |a_\nu|_\nu = 1\}$, the norm-one subgroup of the product of the completions K_ν of K with respect to the infinite place ν. Characters $\eta : F^0 \to \mathbb{C}$ are of the form

$$\eta((a_\nu)_\nu) = \prod_\nu \left(\frac{a_\nu}{|a_\nu|}\right)^{u_\nu} e^{iv_\nu \log |a_\nu|_\nu}, \tag{4}$$

where $v_\nu \in \mathbb{R}$, and $u_\nu \in \mathbb{Z}$ or $u_\nu \in \{0,1\}$ depending on whether ν is complex or real (see [35, §3.3, Eq. 3.3.1]). In all these definitions, the absolute value $|\cdot|_\nu$ equals $|\cdot|^2_\mathbb{C}$ or $|\cdot|_\mathbb{R}$ depending on whether ν is complex or real.

Since there is the map $\iota : F^0 \to \mathrm{Pic}^0_K, (a_\nu)_\nu \longmapsto \sum_\nu \log |a_\nu|_\nu \cdot (\!|\nu|\!)$, we must have that $\chi \circ \iota$ is of the form described in Eq. (4) for all $\chi \in \mathrm{Pic}^0_K$. This leads to the following definition.

Definition 3.9 (Local parameters of a character on Pic^0_K). *For a character* $\chi : \mathrm{Pic}^0_K \to \mathbb{C}$, *the numbers* $k_\nu(\chi) = |u_\nu| + iv_\nu$ *(for all infinite places ν) are called the* local parameters *of χ, where u_ν and v_ν are the numbers appearing in the formula of $\chi \circ \iota : F^0 \to \mathbb{C}$ in Eq. (4).*

As characters on the Arakelov class group are actually very special Hecke characters[3], the local parameters are very restricted. This is described in the following lemma.

Lemma 3.10. *Let $\chi \in \widehat{\mathrm{Pic}^0_K}$ and let $\ell^* \in \Lambda^*_K$ such that $\chi|_T = \chi_{\ell^*} = e^{2\pi i \langle \ell^*, \cdot \rangle}$. Then we have $k_\nu(\chi) = 2\pi i \ell^*_{\sigma_\nu}$, where σ_ν is an embedding associated with the place ν.*

Proof. As the map $\iota : F^0 \to \mathrm{Pic}^0_K$ only depends on the absolute values of $(a_\nu)_\nu$, it is clear that $u_\nu = 0$ in the decomposition of $\chi \circ \iota$ as in Eq. (4). It remains to prove that $v_\nu = 2\pi i \ell^*_{\sigma_\nu}$. The units $\mathcal{O}^*_K \subseteq F^0$ map to one under $\chi \circ \iota$, since any principal divisor maps to one. Here, the inclusion $\mathcal{O}^*_K \to F^0$ is defined by $\eta \mapsto (\sigma_\nu(\eta))_\nu$, where σ_ν is a fixed embedding associated with the infinite place ν. This means that

$$\chi \circ \iota(\eta) = \prod_\nu e^{iv_\nu \log |\sigma_\nu(\eta)|_\nu} = \exp\left(i\sum_\sigma v_{\nu_\sigma} \log |\sigma(\eta)|_\mathbb{C}\right) = 1 \text{ for all } \eta \in \mathcal{O}^*_K, \tag{5}$$

---

[3] Hecke characters of K are characters on the idèle class group of K. As the Arakelov class group is a specific quotient of the idèle class group [37, Ch. VI, pp. 360], the characters on the Arakelov class group are essentially Hecke characters whose kernel contains the kernel of the quotient map sending the idèle class group to the Arakelov class group.

where the last sum is over all embeddings $\sigma : K \to \mathbb{C}$, where ν_σ is the place associated with the embedding σ, and where $|\cdot|_\mathbb{C}$ is the standard absolute value on $\mathbb{C}$. Vectors of the form $(v_{\nu_\sigma})_\sigma$ satisfying Eq. (5) are precisely the vectors $(v_{\nu_\sigma})_\sigma \in 2\pi\Lambda_K^* \subseteq \log K_\mathbb{R}$. By Definition 3.9, one directly obtains $k_\nu(\chi) = 2\pi i \ell_{\sigma_\nu}^*$. $\square$

Definition 3.11 (The infinite part of the analytic conductor). *Let $\chi \in \widehat{\mathrm{Pic}_K^0}$ be a character with local parameters $k_\nu(\chi)$, where ν ranges over the infinite places of K. Then, we define the infinite part of the analytic conductor to be*

$$\mathfrak{q}_\infty(\chi) = \prod_{\nu \ real} (3 + |k_\nu|) \prod_{\nu \ complex} (3 + |k_\nu|)(3 + |k_\nu + 1|)$$

Remark 3.12. Above definition of the infinite part of the analytic conductor is obtained from [21, p. 95, eq. (5.6) with $s = 0$], where it is described in a slightly different form. In [21], the functional equation lacks the complex L-functions $L_\mathbb{C}$. Instead, those are replaced by $L_\mathbb{R}(s)L_\mathbb{R}(s+1) = L_\mathbb{C}(s)$ (see [37, Ch. 7, Prop 4.3 (iv)]). This means that the local parameters $\kappa_\sigma, \kappa_{\bar\sigma}$ as in [21, p. 93, eq. (5.3)] must equal $k_\nu, k_\nu + 1$ for the embeddings $\{\sigma, \bar\sigma\}$ associated with the complex place ν (cf. [21, p. 125]).

Lemma 3.13. *Let $\mathfrak{q}_\infty(\chi)$ be the infinite part of the analytic conductor of the character $\chi \in \widehat{\mathrm{Pic}_K^0}$, and let $\ell^* \in \Lambda_K^*$ be such that $\chi|_T = \chi_{\ell^*}$, where Λ_K^* is the dual lattice of the log-unit lattice. Then we have*

$$\mathfrak{q}_\infty(\chi) \le \left(4 + 2\pi \|\ell^*\|/\sqrt{n}\right)^n$$

Proof. Let $|\ell^*|$ denote the vector ℓ^* where all entries are replaced by their absolute value. Then, by applying subsequently the triangle inequality, the inequality between $\|\cdot\|_1$ and $\|\cdot\|_2$ and the arithmetic-geometric mean inequality, one obtains

$$4\sqrt{n} + 2\pi \|\ell^*\|_2 \ge \|4 + 2\pi|\ell^*|\|_2 \ge \frac{1}{\sqrt{n}}\|4 + 2\pi|\ell^*|\|_1 \ge \sqrt{n}\left(\prod_\sigma (4 + 2\pi|\ell_\sigma^*|)\right)^{1/n}$$

$$\ge \sqrt{n}\,\mathfrak{q}_\infty(\chi_{\ell^*})^{1/n}.$$

Dividing by $\sqrt{n}$ and raising to the power n yields the claim. $\square$

3.5   Fourier Analysis on the Hypertorus

Definition 3.14. *Let $H \subseteq \mathrm{Log}\,K_\mathbb{R}$ be the hyperplane where the log unit lattice $\Lambda_K = \mathrm{Log}(\mathcal{O}_K^*)$ lives in. Recall the Gaussian function $\rho_s : H \to \mathbb{R}, x \mapsto e^{-\pi\|x\|^2/s^2}$. Denoting $T = H/\Lambda_K$, we put $\rho_s|^T : T \to \mathbb{R}, x \mapsto \sum_{\ell \in \Lambda_K} \rho_s(x + \ell)$.*

As we have (see Lemma A.2 of the full version [7]) $\|s^{-\ell}\rho_s\|_{H,1} = \int_H s^{-\ell}\rho_s(x)dx = 1$, and $\|s^{-\ell}\rho_s|^T\|_{T,1} = \int_T s^{-\ell}\rho_s|^T(x)dx = 1$, both functions $s^{-\ell}\rho_s$ and $s^{-\ell}\rho_s|^T$ can be seen as probability distributions on their respective domains $\mathbb{R}^m$ and T.

Lemma 3.15 (Fourier coefficients of the periodized Gaussian). *The function $s^{-\ell}\rho_s|^T \in L^2(T)$ satisfies*

$$s^{-\ell}\rho_s|^T = \sum_{\ell^* \in \Lambda_K^*} a_{\ell^*}\chi_{\ell^*}$$

where $a_{\ell^*} = \frac{1}{\mathrm{Vol}(T)}\rho_{1/s}(\ell^*)$, where Λ_K^* is the dual lattice of the log unit lattice Λ_K, and where $\chi_{\ell^*}(x) = e^{-2\pi i\langle x, \ell^*\rangle}$.

Proof. Note that $\langle \chi_{\ell_1^*}, \chi_{\ell_2^*}\rangle = \mathrm{Vol}(T)\cdot\delta_{\ell_1^*,\ell_2^*}$. Identifying $\hat{T}$ and Λ_K^* via the map $\chi_{\ell^*} \mapsto \ell^*$, taking a fundamental domain F of Λ_K and spelling out the definition of $\rho_s|^T$, we obtain, for all $\ell^* \in \Lambda_K^*$,

$$a_{\ell^*} = \frac{1}{\mathrm{Vol}(T)}\langle s^{-\ell}\rho_s|^T, \chi_{\ell^*}\rangle = \frac{1}{\mathrm{Vol}(T)}\int_{x\in F}\sum_{\ell\in\Lambda_K} s^{-\ell}\rho_s(x+\ell)\overline{\chi_{\ell^*}(x)}dx$$

$$= \frac{1}{\mathrm{Vol}(T)}\int_{x\in H} s^{-\ell}\rho_s(x)\overline{\chi_{\ell^*}(x)}dx = \frac{1}{\mathrm{Vol}(T)}\mathcal{F}_H(s^{-\ell}\rho_s)(\ell^*) = \frac{1}{\mathrm{Vol}(T)}\rho_{1/s}(\ell^*).$$

$\square$

3.6   Conclusion

Theorem 3.16 (ERH). *Let $\mathcal{P}$ be the set of primes of K of norm at most B, and let $H = H_{\mathcal{P}}$ the Hecke operator for this set of primes. Then, for all $r, s > 0$ with $rs > \sqrt{\frac{\ell}{4\pi}}$, we have*

$$\left\|H^N(s^{-n}\rho_s) - \frac{1}{\mathrm{Vol}(\mathrm{Pic}_K^0)}\mathbf{1}_{\mathrm{Pic}_K^0}\right\|_2^2 \le \frac{\rho_{\frac{1}{\sqrt{2}s}}(\Lambda_K^*)}{\mathrm{Vol}(T)}\left(c^{2N} + \beta_{\sqrt{2}rs}^{(\ell)}\right) \qquad (6)$$

with $c = O\left(\frac{\log(B)\log(B^n\cdot\Delta\cdot(4+2\pi r/\sqrt{n})^n)}{B^{1/2}}\right)$.

Proof. As $s^{-\ell}\rho_s = \frac{1}{\mathrm{Vol}(T)}\sum_{\chi\in\hat{T}}\rho_{1/s}(\ell^*)\chi_{\ell^*}$ (see Lemma 3.15), $\mathrm{Vol}(\mathrm{Pic}_K^0) = h_K\mathrm{Vol}(T)$, and every $\chi \in \hat{T}$ has exactly h_K extensions [13, Cor. 3.6.2] to characters on Pic_K^0, we directly deduce that

$$s^{-\ell}\rho_s = \frac{1}{\mathrm{Vol}(\mathrm{Pic}_K^0)}\sum_{\chi_{\ell^*}\in\hat{T}}\sum_{\chi'|_T=\chi_{\ell^*}}\rho_{1/s}(\ell^*)\chi',$$

where χ' ranges over all characters of Pic_K^0. Therefore, by the fact that the characters χ' are eigenfunctions of the operator $H = H_{\mathcal{P}}$ (see Lemma 3.7),

$$H^N(s^{-\ell}\rho_s) = \frac{1}{\mathrm{Vol}(\mathrm{Pic}_K^0)}\sum_{\chi_{\ell^*}\in\hat{T}}\rho_{1/s}(\ell^*)\sum_{\chi'|_T=\chi_{\ell^*}}\lambda_{\chi'}^N\chi'$$

where χ' ranges over all characters of Pic_K^0. By the fact that $s^{-\ell}\rho_s$ is a probability distribution, we obtain that the eigenvalue of the unit character $\mathbf{1} = \mathbf{1}_{\text{Pic}_K^0}$ satisfies $\lambda_{\mathbf{1}} = 1$. Therefore, by Parseval's theorem (see Eq. (1)) and the fact that $\rho_{1/s}^2 = \rho_{\frac{1}{\sqrt{2}s}}$,

$$\left\| H^N(s^{-\ell}\rho_s) - \frac{1}{\text{Vol}(\text{Pic}_K^0)}\mathbf{1} \right\|_2^2 = \frac{1}{\text{Vol}(\text{Pic}_K^0)} \sum_{\chi_{\ell^*} \in \widehat{T}} \rho_{\frac{1}{\sqrt{2}s}}(\ell^*) \sum_{\substack{\chi'|_T = \chi_{\ell^*} \\ \chi' \neq \mathbf{1}}} |\lambda_{\chi'}|^{2N},$$

where χ' ranges over all characters of Pic_K^0. In order to bound the quantity above, we split up the sum into a part where $\|\ell^*\| > r$, and a part where $\|\ell^*\| \leq r$. For the former part we can namely bound the Gaussian $\rho_{\frac{1}{\sqrt{2}s}}(\ell^*)$ whereas for the latter part we can bound the eigenvalues $\lambda_{\chi'}$ (see Proposition 3.8). For the part where $\|\ell^*\| > r$, we use the assumption $\sqrt{2}sr > \sqrt{\ell/(2\pi)}$ to apply Banaszczyk's bound (see Lemma 2.10), and the fact that $|\lambda_{\chi'}| \leq 1$.

$$\frac{1}{\text{Vol}(\text{Pic}_K^0)} \sum_{\|\ell^*\| > r} \rho_{\frac{1}{\sqrt{2}s}}(\ell^*) \underbrace{\sum_{\chi'|_T = \chi_{\ell^*}} |\lambda_{\chi'}|^{2N}}_{\leq h_K} \leq \frac{\rho_{\frac{1}{\sqrt{2}s}}(\Lambda_K^* \setminus r\mathcal{B})}{\text{Vol}(T)} \leq \frac{\beta_{\sqrt{2}rs}^{(\ell)} \cdot \rho_{\frac{1}{\sqrt{2}s}}(\Lambda_K^*)}{\text{Vol}(T)}$$

$$(7)$$

For the part where $\|\ell^*\| < r$, we have, by Lemma 3.13 that $\mathfrak{q}_\infty(\chi) \leq (4 + 2\pi r/\sqrt{n})^n$, and therefore, by Proposition 3.8, we have the bound $|\lambda_{\chi'}| \leq c = O\left(\frac{\log(B)\log(B^n \cdot \Delta \cdot (4+2\pi r/\sqrt{n})^n)}{B^{1/2}}\right)$. So,

$$\frac{1}{\text{Vol}(\text{Pic}_K^0)} \sum_{\|\ell^*\| \leq r} \rho_{\frac{1}{\sqrt{2}s}}(\ell^*) \underbrace{\sum_{\chi'|_T = \chi_{\ell^*}} |\lambda_{\chi'}|^{2N}}_{\leq h_K \cdot c^{2N}} \leq \frac{c^{2N} \cdot \rho_{\frac{1}{\sqrt{2}s}}(\Lambda_K^*)}{\text{Vol}(T)} \qquad (8)$$

Combining Eqs. (7) and (8), we obtain the result.   □

Proof (of Theorem 3.3*).* Let $1 > \varepsilon > 0$, $s > 0$ and $k \in \mathbb{N}_{>0}$ be given. As $1/\tilde{s} = \max(\frac{1}{\sqrt{2}s}, \eta_1(\Lambda_K^*)) \geq \eta_1(\Lambda_K^*)$, the smoothing parameter of Λ_K^*, we have

$$\rho_{\frac{1}{\sqrt{2}s}}(\Lambda_K^*)/\text{Vol}(T) \leq \rho_{1/\tilde{s}}(\Lambda_K^*)/\text{Vol}(T) \leq 2 \cdot \tilde{s}^{-\ell}. \qquad (9)$$

By applying subsequently Hölder's inequality (i.e., $\|f \cdot 1\|_1 \leq \|f\|_2\|1\|_2$) and the inequality $\rho_{1/s}(\Lambda_K^*)/\text{Vol}(T) \leq 2\tilde{s}^{-\ell}$ in Eq. (6), we obtain (for $rs \geq \sqrt{\frac{\ell}{4\pi}}$)

$$\left\| H^N(s^{-n}\rho_s) - U(\text{Pic}_K^0) \right\|_1^2 \leq 2\,\text{Vol}(\text{Pic}_K^0) \cdot \tilde{s}^{-\ell}(c^{2N} + \beta_{\sqrt{2}rs}^{(\ell)}) \qquad (10)$$

In the following, we will bound the two summands in Eq. (10) separately. Putting[4]

$$r = \frac{1}{\sqrt{2}s} \cdot \max\left(\sqrt{\ell}, \sqrt{2 + \ell \log(1/\tilde{s}) + 2\log(1/\varepsilon) + \log(\mathrm{Vol}(\mathrm{Pic}_K^0))}\right),$$

implies $2 \cdot \mathrm{Vol}(\mathrm{Pic}_K^0) \cdot \tilde{s}^{-\ell} \cdot \beta_{\sqrt{2}rs}^{(\ell)} \leq \varepsilon^2/2$. Subsequently, choose[5]

$$B = \tilde{O}\left(n^{2k} \cdot [\log(\Delta)^2 + n^2 \log(1/\tilde{s})^2 + n^2 \log(\log(1/\varepsilon))^2]\right),$$

such that $c \leq 1/n^k$, where $c = O\left(\frac{\log(B)\log(B^n \cdot \Delta \cdot (4 + 2\pi r/\sqrt{n})^n)}{B^{1/2}}\right)$, as in Theorem 3.16. Finally, taking any $N \geq \frac{\ell/2 \cdot \log(1/\tilde{s}) + \log(1/\varepsilon) + \frac{1}{2}\log(\mathrm{Vol}(\mathrm{Pic}_K^0)) + 1}{k \log n}$ and noting that $c^{\frac{1}{k \log n}} \leq 1/e$, we deduce $2\,\mathrm{Vol}(\mathrm{Pic}_K^0) \cdot \tilde{s}^{-\ell} c^{2N} \leq \frac{1}{2}\varepsilon^2$.

Combining above two bounds, we can bound the right-hand side of Eq. (10) by ε^2. Taking square roots gives the final result. □

4 Worst-Case to Average-Case Reduction

In this section, we give a worst-case to average-case reduction for approx-Hermite-SVP in fractional ideal lattices. In the case of prime power cyclotomic number fields (under the assumption that $h_k^+ \leq (\log n)^n$), our reduction increases the approximation factor by a factor $\tilde{O}(\sqrt{n})$. In the more general case, the approximation factor increases by a factor $\tilde{O}(n \cdot \Delta^{1/(2n)})$.

Our reduction works as follows. Given as input a fractional ideal $\mathfrak{a}$, we randomize it using the random walk of the previous section, in order to obtain something uniform in the Arakelov class group. More formally, we multiply $\mathfrak{a}$ by N prime ideals $\mathfrak{p}_i$ chosen uniformly among the prime ideals of norm smaller than B (where N and B are the ones of Theorem 3.3). We then multiply the resulting ideal $\mathfrak{a}\prod_i \mathfrak{p}_i$ by an element $x \in K_\mathbb{R}$ sampled such that $\mathrm{Log}(x)$ follows a Gaussian distribution of small standard deviation. Observe that this means that the coordinates of x are somehow balanced and so multiplication by x does not change the geometry of the ideal that much. Using Theorem 3.3, the obtained ideal lattice $L = x\mathcal{L}(\mathfrak{a} \cdot \prod_i \mathfrak{p}_i)$ has a uniform class in the Arakelov class group. This will essentially be our average-case distribution for ideals.[6]

Assume now that one can efficiently find a small vector v in the randomized ideal $x \cdot \mathcal{L}(\mathfrak{a} \cdot \prod_i \mathfrak{p}_i)$. Then $x^{-1} \cdot v$ is an element of $\mathcal{L}(\mathfrak{a})$ (because $\mathcal{L}(\mathfrak{a} \cdot \prod_i \mathfrak{b}_i)$ is a subset of $\mathcal{L}(\mathfrak{a})$). Since x does not distort the geometry too much, this element

---

[4] We use the bound $\beta_\alpha^{(\ell)} \leq e^{-\alpha^2}$ for $\alpha \geq \sqrt{\ell}$.

[5] In this bound on B one would expect an additional $\log(\log(\mathrm{Vol}(\mathrm{Pic}_K^0)))$. But as it is bounded by $\log(\log(\Delta))$ (see Lemma 2.3), it can be put in the hidden polylogarithmic factors.

[6] One can observe that this randomization process outputs an ideal lattice instead of a fractional ideal. This will be solved by rounding the ideal lattice to a fractional lattice with close geometry.

$x^{-1} \cdot v$ is still small compared to $\mathrm{Vol}(\mathcal{L}(\mathfrak{a} \cdot \prod_i \mathfrak{p}_i))^{1/n} = \mathrm{Vol}(\mathcal{L}(\mathfrak{a}))^{1/n} \cdot \mathcal{N}(\prod_i \mathfrak{p}_i)^{1/n}$. The approximation factor we get is then roughly equal to $\mathcal{N}(\prod_i \mathfrak{p}_i)^{1/n} \leq B^{N/n}$. Using the values of N and B in Corollaries 3.4 and 3.5, we obtain the claimed upper bound on the increase of the approximation factors.

In this overview, we assumed for simplicity that the average-case distribution is the uniform distribution over ideal lattices. In reality, however, for computational reasons, we will instead use a close, 'rounded', fractional version of this uniform distribution. This is because general ideal lattices (i.e., Arakelov class group elements) can't be represented efficiently and uniquely on a computer. In order to make the reduction computable, we therefore resort to computing with fractional ideals only, which can be efficiently represented, for instance by a basis with rational coefficients. To be clear, elements of the Arakelov class group are thus only used theoretically and are never actually represented on a computer.

The first subsection below describes the average-case distribution we consider, and gives some insight on why we have to modify slightly the simple 'uniform in the Arakelov class group' distribution. In the second subsection, we show that the randomization procedure described above indeed produces an ideal of the desired average-case distribution. Finally, we prove the reduction in the last subsection.

4.1 The Average-Case Distribution

As mentioned above, the average-case distribution we would like to use is the one obtained by sampling a uniformly distributed Arakelov class [a], and then considering the associated ideal lattice L (defined up to K-isometries, see Lemma 2.7). This distribution however, suffers from the following difficulty: we don't have a nice way of representing ideal lattices. First of all, these lattices involve real numbers, which cannot be represented on a computer; but even if it was possible to represent real numbers, we do not have a canonical way of representing an ideal lattice. For instance, the natural representation of the ideal lattice $L = x\mathcal{L}(\mathfrak{a})$ as a pair $(x, \mathcal{L}(\mathfrak{a}))$ is highly non-unique and it may leak some information on the random walk that was performed to obtain L.

We solve both problems by introducing a specific rounding procedure, that maps an ideal lattice to a fractional ideal lattice with almost the same geometry. Once we have a fractional ideal lattice, we can compute the Hermite Normal Form (HNF) of one of its bases. This provides us a unique representation of the lattice, which can be efficiently represented by a matrix with rational coefficients.

The ideas behind the rounding procedure are the following. First, we observe that dividing L by any element $v \in L$ provides an ideal lattice $v^{-1} \cdot L$ which is fractional. Hence, to round the ideal lattice L, it is sufficient to find an element $v \in L$ such that multiplication by v^{-1} does not distort too much the geometry of L (this idea was already exploited by [19]). We find such a good v by sampling it from a Gaussian distribution in L centered in $(M, M, \cdots, M)$ for some M significantly larger than the standard deviation. This choice of center ensures that v has all its coordinates close to M, hence v and v^{-1} are well balanced and so multiplication by v^{-1} does not distort the geometry too much. To conclude,

Algorithm 1. Randomized function $\mathrm{Extract}_{\varsigma,M} : \mathrm{IdLat}_K^0 \to \mathcal{I}_K$
___

Require: An ideal lattice $L \in \mathrm{IdLat}_K^0$
Ensure: A fractional ideal lattice $\mathcal{L}(\mathfrak{b})$
1: Sample $c = (c_\sigma)_\sigma$ uniformly in $\{(x_\sigma)_\sigma : |x_\sigma| = M, \forall \sigma\}$.
2: Sample $v \leftarrow \mathcal{G}_{L,\varsigma,c}$.
3: **return** $\mathcal{L}(\mathfrak{b}) = v^{-1} \cdot L \subset K_\mathbb{R}$.
___

we finally consider the ideal $v^{-1}L$, whose geometry is close to the one of L, and which is a fractional ideal.

In this subsection, our only goal is to describe the average-case distribution, from a mathematical point of view. This means that none of the functions described here needs to be efficiently computable, and none of the elements involved needs to be efficiently representable.

Let us start by describing a randomized function $\mathrm{Extract}_{\varsigma,M}$ (parameterized by some $\varsigma > 0$ and $M > 0$), that extracts from an Arakelov class $[\mathbf{a}]$ a fractional ideal $\mathfrak{b}$, such that the distribution of $\mathfrak{b}$ is independent from the representation of $[\mathbf{a}]$. We first describe the function $\mathrm{Extract}_{\varsigma,M}$ from ideal lattices of norm 1 to fractional ideals, and we will later extend it to Arakelov classes.[7]

Lemma 4.1. *The function $\mathrm{Extract}_{\varsigma,M}$ described in Algorithm 1 outputs a fractional ideal lattice of the form $\mathcal{L}(\mathfrak{b})$ for a fractional ideal $\mathfrak{b} \subset K$. More precisely, $\mathfrak{b}$ is the inverse of an integral ideal and has an algebraic norm larger than $(\sqrt{n}\varsigma + M)^{-n}$ with overwhelming probability (i.e., probability at least $1 - 2^{-\Omega(n)}$).*

Proof. Let us write the ideal lattice L as $L = x\mathcal{L}(\mathfrak{c})$ for some fractional ideal $\mathfrak{c}$. The element v is in L, so it is of the form $x \Psi(w)$ for some $w \in \mathfrak{c}$. In particular, there exists an (integral) ideal $\mathfrak{d}$ such that $(w) = \mathfrak{c}\mathfrak{d}$. Putting everything together we obtain that $v^{-1}L = \Psi(w)^{-1}\mathcal{L}(\mathfrak{c}) = \mathcal{L}(\mathfrak{d}^{-1})$. To conclude the proof, we need an upper-bound on the algebraic norm of $\mathfrak{d}$. Since L in is IdLat_K^0, we know that $|\mathcal{N}(x)| \cdot \mathcal{N}(\mathfrak{c}) = 1$. We also know that with overwhelming probability, every coordinate of v is smaller (in absolute value) than $\sqrt{n}\varsigma + M$, and so $|\mathcal{N}(v)| \leq (\sqrt{n}\varsigma + M)^n$. We conclude by using the fact that $|\mathcal{N}(v)| = |\mathcal{N}(x)| \cdot \mathcal{N}(\mathfrak{c}) \cdot \mathcal{N}(\mathfrak{d})$. $\square$

Let us now show that the function $\mathrm{Extract}_{\varsigma,M}$ is constant (as a probability distribution) over K-isometric ideal lattices.

Lemma 4.2. *Let L and L' be two ideal lattices such that $L \sim L'$ (i.e., there exists $(\xi_\sigma)_\sigma \in K_\mathbb{R}$, with $|\xi_\sigma| = 1$ for all σ, such that $(\xi_\sigma)_\sigma \cdot L = L'$). Then the two probability distributions $\mathrm{Extract}_{\varsigma,M}(L)$ and $\mathrm{Extract}_{\varsigma,M}(L')$ are identical.*

Proof. Let $\xi = (\xi_\sigma) \in K_\mathbb{R}$ be as in the lemma. Observe that the multiplication by ξ is an isometry. This means that for any $v \in L$ and $c \in K_\mathbb{R}$, the probability

___
[7] Observe that contrary to the high level overview, the center c of the Gaussian distribution has been randomized (but it still holds that the sampled element v will be balanced). This is needed in Lemma 4.2, to show that the $\mathrm{Extract}_{\varsigma,M}(\cdot)$ distributions are identical when applied to K-isomorphic ideal lattices.

that $\mathcal{G}_{L,\varsigma,c}$ outputs v is the same as the one that $\mathcal{G}_{L',\varsigma,\xi c}$ outputs ξv. In both cases, the ideal output by the $\mathrm{Extract}_{\varsigma,M}$ function will be $v^{-1} \cdot L = (\xi v)^{-1} \cdot L'$. Due to the random choice of c (uniform among $\{(x_\sigma)_\sigma : |x_\sigma| = M$ for all $\sigma\}$), the distribution of ξc is the same as the one of c . We then conclude that both final distributions must be identical.   □

Since $\mathrm{Extract}_{\varsigma,M}$ is constant over all classes of ideal lattices modulo $\mathrm{Iso}_K = \{L \in \mathrm{IdLat}_K^0 \mid L \sim \mathcal{L}(\mathcal{O}_K)\} \subset \mathrm{IdLat}_K^0$, we can view it as a randomized function from $\mathrm{IdLat}_K^0 / \mathrm{Iso}_K$ to $\mathcal{I}_K$. But recall that we have an isomorphism between $\mathrm{IdLat}_K^0 / \mathrm{Iso}_K$ and Pic_K^0. Using this isomorphism, we can finally define a function $\mathrm{Extract}_{\varsigma,M}$ from Pic_K^0 to $\mathcal{I}_K$, such that for any ideal lattice L, it holds that the distributions $\mathrm{Extract}_{\varsigma,M}(L)$ and $\mathrm{Extract}_{\varsigma,M}(P(L))$ are identical (where $P : \mathrm{IdLat}_K^0 \to \mathrm{Pic}_K^0$ is the map defined in Lemma 2.7).

We now describe our average-case distribution, which we will refer to as $\mathcal{D}_{\varsigma,M}^{\mathrm{perfect}}$ (parameterized by two parameters $\varsigma, M > 0$):

$$\mathcal{D}_{\varsigma,M}^{\mathrm{perfect}} := \mathrm{Extract}_{\varsigma,M}(\mathcal{U}(\mathrm{Pic}_K^0)), \tag{11}$$

where $\mathcal{U}(\mathrm{Pic}_K^0)$ is the uniform distribution over Pic_K^0. Once again, this is only the mathematical definition of the distribution $\mathcal{D}_{\varsigma,M}^{\mathrm{perfect}}$, and this does not provide an efficient algorithm for sampling from this distribution (in particular because we cannot sample from $\mathcal{U}(\mathrm{Pic}_K^0)$). In the next subsection, we will explain how one can sample efficiently from a distribution statistically close to $\mathcal{D}_{\varsigma,M}^{\mathrm{perfect}}$, when the parameter ς is large enough (this is possible since the output of $\mathcal{D}_{\varsigma,M}^{\mathrm{perfect}}$ are fractional ideals of bounded algebraic norm, which can be efficiently represented).

4.2   Sampling from the Average-Case Distribution

In this section, we explain how one can efficiently sample from a distribution $\mathcal{D}_{\varsigma,M}^{\mathrm{sample}}$ that is statistically close to the distribution $\mathcal{D}_{\varsigma,M}^{\mathrm{perfect}}$. Let us start by describing a tool distribution $\mathcal{D}^{\mathrm{round}}$, which should be efficiently samplable. In order to use our random walk theorem, we need to be able to sample elements $x \in K_\mathbb{R}$ such that $\mathrm{Log}(x)$ follows a continuous Gaussian distribution of parameter s in $H = \mathrm{Log}(K_\mathbb{R}^*)$. This distribution however cannot be sampled efficiently on a computer, as it is a continuous distribution. The objective of the distribution $\mathcal{D}^{\mathrm{round}}$ is to compute efficiently a rounded version of this distribution, where the output x lies in $\Psi(K) \subset K_\mathbb{R}$. This is formalized in the lemma below. The proof is rather technical and is available in the full version [7].

Lemma 4.3. *For any $\varepsilon_1, \varepsilon_2 > 0$, there exists a deterministic function[8] $E_{\varepsilon_1} : H \to \Psi(K)$ such that for any $y \in H$ it holds that*

$$\|E_{\varepsilon_1}(y) \cdot (e^{-y_\sigma})_\sigma - 1\|_\infty \leq \varepsilon_1.$$

---

[8] The function E_{ε_1} plays the role of the exponential function, rounded to a near element of K.

Algorithm 2. Distribution $\mathcal{D}_{\varsigma,M,\mathfrak{a}}^{\text{sample}}$

Require: A fractional ideal $\mathfrak{a} \subset K$ and two parameters $\varsigma, M > 0$.
Ensure: A fractional ideal lattice $\mathcal{L}(\mathfrak{b}) \subset \Psi(K)$.
1: Let $s = 1/(\log n)^2$ and N, B be the smallest integers satisfying the conditions of Corollary 3.5 (if K is a prime-power cyclotomic field) or Corollary 3.4 (in the generic case).
2: Sample $\mathfrak{p}_1, \cdots, \mathfrak{p}_N$ uniformly among all prime ideals of norm $\leq B$.
3: Sample $(x_\sigma)_\sigma \leftarrow \mathcal{D}_{\varepsilon_1,\varepsilon_2,s}^{\text{round}}$ for $\varepsilon_1 = 2^{-n}/M$ and $\varepsilon_2 = 2^{-n}$.
4: Define $L \in \text{IdLat}_K$ to be $L = (x_\sigma)_\sigma \cdot \mathcal{L}(\prod_{i=1}^N \mathfrak{p}_i \cdot \mathfrak{a})$.
5: Sample $c = (c_\sigma)_\sigma$ uniformly in $\{(x_\sigma)_\sigma : |x_\sigma| = M, \forall \sigma\}$.
6: Let $\varsigma' = \mathcal{N}(\prod_{i=1}^N \mathfrak{p}_i \cdot \mathfrak{a})^{1/n} \cdot \varsigma$ and $c' = \mathcal{N}(\prod_{i=1}^N \mathfrak{p}_i \cdot \mathfrak{a})^{1/n} \cdot c$.
7: Sample $v \leftarrow \widehat{\mathcal{G}}_{L,\varsigma',c'}$.
8: **return** $\mathcal{L}(\mathfrak{b}) = v^{-1} \cdot L \subset \Psi(K)$.

Furthermore, for any $s > 0$, one can sample in time polynomial in n, $\max_i \log \|b_i\|$, s, $\log(1/\varepsilon_1)$ and $\log(1/\varepsilon_2)$ from a distribution $\mathcal{D}_{\varepsilon_1,\varepsilon_2,s}^{\text{round}}$ that is ε_2 close in statistical distance to $E_{\varepsilon_1}(\mathcal{G}_{H,s})$. Here, $(b_1, \cdots, b_n)$ is a known basis of $\mathcal{L}(\mathcal{O}_K)$.

We can now describe the distribution $\mathcal{D}_{\varsigma,M,\mathfrak{a}}^{\text{sample}}$, which we will use as a samplable replacement of $\mathcal{D}_{\varsigma,M}^{\text{perfect}}$. Observe that the distribution $\mathcal{D}_{\varsigma,M,\mathfrak{a}}^{\text{sample}}$ is parameterized by parameters $\varsigma, M > 0$ (the same as for $\mathcal{D}_{\varsigma,M}^{\text{perfect}}$), but also by a fractional ideal $\mathfrak{a} \subset K$. We will show that whatever the choice of $\mathfrak{a}$ is, the distribution $\mathcal{D}_{\varsigma,M,\mathfrak{a}}^{\text{sample}}$ is statistically close to $\mathcal{D}_{\varsigma,M}^{\text{perfect}}$. Looking forward, the distribution $\mathcal{D}_{\varsigma,M,\mathfrak{a}}^{\text{sample}}$ will be the one obtained by randomizing the ideal $\mathfrak{a}$ in the worst-case to average-case reduction.

Let $\mathfrak{a} \subset K$ be any fractional ideal and $\varsigma, M > 0$ be some parameters. Recall that $\widehat{\mathcal{G}}_{L,\varsigma,c}$ refers to the distribution obtained by running Klein's Gaussian sampling algorithm on lattice L with parameter ς and center c (see Proposition 2.14). The distribution $\mathcal{D}_{\varsigma,M,\mathfrak{a}}^{\text{sample}}$ is obtained by running the following algorithm (Algorithm 2).

Theorem 4.4. *Let $\mathfrak{a} \subset K$ be any fractional ideal and $\varsigma \geq 2^{n+1}\sqrt{n} \cdot \Delta^{1/(2n)} \cdot \lambda_n(\mathcal{L}(\mathcal{O}_K))$. Assume we know a basis $(b_1, \cdots, b_n)$ of $\mathcal{L}(\mathcal{O}_K)$ and an LLL reduced basis of $\mathcal{L}(\mathfrak{a})$, then there exists an algorithm sampling from the distribution $\mathcal{D}_{\varsigma,M,\mathfrak{a}}^{\text{sample}}$ in time polynomial in $\text{size}(\mathcal{N}(\mathfrak{a}))$, $\log \Delta$, $\max_i \log \|b_i\|$, $\log M$ and $\log \varsigma$.*

Furthermore, the statistical distance between the distributions $\mathcal{D}_{\varsigma,M,\mathfrak{a}}^{\text{sample}}$ and $\mathcal{D}_{\varsigma,M}^{\text{perfect}}$ is at most 2^{-cn} for some absolute constant $c > 0$.

The proof of this theorem is available in the full version [7].

4.3 The Reduction

We can now prove our worst-case to average-case reduction, where the average-case distribution we consider is $\mathcal{D}_{\varsigma,M}^{\text{perfect}}$ (for some well chosen parameters ς and M). The proof of this theorem is available in the full version [7].

Theorem 4.5. *Let $\varsigma \geq 2^{n+1}\sqrt{n} \cdot \Delta^{1/(2n)} \cdot \lambda_n(\mathcal{L}(\mathcal{O}_K))$ and $M \geq 2\sqrt{n}\varsigma$. Assume we have a (randomized) algorithm $\mathcal{A}$ and real numbers $\gamma \geq 1$ and $p > 0$ such that $\mathcal{A}$ solves γ-Hermite-SVP with probability at least p when given as input $\mathcal{L}(\mathfrak{a}) \leftarrow \mathcal{D}_{\varsigma,M}^{perfect}$ (where the probability is taken over the choice of $\mathfrak{a}$ and over the randomness of $\mathcal{A}$). Let T be an upper bound on the run time of $\mathcal{A}$ on any input.*

Then there exists a randomized algorithm $\mathcal{A}'$ solving γ'-Hermite-SVP in any fractional ideal $\mathcal{L}(\mathfrak{a})$ with probability at least $p - n^{-\omega(1)}$ (where the probability is taken over the randomness of $\mathcal{A}'$), for an approximation factor

$$\gamma' = O(B^{N/n}) \cdot \gamma \leq \begin{cases} \widetilde{O}\left(n^{1/2}\right) \cdot \gamma & \text{for prime power cyclotomic fields} \\ & (\text{assuming } h_K^+ \leq (\log n)^n) \\ \widetilde{O}\left(n^{1-n_{\mathbb{C}}/n} \cdot \Delta^{1/(2n)}\right) \cdot \gamma & \text{for arbitrary number fields.} \end{cases}$$

The run time of $\mathcal{A}'$ is bounded by $T + \mathsf{poly}(\log \Delta, \max_i \log \|b_i\|, \mathrm{size}\,\mathcal{N}(\mathfrak{a}), \log \varsigma, \log M)$, where $(b_1, \cdots, b_n)$ is a known basis of $\mathcal{L}(\mathcal{O}_K)$.

Remark 4.6. Observe that from Theorem 4.4, one can sample in time polynomial in $\log \Delta$, $\max_i \log \|b_i\|$, $\log s$ and $\log M$ from a distribution $\mathcal{D}_{\varsigma,M,\mathcal{O}_K}^{\mathrm{sample}}$ whose statistical distance to $\mathcal{D}_{\varsigma,M}^{\mathrm{perfect}}$ is at most $2^{-\Omega(n)}$.

Remark 4.7. Recall from Lemma 2.8 that $\lambda_n(\mathcal{L}(\mathcal{O}_K)) \leq \sqrt{n\Delta}$. Hence, if one chooses ς and M minimal (still satisfying the conditions of Theorem 4.5) and if we are given an LLL reduced basis of $\mathcal{L}(\mathcal{O}_K)$ (which can always be computed from any other basis), then the run time of Algorithm $\mathcal{A}'$ in Theorem 4.5 is of the form $T + \mathsf{poly}\left(\log \Delta, \mathrm{size}(\mathcal{N}(\mathfrak{a}))\right)$.

Acknowledgments. The authors are grateful to René Schoof for valuable feedback on a preliminary version of this work. Part of this work was done while the authors were visiting the Simons Institute for the Theory of Computing.

L.D. is supported by the European Union Horizon 2020 Research and Innovation Program Grant 780701 (PROMETHEUS), and by a Fellowship from the Simons Institute. K.d.B. was supported by the ERC Advanced Grant 740972 (ALGSTRONGCRYPTO) and by the European Union Horizon 2020 Research and Innovation Program Grant 780701 (PROMETHEUS). A.P. was supported in part by CyberSecurity Research Flanders with reference number VR20192203 and by the Research Council KU Leuven grant C14/18/067 on Cryptanalysis of post-quantum cryptography. Part of this work was done when A.P. was visiting CWI, under the CWI PhD internship program. Part of this work was done when B.W. was at the Cryptology Group, CWI, Amsterdam, The Netherlands, supported by the ERC Advanced Grant 740972 (ALGSTRONGCRYPTO).

References

1. Ajtai, M.: Generating hard instances of the short basis problem. In: Wiedermann, J., van Emde Boas, P., Nielsen, M. (eds.) ICALP 1999. LNCS, vol. 1644, pp. 1–9. Springer, Heidelberg (1999). https://doi.org/10.1007/3-540-48523-6_1

2. Bach, E., Shallit, J.O.: Algorithmic Number Theory: Efficient Algorithms, vol. 1. MIT Press, Cambridge (1996)
3. Banaszczyk, W.: New bounds in some transference theorems in the geometry of numbers. Math. Ann. **296**(4), 625–636 (1993). https://doi.org/10.1007/BF01445125
4. Biasse, J.-F., Espitau, T., Fouque, P.-A., Gélin, A., Kirchner, P.: Computing generator in cyclotomic integer rings. In: Coron, J.-S., Nielsen, J.B. (eds.) EUROCRYPT 2017, Part I. LNCS, vol. 10210, pp. 60–88. Springer, Cham (2017). https://doi.org/10.1007/978-3-319-56620-7_3
5. Biasse, J.-F., Fieker, C.: Subexponential class group and unit group computation in large degree number fields. LMS J. Comput. Math. **17**(A), 385–403 (2014)
6. Biasse, J.-F., Song, F.: A polynomial time quantum algorithm for computing class groups and solving the principal ideal problem in arbitrary degree number fields. In: SODA (2016)
7. de Boer, K., Ducas, L., Pellet-Mary, A., Wesolowski, B.: Random self-reducibility of ideal-SVP via Arakelov random walks. Cryptology ePrint Archive, report 2020/297 (2020). https://eprint.iacr.org/2020/297
8. de Boer, K., Pagano, C.: Calculating the power residue symbol and Ibeta. In: ISSAC, vol. 68, pp. 923–934 (2017)
9. Buhler, J., Pomerance, C., Robertson, L.: Heuristics for class numbers of prime-power real cyclotomic fields. In: High Primes and Misdemeanours: Lectures in Honour of the 60th Birthday of Hugh Cowie Williams, Fields Institute Communications, pp. 149–157. American Mathematical Society (2004)
10. Campbell, P., Groves, M., Shepherd, D.: Soliloquy: a cautionary tale. In: ETSI 2nd Quantum-Safe Crypto Workshop (2014)
11. Cramer, R., Ducas, L., Peikert, C., Regev, O.: Recovering short generators of principal ideals in cyclotomic rings. In: Fischlin, M., Coron, J.-S. (eds.) EUROCRYPT 2016, Part II. LNCS, vol. 9666, pp. 559–585. Springer, Heidelberg (2016). https://doi.org/10.1007/978-3-662-49896-5_20
12. Cramer, R., Ducas, L., Wesolowski, B.: Short stickelberger class relations and application to ideal-SVP. In: Coron, J.-S., Nielsen, J.B. (eds.) EUROCRYPT 2017, Part I. LNCS, vol. 10210, pp. 324–348. Springer, Cham (2017). https://doi.org/10.1007/978-3-319-56620-7_12
13. Deitmar, A., Echterhoff, S.: Principles of Harmonic Analysis, 2nd edn. Springer, Cham (2016)
14. Dobrowolski, E.: On a question of Lehmer and the number of irreducible factors of a polynomial. Acta Arithmetica **34**(4), 391–401 (1979)
15. Ducas, L., Plançon, M., Wesolowski, B.: On the shortness of vectors to be found by the ideal-SVP quantum algorithm. In: Boldyreva, A., Micciancio, D. (eds.) CRYPTO 2019, Part I. LNCS, vol. 11692, pp. 322–351. Springer, Cham (2019). https://doi.org/10.1007/978-3-030-26948-7_12
16. Eisenträger, K., Hallgren, S., Kitaev, A., Song, F.: A quantum algorithm for computing the unit group of an arbitrary degree number field. In: STOC, pp. 293–302. ACM (2014)
17. Gentry, C.: A fully homomorphic encryption scheme. Ph.D. thesis, Stanford University (2009). http://crypto.stanford.edu/craig
18. Gentry, C.: Fully homomorphic encryption using ideal lattices. In: STOC, pp. 169–178 (2009)
19. Gentry, C.: Toward basing fully homomorphic encryption on worst-case hardness. In: Rabin, T. (ed.) CRYPTO 2010. LNCS, vol. 6223, pp. 116–137. Springer, Heidelberg (2010). https://doi.org/10.1007/978-3-642-14623-7_7

20. Gentry, C., Peikert, C., Vaikuntanathan, V.: Trapdoors for hard lattices and new cryptographic constructions. In: STOC, pp. 197–206 (2008)
21. Iwaniec, H., Kowalski, E.: Analytic Number Theory. American Mathematical Society, Providence (2004)
22. Jao, D., Miller, S.D., Venkatesan, R.: Expander graphs based on GRH with an application to elliptic curve cryptography. J. Number Theory **129**, 1491–1504 (2009)
23. Jetchev, D., Wesolowski, B.: On graphs of isogenies of principally polarizable abelian surfaces and the discrete logarithm problem. CoRR, abs/1506.00522 (2015)
24. Kessler, V.: On the minimum of the unit lattice. Séminaire de Théorie des Nombres de Bordeaux **3**(2), 377–380 (1991)
25. Klein, P.N.: Finding the closest lattice vector when it's unusually close. In: SODA, pp. 937–941 (2000)
26. Lee, C., Pellet-Mary, A., Stehlé, D., Wallet, A.: An LLL algorithm for module lattices. In: Galbraith, S.D., Moriai, S. (eds.) ASIACRYPT 2019, Part II. LNCS, vol. 11922, pp. 59–90. Springer, Cham (2019). https://doi.org/10.1007/978-3-030-34621-8_3
27. Louboutin, S.: Explicit bounds for residues of Dedekind zeta functions, values of l-functions at s=1, and relative class numbers. J. Number Theory **85**, 263–282 (2000)
28. Lyubashevsky, V., Micciancio, D.: Generalized compact knapsacks are collision resistant. In: Bugliesi, M., Preneel, B., Sassone, V., Wegener, I. (eds.) ICALP 2006, Part II. LNCS, vol. 4052, pp. 144–155. Springer, Heidelberg (2006). https://doi.org/10.1007/11787006_13
29. Lyubashevsky, V., Peikert, C., Regev, O.: On ideal lattices and learning with errors over rings. J. ACM **60**(6), 43:1–43:35 (2013). Preliminary version in Eurocrypt 2010
30. Micciancio, D.: Generalized compact knapsacks, cyclic lattices, and efficient one-way functions. Comput. Complex. **16**(4), 365–411 (2007). https://doi.org/10.1007/s00037-007-0234-9. Preliminary version in FOCS 2002
31. Micciancio, D., Regev, O.: Worst-case to average-case reductions based on Gaussian measures. SIAM J. Comput. **37**(1), 267–302 (2007)
32. Miller, J.C.: Real cyclotomic fields of prime conductor and their class numbers. Math. Comput. **84**(295), 2459–2469 (2015)
33. Miller, S.D., Stephens-Davidowitz, N.: Generalizations of Banaszczyk's transference theorems and tail bound. arXiv preprint arXiv:1802.05708 (2018)
34. Minkowski, H.: Gesammelte Abhandlungen. Chelsea, New York (1967)
35. Miyake, T.: Modular Forms. Springer Monographs in Mathematics. Springer, Heidelberg (1989). https://doi.org/10.1007/3-540-29593-3
36. Neukirch, J.: Algebraic Number Theory, vol. 322. Springer, Heidelberg (2013). https://doi.org/10.1007/978-3-662-03983-0d
37. Neukirch, J., Schappacher, N.: Algebraic Number Theory. Grundlehren der mathematischen Wissenschaften. Springer, Heidelberg (2013)
38. Peikert, C., Rosen, A.: Efficient collision-resistant hashing from worst-case assumptions on cyclic lattices. In: Halevi, S., Rabin, T. (eds.) TCC 2006. LNCS, vol. 3876, pp. 145–166. Springer, Heidelberg (2006). https://doi.org/10.1007/11681878_8
39. Pellet-Mary, A., Hanrot, G., Stehlé, D.: Approx-SVP in ideal lattices with preprocessing. In: Ishai, Y., Rijmen, V. (eds.) EUROCRYPT 2019, Part II. LNCS, vol. 11477, pp. 685–716. Springer, Cham (2019). https://doi.org/10.1007/978-3-030-17656-3_24
40. Regev, O.: On lattices, learning with errors, random linear codes, and cryptography. J. ACM **56**(6), 1–40 (2009). Preliminary version in STOC 2005

41. Schoof, R.: Computing Arakelov class groups. In: Algorithmic Number Theory: Lattices, Number Fields, Curves and Cryptography, pp. 447–495. Cambridge University Press (2008)
42. Shoup, V.: A new polynomial factorization algorithm and its implementation. J. Symb. Comput. **20**(4), 363–397 (1995)
43. Stehlé, D., Steinfeld, R., Tanaka, K., Xagawa, K.: Efficient public key encryption based on ideal lattices. In: Matsui, M. (ed.) ASIACRYPT 2009. LNCS, vol. 5912, pp. 617–635. Springer, Heidelberg (2009). https://doi.org/10.1007/978-3-642-10366-7_36
44. von zur Gathen, J., Panario, D.: Factoring polynomials over finite fields: a survey. J. Symb. Comput. **31**(1), 3–17 (2001)

Slide Reduction, Revisited—Filling the Gaps in SVP Approximation

Divesh Aggarwal[1][(✉)], Jianwei Li[2][(✉)], Phong Q. Nguyen[3,4][(✉)], and Noah Stephens-Davidowitz[5][(✉)]

[1] National University of Singapore, Singapore, Singapore
dcsdiva@nus.edu.sg
[2] Information Security Group, Royal Holloway, University of London, Egham, UK
lijianweithu@sina.com
[3] Inria, Paris, France
pnguyen@inria.fr
[4] Département d'informatique de l'ENS, ENS, CNRS, PSL University, Paris, France
[5] Cornell University, Ithaca, USA
noahsd@gmail.com

Abstract. We show how to generalize Gama and Nguyen's slide reduction algorithm [STOC '08] for solving the approximate Shortest Vector Problem over lattices (SVP) to allow for arbitrary block sizes, rather than just block sizes that divide the rank n of the lattice. This leads to significantly better running times for most approximation factors. We accomplish this by combining slide reduction with the DBKZ algorithm of Micciancio and Walter [Eurocrypt '16].

We also show a different algorithm that works when the block size is quite large—at least half the total rank. This yields the first non-trivial algorithm for sublinear approximation factors.

Together with some additional optimizations, these results yield significantly faster provably correct algorithms for δ-approximate SVP for all approximation factors $n^{1/2+\varepsilon} \leq \delta \leq n^{O(1)}$, which is the regime most relevant for cryptography. For the specific values of $\delta = n^{1-\varepsilon}$ and $\delta = n^{2-\varepsilon}$, we improve the exponent in the running time by a factor of 2 and a factor of 1.5 respectively.

Keywords: Lattice reduction · Slide reduction · DBKZ · SVP

The first author was partially funded by the Singapore Ministry of Education and the National Research Foundation under grant R-710-000-012-135, and supported by the grant MOE2019-T2-1-145 "Foundations of quantum-safe cryptography". The second author was funded by EPSRC grant EP/S020330/1. This project has received funding from the European Research Council (ERC) under the European Union's Horizon 2020 research and innovation programme (grant agreement No 885394). Parts of this work were done while the fourth author was visiting the Massachusetts Institute of Technology, the Centre for Quantum Technologies at the National University of Singapore, and the Simons Institute in Berkeley.

D. Micciancio and T. Ristenpart (Eds.): CRYPTO 2020, LNCS 12171, pp. 274–295, 2020.
https://doi.org/10.1007/978-3-030-56880-1_10

1   Introduction

A lattice $\mathcal{L} \subset \mathbb{R}^m$ is the set of integer linear combinations

$$\mathcal{L} := \mathcal{L}(\mathbf{B}) = \{z_1 \boldsymbol{b}_1 + \cdots + z_n \boldsymbol{b}_n \ : \ z_i \in \mathbb{Z}\}$$

of linearly independent basis vectors $\mathbf{B} = (\boldsymbol{b}_1, \ldots, \boldsymbol{b}_n) \in \mathbb{R}^{m \times n}$. We call n the *rank* of the lattice.

The Shortest Vector Problem (SVP) is the computational search problem in which the input is (a basis for) a lattice $\mathcal{L} \subseteq \mathbb{Z}^m$, and the goal is to output a non-zero lattice vector $\boldsymbol{y} \in \mathcal{L}$ with minimal length, $\|\boldsymbol{y}\| = \lambda_1(\mathcal{L}) := \min_{\boldsymbol{x} \in \mathcal{L}_{\neq 0}} \|\boldsymbol{x}\|$. For $\delta \geq 1$, the δ-approximate variant of SVP (δ-SVP) is the relaxation of this problem in which any non-zero lattice vector $\boldsymbol{y} \in \mathcal{L}_{\neq 0}$ with $\|\boldsymbol{y}\| \leq \delta \cdot \lambda_1(\mathcal{L})$ is a valid solution.

A closely related problem is δ-*Hermite SVP* (δ-HSVP, sometimes also called Minkowski SVP), which asks us to find a non-zero lattice vector $\boldsymbol{y} \in \mathcal{L}_{\neq 0}$ with $\|\boldsymbol{y}\| \leq \delta \cdot \mathrm{vol}(\mathcal{L})^{1/n}$, where $\mathrm{vol}(\mathcal{L}) := \det(\mathbf{B}^T \mathbf{B})^{1/2}$ is the covolume of the lattice. *Hermite's constant* γ_n is (the square of) the minimal possible approximation factor that can be achieved in the worst case. I.e.,

$$\gamma_n := \sup \frac{\lambda_1(\mathcal{L})^2}{\mathrm{vol}(\mathcal{L})^{2/n}} \ ,$$

where the supremum is over lattices $\mathcal{L} \subset \mathbb{R}^n$ with full rank n. Hermite's constant is only known exactly for $1 \leq n \leq 8$ and $n = 24$, but it is known to be asymptotically linear in n, i.e., $\gamma_n = \Theta(n)$. HSVP and Hermite's constant play a large role in algorithms for δ-SVP.

Starting with the celebrated work of Lenstra, Lenstra, and Lovász in 1982 [LLL82], algorithms for solving δ-(H)SVP for a wide range of parameters δ have found innumerable applications, including factoring polynomials over the rationals [LLL82], integer programming [Len83, Kan83, DPV11], cryptanalysis [Sha84, Odl90, JS98, NS01], etc. More recently, many cryptographic primitives have been constructed whose security is based on the (worst-case) hardness of δ-SVP or closely related lattice problems [Ajt96, Reg09, GPV08, Pei09, Pei16]. Such lattice-based cryptographic constructions are likely to be used on massive scales (e.g., as part of the TLS protocol) in the not-too-distant future [NIS18], and in practice, the security of these constructions depends on the fastest algorithms for δ-(H)SVP, typically for $\delta = \mathrm{poly}(n)$.

Work on δ-(H)SVP has followed two distinct tracks. There has been a long line of work showing progressively faster algorithms for exact SVP (i.e., $\delta = 1$) [Kan83, AKS01, NV08, PS09, MV13]. However, even the fastest such algorithm (with proven correctness) runs in time $2^{n + o(n)}$ [ADRS15, AS18]. So, these algorithms are only useful for rather small n.

This paper is part of a separate line of work on *basis reduction algorithms* [LLL82, Sch87, SE94, GHKN06, GN08a, HPS11, MW16]. (See [NV10] and [MW16] for a much more complete list of works on basis reduction.) At a high level, these are reductions from δ-(H)SVP on lattices with rank n to exact SVP on lattices with rank $k \leq n$. More specifically, these algorithms divide a basis $\mathbf{B}$ into projected blocks $\mathbf{B}_{[i,i+k-1]}$ with *block size* k, where

$$\mathbf{B}_{[i,j]} = (\pi_i(\mathbf{b}_i), \pi_i(\mathbf{b}_{i+1}), \dots, \pi_i(\mathbf{b}_j))$$

and π_i is the orthogonal projection onto the subspace orthogonal to $\boldsymbol{b}_1, \dots, \boldsymbol{b}_{i-1}$. Basis reduction algorithms use their SVP oracle to find short vectors in these (low-rank) blocks and incorporate these short vectors into the lattice basis $\mathbf{B}$. By doing this repeatedly (at most $\text{poly}(n, \log \|\mathbf{B}\|)$ times) with a cleverly chosen sequence of blocks, such algorithms progressively improve the "quality" of the basis $\mathbf{B}$ until $\boldsymbol{b}_1$ is a solution to δ-(H)SVP for some $\delta \geq 1$. The goal, of course, is to take the block size k to be small enough that we can actually run an exact algorithm on lattices with rank k in reasonable time while still achieving a relatively good approximation factor δ.

For HSVP, the DBKZ algorithm due to Micciancio and Walter yields the best proven approximation factor for all ranks n and block sizes k [MW16], which was previously obtained by [GN08a] only when n is divisible by k. Specifically, the approximation factor corresponds to Mordell's inequality:

$$\delta_{\mathsf{MW},H} := \gamma_k^{\frac{n-1}{2(k-1)}} . \tag{1}$$

(Recall that $\gamma_k = \Theta(k)$ is Hermite's constant. Here and throughout the introduction, we have left out low-order factors that can be made arbitrarily close to one.) Using a result due to Lovász [Lov86], this can be converted into an algorithm for $\delta_{\mathsf{MW},H}^2$-SVP. However, the slide reduction algorithm of Gama and Nguyen [GN08a] achieves a better approximation factor for SVP. It yields

$$\delta_{\mathsf{GN},H} := \gamma_k^{\frac{\lceil n \rceil_k - 1}{2(k-1)}} \qquad \delta_{\mathsf{GN},S} := \gamma_k^{\frac{\lceil n \rceil_k - k}{k-1}} , \tag{2}$$

for HSVP and SVP respectively, where we write $\lceil n \rceil_k := k \cdot \lceil n/k \rceil$ for n rounded up to the nearest multiple of k. (We have included the result for HSVP in Eq. (2) for completeness, though it is clearly no better than Eq. (1).)

The discontinuous approximation factor in Eq. (2) is the result of an unfortunate limitation of slide reduction: it only works when the block size k divides the rank n. If n is not divisible by k, then we must artificially pad our basis so that it has rank $\lceil n \rceil_k$, which results in the rather odd expressions in Eq. (2). Of course, for $n \gg k$, this rounding has little effect on the approximation factor. But, for cryptographic applications, we are interested in small polynomial approximation factors $\delta \approx n^c$ for relatively small constants c, i.e., in the case when $k = \Theta(n)$. For such values of k and n, this rounding operation can cost us a constant factor in the exponent of the approximation factor, essentially changing n^c to $n^{\lceil c \rceil}$. Such constants in the exponent have a large effect on the theoretical security of lattice-based cryptography.[1]

---

[1] The concrete security of lattice-based cryptography is assessed using HSVP and a heuristic version of Eq. (2) where Hermite's constant is replaced by a Gaussian heuristic estimate. In this work, we restrict our attention to what we can prove, and we focus on SVP rather than HSVP.

1.1   Our Results

Our first main contribution is a generalization of Gama and Nguyen's slide reduction [GN08a] without the limitation that the rank n must be a multiple of the block size k. Indeed, we achieve exactly the approximation factor shown in Eq. (2) without any rounding, as we show below.

As a very small additional contribution, we allow for the possibility that the underlying SVP algorithm for lattices with rank k only solves δ-approximate SVP for some $\delta > 1$. This technique was already known to folklore and used in practice, and the proof requires no new ideas. Nevertheless, we believe that this work is the first to formally show that a δ-SVP algorithm suffices and to compute the exact dependence on δ. (This minor change proves quite useful when we instantiate our δ-SVP subroutine with the $2^{0.802k}$-time δ-SVP algorithm for some large constant $\delta \gg 1$ due to Liu, Wang, Xu, and Zheng [LWXZ11, WLW15]. See Table 1 and Figure 1.)

Theorem 1 (Informal, slide reduction for $n \geq 2k$). *For any approximation factor $\delta \geq 1$ and block size $k := k(n) \geq 2$, there is an efficient reduction from δ_H-HSVP and δ_S-SVP on lattices with rank $n \geq 2k$ to δ-SVP on lattices with rank k, where*

$$\delta_H := (\delta^2 \gamma_k)^{\frac{n-1}{2(k-1)}} \qquad \delta_S := \delta(\delta^2 \gamma_k)^{\frac{n-k}{k-1}} \ .$$

Notice in particular that this matches Eq. (2) in the case when $\delta = 1$ and k divides n. (This is not surprising, since our algorithm is essentially identical to the original algorithm from [GN08a] in this case.) Theorem 1 also matches the approximation factor for HSVP achieved by [MW16], as shown in Eq. (1), so that the best (proven) approximation factor for both problems is now achieved by a single algorithm: in other words, we get the best of both algorithms [GN08a] and [MW16].

However, Theorem 1 only applies for $n \geq 2k$. Our second main contribution is an algorithm that works for $k \leq n \leq 2k$. To our knowledge, this is the first algorithm that provably achieves sublinear approximation factors for SVP and is asymptotically faster than, say, the fastest algorithm for $O(1)$-SVP. (We overcame a small barrier here. See the discussion in Sect. 3.)

Theorem 2 (Informal, slide reduction for $n \leq 2k$). *For any approximation factor $\delta \geq 1$ and block size $k \in [n/2, n]$, there is an efficient reduction from δ_S-SVP on lattices with rank n to δ-SVP on lattices with rank k, where*

$$\delta_S := \delta^2 \sqrt{\gamma_k} (\delta^2 \gamma_q)^{\frac{q+1}{q-1} \cdot \frac{n-k}{2k}} \lesssim \delta(\delta^2 \gamma_k)^{\frac{n}{2k}} \ ,$$

and $q := n - k \leq k$.

Together, these algorithms yield the asymptotically fastest proven running times for δ-SVP for all approximation factors $n^{1/2+\varepsilon} \leq \delta \leq n^{O(1)}$—with a particularly large improvement when $\delta = n^c$ for $1/2 < c < 1$ or for any c slightly smaller than an integer. Table 1 and Fig. 1 summarize the current state of the art.

Table 1. Provable algorithms for solving SVP. We write [A] + [B] to denote the algorithm that uses basis reduction from [A] with the exact/near-exact SVP algorithm from [B], and we write [*] for this work. The "folklore" column represents a result that was likely known to many experts in the field but apparently never published.

Approximation factor	Previous best	Folklore	This work
Exact	2^n [ADRS15]	—	—
$\Omega(1) \leq \delta \leq \sqrt{n}$	$2^{0.802n}$ [WLW15]	—	—
n^c for $c \in [\frac{1}{2}, 1)$	$2^{0.802n}$ [WLW15]	—	$2^{\frac{0.802n}{2c}}$ [*] + [WLW15]
n^c for $c \geq 1$	$2^{\frac{n}{\lfloor c+1 \rfloor}}$ [GN08a] + [ADRS15]	$2^{\frac{0.802n}{\lfloor c+1 \rfloor}}$ [GN08a] + [WLW15]	$2^{\frac{0.802n}{c+1}}$ [*] + [WLW15]

Table 2. Heuristic algorithms for solving SVP.

Approximation factor	Previous best	This work
$1 \leq \delta \leq \sqrt{n}$	$2^{0.292n}$ [BDGL16]	—
n^c for $c \in [\frac{1}{2}, 1)$	$2^{0.292n}$ [BDGL16]	$2^{\frac{0.292n}{2c}}$ [*] + [BDGL16]
n^c for $c \geq 1$	$2^{\frac{0.292n}{\lfloor c+1 \rfloor}}$ [GN08a] + [BDGL16]	$2^{\frac{0.292n}{c+1}}$ [*] + [BDGL16]

For example, one can solve $O(n^{1.99})$-SVP in $2^{0.269n+o(n)}$-time and $O(n^{0.99})$-SVP in $2^{0.405n+o(n)}$ instead of the previously best $2^{0.401n+o(n)}$-time and $2^{0.802n+o(n)}$, respectively.

It is worthwhile to mention that, though our focus is on provable algorithms, any heuristic algorithm can be plugged into our reduction giving us the same improvement for these algorithms (see Table 2). Our reduction just shows how to "recycle" one's favourite algorithm for exact (or near-exact) SVP to tackle higher dimension, provided that one is interested in approximating SVP rather than HSVP. Our results further our understanding of the hardness of SVP but they do not impact usual security estimates, such as those of lattice-based candidates to NIST's post-quantum standardization: this is because current security estimates actually rely on HSVP estimates, following [GN08b]. The problem of approximating SVP is essentially the same as that of approximating HSVP, except for lattices with an extremely small first minimum: such lattices exist but typically do not arise in real-world cryptographic constructions (see [GN08b, §3.2]). For the same reason, implementing our algorithm has limited value in practice at the moment: running the algorithm would only be meaningful if one was interested in approximating SVP on ad-hoc lattices with an extremely small first minimum.

1.2   Our Techniques

We first briefly recall some of the details of Gama and Nguyen's slide reduction. Slide reduction divides the basis $\mathbf{B} = (\boldsymbol{b}_1, \ldots, \boldsymbol{b}_n) \in \mathbb{R}^{m \times n}$ evenly into disjoint "primal blocks" $\mathbf{B}_{[ik+1,(i+1)k]}$ of length k. (Notice that this already requires n to be divisible by k.) It also defines certain "dual blocks" $\mathbf{B}_{[ik+2,(i+1)k+1]}$, which are the primal blocks shifted one to the right. The algorithm then tries to simultaneously satisfy certain primal and dual conditions on these blocks. Namely, it tries to *SVP-reduce* each primal block—i.e., it tries to make the first vector

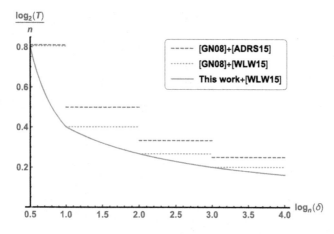

Fig. 1. Provable running time T as a function of approximation factor δ for δ-SVP. The y-axis is $\log_2(T)/n$, and the x-axis is $\log_n \delta$.

in the block $\boldsymbol{b}^*_{ik+1}$ a shortest vector in $\mathcal{L}(\mathbf{B}_{[ik+1,(i+1)k]})$, where $\boldsymbol{b}^*_j := \pi_j(\boldsymbol{b}_j)$. Simultaneously, it tries to *dual SVP-reduce* (DSVP-reduce) the dual blocks. (See Sect. 2.3 for the definition of DSVP reduction.) We call a basis that satisfies all of these conditions simultaneously *slide-reduced* (Fig. 2).

An SVP oracle for lattices with rank k is sufficient to enforce all primal conditions or all dual conditions separately. (E.g., we can enforce the primal conditions by simply finding a shortest non-zero vector in each primal block and including this vector in an updated basis for the block.) Furthermore, if all primal and dual conditions hold simultaneously, then $\|\boldsymbol{b}_1\| \leq \delta_{\mathsf{GN},S}\lambda_1(\mathcal{L})$ with $\delta_{\mathsf{GN},S}$ as in Eq. (2), so that $\|\boldsymbol{b}_1\|$ yields a solution to $\delta_{\mathsf{GN},S}$-SVP. This follows from repeated application of a "gluing" lemma on such bases, which shows how to "glue together" two reduced block to obtain a larger reduced block. (See Lemma 1.) Finally, Gama and Nguyen showed that, if we alternate between SVP-reducing the primal blocks and DSVP-reducing the dual blocks, then the basis will converge quite rapidly to a slide-reduced basis (up to some small slack) [GN08a]. Combining all of these facts together yields the main result in [GN08a]. (See Sect. 4.)

The case $n > 2k$. We wish to extend slide reduction to the case when $n = pk + q$ for $1 \leq q < k$. So, intuitively, we have to decide what to do with "the extra q vectors in the basis." To answer this, we exploit a "gluing" property, which is implicit in LLL and slide reduction, but which we make explicit: given an integer $\ell \in \{1, \ldots, n\}$, any basis B of a lattice L defines two blocks $B_1 = B_{[1,\ell]}$ and $B_2 = B_{[\ell+1,n]}$. The first block B_1 is a basis of a (primitive) sublattice L_1 of L, and the second block B_2 is a basis of another lattice L_2 which can be thought as the quotient L/L_1. Intuitively, the basis B glues the two blocks B_1 and B_2 together: a gluing property (Lemma 1) provides sufficient conditions on the two blocks B_1 and B_2 to guarantee that the basis B is (H)SVP-reduced. Crucially, the gluing property shows that there is an asymmetry between B_1 and B_2: B can be SVP-reduced without requiring both B_1 and B_2 to be SVP-reduced. Namely,

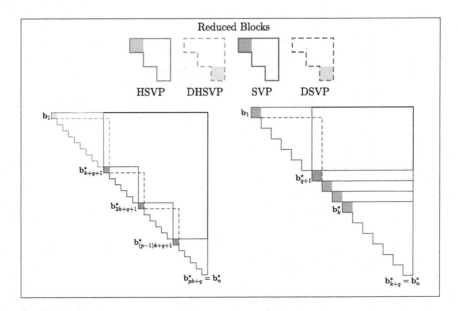

Fig. 2. Slide reduction of an upper-triangular matrix for $n = pk + q \geq 2k$ (left) and $n = k + q \leq 2k$ (right). (The original notion of slide reduction in [GN08a] used only SVP-reduced and DSVP-reduced blocks of fixed size k.)

it suffices that B_1 is HSVP-reduced, B_2 is SVP-reduced together with a gluing condition relating the first vectors of B_1 and B_2.[2]

The HSVP reduction of B_1 can be handled by the algorithm from [MW16], irrespective of the rank of B_1. The SVP reduction of B_2 can be handled by our SVP oracle if the rank of B_2 is chosen to be k, or by slide reduction [GN08a] if the rank of B_2 is chosen to be a multiple of k. Finally, the gluing condition can be achieved by duality, by reusing the main idea of [GN08a]. Thus, "the extra q vectors in the basis" can simply be included in the first block B_1.

Interestingly, the HSVP approximation factor achieved by [MW16] (which we use for B_1) and the SVP approximation factor achieved by [GN08a] (which we can use for B_2) are exactly what we need to apply our gluing lemma. (This is not a coincidence, as we explain in Sect. 4.) The result is Theorem 1.

The case $n < 2k$. For $n = k + q < 2k$, the above idea cannot work. In particular, a "big block" of size $k + q$ in this case would be our entire basis! So, instead of working with one big block and some "regular blocks" of size k, we work with a

---

[2] We are ignoring a certain degenerate case here for simplicity. Namely, if all short vectors happen to lie in the span of the first block, and these vectors happen to be very short relative to the volume of the first block, then calling an HSVP oracle on the first block might not be sufficient to solve approximate SVP. Of course, if we know a low-dimensional subspace that contains the shortest non-zero vector, then finding short lattice vectors is much easier. This degenerate case is therefore easily handled separately (but it does in fact need to be handled separately).

"small block" of size q and one regular block of size k. We then simply perform slide reduction with (primal) blocks $\mathbf{B}_{[1,q]}$ and $\mathbf{B}_{[q+1,n]} = \mathbf{B}_{[n-k+1,n]}$. If we were to stop here, we would achieve an approximation factor of roughly γ_q (see [LW13, Th. 4.3.1]), which for $q = \Theta(k)$ is essentially the same as the approximation factor of roughly γ_k that we get when the rank is $2k$. I.e., we would essentially "pay for two blocks of length k," even though one block has size $q < k$.

However, we notice that a slide-reduced basis guarantees more than just a short first vector. It also promises a very strong bound on $\mathrm{vol}(\mathbf{B}_{[1,q]})$. In particular, since $q < k$ and since we have access to an oracle for lattices with rank k, it is natural to try to extend this small block $\mathbf{B}_{[1,q]}$ with low volume to a larger block $\mathbf{B}_{[1,k]}$ of length k that still has low volume. Indeed, we can use our SVP oracle to guarantee that $\mathbf{B}_{[q+1,k]}$ consists of relatively short vectors so that $\mathrm{vol}(\mathbf{B}_{[q+1,k]})$ is relatively small as well. (Formally, we SVP-reduce $\mathbf{B}_{[i,n]}$ for $i \in [q+1, k]$. Again, we are ignoring a certain degenerate case, as in Footnote 2.) This allows us to upper bound $\mathrm{vol}(\mathbf{B}_{[1,k]}) = \mathrm{vol}(\mathbf{B}_{[1,q]}) \cdot \mathrm{vol}(\mathbf{B}_{[q+1,k]})$, which implies that $\lambda_1(\mathcal{L}(\mathbf{B}_{[1,k]}))$ is relatively short. We can therefore find a short vector by making an additional SVP oracle call on $\mathcal{L}(\mathbf{B}_{[1,k]})$. (Micciancio and Walter used a similar idea in [MW16].)

1.3   Open Questions and Directions for Future Work

Table 1 suggests an obvious open question: can we find a non-trivial basis reduction algorithm that provably solves δ-SVP for $\delta \leq O(\sqrt{n})$? More formally, can we reduce $O(\sqrt{n})$-SVP on lattices with rank n to exact SVP on lattices with rank $k = cn$ for some constant $c < 1$. Our current proof techniques seem to run into a fundamental barrier here in that they seem more-or-less incapable of achieving $\delta \ll \sqrt{\gamma_k}$. This setting is interesting in practice, as many record lattice computations use block reduction with $k \geq n/2$ as a subroutine, such as [CN12]. (One can provably achieve approximation factors $\delta \ll \sqrt{\gamma_k}$ when $k = (1-o(1))n$ with a bit of work,[3] but it is not clear if these extreme parameters are useful.)

Next, we recall that this work shows how to exploit the existing very impressive algorithms for HSVP (in particular, DBKZ [MW16]) to obtain better algorithms for SVP. This suggests two closely related questions for future work: (1) can we find better algorithms for HSVP (e.g., for δ-HSVP with $\delta \approx \sqrt{\gamma_n}$—i.e., "near-exact" HSVP); and (2) where else can we profitably replace SVP oracles with HSVP oracles? Indeed, most of our analysis (and the analysis of other basis reduction algorithms) treats the δ-SVP oracle as a $\delta\sqrt{\gamma_k}$-HSVP oracle. We identified one way to exploit this to actually get a faster algorithm, but perhaps more can be done here—particularly if we find faster algorithms for HSVP.

Finally, we note that we present two distinct (though similar) algorithms: one for lattices with rank $n \leq 2k$ and one for lattices with rank $n \geq 2k$. It is

---

[3] For example, it is immediate from the proof of Theorem 5 that the (very simple) notion of a slide-reduced basis for $n \leq 2k$ in Definition 1 is already enough to obtain $\delta \approx \gamma_{n-k} \approx n-k$. So, for $n \lesssim k + \sqrt{k}$, this already achieves $\delta \lesssim \sqrt{n}$. With a bit more work, one can show that an extra oracle call like the one used in Corollary 1 can yield a still better approximation factor in this rather extreme setting of $k = (1-o(1))n$.

natural to ask whether there is a single algorithm that works in both regimes. Perhaps work on this question could even lead to better approximation factors.

2   Preliminaries

We denote column vectors $x \in \mathbb{R}^m$ by bold lower-case letters. Matrices $\mathbf{B} \in \mathbb{R}^{m \times n}$ are denoted by bold upper-case letters, and we often think of a matrix as a list of column vectors, $\mathbf{B} = (b_1, \ldots, b_n)$. For a matrix $\boldsymbol{B} = (\mathbf{b}_1, \ldots, \mathbf{b}_n)$ with n linearly independent columns, we write $\mathcal{L}(\boldsymbol{B}) := \{z_1 b_1 + \cdots + z_n b_n \; : \; z_i \in \mathbb{Z}\}$ for the lattice generated by $\mathbf{B}$ and $\|\boldsymbol{B}\| = \max\{\|\mathbf{b}_1\|, \ldots, \|\mathbf{b}_n\|\}$ for the maximum norm of a column. We often implicitly assume that $m \geq n$ and that a basis matrix $\mathbf{B} \in \mathbb{R}^{m \times n}$ has rank n (i.e., that the columns of $\mathbf{B}$ are linearly independent). We use the notation $\log := \log_2$ to mean the logarithm with base two.

2.1   Lattices

For any lattice $\mathcal{L}$, its *dual lattice* is

$$\mathcal{L}^\times = \{\mathbf{w} \in \mathrm{span}(\mathcal{L}) : \; \langle \mathbf{w}, \mathbf{y} \rangle \in \mathbb{Z} \text{ for all } \boldsymbol{y} \in \mathcal{L}\} \,.$$

If $\mathbf{B} \in \mathbb{R}^{m \times n}$ is a basis of $\mathcal{L}$, then $\mathcal{L}^\times$ has basis $\mathbf{B}^\times := \mathbf{B}(\mathbf{B}^T \mathbf{B})^{-1}$, called the *dual basis* of $\mathbf{B}$. The *reversed dual basis* $\mathbf{B}^{-s}$ of $\mathbf{B}$ is simply $\mathbf{B}^\times$ with its columns in reversed order [GHN06].

2.2   Gram-Schmidt Orthogonalization

For a basis $\mathbf{B} = (b_1, \ldots, b_n) \in \mathbb{R}^{m \times n}$, we associate a sequence of projections $\pi_i := \pi_{\{b_1, \ldots, b_{i-1}\}^\perp}$. Here, $\pi_{W^\perp}$ means the orthogonal projection onto the subspace $W^\perp$ orthogonal to W. As in [GN08a], $\mathbf{B}_{[i,j]}$ denotes the projected block $(\pi_i(b_i), \pi_i(b_{i+1}), \ldots, \pi_i(b_j))$.

We also associate to $\mathbf{B}$ its Gram-Schmidt orthogonalization (GSO) $\boldsymbol{B}^* := (\mathbf{b}_1^*, \ldots, \mathbf{b}_n^*)$, where $\boldsymbol{b}_i^* := \pi_i(\boldsymbol{b}_i) = \boldsymbol{b}_i - \sum_{j<i} \mu_{i,j} \boldsymbol{b}_j^*$, and $\mu_{i,j} = \langle \boldsymbol{b}_i, \boldsymbol{b}_j^* \rangle / \|\boldsymbol{b}_j^*\|^2$.

We say that $\mathbf{B}$ is *size-reduced* if $|\mu_{i,j}| \leq \frac{1}{2}$ for all $i \neq j$: then $\|\mathbf{B}\| \leq \sqrt{n}\|\mathbf{B}^*\|$. Transforming a basis into this form without modifying $\mathcal{L}(\mathbf{B})$ or $\mathbf{B}^*$ is called *size reduction*, and this can be done easily and efficiently.

2.3   Lattice Basis Reduction

LLL reduction. Let $\boldsymbol{B} = (\mathbf{b}_1, \ldots, \mathbf{b}_n)$ be a size-reduced basis. For $\varepsilon \in [0, 1]$, we say that $\boldsymbol{B}$ is *ε-LLL-reduced* [LLL82] if every rank-two projected block $\boldsymbol{B}_{[i,i+1]}$ satisfies Lovász's condition: $\|\mathbf{b}_i^*\|^2 \leq (1+\varepsilon)\|\mu_{i,i-1}\mathbf{b}_{i-1}^* + \mathbf{b}_i^*\|^2$ for $1 < i \leq n$. For $\varepsilon \geq 1/\mathrm{poly}(n)$, one can efficiently compute an ε-LLL-reduced basis for a given lattice.

SVP reduction and its extensions. Let $B = (\mathbf{b}_1, \ldots, \mathbf{b}_n)$ be a basis of a lattice $\mathcal{L}$ and $\delta \geq 1$ be an approximation factor.

We say that B is *δ-SVP-reduced* if $\|\mathbf{b}_1\| \leq \delta \cdot \lambda_1(\mathcal{L})$. Similarly, we say that B is *δ-HSVP-reduced* if $\|\mathbf{b}_1\| \leq \delta \cdot \mathrm{vol}(\mathcal{L})^{1/n}$.

B is *δ-DSVP-reduced* [GN08a] (where D stands for dual) if the reversed dual basis B^{-s} is δ-SVP-reduced and B is $\frac{1}{3}$-LLL-reduced. Similarly, we say that B is *δ-DHSVP-reduced* if B^{-s} is δ-HSVP-reduced.

The existence of such δ-DSVP-reduced bases is guaranteed by a classical property of LLL that $\|b_n^*\|$ never decreases during the LLL-reduction process [LLL82].

We can efficiently compute a δ-(D)SVP-reduced basis for a given rank n lattice $\mathcal{L} \subseteq \mathbb{Z}^m$ with access to an oracle for δ-SVP on lattices with rank at most n. Furthermore, given a basis $\mathbf{B} = (\mathbf{b}_1, \ldots, \mathbf{b}_n) \in \mathbb{Z}^{m \times n}$ of $\mathcal{L}$ and an index $i \in [1, n - k + 1]$, we can use a δ-SVP oracle for lattices with rank at most k to efficiently compute a size-reduced basis $\mathbf{C} = (\mathbf{b}_1, \ldots, \mathbf{b}_{i-1}, \mathbf{c}_i, \ldots, \mathbf{c}_{i+k-1}, \mathbf{b}_{i+k}, \ldots, \mathbf{b}_n)$ of $\mathcal{L}$ such that the block $\mathbf{C}_{[i,i+k-1]}$ is δ-SVP reduced or δ-DSVP reduced:

- If $\mathbf{C}_{[i,i+k-1]}$ is δ-SVP-reduced, the procedures in [GN08a, MW16, LN19] equipped with δ-SVP-oracle ensure that $\|\mathbf{C}^*\| \leq \|\mathbf{B}^*\|$;
- If $\mathbf{C}_{[i,i+k-1]}$ is δ-DSVP-reduced, the inherent LLL reduction implies $\|\mathbf{C}^*\| \leq 2^k \|\mathbf{B}^*\|$. Indeed, the GSO of $\mathbf{C}_{[i,i+k-1]}$ satisfies

$$\|(\mathbf{C}_{[i,i+k-1]})^*\| \leq 2^{k/2} \lambda_k(\mathcal{L}(\mathbf{C}_{[i,i+k-1]}))$$

(by [LLL82, p. 518, Line 27]) and $\lambda_k(\mathcal{L}(\mathbf{C}_{[i,i+k-1]})) \leq \sqrt{k} \|\mathbf{B}^*\|$. Here, $\lambda_k(\cdot)$ denotes the k-th minimum.

With size-reduction, we can iteratively perform $\mathrm{poly}(n, \log \|\mathbf{B}\|)$ many such operations efficiently. In particular, doing so will not increase $\|\mathbf{B}^*\|$ by more than a factor of $2^{\mathrm{poly}(n, \log \|\mathbf{B}\|)}$, and therefore the same is true of $\|\mathbf{B}\|$. That is, all intermediate entries and the total cost during execution (excluding oracle queries) remain polynomially bounded in the initial input size; See, e.g., [GN08a, LN14] for the evidence. Therefore, to bound the running time of basis reduction, it suffices to bound the number of calls to these block reduction subprocedures.

Twin reduction and gluing. We define the following notion, which was implicit in [GN08a] and will arise repeatedly in our proofs. $B = (\mathbf{b}_1, \ldots, \mathbf{b}_{d+1})$ is δ-*twin-reduced* if $\mathbf{B}_{[1,d]}$ is δ-HSVP-reduced and $\mathbf{B}_{[2,d+1]}$ is δ-DHSVP-reduced. The usefulness of twin reduction is illustrated by the following fact, which is the key idea behind Gama and Nguyen's slide reduction (and is remarkably simple in hindsight).

Fact 3. *If* $\mathbf{B} := (\mathbf{b}_1, \ldots, \mathbf{b}_{d+1}) \in \mathbb{R}^{m \times (d+1)}$ *is* δ-*twin-reduced, then*

$$\|\mathbf{b}_1\| \leq \delta^{2d/(d-1)} \|\mathbf{b}_{d+1}^*\| . \tag{3}$$

Furthermore,

$$\delta^{-d/(d-1)} \|\mathbf{b}_1\| \leq \mathrm{vol}(\mathbf{B})^{1/(d+1)} \leq \delta^{d/(d-1)} \|\mathbf{b}_{d+1}^*\| . \tag{4}$$

Proof. By definition, we have $\|\boldsymbol{b}_1\|^d \leq \delta^d \mathrm{vol}(\mathbf{B}_{[1,d]})$, which is equivalent to

$$\|\boldsymbol{b}_1\|^{d-1} \leq \delta^d \mathrm{vol}(\mathbf{B}_{[2,d]}) \ .$$

Similarly,

$$\mathrm{vol}(\mathbf{B}_{[2,d]}) \leq \delta^d \|\boldsymbol{b}_{d+1}^*\|^{d-1} \ .$$

Combining these two inequalities yields Eq. (3).

Finally, we have $\|\boldsymbol{b}_1\|^d \|\boldsymbol{b}_{d+1}^*\| \leq \delta^d \mathrm{vol}(\mathbf{B})$. Applying Eq. (3) implies the first inequality in Eq. (4), and similar analysis yields the second inequality.   □

The following gluing lemma, which is more-or-less implicit in prior work, shows conditions on the blocks $\mathbf{B}_{[1,d]}$ and $\mathbf{B}_{[d+1,n]}$ that are sufficient to imply (H)SVP reduction of the full basis $\mathbf{B}$. Notice in particular that the decay of the Gram-Schmidt vectors guaranteed by Eq. (3) is what is needed for Item 2 of the lemma below, when $\eta = \delta^{1/(d-1)}$. And, with this same choice of η, the HSVP reduction requirement on $\mathbf{B}_{[1,d]}$ in Fact 3 is the same as the one in Item 2 of Lemma 1.

Lemma 1 (The gluing lemma). *Let* $\mathbf{B} := (\boldsymbol{b}_1, \ldots, \boldsymbol{b}_n) \in \mathbb{R}^{m \times n}$, $\alpha, \beta, \eta \geq 1$, *and* $1 \leq d \leq n$.

1. *If* $\mathbf{B}_{[d+1,n]}$ *is* β-SVP-reduced, $\|\boldsymbol{b}_1\| \leq \alpha \|\boldsymbol{b}_{d+1}^*\|$, *and* $\lambda_1(\mathcal{L}(\mathbf{B})) < \lambda_1(\mathcal{L}(\mathbf{B}_{[1,d]}))$, *then* $\mathbf{B}$ *is* $\alpha\beta$-SVP-reduced.
2. *If* $\mathbf{B}_{[1,d]}$ *is* η^{d-1}-HSVP-reduced, $\mathbf{B}_{[d+1,n]}$ *is* η^{n-d-1}-HSVP-reduced, *and* $\|\boldsymbol{b}_1\| \leq \eta^{2d}\|\boldsymbol{b}_{d+1}^*\|$, *then* $\mathbf{B}$ *is* η^{n-1}-HSVP-reduced.

Proof. For Item 1, since $\lambda_1(\mathcal{L}(\mathbf{B})) < \lambda_1(\mathcal{L}(\mathbf{B}_{[1,d]}))$, there exists a shortest nonzero vector $\boldsymbol{u} \in \mathcal{L}(\mathbf{B})$ with $\|\boldsymbol{u}\| = \lambda_1(\mathcal{L}(\mathbf{B}))$ and $\pi_d(\boldsymbol{u}) \neq 0$. Since $\mathbf{B}_{[d+1,n]}$ is β-SVP-reduced, it follows that $\|\boldsymbol{b}_{d+1}^*\|/\beta \leq \|\pi_d(\boldsymbol{u})\| \leq \|\boldsymbol{u}\| = \lambda_1(\mathcal{L}(\mathbf{B}))$. Finally, we have $\|\boldsymbol{b}_1\| \leq \alpha\|\boldsymbol{b}_{d+1}^*\| \leq \alpha\beta\lambda_1(\mathcal{L})$ as needed.

Turning to Item 2, we note that the HSVP conditions imply that $\|\boldsymbol{b}_1\|^d \leq \eta^{d(d-1)}\mathrm{vol}(\mathbf{B}_{[1,d]})$ and $\|\boldsymbol{b}_{d+1}^*\|^{n-d} \leq \eta^{(n-d)(n-d-1)}\mathrm{vol}(\mathbf{B}_{[d+1,n]})$. Using the bound on $\|\boldsymbol{b}_1\|$ relative to $\|\boldsymbol{b}_{d+1}^*\|$, we have

$$\begin{aligned}
\|\boldsymbol{b}_1\|^n &\leq \eta^{2d(n-d)}\|\boldsymbol{b}_1\|^d \cdot \|\boldsymbol{b}_{d+1}^*\|^{n-d} \\
&\leq \eta^{2(n-d)d + d(d-1) + (n-d)(n-d-1)}\mathrm{vol}(\mathbf{B}) \\
&= \eta^{n(n-1)}\mathrm{vol}(\mathbf{B}) \ ,
\end{aligned}$$

as needed.   □

2.4   The Micciancio-Walter DBKZ Algorithm

We recall Micciancio and Walter's elegant DBKZ algorithm [MW16], as we will need it later. Formally, we slightly generalize DBKZ by allowing for the use of a δ-SVP-oracle. We provide only a high-level sketch of the proof of correctness, as the full proof is the same as the proof in [MW16], with Hermite's constant γ_k replaced by $\delta^2 \gamma_k$.

Algorithm 1. The Micciancio-Walter DBKZ algorithm [MW16, Algorithm 1]

Input: A block size $k \geq 2$, number of tours N, a basis $\mathbf{B} = (\mathbf{b}_1, \cdots, \mathbf{b}_n) \in \mathbb{Z}^{m \times n}$, and access to a δ-SVP oracle for lattices with rank k.

Output: A new basis of $\mathcal{L}(\mathbf{B})$.

1: **for** $\ell = 1$ **to** N **do**
2:     **for** $i = 1$ **to** $n - k$ **do**
3:         δ-SVP-reduce $\mathbf{B}_{[i,i+k-1]}$.
4:     **end for**
5:     **for** $j = n - k + 1$ **to** 1 **do**
6:         δ-DSVP-reduce $\mathbf{B}_{[j,j+k-1]}$
7:     **end for**
8: **end for**
9: δ-SVP-reduce $\mathbf{B}_{[1,k]}$.
10: **return** $\mathbf{B}$.

Theorem 4. *For integers $n > k \geq 2$, an approximation factor $1 \leq \delta \leq 2^k$, an input basis $\mathbf{B}_0 \in \mathbb{Z}^{m \times n}$ for a lattice $\mathcal{L} \subseteq \mathbb{Z}^m$, and $N := \lceil (2n^2/(k-1)^2) \cdot \log(n \log(5\|\mathbf{B}_0\|)/\varepsilon) \rceil$ for some $\varepsilon \in [2^{-\mathrm{poly}(n)}, 1]$, Algorithm 1 outputs a basis $\mathbf{B}$ of $\mathcal{L}$ in polynomial time (excluding oracle queries) such that*

$$\|\boldsymbol{b}_1\| \leq (1 + \varepsilon) \cdot (\delta^2 \gamma_k)^{\frac{n-1}{2(k-1)}} \mathrm{vol}(\mathcal{L})^{1/n}$$

by making $N \cdot (2n - 2k + 1) + 1$ calls to the δ-SVP oracle for lattices with rank k.

Proof (Proof sketch). We briefly sketch a proof of the theorem, but we outsource the most technical step to a claim from [MW16], which was originally proven in [Neu17]. Let $\mathbf{B}^{(\ell)}$ be the basis immediately after the ℓth tour, and let $x_i^{(\ell)} := \log \mathrm{vol}(\mathbf{B}^{(\ell)}_{[1,k+i-1]}) - \frac{k+i-1}{n} \log \mathrm{vol}(\mathcal{L})$ for $i = 1, \ldots, n - k$. Let

$$y_i := \frac{(n - k - i + 1)(k + i - 1)}{k - 1} \cdot \log(\delta\sqrt{\gamma_k}) \quad \text{for} \quad i = 1, \ldots, n - k .$$

By [MW16, Claim 3] (originally proven in [Neu17]), we have

$$\max_{1 \leq i \leq n-k} \left| x_i^{(\ell)}/y_i - 1 \right| \leq (1 - \xi) \max_{1 \leq i \leq n-k} \left| x_i^{(\ell-1)}/y_i - 1 \right| ,$$

where $\xi := 1/(1 + n^2/(4k(k-1))) \geq 4(k-1)^2/(5n^2)$. Furthermore, notice that

$$\max_{1 \leq i \leq n-k} \left| x_i^{(0)}/y_i - 1 \right| \leq \frac{k(n-k) \log(5\|\mathbf{B}^{(0)}\|)}{y_1} .$$

It follows that

$$\frac{x_1^{(N)} - y_1}{y_1} \leq (1 - \xi)^N \max_{1 \leq i \leq n-k} \left| x_i^{(0)}/y_i - 1 \right|$$

$$\leq e^{-4(k-1)^2 N/(5n^2)} \cdot \frac{k(n-k) \log(5\|\mathbf{B}^{(0)}\|)}{y_1}$$

$$\leq \frac{k \log(1 + \varepsilon)}{y_1} .$$

In other words,

$$\text{vol}\big(\mathbf{B}_{[1,k]}^{(N)}\big) \le (1+\varepsilon)^k \cdot (\delta^2 \gamma_k)^{\frac{(n-k)k}{2(k-1)}} \text{vol}(\mathcal{L})^{k/n} .$$

Notice that the first vector $\boldsymbol{b}_1$ of the output basis is a δ-approximate shortest vector in $\mathcal{L}\big(\mathbf{B}_{[1,k]}^{(N)}\big)$. Therefore,

$$\|\boldsymbol{b}_1\| \le \delta\sqrt{\gamma_k} \cdot \text{vol}\big(\mathbf{B}_{[1,k]}^{(N)}\big)^{1/k} \le (1+\varepsilon)(\delta^2 \gamma_k)^{\frac{n-1}{2(k-1)}} \text{vol}(\mathcal{L})^{1/n} ,$$

as needed.   □

3   Slide Reduction for $n \le 2k$

In this section, we consider a generalization of Gama and Nguyen's slide reduction that applies to the case when $k < n \le 2k$ [GN08a]. Our definition in this case is not particularly novel or surprising, as it is essentially identical to Gama and Nguyen's except that our blocks are not the same size.[4]

What *is* surprising about this definition is that it allows us to achieve sublinear approximation factors for SVP when the rank is $n = k + q$ for $q = \Theta(k)$. Before this work, it seemed that approximation factors less than roughly $\gamma_q \approx n$ could not be achieved using the techniques of slide reduction (or, for that matter, any other known techniques with formal proofs). Indeed, our slide-reduced basis only achieves $\|\boldsymbol{b}_1\| \lesssim \gamma_q \lambda_1(\mathcal{L})$ (see [LW13, Th. 4.3.1]), which is the approximation factor resulting from the gluing lemma, Lemma 1. (This inequality is tight.) We overcome this barrier by using our additional constraints on the primal together with some additional properties of slide-reduced bases (namely, Eq. (4)) to bound $\lambda_1(\mathcal{L}(\mathbf{B}_{[1,k]}))$. Perhaps surprisingly, the resulting bound is much better than the bound on $\|\boldsymbol{b}_1\|$, which allows us to find a much shorter vector with an additional oracle call.

Definition 1 (Slide reduction). *Let $n = k + q$ where $1 \le q \le k$ are integers. A basis $\mathbf{B}$ of a lattice with rank n is (δ, k)-slide-reduced (with block size $k \ge 2$ and approximation factor $\delta \ge 1$) if it is size-reduced and satisfies the following set of conditions.*

1. *Primal conditions: The blocks $\mathbf{B}_{[1,q]}$ and $\mathbf{B}_{[i,n]}$ for $i \in [q+1, \max\{k, q+1\}]$ are δ-SVP-reduced.*
2. *Dual condition: The block $\mathbf{B}_{[2,q+1]}$ is δ-DSVP-reduced.*

---

[4] The only difference, apart from the approximation factor δ, is that we use SVP reduction instead of HKZ reduction for the primal. It is clear from the proof in [GN08a] that only SVP reduction is required, as was observed in [MW16]. We *do* require that additional blocks $\mathbf{B}_{[i,n]}$ for $q + 1 \le i \le k$ are SVP-reduced, which is quite similar to simply HKZ-reducing $\mathbf{B}_{[q+1,n]}$, but this requirement plays a distinct role in our analysis, as we discuss below.

A reader familiar with the slide reduction algorithm from [GN08a] will not be surprised to learn that such a basis can be found (up to some small slack) using polynomially many calls to a δ-SVP oracle on lattices with rank at most k. Before presenting and analyzing the algorithm, we show that such a slide-reduced basis is in fact useful for approximating SVP with sub-linear factors. (We note in passing that a slight modification of the proof of Theorem 5 yields a better result when $q = o(k)$. This does not seem very useful on its own, though, since when $q = o(k)$, the running times of our best SVP algorithms are essentially the same for rank k and rank $k + q$.)

Theorem 5. *Let $\mathcal{L}$ be a lattice with rank $n = k+q$ where $2 \leq q \leq k$ are integers. For any $\delta \geq 1$, if a basis $\mathbf{B}$ of $\mathcal{L}$ is (δ, k)-slide-reduced, then,*

$$\lambda_1(\mathcal{L}(\mathbf{B}_{[1,k]})) \leq \delta\sqrt{\gamma_k}(\delta^2\gamma_q)^{\frac{q+1}{q-1}\cdot\frac{n-k}{2k}}\lambda_1(\mathcal{L}) \ .$$

Proof. Let $\mathbf{B} = (\mathbf{b}_1, \ldots, \mathbf{b}_n)$. We distinguish two cases.

First, suppose that there exists an index $i \in [q + 1, \max\{k, q + 1\}]$ such that $\|\mathbf{b}_i^*\| > \delta\lambda_1(\mathcal{L})$. Let $\mathbf{v}$ be a shortest non-zero vector of $\mathcal{L}$. We claim that $\pi_i(\mathbf{v}) = 0$, i.e., that $\mathbf{v} \in \mathcal{L}(\mathbf{B}_{[1,i-1]})$. If this is not the case, since $\mathbf{B}_{[i,n]}$ is δ-SVP-reduced, we have that

$$\|\mathbf{b}_i^*\|/\delta \leq \|\pi_i(\mathbf{v})\| \leq \|\mathbf{v}\| = \lambda_1(\mathcal{L}),$$

which is a contradiction. Thus, we see that $\mathbf{v} \in \mathcal{L}(\mathbf{B}_{[1,i-1]}) \subseteq \mathcal{L}(\mathbf{B}_{[1,k]})$, and hence $\lambda_1(\mathcal{L}(\mathbf{B}_{[1,k]})) = \lambda_1(\mathcal{L})$ (which is much stronger than what we need).

Now, suppose that $\|\mathbf{b}_i^*\| \leq \delta\lambda_1(\mathcal{L})$ for all indices $i \in [q + 1, \max\{k, q + 1\}]$. By definition, the primal and dual conditions imply that $\mathbf{B}_{[1,q+1]}$ is $\delta\sqrt{\gamma_q}$-twin-reduced. Therefore, by Eq. (4) of Fact 3, we have

$$\text{vol}(\mathbf{B}_{[1,k]}) = \text{vol}(\mathbf{B}_{[1,q]}) \cdot \prod_{i=q+1}^{k} \|\mathbf{b}_i^*\|$$

$$\leq (\delta\sqrt{\gamma_q})^{q(q+1)/(q-1)}\|\mathbf{b}_{q+1}^*\|^q \cdot \prod_{i=q+1}^{k} \|\mathbf{b}_i^*\|$$

$$\leq (\delta^2\gamma_q)^{\frac{q+1}{q-1}\cdot\frac{n-k}{2}}(\delta\lambda_1(\mathcal{L}))^k \ ,$$

where we have used the assumption that $\|\mathbf{b}_i^*\| \leq \delta\lambda_1(L)$ for all indices $i \in [q+1, \max\{k, q+1\}]$ (and by convention we take the product to equal one in the special case when $q = k$). By the definition of Hermite's constant, this implies that

$$\lambda_1(\mathcal{L}(\mathbf{B}_{[1,k]})) \leq \sqrt{\gamma_k}\text{vol}(\mathbf{B}_{[1,k]})^{1/k} \leq \delta\sqrt{\gamma_k}(\delta^2\gamma_q)^{\frac{q+1}{q-1}\cdot\frac{n-k}{2k}}\lambda_1(\mathcal{L}) \ ,$$

as needed. $\square$

Algorithm 2. The slide reduction algorithm for $n \leq 2k$ (adapted from [GN08a, Algorithm 1])

Input: Block size k, slack $\varepsilon > 0$, approximation factor $\delta \geq 1$, a basis $\mathbf{B} = (\mathbf{b}_1, \ldots, \mathbf{b}_n) \in \mathbb{Z}^{m \times n}$ of a lattice $\mathcal{L}$ with rank $n = k + q$ where $2 \leq q \leq k$, and access to a δ-SVP oracle for lattices with rank at most k.

Output: A $((1 + \varepsilon)\delta, k)$-slide-reduced basis of $\mathcal{L}$.

1: **while** $\text{vol}(\mathbf{B}_{[1,q]})^2$ is modified by the loop **do**
2:    δ-SVP-reduce $\mathbf{B}_{[1,q]}$.
3:    **for** $i = q + 1$ **to** $\max\{k, q + 1\}$ **do**
4:       δ-SVP reduce $\mathbf{B}_{[i,n]}$.
5:    **end for**
6:    Find a new basis $C := (\mathbf{b}_1, \mathbf{c}_2, \ldots, \mathbf{c}_{q+1}, \mathbf{b}_{q+2}, \ldots, \mathbf{b}_n)$ of $\mathcal{L}$ by δ-DSVP-reducing $\mathbf{B}_{[2,q+1]}$.
7:    **if** $(1 + \varepsilon)\|\mathbf{b}_{q+1}^*\| < \|\mathbf{c}_{q+1}^*\|$ **then**
8:       $\mathbf{B} \leftarrow C$.
9:    **end if**
10: **end while**
11: **return** B.

3.1   The Slide Reduction Algorithm for $n \leq 2k$

We now present our slight generalization of Gama and Nguyen's slide reduction algorithm that works for all $k + 2 \leq n \leq 2k$.

Our proof that Algorithm 2 runs in polynomial time (excluding oracle calls) is essentially identical to the proof in [GN08a].

Theorem 6. *For $\varepsilon \geq 1/\text{poly}(n)$, Algorithm 2 runs in polynomial time (excluding oracle calls), makes polynomially many calls to its δ-SVP oracle, and outputs a $((1 + \varepsilon)\delta, k)$-slide-reduced basis of the input lattice $\mathcal{L}$.*

Proof. First, notice that if Algorithm 2 terminates, then its output must be $((1 + \varepsilon)\delta, k)$-slide-reduced. So, we only need to argue that the algorithm runs in polynomial time (excluding oracle calls).

Let $\mathbf{B}_0 \in \mathbb{Z}^{m \times n}$ be the input basis and let $\mathbf{B} \in \mathbb{Z}^{m \times n}$ denote the current basis during the execution of the algorithm. As is common in the analysis of basis reduction algorithms [LLL82, GN08a, LN14], we consider an integral potential of the form

$$P(\mathbf{B}) := \text{vol}(\mathbf{B}_{[1,q]})^2 \in \mathbb{Z}^+ .$$

The initial potential satisfies $\log P(\mathbf{B}_0) \leq 2q \cdot \log \|\mathbf{B}_0\|$, and every operation in Algorithm 2 either preserves or significantly decreases $P(\mathbf{B})$. More precisely, if the δ-DSVP-reduction step (i.e., Step 8) occurs, then the potential $P(\mathbf{B})$ decreases by a multiplicative factor of at least $(1 + \varepsilon)^2$. No other step changes $\mathcal{L}(\mathbf{B}_{[1,q]})$ or $P(\mathbf{B})$.

Therefore, Algorithm 2 updates $\mathcal{L}(\mathbf{B}_{[1,q]})$ at most $\frac{\log P(\mathbf{B}_0)}{2 \log(1+\varepsilon)}$ times, and hence it makes at most $\frac{qk \log \|\mathbf{B}_0\|}{\log(1+\varepsilon)}$ calls to the δ-SVP-oracle. From the complexity statement in Sect. 2.3, it follows that Algorithm 2 runs efficiently (excluding the running time of oracle calls). $\qquad\square$

Corollary 1. *For any constant $c \in (1/2, 1]$ and $\delta := \delta(n) \geq 1$, there is an efficient reduction from $O(\delta^{2c+1} n^c)$-SVP on lattices with rank n to δ-SVP on lattices with rank $k := \lceil n/(2c) \rceil$.*

Proof. On input (a basis for) an integer lattice $\mathcal{L} \subseteq \mathbb{Z}^m$ with rank n, the reduction first calls Algorithm 2 to compute a $((1 + \varepsilon)\delta, k)$-slide-reduced basis $\mathbf{B}$ of $\mathcal{L}$ with, say, $\varepsilon = 1/n$. The reduction then uses its δ-SVP oracle once more on $\mathbf{B}_{[1,k]}$ and returns the resulting nonzero short lattice vector.

It is immediate from Theorem 6 that this reduction is efficient, and by Theorem 5, the output vector is a δ'-approximate shortest vector, where

$$\delta' = \delta^2 \sqrt{\gamma_k} ((1 + \varepsilon)^2 \delta^2 \gamma_q)^{\frac{q+1}{q-1} \cdot \frac{n-k}{2k}} \leq O(\delta^{2c+1} n^c) \,,$$

as needed. □

4   Slide Reduction for $n \geq 2k$

We now introduce a generalized version of slide reduction for lattices with any rank $n \geq 2k$. As we explained in Sect. 1.2, at a high level, our generalization of the definition from [GN08a] is the same as the original, except that (1) our first block $\mathbf{B}_{[1,k+q]}$ is bigger than the others (out of necessity, since we can no longer divide our basis evenly into disjoint blocks of size k); and (2) we only η-HSVP reduce the first block (since we cannot afford to δ-SVP reduce a block with size larger than k). Thus, our notion of slide reduction can be restated as "the first block and the first dual block are η-(D)HSVP reduced and the rest of the basis $\mathbf{B}_{[k+q+1,n]}$ is slide-reduced in the sense of [GN08a]."[5]

However, the specific value of η that we choose in our definition below might look unnatural at first. We first present the definition and then explain where η comes from.

Definition 2 (Slide reduction). *Let n, k, p, q be integers such that $n = pk + q$ with $p, k \geq 2$ and $0 \leq q \leq k - 1$, and let $\delta \geq 1$. A basis $\mathbf{B} \in \mathbb{R}^{m \times n}$ is (δ, k)-slide-reduced if it is size-reduced and satisfies the following three sets of conditions.*

1. *Mordell conditions: The block $\mathbf{B}_{[1,k+q]}$ is η-HSVP-reduced and the block $\mathbf{B}_{[2,k+q+1]}$ is η-DHSVP-reduced for $\eta := (\delta^2 \gamma_k)^{\frac{k+q-1}{2(k-1)}}$.*
2. *Primal conditions: for all $i \in [1, p-1]$, the block $\mathbf{B}_{[ik+q+1,(i+1)k+q]}$ is δ-SVP-reduced.*
3. *Dual conditions: for all $i \in [1, p-2]$, the block $\mathbf{B}_{[ik+q+2,(i+1)k+q+1]}$ is δ-DSVP-reduced.[6]*

---

[5] Apart from the approximation factor δ, there is one minor difference between our primal conditions and those of [GN08a]. We only require the primal blocks to be SVP-reduced, while [GN08a] required them to be HKZ-reduced, which is a stronger condition. It is clear from the proof in [GN08a] that only SVP reduction is required, as was observed in [MW16].

[6] When $p = 2$, there are simply no dual conditions.

There are two ways to explain our specific choice of η. Most simply, notice that the output of the DBKZ algorithm—due to [MW16] and presented in Sect. 2.4—is η-HSVP reduced when the input basis has rank $k + q$ (up to some small slack ε). In other words, one reason that we choose this value of η is because we actually can η-HSVP reduce a block of size $k + q$ efficiently with access to a δ-SVP oracle for lattices with rank k. If we could do better, then we would in fact obtain a better algorithm, but we do not know how. Second, this value of η is natural in this context because it is the choice that "makes the final approximation factor for HSVP match the approximation factor for the first block". I.e., the theorem below shows that when we plug in this value of η, a slide-reduced basis of rank n is $(\delta^2 \gamma_k)^{\frac{n-1}{2(k-1)}}$-HSVP, which nicely matches the approximation factor of $\eta = (\delta^2 \gamma_k)^{\frac{k+q-1}{2(k-1)}}$-HSVP that we need for the first block (whose rank is $k + q$). At a technical level, this is captured by Fact 3 and Lemma 1.

Of course, the fact that these two arguments suggest the same value of η is not a coincidence. Both arguments are essentially disguised proofs of Mordell's inequality, which says that $\gamma_n \leq \gamma_k^{(n-1)/(k-1)}$ for $2 \leq k \leq n$. E.g., with $\delta = 1$ the primal Mordell condition says that b_1 yields a witness to Mordell's inequality for $\mathbf{B}_{[1,k+q]}$.

Theorem 7. *For any $\delta \geq 1$, $k \geq 2$, and $n \geq 2k$, if $\mathbf{B} = (b_1, \ldots, b_n) \in \mathbb{R}^{m \times n}$ is a (δ, k)-slide-reduced basis of a lattice $\mathcal{L}$, then*

$$\|b_1\| \leq (\delta^2 \gamma_k)^{\frac{n-1}{2(k-1)}} \operatorname{vol}(\mathcal{L})^{1/n} . \tag{5}$$

Furthermore, if $\lambda_1(\mathcal{L}(\mathbf{B}_{[1,k+q]})) > \lambda_1(\mathcal{L})$, then

$$\|b_1\| \leq \delta(\delta^2 \gamma_k)^{\frac{n-k}{k-1}} \lambda_1(\mathcal{L}) , \tag{6}$$

where $0 \leq q \leq k - 1$ is such that $n = pk + q$.

Proof. Let $d := k + q$. Theorem 9 of Appendix A shows that $\mathbf{B}_{[d+1,n]}$ is both $(\delta^2 \gamma_k)^{\frac{n-d-1}{2(k-1)}}$-HSVP-reduced and $(\delta^2 \gamma_k)^{\frac{n-d-k}{(k-1)}}$-SVP-reduced. (We relegate this theorem and its proof to the appendix because it is essentially just a restatement of [GN08a, Theorem 1], since $\mathbf{B}_{[d+1,n]}$ is effectively just a slide-reduced basis in the original sense of [GN08a].) Furthermore, $\mathbf{B}_{[1,d+1]}$ is $(\delta^2 \gamma_k)^{\frac{d-1}{2(k-1)}}$-twin-reduced, so that $\|b_1\| \leq (\delta^2 \gamma_k)^{\frac{d}{k-1}} \|b_{d+1}^*\|$. Applying Lemma 1 then yields both Eq. (5) and Eq. (6). □

4.1 The Slide Reduction Algorithm for $n \geq 2k$

We now present our slight generalization of Gama and Nguyen's slide reduction algorithm that works for all $n \geq 2k$. Our proof that the algorithm runs in polynomial time (excluding oracle calls) is essentially identical to the proof in [GN08a].

Algorithm 3. The slide-reduction algorithm for $n \geq 2k$

Input: Block size $k \geq 2$, slack $\varepsilon > 0$, approximation factor $\delta \geq 1$, basis $\mathbf{B} = (\mathbf{b}_1, \ldots, \mathbf{b}_n) \in \mathbb{Z}^{m \times n}$ of a lattice $\mathcal{L}$ of rank $n = pk + q \geq 2k$ for $0 \leq q \leq k - 1$, and access to a δ-SVP oracle for lattices with rank k.
Output: A $((1 + \varepsilon)\delta, k)$-slide-reduced basis of $\mathcal{L}(\mathbf{B})$.
 1: **while** $\mathrm{vol}(\mathbf{B}_{[1,ik+q]})^2$ is modified by the loop for some $i \in [1, p-1]$ **do**
 2:     $(1 + \varepsilon)\eta$-HSVP-reduce $\mathbf{B}_{[1,k+q]}$ using Alg. 1 for $\eta := (\delta^2 \gamma_k)^{\frac{k+q-1}{2(k-1)}}$.
 3:     **for** $i = 1$ to $p - 1$ **do**
 4:         δ-SVP-reduce $\mathbf{B}_{[ik+q+1,(i+1)k+q]}$.
 5:     **end for**
 6:     **if** $\mathbf{B}_{[2,k+q+1]}$ is not $(1 + \varepsilon)\eta$-DHSVP-reduced **then**
 7:         $(1 + \varepsilon)^{1/2}\eta$-DHSVP-reduce $\mathbf{B}_{[2,k+q+1]}$ using Alg. 1.
 8:     **end if**
 9:     **for** $i = 1$ to $p - 2$ **do**
10:         Find a new basis $\mathbf{C} := (\mathbf{b}_1, \ldots, \mathbf{b}_{ik+q+1}, \mathbf{c}_{ik+q+2}, \ldots, \mathbf{c}_{(i+1)k+q+1}, \mathbf{b}_{ik+q+2}, \ldots, \mathbf{b}_n)$
          of $\mathcal{L}$ by δ-DSVP-reducing $\mathbf{B}_{[ik+q+2,(i+1)k+q+1]}$.
11:         **if** $(1 + \varepsilon)\|\mathbf{b}^*_{(i+1)k+q+1}\| < \|\mathbf{c}^*_{(i+1)k+q+1}\|$ **then**
12:             $\mathbf{B} \leftarrow \mathbf{C}$.
13:         **end if**
14:     **end for**
15: **end while**
16: **return** $\mathbf{B}$.

Theorem 8. *For $\varepsilon \in [1/\mathrm{poly}(n), 1]$, Algorithm 3 runs in polynomial time (excluding oracle calls), makes polynomially many calls to its δ-SVP oracle, and outputs a $((1 + \varepsilon)\delta, k)$-slide-reduced basis of the input lattice $\mathcal{L}$.*

Proof. First, notice that if Algorithm 3 terminates, then its output is $((1+\varepsilon)\delta, k)$-slide-reduced. So, we only need to argue that the algorithm runs in polynomial time (excluding oracle calls).

Let $\mathbf{B}_0 \in \mathbb{Z}^{m \times n}$ be the input basis and let $\mathbf{B} \in \mathbb{Z}^{m \times n}$ denote the current basis during the execution of Algorithm 3. As is common in the analysis of basis reduction algorithms [LLL82, GN08a, LN14], we consider an integral potential of the form

$$P(\mathbf{B}) := \prod_{i=1}^{p-1} \mathrm{vol}(\mathbf{B}_{[1,ik+q]})^2 \in \mathbb{Z}^+.$$

The initial potential satisfies $\log P(\mathbf{B}_0) \leq 2n^2 \cdot \log \|\mathbf{B}_0\|$, and every operation in Algorithm 3 either preserves or significantly decreases $P(\mathbf{B})$. In particular, the potential is unaffected by the primal steps (i.e., Steps 2 and 4), which leave $\mathrm{vol}(\mathbf{B}_{[1,ik+q]})$ unchanged for all i. The dual steps (i.e., Steps 7 and 12) either leave $\mathrm{vol}(\mathbf{B}_{[1,ik+q]})$ for all i or decrease $P(\mathbf{B})$ by a multiplicative factor of at least $(1 + \varepsilon)$.

Therefore, Algorithm 2 updates $\mathrm{vol}(\mathbf{B}_{[1,ik+q]})$ for some i at most $\log P(\mathbf{B}_0)/\log(1+\varepsilon)$ times. Hence, it makes at most $4pn^2 \log \|\mathbf{B}_0\| / \log(1+\varepsilon)$ calls to the SVP oracle in the SVP and DSVP reduction steps (i.e., Steps 4 and 12), and similarly at most $4n^2 \log \|\mathbf{B}_0\| / \log(1+\varepsilon)$ calls to Algorithm 1. From the complexity statement in Sect. 2.3, it follows that Algorithm 2 runs efficiently (excluding the running time of oracle calls), as needed.

$\square$

Corollary 2. *For any constant $c \geq 1$ and $\delta := \delta(n) \geq 1$, there is an efficient reduction from $O(\delta^{2c+1}n^c)$-SVP on lattices with rank n to δ-SVP on lattices with rank $k := \lfloor n/(c+1) \rfloor$.*

Proof. On input (a basis for) an integer lattice $\mathcal{L} \subseteq \mathbb{Z}^m$ with rank n, the reduction first calls Algorithm 3 to compute a $((1 + \varepsilon)\delta, k)$-slide-reduced basis $\mathbf{B} = (\mathbf{b}_1, \cdots, \mathbf{b}_n)$ of $\mathcal{L}$ with, say, $\varepsilon = 1/n$. Then, the reduction uses the procedure from Corollary 1 on the lattice $\mathcal{L}(\mathbf{B}_{[1,2k]})$ with $c = 1$ (i.e., slide reduction on a lattice with rank $2k$), to find a vector $\boldsymbol{v} \in \mathcal{L}(\mathbf{B}_{[1,2k]})$ with $0 < \|\boldsymbol{v}\| \leq O(\delta^3 n)\lambda_1(\mathcal{L}(\mathbf{B}_{[1,2k]}))$. Finally, the reduction outputs the shorter of the two vectors $\mathbf{b}_1$ and $\boldsymbol{v}$.

It is immediate from Corollary 1 and Theorem 8 that this reduction is efficient. To prove correctness, we consider two cases.

First, suppose that $\lambda_1(\mathcal{L}(\mathbf{B}_{[1,k+q]})) = \lambda_1(\mathcal{L})$. Then,

$$\|\boldsymbol{v}\| \leq O(\delta^3 n)\lambda_1(\mathcal{L}(\mathbf{B}_{[1,2k]})) \leq O(\delta^{2c+1}n^c)\lambda_1(\mathcal{L}) ,$$

so that the algorithm will output a $O(\delta^{2c+1}n^c)$-approximate shortest vector.

On the other hand, if $\lambda_1(\mathcal{L}(\mathbf{B}_{[1,k+q]})) > \lambda_1(\mathcal{L})$, then by Theorem 7, we have

$$\|\boldsymbol{b}_1\| \leq (1 + \varepsilon)\delta((1 + \varepsilon)^2\delta^2\gamma_k)^{\frac{n-k}{k-1}}\lambda_1(\mathcal{L}) \leq O(\delta^{2c+1}n^c) ,$$

so that the algorithm also outputs a $O(\delta^{2c+1}n^c)$-approximate shortest vector in this case.

$\square$

A   Properties of Gama and Nguyen's Slide Reduction

In the theorem below, $\mathbf{B}_{[d+1,n]}$ is essentially just a slide-reduced basis in the sense of [GN08a]. So, the following is more-or-less just a restatement of [GN08a, Theorem 1].

Theorem 9. *Let $\mathbf{B} = (\boldsymbol{b}_1, \ldots, \boldsymbol{b}_n) \in \mathbb{R}^{m \times n}$ with $n = pk + d$ for some $p \geq 1$ and $d \geq k$ be (δ, k)-slide reduced in the sense of Definition 2. Then,*

$$\|\mathbf{b}_{d+1}^*\| \leq (\delta^2\gamma_k)^{ik/(k-1)}\|\mathbf{b}_{ik+d+1}^*\| \text{ for } 0 \leq i \leq p-1 , \tag{7}$$

$$\|\mathbf{b}_{d+1}^*\| \leq (\delta^2\gamma_k)^{\frac{n-d-1}{2(k-1)}}\text{vol}(\mathbf{B}_{[d+1,n]})^{1/(n-d)} , \text{ and} \tag{8}$$

$$\|\mathbf{b}_{d+1}^*\| \leq \delta(\delta^2\gamma_k)^{\frac{n-d-k}{k-1}}\lambda_1(\mathcal{L}(\mathbf{B}_{[d+1,n]})) . \tag{9}$$

Proof. By definition, for each $i \in [0, p-2]$, the block $\mathbf{B}_{[ik+d+1,(i+1)k+d+1]}$ is $\delta\sqrt{\gamma_k}$-twin-reduced. By Eq. (3) of Fact 3, we see that

$$\|\boldsymbol{b}_{ik+d+1}^*\| \leq (\delta\sqrt{\gamma_k})^{2k/(k-1)}\|\boldsymbol{b}_{(i+1)k+d+1}^*\| ,$$

which implies (7) by induction.

We prove (8) and (9) by induction over p. If $p = 1$, then both inequalities hold as $\mathbf{B}_{[d+1,n]}$ is δ-SVP reduced by the definition of slide reduction. Now, assume that Eqs. (8) and (9) hold for some $p \geq 1$. Let $n = (p+1)k + d$. Then $\mathbf{B}$ satisfies the requirements of the theorem with $d' := d + k$. Therefore, by the induction hypothesis, we have

$$\|\mathbf{b}^*_{d+k+1}\| \leq (\delta^2 \gamma_k)^{\frac{n-d-k-1}{2(k-1)}} \operatorname{vol}(\mathbf{B}_{[d+k+1,n]})^{1/(n-d-k)} \text{ , and}$$

$$\|\mathbf{b}^*_{d+k+1}\| \leq \delta(\delta^2 \gamma_k)^{\frac{n-d-2k}{k-1}} \lambda_1(\mathcal{L}(\mathbf{B}_{[d+k+1,n]})) \text{ .}$$

Since $\mathbf{B}_{[d+1,d+k]}$ is $\delta\sqrt{\gamma_k}$-HSVP reduced, we may apply Lemma 1.2 with $\eta = (\delta^2 \gamma_k)^{\frac{1}{2(k-1)}}$, which proves (8) for $\mathbf{B}_{[d+1,n]}$.

Furthermore, if $\lambda_1(\mathcal{L}(\mathbf{B}_{[d+1,n]})) < \lambda_1(\mathcal{L}(\mathbf{B}_{[d+1,d+k]}))$, it follows from Lemma 1.1 that $\mathbf{B}_{[d+1,n]}$ is δ'-SVP-reduced for

$$\delta' = (\delta^2 \gamma_k)^{k/(k-1)} \cdot \delta(\delta^2 \gamma_k)^{\frac{n-d-2k}{k-1}} = \delta(\delta^2 \gamma_k)^{\frac{n-d-k}{k-1}} \text{ ,}$$

as needed. If not, then $\lambda_1(\mathcal{L}(\mathbf{B}_{[d+1,n]})) = \lambda_1(\mathcal{L}(\mathbf{B}_{[d+1,d+k]}))$, and $\|\mathbf{b}^*_{d+1}\| \leq \delta\lambda_1(\mathcal{L}(\mathbf{B}_{[d+1,n]}))$ because $\mathbf{B}_{[d+1,d+k]}$ is δ-SVP reduced. In all cases, we proved (9). This completes the proof of Theorem 9. □

References

[ADRS15] Aggarwal, D., Dadush, D., Regev, O., Stephens-Davidowitz, N.: Solving the shortest vector problem in 2^n time via discrete gaussian sampling. In: STOC (2015). http://arxiv.org/abs/1412.7994

[Ajt96] Ajtai, M.: Generating hard instances of lattice problems. In: STOC (1996)

[AKS01] Ajtai, M., Kumar, R., Sivakumar, D.: A sieve algorithm for the shortest lattice vector problem. In: STOC (2001)

[AS18] Aggarwal, D., Stephens-Davidowitz, N.: Just take the average! An embarrassingly simple 2^n-time algorithm for SVP (and CVP). In: SOSA (2018). http://arxiv.org/abs/1709.01535

[BDGL16] Becker, A., Ducas, L., Gama, N., Laarhoven, T.: New directions in nearest neighbor searching with applications to lattice sieving. In: SODA (2016)

[CN12] Chen, Y., Nguyen, P.Q.: Faster algorithms for approximate common divisors: breaking fully-homomorphic-encryption challenges over the integers. In: Pointcheval, D., Johansson, T. (eds.) EUROCRYPT 2012. LNCS, vol. 7237, pp. 502–519. Springer, Heidelberg (2012). https://doi.org/10.1007/978-3-642-29011-4_30

[DPV11] Dadush, D., Peikert, C., Vempala, S.: Enumerative lattice algorithms in any norm via M-ellipsoid coverings. In: FOCS (2011)

[GHKN06] Gama, N., Howgrave-Graham, N., Koy, H., Nguyen, P.Q.: Rankin's constant and blockwise lattice reduction. In: Dwork, C. (ed.) CRYPTO 2006. LNCS, vol. 4117, pp. 112–130. Springer, Heidelberg (2006). https://doi.org/10.1007/11818175_7

[GHN06] Gama, N., Howgrave-Graham, N., Nguyen, P.Q.: Symplectic lattice reduction and NTRU. In: Vaudenay, S. (ed.) EUROCRYPT 2006. LNCS, vol. 4004, pp. 233–253. Springer, Heidelberg (2006). https://doi.org/10.1007/11761679_15

[GN08a] Gama, N., Nguyen, P.Q.: Finding short lattice vectors within Mordell's inequality. In: STOC (2008)

[GN08b] Gama, N., Nguyen, P.Q.: Predicting lattice reduction. In: Smart, N. (ed.) EUROCRYPT 2008. LNCS, vol. 4965, pp. 31–51. Springer, Heidelberg (2008). https://doi.org/10.1007/978-3-540-78967-3_3

[GPV08] Gentry, C., Peikert, C., Vaikuntanathan, V.: Trapdoors for hard lattices and new cryptographic constructions. In: STOC (2008). https://eprint.iacr.org/2007/432

[HPS11] Hanrot, G., Pujol, X., Stehlé, D.: Analyzing blockwise lattice algorithms using dynamical systems. In: Rogaway, P. (ed.) CRYPTO 2011. LNCS, vol. 6841, pp. 447–464. Springer, Heidelberg (2011). https://doi.org/10.1007/978-3-642-22792-9_25

[JS98] Joux, A., Stern, J.: Lattice reduction: a toolbox for the cryptanalyst. J. Cryptol. 11(3), 161–185 (1998). https://doi.org/10.1007/s001459900042

[Kan83] Kannan, R.: Improved algorithms for integer programming and related lattice problems. In: STOC (1983)

[Len83] Lenstra Jr., H.W.: Integer programming with a fixed number of variables. Math. Oper. Res. 8(4), 538–548 (1983)

[LLL82] Lenstra, A.K., Lenstra Jr., H.W., Lovász, L.: Factoring polynomials with rational coefficients. Math. Ann. 261(4), 515–534 (1982)

[LN14] Li, J., Nguyen, P.Q.: Approximating the densest sublattice from Rankin's inequality. LMS J. Comput. Math. 17(Special Issue A) (2014). Contributed to ANTS-XI, 2014

[LN19] Li, J., Nguyen, P.Q.: Computing a lattice basis revisited. In: ISSAC (2019)

[Lov86] Lovász, L.: An Algorithmic Theory of Numbers, Graphs and Convexity. Society for Industrial and Applied Mathematics, Philadelphia (1986)

[LW13] Li, J., Wei, W.: Slide reduction, successive minima and several applications. Bull. Aust. Math. Soc. 88, 390–406 (2013)

[LWXZ11] Liu, M., Wang, X., Xu, G., Zheng, X.: Shortest lattice vectors in the presence of gaps (2011). http://eprint.iacr.org/2011/139

[MV13] Micciancio, D., Voulgaris, P.: A deterministic single exponential time algorithm for most lattice problems based on Voronoi cell computations. SIAM J. Comput. 42(3), 1364–1391 (2013)

[MW16] Micciancio, D., Walter, M.: Practical, predictable lattice basis reduction. In: Fischlin, M., Coron, J.-S. (eds.) EUROCRYPT 2016. LNCS, vol. 9665, pp. 820–849. Springer, Heidelberg (2016). https://doi.org/10.1007/978-3-662-49890-3_31. http://eprint.iacr.org/2015/1123

[Neu17] Neumaier, A.: Bounding basis reduction properties. Des. Codes Cryptogr. 84(1), 237–259 (2016). https://doi.org/10.1007/s10623-016-0273-9

[NIS18] Computer Security Division NIST: Post-quantum cryptography (2018). https://csrc.nist.gov/Projects/Post-Quantum-Cryptography

[NS01] Nguyen, P.Q., Stern, J.: The two faces of lattices in cryptology. In: Silverman, J.H. (ed.) CaLC 2001. LNCS, vol. 2146, pp. 146–180. Springer, Heidelberg (2001). https://doi.org/10.1007/3-540-44670-2_12

[NV08] Nguyen, P.Q., Vidick, T.: Sieve algorithms for the shortest vector problem are practical. J. Math. Cryptol. 2(2), 181–207 (2008)

[NV10] Nguyen, P.Q., Vallée, B. (eds.): The LLL Algorithm: Survey and Applications. Springer, Heidelberg (2010). https://doi.org/10.1007/978-3-642-02295-1

[Odl90] Odlyzko, A.M.: The rise and fall of knapsack cryptosystems. Cryptol. Comput. Number Theory **42**, 75–88 (1990)

[Pei09] Peikert, C.: Public-key cryptosystems from the worst-case shortest vector problem. In: STOC (2009)

[Pei16] Peikert, C.: A decade of lattice cryptography. Found. Trends Theor. Comput. Sci. **10**(4), 283–424 (2016)

[PS09] Pujol, X., Stehlé, D.: Solving the shortest lattice vector problem in time $2^{2.465n}$ (2009). http://eprint.iacr.org/2009/605

[Reg09] Regev, O.: On lattices, learning with errors, random linear codes, and cryptography. J. ACM **56**(6), 1–40 (2009)

[Sch87] Schnorr, C.-P.: A hierarchy of polynomial time lattice basis reduction algorithms. Theor. Comput. Sci. **53**(23), 201–224 (1987)

[SE94] Schnorr, C.-P., Euchner, M.: Lattice basis reduction: improved practical algorithms and solving subset sum problems. Math. Program. **66**, 181–199 (1994). https://doi.org/10.1007/BF01581144

[Sha84] Shamir, A.: A polynomial-time algorithm for breaking the basic Merkle-Hellman cryptosystem. IEEE Trans. Inform. Theory **30**(5), 699–704 (1984)

[WLW15] Wei, W., Liu, M., Wang, X.: Finding shortest lattice vectors in the presence of gaps. In: Nyberg, K. (ed.) CT-RSA 2015. LNCS, vol. 9048, pp. 239–257. Springer, Cham (2015). https://doi.org/10.1007/978-3-319-16715-2_13

Rounding in the Rings

Feng-Hao Liu and Zhedong Wang$^{(\boxtimes)}$

Florida Atlantic University, Boca Raton, FL, USA
{fenghao.liu,wangz}@fau.edu

Abstract. In this work, we conduct a comprehensive study on establishing hardness reductions for (Module) Learning with Rounding over rings (RLWR). Towards this, we present an algebraic framework of LWR, inspired by a recent work of Peikert and Pepin (TCC '19). Then we show a search-to-decision reduction for Ring-LWR, generalizing a result in the plain LWR setting by Bogdanov et al. (TCC '15). Finally, we show a reduction from Ring-LWE to Module Ring-LWR (even for leaky secrets), generalizing the plain LWE to LWR reduction by Alwen et al. (Crypto '13). One of our central techniques is a new ring leftover hash lemma, which might be of independent interests.

1 Introduction

Lattice-based cryptography has attracted significant attention due to its nice mathematical structure and versatility – first it is one of very few promising candidates against quantum algorithms [42], and moreover, it serves as a solid foundation on which a wide range of (advanced) crypto systems can be based, e.g., [36]. Particularly, many lattice-based crypto systems are directly based on the *learning with error* (LWE) problem [40], which enjoys search-to-decision reductions [29,30,33,40] and as well worst-case hardness from some lattice problems, under quantum or classical reductions [10,33,40]. With these results, we are more confident in the hardness of LWE, both the decision and search forms, and thus the derived LWE-based crypto systems.

However, the "plain" LWE-based solutions are usually considered impractical due to the large keys/parameters and the requirement of performing rather complicated Gaussian samplings (albeit significant improvements in recent years [23–25,30,31,34]). To tackle these two technical challenges, researchers have proposed other efficient variants of LWE:

- LWE over rings (Ring-LWE). This problem [26] is a compact variant of the plain LWE specialized in some ring in a number field. This Ring-LWE based schemes have significantly smaller keys, and computation of ring multiplications can be further accelerated by Fast Fourier Transform [27]. These advantages make Ring-LWE one of the most competitive candidates for developing practical post-quantum crypto schemes.
- Learning with rounding (LWR). This problem [6] is a de-randomized variant of the plain LWE, where random errors are replaced by the deterministic

© International Association for Cryptologic Research 2020
D. Micciancio and T. Ristenpart (Eds.): CRYPTO 2020, LNCS 12171, pp. 296–326, 2020.
https://doi.org/10.1007/978-3-030-56880-1_11

rounding. Many crypto systems can be naturally derived from LWR, such as pseudorandom functions [6], lossy trapdoor functions, reusable extractors, and deterministic encryption [3]. As these systems do not require Gaussian samplings, they are in general much easier to implement and more efficient.

A natural combination of these two is *learning with rounding over rings* (Ring-LWR), which in fact has been proposed in the original LWR work [6] as a more efficient version of the plain LWR. Moreover, several submissions to the NIST's post-quantum competition have built their schemes with competitive efficiency from Ring-LWR (or a more general Module Ring-LWR), such as [7,18] (round 2 submissions). Thus, Ring-LWR is also a promising direction towards developing practical post-quantum solutions.

Even though Ring-LWR provides substantial efficiency gains, our understanding about its hardness is rather limited, compared with what we have developed in the Ring-LWE [26,38] and plain LWR [3,5,6,8] settings. To fully enjoy the efficiency brought from the ring structure, it is necessary to determine whether the additional structure would weaken the underlying hard problem. Toward this goal, this work focuses on the following endeavor:

Main Task: Determine the hardness of Ring-LWR.

While Ring-LWE/LWR and plain LWE/LWR share many nice mathematical features, establishing hardness results in the ring settings is however tricky. As there are several ad-hoc instantiations of Ring-LWE that can be broken by relatively simple attacks [11–13,20,21], the selection of parameters can be much subtler than in the plain LWE/LWR setting. To handle this, the work [35] conducted a comprehensive research about the existing attacks and hardness results, and then pointed out that several instantiations of Ring-LWE that have security reductions (e.g., from some worst-case ideal lattice problems [26,38]) avoid all the known attacks. Thus, establishing meaningful security reductions would not only guarantee theoretic hardness but also provide important guidance of how to avoid vulnerabilities, which is significant in practical applications. Motivated by this, we then focus on how to build meaningful reductions for Ring-LWR.

Challenges for Ring-LWR. We know a simple reduction from (Ring)-LWE to (Ring)-LWR if the ratio of the moduli q/p is super-polynomial [6]. This parameter setting however, requires larger dimension n for the security need of the underlying (Ring)-LWE [1] (and its derived schemes). To achieve better efficiency, the community then turned to determine the hardness of LWR for polynomial moduli, and in subsequent work [3,5,8] several significant reductions have been developed for plain LWR. Unfortunately, these results cannot be generalized to the ring setting for various technical reasons as we summarize below.

– The work [8] derived a search-to-decision reduction for LWR, meaning that LWR is pseudorandom as long as it is one-way. This reduction relies on the ability to predict a random linear function over the secret given the help of the distinguisher of LWR. This property however, does not hold in the ring setting, as there are super-polynomially many possibilities of $r \cdot s$ for some random ring element r (as a random function) and secret s. Even though there is a reduction of search Ring-LWE to search Ring-LWR via Rényi Distance (RD) [8], there is still a disconnection for proving pseudorandom of Ring-LWR from Ring-LWE, even for bounded samples.

- The work [3] takes another approach, proving that the plain LWR remains pseudorandom (for bounded samples), even if the secret comes from an imperfect source (yet with sufficient min entropy). Their result relies on the leftover hash lemma over $\mathbb{Z}_q$ (i.e., inner product in $\mathbb{Z}_q$ is a strong extractor), which does not generalize to the ring setting. This is a critical technical obstacle for porting the LWR results [3] to the ring setting. How to analyze the ring setting was explicitly left as an open interesting question [3].

To mitigate the gap between plain LWR and Ring-LWR, a recent work [14] introduced a new variant called Computational Ring-LWR, which captures security of the following concept – an adversary's winning probability remains similar in a computation game (of some search problem), no matter whether the challenge is generated by using Ring-LWR samples as randomness or truly random samples. The work [14] showed that security of Computational Ring-LWR can be based on Search Ring-LWE via an RD analysis, and can be used to analyze security of several NIST submissions.

This approach still leaves several fundamental questions. For example, whether Ring-LWR is pseudorandom under some more well-studied assumptions remains elusive. As a result, we do not know the core reason why the computational Ring-LWR is hard – maybe Ring-LWR is already pseudorandom, or maybe it is not pseudorandom yet just does not give significant help to solve other computational problems. Additionally, the computational nature of the problem is usually inconvenient to analyze indistinguishability-based security (e.g., security of an encryption scheme or a PRF), as we need to reduce indistinguishability from the search problem. Usually, this is not an easy task, and might require the help of random oracles as the examples in the work [14]. It remains unclear whether the computational Ring-LWR can be used *natively* to analyze indistinguishability-based security in the plain model.

1.1   Our Contributions

In this work, we conduct a systematic study on the (Module) Ring-LWR problem (and its generalizations), even in the presence of leakage (weak secret). The problem can be described in the following form: determine whether samples of $(\boldsymbol{a}, \lfloor \boldsymbol{a} \cdot \boldsymbol{s} \rceil)$ are pseudorandom, where $\lfloor \cdot \rceil$ is some rounding function from modulo q to modulo p, and $\boldsymbol{a}, \boldsymbol{s}$ are vectors of size k from some appropriate spaces (e.g., the ring of integers of some number field). For an appropriate ring and $k = 1$, the problem is specialized to Ring-LWR, and for general $k > 1$, Module Ring-LWR. Below we describe our contributions.

Contribution 1. As a warm up, we show that the algebraic LWE framework of Peikert and Pepin [37] is portable to the setting of LWR while preserving many important reduction results. Below we elaborate.

Following the notion of Module $\mathcal{L}$-LWE, we define Module $\mathcal{L}$-LWR for a certain number field lattice $\mathcal{L}$ – in this case, we have $s \in (\mathcal{L}_q^\vee)^k$ and $a \in (\mathcal{O}_q^{\mathcal{L}})^k$ where $\mathcal{L}^\vee$ denotes the dual of $\mathcal{L}$, $\mathcal{O}^{\mathcal{L}}$ denotes the coefficient ring, and q is some modulus. By using this notion, we are able to express Ring-, Module-, Order-, and Poly-LWR in a natural way, similar to the Module $\mathcal{L}$-LWE framework [37]. (We refer the readers to the work [37] for more discussions for why we use the dual lattice space $\mathcal{L}^\vee$.) Next, we prove the following two $\mathcal{L}$-LWR reductions similar to those for $\mathcal{L}$-LWE [37]:

- a reduction from Module $\mathcal{L}$-LWR to Module $\mathcal{L}'$-LWR for $\mathcal{L}' \subseteq \mathcal{L}$, assuming the modulus q is co-prime with the index $|\mathcal{L}/\mathcal{L}'|$, and
- a reduction from $\mathcal{O}$-LWR to Middle-product-LWR for an order $\mathcal{O}$ with a (tweaked) power basis.

As the ring of integers $\mathcal{O}_K$ is the maximal Order in a number field K, via these reductions the hardness of (Module) Ring-LWR would imply that of (Module) $\mathcal{O}'$-LWR for any other Order $\mathcal{O}'$ as well as that of the Middle-Product-LWR [4]. Thus, our main focus would be the hardness of (Module) Ring-LWR, as it would imply hardness of many other variants.

An important add-on. In addition to the above generalization to $\mathcal{L}$-LWR from the work [37], we add an *important* specification to the procedure of rounding a ring element – we must specify a basis $\mathbf{B} = \{b_i\}_{i \in [n]}$ to which the ring element is rounded with respect. More specifically, we define rounding a ring element α with respect to $\mathbf{B}$ as the following steps:

1. Interpret $\alpha = \sum_{i \in [n]} a_i b_i$ for $a_i \in \mathbb{Z}_q$.
2. Output $\lfloor \alpha \rceil = \sum_{i \in [n]} \lfloor a_i \rceil b_i$.

As the selection of basis can affect our reduction results, either in parameter quality or even feasibility, this specification is critical. While all known prior work [2,6,8] (to our knowledge) used the coefficient embedding (the power basis), our hardness results would suggest to work with alternative bases for certain parameters as required by the reductions.

Below we do two important case studies: (1) Ring-LWR without leakage, and (2) (Module) Ring-LWR with leakage. These results will provide as hardness foundations for further algebraic structured LWR via the reduction above, such as Order-, Poly-, Middle-Product-, and many other possible variants of LWR.

Contribution 2. We identify a sufficient condition and prove a search-to-decision reduction for Ring-LWR. Thus under this condition, Ring-LWR is pseudorandom as long as it is one-way, generalizing a plain LWR result of [8].

Particularly, let $R = \mathcal{O}_K$ be the ring of integers over some Galois extension K, and p be a polynomial-sized modulus such that $p|q$ and $\langle p \rangle$ completely splits[1] over $\mathcal{O}_K$, i.e., $p\mathcal{O}_K = \mathfrak{p}_1 \mathfrak{p}_2 \ldots \mathfrak{p}_n$ for n being the dimension of $K/\mathbb{Q}$, and $\mathbf{B}$ be a *normal integral basis* of K. Then there exists a search-to-decision reduction

---

[1] Actually the result is more general, as the reduction only requires that $\langle p \rangle$ splits into a product of *small* ideals.

for Ring-LWR when rounding is with respect to the basis **B**. Furthermore, the quality/parameters of the reduction depend on a certain "norm" of **B**, which is the shorter the better.

We next derive a search Ring-LWE to search Ring-LWR reduction via an RD analysis[2], yet this only holds for a bounded number of samples. Our search-to-decision Ring-LWR however, is not sample preserving, as the number of samples depends on the advantage of the decision Ring-LWR distinguisher. Thus, combining the two reductions can only derive a search Ring-LWE to $1/\lambda^c$-secure decision Ring-LWR, i.e., hardness of Ring-LWE can only guarantee weak pseudorandomness of Ring-LWR. Nevertheless, we can apply the hardness amplification technique of [43] to achieve $\mathsf{negl}(\lambda)$-security by a parallel repetition up to $\omega(1)$ times. This would give us a modular way to design fully secure schemes such as PRFs from Ring-LWR, based on the hardness of Ring-LWE.

On the other hand, by the Hilbert-Speiser and Kronecker-Weber theorems, normal integral bases only exist for certain cyclotomic fields (and their subfields), and moreover, a field K might have multiple normal integral bases [22]. We can choose a good one using the idea of [27]. Moreover, by selecting appropriate rounding functions, the hardness result can be generalized to the case of cyclotomic fields of power of 2, which do not have normal integer bases. We discuss these in details in Sect. 4.3.

Contribution 3. Next we study whether Ring-LWR holds under leakage. Towards this goal, we show a negative result for Ring-LWR (i.e., $k = 1$). Next, we prove some positive results for Module Ring-LWR (for bounded samples) of larger dimensions k's.

For Ring-LWR such that $\langle p \rangle$ completely splits, we do have a search-to-decision reduction, and a hardness guarantee from Ring-LWR (even just $1/\lambda^c$-security) as Contribution 2. However, if information of $\{s \bmod \mathfrak{p}_i\}$'s for a constant fraction of the ideals is leaked, then one can apply a similar attack as [9] to break search LWR completely given only one sample, with a significant probability. Thus, only an entropy lower bound is not sufficient to derive hardness of Ring-LWR against general leakage of say $0.1 \cdot n \log q$ bits.

On the other hand for larger k's, we show that Module Ring-LWR remains pseudorandom under leakage assuming (Module) Ring-LWE (in some cases, $k = 1$, namely Ring-LWE, is sufficient!). Towards this goal, we prove a general ring leftover hash lemma, showing that the inner product over ring elements is a strong extractor, as long as the source, when taken modulo over *any ideal factor* of $p\mathcal{O}_K$, has sufficient entropy. The leftover hash lemma holds regardless of how $p\mathcal{O}_K$ factors, as its factoring only affects the parameters but not feasibility. More interestingly, it also does not require K to be Galois extension as required by

---

[2] A similar reduction appeared in the work [8], but their Ring-LWE* adds errors in the coefficient-embedding space. "The" Ring-LWE of [26] suggests to add errors in the canonical-embedding space. A direct application of the analysis [8] to "the" Ring-LWE setting would result in significantly worse parameters, e.g., [14] took this approach and can only analyze the case with a constant number of samples.

the search-to-decision reduction in Contribution 2. By using this new leftover hash lemma, we generalize the plain LWR result [3] to the Ring setting, showing Module Ring-LWR is pseudorandom, even for entropic secrets under certain appropriate conditions. Similar to the result of [3], our analysis requires the number of samples to be smaller to the modulus q, and thus the reduction holds for a fixed number of samples.

Our ring leftover hash lemma generalizes prior work [27–29], and might be of independent interests. We further elaborate on our improvements over prior results in the next section.

1.2   Technical Overview

We overview the most interesting techniques in Contributions 2 and 3.

Search-to-decision Reduction for Ring-LWR. We first give an overview of our first reduction when $\langle q \rangle$ completely splits. Our reduction follows the search-to-decision framework of Ring-LWE [26], but makes several important changes.

Let K be a Galois extension over $\mathbb{Q}$ with dimension n, $\mathbf{B}$ be a normal integral basis of K, $p|q$ such that the rounding $\lfloor \cdot \rceil$ maps ring elements from modulo q to modulo p, and $\langle p \rangle = \mathfrak{p}_1 \ldots \mathfrak{p}_n$. Our reduction uses two intermediate problems: (W)-$\mathfrak{p}_i$-RLWR and (W)-D-RLWR^i, where the former is the problem of finding s mod $\mathfrak{p}_i$ (for worst-case secret s), and the latter is to distinguish $(a, \lfloor a \cdot s \rceil + h_i)$ from $(a, \lfloor a \cdot s \rceil + h_{i+1})$ for h_j being a distribution that is uniformly random over modulo $\mathfrak{p}_1 \ldots \mathfrak{p}_j$ and 0 over modulo $\mathfrak{p}_{j+1} \ldots \mathfrak{p}_n$, for the worst-case secret. Then, our reduction follows the path below:

$$\text{Search-RLWR} \xrightarrow{(1)} \text{(W)-}\mathfrak{p}_i\text{-RLWR} \xrightarrow{(2)} \text{(W)-D-RLWR}^i \xrightarrow{(3)} \text{Decision-RLWR.}$$

We first note that (3) follows from a simple hybrid argument and a worst-case to average-case re-randomization (as the work [8]); (2) can be derived by a similar technique use in the work [26]. Thus in this section, we just overview the most interesting part (1).

Essentially, we would like to show that suppose one can find s mod $\mathfrak{p}_i$ for some ideal $\mathfrak{p}_i$, then he can find s mod $\mathfrak{p}_j$ for all the other ideals, and thus by the Chinese Remainder Theorem, find s mod $\langle p \rangle$. This idea can be achieved in the Ring-LWE case [26] by using the fact that automorphisms in Galois extensions permutes ideals, i.e., for every $i, j \in [n]$, there exists an automorphism σ such that $\mathfrak{p}_i = \sigma(\mathfrak{p}_j)$. Fixed such i, j and σ, the reduction works as follows: given a sample $(a, b = as + e)$, the reduction computes $a' = \sigma(a), b' = \sigma(b) = \sigma(a) \cdot \sigma(s) + \sigma(e)$, by the homomorphic property of the automorphism. The work [26] chooses e in the canonical embedding space such that the distribution of $\sigma(e)$ remains the same for every automorphism. Therefore, the (W)-$\mathfrak{p}_i$-RLWE solver on input (a', b') would return $s' = \sigma(s)$ mod $\mathfrak{p}_i$. Then by a simple calculation we have $\sigma^{-1}(s') = s$ mod $\mathfrak{p}_j$.

In the RLWR case, we have $(a, b = \lfloor as \rceil)$, and can still compute $(a' = \sigma(a), b' = \sigma(b))$. However, the required equation $\sigma(b) = \lfloor \sigma(s)\sigma(a) \rceil$ might not hold as σ and $\lfloor \cdot \rceil$ might not commute in general. Consequently, (a', b') might not be a valid RLWR instance, which the underlying (W)-$\mathfrak{p}_i$-RLWR solver might fail to solve. Thus, the straight-forward analysis would break down.

To tackle this issue, we prove a key fact that as long as the rounding is with respect to a normal integral basis **B**, then rounding and automorphisms commute. This suffices to bring the Ring-LWE result to the Ring-LWR. Below we describe our insights.

Recall that **B** is a normal integral basis if it is $\mathbb{Z}$-bases that can be represented as $\{b_i = \sigma_i(\gamma)\}_{i \in [n]}$ for some $\gamma \in \mathcal{O}_K$. Every element $x \in \mathcal{O}_K$ can be written as $\sum_{i \in [n]} x_i b_i$ for $x_i \in \mathbb{Z}$. If rounding is with respect to **B**, we have:

$$\sigma(\lfloor x \rceil) = \sigma\Big(\sum_{i \in [n]} \lfloor x_i \rceil b_i \Big) = \sum_{i \in [n]} \lfloor x_i \rceil \sigma(b_i).$$

We next observe that $\sigma(\mathbf{B}) = \mathbf{B}$ (up to some re-ordering), as σ just permutes the normal integral basis. Thus we can further re-write the above equation as:

$$\Big\lfloor \sum_{i \in [n]} x_i \sigma(b_i) \Big\rceil = \Big\lfloor \sigma\Big(\sum_{i \in [n]} x_i b_i \Big) \Big\rceil = \lfloor \sigma(x) \rceil.$$

This proves what we desired.

Module Ring-LWR Under Leakage. Next we overview how to prove pseudorandom of Module Ring-LWR even for entropic secrets. Briefly speaking, the (Module, Ring)-LWR samples have the form $(\mathbf{A}, \lfloor \mathbf{A} \cdot \mathbf{s} \rceil_{q \to p})$ for matrix $\mathbf{A} \in R_q^{\ell \times k}$ and $\mathbf{s} \in R_q^k$. Here for simplicity of exposition, we use R_q for both the secret and randomness spaces. More general results on $R_q^\vee$ can be obtained via isomorphisms, such as $R/qR \cong R^\vee/qR^\vee$.

To achieve this, we first take a look at a prior approach [3] who successfully achieved the task in the plain LWR setting. Their proof framework can be summarized as the following.

1. We first break $\mathbf{A} = (\mathbf{A}', \mathbf{a})$ where $\mathbf{A}'$ is the first $\ell - 1$ rows.
2. We switch $\mathbf{A}'$ into some lossy matrix $\tilde{\mathbf{A}}'$.
3. Then we show that the conditional entropy $H(\mathbf{s}|\tilde{\mathbf{A}}', \lfloor \tilde{\mathbf{A}}' \cdot \mathbf{s} \rceil_{q \to p})$ is still high.
4. Thus, from a leftover hash lemma we have $(\tilde{\mathbf{A}}', \lfloor \tilde{\mathbf{A}}' \cdot \mathbf{s} \rceil_{q \to p}), \mathbf{a}, \lfloor \mathbf{a} \cdot \mathbf{s} \rceil_{q \to p}) \approx (\tilde{\mathbf{A}}', \lfloor \tilde{\mathbf{A}}' \cdot \mathbf{s} \rceil_{q \to p}), \mathbf{a}, \lfloor u \rceil_{q \to p})$, as $\mathbf{a}$ acts as a fresh random seed.
5. We switch back $\tilde{\mathbf{A}}'$ to $\mathbf{A}'$.

We can prove that LWR (even for entropic secrets) is pseudorandom by repeatedly applying Steps 2–5 on all rows of $\mathbf{A}$ as [3].

Steps 1, 2, 3, 5 are portable to the ring setting, even though we need to take care of some mathematical subtleties in the ring. The major barrier in the ring setting comes from the lack of a ring leftover hash lemma, i.e., showing inner product of ring elements is a strong extractor, namely $(\mathbf{a}, \langle \mathbf{a}, \mathbf{s} \rangle) \approx (\mathbf{a}, u)$. For this task, we only know some partial results: the lemma holds (1) if each element in s is uniform from a fixed domain [28]; (2) or if each element of s comes from the Gaussian distribution [27] or some specific noisy leaky Gaussian [17]. Under more general leakage functions, it was unclear how inner product over rings behaves. Therefore, it is not inferred from the prior results [17,27,28] whether (Module) Ring-LWR remains hard against more general leakage functions.

A Ring Leftover Hash Lemma. Next we describe our new ideas to tackle the challenge. We start with the approach of [29], which proved that the leftover hash lemma follows if one can bound the collision probability of $\mathcal{D} = (\boldsymbol{a}, \boldsymbol{s})$. Let $(\boldsymbol{a}, \boldsymbol{a}')$ and $(\boldsymbol{s}, \boldsymbol{s}')$ be two independent samples, and we are interested in the following quantity.

$$
\begin{aligned}
\mathsf{Col}(\mathcal{D}) &= \Pr[(\boldsymbol{a} = \boldsymbol{a}') \wedge (\boldsymbol{a} \cdot \boldsymbol{s} = \boldsymbol{a}' \cdot \boldsymbol{s}' \bmod qR)] \\
&= \Pr[\boldsymbol{a} = \boldsymbol{a}'] \cdot \Pr[\boldsymbol{a} \cdot \boldsymbol{s} - \boldsymbol{a}' \cdot \boldsymbol{s}' = 0 \bmod qR | \boldsymbol{a} = \boldsymbol{a}'] \\
&= \frac{1}{q^{n\ell}} \cdot \Pr[\boldsymbol{a} \cdot (\boldsymbol{s} - \boldsymbol{s}') = 0 \bmod qR].
\end{aligned}
$$

To further bound this quantity, in the integer case ($R = \mathbb{Z}$) the work [29] partitions the space using $\gcd(\boldsymbol{s} - \boldsymbol{s}') = d$ for every factor d of q. For each factor d, the distribution $\boldsymbol{a} \cdot (\boldsymbol{s} - \boldsymbol{s}')$ would be uniformly random over $\mathbb{Z}_d / \mathbb{Z}_q$, allowing us to compute the exact probability of $\Pr[\boldsymbol{a} \cdot (\boldsymbol{s} - \boldsymbol{s}') = 0 \bmod qR | \gcd = d] = d/q$. Furthermore, $\Pr[\gcd(\boldsymbol{s} - \boldsymbol{s}') = d] \leq \Pr[\boldsymbol{s} = \boldsymbol{s}' \bmod d] = \mathsf{Col}(\boldsymbol{s} \bmod d)$. Thus, if the collision probability of $\boldsymbol{s} \bmod d$ is small for any factor of q, then we are able to bound the collision probability of $\mathsf{Col}(\mathcal{D})$, implying the desired leftover hash lemma.

In the ring setting however, a ring element might have multiple factorizations, so it is not clear how GCD of ring elements should be. As R might not even be a GCD domain, a general proof cannot rely on this fact. To tackle this issue, we move to *ideal factorization* instead of ring element factorization. By a classic algebraic number theory result (thanks to Dedekind, Kummer, and others), each proper ideal of ring of integers (i.e., $R = \mathcal{O}_K$) factors into a product of prime ideals (or their power), and the factorization is unique up to permutation. Therefore, we can write $q\mathcal{O}_K = \mathfrak{q}_1^{e_1} \mathfrak{q}_2^{e_2} \ldots \mathfrak{q}_g^{e_g}$ without loss of generality. This result holds for a general number field K, not just Galois extensions.

Next we define a notion *maximal belonging* for a vector $\boldsymbol{x} \in R_q^k$, generalizing the spirit of GCD in the view of *ideals*. Let $\mathcal{I}$ be an ideal factor of qR, and we denote $\boldsymbol{x} \in_{\max} \mathcal{I}$ if (i) every element in the vector belongs to the ideal $\mathcal{I}$, and (ii) for every ideal $\mathcal{J}$ such that $\mathcal{I} | \mathcal{J}$, there exists one element of $\boldsymbol{x}$, say x_j that $x_j \notin \mathcal{J}$. With this notion, we show that if $\boldsymbol{x} \in_{\max} \mathcal{I}$ for some factor $\mathcal{I}$ of qR, then the distribution of $\boldsymbol{a} \cdot \boldsymbol{x}$ is uniform over $\mathcal{I}$ for a uniformly random $\boldsymbol{a}$. This allows us to calculate $\Pr[\boldsymbol{a} \cdot (\boldsymbol{s} - \boldsymbol{s}') = 0 \bmod qR | (\boldsymbol{s} - \boldsymbol{s}') \in_{\max} \mathcal{I}] = N(\mathcal{I})/q^n$, and $\Pr[(\boldsymbol{s} - \boldsymbol{s}') \in_{\max} \mathcal{I}] \leq \Pr[\boldsymbol{s} = \boldsymbol{s}' \bmod \mathcal{I}] = \mathsf{Col}(\boldsymbol{s} \bmod \mathcal{I})$. From these facts, we are able to show, suppose the collision probability of $\boldsymbol{s} \bmod \mathcal{I}$ is small for any ideal factor $\mathcal{I}$ of qR, then the leftover hash lemma holds. This translates into an entropy requirement of $H(\boldsymbol{s} \bmod \mathcal{I})$ for every ideal factor $\mathcal{I}$.

We note that proving these results requires to tackle non-trivial mathematical arguments in the ring setting. Particularly, we use some important observations:

(1) $\mathcal{I}/\langle q \rangle \cong \mathfrak{q}^{x_1}/\mathfrak{q}^{e_1} \times \mathfrak{q}^{x_2}/\mathfrak{q}^{e_2} \times \cdots \times \mathfrak{q}^{x_g}/\mathfrak{q}^{e_g}$ for some $x_i \in [e_i]$ where $\mathcal{I}$ factors into $\prod_{i \in [g]} \mathfrak{q}_i^{x_i}$, and (2) each $\mathfrak{q}_i^{x_i}/\mathfrak{q}_i^{e_i} \cong \left(\mathfrak{q}_i^{x_i}/\langle q \rangle\right)/\left(\mathfrak{q}_i^{e_i}/\langle q \rangle\right)$ is further isomorphic to a principle ideal to some power quotient the principle ideal to another larger power. (1) is from the fact of unique ideal factorization and the Chinese Remainder Theorem; (2) is from a theorem of Dedekind that each $\mathfrak{q}_i$ is a prime ideal isomorphic to $\langle q, f_i(\alpha) \rangle$ for some monic irreducible polynomial f_i in $\mathbb{Z}_q[x]$. We refer the details in Sect. 5.2.

Parameters and Implications. By using the leftover hash lemma, we are able to derive some interesting entropy requirements: the lemma holds if $H(s \bmod \mathcal{I}) \geq n \log q + O(\log(1/\varepsilon)) + \delta$ (for every ideal factor $\mathcal{I}$). For a general field K, we would need $\delta = n \log q$, resulting a more strict requirement on entropy. For special cases such as (1) K is a cyclotomic field, or (2) each prime ideal of qR has large norm, we can derive a sharper parameter $\delta = O(\log q)$ or even $O(1)$. Intuitively, the leftover hash lemma anyway needs to extract a ring element (entropy $n \log q$), and thus the term $n \log q + O(\log(1/\varepsilon))$ is necessary similar to the regular leftover hash lemma in $\mathbb{Z}_q$. The extra term δ may depend on the structure of the ring and/or how $q\mathcal{O}_K$ factors.

The next natural question is, how small can k (the dimension of the vector a and s) be to reach the lemma's requirement for extraction? Clearly, $k = 1$ is not possible as a one dimension s cannot provide sufficient entropy. Suppose $q\mathcal{O}_K$ only has ideals with large norms, i.e., each $N(\mathfrak{q}_i)$ is large, say $q^{n/2}$, then a constant ℓ might suffice for s to reach the entropy requirement. On the other hand, if each $N(\mathfrak{q}_i)$ is small, say q, then each coordinate of s modulo $\mathfrak{q}_i$ can only provide $\log q$ bits of entropy. To reach the entropy bound, it would require at least $k = \Omega(n)$. Therefore, a completely-split $q\mathcal{O}_K$ would be less favorable for randomness extraction compared with a low-split $q\mathcal{O}_K$, e.g., $q\mathcal{O}_K = \mathfrak{q}_1\mathfrak{q}_2$, where each $N(\mathfrak{q}_i) = q^{n/2}$. Our new leftover hash lemma would suggest to use an appropriate q (such that $q\mathcal{O}_K$ factors in a nice way) in future Ring-LWE/R applications.

Open Directions. Our leftover hash lemma, together with [3], shows Module-Ring-LWR (for sufficiently large k) remains pseudorandom for bounded samples. An interesting open question is to determine whether Ring-LWR ($k = 1$) is hard if $s \bmod \mathcal{I}$ has sufficient entropy for every ideal factor $\mathcal{I}$. Proving or disproving this would require new ideas beyond the current techniques: we cannot use leftover hash lemma in the $k = 1$ case as argued above. On the other hand, the attack of [9] does not work either, as it requires to leak completely $s \bmod \mathcal{I}$ for some ideal factor $\mathcal{I}$. Another interesting question is to extend the result to the case of unbounded samples, which is a significant open question since [6].

2   Preliminaries

Notations. Let λ denote the security parameter. For an integer n, let $[n]$ denote the set $\{1, ..., n\}$. We use bold lowercase letters (e.g. a) to denote vectors and bold capital letters (e.g. $\mathbf{A}$) to denote matrices. For a positive integer $q \geq 2$, let $\mathbb{Z}_q$ be the ring of integers modulo q. For a distribution on a set X, we write $x \xleftarrow{\$} X$ to denote the operation of sampling a random x according to X. For distributions X, Y, we let $\mathsf{SD}(X, Y)$ denote their statistical distance. We write $X \overset{s}{\approx} Y$ or $X \overset{c}{\approx} Y$ to denote statistical closeness or computational indistinguishability, respectively. We use $\mathsf{negl}(\lambda)$ to denote the set of all negligible functions $\mu(\lambda) = \lambda^{-\omega(1)}$.

2.1   Rounding Function in $\mathbb{Z}_q$

For any integer modulus $q \geq 2$, we use the 'rounding' function defined in [6] – for $q \geq p \geq 2$, let $\lfloor \cdot \rceil_p : \mathbb{Z}_q \to \mathbb{Z}_p$ be the function as $\lfloor x \rceil_p = \lfloor (p/q) \cdot \bar{x} \rceil_p \bmod p$, where $\bar{x} \in \mathbb{Z}$ is any integer congruent to $x \bmod q$.

2.2   The Space H

When working with number fields and algebraic number theory, it is convenient to work with a certain linear subspace $H \subseteq \mathbb{R}^{s_1} \times \mathbb{C}^{2s_2}$ for some integers $s_1, s_2 > 0$ such that $s_1 + 2s_2 = n$, defined as

$$H = \{(x_1, \cdots x_n) \in \mathbb{R}^{s_1} \times \mathbb{C}^{2s_2} | x_{s_1+s_2+j} = \overline{x_{s_1+j}}, \forall j \in [s_2]\}.$$

As described in the work [26], we can equip H with norms, which would naturally define norms of elements in a number field or ideal lattice via an embedding that maps field elements into H. We will present more details next.

It is not hard to verify that H equipped with the inner product induced by $\mathbb{C}^n$, is isomorphic to $\mathbb{R}^n$ as an inner product space. This can be seen via the orthonormal basis $\{h_i\}_{i \in [n]}$ defined as: for $j \in [n]$, let $e_i \in \mathbb{C}^n$ be the vector with 1 in its jth coordinate, and 0 elsewhere; then for $j \in [s_1]$, we define $h_j = e_j \in \mathbb{C}^n$, and for $s_1 < j < s_1 + s_2$ we take $h_j = \frac{1}{\sqrt{2}}(e_j + e_{j+s_2})$ and $h_{j+s_2} = \frac{1}{\sqrt{-2}}(e_j - e_{j+s_2})$.

We can equip H with the ℓ_2 and ℓ_∞ norms induced on it from $\mathbb{C}^n$. Namely, for $x \in H$ we have $\|x\|_2 = \sum_i (|x_i|^2)^{1/2} = \sqrt{\langle x, x \rangle}$ and $\|x\|_\infty = \max_i |x_i|$. ℓ_p norms can be defined similarly.

2.3   Algebraic Number Theory Background

Algebraic number theory is the study of number fields. Below we present the requisite concepts and notations used in this work. More backgrounds and complete proofs can be found in any introductory book on the subject, e.g., [15,44].

Number Fields and Their Geometry

A *number field* can be defined as a field extension $K = \mathbb{Q}(\alpha)$ obtained by adjoining an abstract element α to the field of rationals, where α satisfies the relation $f(\alpha) = 0$ for some irreducible polynomial $f(x) \in \mathbb{Q}[x]$, called *minimal polynomial* of α, which is monic without loss of generality. The *degree* n of the number field is the degree of f.

A number field $K = \mathbb{Q}(\alpha)$ of degree n has exactly n field embeddings (injective homomorphisms) $\sigma_i : K \rightarrow \mathbb{C}$. Concretely, these embeddings map α to each of the complex roots of its minimal polynomial f. An embedding whose images lies in $\mathbb{R}$ is said to be *real*, or otherwise it is *complex*. Because roots of f come in conjugate pairs, so do the complex embeddings. The number of real embeddings is denoted as s_1 and the number of pairs of complex embeddings is denoted as s_2, satisfying $n = s_1 + 2s_2$ with σ_i for $1 < i < s_1$ being the real embeddings and $\sigma_{s_1+s_2+i} = \overline{\sigma_{s_1+i}}$ for $1 \leq i \leq s_2$ being the conjugate pairs of complex embeddings.

The *canonical embedding* $\sigma : K \leftarrow \mathbb{R}^{s_1} \times \mathbb{C}^{2s_2}$ is then defined as $\sigma(x) = (\sigma_1(x), \cdots \sigma_n(x))$. Note that σ is a ring homomorphism from K to H, where multiplication and addition in H are both component-wise.

By identifying elements of K and their canonical embeddings on H, we can define the norms on K. For any $x \in K$ and any $p \in [1, \infty]$, the ℓ_p norm of x is simply $\|x\|_p = \|\sigma(x)\|_p$. Then we have that $\|xy\|_p \leq \|x\|_\infty \cdot \|y\|_p \leq \|x\|_p \cdot \|y\|_p$, for any $x, y \in K$ and $p \in [1, \infty]$.

The canonical embedding also allows us to view Gaussian distribution D_r over H, or their discrete analogues over a lattice $\mathcal{L} \subset H$, as distributions over K. Formally, the continuous distribution D_r is actually over the field tensor product $K_\mathbb{R} = K \otimes_\mathbb{Q} \mathbb{R}$, which is isomorphic to H.

The *trace* $\mathrm{Tr} = \mathrm{Tr}_{K/\mathbb{Q}} : K \rightarrow \mathbb{Q}$ of an element $a \in K$ can be defined as the sum of the embeddings: $\mathrm{Tr}(a) = \sum_i \sigma_i(a)$. The *norm* $N = N_{K/\mathbb{Q}} : K \rightarrow \mathbb{Q}$ can be defined as the product of all the embeddings: $N(a) = \prod_i \sigma_i(a)$. Clearly, the trace is $\mathbb{Q}$-linear, and also notice that $\mathrm{Tr}(a \cdot b) = \sum_i \sigma_i(a)\sigma_i(b) = \langle \sigma(a), \overline{\sigma(b)} \rangle$, so $\mathrm{Tr}(a \cdot b)$ is a symmetric bilinear form akin to the inner product of the embeddings of a and b. The norm N is multiplicative.

Ring of Integers and Ideals

An *algebraic integer* is an algebraic number whose minimal polynomial over the rationals has integer coefficients. For a number field K, we denote its subset of algebraic integers by $\mathcal{O}_K$. This set forms a ring, called the *ring of integers* of the number field. The norm of any algebraic integer is in $\mathbb{Z}$.

An *(integer) ideal* $\mathcal{I} \subseteq \mathcal{O}_K$ is an additive subgroup that is closed under multiplication by R. Every ideal in $\mathcal{O}_K$ is the set of all $\mathbb{Z}$-linear combinations of some basis $\{b_1, \cdots, b_n\} \subset \mathcal{I}$. The *norm* of an ideal $\mathcal{I}$ is its index as a subgroup of $\mathcal{O}_K$, i.e., $N(\mathcal{I}) = |\mathcal{O}_K/\mathcal{I}|$. The sum of two ideals $\mathcal{I}, \mathcal{J}$ is the set of all $x + y$ for $x \in \mathcal{I}, y \in \mathcal{J}$, and the product ideal $\mathcal{I}\mathcal{J}$ is the set of all sums of terms xy. We also have that $N(\langle a \rangle) = |N(a)|$ for any $a \in \mathcal{O}_K$, and $N(\mathcal{I}\mathcal{J}) = N(\mathcal{I}) \cdot N(\mathcal{J})$. The following lemma states the condition of an element not belonging to an ideal, we put the proof in full version of this paper.

Lemma 2.1. *Let $a \in \mathcal{O}_K$ be an element, $\mathcal{I} \subset \mathcal{O}_K$ be an ideal. If $\|a\|_2 < \sqrt{n} \cdot N(\mathcal{I})^{\frac{1}{n}}$, then $a \notin \mathcal{I}$.*

An ideal $\mathfrak{p} \subsetneq \mathcal{O}_K$ is prime if $ab \in \mathfrak{p}$ for some $a, b \in \mathcal{O}_K$, then $a \in \mathfrak{p}$ or $b \in \mathfrak{p}$ (or both). In $\mathcal{O}_K$, an ideal $\mathfrak{p}$ is prime if and only if it is maximal, which implies that the quotient ring $\mathcal{O}_K/\mathfrak{p}$ is a finite field of order $N(\mathfrak{p})$. An ideal $\mathcal{I}$ is called to *divide* ideal $\mathcal{J}$, which is written as $\mathcal{I}|\mathcal{J}$, if there exists another ideal $\mathcal{H} \in \mathcal{O}_K$ such that $\mathcal{J} = \mathcal{H}\mathcal{I}$. Two ideal $\mathcal{I}, \mathcal{J} \subseteq \mathcal{O}_K$ are *coprime* if $\mathcal{I} + \mathcal{J} = \mathcal{O}_K$. The following lemma states the coprime condition of the power of primes, we put the proof in the full version of this paper.

Lemma 2.2. *Let $\mathcal{I}, \mathcal{J} \subseteq \mathcal{O}_K$ be two ideals, and $\mathcal{I}$ is coprime to $\mathcal{J}$, then $\mathcal{I}^x$ is coprime to $\mathcal{J}^y$ for any integers $x, y \geq 1$.*

A *fraction ideal* $\mathcal{I} \subset K$ is a set such that $d\mathcal{I} \subseteq \mathcal{O}_K$ is an integral ideal for some $d \in \mathcal{O}_K$. Its norm is defined as $N(\mathcal{I}) = N(d\mathcal{I})/|N(d)|$. A fractional ideal $\mathcal{I}$ is *invertible* if there exists a fractional ideal $\mathcal{J}$ such that $\mathcal{I} \cdot \mathcal{J} = \mathcal{O}_K$, which is unique and denoted as $\mathcal{I}^{-1}$. The set of fractional ideals form a group under multiplication, and the norm is multiplicative homomorphism on this group.

An *order* $\mathcal{O}$ of K is a subring with unity, i.e., $1 \in \mathcal{O}$ and $\mathcal{O}$ is closed under multiplication, and the $\mathbb{Q}$ span of $\mathcal{O}$ is equal to K. It's easy to see that $\mathcal{O}_K$ is an order, and it is the maximal order: every order $\mathcal{O} \subseteq \mathcal{O}_K$. For any order $\mathcal{O}$ of K, we have $\mathcal{O} \cdot \mathcal{O}^\vee = \mathcal{O}^\vee$ and $\mathrm{Tr}((\mathcal{O} \cdot \mathcal{O}^\vee) \cdot \mathcal{O}) = \mathrm{Tr}(\mathcal{O}^\vee \cdot \mathcal{O}) \subseteq \mathbb{Z}$.

2.4   Duality

For any lattice $\mathcal{L} \subseteq K$ (i.e., for the $\mathbb{Z}$-span of any $\mathbb{Q}$-basis of K), its *dual* is defined as $\mathcal{L}^\vee = \{x \in K : \mathrm{Tr}(x\mathcal{L}) \subseteq \mathbb{Z}\}$.

Then $\mathcal{L}^\vee$ embeds as the complex conjugate of the dual lattice, i.e., $\sigma(\mathcal{L}^\vee) = \overline{\sigma(\mathcal{L})^*}$ due to the fact that $\mathrm{Tr}(xy) = \sum_i \sigma_i(x)\sigma_i(y) = \langle \sigma(x), \overline{\sigma(y)} \rangle$. It is easy to check that $(\mathcal{L}^\vee)^\vee = \mathcal{L}$, and that if $\mathcal{L}$ is a fractional ideal, then $\mathcal{L}^\vee$ is one as well.

We point out that the ring of integers $R = \mathcal{O}_K$ is not self-dual, nor are an ideal and its inverse dual to each other. For any fractional ideal $\mathcal{I}$, its dual ideal is $\mathcal{I}^\vee = \mathcal{I}^{-1} \cdot R^\vee$. The factor $R^\vee$ is a fractional ideal whose inverse $(R^\vee)^{-1}$, called the *different ideal*, is integral and of norm $N((R^\vee)^{-1}) = \Delta_K$. The fractional ideal $R^\vee$ itself is often called the *codifferent*.

For any $\mathbb{Q}$-basis $\mathbf{B} = \{b_j\}$ of K, we denote its dual basis by $\mathbf{B}^\vee = \{b_j^\vee\}$, which is characterized by $\mathrm{Tr}(b_i \cdot b_j^\vee) = \delta_{ij}$, the Kronecker delta. It is immediate that $(\mathbf{B}^\vee)^\vee = \mathbf{B}$, and if $\mathbf{B}$ is a $\mathbb{Z}$-basis of some fractional ideal $\mathcal{I}$, then $\mathbf{B}^\vee$ is a $\mathbb{Z}$-basis of its dual ideal $\mathcal{I}^\vee$. If $a = \sum_j a_j \cdot b_j$ for $a_j \in \mathbb{R}$ is the unique presentation of $a \in K_\mathbb{R}$ in basis $\mathbf{B}$, then $a_j = \mathrm{Tr}(a \cdot b^\vee)$.

The following lemma generalized Lemma 4.4 of [28] determines the distribution of $\langle a, s \rangle$ for random $a \in (R/\mathcal{I}R)^\ell$ and fixed $s \in (R^\vee/\mathcal{I}R^\vee)^\ell$, we put the proof in full version of this paper.

Lemma 2.3 ([28]). *Let $R = \mathcal{O}_K$ be the ring of integers of a number field K, $\mathcal{I}$ be an ideal of R, and $s = (s_1, \cdots, s_\ell) \in (R^\vee/\mathcal{I}R^\vee)^\ell$ be a vector of ring elements. If $a = (a_1, \cdots, a_\ell) \in (R/\mathcal{I}R)^\ell$ are uniformly random, then $\sum_i a_i \cdot s_i \bmod \mathcal{I}R^\vee$ is uniformly random over the ideal $\langle s_1, \cdots, s_\ell \rangle / \mathcal{I}R^\vee$. In particular, $\Pr\left[\sum_i a_i \cdot s_i = 0 \bmod \mathcal{I}R^\vee\right] = 1/|\langle s_1, \cdots, s_\ell \rangle / \mathcal{I}R^\vee|$.*

2.5   Prime Splitting and Chinese Remainder Theorem

For an integer prime $p \in \mathbb{Z}$, the factorization of the principal ideal $\langle p \rangle \subset R = \mathcal{O}_K$ for a number field K (where $K/\mathbb{Q}$ is a field extension with degree n) is as follows.

Lemma 2.4 (Dedekind [16]). *Let* $K = \mathbb{Q}(\alpha)$ *be a number field for* $\alpha \in \mathcal{O}_K$, *and* $F(x)$ *be the minimal polynomial of* α *in* $\mathbb{Z}[x]$. *For any prime* p, *the ideal* $p\mathcal{O}_K$ *factors into prime ideals as* $\langle p \rangle = \mathfrak{p}_1^{e_1} \cdots \mathfrak{p}_g^{e_g}$, *where* $N(\mathfrak{p}_i) = p^{f_i}$ *for* $f_i = [\mathcal{O}_K/\mathfrak{p}_i : \mathbb{Z}_p]$, *and* $n = \sum_{i=1}^{g} e_i f_i$.
Moreover if p *does not divide the index of* $[\mathcal{O}_K : \mathbb{Z}[\alpha]]$, *then we have further structures as following. We can express* $F(x) = f_1(x)^{e_1} \ldots f_g(x)^{e_g} \mod p$, *where each* $f_i(x)$ *is a monic irreducible polynomial in* $\mathbb{Z}_p[x]$. *There exists a bijection between* $\mathfrak{p}_i$'s *and* $f_i(x)$'s *such that* $\mathfrak{p}_i = \langle p, f_i(\alpha) \rangle$, *and* $f_i = \deg f_i(x)$.

For each $\mathfrak{p}_i$, we have $\mathfrak{p}_i | p\mathcal{O}_K$, which can be written as $\mathfrak{p}_i | \langle p \rangle$, and call $\mathfrak{p}_i$ a factor of $\langle p \rangle$. Next we recall the Chinese Remainder Theorem (CRT) for the fraction ideal over a number field K.

Lemma 2.5 (Chinese Remainder Theorem [9]). *Let* $\mathcal{I}$ *be a fractional in over* K, *and let* $\mathfrak{p}_i$ *be pairwise coprime ideals in* $R = \mathcal{O}_K$, *then natural ring homomorphism is an isomorphism:* $\mathcal{I}/\left(\prod_i \mathfrak{p}_i \right)\mathcal{I} \to \bigoplus_i (\mathcal{I}/\mathfrak{p}_i\mathcal{I})$.

As a corollary of Chinese Remainder Theorem above, the following lemma states the equivalence of prime ideal factors of qR and $qR^\vee$ under isomorphism.

Lemma 2.6 (Lemma 2.35 of [9]). *Let* $\mathcal{I}, \mathcal{J}$ *be integral ideals in an order* $\mathcal{O}$ *and let* $\mathcal{M}$ *be a fractional* $\mathcal{O}$-*ideal. Assume that* $\mathcal{I}$ *is invertible. Given the associated primes of* $\mathcal{J}, \mathfrak{p}_1, \mathfrak{p}_2, \ldots, \mathfrak{p}_k$, *and an element* $t \in \mathcal{I} \setminus \bigcup_{j=1}^{k} \mathfrak{p}_j\mathcal{I}$ *the map*

$$\theta_t : \mathcal{M}/\mathcal{J}\mathcal{M} \to \mathcal{I}\mathcal{M}/\mathcal{I}\mathcal{J}\mathcal{M}$$
$$x \mapsto t \cdot x$$

induces an isomorphism of $\mathcal{O}$-*modules. Moreover,* θ_t *is efficiently inverted given* $\mathcal{I}, \mathcal{J}, \mathcal{M}$ *and* t, *and* t *can be computed given* $\mathcal{I}$ *and* $\mathfrak{p}_1, \cdots, \mathfrak{p}_k$.

In particular, let $\mathcal{I} = (R^\vee)^{-1}, \mathcal{J} = qR, \mathcal{M} = R^\vee$, then $R/qR \cong R^\vee/qR^\vee$.

2.6   The Ring-LWE Problem

We now provide the formal definition of the ring-LWE problem and describe the hardness result shown in [26,38].

Definition 2.7 (Ring-LWE Distribution). *For a secret* $s \in R_q^\vee$ $(R = \mathcal{O}_K)$ *and a distribution* ϕ *over* $K_\mathbb{R}$, *a sample from the Ring-LWE distribution* $A_{s,\phi}$ *over* $R_q \times (K_\mathbb{R}/qR^\vee)$ *is generated by choosing* $a \leftarrow R_q$ *uniformly random, choosing* $e \leftarrow \phi$, *and outputting* $(a, b = a \cdot s + e \mod qR^\vee)$.

Definition 2.8 (Ring-LWE, Average-case Decision Problem). *The average-case decision version of the Ring-LWE problem, denoted R-DLWE$_{\ell,q,\phi}$ is to distinguish between ℓ independent samples from $A_{s,\phi}$ for a random choice of a secret $s \leftarrow R_q^\vee$ of degree n, and the same number of uniformly random and independent samples from $R_q \times (K_\mathbb{R}/qR^\vee)$.*

The subscript ℓ of the number of samples is usually omitted if there is no special explanation. The hardness of RLWE can be reduced from the hardness of hard problems over ideal lattices, ref. Full version of this paper.

3   Generalized Learning with Rounding

In this section, we present a new algebraic framework of LWR that generalizes previous RLWR notions [6,8,14], which mainly focused on primal ring elements and rounding over their polynomial coefficient representations. Essentially, we show that the unified framework of algebraic LWE in a recent work [37] can be portable to the LWR setting while maintaining important features. Under our algebraic LWR framework, we can naturally express several variants of Ring-, Order-, and Poly-LWR in a single problem parameterized by a number field lattice, and derive hardness results for these variants of LWRs and as well middle-product LWR based on RLWR.

Moreover, we can derive new and tighter hardness results for (Module) RLWR based on RLWE, even in the entropic secret cases. Thus, the hardness of RLWE would provide a foundation for RLWR and these algebraic variants via our new framework. In the rest of this section, we present the algebraic framework of LWR and relate the hardness of RLWR to the other variants of LWRs. Later in Sects. 4 and 5, we present our new hardness results.

3.1   Rounding with Respect to Specific Basis

Recall that for a monogenic field K (e.g., cyclotomic fields), an element $a \in R_q = (\mathcal{O}_K)_q$ can be treated as a polynomial of integer coefficients, as $(\mathcal{O}_K)_q = \mathbb{Z}_q[\alpha] \cong \mathbb{Z}_q[x]/f(x)$, where $f(x)$ is the minimal polynomial of α. Let $a(x) = a_0 + a_1 x + \cdots + a_{n-1}x^{n-1} \in \mathbb{Z}_q[x]/f(x)$, and we can naturally define *rounding* $\lfloor \cdot \rceil_p$ of $a(x)$ as:

$$\lfloor a(x) \rceil_p =: \lfloor a_0 \rceil_p + \lfloor a_1 \rceil_p x + \cdots + \lfloor a_{n-1} \rceil_p x^{n-1}.$$

To our knowledge, all prior work [6,8,14] use this coefficient embedding in the primal R_q when studying rounding in the ring. This choice however, is not optimal for ideal lattices. As "the" RLWE problem is defined in the dual form for several analytical advantages as argued in [26], i.e., the secret and the inner products are in the dual space $R_q^\vee = (\mathcal{O}_K)_q^\vee$, the natural analog RLWR of RLWE should be defined in the dual form. However, an element in the dual in general might not be able to described as an integral polynomial, and thus it is not clear how to define rounding in this case. One might consider to use the relation $R_q^\vee = t^{-1}R_q$ for some $t^{-1} \in R_q^\vee$ to move elements from the dual to the primal (e.g., see [35,41]). This approach goes back to the primal RLWR (RLWE) case, which would lose some analytical advantages, e.g., tightness of parameters in our reduction. We explain this further in Sect. 4. Thus, we would like to stick to the dual form of RLWR, similar to the RLWE setting [26].

To tackle the above issue, we observe that an element $a \in R^\vee$ (also $R_q^\vee$) can also be uniquely represented as integer linear combinations of a certain $\mathbb{Z}$-basis of $R^\vee$, say $\mathbf{B} = \{b_1, \cdots, b_n\}$, i.e., $a = x_1 b_1 + \cdots + x_n b_n$, where all $x_i \in \mathbb{Z}$. Under this basis, rounding an element can be easily defined. Since there are multiple possible bases, it is important to specify to which basis the rounding is with respect. Thus, below we explicitly define a rounding function that is also parameterized by a basis.

Definition 3.1. *Let $K = \mathbb{Q}(\alpha)$ be a number field with degree n, and $\mathcal{I}$ be a fractional ideal over K with a $\mathbb{Z}$-basis $\mathbf{B} = \{b_1, \cdots, b_n\}$. Then for any integers $q \geq p \geq 2$, we define the rounding function (with respect to basis $\mathbf{B}$) $\lfloor \cdot \rceil_{\mathbf{B},p}$: $\mathcal{I}_q \rightarrow \mathcal{I}_p$ as*

$$\lfloor a \rceil_{\mathbf{B},p} = \lfloor x_1 \rceil_p b_1 + \cdots + \lfloor x_n \rceil_p b_n \mod p\mathcal{I},$$

where $\mathcal{I}_q$ (similarly $\mathcal{I}_p$) is the quotient groups $\mathcal{I}/q\mathcal{I}$, and $a = x_1 b_1 + \cdots + x_n b_n \in \mathcal{I}_q, x_1, \cdots, x_n \in \mathbb{Z}_q$. The rounding function for $\mathbb{Z}_q \rightarrow \mathbb{Z}_p$, i.e., $\lfloor \cdot \rceil_p$, is the same as we described in Sect. 2.1.

Throughout this paper, when we define a rounding function of a ring elements, there must be a reference basis associated with it. In situations where the basis $\mathbf{B}$ is clear, we might omit it in the subscript for succinctness of notion.

3.2 $\mathcal{L}$-LWR and MP-LWR Problems

Following the framework of [37], we next present an algebraic form of LWR that captures Ring-, Order-, Poly-LWR. Similar to the work [37], we derive two hardness results: (1) we prove a reduction from $\mathcal{L}$-LWR to $\mathcal{L}'$-LWR for $\mathcal{L}' \subseteq \mathcal{L}$, and (2) we prove hardness of middle-product LWR (namely, MP-LWR) and a variant multivariate MP-LWR (denoted as MV-MP-LWR), based on the hardness of Order-LWR. Due to the limitation of space, the definitions and reductions of MP-LWR are in full version of this paper. As $\mathcal{O}_K$ is the maximal order, the hardness of Order-, MP-, and Poly-LWR can be based on the hardness of RLWR.

Next we define Coefficient Ring $\mathcal{O}^\mathcal{L}$ of a lattice $\mathcal{L}$ in a number field K, following the framework of [37]. Intuitively, we have the secret vector $s \in \mathcal{L}^\vee$, and the public random element $a \in \mathcal{O}^\mathcal{L}$. Then the product $s \cdot a$ will lie in the space $\mathcal{L}^\vee$, consistent with the prior RLWE structure.

Coefficient Ring

Definition 3.2 (Coefficient Ring). *For a lattice $\mathcal{L} \subseteq K$, we define the coefficient ring of it as $\mathcal{O}^\mathcal{L} := \{x \in K : x\mathcal{L} \subseteq \mathcal{L}\}$.*

Then, the following lemmas can be derived.

Lemma 3.3 ([37]). $\mathcal{O}^{\mathcal{L}} = (\mathcal{L} \cdot \mathcal{L}^\vee)^\vee$, $\mathcal{L}$ and $\mathcal{L}^\vee$ have the same coefficient ring $\mathcal{O}^{\mathcal{L}} = \mathcal{O}^{\mathcal{L}^\vee}$. Particularly, if $\mathcal{L}$ is an order $\mathcal{O}$ or it dual $\mathcal{O}^\vee$ of K, then $\mathcal{O}^{\mathcal{L}} = \mathcal{O}$.

Lemma 3.4 ([37]). The coefficient ring $\mathcal{O}^{\mathcal{L}}$ is an order of K, and $\mathcal{O}^{\mathcal{L}} \subseteq \mathcal{O}_K$.

$\mathcal{L}$-LWR Problem

With the definition above, we define a general algebraic LWR problem as follows.

Definition 3.5 ($\mathcal{L}$-LWR distribution). Let $\mathcal{L}$ be a lattice in a number field K, $\mathcal{O}^{\mathcal{L}}$ be the coefficient ring of $\mathcal{L}$, $q \geq p \geq 2$, $k \geq 1$ be positive integers, and $\mathbf{B}$ be a basis of $\mathcal{L}^\vee$. For $s \in (\mathcal{L}_q^\vee)^k$, a sample from the $\mathcal{L}$-LWR distribution $L_{s,q,p}^k(\mathcal{L}, \mathbf{B})$ over $(\mathcal{O}_q^{\mathcal{L}})^k \times \mathcal{L}_p^\vee$ is generated by choosing $\mathbf{a} \leftarrow (\mathcal{O}_q^{\mathcal{L}})^k$ uniformly at random, outputting $(\mathbf{a}, b = \lfloor \langle \mathbf{a}, s \rangle \rceil_{\mathbf{B},p})$.

Definition 3.6 ($\mathcal{L}$-LWR problem, decision). The decision problem D-$\mathcal{L}$-$\mathrm{LWR}_{\mathbf{B},q,p,\ell,\psi}^k$ is to distinguish between ℓ samples from $L_{s,q,p}^k(\mathcal{L}, \mathbf{B})$ where $s \leftarrow \psi$, and ℓ samples from $U((\mathcal{O}_q^{\mathcal{L}})^k \times \mathcal{L}_p^\vee)$.

Definition 3.7 ($\mathcal{L}$-LWR problem, search). The decision problem S-$\mathcal{L}$-$\mathrm{LWR}_{\mathbf{B},q,p,\ell,\psi}^k$ is given ℓ samples from $L_{s,q,p}^k(\mathcal{L}, \mathbf{B})$ for $s \leftarrow \psi$, find s.

For simplicity of notation, we omit the subscript ψ for the uniform distribution for the above two definitions. Below the computational problems are all *average-case*, where distinguishability/solvability is referred to the case when the secret s comes from some distribution. We also define their *worst-case* variants by adding (W), i.e., (W)-S-$\mathcal{L}$-LWR, where solvability means finding solutions for any s in the support of ψ, i.e., for any $s \in \mathsf{Supp}(\psi)$.

The definitions above generalize the algebraic LWR variants defined over number fields or polynomial rings. Let $k = 1$. If $\mathcal{L}$ is an order $\mathcal{O}$ of K or its dual $\mathcal{O}^\vee$, then $\mathcal{O}^{\mathcal{L}} = \mathcal{O}$. Therefore, by taking $\mathcal{L} = O_K$, we obtain the original Ring-LWR problems defined in [6]. Alternatively, by taking $\mathcal{L} = \mathcal{O}^\vee$, we get the "primal" form of Order-LWR over $\mathcal{O}$, which is corresponding to the Poly-LWR problem if further taking $\mathcal{O} = \mathbb{Z}[\alpha]$ for some $\alpha \in \mathcal{O}_K$. Furthermore, if we take $\mathcal{L} = \mathcal{O}$, a natural "dual" variant of Order-LWR is obtained, where $s \in \mathcal{O}^\vee/q\mathcal{O}^\vee$ and $\lfloor s \cdot a \rceil_p \in \mathcal{O}^\vee/p\mathcal{O}^\vee$. We also get other problems that are not covered by above ones if we take $\mathcal{L}$ to be neither an order nor its dual. For $k \geq 2$, this generalizes the Module RLWR to arbitrary lattices.

3.3 Reductions and Hardness Results

Below we present a $\mathcal{L}$-LWR to $\mathcal{L}'$-LWR reduction. Due to space limit, we present another reduction about MP-RLWR in full version of this paper.

Reduction from $\mathcal{L}$-LWR to $\mathcal{L}'$-LWR

For any lattices $\mathcal{L}' \subseteq \mathcal{L}$ in K, we define the *natural inclusion map* $h : \mathcal{L}'_q \rightarrow \mathcal{L}_q$ as the map that sends $x + q\mathcal{L}'$ to $x + q\mathcal{L}$ for any $x \in \mathcal{L}'$. Similarly, the *natural inclusion map* $g : \mathcal{O}_q^{\mathcal{L}'} \rightarrow \mathcal{O}_q^{\mathcal{L}}$ sends $x + q\mathcal{O}^{\mathcal{L}'}$ to $x + q\mathcal{O}^{\mathcal{L}}$. The following lemmas presents the conditions under which maps of this kind are bijections.

Lemma 3.8 ([37]). *Let $\mathcal{L}' \subseteq \mathcal{L}$ be lattices in number field K and q be a positive integer. Then the natural inclusion map $h : \mathcal{L}'_q \rightarrow \mathcal{L}_q$ is a bijection if and only if q is coprime with the index $|\mathcal{L}/\mathcal{L}'|$; in this case, h is efficient computable and invertible given an arbitrary basis of $\mathcal{L}'$ relative to a basis of $\mathcal{L}$. The same conclusions holds for the natural inclusion map $\bar{h} : \mathcal{L}_q^{\vee} \rightarrow (\mathcal{L}'_q)^{\vee}$.*

Lemma 3.9 ([37]). *Let $\mathcal{L}' \subseteq \mathcal{L}$ be lattices in number field K and q be a positive integer that is coprime with the index $|\mathcal{L}/\mathcal{L}'|$. If $\mathcal{O}^{\mathcal{L}'} \subseteq \mathcal{O}^{\mathcal{L}}$, then the natural inclusion map $g : \mathcal{O}_q^{\mathcal{L}'} \rightarrow \mathcal{O}_q^{\mathcal{L}}$ is a bijection.*

The following Theorem presents the reduction from $\mathcal{L}$-LWR to $\mathcal{L}'$-LWR, due to the limitation of space, we put the full proof of it in full version of this paper.

Theorem 3.10. *Let $\mathcal{L}' \subseteq \mathcal{L}$ be lattices in a number field K with degree n, $q \geq p \geq 2$, $k \geq 1$ be positive integers where $p|q$, and $\mathbf{B}$ be a basis of $\mathcal{L}^{\vee}$. If $\mathcal{O}^{\mathcal{L}'} \subseteq \mathcal{O}^{\mathcal{L}}$, and the natural inclusion maps $g : \mathcal{O}_q^{\mathcal{L}'} \rightarrow \mathcal{O}_q^{\mathcal{L}}$ is an efficiently invertible bijection, then there is an efficient deterministic transformation which:*

- *maps distribution $U((\mathcal{O}_q^{\mathcal{L}})^k \times \mathcal{L}_p^{\vee})$ to distribution $U((\mathcal{O}_q^{\mathcal{L}'})^k \times \mathcal{L}'_p{}^{\vee})$*
- *maps distribution $L_{s,q,p}^k(\mathcal{L}, \mathbf{B})$ to distribution $L_{s',q,p}^k(\mathcal{L}', \mathbf{B}')$, where $s' = s$ mod $q(\mathcal{L}')^{\vee}$, $\mathbf{B}' = \mathbf{B}$ mod $q(\mathcal{L}')^{\vee}$.*

Corollary 3.11. *Adopt the notations from Theorem 3.10, and assume that $|\mathcal{L}/\mathcal{L}'|$ is coprime with q, that $\mathcal{O}^{\mathcal{L}'} \subseteq \mathcal{O}^{\mathcal{L}}$, and that bases of $\mathcal{L}', \mathcal{O}^{\mathcal{L}'}$ relative to bases of $\mathcal{L}, \mathcal{O}^{\mathcal{L}'}$ (respectively) are known. Then there is an efficient deterministic reduction from $\mathcal{L}$-LWR$_{\mathbf{B},q,p,\ell,U}^k$ to $\mathcal{L}'$-LWR$_{\mathbf{B}',q,p,\ell,U'}^k$ for both the search and decision versions, where U and U' are the uniformly random distributions over $\mathcal{L}_q^{\vee}$ and $(\mathcal{L}'_q)^{\vee}$ respectively, $\mathbf{B}$ and $\mathbf{B}'$ are $\mathbb{Z}_q$-bases of $\mathcal{L}_q^{\vee}$ and $(\mathcal{L}'_q)^{\vee}$ respectively, and $\mathbf{B}' = \mathbf{B}$ mod $q(\mathcal{L}')^{\vee}$.*

4   New Hardness Results of Ring-LWR

4.1   Search RLWR to Decision RLWR

Definition 4.1 (Normal Integral Basis). *Let $K/\mathbb{Q}$ be a finite Galois extension with Galois group G. We say that $K/\mathbb{Q}$ has a normal integral basis (NIB) if there exists an element $\alpha \in \mathcal{O}_K$ such that the Galois conjugates of α form an $\mathbb{Z}$-basis of $\mathcal{O}_K$.*

We denote R_q^* (or $(R_q^\vee)^*$) as the set that consists of all invertible elements in R_q (or $R_q^\vee$). Next, we present a hardness result of decision RLWR based on search RLWR under appropriate parameters.

Theorem 4.2. *Let* **B** *be a normal integral basis of a Galois extension $K/\mathbb{Q}$ of degree $\varphi(m) = n$, $q \ge p \ge 2$ be integers where $p|q$, p is a prime, and $p\mathcal{O}_K = \mathfrak{p}_1 \cdots \mathfrak{p}_g$ where $g = n/c$ for a constant $c \in \mathbb{Z}$. Then there exists an efficient reduction from $S\text{-RLWR}_{\mathbf{B},q,p,\ell',\psi}$ to $D\text{-RLWR}_{\mathbf{B},q,p,\ell,\psi'}$, where ψ denotes the uniform distribution over $R_p^\vee \cap (R_q^\vee)^*$, ψ' denotes the uniform distribution over $U\big((R_q^\vee)^*\big)$, $\ell' = gp^c\ell \cdot \mathsf{poly}(1/\varepsilon)$, and ε is the advantage of $D\text{-RLWR}_{\mathbf{B},q,p,\ell,\psi'}$ oracle.*

At a high level, the proof of Theorem 4.2 consists of three reductions following the approach of [26]. We summarize the reduction route as follows, and explain the parameters later:

$$S\text{-RLWR}_{\mathbf{B},q,p,\ell',\psi} \xrightarrow{(1)} (\text{W})\text{-}\mathfrak{p}_i\text{-RLWR}_{\mathbf{B},q,p,\ell'',\psi} \xrightarrow{(2)} (\text{W})\text{-}D\text{-RLWR}^i_{\mathbf{B},q,p,\ell,\psi'} \xrightarrow{(3)} D\text{-RLWR}_{\mathbf{B},q,p,\ell,\psi'}.$$

We note that the above step (3) consists of two sub-steps: one is a reduction from $(\text{W})\text{-}D\text{-RLWR}^i_{\mathbf{B},q,p,\ell,\psi}$ to average case $D\text{-RLWR}^i_{\mathbf{B},q,p,\ell,\psi'}$, followed by another reduction from average case $D\text{-RLWR}^i_{\mathbf{B},q,p,\ell,\psi}$ to (average case) $D\text{-RLWR}_{\mathbf{B},q,p,\ell,\psi'}$.

S-RLWR$_{\mathbf{B},q,p,\ell',\psi}$ to (W)-$\mathfrak{p}_i$-RLWR$_{\mathbf{B},q,p,\ell'',\psi}$

Definition 4.3 ((W)-$\mathfrak{p}_i$-RLWR$_{\mathbf{B},q,p,\ell'',\psi}$). *The worst-case (W)-$\mathfrak{p}_i$-RLWR$_{\mathbf{B},q,p,\ell'',\psi}$ problem is: given ℓ'' samples from $L_{s,q,p}(R, \mathbf{B})$ for some arbitrary $s \in \mathsf{Supp}(\psi)$, find $s \bmod \mathfrak{p}_i R^\vee$.*

Lemma 4.4 (S-RLWR$_{\mathbf{B},q,p,\ell',\psi}$ to (W)-$\mathfrak{p}_i$-RLWR$_{\mathbf{B},q,p,\ell'',\psi}$). *Let* **B** *be a normal integral basis as used in* RLWR. *Then for every $i \in \{1, \cdots, g\}$, there exists a deterministic poly-time reduction from $S\text{-RLWR}_{\mathbf{B},q,p,\ell',\psi}$ to (W)-$\mathfrak{p}_i$-RLWR$_{\mathbf{B},q,p,\ell'',\psi}$, where $\psi = R_p^\vee \cap (R_q^\vee)^*$, $\ell' = g\ell''$.*

Proof. To prove this theorem, we will work on an arbitrary $i \in \{1, \cdots, g\}$. The same argument can be extended to all the other i's. Throughout the rest of the poof, we will view i as an arbitrary fixed index.

We first observe a simple fact. For $k \in \{1, \cdots, g\}$, let σ_k be an automorphism that maps $\mathfrak{p}_k$ to $\mathfrak{p}_i$. We know that all these automorphisms exist as K is a Galois extension. Then the reduction proceeds as follow.

- For each $k \in \{1, \cdots, g\}$, the reduction runs through the following steps.
  - Make ℓ'' queries to the oracle $L_{s,q,p}(R, \mathbf{B})$.
  - For each given sample (a, b), transform it to $(\sigma_k(a), \sigma_k(b))$.
  - Send the ℓ'' transformed samples to the $\mathfrak{p}_i$-RLWR$_{\mathbf{B},q,p,\ell'',\psi}$ oracle
  - Upon receiving the answer $x \in R^\vee/\mathfrak{p}_i R^\vee$, store $\sigma_k^{-1}(x) \in R^\vee/\mathfrak{p}_k R^\vee$.
- Next, the reduction combines all $\{\sigma_k^{-1}(x)\}_{k \in \{1,\cdots,g\}}$ by the Chinese Remainder Theorem. Then it outputs the combined value $s' \in R_p^\vee$.

We now show that for each $k \in [g]$, $\sigma_k^{-1}(x) = s \bmod \mathfrak{p}_k R^\vee$. To show this, we prove that the distribution of the transformed samples is correctly distributed as the $\mathfrak{p}_i$-$\mathrm{RLWR}_{\mathbf{B},q,p,\ell'',\psi}$ oracle requires. Particularly, for each $(a,b) \leftarrow L_{s,q,p}(R,\mathbf{B})$, $\sigma_k(a)$ is uniformly random in $\sigma_k(R_q) = R_q$ as σ_k is an automorphism. Next we would like to show that $\sigma_k(b) = \lfloor \sigma_k(a) \cdot \sigma_k(s) \rceil_{\mathbf{B},p}$. If this holds, then $(\sigma_k(a), \sigma_k(b))$ would be the correct distribution that the $\mathfrak{p}_i$-$\mathrm{RLWR}_{\mathbf{B},q,p,\ell'',\psi}$ oracle expects, and then the oracle would return $x = \sigma_k(s) \bmod \mathfrak{p}_i R^\vee$ (with a non-negligible probability). Thus, we have $\sigma_k^{-1}(x) = s \bmod \mathfrak{p}_k R^\vee$. Now we focus on proving $\sigma_k(b) = \lfloor \sigma_k(a) \cdot \sigma_k(s) \rceil_{\mathbf{B},p}$.

We analyze the term $b = \lfloor a \cdot s \rceil_{\mathbf{B},p}$. Without loss of generality, we write $a \cdot s \bmod qR^\vee = \sum_{i=1}^n \alpha_i b_i$ under the $\mathbb{Z}_q$-basis $\mathbf{B} = \{b_1, \cdots, b_n\}$ for $\alpha_i \in \mathbb{Z}_q$, $i \in [n]$. When rounding with respect to this basis, we can write $b = \sum_{i=1}^n \lfloor \alpha_i \rceil_p b_i \in R_p^\vee$. By taking the automorphism σ_k, we have $\sigma_k(b) = \sigma_k\left(\sum_{i=1}^n \lfloor \alpha_i \rceil_p b_i \right) = \sum_{i=1}^n \lfloor \alpha_i \rceil_p \sigma_k(b_i)$. Next we observe that $\sigma_k(a \cdot s \bmod qR^\vee) = \sigma_k(a) \cdot \sigma_k(s) \bmod qR^\vee$, which is also equal to $\sigma_k\left(\sum_{i=1}^n \alpha_i b_i \right)$. Then we have $\lfloor \sigma_k(a) \cdot \sigma_k(s) \rceil_{\mathbf{B},p} = \lfloor \sigma_k\left(\sum_{i=1}^n \alpha_i b_i \right) \rceil_{\mathbf{B},p} = \lfloor \sum_{i=1}^n \alpha_i \sigma_k(b_i) \rceil_{\mathbf{B},p}$.

As $\mathbf{B}$ is a normal integer basis, we know that σ_k acts as a permutation over the basis, i.e., $\sigma_k(\mathbf{B})$ is equivalent to $\mathbf{B}$ up to a permutation. Thus,

$$\lfloor \sigma_k(a) \cdot \sigma_k(s) \rceil_{\mathbf{B},p} = \lfloor \sum_{i=1}^n \alpha_i \sigma_k(b_i) \rceil_{\mathbf{B},p} = \sum_{i=1}^n \lfloor \alpha_i \rceil_p \sigma_k(b_i) = \sigma_k(b).$$

Finally, by the Chinese Reminder Theorem, $s \bmod pR^\vee$ can be reconstructed from $\{s \bmod \mathfrak{p}_k R^\vee\}_{k=1}^g$. Since the secret distribution ψ has support over $R_p^\vee \cap (R_q^\vee)^*$, we have $s = s \bmod pR^\vee$. This completes the proof.   □

(W)-$\mathfrak{p}_i$-$\mathrm{RLWR}_{\mathbf{B},q,p,\ell'',\psi}$ to (W)-D-$\mathrm{RLWR}_{\mathbf{B},q,p,\ell,\psi}^i$

Definition 4.5 (Hybrid RLWR distribution). *For $i \in \{1, \cdots, g\}$, $s \in R_p^\vee$, we define the distribution $L_{s,q,p}^i(R,\mathbf{B})$ over $R_q \times R_p^\vee$ as: sample $(a,b) \leftarrow L_{s,q,p}(R,\mathbf{B})$ and output $(a, b+h)$ where $h \in R_p^\vee$ is uniformly random over mod $\mathfrak{p}_j R^\vee$ for all $j \leq i$, and 0 over mod all the other ideals, i.e., $\mathfrak{p}_j R^\vee$'s for $j > i$.*

We note that $L_{s,q,p}^0(R,\mathbf{B})$ is the same as $L_{s,q,p}(R,\mathbf{B})$, $L_{s,q,p}^g(R,\mathbf{B})$ is the uniformly random distribution over $R_q \times R_p^\vee$, and the other $L_{s,q,p}^i(R,\mathbf{B})$'s are intermediate hybrids, which will be used via a hybrid argument later.

Definition 4.6 ((W)-D-$\mathrm{RLWR}_{\mathbf{B},q,p,\ell,\psi'}^i$). *The worst-case D-$\mathrm{RLWR}_{\mathbf{B},q,p,\ell,\psi'}^i$ problem is defined as follows: given ℓ samples from $L_{s,q,p}^j(R,\mathbf{B})$ for arbitrary $s \in \mathsf{Supp}(\psi')$ and $j \in \{i-1, i\}$, determine j.*

Lemma 4.7 ($\mathfrak{p}_i$-$\mathrm{RLWR}_{\mathbf{B},q,p,\ell'',\psi}$ to (W)-D-$\mathrm{RLWR}_{\mathbf{B},q,p,\ell,\psi'}^i$). *For any $i \in \{1, \cdots, g\}$, and ideal $\mathfrak{p}_i$ with $N(\mathfrak{p}_i) = p^{n/g} = p^c$ where $c \geq 1$ is a constant integer, there exists a probabilistic polynomial time reduction from $\mathfrak{p}_i$-$\mathrm{RLWR}_{\mathbf{B},q,p,\ell'',\psi}$ to (W)-D-$\mathrm{RLWR}_{\mathbf{B},q,p,\ell,\psi'}$ where $\psi = R_p^\vee \cap (R_q^\vee)^*$, $\psi' = (R_q^\vee)^*$, $\ell'' = p^c \ell \cdot \mathrm{poly}(1/\varepsilon)$, and ε is the advantage of the (W)-D-$\mathrm{RLWR}_{\mathbf{B},q,p,\ell,\psi'}^i$ oracle.*

The proof of this lemma is similar to that of Lemma 5.9 in [26]. Due to the space limit, we put it in full version of this paper.

(W)-D-RLWR$^i_{\mathbf{B},q,p,\ell,\psi'}$ to D-RLWR$_{\mathbf{B},q,p,\ell,\psi'}$

Definition 4.8 (D-RLWR$^i_{\mathbf{B},q,p,\ell,\psi'}$). *The average-case D-RLWR$^i_{\mathbf{B},q,p,\ell,\psi'}$ problem is defined as follows: given ℓ samples from $L^j_{s,q,p}(R, \mathbf{B})$ for $s \leftarrow U(\psi')$ and $j \in \{i-1, i\}$, determine j.*

Lemma 4.9 (Worst-case to average-case). *For every $i \in \{1, \cdots, g\}$ and the uniform distribution ψ' over $(R^\vee_q)^*$, there exists a randomized poly-time reduction from worst-case (W)-D-RLWR$^i_{\mathbf{B},q,p,\ell,\psi'}$ to average-case D-RLWR$^i_{\mathbf{B},q,p,\ell,\psi'}$.*

The lemma can be proved by the technique of re-randomization of the secret. Due to the space limit, we put the proof in full version of this paper.

Lemma 4.10 (D-RLWR$^i_{\mathbf{B},q,p,\ell,\psi'}$ to D-RLWR$_{\mathbf{B},q,p,\ell,\psi'}$). *For any oracle solving the D-RLWR$_{\mathbf{B},q,p,\ell,\psi'}$ problem with advantage ε, there exists an $i \in \{1, \cdots, g\}$ and an efficient algorithm that solves D-RLWR$^i_{\mathbf{B},q,p,\ell,\psi'}$ with advantage ε/g using this oracle.*

The lemma can be proved by a simple hybrid argument. We put the proof in full version of this paper.

The proof of Theorem 4.2 follows from Lemmas 4.4, 4.7, 4.9, and 4.10.

4.2 Search RLWE to Search RLWR

Before presenting the main theorem, we describe some notations that will be used later. First, the ring LWE problem will take parameters to specify the modulus, and the distributions of secret and the error. We will use ϕ to denote the error distribution, ψ to denote the secret distribution (same as RLWR). Thus, RLWE$_{q,\phi,\ell,\psi}$ means the ring LWE problem with modulus q, error distribution ϕ, ℓ samples, and secret distribution ψ. Next, we use $U_\beta(\mathbf{B})$ to denote the distribution over $R^\vee_q$ that each coefficient with respect to the basis $\mathbf{B}$ over $R^\vee$ is sampled uniformly at random in the interval $[-\beta, \beta]$.

Theorem 4.11 (S-RLWE$_{q,\phi,\ell,\psi}$ to S-RLWR$_{\mathbf{B},q,p,\ell,\psi}$). *Let ϕ be a B_e-bounded distribution over the canonical imbedding space H, $\mathbf{B}$ be a basis of $R^\vee$ with dual basis $\mathbf{B}'$ such that $\|\sigma(b'_j)\|_2 \leq B_d$, and $q \geq 18pB_dB_e\ell n$. Then there exists a poly-time reduction from S-RLWE$_{q,\phi,\ell,\psi}$ to S-RLWR$_{\mathbf{B},q,p,\ell,\psi}$, where $\psi = R^\vee_p \cap (R^\vee_q)^*$.*

Our reduction can be obtained by the following two steps:

$$S\text{-RLWE}_{q,\phi,\ell,\psi} \xrightarrow{(1)} S\text{-RLWE}_{q,\phi+U_\beta(\mathbf{B}),\ell,\psi} \xrightarrow{(2)} S\text{-RLWR}_{\mathbf{B},q,p,\ell,\psi}.$$

The first reduction is straight-forward. The second reduction uses an RD analysis similar to the work [8]. We note that it is possible to use bound the Rènyi

Divergence of the instances from the first and the third problems. However, this will incur large parameter loss, e.g., the work [14] takes this approach, and they are only able to analyze a constant number of samples, i.e., $\ell = O(1)$.

Due to space limit, we put the proof in full version of this paper.

4.3   On Normal Integer Basis and Cyclotomic Fields of Power of 2

Our hardness results require a short normal integral basis by combining Theorem 4.2 and Theorem 4.11. As we discussed in the introduction, by Hilbert-Speiser and Kronecker-Weber theorems, normal integral bases exist for cyclotomic fields with prime-power-free periods and their subfields. It's not hard to determine such a basis in squared-free fields using the idea of [27]. We describe the selection of the bases in full version of this paper.

One very special type of cyclotomic fields is the case of power of 2. This field does not have normal integer basis, but our main Theorem 4.2 can be generalized to this setting *if* we select specify types of rounding function $\lfloor \cdot \rceil$. Note: for normal integer bases (NIB), Theorem 4.2 holds with respect to *any* rounding function. With a careful inspection, the most significant property we need for the theorem is that rounding commutes with automorphisms, which is true if $\mathbf{B}$ is an NIB. However, for cyclotomic fields of power of 2, we know that there is a case where $\sigma(x) = -x$, in which $\lfloor \sigma(x) \rceil$ might be different from $\sigma(\lfloor x \rceil)$ for a general rounding function $\lfloor \cdot \rceil$. Nevertheless, if we use specific rounding function that imposes this constraint, then Theorem 4.2 also holds. A particular example is to round coefficients in the following way: for $z \in \mathbb{R}$, define $\lfloor z \rceil = \mathsf{Sign}(z) \cdot \mathsf{round}(|z|)$ for any rounding function $\mathsf{round} : \mathbb{R}^+ \cup \{0\} \to \mathbb{Z}^+ \cup \{0\}$.

5   Module Ring-LWR Under Leakage

In this section, we study whether (Module) Ring-LWR is hard in the presence of leakage. As discussed in the introduction, we first present a negative result for Ring-LWR, and thus simply an entropy lower bound is not sufficient to derive leakage resilience over Ring-LWR. Next we show general positive results for Module Ring-LWR, for sufficiently large dimensions. As a key technical building block, we prove a general ring leftover hash lemma.

5.1   A Negative Result for Ring-LWR Under Leakage

First, we show that Ring-LWR might be completely insecure if the attacker obtains some leakage of the secret. The idea of our attack is similar to that of Ring-LWE by Bolboceanu et al. [9]. Below we present the details.

Let $\mathfrak{q} \supset qR$ be an integral ideal in R, we let $\bar{\mathfrak{q}} = q\mathfrak{q}^{-1}$ denote its complement with respect to qR. Then we have that $\bar{\mathfrak{q}}^\vee = (q\mathfrak{q}^{-1})^\vee = \frac{1}{q}(\mathfrak{q}^{-1})^\vee = \frac{1}{q}\mathfrak{q}R^\vee$ with respect to $R^\vee$. Before presenting the attack on Ring-LWR, we first recall the attack of Ring-LWE in [9].

Lemma 5.1 ([9]). *Let K, R be a degree n number field and its ring of integers, $\mathfrak{q} \supset qR$ be an integral R-ideal, and $\bar{\mathfrak{q}} = q\mathfrak{q}^{-1}$ be its complement. There exists a non-uniform algorithm such that for any secret distribution ψ, any error distribution ϕ satisfying that $\mathsf{Pr}_{e \leftarrow \phi}[\|e\|_2 < 1/(2\lambda_n(\bar{\mathfrak{q}}))]$ is non-negligible, the algorithm solves search $\mathsf{RLWE}_{q,\phi,1,\psi}$ with a non-negligible probability.*

Then the attack can be described by the the the corollary below.

Corollary 5.2 (Attack for RLWR with Entropic Secrets). *Let K, R be a degree n cyclotomic field and its ring of integers, $\mathbf{B}$ be a basis of R with B_d-bounded ℓ_∞ norm for all its elements, $q = pp'$ where p is a prime such that pR completely splits as prime ideals over R.*

Then for every integer $\eta \in [n]$, letting $\epsilon = \eta/n$, if $p^\epsilon > 2n^{5/2}p'B_d$, there exists a distribution ψ over $R_p^\vee$ with entropy $(1 - \epsilon)n \log p$ such that $\mathsf{RLWR}_{\mathbf{B},q,p,1,\psi}$ can be solved with a non-negligible probability.

Proof. Let $qR = pp'R = \prod_i^n \mathfrak{p}_i \cdot p'R$, where $pR = \prod_i^n \mathfrak{p}_i$. We define the distribution ψ as follows: given a parameter $\eta \in [n]$, set ideal $\mathcal{I} = \prod_i^\eta \mathfrak{p}_i$. Then a sample from ψ is generated by choosing $s \leftarrow \mathcal{I}R^\vee/pR^\vee$ uniformly random in this ideal.

For a given $L_{s,q,p}(R, \mathbf{B})$ sample $(a, b = \lfloor a \cdot s \rceil_{\mathbf{B},p}), s \leftarrow \psi$, b can be written as $b = \frac{p}{q}a \cdot s + \delta$, where $\delta = \lfloor a \cdot s \rceil_{\mathbf{B},p} - \frac{p}{q}a \cdot s$ can be viewed as the deterministic noise induced by rounding. The coefficients of the noise with respect to $\mathbf{B}$ belong to $[-1, 1]$ (real numbers). First we set $b' = \frac{1}{p}b = \frac{1}{q}a \cdot s + \frac{1}{p}\delta$ (as an element in $K_\mathbb{R}$). By Lemma 5.1, we know that if $\|\frac{1}{p}\delta\|_2 < 1/(2\lambda_n(\bar{\mathfrak{q}}))$ with non-negligible probability, s can be recovered by non-negligible probability.

It remains to bound the ℓ_2 norm of $\frac{1}{p}\delta$. According the definition of δ, the coefficients of $\frac{1}{p}\delta$ with respect to $\mathbf{B}$ belong to $[-\frac{1}{p}, \frac{1}{p}]$. Writing $\frac{1}{p}\delta = \langle \mathbf{B}, c \rangle$, then by Cauchy-Schwarz inequality: $\|\frac{1}{p}\delta\|_2 \leq \|\sum_{i=1}^n c_i\sigma(b_i)\|_2 \leq \sum_{i=1}^n |c_i| \cdot \|\sigma(b_i)\|_2 \leq \frac{1}{p}\sum_{i=1}^n \|\sigma(b_i)\|_2$. Furthermore $\|\sigma(b_i)\|_2 = (\sum_{i=1}^n |\sigma(b_i)|^2)^{1/2} \leq \sqrt{n}B_d$. We can bound the ℓ_2 norm of $\frac{1}{p}\delta$ by $\frac{1}{p}n^{3/2}B_d$.

On the other hand, by similar calculation as [9], we know that $\lambda_n(\bar{\mathfrak{q}}) \leq \frac{nq}{p^{n/n}} = np'p^{1-\epsilon}$. By the parameters setting, we have that $\|\frac{1}{p}\delta\| < \frac{1}{2\lambda_n(\bar{\mathfrak{q}})}$, as desired. $\qquad\square$

Remark 5.3. *Corollary 5.2 can be easily generalized to the case where the secret is uniformly random over $R^\vee/pR^\vee$, yet the attacker learns the information of $s' = s \mod \mathcal{I}R^\vee$ for $\mathcal{I} = \prod_{i=1}^\eta \mathfrak{p}_i$. We can set $b' = \frac{1}{p}b - \frac{1}{q}as' = \frac{1}{q}a \cdot (s - s') + \frac{1}{p}\delta$. Then this reduces back to the entropic secret as $s - s' \in \mathcal{I}$. By applying Corollary 5.2, the attacker learns $s - s'$, and then he can recover s.*

5.2   Towards Leakage Resilience of Module Ring-LWR

Next, we proceed to prove that Module Ring-LWR is pseudorandom for entropic secrets (under some entropy requirements) for larger dimensions. To achieve this, we first prove a general leftover hash lemma in the ring setting as a new tool. By using the leftover hash lemma, we are able to generalize the plain LWR hardness result of [3] to the ring setting. Depending on the splitting of qR, we are able to achieve different range of parameters. We present two important case studies: (1) qR is low-splitting, i.e., it splits into fewer but larger ideals, and (2) general cases where qR can be arbitrary. In the former case, we are able to achieve smaller parameters, as low-splitting is in favor of randomness extraction by the leftover hash lemma. We will elaborate further below.

New Tool: A New Algebraic Leftover Hash Lemma

Definition 5.4 (Hash Family over (Algebraic) Lattice). *Let $q, k \geq 2$ be integers, $\mathcal{L}$ be lattice over the number field K, and $\mathcal{O}^{\mathcal{L}}$, $\mathcal{L}^{\vee}$ be its coefficient ring and dual lattice, respectively. We define the following hash function family $\mathcal{H}(\mathcal{O}^{\mathcal{L}}, \mathcal{X}, q, k) = \{f_a : (\mathcal{L}_q^{\vee})^k \to \mathcal{L}_q^{\vee}\}_{a \in (\mathcal{O}_q^{\mathcal{L}})^k}$ as $f_a(\boldsymbol{x}) = \sum_{i=1}^{k} x_i \cdot a_i \bmod q(\mathcal{L})^{\vee}$, for all $\boldsymbol{x} \in \mathcal{X} \subseteq (\mathcal{L}_q^{\vee})^k$, where $\sum_i x_i \cdot a_i$ is computed by using the field addition and multiplication over K.*

In this paper, we consider $\mathcal{L} = R = \mathcal{O}_K$ and $\mathcal{L} = \mathcal{O}$ for an arbitrary order of $K = \mathbb{Q}(\alpha)$ (or their dual $R^{\vee}$ and $\mathcal{O}^{\vee}$). We remark that for any $\mathcal{O} \subseteq \mathcal{O}_K$, there exists an isomorphism between $\mathcal{O}_q$ and R_q as long as $|\mathcal{O}/R|$ is coprime with q [37]. For brevity, we focus on the case of $\mathcal{L} = R = \mathcal{O}_K$, and analogous properties of $\mathcal{O}$ will follow by which of $\mathcal{O}_K$ according to the isomorphism.

Next we introduce the following variant of the Leftover Hash Lemma [19], generalized to the ring of integers of any arbitrary number field K (not necessarily a Galois extension). Before presenting the description of the lemma, we first define the distribution as follows

$$\mathcal{D}(\mathcal{H}, R_q^{\vee}) = \{(f_a, b) | f_a \xleftarrow{\$} \mathcal{H}(R, \mathcal{X}, q, k), b = f_a(\boldsymbol{x}) \text{ for } \boldsymbol{x} \leftarrow \mathcal{X}\}.$$

For simplicity, we will use $\boldsymbol{a}$ to stand for the description of f_a in the distribution $\mathcal{D}(\mathcal{H}, R_q^{\vee})$, and then $\mathcal{D}(\mathcal{H}, R_q^{\vee})$ can be simply denoted as $\mathcal{D}((R_q)^k, R_q^{\vee}) = \{(\boldsymbol{a}, b) | \boldsymbol{a} \xleftarrow{\$} (R_q)^k, b = f_a(\boldsymbol{x}) \text{ for } \boldsymbol{x} \leftarrow \mathcal{X}\}$. Our goal is to prove that $\mathcal{D}(\mathcal{H}, R_q^{\vee})$ is statistically close to the uniform distribution if the input distribution $\mathcal{X}$ satisfies a certain entropy condition.

To achieve this, we need some preparation of the following definition: we say that vector $\boldsymbol{r} \in (R^{\vee})^k$ *maximal belongs* to a factor $\mathcal{I}$ of qR, abbreviated as $\boldsymbol{r} \in_{\max} \mathcal{I}R^{\vee}$ if the following conditions hold.

- For every coordinate r_i of $\boldsymbol{r}$, we have $r_i \in \mathcal{I}R^{\vee}$.
- For any ideal $\mathcal{J}|qR$ such that $\mathcal{I}|\mathcal{J}$, there exists at least one coordinate r_j such that $r_j \notin \mathcal{J}R^{\vee}$.

Now we present our main result as follows:

Theorem 5.5 (Algebraic Leftover Hash Lemma). *For any hash function family $\mathcal{H}(R, \mathcal{X}, q, k)$ over a number field $K = \mathbb{Q}(\alpha)$ with degree n and $\gcd(q, [\mathcal{O}_K : \mathbb{Z}[\alpha]]) = 1$, we have*

$$\Delta\big(\mathcal{D}(\mathcal{H}, R_q^{\vee}), U(\mathcal{H}, R_q^{\vee})\big) \leq \frac{1}{2} \sqrt{\sum_{\substack{\mathfrak{q} \neq \langle 1 \rangle \\ \mathfrak{q} | qR}} N(\mathfrak{q}) \mathsf{Col}(\mathcal{X}_{\mathfrak{q}})},$$

where $\mathcal{X}_{\mathsf{q}} = \{\boldsymbol{x} \bmod \mathsf{q}R^\vee | \boldsymbol{x} \leftarrow \mathcal{X}\}$, $\mathsf{Col}(\mathcal{X}_{\mathsf{q}})$ is the collision probability of $\mathcal{X}_{\mathsf{q}}$, and q ranges over all divisors (except $\langle 1 \rangle$) of the ideal $\langle q \rangle = qR$.

Proof. As discussed above, we need to bound $\Delta\big(\mathcal{D}((R_q)^k, R_q^\vee), U((R_q)^k, R_q^\vee)\big)$. To do this, we first derive an upper bound on the statistical distance between $\mathcal{D}((R_q)^k, R_q^\vee)$ and $U((R_q)^k, R_q^\vee)$ (which are written as $\mathcal{D}$ and U for simplicity) in terms of the collision probability $\mathsf{Col}(\mathcal{D})$.

$$
\begin{aligned}
\Delta(\mathcal{D}, U) &= \frac{1}{2} \sum_{(a,b) \in U} \left| \Pr[(\boldsymbol{a}, b) \leftarrow \mathcal{D}] - \frac{1}{|U|} \right| \\
&\le \frac{1}{2} \sqrt{|U|} \sqrt{\sum_{(a,b) \in U} \left(\Pr[(\boldsymbol{a}, b) \leftarrow \mathcal{D}] - \frac{1}{|U|} \right)^2} \\
&= \frac{1}{2} \sqrt{|U|} \sqrt{-\frac{1}{|U|} + \sum_{(a,b) \in U} \Pr[(\boldsymbol{a}, b) \leftarrow \mathcal{D}]^2} \\
&\le \frac{1}{2} \sqrt{|U| \cdot \mathsf{Col}(\mathcal{D}) - 1}.
\end{aligned}
\tag{1}
$$

Next we bound $\mathsf{Col}(\mathcal{D})$ as follows, where all probabilities run through two independently copies of $\boldsymbol{a}, \boldsymbol{a}' \leftarrow (R_q)^k$ and $\boldsymbol{x}, \boldsymbol{y} \leftarrow \mathcal{X}$:

$$
\begin{aligned}
\mathsf{Col}(\mathcal{D}) &= \Pr[(\boldsymbol{a} = \boldsymbol{a}') \wedge (\boldsymbol{a} \cdot \boldsymbol{x} = \boldsymbol{a}' \cdot \boldsymbol{y} \bmod qR^\vee)] \\
&= \Pr[\boldsymbol{a} = \boldsymbol{a}'] \cdot \Pr[\boldsymbol{a} \cdot \boldsymbol{x} - \boldsymbol{a}' \cdot \boldsymbol{y} = 0 \bmod qR^\vee | \boldsymbol{a} = \boldsymbol{a}'] \\
&= \frac{1}{q^{nk}} \cdot \Pr[\boldsymbol{a} \cdot (\boldsymbol{x} - \boldsymbol{y}) = 0 \bmod qR^\vee].
\end{aligned}
\tag{2}
$$

Now we further bound the probability $\Pr[\boldsymbol{a} \cdot (\boldsymbol{x} - \boldsymbol{y}) = 0 \bmod qR^\vee]$. To do this, we first let $q = p_1^{r_1} \cdots p_t^{r_t}$ be the prime (integer) factorization, and the consider the (ideal) decomposition of qR. Since $\gcd(q, [\mathcal{O}_K : \mathbb{Z}[\alpha]]) = 1$, we can apply Lemma 2.4 on each prime factor and obtain $p_i R = \prod_{j \in [g_i]} \mathfrak{p}_{i,j}^{e'_{i,j}}$ where $\mathfrak{p}_{i,j} = \langle p_i, f_{i,j}(\alpha) \rangle$ for some monic irreducible polynomial $f_{i,j}(x) \in \mathbb{Z}_{p_i}[x]$, for $i \in [t]$. Thus, $qR = p_1^{r_1} \cdots p_t^{r_t} R = \prod_{i,j} \mathfrak{p}_{i,j}^{e_{i,j}}$, where $e_{i,j} = e'_{i,j} r_i$ for every $i \in [t], j \in [g_i]$. We also have $qR^\vee = \prod_{i,j} \mathfrak{p}_{i,j}^{e_{i,j}} R^\vee$ by Lemma 2.6.

Then we observe a simple fact that any possible $\boldsymbol{x} - \boldsymbol{y}$ in the range must maximal belong to $\mathcal{J}R^\vee$ for only one ideal factor $\mathcal{J}|qR$. We sketch a simple proof by contradiction. Assume there are $\mathcal{J}_1 \neq \mathcal{J}_2$ that a vector $\boldsymbol{x} \in_{\max} \mathcal{J}_1$ and $\boldsymbol{x} \in_{\max} \mathcal{J}_2$. Then it is not hard to see that $\boldsymbol{x}$ maximal belongs to their LCM, i.e., $\mathcal{J}_1 \cap \mathcal{J}_2$, a strictly smaller ideal. Then we know that $\mathcal{J}_1 | \mathcal{J}_1 \cap \mathcal{J}_2$, and every element of $\boldsymbol{x}$ belongs to $\mathcal{J}_1 \cap \mathcal{J}_2$, reaching a contradiction to $\boldsymbol{x} \in_{\max} \mathcal{J}_1$.

As $\{(\boldsymbol{x} - \boldsymbol{y}) \in_{\max} \mathcal{J}\}_{\mathcal{J}|qR^\vee}$ forms a partition (as argued above), we can use the total probability to re-write the following equation:

$$
\begin{aligned}
&\Pr[\boldsymbol{a} \cdot (\boldsymbol{x} - \boldsymbol{y}) = 0 \bmod qR^\vee] \\
&= \sum_{\mathcal{J}|qR^\vee} \Pr[\boldsymbol{a} \cdot (\boldsymbol{x} - \boldsymbol{y}) = 0 \bmod qR^\vee | \boldsymbol{x} - \boldsymbol{y} \in_{\max} \mathcal{J}R^\vee] \cdot \Pr[\boldsymbol{x} - \boldsymbol{y} \in_{\max} \mathcal{J}R^\vee].
\end{aligned}
\tag{3}
$$

We know the probability $\Pr[\boldsymbol{x} - \boldsymbol{y} \in_{\max} \mathcal{J}R^\vee] \le \Pr[\boldsymbol{x} - \boldsymbol{y} = 0 \bmod \mathcal{J}R^\vee] = \mathrm{Col}(\mathcal{X}_\mathcal{J})$ for every $\mathcal{J}|qR$. Thus, it remains to compute

$$\Pr\left[\boldsymbol{a} \cdot (\boldsymbol{x} - \boldsymbol{y}) = 0 \bmod qR^\vee \,|\, \boldsymbol{x} - \boldsymbol{y} \in_{\max} \mathcal{J}R^\vee\right].$$

Without loss of generality, we let $\mathcal{J} = \prod_{i,j} \mathfrak{p}_{i,j}^{x_{i,j}}, 0 \le x_{i,j} \le e_{i,j}$. By Chinese Reminder Theorem 2.5, we have $R^\vee/qR^\vee \cong \bigoplus_{i,j} R^\vee/\mathfrak{p}_{i,j}^{e_{i,j}}$. Thus, we can view a random ring element in $R^\vee/qR^\vee$ as independently random coordinates in $\{R^\vee/\mathfrak{p}_{i,j}^{e_{i,j}}\}_{i,j}$. Therefore, we write:

$$\begin{aligned}
&\Pr[\boldsymbol{a} \cdot (\boldsymbol{x} - \boldsymbol{y}) = 0 \bmod qR^\vee \,|\, \boldsymbol{x} - \boldsymbol{y} \in_{\max} \mathcal{J}R^\vee] \\
&= \prod_{i,j} \Pr[\boldsymbol{a} \cdot (\boldsymbol{x} - \boldsymbol{y}) = 0 \bmod \mathfrak{p}_{i,j}^{e_{i,j}} R^\vee \,|\, \boldsymbol{x} - \boldsymbol{y} \in_{\max} \mathcal{J}R^\vee] \\
&= \prod_{i,j} \Pr[\boldsymbol{a}_{i,j} \cdot (\boldsymbol{x} - \boldsymbol{y})_{i,j} = 0 \bmod \mathfrak{p}_{i,j}^{e_{i,j}} R^\vee \,|\, \boldsymbol{x} - \boldsymbol{y} \in_{\max} \mathcal{J}R^\vee],
\end{aligned} \tag{4}$$

where $\boldsymbol{a}_{i,j} = \boldsymbol{a} \bmod \mathfrak{p}_{i,j}^{e_{i,j}}, (\boldsymbol{x} - \boldsymbol{y})_{i,j} = \boldsymbol{x} - \boldsymbol{y} \bmod \mathfrak{p}_{i,j}^{e_{i,j}} R^\vee$.

Next we will determine the ideal generated by the vector $(\boldsymbol{x} - \boldsymbol{y})_{i,j} = ((\boldsymbol{x} - \boldsymbol{y})_{i,j}[1], \cdots, (\boldsymbol{x} - \boldsymbol{y})_{i,j}[k])$, so that we can apply Lemma 2.3 to bound the probability $\Pr[\boldsymbol{a}_i \cdot (\boldsymbol{x} - \boldsymbol{y})_i = 0 \bmod \mathfrak{p}_{i,j}^{e_{i,j}} R^\vee \,|\, \boldsymbol{x} - \boldsymbol{y} \in_{\max} \mathcal{J}R^\vee]$ for each i, j.

Claim 5.6. *The ideal generated by vector $(\boldsymbol{x} - \boldsymbol{y})_{i,j}$ is $\mathfrak{p}_{i,j}^{x_{i,j}} R^\vee$.*

Proof. Below we will use r_p to denote a ring element r modulo an integer p, i.e., $r_p = r \bmod p$, for short.

By definition of $(\boldsymbol{x} - \boldsymbol{y}) \in_{\max} \mathcal{J}$, we know that for each $\eta \in [k]$, $(\boldsymbol{x} - \boldsymbol{y})_{i,j}[\eta] \in \mathfrak{p}_{i,j}^{x_{i,j}} R^\vee/\mathfrak{p}_{i,j}^{e_{i,j}} R^\vee$. Therefore, the ideal $\langle (\boldsymbol{x} - \boldsymbol{y})_{i,j} \rangle$ generated by vector $(\boldsymbol{x} - \boldsymbol{y})_{i,j}$ satisfies $\langle (\boldsymbol{x} - \boldsymbol{y})_{i,j} \rangle \subseteq \mathfrak{p}_{i,j}^{x_{i,j}} R^\vee$.

On the other hand, there exists $k' \in [k]$ such that $(\boldsymbol{x} - \boldsymbol{y})_{i,j}[k'] \notin \mathfrak{p}_{i,j}^{x_{i,j}+1} R^\vee/\mathfrak{p}_{i,j}^{e_{i,j}} R^\vee$. It is clear that the principle ideal $\langle (\boldsymbol{x} - \boldsymbol{y})_{i,j}[k'] \rangle$ generated by $(\boldsymbol{x} - \boldsymbol{y})_{i,j}[k']$ satisfies that $\langle (\boldsymbol{x} - \boldsymbol{y})_{i,j}[k'] \rangle \subseteq \langle (\boldsymbol{x} - \boldsymbol{y})_{i,j} \rangle$. Thus in order to show $\langle (\boldsymbol{x} - \boldsymbol{y})_{i,j} \rangle = \mathfrak{p}_{i,j}^{x_{i,j}} R^\vee$, it suffices to show $\mathfrak{p}_{i,j}^{x_{i,j}} R^\vee \subseteq \langle (\boldsymbol{x} - \boldsymbol{y})_{i,j}[k'] \rangle$.

According to Lemma 2.6 and the isomorphism theorem, we have

$$\mathfrak{p}_{i,j}^{x_{i,j}} R^\vee/\mathfrak{p}_{i,j}^{e_{i,j}} R^\vee \cong \mathfrak{p}_{i,j}^{x_{i,j}} R/\mathfrak{p}_{i,j}^{e_{i,j}} R \cong (\mathfrak{p}_{i,j}^{x_{i,j}}/\langle p_i \rangle)/(\mathfrak{p}_{i,j}^{e_{i,j}}/\langle p_i \rangle) = \langle f_{i,j}^{x_{i,j}}(\alpha)_{p_i} \rangle/\langle f_{i,j}^{e_{i,j}}(\alpha)_{p_i} \rangle,$$

and as well

$$\mathfrak{p}_{i,j}^{x_{i,j}+1} R^\vee/\mathfrak{p}_{i,j}^{e_{i,j}} R^\vee \cong \mathfrak{p}_{i,j}^{x_{i,j}+1} R/\mathfrak{p}_{i,j}^{e_{i,j}} R \cong \langle f_{i,j}^{x_{i,j}+1}(\alpha)_{p_i} \rangle/\langle f_{i,j}^{e_{i,j}}(\alpha)_{p_i} \rangle.$$

Then we can see that, there exists an element $r \cdot f_{i,j}^{x_{i,j}}(\alpha)_{p_i} \in \langle f_{i,j}^{x_{i,j}}(\alpha)_{p_i} \rangle/\langle f_{i,j}^{e_{i,j}}(\alpha)_{p_i} \rangle$ that is equivalent to $(\boldsymbol{x} - \boldsymbol{y})_{i,j}[k']$ under the isomorphism, satisfying $r \in R, r \notin \langle f_{i,j}(\alpha)_{p_i} \rangle$. Therefore, $\mathfrak{p}_{i,j}^{x_{i,j}} R^\vee \subseteq \langle (\boldsymbol{x} - \boldsymbol{y})_{i,j}[k'] \rangle$ is equivalent to $\langle f_{i,j}^{x_{i,j}}(\alpha)_{p_i} \rangle \subseteq \langle r \cdot f_{i,j}^{x_{i,j}}(\alpha)_{p_i} \rangle$, under the view of the isomorphism. It remains to show $\langle f_{i,j}^{x_{i,j}}(\alpha)_{p_i} \rangle \subseteq \langle r \cdot f_{i,j}^{x_{i,j}}(\alpha)_{p_i} \rangle$.

To see this, we denote $u = r \bmod f_{i,j}(\alpha)_{p_i} \in R_{p_i}/\langle f_{i,j}(\alpha)_{p_i} \rangle$. We notice that $R_{p_i}/\langle f_{i,j}(\alpha)_{p_i} \rangle \cong R/\mathfrak{p}_{i,j}$, which is a field as $\mathfrak{p}_{i,j}$ is a prime ideal according to

Lemma 2.4. Therefore, $u \neq 0$ is invertible over $R_{p_i}/\langle f_{i,j}(\alpha)_{p_i}\rangle$, and hence there is an element $v \in R_{p_i}/\langle f_{i,j}(\alpha)_{p_i}\rangle$ such that $vr = 1 \bmod f_{i,j}(\alpha)_{p_i}$. From this, there exist $vr \in \langle r \rangle, tf_{i,j}(\alpha)_{p_i} \in \langle f_{i,j}(\alpha)_{p_i}\rangle$ such that $vr + tf_{i,j}(\alpha)_{p_i} = 1$, so $\langle r \rangle$ is coprime to $\langle f_{i,j}(\alpha)_{p_i}\rangle$. Furthermore, according to Lemma 2.2, $\langle r \rangle$ is coprime to $\langle f_{i,j}^{e_{i,j}}(\alpha)_{p_i}\rangle$, and thus r is invertible over $R_{p_i}/\langle f_{i,j}^{e_{i,j}}(\alpha)_{p_i}\rangle$. Therefore, any element $\mu \cdot f_{i,j}^{x_{i,j}}(\alpha)_{p_i} = \mu \cdot r^{-1} r \cdot f_{i,j}^{e_{i,j}}(\alpha)_{p_i} \in \langle f_{i,j}^{e_{i,j}}(\alpha)_{p_i}\rangle$ also belongs to $\langle r \cdot f_{i,j}^{x_{i,j}}(\alpha)_{p_i}\rangle$. This reaches our desired conclusion that $\langle f_{i,j}^{x_{i,j}}(\alpha)_{p_i}\rangle \subseteq \langle r \cdot f_{i,j}^{x_{i,j}}(\alpha)_{p_i}\rangle$. □

From Lemma 2.3 and Claim 5.6, we know that $\Pr[\boldsymbol{a}_i \cdot (\boldsymbol{x}-\boldsymbol{y})_i = 0 \bmod \mathfrak{p}_{i,j}^{e_{i,j}} R^\vee | \boldsymbol{x} - \boldsymbol{y} \in_{\max} \mathcal{J}R^\vee] = \dfrac{N(\mathfrak{p}_{i,j}^{x_{i,j}})}{N(\mathfrak{p}_{i,j}^{e_{i,j}})}$. Then we continue to compute Eq. (4):

$$
\prod_{i,j} \Pr[\boldsymbol{a}_i \cdot (\boldsymbol{x} - \boldsymbol{y})_i = 0 \bmod \mathfrak{p}_{i,j}^{e_{i,j}} | \boldsymbol{x} - \boldsymbol{y} \in_{\max} \mathcal{J}R^\vee]
$$
$$
= \prod_{i,j} \frac{N(\mathfrak{p}_{i,j}^{x_{i,j}})}{N(\mathfrak{p}_{i,j}^{e_{i,j}})} = \prod_{i,j} \frac{N(\mathfrak{p}_{i,j})^{x_{i,j}}}{N(\mathfrak{p}_{i,j}^{e_{i,j}})} = \frac{N(\mathcal{J})}{\prod_i N(p_i)} = \frac{N(\mathcal{J})}{q^n}.
\tag{5}
$$

Combine Eqs. (1), (2), (3), and using the facts $N(R) = 1$, $\mathsf{Col}(\mathcal{X}_R) = 1$, yields the bound in the lemma. □

From our leftover hash lemma, we can derive the following corollaries for three important cases: (1) the general case, (2) K is a cyclotomic field, and (3) qR does not have a "small" ideal factor (in the norm). Due to the limitation of space, we defer the proof to full version of this paper.

Corollary 5.7. *Let k, e, q be integers, $\varepsilon \in (0, 1)$, and $R = \mathcal{O}_K$ be the ring of integers of a number field $K = \mathbb{Q}(\alpha)$ with degree n, such that $\gcd(q, [\mathcal{O}_K : \mathbb{Z}[\alpha]]) = 1$ and $e \geq 2\log\left(\frac{1}{\varepsilon}\right) + 2n\log q - 2$. Suppose $\boldsymbol{s}$ is chosen from some distribution $\mathcal{X}$ over $(R_q^\vee)^k$ such that $H_\infty(\boldsymbol{s} \bmod \mathfrak{q}) \geq e$ for any ideal $\mathfrak{q}|qR$, and $\boldsymbol{a} \overset{\$}{\leftarrow} (R_q)^k, u \overset{\$}{\leftarrow} R_q^\vee$ are uniformly random and independent of $\boldsymbol{s}$. Then we have that $\Delta\big[(\boldsymbol{a}, \langle \boldsymbol{a}, \boldsymbol{s}\rangle \bmod qR^\vee), (\boldsymbol{a}, u)\big] \leq \varepsilon$.*

Corollary 5.8 (Cyclotomic Fields). *Adopt the notations in Corollary 5.7. Let K be a cyclotomic number field of degree n. The conclusion holds for $e \geq 2\log\left(\frac{1}{\varepsilon}\right) + (n+2)\log q - 2$.*

Corollary 5.9 (Large Ideal Factors). *Adopt the notations in Corollary 5.7. The conclusion holds if for any prime ideal factor $\mathfrak{p}_{i,j}$ of qR, we have $N(\mathfrak{p}_{i,j}) \geq n\log q + 1$, and $e \geq 2\log\left(\frac{1}{\varepsilon}\right) + n\log q$.*

5.3   Hardness of Module-RLWR

In this section, we present hardness results of Module Ring-LWR, by applying our new leftover hash lemma to the proof framework of [3]. We first present a definition of module-RLWR under weak secrets, a generalization of the plain weak LWR in the work [3].

Definition 5.10 (Weak Module-RLWR). *Let n, p, q, ℓ, k be positive integers, $R = \mathcal{O}_K$ be the ring of integers of a number field K with degree n, $\mathbf{B}$ be a basis of $R^\vee$, and the decomposition of qR be $\mathfrak{q}_1^{e_1} \cdots \mathfrak{q}_g^{e_g}$ where each $\mathfrak{q}_i$ is a prime ideal over $R^\vee$. The (decision) $\mathsf{wRLWR}^k_{\mathbf{B},q,p,\ell,\gamma,e}$ assumption is defined as: let $(\mathbf{s}, \mathsf{aux})$ be a pair of correlated random variable where*

- *each coefficient $s_i[j]$ of each s_i relative to $\mathbf{B}$ has range in $[-\gamma, \gamma]$ for $i \in [k], j \in [n]$;*
- *$H_\infty(\mathbf{s} \bmod \mathfrak{q}_j | \mathsf{aux}) \geq e$ for each prime ideal factor $\mathfrak{q}_j$ of qR.*

The task is to distinguish the following two distributions:

$$(\mathsf{aux}, \mathbf{A}, \lfloor \mathbf{A} \cdot \mathbf{s} \rceil_{\mathbf{B},p}) \text{ versus } (\mathsf{aux}, \mathbf{A}, \lfloor \mathbf{u} \rceil_{\mathbf{B},p}),$$

where $\mathbf{A} \xleftarrow{\$} (R_q)^{\ell \times k}$, $\mathbf{u} \xleftarrow{\$} (R_q^\vee)^\ell$ are uniform and independent of $(\mathbf{s}, \mathsf{aux})$.

Below we describe two interesting case studies: (1) when qR is low-splitting, i.e., it factors into fewer but larger ideals (in norm), and (2) the general case. For the low-splitting case, we are able to achieve the following theorem.

Theorem 5.11 (Hardness of Module-RLWR for Low-splitting Case). *Let $\lambda, n, p, q, \ell, k, \gamma$ be positive integers, $R = \mathcal{O}_K$ be the ring of integers of a number field $K = \mathbb{Q}(\alpha)$ with degree n, $\mathbf{B}$ be a basis of $R^\vee$ with B_{d_1} bounded ℓ_∞ norm for all entries, all entries of its dual basis $\mathbf{B}'$ be B_{d_2}-bounded in ℓ_∞ norm, $t \in (R^\vee)^{-1}$ such that $tR^\vee + qR = R$, ϕ be a β-bounded distribution over $K_\mathbb{R}$ for some real $\beta > 0$, such that $q \geq 2B_{d_1}B_{d_2}\beta\gamma k\ell pn^{\frac{5}{2}}$ and $\gcd(q, [\mathcal{O}_K : \mathbb{Z}[\alpha]]) = 1$.*

Assume that the decomposition of qR can be expressed as $\prod_{i,j} \mathfrak{p}_{i,j}^{e_{i,j}}$, where each $\mathfrak{p}_{i,j}$ is a prime ideal over R, and $N(\mathfrak{p}_{i,j}) \geq 2^\lambda \geq n\log q + 1$. Then we have the following:

- *(High entropy secret) There exists a poly-time reduction from $\mathsf{RLWE}_{q,t^{-1}\cdot\phi,\ell}$ to $\mathsf{wRLWR}^k_{\mathbf{B},q,p,\ell,\gamma,e}$, where $e \geq (2n+\lambda)\log q + 2\lambda$.*
- *(Uniform secret) There exists a poly-time reduction from $\mathsf{RLWE}_{q,t^{-1}\cdot\phi,\ell}$ to $\mathsf{RLWR}^k_{\mathbf{B},q,p,\ell}$, where $k \geq \frac{\log q}{\lambda \log(2\gamma)}\left((2n+\lambda)\log q + 2\lambda\right)$.*

The theorem can be proved by similar techniques as [3] together with Theorem 5.5. As the proof structure is similar to that in the prior work, for completeness we describe the proof in full version of this paper.

Theorem 5.12 (Hardness of Module-RLWR for General Cases). *Let $\lambda, n, p, q, \ell, f, k, \gamma$ be positive integers, $R = \mathcal{O}_K$ be the ring of integers of a field extension $K = \mathbb{Q}(\alpha)$ with degree n, K' be a number field and R' be the ring of integers of K' that is a rank-f free R-module with known basis, $\mathbf{B}$ be a basis of $R^\vee$ with B_{d_1} bounded ℓ_∞ norm for all entries, and also all entries of its dual basis $\mathbf{B}'$ be with B_{d_2}-bounded ℓ_∞ norm, $t \in (R'^\vee)^{-1}$ such that $tR'^\vee + qR' = R'$, ϕ be a β-bounded distribution over $K_\mathbb{R}$ for some real $\beta > 0$, such that $q \geq 2B_{d_1}B_{d_2}\beta\gamma k\ell pn^{\frac{5}{2}}$ and $\gcd(q, [\mathcal{O}_K : \mathbb{Z}[\alpha]]) = 1$. Then we have the following:*

- *(High entropy secret) There exists a poly-time reduction from* $\mathsf{RLWE}_{q,t^{-1}\phi',\ell}$ *to* $\mathsf{wRLWR}^k_{\mathbf{B},q,p,\ell,\gamma,e}$, *where* ϕ' *is a distribution over* $K'_{\mathbb{R}}$ *such that* $\phi = \mathrm{Tr}_{K'_{\mathbb{R}}/K_{\mathbb{R}}}(\phi')$ *and* $e \geq ((f+2)n + \lambda)\log q + 2\lambda - 2$.
- *(Uniform secret) There exists a poly-time reduction from* $\mathsf{RLWE}_{q,t^{-1}\phi',\ell}$ *to* $\mathsf{RLWR}^k_{\mathbf{B},q,p,\ell}$, *where* ϕ' *is as above and* $k \geq \frac{\log q}{\log(N(\mathfrak{q}_i)_{\min})\log(2\gamma)}(((f+2)n + \lambda)\log q + 2\lambda - 2)$.

The proof of this theorem is similar to that of Theorem 5.11, we detail it in full version of this paper.

For the case of cyclotomic fields, according to Corollary 5.8, we have the following tighter result.

Corollary 5.13. *Adopt the notations of Theorem 5.12. Let K be a cyclotomic field of degree n, then*

- *(High entropy secret) There exists a poly-time reduction from* $\mathsf{RLWE}_{q,t^{-1}\phi',\ell}$ *to* $\mathsf{wRLWR}^k_{\mathbf{B},q,p,\ell,\gamma,e}$, *where* $k \geq ((f+1)n + \lambda + 2)\log q + 2\lambda - 2$.
- *(Uniform secret) There exists a poly-time reduction from* $\mathsf{RLWE}_{q,t^{-1}\phi',\ell}$ *to* $\mathsf{RLWR}^k_{\mathbf{B},q,p,\ell}$, *where* $k \geq \frac{\log q}{\log(N(\mathfrak{q}_i)_{\min})\log(2\gamma)}(((f+1)n + \lambda + 2)\log q + 2\lambda - 2)$.

Acknowledgement. The authors would like to thank Han Wang for insightful discussions and anonymous reviewers of Crypto 2020 for their comments. This work is supported by NSF Awards CNS-1657040 and CNS-1942400. Any opinions, findings, and conclusions or recommendations expressed in this material are those of the author(s) and do not necessarily reflect the views of the sponsors.

References

1. Albrecht, M.R., Player, R., Scott, S.: On the concrete hardness of learning with errors. J. Math. Cryptol. **9**(3), 169–203 (2015)
2. Alperin-Sheriff, J., Apon, D.: Dimension-preserving reductions from LWE to LWR
3. Alwen, J., Krenn, S., Pietrzak, K., Wichs, D.: Learning with rounding, revisited. In: Canetti, R., Garay, J.A. (eds.) CRYPTO 2013, Part I. LNCS, vol. 8042, pp. 57–74. Springer, Heidelberg (2013). https://doi.org/10.1007/978-3-642-40041-4_4
4. Bai, S., Boudgoust, K., Das, D., Roux-Langlois, A., Wen, W., Zhang, Z.: Middle-product learning with rounding problem and its applications. In: Galbraith, S.D., Moriai, S. (eds.) ASIACRYPT 2019, Part I. LNCS, vol. 11921, pp. 55–81. Springer, Cham (2019). https://doi.org/10.1007/978-3-030-34578-5_3
5. Bai, S., Langlois, A., Lepoint, T., Stehlé, D., Steinfeld, R.: Improved security proofs in lattice-based cryptography: using the Rényi divergence rather than the statistical distance. In: Iwata, T., Cheon, J.H. (eds.) ASIACRYPT 2015, Part I. LNCS, vol. 9452, pp. 3–24. Springer, Heidelberg (2015). https://doi.org/10.1007/978-3-662-48797-6_1
6. Banerjee, A., Peikert, C., Rosen, A.: Pseudorandom functions and lattices. In: Pointcheval and Johansson [39], pp. 719–737
7. Bhattacharya, S., et al.: Round5: compact and fast post-quantum public-key encryption. IACR Cryptology ePrint Archive 2018:725 (2018)

8. Bogdanov, A., Guo, S., Masny, D., Richelson, S., Rosen, A.: On the hardness of learning with rounding over small modulus. In: Kushilevitz, E., Malkin, T. (eds.) TCC 2016, Part I. LNCS, vol. 9562, pp. 209–224. Springer, Heidelberg (2016). https://doi.org/10.1007/978-3-662-49096-9_9

9. Bolboceanu, M., Brakerski, Z., Perlman, R., Sharma, D.: Order-LWE and the hardness of Ring-LWE with entropic secrets. In: Galbraith, S.D., Moriai, S. (eds.) ASIACRYPT 2019, Part II. LNCS, vol. 11922, pp. 91–120. Springer, Cham (2019). https://doi.org/10.1007/978-3-030-34621-8_4

10. Brakerski, Z., Langlois, A., Peikert, C., Regev, O., Stehlé, D.: Classical hardness of learning with errors. In: Boneh, D., Roughgarden, T., Feigenbaum, J. (eds.) 45th ACM STOC, pp. 575–584. ACM Press, June 2013

11. Castryck, W., Iliashenko, I., Vercauteren, F.: Provably weak instances of Ring-LWE revisited. In: Fischlin, M., Coron, J.-S. (eds.) EUROCRYPT 2016, Part I. LNCS, vol. 9665, pp. 147–167. Springer, Heidelberg (2016). https://doi.org/10.1007/978-3-662-49890-3_6

12. Chen, H., Lauter, K., Stange, K.E.: Attacks on search RLWE (2015)

13. Chen, H., Lauter, K.E., Stange, K.E.: Vulnerable Galois RLWE families and improved attacks. IACR Cryptology ePrint Archive 2016:193 (2016)

14. Chen, L., Zhang, Z., Zhang, Z.: On the hardness of the computational Ring-LWR problem and its applications. In: Peyrin, T., Galbraith, S. (eds.) ASIACRYPT 2018, Part I. LNCS, vol. 11272, pp. 435–464. Springer, Cham (2018). https://doi.org/10.1007/978-3-030-03326-2_15

15. Conrad, K.: The different ideal. Expository papers. https://www.math.uconn.edu/~kconrad/blurbs/gradnumthy/different.pdf

16. Conrad, K.: Factoring ideals after Dedekind. Expository papers/Lecture notes. https://kconrad.math.uconn.edu/blurbs/gradnumthy/dedekindf.pdf

17. Dachman-Soled, D., Gong, H., Kulkarni, M., Shahverdi, A.: Partial key exposure in Ring-LWE-based cryptosystems: attacks and resilience. IACR Cryptology ePrint Archive 2018:1068 (2018)

18. D'Anvers, J.-P., Karmakar, A., Sinha Roy, S., Vercauteren, F.: Saber: module-LWR based key exchange, CPA-secure encryption and CCA-secure KEM. In: Joux, A., Nitaj, A., Rachidi, T. (eds.) AFRICACRYPT 2018. LNCS, vol. 10831, pp. 282–305. Springer, Cham (2018). https://doi.org/10.1007/978-3-319-89339-6_16

19. Dodis, Y., Ostrovsky, R., Reyzin, L., Smith, A.: Fuzzy extractors: how to generate strong keys from biometrics and other noisy data. SIAM J. Comput. 38(1), 97–139 (2008)

20. Eisenträger, K., Hallgren, S., Lauter, K.: Weak instances of PLWE. In: Joux, A., Youssef, A. (eds.) SAC 2014. LNCS, vol. 8781, pp. 183–194. Springer, Cham (2014). https://doi.org/10.1007/978-3-319-13051-4_11

21. Elias, Y., Lauter, K.E., Ozman, E., Stange, K.E.: Provably weak instances of Ring-LWE. In: Gennaro, R., Robshaw, M. (eds.) CRYPTO 2015, Part I. LNCS, vol. 9215, pp. 63–92. Springer, Heidelberg (2015). https://doi.org/10.1007/978-3-662-47989-6_4

22. Fröhlich, A.: A normal integral basis theorem. J. Algebra 39(1), 131–137 (1976)

23. Genise, N., Micciancio, D.: Faster Gaussian sampling for trapdoor lattices with arbitrary modulus. In: Nielsen and Rijmen [32], pp. 174–203

24. Genise, N., Micciancio, D., Polyakov, Y.: Building an efficient lattice gadget toolkit: subgaussian sampling and more. In: Ishai, Y., Rijmen, V. (eds.) EUROCRYPT 2019, Part II. LNCS, vol. 11477, pp. 655–684. Springer, Cham (2019). https://doi.org/10.1007/978-3-030-17656-3_23

25. Gentry, C., Peikert, C., Vaikuntanathan, V.: Trapdoors for hard lattices and new cryptographic constructions. In: Ladner, R.E., Dwork, C. (eds.) 40th ACM STOC, pp. 197–206. ACM Press, May 2008

26. Lyubashevsky, V., Peikert, C., Regev, O.: On ideal lattices and learning with errors over rings. In: Gilbert, H. (ed.) EUROCRYPT 2010. LNCS, vol. 6110, pp. 1–23. Springer, Heidelberg (2010). https://doi.org/10.1007/978-3-642-13190-5_1

27. Lyubashevsky, V., Peikert, C., Regev, O.: A toolkit for Ring-LWE cryptography. In: Johansson, T., Nguyen, P.Q. (eds.) EUROCRYPT 2013. LNCS, vol. 7881, pp. 35–54. Springer, Heidelberg (2013). https://doi.org/10.1007/978-3-642-38348-9_3

28. Micciancio, D.: Generalized compact knapsacks, cyclic lattices, and efficient one-way functions from worst-case complexity assumptions. In: 43rd FOCS, pp. 356–365. IEEE Computer Society Press, November 2002

29. Micciancio, D., Mol, P.: Pseudorandom knapsacks and the sample complexity of LWE search-to-decision reductions. In: Rogaway, P. (ed.) CRYPTO 2011. LNCS, vol. 6841, pp. 465–484. Springer, Heidelberg (2011). https://doi.org/10.1007/978-3-642-22792-9_26

30. Micciancio, D., Peikert, C.: Trapdoors for lattices: simpler, tighter, faster, smaller. In: Pointcheval and Johansson [39], pp. 700–718

31. Micciancio, D., Walter, M.: Gaussian sampling over the integers: efficient, generic, constant-time. In: Katz, J., Shacham, H. (eds.) CRYPTO 2017, Part II. LNCS, vol. 10402, pp. 455–485. Springer, Cham (2017). https://doi.org/10.1007/978-3-319-63715-0_16

32. Nielsen, J.B., Rijmen, V. (eds.): EUROCRYPT 2018, Part I. LNCS, vol. 10820. Springer, Cham (2018). https://doi.org/10.1007/978-3-319-78381-9

33. Peikert, C.: Public-key cryptosystems from the worst-case shortest vector problem: extended abstract. In: Mitzenmacher, M. (ed.) 41st ACM STOC, pp. 333–342. ACM Press, May/June 2009

34. Peikert, C.: An efficient and parallel Gaussian sampler for lattices. In: Rabin, T. (ed.) CRYPTO 2010. LNCS, vol. 6223, pp. 80–97. Springer, Heidelberg (2010). https://doi.org/10.1007/978-3-642-14623-7_5

35. Peikert, C.: How (not) to instantiate Ring-LWE. In: Zikas, V., De Prisco, R. (eds.) SCN 2016. LNCS, vol. 9841, pp. 411–430. Springer, Cham (2016). https://doi.org/10.1007/978-3-319-44618-9_22

36. Peikert, C., et al.: A decade of lattice cryptography. Found. Trends® Theoret. Comput. Sci. 10(4), 283–424 (2016)

37. Peikert, C., Pepin, Z.: Algebraically structured LWE, revisited. In: Hofheinz, D., Rosen, A. (eds.) TCC 2019, Part I. LNCS, vol. 11891, pp. 1–23. Springer, Cham (2019). https://doi.org/10.1007/978-3-030-36030-6_1

38. Peikert, C., Regev, O., Stephens-Davidowitz, N.: Pseudorandomness of Ring-LWE for any ring and modulus. In: Hatami, H., McKenzie, P., King, V. (eds.) 49th ACM STOC, pp. 461–473. ACM Press, June 2017

39. Pointcheval, D., Johansson, T. (eds.): EUROCRYPT 2012. LNCS, vol. 7237. Springer, Heidelberg (2012). https://doi.org/10.1007/978-3-642-29011-4

40. Regev, O.: On lattices, learning with errors, random linear codes, and cryptography. In: Gabow, H.N., Fagin, R. (eds.) 37th ACM STOC, pp. 84–93. ACM Press, May 2005

41. Rosca, M., Stehlé, D., Wallet, A.: On the Ring-LWE and polynomial-LWE problems. In: Nielsen and Rijmen [32], pp. 146–173

42. Shor, P.W.: Algorithms for quantum computation: discrete logarithms and factoring. In: 35th FOCS, pp. 124–134. IEEE Computer Society Press, November 1994

43. Tessaro, S.: Security amplification for the cascade of arbitrarily weak PRPs: tight bounds via the interactive hardcore lemma. In: Ishai, Y. (ed.) TCC 2011. LNCS, vol. 6597, pp. 37–54. Springer, Heidelberg (2011). https://doi.org/10.1007/978-3-642-19571-6_3
44. Stein, W.: A brief introduction to classical and adelic algrbraic number theory (2004). https://modular.math.washington.edu/papers/ant/. Accessed 12 Oct 2009

Lattice-Based and Post-quantum Cryptography

LWE with Side Information: Attacks and Concrete Security Estimation

Dana Dachman-Soled[1]($\boxtimes$), Léo Ducas[2]($\boxtimes$), Huijing Gong[1]($\boxtimes$), and Mélissa Rossi[3,4,5,6]($\boxtimes$)

[1] University of Maryland, College Park, USA
danadach@ece.umd.edu, gong@cs.umd.edu
[2] CWI, Amsterdam, The Netherlands
l.ducas@cwi.nl
[3] ANSSI, Paris, France
[4] ENS Paris, CNRS, PSL University, Paris, France
melissa.rossi@ens.fr
[5] Thales, Gennevilliers, France
[6] Inria, Paris, France

Abstract. We propose a framework for cryptanalysis of lattice-based schemes, when side information—in the form of "hints"—about the secret and/or error is available. Our framework generalizes the so-called primal lattice reduction attack, and allows the progressive integration of hints before running a final lattice reduction step. Our techniques for integrating hints include sparsifying the lattice, projecting onto and intersecting with hyperplanes, and/or altering the distribution of the secret vector. Our main contribution is to propose a toolbox and a methodology to integrate such hints into lattice reduction attacks and to predict the performance of those lattice attacks with side information.

While initially designed for side-channel information, our framework can also be used in other cases: exploiting decryption failures, or simply exploiting constraints imposed by certain schemes (LAC, Round5, NTRU).

We implement a Sage 9.0 toolkit to actually mount such attacks with hints when computationally feasible, and to predict their performances on larger instances. We provide several end-to-end application examples, such as an improvement of a single trace attack on Frodo by Bos et al. (SAC 2018). In particular, our work can estimates security loss even given very little side information, leading to a smooth measurement/computation trade-off for side-channel attacks.

The research of L. Ducas and M. Rossi was supported by the European Union's H2020 Programme under PROMETHEUS project (grant 780701). The research of M. Rossi was also supported by ANRT under the programs CIFRE N 2016/1583. It was also supported by the French Programme d'Investissement d'Avenir under national project RISQ P14158. The research of D. Dachman-Soled and H. Gong was supported in part by NSF grants #CNS-1933033, #CNS-1840893, #CNS-1453045 (CAREER), by a research partnership award from Cisco and by financial assistance award 70NANB15H328 and 70NANB19H126 from the U.S. Department of Commerce, National Institute of Standards and Technology.

D. Micciancio and T. Ristenpart (Eds.): CRYPTO 2020, LNCS 12171, pp. 329–358, 2020.
https://doi.org/10.1007/978-3-030-56880-1_12

$$\text{LWE/BDD} \xrightarrow{\text{Kannan}} \text{uSVP}_{\Lambda'} \xrightarrow{\text{Sec 3.4}} \begin{array}{c} \text{Lattice} \\ \text{reduction} \end{array}$$

Fig. 1. Primal attack without hints (prior art).

Keywords: LWE · NTRU · Lattice reduction · Cryptanalysis · Side-channels analysis · Decryption failures

1 Introduction

A large effort is currently underway to replace standardized public key cryptosystems, which are quantum-insecure, with newly developed "post-quantum" cryptosystems, conjectured to be secure against quantum attack. Lattice-based cryptography has been widely recognized as a foremost candidate for practical, post-quantum security and accordingly, a large effort has been made to develop and analyze lattice-based cryptosystems. The ongoing standardization process and anticipated deployment of lattice-based cryptography raises an important question: How resilient are lattices to side-channel attacks or other forms of side information? While there are numerous works addressing this question for specific cryptosystems (See [2,9,17,18,32,33] for side channel attacks targeting lattice-based NIST candidates), these works use rather ad-hoc methods to reconstruct the secret key, requiring new techniques and algorithms to be developed for each setting. For example, the work of [9] uses brute-force methods for a portion of the attack, while [7] exploits linear regression techniques. Moreover, ad-hoc methods do not allow (1) to take advantage of decades worth of research and (2) optimization of standard lattice attacks. Second, most of the side-channel attacks from prior work consider substantial amounts of information leakage and show that it leads to feasible recovery of the entire key, whereas one may be interested in more precise tradeoffs in terms of information leakage versus concrete security of the scheme. The above motivates the focus of this work: Can one integrate side information into a standard lattice attack, and if so, by how much does the information reduce the cost of this attack? Given that side-channel resistance is the next step toward the technological readiness of lattice-based cryptography, and that we expect numerous works in this growing area, we believe that a general framework and a prediction software are in order.

Contributions. First, we propose a framework that generalizes the so-called primal lattice reduction attack, and allows the progressive integration of "hints" (i.e. side information that takes one of several forms) before running the final lattice reduction step. This contribution is summarized in Figs. 1 and 2 and developed in Sect. 3.

Second, we implement a Sage 9.0 toolkit to actually mount such attacks with hints when computationally feasible, and to predict their performance on larger instances. Our predictions are validated by extensive experiments. Our tool and these experiments are described in Sect. 5. Our toolkit is open-source, available at: https://github.com/lducas/leaky-LWE-Estimator.

Third, we demonstrate the usefulness of our framework and tool via three example applications. Our main example (Sect. 6.1) revisits the side channel information obtained from the first side-channel attack of [9] against Frodo. In that article, it was concluded that a divide-and-conquer side-channel template attack would not lead to a meaningful attack using standard combinatorial search for reconstruction of the secret. Our technique allows to integrate this side-channel information into lattice attacks, and to predict the exact security drop. For example, the CCS2 parameter set very conservatively aims for 128-bits of post-quantum security (or 448 "bikz" as defined in Sect. 3.4); but after the leakage of [9] we predict that its security drops to 29 "bikz", i.e. that it can be broken with BKZ-29, a computation that should be more than feasible, but would require a dedicated re-implementation of our framework.

Interestingly, we note that our framework is not only useful in the side-channel scenario; we are for example also able to model decryption failures as hints fitting our framework. This allows us to reproduce some predictions from [14]. This is discussed in Sect. 6.2.

Perhaps more surprisingly, we also find a novel improvement to attack a few schemes (LAC [25], Round5 [16], NTRU [35]) without any side-channel or oracle queries. Indeed, such schemes use ternary distribution for secrets, with a prescribed numbers of 1 and -1: this hint fits our framework, and lead to a (very) minor improvement, discussed in Sect. 6.3.

Lastly, our framework also encompasses and streamlines existing tweaks of the primal attack: the choice of ignoring certain LWE equations to optimize the volume-dimension trade-off, as well as the re-centering [30] and isotropization [12,19] accounting for potential a-priori distortions of the secret. It also implicitly solves the question of the optimal choice of the coefficient for Kannan's Embedding from the Bounded Distance Decoding problem (BDD) to the unique Shortest Vector Problem (uSVP) [21] (See Remark 22).

As a side contribution, we also propose in the full version of our paper [13] a refined method to estimate the required blocksize to solve an LWE/BDD/uSVP instance. This refinement was motivated by the inaccuracy of the standard method from the literature [3,4] in experimentally reachable blocksizes, which was making the validation of our contribution difficult. While experimentally much more accurate, this new methodology certainly deserves further scrutiny.

Technical overview. Our work is based on a generalization of the Bounded Distance Decoding problem (BDD) to a Distorted version (DBDD), which allows to account for the potentially non-spherical covariance of the secret vector to be found.

Each hint will affect the lattice itself, the mean and/or the covariance parameter of the DBDD instance, making the problem easier (see Fig. 2). At last, we make the distribution spherical again by applying a well-chosen linear transformation, reverting to a spherical BDD instance before running the attack. Thanks to the hints, this new instance will be easier than the initial one. Let us assume

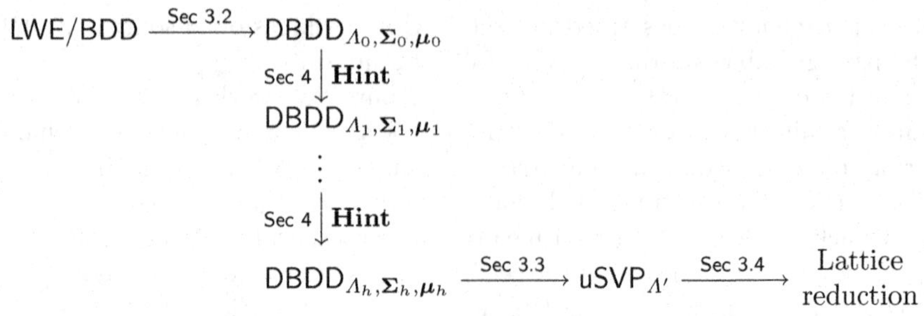

LWE/BDD $\xrightarrow{\text{Sec 3.2}}$ $\text{DBDD}_{\Lambda_0, \Sigma_0, \mu_0}$

Sec 4 $\bigg|$ **Hint**

$\text{DBDD}_{\Lambda_1, \Sigma_1, \mu_1}$

$\vdots$

Sec 4 $\bigg|$ **Hint**

$\text{DBDD}_{\Lambda_h, \Sigma_h, \mu_h}$ $\xrightarrow{\text{Sec 3.3}}$ $\text{uSVP}_{\Lambda'}$ $\xrightarrow{\text{Sec 3.4}}$ Lattice reduction

Fig. 2. The primal attack with hints (our work).

that $\mathbf{v}$, l, k and σ are parameters known by the attacker. Our framework can handle four types of hints on the secret $\mathbf{s}$ or on the lattice Λ.

- Perfect hints: $\langle \mathbf{s}, \mathbf{v} \rangle = l$ *intersect the lattice with an hyperplane.*
- Modular hints: $\langle \mathbf{s}, \mathbf{v} \rangle = l \bmod k$ *sparsify the lattice.*
- Approximate hints: $\langle \mathbf{s}, \mathbf{v} \rangle = l + \epsilon_\sigma$ *decrease the covariance of the secret.*
- Short vector hints: $\mathbf{v} \in \Lambda$ *project orthogonally to $\mathbf{v}$.*

While the first three hints are clear wins for the performance of lattice attacks, the last one is a trade-off between the dimension and the volume of the lattice. This last type of hint is in fact meant to generalize the standard trick consisting of 'ignoring' certain LWE equations; ignoring such an equation can be interpreted geometrically as such a projection orthogonally to a so-called q-vector.

All the transformations of the lattice above can be computed in polynomial time. However, computing with general distribution in large dimension is not possible; we restrict our study to the case of Gaussian distributions of arbitrary covariance, for which such computations are also poly-time.

Some of these transformations remain quite expensive, in particular because they involve rational numbers with very large denominators, and it remains rather impractical to run them on cryptographic-grade instances. Fortunately, up to a necessary hypothesis of primitivity of the vector $\mathbf{v}$ (with respect to either Λ or its dual depending on the type of hint), we can also predict the effect of each hint on the lattice parameters, and therefore run faster predictions of the attack cost.

From Leaks to Hints. At first, it may not be so clear that the types of hints above are so useful in realistic applications, in particular since they need to be linear on the secret. Of course our framework can handle rather trivial hints such as the perfect leak of a secret coefficient $\mathbf{s}_i = l$. Slightly less trivial is the case where the only the low-order bits leaks, a hint of the form $\mathbf{s}_i = l \bmod 2$.

We note that most of the computations done during an LWE decryption are linear: leaking any intermediate register during a matrix vector product leads to a hint of the same form (possibly $\bmod q$). Similarly, the leak of a NTT coefficient of a secret in a Ring/Module variant can also be viewed as such.

Admittedly, such ideal leaks of a full register are not the typical scenario and leaks are typically not linear on the content of the register. However, such non-linearities can be handled by approximate hints. For instance, let s_0 be a secret coefficient (represented by a signed 16-bits integer), whose a priori distribution is supported by $\{-5, \ldots, 5\}$. Consider the case where we learn the Hamming weight of s_0, say $H(s_0) = 2$. Then, we can narrow down the possibilities to $s_0 \in \{3, 5\}$. This leads to two hints:

- a modular hint: $s_0 = 1 \bmod 2$,
- an approximate hint: $s_0 = 4 + \epsilon_1$, where ϵ_1 has variance 1.

While closer to a realistic scenario, the above example remains rather simplified. A detailed example of how realistic leaks can be integrated as hint will be given in Sect. 6.1, based on the leakage data from [9].

2 Preliminaries

2.1 Linear Algebra

We use bold lower case letters to denote vectors, and bold upper case letters to denote matrices. We use row notations for vectors, and start indexing from 0. Let $\mathbf{I}_d$ denote the d-dimensional identity matrix. Let $\langle \cdot, \cdot \rangle$ denote the inner product of two vectors of the same size. Let us introduce the row span of a matrix (denoted $\mathrm{Span}(\cdot)$) as the subspace generated by all $\mathbb{R}$-linear combinations of the rows of its input.

Definition 1 (Positive Semidefinite). *A $n \times n$ symmetric real matrix $\mathbf{M}$ is positive semidefinite if scalar $\mathbf{x}\mathbf{M}\mathbf{x}^T \geq 0$ for all $\mathbf{x} \in \mathbb{R}^n$; if so we write $\mathbf{M} \geq 0$. Given two $n \times n$ real matrix $\mathbf{A}$ and $\mathbf{B}$, we note $\mathbf{A} \geq \mathbf{B}$ if $\mathbf{A} - \mathbf{B}$ is positive semidefinite.*

Definition 2. *A matrix $\mathbf{M}$ is a square root of Σ, denoted $\sqrt{\Sigma}$, if*

$$\mathbf{M}^T \cdot \mathbf{M} = \Sigma,$$

Our techniques involve keeping track of the covariance matrix Σ of the secret and error vectors as hints are progressively integrated. The covariance matrix may become singular during this process and will not have an inverse. Therefore, in the following we introduce some degenerate notions for the inverse and the determinant of a square matrix. Essentially, we restrict these notions to the row span of their input. For $\mathbf{X} \in \mathbb{R}^{d \times k}$ (with any $d, k \in \mathbb{N}$), we will denote $\mathbf{\Pi}_{\mathbf{X}}$ the orthogonal projection matrix onto $\mathrm{Span}(\mathbf{X})$. More formally, let $\mathbf{Y}$ be a maximal set of independent row-vectors of $\mathbf{X}$; the orthogonal projection matrix is given by $\mathbf{\Pi}_{\mathbf{X}} = \mathbf{Y}^T \cdot (\mathbf{Y} \cdot \mathbf{Y}^T)^{-1} \cdot \mathbf{Y}$. Its complement (the projection orthogonally to $\mathrm{Span}(\mathbf{X})$) is denoted $\mathbf{\Pi}_{\mathbf{X}}^{\perp} := \mathbf{I}_d - \mathbf{\Pi}_{\mathbf{X}}$. We naturally extend the notation $\mathbf{\Pi}_F$ and $\mathbf{\Pi}_F^{\perp}$ to subspaces $F \subset \mathbb{R}^d$. By definition, the projection matrices satisfy $\mathbf{\Pi}_F^2 = \mathbf{\Pi}_F$, $\mathbf{\Pi}_F^T = \mathbf{\Pi}_F$ and $\mathbf{\Pi}_F \cdot \mathbf{\Pi}_F^{\perp} = \mathbf{\Pi}_F^{\perp} \cdot \mathbf{\Pi}_F = \mathbf{0}$.

Definition 3 (Restricted inverse and determinant). *Let Σ be a symmetric matrix. We define a* restricted inverse *denoted $\Sigma^{\sim}$ as*

$$\Sigma^{\sim} := (\Sigma + \Pi_{\Sigma}^{\perp})^{-1} - \Pi_{\Sigma}^{\perp}.$$

It satisfies $\mathrm{Span}(\Sigma^{\sim}) = \mathrm{Span}(\Sigma)$ *and* $\Sigma \cdot \Sigma^{\sim} = \Pi_{\Sigma}$.
We also denote $\mathrm{rdet}(\Sigma)$ *as the* restricted determinant *defined as follows.*

$$\mathrm{rdet}(\Sigma) := \det(\Sigma + \Pi_{\Sigma}^{\perp}).$$

The idea behind Definition 3 is to provide an (artificial) invertibility property to the input Σ by adding the missing orthogonal part and to remove it afterwards. For example, if $\Sigma = \begin{bmatrix} \mathbf{A} & 0 \\ 0 & 0 \end{bmatrix}$ where $\mathbf{A}$ is invertible,

$$\Sigma^{\sim} = \left(\begin{bmatrix} \mathbf{A} & 0 \\ 0 & 0 \end{bmatrix} + \begin{bmatrix} 0 & 0 \\ 0 & 1 \end{bmatrix} \right)^{-1} - \begin{bmatrix} 0 & 0 \\ 0 & 1 \end{bmatrix} = \begin{bmatrix} \mathbf{A}^{-1} & 0 \\ 0 & 0 \end{bmatrix} \text{ and } \mathrm{rdet}\, \Sigma = \det(\mathbf{A}).$$

2.2 Statistics

Random variables, i.e. variables whose values depend on outcomes of a random phenomenon, are denoted in lowercase calligraphic letters e.g. a, b, e. Random vectors are denoted in uppercase calligraphic letters e.g. C, X, Z.

Before hints are integrated, we will assume that the secret and error vectors follow a multidimensional normal (Gaussian) distribution. Hints will typically correspond to learning a (noisy, modular or perfect) linear equation on the secret. We must then consider the altered distribution on the secret, conditioned on this information. Fortunately, this will also be a multidimensional normal distribution with an altered covariance and mean. In the following, we present the precise formulae for the covariance and mean of these conditional distributions.

Definition 4 (Multidimensional normal distribution). *Let $d \in \mathbb{Z}$, for $\mu \in \mathbb{Z}^d$ and Σ being a symmetric matrix of dimension $d \times d$, we denote by $D_{\Sigma,\mu}^d$ the multidimensional normal distribution supported by $\mu + \mathrm{Span}(\Sigma)$ by the following*

$$\mathbf{x} \mapsto \frac{1}{\sqrt{(2\pi)^{\mathrm{rank}(\Sigma)} \cdot \mathrm{rdet}(\Sigma)}} \exp\left(-\frac{1}{2} (\mathbf{x} - \mu) \cdot \Sigma^{\sim} \cdot (\mathbf{x} - \mu)^T \right).$$

The following states how a normal distribution is altered under linear transformation.

Lemma 5. *Suppose X has a $D_{\Sigma,\mu}^d$ distribution. Let $\mathbf{A}$ be a $n \times d$ matrix. Then $X\mathbf{A}^T$ has a $D_{\mathbf{A}\Sigma\mathbf{A}^T, \mu\mathbf{A}^T}^n$ distribution.*

Lemma 6 shows the altered distribution of a normal random variable conditioned on its noisy linear transformation value, following from [24, Equations (6) and (7)].

Lemma 6 (Conditional distribution $X|X\mathbf{A}^T + \mathbf{b}$ from [24]). *Suppose that $X \in \mathbb{Z}^d$ has a $D^d_{\Sigma,\mu}$ distribution, and $\mathbf{b} \in \mathbb{Z}^n$ has a $D^n_{\Sigma_b,0}$ distribution. Let us fix $\mathbf{A}$ as a $n \times d$ matrix and $\mathbf{z} \in \mathbb{Z}^n$. The conditional distribution of $X\Big|\left(X\mathbf{A}^T + \mathbf{b} = \mathbf{z}\right)$ is $D^d_{\Sigma',\mu'}$, where*

$$\boldsymbol{\mu}' = \boldsymbol{\mu} + (\mathbf{z} - \boldsymbol{\mu}\mathbf{A}^T)(\mathbf{A}\boldsymbol{\Sigma}\mathbf{A}^T + \boldsymbol{\Sigma}_b)^{-1}\mathbf{A}\boldsymbol{\Sigma}$$
$$\boldsymbol{\Sigma}' = \boldsymbol{\Sigma} - \boldsymbol{\Sigma}\mathbf{A}^T(\mathbf{A}\boldsymbol{\Sigma}\mathbf{A}^T + \boldsymbol{\Sigma}_b)^{-1}\mathbf{A}\boldsymbol{\Sigma}.$$

Corollary 7 (Conditional distribution $X|\langle X, \mathbf{v}\rangle + e$). *Suppose that $X \in \mathbb{Z}^d$ has a $D^d_{\Sigma,\mu}$ distribution and e has a $D^1_{\sigma_e^2,0}$ distribution. Let us fix $\mathbf{v} \in \mathbb{R}^d$ as a nonzero vector and $z \in \mathbb{Z}$. We define the following scalars:*

$$y = \langle X, \mathbf{v}\rangle + e, \ \mu_2 = \langle \mathbf{v}, \boldsymbol{\mu}\rangle \ and \ \sigma_2 = \mathbf{v}\boldsymbol{\Sigma}\mathbf{v}^T + \sigma_e^2$$

If $\sigma_2 \neq 0$, the conditional distribution of $X\Big|\left(y = z\right)$ is $D^d_{\Sigma',\mu'}$, where

$$\boldsymbol{\mu}' = \boldsymbol{\mu} + \frac{(z - \mu_2)}{\sigma_2}\mathbf{v}\boldsymbol{\Sigma}, \qquad \boldsymbol{\Sigma}' = \boldsymbol{\Sigma} - \frac{\boldsymbol{\Sigma}\mathbf{v}^T\mathbf{v}\boldsymbol{\Sigma}}{\sigma_2}. \tag{1}$$

If $\sigma_2 = 0$, the conditional distribution of $X\Big|\left(y = z\right)$ is $D^d_{\Sigma,\mu}$.

Remark 8. We note that Corollary 7 is also useful to describe for $X|\langle X, \mathbf{v}\rangle$ by letting $\sigma_e = 0$.

2.3 Lattices

A *lattice*, denoted as Λ, is a discrete additive subgroup of $\mathbb{R}^m$, which is generated as the set of all linear integer combinations of n $(m \geq n)$ linearly independent basis vectors $\{\mathbf{b}_j\} \subset \mathbb{R}^m$, namely,

$$\Lambda := \left\{\sum_j z_j\mathbf{b}_j : z_j \in \mathbb{Z}\right\},$$

We say that m is the *dimension* of Λ and n is its rank. A lattice is *full rank* if $n = m$. A matrix $\mathbf{B}$ having the basis vectors as rows is called a *basis*. The *volume* of a lattice Λ is defined as $\mathrm{Vol}(\Lambda) := \sqrt{\det(\mathbf{B}\mathbf{B}^T)}$. The *dual lattice* of Λ in $\mathbb{R}^n$ is defined as follows.

$$\Lambda^* := \{\mathbf{y} \in \mathrm{Span}(\mathbf{B}) \mid \forall \mathbf{x} \in \Lambda, \langle \mathbf{x}, \mathbf{y}\rangle \in \mathbb{Z}\}.$$

Note that, $(\Lambda^*)^* = \Lambda$, and $\mathrm{Vol}(\Lambda^*) = 1/\mathrm{Vol}(\Lambda)$.

Lemma 9 ([26, **Proposition 1.3.4**]). *Let Λ be a lattice and let F be a subspace of $\mathbb{R}^n$. If $\Lambda \cap F$ is a lattice, then the dual of $\Lambda \cap F$ is the orthogonal projection onto F of the dual of Λ. In other words, each element of Λ^* is multiplied by the projection matrix $\mathbf{\Pi}_F$:*

$$(\Lambda \cap F)^* = \Lambda^* \cdot \mathbf{\Pi}_F.$$

Definition 10 (Primitive vectors). *A set of vector $\mathbf{y}_1, \ldots, \mathbf{y}_k \in \Lambda$ is said primitive with respect to Λ if $\Lambda \cap \mathrm{Span}(\mathbf{y}_1, \ldots, \mathbf{y}_k)$ is equal to the lattice generated by $\mathbf{y}_1, \ldots, \mathbf{y}_k$. Equivalently, it is primitive if it can be extended to a basis of Λ. If $k = 1$, $\mathbf{y}_1$, this is equivalent to $\mathbf{y}_1/i \notin \Lambda$ for any integer $i \geq 2$.*

To predict the hardness of the lattice reduction on altered instances, we must compute the volume of the final transformed lattice. We devise a highly efficient way to do this, by observing that each time a hint is integrated, we can update the volume of the transformed lattice, given only the volume of the previous lattice and information about the current hint (under mild restrictions on the form of the hint). Lemmas 11 and 12 are proved in the full version of our paper [13].

Lemma 11 (Volume of a lattice slice). *Given a lattice Λ with volume $\mathrm{Vol}(\Lambda)$, and a primitive vector $\mathbf{v}$ with respect to Λ^*. Let $\mathbf{v}^\perp$ denote subspace orthogonal to $\mathbf{v}$. Then $\Lambda \cap \mathbf{v}^\perp$ is a lattice with volume $\mathrm{Vol}(\Lambda \cap \mathbf{v}^\perp) = \|\mathbf{v}\| \cdot \mathrm{Vol}(\Lambda)$.*

Lemma 12 (Volume of a sparsified lattice). *Let Λ be a lattice, $\mathbf{v} \in \Lambda^*$ be a primitive vector of Λ^*, and $k > 0$ be an integer. Let $\Lambda' = \{\mathbf{x} \in \Lambda \mid \langle \mathbf{x}, \mathbf{v} \rangle = 0 \bmod k\}$ be a sublattice of Λ. Then $\mathrm{Vol}(\Lambda') = k \cdot \mathrm{Vol}(\Lambda)$.*

Fact 13 (Volume of a projected lattice). *Let Λ be a lattice, $\mathbf{v} \in \Lambda$ be a primitive vector of Λ. Let $\Lambda' = \Lambda \cdot \mathbf{\Pi}_{\mathbf{v}}^\perp$ be a sublattice of Λ. Then $\mathrm{Vol}(\Lambda') = \mathrm{Vol}(\Lambda)/\|\mathbf{v}\|$. More generally, if $\mathbf{V}$ is a primitive set of vectors of Λ, then $\Lambda' = \Lambda \cdot \mathbf{\Pi}_{\mathbf{V}}^\perp$ has volume $\mathrm{Vol}(\Lambda') = \mathrm{Vol}(\Lambda)/\sqrt{\det(\mathbf{V}\mathbf{V}^T)}$.*

Fact 14 (Lattice volume under linear transformations). *Let Λ be a lattice in $\mathbb{R}^n$, and $\mathbf{M} \in \mathbb{R}^{n \times n}$ a matrix such that $\ker \mathbf{M} = \mathrm{Span}(\Lambda)^\perp$. Then we have $\mathrm{Vol}(\Lambda \cdot \mathbf{M}) = \mathrm{rdet}(\mathbf{M}) \, \mathrm{Vol}(\Lambda)$.*

3 Distorted Bounded Distance Decoding

3.1 Definition

We first recall the definition of the (search) LWE problem, in its short-secret variant which is the most relevant to practical LWE-based encryption.

Definition 15 (Search LWE problem with short secrets). *Let n, m and q be positive integers, and let χ be a distribution over $\mathbb{Z}$. The search LWE problem (with short secrets) for parameters (n, m, q, χ) is:*

   ***Given** the pair $\left(\mathbf{A} \in \mathbb{Z}_q^{m \times n}, \mathbf{b} = \mathbf{z}\mathbf{A}^T + \mathbf{e} \in \mathbb{Z}_q^m\right)$ **where**:*

1. $\mathbf{A} \in \mathbb{Z}_q^{m \times n}$ *is sampled uniformly at random,*
2. $\mathbf{z} \leftarrow \chi^n$, *and* $\mathbf{e} \leftarrow \chi^m$ *are sampled with independent and identically distributed coefficients following the distribution* χ.

Find z.

The primal attack (See for example [3]) against (search)-LWE proceeds by viewing the LWE instance as an instance of a Bounded Distance Decoding (BDD) problem, converting it to a uSVP instance (via Kannan's embedding [21]), and finally applying a lattice reduction algorithm to solve the uSVP instance. The central tool of our framework is a generalization of BDD that accounts for potential distortion in the distribution of the secret noise vector that is to be recovered.

Definition 16 (Distorted Bounded Distance Decoding problem). *Let* $\Lambda \subset \mathbb{R}^d$ *be a lattice,* $\mathbf{\Sigma} \in \mathbb{R}^{d \times d}$ *be a symmetric matrix and* $\boldsymbol{\mu} \in \mathrm{Span}(\Lambda) \subset \mathbb{R}^d$ *such that*

$$\mathrm{Span}(\mathbf{\Sigma}) \subsetneq \mathrm{Span}(\mathbf{\Sigma} + \boldsymbol{\mu}^T \cdot \boldsymbol{\mu}) = \mathrm{Span}(\Lambda). \tag{2}$$

The Distorted Bounded Distance Decoding problem $DBDD_{\Lambda,\boldsymbol{\mu},\mathbf{\Sigma}}$ *is the following problem:*

Given $\boldsymbol{\mu}, \mathbf{\Sigma}$ *and a basis of* Λ.
Find the unique vector $\mathbf{x} \in \Lambda \cap E(\boldsymbol{\mu}, \mathbf{\Sigma})$

where $E(\boldsymbol{\mu}, \mathbf{\Sigma})$ *denotes the ellipsoid*

$$E(\boldsymbol{\mu}, \mathbf{\Sigma}) := \{\mathbf{x} \in \boldsymbol{\mu} + \mathrm{Span}(\mathbf{\Sigma}) | (\mathbf{x} - \boldsymbol{\mu}) \cdot \mathbf{\Sigma}^{\sim} \cdot (\mathbf{x} - \boldsymbol{\mu})^T \leq \mathrm{rank}(\mathbf{\Sigma})\}.$$

We will refer to the triple $\mathcal{I} = (\Lambda, \boldsymbol{\mu}, \mathbf{\Sigma})$ *as the instance of the* $DBDD_{\Lambda,\boldsymbol{\mu},\mathbf{\Sigma}}$ *problem.*

Intuitively, Definition 16 corresponds to knowing that the secret vector $\mathbf{x}$ to be recovered follows a distribution of variance $\mathbf{\Sigma}$ and average $\boldsymbol{\mu}$. The quantity $(\mathbf{x} - \boldsymbol{\mu}) \cdot \mathbf{\Sigma}^{\sim} \cdot (\mathbf{x} - \boldsymbol{\mu})^T$ can be interpreted as a non-canonical Euclidean squared distance $\|\mathbf{x} - \boldsymbol{\mu}\|_{\mathbf{\Sigma}}^2$, and the expected value of such a distance for a Gaussian $\mathbf{x}$ of variance $\mathbf{\Sigma}$ and average $\boldsymbol{\mu}$ is $\mathrm{rank}(\mathbf{\Sigma})$. One can argue that, for such a Gaussian, there is a constant probability that $\|\mathbf{x} - \boldsymbol{\mu}\|_{\mathbf{\Sigma}}^2$ is slightly greater than $\mathrm{rank}(\mathbf{\Sigma})$. Since we are interested in the average behavior of our attack, we ignore this benign technical detail. In fact, we will typically interpret DBDD as the promise that the secret follows a Gaussian distribution of center $\boldsymbol{\mu}$ and covariance $\mathbf{\Sigma}$.

The ellipsoid can be seen as an affine transformation (that we call "distortion") of the centered hyperball of radius $\mathrm{rank}(\mathbf{\Sigma})$. Let us introduce a notation for the hyperball; for any $d \in \mathbb{N}$

$$B_d := \{\mathbf{x} \in \mathbb{R}^d \mid \|\mathbf{x}\|_2 \leq d\}. \tag{3}$$

One can thus write using Definition 2:

$$E(\boldsymbol{\mu}, \mathbf{\Sigma}) = B_{\mathrm{rank}(\mathbf{\Sigma})} \cdot \sqrt{\mathbf{\Sigma}} + \boldsymbol{\mu}. \tag{4}$$

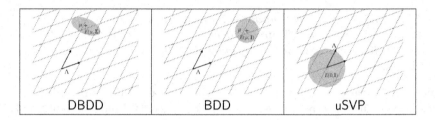

Fig. 3. Graphical intuition of DBDD, BDD and uSVP in dimension two: the problem consists in finding a nonzero element of Λ in the colored zone. The identity hyperball is larger for uSVP to represent the fact that, during the reduction, the uSVP lattice has one dimension more than for BDD.

From the Span inclusion in Eq. (2), one can deduce that the condition is equivalent to requiring $\boldsymbol{\mu} \notin \mathrm{Span}(\boldsymbol{\Sigma})$ and $\mathrm{rank}(\boldsymbol{\Sigma} + \boldsymbol{\mu}^T \cdot \boldsymbol{\mu}) = \mathrm{rank}(\boldsymbol{\Sigma}) + 1 = \mathrm{rank}(\Lambda)$. This technical detail is necessary for embedding it properly into a uSVP instance (See later in Sect. 3.3).

Particular cases of Definition 16. Let us temporarily ignore the condition in Eq. (2) to study some particular cases. As shown in Fig. 3, when $\boldsymbol{\Sigma} = \mathbf{I}_d$, $\mathrm{DBDD}_{\Lambda,\boldsymbol{\mu},\mathbf{I}_d}$ is BDD instance. Indeed, the ellipsoid becomes a shifted hyperball $E(\boldsymbol{\mu}, \mathbf{I}_d) = \{\mathbf{x} \in \boldsymbol{\mu} + \mathbb{R}^{d \times d} \mid \|\mathbf{x} - \boldsymbol{\mu}\|_2 \leq d\} = B_d + \boldsymbol{\mu}$. If in addition $\boldsymbol{\mu} = 0$, $\mathrm{DBDD}_{\Lambda,0,\mathbf{I}_d}$ becomes a uSVP instance on Λ.

3.2   Embedding **LWE** into **DBDD**

In the typical primal attack framework (Fig. 1), one directly views LWE as a BDD instance of the same dimension. For our purposes, however, it will be useful to apply Kannan's Embedding at this stage and therefore increase the dimension of the lattice by 1. While it could be delayed to the last stage of our attack, this extra fixed coefficient 1 will be particularly convenient when we integrate hints (see Remark 22 in Sect. 4). It should be noted that no information is lost through this transformation, since the parameters $\boldsymbol{\mu}$ and $\boldsymbol{\Sigma}$ allow us to encode the knowledge that the solution we are looking for has its last coefficient set to 1 and nothing else. In more details, the solution $\mathbf{s} := (\mathbf{e}, \mathbf{z})$ of an LWE instance is extended to

$$\bar{\mathbf{s}} := (\mathbf{e}, \mathbf{z}, 1) \qquad (5)$$

which is a short vector in the lattice $\Lambda = \{(\mathbf{x}, \mathbf{y}, w) \mid \mathbf{x} + \mathbf{y}\mathbf{A}^T - \mathbf{b}w = 0 \mod q\}$. A basis of this lattice is given by the row vectors of

$$\begin{bmatrix} q\mathbf{I}_m & 0 & 0 \\ \mathbf{A}^T & -\mathbf{I}_n & 0 \\ \mathbf{b} & 0 & 1 \end{bmatrix}.$$

Denoting μ_χ and σ_χ^2 the average and variance of the LWE distribution χ (See Definition 15), we can convert this LWE instance to a $\mathrm{DBDD}_{\Lambda,\boldsymbol{\mu},\boldsymbol{\Sigma}}$ instance with

$\boldsymbol{\mu} = [\mu_{\chi} \cdots \mu_{\chi} \; 1]$ and $\boldsymbol{\Sigma} = \begin{bmatrix} \sigma_{\chi}^2 \mathbf{I}_{m+n} & 0 \\ 0 & 0 \end{bmatrix}$. The lattice Λ is of full rank in $\mathbb{R}^d$ where $d := m + n + 1$, and its volume is q^m. Note that the rank of $\boldsymbol{\Sigma}$ is only $d - 1$: the ellipsoid has one less dimension than the lattice. It then validates the requirement of Eq. (2).

Remark 17. Typically, Kannan's embedding from BDD to uSVP leaves the bottom right matrix coefficient as a free parameter, say c, to be chosen optimally. The optimal value is the one maximizing

$$\frac{\|(\mathbf{z}; c)\|}{\det(\Lambda)^{1/d}} = \frac{(m+n)\sigma_{\chi} + c}{(c \cdot q^m)^{1/d}},$$

namely, $c = \sigma_{\chi}$ according to the arithmetic-geometric mean inequality. Some prior works [3,5] instead chose $c = 1$. While this is benign since σ_{χ} is typically not too far from 1, it remains a sub-optimal choice. Looking ahead, in our DBDD framework, this choice becomes irrelevant thanks to the *isotropization* step introduced in the next section; we can therefore choose $c = 1$ without worsening the attack.

3.3   Converting DBDD to uSVP

In this Section, we explain how a DBDD instance $(\Lambda, \boldsymbol{\mu}, \boldsymbol{\Sigma})$ is converted into a uSVP one. Two modifications are necessary. First, we need to homogeneize the problem. Let us show that the ellipsoid in Definition 16 is contained in a larger centered ellipsoid (with one more dimension) as follows:

$$E(\boldsymbol{\mu}, \boldsymbol{\Sigma}) \subset E(\mathbf{0}, \boldsymbol{\Sigma} + \boldsymbol{\mu}^T \cdot \boldsymbol{\mu}). \tag{6}$$

Using Eq. (4), one can write

$$E(\boldsymbol{\mu}, \boldsymbol{\Sigma}) = B_{\mathrm{rank}(\boldsymbol{\Sigma})} \cdot \sqrt{\boldsymbol{\Sigma}} + \boldsymbol{\mu} \subset B_{\mathrm{rank}(\boldsymbol{\Sigma})} \cdot \sqrt{\boldsymbol{\Sigma}} \pm \boldsymbol{\mu},$$

where $B_{\mathrm{rank}(\boldsymbol{\Sigma})}$ is defined in Eq. (3). And, with Eq. (2), one can deduce $\mathrm{rank}(\boldsymbol{\Sigma} + \boldsymbol{\mu}^T \cdot \boldsymbol{\mu}) = \mathrm{rank}(\boldsymbol{\Sigma}) + 1$, then:

$$B_{\mathrm{rank}(\boldsymbol{\Sigma})} \cdot \sqrt{\boldsymbol{\Sigma}} \pm \boldsymbol{\mu} \subset B_{\mathrm{rank}(\boldsymbol{\Sigma})+1} \cdot \begin{bmatrix} \sqrt{\boldsymbol{\Sigma}} \\ \boldsymbol{\mu} \end{bmatrix}.$$

We apply Definition 2 which confirms the inclusion of Eq. (6):

$$E(\boldsymbol{\mu}, \boldsymbol{\Sigma}) \subset B_{\mathrm{rank}(\boldsymbol{\Sigma})+1} \cdot \begin{bmatrix} \sqrt{\boldsymbol{\Sigma}} \\ \boldsymbol{\mu} \end{bmatrix} = E(\mathbf{0}, \boldsymbol{\Sigma} + \boldsymbol{\mu}^T \cdot \boldsymbol{\mu}).$$

Thus, we can homogenize and transform the instance into a centered one with $\boldsymbol{\Sigma}' := \boldsymbol{\Sigma} + \boldsymbol{\mu}^T \cdot \boldsymbol{\mu}$.

Secondly, to get an isotropic distribution (i.e. with all its eigenvalues being 1), one can just multiply every element of the lattice with the pseudoinverse of $\sqrt{\mathbf{\Sigma'}}$. We get a new covariance matrix $\mathbf{\Sigma''} = \sqrt{\mathbf{\Sigma'}}^{\sim} \cdot \mathbf{\Sigma'} \cdot \sqrt{\mathbf{\Sigma'}}^{\sim T} = \mathbf{\Pi}_{\mathbf{\Sigma'}} \cdot \mathbf{\Pi}_{\mathbf{\Sigma'}}{}^T$. And with orthogonal projection properties (see Sect. 2.1), $\mathbf{\Sigma''} = \mathbf{\Pi}_{\mathbf{\Sigma'}} = \mathbf{\Pi}_{\Lambda}$, the last equality coming from Eq. (2).

In summary, one must make by the two following changes:

$$\text{homogenize: } (\Lambda, \boldsymbol{\mu}, \mathbf{\Sigma}) \mapsto (\Lambda, \mathbf{0}, \mathbf{\Sigma'} := \mathbf{\Sigma} + \boldsymbol{\mu}^T \cdot \boldsymbol{\mu})$$
$$\text{isotropize: } (\Lambda, \mathbf{0}, \mathbf{\Sigma'}) \mapsto (\Lambda \cdot \mathbf{M}, \mathbf{0}, \mathbf{\Pi}_{\Lambda})$$

where $\mathbf{M} := (\sqrt{\mathbf{\Sigma'}})^{\sim}$. From the solution $\mathbf{x}$ to the uSVP$_{\Lambda \cdot \mathbf{M}}$ problem, one can derive $\mathbf{x'} = \mathbf{x}\mathbf{M}^{\sim}$ the solution to the DBDD$_{\Lambda, \boldsymbol{\mu}, \mathbf{\Sigma}}$ problem.

Remark 18. One may note that we could solve a DBDD instance without isotropization simply by including the ellipsoid in a larger ball, and directly apply lattice reduction before the second step. This leads, however, to less efficient attacks. One may also note that the first homogenization step "forgets" some information about the secret's distribution. This, however, is inherent to the conversion to a unique-SVP problem which is geometrically homogeneous, and is already present in the original primal attack.

3.4   Security Estimates of uSVP: Bikz versus Bits

The attack on a uSVP instance consists of applying BKZ-β on the uSVP lattice Λ for an appropriate block size parameter β. The cost of the attack grows with β, however, modeling this cost precisely is at the moment rather delicate, as the state of the art seems to still be in motion. Numerous NIST candidates choose to underestimate this cost, keeping a margin to accommodate future improvements, and there seems to be no clear consensus on which model to use (see [1] for a summary of existing cost models).

While this problem is orthogonal to our work, we still wish to be able to formulate quantitative security losses. We therefore express all concrete security estimates using the blocksize β as our measure of the level of security, and treat the latter as a measurement of the security level in a unit called the *bikz*. We thereby leave the question of the exact bikz-to-bit conversion estimate outside the scope of this paper, and recall that those conversion formulae are not necessarily linear, and may have small dependency in other parameters. For the sake of concreteness, we note that certain choose, for example, to claim 128 bits of security for 380 bikz, and in this range, most models suggest a security increase of one bit every 2 to 4 bikz.

Remark 19. We also clarify that the estimates given in this paper only concern the pure lattice attack via the uSVP embedding discussed above. In particular, we note that some NIST candidates with ternary secrets [25] also consider the hybrid attack of [20], which we ignore in this work. We nevertheless think that the compatibility with our framework is plausible, with some effort.

Predicting β from a uSVP instance. The state-of-the-art predictions for solving uSVP instances using BKZ were given in [3,4]. Namely, for Λ a lattice of dimension $\dim(\Lambda)$, it is predicted that BKZ-β can solve a uSVP$_\Lambda$ instance with secret **s** when

$$\sqrt{\beta/\dim(\Lambda)} \cdot \|\mathbf{s}\| \leq \delta_\beta^{2\beta-\dim(\Lambda)-1} \cdot \mathrm{Vol}(\Lambda)^{1/\dim(\Lambda)} \tag{7}$$

where δ_β is the so called root-Hermite-Factor of BKZ-β. For $\beta \geq 50$, the Root-Hermite-Factor is predictable using the Gaussian Heuristic [11]:

$$\delta_\beta = \left((\pi\beta)^{\frac{1}{\beta}} \cdot \frac{\beta}{2\pi e} \right)^{1/(2\beta-2)} . \tag{8}$$

Note that the uSVP instances we generate are isotropic and centered so that the secret has covariance $\mathbf{\Sigma} = \mathbf{I}$ (or $\mathbf{\Sigma} = \mathbf{\Pi}_\Lambda$ if Λ is not of full rank) and $\mu = \mathbf{0}$. Thus, on average, we have $\|\mathbf{s}\|^2 = \mathrm{rank}(\mathbf{\Sigma}) = \dim(\Lambda)$. Therefore, β can be estimated as the minimum integer that satisfies

$$\sqrt{\beta} \leq \delta_\beta^{2\beta-\dim(\Lambda)-1} \cdot \mathrm{Vol}(\Lambda)^{1/\dim(\Lambda)}. \tag{9}$$

While β must be an integer as a BKZ parameter, we nevertheless provide a continuous value, for a finer comparison of the difficulty of an instance. Below, we will call this method the "GSA-Intersect" method.

Remark 20. To predict security, one does not need the basis of Λ, but only its dimension and its volume. Similarly, it is not necessary to explicitly compute the isotropization matrix **M** of Sect. 3.3, thanks to Fact 14: $\mathrm{Vol}(\Lambda \cdot \mathbf{M}) = \mathrm{rdet}(\mathbf{M})\,\mathrm{Vol}(\Lambda) = \mathrm{rdet}(\mathbf{\Sigma}')^{-1/2}\,\mathrm{Vol}(\Lambda)$. These two shortcuts will allow us to efficiently make predictions for cryptographically large instances, in our *lightweight* implementation of Sect. 5.

Refined prediction for small blocksizes. For experimental validation purposes of our work, we prefer to have accurate prediction even for small blocksizes; a regime where those predictions are not accurate with the current state of the art. We therefore present a refined strategy using BKZ-simulation and a probabilistic model in the full version of our paper [13].

As depicted in Fig. 4, this methodology (coined Probabilistic-simulation) leads to much more satisfactory estimates compared to the model from the literature [3,4]. In particular, for low blocksize the literature widely underestimates the required blocksize, which is due to only considering detectability at position $d - \beta$. For large blocksize, it somewhat overestimates it, which could be attributed to the fact that it does not account for luck. On the contrary, our new methodology seems quite precise in all regimes, making errors of at most 1 bikz. This new methodology certainly deserves further study and refinement, which we leave to future work.

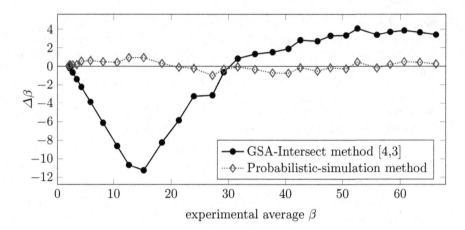

Fig. 4. The difference $\Delta\beta = \text{real} - \text{predicted}$, as a function of the average experimental beta β. The experiment consists in running a single tour of BKZ-β for $\beta = 2, 3, 4, \ldots$ until the secret short vector is found. This was averaged over 256 many LWE instances per data-point, for parameters $q = 3301$, $\sigma = 20$ and $n = m \in \{30, 32, 34, \ldots, 88\}$.

4   Hints and Their Integration

In this Section, we define several categories of hints—**perfect hints, modular hints, approximate hints (conditioning** and *a posteriori*), and **short vector hints**—and show that these types of hints can be integrated into a DBDD instance. Hints belonging to these categories typically have the form of a linear equation in **s** (and possibly additional variables). As emphasized in Sect. 1, these hints have lattice-friendly forms and their usefulness in realistic applications may not be obvious. We refer to Sect. 6 for detailed applications of these hints.

The technical challenge, therefore, is to characterize the effect of such hints on the DBDD instance—i.e. determine the resulting $(\Lambda', \boldsymbol{\mu}', \boldsymbol{\Sigma}')$ of the new DBDD instance, after the hint is incorporated.

Henceforth, let $\mathcal{I} = \text{DBDD}_{\Lambda, \boldsymbol{\mu}, \boldsymbol{\Sigma}}$ be a fixed instance constructed from an LWE instance with secret $\mathbf{s} = (\mathbf{z}, \mathbf{e})$. Each hint will introduce new constraints on $\mathbf{s}$ and will ultimately decrease the security level.

Non-Commutativity. It should be noted that many types of hints commute: Integrating them in any order will lead to the same DBDD instance. Potential exceptions are **non-smooth modular hints** (See later in Sect. 4.2) and *a posteriori* **approximate hints** (See later in Sect. 4.4): they do not always commute with the other types of hints, and do not always commute between themselves, unless the vectors **v**'s of those hints are all orthogonal to each other. The reason is: in these cases, the distribution in the direction of **v** is redefined which erases the prior information.

4.1   Perfect Hints

Definition 21 (Perfect hint). *A perfect hint on the secret* **s** *is the knowledge of* $\mathbf{v} \in \mathbb{Z}^{d-1}$ *and* $l \in \mathbb{Z}$, *such that*

$$\langle \mathbf{s}, \ \mathbf{v} \rangle = l.$$

A perfect hint is quite strong in terms of additional knowledge. It allows decreasing the dimension of the lattice by one and increases its volume. One could expect such hints to arise from the following scenarios:

- The full leak without noise of an original coefficient, or even an unreduced intermediate register since most of the computations are linear. For the second case, one may note that optimized implementations of NTT typically attempt to delay the first reduction modulo q, so leaking a register on one of the first few levels of the NTT would indeed lead to such a hint.
- A noisy leakage of the same registers, but with still a rather high guessing confidence. In that case it may be worth making the guess while decreasing the success probability of the attack.[1] This could happen in a cold-boot attack scenario. This is also the case in the single trace attack on Frodo [9] that we will study as one of our examples in Sect. 6.1.
- More surprisingly, certain schemes, including some NIST candidates offer such a hint 'by design'. Indeed, LAC, Round5 and NTRU-HPS all choose ternary secret vectors with a prescribed number of 1's and -1's, which directly induce one or two such perfect hints. This will be detailed in Sect. 6.3.

Integrating a perfect hint into a DBDD instance. Let $\mathbf{v} \in \mathbb{Z}^{d-1}$ and $l \in \mathbb{Z}$ be such that $\langle \mathbf{s}, \mathbf{v} \rangle = l$. Note that the hint can also be written as

$$\langle \bar{\mathbf{s}}, \ \bar{\mathbf{v}} \rangle = 0,$$

where $\bar{\mathbf{s}}$ is the extended LWE secret as defined in Eq. (5) and $\bar{\mathbf{v}} := (\mathbf{v} \, ; \, -l)$.

Remark 22. Here we understand the interest of using Kannan's embedding *before* integrating hints rather than after: it allows to also homogenize the hint, and therefore to make Λ' a proper lattice rather than a lattice coset (i.e. a shifted lattice).

Including this hint is done by modifying the $\mathrm{DBDD}_{\Lambda,\mu,\Sigma}$ to $\mathrm{DBDD}_{\Lambda',\mu',\Sigma'}$, where:

$$\Lambda' = \Lambda \cap \left\{ \mathbf{x} \in \mathbb{Z}^d \mid \langle \mathbf{x}, \bar{\mathbf{v}} \rangle = 0 \right\}$$

$$\Sigma' = \Sigma - \frac{(\bar{\mathbf{v}}\Sigma)^T \bar{\mathbf{v}}\Sigma}{\bar{\mathbf{v}}\Sigma\bar{\mathbf{v}}^T} \tag{10}$$

$$\mu' = \mu - \frac{\langle \bar{\mathbf{v}}, \mu \rangle}{\bar{\mathbf{v}}\Sigma\bar{\mathbf{v}}^T} \bar{\mathbf{v}}\Sigma \tag{11}$$

---

[1] One may then re-amplify the success probability by retrying the attack making guesses at different locations.

We now explain how to derive the new mean μ' and the new covariance Σ'. Let y be the random variable $\langle \bar{\mathbf{s}}, \bar{\mathbf{v}} \rangle$, where $\bar{\mathbf{s}}$ has mean μ and covariance Σ. Then μ' is the mean of $\bar{\mathbf{s}}$ conditioned on $y = 0$, and Σ' is the covariance of $\bar{\mathbf{s}}$ conditioned on $y = 0$. Using Corollary 7, we obtain the corresponding conditional mean and covariance.

We note that lattice Λ' is an intersection of Λ and a hyperplane orthogonal to $\bar{\mathbf{v}}$. Given $\mathbf{B}$ as basis of Λ, by Lemma 9 a basis of Λ' can be computed as follows:

1. Let $\mathbf{D}$ be dual basis of $\mathbf{B}$. Compute $\mathbf{D}_\perp := \mathbf{D} \cdot \mathbf{\Pi}_{\bar{\mathbf{v}}}^\perp$.
2. Apply the LLL algorithm on $\mathbf{D}_\perp$ to eliminate linear dependencies. Then delete the first row of $\mathbf{D}_\perp$ (which is $\mathbf{0}$ because with the hyperplane intersection, the dimension of the lattice is decremented).
3. Output the dual of the resulting matrix.

While polynomial time, the above computation is quite heavy, especially as there is no convenient library offering a parallel version of LLL. Fortunately, for predicting attack costs, one only needs the dimension of the lattice Λ and its volume. These can easily be computed assuming $\bar{\mathbf{v}}$ is a primitive vector (see Definition 10) of the dual lattice: the dimension decreases by 1, and the volume increases by a factor $\|\bar{\mathbf{v}}\|$. This is stated and proved in Lemma 11. Intuitively, the primitivity condition is needed since then one can scale the leak to $\langle \mathbf{s}, f\mathbf{v} \rangle = fl$ for any non-zero factor $f \in \mathbb{R}$ and get an equivalent leak; however there is only one factor f that can ensure that $f\bar{\mathbf{v}} \in \Lambda^*$, and is primitive in it.

Remark 23. Note that if $\bar{\mathbf{v}}$ is not in the span of Λ—as typically occurs if other non-orthogonal perfect hints have already been integrated—Lemma 11 should be applied to the orthogonal projection $\bar{\mathbf{v}}' = \bar{\mathbf{v}} \cdot \mathbf{\Pi}_\Lambda$ of $\bar{\mathbf{v}}$ onto Λ. Indeed, the perfect hint $\langle \bar{\mathbf{s}}, \bar{\mathbf{v}}' \rangle = 0$ replacing $\bar{\mathbf{v}}$ by $\bar{\mathbf{v}}'$ is equally valid.

4.2   Modular Hints

Definition 24 (Modular hint). *A modular hint on the secret $\mathbf{s}$ is the knowledge of $\mathbf{v} \in \mathbb{Z}^{d-1}$, $k \in \mathbb{Z}$ and $l \in \mathbb{Z}$, such that*

$$\langle \mathbf{s}, \mathbf{v} \rangle = l \mod k.$$

We can expect such hints to arise from several scenarios:

- obtaining the value of an intermediate register during LWE decryption would likely correspond to giving such a modular equation modulo q. This is also the case if an NTT coefficient leaks in a Ring-LWE scheme. It can also occur "by design" if the LWE secret is chosen so that certain NTT coordinates are fixed to 0 modulo q, as is the case in some instances of Order LWE [6].
- obtaining the absolute value $a = |s|$ of a coefficient s implies $s = a \mod 2a$, and such a hint could be obtained by a timing attack on an unprotected implementation of a table-based sampler, in the spirit of [17].

– obtaining the Hamming weight of the string $b_1 b_2 \ldots b_1' b_2' \ldots$ used to sample a centered binomial coefficient $s = \sum b_i - \sum b_i'$ (as done in NewHope and Kyber [31,34]) reveals in particular $s \bmod 2$. Indeed, the latter string (or at least some parts of it) is more likely to be leaked than the Hamming weight of s.

Integrating a modular hint into a DBDD instance. Let $\mathbf{v} \in \mathbb{Z}^{d-1}$; $k \in \mathbb{Z}$ and $l \in \mathbb{Z}$ be such that $\langle \mathbf{s}, \mathbf{v} \rangle = l \bmod k$. Note that the hint can also be written as

$$\langle \bar{\mathbf{s}}, \bar{\mathbf{v}} \rangle = 0 \mod k \tag{12}$$

where $\bar{\mathbf{s}}$ is the extended LWE secret as defined in Eq. 5 and $\bar{\mathbf{v}} := (\mathbf{v} ; -l)$. We refer to Remark 22 for the legitimacy of such dimension increase.

Smooth case. Intuitively, such a hint should only sparsify the lattice, and leave the average and the variance unchanged. This is not entirely true, this is only (approximately) true when the variance is sufficiently large in the direction of $\mathbf{v}$ to ensure smoothness, i.e. when $k^2 \ll \mathbf{v}\mathbf{\Sigma}\mathbf{v}^T$; one can refer to [28, Lemma 3.3 and Lemma 4.2] for the quality of that approximation. In this smooth case, we therefore have:

$$\Lambda' = \Lambda \cap \{ \mathbf{x} \in \mathbb{Z}^d \mid \langle \mathbf{x}, \bar{\mathbf{v}} \rangle = 0 \mod k \} \tag{13}$$
$$\boldsymbol{\mu}' = \boldsymbol{\mu} \tag{14}$$
$$\mathbf{\Sigma}' = \mathbf{\Sigma} \tag{15}$$

On the other hand, if $k^2 \gg \mathbf{v}\mathbf{\Sigma}\mathbf{v}^T$, then the residual distribution will be highly concentrated on a single value, and one should therefore instead use a perfect $\langle \mathbf{s}, \mathbf{v} \rangle = l + ik$ for some i.

General case. In the general case, one can resort to a numerical computation of the average μ_c and the variance σ_c^2 of the one-dimensional centered discrete Gaussian of variance $\sigma^2 = \mathbf{v}\mathbf{\Sigma}\mathbf{v}^T$ over the coset $l+k\mathbb{Z}$, and apply the corrections:

$$\boldsymbol{\mu}' = \boldsymbol{\mu} + \frac{\mu_c - \langle \bar{\mathbf{v}}, \boldsymbol{\mu} \rangle}{\bar{\mathbf{v}}\mathbf{\Sigma}\bar{\mathbf{v}}^T} \bar{\mathbf{v}}\mathbf{\Sigma} \tag{16}$$

$$\mathbf{\Sigma}' = \mathbf{\Sigma} + \left(\frac{\sigma_c^2}{(\bar{\mathbf{v}}\mathbf{\Sigma}\bar{\mathbf{v}}^T)^2} - \frac{1}{\bar{\mathbf{v}}\mathbf{\Sigma}\bar{\mathbf{v}}^T} \right) (\bar{\mathbf{v}}\mathbf{\Sigma})^T (\bar{\mathbf{v}}\mathbf{\Sigma}) \tag{17}$$

Intuitively, these formulae completely erase prior information on $\langle \mathbf{s}, \bar{\mathbf{v}} \rangle$, before it is replaced by the new average and variance in the adequate direction. Both can be derived[2] using Corollary 7.

As for perfect hints, the computation of Λ' can be done by working on the dual lattice. More specifically:

---

[2] We are thankful to Thibauld Feneuil for pointing out an incorrect equation in a previous version of this paper.

1. Let $\mathbf{D}$ be dual basis of $\mathbf{B}$.
2. Redefine $\bar{\mathbf{v}} \leftarrow \bar{\mathbf{v}} \cdot \mathbf{\Pi}_\Lambda$, noting that this does not affect the validity of the hint.
3. Append $\bar{\mathbf{v}}/k$ to $\mathbf{D}$ and obtain $\mathbf{D}'$
4. Apply the LLL algorithm on $\mathbf{D}'$ to eliminate linear dependencies. Then delete the first row of $\mathbf{D}'$ (which is $\mathbf{0}$ since we introduced a linear dependency).
5. Output the dual of the resulting matrix.

Also, as for perfect hints the parameters of the new lattice Λ' can be predicted: the dimension is unchanged, and the volume increases by a factor k under a primitivity condition, which is proved by Lemma 12.

4.3   Approximate Hints (conditioning)

Definition 25 (Approximate hint). *An approximate hint on the secret* $\mathbf{s}$ *is the knowledge of* $\mathbf{v} \in \mathbb{Z}^{d-1}$ *and* $l \in \mathbb{Z}$, *such that*

$$\langle \mathbf{s}, \ \mathbf{v} \rangle + e = l,$$

where e *models noise following a distribution* $N_1(0, \sigma_e^2)$, *independent of* $\mathbf{s}$.

One can expect such hints from:

- any noisy side channel information about a secret coefficient. This is the case of our study in Sect. 6.1.
- decryption failures. In Sect. 6.2, we show how this type of hint can represent the information gained by a decryption failure.

To include this knowledge in the DBDD instance, we must combine this knowledge with the prior knowledge on the solution $\mathbf{s}$ of the instance.

Integrating an approximate hint into a DBDD instance. Let $\mathbf{v} \in \mathbb{Z}^{d-1}$ and $l \in \mathbb{Z}$ be such that $\langle \mathbf{s}, \mathbf{v} \rangle \approx l$. Note that the hint can also be written as

$$\langle \bar{\mathbf{s}}, \ \bar{\mathbf{v}} \rangle + e = 0 \tag{18}$$

where $\bar{\mathbf{s}}$ is the extended LWE secret as defined in Eq. (5), $\bar{\mathbf{v}} := (\mathbf{v} ; -l)$, and e has $N_1(0, \sigma_e^2)$ distribution. The unique shortest non-zero solution of $\mathrm{DBDD}_{\Lambda, \mu, \Sigma}$, is also the unique solution of the instance $\mathrm{DBDD}_{\Lambda', \mu', \Sigma'}$ where

$$\Lambda' = \Lambda \tag{19}$$

$$\Sigma' = \Sigma - \frac{(\bar{\mathbf{v}} \Sigma)^T \bar{\mathbf{v}} \Sigma}{\bar{\mathbf{v}} \Sigma \bar{\mathbf{v}}^T + \sigma_e^2} \tag{20}$$

$$\mu' = \mu - \frac{\langle \bar{\mathbf{v}}, \mu \rangle}{\bar{\mathbf{v}} \Sigma \bar{\mathbf{v}}^T + \sigma_e^2} \bar{\mathbf{v}} \Sigma \tag{21}$$

We note that Eq. (19) comes from

$$\Lambda' := \Lambda \cap \left\{ \mathbf{x} \in \mathbb{Z}^d \mid \langle \mathbf{x}, \bar{\mathbf{v}} \rangle + e = 0, \text{ for all possible } e \sim N_1(0, \sigma_e^2) \right\} = \Lambda.$$

The new covariance and mean follow from Corollary 7.

Consistency with Perfect Hint. Note that if $\sigma_e = 0$, we fall back to a perfect hint $\langle \mathbf{s}, \mathbf{v} \rangle = l$. The above computation of $\mathbf{\Sigma}'$ (20) (resp. $\boldsymbol{\mu}'$ (21)) is indeed equivalent to Eq. (10) (resp. Eq. (11)) from Sect. 4.1. Note however, in our implementation, that to avoid singularities, we require the span of $\mathrm{Span}(\mathbf{\Sigma} + \boldsymbol{\mu}^T \boldsymbol{\mu}) = \mathrm{Span}(\Lambda)$ (See the requirement in Eq. (2)): If $\sigma_e = 0$, one *must* instead use a Perfect hint.

Multi-dimensional approximate hints. The formulae of [24] are even more general, and one could consider a multidimensional hint of the form $\mathbf{s}\mathbf{V} + \mathbf{e} = \mathbf{l}$, where $\mathbf{V} \in \mathbb{R}^{n \times k}$ and $\mathbf{e}$ a gaussian noise of any covariance $\mathbf{\Sigma_e}$. However, those general formulae require explicit matrix inversion which becomes impractical in large dimension. We therefore only implemented full-dimensional ($k = n$) hint integration in the *super-lightweight* version of our tool, which assumes all covariance matrices to be diagonal. These will be used for hints obtained from decryption failures in Sect. 6.2.

4.4 Approximate Hint (*a posteriori*)

In certain scenarios, one may more naturally obtain directly the a posteriori distribution of $\langle \mathbf{s}, \mathbf{v} \rangle$, rather than a hint $\langle \mathbf{s}, \mathbf{v} \rangle + e = l$ for some error e independent of $\mathbf{s}$. Such a scenario is typical in template attacks, as we exemplify via the single trace attack on Frodo from [9], which we study in Sect. 6.1.

Given the a posteriori distribution of $\langle \bar{\mathbf{s}}, \bar{\mathbf{v}} \rangle$, one can derive its mean μ_{ap} and variance σ_{ap}^2 and apply the corrections to compute the new mean and covariance exactly as in Eqs. (16) and (17).

4.5 Short Vector Hints

Definition 26 (Short vector hint). *A short vector hint on the lattice Λ is the knowledge of a short vector $\bar{\mathbf{v}}$ such that*

$$\bar{\mathbf{v}} \in \Lambda.$$

Note that such hints are not related to the secret, and are not expected to be obtained by side-channel information, but rather by the very design of the scheme. In particular, the lattice Λ underlying LWE instance modulo q contains the so-called q-vectors, i.e. the vectors $(q, 0, 0, \ldots, 0)$ and its permutations. These vectors are in fact implicitly exploited in the literature on the cryptanalysis of LWE since at least [23]. Indeed, in some regimes, the best attacks are obtained by 'forgetting' certain LWE equations, which can be geometrically interpreted as a projection orthogonally to a q-vector. Note that, among all hints, the short vector hints should be the last to be integrated. In our context, we need to generalize this idea beyond q-vector because the q-vectors may simply disappear after the integration of a perfect or modular hint. For example, after the integration of a perfect hint $\langle \mathbf{s}, (1, 1, \ldots, 1) \rangle = 0$, all the q-vectors are no longer in the lattice, but $(q, -q, 0, \ldots, 0)$ still is, and so are all its permutations.

Resolving the DBDD problem resulting from this projection will not directly lead to the original secret, as projection is not injective. However, as long as we keep $n + 1$ dimensions out of the $n + m + 1$ dimensions of the original LWE instance, we can still efficiently reconstruct the full LWE secret by solving a linear system over the rationals.

Integrating a short vector hint into a DBDD instance. It is the case when the secret vector is short enough to be a solution after applying projection $\Pi_{\bar{\mathbf{v}}}^{\perp}$ on $\mathsf{DBDD}_{\Lambda, \Sigma, \mu}$.

$$\Lambda' = \Lambda \cdot \Pi_{\bar{\mathbf{v}}}^{\perp} \tag{22}$$

$$\Sigma' = (\Pi_{\bar{\mathbf{v}}}^{\perp})^T \cdot \Sigma \cdot \Pi_{\bar{\mathbf{v}}}^{\perp} \tag{23}$$

$$\mu' = \mu \cdot \Pi_{\bar{\mathbf{v}}}^{\perp} \tag{24}$$

To compute a basis of Λ' one can simply apply the projection to all the vectors of its current basis, and then eliminate linear dependencies in the resulting basis using LLL.

Remark 27. Once a short vector hint $\bar{\mathbf{v}} \in \Lambda$ has been integrated, Λ has been transformed into Λ'. And, if one has to perform another short vector hint integration $\bar{\mathbf{v}}_1 \in \Lambda$, $\bar{\mathbf{v}}_1$ should be projected onto Λ' with $\bar{\mathbf{v}} \cdot \Pi_{\Lambda'} \in \Lambda'$. In our implementation however, this has been taken into account and one can simply apply the same transformation as above, replacing a single vector $\bar{\mathbf{v}}$ by a matrix $\mathbf{V}$.

The dimension of the lattice decreases by one (or by k, if one directly integrates a matrix of k vectors) and the volume of the lattice also decreases according to Fact 13. One can also predict the decrease of the determinant of Σ via the identity:

$$\mathrm{rdet}(\Sigma') = \mathrm{rdet}(\Sigma) \cdot \frac{\|\bar{\mathbf{v}}\|^2}{\bar{\mathbf{v}} \Sigma \bar{\mathbf{v}}^T}, \quad \text{or } \mathrm{rdet}(\Sigma') = \mathrm{rdet}(\Sigma) \cdot \frac{\det(\mathbf{V}\mathbf{V}^T)}{\det(\mathbf{V}\Sigma\mathbf{V}^T)}. \tag{25}$$

Worthiness and choice of short vector hints. Integrating such a hint induces a trade-off between the dimension and the volume, and therefore it is not always advantageous to integrate.

This raises the following potentially hard problem: given a set $\mathbf{W}$ of short vectors of Λ (viewed as a matrix), which subset $\mathbf{V} \subset \mathbf{W}$ of size k lead to the easiest DBDD instance? Because the hardness of the new problem grows with

$$\frac{\mathrm{rdet}(\Sigma')}{\mathrm{Vol}(\Lambda')^2} = \frac{\mathrm{rdet}(\Sigma)}{\mathrm{Vol}(\Lambda)^2} \cdot \frac{\det(\mathbf{V}\mathbf{V}^T)^2}{\det(\mathbf{V}\Sigma\mathbf{V}^T)} \tag{26}$$

In the case of an un-hinted DBDD instance directly obtained from the LWE problem, for $\mathbf{V}$ being the set of (primitive) q-vectors, the problem is easier: all subsets of size k lead to instances with the same parameters.

But this is not true anymore as soon as $\boldsymbol{\Sigma}$ has been altered or if the set $\mathbf{W}$ is arbitrary. For example, setting $\boldsymbol{\Sigma} = \mathbf{I}$, one simply wishes to minimize $\det(\mathbf{VV}^T)$; but for an arbitrary set $\mathbf{W}$ the problem of finding the optimal subset $\mathbf{V} \subset \mathbf{W}$ is NP-hard [22], and remains NP-hard up to exponential approximation factors.

A natural approach to try to get an approximate solution in polynomial time consists in making sequential greedy choices. This involves computing $|\mathbf{V}| \cdot |\mathbf{W}|$ many matrix-vector products over increasingly large rationals, and appeared painfully slow in practice for making prediction on cryptographically large instances. Fortunately, in the typical cases where the vectors of $\mathbf{W}$ are the q-vectors, this can be made somewhat practical (See Sect. 6.3 for example).

Remark 28. When the basis of an LWE-lattice is given in its systematic form, the q-vectors are already explicitly given to lattice reduction algorithms, and these algorithms will implicitly make use of them when they are worthy, as if we had integrated them. The reason is that lattice reduction algorithm naturally work with projected sublattices, and if a q-vector is shorter than what the algorithm can produce, those q-vectors will remain untouched at the beginning of the basis; the reduction algorithm will effectively work on the lattice projected orthogonally to them. In other words, integrating q-vectors is important to understand and predict how lattice reduction algorithm will work, but, in certain cases they may be automatically detected and exploited by lattice reduction algorithms themselves.

5   Implementation

5.1   Our Sage Implementation

We propose three implementations of our framework, all following the same python/sage 9.0 API.[3] More specifically, the API and some common functions are defined in DBDD_generic.sage, as a class DBDD_Generic. Three derived classes are then given:

1. The class DBDD (provided in DBDD.sage) is the *full-fledged* implementation: i.e. it fully maintains all information about a DBDD instance as one integrates hints: the lattice Λ, the covariance matrix $\boldsymbol{\Sigma}$ and the average $\boldsymbol{\mu}$. While polynomial time, maintaining the lattice information can be quite slow, especially since consecutive intersections with hyperplanes can lead to manipulations on rationals with large denominators. It also allows to finalize the attack, running the homogenization, isotropization and lattice reduction, based on the fplll [15] library available through sage.

   We note that if one were to repeatedly use perfect or modular hints, a lot of effort would be spent on uselessly alternating between the primal and the dual lattice. Instead, we implement a caching mechanism for the primal and dual basis, and only update them when necessary.

---

[3] While we would have preferred a full python implementation, we are making a heavy use of linear algebra over the rationals for which we could find no convenient python library.

2. The class `DBDD_predict` (provided in `DBDD_predict.sage`) is the *lightweight* implementation: it only fully maintains the covariance information, and the parameters of the lattice (dimension, volume). It must therefore work under assumptions about the primitivity of the vector $\mathbf{v}$; in particular, it cannot detect hints that are redundant. If one must resort to this faster variant on large instances, it is advised to consider potential (even partial) redundancy between the given hints, and to run a comparison with the previous on small instances with similarly generated hints.

3. The class `DBDD_predict_diag` (provided in `DBDD_predict_diag.sage`) is the *super-lightweight* implementation. It maintains the same information as the above, but requires the covariance matrix to remain diagonal at all times. In particular, one can only integrate hints for which the directional vector $\mathbf{v}$ is colinear with a canonical vector.

5.2 Tests and Validation

In the full version of our paper, we present a demonstration of our tool with some extracts of Sage 9.0 code. We implement two tests to verify the correctness of our scripts, and more generally the validity of our predictions.

Consistency checks. Our first test (`check_consistency.sage`) simply verifies that all three classes always agree perfectly. More specifically we run all three versions on a given instances, integrating the same random hint in all of them, and compare their hardness prediction. We first test using the full-fledged version that the primitivity condition does hold, and discard the hint if not, as we know that predictions cannot be correct on such hints. This verification passes.

Prediction verifications. We now verify experimentally the prediction made by our tool for various types of hints, by comparing those predictions to actual attack experiments (see `compare_usvp_models.sage` for the prediction without hints and `prediction_verifications.sage` for the prediction with hints). This is done for a given set of LWE parameters, and increasing the number of hints. The details of the experiments and the results are given in Fig. 5.

While our predictions seem overall accurate, we still note a minor discrepancy of up to 2 or 3 bikz in the low blocksize regime. This exceeds the error made by prediction on the attack without any hint, which was below 1 bikz, even in the same low blocksize regime. We suspected that this discrepancy is due to residual q-vectors, or small combinations of them, that are hard to predict for randomly generated hints, but would still benefit by lattice reduction. We tested that hypothesis by running similar experiments, but leaving certain coordinates untouched by hints, so to still explicitly know some q-vectors for short-vector hint integration, if they are "worthy". This didn't to improve the accuracy of our prediction, which infirms our suspected explanation. We are at the moment unable to explain this inaccuracy. We nevertheless find our predictions satisfactory, considering that even without hints, previous predictions [3] were much less accurate (see Fig. 4).

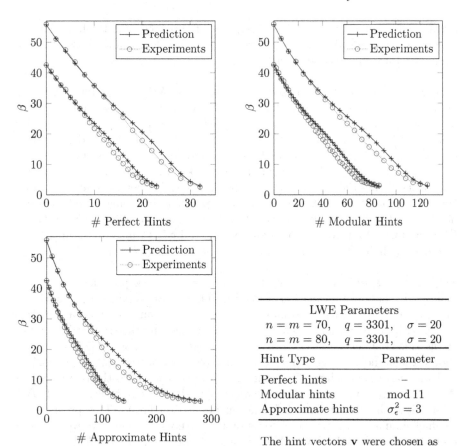

The hint vectors **v** were chosen as random ternary vectors of weight 5.

Fig. 5. Experimental verification of the security decay predictions for each type of hints. Each data point was averaged over 256 samples.

6 Applications Examples

6.1 Hints from Side Channels

In [9], W. Bos et al. study the feasibility of a single-trace power analysis of the Frodo Key Encapsulation Mechanism (FrodoKEM) [29]. Specifically, in the first approach, they analyze the possibility of a divide-and-conquer attack targeting a multiplication in the key generation. This attack was claimed unsuccessful in [9] because the bruteforce phase after recovering a candidate for the private key was too expensive. Along with this unsuccessful result, a successful powerful extend-and-prune attack is provided in [9].

We emphasize that the purpose of this section is to exemplify our tool on a standard side-channel attack, and this is why we choose the former unsuccessful divide-and-conquer attack of [9]. The point of this section is to show that our framework can indeed lead to improvements in the algorithmic phase of a side-channel attack, once the leak has been fixed.

FrodoKEM. FrodoKEM is based on small-secret-LWE; we outline here some details necessary to understand the attack. Note that we use different letter notations from [29] for consistency. For parameters n and q, the private key is $(z \in \mathbb{Z}_q^n, e \in \mathbb{Z}_q^n)$ where the coefficients of z and e, denoted z_i and e_i, can take several values in a small set that we denote L. The public key is $(A \in \mathbb{Z}_q^{n \times n}, b = zA + e)$. The goal of the attack is to recover z by making measurements during the multiplication between z and A when computing b in the key generation. Note that there is no multiplication involving e and thus it is not targeted in this attack. Six sets of parameters are considered: CCS1, CCS2, CCS3 and CCS4 introduced in [8] and NIST1 and NIST2 introduced in [29]. For example, with NIST1 parameters, $n = 640$, $q = 2^{15}$ and $L = \{-11, \cdots, 11\}$.

Side-channel simulation. The divide-and-conquer attack provided by [9] simulates side-channel information using ELMO, a power simulator for a Cortex M0 [27]. This tool outputs simulated power traces using an elaborate leakage model with Gaussian noise. Thus, it is parametrized by the standard deviation of the side-channel noise. For proofs of concept, the authors of [27] suggest to choose the standard deviation of the simulated noise as $\sigma_{\text{SimNoise}} := 0.0045$ for realistic leakage modeling. This standard deviation was also the one chosen in [9, Fig. 2b] and W. Bos et al. implemented a Matlab script that calls ELMO to simulate the side-channel information applied on Frodo. This precise side-channel simulator was provided to us by the authors of [9] and we were able to re-generate all their data with Matlab, again using $\sigma_{\text{SimNoise}} = 0.0045$.

Template attack. The divide-and-conquer side-channel attack proposed by W. Bos et al. belongs in the template attack family. Template attacks were introduced in [10]. In a nutshell, these attacks include a profiling phase and an online phase. Let us detail the template attack for Frodo implemented in [9].

1. The profiling phase consists in using a copy of the device and recording a large number of traces using many different known secret values. From these measures, the attacker can derive the multidimensional distribution of several points of interest when the traces share the same secret coefficient. More precisely, in the case of FrodoKEM, for a given index $i \in [0, n - 1]$, the points of interest will be the instants in the trace when z_i is multiplied by the coefficients of A(n interest points in total). Let us define

$$c_i := (T[t_{i,0}], \dots, T[t_{i,n-1}]) \quad c \in \mathbb{R}^n, \tag{27}$$

where T denotes the trace measurement and $(t_{i,k})$ denotes the instants of the multiplication of z_i with the coefficients $A_{i,k}$ for $(i, k) \in [0, n-1]$. The random variable vector associated to c_i is denoted by C_i. For each $i \in [0, n - 1]$ and

$x \in L$, the goal of the profiling phase is to learn the center of the probability distribution

$$A_{i,x}(\mathbf{c}) := P\left[C_i = \mathbf{c} \mid \mathbf{z}_i = x\right].$$

By hypothesis, for template attacks (see [10, Section 2.1]), $A_{i,x}$ is assumed to follow a multidimenstional normal distribution of standard deviation $\sigma_{\text{SimNoise}} \cdot \mathbf{I}_n$. Thus, the attacker recovers the center of $A_{i,x}$ for each $i \in [0, n-1]$ and $x \in L$ by averaging all the measured $\mathbf{c}_i$ that validate $\mathbf{z}_i = x$. The center of $A_{i,x}$ is denoted $\mathbf{t}_{i,x}$ and we call it a *template*. W. Bos et al. [9] actually assume that $\mathbf{t}_{i,x}$ depends only on x and is independent from the index i. Thus, $\mathbf{t}_{i,x} = \mathbf{t}_x$. Essentially, this common assumption implies that the index $i \in [0, n-1]$ of the target coefficient does not influence the leakage. Consequently, the attacker only has to derive $\mathbf{t}_{0,x}$, for example.

2. In a second step, the attacker knows the templates $\mathbf{t}_x$ for all $x \in L$. She also knows the points of interest $t_{i,k}$ as defined above in Eq. 27. She will construct a candidate $\tilde{\mathbf{z}}$ for the secret $\mathbf{z}$ by recovering the coefficients one by one. For each unknown secret coefficient $\mathbf{z}_i$, she takes the measurement $\mathbf{c}_i$ as defined in Eq. 27. Using this measurement, she can derive an a posteriori probability distribution: With her fixed $i \in [0, n-1]$ and measured $\mathbf{c}_i \in \mathbb{R}$, she computes for all $x \in L$,

$$P\left[\mathbf{z}_i = x \mid C_i = \mathbf{c}_i\right] = \frac{P\left[\mathbf{z}_i = x\right]}{P\left[C_i = \mathbf{c}_i\right]} \cdot P\left[C_i = \mathbf{c}_i \mid \mathbf{z}_i = x\right] \tag{28}$$

$$\propto P\left[\mathbf{z}_i = x\right] \cdot \exp\left(-\frac{\|\mathbf{c}_i - \mathbf{t}_x\|_2^2}{2\sigma_{\text{SimNoise}}^2}\right) \tag{29}$$

In [9], a score table, denoted $(S_i[x])_{x \in L}$ is derived from the a posteriori distribution as follows,

$$S_i[x] := \ln\left(P\left[\mathbf{z}_i = x \mid C_i = \mathbf{c}_i\right]\right) \tag{30}$$

$$= \ln\left(P\left[\mathbf{z}_i = x\right]\right) - \frac{\|\mathbf{c}_i - \mathbf{t}_x\|_2^2}{2\sigma_{\text{SimNoise}}^2}. \tag{31}$$

Finally, the output candidate for $\mathbf{z}_i$ is $\tilde{\mathbf{z}}_i := \operatorname{argmax}_{x \in L}(S_i[x])$.

One can use the presented attack as a "black-box" to generate the score tables using the script from [9]. As an example, using the NIST1 parameters, we show several measured scores $(S[-11], \cdots, S[11])$ corresponding to several secret coefficients in Table 1. The first line corresponds to a secret equal to 0, the second line to 1 and the third and fourth line to -1. The last line is an example of failed guessing because we see that the outputted candidate is not -1. We remark that the values having the opposite sign are assigned a very low score, we conjecture that it is because the sign is filling the register and then the Hamming weight of the register will be very far from the correct one.

Table 1. Examples of scores associated to the secret values $s_i \in \{0, \pm 1\}$, after the side-channel analysis of [9] for NIST1 parameters. The best score in each score table is highlighted. This best guess is correct for the first 3 score table, but incorrect for the last one.

z_i	S											
	-11	-10	-9	-8	-7	-6	-5	-4	-3	-2	-1	0
0	-4098	-3918	-4344	-2580	-3212	-3108	-3758	-3155	-3583	-3498	-3900	$\mathbf{-340}$
1	-3273	-3114	-3491	-1951	-2495	-2405	-2972	-2445	-2819	-2744	-3098	-365
-1	-341	-335	-352	-465	-358	-369	-329	-362	-331	-334	$\mathbf{-328}$	-3712
-1	-306	-298	-319	-414	-314	-323	$\mathbf{-290}$	-317	-291	-293	-291	-3608

z_i	$\ldots$	1	2	3	4	5	6	7	8	9	10	11
0	$\ldots$	-380	-367	-452	-818	-975	-933	-1084	-368	-459	-453	-592
1	$\ldots$	$\mathbf{-325}$	-328	-338	-546	-657	-627	-737	-333	-344	-342	-407
-1	$\ldots$	-3079	-3195	-2656	-1696	-1461	-1521	-1329	-3231	-2648	-2685	-2201
-1	$\ldots$	-2982	-3097	-2564	-1617	-1385	-1444	-1256	-3132	-2556	-2593	-2115

With this template attack, one can recover $\tilde{\mathbf{z}} \approx \mathbf{z}$. However, W. Bos et al. [9] could not conclude the attack with a key recovery even though much information leaked about the secret. Frustratingly, a bruteforce phase to derive $\mathbf{z}$ from $\tilde{\mathbf{z}}$ did not lead to any security threat as stated in [9, Section 3]. They actually pointed out an interesting open question of whether "novel lattice reduction algorithms [can] take into account side-channel information". Our work solves this open question by combining the knowledge obtained in the divide-and-conquer template attack of [9] with our framework.

From scores to hints. We first instantiate a DBDD instance with a chosen set of parameters. Then we assume that, for each secret coefficient $\mathbf{z}_i$, we are given the associated score table S_i, thanks to the template attack that has already been carried out. We go back to the a posteriori distribution in Eq. 29 by applying the exp() function and renormalizing the score table. As an example, we show the probability distributions derived from Table 1, along with their variances and centers, in Table 2.

Finally, we use our framework to introduce n a posteriori *approximate hints* to our DBDD instance with the derived centers and variances for each score table. When the variance is exactly 0, we integrate perfect hints instead.

Results. One can reproduce this attack using the Sage 9.0 script exploiting_SCA_from_Bos_et_al.sage. The experimentally derived data containing the score tables is in the folder Scores_tables_SCA for which, as mentioned earlier, was generated with a simulated noise variance of 0.0045. One can note that the obtained security fluctuates a bit from instance to instance, as it depends on the strength of the hints, which themselves depend on the randomness of the scheme. In the first two lines of Table 3, we show the new security with the inclusion of the approximate hints averaged on 50 tests per set of parameters.

Table 2. Probability distributions derived from Table 1, along with variances and centers.

z_i	-11	-10	-9	-8	-7	-6	-5	-4	-3	-2	-1	0
						A posteriori distribution						
0	0	0	0	0	0	0	0	0	0	0	0	1
1	0	0	0	0	0	0	0	0	0	0	0	0
-1	0	0	0	0	0	0	0.26	0	0.04	0.00	0.70	0
-1	0	0	0	0	0	0	0.56	0	0.21	0.03	0.21	0

	...	1	2	3	4	5	6	7	8	9	10	11	center	variance
0	...	0	0	0	0	0	0	0	0	0	0	0	0	0
1	...	0.95	0.04	0	0	0	0	0	0.01	0	0	0	1.05	0.06
-1	...	0	0	0	0	0	0	0	0	0	0	0	-2.11	3.11
-1	...	0	0	0	0	0	0	0	0	0	0	0	-3.68	2.63

Table 3. Cost of the attacks without/with hints without/with guesses.

		NIST1	NIST2	CCS1	CCS2	CCS3	CCS4
Attack without hints	(bikz)	487	708	239	448	492	584
Attack with hints	(bikz)	**330**	**423**	**128**	**123**	**219**	**230**
Attack with hints & guesses	(bikz)	**292**	**298**	**70**	**29**	**124**	**129**
Number of guesses g		100	250	200	300	250	250
Success probability		0.86	0.64	0.87	0.77	0.81	0.84

Guessing. To improve the attack further, one can note from Table 2 that certain key values have a very high probability of being correct, and assuming each of these values are correct, one can replace an approximate hint with a perfect one. For example, considering the second line of Table 2, the secret has a probability of 0.95 to be 1 and thus guessing it trades a perfect hint for a decrease of the success probability of the attack by 5%. This hybrid attack exploiting hints, guesses and lattice reduction, works as follows. Let g be a parameter.

1. Include all the approximate and perfect hints given by the score tables,
2. Order the coefficients of the secret z_i according to the maximum value of their a posteriori distribution table,
3. Include perfect hints for the g first coefficients and then solve and check the solution.

Increasing the number of guesses g leads to a trade-off between the cost of the attack and its success probability. We have chosen here a success probability larger than 0.6, while reducing the attack cost by 38 to 145 bikz depending on the parameter set. Given that 1 bit of security corresponds roughly to 3 or 4 bikz, this is undoubtedly advantageous.

Remark 29. The refinement presented above are very recent (lastly improved on June 2020). We are grateful to the authors of [9] of for helping us reconstructing distributions from the score table.

We remark that, with these results, the attacks with guesses on the parameters CCS1 and CCS2 seem doable in practice while it was not the case with our original results. However, some improvements of the implementation remain to be done in order to actually mount the attack. The full-fledged implementation cannot handle in reasonable time the large matrices of the original DBDD instance. We require another class of implementation which fully maintains all information about the instance, like the DBDD class, and assumes that the covariance matrix Σ is diagonal to simplify the computations, like the DBDD_predict_diag class. We hope to report on such an implementation in a future update of this report.

Remark 30. It should be noted that, given a single trace, one cannot naively retry the attack to boost its success probability. Indeed, the "second-best" guess may already have a much lower success probability than the first. Setting up such an hybrid attack mixing lattice reduction within our framework and key-ranking appears to be an interesting problem.

6.2   Hints from Decryption Failures

Another kind of hint our framework can model are hints provided by decryption failures. Using our framework, we produce prediction on a decryption failure attack on FrodoKEM-976 that match very closely the ad-hoc analysis of [14]. Our analysis is deferred to the full version of this paper [13].

6.3   Structural Hints from Design

Interestingly, we can also incorporate structural information on the secret or error that is present in certain schemes. We present (slightly) improved attacks on several Round 2 NIST submissions (such as LAC, Round5, and NTRU) which use ternary distribution for secrets, with a prescribed numbers of 1's and −1's in the full version of our paper [13].

Acknowledgments. The authors would like to thank Marco Martinoli and his co-authors [9] for sharing their source code. We express our gratitude to Jan-Pieter D'anvers for sharing precious insights and intuitions, guiding toward the proper formalization of decryption failures as approximate hints. We also thank John Schanck for valuable references and discussions that lead to refinements of the section on NTRU. We are also grateful to Martin Albrecht, Henri Gilbert, Ange Martinelli, Thomas Prest and Thibauld Feneuil and to the anonymous CRYPTO'2020 reviewers for valuable feedback on a preliminary version of this work.

References

1. Albrecht, M.R., et al.: Estimate all the {LWE, NTRU} schemes! In: Catalano, D., De Prisco, R. (eds.) SCN 2018. LNCS, vol. 11035, pp. 351–367. Springer, Cham (2018). https://doi.org/10.1007/978-3-319-98113-0_19
2. Albrecht, M.R., Deo, A., Paterson, K.G.: Cold boot attacks on ring and module LWE keys under the NTT. IACR TCHES **2018**, 173–213 (2018)
3. Albrecht, M.R., Göpfert, F., Virdia, F., Wunderer, T.: Revisiting the expected cost of solving uSVP and applications to LWE. In: Takagi, T., Peyrin, T. (eds.) ASIACRYPT 2017. LNCS, vol. 10624, pp. 297–322. Springer, Cham (2017). https://doi.org/10.1007/978-3-319-70694-8_11
4. Alkim, E., Ducas, L., Pöppelmann, T., Schwabe, P.: Post-quantum key exchange—a new hope. In: 25th USENIX Security Symposium (USENIX Security 2016), pp. 327–343 (2016)
5. Bai, S., Miller, S., Wen, W.: A refined analysis of the cost for solving LWE via uSVP. Cryptology ePrint Archive, Report 2019/502 (2019)
6. Bolboceanu, M., Brakerski, Z., Perlman, R., Sharma, D.: Order-LWE and the hardness of ring-LWE with entropic secrets. In: Galbraith, S.D., Moriai, S. (eds.) ASIACRYPT 2019. LNCS, vol. 11922, pp. 91–120. Springer, Cham (2019). https://doi.org/10.1007/978-3-030-34621-8_4
7. Bootle, J., Delaplace, C., Espitau, T., Fouque, P.-A., Tibouchi, M.: LWE without modular reduction and improved side-channel attacks against BLISS. In: Peyrin, T., Galbraith, S. (eds.) ASIACRYPT 2018. LNCS, vol. 11272, pp. 494–524. Springer, Cham (2018). https://doi.org/10.1007/978-3-030-03326-2_17
8. Bos, J.W., et al.: Frodo: take off the ring! Practical, quantum-secure key exchange from LWE, pp. 1006–1018 (2016)
9. Bos, J.W., Friedberger, S., Martinoli, M., Oswald, E., Stam, M.: Assessing the feasibility of single trace power analysis of Frodo. In: Cid, C., Jacobson Jr., M. (eds.) SAC 2018. LNCS, vol. 11349, pp. 216–234. Springer, Cham (2019). https://doi.org/10.1007/978-3-030-10970-7_10
10. Chari, S., Rao, J.R., Rohatgi, P.: Template attacks. In: Kaliski, B.S., Koç, K., Paar, C. (eds.) CHES 2002. LNCS, vol. 2523, pp. 13–28. Springer, Heidelberg (2003). https://doi.org/10.1007/3-540-36400-5_3
11. Chen, Y., Nguyen, P.Q.: BKZ 2.0: better lattice security estimates. In: Lee, D.H., Wang, X. (eds.) ASIACRYPT 2011. LNCS, vol. 7073, pp. 1–20. Springer, Heidelberg (2011). https://doi.org/10.1007/978-3-642-25385-0_1
12. Cheon, J.H., Kim, D., Lee, J., Song, Y.: Lizard: cut off the tail! A practical post-quantum public-key encryption from LWE and LWR. In: Catalano, D., De Prisco, R. (eds.) SCN 2018. LNCS, vol. 11035, pp. 160–177. Springer, Cham (2018). https://doi.org/10.1007/978-3-319-98113-0_9
13. Dachman-Soled, D., Ducas, L., Gong, H., Rossi, M.: LWE with side information: attacks and concrete security estimation. Cryptology ePrint Archive, Report 2020/292 (2020). https://eprint.iacr.org/2020/292
14. D'Anvers, J.-P., Vercauteren, F., Verbauwhede, I.: On the impact of decryption failures on the security of LWE/LWR based schemes. IACR Cryptology ePrint Archive, 2018:1089 (2018)
15. The FPLLL Development Team: FPLLL, a lattice reduction library (2016). https://github.com/fplll/fplll
16. Garcia-Morchon, O., et al.: Round5. Technical report, NIST (2019)

17. Groot Bruinderink, L., Hülsing, A., Lange, T., Yarom, Y.: Flush, gauss, and reload–a cache attack on the BLISS lattice-based signature scheme. In: Gierlichs, B., Poschmann, A.Y. (eds.) CHES 2016. LNCS, vol. 9813, pp. 323–345. Springer, Heidelberg (2016). https://doi.org/10.1007/978-3-662-53140-2_16

18. Groot Bruinderink, L., Pessl, P.: Differential fault attacks on deterministic lattice signatures. IACR TCHES **2018**, 21–43 (2018)

19. Hoffstein, J., Howgrave-Graham, N., Pipher, J., Whyte, W.: Practical lattice-based cryptography: NTRUEncrypt and NTRUSign. In: Nguyen, P., Vallée, B. (eds.) The LLL Algorithm. ISC, pp. 349–390. Springer, Heidelberg (2009). https://doi.org/10.1007/978-3-642-02295-1_11

20. Howgrave-Graham, N.: A hybrid lattice-reduction and meet-in-the-middle attack against NTRU. In: Menezes, A. (ed.) CRYPTO 2007. LNCS, vol. 4622, pp. 150–169. Springer, Heidelberg (2007). https://doi.org/10.1007/978-3-540-74143-5_9

21. Kannan, R.: Minkowski's convex body theorem and integer programming. Math. Oper. Res. **12**, 415–440 (1987)

22. Khachiyan, L.: On the complexity of approximating extremal determinants in matrices. J. Complex. **11**, 138–153 (1995)

23. Lindner, R., Peikert, C.: Better key sizes (and attacks) for LWE-based encryption. In: Kiayias, A. (ed.) CT-RSA 2011. LNCS, vol. 6558, pp. 319–339. Springer, Heidelberg (2011). https://doi.org/10.1007/978-3-642-19074-2_21

24. Liu, L.-P.: Linear transformation of multivariate normal distribution: marginal, joint and posterior. http://www.cs.columbia.edu/~liulp/pdf/linear_normal_dist.pdf. Accessed Sept 2019

25. Lu, X., et al.: PQC round-2 candidate: LAC. Technical report, NIST (2019). https://csrc.nist.gov/projects/post-quantum-cryptography/round-2-submissions

26. Martinet, J.: Perfect Lattices in Euclidean Spaces, vol. 327. Springer, Heidelberg (2013). https://doi.org/10.1007/978-3-662-05167-2

27. McCann, D., Oswald, E., Whitnall, C.: Towards practical tools for side channel aware software engineering: 'grey box' modelling for instruction leakages. In: 26th USENIX Security Symposium (USENIX Security 2017), Vancouver, BC, pp. 199–216. USENIX Association, August 2017

28. Micciancio, D., Regev, O.: Worst-case to average-case reductions based on Gaussian measures. SIAM J. Comput. **37**, 267–302 (2007)

29. Naehrig, M., et al.: FrodoKEM. Technical report, National Institute of Standards and Technology (2017). https://csrc.nist.gov/projects/post-quantum-cryptography/round-1-submissions

30. Nguyen, P.: Giophanthus and *LWR-based submissions (2019). Comment on the NIST PQC forum. https://groups.google.com/a/list.nist.gov/d/msg/pqc-forum/nZBIBvYmmUI/J0pug16CBgAJ

31. Pöppelmann, T., et al.: NewHope. Technical report, NIST (2019)

32. Ravi, P., Jhanwar, M.P., Howe, J., Chattopadhyay, A., Bhasin, S.: Side-channel assisted existential forgery attack on Dilithium - a NIST PQC candidate. Cryptology ePrint Archive, Report 2018/821 (2018)

33. Ravi, P., Jhanwar, M.P., Howe, J., Chattopadhyay, A., Bhasin, S.: Exploiting determinism in lattice-based signatures: practical fault attacks on pqm4 implementations of NIST candidates. In: Asia CCS 2019, pp. 427–440. Association for Computing Machinery (2019)

34. Schwabe, P., et al.: CRYSTALS-KYBER. Technical report, NIST (2019)

35. Zhang, Z., et al.: PQC round-2 candidate: NTRU. Technical report, NIST (2019). https://csrc.nist.gov/projects/post-quantum-cryptography/round-2-submissions

A Key-Recovery Timing Attack on Post-quantum Primitives Using the Fujisaki-Okamoto Transformation and Its Application on FrodoKEM

Qian Guo[1,2(✉)], Thomas Johansson[1(✉)], and Alexander Nilsson[1,3(✉)]

[1] Department of Electrical and Information Technology,
Lund University, Lund, Sweden
{qian.guo,thomas.johansson,alexander.nilsson}@eit.lth.se
[2] Selmer Center, Department of Informatics, University of Bergen, Bergen, Norway
[3] Advenica AB, Malmö, Sweden

Abstract. In the implementation of post-quantum primitives, it is well known that all computations that handle secret information need to be implemented to run in constant time. Using the Fujisaki-Okamoto transformation or any of its different variants, a CPA-secure primitive can be converted into an IND-CCA secure KEM. In this paper we show that although the transformation does not handle secret information apart from calls to the CPA-secure primitive, it has to be implemented in constant time. Namely, if the ciphertext comparison step in the transformation is leaking side-channel information, we can launch a key-recovery attack.

Several proposed schemes in round 2 of the NIST post-quantum standardization project are susceptible to the proposed attack and we develop and show the details of the attack on one of them, being FrodoKEM. It is implemented on the reference implementation of FrodoKEM, which is claimed to be secure against all timing attacks. Experiments show that the attack code is able to extract the secret key for all security levels using about 2^{30} decapsulation calls.

Keywords: Lattice-based cryptography · NIST post-quantum standardization · LWE · Timing attacks · Side-channel attacks

1 Introduction

Post-Quantum Cryptography is the area of cryptographic research in the presence of an, assumed to be practical, quantum computer. It is well known that most of today's public-key solutions are insecure under this assumption since they are based on the difficulty of factoring or the discrete log problem. These two problems can be solved in polynomial time if a large enough quantum computer exists [30]. Instead, post-quantum cryptography is based on other hard problems, not known to be broken by a quantum computer. The two most popular areas are lattice-based schemes and code-based schemes.

© International Association for Cryptologic Research 2020
D. Micciancio and T. Ristenpart (Eds.): CRYPTO 2020, LNCS 12171, pp. 359–386, 2020.
https://doi.org/10.1007/978-3-030-56880-1_13

Learning with errors (LWE) is a hard problem that is closely connected to difficult problems in lattices, such as the shortest vector problem. Learning with errors, or some version of the problem, is used in many of the recently proposed schemes to build public-key encryption schemes (PKE) and key encapsulation mechanisms (KEM).

Code-based schemes are similar to LWE schemes, but rely instead on difficult coding theory problems, like finding a minimum (Hamming) weight codeword in a binary code. Code-based schemes date back to 1978 and the McEliece PKE scheme [26].

The importance of post-quantum cryptography is highlighted by the fact that NIST is currently running a standardization project on post-quantum cryptography [1] which is in the second round. Most KEM- and PKE-schemes remaining in the NIST post-quantum cryptography standardization project (NIST PQ project) are either lattice-based or code-based schemes.

A very common approach for the above mentioned types of schemes is to construct a public-key encryption scheme that is secure in the chosen plaintext model (CPA) and then use a generic transformation to transform the scheme into a IND-CCA secure KEM. An IND-CCA secure primitive is secure in the model of indistinguishability under chosen ciphertext attacks. For definitions of these models, we refer to any textbook on the subject [31]. The most common generic transformation is the Fujisaki-Okamoto (FO) transformation [19] or any of its many different variants [21]. It gives IND-CCA security in the random oracle model, and there is also a post-quantum secure version [21]. This is also the way lattice-based and code-based KEM schemes in the NIST PQ project are constructed. They all use some version of the FO transformation.

In the implementation of post-quantum primitives, it is well known that all computations that handle secret information need to be implemented to run in constant time. Leakage of timing information can give information about secret values. This is a hard problem in practice, as we might not trust just any programmer to pay enough attention to such issues. There is now much focus on constant time implementations for the remaining candidates in the NIST PQ project and much research is devoted to examine cryptanalysis on so called side-channels [14,24]. This includes work showing attacks on schemes with implementations that leak timing information when processing secret data, such as the step of decoding an error correcting code inside the decryption scheme.

In this paper we show that even though the FO transformation itself does not handle secret information apart from calls to the CPA-secure PKE (running in constant time), it still has to be implemented in constant time. Namely, if the ciphertext comparison step in the FO transformation is leaking side-channel information, we can launch a key-recovery attack. The attack is based on generating decryption failures in the CPA-secure primitive by modifying the ciphertext. Through timing information we can learn whether a modified ciphertext is decrypted to the same message as the original ciphertext, or not.

This kind of attack has not been observed before, as several of the NIST candidates provide implementations that are directly susceptible to the proposed attack. We mention that at least the round 2 candidates FrodoKEM, LAC,

BIKE, HQC, ROLLO and RQC have all submitted reference implementations that potentially leaked timing information in the ciphertext comparison step, and thus they might be susceptible to this attack.

We decided to develop and show the details of the attack on one of them, being FrodoKEM. FrodoKEM is a lattice-based KEM where the security is based on the LWE problem. It is a very conservative design with strong security proofs and its design team contains many very distinguished cryptographers. In the document [27] submitted to NIST, it is claimed that "All our implementations avoid the use of secret address accesses and secret branches and, hence, are protected against timing and cache attacks." An implementation of FrodoKEM that can be attacked also appears in Open Quantum Safe [3].

The attack on FrodoKEM is detailed in the paper and then implemented on the reference implementation of FrodoKEM. Using experiments, we show that the attack code, by measuring the execution time of full decapsulations, is able to collect enough data for a complete secret key recovery using about 2^{30} decapsulation queries. We target the FrodoKEM parameters for the highest security level.

Previous work: Some previous work on using decryption failures in cryptanalysis appeared in [22,23]. More recent attacks using decryption failures on lattice-based schemes are to be found in [8–10,18]. None of these attacks apply to CCA-secure schemes unless there is some misuse of the scheme.

Attacks on CCA secure schemes based on failures were modelled in [15] and a complex attack on an NTRU version was presented. An attack on LAC [25] using decryption errors was given in [20].

Side-channel attacks were first proposed by Kocher in [24]. In such an attack, information obtained through physical measurements is used in the attack, being timing information, power measurements, electromagnetic radiation or other means. Brumley and Boneh attacked OpenSSL in [14], showing that remote timing attacks are practical. Side-channel attacks on post-quantum primitives have been proposed on signature schemes like BLISS [13]. Side-channel attacks on encryption/KEM primitives have been less successful, but include [17] measuring the robustness of the candidates in the NIST PQ project against cache-timing attacks. An attack on LWE schemes that use error correcting codes for which decoding is not implemented in constant time was given in [16] and the same for code-based schemes are given in [32] and [33].

Paper organization: The remaining parts of the paper are organized as follows. Section 2 gives basic notation and definitions used later in the paper. In Sect. 3 we give a high-level description of the attack and describe the general underlying ideas used to achieve success in building the key parts of the attack. In Sect. 4 we describe the FrodoKEM scheme and briefly highlight the weakness in its reference implementation. In Sect. 5 we give the full details on how to apply the attack on FrodoKEM and recover the secret key. Results on implementing the attack on the FrodoKEM reference implementation are given. Finally, we discuss in Sect. 6 a few other round 2 NIST schemes where the reference implementations can be attacked, including LWE schemes using error correction and pure code-based schemes. Further details on how the attack could be adapted to LAC is found in the appendix.

2 Preliminary

We start by defining some useful notations used throughout the rest of the paper. In post-quantum cryptography with emphasis on lattice-based or code-based schemes, it makes sense to consider the message $\mathbf{m} \in \mathcal{M}$ and ciphertext $\mathbf{c} \in \mathcal{C}$ as being vectors with entries in some alphabet $\mathbb{Z}_q$. A PKE is then a triple of algorithms (KeyGen, Enc, Dec), where KeyGen generates the secret key sk $\in \mathcal{SK}$ and the public key pk $\in \mathcal{PK}$. The encryption algorithm Enc maps the message to a ciphertext using the public key and the decryption algorithm Dec maps the ciphertext back to a message using the secret key. Encryption may also use some randomness denoted $\mathbf{r} \in \mathcal{R}$, that can be viewed as part of the input to the algorithm. If $\mathbf{c} = \mathsf{Enc}(\mathsf{pk}, \mathbf{m}; \mathbf{r})$, then decrypting such a ciphertext, i.e., computing $\mathsf{Dec}(\mathsf{sk}, \mathsf{pk}, \mathbf{c})$, returns the ciphertext $\mathbf{m}$. Some schemes may have a small failure probability, meaning that the decryption algorithm fails to return a correctly encrypted message when decrypted.

A KEM is similarly defined as a triple of algorithms (KeyGen, Encaps, Decaps), where KeyGen generates the secret key sk $\in \mathcal{SK}$ and the public key pk $\in \mathcal{PK}$. The encapsulation algorithm Encaps generates a random session key, denoted as $\mathbf{s} \in \mathcal{S}$, and computes a ciphertext $\mathbf{c}$ using the public key. Applying the decapsulation algorithm Decaps on a ciphertext using the secret key returns the chosen session key $\mathbf{s}$, or possibly a random output in case the ciphertext does not fully match a possible output of the encapsulation algorithm.

Security can be defined in many different models, but most commonly the analysis is done in the CPA model, where the adversary essentially only have access to the public key pk and the public encryption/encapsulation calls. In a CCA model, the adversary is allowed to ask for decryptions/decapsulations of her choice. So for example, the notion of IND-CCA for a KEM is defined through the following game: Let the ciphertext $\mathbf{c}$ be the encapsulation of the secret key $\mathbf{s}_0 \in \mathcal{S}$. Consider another randomly selected key $\mathbf{s}_1 \in \mathcal{S}$. The adversary gets the ciphertext $\mathbf{c}$ as well as $\mathbf{s}_b$, where $b \in \{0, 1\}$ is randomly chosen. The adversarial task is to correctly predict b with as large probability as possible and access to the decapsulation oracle is allowed for all ciphertext inputs except $\mathbf{c}$. For more detailed definitions of these different security models, we refer to any textbook on the subject, for example [31].

A very common approach is to construct a public-key primitive that is secure in the CPA model and then use a generic transformation to transform the scheme into a IND-CCA secure primitive. A common such generic transformation is the FO transformation [19], which has also many different variants [21]. It gives IND-CCA security in the random oracle model and include a post-quantum secure version [21]. This is also the way lattice-based and code-based KEM schemes in the NIST PQ project are constructed. They use some version of the FO transformation. We will introduce and investigate the FO transformation in relation to side-channel leakage in the next section.

3   A General Description of the Proposed Attack

We describe the attack for post-quantum primitives in the form of KEMs, although the attack could work for other types of PKC primitives as well.

Let PKE.CPA.Enc($pk, \mathbf{m}; \mathbf{r}$) denote a public key encryption algorithm which is secure in the CPA model. Here pk is the public key, $\mathbf{m}$ is the message to be encrypted, and $\mathbf{r}$ is the randomness used in the scheme. The algorithm returns a ciphertext $\mathbf{c}$. Furthermore, let PKE.CPA.Dec($sk, pk, \mathbf{c}$) denote the corresponding decryption algorithm. This algorithm returns a message, again denoted $\mathbf{m}$.

We will now assume that the PKE.CPA.Dec($\cdot$) call is implemented in constant-time and is not leaking any side-channel information.

The CCA-secure KEM is assumed to be obtained through some variant of the FO transformation, resulting in algorithms for encapsulation and decapsulation similar to Algorithms 1 and 2 shown here.

Algorithm 1. KEM.CCA.Encaps

Input: pk
Output: $\mathbf{c}$ and $\mathbf{s}$
  1: pick a random $\mathbf{m}$
  2: $(\mathbf{r}, \mathbf{k}) \leftarrow H_1(\mathbf{m}, pk)$
  3: $\mathbf{c} \leftarrow$ PKE.CPA.Enc($pk, \mathbf{m}; \mathbf{r}$)
  4: $\mathbf{s} \leftarrow H_2(\mathbf{c}, \mathbf{k})$
  5: **Return** $(\mathbf{c}, \mathbf{s})$

Algorithm 2. KEM.CCA.Decaps

Input: $sk, pk, \mathbf{c}$
Output: $\mathbf{s}'$
  1: $\mathbf{m}' \leftarrow$ PKE.CPA.Dec($sk, \mathbf{c}$)
  2: $(\mathbf{r}', \mathbf{k}') \leftarrow H_1(\mathbf{m}', pk)$
  3: $\mathbf{c}' \leftarrow$ PKE.CPA.Enc($pk, \mathbf{m}'; \mathbf{r}'$)
  4: **if** $(\mathbf{c}' = \mathbf{c})$ **then Return** $\mathbf{s}' \leftarrow H_2(\mathbf{c}, \mathbf{k}')$
  5: **else   Return** $\mathbf{s}' \leftarrow H_2(\mathbf{c}, sk_r)$, where sk_r is a random seed in sk
  6: **end if**

Here $\mathbf{k} \in \mathcal{K}$ and H_1 and H_2 are pseudo-random functions generating values indistinguishable from true randomness, with images $\mathcal{R} \times \mathcal{K}$ and $\mathcal{S}$, respectively. Also, $(\mathbf{r}', \mathbf{k}') = (\mathbf{r}, \mathbf{k})$ if $\mathbf{m}' = \mathbf{m}$. The key generation algorithm, denoted

KEM.CCA.KeyGen, randomly selects a secret key sk and computes the corresponding public key pk, and returns both of them. We note that essentially all KEM candidates in the NIST PQ project can be written in the above form or in some similar way.

The side-channel attack is now described using calls to an oracle that determines whether, in the PKE.CPA.Dec($\cdot$) call, a modified ciphertext decrypts to the same "message" or not. To be a bit more precise, we follow the steps in the public KEM.CCA.Encaps algorithm and record the values of a chosen $\mathbf{m}$, and the corresponding computed $\mathbf{r}$ and ciphertext $\mathbf{c}$. Then we modify the ciphertext to $\mathbf{c}' = \mathbf{c} + \mathbf{d}$, where $\mathbf{d}$ denotes a predetermined modification to the ciphertext. Finally, we require that the oracle can tell us if the modified ciphertext is still decrypted to the same message, i.e., whether $\mathbf{m} = $ PKE.CPA.Dec(sk, $\mathbf{c}'$). If so, the oracle returns 0. But if PKE.CPA.Dec(sk, $\mathbf{c}'$) returns a different message, the oracle returns 1. Finally, we assume that an oracle output of -1 represents a situation when the oracle cannot decisively give an answer. The high-level construction of the oracle is given in Algorithm 3.

Algorithm 3. Decryption.Error.In.CPAcall.Oracle

Input: $\mathbf{m}$, a ciphertext modification $\mathbf{d}$
Output: b (decryption failure or not)
1: $(\mathbf{r}, \mathbf{k}) \leftarrow H_1(\mathbf{m}, \mathsf{pk})$
2: $\mathbf{c} \leftarrow$ PKE.CPA.Enc(pk, $\mathbf{m}$; $\mathbf{r}$)
3: $\mathbf{c}' \leftarrow \mathbf{c} + \mathbf{d}$
4: $t \leftarrow$ Side-channel.information[KEM.CCA.Decaps($\mathbf{c}'$)]
5: $b \leftarrow F(t)$, where $F(t)$ uses the side.channel information to determine
   whether PKE.CPA.Dec($\mathbf{c}'$) returns $\mathbf{m}$ or not ($b = 0$ means returning $\mathbf{m}$,
   $b = 1$ means not returning $\mathbf{m}$, and $b = -1$ means inconclusive)
6: **Return** b

The notation $t = $ Side-channel.information[X] means that side-channel information of some kind is collected when executing algorithm X. This information is then analyzed in the $F(t)$ analysis algorithm. In our case we are collecting the time of execution through the number of clock cycles and this is the assumed type of side-channel information. At the end of the paper we discuss and argue for the fact that other types of side-channel information can also be used, for example analysis of power or electromagnetic emanations in case of microcontroller or pure hardware implementations.

The design of $F(t)$ is clearly a key part of the attack. Assuming we have found an oracle that can give us decisive answers for some choices of $\mathbf{m}$ and ciphertext modifications $\mathbf{d}$, the final step is to extract information about the secret key used in the PKE.CPA.Dec algorithm. This part will be highly dependent on the actual scheme considered, but a general summary is given in Algorithm 4.

Algorithm 4. Secret key recovery

Input: n_1
Output: the secret key sk
1: **for** $i = 0; i < n_1; i \leftarrow i + 1$ **do**
2:     find $(\mathbf{m}_i, \mathbf{d}_i)$ such that Decryption.Error.In.CPAcall.Oracle$(\mathbf{m}_i, \mathbf{d}_i) \in \{0, 1\}$
3: **end for**
4: Use the determined set $\{((\mathbf{m}_i, \mathbf{d}_i), 0 \leq i < n)\}$ to extract the secret key, by exploring the relation between the secret key and modifications that cause decryption errors in PKE.CPA.Dec.
5: **Return** sk

3.1 Designing the Oracle for LWE-Based Schemes

The main question is how to find $\mathbf{m}$ and ciphertext modifications $\mathbf{d}$ such that the measured timing information may reveal whether PKE.CPA.Dec$(\mathbf{c}+\mathbf{d})$ inside the KEM.CCA.Decaps$(\mathbf{c} + \mathbf{d})$ is returning the same message $\mathbf{m}$ or not. The general idea is the following.

The side-channel information $t \leftarrow$ timing.information[X] is simply the time (clock cycles) it takes to execute X. The ciphertext of an LWE-based scheme, created in PKE.CPA.Enc(pk, $\mathbf{m}$; $\mathbf{r}$) may consist of several parts, but at a general level we may describe it as

$$\mathbf{c} = g(\mathsf{pk}, \mathbf{m}; \mathbf{r}) + e(\mathbf{r}),$$

where $e(\mathbf{r})$ is a vector of small error values, and $g(\mathsf{pk}, \mathbf{m}; \mathbf{r})$ represents the remaining part of the ciphertext generation in the scheme. Unique for post-quantum schemes is the property that the error vector $e(\mathbf{r})$ may vary a bit without affecting the ability to decrypt the ciphertext to the correct message. So if we introduce a modified ciphertext $\mathbf{c}' = \mathbf{c} + \mathbf{d}$, then the new ciphertext $\mathbf{c}' = g(\mathsf{pk}, \mathbf{m}; \mathbf{r}) + e(\mathbf{r}) + \mathbf{d}$. Two things can then happen. Either the modification $\mathbf{d}$ is small enough so that it does not cause an error in decryption and $\mathbf{m} \leftarrow$ PKE.CPA.Dec(sk, $\mathbf{c}'$); or the modification $\mathbf{d}$ is big enough to cause an error in decryption and $\mathbf{m} \neq \mathbf{m}' \leftarrow$ PKE.CPA.Dec(sk, $\mathbf{c}'$);

An observation is that when we have an error in decryption of $\mathbf{c}'$, receiving $\mathbf{m}'$ ($\neq \mathbf{m}$), then re-encrypting $\mathbf{m}'$ in the decapsulation (line 3 of Algorithm 2) results in a completely different ciphertext, which is not at all similar to $\mathbf{c}'$. The attack relies on the fact that the side-channel information can be used to distinguish between the two cases.

The key observation used in the paper is now that if we adopt a ciphertext modification of the form

$$\mathbf{d} = (\underbrace{00 \cdots 0}_{n-l} d_{n-l} d_{n-l+1} \cdots d_{n-1}),$$

i.e., we only modify the last l entries of the ciphertext, we have the two different cases:

Either there is no decryption error, which leads to $\mathbf{m} = \mathbf{m}' \leftarrow$ PKE.CPA. Dec(sk, $\mathbf{c}'$), $(\mathbf{r}, \mathbf{k}) = (\mathbf{r}', \mathbf{k}')$, and $\mathbf{c} =$ PKE.CPA.Enc(pk, $\mathbf{m}'; \mathbf{r}'$). So in the check in line 4 of Algorithm 2, ($\mathbf{c}' = \mathbf{c}$), we see that $\mathbf{c}'$ and $\mathbf{c}$ are guaranteed identical except for the last l positions.

If there is a decryption error, on the other hand, i.e., $\mathbf{m} \neq \mathbf{m}' \leftarrow$ PKE.CPA. Dec(sk, $\mathbf{c}'$), then the next step in the decapsulation, $(\mathbf{r}', \mathbf{k}') \leftarrow H_1(\mathbf{m}', \text{pk})$ leads to completely different values of $(\mathbf{r}', \mathbf{k}')$, which in turn will give a completely different ciphertext $\mathbf{c}$. In particular $\mathbf{c}'$ and $\mathbf{c}$ will most likely have different values already in the beginning of the vectors.

Finally, how can we separate the two cases using timing information? This is possible since the check in line 4 of Algorithm 2, ($\mathbf{c}' = \mathbf{c}$), involves checking the equality of two long vectors and a standard implementation would terminate after finding a position for which equality does not hold. In the first case above, the first $n - l$ positions are equal and we would have to run through and check all of them before we terminate. In the second case, however, it is very likely to terminate the check very quickly. Typical instructions for which this assumption is true is the use of the memcmp function in C or the java.util.Arrays.equals function in Java. The analysis function $F(t)$, in its simplest form, is assumed to have made some initial measurements to establish intervals $\mathcal{I}_0, \mathcal{I}_1$ for the time of execution in the two cases and returns $F(t) = 0$ if the number of clock cycles is in $\mathcal{I}_0$, $F(t) = 1$ if it is in $\mathcal{I}_1$ and $F(t) = -1$ otherwise. In practice, timing measurements are much more complicated and more advanced methods to build $F(t)$ should be considered.

4   The FrodoKEM Design and Implementation

In the next section, we will apply our general attack on the FrodoKEM scheme, a main candidate of round 2 in the NIST PQ project. FrodoKEM is a lattice-based KEM with security based on the standard LWE problem. It is a conservative design with security proofs. In the document [27] submitted to NIST, it is claimed that *"All our implementations avoid the use of secret address accesses and secret branches and, hence, are protected against timing and cache attacks."* An implementation of FrodoKEM that can be attacked also appears in Open Quantum Safe [3].

4.1   The FrodoKEM Design

FrodoKEM was firstly published in [12]. We describe the different algorithms in FrodoKEM (from [27]) for the key generation, the key encapsulation, and the key decapsulation in Algorithm 5–7. We refer to the design document [27] for all the design details and provide only algorithmic descriptions of the relevant parts in the design. We now also use the notation from the design paper.

Briefly, from an initial seed the key generation FrodoKEM.KeyGen generates the secret and public keys. Note that from $\mathsf{pk} = (\mathsf{seed_A}, \mathbf{B})$, we generate $\mathbf{A} = \mathsf{Frodo.Gen}(\mathsf{seed_A})$. We have the following equation for a key pair $(\mathsf{pk}, \mathsf{sk})$,

$$\mathbf{B} = \mathbf{AS} + \mathbf{E}, \tag{1}$$

where $\mathbf{B}, \mathbf{E}, \mathbf{S} \in \mathbb{Z}_q^{n \times \bar{n}}$ and $\mathbf{A} \in \mathbb{Z}_q^{n \times n}$. Note that while $\mathbf{A}$ and $\mathbf{B}$ are publicly known both $\mathbf{S}$ and $\mathbf{E}$ are secrets and $\mathbf{S}$ is saved as part of sk to be used in the decapsulation process, later. Here $\mathbf{E}, \mathbf{S}$ are error matrices and by this we mean that the entries in the matrices are small values (compared to $\mathbb{Z}_q$) and distributed according to some predetermined distribution χ.

Algorithm 5. FrodoKEM.KeyGen

Input: None.
Output: Key pair $(\mathsf{pk}, \mathsf{sk}')$ with $\mathsf{pk} \in \{0, 1\}^{\mathsf{len_{seed_A}} + D \cdot n \cdot \bar{n}}$,
$\mathsf{sk}' \in \{0, 1\}^{\mathsf{len_s} + \mathsf{len_{seed_A}} + D \cdot n \cdot \bar{n}} \times \mathbb{Z}_q^{n \times \bar{n}} \times \{0, 1\}^{\mathsf{len_{pkh}}}$.

1: Choose uniformly random seeds $\mathsf{s}\|\mathsf{seed_{SE}}\|\mathbf{z} \leftarrow_{\$} U(\{0, 1\}^{\mathsf{len_s} + \mathsf{len_{seed_{SE}}} + \mathsf{len_z}})$
2: Generate pseudorandom seed $\mathsf{seed_A} \leftarrow \mathrm{SHAKE}(\mathbf{z}, \mathsf{len_{seed_A}})$
3: Generate the matrix $\mathbf{A} \in \mathbb{Z}_q^{n \times n}$ via $\mathbf{A} \leftarrow \mathsf{Frodo.Gen}(\mathsf{seed_A})$
4: Generate pseudorandom bit string
   $(\mathbf{r}^{(0)}, \ldots, \mathbf{r}^{(2n\bar{n}-1)}) \leftarrow \mathrm{SHAKE}(\mathrm{0x5F}\|\mathsf{seed_{SE}}, 2n\bar{n} \cdot \mathsf{len_\chi})$
5: Sample error matrix $\mathbf{S} \leftarrow \mathsf{Frodo.SampleMatrix}((\mathbf{r}^{(0)}, \ldots, \mathbf{r}^{(n\bar{n}-1)}), n, \bar{n}, T_\chi)$
6: Sample error matrix
   $\mathbf{E} \leftarrow \mathsf{Frodo.SampleMatrix}((\mathbf{r}^{(n\bar{n})}, \ldots, \mathbf{r}^{(2n\bar{n}-1)}), n, \bar{n}, T_\chi)$
7: Compute $\mathbf{B} \leftarrow \mathbf{AS} + \mathbf{E}$
8: Compute $\mathbf{b} \leftarrow \mathsf{Frodo.Pack}(\mathbf{B})$
9: Compute $\mathsf{pkh} \leftarrow \mathrm{SHAKE}(\mathsf{seed_A}\|\mathbf{b}, \mathsf{len_{pkh}})$
10: **Return** public key $\mathsf{pk} \leftarrow \mathsf{seed_A}\|\mathbf{b}$ and secret key $\mathsf{sk}' \leftarrow (\mathsf{s}\|\mathsf{seed_A}\|\mathbf{b}, \mathbf{S}, \mathsf{pkh})$

In an encapsulation, a uniformly random key $\mu \leftarrow_{\$} U(\{0, 1\}^{\mathsf{len_\mu}})$ is first chosen. It is then used to generate a pseudorandom bit string that in turn determines error matrices $\mathbf{S}', \mathbf{E}', \mathbf{E}''$. A ciphertext now contains two parts, one being $\mathbf{S}'\mathbf{A} + \mathbf{E}'$ and the second part being $\mathbf{S}'\mathbf{B} + \mathbf{E}'' + \mathsf{Frodo.Encode}(\mu)$. These matrices are converted to bitstrings using the Frodo.Pack and Frodo.UnPack algorithms. The shared key ss is computed using the pseudorandomness generator SHAKE.

Algorithm 6. FrodoKem.Encaps

Input: Public Key $\mathsf{pk} = \mathsf{seed}_\mathbf{A} || \mathbf{b} \in \{0,1\}^{\mathsf{len}_{\mathsf{seed}_\mathbf{A}} + D \cdot n \cdot \bar{n}}$.
Output: Ciphertext $\mathbf{c}_1 || \mathbf{c}_2 \in \{0,1\}^{(\bar{m} \cdot n + \bar{m} \cdot \bar{n})D}$ and shared secret
$\mathsf{ss} \in \{0,1\}^{\mathsf{len}_{\mathsf{ss}}}$.

1: Choose a uniformly random key $\mu \leftarrow_\$ U(\{0,1\}^{\mathsf{len}_\mu})$
2: Compute $\mathsf{pkh} \leftarrow \mathsf{SHAKE}(\mathsf{pk}, \mathsf{len}_{\mathsf{pkh}})$
3: Generate pseudorandom values
   $\mathsf{seed}_{\mathbf{SE}} || \mathbf{k} \leftarrow \mathsf{SHAKE}(\mathsf{pkh} || \mu, \mathsf{len}_{\mathsf{seed}_{\mathbf{SE}}} + \mathsf{len}_\mathbf{k})$
4: Generate pseudorandom bit string
   $(\mathbf{r}^{(0)}, \ldots, \mathbf{r}^{(2\bar{m}n + \bar{m}\bar{n}-1)}) \leftarrow \mathsf{SHAKE}(\mathsf{0x96} || \mathsf{seed}_{\mathbf{SE}}, (2\bar{m}n + \bar{m}\bar{n}) \cdot \mathsf{len}_\chi)$
5: Sample error matrix
   $\mathbf{S}' \leftarrow \mathsf{Frodo.SampleMatrix}((\mathbf{r}^{(0)}, \ldots, \mathbf{r}^{(\bar{m}n-1)}), \bar{m}, n, T_\chi)$
6: Sample error matrix
   $\mathbf{E}' \leftarrow \mathsf{Frodo.SampleMatrix}((\mathbf{r}^{(\bar{m}n)}, \ldots, \mathbf{r}^{(2\bar{m}n-1)}), \bar{m}, n, T_\chi)$
7: Generate $\mathbf{A} \leftarrow \mathsf{Frodo.Gen}(\mathsf{seed}_\mathbf{A})$
8: Compute $\mathbf{B}' \leftarrow \mathbf{S}'\mathbf{A} + \mathbf{E}'$
9: Compute $\mathbf{c}_1 \leftarrow \mathsf{Frodo.Pack}(\mathbf{B}')$
10: Sample error matrix
    $\mathbf{E}'' \leftarrow \mathsf{Frodo.SampleMatrix}((\mathbf{r}^{(2\bar{m}n)}, \ldots, \mathbf{r}^{(2\bar{m}n + \bar{m}\bar{n}-1)}), \bar{m}, \bar{n}, T_\chi)$
11: Compute $\mathbf{B} \leftarrow \mathsf{Frodo.UnPack}(\mathbf{b}, n, \bar{n})$
12: Compute $\mathbf{V} \leftarrow \mathbf{S}'\mathbf{B} + \mathbf{E}''$
13: Compute $\mathbf{C} \leftarrow \mathbf{V} + \mathsf{Frodo.Encode}(\mu)$
14: Compute $\mathbf{c}_2 \leftarrow \mathsf{Frodo.Pack}(\mathbf{C})$
15: Compute $\mathsf{ss} \leftarrow \mathsf{SHAKE}(\mathbf{c}_1 || \mathbf{c}_2 || \mathbf{k}, \mathsf{len}_{\mathsf{ss}})$
16: **Return** ciphertext $\mathbf{c}_1 || \mathbf{c}_2$ and shared secret ss

---

In decapsulation, the step $\mathbf{M} \leftarrow \mathbf{C} - \mathbf{B}'\mathbf{S}$ actually computes Frodo.Encode$(\mu') + \mathbf{S}'\mathbf{E} - \mathbf{E}'\mathbf{S} + \mathbf{E}''$. Since $\mathbf{S}, \mathbf{S}', \mathbf{E}, \mathbf{E}', \mathbf{E}''$ all have small entries, also $\mathbf{S}'\mathbf{E} - \mathbf{E}'\mathbf{S} + \mathbf{E}''$ will have somewhat small entries and is regarded as noise. The Frodo.Decode algorithm removes this noise and returns the initial seed μ'. The decapsulation then continues by re-encrypting using this seed to get the corresponding ciphertext $\mathbf{B}'' || \mathbf{C}'$. In line 16 the two ciphertexts are compared to check equality. If they are equal, the correct shared key ss is returned.

Algorithm 7. FrodoKEM.Decaps

Input: Ciphertext $c_1 \| c_2 \in \{0,1\}^{(\bar{m} \cdot n + \bar{m} \cdot \bar{n})D}$, secret
$sk' \in \{0,1\}^{len_s + len_{seed_A} + D \cdot n \cdot \bar{n}} \times \mathbb{Z}_q^{n \times \bar{n}} \times \{0,1\}^{len_{pkh}}$.
Output: Shared secret $ss \in \{0,1\}^{len_{ss}}$.

1: $\mathbf{B'} \leftarrow$ Frodo.UnPack(c_1)
2: $\mathbf{C} \leftarrow$ Frodo.UnPack(c_2)
3: Compute $\mathbf{M} \leftarrow \mathbf{C} - \mathbf{B'S}$
4: Compute $\mu' \leftarrow$ Frodo.Decode$(\mathbf{M})$
5: Parse $pk \leftarrow seed_A \| b$
6: Generate pseudorandom values
   $seed_{SE'} \| k' \leftarrow$ SHAKE$(pkh \| \mu', len_{seed_{SE}} + len_k)$
7: Generate pseudorandom bit string
   $(\mathbf{r}^{(0)}, \ldots, \mathbf{r}^{(2\bar{m}n + \bar{m}\bar{n} - 1)}) \leftarrow$ SHAKE$(0x96 \| seed_{SE'}, (2\bar{m}n + \bar{m}\bar{n}) \cdot len_\chi)$
8: Sample error matrix
   $\mathbf{S'} \leftarrow$ Frodo.SampleMatrix$((\mathbf{r}^{(0)}, \ldots, \mathbf{r}^{(\bar{m}n-1)}), \bar{m}, n, T_\chi)$
9: Sample error matrix
   $\mathbf{E'} \leftarrow$ Frodo.SampleMatrix$((\mathbf{r}^{(\bar{m}n)}, \ldots, \mathbf{r}^{(2\bar{m}n-1)}), \bar{m}, n, T_\chi)$
10: Generate $\mathbf{A} \leftarrow$ Frodo.Gen$(seed_A)$
11: Compute $\mathbf{B''} \leftarrow \mathbf{S'A} + \mathbf{E'}$
12: Sample error matrix
    $\mathbf{E''} \leftarrow$ Frodo.SampleMatrix$((\mathbf{r}^{(2\bar{m}n)}, \ldots, \mathbf{r}^{(2\bar{m}n + \bar{m}\bar{n} - 1)}), \bar{m}, \bar{n}, T_\chi)$
13: Compute $\mathbf{B} \leftarrow$ Frodo.UnPack$(b, n, \bar{n})$
14: Compute $\mathbf{V} \leftarrow \mathbf{S'B} + \mathbf{E''}$
15: Compute $\mathbf{C'} \leftarrow \mathbf{V} +$ Frodo.Encode(μ')
16: **if** $\mathbf{B'} \| \mathbf{C} = \mathbf{B''} \| \mathbf{C'}$ **then**
17:     **Return** shared secret $ss \leftarrow$ SHAKE$(c_1 \| c_2 \| k', len_{ss})$
18: **else**
19:     **Return** shared secret $ss \leftarrow$ SHAKE$(c_1 \| c_2 \| s, len_{ss})$
20: **end if**

The Frodo.SampleMatrix algorithm constructs the matrices with small values from a distribution described by a table T_χ, as given in Algorithms 8 and 9. Algorithms 10 and 11 gives the encoding and decoding procedures.

Algorithm 8. Frodo.Sample

Input: A (random) bit string $\mathbf{r} = (\mathbf{r}_0, \ldots, \mathbf{r}_{\mathsf{len}_\chi - 1}) \in \{0,1\}^{\mathsf{len}_\chi}$, the table $T_\chi = (T_\chi(0), \ldots, T_\chi(s))$.

Output: A sample $e \in \mathbb{Z}$.

1: $t \leftarrow \sum_{i=1}^{\mathsf{len}_\chi - 1} \mathbf{r}_i \cdot 2^{i-1}$
2: $e \leftarrow 0$
3: **for** $z = 0; z < s; z \leftarrow z + 1$ **do**
4:     **if** $t > T_\chi(z)$ **then**
5:         $e \leftarrow e + 1$
6:     **end if**
7: **end for**
8: $e \leftarrow (-1)^{\mathbf{r}_0} \cdot e$
9: **Return C**

Algorithm 9. Frodo.SampleMatrix

Input: A (random) bit string $\mathbf{r} = (\mathbf{r}^{(0)}, \ldots, \mathbf{r}^{(n_1 \times n_2 - 1)}) \in \{0,1\}^{n_1 n_2 \cdot \mathsf{len}_\chi}$, the table T_χ.

Output: A sample $\mathbf{E} \in \mathbb{Z}^{n_1 \times n_2}$.

1: **for** $i = 0; i < n_1; i \leftarrow i + 1$ **do**
2:     **for** $j = 0; j < n_2; j \leftarrow j + 1$ **do**
3:         $\mathbf{E}_{i,j} \leftarrow \mathsf{Frodo.Sample}(\mathbf{r}^{(i \cdot n_2 + j)}, T_\chi)$
4:     **end for**
5: **end for**
6: **Return E**

Algorithm 10. Frodo.Encode

Input: Bit string $\mathbf{k} \in \{0,1\}^l$, $l = B \cdot \bar{m} \cdot \bar{n}$.

Output: Matrix $\mathbf{K} \in \mathbb{Z}_q^{\bar{m} \times \bar{n}}$.

1: **for** $i = 0; i < \bar{m}; i \leftarrow i + 1$ **do**
2:     **for** $j = 0; j < \bar{n}; j \leftarrow j + 1$ **do**
3:         $k = \sum_{l=0}^{B-1} \mathbf{k}_{(i \cdot \bar{n} + j)B + l} \cdot 2^l$
4:         $\mathbf{K}_{i,j} \leftarrow \mathsf{ec}(k) = k \cdot q/2^B$
5:     **end for**
6: **end for**
7: **Return** $\mathbf{K} = (\mathbf{K}_{i,j})_{0 \leq i \leq \bar{m}, 0 \leq j \leq \bar{n}}$

Algorithm 11. Frodo.Decode

Input: Matrix $\mathbf{K} \in \mathbb{Z}_q^{\bar{m} \times \bar{n}}$.

Output: Bit string $\mathbf{k} \in \{0,1\}^l$, $l = B \cdot \bar{m} \cdot \bar{n}$.

1: **for** $i = 0; i < \bar{m}; i \leftarrow i + 1$ **do**
2:     **for** $j = 0; j < \bar{n}; j \leftarrow j + 1$ **do**
3:         $k \leftarrow \mathrm{dc}(\mathbf{K}_{i,j}) = \lfloor \mathbf{K}_{i,j} \cdot 2^B / q \rceil \mod 2^B$
4:         $k = \sum_{l=0}^{B-1} k_l \cdot 2^l$ where $k_l \in \{0,1\}$
5:         **for** $l = 0; l < D; l \leftarrow l + 1$ **do**
6:             $\mathbf{k}_{(i \cdot \bar{n} + j)B + l} \leftarrow k_l$
7:         **end for**
8:     **end for**
9: **end for**
10: **Return k**

Algorithm 12. Frodo.Pack

Input: Matrix $\mathbf{C} \in \mathbb{Z}_q^{n_1 \times n_2}$

Output: Bit string $\mathbf{b} \in \{0,1\}^{D \cdot n_1 \cdot n_2}$

1: **for** $i = 0; i < n_1; i \leftarrow i + 1$ **do**
2:     **for** $j = 0; j < n_2; j \leftarrow j + 1$ **do**
3:         $\mathbf{C}_{i,j} = \sum_{l=0}^{D-1} c_l \cdot 2^l$ where $c_l \in \{0,1\}$
4:         **for** $l = 0; l < D; l \leftarrow l + 1$ **do**
5:             $\mathbf{b}_{(i \cdot n_2 + j)D + l} \leftarrow c_{D-1-l}$
6:         **end for**
7:     **end for**
8: **end for**
9: **Return b**

Finally, Frodo designs packing and unpacking algorithms to transform matrices with entries in $\mathbb{Z}_q$ to bit strings and vice versa, as described in Algorithm 12 and Algorithm 13.

The security parameters of FrodoKEM are listed in Table 1.

4.2 A Useful Observation

A useful observation is that Line 16 in Frodo.Decaps (i.e., Algorithm 7) is, in the reference implementation, implemented in a standard way using the following code block.

```
1  // Is (Bp == BBp & C == CC) = true
2  if (memcmp(Bp, BBp, 2*PARAMS_N*PARAMS_NBAR) == 0 && memcmp(C,
       CC, 2*PARAMS_NBAR*PARAMS_NBAR) == 0) {
```

Algorithm 13. Frodo.Unpack

Input: Bit string $\mathbf{b} \in \{0,1\}^{D \cdot n_1 \cdot n_2}$, n_1, n_2.
Output: Matrix $\mathbf{C} \in \mathbb{Z}_q^{n_1 \times n_2}$
1: **for** $i = 0; i < n_1; i \leftarrow i + 1$ **do**
2:     **for** $j = 0; j < n_2; j \leftarrow j + 1$ **do**
3:        $\mathbf{C}_{i,j} = \sum_{l=0}^{D-1} \mathbf{b}_{(i \cdot n_2 + j)D + l} \cdot 2^{D-1-l}$
4:     **end for**
5: **end for**
6: **Return C**

Table 1. Proposed parameters in FrodoKEM.

	n	q	σ	support of χ	B	$\bar{m} \times \bar{n}$	Security
Frodo-640	640	2^{15}	2.8	$[-12 \dots 12]$	2	8×8	1
Frodo-976	976	2^{16}	2.3	$[-10 \dots 10]$	3	8×8	3
Frodo-1344	1344	2^{16}	1.4	$[-6 \dots 6]$	4	8×8	5

```
3     memcpy(Fin_k, kprime, CRYPTO_BYTES);
4  } else {
5     memcpy(Fin_k, sk_s, CRYPTO_BYTES);
6  }
```

We follow the attack strategy from the previous section and assume that the attacker modifies the $\mathbf{c}_2$ part in the ciphertext. If the modification does not affect the output of Frodo.Decode, the re-encryption procedure will generate the same tuple $(\mathbf{S}', \mathbf{E}', \mathbf{E}'')$ and the check

```
1  memcmp(Bp, BBp, 2*PARAMS_N*PARAMS_NBAR) == 0
```

will be satisfied. Thus,

```
1  memcmp(C, CC, 2*PARAMS_NBAR*PARAMS_NBAR) == 0
```

will be further executed. On the other hand, if Frodo.Decode outputs a different message μ', the first check will fail and the second check after the && operation will be ignored. This type of mechanics is referred to as Short Circuit Evaluation, and should not be employed to handle sensitive data. This could lead to a significant difference when comparing the executed time.

More importantly though, the function memcmp is not implemented in a constant time manner, meaning that if we change only the last part of $\mathbf{C}$ it will lead to a longer execution time. We further explore this feature by only changing the last part of $\mathbf{C}$ to enlarge the timing gap.

5   The Attack Applied on FrodoKEM

We first mention the adversary model, which is a CCA attack model with timing leakage. In this model, the adversary $\mathcal{A}$ sends a series of (valid or invalid) ciphertexts to the decapsulation oracle $\mathcal{O}$ and could obtain the corresponding decapsulation time information. He then performs further analysis to recover the secret key $\mathbf{S}$.

5.1 The Details of the Attack

With a call to the PKE decryption function Frodo.Decode, FrodoKEM.Decaps computes

$$\mathbf{M} = \mathbf{C} - \mathbf{B}'\mathbf{S} = \text{Frodo.Encode}(\mu) + \mathbf{S}'\mathbf{E} - \mathbf{E}'\mathbf{S} + \mathbf{E}''.$$

The next lemma from [27] states the error size that can be handled by the Frodo decode algorithm Frodo.Decode.

Lemma 1. *Let $q = 2^D$, $B \leq D$. Then $\text{dc}(\text{ec}(k) + e) = k$ for any $k, e \in \mathbb{Z}$, such that $0 \leq k \leq 2^B$ and $-q/2^{B+1} \leq e < q/2^{B+1}$. Here dc is the decoding function and ec is the encoding function.*

We start by generating a valid ciphertext $(\mathbf{c}_1 \| \mathbf{c}_2)$, which will be successfully decrypted. This event happens with probability close to one since the designed decryption failure probability of the CCA version of Frodo is very low. Let $\mathbf{E}'''$ denote the noise matrix, i.e.,

$$\mathbf{E}''' = \mathbf{S}'\mathbf{E} - \mathbf{E}'\mathbf{S} + \mathbf{E}''. \tag{2}$$

Note that $\mathbf{S}', \mathbf{E}', \mathbf{E}''$ are known values and $\mathbf{E} = \mathbf{B} - \mathbf{AS}$ due to Eq. (1). If we can determine $\mathbf{E}'''$, we will have linear equations in the secret key value $\mathbf{S}$. We know that all the $\bar{m} \times \bar{n}$ entries in the matrix $\mathbf{E}'''$ belong to the interval $[-q/2^{B+1}, q/2^{B+1}) = [-2^{D-B-1}, 2^{D-B-1})$ because the decryption succeed.

We now show how to recover $\mathbf{E}'''_{i,j}$, the element of the i-th row and j-th column of $\mathbf{E}'''$. We first unpack $\mathbf{c}_2$ to $\mathbf{C}$ by applying Frodo.UnPack($\mathbf{c}_2$) and our goal is to decide the value x_0 such that

$$\mathbf{E}'''_{i,j} + x_0 = 2^{D-B-1}.$$

If we add a positive value x to the element of the i-th row and j-th column of $\mathbf{C}$ to form $\mathbf{C}'$, then this operation is equivalent to adding x to $\mathbf{E}'''_{i,j}$. We pack $\mathbf{C}'$ to $\mathbf{c}'_2$ and send the new ciphertext $(\mathbf{c}_1 \| \mathbf{c}'_2)$ to the decapsulation procedure. If we detect a fast execution, we know that a decryption failure occurred and the value $\mathbf{E}'''_{i,j} + x$ should be outside the interval $[-2^{D-B-1}, 2^{D-B-1})$. Since x is picked to be positive, then we know that

$$\mathbf{E}'''_{i,j} + x \geq 2^{D-B-1}.$$

Otherwise, for a slow execution, we know that

$$\mathbf{E}'''_{i,j} + x < 2^{D-B-1}.$$

Since it will definitely lead to a decryption failure if choosing $x = 2^{D-B}$, we could start the binary search by setting the initial interval as $[0, 2^{D-B}]$ and determine x_0 by $(D - B - 1)$ different choices[1] of x.

Due to the implementation of the memcmp function, we intend to introduce the added noise at the tail part of c_2, to enlarge the time difference. Therefore, we aim to recover $\mathbf{E}'''_{\bar{m}-1,j}$, where $0 \le j < \bar{n}$, for one valid ciphertext $(\mathbf{c}_1 || \mathbf{c}_2)$. For such $\bar{n}$ entries, the changes in the ciphertext are limited to the last $\bar{n}$ positions. Thus, if a decryption error is triggered and the re-encrypted ciphertext is a totally different one, the timing difference could be large.

Let N denote the number of valid ciphertexts generated. One pair of generated valid ciphertexts could provide us $\bar{m} \times \bar{n}$ linear equations. For the Frodo parameters, we always have $\bar{m} = \bar{n} = 8$. As described before, we only select $\bar{n}$ equations corresponding to the last $\bar{n}$ entries in $\mathbf{E}'''$ with the largest time difference. Since we have $n \times \bar{n}$ unknown entries in $\mathbf{S}$, we need roughly $N \approx n$ valid ciphertexts for a full key-recovery if all the collected linear equations are independent[2]. Then, the complexity can be roughly estimated as $N \times \bar{n} \times (D-B-1) \times N_{\text{dis}}$, where N_{dis} is the required number of decryption attempts to decide if it is a fast execution or not.

Last, we point out that if errors occur in the process of recovering the value of x_0, one could use a post-processing step like lattice reduction algorithms to handle these errors and to fully recover the secret key. In this case, it would be helpful to reduce the post-processing complexity if a few more equations are collected.

A summary of the attack procedure against FrodoKEM is given in Algorithm 14.

Algorithm 14. Timing attack on Frodo.KEM

Input: The public key pk $\leftarrow$ (seed$_\mathbf{A}$, $\mathbf{B}$).
Output: The secret key $\mathbf{S}$.

1: **for** $t = 0; t < N; t \leftarrow t + 1$ **do**
2:     Generate a valid ciphertext $(\mathbf{c}_1 || \mathbf{c}_2)$
3:     **for** $i = 0; i < \bar{n}; i \leftarrow i + 1$ **do**
4:         Use the binary search to recover $\mathbf{E}'''_{(\bar{m}-1),i}$
5:     **end for**
6: **end for**
7: Recover $\mathbf{S}$ from $\mathbf{E}'''_{(\bar{m}-1),i}$ values by solving linear equations
8: **Return** $\mathbf{S}$

---

[1] Due to the distribution of $\mathbf{E}'''_{i,j}$ a minor optimization is possible; The binary search midpoint selection is can be skewed towards the more likely values closer to the middle of the range. This makes a small reduction in the average number of necessary binary search evaluations.

[2] As q is a large integer, the probability for a matrix to be full-rank is high. One could also collect slightly more than n ciphertexts to ensure that a full-rank matrix will be obtained.

5.2   Simulation Method

To increase the chances of successfully distinguishing the two outcomes for each step of the binary search algorithm, the following actions were taken to minimize the noise in our experiment and improving the accuracy of the measurements.

- Hyper Threading was turned off in BIOS.
- Intel SpeedStep was turned off in BIOS.
- Linux kernel's scheduling governor was set to 'performance'.
- All unnecessary processes in the system were turned off for the duration of the measurements.
- The measurement program's affinity was set to a single core.
- The remaining system processes' CPU core affinity were set to the other remaining cores.
- The measurement program's priority was set to the highest value.
- The `rdtscp` instruction were used for measurements. This is a serializing version of the `rdtsc` instruction which forces every preceding instruction to complete before allowing the program to continue. This prevents the CPU out-of-order execution from interfering with the measurements.
- Before starting the timer the decapsulation function is executed once, without being measured, to warm up the data and instruction caches.

Despite the actions listed above the noise in the measurements are considerable, and critically, the amount of noise and the shape of the histogram seems to be non-constant. We compensate both by increasing the number of samples and also by attempting a reliability estimation of each set of measurements and discard if they do not seem to match what we expect. The rest of this section will be dedicated to explaining how this has been done in the experiment.

Before running the binary search a warmup-phase is executed which ensures that the CPU frequency stabilizes, branch prediction buffers are populated and the cache is filled. These measurements are also used to calculate a very rough "cutoff" limit above which no timing values will be recorded, as they are deemed too noisy to be of any interest.

We begin by observing that the most significant measurements are those which are closest to the minimum, since these are the values least affected by noise. In our experiments, the most effective strategy to distinguish the two distributions was to simply count the number of measurements whose values are lower than a certain small threshold.

We establish a good threshold by profiling with a high number of iterations I_p in 2 stages.

First we generate a set of measurements M_{low}, with $|M_{low}| = I_p$, as the first part of the profiling step by repeatedly measuring with a single ciphertext modified by a low amount ($x = 1$). The subset $T_{low} \subset M_{low}$ is the fraction F_{low} of the values in M_{low} whose measurements are smallest, i.e. $|T_{low}| = |M_{low}| * F_{low}$. F_{low} is a fixed value in the interval $(0..1)$ and has been determined by experimentation (see Sect. 5.3).

$L_{\text{low}} = \max(T_{\text{low}})$ is used to determine the similar fraction F_{high} of values from the second profiling stage M_{high}, whose values were generated by a high amount of modification ($x = 2^{D-B}$). That is to say

$$T_{\text{high}} = \{t | t \in M_{\text{high}}, t \leq L_{\text{low}}\}$$

and

$$F_{\text{high}} = \frac{|T_{\text{high}}|}{|M_{\text{high}}|}.$$

F_{low} (fixed) and F_{high} (dynamic) are used in the next measurement phase where the binary search algorithm decides whether or not it is experiencing a "fast" or "slow" execution for the particular modification x under evaluation.

We use the set of measurements M_x (where $|M_x| = I_m$) to denote the measurements for a certain value of x and T_x the subset of measurements whose values are lower than L_{low}, so

$$T_x = \{t | t \in M_x, t \leq L_{\text{low}}\}.$$

If

$$F_x = \frac{|T_x|}{|M_x|}$$

is closer to F_{high} than to F_{low} then we assume $\mathbf{E}'''_{i,j} + x \geq 2^{D-B-1}$. Likewise if F_x is closer to F_{low} than to F_{high} then we assume $\mathbf{E}'''_{i,j} + x < 2^{D-B-1}$.

Reliability estimation. As previously mentioned, the measurement noise is considerable, due to the total run-time of the decapsulation routine being so large relative to the difference we wish to measure. The probability of making the wrong decision in each step of the binary search algorithm is non-negligible and therefore some additional checks are added, as detailed below.

If

$$F_{\text{low}} + \frac{\Delta F}{4} \leq F_x \leq F_{\text{high}} - \frac{\Delta F}{4},$$

where $\Delta F = F_{\text{high}} - F_{\text{low}}$, then we deem F_x as too uncertain for us to draw any conclusions. In such a case we do another round of measurements until either F_x move beyond one of the limits or we give up. In the latter case we restart the profiling phase and start over for that particular set of indexes (i, j).

Furthermore we additionally redo the binary search steps when they a) have not changed direction[3] in a number of steps or b) when we have narrowed the possible range down to a single value and we wish to confirm our findings. For case a) this helps with detection and recovery of bad early decisions. Case b) is a way to lower the probability of finding an erroneous value due to a bad decision later in the binary search.

---

[3] i.e. if we either continuously lower the upper limit or continuously raise the lower limit for a number of consecutive steps, then we retry the last step to guard against an earlier erroneous decision.

Lastly we make sure $F_x \leq F_{high} + \Delta F$, otherwise we discard the measurements since they indicates that the profile is no longer valid. In that case we restart with a new profiling phase for the indexes i, j.

5.3   Results

The results documented in this section were generated[4] on a i5–4200U CPU running at 1.6 GHz using the FrodoKEM-1344-AES variant as implemented in the Open Quantum Safe software library[5] (liboqs) and compiled with default compiler flags.

In Fig. 1 we see that the timing difference is in the order of $\approx$4800 reference clock cycles, as measured on our machine. In contrast, the entire FrodoKEM.Decaps function requires $\approx$12.7M clock cycles, in average, to complete when running on the same machine. Thus we need to distinguish differences in the running time of less than 0.04% of the total run-time of a single decapsulation.

Using the method previously described and with $F_{low} = 1\%$ (see the L_{low} indication in Fig. 1) we get 85000 measured decapsulations per $\mathbf{E}'''_{i,j}$ value, split between 10000×2 for profiling each index of $\mathbf{E}'''_{i,j}$ and 5000 for each step of the binary search and confirmation stage. Factoring in retries of the binary search the average number of decapsulations ends up at $\approx$97000. Using these settings no incorrect values of $\mathbf{E}'''_{i,j}$ were obtained after collecting data for >3000 out of the $1344 \times 8 = 10752$ equations necessary for complete key recovery.

5.4   Summary

For FrodoKEM-1344-AES $\mathbf{E}'''$ is a matrix of size 1344×8 and the attack as implemented requires $97000 \times 1344 \times 8 \approx 2^{30}$ measured decapsulations to complete. With an average runtime of 3.3 positions of $\mathbf{E}'''_{i,j}$ per hour (on the limited hardware described above) we can make a complete key recovery in approximately 136 core-days. This is only taking the data collection phase into account, additional computation for solving the linear equations is considered negligible in comparison.

A strategy to lower the sample complexity would be to improve upon our admittedly simple distinguisher for the two timing distributions. Another source of potentially unnecessary samples is the repetition of the profiling phase for each set of indexes and ciphertexts. It can be argued that a simple timing model could be developed which would allow for a reuse of information from a single or smaller number of profiling steps.

The sample complexity can be even lower if we increase the complexity of the post-processing step using lattice reduction algorithms to deal with any decision errors that would follow a reduced number of measured decapsulations.

---

[4] Proof of concept implementation available at: https://github.com/atneit/open-quantum-safe-attacks.

[5] The latest official reference implementation at https://github.com/Microsoft/PQCrypto-LWEKE appear to be identical to the implementation in liboqs.

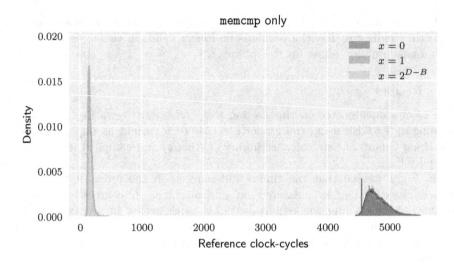

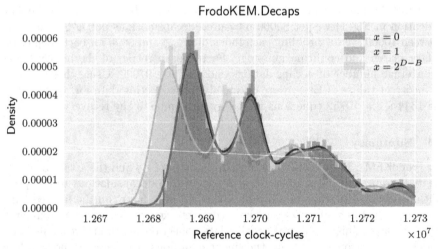

Fig. 1. Histograms of timing measurements of only the memcmp function-call (the $\mathbf{C} = \mathbf{C'}$ check) and the entire decapsulation function, respectively. The same ciphertext was sent to the decapsulation function modified in the last position ($i = j = \bar{n} - 1$) of $\mathbf{C}_{i,j}$ by the amount x according to the legend. The curves are the Kernel Density Estimate over the raw measurements. The vertical bar indicates the L_{low} value where $F_1 = 1\%$. In this graph we see that the cutoff limits are at 5500 and 12730000 respectively, above which no values were recorded. 10000 decapsulations each were measured to generate the two figures.

Last, the complexity for attacking Frodo-640 and Frodo-976 will be lower due to the smaller size of n. The reason is two-folds; we need to collect less equations and also for a fixed post-process cost (again using lattice reduction techniques), we can handle larger decision errors in the binary search.

6   Discussion on Attacking Other Schemes

The new timing attack could also be applied on the NIST PQC round-2 implementations of LAC [25], HQC [4], BIKE[6] [6], Rollo [7], and RQC [5], where the non constant-time function memcmp or a short circuit evaluation is employed in the implementation of the FO transform to check the re-encrypted ciphertexts. The similar designs indicate that they should be vulnerable to the newly proposed attack and the leaked timing information allows a key recovery.

The attack should be slightly adjusted when being applied to schemes like LAC and HQC where additional error-correcting codes are implemented to further reduce the decryption failure probability. In their published implementations, efforts have been made to ensure the BCH decoding to be constant-time in LAC and the recently revised HQC implementation, but a constant-time implementation for the FO transform do not appear to be considered. This knowledge-gap could lead to severe security issues. We refer the interested readers to the appendix for more details on a proposed adaptation of the attack for LAC. The attack on HQC is similar.

We also noted a similar problem in a java implementation of NTRUEncrypt in the NTRU Open Source Project [2], using a non constant-time comparison java.util.Arrays.equals for implementing the FO transform.

For all of the schemes mentioned in this paper we suggest to use the constant-time counterpart to memcmp (or similar). To do so should not impact the performance of the schemes in any way.

7   Conclusions and Future Works

We have presented a novel timing attack that can be applied to lattice-based or code-based schemes that use the FO transformation. It uses timing leakage in the ciphertext comparison step of the FO transformation and it can potentially recover the secret key. We applied it on FrodoKEM and implemented the attack with the result that we, with experiments, extrapolated that enough information to determine the secret key can be obtained by measuring about 2^{30} decapsulation calls. Additionally we derived some details of how the attack can be adapted to work on LAC, see appendix.

The attack applies also a number of other round 2 candidates, although we did not fully derive the details of the attack for other schemes, nor did we implement the attack on them.

---

[6] The attack discussed using the memcmp function appears to not be applicable to BIKE's implementation in the Open Quantum Safe project nor the latest reference implementation (available on https://bikesuite.org).

Note that the current attack could not directly be applied to the submitted reference implementations of, for example, NewHope [28], Kyber [29], classic McEliece [11], or the latest implementation of BIKE (including the BIKE implementation in Open Quantum Safe).

Following the basic idea of the attack on FrodoKEM, one can note that the bitwise sum of the two ciphertexts to be compared have quite different Hamming weights in the two cases of generating a decryption failure or not in the call to the CPA-secure primitive. If a modified ciphertext is decrypted to the same message, the Hamming weights of the xor differences is very low. Such a scenario opens up for other types of side-channel attacks like power analysis, since operations on binary data with different Hamming weight is a typical source of leakage in power analysis.

Acknowledgements. The authors would like to thank the anonymous reviewers from CRYPTO 2020 for their helpful comments. This work was partially supported by the Wallenberg AI, Autonomous Systems and Software Program (WASP) funded by the Knut and Alice Wallenberg Foundation, by the Norwegian Research Council (Grant No. 247742/070), by the SSF SURPRISE project and the Swedish Research Council (Grant No. 2019-04166).

A   The Attack on LAC

In this section, we focus on applying the new attack on LAC [25]. Similar procedures can also be used in attacking HQC after some minor modifications, and the framework is the same as we described here for general schemes with ECC.

LAC is a lattice-based proposal to the NIST Post-quantum Standardization project that has advanced to the second round. It includes three different versions, LAC128-v2, LAC192-v2, and LAC256-v2, aiming for the security levels of 128, 192, and 256 bits, respectively. We take LAC128-v2 as an instance to describe how the new timing attacks can be applied to the LAC proposal. The concrete parameters of LAC128-v2 are shown in Table 2.

Table 2. Proposed parameters of LAC128-v2.

n	q	$\mathcal{R}$	h	η	Distribution	ecc	bit-er	DFR	Security
512	251	$\frac{\mathbb{Z}_q[x]}{(x^n+1)}$	256	400	$\Psi_1, \Psi_1^{n,h}$	BCH[511, 256, 33]	$2^{-12.61}$	2^{-116}	I

Notations. Let the modulus be q, and the underlying polynomial ring be $\mathcal{R} = \mathbb{Z}_q/(x^n + 1)$. The distribution Ψ_1 randomly outputs 0 with probability $1/2$ and outputs 1 (or -1) with probability $1/4$. For a positive integer h, the distribution $\Psi_1^{n,h}$ outputs a length-n vector with $h/2$ ones, $h/2$ minus-ones, and $(n-h)$ zeros.

The LAC design. The LAC scheme has an extreme design with a very small q and therefore the position-wise error probability (denoted as bit-er in Table 2) is rather large. It uses an error correcting codes (ECC) to further reduce the overall decryption error probability. The concrete code used is a BCH code with length 511, dimension 256, and minimum distance 33. Thus, the error correcting capability of the employed BCH code is 16. This code is a shorten code and the parameter η denotes the size of the information and the redundant data. In the second round submission, the designers employ a compression function to reduce the ciphertext size in transmission.

The algorithms in the LAC proposal for key generation, key encapsulation, and key decapsulation can be found in [25]. We list them here for completeness.

Algorithm 1. LAC.KeyGen()

Output: A pair of public key and secret key (pk, sk).

1: $\mathsf{seed_a} \xleftarrow{\$} \mathcal{S}$;
2: $\mathbf{a} \leftarrow \mathsf{Samp}(U(\mathcal{R}); \mathsf{seed_a}) \in \mathcal{R}$;
3: $\mathbf{s} \xleftarrow{\$} \Psi_\sigma^n$;
4: $\mathbf{e} \xleftarrow{\$} \Psi_\sigma^n$;
5: $\mathbf{b} \leftarrow \mathbf{as} + \mathbf{e} \in \mathcal{R}$;
6: **return** $(pk := (\mathsf{seed_a}, \mathbf{b}), sk := \mathbf{s})$;

Algorithm 2. LAC.CCA.Enc($pk; \mathsf{seed_m}$)

Output: A ciphertext and encapsulation key pair $(\mathbf{c}, K)$.

1: $\mathbf{m} \leftarrow \mathsf{Samp}(U(\mathcal{M}); \mathsf{seed_m}) \in \mathcal{M}$;
2: $\mathsf{seed} \leftarrow G(\mathbf{m}) \in \mathcal{S}$;
3: $\mathbf{c} \leftarrow \mathsf{LAC.CPA.Enc}(pk, \mathbf{m}; \mathsf{seed})$;
4: $K \leftarrow H(\mathbf{m}, \mathbf{c}) \in \{0,1\}^{l_k}$;
5: **return** $(\mathbf{c}, K)$;

A general approach for attacking schemes with ECC. We now describe the general attacking framework. Similar to the FrodoKEM, the ciphertext is generally of the form $(\mathbf{c_1} \| \mathbf{c_2})$ and the decoding is done by computing $\mathbf{c_2} - \mathbf{c_1 s}$, where $\mathbf{s}$ is the secret key. In the schemes with ECC, however, the ambient space is a polynomial ring where a vector can be also treated as a polynomial. Thus, we could mix the use of the notations of $s(x)$ and $\mathbf{s}$ if there is no ambiguity.

The main tool is still to introduce additional noise in the last part of $\mathbf{c_2}$, which can be done by adding a large value to a position in the Euclidean case

---

Algorithm 3. LAC.CCA.Dec$(sk; \mathbf{c})$

Output: An encapsulation key (K).

1: $\mathbf{m} \leftarrow$ LAC.CPA.Dec$(sk, \mathbf{c})$;
2: $K \leftarrow H(\mathbf{m}, \mathbf{c})$;
3: $\mathbf{seed} \leftarrow G(\mathbf{m}) \in \mathcal{S}$;
4: $\mathbf{c}' \leftarrow$ LAC.CPA.Enc$(pk, \mathbf{m}; \mathbf{seed})$;
5: **if** $\mathbf{c}' \neq \mathbf{c}$ **then**
6:     $K \leftarrow H(H(sk), \mathbf{c})$;
7: **end if**
8: **return** K;

Algorithm 4. LAC.CPA.Enc$(pk = (\mathbf{seed_a}, \mathbf{b}), \mathbf{m} \in \mathcal{M}; \mathbf{seed} \in \mathcal{S})$

Output: A ciphertext $\mathbf{c}$.

1: $\mathbf{a} \leftarrow$ Samp$(U(\mathcal{R}); \mathbf{seed_a}) \in \mathcal{R}$;
2: $\mathbf{c_m} \leftarrow$ ECCEnc$(\mathbf{m}) \in \{0, 1\}^{l_v}$;
3: $(\mathbf{r}, \mathbf{e_1}, \mathbf{e_2}) \leftarrow$ Samp$(\Psi_\sigma^n, \Psi_\sigma^n, \Psi_\sigma^{l_v}; \mathbf{seed})$;
4: $\mathbf{c_1} \leftarrow \mathbf{ar} + \mathbf{e_1} \in \mathcal{R}$;
5: $\mathbf{c_2} \leftarrow (\mathbf{br})_{l_v} + \mathbf{e_2} + \lfloor \frac{q}{2} \rfloor \cdot \mathbf{c_m} \in \mathbb{Z}_q^{l_v}$;
6: **return** $\mathbf{c} := (\mathbf{c_1}, \mathbf{c_2}) \in \mathcal{R} \times \mathbb{Z}_q^{l_v}$;

(for LAC) or by filliping many bits within a small chunk of positions in the Hamming case (for HQC). The aim is then to recover the noise variables w.r.t. certain positions, which are linear functions of the secret key by testing the minimal added noise size that could lead to a decryption error. The decryption will lead to a fast checking in the non constant-time FO implementation since the re-encrypted ciphertext are random vectors leading to a difference at the beginning part of the ciphertexts $\mathbf{c_1}$, as described. However, since the overall decryption error happen only if strictly more than δ_0 position errors occur in the decryption phase, the attack strategy is less straightforward.

Since one could trigger a position error using the described process of introducing a rather large noise, the attacker is capable of adding position errors at the last positions to ensure the number of position errors to be exactly δ_0. The attacker is then capable of detecting if an uncontrolled position is erroneous or error-free — he could add a big noise to that position and this will lead to a decryption error if the position is error-free.

The attacker picks a position close to the controlled error positions that are error-free and tests the error value in that position by the binary search as discussed in the previous section for FrodoKEM. The error term is generally in

---

Algorithm 5. LAC.CPA.Dec($sk = \mathbf{s}; \mathbf{c} = (\mathbf{c}_1, \mathbf{c}_2)$)

Output: A plaintext $\mathbf{m}$.

1: $\mathbf{u} \leftarrow \mathbf{c}_1\mathbf{s} \in \mathcal{R}$;
2: $\mathbf{c}'_m \leftarrow \mathbf{c}_2 - (\mathbf{u})_{l_v} \in \mathbb{Z}_q^{l_v}$;
3: **for** $i = 0$ to $l_v - 1$ **do**
4:    **if** $\frac{q}{4} \le \mathbf{c}'_{mi} < \frac{3q}{4}$ **then**
5:       $\mathbf{c}_{mi} \leftarrow 1$
6:    **else**
7:       $\mathbf{c}_{mi} \leftarrow 0$
8:    **end if**
9: **end for**
10: $\mathbf{m} \leftarrow \mathsf{ECCDec}(\mathbf{c}_m)$;
11: **return** $\mathbf{m}$;

---

the form of $w(x) = e(x)r(x) - e_1(x)s(x) + e_2(x)$, where $e(x)$ and $s(x)$ contain the secret key information, and $r(x)$, $e_1(x)$, and $e_2(x)$ could be known from the encapsulation algorithm. Thus, we can obtain one linear equation whose unknowns are the coefficients of $e(x)$ and $s(x)$ from the detected one coefficient (position) of $w(x)$. Also, note that we already know n linear equations w.r.t. the coefficients of $e(x)$ and $s(x)$ from the key generation procedure. The attack proceeds by generating more ciphertexts until a sufficient number of equations are collected for a full key-recovery.

Dealing with the compression function. In the round-2 submission of LAC, a ciphertext compression technique is employed, introducing an additional rounding error. Thus, the general attack approach should be tweaked to handle this unknown noise part.

In the reference implementation of LAC128-v2, the comparison between the ciphertext and the re-encrypted one is implemented as follows.

```
//verify
if(memcmp(c,c_v,CIPHER_LEN)!=0)
{
    //k=hash(hash(sk)|c)
    hash((unsigned char*)sk,DIM_N,buf);
    hash(buf,MESSAGE_LEN+CIPHER_LEN,k);
}
```

Here, $\mathbf{c} = (\mathbf{c}_1 \| \mathbf{c}_{2,\text{compressed}})$, where $\mathbf{c}_1$ is a length-512 vector (or polynomial) and $\mathbf{c}_{2,\text{compressed}}$ is the compressed ciphertext part of length 200, and $\mathbf{c}_v$ is the re-encrypted ciphertext of the same size. Each byte in $\mathbf{c}_{2,\text{compressed}}$ is the concatenation of the 4 most significant bits in the two corresponding positions in $\mathbf{c}_2$. Thus, the final noise term should include a new polynomial $e_3(x)$ from the compression operation. Since this polynomial is from a rounding operation and unknown to us, the above general approach can not be directly applied.

On the other hand, it is already shown in [15] that if one can detect if a position is erroneous, then a few thousand such erroneous positions could lead to a full recovery. We next show in detail the procedure of determining the erroneous positions, which is an elaboration of the method described in the general attack.

For LAC128-v2, the position-wise decoding is successful if the error variable corresponding to that position lies in the interval of $[-62, 62]$, and in this case, the value has a small absolute value with high probability. Let c_2 be the vector of length 400, which will be compressed to $c_{2,\text{compressed}}$ of length 200 in the ciphertext. Then, it will cause a position error with high probability if adding 125 to a position in c_2 and compressing the new c_2 to $c'_{2,\text{compressed}}$ by the compression function. Since the position error probability for LAC128-v2 is only $2^{-12.61}$ (see Table 2), it will have $\delta_0 = 16$ position errors with high probability if one adds 125 to the last 16 entries in c_2. The threshold δ_0 is set to be 16 since the error correcting capability of the employed BCH codes is exactly 16. With some probability (of about $384/2^{12.6}$), one could find one position error originally occurs in the first 384 positions of c_2. Thus, it will lead to a different re-encryption if one adds 125 to the last 16 positions of c_2, but not if only 15 positions are changed. After finding this state, the attacker can keep the last 15 positions of c_2 added by 125 and also add the i-th position in c_2 by 125. He then compresses the invalid ciphertext and sends it to the decryption oracle. If the i-th position is already erroneous, the number of position errors will not be increased and a fast check cannot be detected via the timing channel. All additions are operated over $\mathbb{Z}_q$.

The other LAC versions can be attacked in a similar manner, and the attack version on LAC256-v2 with the D2 encoding would need a slight adjustment.

References

1. NIST post-quantum cryptography standardization. https://csrc.nist.gov/Projects/Post-Quantum-Cryptography/Post-Quantum-Cryptography-Standardization. Accessed 24 Sept 2018
2. NTRU Open Source Project. https://github.com/NTRUOpenSourceProject. Accessed 10 Feb 2020
3. Open quantum safe. https://openquantumsafe.org. Accessed 21 Jan 2020
4. Aguilar Melchor, C., et al.: HQC. Technical report, National Institute of Standards and Technology (2019). https://csrc.nist.gov/projects/post-quantum-cryptography/round-2-submissions
5. Aguilar Melchor, C., et al.: RQC. Technical report, National Institute of Standards and Technology (2019). https://csrc.nist.gov/projects/post-quantum-cryptography/round-2-submissions
6. Aragon, N., et al.: BIKE. Technical report, National Institute of Standards and Technology (2019). https://csrc.nist.gov/projects/post-quantum-cryptography/round-2-submissions

7. Aragon, N., et al.: ROLLO. Technical report, National Institute of Standards and Technology (2019). https://csrc.nist.gov/projects/post-quantum-cryptography/round-2-submissions

8. Băetu, C., Durak, F.B., Huguenin-Dumittan, L., Talayhan, A., Vaudenay, S.: Misuse attacks on post-quantum cryptosystems. In: Ishai, Y., Rijmen, V. (eds.) EUROCRYPT 2019, Part II. LNCS, vol. 11477, pp. 747–776. Springer, Cham (2019). https://doi.org/10.1007/978-3-030-17656-3_26

9. Bauer, A., Gilbert, H., Renault, G., Rossi, M.: Assessment of the key-reuse resilience of NewHope. In: Matsui, M. (ed.) CT-RSA 2019. LNCS, vol. 11405, pp. 272–292. Springer, Cham (2019). https://doi.org/10.1007/978-3-030-12612-4_14

10. Bernstein, D.J., Bruinderink, L.G., Lange, T., Panny, L.: HILA5 pindakaas: on the CCA security of lattice-based encryption with error correction. Cryptology ePrint Archive, Report 2017/1214 (2017). https://eprint.iacr.org/2017/1214

11. Bernstein, D.J., et al.: Classic McEliece. Technical report, National Institute of Standards and Technology (2019). https://csrc.nist.gov/projects/post-quantum-cryptography/round-2-submissions

12. Bos, J.W., et al.: Frodo: take off the ring! Practical, quantum-secure key exchange from LWE. In: Weippl, E.R., Katzenbeisser, S., Kruegel, C., Myers, A.C., Halevi, S. (eds.) ACM CCS 2016: 23rd Conference on Computer and Communications Security, Vienna, Austria, 24–28 October 2016, pp. 1006–1018. ACM Press (2016). https://doi.org/10.1145/2976749.2978425

13. Bruinderink, L.G., Hülsing, A., Lange, T., Yarom, Y.: Flush, gauss, and reload – a cache attack on the BLISS lattice-based signature scheme. In: Gierlichs, B., Poschmann, A.Y. (eds.) CHES 2016. LNCS, vol. 9813, pp. 323–345. Springer, Heidelberg (2016). https://doi.org/10.1007/978-3-662-53140-2_16

14. Brumley, D., Boneh, D.: Remote timing attacks are practical. In: USENIX Security 2003: 12th USENIX Security Symposium, Washington, DC, USA, 4–8 August 2003. USENIX Association (2003)

15. D'Anvers, J.-P., Guo, Q., Johansson, T., Nilsson, A., Vercauteren, F., Verbauwhede, I.: Decryption failure attacks on IND-CCA secure lattice-based schemes. In: Lin, D., Sako, K. (eds.) PKC 2019, Part II. LNCS, vol. 11443, pp. 565–598. Springer, Cham (2019). https://doi.org/10.1007/978-3-030-17259-6_19

16. D'Anvers, J.P., Tiepelt, M., Vercauteren, F., Verbauwhede, I.: Timing attacks on error correcting codes in post-quantum secure schemes. IACR Cryptology ePrint Archive 2019, 292 (2019)

17. Facon, A., Guilley, S., Lec'Hvien, M., Schaub, A., Souissi, Y.: Detecting cache-timing vulnerabilities in post-quantum cryptography algorithms. In: 2018 IEEE 3rd International Verification and Security Workshop (IVSW), pp. 7–12. IEEE (2018)

18. Fluhrer, S.: Cryptanalysis of ring-LWE based key exchange with key share reuse. Cryptology ePrint Archive, Report 2016/085 (2016). http://eprint.iacr.org/2016/085

19. Fujisaki, E., Okamoto, T.: Secure integration of asymmetric and symmetric encryption schemes. In: Wiener, M.J. (ed.) CRYPTO 1999. LNCS, vol. 1666, pp. 537–554. Springer, Heidelberg (1999). https://doi.org/10.1007/3-540-48405-1_34

20. Guo, Q., Johansson, T., Yang, J.: A novel CCA attack using decryption errors against LAC. In: Galbraith, S.D., Moriai, S. (eds.) ASIACRYPT 2019, Part I. LNCS, vol. 11921, pp. 82–111. Springer, Cham (2019). https://doi.org/10.1007/978-3-030-34578-5_4

21. Hofheinz, D., Hövelmanns, K., Kiltz, E.: A modular analysis of the Fujisaki-Okamoto transformation. In: Kalai, Y., Reyzin, L. (eds.) TCC 2017, Part I. LNCS, vol. 10677, pp. 341–371. Springer, Cham (2017). https://doi.org/10.1007/978-3-319-70500-2_12

22. Howgrave-Graham, N., et al.: The impact of decryption failures on the security of NTRU encryption. In: Boneh, D. (ed.) CRYPTO 2003. LNCS, vol. 2729, pp. 226–246. Springer, Heidelberg (2003). https://doi.org/10.1007/978-3-540-45146-4_14

23. Howgrave-Graham, N., Silverman, J.H., Singer, A., Whyte, W.: NAEP: provable security in the presence of decryption failures. Cryptology ePrint Archive, Report 2003/172 (2003). http://eprint.iacr.org/2003/172

24. Kocher, P.C.: Timing attacks on implementations of Diffie-Hellman, RSA, DSS, and other systems. In: Koblitz, N. (ed.) CRYPTO 1996. LNCS, vol. 1109, pp. 104–113. Springer, Heidelberg (1996). https://doi.org/10.1007/3-540-68697-5_9

25. Lu, X., et al.: LAC. Technical report, National Institute of Standards and Technology (2019). https://csrc.nist.gov/projects/post-quantum-cryptography/round-2-submissions

26. McEliece, R.J.: A public-key cryptosystem based on algebraic. Coding Thv **4244**, 114–116 (1978)

27. Naehrig, M., et al.: FrodoKEM. Technical report, National Institute of Standards and Technology (2019). https://csrc.nist.gov/projects/post-quantum-cryptography/round-2-submissions

28. Poppelmann, T., et al.: NewHope. Technical report, National Institute of Standards and Technology (2019). https://csrc.nist.gov/projects/post-quantum-cryptography/round-2-submissions

29. Schwabe, P., et al.: CRYSTALS-KYBER. Technical report, National Institute of Standards and Technology (2019). https://csrc.nist.gov/projects/post-quantum-cryptography/round-2-submissions

30. Shor, P.W.: Algorithms for quantum computation: discrete logarithms and factoring. In: 35th Annual Symposium on Foundations of Computer Science, Santa Fe, NM, USA, 20–22 November 1994, pp. 124–134. IEEE Computer Society Press (1994). https://doi.org/10.1109/SFCS.1994.365700

31. Smart, N.P.: Cryptography Made Simple. Information Security and Cryptography. Springer, Heidelberg (2016). https://doi.org/10.1007/978-3-319-21936-3

32. Strenzke, F.: A timing attack against the secret permutation in the McEliece PKC. In: Sendrier, N. (ed.) PQCrypto 2010. LNCS, vol. 6061, pp. 95–107. Springer, Heidelberg (2010). https://doi.org/10.1007/978-3-642-12929-2_8

33. Strenzke, F.: Timing attacks against the syndrome inversion in code-based cryptosystems. In: Gaborit, P. (ed.) PQCrypto 2013. LNCS, vol. 7932, pp. 217–230. Springer, Heidelberg (2013). https://doi.org/10.1007/978-3-642-38616-9_15

Efficient Pseudorandom Correlation Generators from Ring-LPN

Elette Boyle[1]([✉]), Geoffroy Couteau[2]([✉]), Niv Gilboa[3]([✉]), Yuval Ishai[4]([✉]),
Lisa Kohl[4]([✉]), and Peter Scholl[5]([✉])

[1] IDC Herzliya, Herzliya, Israel
eboyle@alum.mit.edu
[2] IRIF, Paris, France
couteau@irif.fr
[3] Ben-Gurion University of the Negev, Beersheba, Israel
gilboan@bgu.ac.il
[4] Technion, Haifa, Israel
{yuvali,lisa.kohl}@cs.technion.ac.il
[5] Aarhus University, Aarhus, Denmark
peter.scholl@cs.au.dk

Abstract. Secure multiparty computation can often utilize a trusted source of correlated randomness to achieve better efficiency. A recent line of work, initiated by Boyle et al. (CCS 2018, Crypto 2019), showed how useful forms of correlated randomness can be generated using a cheap, one-time interaction, followed by only "silent" local computation. This is achieved via a *pseudorandom correlation generator* (PCG), a deterministic function that stretches short correlated seeds into long instances of a target correlation. Previous works constructed concretely efficient PCGs for simple but useful correlations, including random oblivious transfer and vector-OLE, together with efficient protocols to distribute the PCG seed generation. Most of these constructions were based on variants of the Learning Parity with Noise (LPN) assumption. PCGs for other useful correlations had poor asymptotic and concrete efficiency.

In this work, we design a new class of efficient PCGs based on different flavors of the *ring-LPN* assumption. Our new PCGs can generate OLE correlations, authenticated multiplication triples, matrix product correlations, and other types of useful correlations over large fields. These PCGs are more efficient by orders of magnitude than the previous constructions and can be used to improve the preprocessing phase of many existing MPC protocols.

1 Introduction

Correlated secret randomness is a commonly used resource for secure multiparty computation (MPC) protocols. Indeed, simple kinds of correlations enable lightweight MPC protocols even when there is no honest majority. For instance, an *oblivious transfer* (OT) correlation supports MPC for Boolean

D. Micciancio and T. Ristenpart (Eds.): CRYPTO 2020, LNCS 12171, pp. 387–416, 2020.
https://doi.org/10.1007/978-3-030-56880-1_14

circuits [29,35,40,46], while oblivious linear-function evaluation[1] (OLE), an arithmetic variant of OT, supports MPC for arithmetic circuits [36,45]. Other useful types of correlations include multiplication triples [4] and truth-table correlations [21,23,33]. Finally, *authenticated* multiplication triples serve as a powerful resource for achieving security against malicious parties [6,25].

A common paradigm in modern MPC protocols is to utilize the above kinds of correlations in the following way. In a preprocessing phase, before the inputs are known, the parties use an *offline protocol* to generate many instances of the correlation. These instances are then consumed by an *online protocol* to securely compute a function of the secret inputs. This approach is appealing because of the high efficiency of the online protocol. Indeed, with the above simple correlations, the online communication and computation costs are comparable to the size of the circuit being evaluated. The price one pays for the fast online protocol is a much slower and higher-bandwidth offline protocol. Even simple types of correlated randomness are expensive to generate in a secure way. This high cost becomes even higher when aiming for security against malicious parties.

Recently, a promising approach for instantiating the preprocessing phase of MPC protocols was suggested in [9,11], relying on a new primitive called a *pseudorandom correlation generator* (PCG). Consider a target two-party correlation $\mathcal{C}$, typically consisting of many independent instances of a simple correlation as above. A PCG for $\mathcal{C}$ consists of two algorithms: $\mathsf{Gen}(1^\lambda)$, which given a security parameter λ generates a pair of short, correlated seeds $(\mathsf{k}_0, \mathsf{k}_1)$, and $\mathsf{Expand}(\mathsf{k}_\sigma)$, which deterministically stretches a seed k_σ to a long output R_σ. The intuitive security requirement is that the joint outputs (R_0, R_1) of the above process cannot be distinguished from $\mathcal{C}$ not only by an outsider, but also by an insider who learns one of the two seeds. PCGs naturally lead to protocols with an appealing *silent preprocessing* feature, by breaking the offline phase into two parts:

1. SETUP. The parties run a secure protocol to distribute the seed generation of Gen. Since Gen has low computational cost and short outputs, this protocol only involves a small amount of communication, much smaller than the output of $\mathcal{C}$. Each party stores its own short seed k_σ for later use.
2. SILENT EXPANSION. Shortly before the online phase, the parties use Expand to generate long pseudorandom correlated strings (R_0, R_1) to be used by the online protocol. This part is referred to as *silent*, since it involves no communication.

Beyond the potential improvement in the total offline communication and computation, this blueprint has two additional advantages. First, it can substantially reduce the *storage* cost of correlated randomness by enabling efficient compression. Indeed, the parties can afford to generate and store many correlated seeds, possibly with different sets of parties, and expand them just before they are needed. Second, the cost of protecting the offline protocol against malicious parties is "amortized away," since it is only the small setup part that needs to be protected. A malicious execution of Expand is harmless.

---

[1] An OLE correlation over a finite field $\mathbb{F}$ is a two-party correlation (r_0, r_1) where $r_0 = (a, b)$ is uniform over $\mathbb{F}^2$ and $r_1 = (x, ax + b)$ for $x \in_R \mathbb{F}$.

The work of Boyle et al. [11] constructed efficient PCGs for several kinds of useful correlations based on different assumptions that include variants of Learning Parity with Noise (LPN) [8] and Learning With Errors (LWE) [47]. While the LPN-based PCG for OT from [11] has very good concrete efficiency, making it a practically appealing approach for generating many OTs [10], this is not the case for other useful correlations such as OLE or authenticated multiplication triples. For these correlations, two different constructions were proposed in [10]. Both are "practically feasible" but quite inefficient. In the first construction, based on homomorphic secret sharing from ring-LWE [12,14,16,18], the seed expansion can be at most quadratic due to the use of a pseudorandom generator with algebraic degree 2. In concrete terms, the seeds are several GBs long and can only be expanded by around 6x, giving far too much overhead for most applications. Their second construction is based directly on LPN, and has computational cost of at least $\Omega(N^2)$ for output length N, which is impractical for large N.

1.1 Our Contributions

In this work, we present efficient new PCG constructions for several widely used correlations for which previous techniques had poor concrete efficiency.

Silent OLE and silent triple generation. Our main construction gives the first concretely efficient PCG for OLE over big finite fields $\mathbb{F}$. This PCG is based on a variant of the *ring-LPN* assumption over $\mathbb{F}$, makes a black-box use of $\mathbb{F}$, and has $\mathsf{poly}(\lambda) \cdot \log N$ seed size and $\mathsf{poly}(\lambda) \cdot \tilde{O}(N)$ computational cost for expanding the seeds into N instances of OLE. This PCG gives both an asymptotic and concrete improvement over the LPN-based construction from [11].

We also show how to modify our PCG for OLE to produce multiplication triples and authenticated triples, used in maliciously secure MPC protocols like SPDZ [25]. This incurs an extra overhead of only around a factor of two in seed size, seed generation, and silent expansion time. Finally, we extend the main construction to other types of useful correlations, including matrix products and circuit-dependent correlations.

Technically, one of our main innovations here is showing how to avoid the $\Omega(N^2)$ blowup from the previous LPN-based PCG for OLE from [11]. Our method of doing this requires switching from unstructured LPN to ring-LPN over a certain kind of polynomial rings. This is analogous to early fully homomorphic encryption schemes, where switching from a construction based on LWE [19] to one based on ring-LWE [20] reduced the ciphertext expansion in multiplication from quadratic to linear. A key difference between LWE-based constructions and LPN-based constructions over a big field $\mathbb{F}$ is the noise distribution: Gaussian in the former and low Hamming weight noise in the latter. With LPN-style noise distribution more care is needed, and some natural PCG candidates based on Reed-Solomon codes can be broken using algebraic decoding techniques.

Concrete efficiency. Our PCGs have attractive concrete efficiency features. To give a couple of data points, in the case of OLE the parties can store a pair of seeds of size 1.25 MB each, and expand them on demand to produce over a million OLEs (of size 32 MB, 26x larger than the seeds) in $\mathbb{Z}_q$, where q is the product of two 62-bit primes,[2] with 128-bit security. When running on a single core of a modern laptop, we estimate this takes under 10 s, resulting in a throughput of over 100 thousand OLEs per second. To produce authenticated triples instead of OLE, the expansion cost roughly doubles, giving 50 thousand triples per second, while the seed size increases to 2.6 MB. For comparison, estimates from [11] for their PCG for producing authenticated triples gave a throughput of up to 7 thousand per second, but this was only possible when generating an enormous batch of 17 GB worth of triples, with 3 GB seeds. See below for comparison with non-silent correlation generation techniques.

Efficient setup protocols. Recall that to avoid a trusted setup, one typically needs a setup protocol to securely distribute the PCG seed generation. We present concretely efficient setup protocols for OLE and authenticated triples, with both semi-honest and malicious security. The protocols make black-box use of lightweight cryptographic primitives, as well as of generic MPC protocols for performing binary and arithmetic computations on secret-shared values.

In practice, our PCGs and setup protocols can be used in a *bootstrapping mode*, where a portion of the PCG outputs are reserved to be used as correlated randomness for the setup procedure of the next PCG seeds. This means that the vast majority of the setup cost is amortized away over multiple instances. Concretely, we estimate that when bootstrapped in this way, the setup phase for a PCG of one million authenticated triples requires only around 4.2 MB of communication per party, to produce 32 MB worth of triples. The initial setup protocol for the first PCG (before bootstrapping can take place) requires around 25000 authenticated triples, plus some additional correlated randomness (OT and VOLE). This should be feasible to produce in under a minute (although with high communication cost) using standard protocols such as MASCOT [38] or Overdrive [39], and previous PCG protocols for OT and VOLE with malicious security [10].

Compared with non-silent secure correlation generation protocols, we expect the overall *computational* cost of our approach to be comparable with state-of-the-art protocols based on homomorphic encryption [31,37,39], but with much lower *communication* costs. For instance, in the case of authenticated multiplication triples, the Overdrive protocol [39] can produce around 30 thousand triples per second with malicious security. This is similar to our PCG expansion phase (modulo different hardware, environment, and so on), with the significant difference that Overdrive requires almost 2 GB of communication to produce the triples. In comparison, our amortized 4.2 MB communication complexity is over two orders of magnitude smaller, with the additional benefit that our short correlated seeds can be easily stored for on-demand silent expansion.

---

[2] Our construction works in any sufficiently large finite field, or modulus that is a product of primes via the CRT. We estimated costs with a product of two primes due to better software support.

Extension to other correlations and multiple parties. Beyond multiplication triples, it can be useful to have more general "degree-two" correlations, such as inner-product triples, matrix-multiplication triples, or circuit-dependent multiplication triples [5,17,21]. We use our PCG for OLE to obtain PCGs for these kinds of correlations, by exploiting a special "programmability" feature that enables reusing the same PCG output in multiple instances [11]. This gives us a way to produce many independent instances of any degree-two correlation (a vast generalization of OLE and multiplication triples), with seed size that grows sublinearly with the total number of instances. Useful special cases include the types of correlations mentioned above. This construction has a bigger overhead than our PCG for OLE, and in practice seems mainly suited for small correlations such as low-dimensional matrix products. However, these can still be useful in larger computations which involve a lot of linear algebra or other repeated sub-computations.

We can also use same programmability feature of our 2-party PCGs to extend them to the *multi-party setting*. This yields practical multi-party PCGs for multiplication triples that enable an online passively-secure MPC protocol for arithmetic circuits whose cost scales linearly (rather than quadratically) with the number of parties. This transformation to the multi-party case, which originates from [11], does not scale well to correlations with degree higher than 2. As a result, we do not get a multi-party PCG for authenticated triples (a degree-three correlation) with the same level of efficiency.

Security of ring-LPN. Our constructions rely on variants of the ring-LPN assumption [32] over non-binary fields. Binary ring-LPN is a fairly standard assumption that withstood a significant amount of cryptanalysis. However, since we also use relatively unexplored variants over different rings, we give a thorough survey of known attacks, and analyze the best strategies that apply to our setting. We find that there are only one or two additional attack possibilities from the additional structure we introduce, and these are easily countered with a small increase in the number of errors.

More precisely, settling for a PCG that generates a single OLE instance over a large ring of degree-N polynomials, our construction can be based on a conservative variant of ring-LPN where the modulus is irreducible. A big ring-OLE correlation can then be converted into N independent instances of standard OLE by communicating $O(N)$ field elements. For generating *silent* OLE over $\mathbb{F}_p$, we instead rely on a variant of ring-LPN where the modulus splits completely into N linear factors. In practice, this requires using larger parameters and increases the cost of our protocols by around a factor of two, compared with irreducible ring-LPN.

1.2 Technical Overview

Construction from [11]. Before describing our PCG for OLE, it is instructive to recall the PCG for general degree-two correlations by Boyle et al. [11], based on LPN. The goal is to build a PCG for the correlation which gives each party a random vector $\mathbf{x}_i$, together with an additive secret share of the tensor product $\mathbf{x}_0 \otimes \mathbf{x}_1$. They used the dual form of LPN over a ring $\mathbb{Z}_p$, which states that the distribution

$$\left\{ H, H \cdot \mathbf{e} \,\middle|\, H \xleftarrow{\$} \mathbb{Z}_p^{m \times n}, \mathbf{e} \xleftarrow{\$} \mathbb{Z}_p^n \text{ s.t. wt}(\mathbf{e}) = t \right\}$$

is computationally indistinguishable from uniform, where $\mathbf{e}$ is a sparse random vector with only t non-zero coordinates, for some $t \ll n$, and $m < n$.

The idea of the construction is that the setup algorithm gives each party a random sparse $\mathbf{e}_0$ or $\mathbf{e}_1$, and computes the tensor product $\mathbf{e}_0 \otimes \mathbf{e}_1$, which has at most t^2 non-zero coordinates. This product is then distributed to the parties via function secret sharing (FSS), by generating a pair of FSS keys for the function that outputs each entry of the product on its respective inputs from 1 to n^2. This function can be written as a sum of t^2 point functions, allowing practical FSS schemes based on distributed point functions [13,15,28]. Note that unlike the case of PCGs for OT or Vector-OLE [10,48], here we cannot replace FSS by the simpler punctured PRF primitive.

Given shares of $\mathbf{e}_0 \otimes \mathbf{e}_1$ and either $\mathbf{e}_0$ or $\mathbf{e}_1$, the parties expand these using LPN, computing:

$$\mathbf{x}_0 = H \cdot \mathbf{e}_0, \quad \mathbf{x}_1 = H \cdot \mathbf{e}_1, \quad \mathbf{z} = (H \cdot \mathbf{e}_0) \otimes (H \cdot \mathbf{e}_1) = (H \otimes H) \cdot (\mathbf{e}_0 \otimes \mathbf{e}_1)$$

where $\mathbf{x}_i$ is computed by party P_i, while $\mathbf{z}$ is computed in secret-shared form, using the shares of $\mathbf{e}_0 \otimes \mathbf{e}_1$ and the formula on the right-hand side.

Notice that both $\mathbf{x}_0$ and $\mathbf{x}_1$ are pseudorandom under LPN, which gives the desired correlation.

Optimizations and additional applications. Boyle et al. state the computational complexity of the above as $O(n^4)$ operations, due to the tensor product of H with itself. We observe that the value of $(H \cdot \mathbf{e}_0) \otimes (H \cdot \mathbf{e}_1)$ can be read directly from $H \cdot (\mathbf{e}_0 \cdot \mathbf{e}_1^{\mathsf{T}}) \cdot H^{\mathsf{T}}$, which requires much less computation and can be made even more efficient if H is a structured matrix, reducing the computational complexity to $\tilde{O}(n^2)$. We also describe two variants of the PCG which allow producing large matrix multiplication correlations with different parameter tradeoffs. As these are much less practical than our main constructions, we refer the interested reader to the full version for details.

An efficient PCG for OLE. The problem with the above construction is that it produces an entire tensor product correlation, which inherently requires $\Omega(n^2)$ computation. Even if we only want to compute the diagonal entries of the tensor product output (that is, n OLEs), we do not see a way to do this any more efficiently.

Instead, we propose to replace the tensor product with a *polynomial product*. Let $R_p = \mathbb{Z}_p[X]/(F(X))$ for some degree N polynomial $F(X)$, and let e, f be two sparse polynomials in R_p. For a random polynomial $a \in R_p$, the pair

$$(a, a \cdot e + f \mod F(X))$$

is pseudorandom under the *ring-LPN* assumption [32].

Now, given two pairs of sparse polynomials (e_0, e_1) and (f_0, f_1), each product $e_i \cdot f_j$ (without reduction modulo F) has degree $< 2N$ and only t^2 non-zero coefficients. These can again be distributed to two parties using FSS, but this time the expanded FSS outputs can be computed in *linear time* in N, instead of quadratic, since the domain size of the function being shared is only $2N$.

Given shares of $e_i \cdot f_j$, similarly to the LPN case, the parties compute expanded outputs by defining

$$x_0 = a \cdot e_0 + f_0, \quad x_1 = a \cdot e_1 + f_1, \quad z = ((1, a) \otimes (1, a)) \cdot ((e_0, f_0) \otimes (e_1, f_1))$$

The main difference here is that each tensor product is only of length 2, and can be computed in $\tilde{O}(N)$ time using fast polynomial multiplication algorithms.

This gives a PCG that compresses a single OLE over the ring R_p. To obtain a PCG for OLE over $\mathbb{Z}_p$, we again take inspiration from the fully homomorphic encryption literature, by using ciphertext-packing techniques [49]. We can carefully choose p and $F(X)$ such that $F(X)$ splits into N distinct, linear factors modulo p. Then R_p is isomorphic to N copies of $\mathbb{Z}_p$, and we can immediately convert a random OLE over R_p into N random OLEs over $\mathbb{Z}_p$. This works particularly well with cyclotomic rings as used in ring-LWE [43], where we can e.g. use N a power of two and easily exploit FFTs for polynomial arithmetic.

Extending to authenticated multiplication triples. We show that our construction extends from OLE to authenticated multiplication triples, as used in the SPDZ protocol for maliciously secure MPC [22,25]. This follows from a simple trick, where we modify the FSS scheme to additionally multiply its outputs by a random MAC key $\alpha \in \mathbb{Z}_p$. Since this preserves sparsity of the underlying shared vector, it adds only at most a factor of two overhead on top of the basic scheme.

Distributed setup. We focus on the case of OLE correlations over R_p (the setup for authenticated triples is very similar). Recall that the seed of the PCG for OLE consists of t-sparse degree-N "error" polynomials e_0, e_1 and f_0, f_1, and FSS keys for secret-shares of the products $e_i \cdot f_j$, each represented as a coefficient vector via the sum of t^2 point functions $f_{\alpha, \beta} \colon [2N] \to \mathbb{Z}_p$. Each point function corresponds to a single monomial product from e_i and f_j. The index $\alpha \in [2N]$ of the nonzero position is the *sum* of the corresponding nonzero indices, and the payload $\beta \in \mathbb{Z}_p$ is the *product* of the corresponding payloads in e_i and f_j.

In the semi-honest setting, secure computation of this PCG generation procedure can be attained directly, using generic 2-PC for simple operations on the α and β values, as well as black-box use of a protocol for secure computation of FSS key generation, such as the efficient protocol of Doerner and shelat [27].

For the malicious setting, we would wish to mimic the same protocol structure with underlying 2-PC components replaced with maliciously secure counterparts. The simple 2-PCs on α, β can be converted to malicious security with relatively minor overhead. The problem is the FSS key generation, for which efficient maliciously secure protocols currently do not exist. Generic 2-PC of the FSS key generation functionality would require expensive secure evaluations of crytographic pseudorandom generators (PRG). The semi-honest protocol of [27] is black-box in a PRG; but, precisely this fact makes it difficult to ensure consistency between different steps in the face of a malicious party.

Note that this is similar to the problem that Boyle et al. faced in [10] for silent OT generation, but their setting was conceptually simpler: There, one party always knew the position α of the non-zero value of the distributed point function (indeed, for their purpose the simpler building block of a puncturable pseudorandom function sufficed). Further, they did not have to assume any correlation between path values, whereas in our setting we require that the parties behave consistently regarding the path positions *and* payloads across several instances.

In this work we show how to extend the approach of [10] to the context of distributed point functions, further addressing the mentioned issues.

Our protocol realizes a PCG-type functionality for a scaled unit vector[3] with leakage: Given authenticated values for the location of the non-zero position $\alpha \in [0..N)$ and the non-zero payload $\beta \in \mathbb{Z}_p$, the functionality allows a corrupt party to choose its output vector $\mathbf{y} \in \mathbb{Z}_p^N$ and delivers to the honest party the correct corresponding output $\mathbf{y} - (0, \dots, \beta, \dots, 0)$, where β is in the α-th position. The leakage on α can be captured by allowing the adversary a predicate guess on α.[4] In the setting of noise generation for (ring-)LPN, as is the case for our PCG constructions (and likely future constructions), such leakage is tolerable as, intuitively, this can be accounted for by slightly increasing the noise rate. Indeed, we prove that this functionality suffices to implement a protocol securely realizing PCG functionalities, such as the corruptible functionality for OLE and authenticated multiplication triples, based on a variant of the ring-LPN assumption that allows small amount of leakage (only 1 bit on average).

Extensions. A downside of the above construction, compared with the one from LPN, is that it is restricted to multiplication triples or OLE. It can be useful to obtain other degree-two correlations such as matrix multiplication triples, which allow multiplying two secret matrices with only $O(n^2)$ communication, instead of $O(n^3)$ from naively using individual triples. Another technique is preprocessing multiplications in a way that depends on the structure of the circuit, which allows reducing the online cost of 2-PC down to communicating just one field element

---

[3] Note that this corresponds to a distributed point function where we do not require the key setup on its own to be secure, but only require the protocol to securely implement the FSS functionality including expansion, as this suffices for using PCGs in the context of secure computation (see also [10]).

[4] In fact, the leakage can be characterized by predicates corresponding to bit-matching with wildcards.

per party, instead of two from multiplication triples [4,5,23]. This type of circuit-dependent preprocessing can also be expressed as a degree two correlation.

Our PCG for OLE satisfies a useful "programmability" feature, introduced by Boyle et al. [11], allowing certain parts of the PCG output to be reused across multiple instances. This is simply due to the fact that we can reuse the polynomials e_0, e_1 or f_0, f_1 in the PCG, without harming security. This allows us to extend the PCG to build more general correlations, by using multiple programmed instances to perform every multiplication in the general correlation.

We in fact present a more general construction, which, loosely speaking, achieves the following. Given a programmable PCG for some bilinear correlation g, let f be another bilinear correlation that is computable using linear combinations of outputs of g applied to its input. Then, we can construct a PCG for f using several copies of the PCG for g, where the number of instances is given by the complexity of f written as a function of g. This gives a general way of combining PCGs to obtain correlations of increasing complexity, while allowing for different complexity tradeoffs by varying the "base" bilinear correlation f.

Multi-party PCGs. As discussed earlier, the programmability feature also immediately allows us to extend our PCGs for OLE and degree-two correlations to the multi-party setting, using the construction from [11]. This does not apply to the PCG for authenticated multiplication triples; in the full version, we sketch a possible alternative solution based on three-party distributed point functions, but these are much less efficient than the two-party setting.

Security analysis of ring-LPN. We use the ring $R_p = \mathbb{Z}_p[X]/F(X)$, for some degree N polynomial $F(X)$. There are two main ring-LPN variants we consider, depending on how the parameters are instantiated. The more conservative is when $F(X)$ is either *irreducible* in R_p (hence, R_p is isomorphic to a finite field), or at least when $F(X)$ has only very few low-degree factors, so R_p has a large subring that is a field. This type of instantiation is similar to previous recommendations for ring-LPN [30,32] and post-quantum encryption schemes from quasi-cyclic codes [44]. The best known attacks are to solve the underlying syndrome decoding problem, and the additional ring structure does not seem to give much advantage. One exception is when a very large number of samples are available, when the ring structure can in some cases be exploited [7]. This does not apply to our setting, however, since our constructions only rely on ring-LPN with one sample[5].

The second variant, which is needed for silent OLE in $\mathbb{F}_p$, is when $F(X)$ splits modulo p into many distinct factors of low degree. Here, the main attack vector that needs to be considered is that if f_i is some degree-d factor of $F(X)$, then reducing a ring-LPN instance modulo f_i gives a new instance in smaller dimension d, albeit with a different noise distribution. The best case for the adversary is when f_i is of the form $X^d + c_i$, when this reduction does not increase the Hamming weight of the noise (although, the corresponding error rate goes

---

[5] Or, two samples if security is based on ring-LPN with a uniform (not sparse) secret.

up). If such sparse factors exist, then, we must also ensure that the underlying ring-LPN instance in dimension d, with new noise weight, is hard to solve.

One way to counter this attack is to choose $F(X)$ to be a product of N random linear factors, ensuring that any factors of F an adversary can find are likely to be very dense. However, to improve computational efficiency, it is better to use a cyclotomic polynomial such as $F(X) = X^N + 1$ with N a power of two, as is common in the ring-LWE setting. In this case, there are many sparse factors of the form $X^{2^i} + c_i$ which can be exploited, and we must take these into account when choosing parameters. The main advantage of performing this reduction is the vector operations in attacks such as information-set decoding become cheaper, since they are all in a smaller dimension. This only has a small overall effect on attack complexity, though, since these algorithms are all exponential in the noise weight. Therefore, to counter the attack, it suffices to ensure there are enough noisy coordinates in a reduced instance, which requires only a small increase in noise weight.

Note that for $p = 2$, this strategy was also considered in Lapin [32], and it was later shown that an optimized version of this over $\mathbb{F}_2$ reduces security of some Lapin parameter sets by ≈ 10 bits [30]. Our analysis over $\mathbb{F}_p$ is roughly consistent with this.

2   Preliminaries

Notation. We let λ denote a security parameter, and use the standard definitions of negligible functions, computational indistinguishability (with respect to nonuniform distinguishers), and pseudorandom generators. We use $[0..n)$ to denote the index set $\{0, \cdots, n-1\}$, as well as $[0..n] = \{0, \ldots, n\}$ and $[n] = \{1, \ldots, n\}$.

Vectors, outer sum and outer product. We use column vectors by default. For two vectors $\mathbf{u} = (u_1, \ldots, u_t), \mathbf{v} = (v_1, \ldots, v_t) \in R^t$, for some ring R, we write $\mathbf{u} \boxplus \mathbf{v}$ to mean the *outer sum* given by the length t^2 vector $(u_i + v_j)_{i \in [t], j \in [t]}$. Similarly, we define the flattened outer product (or tensor product) to be $\mathbf{u} \otimes \mathbf{v} = (u_i \cdot v_j)_{i \in [t], j \in [t]}$, that is, the vector $(v_1 \cdot \mathbf{u}, \ldots, v_n \cdot \mathbf{u})$. We denote the inner product of two vectors by $\langle \mathbf{u}, \mathbf{v} \rangle$.

PCG and FSS. We refer to the full version for formal definitions of a *pseudorandom correlation generator* (PCG), *function secret sharing* (FSS) and the special case of *distributed point function*. Here we will use an FSS scheme *SPFSS* for secret-sharing a *sum of point functions* $f_{S,\mathbf{y}}$ defined as follows. For a sequence of inputs $S = (s_1, \ldots, s_t) \in [n]^t$ and outputs $\mathbf{y} = (y_1, \ldots, y_t)$, the function $f_{S,\mathbf{y}}(x)$ returns the sum of the point functions $f_{s_i, y_i}(x)$, where the latter returns y_i if $x = s_i$ and 0 otherwise. For better readability, when generating keys for a scheme SPFSS = (SPFSS.Gen, SPFSS.Eval), we write SPFSS.Gen$(1^\lambda, S, \mathbf{y})$, instead of explicitly writing $f_{S,\mathbf{y}}$. To construct SPFSS for a sum of t point functions, we can simply take t distributed point functions and sum up their outputs. Alternatively, more efficient constructions with optimized full-domain evaluation can be obtained using (randomized) batch codes [9,48].

3   Ring-LPN Assumption

In this section, we recall the ring-LPN assumption, which was first introduced in [32] to build efficient authentication protocols. Since then, it has received some attention from the cryptography community [7,24,30,42], due to its appealing combination of LPN-like structure, compact parameters, and short runtimes. Below, we also provide a definition of module-LPN, which generalizes ring-LPN in the same way that the more well-known module-LWE generalizes ring-LWE.

3.1   Ring-LPN

Definition 1 (Ring-LPN). *Let $R = \mathbb{Z}_p[X]/(F(X))$ for some prime p and degree-N polynomial $F(X) \in \mathbb{Z}[X]$, and let $m, t \in \mathbb{N}$. Let $\mathcal{HW}_t$ be the distribution over R_p that is obtained via sampling t noise positions $A \leftarrow [0..N)^t$ as well as t payloads $\mathbf{b} \leftarrow \mathbb{Z}_p^t$ uniformly at random, and outputting $e(X) := \sum_{j=0}^{t-1} \mathbf{b}[j] \cdot X^{A[j]}$. The R-LPN$_{p,m,t}$ problem is hard if for any PPT adversary $\mathcal{A}$, it holds that*

$$\left| \Pr[\mathcal{A}((a^{(i)}, a^{(i)} \cdot e + f^{(i)})_{i=1}^m) = 1] - \Pr[\mathcal{A}((a^{(i)}, u^{(i)})_{i=1}^m) = 1] \right| \leq \mathsf{negl}(\lambda)$$

where the probabilities are taken over $a^{(1)}, \ldots, a^{(m)}, u^{(1)}, \ldots, u^{(m)} \leftarrow R_p$, e, $f^{(1)}, \ldots, f^{(m)} \leftarrow \mathcal{HW}_t$ and the randomness of $\mathcal{A}$.

Remark 2. Note that sampling t noise positions individually can lead to collisions, and thus negatively affect the entropy introduced by the payloads. The reason we decided in favor of this definition is that this entropy loss is minor in the regime of parameters we care about—as for $t \ll N$ the probability of collisions is very small—and this choice helps to simplify the analysis.

Note that our restriction to $\mathbb{Z}_p$ with p prime as the underlying field is only for simplicity; in fact, R-LPN can be defined equivalently over any other field, or even over rings (e.g. $\mathbb{Z}_{2^k}$ or $\mathbb{Z}_{pq}$ for primes p, q); these alternative choices are not known to introduce any significant weakness or structural difference compared to the version over $\mathbb{Z}_p$.

In this work, we will also use a natural generalization of R-LPN, where we replace $a^{(i)} \cdot e$ by the inner product $\langle \mathbf{a}^{(i)}, \mathbf{e} \rangle$ between length-$(c-1)$ vectors over R, for some constant c. We call this *module-LPN*, analagously to module-LWE. This will allow for more efficient instantiations, as according to our security analysis it will be enough to choose the total number of noise positions $w = c \cdot t = O(\lambda)$, and therefore increasing c allows to choose a smaller t.

Definition 3 (Module-LPN). *Let $R = \mathbb{Z}_p[X]/(F(X))$ for some prime p and degree-N polynomial $F(X) \in \mathbb{Z}[X]$, and let $c, m, t \in \mathbb{N}$ with $c \geq 2$. Let $\mathcal{HW}_t$ be the distribution of uniformly random polynomials in R_p with exactly t non-zero coefficients. The R^c-LPN$_{p,m,t}$ problem is hard if for any PPT adversary $\mathcal{A}$, it holds that*

$$\left| \Pr[\mathcal{A}((\mathbf{a}^{(i)}, \langle \mathbf{a}^{(i)}, \mathbf{e} \rangle + f^{(i)})_{i=1}^m) = 1] - \Pr[\mathcal{A}((\mathbf{a}^{(i)}, u^{(i)})_{i=1}^m) = 1] \right| \leq \mathsf{negl}(\lambda)$$

where the probabilities are taken over $\mathbf{a}^{(1)}, \ldots, \mathbf{a}^{(m)} \leftarrow R_p^{c-1}$, $u^{(1)}, \cdots, u^{(m)} \leftarrow R_p$ $\mathbf{e} \leftarrow \mathcal{HW}_t^{c-1}$, $f^{(1)}, \ldots, f^{(m)} \leftarrow \mathcal{HW}_t$, and the randomness of $\mathcal{A}$.

Equivalence to module-LPN with uniform secret. We observe that, by the same argument as for standard LWE [2], the R-LPN (resp. module-LPN) problem with a secret chosen from the error distribution is at least as hard as the corresponding R-LPN (resp. module-LPN) problem where the secret is chosen uniformly at random, if the adversary is given one additional sample. For a proof we refer to the full version.

Lemma 4. *For any $c \geq 2$, let R^c-uLPN$_{p,m,t}$ denote the variant of R^c-LPN where the secret e is sampled uniformly at random. Then, for $m \geq c$, R^c-uLPN$_{p,m,t}$ is at least as hard as R^c-LPN$_{p,m-c,t}$.*

Relation to syndrome decoding. In our constructions, we typically consider module-LPN with a single sample ($m = 1$). To simplify notation and emphasize that the secret comes from the error distribution, we often combine the two into a single vector, writing

$$\left\{ (\mathbf{a}, \langle \mathbf{a}, \mathbf{e} \rangle) \;\middle|\; \mathbf{a} = (1, \mathbf{a}'), \mathbf{a}' \xleftarrow{\$} R_p^{c-1}, \mathbf{e} \xleftarrow{\$} \mathcal{HW}_t^c \right\}.$$

This formulation of module-LPN is equivalent to a variant of the syndrome decoding problem in random polynomial codes. To see this, let M_i be the $N \times N$ matrix over $\mathbb{Z}_p$ representing multiplication with the fixed element $a_i' \in R_p$, for $i = 1$ to $c - 1$. Define the matrix

$$H = [\mathsf{Id}_N || M_1 || \cdots || M_{c-1}].$$

H is a parity-check matrix in systematic form for a polynomial code defined by the random elements $a_i' \in R_p$. Module-LPN can be seen as a decisional version of syndrome decoding for this code, where we assume that $H\mathbf{e}$ is pseudorandom for an error vector $\mathbf{e} = (e_1, \ldots, e_c)$ with a regular structure, where each of the length-N blocks e_i have exactly t non-zero entries. The code has length $N \cdot c$ and dimension $N \cdot (c - 1)$; the rate of the code is therefore $(c - 1)/c$. With this formulation, c can be viewed as the compression factor of the linear map $\mathbf{e} \to H \cdot \mathbf{e}$. Therefore, we generally refer to c as the *syndrome compression factor*.

3.2 Choice of the Polynomial F

The ring-LPN assumption (and more generally, the module-LPN assumption) is dependent of the choice of the underlying polynomial F. We discuss possible choices for the polynomial F, and their implications for the security of ring-LPN/module-LPN over the corresponding ring R.

Irreducible $F(X)$. The most conservative instantiation is when $F(X)$ is irreducible over $\mathbb{Z}_p$, and so R_p is a field. In this setting, no attacks are known that perform significantly better than for standard LPN.

Reducible $F(X)$. We also consider when $F(X)$ is reducible over $\mathbb{Z}_p$, and splits into several distinct factors. Here we have a few different instantiations.

Cyclotomic $F(X)$. Let $F(X)$ be the m-th cyclotomic polynomial of degree $N = \phi(m)$. Then, $F(X)$ splits modulo p into N/d distinct factors f_i, where each f_i is of degree d, and d is the smallest integer satisfying $p^d = 1 \bmod m$. We are particularly interested in the following cases.

- *Two-power N.* Let N be a power of two and p a large prime such that $p = 1 \bmod (2N)$ (here, $m = 2N$). Then $F(X)$ splits completely into N linear factors modulo p, so R_p is isomomorphic to $\mathbb{Z}_p^N$.
- $p = 2$. Here, each degree-d subring $\mathbb{Z}_p[X]/(f_i(X))$ is isomorphic to the finite field $\mathbb{F}_{2^d}$, hence $R_p \cong \mathbb{F}_{2^d}^{N/d}$.

Random factors. A more conservative option is to choose an $F(X)$ that splits completely into d distinct, *random* factors. For instance, for a large prime p we can pick (distinct) random elements $\alpha_1, \ldots, \alpha_N \leftarrow \mathbb{Z}_p$ and let

$$F(X) = \prod_{i=1}^{N} (X - \alpha_i)$$

Just as with the two-power cyclotomic case, R_p is isomorphic to $\mathbb{Z}_p^N$. Now, however, the problem may be harder since we are avoiding the structure given by roots of unity. On the other hand, the isomorphism is more expensive to compute as we can no longer use the FFT, and polynomial interpolation algorithms cost $O(N \log^2 N)$ instead of $O(N \log N)$.

4 PCGs for OLE and Authenticated Triples

In this section, we construct PCGs for OLE and authenticated multiplication triples, based on the R^c-LPN assumption. The constructions can achieve an arbitrary (a priori bounded) polynomial stretch, that is, the seed size scales logarithmically with the output length.

Construction G_{OLE}

PARAMETERS: Security parameter 1^λ, noise weight t, compression factor c, modulus p, and the ring $R = \mathbb{Z}[X]/(F(X))$, where $F(X)$ has degree N.
An FSS scheme (SPFSS.Gen, SPFSS.FullEval) for sums of t^2 point functions, with domain $[0..2N-1)$ and range $\mathbb{Z}_p$.
PUBLIC INPUT: random polynomials $a_1, \ldots, a_{c-1} \in R_p$, used for R^c-LPN
CORRELATION: After expansion, outputs $(x_0, z_0) \in R_p^2$ and $(x_1, z_1) \in R_p^2$, where $z_0 + z_1 = x_0 \cdot x_1$.

Gen: On input 1^λ:

1. For $\sigma \in \{0,1\}$ and $i \in [0..c)$, sample random vectors $A_\sigma^i \leftarrow [0..N)^t$ and $\mathbf{b}_\sigma^i \leftarrow \mathbb{Z}_p^t$.
2. For each $i, j \in [0..c)$, sample FSS keys $(K_0^{i,j}, K_1^{i,j}) \xleftarrow{\$} \mathsf{SPFSS.Gen}(1^\lambda, A_0^i \boxplus A_1^j, \mathbf{b}_0^i \otimes \mathbf{b}_1^j)$.
3. Let $\mathsf{k}_\sigma = \big((K_\sigma^{i,j})_{i,j \in [0..c)}, (A_\sigma^i, \mathbf{b}_\sigma^i)_{i \in [0..c)}\big)$.
4. Output $(\mathsf{k}_0, \mathsf{k}_1)$.

Expand: On input $(\sigma, \mathsf{k}_\sigma)$:

1. Parse k_σ as $\big((K_\sigma^{i,j})_{i,j \in [0..c)}, (A_\sigma^i, \mathbf{b}_\sigma^i)_{i \in [0..c)}\big)$.
2. Define (over $\mathbb{Z}_p$) the degree $< N$ polynomials, for $i \in [0..c)$

$$e_\sigma^i(X) = \sum_{j \in [0..t)} \mathbf{b}_\sigma^i[j] \cdot X^{A_\sigma^i[j]}$$

3. Compute $x_\sigma = \langle \mathbf{a}, \mathbf{e}_\sigma \rangle \mod F(X)$, where $\mathbf{a} = (1, a_1, \ldots, a_{c-1})$, $\mathbf{e}_\sigma = (e_\sigma^0, \ldots, e_\sigma^{c-1})$.
4. For $i, j \in [0..c)$, compute $u_{\sigma, i+cj} \leftarrow \mathsf{SPFSS.FullEval}(\sigma, K_\sigma^{i,j})$ and view this as a degree $< 2N$ polynomial, defining the length-c^2 vector $\mathbf{u}_\sigma$
5. Compute $z_\sigma = \langle \mathbf{a} \otimes \mathbf{a}, \mathbf{u}_\sigma \rangle \mod F(X)$.
6. Output (x_σ, z_σ)

Fig. 1. PCG for OLE over the ring R_p, based on ring-LPN

4.1 PCG for OLE over R_p

We build a PCG for producing a single OLE over the ring R_p. When R_p splits appropriately, as described in Sect. 3, this can be locally transformed into a PCG for a large batch of OLEs or authenticated triples over a finite field $\mathbb{F}_{p^d}$ or $\mathbb{F}_p$. The OLE correlation over R_p outputs a single sample from the distribution

$$\left\{ (x_0, z_0), (x_1, z_1) \,\Big|\, x_0, x_1, z_0 \xleftarrow{\$} R_p, z_1 = x_0 \cdot x_1 - z_0 \right\}$$

This is equivalent to a simple bilinear correlation for multiplication in R_p.

Below is an informal presentation of the construction, which is described formally in Fig. 1.

The high-level idea is to first give each of the two parties a random vector $\mathbf{e}_0$ or $\mathbf{e}_1 \in R_p^c$, consisting of sparse polynomials, together with a random, additive secret sharing of the tensor product $\mathbf{e}_0 \otimes \mathbf{e}_1$ over R_p.

We view e_0, e_1 as R^c-LPN error vectors (whose first entry is implicitly the R^c-LPN secret), which will be expanded to produce outputs $x_\sigma = \langle a, e_\sigma \rangle$ by each party P_σ for a random, public $a = (1, \hat{a})$. This defines two R^c-LPN instances with independent secrets but the same a value, which are pseudorandom by a standard reduction to R^c-LPN with a single sample. To obtain shares of $x_0 \cdot x_1$, observe that when a is fixed, this is a degree 2 function in (e_0, e_1), so can be computed locally by the parties given their shares of $e_0 \otimes e_1$.

The only part that remains, then, is to distribute shares of this tensor product. Recall that each entry of e_σ is a polynomial of degree less than N with at most t non-zero coordinates. We write these coefficients as a set of indices $A \in [0..N)^t$ and corresponding non-zero values $b \in \mathbb{Z}_p^t$. Taking two such sparse polynomials (A, b) and (A', b'), notice that the product of the two polynomials is given by

$$\left(\sum_{i \in [0..t)} b[i] \cdot X^{A[i]} \right) \cdot \left(\sum_{j \in [0..t)} b'[j] \cdot X^{A'[j]} \right) = \sum_{i,j \in [0..t)} b[i] \cdot b'[j] \cdot X^{A[i]+A'[j]}$$

We can therefore express the coefficient vector of the product as a *sum of t^2 point functions*, where the (i, j)-th point function evaluates to $b[i] \cdot b'[j]$ at input $A[i] + A'[j]$, and zero elsewhere. This means the parties can distribute this product using a function secret sharing scheme SPFSS for sums of point functions. Each SPFSS takes a set of t^2 points and associated vector of values, and produces two keys that represent shares of the underlying sum of point functions. If each party locally evaluates its key at every point in the domain, then it obtains a pseudorandom secret-sharing of the entire sparse polynomial.

There are c^2 polynomials in the tensor product, so overall we need c^2 instances of SPFSS, where each SPFSS uses t^2 point functions. Instantiating this naively using t^2 distributed point functions, we get a seed size of $\tilde{O}(\lambda(ct)^2 \log N)$ bits. Note that to achieve exponential security against the best known attacks on R^c-LPN, it is enough to choose $ct = O(\lambda)$. By increasing N, we can therefore obtain an arbitrary polynomial stretch for the PCG, where the stretch is defined as the ratio of its output length to the seed size.

More concretely, we have the following theorem. For a proof we refer to the full version.

Theorem 5. *Suppose that SPFSS is a secure FSS scheme, and the R^c-LPN$_{p,1,t}$ assumption (Definition 3) holds. Then the construction in Fig. 1 is a secure PCG for OLE over R_p.*

When instantiating SPFSS using DPFs from a PRG : $\{0,1\}^\lambda \to \{0,1\}^{2\lambda+2}$, we have:

- *Each party's seed has size at most $(ct)^2 \cdot ((\log N + 1) \cdot (\lambda + 2) + \lambda + \log p) + ct(\log N + \log p)$ bits.*
- *The computation of Expand can be done with at most $(4 + 2\lfloor (\log p)/\lambda \rfloor)N(ct)^2$ PRG operations, and $O(c^2 N \log N)$ operations in $\mathbb{Z}_p$.*

We remark that assuming R^c-LPN holds for *regular error distributions*, the seed size can be reduced to $(ct)^2 \cdot ((\log N - \log t + 1) \cdot (\lambda + 2) + \lambda + \log p) + ct(\log N + \log p)$ bits, and the number of PRG calls in Expand down to $(4 + 2\lfloor(\log p)/\lambda\rfloor)Nc^2t$. Furthermore, implementing SPFSS using batch codes reduces the number of PRG calls to $O(Nc^2)$.

Obtaining OLEs over $\mathbb{F}_p$. As mentioned previously, when R and p are chosen appropriately, an OLE over R_p is locally equivalent to N OLEs over $\mathbb{F}_p$ or $\mathbb{F}_{p^d}$. Hence, this PCG immediately implies PCGs over $\mathbb{F}_{p^d}$, with the same seed size and complexity.

If we want to rely on the (apparently) more conservative version of R^c-LPN, where $F(X)$ is *irreducible* in $\mathbb{Z}_p[X]$, the parties can still use our PCG over R_p to obtain OLEs over $\mathbb{Z}_p$, but this requires $O(N)$ interaction. To do this, the parties each sample random polynomials $a, b \in \mathbb{Z}_p[X]$, each of degree $< N/2$. They then use the OLE over R_p to multiply a and b, which can be done by sending N elements of $\mathbb{Z}_p$.[6] This gives shares of $c = ab$ in R_p, which equals ab over $\mathbb{Z}_p[X]$, since no overflow occurs modulo $F(X)$ (which has degree N). Each party then locally computes evaluations of its shares of a, b and c at $N/2$ fixed, distinct, non-zero points, which gives $N/2$ secret-shared products over $\mathbb{Z}_p$ (this can be done as long as $p > N/2$).

Optimizations. We now discuss a few optimizations which apply to the basic scheme.

Optimizing the MPFSS evaluation. Naively, the computational cost of the FSS full-domain evaluation is $O((ct)^2N)$ PRG operations. Using a regular error distribution, we can bring this down to $O(c^2tN)$ (see below). With batch codes [34] or randomized batch codes [48], the full evaluation cost can be brought down to $O(c^2N)$ operations. However, if the seed generation phase has to be created by a secure distributed protocol, this may introduce further complexity.

Using regular errors. Suppose two sparse polynomials $e_0, e_1 \in \mathbb{Z}_p^N$ are regular, that is $e_b = (e_{b,1}, \ldots, e_{b,t})$, where each $e_{b,j} \in \mathbb{Z}_p^{N/t}$ has weight 1, and defines a coefficient in the range $[(j-1) \cdot (N/t), j \cdot (N/t) - 1]$. Each pair $(e_{0,i}, e_{1,j})$ gives rise to an index in $[(i+j-2) \cdot (N/t), (i+j) \cdot (N/t) - 2]$, so the product of two regular error polynomials can be represented by a t^2-point SPFSS of domain size $2N/t$. This leads to a total expansion cost of $O(c^2tN)$ PRG operations.

Extension to higher degree correlations. We can naturally extend this construction from OLE over R_p to general degree-D correlations (over R_p), for any constant D, by sharing D-way products of sparse polynomials instead of just pairwise products. However, this comes at a high cost: the seed size increases to $O((ct)^D \log N\lambda)$, and the computational cost becomes $\tilde{O}((ct)^D \cdot N)$.

---

[6] This can be reduced to $N/2$, by defining a, b to be the first $N/2$ coefficients of the polynomials x_0, x_1 produced by the OLE, so that only the second half of the coefficients need to be sent in the multiplication protocol.

4.2 Authenticated Multiplication Triples

We now show how to modify the PCG for OLE to produce *authenticated multiplication triples*, which are often used in maliciously secure MPC protocols such as the BDOZ [6] and SPDZ [22,25] line of work. Note that although OLE can be used to build authenticated triples in a black-box way, doing this requires several OLEs and some interaction, for every triple. Our PCG avoids this interaction, with only a small overhead on top of the previous construction: the seeds are less than 2x larger, while the expansion phase has around twice the computational cost.

Secret-sharing with MACs. We use authenticated secret-sharing based on SPDZ MACs between n parties, where a secret-sharing of $x \in \mathbb{Z}_p$ is defined as:

$$[\![x]\!] = (\alpha_i, x_i, m_{x,i})_{i=1}^n \quad \text{such that} \quad \sum_i x_i = x, \sum_i m_{x,i} = x \cdot \sum_i \alpha_i$$

Note that the MAC key shares α_i are fixed for every shared x. The MAC shares $m_{x,i}$ are used to prevent a sharing from being opened incorrectly, via a MAC check procedure from [22]. An *authenticated multiplication triple* is a tuple of random sharings $([\![x]\!], [\![y]\!], [\![z]\!])$, where $x, y \xleftarrow{\$} \mathbb{Z}_p$ and $z = x \cdot y$. Our PCG outputs a single multiplication triple over the ring R_p, for $n = 2$ parties, together with additive shares of the MAC key $\alpha \in \mathbb{Z}_p$. When using the fully-reducible variant of ring-LPN, this is equivalent to N triples over $\mathbb{F}_{p^d}$ (where for suitably chosen p we can have $d = 1$).

PCG construction. The construction is remarkably simple. Recall that our previous construction for OLE uses FSS keys which are expanded into shares of sparse polynomials $u_{i,j} = e_i \cdot e_j \in \mathbb{Z}_p[X]$. The FSS payload was defined by some (column) vector $\mathbf{v} \in \mathbb{Z}_p^{t^2}$, which defines the t^2 values of the non-zero coefficients in $u_{i,j}$. We can modify this to produce *authenticated OLE* by extending the FSS range from $\mathbb{Z}_p$ to $\mathbb{Z}_p^2$, and letting the payload be $\mathbf{v} \cdot (1, \alpha) \in \mathbb{Z}_p^{2N \times 2}$, for a random $\alpha \in \mathbb{Z}_p$. Evaluating the FSS keys at some input k now produces shares of $(\mathbf{v}[k], \alpha \cdot \mathbf{v}[k])$. Hence, these can be used to obtain authenticated shares of $x_0 \cdot x_1$, as well as the OLE.

To extend the above to authenticated triples, the seed generation phase will now produce three sets of FSS keys. The first two sets, $(K_{x,0}^i, K_{x,1}^i)$ and $(K_{y,0}^i, K_{y,1}^i)$, are used to compress shares of the $2c$ sparse polynomials defined by $(A_0^i, \mathbf{b}_0^i)$ and $(A_1^i, \mathbf{b}_1^i)$. These have sparsity t, so can be compressed using t-point SPFSS, and are later expanded to produce shares and MAC shares for R_p elements x and y. The third set, $(K_{z,0}^i, K_{z,1}^i)$, compresses pairwise products of the previous sparse polynomials, so each of these can be defined using t^2-point SPFSS, as in the previous construction. This gives the shares and MAC shares for the product term $z = x \cdot y$. For the full protocol description we refer to the full version of this paper.

We omit the proof of the following theorem, which is very similar to that of Theorem 5. Recall that to achieve exponential security against the best known attacks on R^c-LPN, it is enough to choose $ct = O(\lambda)$, therefore choosing a larger c allows to decrease the size of t. For more details on concrete parameter choices we refer to Sect. 7.

Theorem 6. *Suppose that the R^c-LPN$_{p,1,t}$ assumption holds and given a PRG PRG : $\{0,1\}^\lambda \to \{0,1\}^{2\lambda+2}$. Then there exists a secure PCG for two-party authenticated multiplication triples over R_p with the following complexities:*

- *Each party's seed has size at most $2(2ct + (ct)^2) \cdot ((\log N + 1) \cdot (\lambda + 2) + \lambda + \log p) + \log p$ bits.*
- *The computation of* Expand *can be done with at most $(8 + 4\lfloor(\log p)/\lambda\rfloor) N(2ct + (ct)^2)$ PRG operations, and $O(c^2 N \log N)$ operations in $\mathbb{Z}_p$.*

5   Distributed Setup Protocols

Up to this point, exposition has focused on how to obtain and use pseudorandom correlation generators (PCG), abstracted in an idealized model where the short PCG seeds are sampled by a third-party trusted dealer. In this section, we address solutions for parties to *jointly* generate the desired PCG correlations, via secure distributed setup protocols.

In Sect. 5.1, we show how to securely realize (against a semi-honest adversary) the randomized functionality $\mathcal{F}_{\mathsf{OLE\text{-}Setup}}$ that executes the seed generation for our PCG construction PCG$_{\mathsf{OLE}}$ constructed in Sect. 4, and outputs the corresponding PCG seeds to each party. This can in turn be used to realize a functionality for the secure generation of OLE correlations, by having the parties simply expand their received PCG seeds locally. Our protocol to implement $\mathcal{F}_{\mathsf{OLE\text{-}Setup}}$ makes black-box use of sub-protocols for simple secure computations over $\mathbb{Z}_p$ and $\{0,1\}^\ell$, and for secure computation of DPF key generation where the position and payload values are held secret shared across the two parties. In particular, the latter can be implemented with the efficient DPF key generation protocol of Doerner and shelat [27].

In the full version, for the malicious case we present a protocol securely realizing the randomized functionality $\mathcal{F}_{\mathsf{mal\text{-}OLE}}$, in which a corrupt adversary can choose his output $(x_\sigma, z_\sigma) \in R_p^2$ and the honest party receives a random consistent value $(x_{1-\sigma}, z_{1-\sigma})$, i.e. for which $z_0 + z_1 = x_0 \cdot x_1$ (or the parties receive a random sample from the correlation given honest behavior; see the full version for details). As discussed in [11], such a protocol can *directly* serve as a substitute for ideal OLE correlations in a wide range of higher-level applications, already proven to remain secure given this functionality. Further, we give a protocol realizing an analogous functionality for *authenticated multiplication triples* in the malicious model at little extra cost. Achieving security in the malicious setting poses further challenges, including managing potential leakage on the secret noise positions from the [27] protocol in the face of malicious behavior, while simultaneously enforcing consistency.

For a detailed listing of efficiency of our protocols we refer to the full version. For an overview of concrete efficiency we refer to Table 2 in Sect. 7.

5.1   Semi-honest Distributed Setup

We present a protocol for securely executing the seed-generation functionality respective to our PCG construction $\mathsf{PCG}_{\mathsf{OLE}}$ from Sect. 4. For a description of the functionality $\mathcal{F}_{\mathsf{OLE\text{-}Setup}}$ we refer to the full version.

Recall that in the $\mathsf{PCG}_{\mathsf{OLE}}.\mathsf{Gen}$ procedure (see Fig. 1), each party receives a succinct description $(A_\sigma^i, \mathbf{b}_\sigma^i)_{i \in [0..c)}$ of t-sparse "noise vectors" $e_\sigma^0, \ldots, e_\sigma^{c-1}$ each of length N, as well as a collection of $(ct)^2$ distributed point function (DPF) keys as a compact representation of all possible products $e_0^i \cdot e_1^j$. A secure distributed realization of this procedure can then be achieved given access to two secure sub-protocols:

- Secure computation of DPF key generation for a "path" α and "payload" β held secret shared across the parties. Concretely, this can be instantiated by the DPF-generation protocol of Doerner and shelat [27], given *bitwise* additive shares of the path $\alpha \in \mathbb{Z}_{2N}$ and $\mathbb{Z}_p$-additive shares of the nonzero payload β. For the functionality $\mathcal{F}_{\mathsf{DPF}}$ and a high-level description of the protocol by Doerner and shelat [27], we refer to the full version of this paper.
- Generic secure computation of simple computations over $\mathbb{Z}_2$ or $\mathbb{Z}_p$, used to securely compute secret shares of the products $(\mathbf{b}_0^i[k] \cdot \mathbf{b}_1^j[l])$ over $\mathbb{Z}_p$, and shares of the $\mathbb{Z}_p$-sums $(A_0^i[k] + A_1^j[l]) \in [0..2N-1)$. Note that the latter computation is nontrivial, as the parties must hold *bitwise* additive shares of $(A_0^i[k] + A_1^j[l])$ for the [27] protocol, but the sum itself is with respect to $\mathbb{Z}_N$. This "grade school addition" over bits can be implemented via a binary circuit for integer addition with $\log N$ AND gates, similar to previous (e.g., garbled circuit based [41]) protocols. For more details on the functionality $\mathcal{F}_{\mathsf{2\text{-}PC}}$, an implementation of $\mathcal{F}_{\mathsf{2\text{-}PC}}$ and efficiency considerations we refer to the full version.

The protocol Π_{OLE} for securely realizing $\mathcal{F}_{\mathsf{OLE\text{-}Setup}}$ in the $(\mathcal{F}_{\mathsf{2\text{-}PC}}, \mathcal{F}_{\mathsf{DPF}})$-hybrid model is given in Fig. 2.

Theorem 7. *Assuming hardness of $R^c\text{-}\mathsf{LPN}_{p,1,t}$, the protocol $\Pi_{\mathsf{OLE\text{-}Setup}}$ (Fig. 2) securely realizes the OLE generation functionality $\mathcal{F}_{\mathsf{OLE\text{-}Setup}}$ with security against semi-honest adversaries in the $(\mathcal{F}_{\mathsf{2\text{-}PC}}, \mathcal{F}_{\mathsf{DPF}})$-hybrid model.*

Proof. Observe that the protocol $\Pi_{\mathsf{OLE\text{-}Setup}}$ is directly a secure evaluation of the computation steps of $\mathcal{F}_{\mathsf{OLE\text{-}Setup}}$ (see description of $\mathsf{PCG}_{\mathsf{OLE}}.\mathsf{Gen}$ as given in Fig. 1 within Sect. 4), with the exception that the FSS key generation

---

Protocol $\Pi_{\text{OLE-Setup}}$

PARAMETERS: Security parameter 1^λ, natural number $N = 2^k$, prime p, distributed point function $\text{DPF} = (\text{DPF.Gen}, \text{DPF.Eval})$ with domain $[0..2N)$ and range $\mathbb{Z}_p$.

We assume access to a functionality $\mathcal{F}_{\text{2-PC}}$ as follows: $\textbf{Input}(P_\sigma, x)$ receives a value $x \in \{0,1\}^\ell$ or $x \in \mathbb{Z}_p$ from party P_σ and stores an identifier $[\![x]\!]$, $\textbf{BitAdd}([\![x]\!]_2, [\![y]\!]_2)$ (for $x, y \in \{0,1\}^\ell$) computes $z = x + y \in \{0,1\}^{\ell+1}$ via arithmetic addition and stores $[\![z]\!]_2$, and $\textbf{Mult}([\![x]\!]_p, [\![y]\!]_p)$ (for $x, y \in \mathbb{Z}_p$) computes $z = x \cdot y \mod p$ and stores $[\![z]\!]_p$.

PROTOCOL:

1. For $\sigma \in \{0,1\}, i \in [0..c)$, party P_σ samples random vectors $A_\sigma^i \leftarrow [0..N)^t$ (where each entry of A_σ^i is viewed as a length-$\log N$ bit-string) and $\mathbf{b}_\sigma^i \leftarrow \mathbb{Z}_p^t$. Note that as outlined in Figure 1, each pair $A_\sigma^i, \mathbf{b}_\sigma^i$ defines a t-sparse polynomial $e_\sigma^i \in R_p$.
2. For $\sigma \in \{0,1\}, i \in [0..c)$ and $k \in [0..t)$:
   //P_σ inputs the k-th non-zero position and corresponding payload of e_σ^i.

   $$[\![A_\sigma^i[k]]\!]_2 \leftarrow \textbf{Input}(P_\sigma, A_\sigma^i[k]) \text{ and } [\![\mathbf{b}_\sigma^i[k]]\!]_p \leftarrow \textbf{Input}(P_\sigma, \mathbf{b}_\sigma^i[k])$$

3. For every $i, j \in [0..c)$ and $k, l \in [0..t)$ (in parallel) the parties do the following:
   (a) $[\![\alpha_{k,l}^{i,j}]\!]_2 \leftarrow \textbf{BitAdd}([\![A_0^i[k]]\!]_2, [\![A_1^j[l]]\!]_2)$ //Compute the $k + tl$-th position of $e_0^i \cdot e_1^j$.
   (b) $[\![\beta_{k,l}^{i,j}]\!]_p \leftarrow \textbf{Mult}([\![\mathbf{b}_0^i[k]]\!]_p, [\![\mathbf{b}_1^j[l]]\!]_p)$ //Compute the $k + tl$-th payload of $e_0^i \cdot e_1^j$.
   (c) For each $i, j \in [0..c)$ and $k, l \in [0..t)$, call $\mathcal{F}_{\text{DPF}}$ with domain size $[0..2N)$ on input $[\![\alpha_{k,l}^{i,j}]\!]_2$ and $[\![\beta_{k,l}^{i,j}]\!]_p$, and let $K_{\sigma,k,l}^{i,j}$ denote the output to party P_σ.
      //Compute compressed additive secret shares of $e_0^i \cdot e_1^j$.
4. Party P_σ outputs $\mathsf{k}_\sigma = \left((K_{\sigma,k,l}^{i,j})_{i,j \in [0..c), k,l \in [0..t)}, (A_\sigma^i, \mathbf{b}_\sigma^i)_{i \in [0..c)} \right)$.

Fig. 2. Distributed setup of OLE seeds in $(\mathcal{F}_{\text{2-PC}}, \mathcal{F}_{\text{DPF}})$-hybrid model, against semi-honest adversaries. $[\![x]\!]_2, [\![x]\!]_p$ denote additive shares of bit-strings or $\mathbb{Z}_p$ elements.

for the sum of point functions $\text{SPFSS.Gen}(1^\lambda, A_0^i \boxplus A_1^j, \mathbf{b}_0^i \otimes \mathbf{b}_1^j)$ is instantiated directly by the DPF key generation for every individual nonzero component. As this is a valid instantiation of SPFSS, the claim holds.

6 Extensions and Applications

In this section we extend our PCG for OLE in several directions. First, we build PCGs for inner product correlations from OLE over R_p, with the advantage that we do not need to rely on the full reducibility of $F(X)$, and can also obtain correlations over $\mathbb{F}_2$. Secondly, we present a method for building PCGs for general bilinear correlations, such as matrix multiplication, in a black-box way from our previous PCG. Finally, we show that all of these PCGs for degree two correlations can be extended in a natural way to the multi-party setting.

6.1 Bilinear Correlations

The class of bilinear correlations we consider is as follows.

Definition 8 (Simple Bilinear Correlation). *Let* $\mathbb{G}_1, \mathbb{G}_2, \mathbb{G}_T$ *be Abelian groups and* $e \colon \mathbb{G}_1 \times \mathbb{G}_2 \to \mathbb{G}_T$ *be a bilinear map. We define the simple bilinear correlation for* e *by the distribution* $\mathcal{C}_e$ *over* $(\mathbb{G}_1 \times \mathbb{G}_T) \times (\mathbb{G}_2 \times \mathbb{G}_T)$ *of the form*

$$\mathcal{C}_e = \{((r_0, s_0), (r_1, s_1)) \mid r_0 \leftarrow \mathbb{G}_1, r_1 \leftarrow \mathbb{G}_2, s_0 \leftarrow \mathbb{G}_T, s_1 = e(r_0, r_1) - s_0\}.$$

We denote by $\mathcal{C}_e^n$ *the correlation that outputs* n *independent samples from* $\mathcal{C}_e$.

This covers several common correlations like OT and OLE, for example, OLE over a ring R can be obtained with $\mathbb{G}_1 = \mathbb{G}_2 = \mathbb{G}_T = (R, +)$ and $e(x, y) = x \cdot y$. Also, note that two independent bilinear correlations can be locally converted to produce an additively secret-shared instance of the correlation—for example, two OLEs are locally equivalent to one multiplication triple.

6.2 Inner Product Correlations

An inner product correlation is a simple bilinear correlation with the inner product map over $\mathbb{F}_p$. These can be used to compute inner products in an MPC online phase, in a similar way to using multiplication triples. Inner products are common in tasks involving linear algebra, like privately evaluating or training machine learning models such as SVMs and neural networks, and a single inner product can also be used to measure the similarity between two input vectors.

We remark that given n random OLEs in $\mathbb{F}_p$, it is easy to locally convert these into an length-n inner product correlation, so we can build a PCG for inner products of any length using a PCG for OLE. However, the constructions in this section *do not* rely on the fully-reducible ring-LPN assumption that is needed for OLE in $\mathbb{F}_p$; instead, we use the ring-OLE construction from Fig. 1 over more conservative rings, which do not split completely into linear factors.

For the proof of the following lemma, we refer to our full version.

Lemma 9. *Let* $R_p = \mathbb{Z}_p[X]/(F(X))$, *where* $F(X)$ *is a degree-N polynomial with non-zero constant coefficient. Then, a single OLE over* R_p *can be locally converted into an inner product correlation over* $\mathbb{F}_p^N$.

Note that, for the special case of $F(X) = X^n + 1$, the vector $M_a[0]$ can be computed as $(a_0, -a_{n-1}, \dots, -a_1)$, without any modular reductions.

Corollary 10 (Large inner product from irreducible ring-LPN). *Suppose the* R-$\mathsf{LPN}_{p,1,t}$ *assumption holds for* $R = \mathbb{Z}_p[X]/(F(X))$, *where* $F(X)$ *is degree N and irreducible over* $\mathbb{Z}_p$. *Then there is a PCG for the length-N inner product correlation, where the seeds have size* $O(\lambda t^2 \log N)$ *bits, and the computational complexity of the* Expand *operation is* $\tilde{O}(N)$ *operations in* $\mathbb{Z}_p$, *plus* $O(t^2 N)$ *PRG operations.*

Corollary 11 (Small inner products from reducible ring-LPN). *Suppose the R-LPN$_{p,1,t}$ assumption holds for $R = \mathbb{Z}_p[X]/(F(X))$, where $F(X)$ is degree N and splits into N/d distinct factors of degree d. Then there is a PCG for producing N/d instances of length-d inner product correlations, with the same seed size and complexity as above.*

The latter construction has two benefits over naively using OLE over $\mathbb{F}_p$ to generate an inner product. Firstly, OLE in $\mathbb{F}_p$ requires that R splits fully into *linear factors*, whereas for inner products the factors can be degree-d (and irreducible), which is a much more conservative assumption; in particular, the dimension-reduction attack we consider in the full version is less effective. Secondly, we can also use this to generate inner products over small fields such as $\mathbb{F}_2$, whereas we cannot efficiently obtain OLEs over $\mathbb{F}_2$ with our present constructions.

6.3 Bilinear Correlations from Programmable PCG for OLE

We can build a PCG to create a large batch of samples from *any* simple bilinear correlation, using the PCG for OLE from Sect. 4. To do this, we exploit the fact that this PCG is *programmable*, which, roughly speaking, means that one party can "reuse" its input a or b in several instances of the PCG, while maintaining security. Boyle et al. [11] previously used this property to construct multi-party PCGs from several instances of programmable two-party PCGs; unlike their work, we exploit the property for a different purpose in the two-party setting.

In the full version, we recall the definition of programmability, and show that our PCG for OLE satisfies this definition.

Below we describe the main result, and some applications.

Decomposition of bilinear maps. Let $f : \mathbb{G}_1 \times \mathbb{G}_2 \to \mathbb{G}_T$ and $g : \mathbb{G}_1^u \times \mathbb{G}_2^v \to \mathbb{G}_T^w$ be bilinear maps. We will consider ways of computing g that are restricted to a fixed number of calls to f on the components of the inputs to g, followed by linear combinations in $\mathbb{G}_T$ of the results of the f evaluations.

Definition 12 (Simple f-decomposition). *Let $\mathbb{G}_1, \mathbb{G}_2, \mathbb{G}_T$ be additive abelian groups, viewed as $\mathbb{Z}$-modules. Let $f : \mathbb{G}_1 \times \mathbb{G}_2 \to \mathbb{G}_T$ and $g : \mathbb{G}_1^u \times \mathbb{G}_2^v \to \mathbb{G}_T^w$ be non-degenerate bilinear maps. We say that g has a simple f-decomposition if there exist $\gamma \in \mathbb{N}$, $W \in \mathbb{Z}^{w \times \gamma}$ and $\alpha_i \in [u], \beta_i \in [v]$, for $i \in [\gamma]$, such that for all $x = (x_1, \ldots, x_u) \in \mathbb{G}_1^u$ and $y = (y_1, \ldots, y_v) \in \mathbb{G}_2^v$, it holds that*

$$g(x,y) = W \cdot \begin{pmatrix} f(x_{\alpha_1}, y_{\beta_1}) \\ \vdots \\ f(x_{\alpha_\gamma}, y_{\beta_\gamma}) \end{pmatrix}$$

We say that the f-complexity of this decomposition of g is given by $n_f(g) := \gamma$.

Note that if $\mathbb{G}_1, \mathbb{G}_2, \mathbb{G}_T$ are all a (commutative) ring R and f is multiplication in R, then any g has a simple f-decomposition of complexity $u \cdot v$. However, it can still be useful to find a different f that achieves lower complexity.

We now show that any map g with a simple f-decomposition can be used to construct a PCG for the simple bilinear correlation $\mathcal{C}_g$, given a programmable PCG for $\mathcal{C}_f$.

For the construction and its security proof we refer to the full version. There, we further show that the new PCG also satisfies the programmability property.

Theorem 13. *Let f and g be bilinear maps as above, and suppose that g has a simple f-decomposition with f-complexity $n_f(g)$. Furthermore, let $\mathsf{PCG}_f = (\mathsf{PCG}_f.\mathsf{Gen}, \mathsf{PCG}_f.\mathsf{Expand})$ be a programmable PCG for $\mathcal{C}_f^n$. Then there exists a PCG $\mathsf{PCG}_g = (\mathsf{PCG}_g.\mathsf{Gen}, \mathsf{PCG}_g.\mathsf{Expand})$ for $\mathcal{C}_g^n$, with the following properties:*

- *$\mathsf{PCG}_g.\mathsf{Gen}$ runs $n_f(g)$ executions of $\mathsf{PCG}_f.\mathsf{Gen}$, and its key sizes are $n_f(g)$ times that of PCG_f.*
- *$\mathsf{PCG}_g.\mathsf{Expand}$ runs $n_f(g)$ executions of $\mathsf{PCG}_f.\mathsf{Expand}$, and n evaluations of the linear map W from the f-decomposition of g.*

6.4   Applications

In the following we will give a brief overview of applications of the general bilinear construction. For a more detailed discussion we refer to the full version.

Matrix multiplication triples. Multiplication of $n_1 \times n_2$ and $n_2 \times n_3$ matrices is easily decomposed as a sequence of $n_1 \cdot n_3$ inner products of length n_2, where each inner product is taken from a consecutive portion of the two inputs. Therefore, the matrix multiplication map g has a linear f-decomposition with f-complexity $n_1 \cdot n_3$.

This results in a matrix multiplication triple with seed size around $n_1 \cdot n_3$ times larger than the PCG seed for OLE, which will likely be practical for small-to-medium matrices. Note that using a programmable PCG for OLE directly to build matrix multiplications would require $n_1 \cdot n_2 \cdot n_3$ instances of the base PCG, giving a much worse expansion factor.

Circuit-dependent MPC preprocessing. Circuit-dependent preprocessing is a variation on the standard multiplication triples technique, which is based on Beaver's circuit randomization technique [4] and extended in more recent works [5,23]. The idea is to preprocess multiplications in a way that depends on the structure of the circuit, and leads to an online phase that requires just *one opening per multiplication gate*, instead of two when using multiplication triples.

With the PCG for general bilinear correlations, we can generate circuit-dependent preprocessing for a large batch of identical circuits. This can be useful, for instance, when executing the same function many times on different inputs, or when a larger computation contains many small, repeated instances of a particular sub-circuit. For more details we refer to the full version.

Multi-party PCGs for bilinear correlations. In [11] [Theorem 41], Boyle et al. showed that any two-party, programmable PCG for a simple bilinear correlation can be used to build a multi-party PCG for an additively secret-shared version of the same correlation.

Using that the PCG for bilinear correlations from Theorem 13 is programmable and the results of the previous section, we obtain N-party PCGs for (unauthenticated) multiplication triples, matrix triples and circuit-dependent preprocessing over $\mathbb{Z}_p$ based on ring-LPN, for any polynomial number of parties N. Each party's seed contains $2(N-1)$ seeds of the underlying two-party PCG, plus $N-1$ seeds for a PRG. The expansion procedure of the PCG consists of expanding the $2(N-1)$ PCG seeds, as well as the PRG seeds.

7   Efficiency Analysis

In the full version, we provide a detailed security analysis of the flavors of the R-LPN assumption which we use. In this section, based on our security analysis, we discuss concrete choices of parameters for which the corresponding ring-LPN problems are secure against the attacks we considered, and analyse the concrete efficiency of our PCGs. In all instances, we assume the noise vectors to have a regular structure (as was done e.g. in [9–11]), since this does not introduce any known weakness, but significantly increases the efficiency of Expand. For large fields, we focus on the statistical decoding and information set decoding (ISD) families of attacks (the latter being always at least as efficient as the Gaussian elimination attack), combined with the speedup obtained with the DOOM attack against quasi-cyclic codes. For statistical decoding, we compute our estimations with a conservative lower bound of $n \cdot (cN/(N-1))^w$ arithmetic operations. For ISD, we used LEDA's public domain software implementation of an automated procedure for the design of tight and optimal sets of parameters, developed in the context of the LEDA candidate [3] for the NIST post-quantum competition[7]. This software takes as input the parameters (dimension, number of sample, number of noisy coordinates, block-size of the quasi-cyclic matrices) of the instance, and outputs the complexity of attacking the instance with several ISD variants.

Theoretical Analysis for Reducible Ring-LPN. We consider a field $\mathbb{F} = \mathbb{Z}_p$ of size $|\mathbb{F}| \approx 2^{128}$. As in our applications, we focus on the case where there is a factor f_i of degree $n = N/k$, for some k, which has sparsity 1, such as when N is a power of two and $F(X) = X^N + 1$ splits completely into N linear factors modulo p. From the analysis in the full version, we can reduce an instance modulo a 1-sparse factor f_i of degree $n = 2^i$, reducing the expected number of noisy coordinates to

$$w_i = w - cn + (c(n-1) + w) \cdot \left(1 - \frac{1}{n}\right)^{w/c-1},$$

---

[7] https://github.com/LEDAcrypt/LEDAtools.

the dimension to $n_i = (c-1) \cdot 2^i$, and the number of samples to $q_i = c \cdot 2^i$. In our experiments, we found that the optimal behavior for the adversary was always to pick the smallest i such that the new weight w_i of the noise is not higher than the dimension n_i (such that the reduced instance is still uniquely decodable and is not statistically close to random). For security parameter $\lambda = 80$ (resp. $\lambda = 128$), the smallest such i is $i = 6$ (resp. $i = 7$). In Table 1, we provide various choices of parameters (λ, N, c, w) such that the best attack on any reduced instance requires at least 2^λ multiplications over a field $\mathbb{F}$ of size $|\mathbb{F}| \approx 2^{128}$. The table also presents the concrete seed sizes and computational requirements for our PCG for OLE, based on Theorem 5 (and with optimizations due to the regular error distribution).

Our conservative estimates of the running time of the statistical decoding attack have better asymptotic complexity than the ISD attacks, according to our analysis in the full version; and indeed, we found statistical decoding to always give the best available attack. Given that statistical decoding should not generally perform better than ISD [26], this suggests that our estimation of the cost of statistical decoding might be overly conservative, meaning that our parameters are slightly pessimistic.

Estimated Runtimes for OLE and Triple Generation. We estimate the computational cost of expanding a PCG seed to produce $N = 2^{20}$ OLEs over $\mathbb{Z}_p$, using our PCG over a ring R_p which splits fully into linear factors. The main costs in the expansion step are the DPF full-domain evaluations, and polynomial operations over R_p. We separately benchmarked these using the DPF code from [10], and NFLLib [1] for polynomial arithmetic with a 124-bit modulus p, which is a product of two 62-bit primes (such that R_p splits completely into linear factors, by the CRT). We also estimated the communication complexity required to distribute the PCG seeds with active security, based on the analysis provided in the full version.

The results are in Table 2 for OLE, and Table 3 for authenticated triples. Note that compared with Table 1, the noise weight w has been rounded so it is divisible by c, so that $t = w/c$ is an integer. We see that as the module-LPN compression parameter c increases, the polynomial arithmetic gets more expensive, while the DPF cost first decreases at $c = 4$, and then goes back up at $c = 8$. This is because the DPF complexity scales with $c^2 t$, so doubling c only reduces its cost if t can be reduced by more than a factor of 4. The best choice for speed seems to be $c = 4$, where we are able to silently expand over 100 thousand OLEs per second at the 128-bit security level, with a seed size of around 1 MB. When generating authenticated triples instead of OLEs, the seed size and runtimes increase by roughly a factor of two, while the setup communication cost is only slightly larger.

Table 1. Concrete parameters and seed size (per party, counted as equivalent number of field elements) for our PCG for OLE over $R_p = \mathbb{Z}_p[X]/F(X)$, where $p = 1 \bmod 2N$, $\log p \approx 128$ and $F = X^N + 1$ is the $2N$-th cyclotomic polynomial which fully splits over $\mathbb{Z}_p$, for various λ, N, syndrome compression factor c, and number of noisy coordinates w. 'Stretch', computed as $2N/(\text{seed size})$, is the ratio between storing a full random OLE (i.e., $2N$ field elements) and the smaller PCG seed. Parameters are chosen such that the best-known distinguishing attacks, over any instance reduced modulo a sparse factor of F, require T field multiplications over $\mathbb{Z}_p$ to have distinguishing advantage $T/2^\lambda$. This setting is useful for generating batches of N OLE correlations or authenticated triples over $\mathbb{Z}_p$, or small inner-product correlations (Sect. 6.2). When using a smaller field $\mathbb{F}'$, the bit-length of the seed stays roughly the same but increases by a factor of $\approx \log_2 |\mathbb{F}|/\log_2 |\mathbb{F}'|$ in field elements, the stretch decreases by the same factor, (e.g. about a factor 2 when using $\mathbb{F}$ with $\log_2 |\mathbb{F}'| \approx 64$), and all other entries remain the same.

λ	N	c	w	(i, w_i)	Seed size	Stretch	$\# R$-mults	#PRG calls
80	2^{20}	2	97	$(6, 74)$	$2^{17.4}$	12	4	$2^{29.6}$
80	2^{20}	4	40	$(6, 37)$	$2^{15.0}$	65	16	$2^{29.3}$
80	2^{20}	8	26	$(6, 25)$	$2^{13.9}$	139	64	$2^{29.7}$
128	2^{20}	2	152	$(7, 121)$	$2^{18.6}$	5	4	$2^{30.2}$
128	2^{20}	4	64	$(7, 60)$	$2^{16.3}$	27	16	$2^{30.0}$
128	2^{20}	8	41	$(7, 40)$	$2^{15.1}$	59	64	$2^{30.4}$
80	2^{25}	2	97	$(6, 74)$	$2^{17.7}$	306	4	$2^{34.6}$
80	2^{25}	4	40	$(6, 37)$	$2^{15.3}$	1654	16	$2^{34.3}$
80	2^{25}	8	26	$(6, 25)$	$2^{14.2}$	3623	64	$2^{34.7}$
128	2^{25}	2	152	$(7, 121)$	$2^{19.0}$	130	4	$2^{35.2}$
128	2^{25}	4	64	$(7, 60)$	$2^{16.6}$	673	16	$2^{35.0}$
128	2^{25}	8	41	$(7, 40)$	$2^{15.4}$	1513	64	$2^{35.4}$

Table 2. Estimated costs for our PCG for producing $N = 2^{20}$ OLEs in $\mathbb{Z}_p$, with $\log p \approx 124$. Setup comm. measures the per-party communication required to setup the PCG seeds with active security (ignoring costs for correlated randomness that can come from a previous PCG).

λ	c	w	Seed size (MB)	Setup comm. (MB)	Runtimes for **Expand** (s)		
					R-mult (s)	DPF eval. (s)	Total (s)
80	2	96	2.69	7.43	0.4	9.8	10.2
80	4	40	0.52	1.41	1.4	7.5	8.9
80	8	32	0.35	0.94	5.3	9.3	14.6
128	2	152	6.37	17.77	0.4	12.6	13.0
128	4	64	1.26	3.45	1.4	8.6	10.0
128	8	40	0.55	1.47	5.3	14.4	19.7

Table 3. Estimated costs for our PCG for producing $N = 2^{20}$ authenticated triples in $\mathbb{Z}_p$, with $\log p \approx 124$. Setup comm. measures the per-party communication required to setup the PCG seeds with active security (ignoring costs for correlated randomness that can come from a previous PCG).

λ	c	w	Seed size (MB)	Setup comm. (MB)	Runtimes for Expand (s)		
					R-mult (s)	DPF eval. (s)	Total (s)
80	2	96	5.49	9.07	0.8	19.6	20.4
80	4	40	1.09	1.74	2.8	15.0	17.8
80	8	32	0.74	1.16	10.6	18.6	29.2
128	2	152	12.91	21.73	0.8	25.2	26.0
128	4	64	2.60	4.22	2.8	17.2	20.0
128	8	40	1.14	1.80	10.6	28.8	39.4

Acknowledgements. We would like to thank Vadim Lyubashevsky, Chris Peikert, Ronny Roth and Jean-Pierre Tillich for helpful discussions and pointers.

E. Boyle, N. Gilboa, and Y. Ishai, and L. Kohl supported by ERC Project NTSC (742754). E. Boyle additionally supported by ISF grant 1861/16 and AFOSR Award FA9550-17-1-0069. G. Couteau supported by ERC Project PREP-CRYPTO (724307). N. Gilboa additionally supported by ISF grant 1638/15, ERC grant 876110, and a grant by the BGU Cyber Center. Y. Ishai additionally supported by NSF-BSF grant 2015782, BSF grant 2018393, and a grant from the Ministry of Science and Technology, Israel and Department of Science and Technology, Government of India. Work of L. Kohl was done in part while at Karlsruhe Institute of Technology, supported by ERC Project PREP-CRYPTO (724307) and DFG grant HO 4534/2-2. P. Scholl supported by the Danish Independent Research Council under Grant-ID DFF-6108-00169 (FoCC) and an Aarhus University Research Foundation starting grant.

References

1. Aguilar-Melchor, C., Barrier, J., Guelton, S., Guinet, A., Killijian, M.-O., Lepoint, T.: NFLlib: NTT-based fast lattice library. In: Sako, K. (ed.) CT-RSA 2016. LNCS, vol. 9610, pp. 341–356. Springer, Cham (2016). https://doi.org/10.1007/978-3-319-29485-8_20
2. Applebaum, B., Cash, D., Peikert, C., Sahai, A.: Fast cryptographic primitives and circular-secure encryption based on hard learning problems. In: Halevi, S. (ed.) CRYPTO 2009. LNCS, vol. 5677, pp. 595–618. Springer, Heidelberg (2009). https://doi.org/10.1007/978-3-642-03356-8_35
3. Baldi, M., Barenghi, A., Chiaraluce, F., Pelosi, G., Santini, P.: Design of LEDAkem and LEDApkc instances with tight parameters and bounded decryption failure rate (2019). https://www.ledacrypt.org/archives/official_comment.pdf
4. Beaver, D.: Efficient multiparty protocols using circuit randomization. In: Feigenbaum, J. (ed.) CRYPTO 1991. LNCS, vol. 576, pp. 420–432. Springer, Heidelberg (1992). https://doi.org/10.1007/3-540-46766-1_34

5. Ben-Efraim, A., Nielsen, M., Omri, E.: Turbospeedz: double your online SPDZ! improving SPDZ using function dependent preprocessing. In: Deng, R.H., Gauthier-Umaña, V., Ochoa, M., Yung, M. (eds.) ACNS 2019. LNCS, vol. 11464, pp. 530–549. Springer, Cham (2019). https://doi.org/10.1007/978-3-030-21568-2_26

6. Bendlin, R., Damgård, I., Orlandi, C., Zakarias, S.: Semi-homomorphic encryption and multiparty computation. In: Paterson, K.G. (ed.) EUROCRYPT 2011. LNCS, vol. 6632, pp. 169–188. Springer, Heidelberg (2011). https://doi.org/10.1007/978-3-642-20465-4_11

7. Bernstein, D.J., Lange, T.: Never trust a bunny. In: Hoepman, J.-H., Verbauwhede, I. (eds.) RFIDSec 2012. LNCS, vol. 7739, pp. 137–148. Springer, Heidelberg (2013). https://doi.org/10.1007/978-3-642-36140-1_10

8. Blum, A., Furst, M., Kearns, M., Lipton, R.J.: Cryptographic primitives based on hard learning problems. In: Stinson, D.R. (ed.) CRYPTO 1993. LNCS, vol. 773, pp. 278–291. Springer, Heidelberg (1994). https://doi.org/10.1007/3-540-48329-2_24

9. Boyle, E., Couteau, G., Gilboa, N., Ishai, Y.: Compressing vector OLE. In: ACM CCS 2018, pp. 896–912. ACM Press (2018)

10. Boyle, E., et al.: Efficient two-round OT extension and silent non-interactive secure computation. In: ACM CCS 2019, pp. 291–308. ACM Press (2019)

11. Boyle, E., Couteau, G., Gilboa, N., Ishai, Y., Kohl, L., Scholl, P.: Efficient pseudorandom correlation generators: silent OT extension and more. In: Boldyreva, A., Micciancio, D. (eds.) CRYPTO 2019. LNCS, vol. 11694, pp. 489–518. Springer, Cham (2019). https://doi.org/10.1007/978-3-030-26954-8_16

12. Boyle, E., Couteau, G., Gilboa, N., Ishai, Y., Orrù, M.: Homomorphic secret sharing: optimizations and applications. In: ACM CCS 2017, pp. 2105–2122. ACM Press (2017)

13. Boyle, E., Gilboa, N., Ishai, Y.: Function secret sharing. In: Oswald, E., Fischlin, M. (eds.) EUROCRYPT 2015. LNCS, vol. 9057, pp. 337–367. Springer, Heidelberg (2015). https://doi.org/10.1007/978-3-662-46803-6_12

14. Boyle, E., Gilboa, N., Ishai, Y.: Breaking the circuit size barrier for secure computation under DDH. In: Robshaw, M., Katz, J. (eds.) CRYPTO 2016, Part I. LNCS, vol. 9814, pp. 509–539. Springer, Heidelberg (2016). https://doi.org/10.1007/978-3-662-53018-4_19

15. Boyle, E., Gilboa, N., Ishai, Y.: Function secret sharing: improvements and extensions. In: ACM CCS 2016, pp. 1292–1303. ACM Press (2016)

16. Boyle, E., Gilboa, N., Ishai, Y.: Group-based secure computation: optimizing rounds, communication, and computation. In: Coron, J.-S., Nielsen, J.B. (eds.) EUROCRYPT 2017. LNCS, vol. 10211, pp. 163–193. Springer, Cham (2017). https://doi.org/10.1007/978-3-319-56614-6_6

17. Boyle, E., Gilboa, N., Ishai, Y.: Secure computation with preprocessing via function secret sharing. In: Hofheinz, D., Rosen, A. (eds.) TCC 2019. LNCS, vol. 11891, pp. 341–371. Springer, Cham (2019). https://doi.org/10.1007/978-3-030-36030-6_14

18. Boyle, E., Kohl, L., Scholl, P.: Homomorphic secret sharing from lattices without FHE. In: Ishai, Y., Rijmen, V. (eds.) EUROCRYPT 2019. LNCS, vol. 11477, pp. 3–33. Springer, Cham (2019). https://doi.org/10.1007/978-3-030-17656-3_1

19. Brakerski, Z., Vaikuntanathan, V.: Efficient fully homomorphic encryption from (standard) LWE. In: Ostrovsky, R. (ed.) 52nd FOCS, pp. 97–106. IEEE Computer Society Press, October 2011

20. Brakerski, Z., Vaikuntanathan, V.: Fully homomorphic encryption from ring-LWE and security for key dependent messages. In: Rogaway, P. (ed.) CRYPTO 2011. LNCS, vol. 6841, pp. 505–524. Springer, Heidelberg (2011). https://doi.org/10.1007/978-3-642-22792-9_29
21. Couteau, G.: A note on the communication complexity of multiparty computation in the correlated randomness model. In: Ishai, Y., Rijmen, V. (eds.) EUROCRYPT 2019. LNCS, vol. 11477, pp. 473–503. Springer, Cham (2019). https://doi.org/10.1007/978-3-030-17656-3_17
22. Damgård, I., Keller, M., Larraia, E., Pastro, V., Scholl, P., Smart, N.P.: Practical covertly secure MPC for dishonest majority – or: breaking the SPDZ limits. In: Crampton, J., Jajodia, S., Mayes, K. (eds.) ESORICS 2013. LNCS, vol. 8134, pp. 1–18. Springer, Heidelberg (2013). https://doi.org/10.1007/978-3-642-40203-6_1
23. Damgård, I., Nielsen, J.B., Nielsen, M., Ranellucci, S.: The TinyTable protocol for 2-party secure computation, or: gate-scrambling revisited. In: Katz, J., Shacham, H. (eds.) CRYPTO 2017. LNCS, vol. 10401, pp. 167–187. Springer, Cham (2017). https://doi.org/10.1007/978-3-319-63688-7_6
24. Damgård, I., Park, S.: How practical is public-key encryption based on LPN and ring-LPN? Cryptology ePrint Archive, Report 2012/699 (2012). http://eprint.iacr.org/2012/699
25. Damgård, I., Pastro, V., Smart, N., Zakarias, S.: Multiparty computation from somewhat homomorphic encryption. In: Safavi-Naini, R., Canetti, R. (eds.) CRYPTO 2012. LNCS, vol. 7417, pp. 643–662. Springer, Heidelberg (2012). https://doi.org/10.1007/978-3-642-32009-5_38
26. Debris-Alazard, T., Tillich, J.P.: Statistical decoding. In: 2017 IEEE International Symposium on Information Theory (ISIT), pp. 1798–1802. IEEE (2017)
27. Doerner, J., Shelat, A.: Scaling ORAM for secure computation. In: ACM CCS 2017, pp. 523–535. ACM Press (2017)
28. Gilboa, N., Ishai, Y.: Distributed point functions and their applications. In: Nguyen, P.Q., Oswald, E. (eds.) EUROCRYPT 2014. LNCS, vol. 8441, pp. 640–658. Springer, Heidelberg (2014). https://doi.org/10.1007/978-3-642-55220-5_35
29. Goldreich, O., Micali, S., Wigderson, A.: How to play any mental game or a completeness theorem for protocols with honest majority. In: Aho, A. (ed.) 19th ACM STOC, pp. 218–229. ACM Press, May 1987
30. Guo, Q., Johansson, T., Löndahl, C.: A new algorithm for solving ring-LPN with a reducible polynomial. IEEE Trans. Inf. Theory 61(11), 6204–6212 (2015)
31. Hazay, C., Ishai, Y., Marcedone, A., Venkitasubramaniam, M.: LevioSA: lightweight secure arithmetic computation. In: ACM CCS 2019, pp. 327–344. ACM Press (2019)
32. Heyse, S., Kiltz, E., Lyubashevsky, V., Paar, C., Pietrzak, K.: Lapin: an efficient authentication protocol based on ring-LPN. In: Canteaut, A. (ed.) FSE 2012. LNCS, vol. 7549, pp. 346–365. Springer, Heidelberg (2012). https://doi.org/10.1007/978-3-642-34047-5_20
33. Ishai, Y., Kushilevitz, E., Meldgaard, S., Orlandi, C., Paskin-Cherniavsky, A.: On the power of correlated randomness in secure computation. In: Sahai, A. (ed.) TCC 2013. LNCS, vol. 7785, pp. 600–620. Springer, Heidelberg (2013). https://doi.org/10.1007/978-3-642-36594-2_34
34. Ishai, Y., Kushilevitz, E., Ostrovsky, R., Sahai, A.: Batch codes and their applications. In: Babai, L. (ed.) 36th ACM STOC, pp. 262–271. ACM Press, June 2004
35. Ishai, Y., Prabhakaran, M., Sahai, A.: Founding cryptography on oblivious transfer – efficiently. In: Wagner, D. (ed.) CRYPTO 2008. LNCS, vol. 5157, pp. 572–591. Springer, Heidelberg (2008). https://doi.org/10.1007/978-3-540-85174-5_32

36. Ishai, Y., Prabhakaran, M., Sahai, A.: Secure arithmetic computation with no honest majority. In: Reingold, O. (ed.) TCC 2009. LNCS, vol. 5444, pp. 294–314. Springer, Heidelberg (2009). https://doi.org/10.1007/978-3-642-00457-5_18
37. Juvekar, C., Vaikuntanathan, V., Chandrakasan, A.: GAZELLE: a low latency framework for secure neural network inference. In: USENIX 2018, pp. 1651–1669 (2018)
38. Keller, M., Orsini, E., Scholl, P.: MASCOT: faster malicious arithmetic secure computation with oblivious transfer. In: ACM CCS 2016, pp. 830–842. ACM Press (2016)
39. Keller, M., Pastro, V., Rotaru, D.: Overdrive: making SPDZ great again. In: Nielsen, J.B., Rijmen, V. (eds.) EUROCRYPT 2018. LNCS, vol. 10822, pp. 158–189. Springer, Cham (2018). https://doi.org/10.1007/978-3-319-78372-7_6
40. Kilian, J.: Founding cryptography on oblivious transfer. In: 20th ACM STOC, pp. 20–31. ACM Press, May 1988
41. Kolesnikov, V., Sadeghi, A.-R., Schneider, T.: Improved garbled circuit building blocks and applications to auctions and computing minima. In: Garay, J.A., Miyaji, A., Otsuka, A. (eds.) CANS 2009. LNCS, vol. 5888, pp. 1–20. Springer, Heidelberg (2009). https://doi.org/10.1007/978-3-642-10433-6_1
42. Lipmaa, H., Pavlyk, K.: Analysis and implementation of an efficient ring-LPN based commitment scheme. In: Reiter, M., Naccache, D. (eds.) CANS 2015. LNCS, vol. 9476, pp. 160–175. Springer, Cham (2015). https://doi.org/10.1007/978-3-319-26823-1_12
43. Lyubashevsky, V., Peikert, C., Regev, O.: A toolkit for ring-LWE cryptography. In: Johansson, T., Nguyen, P.Q. (eds.) EUROCRYPT 2013. LNCS, vol. 7881, pp. 35–54. Springer, Heidelberg (2013). https://doi.org/10.1007/978-3-642-38348-9_3
44. Melchor, C.A., Blazy, O., Deneuville, J., Gaborit, P., Zémor, G.: Efficient encryption from random quasi-cyclic codes. IEEE Trans. Inf. Theory 64(5), 3927–3943 (2018). https://doi.org/10.1109/TIT.2018.2804444
45. Naor, M., Pinkas, B.: Oblivious transfer and polynomial evaluation. In: 31st ACM STOC, pp. 245–254. ACM Press, May 1999
46. Nielsen, J.B., Nordholt, P.S., Orlandi, C., Burra, S.S.: A new approach to practical active-secure two-party computation. In: Safavi-Naini, R., Canetti, R. (eds.) CRYPTO 2012. LNCS, vol. 7417, pp. 681–700. Springer, Heidelberg (2012). https://doi.org/10.1007/978-3-642-32009-5_40
47. Regev, O.: On lattices, learning with errors, random linear codes, and cryptography. In: Gabow, H.N., Fagin, R. (eds.) 37th ACM STOC, pp. 84–93. ACM Press, May 2005
48. Schoppmann, P., Gascón, A., Reichert, L., Raykova, M.: Distributed vector-OLE: improved constructions and implementation. In: ACM CCS 2019, pp. 1055–1072. ACM Press (2019)
49. Smart, N.P., Vercauteren, F.: Fully homomorphic simd operations. Des. Codes Cryptogr. 71(1), 57–81 (2014)

Scalable Pseudorandom Quantum States

Zvika Brakerski[1](✉) and Omri Shmueli[2](✉)

[1] Weizmann Institute of Science, Rehovot, Israel
zvika.brakerski@weizmann.ac.il
[2] Tel-Aviv University, Tel Aviv, Israel
omrishmueli@mail.tau.ac.il

Abstract. Efficiently sampling a quantum state that is hard to distinguish from a truly random quantum state is an elementary task in quantum information theory that has both computational and physical uses. This is often referred to as pseudorandom (quantum) state generator, or PRS generator for short.

In existing constructions of PRS generators, security scales with the number of qubits in the states, i.e. the (statistical) security parameter for an n-qubit PRS is roughly n. Perhaps counter-intuitively, n-qubit PRS are not known to imply k-qubit PRS even for $k < n$. Therefore the question of *scalability* for PRS was thus far open: is it possible to construct n-qubit PRS generators with security parameter λ for all n, λ. Indeed, we believe that PRS with tiny (even constant) n and large λ can be quite useful.

We resolve the problem in this work, showing that any quantum-secure one-way function implies scalable PRS. We follow the paradigm of first showing a *statistically* secure construction when given oracle access to a random function, and then replacing the random function with a quantum-secure (classical) pseudorandom function to achieve computational security. However, our methods deviate significantly from prior works since scalable pseudorandom states require randomizing the amplitudes of the quantum state, and not just the phase as in all prior works. We show how to achieve this using Gaussian sampling.

1 Introduction

Quantum mechanics asserts that the state of a physical system is characterized by a vector in complex Hilbert space, whose dimension corresponds to the number of degrees of freedom of the system. Specifically, a system with 2^n possible degrees of freedom (such as an n-qubit system, the quantum analogue to an n

The full version of this paper is available at https://arxiv.org/abs/2004.01976.

Supported by the Binational Science Foundation (Grant No. 2016726), and by the European Union Horizon 2020 Research and Innovation Program via ERC Project REACT (Grant 756482) and via Project PROMETHEUS (Grant 780701).

Supported by the European Union Horizon 2020 Research and Innovation Program via ERC Project REACT (Grant 756482), by the Israel Science Foundation Grant No. 18/484, and by Len Blavatnik and the Blavatnik Family Foundation.

D. Micciancio and T. Ristenpart (Eds.): CRYPTO 2020, LNCS 12171, pp. 417–440, 2020.
https://doi.org/10.1007/978-3-030-56880-1_15

bit system) is represented as a unit vector over $\mathbb{C}^{2^n}$. The ability to sample a random state of a system is a fundamental task when attempting to provide a computational description of the physical world.

Since the description length of a quantum state is infinite (and very long even when taken to a finite precision), relaxed notions for random state sampling are considered in the literature. Most commonly (and in this work) we consider restricting the *number of copies* of the sampled state that are given to the adversary.[1] The notion of quantum t-designs [AE07] considers computationally unbounded adversaries that are given t copies of the sampled state, and the requirement is that this input is (statistically) indistinguishable from t copies of a true random state. The resources of generating t-designs scale at least linearly with t, and therefore if efficient generation is sought, t designs can only be constructed for polynomial t.[2] Recently, a computational variant known as Pseudorandom Quantum State (PRS) was proposed by Ji, Liu and Song [JLS18]. In a PRS, the adversary is allowed to request an a-priori unbounded polynomial number of samples t, but the guarantee of indistinguishability only holds against *computationally bounded* adversaries. PRS have applications in quantum-cryptography (e.g. quantum money [JLS18]) and computational physics (e.g. simulation of thermalized quantum states [PSW06]).

It was shown in [JLS18, BS19] that PRS can be constructed from any quantum-secure one-way function. The design paradigm in both works is as follows. First, assume you are given (quantum) oracle access to a (classical) random function, and show how to efficiently construct a PRS which is secure even against computationally unbounded adversaries, a notion that [BS19] calls Asymptotically Random State (ARS). Then, replace the random function with a post-quantum pseudorandom function (PRF) to obtain computational security. Since only a fixed number of calls to the PRF is required in order to generate each PRS copy, this paradigm also leads to new constructions of t-designs, as observed in [BS19].

The previous works [JLS18, BS19] showed how to construct an n-qubit PRS, which is secure against any poly(n) time adversary. To be more precise, they constructed ARS whose distinguishing advantage is bounded by $4t^2 \cdot 2^{-n}$, and converted it into a PRS using a PRF as described above. We can therefore say that the *statistical security parameter* of the scheme is (essentially) n, and there is an additional computational security parameter that comes from the hardness of the PRF. Indeed, a security parameter of n seems quite sufficient since the complexity of the construction is poly(n) so it is possible to choose n as large as needed in order to provide sufficient security. Alas it is not possible to convert an n-qubit state generator into one that produces a random state over a smaller

---

[1] Recall that in the quantum setting, due to the no-cloning property, providing additional copies of the same state allows to recover more information about it. In utmost generality, any additional copy provides additional information, and a complete recovery of a quantum state requires infinitely many copies.

[2] As usual, we use the notion of security parameter λ that indicates the power of honest parties and of adversaries. We assume that honest parties run in time poly(λ) for a *fixed* polynomial, whereas the advantage of the adversary needs to scale super-polynomially, and preferably exponentially, with λ.

number of qubits, say $k < n$. This may be quite surprising as one would imagine that we can simply generate an n-qubit state, and just take its k-qubit prefix. However, recall that the n-qubits are in superposition, and taking a prefix is equivalent to measurement of the remaining $(n - k)$ qubits. For each of the t copies, this measurement has a different outcome and therefore each of the t copies will produce a different k-qubit states, as opposed to t copies of the same state as we wanted.

This peculiar state of affairs means that prior to this work it was not known, for example, how to construct ARS/PRS of n qubits, but with adversarial advantage bounded by 2^{-2n}. This issue is also meaningful when considering the concrete (non-asymptotic) security guarantees of PRS, where we wish to obtain for example 128 bits of security against an adversary that obtains at most 2^{20} copies of a PRS over 70 qubits.

This Work: Scalable ARS/PRS. In this light, it is desirable to introduce ARS/PRS constructions where the security parameter is in fact a parameter which is tunable independently of the length of the generated state. We call this notion *scalable* ARS/PRS. We notice that the approaches of [JLS18, BS19] are inherently not scalable since they can only generate states in which all computational-basis elements have the same amplitude, and the randomness only effects the phase. Such vectors are inherently distinguishable from uniform unless the dimension is very large (hence their dependence between length and security). In this work, we present new techniques for constructing ARS/PRS and in particular present a scalable construction under the same cryptographic assumptions as previous works.

1.1 Our Results

Our main technical result, as in all previous works, is concerned with constructing an ARS generator which is efficient given oracle access to a random function.[3]

Lemma 1.1 (Main Technical Lemma). *There exists a scalable ARS generator.*

Furthermore, for every length n of a quantum state and security parameter λ, running the generator t times (for any t) produces an output distribution that is $O\left(\frac{t}{e^{\lambda}}\right)$-indistinguishable from t copies of a random quantum state of n qubits.

We note that in previous works that construct ARS generators [JLS18, BS19] the dependence on t in the bound on the trace distance is quadratic, that is, previous ARS generators are known to achieve a bound of $\frac{t^2}{2^n}$ on the trace distance between t-copies of the ARS and a random quantum (n-qubit) state, whereas in this work the trace distance bound only scales up linearly with t.

---

[3] Note that this is not the quantum random oracle model since the random oracle is "private" and the adversary does not get access to it.

As immediate corollaries and similarly to [JLS18, BS19], we derive the existence of a scalable PRS generator (assuming post-quantum one-way functions) and scalable t-design generators (unconditionally). Unlike scalable PRS generators, scalable state t-design generators were known to exist before this work, however their depth was known to scale up linearly with t (and polynomially in n), and in our construction the depth scales logarithmically with t (and polynomially in n, λ).

Corollary 1.2. *If post-quantum one-way functions exist, then scalable PRS generators exist.*

Corollary 1.3. *For any polynomial $t(\cdot) : \mathbb{N} \to \mathbb{N}$, scalable state $t(\lambda)$-design generators exist where the circuit depth is $\mathrm{poly}(n, \lambda, \log t)$.*

Our ARS construction requires a random oracle with n bits of input (where n is the length of the generated state) and $\mathrm{poly}(\lambda)$ bits of output, it therefore follows that if $n = O(\log \lambda)$, then it is possible to instantiate the construction with a completely random string of length $2^n \cdot \mathrm{poly}(\lambda) = \mathrm{poly}(\lambda)$, and obtain statistically secure PRS. We view this consequence as not very surprising in hindsight.

Recently Alagic, Majenz and Russell [AMR19] proposed the notion of random state simulators. Simulators are stateful, and their local state grows with the number of copies t, however, there is no a-priori bound on the number of copies that the simulator can produce, and the guarantee is information-theoretic rather than computational. One can observe that a scalable ARS generator also implies efficient state simulators, by using the random-oracle simulation technique of Zhandry [Zha19]. The state simulators of [AMR19] follow a different approach, which is not known to imply ARS, and achieve simulators with perfect security (and thus straightforwardly scalable), but our ARS provides a different avenue for scalable random quantum state simulators as well.

1.2   Paper Organization

We provide a detailed technical overview of our results in Sect. 2. Preliminaries appear in Sect. 3, and in particular we formally state the derivation of the corollaries from the main theorem (which were implicit in previous work) in Sect. 3.3. Our technical results are presented in the following two sections. In Sect. 4 we present quantum information-theoretic tools which are required for our construction but may also find other uses. Then Sect. 5 contains our actual construction.

2   Technical Overview

We now provide a technical outline of how we achieve our main result in Lemma 1.1. Deriving the corollaries is straightforward using known techniques.[4]

As Lemma 1.1 states, we design an algorithm that has oracle access to a random function f, takes as input a bit length n and a security parameter λ, runs in time $\text{poly}(n, \lambda)$, and produces a quantum state over n-qubits $|\psi_{f,n,\lambda}\rangle$ (note that even though our algorithm is randomized, it can either output the state $|\psi_{f,n,\lambda}\rangle$ or $\bot$ and will never output the "wrong" state). It furthermore holds that the distribution that samples a random function f and outputs $|\psi_{f,n,\lambda}\rangle^{\otimes t}$ (i.e. t copies of the state $|\psi_{f,n,\lambda}\rangle$), is within trace distance at most $\text{poly}(t)/2^\lambda$ from the distribution that produces t copies of a truly randomly sampled n-qubit state.

We recall the standard Dirac notation for vectors in Hilbert space. An n-qubit state is generically denoted by a unit vector in $\mathbb{C}^{2^n}$ of the form $|\alpha\rangle = \sum_{x \in \{0,1\}^n} \alpha_x |x\rangle$. Throughout this overview we wish to refer to normalized as well as non-normalized vectors. We will use the convention that a vector $|\alpha\rangle$ is not necessarily normalized unless explicitly noted that it represents a quantum state (or a unit vector), and will denote its normalization

$$|\hat{\alpha}\rangle = \sum_{x \in \{0,1\}^n} \hat{\alpha}_x |x\rangle := \frac{1}{\sqrt{\langle \alpha | \alpha \rangle}} \sum_{x \in \{0,1\}^n} \alpha_x |x\rangle \,,$$

where $\langle \alpha | \alpha \rangle = \sum_x |\alpha_x|^2$.

As explained above, prior works generated quantum states where in the standard basis all coefficients had the same amplitude, i.e. their ARS could be represented by $|\alpha\rangle$ s.t. $|\alpha_x| = 1$ for all x. We abandon this approach, which as we explained cannot lead to a scalable ARS construction. Instead, we will show how to interpret a random function f as an implicit representation of a random unit vector in $\mathbb{C}^{2^n}$. Moreover, we want this interpretation to be *locally computable* in the sense that the value α_x only depends on $f(x)$. Our approach, therefore, is more direct and also more involved than the approach taken in previous works, since we will try to sample from a space that most closely resembles the uniform distribution over quantum states.

2.1   Our Approach: Implicit Random Gaussian Vector

Assume that we had an efficiently computable classical function $g(\cdot)$ s.t. if we set $v_x = g(f(x))$ and consider the vector $|v\rangle = \sum_x v_x |x\rangle$, then the distribution on $|v\rangle$ (induced by sampling the function f randomly) is *spherically symmetric*, i.e. invariant to unitary transformations ("rotations" in $\mathbb{C}^{2^n}$). In this case, the normalized vector $|\hat{v}\rangle$ is a uniform unit vector. In other words, we will show how

---

[4] We note that this standard transition from ARS with oracle to PRS and to t-designs was not formally stated in its generic form in previous works. In this work we also provide the generic derivations in Sect. 3.3.

to use the random function f as an implicit representation of a vector $|v\rangle$ such that for all x, v_x can be efficiently *locally* computed given x (and oracle access to f).

Our solution, therefore, needs to address two challenges. The first is to properly define a locally efficiently computable function g with the desirable properties. The second is to efficiently generate the quantum state $|\hat{v}\rangle$ given oracle access to the values v_x. Let us describe how we handle each one of these challenges at a high level, and then expand on the parts that contain the bulk of technical novelty.

First Technique: Multivariate Gaussian Sampling. For the first challenge, we use the multivariate Gaussian distribution, whose spherical symmetry has proven useful for many applications in the literature. Our function g will simply be a Gaussian sampler (or more accurately, a two-dimensional Gaussian sampler, for the real and imaginary parts of v_x). That is, we use the entries of the random function f as random tape for a Gaussian sampling procedure g. Since the Gaussian distribution is spherically symmetric, such a g has the properties that we need.

This approach indeed seems quite suitable but achieving (perfect) spherical symmetry is at odds with achieving computational efficiency, simply because the Gaussian distribution is continuous and has infinite support. Indeed, we will need to show a truncated discretized Gaussian distribution which on one hand can be sampled efficiently, and on the other hand provides approximate spherical symmetry. Note that the notion of approximation we are interested in here is with respect to the trace distance between the quantum state $|\hat{v}\rangle^{\otimes t}$ and a t-repetition of a random unit vector. This requires us to develop tools in order to relate this notion to standard notions such as Euclidean distance. These tools are not particularly complicated but we view them as fundamental and of potential to be used elsewhere.[5] We elaborate more on this in Sect. 2.2 below, and the full details appear in Sect. 4.

Second Technique: Rejection Sampling. The second challenge is addressed using a quantum analog of the *rejection sampling* technique. Recall that in standard probability theory, if it is possible to sample from a distribution p where $\Pr[x] = p_x$, then we can consider the experiment of first sampling from p, and then either outputting the sample received x with probability q_x, or aborting and restarting the process with probability $1 - q_x$. This process constitutes a sampler for the distribution $\frac{p_x q_x}{\sum_x p_x q_x}$. The probability of not aborting is $\sum_x p_x q_x$, and therefore the expected running time of the new sampler is $\frac{1}{\sum_x p_x q_x}$. In the quantum setting, a similar technique can be used for superpositions (Indeed, extensions of these technique were used e.g. in [ORR13]).

In this work we use quantum rejection sampling to generate quantum states from scratch. To create our state $|v\rangle$ we will start with the uniform superposition $|u\rangle = \sum_x |x\rangle$, and via a rejection process we can obtain (not necessarily with

---

[5] We will not be surprised if they were already discovered and used in the literature, but we were unable to find a relevant reference.

good probability), any desired superposition $|v\rangle$. The probability of success in the quantum case is $\frac{1}{d^2} \cdot \frac{\langle v|v\rangle}{\langle u|u\rangle}$, where d is an *a-priori* bound on $\max_x |v_x|$ that needs to be given as a parameter to the rejection sampling procedure. (The algorithm and success probability are analogous to the classical version described above, when replacing q_x with $\frac{v_x}{d}$ and considering ℓ_2 norm instead of ℓ_1.)

On the face of it, the rejection sampling procedure can work to create any state $|v\rangle$ when a bound d is known. However, the probability of success can still be very small (e.g. negligible), so if we wish to use repetition to obtain $|v\rangle$, the expected running time will become very large (e.g. super-polynomial). Fortunately, our vectors $|v\rangle$ are (approximately) Gaussian, which means that they have strong concentration properties that guarantee that with high probability two properties are satisfied. The first is that all entries v_x have roughly the same magnitude, up to a factor of poly(n, λ).[6] This allows us to choose the value d in such a way that the rejection sampling algorithm will operate correctly. The second property is that $\langle v|v\rangle \approx 2^n$ (formally, $\langle v|v\rangle$ is a constant factor away from 2^n), this makes the probability of success noticeable (i.e. $1/\text{poly}(n, \lambda)$). We informally call a vector that maintains the combination of these two properties "balanced". By running in time poly(n, λ) and repeating the process as needed we can amplify the success probability to $1 - 2^{-\lambda}$. We generalize these properties and provide a state generator for any oracle v_x which satisfied the balance property, see Sect. 4.

Lastly, we note that while the first property above (bound on d) can be made to hold for any n, the second one (lower bound on $\langle v|v\rangle$) might not hold with high enough probability. Special care needs to be taken in the case where n is very small, since in that case concentration properties are insufficient to imply that $\langle v|v\rangle$ does not fall far below its expected value with small yet significant probability (we wish to succeed with all but $2^{-\lambda}$ probability, so anything higher than that is already significant). In such a case, the success probability of the rejection sampler might become negligibly small, which will lead to failure in generating a state.[7] Luckily, since the dimension of the vector $|v\rangle$ is 2^n, good concentration kicks in already at $n \gtrsim \log(\lambda)$, so we only need to worry about this issue when $n < \log(\lambda)$. For such small n, the sampling algorithm can store the vector $|v\rangle$ in its entirety, and check whether the norm $\langle v|v\rangle$ is sufficiently close to its expectation (which happens with constant probability). If the norm is not in the required range, we sample a new Gaussian.[8] Repeating this roughly λ times

---

[6] Note that, e.g. tail bounds on the norm of a Gaussians asserts that the probability that its amplitude is beyond k times standard deviation is at most $e^{-c \cdot k^2}$ for some constant c. This means that if we want to find a tail bound that applies to all 2^n components of the vector $|v\rangle$ at the same time via union bound, it suffices to use $k \approx \sqrt{n + \lambda}$.

[7] We stress again that if the success probability becomes negligible with only negligible probability, e.g. $2^{-\sqrt{\lambda}}$, this is still a problem since the state generator will simply fail with this probability and therefore we cannot hope to be $2^{-\lambda}$ close to uniform.

[8] Recall that we think of the values of the function $f(x)$ as the random tape of a Gaussian sampler g. We can consider a function f with output length which is λ times the number of random bits used by the sampler g, so that we have sufficient randomness to re-run g as needed.

guarantees that we generate a "balanced" vector from a spherically symmetric distribution with all but $2^{-\lambda}$ probability.

2.2 Approximate Gaussians Under Tensored Trace Distance

We wish to do approximate sampling from the continuous Gaussian distribution using an efficiently locally sampleable distribution. If we wish to be fully precise, we need to consider Gaussian distributions over the complex regime. However, for the purpose of sampling, one can think of each complex coordinate just as two real-valued coordinates. For the purpose of this overview we will simplify things even further and assume that we wish to sample from a real-valued Gaussian, i.e. a vector in $\mathbb{R}^{2^n}$ instead of $\mathbb{C}^{2^n}$. Everything we discuss here be extended to the complex regime in a natural manner. From this point and on, our goal is to find an efficient sampler g s.t. when sampling v_x i.i.d from the distribution generated by g, and sampling w_x from a continuous Gaussian, it holds that the trace distance (quantum optimal distinguishing probability) between the quantum states $|\hat{v}\rangle^{\otimes t}$ and $|\hat{w}\rangle^{\otimes t}$, is at most $\text{poly}(t) \cdot 2^{-\lambda}$ for all t. For any vectors $|v\rangle, |w\rangle$, we refer to the trace distance between $|\hat{v}\rangle^{\otimes t}$ and $|\hat{w}\rangle^{\otimes t}$ as the "t-tensored trace distance" between $|v\rangle$ and $|w\rangle$.

An efficiently sampleable distribution is necessarily discrete and supported over a finite segment, whereas the Gaussian distribution is continuous and supported over $(-\infty, \infty)$. Indeed, even in the classical setting Gaussian samplers need to handle this discrepancy. Usually, when one says that it is efficient to sample from the Gaussian distribution, they mean that it is possible to sample to within any polynomial precision and from a Gaussian truncated far enough away from the standard deviation that the probability mass that is chopped off is negligible.[9] We adopt a similar approach here. Formally, sampling to within a fixed precision is equivalent to sampling from a *rounded* Gaussian distribution, i.e. the distribution obtained by sampling from a continuous Gaussian and then rounding the result to the nearest multiple of ϵ, where ϵ indicates the required precision. Truncation means that we sample from the distribution obtained by sampling a Gaussian, and if the absolute value of the sampled value x is at most some bound B, then return x, otherwise return 0. Setting B to be sufficiently larger than the standard deviation, say by roughly a factor of k, would imply that the resulting distribution only distorts the Gaussian by e^{-k^2} in total variation distance. We set our sampler g therefore to be a sampler from the B-truncated ε-rounded Gaussian distribution. It is possible to sample from a distribution that's within ε statistical distance from this distribution in time $\text{poly}(\log(1/\epsilon), \log(B))$ by standard Gaussian sampling techniques, and therefore we can set $1/\epsilon$ to be a sufficiently large exponential function in λ, n and maintain the efficient sampling property.

---

[9] An alternative to chopping the ends of the distribution is to construct a sampler that runs only in expected polynomial time and might run for a very long superpolynomial time with small probability. This approach is less suitable for our purposes.

The challenge, as already mentioned above, is to translate this intuitive notion of "approximate Gaussian" to one that is provable under tensored trace distance. In fact, we present a general analysis of the effects of truncation and rounding on tensored trace distance. We do this using a two-phase proof.

Part I: Tensored Trace Distance Respects Statistical Distance. We show that truncating a continuous Gaussian introduces negligible trace distance for *any* number of copies t. This follows quite straightforwardly from the classical total variation distance bound between the distributions. In fact, we show a more general claim (Lemma 4.3): Let $|v\rangle$ and $|w\rangle$ be distributions over n-qubit states, such that their classical distributions as 2^n-dimensional vectors are within classical statistical distance (total variation distance) δ. Then their t-tensored trace distance is at most δ for all t. The intuition here (which can also be translated to a formal proof), is that even given an infinite number of repetitions, a quantum state does not contain more information than its 2^n-dimensional coefficient vector. Therefore, a (computationally unbounded) adversary that attempts to distinguish $|\hat{v}\rangle^{\otimes t}$ and $|\hat{w}\rangle^{\otimes t}$ as quantum states cannot do better than a classical (computationally unbounded) adversary which receives $|v\rangle, |w\rangle$ as explicit vectors.

Part II: Tensored Trace Distance Respects Rounding. We say that a distribution $|v\rangle$ is a rounding of a distribution $|w\rangle$ if $|v\rangle$ can be described as first sampling an element from $|w\rangle$ and then applying some mapping φ s.t. for all w, $\|\varphi(w) - w\|$ is bounded (say be some value δ).[10] We wish to show that if $|v\rangle$ is a rounding of $|w\rangle$ then these vectors are close under tensored trace distance.

Let us start by considering the case $t = 1$, i.e. the distinguisher needs to distinguish between the quantum states $|\hat{v}\rangle$ and $|\hat{w}\rangle$. It is well established that if $|\hat{v}\rangle$ and $|\hat{w}\rangle$ are close in Euclidean distance, then they are also close in trace distance. However, this does not complete the proof since we only have a bound on the Euclidean distance between the unnormalized vectors $|v\rangle$ and $|w\rangle$. Indeed, the notion we care about is the Euclidean distance when projected onto the unit sphere, or in other words the *angular* distance induced by φ. In our case, our distribution $|w\rangle$ (the Gaussian) is such that the norm is quite regular with high probability, and this is preserved also for the rounded version (some straightforward yet fairly elaborate calculation is required in order to establish the exact parameters).[11]

Once we formalize the right notion of approximation (i.e. angular distance), it is possible to state a general lemma (Lemma 4.4) that shows that if φ is s.t. the angular distance between its input and output (over the support of $|v\rangle$) is bounded, then the t-tensored trace distance degrades moderately with t.

---

[10] Note that we call this "rounding" but in general this can be applied in other situations.

[11] This introduces an additional layer of complication into our proof, as we will need to apply the rounding tool to a restriction of the Gaussian distribution for which the norm is well behaved. Since the "regular norm" variant is close in statistical distance to the standard Gaussian, this can be handled by our first technique above.

Therefore, if we start with a short enough angular distance, our trace distance will indeed be bounded by $\mathrm{poly}(t)/2^\lambda$.

3 Preliminaries

3.1 Standard Notions and Notations

During this paper we use standard notations from the literature. For $n \in \mathbb{N}$,

- We denote $[n] := \{1, \cdots, n\}$.
- We denote by $[n]_2$ the $\lceil \log_2(n) \rceil$-bit binary representation of n.
- We denote by ω_n the complex root of unity of order n: $\omega_n := e^{\frac{2\pi i}{n}}$.
- We denote by $\mathcal{S}(n)$ the set of n-qubit pure quantum states, by $\mathcal{D}(n)$ the set of n-qubit mixed quantum states and by $\mathcal{U}(n)$ the set of n-qubit quantum unitary circuits.
- We sometimes denote 2^n with N, when we do that, we explicitly note it.

Vectors and Quantum States. We use standard Dirac notation throughout this paper, vectors are not assumed to be normalized unless explicitly mentioned. Specifically, for a column vector $u \in \mathbb{C}^m$, we denote $|u\rangle := u$, $\langle u| := u^\dagger$, where $u^\dagger$ is the conjugate transposed of u. We usually let $\hat{u}$ denote the normalized version of the vector u, namely: $\hat{u} := \frac{1}{\|u\|} \cdot u$ (where u is a nonzero complex vector). Vectors that represent quantum states have unit norm and therefore are normalized by default.

We make a distinction between a *vector* in a Hilbert space, and the *quantum state* corresponding to this vector. The two objects are related as a complete characterization of a (pure) quantum state over n-qubits is characterized by a vector in a 2^n-dimensional Hilbert space (up to normalization and global phase). However, the vector is not necessarily (and almost always is not) recoverable given the n-qubit state, and quantum states that correspond to different vectors can be indistinguishable (even perfectly).[12] In terms of vector notation, the symbol $|u\rangle$ can refer either to the vector in the Hilbert space of to the quantum state that corresponds to this vector, we will explicitly mention which of the two we refer to when using this notation.

Distributions Over Quantum States as Density Matrices. Density matrices are a mathematical tool to describe mixed quantum states, that is, distributions over quantum states. Formally, let μ a (possibly continuous) probability distribution over n-qubit quantum states, $\mu : \mathcal{S}(2^n) \to [0, 1]$, $\int_{|\psi\rangle \in \mathcal{S}(2^n)} 1 d\mu(|\psi\rangle) = 1$, then the density matrix induced by μ is denoted ρ_μ and defined as:

$$\rho_\mu = \mathbb{E}_{|\psi\rangle \leftarrow \mu}\Big[\big(|\psi\rangle\langle\psi|\big)\Big] := \int_{|\psi\rangle \in \mathcal{S}(2^n)} \big(|\psi\rangle\langle\psi|\big) d\mu(|\psi\rangle). \qquad (1)$$

---

[12] Information theoretically, in the general case, one requires an infinite number of copies of a quantum state in order to precisely recover the vector in the Hilbert space that characterizes this state.

Statistical Distance. We use basic properties of the statistical distance metric (also known as total variation distance). Statistical distance can be described in terms of operations, that is, for two (possibly continuous) distributions D_1, D_2 with corresponding supports S_1, S_2, the statistical distance between D_1, D_2 is the maximal advantage,

$$\left| \Pr_{x \leftarrow D_1} [\mathsf{A}(x) = 1] - \Pr_{x \leftarrow D_2} [\mathsf{A}(x) = 1] \right|$$

taken over all functions $\mathsf{A} : S_1 \cup S_2 \to \{0, 1\}$. We note that we can allow A to be randomized and obtain an equivalent definition. The statistical distance between two random variables is the statistical distance between their associated distributions.

Additionally, throughout the proof of Theorem 5.1 we will use the following fact about the statistical distance between a distribution and a conditional version of it.

Fact 3.1. *Let X be a random variable and E some probabilistic event. Denote $Y = X|\bar{E}$, i.e. the conditional variable of X conditioned on E not happening. Then*

$$\mathrm{SD}(X, Y) \leq \Pr[E] \,.$$

Trace Distance. The trace distance, defined below, is a generalization of statistical distance to the quantum setting and represents the maximal distinguishing probability between distributions over quantum states.

Definition 3.2 (Trace Distance). *Let $\rho_0, \rho_1 \in \mathcal{D}(2^n)$ be two density matrices of n-qubit mixed states. For a projective measurement A with output in $\{0, 1\}$ define*

$$\Delta_{\mathsf{A}, \rho_0, \rho_1} := \left| \Pr\left[\mathsf{A}(\rho_0) = 0 \right] - \Pr\left[\mathsf{A}(\rho_1) = 0 \right] \right| \,.$$

The trace distance between ρ_0, ρ_1 is

$$\mathrm{TD}(\rho_0, \rho_1) := \max_{\{0,1\} \; projective \; measurement \; \mathsf{A}} \Delta_{\mathsf{A}, \rho_0, \rho_1} \,.$$

We note that the trace distance is often equivalently defined as $\frac{1}{2} \|\rho_0 - \rho_1\|_1$, where $\|\cdot\|_1$ refers to the ℓ_1 norm of the vector of eigenvalues of the operand matrix.

A standard fact about trace distance is the following.

Fact 3.3. *Let D_0, D_1 be two distributions over n-qubit states and let $\rho_0, \rho_1 \in \mathcal{D}(2^n)$ be the corresponding density matrices. For a projective measurement A with output in $\{-1, 1\}$ define*

$$\tilde{\Delta}_{\mathsf{A}, \rho_0, \rho_1} := \left| \underset{\substack{|\psi\rangle \leftarrow D_0, \\ Measurement}}{\mathbb{E}} \left[\mathsf{A}(|\psi\rangle) \right] - \underset{\substack{|\psi\rangle \leftarrow D_1, \\ Measurement}}{\mathbb{E}} \left[\mathsf{A}(|\psi\rangle) \right] \right| \,.$$

Then,

$$2 \cdot \mathrm{TD}(\rho_0, \rho_1) = \max_{\{-1,1\} \; projective \; measurement \; \mathsf{A}} \tilde{\Delta}_{\mathsf{A}, \rho_0, \rho_1} \,.$$

The trace distance between pure states is given by the following expression.

Fact 3.4. *For n-qubit pure quantum states $|\psi\rangle, |\phi\rangle$, the trace distance between them is:*

$$\mathrm{TD}\Big(|\psi\rangle\langle\psi|, |\phi\rangle\langle\phi|\Big) = \sqrt{1 - |\langle\psi|\phi\rangle|^2}.$$

Trace distance is an operator on density matrices. In this work we will sometimes use it directly on distributions, that is we denote $\mathrm{TD}(D_1, D_2)$, where D_1, D_2 are distributions over n-qubit quantum states. This notation refers to the trace distance between the two density matrices induced by D_1 and D_2 (as per Eq. (1)). That is,

$$\mathrm{TD}(D_1, D_2) := \mathrm{TD}(\rho_{D_1}, \rho_{D_2}) = \mathrm{TD}\Big(\mathbb{E}_{|\psi\rangle \leftarrow D_1}\big[(|\psi\rangle\langle\psi|)\big], \mathbb{E}_{|\psi\rangle \leftarrow D_2}\big[(|\psi\rangle\langle\psi|)\big]\Big).$$

Quantum Unitary for a Classical Function. Let $f : \{0,1\}^n \to \{0,1\}^m$ be a function. The unitary of f is denoted by U_f, it is a unitary over $n + m$ qubits defined as

$$\forall x \in \{0,1\}^n, y \in \{0,1\}^m : U_f|x, y\rangle := |x, y \oplus f(x)\rangle.$$

Quantum Rejection Sampling. Quantum Rejection Sampling (QRS) is a known efficient procedure for taking one quantum state $|\alpha\rangle$ and outputting with some probability a different quantum state $|\beta\rangle$, given black box access to a circuit that describes their closeness. Formally, the algorithm QRS gets as input an n-qubit quantum state $|\alpha\rangle$ and quantum oracle access to a unitary U on $n + k$ qubits (where k is related to the binary description length for complex numbers that is being used) and have the following correctness and time complexity guarantees.

Theorem 3.5 (Quantum Rejection Sampling). *Let $|\alpha\rangle, |\beta\rangle$ be two n-qubit quantum states and let U be an $(n + k)$-qubit unitary. Assume there exists a positive real number d such that the following hold*

- $d \geq \max_{x \in \{0,1\}^n} \left|\frac{\beta_x}{\alpha_x}\right|$.
- *$\forall x \in \{0,1\}^n$, the complex number $\frac{(\beta_x/\alpha_x)}{d}$ can be described with full precision in k bits.*
- *U is the unitary of the classical function $f : \{0,1\}^n \to \{0,1\}^k$ such that $f(x) := \frac{(\beta_x/\alpha_x)}{d}$.*

Then $\mathsf{QRS}^U(|\alpha\rangle)$ outputs $(\mathsf{success}, |\beta\rangle)$ with probability at least $\frac{1}{d^2}$ and otherwise outputs $(\mathsf{fail}, |0^n\rangle)$.

The algorithm makes a single query to U, and assuming this query takes a single time step, the time complexity of $\mathsf{QRS}^U(|\alpha\rangle)$ is $\mathrm{poly}(n, k)$.

3.2 Pseudorandom Functions and m-Wise Independent Functions

We define pseudorandom functions with quantum security (QPRFs).

Definition 3.6 (Quantum-Secure Pseudorandom Function (QPRF)).
Let $\mathcal{K} = \{\mathcal{K}_n\}_{n \in \mathbb{N}}$ be an efficiently samplable key distribution, and let $\mathsf{PRF} = \{\mathsf{PRF}_n\}_{n \in \mathbb{N}}$, $\mathsf{PRF}_n : \mathcal{K}_n \times \{0,1\}^n \to \{0,1\}^{\mathrm{poly}(n)}$ be an efficiently computable function, where $\mathrm{poly}(\cdot)$ is some polynomial. We say that PRF is a quantum-secure pseudorandom function if for every efficient non-uniform quantum algorithm $A = \{A_n\}_{n \in \mathbb{N}}$ (with quantum advice) that can make quantum queries there exists a negligible function $\mathrm{negl}(\cdot)$ s.t. for every $n \in \mathbb{N}$,

$$\left| \Pr_{k \leftarrow \mathcal{K}_n}[A_n^{\mathsf{PRF}_k} = 1] - \Pr_{f \leftarrow (\{0,1\}^n)^{(\{0,1\}^n)}}[A_n^f = 1] \right| \leq \mathrm{negl}(n).$$

In [Zha12], QPRFs were proved to exist under the assumption that post-quantum one-way functions exist.

We define m-wise independent functions as keyed functions s.t. when the key is sampled from the key distribution, then any m different inputs to the function generate m-wise independent random variables.

Definition 3.7 (m-Wise Independent Function). *Let $n, m, p \in \mathbb{N}$, let $\mathcal{K}$ be a key distribution, and let f, $f : \mathcal{K} \times \{0,1\}^n \to \{0,1\}^p$ a function. $(f, \mathcal{K})$ is an m-wise independent function if for every distinct m input values $x_1, \cdots, x_m \in \{0,1\}^n$,*

$$\forall y_1, \cdots, y_m \in \{0,1\}^p : \Pr_{k \leftarrow \mathcal{K}}[f(k, x_1) = y_1 \wedge \cdots \wedge f(k, x_m) = y_m] = 2^{-p \cdot m}.$$

Based on m-wise independent functions we define efficiently samplable m-wise independent function families.

Definition 3.8 (Efficient $m(n)$-Wise Independent Function). *Let $m(n)$, $p(n) : \mathbb{N} \to \mathbb{N}$ be functions, let $\mathcal{K} = \{\mathcal{K}_n\}_{n \in \mathbb{N}}$ be an efficiently samplable key distribution, and let $f = \{f_n\}_{n \in \mathbb{N}}$, $f_n : \mathcal{K}_n \times \{0,1\}^n \to \{0,1\}^{p(n)}$ be an efficiently computable function. Then, if for every $n \in \mathbb{N}$, $(f_n, \mathcal{K}_n)$ is an $m(n)$-independent function, then $(f, \mathcal{K})$ is an efficient $m(n)$-wise independent function.*

3.3 Quantum Randomness and Pseudorandomness

The Haar Measure. The Haar measure on quantum states is the quantum analogue of the classical uniform distribution over classical bit strings. That is, it is the uniform (continuous) probability distribution on quantum states. Recall that an n-qubit quantum state can be viewed as a unit vector in $\mathbb{C}^{2^n}$, thus the Haar measure on n qubits is the uniform distribution over all unit vectors in $\mathbb{C}^{2^n}$. In this work we denote the n-qubit Haar distribution with μ_n. From this point forward we refer to the uniform distribution over quantum states simply as "random", and don't mention specifically that it is with respect to the Haar distribution.

Scalable Asymptotically Random State Generators. We propose a scalable variant to the notion of Asymptotically Random State (ARS) generators which was implicitly defined in [JLS18] and explicitly in [BS19]. Previous works consider an ARS generator to be an efficient quantum algorithm Gen that gets quantum oracle access to $U_f : |x, y\rangle \to |x, y \oplus f(x)\rangle$ for a random classical function f, along with a parameter $n \in \mathbb{N}$ that denotes the number of desired output qubits. The guarantee of the ARS generator is that for any polynomial $t(n)$ in n, $t(n)$ outputs from Gen^{U_f} (executed with the same function f) have negligible trace distance (*in* n) from $t(n)$-copies of a random n-qubit state This means that n plays two roles, it denotes the number of qubits in the output state but also the security parameter that determines the quality of randomness (i.e. how indistinguishable it is from random).

A *Scalable* ARS generator is one that gets two parameters n, λ instead of one. n, as before, denotes the number of wanted output qubits, and λ is a security parameter, thus a scalable ARS generator eliminates the dependence between state size and security.

Definition 3.9 (Asymptotically Random State (ARS) Generator). *A quantum polynomial-time algorithm* Gen *with input* $(1^n, 1^\lambda)$ *for* $n, \lambda \in \mathbb{N}$ *and quantum oracle access to* $U_f : |x, y\rangle \to |x, y \oplus f(x)\rangle$ *for* $f : \{0, 1\}^n \to \{0, 1\}^{\text{poly}(n, \lambda)}$, *is an ARS generator if there exists a negligible function* $\text{negl}(\cdot)$ *s.t. for every polynomial* $t : \mathbb{N} \to \mathbb{N}$, *for all natural numbers* n, λ,

$$\text{TD}(D_1, D_2) \leq \text{negl}(\lambda),$$

where the distributions D_1, D_2 *are defined as follows.*

- D_1: *Sample* $f \leftarrow (\{0, 1\}^{\text{poly}(n, \lambda)})^{\{0,1\}^n}$, *perform* $t(\lambda)$ *independent executions of* $\text{Gen}^{U_f}(1^n, 1^\lambda)$ *and output the* $t(\lambda)$ *output quantum states.*
- D_2: *Sample* $|\psi\rangle \leftarrow \mu_n$ *a random* n-*qubit quantum state, and output* $t(\lambda)$ *copies of it:* $|\psi\rangle^{\otimes t(\lambda)}$. *Recall that* μ_n *is the Haar measure on* n *qubits.*

We next define (scalable) quantum state t-design generators and (scalable) pseudorandom quantum state (PRS) generators. After defining these, we briefly describe a general and simple reduction structure that shows how to construct t-designs and PRS generators from any ARS generator.

Approximate Quantum State t-Designs. A quantum state t-design [AE07] is a distribution over quantum states that mimics the uniform distribution over quantum states when the number of output copies is restricted to t. A (scalable, approximate) quantum state t-design generator consists of two quantum algorithms K, G. The key sampler algorithm K samples a classical key k given two parameters $1^n, 1^\lambda$ where n denotes the number of qubits and λ denotes the security parameter. The state generation algorithm G gets a key k and outputs an n-qubit state $|\psi\rangle$. Informally, the randomness guarantee of a t-design generator is that if we sample a key k once from $K(1^n, 1^\lambda)$ and then execute $G(k)$ t times and output the t outputs, then this output distribution is going to be indistinguishable from t copies of an n-qubit quantum state, for unbounded quantum distinguishers. The formal definition follows.

Definition 3.10 ($\varepsilon(\lambda)$-Approximate State $t(\lambda)$-Design Generator). *Let $\varepsilon(\lambda) : \mathbb{N} \to [0,1]$, $t(\lambda) : \mathbb{N} \to \mathbb{N}$ be functions. We say that a pair of quantum algorithms (K, G) is an $\varepsilon(\lambda)$-approximate state $t(\lambda)$-design generator if the following holds:*

- *Key Generation. For all $n, \lambda \in \mathbb{N}$, $K(1^n, 1^\lambda)$ always outputs a classical key k.*
- *State Generation. Given k in the support of $K(1^n, 1^\lambda)$ the algorithm $G(1^n, 1^\lambda, k)$ will always output an n-qubit quantum state.*
- *Approximate Quantum Randomness. For all $n, \lambda \in \mathbb{N}$,*

$$\mathrm{TD}\big(D_1, D_2\big) \leq \varepsilon(\lambda),$$

where the distributions D_1, D_2 are defined as follows.

- *D_1: Sample $k \leftarrow K(1^n, 1^\lambda)$, perform $t(\lambda)$ independent executions of $G(1^n, 1^\lambda, k)$ and output the $t(\lambda)$ output quantum states.*
- *D_2: Sample $|\psi\rangle \leftarrow \mu_n$ a random n-qubit quantum state, and output $t(\lambda)$ copies of it: $|\psi\rangle^{\otimes t(\lambda)}$.*

It is not part of the standard definition, but it is usually the case that the algorithms K, G execute in time $\mathrm{poly}(n, \lambda)$, which is going to be the case in this work as well.

Pseudorandom Quantum States. We define scalable Pseudorandom State (PRS) generators. Compared to t-designs, Quantum Pseudorandom State Generators have a slight difference, and formally incomparable randomness guarantee. Mainly, with a PRS we are guaranteed that the output state is going to be indistinguishable for any polynomial number of copies $t(\lambda)$ *without* knowing in advance $t(\lambda)$, however this indistinguishability is only *computational*. That is, it is only guaranteed that computationally bounded distinguishers will be unable to tell the difference between $t(\lambda)$ executions of the generator and $t(\lambda)$ copies of a random quantum state. The scalability property maintains the ability to increase security without increasing the state size n. We remind that the notion of scalability in PRS generators was not considered in previous works [JLS18,BS19] and thus the following definition differs a bit from the previous definition of a PRS, we view this as the more proper definition.

Definition 3.11 (Scalable Pseudorandom Quantum State (PRS) Generator). *We say that a pair of polynomial-time quantum algorithms (K, G) is a Pseudorandom State (PRS) Generator if the following holds:*

- *Key Generation. For all $n, \lambda \in \mathbb{N}$, $K(1^n, 1^\lambda)$ always outputs a classical key k.*

- **State Generation.** *Given k in the support of $K(1^n, 1^\lambda)$ the algorithm $G(1^n, 1^\lambda, k)$ will always output an n-qubit quantum state.*
- **Quantum Pseudorandomness.** *For any polynomial $t(\cdot)$ and a non-uniform polynomial-time quantum algorithm $A = \{A_\lambda\}_{\lambda \in \mathbb{N}}$ (with quantum advice) there exists a negligible function $\mathrm{negl}(\cdot)$ such that for all $n, \lambda \in \mathbb{N}$,*

$$\left| \Pr[A_\lambda(D_1) = 1] - \Pr[A_\lambda(D_2) = 1] \right| \leq \mathrm{negl}(\lambda),$$

where the distributions D_1, D_2 are defined as follows.

- D_1: *Sample $k \leftarrow K(1^n, 1^\lambda)$, perform $t(\lambda)$ independent executions of $G(1^n, 1^\lambda, k)$ and output the $t(\lambda)$ output quantum states.*
- D_2: *Sample $|\psi\rangle \leftarrow \mu_n$ a random n-qubit quantum state, and output $t(\lambda)$ copies of it: $|\psi\rangle^{\otimes t(\lambda)}$.*

Scalable PRS and Quantum State t-Design Generators from Scalable ARS Generators. We recall a generic transformation from previous works that explain how to construct PRS generators and quantum state t-designs from any ARS generator. We start with the paradigm from [JLS18, BS19] that explains a simple way to turn any ARS generator into a PRS generator.

Lemma 3.12. *If there exists a scalable ARS generator and post-quantum one-way functions exist, then there exists a scalable PRS generator.*

Proof (Proof Sketch). The proof follows the same lines as the proof of [BS19, Claim 4, Section 3.1], with the additional scalability property. The key generator $K(1^n, 1^\lambda)$ of the PRS is the key generator of some quantum-secure pseudorandom function PRF with security parameter $n + \lambda$. For a sampled PRF key k, the state generator algorithm G simply executes the ARS generator with the pseudorandom function instead of the truly random function, $G(1^n, 1^\lambda, k) := \mathsf{Gen}^{U_{\mathsf{PRF}_k}}(1^n, 1^\lambda)$. For a polynomial $t(\cdot)$, $t(\lambda)$ copies of the generated distribution are computationally indistinguishable (by quantum adversaries) from $t(\lambda)$ copies of the standard output distribution of the ARS generator, by the security guarantee of the PRF. Additionally, $t(\lambda)$ copies of the output distribution of the ARS is already known to be indistinguishable (by unbounded distinguishers) from $t(\lambda)$ copies of a random quantum state, and our proof is concluded.

Also, we follow the observation from [BS19] that explains how an ARS generator implies the existence of t-designs (with depth that has logarithmic dependence on t).

Lemma 3.13. *Assume there exists a scalable ARS generator with the following properties:*

- *The generator is implemented by a circuit of depth $T(n, \lambda)$.*
- *For all n, λ, t its output is $\varepsilon(n, \lambda, t)$-indistinguishable from a t-tensor of a random n-qubit state.*

Then there exists an $\varepsilon(n, \lambda, t)$-approximate scalable t-design generator, which is implementable by circuits of depth

$$T(n, \lambda) \cdot \log(n) \cdot \log(2 \cdot t \cdot T(n, \lambda)).$$

Proof (Proof Sketch). The proof is similar to the explanation in [BS19, Section 3.2], with slight differences and an additional consideration of the scalability property. The key generator $K(1^n, 1^\lambda)$ of the t-design samples an efficient m-wise independent function $\tilde{f}$, where $m := 2t \cdot T(n, \lambda)$. The state generator algorithm G executes the ARS generator with the function $\tilde{f}$ instead with the truly random function, $G(1^n, 1^\lambda, \tilde{f}) := \mathsf{Gen}^{U_{\tilde{f}}}(1^n, 1^\lambda)$. By [Zha12, Fact 2], The behavior of any quantum algorithm making at most m quantum queries to a $2m$-wise independent function is identical to its behavior when the queries are made to a random function. Therefore if we make t executions of $G(1^n, 1^\lambda, \tilde{f})$, each of which makes at most $T(n, \lambda)$ queries to $U_{\tilde{f}}$, then the output distribution of the algorithm $G(1^n, 1^\lambda, \tilde{f})$ is the same as that produced by the ARS generator (when it uses a truly random function). Since the classical depth of an m-wise independent function on n bits is $\log(n) \cdot \log(m)$, the proof follows (see elaboration on the classical depth of m-wise independent functions in [BS19, Section 3.2]).

3.4   The Continuous Gaussian and Rounded Gaussian Distributions

In this work we will work with distributions related to the Gaussian distribution over $\mathbb{R}$ denoted $\mathcal{N}(0, 1)$, also known as the normal distribution having a mean of 0 and variance of 1. More specifically we will consider the complex Gaussian distribution over $\mathbb{C}$, denoted $\mathcal{N}^{\mathbb{C}}(0, 1)$, where both real and imaginary parts of a complex number are sampled independently from $\mathcal{N}(0, 1)$.

Rounded Gaussian Distribution. The true Gaussian distribution is continuous and we cannot *exactly* sample from it. Instead, we will use a discrete distribution that we can efficiently sample from. There are quite a few versions of distributions that are discretezations of the Gaussian distribution. In this work we use the rounded Gaussian distribution, which we denote by $\mathcal{N}^{\mathbb{C}}_{\mathrm{R}(\varepsilon, B)}(0, 1)$. This distribution is parameterized by $\varepsilon = 2^{-m} > 0$ (for some $m \in \mathbb{N}$) and by $B \in \mathbb{N}$, where B is some integer multiple of ε.

To define the distribution $\mathcal{N}^{\mathbb{C}}_{\mathrm{R}(\varepsilon, B)}(0, 1)$ we first define the rounding function $R_{(\varepsilon, B)}(\cdot)$. For a number $x \in \mathbb{R}$, if $|x| > B$ then $R_{(\varepsilon, B)}(x) := 0$, and otherwise $R_{(\varepsilon, B)}(x)$ rounds x up (in absolute value) to the nearest multiple of ε. Formally, if $|x| \leq B$ then $R_{(\varepsilon, B)}(x)$ is the number $y \in \mathbb{R}$ that has minimal absolute value and s.t. both $|x| \leq |y|, \exists k \in \mathbb{Z} : y = k \cdot \varepsilon$. For a complex number $z \in \mathbb{C}$, $R_{(\varepsilon, B)}(z)$ is just applying $R_{(\varepsilon, B)}(\cdot)$ to both real and imaginary parts of z.

We define $\mathcal{N}^{\mathbb{C}}_{\mathrm{R}(\varepsilon, B)}(0, 1)$ to be the output distribution of the following process: Sample $z \leftarrow \mathcal{N}^{\mathbb{C}}(0, 1)$ and output $R_{(\varepsilon, B)}(z)$. The output of $\mathcal{N}^{\mathbb{C}}_{\mathrm{R}(\varepsilon, B)}(0, 1)$ is specified by a number between 0 and B with precision $\varepsilon = 2^{-m}$, thus the output length in bits is bounded by $m + \lceil \log_2(B) \rceil$.

We use the following standard fact about (classical) Gaussian sampling.

Fact 3.14 (Efficient Rounded Gaussian Sampling). *There is a sampling algorithm $G_{R()}^{\mathbb{C}}$ that takes $1^m, B$ (and random tape) as input, runs in polynomial time, i.e. $\mathrm{poly}(m, \log B)$, and samples from a distribution that has statistical distance at most 2^{-m} from the rounded Gaussian distribution $\mathcal{N}_{R(2^{-m}, B)}^{\mathbb{C}}(0, 1)$.*

4   General Tools for Quantum Information

4.1   State Generation of Balanced Vectors

In this subsection we describe a simple procedure that given quantum oracle access to the entries of some general, not necessarily normalized vector $v \in \mathbb{C}^{2^n}$, generates the n-qubit quantum state $|v\rangle$ that corresponds to (the normalization of) v. More formally, the procedure gets two pieces of information about v:

- Quantum oracle access to U_v, the unitary of the classical function $v : \{0, 1\}^n \to \{0, 1\}^k$ (where k is the description size in bits of each entry of v) that describes the vector v and maps $v(x) := v_x$.
- An upper bound $M \in \mathbb{N}$ on any entry of v, that is, $\max_{x \in [N]} |v_x| \leq M$.

The procedure runs in time $\mathrm{poly}(n, k, \log M)$ and outputs the quantum state $|v\rangle$ as follows.
$\mathrm{BVS}^{U_v}(M)$:

1. Define the quantum unitary $U_{\tilde{v}}$ which is the unitary of the classical function $\tilde{v} : \{0, 1\}^n \to \{0, 1\}^{k + \log(M)}$ that maps $\tilde{v}(x) := v_x \cdot \frac{1}{M}$.
   It's trivial to simulate $U_{\tilde{v}}$ given U_v: Given a query $|x, y\rangle$, we concatenate an ancilla of zeros and apply U_v to get $|x, y, v_x\rangle$, then apply a simple unitary that multiplies by $\frac{1}{M}$ (on the last register as input and on the second register as output) to obtain $|x, y \oplus v_x \cdot \frac{1}{M}, v_x\rangle$, and then use U_v again to uncompute the last register.
2. Execute quantum rejection sampling, $(b, |\hat{v}\rangle) \leftarrow \mathrm{QRS}^{U_{\tilde{v}}}(|+\rangle^{\otimes n})$ (see specification of QRS in Theorem 3.5). If $b = \mathtt{fail}$ then output $\mathtt{fail}$, otherwise output $|\hat{v}\rangle$.

Claim 4.1 (BVS Success Probability). *If $\max_{i \in [N]} |v_i| \leq M$ then the execution $\mathrm{BVS}^{U_v}(M)$ always outputs either $\mathtt{fail}$ or the quantum state $v \cdot \frac{1}{\|v\|} = |\hat{v}\rangle$, furthermore the execution succeeds and outputs the quantum state $|\hat{v}\rangle$ with probability at least $\frac{\|v\|^2}{M^2 \cdot N}$.*

Proof. We need to make sure that we execute the quantum rejection sampling algorithm QRS with correct parameters (specified in Theorem 3.5), and also understand what exactly are the parameters for QRS. As the starting state $|\alpha\rangle$ we input $|+\rangle^{\otimes n}$, our target state $|\beta\rangle$ is $|\hat{v}\rangle = \frac{|v\rangle}{\|v\|}$. As the state transformation unitary U we use $U_{\tilde{v}}$, that is, the unitary of the classical function $f(x) := v_x \cdot \frac{1}{M}$.

It follows that there exists an upper bound $d \geq \max_{x \in \{0, 1\}^n} \left| \frac{\beta_x}{\alpha_x} \right|$ s.t. $\forall x \in \{0, 1\}^n : f(x) := f(x) := v_x \cdot \frac{1}{M} = \frac{\beta_x / \alpha_x}{d}$, by taking $d := \frac{M \cdot \sqrt{N}}{\|v\|}$.

– d is indeed an upper bound:

$$\forall x \in \{0,1\}^n : \left|\frac{\beta_x}{\alpha_x}\right| = \left|\frac{v_x/\|v\|}{1/\sqrt{N}}\right| = \left|v_x \cdot \frac{\sqrt{N}}{\|v\|}\right| \leq \frac{M \cdot \sqrt{N}}{\|v\|}.$$

– $f(\cdot)$ indeed computes $\frac{\beta_x}{\alpha_x}/d$:

$$\forall x \in \{0,1\}^n : f(x) := v_x \cdot \frac{1}{M}$$
$$= v_x \cdot \frac{1}{M} \cdot \frac{\sqrt{N}}{\sqrt{N}} \cdot \frac{\|v\|}{\|v\|}$$
$$= \left(\frac{v_x}{\|v\|} \cdot \sqrt{N}\right) \cdot \left(\frac{1}{M} \cdot \frac{\|v\|}{\sqrt{N}}\right)$$
$$= \frac{\left(\frac{v_x/\|v\|}{1/\sqrt{N}}\right)}{\left(\frac{M \cdot \sqrt{N}}{\|v\|}\right)}$$
$$= \frac{\beta_x/\alpha_x}{d}.$$

The conditions for QRS hold, and thus from the correctness guarantee of quantum rejection sampling we can be sure that the algorithm BVS will always output either fail or $|\beta\rangle := |\hat{v}\rangle$. As for the probability of success in outputting $|\hat{v}\rangle$, again from the success guarantees of QRS this probability is at least $\frac{1}{d^2} = \frac{\|v\|^2}{M^2 \cdot N}$.

The above procedure tries to generate $|\hat{v}\rangle$ once and it will be convenient to have an amplified version of this algorithm as a black box, this is an option because we can always re-generate the state $|+\rangle^{\otimes n}$ efficiently and retry. The amplified version of the algorithm is with the same name and have one more parameter $k \in \mathbb{N}$ (amplification parameter), that is, $\text{BVS}^{U_v}(M, k)$.

The amplified version of BVS executes k (parallel) repetitions of $\text{BVS}^{U_v}(M)$, if all fail it outputs fail, and if either succeeds it outputs the generated state $|\hat{v}\rangle$. The probability of $\text{BVS}^{U_v}(M, k)$ to succeed in generating the state $|\hat{v}\rangle$ follows.

Claim 4.2. (Amplified BVS Success Probability). *If* $\max_{i \in [N]} |v_i| \leq M$ *then the algorithm* $\text{BVS}^{U_v}(M, k)$ *always outputs either* fail *or the quantum state* $v \cdot \frac{1}{\|v\|} = |\hat{v}\rangle$, *furthermore the algorithm succeeds and outputs the quantum state* $|\hat{v}\rangle$ *with probability at least* $1 - e^{-\frac{k \cdot \|v\|^2}{M^2 \cdot N}}$.

Proof.

$$\Pr\left[\mathsf{BVS}^{U_v}(M,k) = \texttt{fail}\right] = \Pr\left[\mathsf{BVS}^{U_v}(M) \text{ failed } k \text{ times in a row}\right]$$

$$= \left(\Pr\left[\mathsf{BVS}^{U_v}(M) = \texttt{fail}\right]\right)^k$$

$$\leq \left(1 - \frac{\|v\|^2}{M^2 \cdot N}\right)^k$$

$$\leq e^{-\frac{k \cdot \|v\|^2}{M^2 \cdot N}}.$$

4.2 Analytic Tools for Distributions

In this subsection we describe some analytic tools for bounding trace norm between two distributions, for multiple output copies. We start with an elementary property of trace distance and classical statistical distance that we will use in our construction.

Lemma 4.3 (Classical Statistical Distance Implies Trace Distance).
Let $n \in \mathbb{N}$ and let D_1, D_2 be two distributions over unit vectors in $\mathbb{C}^{2^n}$. Let $\tilde{D}_1$, $\tilde{D}_2$ be the quantum-state distributions of D_1, D_2, that is, for $b \in \{0,1\}$, a sample from $\tilde{D}_b$ is generated by sampling a vector v from D_b, and outputting an n-qubit register in the state described by v.
Then, if $\mathrm{SD}(D_1, D_2) \leq \varepsilon$, then for every number of copies $t \in \mathbb{N}$,

$$\mathrm{TD}\left(\mathbb{E}_{|v\rangle \leftarrow \tilde{D}_1}\left[(|v\rangle\langle v|)^{\otimes t}\right], \mathbb{E}_{|v\rangle \leftarrow \tilde{D}_2}\left[(|v\rangle\langle v|)^{\otimes t}\right]\right) \leq \varepsilon.$$

Proof. Intuitively, the proof follows from the fact that a computationally unbounded mapping can always capture the computation of an (even unbounded) quantum process, along with the fact that when the classical description of a state is available then there is no advantage in having more than a single copy. Formally, we assume towards contradiction there is a projective measurement A (with output in $\{0,1\}$) that distinguishes between a t-tensor of $\tilde{D}_1$ and a t-tensor of $\tilde{D}_2$ with advantage bigger than ε, and describe a (randomized) distinguisher $\mathsf{A}' : \mathbb{C}^{2^n} \to \{0,1\}$ that distinguishes between D_1, D_2 with advantage bigger than ε. Let A denote the Hermitian matrix that corresponds to the projective measurement A.

The distinguisher A' is defined as follows. Given an input $v \in \mathbb{C}^{2^n}$, consider the vector $|v'\rangle = |v\rangle^{\otimes t}$, and compute the value $p = \langle v'|A|v'\rangle$. We note that this value is exactly the probability that A outputs 1 when input the quantum state $|v\rangle^{\otimes t}$. The distinguisher A' then outputs 1 with probability p and 0 with probability $1-p$. By definition, the advantage of A' in distinguishing D_1 and D_2 is identical to the advantage of A in distinguishing the t-tensored $\tilde{D}_1$ and $\tilde{D}_2$.

Robustness to Small Shifts. Lemma 4.3 asserts that distributions on quantum states are indistinguishable if they are induced by indistinguishable distributions over vectors in the respective Hilbert space. This is a very strict condition and in fact in many cases distributions on quantum states can be indistinguishable even if the respective distributions over vectors are highly distinguishable.

This will be useful in the context of this work since we wish to show indistinguishability between the Haar random distribution, which corresponds to a continuous distribution over the sphere, and an efficiently samplable distribution (with oracle access to a random function), which necessarily produces a discrete distribution over vectors. Hence, the two distributions over vectors are necessarily distinguishable (with advantage 1), and yet we will be able to bound the distinguishing gap between the quantum states.

Technically, we rely on the well known property that quantum states that correspond to vectors with inner product close to 1 are indistinguishable. This is formalized in Lemma 4.4 below, which considers a distribution over vectors, and a small perturbation of this distribution, that does not shift the vector by too much. We show that such perturbation, which in particular captures the case of rounding a continuous distribution into some discrete domain, would be indistinguishable in terms of the resulting quantum state.

Lemma 4.4 (Angular Indistinguishability). *Let $n \in \mathbb{N}$, $\varepsilon \in [0,1]$, let D be a distribution over (not necessarily normalized) vectors in $V \subseteq \mathbb{C}^{2^n}$, let $\varphi : V \to \mathbb{C}^{2^n}$ be a function and let $\hat{\varphi} : V \to \mathbb{C}^{2^n}$ be the normalized version of φ, $\hat{\varphi}(v) := \frac{\varphi(v)}{\|\varphi(v)\|}$. Assume that for every $v \in V$, the normalization of v and its $\hat{\varphi}$-image are close on the unit sphere, that is,*

$$|\langle \hat{v} | \hat{\varphi}(v) \rangle| \geq 1 - \varepsilon,$$

then for all $t \in \mathbb{N}$,

$$\mathrm{TD}\Big(\mathbb{E}_{v \leftarrow D}\big[(|\hat{v}\rangle\langle\hat{v}|)^{\otimes t} \big], \mathbb{E}_{v \leftarrow D}\big[(|\hat{\varphi}(v)\rangle\langle\hat{\varphi}(v)|)^{\otimes t} \big] \Big) \leq \sqrt{2t\varepsilon}. \tag{2}$$

In the original version of this work, the above lemma was proven using a proof different from the one below. We thank the CRYPTO reviewer for suggesting the simplified proof presented below.

Proof. The lemma follows since

$$\mathrm{TD}\Big(\mathbb{E}_{v \leftarrow D}\big[(|\hat{v}\rangle\langle\hat{v}|)^{\otimes t} \big], \mathbb{E}_{v \leftarrow D}\big[(|\hat{\varphi}(v)\rangle\langle\hat{\varphi}(v)|)^{\otimes t} \big] \Big)$$

$$\leq \mathbb{E}_{v \leftarrow D}\Big[\mathrm{TD}\big((|\hat{v}\rangle\langle\hat{v}|)^{\otimes t}, (|\hat{\varphi}(v)\rangle\langle\hat{\varphi}(v)|)^{\otimes t} \big) \Big]$$

$$\leq \mathbb{E}_{v \leftarrow D}\Big[\sqrt{1 - |\langle \hat{v} | \hat{\varphi}(v) \rangle|^{2t}} \Big]$$

$$\leq \mathbb{E}_{v \leftarrow D}\Big[\sqrt{1 - (1 - \varepsilon)^{2t}} \Big]$$

$$\leq \sqrt{2t\varepsilon},$$

where the first inequality follows from the convexity of trace distance, the second follows from the relation between trace distance and fidelity $\mathrm{TD}(\rho, \sigma) \leq$

$\sqrt{1 - F(\rho, \sigma)}$ and the fact that for pure states $|u\rangle, |v\rangle$ the Fidelity is $|\langle u|v\rangle|^2$, and the last inequality follows from Bernoulli's inequality which implies $(1 - \varepsilon)^{2 \cdot t} \geq 1 - 2t\varepsilon$.

5   Scalable Asymptotically Random State (ARS) Generator

In this section we describe a procedure that given quantum oracle access to a random classical function, efficiently samples random quantum states that are arbitrarily random (i.e. we can scale up the randomness of our sampled state and make it increasingly harder to distinguish from a random quantum state, for an increasing number of output copies, without increasing the number of qubits in the state) and can generate multiple copies of a state when executed multiple times with oracle access to the same function. More formally, we describe a sampling procedure with the following inputs:

- 1^n: Number of wanted qubits in the output state.
- 1^λ: Security parameter that measures "how random" the output state is going to be (i.e. how hard will it be to distinguish t copies of the sampled state from t copies of a random quantum state, as a function of λ, t).
- Quantum oracle access to U_f: For a function $f : \{0, 1\}^n \rightarrow \{0, 1\}^{\mathrm{poly}(n, \lambda)}$ (for some polynomial $\mathrm{poly}(\cdot)$, specified later), the sampling procedure gets oracle access to the unitary mapping U_f of f.

The formal statement that explains how to construct a scalable ARS generator follows.

Theorem 5.1 (Scalable ARS Generator Construction). *There exists a scalable ARS generator* Gen *that for every* $n \in \mathbb{N}$ *number of qubits,* $5 \leq \lambda \in \mathbb{N}$ *security parameter and* $t \in \mathbb{N}$ *number of copies, satisfies the following trace distance bound,*

$$\mathrm{TD}\left(D_1, D_2\right) \leq (t + 8) \cdot e^{-\lambda} + \left(5\sqrt{t} + \lambda + 1\right) \cdot 2^{-\lambda} + 2 \cdot \left(\frac{8}{10}\right)^\lambda,$$

where the distributions D_1, D_2 *are defined as follows:*

- D_1: *Sample* $\tilde{f} \leftarrow \left(\{0, 1\}^{\mathrm{poly}(n, \lambda)}\right)^{\{0, 1\}^n}$, *execute* t *times the generation algorithm* $\mathsf{Gen}^{U_{\tilde{f}}}(1^n, 1^\lambda)$ *and output the* t *output states.*
- D_2: *Sample* $|\psi\rangle$ *a random* n-qubit state and output $|\psi\rangle^{\otimes t}$.

Proof. We start with describing the procedure of $\mathsf{Gen}^{U_{\tilde{f}}}(1^n, 1^\lambda)$. First, we denote $\varepsilon := 2^{-n-\lambda}$, $B := \lceil 2\sqrt{n + \lambda} \rceil$ and set the polynomial $\mathrm{poly}(n, \lambda)$ that denotes the output size of $\tilde{f}$ to be $\lambda \cdot r(\varepsilon, B)$, where $r(\varepsilon, B)$ is the randomness complexity of the rounded Gaussian sampler $G^{\mathbb{C}}_{R(\varepsilon, B)}$. Given the oracle access to $\tilde{f} \in \left(\{0,1\}^{\lambda \cdot r(\varepsilon,B)}\right)^{\{0,1\}^n}$, the algorithm starts with deciding on a different function $f \in \left(\{0,1\}^{r(\varepsilon,B)}\right)^{\{0,1\}^n}$ that it is going to use.

In what follows, denote $N := 2^n$, for a function $h \in \left(\{0,1\}^{r(\varepsilon,B)}\right)^{\{0,1\}^n}$ denote by v^h the vector that is created by rounded Gaussian sampling with h, that is, $\forall x \in \{0,1\}^n, v_x^h := G_{R(\varepsilon,B)}^{\mathbb{C}}(h(x))$. We think of $\tilde{f}$, that has an output length of $\lambda \cdot r(\varepsilon,B)$, as λ different functions, each having an output length of $r(\varepsilon,B)$. Specifically, for $i \in [\lambda]$ define the function $f_i \in \left(\{0,1\}^{r(\varepsilon,B)}\right)^{\{0,1\}^n}$ as the function that for input $x \in \{0,1\}^n$ outputs the i-th packet of $r(\varepsilon,B)$ bits from $\tilde{f}(x)$.

The procedure of Gen follows.

1. Decide on a function $f \in \left(\{0,1\}^{r(\varepsilon,B)}\right)^{\{0,1\}^n}$:
   - If $N > \lambda$, we actually use only the first $r(\varepsilon,B)$ bits of the output of $\tilde{f}$. That is, f is simply f_1.
   - If $N \leq \lambda$, iterate for $i \in [\lambda]$:
     - Compute the vector v^{f_i} by applying $G_{R(\varepsilon,B)}^{\mathbb{C}}$ to each of the N outputs of f_i. If $\left\|v^{f_i}\right\| \geq \frac{\sqrt{N}}{2}$, denote $f := f_i$ and halt the loop.[13]

   If you executed all iterations and did not get a function f_i s.t. $\left\|v^{f_i}\right\| \geq \frac{\sqrt{N}}{2}$, halt and output $|0^n\rangle$ (as a sign of failure).
2. Given f execute $\mathsf{BVS}^{U_{v^f}}(\sqrt{2} \cdot B, 8 \cdot \lambda \cdot B^2)$ and output the n-qubit quantum state generated by BVS.

The full analysis and the rest of the proof, showing why a t-tensor of the output of the generator (i.e. the distribution D_1) and a t-tensor of a random quantum state (i.e. the distribution D_2) are indistinguishable, is in the full version of this work[14].

Acknowledgments. We wish to thank the TCC 2019 reviewer of [BS19] who brought the scalability problem in existing PRS constructions to our attention. We thank Crypto 2020 reviewers for their insightful comments on a prior version of this manuscript.

References

[AE07] Ambainis, A., Emerson, J.: Quantum t-designs: t-wise independence in the quantum world. In: Twenty-Second Annual IEEE Conference on Computational Complexity (CCC 2007), pp. 129–140. IEEE (2007)

[AMR19] Alagic, G., Majenz, C., Russell, A.: Efficient simulation of random states and random unitaries. CoRR, abs/1910.05729 (2019)

[BS19] Brakerski, Z., Shmueli, O.: (Pseudo) random quantum states with binary phase. In: Hofheinz, D., Rosen, A. (eds.) TCC 2019, Part I. LNCS, vol. 11891, pp. 229–250. Springer, Cham (2019). https://doi.org/10.1007/978-3-030-36030-6_10

---

[13] Note that all steps here can be done efficiently in λ, because $\lambda \geq N = 2^n$.

[14] The full version of this paper is available at https://arxiv.org/abs/2004.01976.

[JLS18] Ji, Z., Liu, Y.-K., Song, F.: Pseudorandom quantum states. In: Shacham, H., Boldyreva, A. (eds.) CRYPTO 2018, Part III. LNCS, vol. 10993, pp. 126–152. Springer, Cham (2018). https://doi.org/10.1007/978-3-319-96878-0_5

[ORR13] Ozols, M., Roetteler, M., Roland, J.: Quantum rejection sampling. ACM Trans. Comput. Theory (TOCT) 5(3), 1–33 (2013)

[PSW06] Popescu, S., Short, A.J., Winter, A.: Entanglement and the foundations of statistical mechanics. Nat. Phys. 2(11), 754–758 (2006)

[Zha12] Zhandry, M.: How to construct quantum random functions. In: 2012 IEEE 53rd Annual Symposium on Foundations of Computer Science, pp. 679–687. IEEE (2012)

[Zha19] Zhandry, M.: How to record quantum queries, and applications to quantum indifferentiability. In: Boldyreva, A., Micciancio, D. (eds.) CRYPTO 2019, Part II. LNCS, vol. 11693, pp. 239–268. Springer, Cham (2019). https://doi.org/10.1007/978-3-030-26951-7_9

A Non-PCP Approach to Succinct Quantum-Safe Zero-Knowledge

Jonathan Bootle[1,3]($\boxtimes$) (ID), Vadim Lyubashevsky[1]($\boxtimes$),
Ngoc Khanh Nguyen[1,2]($\boxtimes$) (ID), and Gregor Seiler[1,2]($\boxtimes$)

[1] IBM Research – Zurich, Rüschlikon, Switzerland
{vad,nkn}@zurich.ibm.com
[2] ETH Zurich, Zurich, Switzerland
gseiler@inf.ethz.ch
[3] UC Berkeley, Berkeley, USA
jonathan.bootle@berkeley.edu

Abstract. Today's most compact zero-knowledge arguments are based on the hardness of the discrete logarithm problem and related classical assumptions. If one is interested in quantum-safe solutions, then all of the known techniques stem from the PCP-based framework of Kilian (STOC 92) which can be instantiated based on the hardness of any collision-resistant hash function. Both approaches produce asymptotically logarithmic sized arguments but, by exploiting extra algebraic structure, the discrete logarithm arguments are a few orders of magnitude more compact in practice than the generic constructions.

In this work, we present the first (poly)-logarithmic, potentially *post-quantum* zero-knowledge arguments that deviate from the PCP approach. At the core of succinct zero-knowledge proofs are succinct commitment schemes (in which the commitment and the opening proof are sub-linear in the message size), and we propose two such constructions based on the hardness of the (Ring)-Short Integer Solution (Ring-SIS) problem, each having certain trade-offs. For commitments to N secret values, the communication complexity of our first scheme is $\tilde{O}(N^{1/c})$ for any positive integer c, and $O(\log^2 N)$ for the second. Both of these are a significant theoretical improvement over the previously best lattice construction by Bootle et al. (CRYPTO 2018) which gave $O(\sqrt{N})$-sized proofs.

Keywords: Lattices · Zero-knowledge proofs · SNARKS

1 Introduction

Zero-knowledge proofs are a crucial component in many cryptographic protocols. They are essential to electronic voting, verifiable computation, cryptocurrencies, and for adding stronger security and privacy guarantees to digital signature

This work was supported by the SNSF ERC Transfer Grant CRETP2-166734 – FELIC-ITY. The work was done while the first author was at IBM Research – Zurich.

© International Association for Cryptologic Research 2020
D. Micciancio and T. Ristenpart (Eds.): CRYPTO 2020, LNCS 12171, pp. 441–469, 2020.
https://doi.org/10.1007/978-3-030-56880-1_16

and encryption schemes. Across almost all applications, it is important to be able to prove in zero-knowledge that one knows how to open a cryptographic commitment, and to prove that the committed values have particular properties or satisfy some relations.

Recent years have seen an explosion of new zero-knowledge proof techniques, each with improvements in proof-size, proving time, or verification time. These new constructions are based on a variety of cryptographic assumptions, including the discrete logarithm assumption [14], various pairing-based assumptions in the Generic and Algebraic Group Models [26,27], collision-resistant hash functions [7,8], and lattice-based assumptions such as (R)SIS and (R)LWE [3,13,19,20].

Of these, only constructions from hash-functions and lattices stand any chance of being post-quantum secure. At this point in time, general-purpose lattice-based proof systems still lag far behind, both asymptotically and in practice, in proof-size and usability. This may seem somewhat surprising, since unlike hash-functions, lattices are endowed with algebraic structure that allows for constructions of rather efficient encryption [34], signature [17,37], and identity-based encryption schemes [18,24]. One could hope that the additional lattice structure can be also exploited for succinct zero-knowledge proofs as well.

1.1 Our Contribution

In this paper, we present two novel lattice-based commitment schemes with associated zero-knowledge opening protocols which prove knowledge of N secret integers with $\tilde{\mathcal{O}}(N^{1/c})$ and $\tilde{\mathcal{O}}(\log^2 N)$ communication complexity, for any constant c. For the former argument, we sketch out a method for constructing an argument of knowledge of a satisfying assignment for an arithmetic circuit with N gates, with $\tilde{\mathcal{O}}(N^{1/c})$ communication complexity in the full version of this paper. Both arguments of knowledge follow the same basic methodology, which is to replace the homomorphic commitment schemes used in earlier classically-secure protocols with a commitment scheme based on the (Ring)-SIS problem, and adapt the security proofs to match.

Our constructions follow the usual framework of being interactive schemes converted to non-interactive ones using the Fiat-Shamir transform. As with many schemes constructed in this fashion, their security is proven in the ROM rather than the QROM. The latter would be very strong evidence of quantum security,[1] but the former also appears to give strong evidence of quantum security in practice. To this day, there is no example of a practical scheme that has been proven secure in the ROM based on a quantum-safe computational assumption that has shown any weakness when the adversary was given additional quantum access to the random oracle. A recent line of works (e.g. [15,16,28,30]) that prove security in the QROM of schemes using the Fiat-Shamir transform which previously only known to be secure in the ROM give further evidence that security in the ROM based on a quantum-safe assumption is a meaningful security notion in practice.

---

[1] Though still technically heuristic because of the assumption that a concrete hash function acts as a random oracle.

Our first construction extends the classical interactive argument of [25] in which the prover commits to message values using Pedersen commitments, and then commits to those commitments using a pairing-based commitment scheme. The two-level structure means that a clever commitment-opening procedure is possible, giving $\tilde{\mathcal{O}}(N^{1/3})$ communication costs. With a d-level commitment scheme, one could hope to extend the technique and construct an argument with $\tilde{\mathcal{O}}(N^{1/(d+1)})$-sized proofs. However, in [25], Pedersen commitments map finite field elements to source group elements, which are mapped to target group elements by the second commitment scheme. In the classical setting, this is as far as the technique can take us, as no homomorphic, compressing commitment scheme for target group elements is known. In the lattice setting, however, the message space for SIS commitments are small integers and commitments are just made up of larger integers. So there is no fundamental reason not to continue. Using careful manipulation of matrices and moduli, our first new argument extends this technique to any constant number of levels.

The second argument is based on the techniques in the Bulletproofs protocol [14], and an earlier protocol [12], which use Pedersen commitments to commit to long message vectors. The additional structure of the Pedersen commitment scheme allows a neat folding technique, which reduces the length of committed message vectors by a factor of two. The prover and verifier repeatedly employ the technique over logarithmically many rounds of interaction until message vectors are reduced to a single value, which the prover can then easily send to the verifier. This gives logarithmic proof sizes. Our new lattice protocol stems from the observation that a SIS-based commitment scheme has some structure similarity to the Pedersen commitment scheme, and thus can be made compatible with the same folding technique. A technical complication that is unique to the lattice setting is keeping the coefficients of the extracted values from growing (too much) during each fold, as a direct adaptation of the bulletproof technique would result in unconstrained growth for every fold which would make the proof meaningless.

Finally, we make a comparison of these two techniques in terms of commitment/proof sizes as well as sizes of the extracted solutions, alternatively called "slack". Our conclusion is that the Bulletproofs folding argument offers smaller poly-logarithmic proof size at the cost much larger slack. Hence, if one does not necessarily need their extracted solution to be very small, then using Bulletproofs appears to be more suitable. However, in many applications, such as group signatures or verifiable encryption, zero-knowledge proofs are just one part of a more complex scheme. If the extracted witnesses are large, then we must adjust parameters not only for the zero-knowledge proof but also for other components of the scheme. Thus, we believe the leveled commitments can be applied in such scenarios at the cost of slightly larger proofs than lattice-based Bulletproofs.

Discussion and Open Problems. The ultimate goal of the line of research that this paper is pursuing is constructing zero-knowledge proofs with concrete parameters smaller than those that can be achieved following the PCP approach. Our current results achieve parameters that are essentially the same asymptotically, but are larger in practice. The asymptotic equivalence comes from the fact that we succeeded in making the *dimension* of the vector(s) representing the proof be logarithmic in the message size. And while we have also somewhat restricted the *coefficient* growth of the proof vector, the coefficients still grow by some factor with each "folding" of the vector dimension. Finding a technique to even further restrict the coefficient growth is the main open problem stemming from this work.

From experience with other primitives, using the additional algebraic structure of concrete assumptions should (eventually) result in size advantages over the generic PCP-based approaches that have the implicit lower bounds (of around 100–200 KB) posed by using Merkle-tree commitments. While lattice-based constructions may not achieve the extreme compactness of discrete logarithm based approaches (e.g. Bulletproofs, which have proofs sizes of a few kilobytes for reasonably-sized circuits), there is reason to hope that they can be shorter (and faster) than generic constructions. As an analogy, when lattice-based signatures first appeared [24,33], they were significantly larger than the generic quantum-safe signatures that one could construct using techniques, such as one-way functions and Merkle trees, dating back to the 1970s [29,35]. But expanding upon these early lattice constructions via novel algorithms and techniques exploiting the underlying mathematical structure of lattices, the current state-of-the-art lattice-based signatures [17,37] are currently an order of magnitude smaller and two orders of magnitude faster than those stemming from generic constructions [10]. We believe that the techniques of this paper can similarly be the beginning of the path to more practical succinct quantum-safe zero-knowledge.

1.2   Technical Overview

Levelled Commitments. The commitment scheme in [5] arranged N elements of $\mathbb{Z}_q$ to which one wants to commit to, into an $m \times k$ matrix $\mathbf{S}$ and created the commitment

$$\mathbf{A} \cdot \mathbf{S} = \mathbf{T} \bmod q \tag{1}$$

where $\mathbf{A} \leftarrow \mathbb{Z}_p^{n \times m}$ is a random matrix and $p < q$. Notice that $\mathbf{T} \in \mathbb{Z}_q^{n \times k}$, and [5] showed that the proof of knowledge of an $\mathbf{S}$ with small (but larger than the honest prover uses in the proof) coefficients satisfying (1) can be done with λm elements in $\mathbb{Z}_q$[2] where λ is a security parameter. The total size of the proof is therefore the size of $\mathbf{T}$ and the size of the proof of (1), which is $nk + \lambda m$ elements in $\mathbb{Z}_q$. Since $n = \mathcal{O}(\lambda)$, the optimal way to commit to N elements in $\mathbb{Z}_q$ is to arrange them into a matrix $\mathbf{S} \in \mathbb{Z}_q^{m \times k}$, where $m = k = \tilde{\mathcal{O}}(\sqrt{N})$. This makes the total proof size $\tilde{\mathcal{O}}(\sqrt{N})$.

To illustrate our levelled commitment technique, we will describe a commitment scheme and a protocol for achieving a proof size of $\tilde{\mathcal{O}}(N^{1/3})$. We will

---

[2] We provide additional background in Sect. 2.3 for readers not familiar with previous work.

commit to $\mathbf{S} \in \mathbb{Z}^{m_1 \cdot m_2 \times m_3}$ as $\mathbf{A}_1 \cdot ((\mathbf{I}_{m_1} \otimes \mathbf{A}_2) \cdot \mathbf{S} \bmod q_2) \bmod q_1 = \mathbf{T}$ where $\mathbf{A}_1 \leftarrow \mathbb{Z}_{q_1}^{n \times nm_1}, \mathbf{A}_2 \leftarrow \mathbb{Z}_{q_2}^{n \times m_2}$. Our proof will prove knowledge of an $\bar{\mathbf{S}}$ with somewhat larger coefficients than $\mathbf{S}$, and also an $\bar{\mathbf{R}} \in \mathbb{Z}^{n \cdot m_1 \times m_3}$ satisfying

$$\mathbf{A}_1 \cdot ((\mathbf{I}_{m_1} \otimes \mathbf{A}_2) \cdot \bar{\mathbf{S}} \bmod q_2 + \bar{\mathbf{R}} \cdot q_2) \bmod q_1 = \mathbf{T}, \qquad (2)$$

Let us first show that the above extracted commitment of $(\bar{\mathbf{S}}, \bar{\mathbf{R}})$ is binding based on the hardness of SIS when $\|\bar{\mathbf{S}}\| \ll q_2, \|\bar{\mathbf{R}}\| \ll q_1/q_2$ and $q_2 \ll q_1$. Suppose, for contradiction, there are two $(\bar{\mathbf{S}}, \bar{\mathbf{R}}) \neq (\bar{\mathbf{S}}', \bar{\mathbf{R}}')$ satisfying (2). In the first case, suppose that $\bar{\mathbf{R}} \neq \bar{\mathbf{R}}'$. By definition, the coefficients of $(\mathbf{I}_{m_1} \otimes \mathbf{A}_2) \cdot \bar{\mathbf{S}} \bmod q_2$ are smaller than q_2, and thus $\bar{\mathbf{R}} \neq \bar{\mathbf{R}}'$ implies that

$$(\mathbf{I}_{m_1} \otimes \mathbf{A}_2) \cdot \bar{\mathbf{S}} \bmod q_2 + \bar{\mathbf{R}} \cdot q_2 \neq (\mathbf{I}_{m_1} \otimes \mathbf{A}_2) \cdot \bar{\mathbf{S}}' \bmod q_2 + \bar{\mathbf{R}}' \cdot q_2. \qquad (3)$$

If the parameters are set such that the coefficients of both sides of the above equation are less than q_1, then this gives a solution to SIS for $\mathbf{A}_1$. Now assume that $\bar{\mathbf{R}} = \bar{\mathbf{R}}'$, and so $\bar{\mathbf{S}} \neq \bar{\mathbf{S}}'$. If $(\mathbf{I}_{m_1} \otimes \mathbf{A}_2) \cdot \bar{\mathbf{S}} \equiv (\mathbf{I}_{m_1} \otimes \mathbf{A}_2) \cdot \bar{\mathbf{S}}' \pmod{q_2}$, then there must be some $\bar{\mathbf{S}}_i \neq \bar{\mathbf{S}}'_i \in \mathbb{Z}^{m_2 \times m_3}$ such that $\mathbf{A}_2 \cdot \bar{\mathbf{S}}_i \equiv \mathbf{A}_2 \cdot \bar{\mathbf{S}}'_i \pmod{q_2}$, and so we have a SIS solution for $\mathbf{A}_2$. If $(\mathbf{I}_{m_1} \otimes \mathbf{A}_2) \cdot \bar{\mathbf{S}} \not\equiv (\mathbf{I}_{m_1} \otimes \mathbf{A}_2) \cdot \bar{\mathbf{S}}' \pmod{q_2}$, then the inequality in (3) holds and we have a SIS solution for $\mathbf{A}_1$.

We present the basic protocol in Fig. 1. The boxed text contains the parts necessary to make the protocol zero-knowledge. In this overview, we will ignore these and only show that the protocol is a proof of knowledge. First, let us show the correctness of the protocol. Because the coefficients of $\mathbf{S}, \mathbf{C}_1$, and $\mathbf{C}_2$ are small, the coefficients of $\mathbf{Z}$ are also small with respect to q_2. Similarly, because the coefficients of $\mathbf{V}$ consist of a product of a matrix with coefficients less than q_2 with a $0/1$ matrix $\mathbf{C}_1$, parameters can be set such that the coefficients of the product are less than q_1. Thus $\|\mathbf{z}_i\| \leq \beta_z$ and $\|\mathbf{V}\| \leq \beta_v q_2$ can be satisfied with an appropriate choice of parameters. We now move on to showing that the verification equations hold. Note that

$$\mathbf{V} = \begin{bmatrix} \mathbf{V}_1 \\ \vdots \\ \mathbf{V}_{m_1} \end{bmatrix} = \left(\begin{bmatrix} \mathbf{A}_2 \mathbf{S}_1 \\ \vdots \\ \mathbf{A}_2 \mathbf{S}_{m_1} \end{bmatrix} \bmod q_2 \right) \cdot \mathbf{C}_1 \equiv \begin{bmatrix} \mathbf{A}_2 \mathbf{S}_1 \mathbf{C}_1 \\ \vdots \\ \mathbf{A}_2 \mathbf{S}_{m_1} \mathbf{C}_1 \end{bmatrix} \pmod{q_2}, \quad (4)$$

and so one can write $\mathbf{A}_2 \cdot [\mathbf{S}_1 \mathbf{C}_1 \cdots \mathbf{S}_{m_1} \mathbf{C}_1] \equiv [\mathbf{V}_1 \cdots \mathbf{V}_{m_1}] \pmod{q_2}$, and therefore $\mathbf{A}_2 \cdot \mathbf{Z} \equiv \mathbf{A}_2 \cdot [\mathbf{S}_1 \mathbf{C}_1 \cdots \mathbf{S}_{m_1} \mathbf{C}_1] \cdot \mathbf{C}_2 \pmod{q_2}$, which is the first verification equation. For the second verification equation, observe from (4) and (2) that

$$\mathbf{A}_1 \cdot \mathbf{V} = \mathbf{A}_1 \cdot \left(\begin{bmatrix} \mathbf{A}_2 \mathbf{S}_1 \\ \vdots \\ \mathbf{A}_2 \mathbf{S}_{m_1} \end{bmatrix} \bmod q_2 \right) \cdot \mathbf{C}_1 \equiv \mathbf{T} \cdot \mathbf{C}_1 \pmod{q_1}.$$

Finally, ignoring constant terms, the total communication cost (including the statement) can be bounded above by

$$m_3 \cdot (n \log q_1 + \lambda) + m_2 \cdot \lambda \log \beta_z + m_1 \cdot (n\lambda \log(\beta_v q_2) + \lambda^2) + n\lambda \log q_2.$$

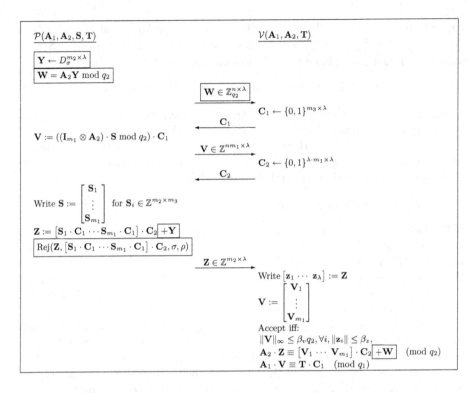

Fig. 1. Levelled commitment with two levels. Here, β_v and β_z are parameters which satisfy $\beta_z \ll q_2, \beta_v \ll q_1/q_2$.

Note that the last term does not depend on m_1, m_2, m_3 hence we ignore it for now. Therefore, in order to minimise the expression above, we want to set m_1, m_2, m_3 such that all three corresponding terms are (almost) equal. We select appropriate n, q_1, q_2 such that both $\mathbf{A}_1$ and $\mathbf{A}_2$ are binding (7) and we get $\log q_2 < \log q_1 = \mathcal{O}(\log N)$ and $n = \mathcal{O}(\lambda)$. Similarly, $\log \beta_v = \mathcal{O}(\log N)$ and $\log \beta_z = \mathcal{O}(\log N)$. Therefore, the total communication cost is approximately $\tilde{\mathcal{O}}(\sqrt[3]{N})$.

In Sect. 3, we extend this approach to more than two levels. Generally, we propose a proof of knowledge for $d \geq 1$ levels with total communication size equal to $\mathcal{O}\left(N^{\frac{1}{d+1}} \cdot (d^3\lambda \log^2 N + d\lambda^2)\right)$. In Sect. 3.3, we also show how to apply techniques similar to previous work [5, 12, 14] in order to extract a relatively short solution to the relaxed equation (e.g. (2) for $d = 2$). Due to space limitations, we skip the details in this overview.

Bulletproofs Folding. Our starting point is the lattice equation:

$$\mathbf{As} = \mathbf{t} \tag{5}$$

where $\mathbf{A} \in R^{1 \times k}, \mathbf{s} \in R^k$ and $R = \mathbb{Z}_q[X]/(X^n + 1)$. Thus, the number of secrets is $N = kn$. In the same vein as [12,14], we are interested in constructing a protocol where proving knowledge of pre-image $\mathbf{s}$ of $\mathbf{t}$ comes down to proving knowledge of some other pre-image, say $\mathbf{s}'$, whose length $k/2$ is half that of $\mathbf{s}$. By recursively applying this argument $\log k$ times, we obtain poly-logarithmic proof size. Concretely, we fold the initial statement (5) as follows. Let us write $\mathbf{A} = [\mathbf{A}_1 \ \mathbf{A}_2]$ and $\mathbf{s} = \begin{bmatrix} \mathbf{s}_1 \\ \mathbf{s}_2 \end{bmatrix}$ where $\mathbf{s}_1, \mathbf{s}_2 \in R^{k/2}$.

Let $\mathbf{l} := \mathbf{A}_1 \mathbf{s}_2 \in R$ and $\mathbf{r} := \mathbf{A}_2 \mathbf{s}_1 \in R$. Then, for all $c \in R$, $(c\mathbf{A}_1 + \mathbf{A}_2)(\mathbf{s}_1 + c\mathbf{s}_2) = c^2 \mathbf{l} + c\mathbf{t} + \mathbf{r}$. We observe that $\mathbf{s}_1 + c\mathbf{s}_2$ has length $k/2$, suggesting the following protocol for proving knowledge of $\mathbf{s}$. First, the prover $\mathcal{P}$ sends $\mathbf{l}, \mathbf{r}$ to the verifier $\mathcal{V}$. Then, $\mathcal{V}$ samples a challenge c uniformly at random from a challenge space $\mathcal{C} \subseteq R$ and sends it to $\mathcal{P}$. Finally, $\mathcal{P}$ sends $\mathbf{z} = \mathbf{s}_1 + c\mathbf{s}_2$ to $\mathcal{V}$. Note that if $\mathcal{P}$ is honest then $\mathbf{z}$ satisfies the new lattice equation $\mathbf{Bz} = \mathbf{t}'$ where $\mathbf{B} = c\mathbf{A}_1 + \mathbf{A}_2$ and $\mathbf{t}' = c^2 \mathbf{l} + c\mathbf{t} + \mathbf{r}$. Therefore, instead of sending $\mathbf{z}$ directly, the prover might repeat the protocol and treat $\mathbf{z}$ as a new secret vector. By folding all the way down to vectors of length 1, we get communication costs of order $\log k$.

Using similar techniques to [12,14], one can extract a solution $\bar{\mathbf{z}}$ to the original equation $\mathbf{A}\bar{\mathbf{z}} = \mathbf{t}$. The problem is that unless we define the challenge space properly, we do not have any information on the size of $\|\bar{\mathbf{z}}\|$. Hence, we let $\mathcal{C}$ be the set of monomials of R, i.e. $\mathcal{C} = \{X^i : i \in \mathbb{Z}\}$. Then, using the fact that polynomials of the form $2/(X^i - X^j) \in R$ have coefficients in $\{-1, 0, 1\}$ [9], we bound the size of an extracted solution. The only drawback of using this approach is that we only obtain a solution for a relaxed equation. Concretely, if we apply the folding technique d times, then we only manage to find a small solution $\bar{\mathbf{z}}$ for the equation $\mathbf{A}\bar{\mathbf{z}} = 8^d \mathbf{t}$ such that $\|\bar{\mathbf{z}}\| = \mathcal{O}(n^{3d} \cdot 12^d \cdot p)$ where $p = \|\mathbf{s}\|_\infty$. For $d = \log k$, the relaxation factor becomes k^3. The communication cost for the $(2d + 1)$-round version of the protocol is equal to $N \log(2^d p)/2^d + 2dn \log q$.

Then, we would just pick q which is a little bit larger than the slack. It is worth mentioning that the protocol in its current state gives us soundness error of order $1/n$, hence we would need to repeat it $\lambda/\log n$ times in order to achieve soundness error $2^{-\lambda}$. Therefore, the total proof size can be bounded by $\mathcal{O}\left(\frac{\lambda N \log(2^d p)}{2^d \log n} + \lambda d^2 n\right)$.

Comparison. We investigate in which applications one technique offers asymptotically smaller proof size than the other (see Sect. 4 for more details). First of all, consider the case when we do not require the extracted solution to be "very small". Then, levelled commitments for $d = \log N - 1$ levels provide proof size of order $\mathcal{O}(\lambda \log^5 N + \lambda^2 \log N)$.

On the other hand, by applying Bulletproofs folding $d = \log k$ times, we obtain proof size[3] $\mathcal{O}(\lambda n \log N \cdot (\log N + 1))$. Consequently, the Bulletproofs approach achieves smaller proof size.

---

[3] We note that more concrete bounds could be computed. However, this non-tight bound already shows that Bulletproofs folding offers smaller proof size.

Next, consider the case when one could only afford limited slack, i.e. the extracted solution is smaller than some set value $B = N^\alpha > N^2$. First, suppose that $N = \lambda^r$ for some $r \geq 3$ (we expect N to be much bigger than λ). Then, we show that levelled commitments and Bulletproofs provide $\tilde{\mathcal{O}}(N^u)$ and $\tilde{\mathcal{O}}(N^v)$ proof sizes respectively, where $u \approx \frac{1}{(\alpha-2)r}$ and $v \approx 1 - \frac{\alpha-1/2}{3\log n + 4}$[4].

Assume the allowed slack is small enough that both u and v are larger than $1/\log N$. Then, we just check which one of u, v is bigger[5]. Since $\log n \geq 1$ and for all $r \geq 3$, the function $f_r(x) := (15 - 2x)(x-2)r - 14$ is positive for $3 \leq x \leq 7$, we deduce that u is smaller than v when $\alpha \leq 7$. This suggests that one should use the levelled commitments protocol when one can only tolerate a limited amount of slack.

1.3   Related Work

In this paper, we investigate techniques from [12,14] and [25] in the lattice world. These papers are the most closely related prior works, along with [14], which forms a key component of the argument in Sect. 3.

We review proof systems which can prove knowledge of a secret with N elements, or prove knowledge of a satisfying assignment to an arithmetic circuit with N gates.

Lattice-Based Arguments. The zero-knowledge argument given in [5] is based on the SIS assumption, and is capable of proving knowledge of commitment openings with proof size $\mathcal{O}(\sqrt{N})$. It was the first and only standard zero-knowledge protocol based on lattice assumptions to achieve a sublinear communication complexity. Previously, the only other lattice-based arguments of knowledge with better asymptotic proof size were lattice-based SNARKs [11,23,36]. Although they offer highly succinct, $\mathcal{O}(1)$-sized proofs, the proofs are only checkable by a designated verifier, and soundness is based on strong, non-falsifiable assumptions.

Hash-Based Arguments. STARKs [6] and Aurora [8] are non-interactive argument systems. Both achieve $\mathcal{O}(\log^2 N)$-sized proofs, with Aurora more efficient by an order of magnitude due to better constants. Ligero [2] achieves $\mathcal{O}(\sqrt{N})$-sized proofs, but is highly efficient in practice.

Classically-Secure Arguments. In the discrete-logarithm setting, Bulletproofs [14] and a related argument [12] give $\mathcal{O}(\log N)$ communication complexity, using Pedersen commitments and the same recursive folding technique that inspired the argument described in Sect. 4. The protocol of [25] gives $\mathcal{O}(N^{1/3})$ proof sizes, and uses a two-tiered commitment scheme, based on Pedersen commitments and a related commitment scheme based on pairings. We extend the same idea to a multi-levelled lattice-based commitment scheme in Sect. 3.

---

[4] Here, n denotes the degree of the underlying cyclotomic polynomial $X^n + 1$.

[5] This would only *asymptotically* tell us which method offers smaller proof size.

There is also a long line of works on succinct non-interactive arguments based on pairings, culminating in protocols including [26] and [27] which have $\mathcal{O}(1)$ proof size, but rely on strong, non-falsifiable assumptions like the Knowledge-of-Exponent assumptions, or have security proofs in idealised models like the Generic Group Model [38] or Algebraic Group Model [21].

2   Preliminaries

Algorithms in our schemes receive a security parameter λ as input (sometimes implicitly) written in unary. Unless stated otherwise, we assume all our algorithms to be probabilistic. We denote by $\mathcal{A}(x)$ the probabilistic computation of the algorithm $\mathcal{A}$ on input x. If $\mathcal{A}$ is deterministic, we write $y := \mathcal{A}(x)$. We write PPT (resp. DPT) for probabilistic (resp. deterministic) polynomial time algorithms. The notation $y \leftarrow \mathcal{A}(x)$ denotes the event that $\mathcal{A}$ on input x returns y. Given two functions $f, g : \mathbb{N} \to [0, 1]$ we write $f(\lambda) \approx g(\lambda)$ when $|f(\lambda) - g(\lambda)| = \lambda^{-\omega(1)}$. We say that f is *negligible* when $f(\lambda) \approx 0$ and that f is *overwhelming* when $f(\lambda) \approx 1$. For $n \in \mathbb{N}$, we write $[n] := \{1, \ldots, n\}$. Regular font letters denote elements in $\mathbb{Z}$ or $\mathbb{Z}_q$, for a prime q, and bold lower-case letters represent column vectors with coefficients in $\mathbb{Z}$ or $\mathbb{Z}_q$. Bold upper-case letters denote matrices. By default, all vectors are column vectors. Let $\mathbf{I}_n \in \mathbb{Z}_q^{n \times n}$ be the $n \times n$ identity matrix. We write a list of objects with square brackets, e.g. $[a_1, \ldots, a_k]$ is a list of k objects: $a_1, \ldots, a_k$. Also, we denote by $[]$ the empty list. For any statement st, we define $[\![st]\!]$ to be equal to 1 if st is true and 0 otherwise.

Sizes of Elements. For an even (resp. odd) positive integer α, we define $r' = r \bmod \alpha$ to be the unique element r' in the range $-\frac{\alpha}{2} < r' \leq \frac{\alpha}{2}$ (resp. $-\frac{\alpha-1}{2} \leq r' \leq \frac{\alpha-1}{2}$) such that $r' = r \bmod \alpha$. For an element $w \in \mathbb{Z}_q$, we write $\|w\|_\infty$ to mean $|w \bmod q|$. Define the ℓ_∞ and ℓ_2 norms for $\mathbf{w} = (w_1, \ldots, w_k) \in \mathbb{Z}_q^k$ as follows:

$$\|\mathbf{w}\|_\infty = \max_i \|w_i\|_\infty, \quad \|\mathbf{w}\| = \sqrt{\|w_1\|_\infty^2 + \ldots + \|w_k\|_\infty^2}.$$

However, if we do not state explicitly that $\mathbf{w} \in \mathbb{Z}_q^k$ but rather treat $\mathbf{w}$ as a vector of integers then the standard notions of L_2 and L_∞ norms apply. We will also consider the operator norm of matrices over $\mathbb{Z}$ defined by $s_1(\mathbf{A}) = \max_{\|\mathbf{x}\| \neq 0} \left(\frac{\|\mathbf{A}\mathbf{x}\|}{\|\mathbf{x}\|} \right)$.

Probability Distributions. Let $\mathcal{D}$ denote a distribution over some set S. Then, $d \leftarrow \mathcal{D}$ means that d was sampled from the distribution $\mathcal{D}$. If we write $d \xleftarrow{\$} S$ for some finite set S without a specified distribution this means that d was sampled uniformly random from S. We let $\Delta(X, Y)$ indicate the statistical distance between two distributions X, Y. Define the function $\rho_\sigma(x) = \exp\left(\frac{-x^2}{2\sigma^2}\right)$ and the discrete Gaussian distribution over the integers, D_σ, as $D_\sigma(x) = \frac{\rho(x)}{\rho(\mathbb{Z})}$ where $\rho(\mathbb{Z}) = \sum_{v \in \mathbb{Z}} \rho(v)$.

We will write $\mathbf{A} \leftarrow D_\sigma^{k \times \ell}$ to mean that every coefficient of the matrix $\mathbf{A}$ is distributed according to D_σ.

Using the tail bounds for the 0-centered discrete Gaussian distribution (cf. [4]), we can show that for any $\sigma > 0$ the norm of $x \leftarrow D_\sigma$ can be upper-bounded using σ. Namely, for any $t > 0$, we have $\mathrm{Pr}_{x \leftarrow D_\sigma}[|x| > t\sigma] \leq 2e^{-t^2/2}$, and when $\mathbf{x}$ is drawn from D_σ^m, we have

$$\Pr_{\mathbf{x} \leftarrow D_\sigma^m}[\|\mathbf{x}\| > \sqrt{2m} \cdot \sigma] < 2^{-m/4}. \tag{6}$$

2.1   Lattice-Based Commitment Schemes

A non-interactive commitment scheme is a pair of PPT algorithms (Gen, Com). The setup algorithm $ck \leftarrow \mathrm{Gen}(1^\lambda)$ generates a commitment key ck, which specifies message, randomness and commitment spaces $\mathsf{M}_{ck}, \mathsf{R}_{ck}, \mathsf{C}_{ck}$. It also specifies an efficiently sampleable probability distribution $D_{\mathsf{R}_{ck}}$ over R_{ck} and a binding set $\mathsf{B}_{ck} \subset \mathsf{M}_{ck} \times \mathsf{R}_{ck}$. The commitment key also specifies a deterministic polynomial-time commitment function $\mathrm{Com}_{ck} : \mathsf{M}_{ck} \times \mathsf{R}_{ck} \to \mathsf{C}_{ck}$. We define $\mathrm{Com}_{ck}(\mathbf{m})$ to be the probabilistic algorithm that given $\mathbf{m} \in \mathsf{M}_{ck}$ samples $\mathbf{r} \leftarrow D_{\mathsf{R}_{ck}}$ and returns $\mathbf{c} = \mathrm{Com}_{ck}(\mathbf{m}; \mathbf{r})$.

The commitment scheme is homomorphic, if the message, randomness and commitment spaces are abelian groups (written additively) and we have for all $\lambda \in \mathbb{N}$, and for all $ck \leftarrow \mathrm{Gen}(1^\lambda)$, for all $\mathbf{m}_0, \mathbf{m}_1 \in \mathsf{M}_{ck}$ and for all $\mathbf{r}_0, \mathbf{r}_1 \in \mathsf{R}_{ck}$:

$$\mathrm{Com}_{ck}(\mathbf{m}_0; \mathbf{r}_0) + \mathrm{Com}_{ck}(\mathbf{m}_1; \mathbf{r}_1) = \mathrm{Com}_{ck}(\mathbf{m}_0 + \mathbf{m}_1; \mathbf{r}_0 + \mathbf{r}_1).$$

Definition 2.1 (Hiding). *The commitment scheme is hiding if for all PPT stateful interactive adversaries $\mathcal{A}$*

$$\Pr\left[\begin{matrix} ck \leftarrow \mathrm{Gen}(1^\lambda); (\mathbf{m}_0, \mathbf{m}_1) \leftarrow \mathcal{A}(ck); b \leftarrow \{0,1\}; \\ \mathbf{r} \leftarrow D_{\mathsf{R}_{ck}}; \mathbf{c} \leftarrow \mathrm{Com}_{ck}(\mathbf{m}_b; \mathbf{r}) : \mathcal{A}(\mathbf{c}) = b \end{matrix}\right] \approx \frac{1}{2},$$

where $\mathcal{A}$ outputs $\mathbf{m}_0, \mathbf{m}_1 \in \mathsf{M}_{ck}$.

Definition 2.2 (Binding). *The commitment scheme is computationally binding if a commitment can only be opened to one value within the binding set B_{ck}. For all PPT adversaries $\mathcal{A}$*

$$\Pr\left[\begin{matrix} ck \leftarrow \mathrm{Gen}(1^\lambda); (\mathbf{m}_0, \mathbf{r}_0, \mathbf{m}_1, \mathbf{r}_1) \leftarrow \mathcal{A}(ck) : \\ \mathbf{m}_0 \neq \mathbf{m}_1 \ and \ \mathrm{Com}_{ck}(\mathbf{m}_0; \mathbf{r}_0) = \mathrm{Com}_{ck}(\mathbf{m}_1; \mathbf{r}_1) \end{matrix}\right] \approx 0,$$

where $\mathcal{A}$ outputs $(\mathbf{m}_0, \mathbf{r}_0), (\mathbf{m}_1, \mathbf{r}_1) \in \mathsf{B}_{ck}$.

The commitment scheme is compressing if the sizes of commitments are smaller than the sizes of the committed values.

Compressing Commitments Based on SIS. We work with the standard SIS (shortest integer solution) commitment scheme, which was already implicit in the aforementioned work of Ajtai [1] and uses uniformly random matrices $\mathbf{A}_1 \in \mathbb{Z}_q^{r \times 2r \log_p q}$ and $\mathbf{A}_2 \in \mathbb{Z}_q^{r \times n}$ as a commitment key, where n is the number of elements that one wishes to commit to and $p < q$. A commitment to a vector $\mathbf{m} \in \mathbb{Z}_p^n$ involves choosing a random vector $\mathbf{r} \in \mathbb{Z}_p^{2r \log_p q}$ and outputting the commitment vector $\mathbf{v} = \mathbf{A}_1 \mathbf{r} + \mathbf{A}_2 \mathbf{m} \bmod q$. By the leftover hash lemma, $(\mathbf{A}_1, \mathbf{A}_1 \mathbf{r} \bmod q)$ is statistically close to uniform, and so the commitment scheme is statistically hiding.[6] To prove binding, note that if there are two different $(\mathbf{r}, \mathbf{m}) \neq (\mathbf{r}', \mathbf{m}')$ such that $\mathbf{v} = \mathbf{A}_1 \mathbf{r} + \mathbf{A}_2 \mathbf{m} \equiv \mathbf{A}_1 \mathbf{r}' + \mathbf{A}_2 \mathbf{m}' \pmod{q}$, then $\mathbf{A}_1(\mathbf{r} - \mathbf{r}') + \mathbf{A}_2(\mathbf{m} - \mathbf{m}') \equiv \mathbf{0} \pmod{q}$ and the non-zero vector $\mathbf{s} = \begin{bmatrix} \mathbf{r} - \mathbf{r}' \\ \mathbf{m} - \mathbf{m}' \end{bmatrix}$ is a solution to the SIS problem for the matrix $\mathbf{A} = [\mathbf{A}_1 \ \mathbf{A}_2]$, i.e. $\mathbf{As} \equiv \mathbf{0} \pmod{q}$. As long as the parameters are set such that $\|\mathbf{s}\|$ is smaller than[7]

$$\min\{q, 2^{2\sqrt{r \log q \log \delta}}\}, \tag{7}$$

the binding property of the commitment is based on an intractable version of the SIS problem [22].

In this paper, we will use the following lattice commitment scheme.

$\mathsf{Gen}(1^\lambda) \rightarrow ck$: Select parameters p, q, r, v, N, B, σ. Pick uniformly random matrices $\mathbf{A}_1 \xleftarrow{\$} \mathbb{Z}_q^{r \times r \log_p q}$ and $\mathbf{A}_2 \xleftarrow{\$} \mathbb{Z}_q^{r \times n}$. Return $ck = (p, q, r, v, \ell, N, \beta, \mathbb{Z}_q, \mathbf{A}_1, \mathbf{A}_2)$. The commitment key defines the message space $\mathsf{M}_{ck} = \mathcal{R}_q^n$, randomness space $\mathsf{R}_{ck} = \mathcal{R}_q^{2r \log_p q}$, commitment space $\mathsf{C}_{ck} = \mathbb{Z}_q^r$, randomness distribution $D_{\mathsf{R}_{ck}} = D_\sigma^r$ and binding space

$$\mathsf{B}_{ck} = \left\{ \mathbf{s} = \begin{bmatrix} \mathbf{m} \\ \mathbf{r} \end{bmatrix} \in \mathcal{R}_q^{n + 2r \log_p q} \mid \|\mathbf{s}\| < B \right\}.$$

$\mathsf{Com}_{ck}(\mathbf{m}; \mathbf{r})$: Given $\mathbf{m} \in \mathbb{Z}_q^n$ and $\mathbf{r} \in \mathbb{Z}_q^{2r \log_p q}$ return $\mathbf{c} = \mathbf{A}_1 \mathbf{r} + \mathbf{A}_2 \mathbf{s}$.

In the following, when we make multiple commitments to vectors $\mathbf{m}_1, \dots, \mathbf{m}_\ell \in \mathsf{M}_{ck}$ we write $\mathbf{C} = \mathsf{Com}_{ck}(\mathbf{M}; \mathbf{R})$ when concatenating the commitment vectors as $\mathbf{C} = [\mathbf{c}_1, \dots, \mathbf{c}_\ell]$. This corresponds to computing $\mathbf{C} = \mathbf{A}_1 \mathbf{R} + \mathbf{A}_2 \mathbf{M}$ with $\mathbf{M} = [\mathbf{m}_1, \dots, \mathbf{m}_\ell]$ and randomness $\mathbf{R} = [\mathbf{r}_1, \dots, \mathbf{r}_\ell]$.

2.2 Arguments of Knowledge

We will now formally define arguments of knowledge. Let R be a polynomial-time-decidable ternary relation. The first input will contain public parameters (a.k.a. common reference string) pp. We define the corresponding language L_{pp}

---

[6] For improved efficiency, one could reduce the number of columns in $\mathbf{A}_1$ and make the commitment scheme computationally-hiding based on the hardness of the LWE problem.

[7] This constant δ is related to the optimal block-size in BKZ reduction [22], which is the currently best way of solving the SIS problem. Presently, the optimal lattice reductions set $\delta \approx 1.005$.

indexed by pp that consists of statement u with a witness w such that $(pp, u, w) \in R$. This is a natural generalisation of standard NP languages, which can be cast as the special case of relations that ignore the first input.

A proof system consists of a PPT parameter generator $\mathcal{K}$, and interactive and stateful PPT algorithms $\mathcal{P}$ and $\mathcal{V}$ used by the prover and verifier. We write $(tr, b) \leftarrow \langle \mathcal{P}(pp), \mathcal{V}(pp, t) \rangle$ for running $\mathcal{P}$ and $\mathcal{V}$ on inputs pp, s, and t and getting communication transcript tr and the verifier's decision bit b. We use the convention that $b = 0$ means reject and $b = 1$ means accept.

Definition 2.3. *Proof system $(\mathcal{K}, \mathcal{P}, \mathcal{V})$ is called an* argument of knowledge *for the relation R if it is complete and knowledge sound as defined below.*

Definition 2.4. *$(\mathcal{K}, \mathcal{P}, \mathcal{V})$ has statistical completeness with completeness error $\rho : \mathbb{N} \to [0; 1]$ if for all adversaries $\mathcal{A}$*

$$\Pr \left[\begin{array}{c} pp \leftarrow \mathcal{K}(1^\lambda); (u, w) \leftarrow \mathcal{A}(pp); (tr, b) \leftarrow \langle \mathcal{P}(pp, u, w), \mathcal{V}(pp, u) \rangle : \\ (pp, u, w) \in R \text{ and } b = 0 \end{array} \right] \leq \rho(\lambda).$$

Definition 2.5. *$(\mathcal{K}, \mathcal{P}, \mathcal{V})$ is knowledge sound with knowledge error $\epsilon : \mathbb{N} \to [0; 1]$ if for all DPT $\mathcal{P}^*$ there exists an expected polynomial time extractor $\mathcal{E}$ such that for all PPT adversaries $\mathcal{A}$*

$$\Pr \left[\begin{array}{c} pp \leftarrow \mathcal{K}(1^\lambda); (u, s) \leftarrow \mathcal{A}(pp); (tr, b) \leftarrow \langle \mathcal{P}^*(pp, u, s), \mathcal{V}(pp, u) \rangle; \\ w \leftarrow \mathcal{E}^{\mathcal{P}^*(pp, u, s)}(pp, u, tr, b) : (pp, u, w) \notin R \text{ and } b = 1 \end{array} \right] \leq \epsilon(\lambda).$$

It is sometimes useful to relax the definition of knowledge soundness by replacing R with a relation $\bar{R}$ such that $R \subset \bar{R}$. For instance, in this work, our zero-knowledge proofs of pre-images will have "slack". Thus, even though $\mathbf{v}$ is constructed using $\mathbf{r}, \mathbf{m}$ with coefficients in $\mathbb{Z}_p$, we will only be able to prove knowledge of vectors $\bar{\mathbf{r}}, \bar{\mathbf{m}}$ with larger norms. This extracted commitment is still binding as long as the parameters are set so that the norm of the vector $\begin{bmatrix} \bar{\mathbf{r}} - \bar{\mathbf{r}}' \\ \bar{\mathbf{m}} - \bar{\mathbf{m}}' \end{bmatrix}$ is smaller than the bound in (7).

We say the proof system is *public coin* if the verifier's challenges are chosen uniformly at random independently of the prover's messages. A proof system is special honest-verifier zero-knowledge if it is possible to simulate the proof without knowing the witness whenever the verifier's challenges are known in advance.

Definition 2.6. *A public-coin argument of knowledge $(\mathcal{K}, \mathcal{P}, \mathcal{V})$ is said to be statistical special honest-verifier zero-knowledge (SHVZK) if there exists a PPT simulator $\mathcal{S}$ such that for all interactive and stateful adversaries $\mathcal{A}$*

$$\Pr \left[\begin{array}{c} pp \leftarrow \mathcal{K}(1^\lambda); (u, w, \varrho) \leftarrow \mathcal{A}(pp); (tr, b) \leftarrow \langle \mathcal{P}(pp, u, w), \mathcal{V}(\sigma, u; \varrho) \rangle : \\ (pp, u, w) \in R \text{ and } \mathcal{A}(tr) = 1 \end{array} \right]$$

$$\approx \Pr \left[\begin{array}{c} pp \leftarrow \mathcal{K}(1^\lambda); (u, w, \varrho) \leftarrow \mathcal{A}(pp); (tr, b) \leftarrow \mathcal{S}(pp, u, \varrho) : \\ (pp, u, w) \in R \text{ and } \mathcal{A}(tr) = 1 \end{array} \right],$$

where ϱ is the randomness used by the verifier.

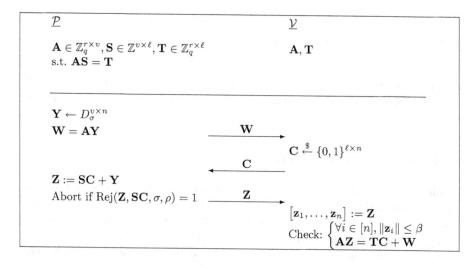

$\mathcal{P}$ $\qquad\qquad\qquad\qquad\qquad\qquad\qquad$ $\mathcal{V}$

$\mathbf{A} \in \mathbb{Z}_q^{r \times v}, \mathbf{S} \in \mathbb{Z}^{v \times \ell}, \mathbf{T} \in \mathbb{Z}_q^{r \times \ell}$ $\qquad\qquad$ $\mathbf{A}, \mathbf{T}$
s.t. $\mathbf{AS} = \mathbf{T}$

$\mathbf{Y} \leftarrow D_\sigma^{v \times n}$
$\mathbf{W} = \mathbf{AY}$ $\qquad\qquad\xrightarrow{\quad \mathbf{W} \quad}$

$\qquad\qquad\qquad\qquad\qquad\qquad\qquad\qquad \mathbf{C} \xleftarrow{\$} \{0,1\}^{\ell \times n}$

$\qquad\qquad\qquad\qquad\xleftarrow{\quad \mathbf{C} \quad}$

$\mathbf{Z} := \mathbf{SC} + \mathbf{Y}$
Abort if $\mathrm{Rej}(\mathbf{Z}, \mathbf{SC}, \sigma, \rho) = 1$ $\qquad\xrightarrow{\quad \mathbf{Z} \quad}$

$\qquad\qquad\qquad\qquad\qquad\qquad [\mathbf{z}_1, \ldots, \mathbf{z}_n] := \mathbf{Z}$
$\qquad\qquad\qquad\qquad\qquad\qquad \mathrm{Check}: \begin{cases} \forall i \in [n], \|\mathbf{z}_i\| \leq \beta \\ \mathbf{AZ} = \mathbf{TC} + \mathbf{W} \end{cases}$

Fig. 2. Amortized proof for ℓ equations.

2.3 Amortized Proofs of Knowledge

Baum et al. [5] give an amortized proof of knowledge for preimages of SIS commitments (see Fig. 2). The prover $\mathcal{P}$ wants to prove knowledge of the secret matrix $\mathbf{S}$ such that $\mathbf{AS} \equiv \mathbf{T} \pmod{q}$, where $\mathbf{A}, \mathbf{T}$ are known to the verifier $\mathcal{V}$.

The protocol begins with $\mathcal{P}$ selecting a "masking" value $\mathbf{Y}$ with small coefficients and sending $\mathbf{W} = \mathbf{AY} \bmod q$. Then $\mathcal{V}$ picks a random challenge matrix $\mathbf{C} \in \{0,1\}^{\ell \times n}$, and sends it to $\mathcal{P}$. Then, $\mathcal{P}$ computes $\mathbf{Z} = \mathbf{SC} + \mathbf{Y}$ and performs a rejection-sampling step (Fig. 3) to make the distribution of $\mathbf{Z}$ independent of $\mathbf{S}$, and if it passes, sends $\mathbf{Z}$ to $\mathcal{V}$. Finally, $\mathcal{V}$ checks that all columns of $\mathbf{Z}$ have small norms and that $\mathbf{AZ} \equiv \mathbf{TC} + \mathbf{W} \pmod{q}$.

$\mathrm{Rej}(\mathbf{Z}, \mathbf{B}, \sigma, \rho)$
01 $u \leftarrow [0,1)$
02 **if** $u > \frac{1}{\rho} \cdot \exp\left(\frac{-2\langle \mathbf{Z}, \mathbf{B} \rangle + \|\mathbf{B}\|^2}{2\sigma^2} \right)$
03   **then return** 0
04 **else**
05   **return** 1

Fig. 3. Rejection sampling [31,32].

This protocol can be proved zero-knowledge using exactly the same techniques as in [31,32], i.e. Lemma 2.7. One proves knowledge-soundness using a standard heavy-row argument (Lemma A.1).

Lemma 2.7 ([32]). *Let $\mathbf{B} \in \mathbb{Z}^{r \times n}$ be any matrix. Consider a procedure that samples $\mathbf{Y} \leftarrow D_\sigma^{r \times n}$ and then returns the output of $\mathrm{Rej}(\mathbf{Z} := \mathbf{Y} + \mathbf{B}, \mathbf{B}, \sigma, \rho)$*

where $\sigma \geq \frac{12}{\ln \rho} \cdot \|\mathbf{B}\|$. *The probability that this procedure outputs* 1 *is within* 2^{-100} *of* $1/\rho$. *The distribution of* $\mathbf{Z}$, *conditioned on the output being* 1, *is within statistical distance of* 2^{-100} *of* $D_\sigma^{r \times n}$.

By choosing appropriate parameters (r, v, n, ℓ), Baum et al. obtain a $\tilde{\mathcal{O}}(\sqrt{N})$ proof size for the standard SIS commitment scheme where $N = v\ell$ is the number of entries in the matrix $\mathbf{S}$.

3   Levelled Commitments

In this section, we define levelled lattice commitments and show how to obtain proofs of knowledge with proof size $\tilde{\mathcal{O}}(N^{1/c})$ where N is the number of secrets and c is a constant. Recall that Baum et al. [5] give an amortized proof of knowledge for statements of the form $\mathbf{T} = \mathbf{AS} \bmod q$. We call this a *level-one commitment*. Roughly speaking, the main idea is to apply lattice commitments $c - 1$ times to the secret $\mathbf{S}$ in a structured way.

In the full version of this paper, we extend this result and sketch out the details of an arithmetic circuit satisfiability argument which uses the proof of knowledge based on levelled commitments as a key component.

From now on, we assume that the secret matrix $\mathbf{S}$ already includes the randomness. This not only significantly improves the readability of our protocol, but also ensures that the standard SIS commitment defined in Sect. 2.1 is both binding and hiding.

3.1   Overview

We define our levelled commitment scheme with d levels for constant d. Let $n, m_0, m_1, ..., m_d, m_{d+1} \in \mathbb{N}$ such that $m_0 = 1$ and $N = m_1 \cdot ... \cdot m_{d+1}$. We denote $M_{i,j} = m_i \cdot m_{i+1} \cdot ... \cdot m_j$ and for simplicity, we write $M_i = M_{0,i}$. Consider d distinct moduli $q_1 > q_2 > ... > q_d$. Let $\mathbf{A}_d, ..., \mathbf{A}_1$ be matrices such that $\mathbf{A}_d \in \mathbb{Z}_{q_d}^{n \times m_d}$ and $\mathbf{A}_i \in \mathbb{Z}_{q_i}^{n \times n \cdot m_i}$ for $i \in [d-1]$. Then, the levelled commitment is a function F defined as follows:

$$F_{i,j}(\mathbf{S}) := \begin{cases} \mathbf{A}_i \mathbf{S} \bmod q_i, & \text{if } i = j \\ F_{i,j-1}\left(\left(\mathbf{I}_{M_{i,j-1}} \otimes \mathbf{A}_j\right) \mathbf{S} \bmod q_j\right) & \text{if } i < j. \end{cases} \tag{8}$$

For example, when $d = 2$, the explicit formula for F is

$$F_{1,2}(\mathbf{S}) = \mathbf{A}_1 \cdot \left(\left(\mathbf{I}_{m_1} \otimes \mathbf{A}_2\right) \cdot \mathbf{S} \bmod q_2\right) \bmod q_1. \tag{9}$$

When $d = 3$, the explicit formula for F is

$$F_{1,3}(\mathbf{S}) = \mathbf{A}_1 \cdot \left(\left(\mathbf{I}_{m_1} \otimes \mathbf{A}_2\right) \left(\left(\mathbf{I}_{m_1 \cdot m_2} \otimes \mathbf{A}_3\right) \cdot \mathbf{S} \bmod q_3\right) \bmod q_2\right) \bmod q_1. \tag{10}$$

Observe that explicit formulae for F written without tensor notation bear some similarity to Merkle trees of SIS commitments. For instance, if $d = 3$ then

$$
\mathbf{T} = F_{1,3}\left(\begin{bmatrix} \mathbf{S}_1 \\ \vdots \\ \mathbf{S}_{m_1 m_2} \end{bmatrix}\right) = \mathbf{A}_1 \cdot \begin{bmatrix} \mathbf{A}_2 \cdot \begin{bmatrix} \mathbf{A}_3 \mathbf{S}_1 \\ \vdots \\ \mathbf{A}_3 \mathbf{S}_{m_2} \end{bmatrix} \\ \vdots \\ \mathbf{A}_2 \cdot \begin{bmatrix} \mathbf{A}_3 \mathbf{S}_{m_1(m_2-1)+1} \\ \vdots \\ \mathbf{A}_3 \mathbf{S}_{m_1 m_2} \end{bmatrix} \end{bmatrix}.
$$

Here, $\mathbf{T}$ represents a commitment to the whole tree. In our protocol, the statement will be $F_{1,d}(\mathbf{S}) \equiv \mathbf{T} \pmod{q_1}$, where $\mathbf{S}$ is a matrix consisting of small elements.

For readability, let us introduce commitments for intermediate vertices in this tree. We start from the leaves and denote them as $\mathbf{S}_{[i_1,\ldots,i_{d-1}]}$ where each $i_k \in [m_k]$. More concretely, write

$$
\mathbf{S} = \begin{bmatrix} \mathbf{S}_{[1,\ldots,1,1]} \\ \mathbf{S}_{[1,\ldots,1,2]} \\ \vdots \\ \mathbf{S}_{[1,\ldots,1,m_{d-1}]} \\ \mathbf{S}_{[1,\ldots,2,1]} \\ \vdots \\ \mathbf{S}_{[m_1,\ldots,m_{d-1}]} \end{bmatrix}, \text{ where } \mathbf{S}_{[i_1,\ldots,i_{d-1}]} \in \mathbb{Z}^{m_d \times m_{d+1}}. \tag{11}
$$

Now we can define commitments for the intermediate vertices in the commitment tree. Fix $k \in [d-2]$ and recursively define

$$
\mathbf{S}_{[i_1,\ldots,i_k]} := (\mathbf{I}_{m_{k+1}} \otimes \mathbf{A}_{k+2}) \begin{bmatrix} \mathbf{S}_{[i_1,\ldots,i_k,1]} \\ \mathbf{S}_{[i_1,\ldots,i_k,2]} \\ \vdots \\ \mathbf{S}_{[i_1,\ldots,i_k,m_{k+1}]} \end{bmatrix} \bmod q_{k+2} \in \mathbb{Z}^{nm_{k+1} \times m_{d+1}}. \tag{12}
$$

Let us also set $\mathbf{S}_{[]} := (\mathbf{I}_{m_1} \otimes \mathbf{A}_2) \begin{bmatrix} \mathbf{S}_{[1]} \\ \vdots \\ \mathbf{S}_{[m_1]} \end{bmatrix} \bmod q_2 \in \mathbb{Z}^{nm_1 \times m_{d+1}}$. Then, we have

$\mathbf{A}_1 \mathbf{S}_{[]} \equiv \mathbf{T} \pmod{q_1}$.

Relaxed Opening. Recall that our protocol aims to prove knowledge of a small matrix $\mathbf{S}$ such that $F_{1,d}(\mathbf{S}) \equiv \mathbf{T} \pmod{q_1}$. However, our extraction algorithm finds a slightly larger (but still small) matrix $\mathbf{S}'$ and additional matrices $\mathbf{R}_1,\ldots,\mathbf{R}_{d-1}$ such that $\tilde{F}_{1,d}(\mathbf{S}';\mathbf{R}_1,\ldots,\mathbf{R}_{d-1}) \equiv \mathbf{T} \pmod{q_1}$ where $\tilde{F}$ is defined by

$$
\tilde{F}_{i,j}(\mathbf{S}';\mathbf{R}_i,\ldots,\mathbf{R}_{j-1}) := \tilde{F}_{i,j-1}(\mathbf{X} \bmod q_j + q_j \mathbf{R}_{j-1}; \mathbf{R}_i,\ldots,\mathbf{R}_{j-2}) \tag{13}
$$

and $\mathbf{X} := (\mathbf{I}_{M_{i-1,j-1}} \otimes \mathbf{A}_j)\mathbf{S}'$ for $i < j$ and $\tilde{F}_{i,i}(\mathbf{S}') := (\mathbf{I}_{m_{i-1}} \otimes \mathbf{A}_i)\mathbf{S}' \bmod q_i$. For example, if $d = 2$ then $\tilde{F}_{1,d}$ is defined to be

$$\tilde{F}_{1,d}(\mathbf{S}'; \mathbf{R}_1) = \mathbf{A}_1 \cdot ((\mathbf{I}_{m_1} \otimes \mathbf{A}_2) \cdot \mathbf{S}' \bmod q_2 + \mathbf{R}_1 \cdot q_2) \bmod q_1 \tag{14}$$

similarly to (2). Clearly, if $\mathbf{R}_1, \ldots, \mathbf{R}_{d-1}$ are all zero matrices then $\tilde{F}_{1,d}(\mathbf{S}'; \mathbf{R}_1 , \ldots, \mathbf{R}_{d-1}) = F_{1,d}(\mathbf{S}')$.

We observe that this is enough for practical applications as long as $\mathbf{A}_1, \ldots, \mathbf{A}_d$ are binding. Indeed, one can show, using similar methods to Sect. 1.2, that $F_{i,j}$ is binding based on the hardness of SIS for appropriate parameter choice $q_1, \ldots, q_d$ (see Sect. 3.4).

Formally, given matrices $\mathbf{A}_d, \ldots, \mathbf{A}_1$ such that $\mathbf{A}_d \in \mathbb{Z}_q^{n \times m_d}$ and $\mathbf{A}_i \in \mathbb{Z}_q^{n \times n \cdot m_i}$ for $i \in [d-1]$, the relation we give a zero-knowledge proof of knowledge for the relation

$$R = \left\{ \begin{array}{c} (pp, u, w) = ((\mathbf{q}, \mathbf{m}, n, B, B_R, \mathbf{A}_1, \ldots, \mathbf{A}_d), \mathbf{T}, (\mathbf{S}', \bar{\mathbf{R}})) \\ [\|\mathbf{s}_i\| \le 2^d B]_{i \in [m_{d+1}]} \wedge [\|\mathbf{R}_i\|_\infty \le B_R]_{i \in [d-1]} \wedge [\mathbf{R}_i \in \mathbb{Z}^{nM_i \times m_{d+1}}]_{i \in [d-1]} \\ \wedge (\mathbf{S}', \mathbf{T}) \in \mathbb{Z}^{M_d \times m_{d+1}} \times \mathbb{Z}_{q_1}^{n \times m_{d+1}} \wedge \tilde{F}_{1,d}(\mathbf{S}'; \bar{\mathbf{R}}) \equiv \mathbf{T} \pmod{q_1} \end{array} \right\}$$

where we denote $\bar{\mathbf{R}} := (\mathbf{R}_1, \ldots, \mathbf{R}_{d-1})$, $\mathbf{S}' := [\mathbf{s}_1 \cdots \mathbf{s}_{m_{d+1}}]$, $\mathbf{q} := (q_1, \ldots, q_d)$ and $\mathbf{m} := (m_0, \ldots, m_{d+1})$.

3.2   The Main Protocol

We present our zero-knowledge proof of knowledge in Fig. 4. First, we describe supporting algorithms that we will use in the protocol. Firstly, BT_i takes a matrix $\mathbf{Z}$ which has a number of rows divisible by m_i and outputs its *block transpose*:

$$\mathsf{BT}_i(\mathbf{Z}) := \begin{bmatrix} \mathbf{Z}_1 \cdots \mathbf{Z}_{m_i} \end{bmatrix}, \text{ where } \mathbf{Z} = \begin{bmatrix} \mathbf{Z}_1 \\ \vdots \\ \mathbf{Z}_{m_i} \end{bmatrix}.$$

On the other hand, Fold_i is a recursive algorithm which takes as input M_i matrices $\mathbf{U}_1, \ldots, \mathbf{U}_{M_i}$ and $i + 1$ challenge matrices $\mathbf{C}_1, \ldots, \mathbf{C}_{i+1}$. If $i = 0$ then it simply outputs $\mathbf{U}_1 \mathbf{C}_1$. Otherwise, it splits the vector $(\mathbf{U}_1, \ldots, \mathbf{U}_{M_i})$ into m_i shorter ones, i.e. $\bar{\mathbf{U}}_j = (\mathbf{U}_{(j-1)M_{i-1}+1}, \ldots, \mathbf{U}_{jM_i})$ and runs $\mathbf{U}'_j = \mathsf{Fold}_{i-1}(\bar{\mathbf{U}}_j; \mathbf{C}_1, \ldots, \mathbf{C}_i)$ for each $j \in [m_i]$. Eventually, it outputs $\begin{bmatrix} \mathbf{U}'_1 \cdots \mathbf{U}'_{m_i} \end{bmatrix} \mathbf{C}_{i+1}$. We show more properties of this algorithm in the correctness section.

The statement is $F_{1,d}(\mathbf{S}) \equiv \mathbf{T} \pmod{q_1}$. The protocol begins with the prover $\mathcal{P}$ selecting a masking value for $\mathbf{Y}$ with small coefficients and sending $\mathbf{W} = \mathbf{A}_d \mathbf{Y} \bmod q_d$. In the i-th round, the verifier $\mathcal{V}$ picks a random challenge $\mathbf{C}_i$ and sends it to $\mathcal{P}$. The prover applies Fold to the intermediate commitments

$$\mathbf{V}_i = (\mathbf{S}_{[1,\ldots,1]}, \mathbf{S}_{[2,1,\ldots,1]}, \ldots, \mathbf{S}_{[m_1,1,\ldots,1]}, \mathbf{S}_{[1,2,\ldots,1]}, \ldots, \mathbf{S}_{[m_1,\ldots,m_{i-1}]})$$

as well as all the previous challenges $\mathbf{C}_1, \ldots, \mathbf{C}_i$ sent by $\mathcal{V}$. If $i = d$ then $\mathcal{P}$ also adds $\mathbf{Y}$ and runs rejection sampling. Next, it returns

$$\mathbf{Z}_i = \mathsf{Fold}_{i-1}(\mathbf{V}_i; \mathbf{C}_1, \ldots, \mathbf{C}_i) + [\![i = d]\!]\mathbf{Y}.$$

Finally, the verifier checks that all the $\mathbf{Z}_i$ are small and for all $i \in [d-1]$:

$$\mathbf{A}_{i+1}\mathbf{Z}_{i+1} \equiv \mathsf{BT}_i(\mathbf{Z}_i)\mathbf{C}_{i+1} + [\![i = d-1]\!]\mathbf{W} \pmod{q_{i+1}}.$$

We assume that $\left(\mathbf{I}_{M_{d-1}} \otimes \mathbf{A}_d\right)\mathbf{S} \bmod q_i$ is public, although this information is not used by the verifier. Consequently, for all $0 \le k < d-1$ and any $i_1, \ldots i_k \in [m_1] \times \ldots \times [m_k]$, $\mathbf{S}_{[i_1, \ldots, i_k]}$ is known as well.

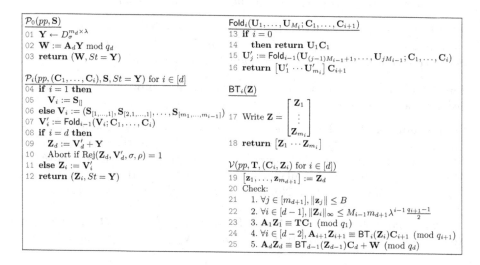

Fig. 4. Levelled lattice commitment protocol.

3.3 Security Analysis

We start by proving certain properties of the Fold algorithm defined in Fig. 4. They will be crucial when proving correctness of our protocol.

Lemma 3.1. *Let* $i \in [d]$ *and* $k, \ell, m \in \mathbb{N}$. *Take arbitrary* $\mathbf{U}_1, \ldots, \mathbf{U}_{M_i} \in \mathbb{Z}^{k \times m_{d+1}}$ *and* $\mathbf{C}_1, \ldots, \mathbf{C}_{i+1}$ *such that* $\mathbf{C}_1 \in \{0, 1\}^{m_{d+1} \times \lambda}$ *and for* $j > 1$, $\mathbf{C}_j \in \{0, 1\}^{m_{j-1}\lambda \times \lambda}$. *Then, the following hold.*

(i) *There exist matrices* $\mathbf{D}_1, \ldots, \mathbf{D}_{M_i} \in \mathbb{Z}^{m_{d+1} \times \lambda}$ *such that* $\|\mathbf{D}_i\|_\infty \le \lambda^i$ *and* $\mathsf{Fold}_i(\mathbf{U}_1, \ldots, \mathbf{U}_{M_i}; \mathbf{C}_1, \ldots, \mathbf{C}_{i+1}) = \sum_{t=1}^{M_i} \mathbf{U}_t \mathbf{D}_t$.

(ii) *For all* $\mathbf{A} \in \mathbb{Z}^{m \times k}$,

$$\mathbf{A} \cdot \mathsf{Fold}_i(\mathbf{U}_1, \ldots, \mathbf{U}_{M_i}; \mathbf{C}_1, \ldots, \mathbf{C}_{i+1}) = \mathsf{Fold}_i(\mathbf{A}\mathbf{U}_1, \ldots, \mathbf{A}\mathbf{U}_{M_i}; \mathbf{C}_1, \ldots, \mathbf{C}_{i+1}).$$

(iii) *Suppose that each* $\mathbf{U}_j$ *can be written as* $\mathbf{U}_j = \begin{bmatrix} \mathbf{U}_{j,1} \\ \vdots \\ \mathbf{U}_{j,\ell} \end{bmatrix}$, *where all matrices*

$\mathbf{U}_{j,j'}$ *have the same dimensions. Then:*

$$\mathsf{Fold}_i(\mathbf{U}_1,\dots,\mathbf{U}_{M_i};\mathbf{C}_1,\dots,\mathbf{C}_{i+1}) = \begin{bmatrix} \mathsf{Fold}_i(\mathbf{U}_{1,1},\dots,\mathbf{U}_{M_i,1};\mathbf{C}_1,\dots,\mathbf{C}_{i+1}) \\ \vdots \\ \mathsf{Fold}_i(\mathbf{U}_{1,\ell},\dots,\mathbf{U}_{M_i,\ell};\mathbf{C}_1,\dots,\mathbf{C}_{i+1}) \end{bmatrix}.$$

Proof. Each part of Lemma 3.1 is proved by induction on i. A detailed proof can be found in the full version of this paper.

We are now ready to prove security properties of our protocol.

Theorem 3.2. *Let* $s \geq \max_{i_1,\dots,i_{d-1}} s_1(\mathbf{S}_{[i_1,\dots,i_{d-1}]})$, $\rho > 1$ *be a constant,* $\sigma \in \mathbb{R}$ *be such that* $\sigma \geq \frac{12}{\ln\rho} M_{d-1} s \lambda^{d-1} \sqrt{m_{d+1}\lambda}$, *and* $B = \sqrt{2m_d}\sigma$. *Then the protocol described in Fig. 4 is a zero-knowledge proof of knowledge for* R.

Proof. We prove correctness and zero-knowledge, and prove knowledge soundness separately in Theorem 3.3.

Correctness. If $\mathcal{P}$ and $\mathcal{V}$ are honest then the probability of abort is exponentially close to $1 - 1/\rho$ (see Lemma 2.7). Indeed, note that by Lemma 3.1 (i) and the triangle inequality we know that $\|V_d'\|$ is bounded above by $M_{d-1} s \lambda^{d-1}\sqrt{m_{d+1}\lambda}$. In a similar manner, one can show that the second verification condition is satisfied. Now, we show that the equations verified by $\mathcal{V}$ are true.

Firstly, note that $\mathbf{A}_1\mathbf{Z}_1 = \mathbf{A}_1\mathsf{Fold}(\mathbf{S}_{[]};\mathbf{C}_1) = \mathbf{A}_1\mathbf{S}_{[]}\mathbf{C}_1 \equiv \mathbf{T}\mathbf{C}_1 \pmod{q_1}$. Now, fix $i \in [d-1]$. We know that $\mathbf{Z}_i = \mathsf{Fold}_{i-1}(\mathbf{V}_i;\mathbf{C}_1,\dots,\mathbf{C}_i)$ (line 7) where

$$\mathbf{V}_i = (\mathbf{S}_{[1,\dots,1]}, \mathbf{S}_{[2,1,\dots,1]}, \dots, \mathbf{S}_{[m_1,1,\dots,1]}, \mathbf{S}_{[1,2,\dots,1]}, \dots, \mathbf{S}_{[m_1,\dots,m_{i-1}]}).$$

By definition, each $\mathbf{S}_{[j_1,\dots,j_{i-1}]}$ is equal to

$$\begin{bmatrix} \mathbf{A}_{i+1}\mathbf{S}_{[j_1,\dots,j_{i-1},1]} \\ \vdots \\ \mathbf{A}_{i+1}\mathbf{S}_{[j_1,\dots,j_{i-1},m_i]} \end{bmatrix}.$$

By Lemma 3.1 (ii) and (iii), we have

$$\mathbf{Z}_i = \begin{bmatrix} \mathbf{A}_{i+1}\mathsf{Fold}_{i-1}(\mathbf{V}_{i,1};\mathbf{C}_1,\dots,\mathbf{C}_i) \\ \vdots \\ \mathbf{A}_{i+1}\mathsf{Fold}_{i-1}(\mathbf{V}_{i,m_i};\mathbf{C}_1,\dots,\mathbf{C}_i) \end{bmatrix},$$

where

$$\mathbf{V}_{i,j} = (\mathbf{S}_{[1,\dots,1,j]}, \mathbf{S}_{[2,1,\dots,1,j]}, \dots, \mathbf{S}_{[m_1,1,\dots,1,j]}, \mathbf{S}_{[1,2,\dots,1,j]}, \dots, \mathbf{S}_{[m_1,\dots,m_{i-1},j]}).$$

Observe that $\mathbf{V}_{i+1}$ is indeed equal to the concatenation of vectors $\mathbf{V}_{i,1}, \ldots \mathbf{V}_{i,m_i}$. Then, by applying the BT function to $\mathbf{Z}_i$ and by definition of Fold, we obtain:

$$
\begin{aligned}
\mathsf{BT}_i(\mathbf{Z}_i)\mathbf{C}_{i+1} &= \left[\mathbf{A}_{i+1}\bar{\mathbf{V}}_1 \cdots \mathbf{A}_{i+1}\bar{\mathbf{V}}_{m_i} \right] \mathbf{C}_{i+1} \\
&= \mathbf{A}_{i+1} \left[\bar{\mathbf{V}}_1 \cdots \bar{\mathbf{V}}_{m_i} \right] \mathbf{C}_{i+1} \\
&= \mathbf{A}_{i+1}\mathsf{Fold}_i(\mathbf{V}_{i+1}; \mathbf{C}_1, \ldots, \mathbf{C}_{i+1}) \\
&= \mathbf{A}_{i+1}\mathbf{Z}_{i+1},
\end{aligned}
\tag{15}
$$

where $\bar{\mathbf{V}}_j := \mathsf{Fold}_{i-1}(\mathbf{V}_{i,j}; \mathbf{C}_1, \ldots, \mathbf{C}_i)$. The last verification equation is also satisfied using the same argument as before and noting that $\mathbf{A}_d\mathbf{Y} = \mathbf{W}$.

Eventually, since each coefficient of $\mathbf{Z}$ is statistically close to D_σ, then according to (6) we have $\|\mathbf{z}_i\| \leq \sqrt{2m_d}\sigma$ with overwhelming probability.

Honest-Verifier Zero-Knowledge. We will now prove that our protocol is honest-verifier zero-knowledge. More concretely, we show that it is zero-knowledge when the prover does not abort prior to sending $\mathbf{Z}_d$. We recall that for all $0 \leq k < d - 1$, $\mathbf{S}_{[i_1, \ldots, i_k]}$ is known to adversaries.

Define a simulator $\mathcal{S}$ as follows. It first selects $\mathbf{C}_1 \xleftarrow{\$} \{0,1\}^{m_{d+1} \times \lambda}$ and $C_j \xleftarrow{\$} \{0,1\}^{m_{j-1}\lambda \times \lambda}$ for $j = 2, \ldots, d$. Next, $\mathcal{S}$ samples $\mathbf{Z}_d \leftarrow D_\sigma^{M_{d-1} \times \lambda}$. Then, for $i \in [d-1]$, the simulator sets $\mathbf{Z}_i := \mathsf{Fold}_{i-1}(\mathbf{V}_i; \mathbf{C}_1, \ldots, \mathbf{C}_i)$ where

$$
\mathbf{V}_i = (\mathbf{S}_{[1, \ldots, 1]}, \mathbf{S}_{[2, 1, \ldots, 1]}, \ldots, \mathbf{S}_{[m_1, 1, \ldots, 1]}, \mathbf{S}_{[1, 2, \ldots, 1]}, \ldots, \mathbf{S}_{[m_1, \ldots, m_{i-1}]}).
$$

Finally, $\mathcal{S}$ sets $\mathbf{W} := \mathbf{A}_d\mathbf{Z}_d - \mathsf{BT}_{d-1}(\mathbf{Z}_{d-1})\mathbf{C}_d$ and outputs $(\mathbf{W}, \mathbf{C}_1, \mathbf{Z}_1, \ldots, \mathbf{C}_d, \mathbf{Z}_d)$.

It is clear that $\mathcal{V}$ verifies with overwhelming probability. We already argued in the section on correctness that in the real protocol when no abort occurs the distribution of $\mathbf{Z}_d$ is within statistical distance 2^{-100} of $D_\sigma^{M_{d-1} \times \lambda}$. Since $\mathbf{W}$ is completely determined by $\mathbf{A}_d, \mathbf{Z}_{d-1}, \mathbf{Z}_d, \mathbf{C}_d$ and additionally, the distribution of $\mathbf{Z}_i$ output by $\mathcal{S}$ is identical to the one in the real protocol for $i \in [d-1]$, the distribution of $(\mathbf{W}, \mathbf{C}_1, \mathbf{Z}_1, \ldots, \mathbf{C}_d, \mathbf{Z}_d)$ output by $\mathcal{S}$ is within 2^{-100} of the distribution of these variables in the actual non-aborting run of the protocol. □

Knowledge Soundness. We describe a knowledge extractor $\mathcal{E}$ which finds small matrices $\mathbf{S}'$ and $\mathbf{R}_1, \ldots, \mathbf{R}_{d-1}$ such that $\mathbf{T} = \tilde{F}_{1,d}(\mathbf{S}'; \mathbf{R}_1, \ldots, \mathbf{R}_{d-1})$.

Theorem 3.3. *For any prover $\mathcal{P}^*$ who succeeds with probability $\varepsilon > 2^{-\lambda+1} \cdot (4dN)^{2d}$ over its random tape $\chi \in \{0,1\}^x$ and the challenge choice $\mathbf{C}_1, \ldots, \mathbf{C}_d$, such that $\mathbf{C}_1 \xleftarrow{\$} \{0,1\}^{m_{d+1} \times \lambda}$ and $\mathbf{C}_j \xleftarrow{\$} \{0,1\}^{m_{j-1}\lambda \times \lambda}$ for $j > 1$, there exists a knowledge extractor $\mathcal{E}$ running in expected time $\mathsf{poly}(\lambda)/\varepsilon$ who can extract $\mathbf{S}'$ and $\mathbf{R}_1, \ldots, \mathbf{R}_{d-1}$ such that $\tilde{F}_{1,d}(\mathbf{S}'; \mathbf{R}_1, \ldots, \mathbf{R}_{d-1}) = \mathbf{T}$. Moreover, each column of $\mathbf{S}'$ has norm at most $2^d B$ and $\forall k \in [d-1]$, we have $\|\mathbf{R}_k\|_\infty \leq 2^k(M_{k-1}m_{d+1}\lambda^{k-1} + 2)$.*

Proof. We provide a sketch of the proof here and include more detail in the full version of this paper. First, the extractor $\mathcal{E}$ constructs a tree $\mathcal{T}$ of partial transcripts similar to [12,14] where each vertex of $\mathcal{T}$ (apart from the root) is created using extraction techniques from [5] based on the heavy-rows argument. The tree-construction algorithm TreeConstruct is given in Fig. 7 in Sect. A. Next, $\mathcal{E}$ computes relaxed openings of the levelled commitments, using the algorithm in Fig. 8 in Sect. A.

We sketch some of the steps of the extraction algorithm. First, we can fix $\alpha \in [m_{d+1}]$ and define an extractor $\mathcal{E}$ which finds small vectors $\mathbf{s}', \mathbf{r}_1, \ldots, \mathbf{r}_{i-1}$ such that $F_{1,d}(\mathbf{s}'; \mathbf{r}_1, \ldots, \mathbf{r}_{d-1}) = \mathbf{t}_\alpha$, where $\mathbf{t}_\alpha$ is the α-th column vector of $\mathbf{T}^8$. Then, using the extraction strategy from [5], we can find $\mathbf{Z}_1', \mathbf{Z}_1''$ such that $\mathbf{A}_1(\mathbf{z}_{1,u}' - \mathbf{z}_{1,u}'') \equiv \mathbf{t}_\alpha \pmod{q_1}$ for some u, where $\mathbf{z}_{1,u}'$ (resp. $\mathbf{z}_{1,u}''$) is the u-th column of $\mathbf{Z}_1'$ (resp. $\mathbf{Z}_1''$). Hence, $\mathcal{E}$ must find a preimage of $\mathbf{z}_{1,u}'$ and $\mathbf{z}_{1,u}''$. We focus on the former. By symmetry, the latter can be obtained analogously.

Suppose that we continue running the prover $\mathcal{P}^*$ given the first response $\mathbf{Z}_1'$. We want to get a preimage of the u-th column of $\mathbf{Z}_1'$. Note that when applying BT_1 to $\mathbf{Z}_1'$, the u-th column vector gets split into the u-th, $u+\lambda$-th,..., $u+(m_1-1)\lambda$-th columns. Take arbitrary $j \in \{u+i\lambda : 0 \leq i < m_1\}$. Then, again by rewinding $\mathcal{P}^*$, we can get $\mathbf{Z}_2', \mathbf{Z}_2''$ such that

$$\mathbf{A}_2\hat{\mathbf{z}}_{2,j} = \mathbf{A}_2(\mathbf{z}_{2,v}' - \mathbf{z}_{2,v}'') \equiv \mathsf{BT}(\mathbf{Z}_1')_j \pmod{q_2}$$

for some v, where $\hat{\mathbf{z}}_{2,j} := \mathbf{z}_{2,v}' - \mathbf{z}_{2,v}''$ and $\mathsf{BT}_1(\mathbf{Z}_1')_j$ denotes the j-th column of $\mathsf{BT}_1(\mathbf{Z}_1')$. By repeating this argument for all possible j, we obtain:

$$(\mathbf{I}_{m_1} \otimes \mathbf{A}_2) \begin{bmatrix} \hat{\mathbf{z}}_{2,u} \\ \vdots \\ \hat{\mathbf{z}}_{2,u+(m_1-1)\lambda} \end{bmatrix} = \begin{bmatrix} \mathsf{BT}_1(\mathbf{Z}_1')_u \\ \vdots \\ \mathsf{BT}_1(\mathbf{Z}_1')_{u+(m_1-1)\lambda} \end{bmatrix} = \mathbf{z}_{1,u}' \pmod{q_2}.$$

Observe how the tree structure appears in the argument. We first find $\mathbf{Z}_1'$ and $\mathbf{Z}_1''$ which correspond to the two children of the root. Then, for each such vertex V, we repeat the same argument m_1 times and add new children $W_1, W_1', \ldots, W_{m_1}, W_{m_1}'$ of V. In general, the tree $\mathcal{T}$ has exactly $2^i M_{i-1}$ vertices on each level $i > 0$.

Eventually, the extracted solution consists of responses which correspond to the leaves of $\mathbf{T}$. We also get additional terms $\mathbf{R}_i$ since each verification equation holds for different moduli. Hence, in order to make any implications from them, we need to first "lift" the previous verification equation and then we can apply it to the next one. The $\mathbf{R}_i$ terms are the result of such lifting. □

3.4 Asymptotic Parameter Choice

In this section, we set parameters for our protocol which minimise the total communication size (see Fig. 5). More concretely, we pick $q_1, \ldots, q_d$ and $m_1, \ldots, m_{d+1}$ (conditioned on the fact that $N = \prod_{i=1}^{d+1} m_i$ is fixed and $N = \mathcal{O}(\lambda^r)$ for some constant, integer r). For readability, we consider asymptotic parameter choice, neglecting constant terms and focussing on the leading terms using "big-$\mathcal{O}$" notation.

---

[8] By collecting extracted solutions for all α, we can merge them and thus obtain the overall solution.

Parameter	Size	Description
λ		Security parameter
p	$\text{poly}(\lambda)$	The largest value of the secrets, i.e. $\|\mathbf{S}\|_\infty$
s		Operator norm of $\mathbf{S}$
N	$m_1 \cdot \ldots \cdot m_{d+1} = \text{poly}(\lambda)$	Number of secrets
n	$d \cdot \mathcal{O}(\log N)$	Number of rows in $\mathbf{A}_1, \ldots, \mathbf{A}_d$
q_i	$\mathcal{O}\left(N^{d-i+2}(2\lambda)^d p^2\right)$	Modulus corresponding to the commitment $\mathbf{A}_i$
m_i	$\left(\mathcal{O}\left(\frac{d \cdot \log N}{d^2 \lambda \cdot \log^2 N + \lambda^2}\right) \cdot N\right)^{\frac{1}{d+1}}$	i–th dimension of $\mathbf{S}$ for $i \in [d-1]$
m_d	$\mathcal{O}\left(\frac{d^2 \cdot \log^2 N + \lambda}{\lambda d \cdot \log N}\right)^{\frac{1}{d+1}} \cdot \left(\frac{N}{\lambda}\right)^{\frac{1}{d+1}}$	d–th dimension of $\mathbf{S}$
m_{d+1}	$\left(\mathcal{O}\left(\frac{\lambda^d d \cdot \log N}{d^2 \cdot \log^2 N + \lambda}\right) \cdot N\right)^{\frac{1}{d+1}}$	$(d+1)$–th dimension of $\mathbf{S}$
σ	$\frac{12}{\ln \rho} M_{d-1} s \lambda^{d-1} \sqrt{m_{d+1} \lambda}$	Standard deviation for rejection sampling
B	$\sqrt{2m_d} \cdot \sigma$	Soundness slack from proof of knowledge
B_R	$(2\lambda)^d N \cdot \sigma$	Infinity norm of extracted matrices $\mathbf{R}_1, \ldots, \mathbf{R}_{d-1}$

Fig. 5. Parameter choice for our protocol.

To begin with, we compute simple upper bounds for the norms of the prover's responses. First, let us assume that secret elements in $\mathbf{S}$ have size at most $p < N$, i.e. $\|\mathbf{S}\|_\infty \leq p$. Using the Cauchy-Schwarz inequality and the definition of an operator norm, we get a bound $s \leq Np^2$. Now, we provide a simple bound on B which is defined in Theorem 3.2:

$$B = \sqrt{2m_d}\sigma = \sqrt{2m_d} \cdot \frac{12}{\ln \rho} M_{d-1} s \lambda^{d-1} \sqrt{m_{d+1}\lambda} = \mathcal{O}(\lambda^d N^2 p^2).$$

We note this bound can be substantially improved. Concretely, $s \leq m_d m_{d+1} p^2$ since we only consider the operator norm of $m_d \times m_{d+1}$ matrices in $\mathbb{Z}_p$. By picking the parameters set below, we get $s = \mathcal{O}(\lambda^2 N^{2/d+1})$. However, for readability, we demonstrate a simpler bound.

We know from Theorem 3.3 that for $k \in [d-1]$ we have

$$\|\mathbf{R}_k\|_\infty \leq 2^k \left(M_{k-1}m_{d+1}\lambda^{k-1} + 2\right) \leq (2\lambda)^d N =: B_R.$$

We are ready to set q_d. In order to make $\mathbf{A}_d$ binding and satisfy (7), one needs to pick $q_d > 2\|\mathbf{s}'_i\|$ where $\mathbf{s}'_i$ is the i-th column of the extracted matrix $\mathbf{S}'$ in Theorem 3.2. We know that $\|\mathbf{s}'_i\| \leq 2^d B$ and therefore choose $q_d = \mathcal{O}\left((2\lambda)^d N^2 p^2\right)$.

Next, let us fix $i \in [d-1]$ and consider the explicit formula for $F_{i,j}$ in (13) without tensor notation. One observes that each copy of the matrix $\mathbf{A}_i$ is multiplied from the right-hand side by a matrix of the form $\mathbf{U} = (\mathbf{V} \bmod q_{i+1}) + q_{i+1}\mathbf{R}$ and we know that $\|\mathbf{R}\|_\infty \leq (2\lambda)^d N$. Thus, we just need to choose q_i which satisfies $q_i > 2N\|\mathbf{U}\|_\infty \geq N \cdot \left(q_{i+1} + 2 \cdot (2\lambda)^d N\right) = Nq_{i+1} + 2 \cdot (2\lambda)^d N^2$. We solve this recursive formula for q_i and obtain

$$\begin{aligned} q_i &= \mathcal{O}\left(N^{d-i}\left((2\lambda)^d N^2 p^2 + \frac{2 \cdot (2\lambda^4)N^2}{N-1}\right) - \frac{2 \cdot (2\lambda^4)N^2}{N-1}\right) \\ &= \mathcal{O}\left(N^{d+2-i}(2\lambda)^d p^2\right). \end{aligned} \quad (16)$$

Hence, we have $\log q_i \leq \log q_1 = d \cdot \mathcal{O}(\log N)$ for $i \in [d]$. Finally, in order to make all commitments $\mathbf{A}_1, \ldots, \mathbf{A}_d$ satisfy (7), we pick $n = d \cdot \mathcal{O}(\log N)$.

Now, let us set $m_1, \ldots, m_{d+1}$ which minimise the total communication cost of our protocol, including the statement $\mathbf{T}$. First, note that the verifier $\mathcal{V}$ sends $\lambda m_{d+1} + \lambda^2 \cdot (m_1 + \ldots + m_{d-1})$ bits as challenges. Next, consider the communication cost from the prover's side. At the beginning, $\mathcal{P}$ sends $\mathbf{W}$ which has $n\lambda \log q_d = \mathcal{O}(d^2\lambda \log^2 N)$ bits. Since it does not contain any $m_1, \ldots, m_{d+1}$, we ignore this term for now. Next, we note that from the second verification equation, each $\mathbf{Z}_i$ sent by $\mathcal{P}$ satisfies:

$$\log\left(2\|\mathbf{Z}_i\|_\infty\right) \leq \log\left(M_{i-1}m_{d+1}\lambda^{i-1}(q_{i+1}-1)\right) \leq \log(N\lambda^d q_{i+1}) = d \cdot \mathcal{O}(\log N)$$

for $i \in [d-1]$. On the other hand, with overwhelming probability we have $\|\mathbf{Z}_d\|_\infty \leq 6\sigma = \mathcal{O}(\lambda^d N^2 p^2)$ and thus

$$\log\left(2\|\mathbf{Z}_d\|_\infty\right) = \mathcal{O}(d\log\lambda + \log N) = d \cdot \mathcal{O}(\log N).$$

Therefore, $\mathcal{P}$ sends in total (excluding $\mathbf{W}$)

$$nm_{d+1}\log q_1 + \sum_{i=1}^{d-1} nm_i\lambda \log\left(2\|\mathbf{Z}_i\|\right) + m_d\lambda \log\left(2\|\mathbf{Z}_d\|_\infty\right)$$

$$\leq \left(nm_{d+1} + \sum_{i=1}^{d-1} nm_i\lambda + m_d\lambda\right) d \cdot \mathcal{O}(\log N) \tag{17}$$

bits. Eventually, this can be upper-bounded by:

$$\sum_{i=1}^{d-1}(n\lambda d \cdot \mathcal{O}(\log N) + \lambda^2) \cdot m_i + \lambda d \cdot \mathcal{O}(\log N) \cdot m_d + (nd \cdot \mathcal{O}(\log N) + \lambda) \cdot m_{d+1}.$$

In order to minimise this expression, we want to set $m_1, \ldots, m_{d+1}$ in such a way that all these $d+1$ terms are (almost) equal. Fix m_{d+1}. Then,

$$m_d = \frac{nd \cdot \mathcal{O}(\log N) + \lambda}{\lambda d \cdot \mathcal{O}(\log N)} \cdot m_{d+1} \text{ and } m_i = \frac{m_{d+1}}{\lambda} \text{ for } i \in [d-1].$$

We compute an exact expression for m_{d+1} as follows:

$$N = \prod_{i=1}^{d+1} m_i = \frac{nd \cdot \mathcal{O}(\log N) + \lambda}{\lambda^d d \cdot \mathcal{O}(\log N)}(m_{d+1})^{d+1}$$

and hence we can set

$$m_{d+1} = \left(\frac{\lambda^d d \cdot \mathcal{O}(\log N)}{nd \cdot \mathcal{O}(\log N) + \lambda} \cdot N\right)^{\frac{1}{d+1}} < \left(\lambda^{d+1}N\right)^{\frac{1}{d+1}} = \lambda \cdot N^{\frac{1}{d+1}}.$$

Then, the total communication cost (now including $\mathbf{W}$) is bounded above by:

$$\mathcal{O}(d^2\lambda \log^2 N) + (d+1)(nd \cdot \mathcal{O}(\log N) + \lambda) \cdot m_{d+1}$$

$$= \mathcal{O}\left(d^2\lambda \log^2 N + (d+1)(d^2 \cdot \log^2 N + \lambda)\lambda N^{\frac{1}{d+1}}\right) \tag{18}$$

$$= \mathcal{O}\left(N^{\frac{1}{d+1}} \cdot (d^3\lambda \log^2 N + d\lambda^2)\right).$$

To obtain logarithmic proof size, set $d+1 = \log N$, giving communication cost $\lambda \cdot \mathcal{O}\left(\log^5 N + \lambda \log N\right)$.

4   Bulletproofs Folding Protocol

In the discrete logarithm setting, one can apply recursive arguments as in [12,14] and thus obtain logarithmic proof sizes. We show how these techniques can also be used in the lattice setting. Concretely, suppose the statement is as usual $\mathbf{As} = \mathbf{t}$ where $\mathbf{A} \in R^{1 \times k}$, $\mathbf{s} \in R^k$ with $\|\mathbf{s}\|_\infty \leq p$ and $R = \mathbb{Z}[X]/(X^n + 1)$. Then the number of secrets N is equal to kn. We highlight that the only variables which are defined the same in this section and the previous one are λ (security parameter), N (number of secrets) and p (the largest coefficient of the secrets).

We fold the initial statement as follows. Let us write $\mathbf{A} = \begin{bmatrix} \mathbf{A}_1 & \mathbf{A}_2 \end{bmatrix}$ and $\mathbf{s} = \begin{bmatrix} \mathbf{s}_1 \\ \mathbf{s}_2 \end{bmatrix}$ where $\mathbf{s}_1, \mathbf{s}_2 \in R^{k/2}$. Hence, if we define $\mathbf{l} = \mathbf{A}_1 \mathbf{s}_2 \in R$ and $\mathbf{r} = \mathbf{A}_2 \mathbf{s}_1 \in R$ then for all $c \in R$, $(c\mathbf{A}_1 + \mathbf{A}_2)(\mathbf{s}_1 + c\mathbf{s}_2) = c^2 \mathbf{l} + c\mathbf{t} + \mathbf{r}$. This gives the following proof of knowledge of $\mathbf{s}$.

$$
\begin{array}{lcr}
\mathcal{P} & & \mathcal{V} \\[1em]
\mathbf{l} = \mathbf{A}_1\mathbf{s}_2, \mathbf{r} = \mathbf{A}_2\mathbf{s}_1 & \xrightarrow{\quad \mathbf{l}, \mathbf{r} \quad} & \\[1em]
 & \xleftarrow{\quad c \quad} & c \xleftarrow{\$} \{X^i : i \in \mathbb{Z}_{2n}\} \subset R \\[1em]
\mathbf{z} = \mathbf{s}_1 + c\mathbf{s}_2 & \xrightarrow{\quad \mathbf{z} \quad} & (c\mathbf{A}_1 + \mathbf{A}_2)\mathbf{z} \overset{?}{=} c^2\mathbf{l} + c\mathbf{t} + \mathbf{r} \\[1em]
 & & \|\mathbf{z}\|_\infty \overset{?}{\leq} 2p
\end{array}
$$

The vector $\mathbf{z}$ has length $k/2$, so this protocol has half the communication cost of simply sending $\mathbf{s}$. We can repeat this protocol for the new statement $\mathbf{Bz} = \mathbf{t}'$ where $\mathbf{B} = c\mathbf{A}_1 + \mathbf{A}_2$ and $\mathbf{t}' = c^2\mathbf{l} + c\mathbf{t} + \mathbf{r}$.

Iterating the folding trick down to vectors of length 1 yields a protocol with communication cost $O(\log k)$. Extraction works in principle as follows. First, let us focus on extracting in the one-round protocol presented above. By rewinding we can get three equations

$$(c_i\mathbf{A}_1 + \mathbf{A}_2)\mathbf{z}_i = c_i^2\mathbf{l} + c_i\mathbf{t} + \mathbf{r}, \qquad i = 1, 2, 3$$

for three different challenges c_i and answers $\mathbf{z}_i$. Combine these to obtain

$$\mathbf{A}_1\left(\sum_{i=1}^{3} \lambda_i c_i \mathbf{z}_i\right) + \mathbf{A}_2\left(\sum_{i=1}^{3} \lambda_i \mathbf{z}_i\right) = \sum_{i=1}^{3} \lambda_i c_i^2 \mathbf{l} + \sum_{i=1}^{3} \lambda_i c_i \mathbf{t} + \sum_{i=1}^{3} \lambda_i \mathbf{r}. \qquad (19)$$

If $\lambda = (\lambda_1, \lambda_2, \lambda_3)^T$ is a solution of the system

$$\begin{pmatrix} c_1^2 & c_2^2 & c_3^2 \\ c_1 & c_2 & c_3 \\ 1 & 1 & 1 \end{pmatrix} \begin{pmatrix} \lambda_1 \\ \lambda_2 \\ \lambda_3 \end{pmatrix} = \begin{pmatrix} 0 \\ 1 \\ 0 \end{pmatrix},$$

then Eq. (19) implies

$$\mathbf{A}_1 \left(\sum_{i=1}^{3} \lambda_i c_i \mathbf{z}_i \right) + \mathbf{A}_2 \left(\sum_{i=1}^{3} \lambda_i \mathbf{z}_i \right) = \mathbf{A} \sum_{i=1}^{3} \lambda_i \begin{bmatrix} c_i \mathbf{z}_i \\ \mathbf{z}_i \end{bmatrix} = \mathbf{t}.$$

Hence, we get a preimage of $\mathbf{t}$ but the problem is that in general it will not be short since λ_i can be large. In order to estimate the size of λ_i, we use the fact that for $i \neq j$, polynomials of the form $2/(X^i - X^j) \in R$ have coefficients in $\{-1, 0, 1\}$ ([9]). Also, we know by the properties of Vandermonde matrices that λ_i are of the form $\pm f \cdot (X^u - X^v)^{-1} \cdot (X^v - X^w)^{-1} \cdot (X^w - X^u)^{-1}$ for some pairwise distinct $u, v, w \in \mathbb{Z}_{2n}$ and $\|f\|_1 \leq 2$. Therefore, we have $\|8\lambda_i\|_\infty \leq 2n^2$. Hence, we have extracted a solution $\bar{\mathbf{z}}$ which satisfies $\mathbf{A}\bar{\mathbf{z}} = 8\mathbf{t}$ and

$$\|\bar{\mathbf{z}}\|_\infty = \left\| \sum_{i=1}^{3} 8\lambda_i \begin{bmatrix} c_i \mathbf{z}_i \\ \mathbf{z}_i \end{bmatrix} \right\|_\infty \leq \sum_{i=1}^{3} \left\| 8\lambda_i \begin{bmatrix} c_i \mathbf{z}_i \\ \mathbf{z}_i \end{bmatrix} \right\|_\infty \leq \sum_{i=1}^{3} 2n^2 \cdot 2np = 12n^3 p.$$

The extractor for the full protocol constructs a tree of partial transcripts similar to [12,14] and applies the strategy we described above at every level. Due to the small soundness error of order $1/n$, the protocol has to be repeated sufficiently many times to achieve negligible soundness error.

Proof Size and Slack. Let us consider the protocol with $d \leq \log k$ rounds. Then, using the same extraction strategy as above recursively, we obtain a relaxed opening $\bar{\mathbf{z}}$ to the modified equation: $\mathbf{A}\bar{\mathbf{z}} = 8^d \mathbf{t}$ such that $\|\bar{\mathbf{z}}\|_\infty = ((6n^3)^d \cdot 2^d \cdot p) = \mathcal{O}\left(n^{3d} \cdot 12^d \cdot p\right)$. Therefore, we set $q = \mathcal{O}\left(n^{3d} \cdot 12^d \cdot p\right)$. The proof size is then equal to $N \log(2^d p)/2^d + 2dn \log q$ which is $\mathcal{O}(N \log(2^d p)/2^d + d^2 n \log n)$.

Since this gives a soundness error of $O(1/n)$, we repeat the protocol $\lambda/\log n$ times in order to get soundness error $2^{-\lambda}$. This gives a total proof size of $\mathcal{O}\left(\frac{\lambda N \log(2^d p)}{2^d \log n} + \lambda d^2 n \right)$.

Suppose that we follow this protocol all the way down to vectors of length 1, i.e. $d = \log k$. Then, we have a "slack"[9] of $\|\bar{\mathbf{z}}\|_\infty = \mathcal{O}\left(n^{3 \log N} N^4 p\right)$ since $k = N/n < N$. The proof size is bounded by $\mathcal{O}\left(\lambda n \log N + \lambda n \log^2 N\right)$.

Comparison. We compare the Bulletproofs approach with levelled commitments introduced in Sect. 3 in terms of both proof sizes and slack. The latter one is not clearly defined in context of levelled commitments since one extracts some secret matrix $\mathbf{S}'$ along with additional terms $\mathbf{R}_1, \mathbf{R}_2, \ldots, \mathbf{R}_{d-1}$ (where d is a number of levels). Therefore, we only focus on the size of $\mathbf{S}'$ and ignore the other terms. We provide a comparison of sizes for both techniques in Fig. 6. Firstly, we observe that none of these methods provide a way to extract an exact solution to the original equation. Indeed, with lattice commitments we only manage to extract $\mathbf{S}'$ along with extra terms $\mathbf{R}_1, \ldots, \mathbf{R}_{d-1}$ which satisfy (13). On the other hand, with Bulletproofs we extract a relaxed opening $\bar{\mathbf{z}}$ such that $\mathbf{A}\bar{\mathbf{z}} = 8^d \mathbf{t}$.

---

[9] Slack here means the Euclidean norm of an extracted solution.

	Bulletproofs	Levelled Commitments
Logarithmic proof size	$\mathcal{O}\left(\lambda n \log N + \lambda n \log^2 N\right)$	$\mathcal{O}\left(\lambda \log^5 N + \lambda^2 \log N\right)$
Corresponding slack	$\mathcal{O}\left(n^{3\log N} N^4 \sqrt{N} p\right)$	$\mathcal{O}(\lambda^{\log N} N^3 p^2)$
poly$(\lambda, N^{1/c})$ proof size	$\mathcal{O}\left(\lambda N^{1/c} \log N + \lambda n \log^2 N\right)$	$\mathcal{O}\left(N^{1/c} \cdot (c^3 \lambda \log^2 N + c\lambda^2)\right)$
Corresponding slack	$\mathcal{O}\left(n^{3(c-1)\log N/c} \cdot N^{4(c-1)/c} \sqrt{N} \cdot p\right)$	$\mathcal{O}\left((2\lambda)^c N^2 p^2\right)$

Fig. 6. Comparison of lattice Bulletproofs and levelled commitments.

In practice, this implies that the slack we have for $\bar{z}$ gets also multiplied by the relaxation factor 8^d in front of $\mathbf{t}$. For $d = \log k$, this factor becomes $k^3 = N^3/n^3$.

From Fig. 6 we deduce that Bulletproofs folding offers smaller proof size at the cost of larger slack. Indeed, if one is not limited with any particular amount of slack then one can achieve quadratic-logarithmic proof size as shown on the top-left part of the table. Now, suppose that we can only tolerate $B = N^\alpha$ of slack for some α. The question would be which method achieves smaller proof size given this condition. Note that if $\alpha = 7.5$ then by the argument above, one would simply use Bulletproofs (by setting $n = 2$). Hence, assume that $3 \le \alpha \le 7$. For readability, from now on we do not write the "big-$\mathcal{O}$" for each expression. Nevertheless, we still consider asymptotic parameters.

Let us first focus on levelled commitments – we find c such that $(2\lambda)^c N^2 p^2 = B$. Then

$$c = \frac{\log(B/N^2 p^2)}{\log(2\lambda)} \approx (\alpha - 2) \cdot \frac{\log N}{\log(2\lambda)} \approx (\alpha - 2)r$$

where $N = \lambda^r$ for some constant r[10]. Then, the levelled commitments achieve $\tilde{\mathcal{O}}(N^{1/(\alpha-2)r})$ proof size. Now consider the Bulletproofs solution. To begin with, we would like to find d such that $n^{3d} \cdot 12^d \cdot \sqrt{N} p = B$. By solving this equation we have

$$d \approx \frac{\log(B/\sqrt{N})}{3\log n + 4} = \frac{(\alpha - 1/2)\log N}{3\log n + 4} = \gamma \log N$$

where $\gamma = (\alpha - 1/2)/(3\log n + 4)$. Then, the Bulletproofs protocol has $\tilde{\mathcal{O}}(N^{1-\gamma})$ proof size. Therefore, we just need to compare $1 - \gamma$ with $1/(\alpha - 2)r$. The main observation is that for $r \ge 3$, the quadratic function $f_r(x) := (15-2x)(x-2)r-14$ is positive when $3 \le x \le 7$. Hence

$$\frac{1}{(\alpha - 2)r} < \frac{15 - 2\alpha}{14} \le 1 - \frac{\alpha - 1/2}{3\log n + 4} = 1 - \gamma.$$

This shows that if one is given only a limited (and relatively small) slack, one should consider using the levelled commitments approach to obtain small sublinear proof sizes.

---

[10] We neglect the $\log p$ term.

A   Knowledge Soundness

In this section, we state the heavy-rows lemma and describe the extraction algorithms used in the proof of Theorem 3.3. A detailed analysis of the extraction algorithms is provided in the full version of this paper.

Lemma A.1. *Let $K > 1$ and $\mathbf{H} \in \{0,1\}^{\ell \times n}$ for some $n, \ell > 1$, such that a fraction ε of the inputs of $\mathbf{H}$ are 1. We say that a row of $\mathbf{H}$ is "heavy" if it contains a fraction at least ε/K of ones. Then less than $1/K$ of the ones in $\mathbf{H}$ are located in heavy rows.*

$\mathsf{TreeConstruct}_i([\mathbf{j}_1, \ldots, \mathbf{j}_i], \mathbf{C}_i, \mathbf{Z}_i, t)$

01 $V = \mathcal{T}[\mathbf{j}_1, \ldots, \mathbf{j}_i]$
02 $\mathsf{chal}(V) = \mathbf{C}_i, \mathsf{resp}(V) = \mathbf{Z}_i, \mathsf{index}(V) = t$
03 $(\mathsf{root}, V_1, \ldots, V_i) :=$ vertices on the path from root to V where $V = V_i$
04 **if** $i = d$ **then**
05   **return**
06 $\mathbf{z}_t := t$-th column vector of $\mathbf{Z}_i$

07 Write $\mathbf{z}_t = \begin{bmatrix} \mathbf{z}_{t,0} \\ \vdots \\ \mathbf{z}_{t,m_i-1} \end{bmatrix}$

08 $t_j := t + (j-1)\lambda$ for $j \in [m_i]$
09 **for** $j \in [m_i]$:
10   Select random $\mathbf{C}'_{i+1}$ and then $\mathbf{C}''_{i+1}$ such that $\forall u \neq t_j, \mathbf{c}'^T_{i+1,u} = \mathbf{c}''^T_{i+1,u}$ and $\mathbf{c}''^T_{i+1,t_j}$ is freshly sampled
11   Run $\mathcal{P}^*$ on the $i+1$-th random challenge $\mathbf{C}'_{i+1}$ until it outputs $\mathbf{Z}'_{i+1}$
12   Rewind $\mathcal{P}^*$ and re-run it on the $i+1$-th challenge $\mathbf{C}''_{i+1}$ until it outputs $\mathbf{Z}''_{i+1}$
13    $T' := (\mathbf{W}, \mathsf{chal}(V_1), \mathsf{resp}(V_1), \ldots, \mathbf{C}'_{i+1}, \mathbf{Z}'_{i+1})$
14    $T'' := (\mathbf{W}, \mathsf{chal}(V_1), \mathsf{resp}(V_1), \ldots, \mathbf{C}''_{i+1}, \mathbf{Z}''_{i+1})$
15    $\mathsf{count} = 0$
16   **while** $i = d - 1$ and $\mathsf{count} < \lambda(4dN)^{2d}/\varepsilon$ and T' is not a valid transcript:
17   Rewind $\mathcal{P}^*$ and run $\mathcal{P}^*$ on the new $\mathbf{C}'_d$ until it outputs $\mathbf{Z}'_d$
18      $T' = (\mathbf{W}, \mathsf{chal}(V_1), \mathsf{resp}(V_1), \ldots, \mathbf{C}'_d, \mathbf{Z}'_d)$
19      $\mathsf{count} = \mathsf{count} + 1$
20   **if** $\mathsf{count} \geq \lambda(4dN)^{2d}/\varepsilon$ **then abort**
21    $\mathsf{count} = 0$
22   **while** $i = d - 1$ and $\mathsf{count} < 2\lambda(4dN)^{2d}/\varepsilon$ and T'' is not a valid transcript:
23   Rewind $\mathcal{P}^*$ and run $\mathcal{P}^*$ on $\mathbf{C}''_{i+1}$ such that $\forall u \neq t_j, \mathbf{c}'^T_{i+1,u} = \mathbf{c}''^T_{i+1,u}$ and $\mathbf{c}''^T_{i+1,t_j}$ is freshly sampled
24   Get response $\mathbf{Z}''_d$
25      $T'' = (\mathbf{W}, \mathsf{chal}(V_1), \mathsf{resp}(V_1), \ldots, \mathbf{C}''_d, \mathbf{Z}''_d)$
26      $\mathsf{count} = \mathsf{count} + 1$
27   **if** $\mathsf{count} \geq 2\lambda(4dN)^{2d}/\varepsilon$ **then abort**
28   Let ℓ be an index where $\mathbf{c}'^T_{i+1,u}[\ell] \neq \mathbf{c}''^T_{i+1,u}[\ell]$ (w.l.o.g. $\mathbf{c}'^T_{i+1,u}[\ell] - \mathbf{c}''^T_{i+1,u}[\ell] = 1$, otherwise swap)
29    $\mathsf{TreeConstruct}_{i+1}([\mathbf{j}_1, \ldots, \mathbf{j}_i, (j, 0)], \mathbf{C}'_{i+1}, \mathbf{Z}'_{i+1}, \ell)$
30    $\mathsf{TreeConstruct}_{i+1}([\mathbf{j}_1, \ldots, \mathbf{j}_i, (j, 1)], \mathbf{C}''_{i+1}, \mathbf{Z}''_{i+1}, \ell)$

Fig. 7. Construction of a tree $\mathcal{T}$ of partial transcripts for $\mathcal{P}^*$. We denote $\mathbf{c}'^T_{i+1,j}$ (resp. $\mathbf{c}'^T_{i+1,j}$) to be the j-th row of $\mathbf{C}'_{i+1}$ (resp. $\mathbf{C}'_{i+1}$).

```
Extract_i(V)
─────────────────────────────────────────────────────────────
01  T[j_1,...,j_i] = V
02  if i = d then return resp_index(V)
03  for j ∈ [m_i]:
04    (s'_{j,0}; r_{j,0,i+2},...,r_{j,0,d-1}) ← Extract_{i+1}(T[j_1,...,j_i,(j,0)])
05    (s'_{j,1}; r_{j,1,i+2},...,r_{j,1,d-1}) ← Extract_{i+1}(T[j_1,...,j_i,(j,1)])
06    if i < d − 1 then
07      w = F_{i+2,d}(s'_{j,b}; r_{j,b,i+2},...,r_{j,b,d-1})
08      r_{j,b,i+1} := (resp_index(T[j_1,...,j_i,(j,b)]) − w)/q_{i+2} for b ∈ {0,1}
09      v_b := (I_{M_{i+1,d-1}} ⊗ A_d)s'_{j,b} mod q_d for b ∈ {0,1}
10      for k = d − 1, d − 2,...,i + 1:
11        u := (v_0 − v_1 − (v_0 − v_1 mod q_k))/q_k
12        r̂_{j,k} := r_{j,0,k} − r_{j,1,k} + u
13        if k > i + 1 then v_b = (I_{M_{i+1,k-1}} ⊗ A_k)(v_b + r_{j,b,k}) mod q_k for b ∈ {0,1}
```

$$
14\ \textbf{return}\ \hat{s} = \begin{bmatrix} s'_{1,0} - s'_{1,1} \\ \vdots \\ s'_{m_i,0} - s'_{m_i,1} \end{bmatrix} \text{ and } \hat{r}_k = \begin{bmatrix} \hat{r}_{1,k} \\ \vdots \\ \hat{r}_{m_i,k} \end{bmatrix} \text{ for } k = i+1,...,d-1
$$

Fig. 8. Extracting relaxed openings of levelled commitments, or more concretely, preimages of $F_{i+1,d}$.

References

1. Ajtai, M.: Generating hard instances of lattice problems (extended abstract). In: Proceedings of the Twenty-Eighth Annual ACM Symposium on Theory of Computing, STOC 1996, pp. 99–108 (1996)

2. Ames, S., Hazay, C., Ishai, Y., Venkitasubramaniam, M.: Ligero: lightweight sublinear arguments without a trusted setup. In: Proceedings of the 2017 ACM SIGSAC Conference on Computer and Communications Security, CCS 2017, pp. 2087–2104 (2017)

3. Attema, T., Lyubashevsky, V., Seiler, G.: Practical product proofs for lattice commitments. IACR Cryptology ePrint Archive, 2020:517 (2020)

4. Banaszczyk, W.: New bounds in some transference theorems in the geometry of numbers. Math. Ann. **296**(1), 625–635 (1993)

5. Baum, C., Bootle, J., Cerulli, A., del Pino, R., Groth, J., Lyubashevsky, V.: Sublinear lattice-based zero-knowledge arguments for arithmetic circuits. In: Shacham, H., Boldyreva, A. (eds.) CRYPTO 2018. LNCS, vol. 10992, pp. 669–699. Springer, Cham (2018). https://doi.org/10.1007/978-3-319-96881-0_23

6. Ben-Sasson, E., et al.: Computational integrity with a public random string from quasi-linear PCPs. In: Coron, J.-S., Nielsen, J.B. (eds.) EUROCRYPT 2017, Part III. LNCS, vol. 10212, pp. 551–579. Springer, Cham (2017). https://doi.org/10.1007/978-3-319-56617-7_19

7. Ben-Sasson, E., Bentov, I., Horesh, Y., Riabzev, M.: Scalable zero knowledge with no trusted setup. In: Boldyreva, A., Micciancio, D. (eds.) CRYPTO 2019, Part III. LNCS, vol. 11694, pp. 701–732. Springer, Cham (2019). https://doi.org/10.1007/978-3-030-26954-8_23

8. Ben-Sasson, E., Chiesa, A., Riabzev, M., Spooner, N., Virza, M., Ward, N.P.: Aurora: transparent succinct arguments for R1CS. In: Ishai, Y., Rijmen, V. (eds.) EUROCRYPT 2019, Part I. LNCS, vol. 11476, pp. 103–128. Springer, Cham (2019). https://doi.org/10.1007/978-3-030-17653-2_4

9. Benhamouda, F., Camenisch, J., Krenn, S., Lyubashevsky, V., Neven, G.: Better zero-knowledge proofs for lattice encryption and their application to group signatures. In: Sarkar, P., Iwata, T. (eds.) ASIACRYPT 2014, Part I. LNCS, vol. 8873, pp. 551–572. Springer, Heidelberg (2014). https://doi.org/10.1007/978-3-662-45611-8_29

10. Bernstein, D.J., Hülsing, A., Kölbl, S., Niederhagen, R., Rijneveld, J., Schwabe, P.: The sphincs+ signature framework. In: CCS, pp. 2129–2146. ACM (2019)

11. Boneh, D., Ishai, Y., Sahai, A., Wu, D.J.: Quasi-optimal SNARGs via linear multi-prover interactive proofs. In: Nielsen, J.B., Rijmen, V. (eds.) EUROCRYPT 2018. LNCS, vol. 10822, pp. 222–255. Springer, Cham (2018). https://doi.org/10.1007/978-3-319-78372-7_8

12. Bootle, J., Cerulli, A., Chaidos, P., Groth, J., Petit, C.: Efficient zero-knowledge arguments for arithmetic circuits in the discrete log setting. In: Fischlin, M., Coron, J.-S. (eds.) EUROCRYPT 2016. LNCS, vol. 9666, pp. 327–357. Springer, Heidelberg (2016). https://doi.org/10.1007/978-3-662-49896-5_12

13. Bootle, J., Lyubashevsky, V., Seiler, G.: Algebraic techniques for short(er) exact lattice-based zero-knowledge proofs. In: Boldyreva, A., Micciancio, D. (eds.) CRYPTO 2019, Part I. LNCS, vol. 11692, pp. 176–202. Springer, Cham (2019). https://doi.org/10.1007/978-3-030-26948-7_7

14. Bünz, B., Bootle, J., Boneh, D., Poelstra, A., Wuille, P., Maxwell, G.: Bulletproofs: short proofs for confidential transactions and more. In: Proceedings of the 39th IEEE Symposium on Security and Privacy, S&P 2018, pp. 315–334 (2018)

15. Don, J., Fehr, S., Majenz, C.: The measure-and-reprogram technique 2.0: multi-round Fiat-Shamir and more. CoRR, abs/2003.05207 (2020)

16. Don, J., Fehr, S., Majenz, C., Schaffner, C.: Security of the Fiat-Shamir transformation in the quantum random-oracle model. In: Boldyreva, A., Micciancio, D. (eds.) CRYPTO 2019. LNCS, vol. 11693, pp. 356–383. Springer, Cham (2019). https://doi.org/10.1007/978-3-030-26951-7_13

17. Ducas, L., et al.: Crystals-dilithium: a lattice-based digital signature scheme. IACR Trans. Cryptogr. Hardw. Embed. Syst. 2018(1), 238–268 (2018)

18. Ducas, L., Lyubashevsky, V., Prest, T.: Efficient identity-based encryption over NTRU lattices. In: Sarkar, P., Iwata, T. (eds.) ASIACRYPT 2014. LNCS, vol. 8874, pp. 22–41. Springer, Heidelberg (2014). https://doi.org/10.1007/978-3-662-45608-8_2

19. Esgin, M.F., Nguyen, N.K., Seiler, G.: Practical exact proofs from lattices: new techniques to exploit fully-splitting rings. IACR Cryptology ePrint Archive, 2020:518 (2020)

20. Esgin, M.F., Steinfeld, R., Liu, J.K., Liu, D.: Lattice-based zero-knowledge proofs: new techniques for shorter and faster constructions and applications. In: Boldyreva, A., Micciancio, D. (eds.) CRYPTO 2019, Part I. LNCS, vol. 11692, pp. 115–146. Springer, Cham (2019). https://doi.org/10.1007/978-3-030-26948-7_5

21. Fuchsbauer, G., Kiltz, E., Loss, J.: The algebraic group model and its applications. In: Shacham, H., Boldyreva, A. (eds.) CRYPTO 2018, Part II. LNCS, vol. 10992, pp. 33–62. Springer, Cham (2018). https://doi.org/10.1007/978-3-319-96881-0_2

22. Gama, N., Nguyen, P.Q.: Predicting lattice reduction. In: Smart, N. (ed.) EUROCRYPT 2008. LNCS, vol. 4965, pp. 31–51. Springer, Heidelberg (2008). https://doi.org/10.1007/978-3-540-78967-3_3

23. Gennaro, R., Minelli, M., Nitulescu, A., Orrù, M.: Lattice-based zk-SNARKs from square span programs. In: Proceedings of the 25th ACM Conference on Computer and Communications Security, CCS 2018, pp. 556–573 (2018)
24. Gentry, C., Peikert, C., Vaikuntanathan, V.: Trapdoors for hard lattices and new cryptographic constructions. In: STOC, pp. 197–206 (2008)
25. Groth, J.: Efficient zero-knowledge arguments from two-tiered homomorphic commitments. In: Lee, D.H., Wang, X. (eds.) ASIACRYPT 2011. LNCS, vol. 7073, pp. 431–448. Springer, Heidelberg (2011). https://doi.org/10.1007/978-3-642-25385-0_23
26. Groth, J.: On the size of pairing-based non-interactive arguments. In: Fischlin, M., Coron, J.-S. (eds.) EUROCRYPT 2016, Part II. LNCS, vol. 9666, pp. 305–326. Springer, Heidelberg (2016). https://doi.org/10.1007/978-3-662-49896-5_11
27. Groth, J., Kohlweiss, M., Maller, M., Meiklejohn, S., Miers, I.: Updatable and universal common reference strings with applications to zk-SNARKs. In: Shacham, H., Boldyreva, A. (eds.) CRYPTO 2018. LNCS, vol. 10993, pp. 698–728. Springer, Cham (2018). https://doi.org/10.1007/978-3-319-96878-0_24
28. Kiltz, E., Lyubashevsky, V., Schaffner, C.: A concrete treatment of Fiat-Shamir signatures in the quantum random-oracle model. In: Nielsen, J.B., Rijmen, V. (eds.) EUROCRYPT 2018. LNCS, vol. 10822, pp. 552–586. Springer, Cham (2018). https://doi.org/10.1007/978-3-319-78372-7_18
29. Lamport, L.: Constructing digital signatures from a one-way function (1979)
30. Liu, Q., Zhandry, M.: Revisiting post-quantum Fiat-Shamir. In: Boldyreva, A., Micciancio, D. (eds.) CRYPTO 2019. LNCS, vol. 11693, pp. 326–355. Springer, Cham (2019). https://doi.org/10.1007/978-3-030-26951-7_12
31. Lyubashevsky, V.: Fiat-Shamir with aborts: applications to lattice and factoring-based signatures. In: Matsui, M. (ed.) ASIACRYPT 2009. LNCS, vol. 5912, pp. 598–616. Springer, Heidelberg (2009). https://doi.org/10.1007/978-3-642-10366-7_35
32. Lyubashevsky, V.: Lattice signatures without trapdoors. In: Pointcheval, D., Johansson, T. (eds.) EUROCRYPT 2012. LNCS, vol. 7237, pp. 738–755. Springer, Heidelberg (2012). https://doi.org/10.1007/978-3-642-29011-4_43
33. Lyubashevsky, V., Micciancio, D.: Asymptotically efficient lattice-based digital signatures. In: Canetti, R. (ed.) TCC 2008. LNCS, vol. 4948, pp. 37–54. Springer, Heidelberg (2008). https://doi.org/10.1007/978-3-540-78524-8_3
34. Lyubashevsky, V., Peikert, C., Regev, O.: On ideal lattices and learning with errors over rings. In: Gilbert, H. (ed.) EUROCRYPT 2010. LNCS, vol. 6110, pp. 1–23. Springer, Heidelberg (2010). https://doi.org/10.1007/978-3-642-13190-5_1
35. Merkle, R.C.: A certified digital signature. In: Brassard, G. (ed.) CRYPTO 1989. LNCS, vol. 435, pp. 218–238. Springer, New York (1990). https://doi.org/10.1007/0-387-34805-0_21
36. Nitulescu, A.: Lattice-based zero-knowledge SNARGs for arithmetic circuits. In: Schwabe, P., Thériault, N. (eds.) LATINCRYPT 2019. LNCS, vol. 11774, pp. 217–236. Springer, Cham (2019). https://doi.org/10.1007/978-3-030-30530-7_11
37. Prest, T., et al.: FALCON. Technical report, National Institute of Standards and Technology (2017). https://csrc.nist.gov/projects/post-quantum-cryptography/round-1-submissions
38. Shoup, V.: Lower bounds for discrete logarithms and related problems. In: Fumy, W. (ed.) EUROCRYPT 1997. LNCS, vol. 1233, pp. 256–266. Springer, Heidelberg (1997). https://doi.org/10.1007/3-540-69053-0_18

Practical Product Proofs for Lattice Commitments

Thomas Attema[1,2,3(✉)], Vadim Lyubashevsky[4(✉)], and Gregor Seiler[4,5(✉)]

[1] CWI – Amsterdam, Amsterdam, The Netherlands
[2] Leiden University, Leiden, The Netherlands
[3] TNO – The Hague, The Hague, The Netherlands
thomas.attema@tno.nl
[4] IBM Research – Zurich, Rüschlikon, Switzerland
vadim.lyubash@gmail.com
[5] ETH Zurich, Zurich, Switzerland
gseiler@inf.ethz.ch

Abstract. We construct a practical lattice-based zero-knowledge argument for proving multiplicative relations between committed values. The underlying commitment scheme that we use is the currently most efficient one of Baum et al. (SCN 2018), and the size of our multiplicative proof (9 KB) is only slightly larger than the 7 KB required for just proving knowledge of the committed values. We additionally expand on the work of Lyubashevsky and Seiler (Eurocrypt 2018) by showing that the above-mentioned result can also apply when working over rings $\mathbb{Z}_q[X]/(X^d+1)$ where X^d+1 splits into low-degree factors, which is a desirable property for many applications (e.g. range proofs, multiplications over $\mathbb{Z}_q$) that take advantage of packing multiple integers into the NTT coefficients of the committed polynomial.

1 Introduction

Commitment schemes, and their associated zero-knowledge proofs of knowledge (ZKPoK) of committed messages, from an important ingredient in the construction of generalized zero-knowledge proofs and advanced cryptographic primitives. An additional feature that's often desirable is being able to prove algebraic relationships among committed values. Very efficient constructions of such primitives exist based on the discrete logarithm problem (e.g. [8]), but the state of affairs is rather different when it comes to quantum-safe assumptions, with the main difficulty being proving multiplicative relations.

There exist generic PCP-type proof techniques [3,4,20,28], which even have asymptotically logarithmic-size proofs, but these proofs have a fixed cost of outputting paths to a Merkle tree in the range of 100–200 KB. One could also think about using fully-homomorphic encryption, which would allow the verifier himself to create additive and multiplicative relations of his choice, thus foregoing the need for a zero-knowledge proof. The main issue with this approach is that one would need to prove that the initial ciphertexts are well-formed, and these

This research was supported by the SNSF ERC starting transfer grant FELICITY and the EU H2020 project No 780701 (PROMETHEUS).

D. Micciancio and T. Ristenpart (Eds.): CRYPTO 2020, LNCS 12171, pp. 470–499, 2020.
https://doi.org/10.1007/978-3-030-56880-1_17

proofs are also currently on the order of a few hundred kilobytes (either using generic techniques or lattice-based proofs [6,31]). There have also been some early lattice-based approaches proposed for this type of problem (e.g. [5,22]), but they result in proofs that are orders of magnitude longer.

1.1 Results Overview and Related Work

The starting point of recent lattice-based constructions that implicitly construct a multiplicative proof system (c.f. [6,14–16,31]) is the commitment scheme from [2], which has a ZK proof that is fairly efficient for proving linear relations among committed polynomials over the ring $\mathcal{R}_q = \mathbb{Z}_q[X]/(X^d + 1)$, where q is prime. All of the aforementioned schemes require that the challenge set in the zero-knowledge proof is such that all pairwise differences of elements are invertible. This restriction imposes a constraint on the underlying $\mathcal{R}_q$ (via e.g. [27]) that the polynomial $X^d + 1$ does not split into many factors. One of the improvements in the current work is the removal of this restriction (we will explain the significance of this below).

Another important improvement in our proofs is of a more technical nature. The prior aforementioned multiplicative proofs create a polynomial function of degree δ whose coefficients include the relation we want to be 0 in the δ-degree term. The goal of the proof is to show by the Schwartz-Zippel lemma that the polynomial is actually of degree $\delta - 1$ and so the highest-order coefficient is indeed 0. Prior works performed this proof by sending masked openings of the committed polynomials and committing to the lower-degree terms of the δ-degree polynomial function (c.f. [6,14–16,31]). In our work we show additional properties of the ZK proof in [2] that imply that it is not necessary to send the masked message openings.

Our construction is very efficient, with the communication complexity of our multiplicative proof being essentially the same as that in [2] for just proving knowledge of the message. Furthermore, removing the restriction that $X^d + 1$ splits into a few high-degree factors is additionally useful because having $X^d + 1$ split into *distinct* linear (or very low-degree) factors allows one to commit to (and independently operate on) many elements in $\mathbb{Z}_q$ by packing them into the NTT coefficients of the committed message. One particular example where this is handy is range proofs where we commit to a number written in binary and want to prove that it is in the range $[0, 2^j)$. We sketch the (folklore) idea below:

Proving that a vector $\vec{v} = v_0 v_1 \ldots v_{d-1} \in \{0,1\}^d$ is binary and the integer represented by it is less than 2^j is equivalent to the statement

$$
\begin{bmatrix} v_0 \\ \cdots \\ v_{j-1} \\ v_j \\ \cdots \\ v_{d-1} \end{bmatrix} \circ \begin{bmatrix} 1 - v_0 \\ \cdots \\ 1 - v_{j-1} \\ v_j \\ \cdots \\ v_{d-1} \end{bmatrix} = 0 \bmod q, \tag{1}
$$

where ∘ is the component-wise product. Thus if we create a commitment to $\vec{v}$ by putting the coefficients of $\vec{v}$ into the NTT coefficients of some polynomial m and can create the polynomial m' corresponding to the right multiplicand in (1), then the proof that $mm' = 0$ would be exactly the range proof we would like since multiplication of NTT slots is component-wise.

Note that the number of NTT slots is the logarithm of the largest integer that can be committed to. As an example, using our multiplicative proofs, range proofs for 32-bit numbers are approximately 5.9 KB in size (see Sect. 5.3). This is about an order of magnitude longer than the discrete logarithm based proofs (c.f. [8, Table 2]), but is shorter than any quantum-safe proof system (e.g. [4,14, 16,19]). In particular, the proofs implicit in [14, Protocol 2] and [16, Section 1.3] used a similar approach of putting elements into NTT coefficients, and had 32-bit proof sizes of around 9 KB [30]. For such range proofs, one only needs to commit to a few polynomials, and so the advantage of our proof system which saves on not sending masked polynomials doesn't manifest itself too much. On the other hand, when applied in the context of proofs of knowledge of a polynomial vector $\vec{s}$ with 2048 small (integer) coefficients satisfying $A\vec{s} = \vec{t}$, our proof technique combined with the additional techniques in [13] result in an order of magnitude reduction in proof size over [6,31].

It should be pointed out that the proofs in [4,8] grow logarithmically in the number of instances, while our proof grows linearly. The results of the current work are thus best suited for non-batched use cases where one wishes to prove knowledge about single instances over $\mathcal{R}_q$ (which actually could be up to d instances over $\mathbb{Z}_q$ when taking advantage of NTT packing.)

1.2   Techniques

We will now provide a somewhat technical overview of the main results of the paper. Prior to getting into them, we recall the commitment scheme of [2] and its zero-knowledge proof.

Overview of [2]. The scheme of [2] commits to a message vector $\vec{m} \in \mathcal{R}_q^k$ by choosing a vector $\vec{r}$ with small coefficients and then outputting the commitment

$$B_0\vec{r} = \vec{t}_0 \tag{2}$$

$$B_1\vec{r} + \vec{m} = \vec{t}_1. \tag{3}$$

The intuition is that if the opening proof can show that $\vec{r}$ is short, then (2) binds the committer to the short $\vec{r}$ (based on the hardness of the SIS problem), and then the message is uniquely determined from (3). Unfortunately, there do not exist very efficient proofs allowing a prover to prove knowledge of such a short $\vec{r}$ satisfying (2), but one can instead give a rather efficient ZKPoK of a vector $\bar{\vec{z}}$ with coefficients somewhat larger than those of $\vec{r}$, and a polynomial $\bar{c}$ with very small coefficients satisfying

$$B_0\bar{\vec{z}} = \bar{c}\vec{t}_0. \tag{4}$$

The proof is a Σ-protocol where the prover picks a small-coefficient masking vector $\vec{y}$ and sends $\vec{w} = \boldsymbol{B}_0 \vec{y}$ to the verifier in the first step. The verifier then selects a challenge polynomial c from the challenge set (which should consist of polynomials with very small coefficients), and the prover responds with $\vec{z} = \vec{y} + c\vec{r}$. Using standard rejection sampling techniques [23, 24], the prover can make the vector $\vec{z}$ independent of $\vec{r}$ to preserve zero-knowledge. The verifier checks that $\boldsymbol{B}_0 \vec{z} = \vec{w} + c\vec{t_0}$ and that $\vec{z}$ has small coefficients. If both of these are satisfied (and c comes from a large-enough domain), then a standard rewinding (where the extractor sends a fresh c' and receives another valid $\vec{z}'$) allows the extractor to obtain $\bar{\vec{z}} = \vec{z} - \vec{z}'$ and $\bar{c} = c - c'$ satisfying (4).

Combining this with the proof that, unless SIS is easy, there can only be a unique opening $(\bar{\vec{z}}, \vec{m}, \bar{c})$ where $\bar{c}$ is invertible in $\mathcal{R}_q$ satisfying (4) and

$$\boldsymbol{B}_1 \bar{\vec{z}} + \vec{m}\bar{c} = \bar{c}\vec{t_1}, \tag{5}$$

it implies that the ZKPoK of (4) uniquely determines $\vec{m}$. It is furthermore shown in [2] (also see [11]) that one can prove that a commitment is to some $\vec{m}$ satisfying $\boldsymbol{U}\vec{m} = \vec{v}$, where $\boldsymbol{U}$ and $\vec{v}$ are an arbitrary public matrix and vector over $\mathcal{R}_q$. Interestingly, this latter proof does not require any extra communication over the basic opening proof, and both the proof and commitment are comfortably under 10 KB for some simple lattice relations (see Table 2 of [2]).

Distribution of the NTT Coefficients. To show that $\bar{c}$ is invertible, it was proposed in [2] to set the modulus q to a prime such that the polynomial $X^d + 1$ does not split too much modulo q – then by the result in [27], it would imply that all elements in the ring with small coefficients are invertible.

In the current paper we show that one no longer needs such a restriction on q. In particular, the prime q can be chosen to allow $X^d + 1$ to fully split into d linear factors. The observation is that we do not need $\bar{c}$ to always be invertible – it suffices to be able to compute the min-entropy of c modulo each NTT coefficient.

An element in $\mathcal{R}_q$ is invertible if and only if all of its NTT coefficients are non-zero. To show that $\bar{c} = c - c'$ is invertible, it would therefore suffice to show that the probability that a random c from the challenge set hits a particular NTT coefficient is smaller than the targeted soundness error.[1] If c were uniformly random in $\mathcal{R}_q$, then this probability would be easy to calculate as each of its NTT coefficients has a $1/q$ probability of being any element in $\mathbb{Z}_q$. But c is chosen from a challenge set that has small coefficients and so the distribution of its NTT coefficients requires different techniques to compute.

As an example, suppose that $X^d + 1 = \prod_{i=1}^{d} (X - r_i) \bmod q$ and that we choose an element $c = \sum_{j=0}^{d-1} c_i X^i$ from $\mathbb{Z}_q[X]/(X^d + 1)$ where $c_i \leftarrow \{-1, 0, 1\}$ with equal

---

[1] We can always amplify the soundness by repetition.

probability. Then

$$\Pr[\boldsymbol{c} \text{ is invertible}] = \Pr[\boldsymbol{c}(r_1) \neq 0 \wedge \ldots \wedge \boldsymbol{c}(r_d) \neq 0].$$

Observe that for any r, $\boldsymbol{c}(r)$ can be written as

$$\sum_{j=0}^{d-1} c_j r^j = c_0 + r\left(c_1 + r\left(c_2 + \ldots + r\left(c_{d-2} + r c_{d-1}\right)\right)\ldots\right),$$

and so the distribution of $\boldsymbol{c}(r)$ is equivalent to the distribution of the random variable Y_0 in the stochastic process $(Y_d, Y_{d-1}, Y_{d-2}, \ldots, Y_0)$ where $Y_d = 0$ and $Y_i = c_i + r Y_{i+1}$ for $i < d$. Fourier analysis is often a useful technique for analyzing certain properties (e.g. min entropy, mixing time, etc.) of stochastic processes, and we show how to efficiently calculate $\max_{y \in \mathbb{Z}_q}[Y_0 = y]$.[2] Calculating the exact probability (or putting a very good bound on it) would require computing sums consisting of q terms, which may be prohibitive when q is on the order of billions, so we furthermore show how certain algebraic symmetries allow us to significantly speed up the computation.

In our applications, we will actually be more interested in a more general case of proving that for a factorization

$$X^d + 1 = \prod_{i=1}^{d/k}(X^k - r_i), \text{ for } r_i \in \mathbb{Z}_q, \tag{6}$$

the value $\boldsymbol{c} \bmod (X^k - r_i)$ is not concentrated on any particular polynomial $c'_0 + c'_1 X + \ldots + c'_{k-1} X^{k-1}$. But proving this is a simple extension of the above case where we were computing $\boldsymbol{c}(r) = \boldsymbol{c} \bmod (X - r)$ because each of the k coefficients $c'_i X^i$ of $c \bmod X^k - r_i$ is only dependent on the coefficients c_{jk+i} for $0 \leq j < d/k$ (i.e. the k coefficients are mutually independent). So the distribution of c'_i has the distribution of the same stochastic process as above, except it consists of d/k steps rather than d.

Proofs of Multiplicative Relations. We now sketch some of the new ingredients of our main result – being able to prove multiplicative relations among committed messages in the commitment scheme defined by (2) and (3). In its most basic form, this involves proving that $\boldsymbol{m}_1 \boldsymbol{m}_2 = \boldsymbol{m}_3$, where $\vec{\boldsymbol{m}} = [\boldsymbol{m}_1 \ \boldsymbol{m}_2 \ \boldsymbol{m}_3]^T$.

We first make a series of observations that show that one can extract more than just (4) from the prover that produces valid transcripts $(\vec{\boldsymbol{w}}, c, \vec{\boldsymbol{z}})$ following

---

[2] In [9], the same techniques were used to show that the statistical distance of Ring-LWE errors is statistically-close to uniform modulo the NTT coefficients. The slight differences are in the distribution of the original polynomial (for our application, it only makes sense to consider polynomials whose coefficients have various distributions over $\{-1, 0, 1\}$) and that we do not need statistical closeness for our application, and obtain tight bounds for a different quantity. We provide more details in Sect. 3.

the protocol of [2]. If we assume, for the moment, that $\bar{c}$ is invertible, then the extractor can extract a unique $\vec{r} = \bar{\vec{z}}/\bar{c}$, not necessarily with small coefficients, satisfying

$$B\vec{r} = \vec{t}. \tag{7}$$

The reason for the uniqueness is that for any small-norm $(\bar{\vec{z}}_1, \bar{c}_1), (\bar{\vec{z}}_2, \bar{c}_2)$ satisfying

$$B\bar{\vec{z}}_1 = \bar{c}_1\vec{t} \qquad B\bar{\vec{z}}_2 = \bar{c}_2\vec{t}, \tag{8}$$

if $\bar{\vec{z}}_1/\bar{c}_1 \neq \bar{\vec{z}}_2/\bar{c}_2$, then (4) implies that

$$B\left(\bar{c}_2\bar{\vec{z}}_1 - \bar{c}_1\bar{\vec{z}}_2\right) = 0. \tag{9}$$

where the vector being multiplied by B has small coefficients. By the assumption, this vector in additionally non-zero, and so it's a solution to SIS. The next observation (see Sect. 4) crucial for keeping our product proof short is that as soon as the (successful) Prover sends $\vec{w}$, he has also committed to a $\vec{y}$ satisfying $B\vec{y} = \vec{w}$. Furthermore, for a challenge c, his response $\vec{z}$ will always be

$$\vec{z} = \vec{y} + c\vec{r}. \tag{10}$$

This is important because of how the product proof works. In previous protocols the prover sends masked openings

$$f_i = a_i + xm_i$$

of the messages with challenge x, sometimes equal to c, and independently uniformly random maskings a_i. Our core approach entails that the message maskings a_i are derived from the randomness masking $\vec{y}$. Hence, since the prover is committed to $\vec{y}$, they are also committed to the a_i. Furthermore, the prover doesn't send the f_i but instead they can be computed by the verifier. We relegate the details to Sect. 5.

After we have established masked openings f_i with fixed maskings a_i, we proceed as in previous works. One makes the observation that one can write

$$f_1f_2 - xf_3 = x^2(m_1m_2 - m_3) + x(a_1m_2 + a_2m_1 - a_3) + a_1a_2, \tag{11}$$

After additionally committing to the "garbage terms" $a_1m_2 + a_2m_1 - a_3$ and a_1a_2, the prover proceeds to show that the above equation is linear in x, which means that the $m_1m_2 - m_3$ term is 0.

An almost immediate consequence of our work would therefore result in a significant reduction of the proofs of [6,31]. We do not discuss this direction further, because with additional techniques, it is shown in [13] how one can use the full product proof of commitments from the current paper to produce an even shorter proof. For this application (and others) we would need to consider the case where $X^d + 1$ fully splits into linear terms in $\mathcal{R}_q$, and therefore we can no longer assume that $\bar{c}$ is invertible. So we continue to describe the ingredients needed here.

If $\bar{c}$ is not invertible, then some NTT coefficient of $\bar{c}$ is 0. In this case we would need to run the protocol in parallel to obtain extractions $(\bar{c}_1, \vec{z}_1), \ldots, (\bar{c}_\ell, \vec{z}_\ell)$ such that for every NTT coefficient, some $\bar{c}_i$ in non-zero in that NTT coefficient. In this case, we can again prove that a valid prover knows a unique $\vec{r}^*$ satisfying (7), and every $\vec{w}$ is similarly a commitment to a $\vec{y}^*$ satisfying (10). One could obtain such $\bar{c}_i$ by sending several challenges in parallel, but for technical reasons (described in Sect. 5) having the challenges c_i related via specific algebraic particular automorphism operations results in smaller proofs. We now explain how the automorphisms are chosen.

When $X^d + 1$ splits into linear terms, one can also write $X^d + 1$ as in (6) where the multiplicative terms $X^k - r_i$ are not irreducible. In particular, we would like to consider such a factorization where $q^k \approx 2^{128}$ to have approximately 128 bits of soundness in the protocol. Then using the results on the distribution of $c \bmod X^k - r_i$, we obtain that except with 2^{-128} probability, two c, c' will not be equivalent modulo $X^k - r_i$. Since $X^k - r_i$ can be further factored as $X^k - r_i = \prod_{j=1}^k (X - r_j)$, this directly implies that one of these NTT coefficients will be distinct – in particular ($c \neq c' \bmod X - r_j$) for some j. Then we define the automorphisms to be exactly those that cycle through the NTT coefficients represented by $X - r_j$, for $j = 1$ to k, and therefore for every NTT coefficient, one of the k automorphisms will result in $\bar{c}$ being non-zero there.

The combination of these techniques, along with several key optimizations that minimize the number of necessary "garbage terms", results in a proof (described in Sect. 5) that is only two kilobytes longer (see Sect. 5.3) than just the opening proof in [2]. Furthermore, if one would like to prove many multiplicative relations, the size of the proof even further approaches the size of the proof from [2] because the extra elements needed in the proof amortize over all the proofs.

2   Preliminaries

2.1   Notation

As is often the case in ring-based lattice cryptography, computation will be performed in the ring $\mathcal{R}_q = \mathbb{Z}_q[X]/(X^d + 1)$, which is the quotient ring of the ring of integers $\mathcal{R}$ of the power-of-two $2d$-th cyclotomic number field modulo a rational prime $q \in Z$.

We use bold letters $\boldsymbol{f}$ for polynomials in $\mathcal{R}$ or $\mathcal{R}_q$, arrows for integer vectors $\vec{v}$ over $\mathbb{Z}_q$, bold letters with arrows $\vec{\boldsymbol{b}}$ for vectors of polynomials over $\mathcal{R}$ or $\mathcal{R}_q$ and capital letters A and $\boldsymbol{A}$ for integer and polynomial matrices, respectively. We write $x \xleftarrow{\$} S$ when $x \in S$ is sampled uniformly at random from the set S and similarly $x \xleftarrow{\$} D$ when x is sampled according to the distribution D.

For $\boldsymbol{f}, \boldsymbol{g} \in \mathcal{R}$, we have the coefficient norm

$$\|\boldsymbol{f}\|_2 = \left(\sum_{i=1}^n |f_i|^2 \right)^{\frac{1}{2}}.$$

The norm is extended to vectors $\vec{v} = (v_1, \ldots, v_k)$ of polynomials in the natural way,

$$\|\vec{v}\|_2 = \left(\sum_{i=1}^{k} \|v_i\|_2^2 \right)^{\frac{1}{2}}.$$

2.2 Prime Splitting and Galois Automorphisms

Let l be a power of two dividing d and suppose $q - 1 \equiv 2l \pmod{4l}$. Then, $\mathbb{Z}_q$ contains primitive $2l$-th roots of unity but no elements with order a higher power of two, and the polynomial $X^d + 1$ factors into l irreducible binomials $X^{d/l} - \zeta$ modulo q where ζ runs over the $2l$-th roots of unity in $\mathbb{Z}_q$ [27, Theorem 2.3].

The ring $\mathcal{R}_q$ has a group of automorphisms $\mathsf{Aut}(\mathcal{R}_q)$ that is isomorphic to $\mathbb{Z}_{2d}^{\times}$,

$$i \mapsto \sigma_i \colon \mathbb{Z}_{2d}^{\times} \to \mathsf{Aut}(\mathcal{R}_q),$$

where σ_i is defined by $\sigma_i(X) = X^i$. In fact, these automorphisms come from the Galois automorphisms of the $2d$-th cyclotomic number field which factor through $\mathcal{R}_q$.

The group $\mathsf{Aut}(\mathcal{R}_q)$ acts transitively on the prime ideals $(X^{d/l} - \zeta)$ in $\mathcal{R}_q$ and every σ_i factors through field isomorphisms

$$\mathcal{R}_q / (X^{d/l} - \zeta) \to \mathcal{R}_q / (\sigma^i(X^{d/l} - \zeta)).$$

Concretely, for $i \in \mathbb{Z}_{2d}^{\times}$ it holds that

$$\sigma_i(X^{d/l} - \zeta) = (X^{id/l} - \zeta) = (X^{d/l} - \zeta^{i^{-1}})$$

To see this, observe that the roots of $X^{d/l} - \zeta^{i^{-1}}$ (in an appropriate extension field of $\mathbb{Z}_q$) are also roots of $X^{id/l} - \zeta$. Then, for $f \in \mathcal{R}_q$,

$$\sigma_i\left(f \bmod (X^{d/l} - \zeta) \right) = \sigma_i(f) \bmod (X^{d/l} - \zeta^{i^{-1}}).$$

The cyclic subgroup $\langle 2l + 1 \rangle \subset \mathbb{Z}_{2d}^{\times}$ generated by $2l + 1$ has order d/l [27, Lemma 2.4] and stabilizes every prime ideal $(X^{d/l} - \zeta)$ since ζ has order $2l$. The quotient group $\mathbb{Z}_{2d}^{\times} / \langle 2l + 1 \rangle$ has order l and hence acts simply transitively on the l prime ideals. Therefore, we can index the prime ideals by $i \in \mathbb{Z}_{2d}^{\times} / \langle 2l + 1 \rangle$ and write

$$\left(X^d + 1 \right) = \prod_{i \in \mathbb{Z}_{2d}^{\times} / \langle 2l+1 \rangle} \left(X^{d/l} - \zeta^i \right)$$

Now, the product of the $k \mid l$ prime ideals $(X^{d/l} - \zeta^i)$ where i runs over $\langle 2l/k + 1 \rangle / \langle 2l + 1 \rangle$ is given by the ideal $(X^{kd/l} - \zeta^k)$. So, we can partition the l prime ideals into l/k groups of k ideals each, and write

$$\left(X^d + 1 \right) = \prod_{j \in \mathbb{Z}_{2d}^{\times} / \langle 2l/k+1 \rangle} \left(X^{kd/l} - \zeta^{jk} \right) = \prod_{j \in \mathbb{Z}_{2d}^{\times} / \langle 2l/k+1 \rangle} \prod_{i \in \langle 2l/k+1 \rangle / \langle 2l+1 \rangle} \left(X^{\frac{d}{k}} - \zeta^{ij} \right).$$

Another way to write this, which we will use in our protocols, is to note that $\mathbb{Z}_{2d}^\times/\langle 2l/k + 1\rangle \cong \mathbb{Z}_{2l/k}^\times$ and the powers $(2l/k + 1)^i$ for $i = 0,\ldots,k-1$ form a complete set of representatives for $\langle 2l/k + 1\rangle/\langle 2l + 1\rangle$. So, if $\sigma = \sigma_{2l/k+1} \in \mathrm{Aut}(\mathcal{R}_q)$, then

$$\left(X^d + 1\right) = \prod_{j\in\mathbb{Z}_{2l/k}^\times} \prod_{i=0}^{k-1} \sigma^i \left(X^{\frac{d}{l}} - \zeta^j\right),$$

and the prime ideals are indexed by $(i,j) \in I = \{0,\ldots,k-1\} \times \mathbb{Z}_{2l/k}^\times$.

2.3   Module SIS/LWE

We employ the computationally binding and computationally hiding commitment scheme from [2] in our protocols, and rely on the well-known Module-LWE (MLWE) and Module-SIS (MSIS) [21,25,26,29] problems to prove the security of our constructions. Both problems are defined over a ring $\mathcal{R}_q$ for a positive modulus $q \in \mathbb{Z}^+$.

Definition 2.1 (MSIS$_{n,m,\beta_{\mathrm{SIS}}}$). *The goal in the Module-SIS problem with parameters $n, m > 0$ and $0 < \beta_{\mathrm{SIS}} < q$ is to find, for a given matrix $A \xleftarrow{\$} \mathcal{R}_q^{n\times m}$, $\vec{x} \in \mathcal{R}_q^m$ such that $A\vec{x} = \vec{0}$ over $\mathcal{R}_q$ and $0 < \|\vec{x}\|_2 \le \beta_{\mathrm{SIS}}$. We say that a PPT adversary $\mathcal{A}$ has advantage ϵ in solving MSIS$_{n,m,\beta_{\mathrm{SIS}}}$ if*

$$\Pr\left[0 < \|\vec{x}\|_2 \le \beta_{\mathrm{SIS}} \wedge A\vec{x} = \vec{0} \ over \ \mathcal{R}_q \,\middle|\, A \xleftarrow{\$} \mathcal{R}_q^{n\times m}; \vec{x} \leftarrow \mathcal{A}(A)\right] \ge \epsilon.$$

Definition 2.2 (MLWE$_{n,m,\chi}$). *In the Module-LWE problem with parameters $n, m > 0$ and an error distribution χ over $\mathcal{R}$, the PPT adversary $\mathcal{A}$ is asked to distinguish $(A, \vec{t}) \xleftarrow{\$} \mathcal{R}_q^{m\times n} \times \mathcal{R}_q^m$ from $(A, A\vec{s} + \vec{e})$ for $A \xleftarrow{\$} \mathcal{R}_q^{m\times n}$, a secret vector $\vec{s} \xleftarrow{\$} \chi^n$ and error vector $\vec{e} \xleftarrow{\$} \chi^m$. We say that $\mathcal{A}$ has advantage ϵ in solving MLWE$_{n,m,\chi}$ if*

$$\left|\Pr\left[b = 1 \,\middle|\, A \xleftarrow{\$} \mathcal{R}_q^{m\times n}; \vec{s} \xleftarrow{\$} \chi^n; \vec{e} \xleftarrow{\$} \chi^m; b \leftarrow \mathcal{A}(A, A\vec{s} + \vec{e})\right]\right. \tag{12}$$
$$\left. - \Pr\left[b = 1 \,\middle|\, A \xleftarrow{\$} \mathcal{R}_q^{m\times n}; \vec{t} \xleftarrow{\$} \mathcal{R}_q^m; b \leftarrow \mathcal{A}(A, \vec{t})\right]\right| \ge \epsilon.$$

For our practical security estimations of these two problems against known attacks, the parameter m in both of the problems does not play a crucial role. Therefore, we sometimes simply omit m and use the notations MSIS$_{n,B}$ and MLWE$_{n,\chi}$. The parameters κ and λ denote the *module ranks* for MSIS and MLWE, respectively.

2.4   Error Distribution, Discrete Gaussians and Rejection Sampling

For sampling randomness in the commitment scheme that we use, and to define the particular variant of the Module-LWE problem that we use, we need to specify the error distribution χ^d on $\mathcal{R}$. In general any of the standard choices in the literature is fine. So, for example, χ can be a narrow discrete Gaussian distribution or the uniform distribution on a small interval. In the numerical examples in Sect. 5.3 we assume that χ is the computationally simple centered binomial distribution on $\{-1, 0, 1\}$ where ± 1 both have probability $5/16$ and 0 has probability $6/16$. This distribution is chosen (rather than the more "natural" uniform one) because it is easy to sample given a random bitstring by computing $a_1 + a_2 - b_1 - b_2 \bmod 3$ with uniformly random bits a_i, b_i.

Rejection Sampling. In our zero-knowledge proof, the prover will want to output a vector $\vec{z}$ whose distribution should be independent of a secret randomness vector $\vec{r}$, so that $\vec{z}$ cannot be used to gain any information on the prover's secret. During the protocol, the prover computes $\vec{z} = \vec{y} + c\vec{r}$ where $\vec{r}$ is the randomness used to commit to the prover's secret, $c \xleftarrow{\$} C$ is a challenge polynomial, and $\vec{y}$ is a "masking" vector. To remove the dependency of $\vec{z}$ on $\vec{r}$, we use the rejection sampling technique by Lyubashevsky [23,24]. In the two variants of this technique the masking vector is either sampled uniformly from some bounded region or using a discrete Gaussian distribution. In the high dimensions we will encounter, the Gaussian variant is far superior as it gives acceptable rejection probabilities for much narrower distributions. We first define the discrete Gaussian distribution and then state the rejection sampling algorithm in Fig. 1, which plays a central role in Lemma 2.4.

Definition 2.3. *The discrete Gaussian distribution on $\mathcal{R}^\ell$ centered around $\vec{v} \in \mathcal{R}^\ell$ with standard deviation $\mathfrak{s} > 0$ is given by*

$$D_{v,\mathfrak{s}}^{\ell d}(\vec{z}) = \frac{e^{-\|\vec{z} - \vec{v}\|_2^2 / 2\mathfrak{s}^2}}{\sum_{\vec{z}' \in \mathcal{R}^\ell} e^{-\|\vec{z}'\|_2^2 / 2\mathfrak{s}^2}}.$$

When it is centered around $\vec{0} \in \mathcal{R}^\ell$ we write $D_\mathfrak{s}^{\ell d} = D_{\vec{0},\mathfrak{s}}^{\ell d}$

Lemma 2.4 (Rejection Sampling). *Let $V \subseteq \mathcal{R}^\ell$ be a set of polynomials with norm at most T and $\rho \colon V \to [0,1]$ be a probability distribution. Also, write $\mathfrak{s} = 11T$ and $M = 3$. Now, sample $\vec{v} \xleftarrow{\$} \rho$ and $\vec{y} \xleftarrow{\$} D_\mathfrak{s}^{\ell d}$, set $\vec{z} = \vec{y} + \vec{v}$, and run $b \leftarrow \mathsf{Rej}(\vec{z}, \vec{v}, \mathfrak{s})$ Then, the probability that $b = 0$ is at least $(1 - 2^{-100})/M$ and the distribution of $(\vec{v}, \vec{z})$, conditioned on $b = 0$, is within statistical distance of $2^{-100}/M$ of the product distribution $\rho \times D_\mathfrak{s}^{\ell d}$.*

We will also use the following tail bound, which follows from [1, Lemma 1.5(i)].

Lemma 2.5. *Let $\vec{z} \xleftarrow{\$} D_\mathfrak{s}^{\ell d}$. Then*

$$\Pr\left[\|\vec{z}\|_2 < \mathfrak{s}\sqrt{2\ell d}\right] > 1 - 2^{-\log(e/2)\ell d/2} > 1 - 2^{-\ell d/8}.$$

$$\text{Rej}(\vec{z}, \vec{v}, \mathfrak{s})$$

01 $u \xleftarrow{\$} [0, 1)$
02 If $u > \frac{1}{M} \cdot \exp\left(\frac{-2\langle \vec{z}, \vec{v}\rangle + \|\vec{v}\|^2}{2\mathfrak{s}^2}\right)$
03   return 0
04 Else
05   return 1

Fig. 1. Rejection sampling [24].

2.5 Commitment Scheme

In our protocol, we use a variant of the commitment scheme from [2] which commits to a vector of messages in $\mathcal{R}_q$. Our basic proof of knowledge of multiplicative relations will prove that $m_1 m_2 = m_3$, so for simplicity, we just describe the commitment scheme for three messages.

The public parameters are a uniformly random matrix $B_0 \in \mathcal{R}_q^{\mu \times (\lambda + \mu + 3)}$ and uniform vectors $\vec{b}_1, \ldots, \vec{b}_3 \in \mathcal{R}_q^{\lambda + \mu + 3}$. To commit to $\vec{m} = (m_1, m_2, m_3)^T \in \mathcal{R}_q^3$, we choose a random short polynomial vector $\vec{r} \xleftarrow{\$} \chi^{(\lambda + \mu + 3)d}$ from the error distribution and output the commitment

$$\vec{t}_0 = B_0 \vec{r},$$
$$t_1 = \langle \vec{b}_1, \vec{r}\rangle + m_1,$$
$$t_2 = \langle \vec{b}_2, \vec{r}\rangle + m_2,$$
$$t_3 = \langle \vec{b}_3, \vec{r}\rangle + m_3.$$

The commitment scheme is computationally hiding under the Module-LWE assumption and computationally binding under the Module-SIS assumption; see [2]. Moreover, the scheme is not only binding for the opening $(\vec{r}, \vec{m})$ known by the prover, but also binding with respect to a relaxed opening $(\bar{c}, \vec{r}*, \vec{m}^*)$. The relaxed opening also includes a short polynomial $\bar{c}$, the randomness vector $\vec{r}^*$ is longer than $\vec{r}$, and the following equations hold,

$$\bar{c}\vec{t}_0 = B_0 \vec{r}^*,$$
$$\bar{c}t_1 = \langle \vec{b}_1, \vec{r}^*\rangle + \bar{c}m_1^*,$$
$$\bar{c}t_2 = \langle \vec{b}_2, \vec{r}^*\rangle + \bar{c}m_2^*,$$
$$\bar{c}t_3 = \langle \vec{b}_3, \vec{r}^*\rangle + \bar{c}m_3^*.$$

The notion of relaxed opening is important since there is an efficient protocol for proving knowledge of a relaxed opening. We do not go into details here since we will define a new notion of a binding relaxed opening and provide a proof of knowledge protocol.

The utility of the commitment scheme for zero-knowledge proof systems stems from the fact that one can compute module homomorphisms on committed messages. For example, let a_1 and a_2 be from $\mathcal{R}_q$. Then

$$a_1 t_1 + a_2 t_2 = \langle a_1 \vec{b}_1 + a_2 \vec{b}_2, \vec{r} \rangle + a_1 m_1 + a_2 m_2$$

is a commitment to the message $a_1 m_1 + a_2 m_2$ with matrix $a_1 \vec{b}_1 + a_2 \vec{b}_2$. This module homomorphic property together with a proof that a commitment is a commitment to the zero polynomial allows to prove linear relations among committed messages over $\mathcal{R}_q$.

3   Distribution in the NTT

In this section we present a way to construct challenge sets $\mathcal{C} \subset \mathcal{R}_q$ so as to be able to compute the (almost exact) probability that $c - c'$ is invertible in $\mathcal{R}_q$, when c and c' are sampled from some distribution C over $\mathcal{C}$. Recall that $d \geq l$ are powers of 2. Moreover,

$$\mathcal{R}_q = \mathbb{Z}_q[X]/(X^d + 1) \cong \prod_{i \in \mathbb{Z}_{2l}^\times} \mathbb{Z}_q[X]/(X^{d/l} - \zeta^i), \tag{13}$$

where $\zeta \in \mathbb{Z}_q$ is a $2l$-th root of unity (in this section, the factors $X^{d/l} - \zeta^i$ are not necessarily irreducible as this doesn't really matter for the results here). The challenge set is defined as all degree d polynomials with coefficients in $\{-1, 0, 1\}$, i.e., $\mathcal{C} = \{-1, 0, 1\}^d \subset \mathcal{R}_q$. The coefficients of a challenge $c \in \mathcal{C}$ are independently and identically distributed, where 0 has probability p and ± 1 both have probability $(1 - p)/2$. For the resulting distribution over $\mathcal{C}$ we write C, and sampling a challenge c from this distribution is written as $c \leftarrow C$.

In the remainder of this section we use Fourier analysis to study the distribution of $c \mod X^{d/l} - \zeta^i$ for $c \leftarrow C$ and $i \in \mathbb{Z}_q^\times$. Lemma 3.1 shows that this distribution does not depend on i.

In [9] a similar analysis is performed. The main differences with our approach is that they sample the coefficients from a binomial distribution centered at 0. In particular, our coefficient distribution with $p = 1/2$ corresponds to a special case of the binomial distribution considered in [9]. For our application it makes sense to consider various distributions over $\{-1, 0, 1\}$. The binomial distribution does allow for the derivation of an elegant upper bound on the maximum probability of $c \mod X^{d/l} - \zeta^i$. However, this upper bound is only applicable when $\sqrt{q} \leq 2d$. For this reason we derive a less elegant but much tighter upper bound on various distributions over $\{-1, 0, 1\}$, that is also applicable when $\sqrt{q} > 2d$.

Lemma 3.1. *Let $x \in \mathcal{R}_q$ be a random polynomial with coefficients independently and identically distributed. Then $\mathcal{R}_q/(X^{d/l} - \zeta^i) \cong \mathcal{R}_q/(X^{d/l} - \zeta^j)$, and $x \mod (X^{d/l} - \zeta^i)$ and $x \mod (X^{d/l} - \zeta^j)$ are identically distributed for all $i, j \in \mathbb{Z}_{2l}^\times$.*

Proof. First suppose that $X^{d/l} - \zeta^i$ is irreducible for all $i \in \mathbb{Z}_{2l}^\times$. Then $\mathfrak{q}_i = (q, X^{d/l} - \zeta^i)$ is prime in $K = \mathbb{Q}[X]/(X^d + 1)$ and for all $i, j \in \mathbb{Z}_{2l}^\times$ there exists an automorphism $\sigma \in \mathrm{Gal}(K/\mathbb{Q})$ such that $\sigma(\mathfrak{q}_i) = \mathfrak{q}_j$. Hence, σ induces an isomorphism between the finite fields $\mathcal{R}_q/(X^{d/l} - \zeta^i)$ and $\mathcal{R}_q/(X^{d/l} - \zeta^j)$.

Since the coefficients of $\boldsymbol{x}$ are i.i.d., it holds that $\sigma(\boldsymbol{x})$ follows the same distribution over $\mathcal{R}_q$ as $\boldsymbol{x}$. Hence, $\boldsymbol{x} \mod (X^{d/l} - \zeta^i)$ follows the same distribution as $\sigma(\boldsymbol{x} \mod (X^{d/l} - \zeta^i)) = \sigma(\boldsymbol{x}) \mod (X^{d/l} - \zeta^j)$ and as $\boldsymbol{x} \mod (X^{d/l} - \zeta^j)$ which proves the lemma for this case.

Now suppose that $X^{d/l} - \zeta^i$ is reducible in $\mathbb{Z}_q$, then so is $X^{d/l} - \zeta^j$. Moreover, since K is Galois both these polynomials split in the same number irreducible factors and for every pair $f(X), g(X)$ of irreducible factors there exists an automorphism $\sigma \in \mathrm{Gal}(K/\mathbb{Q})$ such that $\sigma((q, f(X))) = (q, g(X))$. Using these automorphisms the lemma follows in an analogous manner.

Let us now consider the coefficients of the polynomial $\boldsymbol{c} \mod (X^{d/l} - \zeta)$ for $\boldsymbol{c} \leftarrow C$. Clearly all coefficients follow the same distribution over $\mathbb{Z}_q$. Let us write Y for the random variable over $\mathbb{Z}_q$ that follows this distribution. The following lemma gives an upper bound on the maximum probability of Y.

Lemma 3.2. *Let the random variable Y over $\mathbb{Z}_q$ be defined as above. Then for all $x \in \mathbb{Z}_q$,*

$$\Pr(Y = x) \leq M := \frac{1}{q} + \frac{1}{q} \sum_{j \in \mathbb{Z}_q^\times} \prod_{k=0}^{l-1} \left| p + (1 - p) \cos(2\pi j \zeta^k / q) \right|. \tag{14}$$

The proof of Lemma 3.2 is given in the full version of the paper.

The following lemma shows that, by utilizing certain algebraic symmetries, we can reduce the number of terms in the summation of Lemma 3.2 by a factor $2l$, thereby allowing the maximum probability to be computed more efficiently.

Lemma 3.3. *Let the random variable Y over $\mathbb{Z}_q$ be defined as above. Then for all $x \in \mathbb{Z}_q$,*

$$\Pr(Y = x) \leq M := \frac{1}{q} + \frac{2l}{q} \sum_{j \in \mathbb{Z}_q^\times / \langle \zeta \rangle} \prod_{k=0}^{l-1} \left| p + (1 - p) \cos(2\pi j y \zeta^k / q) \right|. \tag{15}$$

Proof. Let $a, b \in \mathbb{Z}_q^\times$ such that $ab^{-1} \in \langle \zeta \rangle$, i.e., $a = b\zeta^m$ for some m. Now note that $\{1, \zeta, \ldots, \zeta^{l-1}\} = \langle \zeta \rangle / \pm 1 = \zeta^m \langle \zeta \rangle / \pm 1$ for all $m \in \mathbb{Z}$. Since $\cos(x)$ is an even function it therefore follows that $\widehat{P}(a) = \widehat{P}(b)$, from which the lemma immediately follows.

The random variable $Y = Y_l$ corresponds to a random walk of length l over $\mathbb{Z}_q$ defined as follows

$$Y_0 = 0, \quad Y_n = \zeta Y_{n-1} + b_n, \tag{16}$$

where b_n are i.i.d. with distribution $\mu(0) = p$ and $\mu(1) = \mu(-1) = (1-p)/2$. Random walks of this type have been studied extensively [7,10,12,17,18] and convergence is expected in time $O(\log q/H_2(\mu))$ [7], where

$$H_2(\mu) := -\log\left(\sum_{x\in\mathbb{Z}_q}\mu(x)^2\right). \tag{17}$$

However, there exist random walks of this form for which convergence only occurs in time $O(\log q \log\log q)$ [12,17].

Let us consider the following example. Let q be the 32-bit prime $4294962689 = \mod 1 \mod 512$ and $d \mid 256$ the dimension of the ring $\mathcal{R}$. Then, for any d, q splits completely in $\mathbb{Z}[X]/(X^d+1)$, hence in this case $l = d$. Moreover, suppose that the coefficients of challenges are sampled from a uniform distribution over $\{-1,0,1\}$, i.e., $p = 1/3$. Table 1 shows a bound M on the maximum probability $\max_{x\in\mathbb{Z}_q}|\Pr(Y = x)|$, as defined in Lemma 3.2 and Lemma 3.3.

Table 1. Maximum probability for the coefficients of challenges $c \leftarrow C$ when reduced modulo $(X - \zeta)$ ($q = 4294962689$ and $p = 1/3$).

Dimension d	1	2	4	8	16	32	64
$\log_2(M)$	-1.06	-2.13	-4.25	-8.50	-17.01	-31.69	$\approx -\log_2(q)$

4 Opening Proof

Suppose the prover knows an opening to the commitment

$$\vec{t}_0 = \boldsymbol{B}_0\vec{r},$$
$$t_1 = \langle\vec{b}_1, \vec{r}\rangle + m.$$

The standard protocol for proving this, stemming from [2], works by giving an approximate proof for the first equation $\vec{t}_0 = \boldsymbol{B}_0\vec{r}$. So, the prover commits to a short masking vector $\vec{y}$ from a discrete Gaussian distribution by sending $\vec{w} = \boldsymbol{B}_0\vec{y}$. Then the verifier sends a short challenge polynomial $c \in C \subset \mathcal{R}$ and the prover replies with the short vector $\vec{z} = \vec{y} + c\vec{r}$. Here rejection sampling is used to make the distribution of $\vec{z}$ independent from $\vec{r}$. The verifier checks that $\vec{z}$ is short, i.e. $\|\vec{z}\|_2 \leq \beta$, and the equation $\boldsymbol{B}_0\vec{z} = \vec{w} + c\vec{t}_0$.

For suitable instantiations this proves knowledge of a commitment opening because it is possible to extract two prover replies $\vec{z}$ and $\vec{z}'$ for two challenges c and c', respectively, and a message $m^* \in \mathcal{R}_q$ such that

$$\bar{c}\vec{t}_0 = \boldsymbol{B}_0(\vec{z} - \vec{z}'),$$
$$\bar{c}t_1 = \langle\vec{b}_1, \vec{z} - \vec{z}'\rangle + \bar{c}m^*,$$

where $\bar{c} = c - c'$ is the difference of the challenges. In fact, it can be shown [2] that the commitment scheme is binding with respect to the message m^* under the Module-SIS assumption if we have the additional property that $\bar{c}$ is invertible in the ring $\mathcal{R}_q$. Then, it must be that $m^* = m$, unless the prover knows a Module-SIS solution for B_0. The invertibility property is crucial in all previous works that study zero-knowledge proofs for the commitment scheme. It is enforced by choosing the set $\mathcal{C}$ of challenges such that the difference of every two distinct elements is invertible. Unfortunately, depending on how much the prime q splits in the ring $\mathcal{R}$, there will not be sufficiently large sets with this property, and even less so large sets consisting of *short* polynomials. For instance, for both theoretical and practical reasons one often wants q to split completely, but then there can be at most q polynomials which are pairwise different modulo one of the degree 1 prime divisors of q. Even if we let q split slightly less, say in degree 4 prime ideals, then we do not know of large sets of short polynomials that do not collide modulo one of the divisors. This severely restricts the soundness of the protocol and the protocol has to be repeated several times to boost soundness, which blows up the proof size. See [27] for more details about this problem.

The results from Sect. 3 present a way to construct larger challenge sets with the weaker property that $\bar{c}$ is non-invertible only with negligible probability. We generalize the proof further and explain how it is possible to make use of challenge sets where the difference of two elements is non-invertible with non-negligible probability.

So, in the extraction, we drop the assumption that for a pair of accepting transcripts with different challenges c and c', the difference $\bar{c} = c - c'$ is invertible. This essentially means that we can not uniquely interpolate the prover replies $\vec{z}$ and $\vec{z}'$, and obtain vectors $\vec{y}^*$ and $\vec{r}^*$ such that

$$\vec{z} = \vec{y}^* + c\vec{r}^* \quad \text{and} \quad \vec{z}' = \vec{y}^* + c'\vec{r}^*. \tag{18}$$

But we can restore the interpolation by piecing together several transcript pairs that we interpolate locally modulo the various prime ideals dividing q.

Let $X^d + 1 \equiv \varphi_1 \ldots \varphi_l \pmod{q}$ be the factorization of $X^d + 1$ into irreducible polynomials modulo q. Thus, our ring $\mathcal{R}_q$ is the product of the corresponding residue fields $\kappa_i = \mathbb{Z}_q[X]/(\varphi_i)$, i.e.

$$\mathcal{R}_q = \mathbb{Z}_q[X]/(X^d + 1) = \mathbb{Z}_q[X]/(\varphi_1) \times \cdots \times \mathbb{Z}_q[X]/(\varphi_l).$$

Now, what is needed specifically is that for every i there is an accepting transcript pair with nonzero challenge difference $\bar{c}$ modulo φ_i. So, concretely, suppose the extractor $\mathcal{E}$ has obtained l pairs $(\vec{z}_i, \vec{z}_i')$, $i = 1, \ldots, l$, of replies from the prover $\mathcal{P}$ for the challenge pairs (c_i, c_i'), respectively, such that

$$\bar{c}_i = c_i - c_i' \not\equiv 0 \pmod{\varphi_i}.$$

Some of the pairs can be equal and the extractor does not always need really need to compute l pairs as long as the above condition is true. We also assume that all transcripts contain the same prover commitment $\vec{w}$ and are accepting;

that is, in particular, $B_0 \vec{z}_i = \vec{w} + c_i \vec{t}_0$ and $B_0 \vec{z}_i' = \vec{w} + c_i' \vec{t}_0$ for all i. From this data $\mathcal{E}$ computes the local interpolations

$$\vec{z}_i \equiv \vec{y}_i^* + c_i \vec{r}_i^* \quad \text{and} \quad \vec{z}_i' \equiv \vec{y}_i^* + c_i' \vec{r}_i^* \pmod{\varphi_i}.$$

Concretely, we set

$$\vec{r}_i^* = \frac{\vec{z}_i - \vec{z}_i'}{\bar{c}_i} \bmod \varphi_i, \text{ and}$$

$$\vec{y}_i^* = \frac{c_i \vec{z}_i' - c_i' \vec{z}_i}{\bar{c}_i} \bmod \varphi_i.$$

Now, let $\vec{r}^*$ and $\vec{y}^*$ over $\mathcal{R}_q$ be the CRT lifting of the $\vec{r}_i^*$ and $\vec{y}_i^*$. We show it must hold that

$$\vec{z}_i = \vec{y}^* + c_i \vec{r}^* \quad \text{and} \quad \vec{z}_i' = \vec{y}^* + c_i' \vec{r}^*$$

for all i. This restores the global interpolations as in Eq. 18. In fact, we show more than this. Namely, that in every accepting transcript with commitment $\vec{w}$, the prover reply must be precisely of the form in Eq. 18. Also the vectors $\vec{r}^*$ and $\vec{y}^*$ are preimages of $\vec{t}_0$ and $\vec{w}$, respectively, which is what we suspect. So the prover really is committed to $\vec{r}^*$ and $\vec{y}^*$ by $\vec{t}_0$ and $\vec{w}$.

Lemma 4.1. *If we have obtained l pairs of accepting transcripts with commitment $\vec{w}$ as in the preceding paragraph, then every accepting transcript $(\vec{w}, c, \vec{z})$ with commitment $\vec{w}$ must be such that $\vec{z} = \vec{y}^* + c\vec{r}^*$ where $\vec{y}^*$ and $\vec{r}^*$ are the vectors computed above independently from c, or we obtain an $\mathsf{MSIS}_{\mu, 8\kappa\beta}$ solution for B_0 where κ is a bound on the ℓ_1-norm of the challenges. Moreover, we have $B_0 \vec{r}^* = \vec{t}_0$ and $B_0 \vec{y}^* = \vec{w}$.*

Proof. Define $\vec{y}^{*\prime}$ by $\vec{z} = \vec{y}^{*\prime} + c\vec{r}^*$. Fix some $i \in \{1, \ldots, l\}$. Since all transcripts are accepting we get from subtracting the verification equations,

$$B_0(\vec{z}_i - \vec{z}_i') = \bar{c}_i \vec{t}_0, \text{ and}$$
$$B_0(\vec{z} - \vec{z}_i) = (c - c_i) \vec{t}_0.$$

Now, cross-multiplying by $\bar{c}_i$ and $c - c_i$ and subtracting shows that we either have an $\mathsf{MSIS}_{\mu, 8\kappa\beta}$ solution for B_0, or

$$\bar{c}_i(\vec{z} - \vec{z}_i) = (c - c_i)(\vec{z}_i - \vec{z}_i').$$

Suppose the latter case is true. Then we reduce modulo φ_i and substitute the local expressions for $\vec{z}$, $\vec{z}_i$ and $\vec{z}_i'$, which shows

$$\bar{c}_i(\vec{y}^{*\prime} - \vec{y}_i^* + (c - c_i)\vec{r}_i^*) \equiv (c - c_i)\bar{c}_i \vec{r}_i^* \pmod{\varphi_i}$$
$$\Leftrightarrow \bar{c}_i(\vec{y}^{*\prime} - \vec{y}_i^*) \equiv 0 \pmod{\varphi_i}.$$

Since $\bar{c}_i \bmod \varphi_i \neq 0$, $\vec{y}^{*\prime} \equiv \vec{y}_i^* \equiv \vec{y}^*$ modulo φ_i. This holds for all i and hence it follows that $\vec{y}^{*\prime} = \vec{y}^*$.

We come to the statements $B_0 \vec{r}^* = \vec{t}_0$ and $B_0 \vec{y}^* = \vec{w}$. From the construction of $\vec{r}^*$ and the verification equations it follows that

$$
\begin{aligned}
B_0 \vec{r}^* &\equiv B_0 \vec{r}_i^* \\
&\equiv B_0 \frac{\vec{z}_i - \vec{z}_i'}{\bar{c}_i} \\
&\equiv \vec{t}_0 \pmod{\varphi_i}
\end{aligned}
$$

for all i. Similarly, for $\vec{y}^*$,

$$
\begin{aligned}
B_0 \vec{y}^* &\equiv B_0 \vec{y}_i^* \\
&\equiv B_0 \frac{c_i \vec{z}_i' - c_i' \vec{z}_i}{\bar{c}_i} \\
&\equiv \vec{w} \pmod{\varphi_i}.
\end{aligned}
$$

The statements in the lemma follow from the Chinese remainder theorem. □

Finally, the extracted vector $\vec{r}^*$ can be used to define a binding notion of opening for the commitment scheme where the extracted message m^* is simply set to fulfill

$$
t_1 = \langle \vec{b}_1, \vec{r}^* \rangle + m^*.
$$

Then we have found an instance of the following definition.

Definition 4.2. *A weak opening for the commitment $\vec{t} = \vec{t}_0 \,\|\, t_1$ consists of l polynomials $\bar{c}_i \in \mathcal{R}_q$, a randomness vector $\vec{r}^*$ over $\mathcal{R}_q$ and a message $m^* \in \mathcal{R}_q$ such that*

$$
\begin{aligned}
&\|\bar{c}_i\|_1 \leq 2\kappa \text{ and } \bar{c}_i \bmod \varphi_i \neq 0 \text{ for all } 1 \leq i \leq l, \\
&\|\bar{c}_i \vec{r}^*\|_2 \leq 2\beta \text{ for all } 1 \leq i \leq l, \\
&B_0 \vec{r}^* = \vec{t}_0, \\
&\langle \vec{b}_1, \vec{r}^* \rangle + m^* = t_1.
\end{aligned}
$$

It is easy to show that the commitment scheme is binding with respect to these weak openings.

Lemma 4.3. *The commitment scheme is binding with respect to weak openings if $\mathrm{MSIS}_{\mu, 8\kappa\beta}$ is hard. More precisely, from two different weak openings $((\bar{c}_i), \vec{r}^*, m^*)$ and $((\bar{c}_i'), \vec{r}^{*\prime}, m^{*\prime})$ with $m^* \neq m^{*\prime}$ one can immediately compute a Module-SIS solution for B_0 of length at most $8\kappa\beta$.*

Proof. Suppose there are two weak openings $((\bar{c}_i), \vec{r}^*, m^*)$ and $((\bar{c}_i'), \vec{r}^{*\prime}, m^{*\prime})$ with $m^* \neq m^{*\prime}$. Then, $\langle \vec{b}_1, \vec{r}^* \rangle + m^* = t_1 = \langle \vec{b}_1, \vec{r}^{*\prime} \rangle + m^{*\prime}$ implies $\vec{r}^* \neq \vec{r}^{*\prime}$. Therefore, there exists an $i \in \{1, \ldots, l\}$ such that $\vec{r}^* \not\equiv \vec{r}^{*\prime} \pmod{\varphi_i}$. Consequently, $\bar{c}_i \bar{c}_i' (\vec{r}^* - \vec{r}^{*\prime}) = \bar{c}_i' \bar{c}_i \vec{r}^* - \bar{c}_i \bar{c}_i' \vec{r}^{*\prime} \neq 0$ since the polynomials c_i and c_i' are non-zero modulo φ_i. Hence,

$$
B_0 \bar{c}_i \bar{c}_i' (\vec{r}^* - \vec{r}^{*\prime}) = 0
$$

is a non-trivial Module-SIS solution for B_0 of length at most $8\kappa\beta$. □

It remains to explain how we make it possible to arrive at the transcript pairs that we want to piece together. Suppose $\mathcal{R}_q$ factors in the following way,

$$\mathcal{R}_q = \prod_{i \in \mathbb{Z}_{2l}^{\times}} \mathbb{Z}_q[X]/(X^{\frac{d}{l}} - \zeta^i)$$

with l irreducible $\varphi_i = X^{d/l} - \zeta^i$ and ζ a primitive $2l$-th root of unity. Let $\mathcal{C} = \{-1, 0, 1\}^d \subset \mathcal{R}$ and $c \in \mathcal{C}$ be a random element from $\mathcal{C}$ where each coefficient is independently identically distributed with $\Pr(0) = 1/2$ and $\Pr(-1) = \Pr(1) = 1/4$. Then the d/l coefficients of c mod φ_i for a fixed i are mutually independent and Lemma 3.3 gives a bound on their maximum probability over $\mathbb{Z}_q$. We will set parameters such that the maximum probability is not much bigger than $1/q$. Then the probability that a cheating prover can get away with only answering challenges with a particular value modulo φ_i is about $q^{-d/l}$. If this probability is negligible, then, although the projections c mod φ_i for varying i are not independent, we can get several transcript pairs where for each i at least one $\bar{c}$ mod φ_i is non-zero. This works by rewinding the prover l times, once for every i, and sending a challenge that differs from a previous successful challenge modulo φ_i. If otherwise the probability $q^{-d/l}$ is not negligible we can run several, say k, copies of the protocol in parallel and reduce the cheating probability to $q^{-kd/l}$. Then there are k prover commitments $\vec{w}_i$ in the first flow and there won't be l accepting transcript pairs for each of them. Hence this requires a slightly more general analysis than what we have provided in the overview in this section. We handle this case in the security proof of our protocol given in Fig. 2. It turns out that it is still possible to extract unique preimages $\vec{y}_i$ for all commitments $\vec{w}_i$.

In the k parallel repetitions we do not sample the challenges independently. The reason is that when proving relations on the messages and specifically in our product proof we will need more structure. Let $\sigma = \sigma_{2l/k+1} \in \mathrm{Aut}(\mathcal{R}_q) \cong \mathbb{Z}_{2d}^{\times}$ be the automorphism of order kd/l that stabilizes the ideals

$$\left(X^{\frac{kd}{l}} - \zeta^{jk}\right) = \prod_{i=0,\dots,k-1} \sigma^i \left(X^{\frac{d}{l}} - \zeta^j\right) = \prod_{i \in \langle 2l/k+1\rangle / \langle 2l+1\rangle} \left(X^{\frac{d}{l}} - \zeta^{ij}\right)$$

for $j \in \langle -1, 5\rangle / \langle 2l/k + 1\rangle \cong \mathbb{Z}_{2l/k}^{\times}$. Now, we let the challenges in the k parallel executions be the images $\sigma^i(c)$, $i = 0, \dots, k-1$, of a single polynomial $c \in \mathcal{C}$. If parameters are such that the maximum probability of each of the mutually independent coefficients of c mod $(X^{kd/l} - \zeta^{jk})$ is essentially $1/q$, and thus the maximum probability of c mod $(X^{kd/l} - \zeta^{jk})$ is essentially $q^{-kd/l}$, and this is negligible, then the prover must answer two c, c' that differ modulo $X^{kd/l} - \zeta^{jk}$. Hence, $\bar{c} = c - c'$ is non-zero modulo at least one of the divisors, say $(X^{d/l} - \zeta^j)$. Therefore, for every other divisor $\sigma^i(X^{d/l} - \zeta^j)$ we have

$$\sigma^i(\bar{c}) \bmod \sigma^i \left(X^{\frac{d}{l}} - \zeta^j\right) = \sigma^i \left(\bar{c} \bmod \left(X^{\frac{d}{l}} - \zeta^j\right)\right) \neq 0.$$

So we are in the situation where we have an accepting transcript pair with non-zero $\bar{c}$ modulo every prime divisor of $(X^{kd/l} - \zeta^{jk})$. By repeating the argument

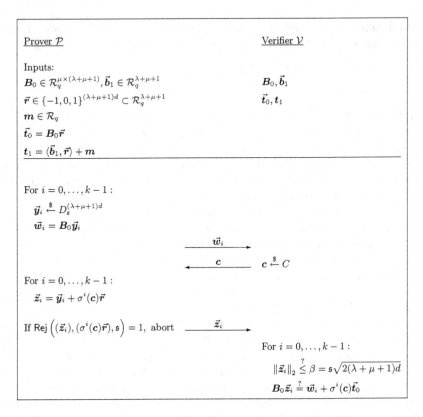

Fig. 2. Automorphism opening proof for the commitment scheme. We assume l, k are powers of two such that $k < l \leq d$, $q - 1 \equiv 2l \pmod{4l}$, and $\sigma = \sigma_{2l/k+1} \in \mathsf{Aut}(\mathcal{R}_q)$. Furthermore, C is the challenge distribution over $\mathcal{R}$ where each coefficient is independently identically distributed with $\Pr(0) = 1/2$ and $\Pr(-1) = \Pr(1) = 1/4$, κ is a bound on the ℓ_1-norm of c, i.e. $\|c\|_1 \leq \kappa$ with overwhelming probability for $c \xleftarrow{\$} C$, and $D_{\mathfrak{s}}$ is the discrete Gaussian distribution on $\mathbb{Z}$ with standard deviation $\mathfrak{s} = 11k\kappa \|\vec{r}\|_2$.

for every $j \in \mathbb{Z}^{\times}_{2l/k}$, we see that we can get an extraction with non-vanishing $\bar{c}$ modulo every prime divisor of $(X^d + 1)$.

The final protocol is given in Fig. 2. It's security is stated in Theorem 4.4. The proof of Theorem 4.4 is given in the full version of the paper.

Theorem 4.4. *The protocol in Fig. 2 is complete, statistical honest verifier zero-knowledge and computational special sound under the Module-SIS assumption. More precisely, let p be the maximum probability over $\mathbb{Z}_q$ of the coefficients of $c \bmod X^{kd/l} - \zeta^k$ as in Lemma 3.3.*

Then, for completeness, unless the honest prover $\mathcal{P}$ aborts due to the rejection sampling, it convinces the honest verifier $\mathcal{V}$ with overwhelming probability.

For zero-knowledge, there exists a simulator $\mathcal{S}$, that, without access to secret information, outputs a simulation of a non-aborting transcript of the protocol between $\mathcal{P}$ and $\mathcal{V}$ which has statistical distance at most 2^{-100} to the actual interaction.

For knowledge-soundness, there is an extractor $\mathcal{E}$ with the following properties. When given rewindable black-box access to a deterministic prover $\mathcal{P}^*$ that convinces $\mathcal{V}$ with probability $\varepsilon > p^{kd/l}$, $\mathcal{E}$ either outputs a weak opening for the commitment $\vec{t}$ or a $\mathsf{MSIS}_{\mu,8\kappa\beta}$ solution for B_0 in expected time at most $1/\varepsilon + (l/k)(\varepsilon - p^{kd/l})^{-1}$ when running $\mathcal{P}^*$ once is assumed to take unit time.

Moreover, the weak opening can be extended to also include k vectors $\vec{y}_i^* \in \mathcal{R}_q^{\lambda+\mu+1}$ such that $B_0 \vec{y}_i^* = \vec{w}_i$, where $\vec{w}_i$ are the prover commitments sent by $\mathcal{P}^*$ in the first flow. Furthermore, for every accepting transcript of an interaction with $\mathcal{P}^*$, the prover replies are given by $\vec{z}_i = \vec{y}_i^* + \sigma^i(c)\vec{r}^*$.

5   Product Proof

In this section we present an efficient protocol for proving multiplicative relations between committed messages. Suppose the prover knows an opening to a commitment $\vec{t}$ to three secret polynomials $m_1, m_2, m_3 \in \mathcal{R}_q$,

$$\vec{t}_0 = B_0\vec{r},$$
$$t_1 = \langle \vec{b}_1, \vec{r} \rangle + m_1,$$
$$t_2 = \langle \vec{b}_2, \vec{r} \rangle + m_2,$$
$$t_3 = \langle \vec{b}_3, \vec{r} \rangle + m_3.$$

His goal is to prove the multiplicative relation $m_1 m_2 = m_3$ in $\mathcal{R}_q$. We recall a simple technique for this, which for example was used in [6,31]. The prover commits to uniformly random masking polynomials $a_1, a_2, a_3 \in \mathcal{R}_q$ and two so-called "garbage polynomials",

$$\vec{t}_0' = B_0'\vec{r}',$$
$$t_1' = \langle \vec{b}_1', \vec{r}' \rangle + a_1,$$
$$t_2' = \langle \vec{b}_2', \vec{r}' \rangle + a_2,$$
$$t_3' = \langle \vec{b}_3', \vec{r}' \rangle + a_3,$$
$$t_4' = \langle \vec{b}_4', \vec{r}' \rangle + a_1 m_2 + a_2 m_1 + a_3,$$
$$t_5' = \langle \vec{b}_5', \vec{r}' \rangle + a_1 a_2.$$

Then $\mathcal{P}$ replies to a challenge polynomial $x \in \mathcal{R}_q$ with masked openings $f_i = a_i + x m_i$ of the messages m_i. Now $\mathcal{P}$ shows that the f_i really open to the committed messages by proving that $t_i' + x t_i - f_i$ is a commitment to zero for $i = 1, 2, 3$. Concretely, in addition to the standard opening proof for all of the commitments where the prover sends

$$\vec{w} = B_0\vec{y},$$
$$\vec{w}' = B_0'\vec{y}',$$
$$\vec{z} = \vec{y} + c\vec{r},$$
$$\vec{z}' = \vec{y}' + c\vec{r}',$$

they will also send

$$v_1 = \langle \vec{b}_1', \vec{y}' \rangle + x\langle \vec{b}_1, \vec{y} \rangle,$$
$$v_2 = \langle \vec{b}_2', \vec{y}' \rangle + x\langle \vec{b}_2, \vec{y} \rangle,$$
$$v_3 = \langle \vec{b}_3', \vec{y}' \rangle + x\langle \vec{b}_3, \vec{y} \rangle.$$

The verifier then checks the equations

$$B_0\vec{z} = \vec{w} + c\vec{t}_0,$$
$$B_0'\vec{z}' = \vec{w}' + c\vec{t}_0',$$
$$\langle \vec{b}_1', \vec{z}' \rangle + x\langle \vec{b}_1, \vec{z} \rangle = v_1 + c(t_1' + xt_1 - f_1),$$
$$\langle \vec{b}_2', \vec{z}' \rangle + x\langle \vec{b}_2, \vec{z} \rangle = v_2 + c(t_2' + xt_2 - f_2),$$
$$\langle \vec{b}_3', \vec{z}' \rangle + x\langle \vec{b}_3, \vec{z} \rangle = v_3 + c(t_3' + xt_3 - f_3).$$

This convinces the verifier that the f_i open to the secret messages m_i. Next, consider the commitment

$$\tau = t_5' + xt_4' - (f_1f_2 - xf_3). \tag{19}$$

The verifier knows that the f_i are of the form $f_i = a_i^* + xm_i^*$ where the polynomials a_i^* and m_i^* are the (extracted) messages in the commitments t_i', t_i. Therefore, $\mathcal{V}$ knows that τ is a commitment to the message

$$\mu = m_5^* + xm_4^* - (a_1^*a_2^* + x(a_1^*m_2^* + a_2^*m_1^*) + x^2m_1^*m_2^* - xa_3^* - x^2m_3^*)$$
$$= (m_5^* - a_1^*a_2^*) + x(m_4^* - a_1^*m_2^* - a_2^*m_1^* + a_3^*) + x^2(m_3^* - m_1^*m_2^*)$$

where m_4^*, m_5^* are the extracted messages from the two garbage commitments. Now the prover completes the product proof by proving that τ is a commitment to zero. We explain why this suffices. The message μ can be viewed as a quadratic polynomial in x with coefficients that are independent from x. If the prover is able to answer three challenges x such that their pairwise differences are invertible, then the polynomial must be the zero polynomial. In particular, the interesting term $m_1^*m_2^* - m_3^*$, which is separated from the other terms as the leading coefficient in the challenge x, must be zero.

There are two main problems with the technique:

1. The prover needs to send a large commitment $\vec{t}'$ to 5 polynomials together with an opening proof for it, and also the three uniform masked openings f_i.

2. Similarly as in the opening proof, the prover can cheat unless it is forced to be able to answer several challenges x with invertible differences. Unlike for the challenge c there is no shortness requirement associated to x. Still, if q splits completely, the soundness error is restricted to $1/q$ even for uniformly random $x \in \mathcal{R}_q$. Repetition is particularly expensive in the case of x since the masking polynomials a_i and corresponding commitments t_i' can not be reused. In fact, sending $f_i = a_i + xm_i$ for different x would break zero-knowledge. This even further increases the cost of the masking and garbage commitment and its opening proof.

Both problems result in concretely quite large communication sizes. We provide solutions to both problems and hereby drastically reduce the proof size.

First Problem. Instead of making the prover send the masked openings f_i and prove their well-formedness by committing to the a_i, we let the verifier compute the f_i from the commitments t_i. Then the proper relation to the messages m_i follows by construction. This is made possible by the results from Sect. 4. Recall that the verifier will be convinced that the vector $\vec{z}$ in the opening proof is of the form $\vec{z} = \vec{y}^* + c\vec{r}^*$ where $\vec{y}^*, \vec{r}^*$ are independent from c and $t_i = \langle \vec{b}_i, \vec{r}^* \rangle + m_i^*$ with binded m_i^*. Hence, the verifier will be convinced that

$$f_i = \langle \vec{b}_i, \vec{z} \rangle - ct_i = \langle \vec{b}_i, \vec{y}^* \rangle - cm_i^*.$$

But this exactly is a masked opening of m_i^* with challenge c and masking polynomial $a_i^* = \langle \vec{b}_i, \vec{y}^* \rangle$.

Now, when we compute the quadratic relation $f_1 f_2 + cf_3$ we need to get rid of the garbage terms. It seems we need to linear combine garbage commitments t_4' and t_5' with the challenge c and hereby construct a new commitment with commitment matrix $b_4' + cb_5'$ depending on c. If we went down this path we would need to send a second fresh opening proof with new challenge to show that $t_4' + ct_5' - (f_1 f_2 + cf_3)$ is a commitment to zero. This would be particularly bad if the garbage commitments are part of the commitment to the messages as one wants to have it in applications.

Instead, we use a new proof technique to achieve the same goal without two-layered opening proof and only one garbage commitment. In a nutshell, we use the masked opening $f_4' = \langle \vec{b}_4', \vec{z}' \rangle - ct_4'$ of the garbage term to reduce $f_1 f_2 + cf_3$ to the polynomial $f_1 f_2 + cf_3 + f_4'$ that is constant in c. Then we show that the prover can just send this polynomial before seeing c without destroying zero-knowledge. The resulting verification equation, which is quadratic in the commitments, can be handled in the extraction proof by making repeated use of the interpolations of $\vec{z}, \vec{z}'$ and the associated expressions for the commitments.

In our protocol we include the single garbage commitment in the commitment to the messages. This has the advantage of saving the separate binding part $\vec{t}_0'$ and the associated cost in the opening proof. Effectively this means that the message commitments become a part of the product proof protocol and this commitment contains an additional commitment to a garbage term,

$$t_4 = \langle \vec{b}_4, \vec{r} \rangle + \langle \vec{b}_3, \vec{y} \rangle - m_1 \langle \vec{b}_2, \vec{y} \rangle - m_2 \langle \vec{b}_2, \vec{y} \rangle.$$

For usual applications this approach is natural. For example when committing to an integer one usually knows that one needs to later provide a range proof for it so one can as well compute the range proof already when doing the commitment.

For concreteness we state the resulting protocol in Fig. 3. It has negligible soundness error when $\bar{c}$ is invertible with overwhelming probability. Otherwise the protocol could be repeated to boost the soundness but this would increase the number of garbage commitments t_4 that need to be transmitted. Instead, we now present a better solution that still only needs a single garbage commitment.

Second Problem. As explained in Sect. 4, we set up parameters so that, for some $j \in \mathbb{Z}_{2l/k+1}^{\times}$, the prover can guess the challenge c modulo each of the k prime ideals $\sigma^i(X^{d/l} - \zeta^j)$, $i = 0, \ldots, k-1$, with non-negligible independent probability of about $1/q^{d/l}$. This means with the above method the prover will prove

$$m_1 m_2 \equiv m_3 \pmod{\sigma^i(X^{d/l} - \zeta^j)}$$

only with non-negligible soundness error. We solve this problem by linear combining all the permutations $\sigma^i(m_1 m_2 - m_3)$ with independently uniformly random challenge polynomials α_i. So we set out to prove

$$\sum_{i=0}^{k-1} \alpha_i \sigma^i(m_1 m_2 - m_3) = 0.$$

Then our proof will show

$$\sum_{i=0}^{k-1} \alpha_i \sigma^i(m_1 m_2 - m_3) \equiv 0 \pmod{\sigma^{i'}(X^{d/l} - \zeta^j)}$$

with independent cheating probability for $i' = 0, \ldots, k-1$. But the last equation for a single i' proves

$$\sigma^i(m_1 m_2 - m_3) \equiv 0 \pmod{\sigma^{i'}(X^{d/l} - \zeta^j)}$$
$$\Rightarrow m_1 m_2 - m_3 \equiv 0 \pmod{\sigma^{i'-i}(X^{d/l} - \zeta^j)}$$

for all $i = 0, \ldots, k-1$ with cheating probability $1/q^{d/l}$ by the Schwartz-Zippel Lemma. A careful analysis will show the success probability of a cheating prover will be reduced to essentially at most

$$\varepsilon = \left(\frac{3}{q^{d/l}} \right)^k.$$

Now we derive the corresponding equation for the masked message openings. Here is where we need the randomness openings $\vec{z}_i$ with the permutations $\sigma^i(c)$

of the challenge. The verifier can compute k masked openings for every message with challenges $\sigma^i(c)$ by setting

$$f_j^{(i)} = \langle \vec{b}_j, \vec{z}_i \rangle - \sigma^i(c)t_j.$$

In the extraction we will have the expressions

$$f_j^{(i)} = \langle \vec{b}_j, \vec{y}_i^* \rangle - \sigma^i(c)m_j^*.$$

Therefore, it follows that

$$\sum_{i=0}^{k-1} \alpha_i \sigma^{-i} \left(f_1^{(i)} f_2^{(i)} + \sigma^i(c) f_3^{(i)} \right)$$

$$= \sum_{i=0}^{k-1} \alpha_i \sigma^{-i} \left(\langle \vec{b}_1, \vec{y}_i^* \rangle \langle \vec{b}_2, \vec{y}_i^* \rangle \right)$$

$$+ c \sum_{i=0}^{k-1} \alpha_i \sigma^{-i} \left(\langle \vec{b}_3, \vec{y}_i^* \rangle - m_1^* \langle \vec{b}_2, \vec{y}_i^* \rangle - m_2^* \langle \vec{b}_1, \vec{y}_i^* \rangle \right)$$

$$+ c^2 \left(\sum_{i=0}^{k-1} \alpha_i \sigma^{-i} \left(m_1^* m_2^* - m_3^* \right) \right)$$

We fold the coefficient of c into the constant coefficient by adding $f_4 = \langle \vec{b}_4, \vec{z}_0 \rangle - ct_4$ computed from the garbage commitment

$$t_4 = \langle \vec{b}_4, \vec{r} \rangle + \sum_{i=0}^{k-1} \alpha_i \sigma^{-i} \left(\langle \vec{b}_3, \vec{y}_i \rangle - m_1 \langle \vec{b}_2, \vec{y}_i \rangle - m_2 \langle \vec{b}_1, \vec{y}_i \rangle \right).$$

Then we arrive at

$$\sum_{i=0}^{k-1} \alpha_i \sigma^{-i} \left(f_1^{(i)} f_2^{(i)} + \sigma^i(c) f_3^{(i)} \right) + f_4$$

$$= \langle \vec{b}_4, \vec{y}_0^* \rangle + \sum_{i=0}^{k-1} \alpha_i \sigma^{-i} \left(\langle \vec{b}_1, \vec{y}_i^* \rangle \langle \vec{b}_2, \vec{y}_i^* \rangle \right)$$

$$+ c \left(\sum_{i=0}^{k-1} \alpha_i \sigma^{-i} \left(\langle \vec{b}_3, \vec{y}_i^* \rangle - m_1 \langle \vec{b}_2, \vec{y}_i^* \rangle - m_2 \langle \vec{b}_1, \vec{y}_i^* \rangle \right) - m_4^* \right)$$

$$+ c^2 \left(\sum_{i=0}^{k-1} \alpha_i \sigma^{-i} \left(m_1^* m_2^* - m_3^* \right) \right).$$

The verifier checks that this is equal to v using the polynomial v that it has received before sending the challenge.

It is important to note that we have departed from a straight-forward repetition of the protocol in Fig. 3. The main advantage being that there is still only one garbage commitment necessary.

5.1   The Protocol

The final protocol is given in Fig. 4. Its security is stated in Theorem 5.1. The proof of the theorem is given in the full version of the paper.

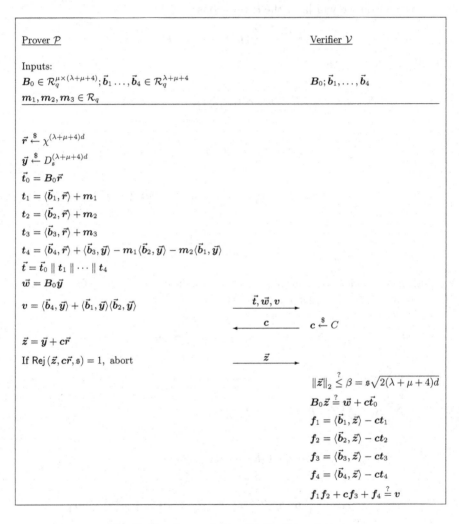

Fig. 3. Simple proof of multiplicative relation.

Theorem 5.1. *The protocol in Fig. 4 is complete, computational honest verifier zero-knowledge under the Module-LWE assumption and computational special sound under the Module-SIS assumption. More precisely, let p be the maximum probability over $\mathbb{Z}_q$ of the coefficients of $\mathbf{c} \bmod X^{kd/l} - \zeta^k$ as in Lemma 3.3.*

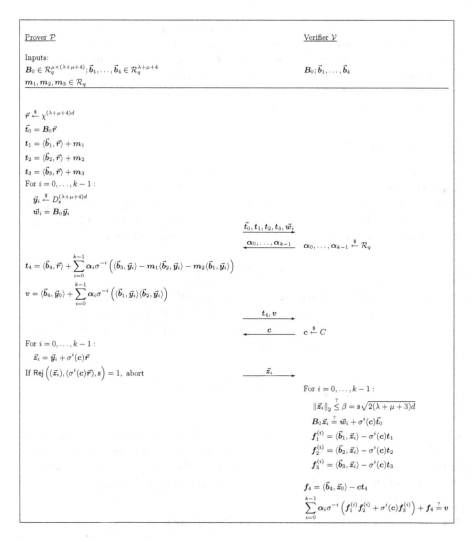

Fig. 4. Automorphism proof of multiplicative relation for automorphism $\sigma \in \mathrm{Aut}(\mathcal{R}_q)$ of order kd/l.

Then, for completeness, in case the honest prover $\mathcal{P}$ does not abort due to rejection sampling, it convinces the honest verifier $\mathcal{V}$ with overwhelming probability.

For zero-knowledge, there exists a simulator $\mathcal{S}$, that, without access to secret information, outputs a simulation of a non-aborting transcript of the protocol between $\mathcal{P}$ and $\mathcal{V}$. Then for every algorithm $\mathcal{A}$ that has advantage ε in distinguishing the simulated transcript from an actual transcript, there is an algorithm $\mathcal{A}'$ with the same running time that has advantage $\varepsilon - 2^{-100}$ in distinguishing $\mathsf{MLWE}_{\lambda,\chi}$.

For soundness, there is an extractor $\mathcal{E}$ with the following properties. When given rewindable black-box access to a deterministic prover $\mathcal{P}^*$ that convinces $\mathcal{V}$ with probability $\varepsilon \geq (3p^{d/l})^k$, $\mathcal{E}$ either outputs a weak opening for the commitment $\vec{t}$ with messages $\boldsymbol{m}_1^*$, $\boldsymbol{m}_2^*$ and $\boldsymbol{m}_3^*$ such that $\boldsymbol{m}_1^*\boldsymbol{m}_2^* = \boldsymbol{m}_3^*$, or a $\mathsf{MSIS}_{\mu,8\kappa\beta}$ solution for $\boldsymbol{B}_0$ in expected time at most $1/\varepsilon + (l/k)(\varepsilon - p^{kd/l})^{-1}$ when running $\mathcal{P}^*$ once is assumed to take unit time.

5.2   Amortized Protocol

The protocol from the last section can be extended into a protocol for the case where the prover wants to prove multiplicative relations between many messages. In this extension there will still only be one garbage commitment necessary for proving all of the relations. So the cost for the garbage commitment is amortized over all relations. Suppose we want to prove n product relations

$$m_1^{(j)} m_2^{(j)} = m_3^{(j)}$$

for $j = 1, \ldots, n$. Then virtually in the same way in which we linear combine the automorphic images of a single relation with uniform challenges, we can use even more challenges and linear combine all the automorphic images of all the relations. Concretely, we want to prove

$$\sum_{i=0}^{k-1} \sum_{j=1}^{n} \alpha_{in+j} \sigma^i \left(m_1^{(j)} m_2^{(j)} - m_3^{(j)} \right) = 0$$

with $\alpha_1, \ldots, \alpha_{nk} \xleftarrow{\$} \mathcal{R}_q$. Now a nice feature of the Schwartz-Zippel lemma is that this does not decrease the soundness. Intuitively, as soon as one of the relations is false, then the linear combination of all of the relations will be uniformly random, and this will be detected with overwhelming probability.

5.3   Non-interactive Protocol and Proof Sizes

In this section we compute the size of a non-interactive proof, where we distinguish between the size for the commitment $\vec{t} = \vec{t}_0 \parallel t_1 \parallel \cdots \parallel t_3$ to the messages and the size for the actual product proof. The message commitment is to be reused in some other protocol. It consists of $\mu + 3$ uniformly random polynomials so its size is $(\mu + 3)d\lceil \log q \rceil$ bits.

The protocol in Fig. 4 is made non-interactive with the help of the standard Fiat-Shamir technique. This means that the challenges are computed by the prover by hashing all previous messages and public information, and the hash function is modeled as a random oracle. To shorten the length of the proof, a standard technique is to not send the input to the hash function, but rather send its output (i.e. the challenge) and let the verifier recompute the input from the later transmitted terms using the verification equation and then test that the hash of these computed input terms is indeed the challenge. Concretely, in the non-interactive version of the product proof, the $k\mu + 1$ full-size polynomials $\vec{w}_i$ and v do not have to be transmitted and only t_4 remains as a non-short polynomial. The polynomials in the vectors $\vec{z}_i$ are short discrete Gaussian vectors with standard deviation $\mathfrak{s}$. Every coefficient is smaller than $6\mathfrak{s}$ in absolute value with probability $1 - 2^{-24}$ [24, Lemma 4.4]. So we can assume this is the case for all coefficients – the non-interactive prover can just restart otherwise. Eventually, we obtain that one non-interactive proof needs

$$d\lceil \log(q) \rceil + k(\lambda + \mu + 4)d\lceil \log(12\mathfrak{s}) \rceil + 256$$

bits.

Example I. Suppose we are given 8 secret polynomials in the ring $\mathcal{R}_q$ of rank $d = 128$ with a prime $q \approx 2^{32}$ that splits completely. So there are 1024 secret NTT coefficients in $\mathbb{Z}_q$ and we need 8 $\mathcal{R}_q$-polynomials to commit to these secret coefficients, not just 3 as before. For this ring the maximum probability over $\mathbb{Z}_q$ of the coefficients of $c \bmod (X^4 - \zeta^4)$ for $c \xleftarrow{\$} C$ is $p = 2^{-31.44}$ according to the formula in Lemma 3.3 when a coefficient of c is zero with probability $1/2$. So $k = 4$ permutations of a challenge under the automorphism $\sigma = \sigma_{64}$ are sufficient to reach negligible soundness error. Further, suppose the commitment scheme uses MLWE rank $\lambda = 10$ and MSIS rank $\mu = 10$. Then, we find $\|c\vec{r}\|_1 \leq 77$ with probability bigger than $1 - 2^{-100}$. If we set the standard deviation of the discrete Gaussian to $\mathfrak{s} = 5 \cdot 77 \cdot \sqrt{(\lambda + \mu + 9)d} = 46913$, we need $\mathsf{MSIS}_{\mu, 8d\beta}$ to be secure for $\beta = \mathfrak{s}\sqrt{2(\lambda + \mu + 9)d}$. We found the root Hermite factor to be approximately 1.0043. Similarly, MLWE_λ with ternary noise has hermite Factor 1.0043. With these parameters the size of the commitment is 9 KB and the size of our product proof is 31.3 KB.

Example II. For a fair comparison to [2, Parameter set I of Table 2], where the polynomial $X^d + 1$ does not necessarily split into linear factors, we modify the previous example and switch to using a prime q that splits into prime ideals of degree 4 (and so there are 32 NTT slots for each polynomial). Then we have negligible soundness error already with $k = 1$ and we don't need parallel repetitions and automorphisms. The protocol is given in Fig. 3 and the product proof size goes down to 8.8 KB.

Example III. In the above comparison to [2], we created a commitment to 256 NTT coefficients each being a polynomial of degree 3. For the 32-bit range proof example stated in the introduction, we only need 32 coefficients and hence only commit to one $\mathcal{R}_q$-polynomial. The size of such a commitment is 5.5 KB and our product proof has size 5.9 KB.

References

1. Banaszczyk, W.: New bounds in some transference theorems in the geometry of numbers. Math. Ann. **296**, 625–635 (1993)
2. Baum, C., Damgård, I., Lyubashevsky, V., Oechsner, S., Peikert, C.: More efficient commitments from structured lattice assumptions. In: Catalano, D., De Prisco, R. (eds.) SCN 2018. LNCS, vol. 11035, pp. 368–385. Springer, Cham (2018). https://doi.org/10.1007/978-3-319-98113-0_20
3. Ben-Sasson, E., Bentov, I., Horesh, Y., Riabzev, M.: Fast Reed-Solomon interactive oracle proofs of proximity. In: ICALP. LIPIcs, vol. 107, pp. 14:1–14:17. Schloss Dagstuhl - Leibniz-Zentrum fuer Informatik (2018)
4. Ben-Sasson, E., Chiesa, A., Riabzev, M., Spooner, N., Virza, M., Ward, N.P.: Aurora: transparent succinct arguments for R1CS. In: Ishai, Y., Rijmen, V. (eds.) EUROCRYPT 2019. LNCS, vol. 11476, pp. 103–128. Springer, Cham (2019). https://doi.org/10.1007/978-3-030-17653-2_4
5. Benhamouda, F., Krenn, S., Lyubashevsky, V., Pietrzak, K.: Efficient zero-knowledge proofs for commitments from learning with errors over rings. In: Pernul, G., Ryan, P.Y.A., Weippl, E. (eds.) ESORICS 2015. LNCS, vol. 9326, pp. 305–325. Springer, Cham (2015). https://doi.org/10.1007/978-3-319-24174-6_16
6. Bootle, J., Lyubashevsky, V., Seiler, G.: Algebraic techniques for short(er) exact lattice-based zero-knowledge proofs. In: Boldyreva, A., Micciancio, D. (eds.) CRYPTO 2019. LNCS, vol. 11692, pp. 176–202. Springer, Cham (2019). https://doi.org/10.1007/978-3-030-26948-7_7
7. Breuillard, E., Varjú, P.P.: Cut-off phenomenon for the ax+b Markov chain over a finite field (2019)
8. Bünz, B., Bootle, J., Boneh, D., Poelstra, A., Wuille, P., Maxwell, G.: Bulletproofs: short proofs for confidential transactions and more. In: IEEE Symposium on Security and Privacy, pp. 315–334 (2018)
9. Chen, H., Lauter, K., Stange, K.E.: Security considerations for Galois non-dual RLWE families. In: Avanzi, R., Heys, H. (eds.) SAC 2016. LNCS, vol. 10532, pp. 443–462. Springer, Cham (2017). https://doi.org/10.1007/978-3-319-69453-5_24
10. Chung, F.R.K., Diaconis, P., Graham, R.L.: Random walks arising in random number generation. Ann. Probab. **15**(3), 1148–1165 (1987)
11. del Pino, R., Lyubashevsky, V., Seiler, G.: Lattice-based group signatures and zero-knowledge proofs of automorphism stability. In: ACM CCS, pp. 574–591. ACM (2018)
12. Diaconis, P.: Group representations in probability and statistics. Lecture Notes-Monograph Series, vol. 11, pp. i–192 (1988)
13. Esgin, M.F., Nguyen, N.K., Seiler, G.: Practical exact proofs from lattices: New techniques to exploit fully-splitting rings (2020). https://eprint.iacr.org/2020/518
14. Esgin, M.F., Steinfeld, R., Liu, J.K., Liu, D.: Lattice-based zero-knowledge proofs: new techniques for shorter and faster constructions and applications. In: Boldyreva, A., Micciancio, D. (eds.) CRYPTO 2019. LNCS, vol. 11692, pp. 115–146. Springer, Cham (2019). https://doi.org/10.1007/978-3-030-26948-7_5
15. Esgin, M.F., Steinfeld, R., Sakzad, A., Liu, J.K., Liu, D.: Short lattice-based one-out-of-many proofs and applications to ring signatures. In: Deng, R.H., Gauthier-Umaña, V., Ochoa, M., Yung, M. (eds.) ACNS 2019. LNCS, vol. 11464, pp. 67–88. Springer, Cham (2019). https://doi.org/10.1007/978-3-030-21568-2_4
16. Esgin, M.F., Zhao, R.K., Steinfeld, R., Liu, J.K., Liu, D.: Matrict: efficient, scalable and post-quantum blockchain confidential transactions protocol. In: CCS, pp. 567–584. ACM (2019)

17. Hildebrand, M.: On the Chung-Diaconis-Graham random process. Electron. Commun. Probab. **11**, 347–356 (2006)
18. Hildebrand, M.V.: Rates of convergence of some random processes on finite groups. Ph.D. thesis, Harvard University (1990)
19. Katz, J., Kolesnikov, V., Wang, X.: Improved non-interactive zero knowledge with applications to post-quantum signatures. In: ACM Conference on Computer and Communications Security, pp. 525–537. ACM (2018)
20. Kilian, J.: A note on efficient zero-knowledge proofs and arguments (extended abstract). In: STOC, pp. 723–732. ACM (1992)
21. Langlois, A., Stehlé, D.: Worst-case to average-case reductions for module lattices. Des. Codes Crypt. **75**(3), 565–599 (2014). https://doi.org/10.1007/s10623-014-9938-4
22. Libert, B., Ling, S., Nguyen, K., Wang, H.: Lattice-based zero-knowledge arguments for integer relations. In: Shacham, H., Boldyreva, A. (eds.) CRYPTO 2018. LNCS, vol. 10992, pp. 700–732. Springer, Cham (2018). https://doi.org/10.1007/978-3-319-96881-0_24
23. Lyubashevsky, V.: Fiat-Shamir with aborts: applications to lattice and factoring-based signatures. In: Matsui, M. (ed.) ASIACRYPT 2009. LNCS, vol. 5912, pp. 598–616. Springer, Heidelberg (2009). https://doi.org/10.1007/978-3-642-10366-7_35
24. Lyubashevsky, V.: Lattice signatures without trapdoors. In: Pointcheval, D., Johansson, T. (eds.) EUROCRYPT 2012. LNCS, vol. 7237, pp. 738–755. Springer, Heidelberg (2012). https://doi.org/10.1007/978-3-642-29011-4_43
25. Lyubashevsky, V., Micciancio, D.: Generalized compact knapsacks are collision resistant. In: Bugliesi, M., Preneel, B., Sassone, V., Wegener, I. (eds.) ICALP 2006. LNCS, vol. 4052, pp. 144–155. Springer, Heidelberg (2006). https://doi.org/10.1007/11787006_13
26. Lyubashevsky, V., Peikert, C., Regev, O.: On ideal lattices and learning with errors over rings. In: Gilbert, H. (ed.) EUROCRYPT 2010. LNCS, vol. 6110, pp. 1–23. Springer, Heidelberg (2010). https://doi.org/10.1007/978-3-642-13190-5_1
27. Lyubashevsky, V., Seiler, G.: Short, invertible elements in partially splitting cyclotomic rings and applications to lattice-based zero-knowledge proofs. In: Nielsen, J.B., Rijmen, V. (eds.) EUROCRYPT 2018. LNCS, vol. 10820, pp. 204–224. Springer, Cham (2018). https://doi.org/10.1007/978-3-319-78381-9_8
28. Micali, S.: Computationally sound proofs. SIAM J. Comput. **30**(4), 1253–1298 (2000)
29. Peikert, C., Rosen, A.: Efficient collision-resistant hashing from worst-case assumptions on cyclic lattices. In: Halevi, S., Rabin, T. (eds.) TCC 2006. LNCS, vol. 3876, pp. 145–166. Springer, Heidelberg (2006). https://doi.org/10.1007/11681878_8
30. Steinfeld, R.: Personal communication (2020)
31. Yang, R., Au, M.H., Zhang, Z., Xu, Q., Yu, Z., Whyte, W.: Efficient lattice-based zero-knowledge arguments with standard soundness: construction and applications. In: Boldyreva, A., Micciancio, D. (eds.) CRYPTO 2019. LNCS, vol. 11692, pp. 147–175. Springer, Cham (2019). https://doi.org/10.1007/978-3-030-26948-7_6

Lattice-Based Blind Signatures, Revisited

Eduard Hauck[1]($\boxtimes$)(iD), Eike Kiltz[1](iD), Julian Loss[2](iD),
and Ngoc Khanh Nguyen[3,4](iD)

[1] Ruhr-Universität Bochum, Bochum, Germany
{eduard.hauck,eike.kiltz}@rub.de
[2] University of Maryland, College Park, USA
julian.loss@gmail.com
[3] ETH Zurich, Zürich, Switzerland
[4] IBM Research, Zurich, Rüschlikon, Switzerland
NKN@zurich.ibm.com

Abstract. We observe that all previously known lattice-based blind signature schemes contain subtle flaws in their security proofs (e.g., Rückert, ASIACRYPT '08) or can be attacked (e.g., BLAZE by Alkadri et al., FC '20). Motivated by this, we revisit the problem of constructing blind signatures from standard lattice assumptions.

We propose a new three-round lattice-based blind signature scheme whose security can be proved, in the random oracle model, from the standard SIS assumption. Our starting point is a modified version of the (insecure) BLAZE scheme, which itself is based Lyubashevsky's three-round identification scheme combined with a new aborting technique to reduce the correctness error. Our proof builds upon and extends the recent modular framework for blind signatures of Hauck, Kiltz, and Loss (EUROCRYPT '19). It also introduces several new techniques to overcome the additional challenges posed by the correctness error which is inherent to all lattice-based constructions.

While our construction is mostly of theoretical interest, we believe it to be an important stepping stone for future works in this area.

Keywords: Blind signatures · Forking lemma · Lattices

1 Introduction

BLIND SIGNATURES. Blind signatures, first proposed by Chaum [18], are a fundamental cryptographic primitive with many applications such as eVoting [54], eCash [18], anonymous credentials [6,8,14–16,19,46], and, as of late, privacy preserving protocols in the context of blockchain protocols [61]. Informally, a blind signature scheme is an interactive protocol between a *signer* S (holding a secret key *sk*) and a *user* U (holding a public key *pk* and a message *m*) with the goal that U obtains a signature σ on *m*. The protocol should satisfy correctness (i.e., σ can be verified using the public key *pk* of S and *m*), unforgeability (i.e., only S can issue signatures), and blindness (i.e., S is not able to link σ to a particular execution of the protocol in which it was created). Blind signatures are among the most well-studied cryptographic primitives and it is well

© International Association for Cryptologic Research 2020
D. Micciancio and T. Ristenpart (Eds.): CRYPTO 2020, LNCS 12171, pp. 500–529, 2020.
https://doi.org/10.1007/978-3-030-56880-1_18

known how to construct blind signatures from general complexity assumptions [22,23,34]. However, achieving *efficient constructions* from *standard assumptions* is known to be a notoriously difficult task with only a handful of constructions being known. To make matters worse, even among these works, some have been pointed out to contain flawed security proofs [2,56]. Effectively, this leaves only the original works due to Pointcheval and Stern [50–53] based on Schnorr [57] and Okomoto-Schnorr [44] signatures. BLIND SIGNATURES FROM LATTICES. In this work, we revisit the problem of constructing blind signatures from standard *lattice assumptions*. This question was first addressed by Rückert [56], who gave a candidate construction based on Lyubashevsky's identification scheme [38] from the SIS assumption. Unfortunately, as we will explain in Sect. 1.2, his security proof contains a subtle flaw. While the recent work of Hauck, Kiltz, and Loss [32] introduces a general framework to obtain blind signatures from (collision resistant) linear hash functions, their framework does not cover the setting of lattice assumptions. Informally, the reason for this is that in the context of lattice-based constructions, most known cryptographic primitives exhibit some form of *noticeable correctness error*. Indeed, this is also true for Lyubashevsky's identification scheme/linear hash function implicitly used in [56]. This makes it impossible to apply the analysis of [32] directly, since it crucially relies on the fact that if both S and U behave honestly, U always obtains a valid signature. Since [56] was published, more lattice-based constructions of blind signatures have been proposed. As we will discuss in detail below, all of these schemes either inherit the proof errors from [56] or introduce new ones. The main goal of our work is to give the first direct lattice-based blind signature scheme with a correct security proof.

1.1 Our Contributions

We construct a blind signature scheme from any linear hash functions [5,32] with noticeable correctness error. We use the aborting technique introduced by Alkadri, El Bansarkhani, and Buchmann [4] to reduce the correctness error of the blind signature scheme. Instantiating our construction with Lyubashevsky's linear hash function [38] we obtain a lattice-based blind signature scheme from the SIS assumption.

While our work offers the first correct proof for a lattice-based blind signature scheme, it comes with several severe drawbacks. First, we can only prove blindness in the weaker *honest signer model* [34] as compared to the *malicious signer model* [23]. We leave the construction of a scheme in the malicious signer setting as an open problem. Second, our construction comes with an exponential security loss in the reduction from the underlying hardness assumption (here, the SIS assumption). This is inherited from the proof technique of Pointcheval and Stern in the discrete logarithm setting [53]. This strongly restricts the number of signatures that can be issued per public key to a poly-logarithmic amount. Indeed, a sub-exponential attack due to Schnorr and Wagner [58,60] resulting from the ROS[1] problem shows that for the Schnorr and Okamoto-Schnorr blind signature schemes, these parameters are optimal. Extending [32,58], we are also able to relate the security of our blind signature to a Generalized ROS problem whose hardness is independent of the SIS problem. However, the sub-exponential attack of Schnorr and Wagner cannot be directly translated to the Generalized ROS problem due to the algebraic structure of our lattice-based instantiation (see Sect. 7). Therefore, an interesting open question is whether our "lattice" variant of the Generalized ROS problem can be solved in sub-exponential time. Nevertheless, we believe that our scheme makes an important first step toward future endeavors in this area by giving the first comprehensive and modular security proof for a blind signature scheme from lattice assumptions. While our scheme might not be practical by itself (our example instantiation has signatures sizes of roughly 36 MB),[2] it seems reasonable to apply similar ideas as in [49] to extend the number of allowed sessions per public key to a polynomial amount at not much overhead (but at the restriction of issuing signatures in a sequential fashion).

1.2   Problems with Existing Schemes

In the following we will first explain in detail the problems in the proof of Rückert's lattice-based blind signature scheme and then sketch how these errors propagate to subsequent schemes. We also list some other lattice-based constructions which have been found to be incorrect.

RÜCKERT'S BLIND SIGNATURE SCHEME. The key idea in the proof of Rückert's lattice-based blind signature scheme [56] is to rewind the forger (with partially different random oracles) so as to obtain two distinct values χ and χ' satisfying $F(\chi) = F(\chi')$, i.e., a collision in the underlying linear hash function. (In the lattice setting, a collision in the hash function directly implies a non-trivial solution $\chi - \chi'$ to the SIS problem.) To argue that $\chi \neq \chi'$, [56] attempts to apply the general forking lemma of Bellare and Neven [9] to the forger and argues that witness indistinguishability alone is sufficient to ensure $\chi \neq \chi'$. Here, [56] relies on Lemma 8 from Pointcheval and Stern's proof [53], who followed a similar approach. However, Lemma 8 does not state that χ and χ' are distinct; only that (by witness indistinguishability of their scheme) there exist two distinct secret keys sk, sk', which can lead to identical transcripts. This is *insufficient* to ensure $\chi \neq \chi'$ in the subsequent rewinding step. In fact, the Generalized ROS attack mentioned above works independently of the concrete secret key that is being used. Using this attack, it is always possible to force an outcome of $\chi = \chi'$ if the number of signatures per public key becomes larger than polylogarithmic in the security parameter. The crucial argument toward proving $\chi \neq \chi'$ only follows from Lemma 9 and the subsequent parts of Pointcheval and Stern's proof and is

---

[1] ROS stands for Random inhomogenities in an Overdetermined, Solvable system of linear equations.

[2] It is not even clear how much better our scheme performs compared to generic constructions using non-interactive zero-knowledge proofs [23].

completely missing from Rückert's proof. It relies on a very subtle probabilistic method argument that only works in a (small) range of parameters for which the ROS problem remains information theoretically hard. Moreover, both Lemma 8 and 9 of [53] apply *exclusively* to the Okamoto-Schnorr scheme and cannot be transferred to other schemes directly. Adapting these lemmas to a setting with correctness error is one of the key novelties in our proof.

BLAZE AND BLAZE$^+$. BLAZE by Alkadri, El Bansarkhani, and Buchmann [3] improves Rückert's construction in the following two aspects. Firstly, BLAZE applies Gaussian rejection sampling [39] instead of uniform [38]. Secondly, it introduces the concept of signed permutations which allows to get rid of rejection sampling on the unblinded challenge values. While BLAZE introduces several interesting new concepts for constructing lattice-based blind signatures, its security analysis reuses the (incorrect) security arguments of Rückert at a crucial point in the reduction, and hence inherits its problems. Concretely, in the one-more unforgeability proof of [3, Theorem 3] it is missing the argument that the candidate solution for the inhomogeneous RSIS problem computed in Case 2 is non-trivial. Even worse and independent of the aforementioned problems with the proof, BLAZE is not one-more unforgeable as we will sketch now. Consider a user U interacting with the signer S in the one-more unforgeability experiment. At the end of the protocol execution, an honest U performs rejection sampling on some values $(\hat{z}_1, \hat{z}_2)$ contained in the signature. (Rejection sampling on U's side is used to ensure blindness.) If rejection sampling rejects, U sends the random coins used for rejection sampling as a proof to S which, upon successful verification, triggers a restart of the protocol. However, even in case rejection sampling rejects, the signature can still be valid and which case a dishonest U can trigger a restart of the protocol while still learning a valid signature. Since by the restart of the protocol U learns another valid signature, this observation can be turned into a simple one-more unforgeability attack. The aforementioned attack on BLAZE actually disappears in the recently proposed BLAZE$^+$ protocol [4] because U performs multiple rejection samplings in parallel and the probability that all of them reject becomes negligible. BLAZE$^+$ introduces a new technique of reducing correctness error by performing multiple rejection samplings in parallel in order to reduce the communication complexity. Unfortunately, the security analysis also reuses the (incorrect) security arguments of Rückert and hence inherits its problems.

FURTHER SCHEMES. Three recent works [13,37,47] propose new lattice-based blind signatures, but they also rely on the same analysis as Rückert to argue that a collision can be found with non-negligible probability when rewinding (see above). Unfortunately, this implies that all of these schemes do not have a valid security proof. There has been a line of research on lattice-based blind signatures using preimage sampleable trapdoor functions [20,28,29,62,63]. As shown by [3], all these schemes are insecure. Concretely, they give attacks which either recover the secret key or solve the underlying lattice problem in at most two executions of the signing protocol.

1.3   Related Work

Three round blind signatures are not achievable in the standard model [25]. We circumvent their result by using (programmable) random oracles and therefore believe that our proof strategies cannot be easily extended to the standard model. Blind signatures are impossible to construct from one-way permutations [35], even in the random oracle model. We circumvent their result by relying on the stronger assumption of collision resistance. A large class of Schnorr-type blind signature schemes cannot be proved secure if the underlying identification scheme has a unique witness [7]. We circumvent their result by requiring our underlying hard problem to have multiple witnesses corresponding to each public key.

As already mentioned, round optimal blind signatures can be constructed from general complexity assumptions beyond one-way permutations [22,23,31, 34]. The impossibility results of [25] are circumvented by either relying on a CRS [23] or using complexity leveraging [22,31]. We refer to [22] for a detailed discussion on the topic of constructing blind signatures from general assumptions.

Several works [2,7,12,26,30,31,45,51,53] show how to construct efficient blind signatures schemes from concrete assumptions in the setting of prime-order groups, in some cases relying on bilinear maps.

1.4   Organization

After establishing some preliminaries in Sect. 2, in Sect. 3 we will introduce the notion of linear hash functions LHF with noticeable correctness error. In Sect. 4 we will define syntax and security of canonical (three-round) blind signature schemes. Figure 5 constructs a blind signature scheme $\mathsf{BS}_\eta[\mathsf{LHF}, \mathsf{H}, \mathsf{G}]$ from any linear hash function LHF and two standard hash functions H and G. This section also contains our main theorems about one-more unforgeability (Theorem 1) and blindness (Theorem 2). As a first step in the proof of Theorem 1, in Sect. 5 we will reduce the one-more unforgeability of $\mathsf{BS}_{\eta,\nu,\mu}[\mathsf{LHF}, \mathsf{H}, \mathsf{G}]$ to one-more man-in-the-middle security of the underlying canonical identification scheme $\mathsf{ID}_{\eta'}[\mathsf{LHF}]$ in the random oracle model. The proof of the one-more man-in-the-middle security of $\mathsf{ID}_{\eta'}[\mathsf{LHF}]$ will be given in the full version [33]. In Sect. 6 we will provide an example instantiation of our framework based on the standard SIS assumption. Finally, Sect. 7 generalizes the ROS attack to our setting and proves that any attack on it also implies an attack on the one-more unforgeability of $\mathsf{BS}_{\eta,\nu,\mu}[\mathsf{LHF}, \mathsf{H}, \mathsf{G}]$.

2   Preliminaries and Notation

SETS AND VECTORS. For $n \in \mathbb{N}$, $[n]$ denotes the set $\{1, \ldots, n\}$. We use bold-faced, lower case letters $\boldsymbol{h}$ to denote a vector of elements and denote the length of $\boldsymbol{h}$ as $|\boldsymbol{h}|$. For $j \geq 1$, we write $\boldsymbol{h}_j$ to denote the j-th element of $\boldsymbol{h}$ and we write $\boldsymbol{h}_{[j]}$ to refer to the first j entries of $\boldsymbol{h}$, i.e., the elements $\boldsymbol{h}_1, ..., \boldsymbol{h}_j$. We use boldface, upper case letters $\mathbf{A}$ to denote matrices. We denote the i-th row of $\mathbf{A}$

as $\mathbf{A}_i$ and the j-th entry of $\mathbf{A}_i$ as $\mathbf{A}_{i,j}$. We let $\Delta(X, Y)$ indicate the statistical distance between two distributions X, Y.

SAMPLING FROM SETS. We write $h \xleftarrow{\$} S$ to denote that the variable h is uniformly sampled from the finite set S. For $1 \leq j \leq Q$ and $\boldsymbol{g} \in S^{j-1}$, we write $\boldsymbol{h}' \xleftarrow{\$} S^Q | \boldsymbol{g}$ to denote that the vector $\boldsymbol{h}'$ is uniformly sampled from S^Q, conditioned on $\boldsymbol{h}'_{[j-1]} = \boldsymbol{g}$. This sampling process can be implemented by copying vector $\boldsymbol{g}$ into the first $j-1$ entries of $\boldsymbol{h}'$ and next sampling the remaining $Q-j+1$ entries of $\boldsymbol{h}$, (i.e., $\boldsymbol{h}'_j, \ldots, \boldsymbol{h}'_Q \xleftarrow{\$} S^{Q-j+1}$).

ALGORITHMS. We use uppercase, serif-free letters A, B to denote algorithms. Unless otherwise stated, algorithms are probabilistic and we write $(y_1, \ldots) \xleftarrow{\$} \mathsf{A}(x_1, \ldots)$ to denote that A returns $(y_1, \ldots)$ when run on input $(x_1, \ldots)$. We write A^B to denote that A has oracle access to B during its execution. To make the randomness ω of an algorithm A on input x explicit, we write $\mathsf{A}(x; \omega)$. Note that in this notation, A is deterministic. For a randomised algorithm A, we use the notation $y \in \mathsf{A}(x)$ to denote that y is a possible output of A on input x.

SECURITY GAMES. We use standard code-based security games [11]. A *game* $\mathbf{G}$ is a probability experiment in which an adversary A interacts with an implicit challenger that answers oracle queries issued by A. $\mathbf{G}$ has one *main procedure* and an arbitrary amount of additional *oracle procedures* which describe how these oracle queries are answered. To distinguish game-related oracle procedures from algorithmic procedures more clearly, we denote the former using monospaced font, e.g., `Oracle`. We denote the (binary) output b of game $\mathbf{G}$ between a challenger and an adversary A as $\mathbf{G}^\mathsf{A} \Rightarrow b$. A is said to *win* $\mathbf{G}$ if $\mathbf{G}^\mathsf{A} \Rightarrow 1$. Unless otherwise stated, the randomness in the probability term $\Pr[\mathbf{G}^\mathsf{A} \Rightarrow 1]$ is over all the random coins in game $\mathbf{G}$.

ALGEBRA. We let $\oplus$ denote the bitwise XOR operation. A module is specified by two sets S and $\mathcal{M}$, where S is a ring with multiplicative identity element 1_S and $\langle \mathcal{M}, +, 0 \rangle$ is an additive Abelian group and a mapping $\cdot : S \times \mathcal{M} \to \mathcal{M}$, s.t. for all $r, s \in S$ and $x, y \in \mathcal{M}$ we have (i) $r \cdot (x + y) = r \cdot x + r \cdot y$; (ii) $(r + s) \cdot x = r \cdot x + s \cdot x$; (iii) $(rs) \cdot x = r \cdot (s \cdot x)$; and (iv) $1_S \cdot x = x$.

SECURITY NOTIONS. We formalize all security notions relative to some fixed parameters *par*. This streamlines the exposition considerably. In doing so, we consider a non-uniform notion of security, as the RSIS problem is not hard for fixed *par*, but only for *par* drawn (uniformly) at random in the security experiment. This is comparable to considerations as in [55]. However, we remark that using the splitting lemma our theorems can easily be made to work in a setting where *par* is indeed chosen at random along with the remaining (random) parts.

3   Linear Hash Functions

In this section we define *linear hash function families with correctness error* which are a generalization of linear (hash) function families with perfect correctness [5, 32].

SYNTAX. A *linear hash function family* LHF is a tuple of algorithms (PGen, F). On input the security parameter, the randomized algorithm PGen returns some parameters *par*, which implicitly define the sets

$$\mathcal{S} = \mathcal{S}(par), \quad \mathcal{D} = \mathcal{D}(par), \quad \text{and } \mathcal{R} = \mathcal{R}(par),$$

where $\mathcal{S}$ is a set of scalars such that $\mathcal{D}$ and $\mathcal{R}$ are modules over $\mathcal{S}$. The parameters *par* also define 9 *filter sets*

$$\mathcal{S}_{\mathrm{xxx}} \subseteq \mathcal{S} \ (\mathrm{xxx} \in \{\beta, c, c'\}) \text{ and } \mathcal{D}_{\mathrm{yyy}} \subseteq \mathcal{D} \ (\mathrm{yyy} \in \{sk, r, s, s', \alpha\}).$$

Throughout the paper, we will assume that *par* is fixed and implicitly given to all algorithms. For linear hash function families with perfect correctness [32], the filter sets are trivial, i.e., $\mathcal{S}_{\mathrm{xxx}} = \mathcal{S}$ and $\mathcal{D}_{\mathrm{yyy}} = \mathcal{D}$.

Algorithm $\mathsf{F}(par, \cdot)$ implements a mapping from $\mathcal{D}$ to $\mathcal{R}$. To simplify our presentation, we will omit *par* from F's input from now on. $\mathsf{F}(\cdot)$ is required to be a *module homomorphism*, meaning that for any $x, y \in \mathcal{D}$ and $s \in \mathcal{S}$:

$$\mathsf{F}(s \cdot x + y) = s \cdot \mathsf{F}(x) + \mathsf{F}(y) . \tag{1}$$

We now define the technical conditions of *torsion-freeness*, *regularity*, *enclosedness*, and *smoothness* of LHF that will be useful for proving correctness and security of blind signatures constructed from LHF.

TORSION-FREENESS AND REGULARITY. We say that LHF has a *torsion-free element from the kernel* if for all *par* generated with PGen, there exist $z^* \in \mathcal{D} \setminus \{0\}$ such that (i) $\mathsf{F}(z^*) = 0$; and (ii) for all $c_1, c_2 \in \mathcal{S}_c$ satisfying $(c_1 - c_2) \cdot z^* = 0$ we have $c_1 - c_2 = 0$. Note that the existence of such an element implies that F is a many-to-one mapping.

We call LHF (ε, Q')-*regular*, if for all *par* generated with PGen, there exist sets $\mathcal{D}'_{sk}, \mathcal{D}'_r$ and a torsion-free element from the kernel z^* s.t.

$$\frac{|\mathcal{D}'_{sk}|}{|\mathcal{D}_{sk}|} \cdot \left(\frac{|\mathcal{D}'_r|}{|\mathcal{D}_r|}\right)^{Q'} \geq 1 - \varepsilon/4,$$

and where

$$\mathcal{D}'_{sk} := \{sk \in \mathcal{D}_{sk} : sk + z^* \in \mathcal{D}_{sk}\}$$

and

$$\mathcal{D}'_r := \{r \in \mathcal{D}_r : \forall c \in \mathcal{S}_c, r + cz^* \in \mathcal{D}_r\}.$$

Similar to the work of Hauck et al. [32], our proof of one-more unforgeability uses torsion-freeness and regularity to argue that a transcript of the scheme with a secret key *sk* can be preserved when switching to a different (valid) secret key $sk' := sk + z^*$, with high probability.

ENCLOSEDNESS ERROR. We say that LHF has *enclosedness errors* $(\delta_1, \delta_2, \delta_3)$ if for all $par \in \mathsf{PGen}(1^\kappa)$, $c' \in \mathcal{S}_{c'}, c \in \mathcal{S}_c, s \in \mathcal{D}_s, sk \in \mathcal{D}_{sk}$,

$$\Pr_{\beta \xleftarrow{\$} \mathcal{S}_\beta} [\beta + c' \notin \mathcal{S}_c] < \delta_1, \quad \Pr_{r \xleftarrow{\$} \mathcal{D}_r} [c \cdot sk + r \notin \mathcal{D}_s] < \delta_2, \quad \text{and} \quad \Pr_{\alpha \xleftarrow{\$} \mathcal{D}_\alpha} [\alpha + s \notin \mathcal{D}_{s'}] < \delta_3.$$

The enclosedness error of LHF is directly linked to the *correctness error* of our schemes. Intuitively, the smaller this error, the easier it is to get a scheme which almost always works correctly.

SMOOTHNESS. We say that LHF is *smooth* if the following conditions hold for all $par \in \mathsf{PGen}(1^\kappa)$:

(S1) For all $s \in \mathcal{D}_s$ and $s' \in \mathcal{D}_{s'}$, we have $\|s' - s\|_\infty \in \mathcal{D}_\alpha$

(S2) For all $s_1, s_2 \in \mathcal{D}_s$ and random variables $\alpha^* \xleftarrow{\$} \{\alpha \in \mathcal{D}_\alpha \mid \alpha + s_1 \in \mathcal{D}_{s'}\}$, $\hat{\alpha} \xleftarrow{\$} \{\alpha \in \mathcal{D}_\alpha \mid \alpha + s_2 \in \mathcal{D}_{s'}\}$ we have that $\hat{\alpha} + s_2$ and $\alpha^* + s_1$ are identically distributed.

(S3) For all $s_1, s_2 \in \mathcal{D}_s$ and random variables $\underline{\alpha}^* \xleftarrow{\$} \{\alpha \in \mathcal{D}_\alpha \mid \alpha + s_1 \notin \mathcal{D}_{s'}\}$, $\underline{\hat{\alpha}} \xleftarrow{\$} \{\alpha \in \mathcal{D}_\alpha \mid \alpha + s_2 \notin \mathcal{D}_{s'}\}$ we have that $\underline{\hat{\alpha}} + s_2$ and $\underline{\alpha}^* + s_1$ are identically distributed.

(S4) For all $c' \in \mathcal{S}_{c'}$ and $c \in \mathcal{S}_c$, we have $\|c - c'\|_\infty \in \mathcal{S}_\beta$.

(S5) For all $c'_1, c'_2 \in \mathcal{S}_{c'}$ and random variables $\beta^* \xleftarrow{\$} \{\beta \in \mathcal{S}_\beta \mid \beta + c'_1 \in \mathcal{S}_c\}$, $\hat{\beta} \xleftarrow{\$} \{\beta \in \mathcal{S}_\beta \mid \beta + c'_2 \in \mathcal{S}_c\}$ we have that $\hat{\beta} + c'_2$ and $\beta^* + c'_1$ are identically distributed.

(S6) For all $c'_1, c'_2 \in \mathcal{S}_{c'}$ and random variables $\underline{\beta}^* \xleftarrow{\$} \{\beta \in \mathcal{S}_\beta \mid \beta + c'_1 \notin \mathcal{S}_c\}$, $\underline{\hat{\beta}} \xleftarrow{\$} \{\beta \in \mathcal{S}_\beta \mid \beta + c'_2 \notin \mathcal{S}_c\}$ we have that $\underline{\hat{\beta}} + c'_2$ and $\underline{\beta}^* + c'_1$ are identically distributed.

Smoothness of LHF will be a crucial tool for proving *blindness* of our schemes. Intuitively, smoothness allows to 'match' any message/signature pair (m_i, σ_i) that was generated via the ith run of the scheme to the transcript T_j of *any run* $j \in \{1, ..., i, ...\}$.

COLLISION RESISTANCE. LHF is (ε, t)-**CR** relative to $par \in \mathsf{PGen}(1^\kappa)$ if for all adversaries running in time at most t,

$$\Pr_{(x_1, x_2) \xleftarrow{\$} A(par)} [(\mathsf{F}(x_1) = \mathsf{F}(x_2)) \wedge (x_1 \neq x_2)] \leq \varepsilon.$$

4 Canonical Blind Signature Schemes

In this section, we recall syntax and security of a special type of blind signature scheme, called *canonical three-move blind signature scheme* [32]. In Sect. 4.1, we first recall the syntax of such schemes and give the proper security definitions. Next, in Sect. 4.3, we give a generic construction that gives a canonical three-move blind signature scheme BS[LHF] from any linear hash function family LHF.

4.1 Definitions

Definition 1 (Canonical Three-Move Blind Signature Scheme). *A canonical three-move blind signature scheme* BS *is a tuple of algorithms* BS = (PGen, KG, S, U, BSVer).

- The *randomised* parameter generation algorithm PGen *returns system parameters par.*
- The *randomised* key generation algorithm KG *takes as input system parameters par and outputs a public key/secret key pair* (pk, sk). *We assume that pk defines a challenge set* $\mathcal{C} := \mathcal{C}(pk)$ *and that pk is known to all parties.*
- The signer algorithm S *is split into two algorithms, i.e.,* $S := (S_1, S_2)$, *where:*
  - *The randomised algorithm* S_1 *takes as input the secret key sk and returns a commitment R and the signer's state stS.*
  - *The deterministic algorithm* S_2 *takes as input the signer's state stS, a secret key sk, a commitment R, and a challenge* $c \in \mathcal{C}$. *It returns the response s.*
- The user algorithm U *is split into two algorithms, i.e.,* $U := (U_1, U_2)$, *where:*
  - *The randomised algorithm* U_1 *takes as input the public key pk, a commitment R, and a message m. It returns the user's state stU and a challenge* $c \in \mathcal{C}$.
  - *The deterministic algorithm* U_2 *takes as input the public key pk, a commitment R, a challenge* $c \in \mathcal{C}$, *a response s, a message m, and the user's state stU. It returns a signature* σ *where, possibly,* $\sigma = \perp$.
- The *deterministic verification algorithm* BSVer *takes as input the public key pk, a signature* σ, *and a message m. It outputs 1 (accept) or 0 (reject). We make the convention that* BSVer *always outputs 0 on input a signature* $\sigma = \perp$.

We note that modeling S_2 and U_2 as deterministic algorithms is w.l.o.g. since randomness can be transmitted through the states.

Consider an interaction $(R, c, s, \sigma) \leftarrow \langle S(sk), U(pk, m) \rangle$ between signer S and user U, as defined in Fig. 1. We say that BS $= (\text{PGen}, \text{KG}, S, U, \text{BSVer})$ has *correctness error* δ, if for all messages $m \in \{0, 1\}^*$, $par \in \text{PGen}(1^\kappa)$, $(pk, sk) \in \text{KG}(par)$,

$$\Pr_{(a, \sigma) \xleftarrow{\$} \langle S(sk), U(pk, m) \rangle} \left[\text{BSVer}(pk, m, \sigma) \neq 1 \right] \leq \delta .$$

Signer $S(sk)$		User $U(pk, m)$
$(R, stS) \xleftarrow{\$} S_1(sk)$	$\xrightarrow{R}$	
	$\xleftarrow{c}$	$(c, stU) \xleftarrow{\$} U_1(pk, R, m)$
$s \leftarrow S_2(sk, R, c, stS)$	$\xrightarrow{s}$	$\sigma \leftarrow U_2(pk, R, c, s, m, stU)$
		Output σ

Fig. 1. Interaction $(R, c, s, \sigma) \leftarrow \langle S(sk), U(pk, m) \rangle$ between signer S and user U.

SECURITY NOTIONS. Security of a Canonical Three-Move Blind Signature Scheme BS is captured by two security notions: *blindness* and *one-more unforgeability.*

Intuitively, blindness ensures that a signer S that issues signatures on two messages (m_0, m_1) of its own choice to a user U, can not tell in what order it issues them. In particular, S is given both resulting signatures σ_0, σ_1, and gets

Game $\mathbf{Blind}_{BS,par}$:	Oracle $U_1(sid, R)$:	Oracle $U_2(sid, s)$:
01 $b \xleftarrow{\$} \{0,1\}$	08 If $sid \notin \{1,2\} \vee \mathsf{sess}_{sid} \neq \mathtt{init}$:	14 If $\mathsf{sess}_{sid} \neq \mathtt{open}$: Return $\bot$
02 $b_1 \leftarrow b;\ b_2 \leftarrow 1 - b$	09 $\quad$ Return $\bot$	15 $\mathsf{sess}_{sid} \leftarrow \mathtt{closed}$
03 $(sk, pk) \xleftarrow{\$} \mathrm{KG}(par)$	10 $\mathsf{sess}_{sid} \leftarrow \mathtt{open}$	16 $s_{sid} \leftarrow s$
04 $b' \xleftarrow{\$} A^{\mathtt{Init},U_1,U_2}(pk, sk)$	11 $R_{sid} \leftarrow R$	17 $\sigma_{b_{sid}} \xleftarrow{\$} U_2(pk, R_{sid}, c_{sid}, s_{sid}, st_{sid})$
05 Return $b = b'$	12 $(c_{sid}, st_{sid}) \xleftarrow{\$} U_1(pk, R_{sid}, m_{b_{sid}})$	18 If $\mathsf{sess}_1 = \mathsf{sess}_2 = \mathtt{closed}$:
Oracle $\mathtt{Init}(\tilde{m}_0, \tilde{m}_1)$: // Once	13 Return (sid, c_{sid})	19 $\quad$ If $\sigma_0 = \bot \vee \sigma_1 = \bot$:
06 $m_0 \leftarrow \tilde{m}_0, m_1 \leftarrow \tilde{m}_1$		20 $\quad\quad$ Return $(\bot, \bot)$
07 $\mathsf{sess}_1 \leftarrow \mathsf{sess}_2 \leftarrow \mathtt{init}$		21 $\quad$ Return (σ_0, σ_1)
		22 Return $(sid, \mathtt{closed})$

Fig. 2. Games defining $\mathbf{Blind}_{BS,par}$ for a canonical three-move blind signature scheme BS, with the convention that adversary A makes exactly one query to $\mathtt{Init}$ at the beginning of its execution.

to keep the transcripts of both interactions with U. We remark that we consider for this work the weaker notion of blindness in the *honest signer model* [34] as compared to the *malicious signer model* [23]. The difference between these two models is that in the honest signer model, the adversary obtains the keys from the experiment, whereas in the malicious signer model, the adversary gets to choose its own keys. Also, our notion does not capture security of blind signatures under aborts, where S or U may stop the interactive signing protocol prematurely [17, 59]. The work of [24] proposes generic transformation to achieve such a stronger notion. We formalize the notion of blindness (for a canonical three-move blind signature scheme BS and for parameters $par \in \mathsf{PGen}$) via game $\mathbf{Blind}_{BS,par}$ depicted in Fig. 2. In $\mathbf{Blind}_{BS,par}$, the game takes the role of the user and A takes the role of the signer. First, the game selects a random bit b which determines the order of adversarially chosen messages in both transcripts. It then runs A on a freshly generated key pair (pk, sk). A is given access to the three oracles $\mathtt{Init}, U_1$ and U_2. By convention, A first has to query oracle $\mathtt{Init}$. Subsequently, A may open at most two sessions. For each of these two sessions, A obtains corresponding transcripts $T_1 = (R_1, c_1, s_1)$ and $T_2 = (R_2, c_2, s_2)$. The game uses m_b and m_{1-b} to generate the transcripts T_1 and T_2, respectively. If A honestly completes both sessions with the game, it obtains signatures σ_b and σ_{1-b} on messages m_b and m_{1-b}. Note that A obtains σ_b and σ_{1-b} by calling U_2 twice. More precisely, the first call to U_2 closes the first session and the second call closes the second session. Once both sessions are closed, the game checks if A acted honestly in both of them and if so, returns the signatures (σ_b, σ_{1-b}). If instead A has behaved dishonestly and, as a result, $\sigma_b = \bot$ or $\sigma_{1-b} = \bot$ at the time of closing the second session, U_2 returns $(\bot, \bot)$. At the end of the experiment, A has to guess the bit b. We define the advantage of adversary A in $\mathbf{Blind}_{BS,par}$ as $\mathbf{Adv}_{BS,par}^{\mathrm{Blind}}(A) := \left| \Pr[\mathbf{Blind}_{BS,par}^A \Rightarrow 1] - \frac{1}{2} \right|$.

Definition 2 (Perfect Blindness). *Let* BS *be a canonical three-move blind signature scheme. We say that* BS *is* perfectly blind *relative to* $par \in \mathsf{PGen}(1^\kappa)$ *if for all adversaries* A, $\mathbf{Adv}_{BS,par}^{\mathrm{Blind}}(A) = 0$.

OMUF OF BLIND SIGNATURE SCHEMES. Intuitively, one-more unforgeability ensures that a user U can not produce even a single signature more than it should be able to learn from its interactions with the signer S. Our notion does not cover the stronger notion of *honest-user unforgeability* but a generic transformation from [59] can be applied to achieve it. We formalize the notion of one-more unforgeability (for a canonical three-move blind signature scheme BS and for all parameter $par \in$ PGen) via game $\mathbf{OMUF}_{BS,par}$ as depicted in Fig. 3. In $\mathbf{OMUF}_{BS,par}$, an adversary A in the role of U is run on input the public key of the signer S and subsequently interacts with oracles that imitate the behaviour of S. A call to S_1 returns a new session identifier sid and sets flag $\mathbf{sess}_{sid}$ to $\mathtt{open}$. A call to $S_2(sid, \cdot)$ with the same sid sets the flag $\mathbf{sess}_{sid}$ to $\mathtt{closed}$. The closed sessions result in (at most) Q_{S_2} transcripts $(\boldsymbol{R}_k, \boldsymbol{c}_k, \boldsymbol{s}_k)$, where the challenges $\boldsymbol{c}_k$ are chosen by A. (The remaining (at most) Q_{S_1} abandoned sessions are of the form $(\boldsymbol{R}_k, \perp, \perp)$ and hence do not contain a complete transcript.) A wins the experiment, if it is able to produce $\ell(A) \geq Q_{S_2}(A) + 1$ signatures (on distinct messages) after having closed $Q_{S_2}(A) \leq Q_{S_2}$ signer sessions (from which it should be able to compute $Q_{S_2}(A)$ signatures). We define the advantage of adversary A in $\mathbf{OMUF}_{BS,par}$ as $\mathbf{Adv}_{BS,par}^{OMUF}(A) := \Pr[\mathbf{OMUF}_{BS,par}^{A} \Rightarrow 1]$ and denote its running time as $\mathbf{Time}_{BS,par}^{OMUF}(A)$.

Game $\mathbf{OMUF}_{BS,par}$:

01 $(sk, pk) \xleftarrow{\$} \mathsf{KG}(par)$
02 $sid \leftarrow 0$ //initialize signer session id
03 $((m_1, \sigma_1), ..., (m_{\ell(A)}, \sigma_{\ell(A)})) \leftarrow A^{S_1, S_2}(pk)$
04 If $\exists i \neq j : m_i = m_j$: Return 0   //all messages have to be distinct
05 If $\exists i \in [\ell(A)] : \mathsf{BSVer}(pk, m_i, \sigma_i) = 0$: Return 0   //All signatures have to be valid
06 $Q_{S_1}(A) \leftarrow \#\{k \mid \mathbf{sess}_k = \mathtt{open}\}$ //#abandoned signer sessions
07 $Q_{S_2}(A) \leftarrow \#\{k \mid \mathbf{sess}_k = \mathtt{closed}\}$ //#closed signer sessions
08 If $\ell(A) \geq Q_{S_2}(A) + 1$: Return 1
09 Return 0

Oracle S_1:

10 $sid \leftarrow sid + 1$
11 $\mathbf{sess}_{sid} \leftarrow \mathtt{open}$
12 $(\boldsymbol{st}_{sid}, \boldsymbol{R}_{sid}) \xleftarrow{\$} S_1(sk)$
13 Return $(sid, \boldsymbol{R}_{sid})$

Oracle $S_2(sid, c)$:

14 If $\mathbf{sess}_{sid} \neq \mathtt{open}$: Return $\perp$
15 $\mathbf{sess}_{sid} = \mathtt{closed}$
16 $\boldsymbol{s}_{sid} \leftarrow S_2(sk, \boldsymbol{st}_{sid}, \boldsymbol{R}_{sid}, c)$
17 Return $\boldsymbol{s}_{sid}$

Fig. 3. Game $\mathbf{OMUF}_{BS,par}$ with adversary A.

We remark that the definition of OMUF security is only meaningful for blind signature schemes with negligible correctness error: If the scheme has noticeable correctness error, then even an honest adversary would not be able to produce even ℓ valid signatures after having interacted with ℓ signing sessions. Thus an adversary may learn less than ℓ signatures, but still has to come up with $\ell + 1$ signatures. This results in a significant weakening of the definition.

Definition 3 (One-More Unforgeability). *Let* BS *be a canonical three-move blind signature scheme. We say that* BS *is* $(\varepsilon, t, Q_{S_1}, Q_{S_2})$-**OMUF** *relative to* $par \in$ PGen *if for all adversaries* A *satisfying*

$$\mathrm{Time}_{\mathsf{BS},par}^{\mathrm{OMUF}}(\mathsf{A}) \leq t, \quad Q_{S_1}(\mathsf{A}) \leq Q_{S_1}, \quad Q_{S_2}(\mathsf{A}) \leq Q_{S_2}, \tag{2}$$

we have $\mathbf{Adv}_{\mathsf{BS},par}^{\mathrm{OMUF}}(\mathsf{A}) \leq \varepsilon$.

4.2   Hash Trees

In this section we define hash trees to build trees of commitments similarly as in [4]. The main advantage of this technique is that it significantly reduces the probability of abort in the signing protocol by performing a rejection sampling [38] multiple times and representing each trial as a leaf of the hash tree.

Let G: $\{0,1\}^* \mapsto \{0,1\}^{2\lambda}$ be a hash function. A hash tree HT[G] associated to G is the tuple of three deterministic algorithms (HashTree, BuildAuth, RootCalc) from Fig. 4. Algorithm HashTree takes as input a list of commitments v and returns a sequence of nodes tree spanning the tree and the root root of the tree; Algorithm BuildAuth takes as input a list of indices as well as a tree and outputs an authentication path auth; Algorithm RootCalc takes as input a node and an authentication path auth and returns the root root of a hash tree.

Note that for all nodes $(v_1, \ldots, v_\ell)$ and for all indices $m \in [\ell]$, we have RootCalc(v_m, auth) = root, where (root, tree) ← HashTree$(v_1, \ldots, v_\ell)$ and auth ← BuildAuth(m, tree).

Algorithm HashTree(v)	Algorithm BuildAuth(m, tree)	Algorithm RootCalc(v, auth)
01 $\ell \leftarrow \|v\|$; $v_0, \ldots, v_{\ell-1} \leftarrow v$	11 $(t_{1,0}, \ldots, t_{h,2^{h-1}-1}) \leftarrow$ tree	21 $(m, a_0, \ldots, a_{h-1}) \leftarrow$ auth
02 $h \leftarrow \lceil \log(\ell) \rceil$	12 For $i \in \{0, \ldots, h-1\}$:	22 $b_0 \leftarrow G(v)$
03 For $j \in \{0, \ldots, \ell-1\}$:	13 $\quad s \leftarrow \lfloor m/2^i \rfloor$	23 For $i \in \{1, \ldots, h\}$:
04 $\quad t_{0,j} \leftarrow G(v_j)$	14 $\quad b \leftarrow s \mod 2$	24 $\quad s \leftarrow \lfloor m/2^{i-1} \rfloor$
05 For $i \in \{1, \ldots, h\}$:	15 $\quad$ If $b = 0$	25 $\quad b \leftarrow s \mod 2$
06 $\quad$ For $j \in \{0, \ldots, 2^{h-i}-1\}$:	16 $\qquad a_i \leftarrow t_{s+1}$	26 $\quad$ If $b = 0$
07 $\qquad t_{i,j} \leftarrow G(t_{i-1,2j}, t_{i-1,2j+1})$	17 $\quad$ Else	27 $\qquad b_i \leftarrow G(b_{i-1}, a_{i-1})$
08 root $\leftarrow t_{h,0}$	18 $\qquad a_i \leftarrow t_{s-1}$	28 $\quad$ Else
09 tree $\leftarrow (t_{1,0}, \ldots, t_{h,2^{h-1}-1})$	19 auth $\leftarrow (m, a_0, \ldots, a_{h-1})$	29 $\qquad b_i \leftarrow G(a_{i-1}, b_{i-1})$
10 Return (root, tree)	20 Return auth	30 Return root $:= b_h$

Fig. 4. Description of the algorithms for HT[G] = (HashTree, BuildAuth, RootCalc) associated to G.

4.3   Blind Signature Schemes from Linear Hash Function Families

Let LHF be a linear hash function family and H: $\{0,1\}^* \rightarrow \mathcal{C}$, G: $\{0,1\}^* \rightarrow \{0,1\}^{2\lambda}$ be hash functions where $\mathcal{C} = \mathcal{S}_{c'}$. Let $\eta, \nu, \mu \in \mathbb{N}$ be repetition parameters. In the following we define mappings which convert a tuple of integers to an unique larger integer and vice versa. We define $2\mathsf{Int}_{\eta,\nu,\mu} : [\eta] \times [\nu] \times [\mu] \rightarrow [\eta\nu\mu]$

as the mapping $(i, j, k) \mapsto i + \eta \cdot (j-1) + \eta \nu \cdot (k-1)$, such that $2\mathsf{Int}_{\eta,\nu,\mu}(1, 1, 1) = 1$ and $2\mathsf{Int}_{\eta,\nu,\mu}(\eta, \nu, \mu) = \eta \nu \mu$.

Figure 5 shows how to construct a canonical three-move blind signature scheme $\mathsf{BS}_{\eta,\nu,\mu}[\mathsf{LHF}, \mathsf{G}, \mathsf{H}]$, where the hashtree algorithms $\mathsf{HT}[\mathsf{G}] = (\mathsf{HashTree}, \mathsf{BuildAuth}, \mathsf{RootCalc})$ are defined in Fig. 4.

Algorithm KG(par):
01 $sk \xleftarrow{\$} \mathcal{D}_{sk}; pk \leftarrow \mathsf{F}(sk)$
02 Return (sk, pk)

Algorithm $\mathsf{S}_1(sk)$:
03 For $i \in [\eta]: r_i \xleftarrow{\$} \mathcal{D}_r; R_i \leftarrow \mathsf{F}(r_i)$
04 $stS \leftarrow (r_1, \ldots, r_\eta); R \leftarrow (R_1, \ldots, R_\eta)$
05 Return (stS, R)

Algorithm $\mathsf{S}_2(sk, R, c, stS)$:
06 $(r_1, \ldots, r_\eta) \leftarrow stS$
07 If $c \notin \mathcal{S}_c$:
08 $\quad$ Return $\perp$
09 For $i \in [\eta]$:
10 $\quad s_i \leftarrow c \cdot sk + r_i$
11 $\quad$ If $s_i \in \mathcal{D}_s$:
12 $\quad\quad$ Return $s \leftarrow s_i$
13 Return $\perp$

Algorithm BSVer(pk, σ, m):
14 $(c', s', \mathsf{auth}) \leftarrow \sigma$
15 $R' \leftarrow \mathsf{F}(s') - c' \cdot pk$
16 $\mathsf{root} \leftarrow \mathsf{RootCalc}(R', \mathsf{auth})$
17 If $(c' = \mathsf{H}(\mathsf{root}, m)) \wedge (s' \in \mathcal{D}_{s'})$:
18 $\quad$ Return 1
19 Return 0

Algorithm $\mathsf{U}_1(pk, R, m)$:
20 $(R_1, \ldots, R_\eta) \leftarrow R$
21 $\alpha_1, \ldots, \alpha_\nu \xleftarrow{\$} \mathcal{D}_\alpha; \beta_1, \ldots, \beta_\mu \xleftarrow{\$} \mathcal{S}_\beta$
22 $\gamma \xleftarrow{\$} \mathbb{Z}_\eta$
23 For $(i, j, k) \in [\eta] \times [\mu] \times [\nu]$:
24 $\quad R'_{i \oplus \gamma, j, k} \leftarrow R_i + \mathsf{F}(\alpha_k) + \beta_j \cdot pk$
25 $(\mathsf{root}, \mathsf{tree}) \leftarrow \mathsf{HashTree}(R'_{1,1,1}, \ldots, R'_{\eta,\mu,\nu})$
26 $c' \xleftarrow{\$} \mathsf{H}(\mathsf{root}, m)$
27 For $j \in [\mu]$:
28 $\quad c_j \leftarrow c' + \beta_j$
29 $\quad$ If $c_j \in \mathcal{S}_c$:
30 $\quad\quad$ Return $(c \leftarrow c_j, stU \leftarrow (\alpha_1, \ldots, \alpha_\nu, c', j, \gamma, \mathsf{tree}))$
31 Return $\perp$

Algorithm $\mathsf{U}_2(pk, R, c, s, m, stU)$:
32 $(R_1, \ldots, R_\eta) \leftarrow R$
33 $(\alpha_1, \ldots, \alpha_\nu, c', j, \gamma, \mathsf{tree}) \leftarrow stU$
34 If $s \notin \mathcal{D}_s$:
35 $\quad$ Return $\perp$
36 Find $i \in [\eta]: \mathsf{F}(s) = c \cdot pk + R_i$
37 Return $\perp$ if i does not exist
38 For $k \in [\nu]$:
39 $\quad s'_k \leftarrow s + \alpha_k$
40 $\quad$ If $s'_k \in \mathcal{D}_{s'}$:
41 $\quad\quad \mathsf{auth} \leftarrow \mathsf{BuildAuth}(2\mathsf{Int}_{\eta,\nu,\mu}(i \oplus \gamma, j, k), \mathsf{tree})$
42 $\quad\quad$ Return $\sigma \leftarrow (c', s', \mathsf{auth})$
43 Return $\perp$

Fig. 5. Construction of the canonical three-move blind signature scheme $\mathsf{BS} := \mathsf{BS}_{\eta,\nu,\mu}[\mathsf{LHF}, \mathsf{G}, \mathsf{H}]$ from a linear hash function family $\mathsf{LHF} = (\mathsf{PGen}, \mathsf{F})$, where $\mathsf{BS} := (\mathsf{PGen}, \mathsf{KG}, \mathsf{S} = (\mathsf{S}_1, \mathsf{S}_2), \mathsf{U} = (\mathsf{U}_1, \mathsf{U}_2), \mathsf{BSVer})$ and challenge set $\mathcal{C} := \mathcal{S}_{c'}$.

We begin by proving correctness of $\mathsf{BS}_{\eta,\nu,\mu}[\mathsf{LHF}, \mathsf{G}, \mathsf{H}]$.

Lemma 1 (Correctness). *Let* LHF *be a linear hash function family, let* $\mathsf{G}: \{0,1\}^* \to \{0,1\}^{2\lambda}$ *and* $\mathsf{H}: \{0,1\}^* \to \mathcal{C}$ *be hash functions and* $\mathsf{HT}[\mathsf{G}]$ *be a hash tree and* $\mathsf{BS} := \mathsf{BS}_{\eta,\nu,\mu}[\mathsf{LHF}, \mathsf{G}, \mathsf{H}]$. *If* LHF *has enclosedness errors* $(\delta_1, \delta_2, \delta_3)$ *then* BS *has correctness error* $\delta_1^\mu + \delta_2^\eta + \delta_3^\nu$.

Proof. Consider an execution of BS defined in Fig. 5. From the definition of *enclosedness errors* $(\delta_1, \delta_2, \delta_3)$ it follows directly that the probability that during the execution lines 13, 31 and 43 abort are δ_2^η, δ_1^μ and δ_3^ν, respectively.

We continue with a statement about OMUF security of $\mathsf{BS}_{\eta,\nu,\mu}[\mathsf{LHF}, \mathsf{G}, \mathsf{H}]$. Its proof will be given in Sect. 5.

Theorem 1 (OMUF). *Let* LHF $= (\mathsf{PGen}, \mathsf{F})$ *be a* $(\varepsilon, \eta\nu\mu Q_{\mathsf{S}_1})$-*regular linear hash function family with a torsion-free element from the kernel, let* $\mathsf{G} \colon \{0,1\}^* \to \{0,1\}^{2\lambda}$ *and* $\mathsf{H} \colon \{0,1\}^* \to \mathcal{C}$ *be random oracles. If* LHF *is* (ε', t')-**CR** *relative to par* $\in \mathsf{PGen}(1^\kappa)$, *then* $\mathsf{BS}_{\eta,\nu,\mu}[\mathsf{LHF}, \mathsf{G}, \mathsf{H}]$ *is* $(\varepsilon, t, Q_{\mathsf{S}_1}, Q_{\mathsf{S}_2}, Q_{\mathsf{G}}, Q_{\mathsf{H}})$-**OMUF** *relative to par in the random oracle model, where*

$$t' = 2t, \quad \varepsilon' = O\left(\left(\varepsilon^2 - \frac{Q_{\mathsf{G}}^2 + Q_{\mathsf{G}}}{2^\lambda} - \frac{(Q_{\mathsf{V}}Q_{\mathsf{P}_1})^{Q_{\mathsf{P}_2}+1}}{|\mathcal{C}|}\right)^2 \frac{1}{Q_{\mathsf{V}}^2 Q_{\mathsf{P}_2}^3}\right),$$

Q_{G} *and* Q_{H} *are the number of queries to random oracles* G *and* H.

Theorem 2 (Blindness). *Let* LHF $= (\mathsf{PGen}, \mathsf{F})$ *be a smooth linear hash function family and let* $\mathsf{G} \colon \{0,1\}^* \to \{0,1\}^{2\lambda}$ *and* $\mathsf{H} \colon \{0,1\}^* \to \mathcal{C}$ *be random oracles. Then* $\mathsf{BS}_{\eta,\nu,\mu}[\mathsf{LHF}, \mathsf{G}, \mathsf{H}]$ *is perfectly blind relative to all par* $\in \mathsf{PGen}(1^\kappa)$.

Let $\mathsf{BS} := \mathsf{BS}_{\eta,\nu,\mu}[\mathsf{LHF}, \mathsf{G}, \mathsf{H}]$. Intuitively the goal of an adversary in the $\mathbf{Blind}_{\mathsf{BS},par}$ experiment is as follows. The adversary interacts twice with the experiment and thus creates two transcripts. At the end of the interaction the adversary learns two message/signature pairs and tries to unblind which message/signature pair was created in which session. Intuitively to prevent the adversary from doing so, any combination of a transcript and a message/signature pair can be explained by some randomness (of the user) which (i) could have been used to create both the transcript and the message/signature pair and (ii) is indistinguishable from uniformly drawn randomness.

Proof. Fix two messages $\boldsymbol{m}_0, \boldsymbol{m}_1$ and let A be an adversary in the $\mathbf{Blind}_{\mathsf{BS},par}$ experiment (cf. Fig. 2).

Given the output of an interaction $(\boldsymbol{R}_1, \ldots, \boldsymbol{R}_\eta, c, s, m, \sigma) \xleftarrow{\$} \langle \mathsf{S}(sk), \mathsf{U}(pk) \rangle$ we define a transcript $T := (\boldsymbol{R}_1, \ldots, \boldsymbol{R}_\eta, c, s)$. Consider A's view in an execution of $\mathbf{Blind}_{\mathsf{BS},par}$, which consists of the two transcripts $(\boldsymbol{T}_1, \boldsymbol{T}_2)$ and the two signatures $(\boldsymbol{\sigma}_0, \boldsymbol{\sigma}_1)$, where signature $\boldsymbol{\sigma}_b$ corresponds to transcript $\boldsymbol{T}_1$, signature $\boldsymbol{\sigma}_{1-b}$ corresponds to transcript $\boldsymbol{T}_2$, and b is the secret choice bit. Note that it is w.l.o.g. that $\boldsymbol{\sigma}_0, \boldsymbol{\sigma}_1 \neq \perp$. Now, the theorem is implied by the following two claims.

(B1) For each of the four combinations $(\boldsymbol{T}_{sid}, \boldsymbol{\sigma}_i)$, where $(sid, i) \in \{1, 2\} \times \{0, 1\}$, there exists randomness $\boldsymbol{rndU}_{sid,i} := (\boldsymbol{\alpha}_{sid,i,1} \ldots, \boldsymbol{\alpha}_{sid,i,\nu}, \boldsymbol{\beta}_{sid,i,1}, \ldots, \boldsymbol{\beta}_{sid,i,\mu}, \boldsymbol{\gamma}_{sid,i})$ of the user algorithm which results in the tuple $(\boldsymbol{T}_{sid}, \boldsymbol{\sigma}_i)$.

(B2) The real randomness $(\boldsymbol{rndU}_{1,b}, \boldsymbol{rndU}_{2,1-b})$ used in $\mathbf{Blind}_{\mathsf{BS},par}$ is identically distributed to the "fake" randomness $(\boldsymbol{rndU}_{1,1-b}, \boldsymbol{rndU}_{2,b})$.

To prove condition (B1) we argue as follows. Let $2\mathsf{Int}^{-1} \colon [\eta\nu\mu] \to [\eta] \times [\nu] \times [\mu]$ be the inverse of $2\mathsf{Int}_{\eta,\nu,\mu}$, defined in Sect. 4.3. Let $(\boldsymbol{c}'_i, \boldsymbol{s}'_i, \mathsf{auth}_i) \leftarrow \boldsymbol{\sigma}_i$. Let $(\boldsymbol{i}_i, \boldsymbol{j}_i, \boldsymbol{k}_i) \leftarrow 2\mathsf{Int}^{-1}(\boldsymbol{n}_i)$, where $(\boldsymbol{n}_i, \boldsymbol{a}_{i,1}, \ldots, \boldsymbol{a}_{i,h}) \leftarrow \mathsf{auth}_i$. Define $\boldsymbol{\alpha}_{sid,i,k_i} := \boldsymbol{s}'_{k_i} - \boldsymbol{s}_{sid}, \boldsymbol{\beta}_{sid,i,j_i} := \boldsymbol{c}_{sid} - \boldsymbol{c}'_{j_i}$ and for all $\ell \in [\nu] \setminus \{\boldsymbol{k}_i\}, \boldsymbol{\alpha}_{sid,i,\ell} \xleftarrow{\$} \{\alpha \in \mathcal{D}_\alpha \mid \alpha + \boldsymbol{s}_{sid} \notin \mathcal{D}_{s'}\}$ for all $\ell \in [\mu] \setminus \{\boldsymbol{j}_i\}, \boldsymbol{\beta}_{sid,i,\ell} \xleftarrow{\$} \{\beta \in \mathcal{S}_\beta \mid \beta + \boldsymbol{c}_{sid} \notin \mathcal{S}_c\}$. Set $\boldsymbol{i}_{sid} \in [\eta]$ to be the smallest value s.t. $\mathsf{F}(\boldsymbol{s}_{sid}) = \boldsymbol{c}_{sid} \cdot pk + \boldsymbol{R}_{sid,i_{sid}}$. Define $\boldsymbol{\gamma}_{sid,i} \leftarrow \boldsymbol{i}_{sid} \oplus \boldsymbol{i}_i$. By smoothness conditions (S1) and (S4) it follows that

$\boldsymbol{\alpha}_{sid,i,k_i} \in \mathcal{D}_\alpha$ and $\boldsymbol{\beta}_{sid,i,j_i} \in \mathcal{S}_\beta$. Clearly, for all $\ell \in [\nu] \setminus \{k_i\}$, $\boldsymbol{\alpha}_{sid,i,\ell} \in \mathcal{D}_\alpha$ for all $\ell \in [\mu] \setminus \{j_i\}$, $\boldsymbol{\beta}_{sid,i,\ell} \in \mathcal{S}_\beta$. Clearly, $\boldsymbol{\gamma}_{sid,i} \in [\eta]$. Let $\boldsymbol{R}'_{sid,i,i_i,j_i,k_i} = \boldsymbol{R}_{sid,i_i} + \boldsymbol{\beta}_{sid,i,j_j} \cdot pk + \mathsf{F}(\boldsymbol{\alpha}_{sid,i,k_i})$. Let $\mathbf{root}_{sid,i} \leftarrow \mathsf{RootCalc}(\boldsymbol{R}'_{sid,i,i_i,j_i,k_i}, \mathsf{auth}_i)$. To show that $c'_i = \mathsf{H}(\mathbf{root}_{sid,i}, \boldsymbol{m}_i)$ we continue as follows. Since $\boldsymbol{T}_{sid}$ is a valid transcript, we have $\mathsf{F}(\boldsymbol{s}_{sid}) = \boldsymbol{R}_{sid,i_i} + c_{sid} \cdot pk$. Therefore,

$$\boldsymbol{R}_{sid,i_i} + \boldsymbol{\beta}_{sid,i,j_i} \cdot pk + \mathsf{F}(\boldsymbol{\alpha}_{sid,i,k_i}) = \boldsymbol{R}_{sid,i_i} + (c_{sid} - c'_i) \cdot pk + \mathsf{F}(\boldsymbol{s}'_i - \boldsymbol{s}_{sid})$$
$$= \boldsymbol{R}_{sid,i_i} + c_{sid} \cdot pk - \mathsf{F}(\boldsymbol{s}_{sid}) + \mathsf{F}(\boldsymbol{s}'_i) - c'_i \cdot pk$$
$$= \mathsf{F}(\boldsymbol{s}'_i) - c'_i \cdot pk .$$

Since $\boldsymbol{\sigma}_i$ is a valid signature we have $c'_i = \mathsf{H}(\mathsf{RootCalc}(\mathsf{F}(\boldsymbol{s}'_i) - c'_i \cdot pk, \mathsf{auth}_i), \boldsymbol{m}_i) = \mathsf{H}(\mathbf{root}_{sid,i}, \boldsymbol{m}_i)$.

To show condition (B2) we continue as follows. By smoothness condition (S2) if follows that $\boldsymbol{\alpha}_{1,b,k_b}$ and $\boldsymbol{\alpha}_{2,1-b,k_{1-b}}$ have the same distribution as $\boldsymbol{\alpha}_{1,1-b,k_{1-b}}$ and $\boldsymbol{\alpha}_{2,b,k_b}$. By smoothness condition (S5) it follows that $\boldsymbol{\beta}_{1,b,j_b}$ and $\boldsymbol{\beta}_{2,1-b,j_{1-b}}$ have the same distribution as $\boldsymbol{\beta}_{1,1-b,j_{1-b}}$ and $\boldsymbol{\beta}_{2,b,j_b}$. By smoothness condition (S3) for all $\ell \in [\nu] \setminus \{k_b, k_{1-b}\}$, $\boldsymbol{\alpha}_{1,b,\ell}$ and $\boldsymbol{\alpha}_{1,1-b,\ell}$ have the same distribution as $\boldsymbol{\alpha}_{2,b,\ell}$ and $\boldsymbol{\alpha}_{2,1-b,\ell}$. By smoothness condition (S6) for all $\ell \in [\mu] \setminus \{j_b, j_{1-b}\}$, $\boldsymbol{\beta}_{1,b,\ell}$ and $\boldsymbol{\beta}_{1,1-b,\ell}$ have the same distribution as $\boldsymbol{\beta}_{2,b,\ell}$ and $\boldsymbol{\beta}_{2,1-b,\ell}$. Clearly, all four $\gamma_{1,0}$, $\gamma_{1,1}$, $\gamma_{2,0}$ and $\gamma_{2,1}$ have the same distribution.

5 Proof of One-More Unforgeability

In this section, we will make a first step to the proof of Theorem 1, the one-more unforgeability of $\mathsf{BS}_{\eta,\nu,\mu}[\mathsf{LHF}, \mathsf{H}, \mathsf{G}]$ defined in Fig. 5. To this end we first define canonical identification schemes and prove in Theorem 3 that one-more unforgeability of $\mathsf{BS}_{\eta,\nu,\mu}[\mathsf{LHF}, \mathsf{H}, \mathsf{G}]$ is implied by one-more man-in-the-middle security of the underlying identification scheme $\mathsf{ID}_{\eta'}[\mathsf{LHF}]$. Next, in Theorem 4 we will state that collision-resistance of LHF implies one-more man-in-the-middle security of the canonical identification scheme $\mathsf{ID}_{\eta'}[\mathsf{LHF}]$.

5.1 Canonical Identification Schemes

We recall syntax of *canonical (three-move) identification schemes* [1].

Definition 4 (Canonical Three-Move Identification Scheme). *A canonical three-move identification scheme is a tuple of algorithms* $\mathsf{ID} = (\mathsf{PGen}, \mathsf{KG}, \mathsf{P} = (\mathsf{P}_1, \mathsf{P}_2), \mathsf{IDVer})$.

- *The randomised parameter generation algorithm* PGen *returns system parameters par.*
- *The randomised key generation algorithm* KG *takes as input system parameters par and returns a public/secret key pair* (pk, sk). *We assume that* pk *implicitly defines a challenge space* $\mathcal{C} := \mathcal{C}(pk)$ *and that* pk *is distributed (and hence known) to all parties.*
- *The prover algorithm* P *is split into two algorithms, i.e.,* $\mathsf{P} := (\mathsf{P}_1, \mathsf{P}_2)$, *where:*

- *The randomised algorithm* P_1 *takes as input a secret key* sk *and returns a commitment* R *and a state* st.
- *The deterministic algorithm* P_2 *takes as input a secret key* sk, *a commitment* R, *a challenge* c, *and a state* st. *It returns a response* s.
- *The deterministic* verification algorithm IDVer *takes as input a public key* pk, *a commitment* R, *a challenge* c, *and a response* s. *It returns 1 (accept) or 0 (reject)*.

Figure 6 shows the interaction between algorithms P_1, P_2, and IDVer. Since we will use ID only for the purpose of simplifying our main security statement, we refrain from giving the standard correctness definition.

Prover: sk		Verifier: pk
$(R, stP) \xleftarrow{\$} P_1(sk)$	$\xrightarrow{R}$	
	$\xleftarrow{c}$	$c \xleftarrow{\$} \mathcal{C}$
$s \leftarrow P_2(sk, R, c, stP)$	$\xrightarrow{s}$	$b \leftarrow$ IDVer(pk, R, c, s)
		Output b

Fig. 6. Interaction $(R, c, s) \leftarrow \langle P(sk), \text{IDVer}(pk) \rangle$ of a canonical three-move identification scheme ID $=$ (PGen, KG, P_1, P_2, IDVer).

We now recall *One-More Man-in-the-Middle* security for canonical identification schemes [32]. The One-More Man-in-the-Middle (**OMMIM**) security experiment for an identification scheme ID and an adversary A is defined in Fig. 7. Adversary A simultaneously plays against a prover (modeled through oracles P_1 and P_2) and a verifier (modeled through oracles V_1 and V_2). Session identifiers $pSid$ and $vSid$ are used to model an interaction with the prover and the verifier, respectively. A call to P_1 returns a new prover session identifier $pSid$ and sets flag $\mathbf{pSess}_{pSid}$ to open. A call to $P_2(pSid, \cdot)$ with the same $pSid$ sets the flag $\mathbf{pSess}_{pSid}$ to closed. Similarly, a call to V_1 returns a new verifier session identifier $vSid$ and sets flag $\mathbf{vSess}_{vSid}$ to open. A call to $V_2(vSid, \cdot)$ with the same $vSid$ sets the flag $\mathbf{vSess}_{vSid}$ to closed. A closed verifier session $vSid$ is successful if the oracle $V_2(vSid, \cdot)$ returns 1. Lines 04–07 define several internal random variables for later reference. Variable $Q_{P_2}(A)$ counts the number of closed prover sessions and $Q_{P_1}(A)$ counts the number of abandoned sessions (i.e., sessions that were opened but never closed). Most importantly, variable $\ell(A)$ counts the number of successful verifier sessions and variable $Q_{P_2}(A)$ counts the number of closed sessions with the prover. Adversary A wins the **OMMIM**$_{\text{ID}, par}$ game, if $\ell(A) \geq Q_{P_2}(A) + 1$, i.e., if A convinces the verifier in at least one more successful verifier sessions than there exist closed sessions with the prover. A's advantage in **OMMIM**$_{\text{ID}, par}$ is defined as $\mathbf{Adv}_{\text{ID}, par}^{\text{OMMIM}}(A) := \Pr[\mathbf{OMMIM}_{\text{ID}, par}^A \Rightarrow 1]$ and we denote its running time as $\mathbf{Time}_{\text{ID}, par}^{\text{OMMIM}}(A)$.

Definition 5 (One-more man-in-the-middle security). *We say that* ID *is* $(\varepsilon, t, Q_V, Q_{P_1}, Q_{P_2})$-**OMMIM** *relative to par* $\in$ PGen(1^κ) *if for all adversaries*

A *satisfying* $\mathbf{Time}_{\mathsf{ID},par}^{\mathsf{OMMIM}}(\mathsf{A}) \leq t$, $Q_{\mathsf{V}}(\mathsf{A}) \leq Q_{\mathsf{V}}$, $Q_{\mathsf{P}_2}(\mathsf{A}) \leq Q_{\mathsf{P}_2}$, *and* $Q_{\mathsf{P}_1}(\mathsf{A}) \leq Q_{\mathsf{P}_1}$, *we have* $\mathbf{Adv}_{\mathsf{ID},par}^{\mathsf{OMMIM}}(\mathsf{A}) \leq \varepsilon$.

Game $\mathbf{OMMIM}_{\mathsf{ID},par}^{\mathsf{A}}$:	
01 $(sk, pk) \leftarrow \mathsf{KG}(par)$	
02 $pSid \leftarrow 0, vSid \leftarrow 0$	
03 $\mathsf{A}^{\mathsf{P}_1,\mathsf{P}_2,\mathsf{V}_1,\mathsf{V}_2}(pk)$	
04 $Q_{\mathsf{ch}}(\mathsf{A}) \leftarrow vSid$	// #total sessions with verifier
05 $Q_{\mathsf{P}_1}(\mathsf{A}) \leftarrow \#\{1 \leq k \leq pSid \mid \mathbf{pSess}_k = \mathbf{open}\}$	// #abandoned prover sessions
06 $Q_{\mathsf{P}_2}(\mathsf{A}) \leftarrow \#\{1 \leq k \leq pSid \mid \mathbf{pSess}_k = \mathbf{closed}\}$	// #closed prover sessions
07 $\ell(\mathsf{A}) \leftarrow \#\{1 \leq k \leq vSid \mid \mathbf{vSess}_k = \mathbf{closed} \wedge b'_k = 1\}$	// #successful verifier sessions
08 If $\ell(\mathsf{A}) \geq Q_{\mathsf{P}_2}(\mathsf{A}) + 1$: Return 1	// A's winning condition
09 Return 0	

Oracle P_1:	Oracle $\mathsf{V}_1(R')$:
10 $pSid \leftarrow pSid + 1$	18 $vSid \leftarrow vSid + 1$
11 $\mathbf{pSess}_{pSid} \leftarrow \mathbf{open}$	19 $\mathbf{vSess}_{vSid} \leftarrow \mathbf{open}$
12 $(\boldsymbol{R}_{pSid}, \boldsymbol{st}_{pSid}) \xleftarrow{\$} \mathsf{P}_1(sk)$	20 $\boldsymbol{R}'_{vSid} \leftarrow R'; c'_{vSid} \xleftarrow{\$} \mathcal{C}$
13 Return $(pSid, \boldsymbol{R}_{pSid})$	21 Return $(vSid, c'_{vSid})$

Oracle $\mathsf{P}_2(pSid, c)$:	Oracle $\mathsf{V}_2(vSid, s')$:
14 If $\mathbf{pSess}_{pSid} \neq \mathbf{open}$: Return $\perp$	22 If $\mathbf{vSess}_{vSid} \neq \mathbf{open}$: Return $\perp$
15 $\mathbf{pSess}_{pSid} \leftarrow \mathbf{closed}$	23 $\mathbf{vSess}_{vSid} \leftarrow \mathbf{closed}$
16 $s \leftarrow \mathsf{P}_2(sk, \boldsymbol{R}_{pSid}, c, \boldsymbol{st}_{pSid})$	24 $b'_{vSid} \leftarrow \mathsf{IDVer}(pk, \boldsymbol{R}'_{vSid}, c'_{vSid}, s')$
17 Return s	25 Return b'_{vSid}

Fig. 7. The One-More Man-in-the-Middle security game $\mathbf{OMMIM}_{\mathsf{ID},par}^{\mathsf{A}}$

We remark that *security against impersonation under active and passive attacks* [1] is a weaker notion than OMMIM security, whereas *man-in-the-middle security* [10] is stronger.

5.2   Identification Schemes from Linear Hash Function Families

Let LHF be a linear hash function family and η' be a repetition parameter. Consider the canonical three-move blind signature scheme $\mathsf{BS}_{\eta,\nu,\mu}[\mathsf{LHF}, \mathsf{H}, \mathsf{G}] = (\mathsf{PGen}, \mathsf{KG}, \mathsf{S} = (\mathsf{S}_1, \mathsf{S}_2), \mathsf{U} = (\mathsf{U}_1, \mathsf{U}_2), \mathsf{BSVer})$ from Fig. 5. BS directly implies a canonical identification scheme $\mathsf{ID}_{\eta'}[\mathsf{LHF}] = (\mathsf{PGen}, \mathsf{KG}, \mathsf{P}, \mathsf{IDVer})$ with challenge set $\mathcal{C} := \mathcal{S}_{c'}$, where prover P plays the role of the signer S, i.e., $\mathsf{P} = (\mathsf{P}_1, \mathsf{P}_2) := (\mathsf{S}_1, \mathsf{S}_2)$ and algorithm IDVer is defined as follows.

Algorithm $\mathsf{IDVer}(pk, \boldsymbol{R}_1, \ldots, \boldsymbol{R}_{\eta'}, c, s)$:
01 For $i \in [\eta']$:
02   If $(\boldsymbol{R}_i = \mathsf{F}(s) - c \cdot pk) \wedge (s \in \mathcal{D}_s)$:
03   Return 1
04 Return 0

The identification scheme $\mathsf{ID}_{\eta'}[\mathsf{LHF}]$ can be seen as the projection of $\mathsf{BS}_{\eta,\nu,\mu}[\mathsf{LHF}, \mathsf{H}, \mathsf{G}]$ to the signer, i.e., all user algorithms (involving the techniques to achieve blindness) are removed. This makes it conceptually much simpler.

We will now show that OMUF security of $\mathsf{BS}_{\eta,\nu,\mu}[\mathsf{LHF}, \mathsf{G}, \mathsf{H}]$ is implied (in the ROM) by OMMIM security of $\mathsf{ID}_{\eta'}[\mathsf{LHF}]$, where $\eta' = \eta\nu\mu$.

Theorem 3. *Let* LHF *be a linear hash function family, let* $\mathsf{G} \colon \{0,1\}^* \to \{0,1\}^{2\lambda}$ *and* $\mathsf{H} \colon \{0,1\}^* \to \mathcal{C}$ *be random oracles and let* $\mathsf{ID} := \mathsf{ID}_{\eta'}[\mathsf{LHF}], \mathsf{BS} := \mathsf{BS}_{\eta,\nu,\mu}[\mathsf{LHF}, \mathsf{G}, \mathsf{H}]$. *If* ID *is* $(\varepsilon', t', Q_\mathsf{V}, Q_{\mathsf{P}_1}, Q_{\mathsf{P}_2})$-**OMMIM** *relative to par* $\in$ $\mathsf{PGen}(1^\kappa)$ *then* BS *is* $(\varepsilon, t, Q_{\mathsf{S}_1}, Q_{\mathsf{S}_2}, Q_\mathsf{G}, Q_\mathsf{H})$-**OMUF** *relative to par in the random oracle model, where*

$$t' \approx t, \quad \varepsilon' = \varepsilon - \frac{Q_\mathsf{G}^2}{2^{2\lambda}} - \frac{Q_\mathsf{G}}{2^{2\lambda}}, \quad \eta' = \eta\nu\mu, \quad Q_\mathsf{V} = Q_\mathsf{H}, \quad Q_{\mathsf{P}_1} = Q_{\mathsf{S}_1}, \quad Q_{\mathsf{P}_2} = Q_{\mathsf{S}_2},$$

Q_G *and* Q_H *are the number of queries to random oracles* G *and* H;

Proof. The technical proof of this theorem is comparable to the proof given in [32] and will be given in the full version [33]. $\qquad\square$

We will now state that $\mathsf{ID}_{\eta'}[\mathsf{LHF}]$ is OMMIM secure.

Theorem 4. *Let* LHF *be a* $(\varepsilon, \eta' Q_{\mathsf{P}_1})$-*regular linear hash function family with a torsion-free element from the kernel. If* LHF *is* (ε', t')-**CR** *relative to par* $\in$ $\mathsf{PGen}(1^\kappa)$ *then* $\mathsf{ID}_{\eta'}[\mathsf{LHF}]$ *is* $(\varepsilon, t, Q_\mathsf{V}, Q_{\mathsf{P}_1}, Q_{\mathsf{P}_2})$-**OMMIM** *relative to par, where*

$$t' = 2t, \quad \varepsilon' = O\left(\left(\varepsilon^2 - \frac{(Q_\mathsf{V} Q_{\mathsf{P}_1})^{Q_{\mathsf{P}_2}+1}}{|\mathcal{C}|}\right)^2 \frac{1}{Q_\mathsf{V}^2 Q_{\mathsf{P}_2}^3}\right).$$

The technical proof of this theorem will be given in the full version [33].

6 Instantiation from Lattices

We now give a lattice-based example of a LHF with noticeable correctness error which is derived from Lyubashevsky's identification scheme [38] and has also been implicitly used in [56].

NOTATION. Let R and R_q denote the rings $\mathbb{Z}[X]/\langle X^n + 1\rangle$ and $\mathbb{Z}_q[X]/\langle X^n + 1\rangle$, for integer $n = 2^r$, where $r \in \mathbb{Z}^+$ and q is an odd integer. Polynomials in R_q have degree at most $n - 1$ and coefficients in range $[-(q-1)/2, (q-1)/2]$. For such coefficients we abuse the notation mod to denote with $x' = x \bmod q$, the unique element x' s.t. for any integer k: $x' = x + kq$ and $x' \in [-(q-1)/2, (q-1)/2]$. Bold lower-case letters denote elements in R_q and bold lower-case letters with a hat denote vectors of vectors with coefficients in ring R_q. To measure the size of elements $\mathbf{x} = x_0 + x_1 X^1 + \cdots + x_{n-1} X^{n-1}$ in ring R_q we define norm p_∞ as $\|\mathbf{x}\|_\infty := \max_i |x_i \bmod q|$. In rings R and R_q, $\|x_i\|_\infty$ represents $|x_i|$ and $|x_i \bmod q|$, respectively. Similarly, for $\hat{\mathbf{x}} = (\mathbf{x}_0, \ldots, \mathbf{x}_{k-1})$, we define norm p_∞ as $\|\hat{\mathbf{x}}\|_\infty := \max_i \|\mathbf{x}_i\|_\infty$. Further we define the p_1 norm as $\|\mathbf{x}\|_1 := \sum_i |\mathbf{x}_i|$ and p_2

norm as $\|\mathbf{x}\|_2 := (\sum_i |\mathbf{x}_i|^2)^{1/2}$. It is not hard to see that for any two polynomials $\mathbf{e}, \mathbf{f} \in R_q$,

$$\|\mathbf{e} \cdot \mathbf{f}\|_\infty \leq \|\mathbf{e}\|_\infty \|\mathbf{f}\|_1 \leq n \|\mathbf{e}\|_\infty \|\mathbf{f}\|_\infty . \tag{3}$$

We now recall the R-SIS$_{q,n,m,d}$ problem over R_q [40, 48].

Definition 6 (R-SIS$_{q,n,m,d}$). *We say that* R-SIS$_{q,n,m,d}$ *is* (ε, t)-*hard if for all adversaries* A *running in time at most* t, *the probability that* A$(\hat{a})$ *(where* $\hat{a} \xleftarrow{\$} R_q^m$*) outputs a non-zero* $\hat{\mathbf{z}} \in R_q^m$ *s.t.* $\sum_{i=1}^m \mathbf{a}_i \cdot \mathbf{z}_i = 0$ *and* $\|\hat{\mathbf{z}}\|_\infty \leq d$, *is bounded by* ε.

Similarly, R-SIS$_{q,n,m,d}$ *is* (ε, t)-*hard relative to* $\hat{a} \in R_q^m$ *if for all adversaries* A *running in time at most* t, *the probability that* A *outputs a non-zero* $\hat{\mathbf{z}} \in R_q^m$ *s.t.* $\sum_{i=1}^m \mathbf{a}_i \cdot \mathbf{z}_i = 0$ *and* $\|\hat{\mathbf{z}}\|_\infty \leq d$, *is bounded by* ε.

Let us first estimate the concrete hardness of solving the R-SIS$_{q,n,m,d}$ problem for uniformly random $\hat{a}$ which is equivalent to finding a short vector in the related lattice

$$\Lambda_q^\perp(\hat{a}) = \{\hat{\mathbf{z}} \in R_q^m : \sum_{i=1}^m \mathbf{a}_i \cdot \mathbf{z}_i = 0\}.$$

Gama and Nguyen [27] classified algorithms for finding short vectors in random lattices in terms of the root Hermite factor δ. Such algorithms compute a vector of length δ^n times the shortest vector of the lattice. Whereas $\delta = 1.01$ can be achieved, it is conjectured that a factor of $\delta = 1.007$ may not be achievable [21].

We use the following estimation from [38, Eqn. 3] to estimate the length of the shortest vector (in p_∞ norm) which can be efficiently found in lattice $\Lambda_q^\perp(\hat{a})$ as

$$\mathsf{sv}_\delta(n, q) := \min\{q, 2^{2\sqrt{n \log(q) \log(\delta)}} (n \log(q) / \log(\delta))^{-1/4}\}.$$

We make the following conjecture about R-SIS$_{q,n,m,d}$ with $\delta = 1.005$.

Conjecture 1. If $d < \mathsf{sv}_{1.005}(n, q)$ then no efficient algorithm can solve R-SIS$_{q,n,m,d}$.

We note that security of our blind signature scheme depends on the hardness of R-SIS$_{q,n,m,d}$ relative to fixed $\hat{a}$. However, as discussed in Sect. 2, our theorems can be easily re-written to work in a setting where $\hat{a} \xleftarrow{\$} R_q^m$ is chosen uniformly at random.

LINEAR HASH FUNCTION. We select the parameters according to Fig. 8. Firstly, variables q, n specify the ring $R_q := \mathbb{Z}_q[X]/\langle X^n + 1 \rangle$, where n is a power of two. Define the sets

$$\mathcal{S} := R_q, \mathcal{D} := \mathcal{B}_q(d)^m, \text{ and } \mathcal{R} := \mathcal{B}_q(d),$$

where $\mathcal{B}_q(w)$ is defined as

$$\mathcal{B}_q(w) := \{\mathbf{s} \in R_q : \|\mathbf{s}\|_\infty \leq w\}.$$

Note that the size of the challenge set $\mathcal{C} = \mathcal{S}_{c'}$ is equal to 3^{1024}, hence $1/|\mathcal{C}|$ is negligible.

For $\hat{e}, \hat{f} \in \mathcal{D}$ and $\mathbf{g} \in \mathcal{S}$ we define addition $\hat{e} + \hat{f} := (\mathbf{e}_1 + \mathbf{f}_1, \ldots, \mathbf{e}_m + \mathbf{f}_m)$, multiplication $\hat{e} \cdot \hat{f} := (\mathbf{e}_1 \mathbf{f}_1, \ldots, \mathbf{e}_m \mathbf{f}_m)$, and scalar multiplication $\mathbf{g} \cdot \hat{e} = (\mathbf{g}\mathbf{e}_1, \ldots, \mathbf{g}\mathbf{e}_m)$. This makes $\mathcal{R}$ and $\mathcal{D}$ modules over $\mathcal{S}$.

Algorithm $\mathsf{PGen}(1^\kappa)$ returns a random element $par = \hat{a} \xleftarrow{\$} \mathcal{R}^m$. Algorithm $\mathsf{F} : \mathcal{D} \mapsto \mathcal{R}$ is defined for any $\hat{z} \in \mathcal{D}$ as,

$$\mathsf{F}(\hat{z}) := \sum_{i=1}^{m} \mathbf{a}_i \cdot \mathbf{z}_i \bmod q .$$

Clearly, F is a module homomorphism since for every $\hat{y}, \hat{z} \in \mathcal{D}$, $\mathbf{c} \in \mathcal{R}$: $\mathsf{F}(\hat{y} + \hat{z}) = \hat{a}(\hat{y} + \hat{z}) = \hat{a}\hat{y} + \hat{a}\hat{z} = \mathsf{F}(\hat{y}) + \mathsf{F}(\hat{z})$ and $\mathsf{F}(\hat{y}\mathbf{c}) = \hat{a}(\mathbf{y}_1\mathbf{c}, \ldots, \mathbf{y}_m\mathbf{c}) = \mathbf{a}_1\mathbf{y}_1\mathbf{c} + \cdots + \mathbf{a}_m\mathbf{y}_m\mathbf{c} = \mathsf{F}(\hat{y})\mathbf{c}$.

For $\mathsf{xxx} \in \{\beta, c, c'\}$ and $\mathsf{yyy} \in \{sk, r, s, s', \alpha\}$, the filter sets are defined as

$$\mathcal{S}_{\mathsf{xxx}} := \mathcal{B}_q(d_{\mathsf{xxx}}) \subseteq \mathcal{S}, \quad \mathcal{D}_{\mathsf{yyy}} := \mathcal{B}_q^m(d_{\mathsf{yyy}}) \subseteq \mathcal{D}.$$

Parameter	Definition	Instantiation
n	integer that is power of 2	1024
m	dimension of a secret key vector	189
q	prime	2^{1890}
ι	# of irreducible factors of $X^n + 1$ modulo q	64
δ	p_∞ of a torsion-free element from the kernel	2^{10}
d_{sk}	p_∞ of a secret key	2^{159}
$d_{c'}$	p_∞ of an output of a random oracle	1
u	integer	4
v	integer	4
w	integer	4
μ	number of β_j	60
η	number of $\mathcal{R}_i$	60
ν	number of $\hat{\alpha}_k$	60
d_β	$ud_{c'}n$	2^{12}
d_c	$d_\beta - d_{c'}$	2^{12}
d_r	$\geq vmn^2 d_{sk}d_c$	2^{211}
d_s	$d_r - nd_{sk}d_c$	2^{211}
d_α	$wd_s nm$	2^{232}
$d_{s'}$	$d_\alpha - d_s$	2^{232}
d	$d < \frac{1}{2}\mathsf{sv}_{1.005}(n, q)$	2^{233}
sig size		36.03 MB

Fig. 8. Definition of parameters for the lattice-based LHF.

To estimate the membership of sums and products of $\hat{e}, \hat{f} \in \mathcal{D}$ to specific subsets of $\mathcal{D}$ we use the lemma proven by Rückert [56].

Lemma 2. *Let* k, d_a, d_b *and* γ *be integers, s.t.* $d_b \geq \gamma k n d_a$. *Then, for all* $\hat{a} \in \mathcal{B}_q^k(d_a)$,

$$\Pr_{\hat{b} \xleftarrow{\$} \mathcal{B}_q^k(d_b)} \left[\left\| \hat{a} + \hat{b} \right\|_\infty \leq d_b - d_a \right] > e^{-1/\gamma} - o(1) .$$

ENCLOSEDNESS ERRORS AND SMOOTHNESS. First, we focus on calculating the enclosedness errors of LHF based on parameters chosen in Fig. 8. Later on, we also show that LHF is smooth.

Lemma 3. *If $d_\beta, d_r, d_\alpha, d_c, d_s, d_{s'}$ are defined as in Fig. 8 and LHF is defined as above, then LHF has enclosedness errors equal to:*

$$\left(1 - e^{-1/u} + o(1), 1 - e^{-1/v} + o(1), 1 - e^{-1/w} + o(1)\right).$$

Proof. The statement follows straightforwardly from Lemma 2 and the way we picked $d_\beta, d_r, d_\alpha, d_c, d_s, d_{s'}$. □

In Fig. 8 we select $u = v = w$. Thus, we need choose appropriate μ, η, ν to make sure that correctness error of our blind signature is negligible. Indeed, we simply pick $\mu = \eta = \nu$ such that

$$(1 - e^{-1/u} + o(1))^\mu < 2^{-130}.$$

Then by Lemma 1, BS[LHF] has correctness error at most $3 \cdot 2^{-130} < 2^{-128}$.

Lemma 4. *If d_s and d_c are defined as in Fig. 8, then LHF is smooth.*

Proof. In the following we prove smoothness conditions (S1) and (S2). Condition (S3) can be proven analogously to (S2). Conditions (S4), (S5) and (S6) can be proven analogously to (S1), (S2) and (S3), respectively.

Since $d_\alpha = d_s + d_{s'}$, for all $\hat{s} \in \mathcal{D}_s$ and $\hat{s}' \in \mathcal{D}_{s'}$, $\|\hat{s}' - \hat{s}\|_\infty \leq d_{s'} + d_s = d_\alpha$ and therefore $\hat{s}' - \hat{s} \in \mathcal{D}_\alpha$. This proves smoothness condition (S1).

To prove (S2), we fix $\hat{s}_1, \hat{s}_2 \in \mathcal{D}_s$ and define sets $\mathcal{D}_{\alpha_1} := \{\hat{\alpha} \in \mathcal{D}_\alpha \mid \hat{\alpha} + \hat{s}_1 \in \mathcal{D}_{s'}\}$ and $\mathcal{D}_{\alpha_2} := \{\hat{\alpha} \in \mathcal{D}_\alpha \mid \hat{\alpha} + \hat{s}_2 \in \mathcal{D}_{s'}\}$. Note that for all $\hat{s}_1, \hat{s}_2 \in \mathcal{D}_s$ and $\hat{s}' \in \mathcal{D}_{s'}$ there exist $\hat{\alpha}_1 \in \mathcal{D}_{\alpha_1}$ and $\hat{\alpha}_2 \in \mathcal{D}_{\alpha_2}$ s.t. $\hat{\alpha}_1 + \hat{s}_1 = \hat{s}'$ and $\hat{\alpha}_2 + \hat{s}_2 = \hat{s}'$. So, $|\mathcal{D}_{\alpha_1}| = |\mathcal{D}_{\alpha_2}| = |\mathcal{D}_{s'}|$.

In the following, fix $\hat{s}_1, \hat{s}_2 \in \mathcal{D}_s$ and define the random variables $\hat{\alpha}' \xleftarrow{\$} \mathcal{D}_{\alpha_2}$ and $\hat{\alpha}^* \xleftarrow{\$} \mathcal{D}_{\alpha_1}$. To prove smoothness condition (S2), it remains to show that

$$\Delta(\hat{\alpha}', \hat{\alpha}^* + \hat{s}_1 - \hat{s}_2) = 0, \tag{4}$$

We have

$$\Delta(\hat{\alpha}', \underline{\hat{\alpha}}) = \frac{1}{2} \sum_{\bar{\alpha} \notin \mathcal{D}_{\alpha_2}} \left| \Pr_{\hat{\alpha}' \xleftarrow{\$} \mathcal{D}_{\alpha_2}} [\hat{\alpha}' = \bar{\alpha}] - \Pr_{\hat{\alpha}^* \xleftarrow{\$} \mathcal{D}_{\alpha_1}} [\hat{\alpha}^* + \hat{s}_1 = \bar{\alpha} + \hat{s}_2] \right|$$

$$= \frac{1}{2} \sum_{\bar{\alpha} \in \mathcal{D}_{\alpha_2}} \left| \Pr_{\hat{\alpha}' \xleftarrow{\$} \mathcal{D}_{\alpha_2}} [\hat{\alpha}' = \bar{\alpha}] - \Pr_{\hat{\alpha}^* \xleftarrow{\$} \mathcal{D}_{\alpha_1}} [\hat{\alpha}^* + \hat{s}_1 = \bar{\alpha} + \hat{s}_2] \right|. \tag{5}$$

To show that (5) amounts to zero, we argue as follows. If $\bar{\alpha} \notin \mathcal{D}_{s'}$ then clearly

$$\Pr_{\hat{\alpha}' \xleftarrow{\$} \mathcal{D}_{\alpha_2}} [\hat{\alpha}' = \bar{\alpha}] = 0 = \Pr_{\hat{\alpha}^* \xleftarrow{\$} \mathcal{D}_{\alpha_1}} [\hat{\alpha}^* + \hat{s}_1 = \bar{\alpha} + \hat{s}_2].$$

Now, suppose $\bar{\hat{\alpha}} \in \mathcal{D}_{s'}$. Since $\hat{\alpha}' \in \mathcal{D}_{\alpha_2}$ and random variable $\hat{\alpha}'$ takes values in $\mathcal{D}_{\alpha_2}$, the probability that random variable $\hat{\alpha}'$ takes value $\bar{\hat{\alpha}}$ is $\frac{1}{|\mathcal{D}_{\alpha_2}|} = \frac{1}{|\mathcal{D}_{s'}|}$. So, $\Pr_{\hat{\alpha}' \in \mathcal{D}_{\alpha_2}}[\hat{\alpha}' = \bar{\hat{\alpha}}] = \frac{1}{|\mathcal{D}_{s'}|}$. Since $\bar{\hat{\alpha}} \in \mathcal{D}_{\alpha_2}$, $\bar{\hat{\alpha}} + \hat{s}_2 \in \mathcal{D}_{s'}$. Also $\hat{\alpha}^* \in \mathcal{D}_{\alpha_1}$ implies $\hat{\alpha}^* + \hat{s}_1 \in \mathcal{D}_{s'}$. So the probability that random variable $\hat{\alpha}^*$ fulfills $\hat{\alpha}^* + \hat{s}_1 = \bar{\hat{\alpha}} + \hat{s}_2$ is $\frac{1}{|\mathcal{D}_{\alpha_1}|} = \frac{1}{|\mathcal{D}_{s'}|}$. Therefore, $\Pr_{\hat{\alpha}^* \in \mathcal{D}_{\alpha_1}}[\hat{\alpha}^* + \hat{s}_1 = \bar{\hat{\alpha}} + \hat{s}_2] = \frac{1}{|\mathcal{D}_{s'}|}$. This completes the proof.

TORSION FREE ELEMENTS FROM THE KERNEL. We first observe that we only need to find a non-zero $\hat{z}^*$ such that $\mathsf{F}(\hat{z}^*) = \mathbf{0}$. Indeed, if d_c is small enough then by selecting appropriate prime q we can apply the main result of Lyubashevsky and Seiler [41].

Lemma 5 ([41] Corollary 1.2). *Let $n \geq \iota > 1$ be powers of 2 and $q \equiv 2\iota + 1$ (mod 4ι) be a prime. Then $X^n + 1$ factors into d irreducible polynomials $X^{n/\iota} - r_j$ modulo q and any $\mathbf{y} \in R_q \setminus \{0\}$ that satisfies*

$$\|\mathbf{y}\|_{\infty} < \frac{1}{\sqrt{\iota}} \cdot q^{1/\iota} \quad or \quad \|\mathbf{y}\|_2 < q^{1/\iota}$$

is invertible in R_q.

Hence, pick $d_c < \frac{1}{2\sqrt{\iota}} \cdot q^{1/\iota}$. Then, for $\mathbf{c}_1, \mathbf{c}_2 \in \mathcal{S}_c$, $(\mathbf{c}_1 - \mathbf{c}_2)\hat{z}^* = \mathbf{0} \implies \mathbf{c}_1 = \mathbf{c}_2$ since otherwise $\mathbf{c}_1 - \mathbf{c}_2$ is invertible and thus $\hat{z}^* = \mathbf{0}$. Therefore, $\hat{z}^*$ is a torsion-free element from the kernel.

Many papers investigate non-existence of a short vector in random module lattices e.g. [36,43]. However, here we are interested in the existence. Concretely, we want to make sure there exists a $\hat{z}^*$ from the kernel with infinity norm at most $\delta < q/2$. Consider the set of vectors $B_\delta \subset R_q^m$ of polynomials with coefficients between 0 and δ. Clearly, for $\hat{y}_1, \hat{y}_2 \in B_\delta$: $\|\hat{y}_1 - \hat{y}_2\|_{\infty} \leq \delta < q/2$. If we select δ such that $|B_\delta| = (\delta + 1)^{nm} > q^n$ then by the pigeonhole principle, there exist two distinct $\hat{y}_1, \hat{y}_2 \in B_\delta$ such that $\mathsf{F}(\hat{y}_1) = \mathsf{F}(\hat{y}_2)$. Hence, we can set $\hat{z}^* = \hat{y}_1 - \hat{y}_2$.

COLLISION RESISTANCE. To estimate the hardness of finding collisions in LHF we state the following simple lemma.

Lemma 6. *If R-SIS$_{q,n,m,2d}$ is (ε, t)-hard relative to $\hat{a} \in R_q^m$ then LHF is (ε, t)-CR relative to par $\in$ PGen, where par contains all the values defined in Fig. 8 along with $\hat{a}$.*

Proof. Adversary A returns distinct values $\hat{x}_1, \hat{x}_2 \in \mathcal{D}$ after being called on parameters *par*. Since $\mathsf{F}(\hat{x}_1) = \mathsf{F}(\hat{x}_2)$ and since F is a module homomorphism, $\mathsf{F}(\hat{x}_2 - \hat{x}_1) = \mathsf{F}(\hat{x}_2) - \mathsf{F}(\hat{x}_1) = 0$. Further, $\|\hat{x}_2 - \hat{x}_1\|_{\infty} \leq 2d$. So $\hat{x}_2 - \hat{x}_1$ is a solution to the R-SIS$_{q,n,m,2d}$ problem relative to $\hat{a}$.

As we described in the previous section, adversary A, which can win the OMUF game, manages to extract $\hat{\chi}_1, \hat{\chi}_2$ so that $\mathsf{F}(\hat{\chi}_1 - \hat{\chi}_2) = 0$. The norm of $\hat{\chi}_1$ (and similarly for $\hat{\chi}_2$) can be simply bounded by:

$$\|\hat{\chi}_1\|_{\infty} \leq d_{s'} + n d_{c'} d_{sk} < 2d_{s'}.$$

Thus, we set $d = 2d_{s'}$. With parameters defined in Fig. 8, $d \approx 2^{233}$ and $\frac{1}{2}$sv$_{1.005}(n,q) \approx 2^{235}$. Therefore, we get $\|\hat{\chi}_1 - \hat{\chi}_2\|_\infty < 2d < $ sv$_{1.005}(n,q)$.

REGULARITY. We now prove that by selecting sizes d_{sk} and d_r as in Fig. 8, our LHF is (ϵ, Q')-regular where $\varepsilon = 2^{-128}$ and $Q' = 7\mu\eta\nu$. Note that we only allow seven signing queries due to a potential lattice variant of the ROS attack (see Sect. 7).

Lemma 7. *Denote $\varepsilon = 2^{-128}$ and $Q' = 7\mu\eta\nu$. Then, for our selection of d_{sk}, d_r, the LHF is (ϵ, Q')-regular, i.e.*

$$\frac{|\mathcal{D}'_{sk}|}{|\mathcal{D}_{sk}|} \cdot \left(\frac{|\mathcal{D}'_r|}{|\mathcal{D}_r|}\right)^{Q'} \geq 1 - 2^{-130} = 1 - \varepsilon/4, \tag{6}$$

where

$$\mathcal{D}'_{sk} := \{\hat{sk} \in \mathcal{D}_{sk} : \hat{sk} + \hat{\mathbf{z}}^* \in \mathcal{D}_{sk}\}$$

and

$$\mathcal{D}'_r := \{\hat{r} \in \mathcal{D}_r : \forall \mathbf{c} \in \mathcal{S}_c, \hat{r} + \mathbf{c}\hat{\mathbf{z}}^* \in \mathcal{D}_r\}.$$

Proof. Indeed, we first picked d_r so that

$$\left(\frac{|\mathcal{D}'_r|}{|\mathcal{D}_r|}\right)^{Q'} \geq 1 - 2^{-131}.$$

Simultaneously, we chose d_{sk} which satisfies: $|\mathcal{D}'_{sk}|/|\mathcal{D}_{sk}| \geq 1 - 2^{-131}$. Also, we check that $d_r \geq \upsilon m n^2 d_{sk} d_c$ for the enclosedness property. Then, Eq. (6) follows by the Bernoulli inequality.

SIZES. We pick prime $q \approx 2^{1890}$ so that $q \equiv 2\iota + 1 \pmod{4\iota}$ where $\iota = 64$ and $X^n + 1$ splits into ι irreducible polynomials modulo q. Hence, we can apply Lemma 5. Unfortunately, such a large prime modulus affects the signing time significantly. The signature consists of three parts: $\hat{s}', \mathbf{c}'$ and auth. The size for $\hat{s}'$ and $\mathbf{c}'$ are respectively $nm \log 2d_{s'}$ and $n \log 2d_{c'}$. Also, auth contains the index of the leaf (which can be represented with at most $\log(\mu\eta\nu)$ bits) and $\log(\mu\eta\nu)$ outputs of the hash function G. If we assume that G $: \{0,1\}^* \to \{0,1\}^{128}$ then auth has at most $\log(\mu\eta\nu) + 128 \cdot \log(\mu\eta\nu)$ bits. For parameters selected in Fig. 8, our signature has size around 36.03 MB. We observe that the main reason of obtaining such large signatures is the size for d_r and d_{sk}, which should satisfy the regularity property.

7   Generalized ROS Problem

The standard ROS (Random inhomogenities in an Overdetermined, Solvable system of linear equations) problem was first introduced by Schnorr [58] in the context of blind signatures. If one can solve the ROS problem then one is also able to break the security of the Schnorr as well as the Okamoto-Schnorr and

Okamoto-Gouillou-Quisquarter blind signature schemes. Later works by Wagner and Minder and Sinclair [42,60] proposed algorithms which solve the ROS problem in sub-exponential time. In this section, we discuss main challenges when translating the ROS problem to general linear hash function families with correctness error. To the best of our knowledge, none of previous works on lattice-based blind signatures (e.g. [3,4,56]) consider this issue.

We start by describing the Generalized ROS (**GROS**) problem for linear hash function families with correctness error. For a linear hash function family LHF, $par \in$ PGen and a positive integer ℓ, let $\mathcal{X}_\ell$ be the set

$$\mathcal{X}_\ell := \{(x_1, ..., x_\ell) \in \mathcal{S}^\ell \mid \forall s \in \mathcal{D}_s^\ell : \boldsymbol{x} \cdot \boldsymbol{s} \in \mathcal{D}_{s'}\}. \tag{7}$$

The game ℓ-$\mathbf{GROS}_{\mathsf{LHF},par}$ is defined via Fig. 9. The advantage of adversary A in ℓ-$\mathbf{GROS}_{\mathsf{LHF},par}$ is defined as $\mathbf{Adv}_{\mathsf{LHF},par}^{\ell\text{-}\mathbf{GROS}}(\mathsf{A}) := \Pr[\ell\text{-}\mathbf{GROS}_{\mathsf{LHF},par}^{\mathsf{A}} \Rightarrow 1]$ and its running time is denoted as $\mathbf{Time}_{\mathsf{LHF},par}^{\ell\text{-}\mathbf{GROS}}(\mathsf{A})$.

Game ℓ-$\mathbf{GROS}_{\mathsf{LHF},par}$:

01 $\left(c \in \mathcal{S}_c^{\ell+1}, \mathbf{A} \in \left(\mathcal{X}_\ell^{\ell+1} \times \mathcal{S}_{c'}^{\ell+1}\right)\right) \xleftarrow{\$} \mathsf{A}^{\mathsf{H}(\cdot)}(par)$

02 If $(c_{\ell+1} = -1) \wedge (\mathbf{Ac} = 0) \wedge (\forall i, j \in [\ell+1] : \mathsf{H}(\mathbf{A}_{i,1}, ..., \mathbf{A}_{i,\ell}) = \mathbf{A}_{i,\ell+1}) \wedge (\mathbf{A}_i \neq \mathbf{A}_j)$: Return 1

03 Return 0

Fig. 9. Game ℓ-$\mathbf{GROS}_{\mathsf{LHF},par}$ with adversary A. $\mathsf{H} : \{0,1\}^* \to \mathcal{S}_{c'}$ is a random oracle.

Definition 7 (ℓ-GROS Hardness). *Let $\ell \in \mathbb{N}, \ell > 0$ and let LHF be a linear function family and let $par \in$ PGen(1^κ). ℓ-**GROS** is said to be $(\varepsilon, t, Q_{\mathsf{H}})$-hard in the random oracle model relative to par and LHF if for all adversaries A satisfying $\mathbf{Time}_{\mathsf{LHF},par}^{\ell\text{-}\mathbf{GROS}}(\mathsf{A}) \leq t$ and making at most Q_{H} queries to H, we have that $\mathbf{Adv}_{\mathsf{LHF},par}^{\ell\text{-}\mathbf{GROS}}(\mathsf{A}) \leq \varepsilon$.*

The following theorem shows that an attack on ℓ-$\mathbf{GROS}_{\mathsf{LHF},par}$ propagates to an attack against $\mathbf{OMUF}_{\mathsf{BS}[\mathsf{LHF},\mathsf{G},\mathsf{H}],par}$.

Theorem 5. *Let LHF be a linear hash function family with enclosedness error $(\delta_1, \delta_2, \delta_3)$, $\mathsf{G} : \{0,1\}^* \to \{0,1\}^{2\lambda}$ and $\mathsf{H} : \{0,1\}^* \to \mathcal{S}_{c'}$ be random oracles and let $\mathsf{BS} := \mathsf{BS}_{\eta,\nu,\mu}[\mathsf{LHF}, \mathsf{G}, \mathsf{H}]$. If BS is $(\varepsilon, t, 0, \ell, Q_{\mathsf{G}}, Q_{\mathsf{H}})$-**OMUF** relative to par in the random oracle model then ℓ-**GROS** is $(\varepsilon/(1-\delta_2)^\ell, t, Q_{\mathsf{H}})$-hard relative to LHF and par in the random oracle model.*

Proof (Sketch). The proof is similar to one for perfect correctness [32,58]. For readability, we assume that $\mu = \nu = 1$ since there is no need to blind challenges/signatures in this scenario (it can, however, be easily generalized to arbitrary μ, ν). We now define an adversary B in $\mathbf{OMUF}_{\mathsf{BS},par}$ that internally runs an adversary A against ℓ-$\mathbf{GROS}_{\mathsf{LHF},par}$ with random oracle H'.

- It simultaneously opens ℓ sessions with S_1, receiving commitments $\boldsymbol{R}_1, ..., \boldsymbol{R}_\ell$. Let us denote $\boldsymbol{R}_i = (\boldsymbol{R}_{i,1}, ..., \boldsymbol{R}_{i,\eta})$ for $i \in [\ell]$.
- Next, it executes $A^{H'}(par)$. When A makes a fresh query $\boldsymbol{a}$ to H', B computes $\boldsymbol{R}'_{\boldsymbol{a},j} := \sum_{i=1}^{\ell} a_i \cdot \boldsymbol{R}_{i,j}$ for all $j \in [\eta]$. It then computes $(\text{root}_{\boldsymbol{a}}, \text{tree}_{\boldsymbol{a}}) \leftarrow \text{HashTree}(\boldsymbol{R}'_{\boldsymbol{a},1}, ..., \boldsymbol{R}'_{\boldsymbol{a},\eta})$ and $c' \leftarrow H(\text{root}_{\boldsymbol{a}}, m_{\boldsymbol{a}})$, for a fresh message $m_{\boldsymbol{a}}$, and then returns $H'(\boldsymbol{a}) := c'$ as the answer. Clearly, c' is independent from commitments $\boldsymbol{R}_i$.
- When A terminates and returns $(\mathbf{A}, \boldsymbol{c})$, B sends the value c_i as the challenge value for the ith session with S_2, where $i \in [\ell]$, and receives an answer s_i. If $R_{i,1} \neq F(s_i) - c_i \cdot pk$ then B aborts. Note that the probability that B does not abort at all is at least $(1 - \delta_2)^\ell$ by definition of the enclosedness error.
- Next, for all $j \in [\ell + 1]$, B computes $s'_j := \sum_{i=1}^{\ell} A_{j,i} \cdot s_i$ and retrieves the values $\text{root}_{A_j}, \text{tree}_{A_j}, m_{A_j}$ used to compute A_j and computes $c'_j \leftarrow H(\text{root}_{A_j}, m_{A_j})$, $\text{auth}_j \leftarrow \text{BuildAuth}((0, 1, 1), \text{tree})$. It sets $\sigma_j := (c'_j, s'_j, \text{auth}_j)$.
- Finally, B returns $\ell + 1$ message/signature pairs $(\sigma_1, m_{A_1}), ..., (\sigma_{\ell+1}, m_{A_{\ell+1}})$.

Correctness of the signatures follows because

$$
F\left(s'_j\right) = F\left(\sum_{i=1}^{\ell} A_{j,i} s_i\right)
$$

$$
= \sum_{i=1}^{\ell} \mathbf{A}_{j,i}(c_i \cdot pk + R_{i,1}) = R'_{A_j,1} + pk \sum_{i=1}^{\ell} \mathbf{A}_{j,i} c_i = R'_{A_j,1} + pk \cdot c'_{A_j}.
$$

Further, by (7) we have $s'_i \in \mathcal{D}_{s'}$ for all $i \in [\ell]$. Correctness of the authentication path can easily be verified. $\square$

One observes that the attack only makes sense for small values of ℓ due to the security loss of $(1 - \delta_2)^\ell$. The reason is that we always force S_2 to accept the first rejection sampling, otherwise B aborts. On interesting point about our attack is that it can be easily be modified to other lattice-based signatures (e.g. [56]) since the signer in such schemes usually outputs only one commitment per session instead of η. The ROS problem in the standard setting is a special case where $\mathcal{S}_{c'} = \mathcal{S}_c = \mathcal{S}$ are finite fields of size q and $\mathcal{X}_\ell = \mathcal{S}^\ell$ [58]. In this setting Schnorr proves that the ℓ-**GROS** problem is solvable with probability at most $\binom{Q_H}{\ell+1}/|\mathcal{S}_{c'}| < Q_H^{\ell+1}/q$. Wagner later proposed an algorithm A in the $(\ell := 2^{2\sqrt{\log q}} - 1, Q)$-**GROS**$_{\text{LHF}}^{A}$ experiment with running time $O(2^{2\sqrt{\log q}})$ [60]. The two main reasons that Wagner's algorithm [60] cannot be translated to the ℓ-**GROS** problem even with the lattice instantiation from Sect. 6 are the following. First, let us recall that in Sect. 6 we select $\mathcal{S} := R_q = \mathbb{Z}_q[X]/\langle X^n + 1\rangle$ to be a cyclotomic ring and $\mathcal{S}_{c'}$ to be a set of short polynomials in R_q. Therefore, we have $\mathcal{S}_{c'} \subsetneq \mathcal{S}_c \subsetneq \mathcal{S}$ and $\mathcal{S}_c, \mathcal{S}_{c'}$ are not finite fields (or even rings). Secondly, compared to the work of Hauck et al. [32], the values s' in a signature have to lie in the set $\mathcal{D}_{s'}$. This imposes a further restriction on the values in the matrix $\mathbf{A}$ and the vector $\boldsymbol{c}$ returned by the **GROS** adversary. We believe that the studying this variant of the **GROS** problem further is an interesting problem for future work.

Acknowledgments. We would like to thank Vadim Lyubashevsky for pointing out the flaw in BLAZE and Dominique Schröder for helping us with previous work on blind signatures. We are furthermore very grateful for the anonymous comments by the CRYPTO 2020 reviewers. Eduard Hauck was supported by DFG SPP 1736 Big Data. Eike Kiltz was supported by the BMBF iBlockchain project, the EU H2020 PROMETHEUS project 780701, DFG SPP 1736 Big Data, and the DFG Cluster of Excellence 2092 CASA. Ngoc Khanh Nguyen was supported by the SNSF ERC Transfer Grant CRETP2-166734 FELICITY. Julian Loss was supported by the financial assistance award 70NANB19H126 from U.S. Department of Commerce, National Institute of Standards and Technology.

References

1. Abdalla, M., An, J.H., Bellare, M., Namprempre, C.: From identification to signatures via the Fiat-Shamir transform: minimizing assumptions for security and forward-security. In: Knudsen, L.R. (ed.) EUROCRYPT 2002. LNCS, vol. 2332, pp. 418–433. Springer, Heidelberg (2002). https://doi.org/10.1007/3-540-46035-7_28

2. Abe, M.: A secure three-move blind signature scheme for polynomially many signatures. In: Pfitzmann, B. (ed.) EUROCRYPT 2001. LNCS, vol. 2045, pp. 136–151. Springer, Heidelberg (2001). https://doi.org/10.1007/3-540-44987-6_9

3. Alkadri, N.A., Bansarkhani, R.E., Buchmann, J.: BLAZE: practical lattice-based blind signatures for privacy-preserving applications. In: Bonneau, J., Heninger, N. (eds.) FC 2020. LNCS, vol. 12059, pp. 484–502. Springer, Cham (2020). https://doi.org/10.1007/978-3-030-51280-4_26

4. Alkadri, N.A., Bansarkhani, R.E., Buchmann, J.: On lattice-based interactive protocols with aborts. Cryptology ePrint Archive, Report 2020/007 (2020). https://eprint.iacr.org/2020/007

5. Backendal, M., Bellare, M., Sorrell, J., Sun, J.: The Fiat-Shamir zoo: relating the security of different signature variants. In: Gruschka, N. (ed.) NordSec 2018. LNCS, vol. 11252, pp. 154–170. Springer, Cham (2018). https://doi.org/10.1007/978-3-030-03638-6_10

6. Baldimtsi, F., Lysyanskaya, A.: Anonymous credentials light. In: Sadeghi, A.-R., Gligor, V.D., Yung, M. (eds.) ACM CCS 2013, pp. 1087–1098. ACM Press, November 2013

7. Baldimtsi, F., Lysyanskaya, A.: On the security of one-witness blind signature schemes. In: Sako, K., Sarkar, P. (eds.) ASIACRYPT 2013, Part II. LNCS, vol. 8270, pp. 82–99. Springer, Heidelberg (2013). https://doi.org/10.1007/978-3-642-42045-0_5

8. Belenkiy, M., Camenisch, J., Chase, M., Kohlweiss, M., Lysyanskaya, A., Shacham, H.: Randomizable proofs and delegatable anonymous credentials. In: Halevi, S. (ed.) CRYPTO 2009. LNCS, vol. 5677, pp. 108–125. Springer, Heidelberg (2009). https://doi.org/10.1007/978-3-642-03356-8_7

9. Bellare, M., Neven, G.: Multi-signatures in the plain public-key model and a general forking lemma. In: Juels, A., Wright, R.N., De Capitani di Vimercati, S. (eds.) ACM CCS 2006, pp. 390–399. ACM Press, October/November 2006

10. Bellare, M., Palacio, A.: GQ and Schnorr identification schemes: proofs of security against impersonation under active and concurrent attacks. In: Yung, M. (ed.) CRYPTO 2002. LNCS, vol. 2442, pp. 162–177. Springer, Heidelberg (2002). https://doi.org/10.1007/3-540-45708-9_11

11. Bellare, M., Rogaway, P.: Code-based game-playing proofs and the security of triple encryption. Cryptology ePrint Archive, Report 2004/331 (2004). http://eprint.iacr.org/2004/331

12. Boldyreva, A.: Threshold signatures, multisignatures and blind signatures based on the gap-Diffie-Hellman-group signature scheme. In: Desmedt, Y.G. (ed.) PKC 2003. LNCS, vol. 2567, pp. 31–46. Springer, Heidelberg (2003). https://doi.org/10.1007/3-540-36288-6_3

13. Bouaziz-Ermann, S., Canard, S., Eberhart, G., Kaim, G., Roux-Langlois, A., Traoré, J.: Lattice-based (partially) blind signature without restart. Cryptology ePrint Archive, Report 2020/260 (2020). https://eprint.iacr.org/2020/260

14. Brands, S.: Untraceable off-line cash in wallet with observers. In: Stinson, D.R. (ed.) CRYPTO 1993. LNCS, vol. 773, pp. 302–318. Springer, Heidelberg (1994). https://doi.org/10.1007/3-540-48329-2_26

15. Camenisch, J., Hohenberger, S., Lysyanskaya, A.: Compact e-cash. In: Cramer, R. (ed.) EUROCRYPT 2005. LNCS, vol. 3494, pp. 302–321. Springer, Heidelberg (2005). https://doi.org/10.1007/11426639_18

16. Camenisch, J., Lysyanskaya, A.: An efficient system for non-transferable anonymous credentials with optional anonymity revocation. In: Pfitzmann, B. (ed.) EUROCRYPT 2001. LNCS, vol. 2045, pp. 93–118. Springer, Heidelberg (2001). https://doi.org/10.1007/3-540-44987-6_7

17. Camenisch, J., Neven, G., Shelat, A.: Simulatable adaptive oblivious transfer. In: Naor, M. (ed.) EUROCRYPT 2007. LNCS, vol. 4515, pp. 573–590. Springer, Heidelberg (2007). https://doi.org/10.1007/978-3-540-72540-4_33

18. Chaum, D.: Blind signatures for untraceable payments. In: Chaum, D., Rivest, R.L., Sherman, A.T. (eds.) CRYPTO 1982, pp. 199–203. Plenum Press, New York (1982)

19. Chaum, D., Fiat, A., Naor, M.: Untraceable electronic cash. In: Goldwasser, S. (ed.) CRYPTO 1988. LNCS, vol. 403, pp. 319–327. Springer, New York (1990). https://doi.org/10.1007/0-387-34799-2_25

20. Chen, L., Cui, Y., Tang, X., Hu, D., Wan, X.: Hierarchical ID-based blind signature from lattices. In: Wang, Y., Cheung, Y., Guo, P., Wei, Y. (eds.) Seventh International Conference on Computational Intelligence and Security, CIS 2011, Sanya, Hainan, China, 3–4 December 2011, pp. 803–807. IEEE Computer Society (2011)

21. Chen, Y., Nguyen, P.Q.: BKZ 2.0: better lattice security estimates. In: Lee, D.H., Wang, X. (eds.) ASIACRYPT 2011. LNCS, vol. 7073, pp. 1–20. Springer, Heidelberg (2011). https://doi.org/10.1007/978-3-642-25385-0_1

22. Döttling, N., Fleischhacker, N., Krupp, J., Schröder, D.: Two-message, oblivious evaluation of cryptographic functionalities. In: Robshaw, M., Katz, J. (eds.) CRYPTO 2016, Part III. LNCS, vol. 9816, pp. 619–648. Springer, Heidelberg (2016). https://doi.org/10.1007/978-3-662-53015-3_22

23. Fischlin, M.: Round-optimal composable blind signatures in the common reference string model. In: Dwork, C. (ed.) CRYPTO 2006. LNCS, vol. 4117, pp. 60–77. Springer, Heidelberg (2006). https://doi.org/10.1007/11818175_4

24. Fischlin, M., Schröder, D.: Security of blind signatures under aborts. In: Jarecki, S., Tsudik, G. (eds.) PKC 2009. LNCS, vol. 5443, pp. 297–316. Springer, Heidelberg (2009). https://doi.org/10.1007/978-3-642-00468-1_17

25. Fischlin, M., Schröder, D.: On the impossibility of three-move blind signature schemes. In: Gilbert, H. (ed.) EUROCRYPT 2010. LNCS, vol. 6110, pp. 197–215. Springer, Heidelberg (2010). https://doi.org/10.1007/978-3-642-13190-5_10

26. Fuchsbauer, G., Hanser, C., Slamanig, D.: Practical round-optimal blind signatures in the standard model. In: Gennaro, R., Robshaw, M.J.B. (eds.) CRYPTO 2015, Part II. LNCS, vol. 9216, pp. 233–253. Springer, Heidelberg (2015). https://doi.org/10.1007/978-3-662-48000-7_12

27. Gama, N., Nguyen, P.Q.: Predicting lattice reduction. In: Smart, N.P. (ed.) EURO-CRYPT 2008. LNCS, vol. 4965, pp. 31–51. Springer, Heidelberg (2008). https://doi.org/10.1007/978-3-540-78967-3_3

28. Gao, W., Hu, Y., Wang, B., Xie, J.: Identity-based blind signature from lattices in standard model. In: Chen, K., Lin, D., Yung, M. (eds.) Inscrypt 2016. LNCS, vol. 10143, pp. 205–218. Springer, Cham (2017). https://doi.org/10.1007/978-3-319-54705-3_13

29. Gao, W., Hu, Y., Wang, B., Xie, J., Liu, M.: Identity-based blind signature from lattices. Wuhan Univ. J. Nat. Sci. **22**(4), 355–360 (2017). https://doi.org/10.1007/s11859-017-1258-x

30. Garg, S., Gupta, D.: Efficient round optimal blind signatures. In: Nguyen, P.Q., Oswald, E. (eds.) EUROCRYPT 2014. LNCS, vol. 8441, pp. 477–495. Springer, Heidelberg (2014). https://doi.org/10.1007/978-3-642-55220-5_27

31. Garg, S., Rao, V., Sahai, A., Schröder, D., Unruh, D.: Round optimal blind signatures. In: Rogaway, P. (ed.) CRYPTO 2011. LNCS, vol. 6841, pp. 630–648. Springer, Heidelberg (2011). https://doi.org/10.1007/978-3-642-22792-9_36

32. Hauck, E., Kiltz, E., Loss, J.: A modular treatment of blind signatures from identification schemes. In: Ishai, Y., Rijmen, V. (eds.) EUROCRYPT 2019, Part III. LNCS, vol. 11478, pp. 345–375. Springer, Cham (2019). https://doi.org/10.1007/978-3-030-17659-4_12

33. Hauck, E., Kiltz, E., Loss, J., Nguyen, N.K.: Lattice-based blind signatures, revisited. Cryptology ePrint Archive, Report 2020 (2020). https://eprint.iacr.org/2020

34. Juels, A., Luby, M., Ostrovsky, R.: Security of blind digital signatures. In: Kaliski Jr., B.S. (ed.) CRYPTO 1997. LNCS, vol. 1294, pp. 150–164. Springer, Heidelberg (1997). https://doi.org/10.1007/BFb0052233

35. Katz, J., Schröder, D., Yerukhimovich, A.: Impossibility of blind signatures from one-way permutations. In: Ishai, Y. (ed.) TCC 2011. LNCS, vol. 6597, pp. 615–629. Springer, Heidelberg (2011). https://doi.org/10.1007/978-3-642-19571-6_37

36. Langlois, A., Stehlé, D.: Worst-case to average-case reductions for module lattices. Des. Codes Cryptogr. **75**(3), 565–599 (2015)

37. Le, H.Q., Susilo, W., Khuc, T.X., Bui, M.K., Duong, D.H.: A blind signature from module latices. In: 2019 IEEE Conference on Dependable and Secure Computing (DSC), pp. 1–8. IEEE (2019)

38. Lyubashevsky, V.: Fiat-Shamir with aborts: applications to lattice and factoring-based signatures. In: Matsui, M. (ed.) ASIACRYPT 2009. LNCS, vol. 5912, pp. 598–616. Springer, Heidelberg (2009). https://doi.org/10.1007/978-3-642-10366-7_35

39. Lyubashevsky, V.: Lattice signatures without trapdoors. In: Pointcheval, D., Johansson, T. (eds.) EUROCRYPT 2012. LNCS, vol. 7237, pp. 738–755. Springer, Heidelberg (2012). https://doi.org/10.1007/978-3-642-29011-4_43

40. Lyubashevsky, V., Micciancio, D.: Generalized compact Knapsacks are collision resistant. In: Bugliesi, M., Preneel, B., Sassone, V., Wegener, I. (eds.) ICALP 2006, Part II. LNCS, vol. 4052, pp. 144–155. Springer, Heidelberg (2006). https://doi.org/10.1007/11787006_13

41. Lyubashevsky, V., Seiler, G.: Short, invertible elements in partially splitting cyclotomic rings and applications to lattice-based zero-knowledge proofs. In: Nielsen, J.B., Rijmen, V. (eds.) EUROCRYPT 2018, Part I. LNCS, vol. 10820, pp. 204–224. Springer, Cham (2018). https://doi.org/10.1007/978-3-319-78381-9_8

42. Minder, L., Sinclair, A.: The extended k-tree algorithm. In: Mathieu, C. (ed.) 20th SODA, pp. 586–595. ACM-SIAM, January 2009

43. Nguyen, N.K.: On the non-existence of short vectors in random module lattices. In: Galbraith, S.D., Moriai, S. (eds.) ASIACRYPT 2019, Part II. LNCS, vol. 11922, pp. 121–150. Springer, Cham (2019). https://doi.org/10.1007/978-3-030-34621-8_5

44. Okamoto, T.: Provably secure and practical identification schemes and corresponding signature schemes. In: Brickell, E.F. (ed.) CRYPTO 1992. LNCS, vol. 740, pp. 31–53. Springer, Heidelberg (1993). https://doi.org/10.1007/3-540-48071-4_3

45. Okamoto, T.: Efficient blind and partially blind signatures without random oracles. In: Halevi, S., Rabin, T. (eds.) TCC 2006. LNCS, vol. 3876, pp. 80–99. Springer, Heidelberg (2006). https://doi.org/10.1007/11681878_5

46. Okamoto, T., Ohta, K.: Universal electronic cash. In: Feigenbaum, J. (ed.) CRYPTO 1991. LNCS, vol. 576, pp. 324–337. Springer, Heidelberg (1992). https://doi.org/10.1007/3-540-46766-1_27

47. Papachristoudis, D., Hristu-Varsakelis, D., Baldimtsi, F., Stephanides, G.: Leakage-resilient lattice-based partially blind signatures. Cryptology ePrint Archive, Report 2019/1452 (2019). https://eprint.iacr.org/2019/1452

48. Peikert, C., Rosen, A.: Efficient collision-resistant hashing from worst-case assumptions on cyclic lattices. In: Halevi, S., Rabin, T. (eds.) TCC 2006. LNCS, vol. 3876, pp. 145–166. Springer, Heidelberg (2006). https://doi.org/10.1007/11681878_8

49. Pointcheval, D.: Strengthened security for blind signatures. In: Nyberg, K. (ed.) EUROCRYPT 1998. LNCS, vol. 1403, pp. 391–405. Springer, Heidelberg (1998). https://doi.org/10.1007/BFb0054141

50. Pointcheval, D., Stern, J.: Provably secure blind signature schemes. In: Kim, K., Matsumoto, T. (eds.) ASIACRYPT 1996. LNCS, vol. 1163, pp. 252–265. Springer, Heidelberg (1996). https://doi.org/10.1007/BFb0034852

51. Pointcheval, D., Stern, J.: Security proofs for signature schemes. In: Maurer, U.M. (ed.) EUROCRYPT 1996. LNCS, vol. 1070, pp. 387–398. Springer, Heidelberg (1996). https://doi.org/10.1007/3-540-68339-9_33

52. Pointcheval, D., Stern, J.: New blind signatures equivalent to factorization (extended abstract). In: Graveman, R., Janson, P.A., Neuman, C., Gong, L. (eds.) ACM CCS 1997, pp. 92–99. ACM Press, April 1997

53. Pointcheval, D., Stern, J.: Security arguments for digital signatures and blind signatures. J. Cryptol. 13(3), 361–396 (2000)

54. Rodriuguez-Henriquez, F., Ortiz-Arroyo, D., Garcia-Zamora, C.: Yet another improvement over the Mu-Varadharajan e-voting protocol. Comput. Stand. Interfaces 29(4), 471–480 (2007)

55. Rogaway, P.: Formalizing human ignorance. In: Nguyen, P.Q. (ed.) VIETCRYPT 2006. LNCS, vol. 4341, pp. 211–228. Springer, Heidelberg (2006). https://doi.org/10.1007/11958239_14

56. Rückert, M.: Lattice-based blind signatures. In: Abe, M. (ed.) ASIACRYPT 2010. LNCS, vol. 6477, pp. 413–430. Springer, Heidelberg (2010). https://doi.org/10.1007/978-3-642-17373-8_24

57. Schnorr, C.-P.: Efficient signature generation by smart cards. J. Cryptol. 4(3), 161–174 (1991)

58. Schnorr, C.P.: Security of blind discrete log signatures against interactive attacks. In: Qing, S., Okamoto, T., Zhou, J. (eds.) ICICS 2001. LNCS, vol. 2229, pp. 1–12. Springer, Heidelberg (2001). https://doi.org/10.1007/3-540-45600-7_1

59. Schröder, D., Unruh, D.: Security of blind signatures revisited. J. Cryptol. 30(2), 470–494 (2017)

60. Wagner, D.: A generalized birthday problem. In: Yung, M. (ed.) CRYPTO 2002. LNCS, vol. 2442, pp. 288–304. Springer, Heidelberg (2002). https://doi.org/10.1007/3-540-45708-9_19

61. Yi, X., Lam, K.-Y., Gollmann, D.: A new blind ECDSA scheme for bitcoin transaction anonymity. Cryptology ePrint Archive, Report 2018/660 (2018). https://eprint.iacr.org/2018/660

62. Zhang, L., Ma, Y.: A lattice-based identity-based proxy blind signature scheme in the standard model. Math. Probl. Eng. 2014 (2014)

63. Zhu, H., Tan, Y., Zhang, X., Zhu, L., Zhang, C., Zheng, J.: A round-optimal lattice-based blind signature scheme for cloud services. Future Gener. Comput. Syst. 73, 106–114 (2017)

Multi-party computation

Round-Optimal Black-Box Commit-and-Prove with Succinct Communication

Susumu Kiyoshima$^{(\boxtimes)}$

NTT Research, Palo Alto, CA, USA
susumu.kiyoshima@ntt-research.com

Abstract. We give a four-round black-box construction of a commit-and-prove protocol with succinct communication. Our construction is WI and has constant soundness error, and it can be upgraded into a one that is ZK and has negligible soundness error by relying on a round-preserving transformation of Khurana et al. (TCC 2018). Our construction is obtained by combining the MPC-in-the-head technique of Ishai et al. (SICOMP 2009) with the two-round succinct argument of Kalai et al. (STOC 2014), and the main technical novelty lies in the analysis of the soundness—we show that, although the succinct argument of Kalai et al. does not necessarily provide soundness for $\mathcal{NP}$ statements, it can be used in the MPC-in-the-head technique for proving the consistency of committed MPC views. Our construction is based on sub-exponentially hard collision-resistant hash functions, two-round PIRs, and two-round OTs.

1 Introduction

In this paper, we obtain a new *commit-and-prove protocol* by relying on techniques in the area of *succinct arguments*. We start by giving some backgrounds.

Succinct arguments. Informally speaking, a *succinct argument* is an argument system with small communication complexity and fast verification time—typically, when a statement about T-time deterministic or non-deterministic computation is proven, the communication complexity and the verification time are required to be polylogarithmic in T. (The security requirements are, as usual, completeness and computational soundness.) Succinct arguments are useful when resources for communication and verification are limited; for example, a direct application of succinct arguments is *delegating computation* [GKR15] (or *verifiable computation* [GGP10]), where a computationally weak client delegates heavy computations to a powerful server and the client uses succinct arguments to verify the correctness of the server's computation efficiently. It was shown that a four-round succinct argument for all statements in $\mathcal{NP}$ can be obtained from collision-resistance hash functions [Kil92]. Since then, succinct arguments have been actively studied, and protocols with various properties have been proposed.

Among existing succinct arguments, the most relevant to this work is the one by Kalai et al. [KRR14] (KRR succinct argument in short), which has several

© International Association for Cryptologic Research 2020
D. Micciancio and T. Ristenpart (Eds.): CRYPTO 2020, LNCS 12171, pp. 533–561, 2020.
https://doi.org/10.1007/978-3-030-56880-1_19

desirable properties such as (1) being *doubly efficient* [GKR15] (i.e., not only the verifier but also the prover is efficient), (2) being a two-round protocol (i.e., the scheme consists of a single query message from the verifier and a single answer message from the prover), and (3) being proven secure under standard assumptions, especially without relying on unfalsifiable assumptions and random oracles. More concretely, when the statement is about the correctness of a T-time computation, the communication complexity and the verifier running time is polylogarithmic in T while the prover running time is polynomial in T, and the security is proven assuming the existence of private information retrieval (PIR) or fully homomorphic encryption (FHE).

Given the powerful properties of KRR succinct argument, it is natural to expect that it has many cryptographic applications. For example, since argument systems have been extensively used in the design of cryptographic protocols, one might expect that the efficiency of such cryptographic protocols can be improved by simply plugging in KRR succinct argument.

However, using KRR succinct argument in cryptographic applications is actually non-trivial. One difficulty is that the soundness of KRR succinct argument is currently proven only for some specific types of $\mathcal{NP}$ statements [KP16,BHK17,BKK18] (originally, its soundness was proven for statements in $\mathcal{P}$ [KRR14]). Another difficulty is that it does not provide any privacy on witnesses when it is used for $\mathcal{NP}$ statements.

Nonetheless, recent works showed that KRR succinct argument can be used in some cryptographic applications. For example, by cleverly combining KRR succinct argument with other cryptographic primitives, Bitansky et al. [BBK16] obtained a three-round zero-knowledge argument against uniform cheating provers, Brakerski and Kalai [BK20] obtained a succinct private access control protocol for the access structures that can be expressed by monotone formulas, and Morgan et al. [MPP20] obtained a succinct non-interactive secure two-party computation protocol.

The number of applications is, however, still limited. A potential reason for this limitation is that the current techniques inherently use cryptographic primitives in non-black-box ways. Concretely, to hide the prover's witness, the current techniques use KRR succinct argument under other cryptographic protocols (such as garbling schemes) and thus require non-black-box accesses to the codes of the cryptographic primitives that underlies KRR succinct argument. Consequently, the current techniques cannot be used for applications where black-box uses of cryptographic protocols are desirable, such as the application to commit-and-prove protocols, which we discuss next.

Commit-and-prove protocols. Informally speaking, a commit-and-prove protocol is a commitment scheme in which the committer can prove a statement about the committed value without opening the commitment. Proofs by the committer are required to be *zero-knowledge* (ZK) or *witness-indistinguishable* (WI), where the former requires that the views of the receiver in the commit and prove phases can be simulated in polynomial time without knowing the committed value, and the latter requires that for any two messages and any statement such that both of the messages satisfy the statement, the receiver cannot tell which of the messages is committed even after receiving a proof on the statement. Commit-and-prove protocols were implicitly used by Goldreich et al. [GMW87] for obtaining a secure multi-party computation protocol with malicious security, and later formalized by Canetti et al. [CLOS02].

A desirable property of commit-and-prove protocols is that they are constructed in a black-box way, i.e., in a way that uses the underlying cryptographic primitives as black-box by accessing them only through their input/output interfaces. Indeed, this black-box construction property is essential when commit-and-prove protocols are used as a tool for enforcing honest behaviors on malicious parties without relying on non-black-box uses of the underlying cryptographic primitives (see, e.g., [GLOV12, LP12, GOSV14]).

Very recently, Hazay and Venkitasubramaniam [HV18] and Khurana et al. [KOS18] gave four-round black-box constructions of ZK commit-and-prove protocols, where the round complexity of a commit-and-prove protocol is defined as the sum of that of the commit phase and that of the prove phase. Their protocols are *round optimal* since the commit and prove phases of their commit-and-prove protocols can be thought of as black-box ZK arguments (where the prover first commits to a witness and then proves the validity of the committed witness) and black-box ZK arguments are known to require at least four rounds [GK96]. Their protocols also have the *delayed-input property*, i.e., the property that statements to be proven on committed values can be chosen adaptively in the last round of the prove phase.

The commit-and-prove protocols by Hazay and Venkitasubramaniam [HV18] and Khurana et al. [KOS18] are not succinct in the sense that when the statement is expressed as a T-time predicate on the committed value, the communication complexity depends at least linearly on T. This is because both of their protocols were obtained via transformations from the three-round constant-sound commit-and-prove protocol of Hazay and Venkitasubramaniam [HV16], which is not succinct in the above sense.

1.1   Our Result

Our main result is a four-round black-box construction of a constant-sound WI commit-and-prove protocol with succinct communication complexity.

Theorem 1. *Assume the existence of sub-exponentially hard versions of the following cryptographic primitives: a collision-resistant hash function family, a two-round oblivious transfer protocol, and a two-round private information retrieval protocol. Then, there exists a constant-sound WI commit-and-prove protocol with the following properties.*

1. *The round complexity is 4, and the protocol satisfies the delayed-input property and uses the above cryptographic primitives in a black-box way.*
2. *When the length of the committed value is n and the statement to be proven on the committed value is a T-time predicate, the communication complexity depends polynomially on $\log n$, $\log T$, and the security parameter.*

Our commit-and-prove protocol uses a variant of KRR succinct argument (which is obtained from the private information retrieval protocol), and succinctness of our commit-and-prove protocol is inherited from that of KRR succinct argument. We assume sub-exponential hardness on the cryptographic primitives since we use complexity leveraging.

ZK and negligible soundness error. Given our constant-sound WI commit-and-prove protocol, we can use (a minor variant of) a transformation of Khurana et al. [KOS18] to transform it into a 4-round ZK commit-and-prove protocol with negligible soundness error. The resultant commit-and-prove protocol still satisfies the delayed-input property, the black-box uses of the underlying primitives, and the succinct communication complexity. (See the full version of this paper for details.)

Verification time. The verification of our commit-and-prove protocol is not succinct, i.e., the verifier running time depends polynomially on T. Although we might be able to make it succinct by appropriately modifying our protocol (see Appendix A for details), we do not explore this possibility in this work so that we can focus on our main purpose, i.e., on showing how to use KRR succinct argument in black-box constructions of commit-and-prove protocols.

Complexity leveraging. As mentioned above, we use complexity leveraging in the proof of Theorem 1. Although we might be able to avoid the use of complexity leveraging by using known techniques (e.g., by relying on extractable commitments [PW09]), we do not explore this possibility in this work for the same reason as above.

Comparison with existing schemes. As explained above, Hazay and Venkitasubramaniam [HV18] and Khurana et al. [KOS18] gave four-round black-box ZK commit-and-prove protocols with the delayed-input property. Their schemes rely on a weak primitive (injective one-way functions) but do not have succinct communication.

Goyal et al. [GOSV14] and Ishai and Weiss [IW14] studied black-box commit-and-prove protocols with succinct communication under slightly different definitions than ours.[1] If their techniques are used to obtain schemes under our definitions, the resultant schemes will rely on a weak primitive (collision-resistant hash functions) but have round complexity larger than 4.[2]

---

[1] For example, the definition in [IW14] considers non-deterministic statements on committed values but the statements are assumed to be fixed in the commit phase, whereas our definition considers deterministic statements but the statements are allowed to be chosen after the commit phase is completed.

[2] Roughly speaking, this is because in a setting where statements to be proven are chosen after the commit phase (e.g., the delayed-input setting), techniques in [GOSV14,IW14] require that (1) the commit phase has 2 rounds as it needs to be succinct and (2) the prove phase has 3 rounds as it has a commit-challenge-response structure.

Kalai and Paneth [KP16] observed that when messages are committed by using Merkle tree-hash, KRR succinct argument can be used for proving statements on the committed messages. The resultant scheme is succinct in terms of both communication complexity and verification time, but uses the underlying hash function in a non-black-box way and does not have privacy properties (which are not needed for the purpose of [KP16]).

1.2 Overview of Our Commit-and-Prove Protocol

The overall approach is to combine KRR succinct argument with the *MPC-in-the-head technique* [IKOS09].

Let us first recall how we can obtain a non-succinct WI commit-and-prove protocol by using the MPC-in-the-head technique. Let $M \in \mathbb{N}$ be an arbitrary constant, Π be any 2-private semi-honest secure M-party computation protocol with perfect completeness,[3] OT be any two-round 1-out-of-M^2 oblivious transfer (OT) protocol, SBCom be any statistically binding commitment scheme, and SHCom be any statistically hiding commitment scheme. We assume that the hiding property of SBCom can be broken in a quasi-polynomial time T_{SB}, and the security of the other primitives holds against $\mathrm{poly}(T_{SB})$-time adversaries.

Commit phase. To commit to a message x_{COM}, the committer (1) chooses random $x^1_{MPC}, \ldots, x^M_{MPC}$ such that $x^1_{MPC} \oplus \cdots \oplus x^M_{MPC} = x_{COM}$, (2) chooses randomness $r^1_{MPC}, \ldots, r^M_{MPC}$ for the M parties of Π, and (3) commits to $st^\mu_0 := (x^\mu_{MPC}, r^\mu_{MPC})$ for each $\mu \in [M]$ by using SHCom. (Note that each st^μ_0 can be thought of as an initial state of a party of Π.) For each $\mu \in [M]$, let dec^μ_{SH} denote the decommitment of SHCom for revealing st^μ_0.

Prove phase. In the first round, the receiver computes a receiver message of OT by using random $(\alpha, \beta) \in [M] \times [M]$ as the input,[4] and sends it to the committer.

In the second round, to prove $f(x_{COM}) = 1$ for a predicate f, the committer does the following. (1) Execute Π in the head by using $st^1_0, \ldots, st^M_0$ as the initial states of the M parties and using $f' : (y^1, \ldots, y^M) \mapsto f(y^1 \oplus \cdots \oplus y^M)$ as the functionality to be computed. Let $view^1, \ldots, view^M$ be the views of the parties in this execution of Π. (2) For each $\mu \in [M]$, compute a commitment to $(dec^\mu_{SH}, view^\mu)$ by using SBCom. Let dec^μ_{SB} be the decommitment of SBCom for revealing $(dec^\mu_{SH}, view^\mu)$. (3) Compute a sender message of OT by using $\{(dec^\mu_{SB}, dec^\nu_{SB})\}_{\mu,\nu \in [M]}$ as the input. (4) Send the commitments and the OT message to the receiver.

In the verification, the receiver (1) recovers $dec^\alpha_{SB}, dec^\beta_{SB}$ from the OT message, (2) checks that they are valid decommitments of SBCom for revealing $dec^\alpha_{SH}, view^\alpha, dec^\beta_{SH}, view^\beta$ and that $dec^\alpha_{SH}, dec^\beta_{SH}$ are valid decommitments of SHCom for revealing st^α_0, st^β_0, and (3) checks the following two conditions on $st^\alpha_0, view^\alpha, st^\beta_0, view^\beta$.

---

[3] Such an MPC protocol can be obtained unconditionally (e.g., the 2-private five-party protocol by Ben-Or et al. [BGW88, AL17]).

[4] We assume that the set $[M] \times [M]$ is identified with the set $[M^2]$ in a canonical way.

1. The views $\text{view}^\alpha, \text{view}^\beta$ are *consistent* in the sense that the messages that the party P^α receives from the party P^β in view^α is equal to the messages that P^β sends to P^α in view^β and vice versa.
2. For each $\xi \in \{\alpha, \beta\}$, the view view^ξ indicates that the initial state of P^ξ is st_0^ξ and the output is 1.

First, the constant soundness follows from the receiver security of OT and the perfect completeness of Π. Roughly speaking, this is because (1) the receiver security of OT guarantees that the committer can convince the verifier with high probability only when it commits to initial states and views that satisfy the above two conditions for every $\alpha, \beta \in [M]$,[5] and (2) when the committed initial states and views satisfy the above two conditions for every $\alpha, \beta \in [M]$, the perfect completeness of Π guarantees $f(x_{\text{COM}}) = 1$, where x_{COM} is derived from the committed initial states. Next, the witness-indistinguishability follows from the receiver security of OT and the 2-privacy of Π. This is because the former guarantees that the receiver only learns the committed initial states and views of two parties and the latter guarantees the committed initial states and views of any two parties do not reveal any information about x_{COM}. Finally, this scheme is not succinct since the committer sends the initial states and views of Π (or more precisely the decommitments to them) via OT.

Now, to make the above scheme succinct, we combine it with KRR succinct argument. The idea is to let the committer send succinct arguments about the initial states and views (instead of the initial states and views themselves) via OT. That is, we let the committer prove that the above two conditions hold on the committed initial states and views of each pair of the parties, where a separate instance of KRR succinct argument is used for each pair of the parties, and let it send the resultant M^2 succinct arguments via OT. (Note that KRR succinct argument can naturally be combined with OT since it is a two-round protocol.) As a minor modification, we also let the committer use a succinct commitment scheme to commit to the initial states and the views.

Unfortunately, although the modifications are intuitive, proving the soundness of the resultant scheme is non-trivial. (In contrast, the WI property can be proven similarly to the WI property of the original scheme. The key point is that, although KRR succinct argument does not provide any witness privacy, we can still prove WI of the whole scheme since in each instance of KRR succinct argument, the witness—initial states and views of a pair of the parties—does not reveal any secret information anyway.)

A natural approach for proving the soundness would be to first prove the soundness of each instance of KRR succinct argument and then derive the soundness of the whole scheme from it. Indeed, if we can show that each of the M^2 instances of KRR succinct argument provides an argument-of-knowledge property (which allows us to extract the committed initial states and views from the cheating committer), we can easily prove the soundness of the whole scheme.

---

[5] Formally, complexity leveraging is required in this argument since the receiver security of OT needs to hold even against adversaries that extract the committed initial states and views by brute force.

The problem of this approach is that KRR succinct argument is not known to provide soundness for all statements in $\mathcal{NP}$, and hence, does not necessarily provide soundness when it is used as above.

Our actual approach is to show that, while each of the instances of KRR succinct argument does not necessarily provide soundness, they as a whole provide a meaningful notion of the soundness, which can be used to prove the soundness of the whole scheme. Specifically, by getting into the security proof of the soundness of KRR succinct argument, we show that when M^2 instances of KRR argument are used in parallel for proving the consistency of each pair of the committed views etc. as above, then they as a whole guarantee that the committed views are mutually consistent etc.

We give more detailed overviews of our approach from Sect. 3 to Sect. 6 after giving necessary definitions in Sect. 2.

2 Preliminaries

2.1 Notations and Conventions

We denote the security parameter by λ. We assume that every algorithm takes the security parameter as input, and often do not write it explicitly.

We identify a bit-string with a function in the following manner: a bit-string $x = (x_1, \ldots, x_n)$ is thought of as a function $x : [n] \to \{0, 1\}$ such that $x(i) = x_i$. More generally, for any finite field $\boldsymbol{F}$, we identify a string over $\boldsymbol{F}$ with a function in the same manner. For a vector $\boldsymbol{v} = (v_1, \ldots, v_n)$ and a set $S \subseteq [n]$, we define $\boldsymbol{v}|_S$ by $\boldsymbol{v}|_S := \{v_i\}_{i \in S}$. Similarly, for a function $f : D \to R$ and a set $S \subseteq D$, we define $f|_S$ by $f|_S := \{f(i)\}_{i \in S}$.

For any two probabilistic interactive Turing machines A and B and any input x_A to A and x_B to B, we denote by $(\mathsf{out}_A, \mathsf{out}_B) \leftarrow \langle A(x_A), B(x_B) \rangle$ that the output of an interaction between $A(x_A)$ and $B(x_B)$ is $(\mathsf{out}_A, \mathsf{out}_B)$, where out_A is the output from A and out_B is the output from B.

2.2 Witness-Indistinguishable Commit-and-Prove Protocols

We give the definition of witness-indistinguishable commit-and-prove protocols. Our definition is based on the definition by Khurana et al. [KOS18] but is slightly different from it; see Appendix B for the differences.

A *witness-indistinguishable (WI) commit-and-prove protocol* $\langle C, R \rangle$ is a protocol between a committer $C = (\mathsf{C.Com}, \mathsf{C.Dec}, \mathsf{C.Prv})$ and a receiver $R = (\mathsf{R.Com}, \mathsf{R.Dec}, \mathsf{R.Prv})$, and it consists of three phases.

1. In the commit phase, $\mathsf{C.Com}$ takes a message $x \in \{0, 1\}^n$ as input and interacts with $\mathsf{R.Com}$ to commit to x.[6] At the end of the interaction, $\mathsf{C.Com}$ outputs its internal state st_C and $\mathsf{R.Com}$ outputs the commitment com, which is the transcript of the commit phase.

---

[6] We assume that the length of the message to be committed, n, is implicitly given to the receiver as input.

2. In the prove phase, C.Prv takes a predicate f as input along with st_C, and interacts with R.Prv to prove that $f(x) = 1$ holds, where R.Prv takes (com, f) as input, At the end of the interaction, R.Prv outputs either 1 (accept) or 0 (reject).
3. In the open phase, C.Dec takes an index $i \in [n]$ as input along with st_C, and interacts with R.Dec to reveal the i-th bit of x, where R.Dec takes (com, i) as input. At the end of the interaction, R.Dec outputs either a bit x_i as the decommitted bit, or $\bot$ (reject).

In this paper, we focus on a WI commit-and-prove protocol such that (1) both the prove phase and the open phase consist of two rounds, (2) the first round of the prove phase does not depend on the commitment com and the predicate f,[7] and (3) the first round of the open phase does not depend on the commitment com. Because of (1) and (2), R.Prv can be split into two algorithms, R.Prv.Q and R.Prv.D, such that the prove phase proceeds as follows: $(Q, \mathsf{st}_R) \leftarrow \mathsf{R.Prv.Q}$; $\pi \leftarrow \mathsf{C.Prv}(\mathsf{st}_C, f, Q)$; $b \leftarrow \mathsf{R.Prv.D}(\mathsf{st}_R, \mathsf{com}, f, \pi)$. Similarly, because of (1) and (3), R.Dec can be split into two algorithms, R.Dec.Q and R.Dec.D, such that the open phase proceeds as follows: $(Q, \mathsf{st}_R) \leftarrow \mathsf{R.Dec.Q}(i)$; $\mathsf{dec} \leftarrow \mathsf{C.Dec}(\mathsf{st}_C, i, Q)$; $b \leftarrow \mathsf{R.Dec.D}(\mathsf{st}_R, \mathsf{com}, \mathsf{dec})$.

WI commit-and-prove protocols need to satisfy the following security notions.

Definition 1 (Completeness). *A commit-and-prove protocol $\langle C, R \rangle$ is complete if for any polynomial $n : \mathbb{N} \rightarrow \mathbb{N}$ and any $\lambda \in \mathbb{N}$, $x \in \{0,1\}^{n(\lambda)}$, and $i \in [n(\lambda)]$,*

$$\Pr\left[x_i = \tilde{x}_i \;\middle|\; \begin{array}{l} (\mathsf{st}_C, \mathsf{com}) \leftarrow \langle \mathsf{C.Com}(x), \mathsf{R.Com} \rangle \\ (\bot, \tilde{x}_i) \leftarrow \langle \mathsf{C.Dec}(\mathsf{st}_C, i), \mathsf{R.Dec}(\mathsf{com}, i) \rangle \end{array} \right] = 1 \; .$$

Definition 2 (Binding). *A commit-and-prove protocol $\langle C, R \rangle$ is (computationally) binding if for any polynomial $n : \mathbb{N} \rightarrow \mathbb{N}$, any PPT cheating committer $C^* = (\mathsf{C.Com}^*, \mathsf{C.Dec}^*)$, and any $\lambda \in \mathbb{N}$, the following binding condition holds with overwhelming probability over the choice of $(\mathsf{st}_C, \mathsf{com}) \leftarrow \langle \mathsf{C.Com}^*, \mathsf{R.Com} \rangle$.*

- **Binding Condition:** *For every $i \in [n(\lambda)]$, it holds $\Pr[b_{\mathrm{BAD}} = 1] \leq \mathsf{negl}(\lambda)$ in the following probabilistic experiment $\mathrm{Exp}^{\mathrm{bind}}(\mathsf{C.Dec}^*, \mathsf{st}_C, \mathsf{com}, i)$.*
  1. *For each $b \in \{0,1\}$, sample Q_b by $(Q_b, \mathsf{st}_b) \leftarrow \mathsf{R.Dec.Q}(i)$.*
  2. *Run $\{\mathsf{dec}_b\}_{b \in \{0,1\}} \leftarrow \mathsf{C.Dec}^*(\mathsf{st}_C, i, \{Q_b\}_{b \in \{0,1\}})$.*
  3. *For each $b \in \{0,1\}$, let $x_b^* \leftarrow \mathsf{R.Dec.D}(\mathsf{st}_b, \mathsf{com}, \mathsf{dec}_b)$.*
  4. *Output $b_{\mathrm{BAD}} := 1$ if and only if $x_0^* \neq \bot \wedge x_1^* \neq \bot \wedge x_0^* \neq x_1^*$ holds.*

Definition 3 (Soundness). *Let $\epsilon : \mathbb{N} \rightarrow [0,1]$ be a function. A commit-and-prove protocol $\langle C, R \rangle$ is (computationally) ϵ-sound if for any constant $c \in \mathbb{N}$, there exists a PPT oracle Turing machine E (called an extractor) such that for any polynomial $n : \mathbb{N} \rightarrow \mathbb{N}$, any PPT cheating committer $C^* = (\mathsf{C.Com}^*, \mathsf{C.Prv}^*)$, and any sufficiently large $\lambda \in \mathbb{N}$, the following soundness condition holds with overwhelming probability over the choice of $(\mathsf{st}_C, \mathsf{com}) \leftarrow \langle \mathsf{C.Com}^*, \mathsf{R.Com} \rangle$.*

---

[7] We assume that $\mathsf{Time}(f)$ is known to the both parties in advance (where f is expressed as, e.g., a Turing machine).

- **Soundness Condition[8]:** *If it holds*

$$\Pr\left[b = 1 \;\middle|\; \begin{array}{l} (Q, \mathsf{st}_R) \leftarrow \mathsf{R.Prv.Q}; \; (f, \pi) \leftarrow \mathsf{C.Prv}^*(\mathsf{st}_C, Q); \\ b \leftarrow \mathsf{R.Prv.D}(\mathsf{st}_R, \mathsf{com}, f, \pi) \end{array}\right] \geq \epsilon(\lambda) + \frac{1}{\lambda^c} \;,$$

then there exists $x^* = (x_1^*, \ldots, x_n^*) \in \{0, 1\}^{n(\lambda)}$ *such that*

$$\forall i \in [n(\lambda)], \Pr\left[x_i = x_i^* \;\middle|\; (\bot, x_i) \leftarrow \langle E^{\mathsf{C.Prv}^*(\mathsf{st}_C, \cdot)}(\mathsf{com}, i), \mathsf{R.Dec}(\mathsf{com}, i)\rangle\right]$$
$$\geq 1 - \mathsf{negl}(\lambda)$$

and

$$\Pr\left[\begin{array}{l} b = 1 \\ \wedge \; f(x^*) = 0 \end{array} \;\middle|\; \begin{array}{l} (Q, \mathsf{st}_R) \leftarrow \mathsf{R.Prv.Q}; \; (f, \pi) \leftarrow \mathsf{C.Prv}^*(\mathsf{st}_C, Q); \\ b \leftarrow \mathsf{R.Prv.D}(\mathsf{st}_R, \mathsf{com}, f, \pi) \end{array}\right]$$
$$\leq \epsilon(\lambda) + \mathsf{negl}(\lambda) \;.$$

$\langle C, R \rangle$ *is said to be* sound *if it is* ϵ*-sound for a negligible function* ϵ.

Definition 4 (Witness Indistinguishability). $\langle C, R \rangle$ *is witness-indistinguishable if for any polynomial* $n : \mathbb{N} \to \mathbb{N}$, *any two sequences* $\{x_\lambda^0\}_{\lambda \in \mathbb{N}}$ *and* $\{x_\lambda^1\}_{\lambda \in \mathbb{N}}$ *such that* $x_\lambda^0, x_\lambda^1 \in \{0, 1\}^{n(\lambda)}$, *any* PPT *cheating receiver* $R^* = (\mathsf{R.Com}^*, \mathsf{R.Prv.Q}^*)$, *the outputs of Experiment 0 and Experiment 1 are computationally indistinguishable.*

- *Experiment* b *(*$b \in \{0, 1\}$*).*
    1. $(\mathsf{st}_C, \mathsf{st}_R) \leftarrow \langle \mathsf{C.Com}(x_\lambda^b), \mathsf{R.Com}^*(x_\lambda^0, x_\lambda^1) \rangle$.
    2. $(f, Q, \mathsf{st}_R') \leftarrow \mathsf{R.Prv.Q}^*(\mathsf{st}_R)$. *If* $f(x_\lambda^0) \neq 1$ *or* $f(x_\lambda^1) \neq 1$, *abort.*
    3. $\pi \leftarrow \mathsf{C.Prv}(\mathsf{st}_C, f, Q)$.
    4. *Output* (st_R', π).

2.3 Secure Multi-party Computation

We recall the definition of secure multi-party computation (MPC) protocols based on the description by Ishai et al. [IKOS09]. (We assume that the readers are familiar with the concept of secure MPC protocols.)

The basic model that is used in this paper is the following. The number of parties is denoted by M. We focus on MPC protocols that realize any deterministic M-party functionality that outputs a single bit (which is obtained by all the parties), given the synchronous communication over secure point-to-point channels. We assume that every party implicitly takes as input the M-party functionality to be computed.

Recall that the *view* of a party in an execution of an MPC protocol consists of its input, its randomness, and all the incoming messages that it received from the other parties during the execution of the protocol. The consistency between a pair of views is defined as follows.

---

[8] Roughly speaking, the soundness condition requires that if a cheating prover convinces the verifier with sufficiently high probability, then there exists a value x^* such that (1) the extractor can decommit com to x^* and (2) the cheating prover cannot prove false statements about x^*.

Definition 5 (Consistent Views). *A pair of views* $\mathsf{view}^i, \mathsf{view}^j$ *is consistent (w.r.t. an MPC protocol Π for a functionality f) if the outgoing messages that are implicitly reported in* view^i *are identical to the incoming messages that are reported in* view^j *and vice versa.*

We consider security against semi-honest adversaries. Concretely, we use the following two security notions.

Definition 6 (Perfect correctness). *We say that an MPC protocol Π satisfies* perfect correctness *if for any deterministic M-party functionality f and for any private inputs to the parties, the probability that the output of some party in an honest execution of Π is different from the output of f is 0.*

Definition 7 (2-privacy). *We say that an MPC protocol Π satisfies* perfect 2-privacy *if for any deterministic M-party functionality f, there exists a* PPT *simulator $\mathcal{S}_{\mathrm{MPC}}$ such that for any private inputs $x_1, \ldots, x_M$ to the parties and every pair of corrupted parties, $T \subset [M]$ such that $|T| = 2$, the joint view $\mathsf{View}_T(x_1, \ldots, x_M)$ of the parties in T is identically distributed with $\mathcal{S}_{\mathrm{MPC}}(T, \{x_i\}_{i \in T}, f(x_1, \ldots, x_M))$.*

2.4   Probabilistically Checkable Proofs (PCPs)

We recall the definition of probabilistically checkable proofs (PCPs) based on the description by Brakerski et al. [BHK17]. Roughly speaking, PCPs are proof systems with which one can probabilistically verify the correctness of statements by reading only a few bits or symbols of the proof strings. A formal definition is given below.

Definition 8. *A κ-query PCP system* (P, V) *for an NP language L, where $\mathsf{V} = (\mathsf{Q}, \mathsf{D})$, satisfies the following.*

- *(**Completeness**) For all $\lambda \in \mathbb{N}$ and $x \in L$ (with witness w) such that $|x| \leq 2^\lambda$,*

$$\Pr\left[\mathsf{D}(\mathsf{st}, x, \pi|_Q) = 1 \;\middle|\; \begin{array}{l} (Q, \mathsf{st}) \leftarrow \mathsf{Q}(1^\lambda) \\ \pi \leftarrow \mathsf{P}(1^\lambda, x, w) \end{array}\right] = 1.$$

The PCP proof π is a string of characters over some alphabet Σ, and it can be thought that this string is indexed by a set Γ (by identifying Γ with $[N]$ in a canonical way, where N is the length of the string) and $Q \subseteq \Gamma$. Alternatively, π can be thought of as a function from Γ to Σ.
- *(**Soundness**) For all $\lambda \in \mathbb{N}$, all $x \notin L$ such that $|x| \leq 2^\lambda$, and all proof string π^*,*

$$\Pr\left[\mathsf{D}(\mathsf{st}, x, \pi^*|_Q) \;\middle|\; (Q, \mathsf{st}) \leftarrow \mathsf{Q}(1^\lambda)\right] \leq \frac{1}{2}.$$

- *(**Query Efficiency**) If $(Q, \mathsf{st}) \leftarrow \mathsf{Q}(1^\lambda)$, then $|Q| \leq \kappa(\lambda)$ and the combined run-time of Q and D is $\mathrm{poly}(\lambda)$.*
- *(**Prover Efficiency**) The prover P runs in polynomial time, where its input is $(1^\lambda, x, w)$.*

2.5   Definitions from Kalai et al. [KRR14] and Subsequent Works

Computational no-signaling (CNS). We recall the definition of *adaptive (computational) no-signaling* [KRR14,BHK17].

Definition 9. *Fix any alphabet* $\{\Sigma_\lambda\}_{\lambda \in \mathbb{N}}$, *any* $\{N_\lambda\}_{\lambda \in \mathbb{N}}$ *such that* $N_\lambda \in \mathbb{N}$, *any function* $\kappa_{\max} : \mathbb{N} \to \mathbb{N}$ *such that* $\kappa_{\max}(\lambda) \leq N_\lambda$, *and any algorithm* Algo *such that for any* $\lambda \in \mathbb{N}$, *on input a subset* $Q \subset [N_\lambda]$ *of size at most* $\kappa_{\max}(\lambda)$, Algo *outputs (the truth table of) a function* $A : Q \to \Sigma \cup \{\bot\}$ *with an auxiliary output* out.

Then, the algorithm Algo *is adaptive* $\kappa_{\max}$-*computational no-signaling (CNS) if for any* PPT *distinguisher* $\mathcal{D}$, *any sufficiently large* $\lambda \in \mathbb{N}$, *any* $Q, S \subset [N_\lambda]$ *such that* $Q \subseteq S$ *and* $|S| \leq \kappa_{\max}(\lambda)$, *and any* $z \in \{0,1\}^{\mathsf{poly}(\lambda)}$,

$$\left| \begin{array}{l} \Pr\left[\mathcal{D}(\mathsf{out}, A, z) = 1 \mid (\mathsf{out}, A) \leftarrow \mathsf{Algo}(Q)\right] \\ - \Pr\left[\mathcal{D}(\mathsf{out}, A|_Q, z) = 1 \mid (\mathsf{out}, A) \leftarrow \mathsf{Algo}(S)\right] \end{array} \right| \leq \mathsf{negl}(\lambda).$$

We remark that the above definition can be naturally extended for the case that Algo takes auxiliary inputs, as well as for the case that Algo takes multiple subsets as input and then outputs multiple functions (see the full version of this paper).

Adaptive local assignment generator. We recall the definition of *adaptive local assignment generators* [PR14,BHK17].

Definition 10. *For any function* $\kappa_{\max} : \mathbb{N} \to \mathbb{N}$, *an adaptive* $\kappa_{\max}$-*local assignment generator* Assign *on variables* $\{V_\lambda\}_{\lambda \in \mathbb{N}}$ *is an algorithm that takes as input a security parameter* 1^λ *and a set of at most* $\kappa_{\max}(\lambda)$ *queries* $W \subseteq \{1, \ldots, |V_\lambda|\}$, *and outputs a 3CNF formula* φ *on variables* V_λ *and assignments* $A : W \to \{0,1\}$ *such that the following two properties hold.*

- ***Everywhere Local Consistency.*** *For every* $\lambda \in \mathbb{N}$ *and every set* $W \subseteq \{1, \ldots, |V_\lambda|\}$ *such that* $|W| \leq \kappa_{\max}(\lambda)$, *with probability at least* $1 - \mathsf{negl}(\lambda)$ *over sampling* $(\varphi, A) \leftarrow \mathsf{Assign}(1^\lambda, W)$, *the assignment* A *is "locally consistent" with the formula* φ. *That is, for any* $i_1, i_2, i_3 \in W$, *if* φ *has a clause whose variables are* $v_{i_1}, v_{i_2}, v_{i_3}$, *then this clause is satisfied with the assignment* $A(i_1), A(i_2), A(i_3)$ *with probability at least* $1 - \mathsf{negl}(\lambda)$.
- ***Computational No-signaling.*** Assign *is adaptive* $\kappa_{\max}$-*CNS.*

No-signaling PCPs. We recall the definition of *(computational) no-signaling PCPs* [KRR14,BHK17]. Essentially, no-signaling PCPs are PCP systems that are sound against no-signaling cheating provers. Specifically, for any function $\kappa_{\max} : \mathbb{N} \to \mathbb{N}$, a PCP system (P, V) for a language L, where $\mathsf{V} = (\mathsf{Q}, \mathsf{D})$, is *adaptive* $\kappa_{\max}$-*no-signaling sound* with negligible soundness error if it satisfies the following.

- **(No-signaling Soundness)** For any adaptive κ_{max}-CNS cheating prover P^* and any $\lambda \in \mathbb{N}$,

$$\Pr\left[x^* \notin L \wedge \mathsf{D}(\mathsf{st}, x^*, \pi^*) = 1 \;\middle|\; \begin{array}{l} (Q, \mathsf{st}) \leftarrow \mathsf{Q}(1^\lambda) \\ (x^*, \pi^*) \leftarrow P^*(1^\lambda, Q) \end{array}\right] \leq \mathsf{negl}(\lambda) \ .$$

3   Outline of Proof of Theorem 1

As mentioned in Sect. 1.2, our commit-and-prove protocol uses the succinct argument of Kalai et al. [KRR14] (KRR succinct argument in short). Unfortunately, we do not use it modularly—we slightly modify a building block of KRR succinct argument (namely, their no-signaling PCP system) when constructing our protocol, and we see low-level parts of the analysis of KRR succinct argument when analyzing our protocol.

At a high level, KRR succinct argument is obtained in three steps, starting from a scheme with a weak soundness notion.

1. Obtain a PCP system such that no CNS adversary can break the soundness with overwhelming success probability.
2. Obtain a PCP system such that no CNS adversary can break the soundness with non-negligible success probability.
3. Obtain a succinct argument such that no adversary can break the soundness with non-negligible success probability.

Somewhat similarly, our commit-and-prove protocol is obtained in five steps, starting from a non-WI scheme with a weak soundness notion.

1. Obtain a non-WI scheme, $\langle C_1, R_1 \rangle$, such that no CNS "well-behaving" adversary can break the soundness with overwhelming success probability. (Well-behaving adversaries is the class of adversaries that we introduce later.)
2. Obtain a non-WI scheme, $\langle C_2, R_2 \rangle$, such that no CNS adversary can break the soundness with overwhelming success probability.
3. Obtain a non-WI scheme, $\langle C_3, R_3 \rangle$, such that no CNS adversary can break the soundness with non-negligible success probability.
4. Obtain a non-WI scheme, $\langle C_4, R_4 \rangle$, such that no adversary can break the soundness with non-negligible success probability.
5. Obtain a WI scheme, $\langle C_5, R_5 \rangle$, such that no adversary can break the soundness with constant success probability.

The most technically interesting step is the first step, and an extensive overview of this step is given in Sect. 4. Overviews of the other steps are given in Sect. 5 and Sect. 6. The formal proof is given in the full version of this paper.

3.1 Building Block: Perfect 2-Private MPC Protocol Π

In addition to the cryptographic primitives that are listed in Theorem 1, we use a 2-private semi-honest secure M-party computation protocol Π with perfect completeness, where M is an arbitrary constant. (Note that such an MPC protocol can be obtained unconditionally; cf. Footnote 3.) We denote the parties of Π by $P^1, \ldots P^M$.

For editorial simplicity, we make several simplifying assumptions on Π.

- The length of the initial state of each party is denoted by $n_{st} = n + n_{MPC}$, where n is the input length and n_{MPC} is the randomness length, and each party has n_{st}-bit internal state at the beginning of each round.
- Every party uses the same next-message function in every round.[9]
- Every party sends a 1-bit message to each party at the end of each round.
- Every party receives dummy incoming messages from all the parties at the beginning of the first round, and every party sends a dummy outgoing message to itself at the end of each round. (This assumption is made so that the next-message function always takes an $(n_{st} + M)$-bit input, where the last M bits are the concatenation of the incoming messages.)
- The first bit of the final state of each party denotes the output of that party.

4 Overview of Step 1 (Non-WI Scheme with Soundness Against CNS Well-Behaving Provers)

We give an extensive overview of our non-WI commit-and-prove protocol $\langle C_1, R_1 \rangle$, which is $(1 - \mathsf{negl})$-sound against CNS "well-behaving" provers. At a high level, we follow the approach that we outline in Sect. 1.2. That is, we implement the MPC-in-the-head technique with the MPC protocol Π and a succinct argument. However, instead of using KRR succinct argument, we use a variant of the no-signaling PCP system $(\mathsf{PCP.P_{KRR}}, \mathsf{PCP.V_{KRR}})$ of Kalai et al. [KRR14] (which is the main building block of KRR succinct argument and is referred to as KRR no-signaling PCP in what follows), and we do not use any cryptographic primitives in this step so that we can focus on information theoretical arguments in the analysis. As a result, we can prove soundness only against very restricted provers, which we define as CNS well-behaving provers.

For simplicity, in this overview, we focus on static soundness, where the statement to be proven by the cheating prover is fixed at the beginning of the prove phase. We will also make several implicit oversimplifications in this overview.

---

[9] The next-message function takes as input an internal state and incoming messages of a round, and it outputs the internal state and outgoing messages of the round. (We assume that the internal state implicitly includes all the incoming messages of the previous rounds.)

4.1 Preliminary: Overview of Analysis of KRR No-Signaling PCP

We start by briefly recalling the analysis of KRR no-signaling PCP (i.e., the analysis of its no-signaling soundness for statements in $\mathcal{P}$), focusing on the parts that are relevant to this work.[10]

We first remark that KRR no-signaling PCP is a PCP system for 3SAT, so at the beginning the statement to be proven is converted into a 3SAT instance. Specifically, given any statement in $\mathcal{P}$ of the form "(f, x) satisfies $f(x) = 1$" for some public function f and input x, first the function f is converted into a carefully designed Boolean circuit C that computes f, and next the statement is converted into a 3SAT instance φ that has the following properties.

1. φ has a variable for each of the wires in C, and the values that are assigned to these variables are interpreted as an assignment to the corresponding wires in C.
2. The clauses of φ checks that (1) for each gate in C, the assignment to its input and output wires is consistent with the computation of the gate, (2) the assignment to the input wires of C is equal to x, and (3) the assignment to the output wire of C is equal to 1.

Now, the analysis of KRR no-signaling PCP roughly consists of three parts.

The first part of the analysis shows that any successful CNS cheating prover for a statement (f, x) can be converted into a local assignment generator for the 3SAT instance φ that is obtained from (f, x) as above. That is, it shows that any successful CNS cheating prover can be converted into a probabilistic algorithm Assign such that (1) Assign takes as input a small-size subset of the variables of φ and it outputs an assignment to these variables, and (2) Assign is guaranteed to satisfy the following everywhere local consistency.

Everywhere local consistency. Assign does not make an assignment that violates any clause of φ. Specifically, when Assign is asked to make an assignment to the three variables that appear in a clause of φ, it makes an assignment that satisfies this clause.

(Actually, Assign is also guaranteed to be CNS, but we ignore it in this overview for simplicity.[11]) We note that Assign does not necessarily comply with a single global assignment, that is, Assign can assign different values to the same variable depending on the randomness and the input. We also note that this part of the analysis holds even for statements in $\mathcal{NP}$. For simplicity, in this overview we assume that Assign does not err (i.e., the everywhere local consistency holds with probability 1).

The second part of the analysis shows that the local assignment generator Assign that is obtained in the first part is guaranteed to comply with a single global "correct" assignment. A bit more precisely, this part shows the following.

---

[10] We follow the modularization by Paneth and Rothblum [PR14].

[11] Concretely, in this overview we assume that Assign is perfect no-signaling, i.e., that the RHS of the equation in Definition 10 is 0 even against computationally unbounded distinguishers.

Let *the correct assignment* to a wire in C (or, equivalently, to a variable in φ) be defined as the assignment that is obtained by evaluating C on x, and let Assign be called *correct* on a wire in C (or variable in φ) if Assign makes the correct assignment to it whenever Assign is asked to make an assignment to it. Then, Assign is correct on any wire in C (or variable in φ), and in particular correct on the output wire of C.

Roughly speaking, the above is shown in two steps.

1. First, it is shown, by relying on a specific structure of C, that Assign is correct on any wire in C if Assign is correct on each input wire of C.
2. Next, it is observed that Assign is indeed correct on each input wire of C due to the everywhere local consistency and the definition of φ (which has clauses that check that the assignment to the input wires of C is equal to x).

Finally, the last part of the analysis obtains the soundness by combining what are shown by the preceding two parts. In particular, it is observed that the existence of Assign as above implies $f(x) = 1$ since (1) on the one hand, Assign always assigns 1 to the output wire of C due to the everywhere local consistency and the definition of φ (which has clauses that check that the assignment to the output wire of C is 1), and (2) on the other hand, Assign always assigns $f(x)$ to the output wire of C since what is shown by the second part implies that Assign is correct on the output wire of C.

Remark 1 (Difficulty in the case of $\mathcal{NP}$ statements). The above analysis does not work in general for statements in $\mathcal{NP}$. A difficulty is that when the statement is in $\mathcal{NP}$, it is unclear how we should define the correct assignment in the second part of the analysis. Indeed, on the one hand, the correct assignment can be naturally defined in the case of statements in $\mathcal{P}$ since there exists a unique assignment that any successful prover is supposed to use (namely the assignment that is derived from x); on the other hand, in the case of statements in $\mathcal{NP}$, there does not exist a single such assignment. Jumping ahead, below we define well-behaving provers so that we can define the correct assignment naturally (while at the same time so that we can use cryptographic primitives later to force any prover to be well-behaving). $\Diamond$

4.2 Protocol Description

In this overview, we consider the following protocol $\langle C_1, R_1 \rangle = (\mathsf{C.Com}_1, \mathsf{C.Prv}_1, \mathsf{R.Com}_1, \mathsf{R.Prv.Q}_1, \mathsf{R.Prv.D}_1)$, which is slightly oversimplified from the actual protocol (see the full version of this paper for the actual protocol). (At this point, we temporarily ignore the open phase.) We warn that $\langle C_1, R_1 \rangle$ is not biding at all in sends no message in the commit phase.

Commit Phase:

Round 1: Given x_{COM} as the value to be committed, $\mathsf{C.Com}_1$ does the following.

1. Sample random $x^1_{\mathrm{MPC}}, \ldots, x^M_{\mathrm{MPC}}$ such that $x^1_{\mathrm{MPC}} \oplus \cdots \oplus x^M_{\mathrm{MPC}} = x_{\mathrm{COM}}$.
2. For each $\mu \in [M]$, define $x^\mu_{1,\mathrm{in}}$ as follows: sample random $r^\mu_{\mathrm{MPC}} \in \{0,1\}^{n_{\mathrm{MPC}}}$ and let $\mathsf{st}^\mu_0 := x^\mu_{\mathrm{MPC}} \parallel r^\mu_{\mathrm{MPC}}$, $\mathsf{i\text{-}msgs}^\mu_1 := 0^M$, $x^\mu_{1,\mathrm{in}} := \mathsf{st}^\mu_0 \parallel \mathsf{i\text{-}msgs}^\mu_1$.
3. Output an empty string as the commitment and store $\{x^\mu_{1,\mathrm{in}}\}_{\mu \in [M]}$ as the internal state.

Prove Phase:

Round 1: R.Prv.Q_1 does the following.
1. For each $\mu, \nu \in [M]$, obtain a set of queries $Q^{\mu,\nu}$ by running the verifier of KRR no-signaling PCP.
2. Output $\{Q^{\mu,\nu}\}_{\mu,\nu \in [M]}$ as the query.

Round 2: Given the statement f and the query $\{Q^{\mu,\nu}\}_{\mu,\nu \in [M]}$ as input, C.Prv$_1$ does the following.
1. Run the MPC protocol Π in the head for functionality f' and initial states $\{(\mathsf{st}^\mu_0, \mathsf{i\text{-}msgs}^\mu_1)\}_{\mu \in [M]}$,[12] where f' is defined as $f' : (y^1, \ldots, y^M) \mapsto f(y^1 \oplus \cdots \oplus y^M)$ and each $(\mathsf{st}^\mu_0, \mathsf{i\text{-}msgs}^\mu_1)$ is recovered from the internal state of the commit phase. Let $\{\mathsf{view}^\mu\}_{\mu \in [M]}$ be the view of the parties in this execution.
2. For each $\mu, \nu \in [M]$, obtain a PCP proof $\pi^{\mu:\nu}$ by running the prover of KRR no-signaling PCP on the 3SAT instance $\varphi^{\mu:\nu}$ that we will carefully design later—roughly speaking, $\varphi^{\mu:\nu}$ takes views of the parties P^μ, P^ν of Π as input, and checks that the views are consistent and that P^μ and P^ν output 1 in the views. (In an honest execution, C.Prv$_1$ uses $(\mathsf{view}^\mu, \mathsf{view}^\nu)$ to obtain a satisfying assignment to $\varphi^{\mu:\nu}$ and then uses it to obtain $\pi^{\mu:\nu}$.)
3. Output $\{\pi^{\mu:\nu}|_{Q^{\mu:\nu}}\}_{\mu,\nu \in [M]}$ as the proof.

Verification: Given the statement f and the proof $\{\pi^{*\mu:\nu}\}_{\mu,\nu \in [M]}$ as input, R.Prv.D_1 does the following.
1. Verify each $\pi^{*\mu:\nu}$ by running the verifier of KRR no-signaling PCP, and let $b^{\mu:\nu}$ be the verification result.
2. Output 1 if and only if $b^{\mu:\nu} = 1$ for every $\mu, \nu \in [M]$.

4.3   Proof of Soundness

We give an overview of the proof of the soundness. To focus on the main technical idea, in this overview we consider a weak version of the soundness where the extractor is only required to extract a committed value (rather than decommit the commitment as required in Definition 3). Thus, for any successful cheating prover, the extractor is required to extract a value such that the cheating prover cannot prove false statements on it.

---

[12] Each $\mathsf{i\text{-}msgs}^\mu_1$ is the dummy incoming messages of the first round (cf. Sect. 3.1).

Overall approach. At a very high level, the proof consists of two parts.

The first part is to obtain an extractor. Toward this end, we first observe that, by borrowing analyses from Kalai et al. [KRR14], we can convert any successful CNS cheating prover against $\langle C_1, R_1 \rangle$ into a *parallel local assignment generator* p-Assign, which gives M^2 local assignments to the 3SAT instances $\{\varphi^{\mu:\nu}\}_{\mu,\nu\in[M]}$ in parallel when it is given M^2 subsets of the variables as input. (To see this, observe that the prove phase of $\langle C_1, R_1 \rangle$ consists of M^2 parallel executions of KRR no-signaling PCP.) Then, we obtain an extractor by using p-Assign as follows.

- Note that since each $\varphi^{\mu:\nu}$ is a 3SAT instance that takes views of P^μ, P^ν as input, for any particular parts of P^μ and P^ν's views, $\varphi^{\mu:\nu}$ has variables that are supposed to be assigned with these parts. In the following, when we say that p-Assign makes an assignment to particular parts of P^μ and P^ν's views in $\varphi^{\mu:\nu}$, we mean that p-Assign makes an assignment to the variables that are supposed to be assigned with these parts in $\varphi^{\mu:\nu}$.
- Now, to extract the i-th bit of the committed value, the extractor obtains the i-th bit of each party's MPC input by asking p-Assign to make an assignment to the i-th bit of P^μ's input in $\varphi^{\mu:\mu}$ for every $\mu \in [M]$, and then takes XOR of the obtained bits.

The second part is to show that any cheating prover cannot prove false statements on the extracted value. In this part, the analysis proceeds similarly to the analysis of KRR no-signaling PCP. That is, we first define the correct assignment for each of $\varphi^{\mu:\nu}$, and next show that p-Assign always makes the correct assignment to any variable in any of $\varphi^{\mu:\nu}$.

Unfortunately, we do not know how to prove the second part against CNS cheating provers in general, and thus, we further restrict the provers to be "well-behaving".

Well-behaving provers. Roughly speaking, we define well-behaving provers as follows. Recall that the extractor is obtained by converting the cheating prover into a parallel local assignment generator. Now, we define well-behaving provers so that when we convert a successful CNS well-behaving prover into a parallel local assignment generator p-Assign, it satisfies the following two consistency properties.

Consistency on the initial states: Once the commit phase is completed, there exists a unique set of MPC initial states $\{(\mathsf{st}_0^\mu, \mathsf{i\text{-}msgs}_1^\mu)\}_{\mu\in[M]}$ such that p-Assign always makes assignments that are consistent with it (i.e., for any $\mu, \nu \in [M]$, when p-Assign is asked to make an assignment to any bit of the initial state of P^μ or P^ν in $\varphi^{\mu:\nu}$, then p-Assign always assigns the corresponding bit of $(\mathsf{st}_0^\mu, \mathsf{i\text{-}msgs}_1^\mu)$ or $(\mathsf{st}_0^\nu, \mathsf{i\text{-}msgs}_1^\nu)$).

Consistency on the views: For every $\mu, \nu, \xi \in [M]$, when p-Assign is asked to make an assignment to any bit of P^μ's view in both $\varphi^{\mu:\nu}$ and $\varphi^{\mu:\xi}$, then the value that p-Assign assigns to it in $\varphi^{\mu:\nu}$ is identical with the value that p-Assign assigns to it in $\varphi^{\mu:\xi}$. (The same holds for $\varphi^{\nu:\mu}$ and $\varphi^{\xi:\mu}$ and for $\varphi^{\mu:\nu}$ and $\varphi^{\xi:\mu}$ etc.)

Remark 2 (Intuition of the two consistency properties of p-Assign). Essentially, the above two consistency properties guarantee that p-Assign behaves as if it were obtained from an honest prover. This is because when p-Assign is indeed obtained from an honest prover, we can show that p-Assign always assigns the same MPC initial states once the commit phase is fixed, and assigns the same P^μ's view in any $\varphi^{\mu:\nu}$ and $\varphi^{\mu:\xi}$. (Roughly speaking, this is because in an honest execution of $\langle C_1, R_1 \rangle$, a set of MPC initial states are fixed in the commit phase, and the same P^μ's view is used for computing PCPs on any $\varphi^{\mu:\nu}$ and $\varphi^{\mu:\xi}$ in the prove phase.)   ◇

Before giving more details on the definition of well-behaving provers, we show that by restricting the provers to be well-behaving, we can complete the second part of the above overall approach, where our goal is to show that any cheating prover cannot prove false statements on the extracted value.

Showing that cheating prover cannot prove false statements. As stated earlier, the analysis proceeds similarly to the analysis of KRR no-signaling PCP. That is, we first define the correct assignment for each of $\varphi^{\mu:\nu}$, and next show that p-Assign always makes the correct assignment to any variable in any of $\varphi^{\mu:\nu}$.

Step 1: Defining the correct assignments. We define the correct assignments for $\{\varphi^{\mu:\nu}\}_{\mu,\nu \in [M]}$ by relying on that p-Assign satisfies the consistency on the initial states. Recall that it guarantees that once the commit phase is completed, there exists a unique set of MPC initial states $\{(\mathsf{st}_0^\mu, \mathsf{i\text{-}msgs}_1^\mu)\}_{\mu \in [M]}$ such that p-Assign always makes local assignments that are consistent with it. Then, we first define *the correct views* $\{\mathsf{view}^\mu\}_{\mu \in [M]}$ as the views that are obtained by executing Π on these unique initial states $\{(\mathsf{st}_0^\mu, \mathsf{i\text{-}msgs}_1^\mu)\}_{\mu \in [M]}$, and then define *the correct assignment* for $\varphi^{\mu:\nu}$ $(\mu, \nu \in [M])$ as the assignment that is derived from the correct views $(\mathsf{view}^\mu, \mathsf{view}^\nu)$ of P^μ, P^ν. (Recall that $\varphi^{\mu:\nu}$ is a 3SAT instance that takes views of P^μ, P^ν as input.)

From the definition, it is clear that p-Assign is correct on the initial states in every $\varphi^{\mu:\nu}$ (i.e., p-Assign always assigns the correct assignment to any bit of the initial states of P^μ, P^ν in $\varphi^{\mu:\nu}$ for every $\mu, \nu \in [M]$). Also, since the extractor extracts the committed value by taking XOR of the MPC inputs that are obtained from p-Assign, p-Assign's correctness on the initial states implies that the value that the extractor extracts is unique and is equal to the XOR of the MPC inputs that are used in the correct views.

Step 2: Showing that p-Assign is correct on every variable. At a high level, our approach is to apply the second part of the analysis of KRR no-signaling PCP (Sect. 4.1) on each party's next-message computation in a "round-by-round" manner. More concretely, our approach is to first show that p-Assign is correct on each of the variables that correspond to the internal states and incoming/outgoing messages of Round 1 of Π in every $\varphi^{\mu:\nu}$, next show it on each of the variables that correspond to those of Round 2 of Π in every $\varphi^{\mu:\nu}$, and so on.

Toward this end, we first remark that we design each 3SAT instance $\varphi^{\mu:\nu}$ carefully so that it has the following specific structure.

1. Let N_{round} be the round complexity of Π. Then, $\varphi^{\mu:\nu}$ has variables that can be partitioned into $4N_{\mathrm{round}}$ sequences of variables, $\boldsymbol{w}^{\xi}_{1,\mathrm{in}}, \boldsymbol{w}^{\xi}_{1,\mathrm{out}}, \ldots, \boldsymbol{w}^{\xi}_{N_{\mathrm{round}},\mathrm{in}}$, $\boldsymbol{w}^{\xi}_{N_{\mathrm{round}},\mathrm{out}}$ for $\xi \in \{\mu, \nu\}$, such that for each $\ell \in [N_{\mathrm{round}}]$:
   - $\boldsymbol{w}^{\xi}_{\ell,\mathrm{in}}$ is a sequence of variables such that the values that are assigned to them are interpreted as an internal state and incoming messages of P^{ξ} at the beginning of Round ℓ.[13]
   - $\boldsymbol{w}^{\xi}_{\ell,\mathrm{out}}$ is a sequence of variables such that the values that are assigned to them are interpreted as an internal state and outgoing messages of P^{ξ} at the end of Round ℓ.
2. $\varphi^{\mu:\nu}$ has clauses that check the following.
   - In each round, for each of P^{μ} and P^{ν}, its end state (i.e., its internal state at the end of the round) and outgoing messages are correctly derived from its start state (i.e., its internal state at the beginning of the round) and incoming messages.
   - In each round, for each of P^{μ} and P^{ν}, its start state is equal to its end state of the previous round.
   - In each round, P^{μ}'s incoming message from P^{ν} at the beginning of the round is equal to P^{ν}'s outgoing message to P^{μ} at the end of the previous round, and vise versa.
   - Both P^{μ} and P^{ν} output 1 in the last round.

We note that given consistent views of P^{μ}, P^{ν} in which they output 1, we can compute a satisfying assignment to the variables in $\varphi^{\mu:\nu}$ efficiently by obtaining each party's end state and outgoing messages of each round through the next-message function.

Now, we first show that if in every $\varphi^{\mu:\nu}$, p-Assign is correct on P^{μ} and P^{ν}'s start states and incoming messages in Round 1, then in every $\varphi^{\mu:\nu}$, p-Assign is also correct on P^{μ} and P^{ν}'s end states and outgoing messages in Round 1. A key observation on this step is that, essentially, what we need to show is that in every $\varphi^{\mu:\nu}$, for each $\xi \in \{\mu, \nu\}$, if p-Assign is correct on the input of P^{ξ}'s next-message computation of Round 1, then p-Assign is also correct on the output of it. Given this observation (and by designing the details of $\varphi^{\mu:\nu}$ appropriately), we can complete this step by just reusing the second part of the analysis of KRR no-signaling PCP, where it is shown that if Assign is correct on the input, then Assign is also correct on the output.

We next show that in every $\varphi^{\mu:\nu}$, if p-Assign is correct on P^{μ} and P^{ν}'s end states and outgoing messages in Round 1, then in every $\varphi^{\mu:\nu}$, p-Assign is also

---

[13] We think that each round of Π starts when each party receives incoming messages from the other parties, and ends when each party sends outgoing messages to the other parties.

correct on P^μ and P^ν's start states and incoming messages in Round 2. In this step, we consider three cases for each $\varphi^{\mu:\nu}$.

Case 1. We first consider the correctness on P^ξ's start state of Round 2 ($\xi \in \{\mu, \nu\}$). This case is easy and we just need to use the everywhere local consistency of p-Assign and the definition of $\varphi^{\mu:\nu}$. Specifically, since $\varphi^{\mu:\nu}$ has clauses that check that P^ξ's start state of Round 2 is equal to its end state of Round 1, the everywhere local consistency of p-Assign guarantees that p-Assign assigns the same value on P^ξ's start state of Round 2 and on P^ξ's end state of Round 1, and thus, if p-Assign is correct on the latter, it is also correct on the former.

Case 2. We next consider the correctness on P^μ's incoming message from P^ν and P^ν's incoming message from P^μ at the beginning of Round 2. Again, this case is easy and we just need to use the everywhere local consistency of p-Assign and the definition of $\varphi^{\mu:\nu}$ (which has clauses that check that the message that P^μ receives from P^ν at the beginning of Round 2 is equal to the one that P^ν sends to P^μ at the end of Round 1, and vise versa).

Case 3. We finally consider the correctness on P^μ and P^ν's incoming messages from the parties other than P^μ and P^ν at the beginning of Round 2. This case is not straightforward, and we rely on that p-Assign satisfies the consistency on the views, which is guaranteed since p-Assign is obtained from a well-behaving prover. Let us consider, for example, P^μ's incoming message from P^ξ ($\xi \notin \{\mu, \nu\}$). Then, since the consistency on the views guarantees that p-Assign assigns the same value in $\varphi^{\mu:\nu}$ and $\varphi^{\mu:\xi}$ as P^μ's incoming message from P^ξ, if p-Assign is correct on it in $\varphi^{\mu:\xi}$, then p-Assign is also correct on it in $\varphi^{\mu:\nu}$. Then, since we showed in Case 2 that p-Assign is indeed correct on it in $\varphi^{\mu:\xi}$, we conclude that p-Assign is correct on it in $\varphi^{\mu:\nu}$.[14]

By proceeding identically (and observing that, by definition, p-Assign is correct on P^μ and P^ν's start states and incoming messages in Round 1 in every $\varphi^{\mu:\nu}$), we conclude that p-Assign is correct on any variable, and in particular correct on P^μ and P^ν's final states in every $\varphi^{\mu:\nu}$.

Step 3: Obtaining soundness. On the one hand, the value that p-Assign assigns as the output of any party P^μ is always 1 due to the everywhere local consistency of p-Assign (recall that $\varphi^{\mu:\nu}$ has a clause that checks that P^μ's output is 1). On the other hand, since p-Assign is correct on the output of P^μ, it is also equal to the value that P^μ outputs in the correct views. Thus, P^μ outputs 1 in the correct view, which means that the statement proven by the prover is true on the XOR of the MPC inputs of the correct views. From the definition of the extractor, it follows that the prover cannot prove false statements on the extracted value.

---

[14] Note that we cannot use this argument if we try to reuse the analysis of Kalai et al. [KRR14] for each $\varphi^{\mu:\nu}$ individually (rather than in the round-by-round manner) since we show the correctness in $\varphi^{\mu:\nu}$ by using the correctness in $\varphi^{\mu:\xi}$.

More details of well-behaving provers. It remains to give an overview of the concrete definition of well-behaving provers. As we mentioned earlier, we define well-behaving provers so that when we convert a CNS well-behaving prover into a parallel local assignment generator p-Assign, then p-Assign has the aforementioned two consistency properties.

Before giving the definition of well-behaving provers, we give a few details about the construction of KRR no-signaling PCP.

- When a PCP proof π for a 3SAT instance φ is created by using a satisfying assignment x to φ, the PCP proof π contains an encoding of x,[15] i.e., there is a set of queries $D(X)$ such that $\pi|_{D(X)}$ is an encoding of x.
- Furthermore, we can make sure that in our protocol, each PCP proof $\pi^{\mu:\nu}$ for $\varphi^{\mu:\nu}$ (where $\pi^{\mu:\nu}$ is created by using $(\mathsf{view}^\mu, \mathsf{view}^\nu)$) contains encodings of $x_{1,\mathsf{in}}^\mu$, $x_{1,\mathsf{in}}^\nu$, view^μ, and view^ν, i.e., there are sets of queries $D(X_{1,\mathsf{in}}^\mu)$, $D(X_{1,\mathsf{in}}^\nu)$, $D(X^\mu)$, $D(X^\nu)$ such that:
  - $\pi^{\mu:\nu}|_{D(X_{1,\mathsf{in}}^\mu)}$ and $\pi^{\mu:\nu}|_{D(X_{1,\mathsf{in}}^\nu)}$ are encodings of $x_{1,\mathsf{in}}^\mu$ and $x_{1,\mathsf{in}}^\nu$, respectively.
  - $\pi^{\mu:\nu}|_{D(X^\mu)}$ and $\pi^{\mu:\nu}|_{D(X^\nu)}$ are encodings of view^μ and view^ν, respectively. (Recall that $x_{1,\mathsf{in}}^\mu := \mathsf{st}_0^\mu \parallel \mathsf{i}\text{-}\mathsf{msgs}_1^\mu$ and $x_{1,\mathsf{in}}^\nu := \mathsf{st}_0^\nu \parallel \mathsf{i}\text{-}\mathsf{msgs}_1^\nu$ are the initial states and dummy incoming messages that are computed in the commit phase.)

Then, informally speaking, a CNS prover is said to be *well-behaving* if it satisfies the following two consistency properties.

Consistency on $D(X_{1,\mathsf{in}}^\mu)$. Once the commit phase is completed, the prover gives the same response to a query in $D(X_{1,\mathsf{in}}^\mu)$ ($\mu \in [M]$) in different invocations. More concretely, for any queries $\{Q_0^{\mu:\nu}\}_{\mu,\nu\in[M]}, \{Q_1^{\mu:\nu}\}_{\mu,\nu\in[M]}$, any $\alpha, \beta, \gamma, \delta \in [M]$ such that $\exists \xi \in \{\alpha, \beta\} \cap \{\gamma, \delta\}$, and any $q \in Q_0^{\alpha:\beta} \cap Q_1^{\gamma:\delta} \cap D(X_{1,\mathsf{in}}^\xi)$, we have $\pi^{*\alpha:\beta}_0(q) = \pi^{*\gamma:\delta}_1(q)$, where $\pi^{*\alpha:\beta}_0$ and $\pi^{*\gamma:\delta}_1$ are generated as follows.

1. $(\mathsf{st}_C, \mathsf{com}) \leftarrow \langle \mathsf{C.Com}_1^*, \mathsf{R.Com}_1 \rangle$
2. $(f_0, \{\pi^{*\mu:\nu}_0\}_{\mu,\nu\in[M]}) \leftarrow \mathsf{C.Prv}_1^*(\mathsf{st}_C, \{Q_0^{\mu:\nu}\}_{\mu,\nu\in[M]})$
3. $(f_1, \{\pi^{*\mu:\nu}_1\}_{\mu,\nu\in[M]}) \leftarrow \mathsf{C.Prv}_1^*(\mathsf{st}_C, \{Q_1^{\mu:\nu}\}_{\mu,\nu\in[M]})$

Consistency on $D(X^\mu)$. The prover gives the same responses to a query in $D(X^\mu)$ ($\mu \in [M]$) in a single invocation. More concretely, for any queries $\{Q^{\mu:\nu}\}_{\mu,\nu\in[M]}$, any $\alpha, \beta, \gamma, \delta \in [M]$ such that $\exists \xi \in \{\alpha, \beta\} \cap \{\gamma, \delta\}$, and any $q \in Q^{\alpha:\beta} \cap Q^{\gamma:\delta} \cap D(X^\xi)$, we have $\pi^{*\alpha:\beta}(q) = \pi^{*\gamma:\delta}(q)$, where π^* is generated as follows.

1. $(\mathsf{st}_C, \mathsf{com}) \leftarrow \langle \mathsf{C.Com}_1^*, \mathsf{R.Com}_1 \rangle$
2. $(f, \{\pi^{*\mu:\nu}\}_{\mu,\nu\in[M]}) \leftarrow \mathsf{C.Prv}_1^*(\mathsf{st}_C, \{Q^{\mu:\nu}\}_{\mu,\nu\in[M]})$

To show that the above definition indeed implies the aforementioned two consistency properties of p-Assign, we need to see the details of p-Assign. Specifically, we rely on that p-Assign obtains local assignments by applying a procedure called *self-correction* on the cheating prover. In this overview, we do not give

---

[15] Concretely, a *low-degree extension* of x.

the details of self-correction, and we just note that p-Assign obtains local assignments in the following manner: p-Assign first creates some queries $Q^{\mu:\nu}$ for each $\mu, \nu \in [M]$ based on its input, next queries $\{Q^{\mu:\nu}\}_{\mu,\nu\in[M]}$ to the prover, and finally obtains the local assignments based on the prover's responses.

Now, at first sight, it seems trivial to show that the above definition of well-behaving provers implies the two consistency properties of p-Assign. Consider, for example, showing that the above definition implies that p-Assign has the consistency on the initial states. Then, since p-Assign obtains local assignments based on the prover's responses, and well-behaving provers are guaranteed to give unique responses to any queries on the initial states (i.e., any queries in $D(X_{1,\text{in}}^{\mu})$ ($\mu \in [M]$)), it seems trivial to show that p-Assign makes unique assignments on the initial states.

However, this intuition is wrong. For example, in the case of showing the consistency on the initial states, the problem is that even when making assignments on the initial states, p-Assign's queries to the prover includes those that are not in $D(X_{1,\text{in}}^{\mu})$ ($\mu \in [M]$), and well-behaving provers' responses to such queries are not necessarily unique.

Fortunately, this problem can be solved relatively easily by using a technique in a previous work [HR18]. Specifically, by letting the verifier of KRR no-signaling PCP do several additional tests on the prover, we can show that it suffices to consider a modified version of p-Assign, which obtains local assignments on the initial states (resp., the views) based solely on the prover's responses to the queries in $D(X_{1,\text{in}}^{\mu})$ (resp., in $D(X^{\mu})$).[16] On this modified version of p-Assign, it is indeed easy to show that the two consistency properties of well-behaving provers imply the two consistency properties of p-Assign by relying on analyses given in [KRR14].

Towards formal proof. Finally, we discuss what modifications are needed to turn the above proof idea into a formal proof.

First, we need to modify the extractor so that it can open the commitment (instead of just extracting a committed value) as required in Definition 3; along the way, we also need to define the open phase of the protocol appropriately. Recall that in the above, the extractor uses the parallel local assignment generator p-Assign to extract a committed value. Motivated by this construction of the extractor, we follow the following overall approach: we define the open phase so that running p-Assign jointly with the receiver is sufficient for the committer to succeed in the open phase. To implement this approach, we rely on that, as mentioned above, p-Assign obtains local assignments in the following manner: p-Assign first creates some queries $Q^{\mu:\nu}$ for each $\mu, \nu \in [M]$ based on its input, next queries $\{Q^{\mu:\nu}\}_{\mu,\nu\in[M]}$ to the prover, and finally obtains the local

---

[16] Concretely, we use *layer-parallel low-degree tests* [HR18] to guarantee that the initial states (resp., the views) that are recovered through self-correction in p-Assign do not change when the queries are sampled from $D(X_{1,\text{in}}^{\mu})$ (resp., from $D(X^{\mu})$) rather than from $D(X)$.

assignments based on the prover's responses. Given this structure of p-Assign, we define the open phase as follows.

1. In the first round, the receiver computes queries as in p-Assign and sends them to the committer.
2. In the second round, the committer gives responses to the queries.
3. Finally, the receiver computes the local assignments from the responses as in p-Assign and then uses them to extract a committed value as in the extractor.

Then, we modify the extractor so that it simply forwards the queries from the receiver to the cheating prover and next forwards the responses from the cheating prover to the receiver. Since the extracted value is computed from the output of p-Assign just as before (the only difference is that now p-Assign is executed jointly between the extractor and the receiver), we can still prove that any CNS well-behaving cheating prover cannot prove false statements on the extracted value. Furthermore, we can show that the above open phase is strong enough to guarantee a meaningful binding property. Specifically, by letting the receiver make additional queries in the open phase,[17] we can prove the binding property against CNS *well-behaving decommitters*, which are defined similarly to CNS well-behaving provers. (The proof of the binding property proceeds essentially in the same way as we show that p-Assign satisfies the consistency on the initial states in the proof of the soundness against well-behaving provers, where we show that once the commit phase is completed, the assignments by p-Assign on the MPC initial states—which define the committed value—are unique.)

Second, we need to consider the case that p-Assign can err (i.e., the everywhere local consistency does not necessarily hold with probability 1). Fortunately, this case is already handled in Kalai et al. [KRR14], and we can handle it identically. (Concretely, when showing that p-Assign is correct on every variable in the round-by-round way, we only show that p-Assign is correct *on average*, i.e., instead of showing that p-Assign is correct on any variables that correspond to, say, the start state and incoming message of a round, we only show that p-Assign is correct on randomly chosen $\omega(\log \lambda)$ such variables. It is shown in [KRR14] that showing such average-case correctness is sufficient to prove the soundness.)

Third, we need to consider adaptive soundness, where the cheating prover chooses the statement to prove at the last round of the prove phase. Fortunately, adaptive soundness is already considered in previous works (e.g., [BHK17]), and we can handle it identically.

5   Overview of Step 2 (Non-WI Scheme with Soundness Against CNS Provers)

We give an overview of our non-WI commit-and-prove protocol $\langle C_2, R_2 \rangle$, which is $(1 - \mathsf{negl})$-sound against CNS provers.

---

[17] Specifically, the receiver make queries for a low-degree test (just like the verifier of KRR succinct argument does) so that we can reuse analyses of Kalai et al. [KRR14] as in the proof of soundness.

Our high-level approach is to upgrade the protocol $\langle C_1, R_1 \rangle$ that we give in Step 1 so that the soundness holds against any (not necessarily well-behaving) CNS provers. Recall that, roughly speaking, an adversary is well-behaving if for every $\mu \in [M]$,

1. it does not give different responses to a query in $D(X_{1,\text{in}}^{\mu})$ in different invocations, and
2. it does not give different responses to a query in $D(X^{\mu})$ in a single invocation,

where $D(X_{1,\text{in}}^{\mu})$ and $D(X^{\mu})$ are sets of queries such that in $\langle C_1, R_1 \rangle$, the prover is supposed to create PCPs $\{\pi^{\mu:\nu}\}_{\mu,\nu \in [M]}$ such that $\pi^{\mu:\nu}|_{D(X_{1,\text{in}}^{\mu})}$ is an encoding of $x_{1,\text{in}}^{\mu}$ and $\pi^{\mu:\nu}|_{D(X^{\mu})}$ is an encoding of view^{μ} for every $\nu \in [M]$, where $x_{1,\text{in}}^{\mu}$ is the value that is fixed in the commit phase and view^{μ} is the view that is fixed in the prove phase. Naturally, we enforce this behavior on the prover by relying on collision-resistant hash functions: we require the prover to publish the roots of the tree-hash of the encodings of $\{x_{1,\text{in}}^{\mu}\}_{\mu \in [M]}$ and $\{\text{view}^{\mu}\}_{\mu \in [M]}$, and also require it to give responses along with appropriate certificates when it is queried on these values.

More concretely, we consider the following protocol (which is slightly oversimplified from the actual protocol). In the following, for a hash function hf, we denote by $\text{TreeHash}_{\text{hf}}$ an algorithm that computes the Merkle tree-hash of the input.

Commit Phase
Round 1: R.Com_2 sends a hash function $\text{hf} \in \mathcal{H}$ to C.Com_2.
Round 2: Given $(x_{\text{COM}}, \text{hf})$ as input, C.Com_2 obtains $\{x_{1,\text{in}}^{\mu}\}_{\mu \in [M]}$ by running $\text{C.Com}_1(x_{\text{COM}})$, computes encodings $\{X_{1,\text{in}}^{\mu}\}_{\mu \in [M]}$ of them, and then outputs $\{\text{rt}_{1,\text{in}}^{\mu} := \text{TreeHash}_{\text{hf}}(X_{1,\text{in}}^{\mu})\}_{\mu \in [M]}$ as the commitment and store $(\text{hf}, \{X_{1,\text{in}}^{\mu}\}_{\mu \in [M]})$ as the internal state.

Prove Phase
Round 1: R.Prv.Q_2 works identically with R.Prv.Q_1. That is, R.Prv.Q_2 obtains $\{Q^{\mu,\nu}\}_{\mu,\nu \in [M]}$ just like R.Prv.Q_1 does, and outputs $\{Q^{\mu,\nu}\}_{\mu,\nu \in [M]}$ as the query.
Round 2: Given the statement f and the query $\{Q^{\mu,\nu}\}_{\mu,\nu \in [M]}$ as input, C.Prv_2 does the following.
1. Obtain $\{\text{view}^{\mu}\}_{\mu \in [M]}$ and $\{\pi^{\mu:\nu}\}_{\mu,\nu \in [M]}$ just like C.Prv_1 does.
2. Compute encodings $\{X^{\mu}\}_{\mu \in [M]}$ of $\{\text{view}^{\mu}\}_{\mu \in [M]}$, and compute $\{\text{rt}^{\mu} := \text{TreeHash}_{\text{hf}}(X^{\mu})\}_{\mu \in [M]}$.
3. Augment each $\pi^{\mu:\nu}$ as follows.
   - Augment each symbol in $\pi^{\mu:\nu}|_{D(X_{1,\text{in}}^{\xi})}$ ($\xi \in \{\mu, \nu\}$) with a certificate for opening $\text{rt}_{1,\text{in}}^{\xi}$ to it.
   - Augment each symbol in $\pi^{\mu:\nu}|_{D(X^{\xi}) \setminus D(X_{1,\text{in}}^{\xi})}$ ($\xi \in \{\mu, \nu\}$) with a certificate for opening rt^{ξ} to it.
4. Output $(\{\text{rt}^{\mu}\}_{\mu \in [M]}, \{\pi^{\mu:\nu}|_{Q^{\mu:\nu}}\}_{\mu,\nu \in [M]})$ as the proof.

Verification: Given the commitment $\{rt_{1,in}^{\mu}\}_{\mu \in [M]}$, the statement f, and the proof $(\{rt^{\mu}\}_{\mu \in [M]}, \{\pi^{*\mu:\nu}\}_{\mu,\nu \in [M]})$ as input, $R.Prv.D_2$ works identically with $R.Prv.D_1$ except that before the verification, each $\pi^{*\mu:\nu}$ is "filtered" as follows.

- Replace each symbol $(x, cert)$ in $\pi^{*\mu:\nu}|_{D(X_{1,in}^{\xi})}$ $(\xi \in \{\mu, \nu\})$ with x if cert is a valid certificate for opening $rt_{1,in}^{\xi}$ to x, and replace it with $\perp$ otherwise.

- Replace each symbol $(x, cert)$ in $\pi^{*\mu:\nu}|_{D(X^{\xi}) \setminus D(X_{1,in}^{\xi})}$ $(\xi \in \{\mu, \nu\})$ with x if cert is a valid certificate for opening rt^{ξ} to x, and replace it with $\perp$ otherwise.

We prove the soundness of $\langle C_2, R_2 \rangle$ by relying on the soundness of $\langle C_1, R_1 \rangle$. Specifically, for any cheating committer-prover $C_2^* = (C.Com_2^*, C.Prv_2^*)$ against $\langle C_2, R_2 \rangle$, we consider the following cheating committer-prover $C_1^* = (C.Com_1^*, C.Prv_1^*)$ against $\langle C_1, R_1 \rangle$.

- **Committer.** $C.Com_1^*$ runs $(st_C, com) \leftarrow \langle C.Com_2^*, R.Com_2 \rangle$ internally, sends an empty string to $R.Com_1$ as the commitment, and stores (com, st_C) as the internal state.

- **Prover.** Given (com, st_C) and $\{Q^{\mu:\nu}\}_{\mu,\nu \in [M]}$ as input, $C.Prv_1^*$ first runs $(f, \{rt^{\mu}\}_{\mu \in [M]}, \{\pi^{*\mu:\nu}\}_{\mu,\nu \in [M]}) \leftarrow C.Prv_2^*(st_C, \{Q^{\mu:\nu}\}_{\mu,\nu \in [M]})$. Then, $C.Prv_1^*$ filters each $\pi^{*\mu:\nu}$ as in the verification of $\langle C_2, R_2 \rangle$, and sends $(f, \{\pi^{*\mu:\nu}\}_{\mu,\nu \in [M]})$ to $R.Prv_1$ as the proof.

It is straightforward to show that (1) C_1^* is successful if C_2^* is successful and (2) C_1^* is well-behaving CNS. (The latter follows from the the binding property of $TreeHash_{hf}$.)

6   Overview of Subsequent Steps of Proof of Theorem 1

In Step 3, we upgrade the soundness to the one with negligible soundness error. Fortunately, this type of soundness amplification is already studied by Kalai et al. [KRR14] as mentioned in Sect. 3, and it suffices to apply their soundness amplification on the protocol $\langle C_2, R_2 \rangle$ that we obtained in Step 2. Concretely, in this step, we just borrow a soundness amplification technique from [KRR14, BHK17], which amplifies soundness by letting the verifier use a smaller threshold parameter for the PCP decision algorithm (i.e., letting the verifier tolerate a smaller number of failures on the tests that it applies on the prover).

In Step 4, we upgrade the soundness to the one against any (not necessarily CNS) adversaries. Again, this type of soundness amplification is already studied by Kalai et al. [KRR14] as mentioned in Sect. 3, and it suffices to apply their soundness amplification on the protocol $\langle C_3, R_3 \rangle$ that we obtained in Step 3. Concretely, in this step, we just borrow a transformation from [KRR14], which enforces CNS behavior on the committer by encrypting the verifier queries by PIR. (Intuitively, encrypting the verifier queries by PIR is helpful to enforce

CNS behavior since it forces the prover to answer each query independently of the other queries.)

In Step 5, we add the WI property while tolerating that the soundness error increases to a constant. Toward this end, we augment the protocol $\langle C_4, R_4 \rangle$ that we obtained in Step 4 with commitment schemes and OT by using these two primitives as in the non-succinct protocol that we sketched in Sect. 1.2. The soundness and WI of the resultant protocol $\langle C_5, R_5 \rangle$ can be shown similarly to those of the non-succinct protocol in Sect. 1.2. That is, the soundness follows from the security of OT and the soundness of $\langle C_4, R_4 \rangle$,[18] and the WI property follows from the 2-*privacy* of $\langle C_4, R_4 \rangle$, which roughly guarantees that the verifier does not learn any secret information if it only obtains one of the M^2 KRR nosignaling PCP strings. (The 2-privacy of $\langle C_4, R_4 \rangle$, in turn, follows immediately from the 2-privacy of the underlying MPC protocol Π.)

A   On Verification Time

The verification of our protocol is not succinct since we use a simpler version of KRR succinct argument where the verifier naively evaluates a low-degree extension (LDE) of the indicator function of a 3CNF formula whose size is polynomially related to the complexity of the statement. In Kalai et al. [KRR14] and subsequent works [BHK17, HR18], the verification is made succinct by observing that when the statement to be proven satisfies some conditions, the evaluation of the LDE can be either recursively delegated to the prover succinctly or locally performed by the verifier efficiently. In our protocol, KRR succinct argument is used for proving statements that are related to the next-message function of the underlying perfect 2-privacy MPC protocol (cf. Sect. 1.2 and Sect. 4). Thus, if we can show that the above-mentioned conditions are satisfied for a specific perfect 2-privacy MPC protocol, the verification of our protocol can be made succinct.

B   On Definition of Commit-and-prove Protocols

B.1   Differences from Definition in Khurana et al. [KOS18]

Our definition of commit-and-prove protocols in Sect. 2.2 has several differences from the definition in Khurana et al. [KOS18]. First, our definition has several syntactical differences.

- Instead of thinking the prove phase as a part of the commit phase, we separate the prove phase from the commit phase.
- We focus on the case that each of the prove phase and the open phase consists of two rounds.

Next, our definition is stronger than the definition of Khurana et al. [KOS18] in the following points.

---

[18] Formally, as in the case of the non-succinct protocol in Sect. 1.2, complexity leveraging is required.

- We explicitly define the soundness and witness indistinguishability in the delayed-input setting, where the statement to be proven is chosen at the last round of the prove phase.
- In the definition of the soundness, we require the extractor to decommit the commitment to a value on which any committer cannot prove false statements. (In the definition in [KOS18], the extractor just outputs such a value without decommitment, with the guarantee that any committer cannot decommit the commitment to a value other than the extracted one.)
  We think that requiring the extractor to decommit the commitment is important, as otherwise the definition would not prevent an attack where the committer gives an accepting proof on an invalid commitment (i.e., a commitment that cannot be opened to any value).[19] (This is because even if such an attack is possible, we can still show that any committer cannot decommit the commitment to a value other than the extracted one, since an invalid commitment cannot be opened to any value.) We remark that such an attack is possible if a commit-and-prove protocol is naively executed in parallel multiple times.

Finally, our definition is weaker than the definition of Khurana et al. [KOS18] in the following points.

- In the definitions of the binding and the soundness, the extractor succeeds only on an overwhelming fraction of the executions of the commit phase, rather than on any execution of the commit phase.
- In the definition of the soundness, the extractor is allowed to depend on the success probability of the cheating committer.

B.2   Rationale Behind Our Definition

Since our definition of commit-and-prove protocols in Sect. 2.2 might look too cumbersome, we explain the rationale behind it.

First, binding and witness-indistinguishability are defined naturally, and the only complication is that we allow the open phase to be interactive in the definition of binding. To guarantee a stronger notion of binding, our definition considers an adversary that obtains two sets of receiver decommitment queries simultaneously (rather than obtain each of them separately).

Next, soundness is defined similarly to proof-of-knowledge of interactive proofs [GMR89]. A complication is that we define it so that it guarantees the adaptive delayed-input property, i.e., it holds against an adversary that chooses the statement to prove at the last round of the prove phase.[20] To guarantee proof-of-knowledge with the adaptive delayed-input property, our definition requires

---

[19] We remark that the schemes by Khurana et al. [KOS18] are designed to prevent such an attack. What we claim is that the definition by Khurana et al. [KOS18] does not prevent such an attack.

[20] The adaptive delayed-input property is required to, e.g., upgrade our WI commit-and-prove protocol to a ZK one by using the transformation of Khurana et al. [KOS18].

that if a cheating prover convinces the verifier for a commitment com with sufficiently high probability, then there exists a value x^* such that (1) the extractor can decommit com to x^* and (2) the cheating prover cannot prove false statements about x^*. (We remark that the extractor is required to succeed in the decommitment of each bit of x^* with overwhelming probability so that we can obtain the whole x^* by repeatedly using the extractor.)

References

[AL17] Asharov, G., Lindell, Y.: A full proof of the BGW protocol for perfectly secure multiparty computation. J. Cryptol. **30**(1), 58–151 (2017). https://doi.org/10.1007/s00145-015-9214-4

[BBK16] Bitansky, N., Brakerski, Z., Kalai, Y., Paneth, O., Vaikuntanathan, V.: 3-message zero knowledge against human ignorance. In: Hirt, M., Smith, A. (eds.) TCC 2016-B, Part I. LNCS, vol. 9985, pp. 57–83. Springer, Heidelberg (2016). https://doi.org/10.1007/978-3-662-53641-4_3

[BGW88] Ben-Or, M., Goldwasser, S., Wigderson, A.: Completeness theorems for non-cryptographic fault-tolerant distributed computation (extended abstract). In: 20th ACM STOC, pp. 1–10. ACM Press, May 1988

[BHK17] Brakerski, Z., Holmgren, J., Kalai, Y.T.: Non-interactive delegation and batch NP verification from standard computational assumptions. In: Hatami, H., McKenzie, P., King, V. (eds.) 49th ACM STOC, pp. 474–482. ACM Press, June 2017

[BK20] Brakerski, Z., Kalai, Y.: Witness indistinguishability for any single-round argument with applications to access control. In: Kiayias, A., Kohlweiss, M., Wallden, P., Zikas, V. (eds.) PKC 2020, Part II. LNCS, vol. 12111, pp. 97–123. Springer, Cham (2020). https://doi.org/10.1007/978-3-030-45388-6_4

[BKK18] Badrinarayanan, S., Kalai, Y.T., Khurana, D., Sahai, A., Wichs, D.: Succinct delegation for low-space non-deterministic computation. In: Diakonikolas, I., Kempe, D., Henzinger, M. (eds.) 50th ACM STOC, pp. 709–721. ACM Press, June 2018

[CLOS02] Canetti, R., Lindell, Y., Ostrovsky, R., Sahai, A.: Universally composable two-party and multi-party secure computation. In: 34th ACM STOC, pp. 494–503. ACM Press May 2002

[GGP10] Gennaro, R., Gentry, C., Parno, B.: Non-interactive verifiable computing: outsourcing computation to untrusted workers. In: Rabin, T. (ed.) CRYPTO 2010. LNCS, vol. 6223, pp. 465–482. Springer, Heidelberg (2010). https://doi.org/10.1007/978-3-642-14623-7_25

[GK96] Goldreich, O., Krawczyk, H.: On the composition of zero-knowledge proof systems. SIAM J. Comput. **25**(1), 169–192 (1996)

[GKR15] Goldwasser, S., Kalai, Y.T., Rothblum, G.N.: Delegating computation: interactive proofs for muggles. J. ACM **62**(4), 27:1–27:64 (2015)

[GLOV12] Goyal, V., Lee, C.-K., Ostrovsky, R., Visconti, I.: Constructing non-malleable commitments: a black-box approach. In: 53rd FOCS, pp. 51–60. IEEE Computer Society Press, October 2012

[GMR89] Goldwasser, S., Micali, S., Rackoff, C.: The knowledge complexity of interactive proof systems. SIAM J. Comput. **18**(1), 186–208 (1989)

[GMW87] Goldreich, O., Micali, S., Wigderson, A.: How to play any mental game or a completeness theorem for protocols with honest majority. In: Aho, A. (ed.) 19th ACM STOC, pp. 218–229. ACM Press, May 1987

[GOSV14] Goyal, V., Ostrovsky, R., Scafuro, A., Visconti, I.: Black-box non-black-box zero knowledge. In: Shmoys, D.B. (ed.) 46th ACM STOC, pp. 515–524. ACM Press, May/June 2014

[HR18] Holmgren, J., Rothblum, R.: Delegating computations with (almost) minimal time and space overhead. In: Thorup, M. (ed.) 59th FOCS, pp. 124–135. IEEE Computer Society Press, October 2018

[HV16] Hazay, C., Venkitasubramaniam, M.: On the power of secure two-party computation. In: Robshaw, M., Katz, J. (eds.) CRYPTO 2016, Part II. LNCS, vol. 9815, pp. 397–429. Springer, Heidelberg (2016). https://doi.org/10.1007/978-3-662-53008-5_14

[HV18] Hazay, C., Venkitasubramaniam, M.: Round-optimal fully black-box zero-knowledge arguments from one-way permutations. In: Beimel, A., Dziembowski, S. (eds.) TCC 2018, Part I. LNCS, vol. 11239, pp. 263–285. Springer, Cham (2018). https://doi.org/10.1007/978-3-030-03807-6_10

[IKOS09] Ishai, Y., Kushilevitz, E., Ostrovsky, R., Sahai, A.: Zero-knowledge proofs from secure multiparty computation. SIAM J. Comput. 39(3), 1121–1152 (2009)

[IW14] Ishai, Y., Weiss, M.: Probabilistically checkable proofs of proximity with zero-knowledge. In: Lindell, Y. (ed.) TCC 2014. LNCS, vol. 8349, pp. 121–145. Springer, Heidelberg (2014). https://doi.org/10.1007/978-3-642-54242-8_6

[Kil92] Kilian, J.: A note on efficient zero-knowledge proofs and arguments (extended abstract). In: 24th ACM STOC, pp. 723–732. ACM Press, May 1992

[KOS18] Khurana, D., Ostrovsky, R., Srinivasan, A.: Round optimal black-box "commit-and-prove". In: Beimel, A., Dziembowski, S. (eds.) TCC 2018, Part I. LNCS, vol. 11239, pp. 286–313. Springer, Cham (2018). https://doi.org/10.1007/978-3-030-03807-6_11

[KP16] Kalai, Y., Paneth, O.: Delegating RAM computations. In: Hirt, M., Smith, A. (eds.) TCC 2016, Part II. LNCS, vol. 9986, pp. 91–118. Springer, Heidelberg (2016). https://doi.org/10.1007/978-3-662-53644-5_4

[KRR14] Kalai, Y.T., Raz, R., Rothblum, R.D.: How to delegate computations: the power of no-signaling proofs. In: Shmoys, D.B. (ed.) 46th ACM STOC, pp. 485–494. ACM Press, May/June 2014

[LP12] Lin, H., Pass, R.: Black-box constructions of composable protocols without set-up. In: Safavi-Naini, R., Canetti, R. (eds.) CRYPTO 2012. LNCS, vol. 7417, pp. 461–478. Springer, Heidelberg (2012). https://doi.org/10.1007/978-3-642-32009-5_27

[MPP20] Morgan, A., Pass, R., Polychroniadou, A.: Succinct non-interactive secure computation. In: Canteaut, A., Ishai, Y. (eds.) EUROCRYPT 2020, Part II. LNCS, vol. 12106, pp. 216–245. Springer, Cham (2020). https://doi.org/10.1007/978-3-030-45724-2_8

[PR14] Paneth, O., Rothblum, G.N.: Publicly verifiable non-interactive arguments for delegating computation. Cryptology ePrint Archive, Report 2014/981 (2014). http://eprint.iacr.org/2014/981

[PW09] Pass, R., Wee, H.: Black-box constructions of two-party protocols from one-way functions. In: Reingold, O. (ed.) TCC 2009. LNCS, vol. 5444, pp. 403–418. Springer, Heidelberg (2009). https://doi.org/10.1007/978-3-642-00457-5_24

Efficient Constant-Round MPC with Identifiable Abort and Public Verifiability

Carsten Baum[1], Emmanuela Orsini[2(✉)], Peter Scholl[1],
and Eduardo Soria-Vazquez[1]

[1] Aarhus University, Aarhus, Denmark
[2] imec-COSIC, KU Leuven, Leuven, Belgium
emmanuela.orsini@kuleuven.be

Abstract. Recent years have seen a tremendous growth in the interest in secure multiparty computation (MPC) and its applications. While much progress has been made concerning its efficiency, many current, state-of-the-art protocols are vulnerable to *Denial of Service attacks*, where a cheating party may prevent the honest parties from learning the output of the computation, whilst remaining anonymous. The security model of *identifiable abort* aims to prevent these attacks, by allowing honest parties to agree upon the identity of a cheating party, who can then be excluded in the future. Several existing MPC protocols offer security with identifiable abort against a dishonest majority of corrupted parties. However, all of these protocols have a round complexity that scales linearly with the depth of the circuit (and are therefore unsuitable for use in high latency networks) or use cryptographic primitives or techniques that have a high computational overhead.

In this work, we present the first efficient MPC protocols with identifiable abort in the dishonest majority setting, which run in a constant number of rounds and make only black-box use of cryptographic primitives. Our main construction is built from highly efficient primitives in a careful way to achieve identifiability at a low cost. In particular, we avoid the use of public-key operations outside of a setup phase, incurring a relatively low overhead on top of the fastest currently known constant-round MPC protocols based on garbled circuits. Our construction also avoids the use of adaptively secure primitives and heavy zero-knowledge machinery, which was inherent in previous works. In addition, we show how to upgrade our protocol to achieve *public verifiability* using a public bulletin board, allowing any external party to verify correctness of the computation or identify a cheating party.

C. Baum—Supported by the European Research Council (ERC) under the European Unions' Horizon 2020 research and innovation programme under grant agreement No 669255 (MPCPRO) as well as the BIU Center for Research in Applied Cryptography and Cyber Security in conjunction with the Israel National Cyber Bureau in the Prime Minister's Office. Part of this work was done while the author was at Bar Ilan University.
E. Orsini—Supported in part by ERC Advanced Grant ERC-2015-AdG-IMPaCT.
P. Scholl—Supported in part by the Danish Independent Research Council under Grant-ID DFF-6108-00169 (FoCC) and an Aarhus University Research Foundation (AUFF) starting grant.
E. Soria-Vazquez—Supported by the Carlsberg Foundation under the Semper Ardens Research Project CF18-112 (BCM).

© International Association for Cryptologic Research 2020
D. Micciancio and T. Ristenpart (Eds.): CRYPTO 2020, LNCS 12171, pp. 562–592, 2020.
https://doi.org/10.1007/978-3-030-56880-1_20

1 Introduction

Secure Multi-Party Computation (MPC) is a general term for techniques which allow a set of n parties to compute a function f on their private inputs such that only the output of the function becomes known. Using MPC as a tool to achieve security generally comes with an inherent slowdown over insecure solutions, so using the right MPC protocol with suitable properties is crucial in order to foster adoption in practice. For certain requirements, it is even known that MPC is impossible to achieve.

For example, while in the *honest majority* setting, where more than half of the parties are honest, MPC for any function is possible, when there is a *dishonest majority* it is well-known that *fairness* for MPC is impossible, in general [15]. The fairness property means that if any corrupted party learns the output then all the honest parties do as well, so a dishonest party cannot withhold the output from the other parties. To work around this impossibility, most MPC protocols for dishonest majority settle for the weaker notion of *security with abort*, which allows the adversary to abort the protocol, possibly after learning the output.

However, a major downside of this model is that it does not protect against denial-of-service attacks. This motivates the stronger model of *MPC with identifiable abort*, or ID-MPC, where if the adversary aborts then the honest parties will agree upon the identity of a cheating party. This allows the honest parties to exclude cheaters and re-run the aborting protocol, and it can also be combined with a distributed ledger (such as in [35]) to achieve monetary fairness (see e.g. [4] for an overview). The concept of ID-MPC was first implicitly considered in the context of covert security, and more formally studied in later works [16,29].

A related, desirable property of an MPC protocol is *public verifiability* [3,45], which allows any external party to verify the correctness of some claimed outputs of the protocol by, for instance, inspecting public values posted to a bulletin board. This is important for settings where the computation is of particular interest to the public, for example, it may be desirable for the results of a research study on private medical data to be publicly verifiable. It is also relevant to the client-server setting, where many clients outsource a computation to a set of non-colluding servers and wish to verify the result, without interacting with the servers.

As well as security properties like the above, an important aspect when choosing an MPC protocol is its efficiency. This can be measured in terms of number of rounds of communication, total communication complexity (i.e. amount of data sent over the network), and computational overhead (compared with computing the function in the clear). In this work, we consider the problem of efficiently constructing MPC in the dishonest majority setting providing security with identifiable abort and public verifiability, in a constant number of rounds of interaction.

1.1 Previous Work on Constant-Round MPC, Identifiable Abort and Public Verifiability

Constant-Round MPC. The main tool for building constant-round MPC is garbled circuits, which were introduced by Yao [49] for 2-party secure computation. Garbled circuits were generalized to the multi-party setting by Beaver, Micali and Rogaway [6], who constructed a constant-round MPC protocol (called "BMR") that can support a dishonest majority of participants. The BMR protocol makes heavy, non-black-box use of a pseudorandom generator, so is inefficient in practice.

Subsequently, constant-round MPC making only *black-box* use of cryptographic primitives was presented by Damgård and Ishai [18], for the honest majority setting, and extended to the case of a dishonest majority by Ishai et al. [30]. Later, more efficient black-box solutions with active security for dishonest majority were introduced by Lindell et al. [36,37], who used somewhat homomorphic encryption in a preprocessing phase of the protocols. Currently, the most efficient protocols are those by Wang et al. [48] and Hazay et al. [26], which use oblivious transfer (OT) instead of homomorphic encryption, and can be instantiated very efficiently using the TinyOT-protocol [21,40] based on fast OT extension techniques [28,31].

ID-MPC in the Dishonest Majority Setting. The seminal MPC protocol of Goldreich, Micali and Wigderson [24] can be combined with any public-coin zero-knowledge proof system to obtain ID-MPC for dishonest majority, and the same holds for the BMR protocol [6] to achieve a constant round complexity. However, the resulting protocols make extensive, non-black-box use of cryptographic primitives and are not practical. Additionally, also [41] implies a constant-round ID-MPC scheme that is not black-box (and secure in the stand-alone setting as observed by [7]. More recently, there has been interest in concretely efficient ID-MPC. Ishai, Ostrovsky and Zikas [29] presented an ID-MPC protocol in the preprocessing model, where a trusted dealer gives the parties some correlated randomness, with information-theoretic security. They also gave a general compiler that allows removing the trusted dealer, leading to the first ID-MPC protocol making only black-box use of cryptographic primitives, namely, an adaptively secure oblivious transfer protocol and a broadcast channel. Concurrent to this work, Brandt et al. [9] studied the feasibility of ID-MPC from lower-cardinality primitives as well as the relation of the conflict graph to identifiable abort. Their work is orthogonal to ours, as we are interested in concrete and practical constructions.

Baum et al. [5] also construct ID-MPC in the preprocessing model, with better concrete efficiency, by combining a variant of the BDOZ protocol [8] with information-theoretic signatures, and homomorphic encryption for the preprocessing. Other works [17,46] have added identifiability to the practical SPDZ protocol [19], obtaining more efficient results in a similar setting. These works, while concretely quite practical, all require a number of rounds of interaction that scales *linearly* with the multiplicative depth of the circuit being evaluated.

MPC with Public Verifiability. The idea of secure computation with public verifiability was first introduced in the two-party setting for covert security by Asharov and Orlandi [2]. Subsequent works [27,33] later improved upon the efficiency of their construction, and in particular the size of the cheating certificate, for which the work of Hong et al. [27] requires <400 bytes for 128 bit security.

The notion of public verifiability for actively secure dishonest majority MPC (with potentially all parties being corrupted) has been introduced independently by Baum et al. [3] and Schoenmakers and Veeningen [45]. Their work ensures privacy if at least one party is honest and correctness for any level of corruption. In subsequent works, [5,17] independently showed how to combine public verifiability and identifiable abort for general computations where either the correctness of the output is attested or a cheater will be found by a third party. Both works rely on expensive tools in a preprocessing phase (lattice-based encryption for large fields), have a circuit depth-dependent round complexity and have not been implemented in practice. Another, more general approach for publicly verifiable MPC with identifiable abort was given in [32] where the authors presented a general compiler based on the approach of [29].

1.2   Contributions

In this work, we present the first *concretely efficient* and *constant-round* MPC protocols that provide security with identifiable abort and public verifiability in the dishonest majority setting. Note that all our protocols are in the setting of static corruptions.

Our results for identifiable abort assume access to a *broadcast channel*, while for public verifiability we need a public *bulletin board*, and in both cases we count round complexity by assuming that their consumes a single round. In practice, if using an authenticated broadcast protocol [20,43] to implement this, each broadcast requires $\Omega(n)$ rounds of point-to-point messages [23]. Alternatively, broadcast can be realized using a bulletin board or blockchain, giving a constant number of rounds of interaction with this functionality. Note that it seems difficult to avoid the use of broadcast, since MPC with identifiable abort itself implies secure broadcast [16].

We first establish the feasibility of ID-MPC with constant round complexity, with black-box use of cryptographic primitives.

Theorem 1.1 (informal). *There exists an ID-MPC protocol for securely realizing any functionality in a constant number of rounds, given black-box access to an adaptively secure oblivious transfer protocol and a pseudorandom function.*

Next, our main result is a more *concretely efficient* protocol, with greatly reduced communication complexity and allowing optimizations like efficient OT extension and free-XOR gates.

Theorem 1.2 (informal). *There exists an ID-MPC protocol for securely realizing any functionality in a constant number of rounds, given black-box access to a statically secure oblivious transfer protocol and a circular 2-correlation robust hash function.*

Interestingly, and unlike the previous result, in this construction we manage to avoid the need for adaptively secure OT, allowing our protocol to use efficient OT extensions [28], which are impossible with adaptive security in the standard model as showed by Lindell and Zarosim [39]. This means that Theorems 1.1 and 1.2 are incomparable from a feasibility perspective, since although constructions of adaptively secure OT are known from standard assumptions, it cannot be built from static OT in a black-box manner [38].

Finally, we show how to upgrade the above protocol to achieve public verifiability using a public bulletin board.

Theorem 1.3 (informal). *Assuming additionally a secure public bulletin board, there is a black-box ID-MPC protocol with public verifiability, with a constant number of rounds of interaction with the bulletin board.*

We obtain our first feasibility result with a variant of the Damgård-Ishai protocol [18] for constant-round honest majority MPC, tailored for the dishonest majority setting using information-theoretic signatures [13]. We then obtain a protocol with identifiable abort by combining this with a transformation from [29], which needs an adaptively secure OT protocol. While our construction achieves static security, we want to remark that it is possible to construct an adaptively secure constant-round ID-MPC protocol by applying the [29] transform to the [30] protocol. This approach, on the other hand, will make non-black box use of the underlying PRF by the [29] compiler whereas our construction is fully black-box.

Our second protocol is much more attractive from a practical perspective, since it builds upon recent, optimized MPC protocols that offer active security with (non-identifiable) abort using BMR-style garbled circuits [26,48]. We also support the free-XOR technique [34], by assuming a suitable circular 2-correlation robust hash function [14]. Our core idea is a lightweight method of adding identifiability to the MPC protocol of Hazay, Scholl and Soria-Vazquez [26], which creates a BMR garbled circuit using OT and any non-constant round MPC protocol[1]. We obtain our efficient method in two steps: firstly, we devise a cheater identification procedure for the online phase, based on opening a circuit-independent number of additively homomorphic commitments. The cheater identification is highly efficient as this is the only necessary interaction and because no heavy cryptographic tools such as zero-knowledge proofs are necessary. Secondly, we show how to modify the preprocessing phase of [26] to produce the necessary committed values in an identifiable way. To achieve the latter, we improve techniques by Ishai, Ostrovsky and Zikas [29] to avoid the use of adaptively secure OT. Our approach in doing so might be of independent interest.

Concrete Efficiency. We now expand on the concrete efficiency of our protocols and compare them with existing constant-round, non-identifiable protocols, as illustrated in Table 1. Note that the current most practical, constant-round MPC protocols are all obtained by combining garbling circuits with the so-called 'TinyOT' protocol [40], which combines OT extension and additive secret sharing with information-theoretic MACs over $\mathbb{F}_2$. The TinyOT part turns out to be the dominant, overall cost in the protocols, in terms of communication complexity. The parameter B in Table 1 is related to a statistical security parameter used in cut-and-choose in TinyOT, and in practice is around 3–6. Using the most efficient multi-party variant of TinyOT [48] has a communication complexity of $O(n^2 B\kappa)$ bits per AND gate. The most efficient constant-round protocols have roughly the same communication complexity as TinyOT.

Our efficient protocol from Sects. 3 and 4 uses TinyOT in a similar way to previous works, with the difference that we also use homomorphic commitments to obtain

---

[1] It is plausible that one could alternatively instantiate [36] with [5] as preprocessing, though this appears to yield a slower protocol as already the non-identifiable preprocessing of [36] has a larger overhead ($4n + 5$ SPDZ multiplications vs. 1 TinyOT-AND) plus the constructed circuit does not benefit from Free-XOR.

Table 1. Efficiency of constant-round MPC protocols with and without identifiable abort, for a circuit with $|C|$ AND gates. ID/PV means identifiability or public verifiability. Communication complexity measured in total number of bits transmitted across the network; $\text{bc}(n)$ is the cost of securely broadcasting $O(n)$ bits. The 'free-XOR' assumption is a circular 2-correlation robust hash function [14]

Protocol	ID/PV	Based on	Assumptions	Communication
[26]	✗	OT + [30]	OT, free-XOR	$O((n^2\kappa + \text{poly}(n))|C|)$
[26]	✗	TinyOT	OT, free-XOR	$O(n^2 B^2 \kappa |C|)$
[48]	✗	Optimized TinyOT	OT, free-XOR	$O(n^2 B\kappa |C|)$
Full version	✓ / ✗	[18] + [29]	adaptive OT, PRF	$\text{bc}(\Omega(n^4 \cdot |C|))$
Sects. 3, 4, 5	✓ / ✓	TinyOT + hom. commit.	OT, free-XOR	$O(n^2 B\kappa |C|) + \text{bc}(n^2\kappa |C|)$

identifiability. While most constructions of publicly verifiable homomorphic commitments use public-key style assumptions like discrete log, we are able to get away with a weaker form of homomorphic commitment that only allows a bounded number of openings. This variant be based on any extractable commitment scheme [12], and the main computational cost is PRG evaluations and encodings of an error-correcting code, which can be implemented very efficiently, so we expect only a small computational overhead on top of the non-identifiable protocols. Additionally, the introduced communication overhead from these commitments (per gate) is expected to be a factor 2–3 over the communication that is necessary to perform the String-Oblivious Transfer required to garble a gate as in [26].

Regarding communication complexity, the main overhead in our protocol comes from creating and broadcasting homomorphic commitments to the $O(n \cdot |C|)$ wire keys in a BMR garbled circuit. We minimize this cost by using the efficient homomorphic commitments mentioned above, which have only a small constant communication overhead. Using this scheme, the overhead of commitments is not much more than the cost incurred from having each party broadcast its shares of the garbled circuit $(4n^2 \cdot \kappa|C|$ bits) at the end of our preprocessing phase. We remark that this broadcast step is not needed in non-identifiable protocols [26,48], which can get away with reconstructing the garbled circuit towards a single party who then sends the sum of all shares.

To compare with existing non-constant round protocols such as [5,46], we remark that these use lattice-based preprocessing. Such preprocessing is much more computationally expensive than our lightweight techniques based on OT extension. In terms of broadcasts, the offline phase of [5] has $O(n^3|C|\kappa)$ broadcast complexity, which is worse than our protocol. [46] does not describe the offline phase in detail, but it likely requires $O(n\kappa|C|)$ broadcasts for threshold decryption of the homomorphic encryption scheme. Regarding round complexity, even with the factor n overhead when implementing broadcast, our protocol likely performs significantly better for complex functionalities with high-depth circuits. In general, [5,17,46] are for arithmetic circuits and likely applicable in different scenarios than ours, making a direct comparison difficult.

1.3   Technical Overview

In this overview, we assume some familiarity with garbled circuits and their use in MPC. For a more thorough introduction, we refer to the full version.

Feasibility of constant-round ID-MPC. To first establish a feasibility result, we use a variant of the garbling scheme from [18] combined with information-theoretic signatures [13,25,47], together with a compiler for sampling functionalities with identifiable abort from [29]. Although this construction is quite natural, we are not aware of it being described before.

In a little more detail, [18] is based on a garbling scheme where, similarly to BMR, when evaluating the garbled circuit, for each wire we obtain a vector of keys $(K_w^1, \ldots, K_w^n)$, where the component K_w^i is known to party P_i. The garbling uses a specialized encryption scheme, which encrypts K_w^i by first producing *verifiable secret shares* (VSS) $(K_w^i[1], \ldots, K_w^i[n])$ of K_w^i, and then encrypting each share $K_w^i[j]$ under the corresponding input wire key components of P_j, as:

$$E_{K_u, K_v}(K_w^i) := \begin{pmatrix} \mathsf{H}(K_u^1, K_v^1) \oplus K_w^i[1] \\ \vdots \\ \mathsf{H}(K_u^n, K_v^n) \oplus K_w^i[n] \end{pmatrix}$$

This is amenable to secure computation in a black-box way, as P_j can input the hash values $H(K_u^j, K_v^j)$ to the protocol, and as long as the majority of these hash values are correct, which is guaranteed by an honest majority, the VSS allows correct reconstruction of K_w^i.

We adapt this to the dishonest majority setting by replacing VSS with additive secret-sharing and information-theoretic signatures. Roughly, we consider a preprocessing functionality which samples additive shares of each K_w^i and augments each share with a signature under a signing key that no-one gets, while also allowing corrupt parties to choose their hash values for each gate. This suffices to obtain ID-MPC in an online phase, since if any corrupt party uses an incorrect hash value then the corresponding signature on their share will no longer verify.

To realize the preprocessing phase which outputs authenticated shares of the garbled circuit, we apply the compiler from [29], which transforms a protocol for any sampling functionality that is secure with abort, into one with identifiable abort. We remark that in the preprocessing functionality, the size of each garbled gate is $O(n^3 \cdot \kappa)$ bits, and the communication complexity of the protocol to generate this is at least $\Omega(n^4 \kappa)$ due to overheads in [29], so this approach is not practical.

For space reasons, the complete description of these protocols can be found in the full version.

Concretely efficient ID-MPC with BMR. As mentioned before, our protocol follows the same approach of [26] ('HSS') based upon BMR garbled circuits. In BMR garbling, the vector of output wire keys $(K_w^1, \ldots, K_w^n)$ of a gate g is directly encrypted under the input wire keys, with

$$E_{K_u,K_v}(K_w) := \bigoplus_{j=1}^{n} H(g, K_u^j, K_v^j) \oplus (K_w^1, \dots, K_w^n)$$

When using free-XOR with BMR, each pair keys on a wire is of the form $(K_{w,0}, K_{w,1} = K_{w,0} \oplus R)$ for some fixed string $R = (R^1, \dots, R^n)$, with R^i known to P_i. When garbling an AND gate with input wires u, v and output wire w, we need to produce the 4 rows

$$\begin{aligned} \mathtt{circ}_{g,a,b} = \bigoplus_{j=1}^{n} \; &H(g, K_{u,a}^j, K_{v,b}^j) \oplus (K_{w,0}^1, \dots, K_{w,0}^n) \\ &\oplus (R^1, \dots, R^n) \cdot ((\lambda_u \oplus a)(\lambda_v \oplus b) \oplus \lambda_w), \end{aligned} \tag{1}$$

for $(a, b) \in \{0, 1\}^2$, where $\lambda_u, \lambda_v, \lambda_w$ are the secret wire masks assigned to each wire.

In the HSS protocol, to generate additive shares of the above, each party P_i first samples all of their key components and global string R^i, as well as secret shares of all the wire masks. Then, a generic MPC protocol for binary circuits is used to compute shares of the wire mask products $\lambda_u \cdot \lambda_v$, and shares of the products between each wire mask and every global string R^i are computed using OT. This allows the parties to obtain additive shares of the entire garbled circuit, since each hash value in (1) can be computed locally by party P_j. If any party uses an incorrect hash value, it was shown in [26] that this would result in an abort in the online phase with overwhelming probability, since each party can check correctness when decrypting a gate by checking for the presence of one of their own key components.

Identifiable online phase. Adding identifiable abort to BMR is more challenging than with [18], since if any error is introduced to the hash values in (1), we have no direct way of knowing which party introduced it. Note that if the parties were committed to *the entirety* of the shares of the garbled circuit (i.e. all of (1)) then this would be straightforward: they could simply broadcast their shares, then attempt to run the online phase; if any party sends an incorrect share then the protocol aborts with overwhelming probability, and in our case everyone could then open their commitments to prove they behaved honestly. Unfortunately, we do *not* know how to efficiently create commitments to all of the shares, since in particular each share contains a hash value $H(g, K_{u,a}^j, K_{v,b}^j)$, and it seems challenging to reliably commit to these without resorting to proving statements about hash function computations in zero-knowledge.

Instead, we observe that it is actually enough if each party is given commitments to *partial shares* of the garbled gates, namely, shares of the whole of (1) *except for* the hash values. To see this, consider that some party aborts at gate g in the computation. If g is the *first* (in topological order) such gate where the parties detect an inconsistency, then it must hold that the *preceding* gates were correctly garbled. This means that the wire keys from the previous gate can be used to compute the correct $H(\cdot)$ values by every party. Hence, we can verify the garbling of g by opening the commitments to the partial shares, then reconstructing the shares that should have been sent by 'filling in' the remaining parts of the garbled gate that were not committed to. Finally, the resulting shares can be compared with the shares that were actually sent, allowing us to detect a cheating party.

We therefore rely on a preprocessing functionality that adds XOR-homomorphic commitments to all the wire keys and shares of the bit-string products. Since the commitments are homomorphic, this easily allows computing commitments to the partial shares as required.

Identifiable preprocessing phase. Our first challenge with the preprocessing is to create the necessary commitments to the bit-string products in a reliable way. We show that without identifiability, this can be done without too much difficulty, using a consistency check based on a technique adapted from [26].

Next, the main challenge is to make the whole preprocessing identifiable. One possible approach would be to simply apply the same IOZ transformation we used for the protocol based on Damgård-Ishai, to convert a protocol Π_{Prep} that realizes the preprocessing functionality $\mathcal{F}_{\mathsf{Prep}}$ with abort into a new protocol $\Pi_{\mathsf{Prep}}^{\mathsf{ID}}$ that is identifiable. Unfortunately, this transformation has two main drawbacks: Firstly, the protocol Π_{Prep} needs to compute not only the outputs of $\mathcal{F}_{\mathsf{Prep}}$, but *authenticated secret shares* of these outputs, where each share has an information-theoretic signature attached to it; since IT signatures have a multiplicative $\Omega(n)$ storage overhead, this adds a significant cost burden to the protocol. Secondly, Π_{Prep} needs to be secure against *adaptive corruptions*, which is in general much harder to achieve than static corruptions; in particular, it rules out the use of efficient OT extensions unless we rely on the programmable random oracle model [10,39].

We work around these issues with careful modifications to the [29] transformation, which are tailored specifically to our preprocessing phase. We first briefly recall the idea behind IOZ. To construct $\Pi_{\mathsf{Prep}}^{\mathsf{ID}}$, first each party commits to its randomness in Π_{Prep}, and then if Π_{Prep} aborts, everyone simply opens their randomness, which is safe as the preprocessing phase is independent of the parties' inputs. The main challenge when proving security of this approach is that if the protocol aborts, the simulator needs to be able to convincingly open the honest parties' random tapes to the adversary, explaining the previously simulated protocol messages. This leads to the above two issues, since (1) if the protocol aborts *after* a corrupt party has seen its outputs, the simulator may not be able to produce honest parties' outputs that match, and (2) the simulator may not be able to come up with convincing honest parties' random tapes, since the previous honest parties' messages were simulated independently of the actual outputs from $\mathcal{F}_{\mathsf{Prep}}^{\mathsf{ID}}$. In IOZ, (1) is resolved by producing an authenticated secret-sharing of the outputs, and (2) is resolved by requiring Π_{Prep} to be adaptively secure.

In our work, we address (1) by ensuring that an abort is only possible in Π_{Prep} *before* the ideal functionality $\mathcal{F}_{\mathsf{Prep}}$ has delivered outputs to the honest parties. This means there is no danger of inconsistencies between the simulated honest parties' outputs and those seen by the distinguisher. Our method of resolving (2) is more complex. First, consider a simulation strategy where when running Π_{Prep} within $\Pi_{\mathsf{Prep}}^{\mathsf{ID}}$, the simulator simply performs an honest run of Π_{Prep} on random inputs. If Π_{Prep} later aborts, there is no problem opening the random tapes of honest parties', since the simulator knows these. The problem now is that the simulator can no longer extract any corrupt parties' inputs which may have to be sent to $\mathcal{F}_{\mathsf{Prep}}$, or ensure the corrupt parties get the corrupt output sent by $\mathcal{F}_{\mathsf{Prep}}$. To work around this, we combine Π_{Prep} with a homomorphic commitment scheme, and require that every party commits to all values used in Π_{Prep};

we ensure consistency of these commitments with the values in Π_{Prep} with a simple test where we open random linear combinations of the commitments, and modify the (reactive) protocol Π_{Prep} to open the same combinations. If the homomorphic commitment scheme is UC secure with identifiable abort, then the simulator can use this to extract and open the values in Π_{Prep}, allow us to prove security of the whole protocol. A suitable commitment scheme can be efficiently constructed, building upon any (non-homomorphic) extractable commitment and a PRG [12].

We apply the above blueprint to the preprocessing phase of HSS, which performs multiplications between random bits, as well as between bits and random, fixed strings, to produce additive shares of the garbled circuit. With our transformation, the parties actually end up producing *homomorphic commitments* to shares of some (but not all) parts of the garbled circuit; namely, they are committed to the wire keys and the shares of the bit-string products from (1).

Achieving public verifiability. Public verifiability with identifiable abort requires not only that a party from the protocol can identify a cheater, but anyone can do so (or verify correctness of the result) by simply inspecting some messages posted to a public bulletin board. Adding this to our efficient construction requires modifying both the preprocessing and online phases of the protocol. First, we modify our preprocessing method so that the underlying protocol that is secure with abort satisfies a property called *public detectability*, which requires that an external verifier, who is given the random tapes of all parties in the protocol and all broadcast messages, can detect whether any cheating occurred and identify a corrupted party if so. This is similar to the concept of $\mathcal{P}$-*verifiability* used in IOZ [29], but removes the requirement that the verifier is also given the view of one honest party. We then show that any suitable, secure protocol can be transformed to be publicly detectable, with a simple transformation that is similar to the $\mathcal{P}$-verifiable transformation from [29]. Using the publicly detectable protocol in our identifiable preprocessing phase, and replacing the broadcast channel with a bulletin board, we obtain a publicly verifiable preprocessing protocol with identifiable abort.

To add public verifiability to the online phase, we need to ensure that an external evaluator can detect any cheating in the garbled circuit, given only the public transcript. It turns out that in case of abort, almost all of the computation done by an honest party when detecting a cheater relies only on public information; the only exception is the 0/1 wire values that are obtained when evaluating the garbled circuit, which each party computes by looking at its private keys. To allow an external verifier to compute these values, we modify the preprocessing with a variant of the point-and-permute technique, which encodes these values as the last bit in the corresponding key on that wire. Now if the protocol aborts, and the entire transcript of broadcast messages has been posted to the public bulletin board, the verifier has all the information that is needed to detect any inconsistency and identify a cheating party.

Notice that our public cheater identification is protocol-specific and does not require heavy NIZK machinery. This differentiates it from [32] who gave a general compiler that achieves publicly verifiable ID-MPC, but where the generated "cheating certificate" is a NIZK that has to re-compute the next-message function of the compiled protocol. That means that compiling a BMR-style protocol using their approach might require

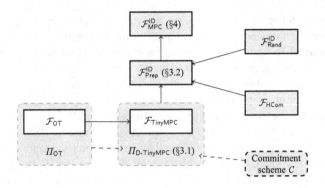

Fig. 1. Illustration of our efficient protocol with identifiable abort.

giving a zero-knowledge proof of correct garbling of the whole circuit, whereas our certificate just requires a few commitments to be opened.

Paper Outline. In Fig. 1 we show the relationship between our protocols and functionalities in our main construction with identifiable abort. Section 3.1 contains our publicly detectable transformation, used for both identifiable abort and public verifiability, and instantiation from the OT-based preprocessing phase of [26]. Section 3.2 describes our identifiable preprocessing protocol, which uses the publicly detectable $\Pi_{\text{D-TinyMPC}}$ in a non-black-box way (but with black-box use of its next-message function), and combines this with homomorphic commitments. In Sect. 4, we present the main MPC protocol with identifiable abort, which uses $\mathcal{F}_{\text{Prep}}^{\text{ID}}$ to create and then evaluate a BMR garbled circuit, with identifiable abort. In Sect. 5, we describe how to modify the previous protocol to additionally obtain public verifiability, using a bulletin board instead of a broadcast channel.

2 Preliminaries

Let κ (resp. s) denote the computational (resp. statistical) security parameter. We let $\mathcal{P} = \{P_1, \ldots, P_n\}$ be the set of parties involved in any particular protocol/functionality, and $\mathcal{V}$ be a verifier which might check $\mathcal{P}$'s computation at a later point. Among those parties, we denote by $\mathcal{I} \subset \mathcal{P}$ the set of corrupted parties and by $\overline{\mathcal{I}} = \mathcal{P} \setminus \mathcal{I}$ the honest parties. Let C_f be a circuit computing the function $f : \mathbb{F}_2^{n_{\text{in}}} \to \mathbb{F}_2^{n_{\text{out}}}$ with n_{in} inputs and n_{out} outputs. To ease the reading, we drop the dependence on f, when it is clear from the context. We will define the disjunct sets $\text{input}_1, \ldots, \text{input}_n \subset [n]$ as the inputs which each party in $\mathcal{P}$ provides to the circuit C, so P_i provides the inputs in input_i. The circuit C has the set of AND gates G, for which we denote the extended set $G^{\text{ext}} := G \times \mathbb{F}_2^2$. For $\tau \in G^{\text{ext}}$, we usually denote $\tau = (g, a, b)$ where g is the AND gate in question and $a, b \in \mathbb{F}_2$ are used to point to a specific entry in g's (garbled) truth table.

2.1 Security Model and Primitives

We will prove security of our protocols in the universal composability (UC) framework [11]. We consider a static, active adversary corrupting up to $n - 1$ parties. To achieve our goals, we will make use of multiple primitives, whose ideal functionalities we now introduce.

Identifiable Abort Version of Functionalities. In order to be able to rigorously discuss our protocols, we now formalize what it is to enhance their ideal functionalities $\mathcal{F}$ to support identifiable abort, which we denote by $\mathcal{F}^{ID}$ and describe in Fig. 2. As showed in [29], the UC composition theorem extends to security with identifiable abort in a straightforward way.

Functionality $\mathcal{F}^{ID}$

Let $\mathcal{F}$ be a functionality which runs with parties $\mathcal{P} = \{P_1, \ldots, P_n\}$ and an adversary $\mathcal{A}$ who corrupts a subset $\mathcal{I} \subset \mathcal{P}$ of parties. $\mathcal{F}^{ID}$ is exactly as $\mathcal{F}$, with the following extra command:

Abort: At any time, $\mathcal{A}$ can send a special command $(\texttt{Abort}, \mathcal{J})$ where $\mathcal{J} \subseteq \mathcal{I}, \mathcal{J} \neq \emptyset$. The functionality then stores $\mathcal{J}$, sends $(\texttt{Abort}, \mathcal{J})$ to parties in $\mathcal{P} \setminus \mathcal{I}$ and terminates the execution of any current command.

Fig. 2. Extending a functionality $\mathcal{F}$ to its identifiable abort version $\mathcal{F}^{ID}$.

An $\mathcal{F}^{ID}$ functionality is exactly as $\mathcal{F}$, but additionally allows the adversary to send a message $(\texttt{Abort}, \mathcal{J})$ at any point of time, where $\mathcal{J}$ denotes a non-empty set of dishonest parties. Upon receiving this message, the functionality ceases all computation and outputs the set $\mathcal{J}$ to all honest parties. The main points of identifiable abort are that (i) The adversary cannot abort without revealing the identity of at least one corrupt party; and (ii) All honest parties interacting with $\mathcal{F}^{ID}$ agree on the revealed corrupted parties.

Coin Tossing. Coin tossing is used by a set of parties to fairly sample a number of coins according to a fixed distribution. In this work we will use an identifiable version of it, $\mathcal{F}^{ID}_{Rand}$, meaning that either all computing parties learn the sampled coins or, otherwise, the honest parties agree on a subset of dishonest parties who cheated in the sampling process. The standard $\mathcal{F}_{Rand}$ functionality is described in the full version.

Secure Broadcast. Our work will crucially rely on the use of *secure* (or, *authenticated*) broadcast, which is a standard functionality given in the full version of the paper. Nevertheless, in order to achieve protocols with identifiable abort, we need to enhance the description of this functionality to $\mathcal{F}^{ID}_{Broadcast}$ as previously described. This is not a problem, as all standard protocols for $\mathcal{F}_{Broadcast}$ such as [20,43] are already identifiable. Under the assumption of a Public Key Infrastructure, implementing $\mathcal{F}_{Broadcast}$ requires $\Omega(n)$ rounds of communication and signatures [23]. If the parties have access to an authenticated bulletin board, $\mathcal{F}_{Broadcast}$ can be achieved with a single call to the board.

Functionality $\mathcal{F}_{\mathsf{HCom}}$

$\mathcal{F}_{\mathsf{HCom}}$ is parameterized by $\kappa \in \mathbb{N}$. $\mathcal{F}_{\mathsf{HCom}}$ interacts with a sender $P_S \in \mathcal{P}$, where the remaining parties $\mathcal{P} \setminus \{P_S\}$ act as receivers. $\mathcal{A}$ may corrupt any subset $\mathcal{I} \subsetneq \mathcal{P}$ and at any point it may send a message $(\mathsf{Abort}, \mathcal{J})$ with $\emptyset \neq \mathcal{J} \subseteq \mathcal{I}$, upon which the functionality sends $(\mathsf{Abort}, \mathcal{J})$ to $\mathcal{P}$ and halts.

Commit: Upon receiving $(\mathsf{Commit}, \mathsf{cid}, M)$ from P_S, where $M \in \mathbb{F}_2^\kappa$, save (cid, M) locally and send $(\mathsf{Commit\text{-}Recorded}, \mathsf{cid})$ to $\mathcal{P}$ and $\mathcal{A}$. Every further message with this cid to **Commit** is ignored.

Add: Upon receiving $(\mathsf{Add}, \mathsf{cid}_1, \mathsf{cid}_2, \mathsf{cid}_3)$ by P_S, where $(\mathsf{cid}_1, M_1), (\mathsf{cid}_2, M_2)$ are stored but not cid_3, add $(\mathsf{cid}_3, M_1 + M_2)$ to the list and send $(\mathsf{Add\text{-}Recorded}, \mathsf{cid}_1, \mathsf{cid}_2, \mathsf{cid}_3)$ to $\mathcal{P}$ and $\mathcal{A}$.

Open: Upon receiving the first $(\mathsf{Open}, \mathsf{cid})$ by P_S where (cid, M) was previously stored, ignore all future messages to **Commit**. Send $(\mathsf{Open}, \mathsf{cid}, M)$ to all parties in $\mathcal{P}$ and $\mathcal{A}$.

Fig. 3. Functionality $\mathcal{F}_{\mathsf{HCom}}$ for homomorphic multiparty commitment with delayed verifiability.

Homomorphic Commitments. In this work, we use homomorphic commitments. These allow a sender to commit to a message M at a certain time, such as to later open M to a set of receivers. The properties required from commitment schemes are that (i) M remains hidden to the receivers until the opening (hiding); and (ii) the sender can only open M and no other value to the receivers, once committed (binding). We further require that the commitment scheme is homomorphic, meaning that the sender can open any linear combination of commitments that it made without revealing anything but the combined output. The functionality $\mathcal{F}_{\mathsf{HCom}}$ is described in Fig. 3.

To efficiently implement $\mathcal{F}_{\mathsf{HCom}}$ we would like to use the homomorphic commitment scheme of Cascudo et al. [12], but it turns out that this is not possible directly. The problem is that $\mathcal{F}_{\mathsf{HCom}}$ (which we use throughout this work) allows to perform multiple rounds of **Add** and **Open**, whereas [12] permits to perform only one call to the interface **Open**. In the full version, we present a slightly weaker functionality $\mathcal{F}_{\mathsf{WHComm}}$ having multiple rounds of **Open** but not **Add**. We show that this is sufficient for our application and also how this weaker functionality can then be implemented using the protocol in [12].

3   Preprocessing Phase

Here we describe our preprocessing phase with identifiable abort. At a high level, we proceed in two steps: first, we describe a protocol with the weaker property of public detectability, and then we bootstrap it to a preprocessing protocol with identifiable abort using homomorphic commitments.

3.1   Publicly Detectable MPC with (Non-identifiable) Abort

We start this section by recalling the notion of the (deterministic) *next message function*, nmf_Π^i, of a party P_i in an n-party protocol Π that is executed in a limited number of rounds, say ρ. Given the VIEW of P_i at the beginning of round h, where $h \leq \rho$, i.e. the set $\text{VIEW}_h^i = (i, X, X_i, \text{Rnd}_i, (M_{i,1}, \ldots, M_{i,h}))$, where i identifies party P_i, X is the common public input, X_i and Rnd_i are P_i's private input and randomness respectively, and $(M_{i,1}, \ldots, M_{i,h})$ are the messages received by P_i in the first h rounds, then $\text{nmf}_\Pi^i(\text{VIEW}_h^i) = M_{h+1}^i$ are the messages that P_i has to send in round $h + 1$. In particular, $\text{nmf}_\Pi^i(\text{VIEW}_\rho^i) = Y_i$, where Y_i is P_i's output, and $\text{VIEW}^i = \text{VIEW}_\rho^i$. In other words, the messages sent by each party P_i at each round are deterministically specified as a function of P_i's inputs and random coins, and messages received by P_i in previous rounds.

We can now introduce the notion of *public detectability*. It is similar to that of $\mathcal{P}$-verifiability given in [29]. However, whereas the notion of $\mathcal{P}$-verifiability in that work was conceived with identifiable abort in mind, public detectability will allow us to implement functionalities not only achieving identifiable abort, but also public verifiability if required (see Sect. 5).

Definition 3.1 (Public detectability). *Let Π be a protocol in the CRS model and $\mathcal{D}$ a deterministic poly-time algorithm, called the* detector, *which takes as inputs the CRS, the inputs and random tape of all parties in $\mathcal{P}$ involved in the execution of Π, and any message sent over an authenticated broadcast channel during the execution of Π. We say that the protocol Π is* publicly detectable *if the detector $\mathcal{D}$ outputs a non-empty subset $\mathcal{J} \subset \mathcal{P}$ corresponding to (some of) the parties that did not honestly execute Π, if any such subset $\mathcal{J}$ exists.*

Notice there is a gap between the public detectability and identifiable abort properties: the latter requires that, upon abort, the adversary does not learn anything about the honest parties' inputs, beyond of what is deducible from the functionalities' output; on the other hand, running the detector requires access to all the input and random tape of $\mathcal{P}$. However, we will show, in Sect. 3.2, that public detectability is almost enough to define our preprocessing with identifiable abort, which we will later on extend to a public verifiable one in Sect. 5. At a high level, the main idea is that, since the goal of the preprocessing phase is to produce random correlated values that will be used in a very efficient online evaluation, during such a phase parties have not yet provided their private inputs, so, if the protocol aborts, it is enough for every party to run the detector on their own. The privacy of the overall MPC protocol is not affected then, due to the absence of the (actual) private inputs.

We now show how to turn any protocol Π that UC-realises an ideal functionality $\mathcal{F}$ in the CRS model with static security, into a protocol Π_V realising the same functionality with public detectability. Given the protocol Π, and a binding and hiding commitment scheme $\mathcal{C} = (\texttt{Commit}, \texttt{Reveal})$, we apply the following changes to Π.

– Before any step of Π is executed, each party securely broadcasts a commitment to their input and random tape using the commitment scheme.[2]

---

[2] This part of the transformation is not actually needed in order to achieve public detectability, but it will simplify the way we use transformed protocols later on in order to achieve identifiable abort and public verifiability.

- In case of any broadcast communication, execute the protocol Π using instead an authenticated broadcast functionality $\mathcal{F}_{\mathsf{Broadcast}}$.
- Each pairwise communication between a sender P_S and a receiver P_R, such that $\{P_S, P_R\} \subseteq \mathcal{P}$, is implemented by first securely broadcasting a commitment $c(M^S)$ to the message M^S that has to be sent, followed by a private opening of it towards the receiving party. If P_R does not receive the correct opening from P_S, then the receiver securely broadcasts a message asking for the opening of $c(M^S)$. The sender has to reply with that information, using also secure broadcast.[3] If the broadcasted reply is a correct opening, parties in $\mathcal{P}$ retake the computation, otherwise they abort.

It is easy to prove that the protocol Π, modified as above, is publicly detectable.

Lemma 3.2. *Let Π be a protocol that realises an ideal functionality $\mathcal{F}$ with static security in the CRS model with broadcast and pairwise communication, and $\mathcal{C}$ a standalone-secure commitment scheme. The protocol Π_V described above is publicly detectable and realises the functionality $\mathcal{F}$ in the $\{\mathrm{CRS}, \mathcal{F}_{\mathsf{Broadcast}}\}$-hybrid model.*

Publicly Detectable Preprocessing. In our preprocessing phase, we use the functionality $\mathcal{F}_{\mathsf{TinyMPC}}$ (Fig. 4), which is a standard functionality for secret sharing-based MPC for binary circuits augmented with the command **MultBitString** that allows multiplying a bit by a fixed string known to one party. This functionality is exactly what is needed to securely preprocess a BMR garbled circuit [26] with abort, where the fixed strings play the roles of the global R^i strings in the garbled circuit; this can be efficiently implemented using a TinyOT-like protocol, for example [21, 26, 40], in the $\mathcal{F}_{\mathsf{OT}}$-hybrid model.

We can apply the transformation above to obtain a publicly detectable protocol $\Pi_{\mathsf{D\text{-}TinyMPC}}$, if we have a protocol Π_{TinyMPC} that implements the functionality $\mathcal{F}_{\mathsf{TinyMPC}}$ in the CRS model. Such a protocol can be efficiently obtained by implementing the OT functionality with OT extension [1, 31], with base OTs realized in the CRS model [42]. Thus, we obtain the following corollary.

Corollary 3.3. *Let $\mathcal{C}$ be a commitment scheme and Π_{TinyMPC} a protocol that UC-realises the functionality $\mathcal{F}_{\mathsf{TinyMPC}}$ in the CRS model. The protocol $\Pi_{\mathsf{D\text{-}TinyMPC}}$ (described in is publicly detectable and it securely realises the functionality $\mathcal{F}_{\mathsf{TinyMPC}}$ in the $\{\mathcal{F}_{\mathsf{Broadcast}}, \mathrm{CRS}\}$-hybrid model.*

3.2 Implementing the Preprocessing with Identifiable Abort

We now combine the detectable protocol $\Pi_{\mathsf{D\text{-}TinyMPC}}$ with homomorphic commitments, $\mathcal{F}_{\mathsf{HCom}}$, to obtain a preprocessing protocol with identifiable abort. Our preprocessing functionality $\mathcal{F}_{\mathsf{Prep}}^{\mathsf{ID}}$ is described in the full version of this work. It essentially performs the same computations as $\mathcal{F}_{\mathsf{TinyMPC}}$, except the output shares of the bit-string multiplication are now committed with homomorphic commitments, modelled in the functionality by allowing them to be added together and opened. Another key difference

---

[3] This does not break security, because such a situation can only occur if P_S or P_R are corrupted, in which case $\mathcal{A}$ would obtain M^S anyway.

Functionality $\mathcal{F}_{\mathsf{TinyMPC}}$

The functionality runs with parties $P_1, \ldots, P_n$ and an adversary $\mathcal{A}$. It has a list of corrupt parties $\mathcal{I}$ which it obtains from $\mathcal{A}$.

Angle brackets $\langle x \rangle$ denote a secret $x \in \mathbb{F}_2$ stored by the functionality, together with a public identifier. The inputs to every command below are public inputs that must be provided by all parties (where in this case, the notation $\langle x \rangle$ refers only to the *identifier* of the secret value x).

Init: On input (Init) from all parties, if (Init) was received before then do nothing. For each $i \in [n]$, if $i \in \mathcal{I}$ then receive $R^i \in \mathbb{F}_2^\kappa$ from $\mathcal{A}$, otherwise sample a random $R^i \leftarrow \mathbb{F}_2^\kappa$. Send R^i to party P_i and store the strings R^i.

Input: On input (Input, $P_i, \langle x \rangle$) from all parties and (Input, $P_i, \langle x \rangle, x$) from P_i, where $x \in \mathbb{F}_2$, store x.

Add: On input (Add, $\langle z \rangle, \langle x \rangle, \langle y \rangle$) from all parties, where the two bits x and y were previously stored, store $z = x + y$

Mult: On input (Multiply, $\mathbb{F}_2, \langle \bar{x} \rangle, \langle x_1 \rangle, \langle x_2 \rangle$) from all parties, where x_1, x_2 were stored previously, store $\bar{x} = x_1 \cdot x_2$.

MultBitString: On input (MultBitString, $\langle x \rangle, P_i$) from all parties, where x was stored previously:

    1. $\mathcal{A}$ inputs $W^j \in \mathbb{F}_2^\kappa$ for each $P_j \in \mathcal{I}$.

    2. Sample $W^j \leftarrow \mathbb{F}_2^\kappa$ for $j \in \bar{\mathcal{I}}$ subject to the constraint that $x \cdot R^i = \sum_{j \in [n]} W^j$.

    3. Send W^j to party P_j.

Open: On input (PublicOutput, $\langle x_1 \rangle, \ldots, \langle x_m \rangle$) from all parties, where $x_i, i \in [m]$, have been stored previously:

    1. Send (Deliver, $x_1, \ldots, x_m$) to $\mathcal{A}$.

    2. If $\mathcal{A}$ sends Abort, forward Abort to all parties and halt. Otherwise send (Output, $x_1, \ldots, x_m$) to all parties.

Fig. 4. Functionality $\mathcal{F}_{\mathsf{TinyMPC}}$ for Bit-MPC.

is that the outputs are only delivered at the very end of the protocol. After the initial outputs are sent to the parties, the only further allowed command is to open values from the homomorphic commitment scheme. This is because in the security proof for our preprocessing protocol, the simulator can always equivocate $\mathcal{F}_{\mathsf{HCom}}$, whereas it cannot equivate the simulation of $\Pi_{\mathsf{D\text{-}TinyMPC}}$ when it is still possible for an abort to occur (which would require opening the honest parties' random tapes to the adversary).

The protocol $\Pi_{\mathsf{Prep}}^{\mathsf{ID}}$, implementing $\mathcal{F}_{\mathsf{Prep}}^{\mathsf{ID}}$ and described in Fig. 5, uses the publicly detectable version of Π_{TinyMPC} (from Corollary 3.3) for all the $\mathbb{F}_2$-arithmetic, i.e. to perform secure additions and multiplications on bits, as well as to obtain secret-shares of the product of secret bits with the strings R^i. The protocol uses two copies of the homomorphic commitment functionality (which we name $\mathcal{F}_{\mathsf{HCom}}$ and $\mathcal{F}_{\mathsf{HCom}}^{\mathsf{Bit}}$). The first copy is used to create commitments to values in $\mathbb{F}_2^\kappa$, such as the fixed strings R^i as well as the additive shares of all the bit-string products of secret bits with R^i. We furthermore employ a consistency check to verify that the committed bit-string shares are correct, which is shown in Fig. 6. The functionality $\mathcal{F}_{\mathsf{HCom}}^{\mathsf{Bit}}$ is used to additionally commit to the bits which are used in $\Pi_{\mathsf{D\text{-}TinyMPC}}$, and we use a second consistency check to verify that these two sets of bits stored in $\Pi_{\text{D-TinyMPC}}$ and $\mathcal{F}_{\text{HCom}}^{\text{Bit}}$ are the same; this can be found in Fig. 7. We also use this functionality to open bit values during the output phase. We remark that the necessity of using $\mathcal{F}_{\text{HCom}}^{\text{Bit}}$ for both of this is an artefact of the proof and we leave it as an interesting open problem to remove $\mathcal{F}_{\text{HCom}}^{\text{Bit}}$ (together with the consistency check Π_{CheckBit}) while retaining a provably-secure protocol.

In the case of abort, we will reveal all random tapes and committed messages of $\Pi_{\text{D-TinyMPC}}$ and test which party has sent inconsistent messages and when. Interestingly, we can do that without requiring adaptive primitives (in comparison to previous works): The simulation of $\Pi_{\text{D-TinyMPC}}$ in the security proof is only ever checked using the public detectability if no output of $\mathcal{F}_{\text{Prep}}^{\text{ID}}$ has been revealed yet. Therefore we do not have to ever equivocate the random tape during the simulation of $\Pi_{\text{D-TinyMPC}}$ - revealing the tape used by the simulator is enough. This is exactly where previous work [29] required adaptivity of the underlying primitives, which we in our case can then avoid. To prove consistency of the committed shares of bit-string products, we use the following lemma. Its statement and proof are very similar to [26, Lemma 3.1] and we only provide it here for completeness. The proof of the lemma is given in the full version.

Lemma 3.4. *If the protocol* $\Pi_{\text{BitStringMult}}$ *does not abort, then the committed values* $R^j, W_{\tau,j}^i$ *produced by* $\Pi_{\text{BitStringMult}}$ *satisfy*

$$\sum_{i=1}^{n} W_{\tau,j}^i = x_\tau \cdot R^j,$$

where R^j *was computed in the* **Init** *phase and* $\langle x_1 \rangle, \ldots, \langle x_m \rangle$ *were input to* $\Pi_{\text{BitStringMult}}$, *except with probability* $\max(\varepsilon, 2^{-s})$.

We use the lemma below to verify that bits committed in both $\mathcal{F}_{\text{HCom}}^{\text{Bit}}$ and $\Pi_{\text{D-TinyMPC}}$ are consistent. We omit the proof, which is essentially a simplified version of the proof of Lemma 3.4.

Lemma 3.5. *If the protocol* Π_{CheckBit} *does not abort, then the inputs* $\langle x_1 \rangle, \ldots, \langle x_m \rangle$, $[x_1^i]_c^{\text{Bit}}, \ldots, [x_m^i]_c^{\text{Bit}}$ *satisfy*

$$\sum_{i=1}^{n} x_j^i = x_j,$$

except with probability $\max(\varepsilon, 2^{-s})$.

These allow us to prove security of our construction.

Theorem 3.6. *Assuming a secure broadcast channel, protocol* $\Pi_{\text{Prep}}^{\text{ID}}$ *implements* $\mathcal{F}_{\text{Prep}}^{\text{ID}}$ *in the* $\{\text{CRS}, \mathcal{F}_{\text{HCom}}, \mathcal{F}_{\text{HCom}}^{\text{Bit}}, \mathcal{F}_{\text{Rand}}\}$*-hybrid model with security against a static, active adversary corrupting at most* $n - 1$ *parties.*

The proof follows a simulation-based argument, along the lines described in Sect. 1.3. It is given in the full version.

The Preprocessing Protocol $\Pi_{\mathsf{Prep}}^{\mathsf{ID}}$

The protocol runs with parties $P_1, \ldots, P_n$. It runs two instances of the homomorphic commitment scheme which we denote as $\mathcal{F}_{\mathsf{HCom}}$ and $\mathcal{F}_{\mathsf{HCom}}^{\mathsf{Bit}}$.

NOTATION: We use $\langle x \rangle$ to denote that $x \in \mathbb{F}_2$ is stored by $\Pi_{\mathsf{D\text{-}TinyMPC}}$, $[x]_i^{\mathsf{Bit}}$ to denote that $x \in \mathbb{F}_2$ is stored in $\mathcal{F}_{\mathsf{HCom}}^{\mathsf{Bit}}$ where P_i is the sender, and $[X]_i$ to denote that $X \in \mathbb{F}_2^\kappa$ is stored in $\mathcal{F}_{\mathsf{HCom}}$ where P_i is the sender. The parties maintain a list PubOutputs which is initially empty.

PHASE I: COMPUTATION

Init: The parties call $\Pi_{\mathsf{D\text{-}TinyMPC}}$ with input (Init) and each obtain a string $R^i \in \mathbb{F}_2^\kappa$. Then they each commit to R^i using $\mathcal{F}_{\mathsf{HCom}}$.

Sample: Party P_i samples $x \leftarrow \mathbb{F}_2$ or $X \leftarrow \mathbb{F}_2^\kappa$. The parties do one of:
- $x \in \mathbb{F}_2$: use the (Input) command of $\Pi_{\mathsf{D\text{-}TinyMPC}}$ to obtain $\langle x \rangle$. P_i then commits to x by calling $\mathcal{F}_{\mathsf{HCom}}^{\mathsf{Bit}}$ on input (Commit, id, x), obtaining $[x]_i^{\mathsf{Bit}}$.
- $X \in \mathbb{F}_2^\kappa$: P_i commits to X by calling $\mathcal{F}_{\mathsf{HCom}}$, to obtain $[X]_i$.

AddBit: To add two bits $\langle x \rangle$ and $\langle y \rangle$, parties use the **Add** command of $\Pi_{\mathsf{D\text{-}TinyMPC}}$. If commitments $\{[x]_i^{\mathsf{Bit}}, [y]_i^{\mathsf{Bit}}\}_i$ are also stored in $\mathcal{F}_{\mathsf{HCom}}^{\mathsf{Bit}}$, use the **Add** command of $\mathcal{F}_{\mathsf{HCom}}^{\mathsf{Bit}}$.

AddString: To add the committed strings $[X]_i$ and $[Y]_i$, the parties use $\mathcal{F}_{\mathsf{HCom}}$.

Mult:
- To multiply two bits $\langle x \rangle$ and $\langle y \rangle$, the parties use the **Multiply** command of $\Pi_{\mathsf{D\text{-}TinyMPC}}$.
- To multiply the bit $\langle x \rangle$ with the strings $R^1, \ldots, R^n$, the parties run the subprotocol $\Pi_{\mathsf{BitStringMult}}$.

Public Output (bit): On input (PublicOutput, $[x]_1^{\mathsf{Bit}}, \ldots, [x]_n^{\mathsf{Bit}}$) from all parties, append $\{[x]_i^{\mathsf{Bit}}\}_i$ to the list PubOutputs.

Delayed Outputs: On input (DelayedOutputs) from all parties:
- Run **Check** of the subprotocol Π_{CheckBit} on input all of the bits committed to during **Sample**, to check their consistency.
- Use the (Open) command of $\mathcal{F}_{\mathsf{HCom}}^{\mathsf{Bit}}$ to output all the x_i values, for every tuple $\{[x]_i^{\mathsf{Bit}}\}_{i=1}^n \in$ PubOutputs, and compute the public value $x = x_1 \oplus \cdots \oplus x_n$.
- Each party P_i outputs the list of public openings, together with all private values that P_i stored during **Sample** or the bit-string **Mult** step.

PHASE II: FINAL OUTPUT

Public Output (String): To output the committed string $[X]_j$, P_j uses the Open command of $\mathcal{F}_{\mathsf{HCom}}$. If P_j fails to open any commitment, the parties output (Abort, P_j).

Abort: If the $\Pi_{\mathsf{D\text{-}TinyMPC}}$ protocol aborts:
1. Every party opens its commitments to its random tape of $\Pi_{\mathsf{D\text{-}TinyMPC}}$.
2. Run the detector $\mathcal{D}$ of $\Pi_{\mathsf{D\text{-}TinyMPC}}$. If $\mathcal{D}$ outputs that $\mathcal{J} \subset [n]$ cheated then output (Abort, $\mathcal{J}$).

Fig. 5. The preprocessing protocol $\Pi_{\mathsf{Prep}}^{\mathsf{ID}}$.

3.3 Efficiency Analysis

The main overhead of our preprocessing protocol, compared with the non-identifiable protocol which we build upon [26], is due to the use of secure broadcast in the

---

Subprotocol $\Pi_{\mathsf{BitStringMult}}^m$

The subprotocol uses the functionalities $\mathcal{F}_{\mathsf{HCom}}$, $\mathcal{F}_{\mathsf{Rand}}$, and the protocol $\Pi_{\mathsf{D\text{-}TinyMPC}}$.
We let s denote a statistical security parameter.
INPUTS: Bits $\langle x_1 \rangle, \ldots, \langle x_m \rangle$, and strings $[R^1]_1, \ldots, [R^n]_n$, where party P_i has R^i.
OUTPUT: Shares of the bit-string products $W_{\tau,j} = x_\tau \cdot R^j$, for $\tau \in [m], j \in [n]$, and commitments to every party's share of $W_{\tau,j}$ under $\mathcal{F}_{\mathsf{HCom}}$.

I: Init: The parties sample s additional random bits.
   1. Each P_i calls **Input** on $\Pi_{\mathsf{D\text{-}TinyMPC}}$ with s random bits $(\hat{x}_1^i, \ldots, \hat{x}_s^i)$. Compute the shared bits $\langle \hat{x}_\tau \rangle = \sum_{i \in [n]} \langle \hat{x}_\tau^i \rangle$ using $\Pi_{\mathsf{D\text{-}TinyMPC}}$.

   2. Write $X = (x_1, \ldots, x_m)$ and $\hat{X} = (\hat{x}_1, \ldots, \hat{x}_s)$ and define $\langle X \rangle, \langle \hat{X} \rangle$ accordingly.

II: Multiply: For each $j \in [n]$, the parties do as follows:
   1. Call $\Pi_{\mathsf{D\text{-}TinyMPC}}$ on input (MultBitString) to obtain random shares $W_{\tau,j}^i$ of $W_{\tau,j} = x_\tau \cdot R^j$, and shares $\hat{W}_{\tau,j}^i$ of $\hat{x}_\tau \cdot R^j$.

   2. Write $W_j^i \in (\mathbb{F}_2^\kappa)^m$ as P_i's shares of $X \cdot R^j$, and $\hat{W}_j^i \in (\mathbb{F}_2^\kappa)^s$ for the shares of $\hat{X} \cdot R^j$.

III: Commit: Each party P_i commits to W_j^i and $\hat{W}_j^i$ using $\mathcal{F}_{\mathsf{HCom}}$, for each $j \in [n]$.

IV: Check: The parties check correctness of the commitments as follows:
   1. The parties call $\mathcal{F}_{\mathsf{Rand}}$ to sample a seed for a uniformly random, ε-almost 1-universal linear hash function, $\mathbf{H} \in \mathbb{F}_2^{s \times m}$.
   2. All parties compute the vector:

$$\langle C_x \rangle = \mathbf{H} \cdot \langle X \rangle + \langle \hat{X} \rangle \in \mathbb{F}_2^s$$

   and open C_x using **Open** of $\Pi_{\mathsf{D\text{-}TinyMPC}}$. If $\Pi_{\mathsf{D\text{-}TinyMPC}}$ aborts, the parties run the **Abort** phase of $\Pi_{\mathsf{Prep}}^{\mathsf{ID}}$.
   3. For each $i \in [n]$, the parties use $\mathcal{F}_{\mathsf{HCom}}$ to obtain commitments to the vectors in $(\mathbb{F}_2^\kappa)^s$:

$$[C_j^i]_i = \mathbf{H} \cdot [W_j^i]_i + [\hat{W}_j^i]_i \text{ for } j \neq i, \text{ and } \quad [C_i^i]_i = \mathbf{H} \cdot [W_i^i]_i + [\hat{W}_i^i]_i + C_x \cdot [R^i]_i.$$

   Each P_i then opens its commitments to C_j^i, for $j \in [n]$.
   4. All parties check that, for each $j \in [n]$, $\sum_{i=1}^n C_j^i = 0$. If any check fails, the parties go to the **Abort** phase below.
   5. The parties output the shares $W_{\tau,j}^i$, and commitments $[W_{\tau,j}^i]_i$.

Abort: If Step 4 of **Check** fails, the parties do as follows:
   1. If $\mathcal{F}_{\mathsf{Rand}}$ outputs $(\mathtt{Abort}, \mathcal{J})$ then all parties output this. If not, continue.
   2. Every party opens its commitments to its random tape of $\Pi_{\mathsf{D\text{-}TinyMPC}}$.
   3. Using the opened random tapes, transcript and CRS of $\Pi_{\mathsf{D\text{-}TinyMPC}}$, compute each party's shares W_j^i and $\hat{W}_j^i$, which were obtained after the **Multiply** step.
   4. Let $\mathcal{J} \subset [n]$ be the set of indices $i \in [n]$ for which $C_j^i \neq \mathbf{H} \cdot W_j^i + \hat{W}_j^i$.
   5. Output $(\mathtt{Abort}, \mathcal{J})$.

Fig. 6. Subprotocol $\Pi_{\mathsf{BitStringMult}}^m$ to check consistency of committed bit-string multiplications.

Subprotocol Π_{CheckBit}

The subprotocol uses the functionalities $\mathcal{F}_{\mathsf{HCom}}^{\mathtt{Bit}}$, $\mathcal{F}_{\mathsf{Rand}}$, and the protocol $\Pi_{\mathsf{D\text{-}TinyMPC}}$.

NOTATION: We use $\langle x \rangle$ to denote that $x \in \mathbb{F}_2$ is stored by $\Pi_{\mathsf{D\text{-}TinyMPC}}$, and $[x]_c^{\mathtt{Bit}}$ to denote $x \in \mathbb{F}_2$ that is stored in $\mathcal{F}_{\mathsf{HCom}}^{\mathtt{Bit}}$. We let s denote a statistical security parameter.

INPUTS: Bits $\langle x_1 \rangle, \ldots, \langle x_m \rangle$ stored using $\Pi_{\mathsf{D\text{-}TinyMPC}}$, and $\mathcal{F}_{\mathsf{HCom}}^{\mathtt{Bit}}$ commitments $[x_1^i]_c^{\mathtt{Bit}}, \cdots, [x_m^i]_c^{\mathtt{Bit}}$, for $i \in [n]$, where P_i committed to the values x_j^i.

OUTPUT: The protocol succeeds if $x_j = \sum_i x_j^i$, for $j \in [m]$.

Check:

1. Each party P_i samples s random bits $\hat{x}_1, \ldots, \hat{x}_s \leftarrow \mathbb{F}_2$.

2. P_i inputs $\hat{x}_j^i$ into $\Pi_{\mathsf{D\text{-}TinyMPC}}$, and commits to $\hat{x}_j^i$ with $\mathcal{F}_{\mathsf{HCom}}^{\mathtt{Bit}}$, for $j \in [m]$.

3. Using $\mathcal{F}_{\mathsf{Rand}}$, the parties sample a random ε-almost 1-universal hash function $\mathbf{H} \in \mathbb{F}_2^{s \times m}$.

4. Writing $[X^i]_c^{\mathtt{Bit}} = ([x_1^i]_c^{\mathtt{Bit}}, \ldots, [x_m^i]_c^{\mathtt{Bit}})$, $[\hat{X}^i]_c^{\mathtt{Bit}} = ([\hat{x}_1^i]_c^{\mathtt{Bit}}, \ldots, [\hat{x}_s^i]_c^{\mathtt{Bit}})$, and similarly for $\langle X \rangle, \langle \hat{X} \rangle$, compute
$$[C_1^i]_c^{\mathtt{Bit}} = \mathbf{H} \cdot [X^i]_c^{\mathtt{Bit}} + [\hat{X}^i]_c^{\mathtt{Bit}}, \quad \langle C_2 \rangle = \mathbf{H} \cdot \langle X \rangle + \langle \hat{X} \rangle$$

5. The parties open C_1^i and C_2 using $\mathcal{F}_{\mathsf{HCom}}^{\mathtt{Bit}}$ and $\Pi_{\mathsf{D\text{-}TinyMPC}}$, respectively, and check that $\sum_i C_1^i = C_2$. If the check fails, the parties go to **Abort**.

Abort:

1. All parties open their $\langle x_j \rangle$-shares as x_j^i using $\Pi_{\mathsf{D\text{-}TinyMPC}}$, and each P_i opens its $[x_j^i]_c^{\mathtt{Bit}}$ values as y_j^i using $\mathcal{F}_{\mathsf{HCom}}^{\mathtt{Bit}}$.

2. Let $\mathcal{J} \subset [n]$ be the set of indices i for which there exists a $j \in [m]$ such that $x_j^i \neq y_j^i$.

3. Output $(\mathtt{Abort}, \mathcal{J})$.

Fig. 7. Subprotocol Π_{CheckBit} to check consistency of committed bits.

compilation with Lemma 3.2, and the use of homomorphic commitments for every wire in the garbled circuit. We now discuss these costs in more detail, and describe an optimization to reduce the use of broadcast.

We first observe that we can run an *optimistic* version of $\Pi_{\mathsf{Prep}}^{\mathsf{ID}}$, without the additional broadcasts in Lemma 3.2. If this optimistic offline protocol ends successfully (i.e. no abort occurs during Phase I), then the online phase will not require the identifiability property of $\Pi_{\mathsf{Prep}}^{\mathsf{ID}}$. In case of an error in the optimistic $\Pi_{\mathsf{Prep}}^{\mathsf{ID}}$ instance, we then re-run the preprocessing with new randomness for each party and using the identifiable version with broadcast. Observe that this may not identify a cheater in case the second protocol succeeds, but this does not contradict the definition of identifiable abort as the adversary now just forces the honest parties to use more resources. At the same time, the fact that the real inputs at this point were not used for any computation and due to the use of new randomness by each party, privacy is preserved.

Regarding the homomorphic commitments, note that the dominating cost is during the bit-string multiplication ($\Pi_{\mathsf{D\text{-}TinyMPC}}$), where each of the n parties must commit to $n \cdot m$ strings of length κ, where m is approximately the number of AND gates. Computationally, this overhead is very cheap. For instance, based on the implementation from [44] (which is similar to the non-interactive scheme we use) as a rough estimate for computation, then for $n = 5$ parties and the AES circuit with 6800 AND gates, we estimate the cost of generating commitments in a WAN setting is around 0.3 s. Compared with [48], this is only around a 10% overhead. Therefore, the main cost introduced in this stage is likely having to securely broadcast these commitments. Since for large circuits this involves the broadcast of very long strings, broadcast "extension" techniques such as [22] may be useful to reduce the complexity.

4   Online Phase

The online phase of our computation is modeled after [26]. For completeness, in the full version we outline the main idea of constant-round MPC, so here we focus on the details necessary in order to achieve identifiable abort. HSS uses a BMR-approach to achieve constant-round MPC, where the parties can identify locally if their output was correct or not. In order to identify a cheater, we will perform a reconstruction of a faulty gate in case of an error in that gate. This reconstruction, as it turns out, does not reveal any information beyond the regular protocol transcript. To be able to perform such a reconstruction we will use the new properties of our enhanced preprocessing functionality $\mathcal{F}_{\mathsf{Prep}}^{\mathsf{ID}}$, namely that it also provides a verification mechanism for keys. This reconstruction consists of opening commitments to the input keys to the gate which all parties used for evaluation as well as the supposed output key using $\mathcal{F}_{\mathsf{Prep}}^{\mathsf{ID}}$.

There are multiple cases in which aborts can happen during the online phase, which entails different ways of how the cheater must be identified. These cases are as follows:

1. *A set of parties can stop to communicate.* As our protocol (apart from $\mathcal{F}_{\mathsf{Prep}}^{\mathsf{ID}}$) only uses broadcast communication, such behaviour identifies cheaters directly.
2. *The adversary can manipulate a gate in such a way that an honest party sees an error.* This is the most straightforward error from garbling and can directly be detected by reconstructing the gate. In the protocol, we detect this in Steps 5, 6 of **Abort**. There, we open the keys which correspond to the output of the gate in $\mathcal{F}_{\mathsf{Prep}}^{\mathsf{ID}}$ that we would expect to see, based on **Init**. We can then compare the opening with the actual outputs which were derived based on share_τ^j (the garbling information) from each party, which directly shows whenever $\mathcal{A}$ garbled a circuit wrongly towards any party.
3. *The adversary may send complaints, even though a gate was garbled correctly.* In this case we reconstruct the gate normally and, as no error occurs, we identify complaining parties as cheaters. This is the end of Step 6 of **Abort**.
4. *The adversary may send complaints about incorrect gates that are outside the "active path".* Here we will show that the honest parties agree on the active path, i.e. on the rows of each garbled table which they decrypt during evaluation or - equivalently - the public values Λ_w. Thus, honest parties can identify complaints outside the active path as cheating, which is done in Step 2 of **Abort**.
5. *The adversary can garble a gate incorrectly for a dishonest party and let that party not report this.* In this case, the protocol will only abort at the next AND gate g' into which the output of the wrongly garbled gate g is fed. In such a case we will see a difference between the keys that the honest parties obtained as input of g and the keys that are opened by the dishonest party that did not send a $\mathsf{Conflict}$-message. We do this by opening the committed input keys $[K_{u,\Lambda_u}^j]_j, [K_{v,\Lambda_v}^j]_j$ in Step 5 via

---

The MPC Protocol - $\Pi_{\mathsf{MPC}}^{\mathsf{ID}}$ (Initialization)

COMMON INPUTS: A hash function $\mathsf{H} : G \times \mathbb{F}_2^{2\kappa} \to \mathbb{F}_2^{n\kappa}$ and a circuit C_f representing the function f. Let the input wires of a gate be labeled u and v, and the output wire be w. Let Λ_u and Λ_v be the public values on the input wires. The protocol uses an instance of $\mathcal{F}_{\mathsf{Prep}}^{\mathsf{ID}}$.
PRIVATE INPUTS: $\rho = (\rho_1, \ldots, \rho_{n_{\mathsf{in}}})$, where $\{\rho_h\}_{h \in \mathsf{input}_i}$ is party P_i's input.
If a set of parties $\mathcal{J}$ does not send messages during the protocol, then each party outputs $(\mathsf{Abort}, \mathcal{J})$ and stops. If $\mathcal{F}_{\mathsf{Prep}}^{\mathsf{ID}}$ at any point outputs $(\mathsf{Abort}, \mathcal{J})$ then each party outputs $(\mathsf{Abort}, \mathcal{J})$ and stops.

Init:

1. Each party P_i sends (Init) to $\mathcal{F}_{\mathsf{Prep}}^{\mathsf{ID}}$, which in turn outputs $[R^1]_1, \ldots, [R^n]_n$.

2. Passing topologically through all the wires $w \in W$ of the circuit:
    - If $w \in \mathsf{input}_h$:
        (a) Each P_i sends $\mathsf{Sample}(\mathbb{F}_2, P_h)$ to $\mathcal{F}_{\mathsf{Prep}}^{\mathsf{ID}}$ which outputs $\langle \lambda_w \rangle$.
        (b) For each $j \in [n]$ each P_i sends $\mathsf{Sample}(\mathbb{F}_2^{\kappa}, P_j)$ to $\mathcal{F}_{\mathsf{Prep}}^{\mathsf{ID}}$ which outputs $[K_{w,0}^j]_j$.
        (c) For each $j \in [n]$ each P_i sends $\mathsf{Add}([K_{w,0}^j]_j, [R^j]_j)$ to $\mathcal{F}_{\mathsf{Prep}}^{\mathsf{ID}}$ which outputs $[K_{w,1}^j]_j$.
    - If w is the output of an AND gate with input wires u, v:
        (a) Each P_i sends $\mathsf{Sample}(\mathbb{F}_2, \perp)$ to $\mathcal{F}_{\mathsf{Prep}}^{\mathsf{ID}}$ which outputs $\langle \lambda_w \rangle$.
        (b) Each P_i sends $\mathsf{Multiply}(\langle \lambda_u \rangle, \langle \lambda_v \rangle)$ to $\mathcal{F}_{\mathsf{Prep}}^{\mathsf{ID}}$ which outputs $\langle \lambda_{uv} \rangle$.
        (c) For each $j \in [n]$ each P_i sends $\mathsf{Sample}(\mathbb{F}_2^{\kappa}, P_j)$ to $\mathcal{F}_{\mathsf{Prep}}^{\mathsf{ID}}$ which outputs $[K_{w,0}^j]_j$.
        (d) For each $j \in [n]$ each P_i sends $\mathsf{Add}([K_{w,0}^j]_j, [R^j]_j)$ to $\mathcal{F}_{\mathsf{Prep}}^{\mathsf{ID}}$ which outputs $[K_{w,1}^j]_j$.
    - If w is the output of a XOR gate, and u and v its input wires:
        (a) Each P_i sends $\mathsf{Add}(\langle \lambda_u \rangle, \langle \lambda_v \rangle)$ to $\mathcal{F}_{\mathsf{Prep}}^{\mathsf{ID}}$ which outputs $\langle \lambda_w \rangle$.
        (b) Each P_i for each $j \in [n]$ sends $\mathsf{Add}([K_{u,0}^j]_j, [K_{v,0}^j]_j)$ to $\mathcal{F}_{\mathsf{Prep}}^{\mathsf{ID}}$ which outputs $[K_{w,0}^j]_j$ and $\mathsf{Add}([K_{w,0}^j]_j, [R^j]_j)$ to $\mathcal{F}_{\mathsf{Prep}}^{\mathsf{ID}}$ which outputs $[K_{w,1}^j]_j$ respectively.

3. For each $\tau \in G^{\mathsf{ext}}$ the parties use **Add** of $\mathcal{F}_{\mathsf{Prep}}^{\mathsf{ID}}$ to compute $\langle d_\tau \rangle = (\langle \lambda_u \rangle \oplus a) \cdot (\langle \lambda_v \rangle \oplus b) \oplus \langle \lambda_w \rangle$ from $\langle \lambda_w \rangle, \langle \lambda_{uv} \rangle, \langle \lambda_u \rangle$ and $\langle \lambda_v \rangle$. Then for each $j \in [n]$ each party P_i sends $\mathsf{MultBitString}(\langle d_\tau \rangle, [R^j]_j)$ to $\mathcal{F}_{\mathsf{Prep}}^{\mathsf{ID}}$ so that the parties obtain $[W_{\tau,j}^1]_1, \ldots, [W_{\tau,j}^n]_n$ respectively.

4. The parties first send $(\mathsf{PublicOutput}, \langle \lambda_w \rangle)$ to $\mathcal{F}_{\mathsf{Prep}}^{\mathsf{ID}}$ for each output wire $w \in \mathsf{out}$ of C_f. Afterwards, the parties send $(\mathsf{DelayedOutputs})$ to $\mathcal{F}_{\mathsf{Prep}}^{\mathsf{ID}}$ so that each party P_i obtains $\{\lambda_w\}_{w \in \mathsf{out}}$ and $\{\lambda_w\}_{w \in \mathsf{input}_i}$ as well as R^i, $K_{w,0}^i$ and $W_{\tau,j}^i$ as defined above.

Fig. 8. The MPC protocol - $\Pi_{\mathsf{MPC}}^{\mathsf{ID}}$ (Initialization).

$\mathcal{F}_{\mathsf{Prep}}^{\mathsf{ID}}$ and comparing these to the keys which are the inputs of the "faulty" gate g as evaluated by every party during the circuit evaluation. This is done in Step 6 of **Abort**.

The MPC Protocol - $\Pi_{\mathsf{MPC}}^{\mathsf{ID}}$ (Computation)

Input:

1. For all input wires $\mathtt{in} \in \mathtt{input}_i$ with input from P_i the party computes $\Lambda_{\mathtt{in}} = \rho_{\mathtt{in}} \oplus \lambda_{\mathtt{in}}$. Then, P_i broadcasts $\Lambda_{\mathtt{in}}$ to all parties.

2. Upon receiving $\Lambda_{\mathtt{in}}$ for all inputs of C_f each party P_i broadcasts $K_{\mathtt{in},\Lambda_{\mathtt{in}}}^i$ for all $\mathtt{in} \in$ input. Denote all these input keys as $\overline{K}_{\mathtt{in},\Lambda_{\mathtt{in}}}^j$ for $j \in [n]$.

Garble:

1. For all $\tau \in G^{\mathsf{ext}}$ with $\tau = (g, a, b)$ each P_i defines

$$\mathtt{share}_\tau^i \leftarrow \mathsf{H}(g, K_{u,a}^i, K_{v,b}^i) \oplus (W_{\tau,1}^i, \dots, W_{\tau,n}^i) \oplus (0, \dots, 0, K_{w,0}^i, \dots, 0).$$

2. Each P_i broadcasts $\mathtt{share}_\tau^i$ to all parties, who set $\mathtt{circ}_\tau = \bigoplus_{j \in [n]} \mathtt{share}_\tau^j$.

Circuit Evaluation: Passing through the circuit topologically, the parties can now locally compute the following operations for each gate g with input wires u, v, public values Λ_u, Λ_v and keys $\overline{K}_{u,\Lambda_u}^j, \overline{K}_{v,\Lambda_v}^j$:

1. If g is a XOR gate, set the public value on the output wire to be $\Lambda_w = \Lambda_u \oplus \Lambda_v$. In addition, for every $j \in [n]$, each party computes $\overline{K}_{w,\Lambda_w}^j = \overline{K}_{u,\Lambda_u}^j \oplus \overline{K}_{v,\Lambda_v}^j$.

2. If g is an AND gate, then each party computes:

$$(\overline{K}_{w,\Lambda_w}^1, \dots, \overline{K}_{w,\Lambda_w}^n) = \mathtt{circ}_{g,\Lambda_u,\Lambda_v} \oplus \left(\bigoplus_{j \in [n]} \mathsf{H}(g, \overline{K}_{u,\Lambda_u}^j, \overline{K}_{v,\Lambda_v}^j) \right)$$

3. If $\overline{K}_{w,\Lambda_w}^i \notin \{K_{w,0}^i, K_{w,1}^i\}$, then P_i broadcasts $(\mathtt{Conflict}, g, \Lambda_u, \Lambda_v)$ and enters **Abort**. Otherwise, it sets $\Lambda_w = c$ if $\overline{K}_{w,\Lambda_w}^i = K_{w,c}^i$.

4. The output key of g is defined to be $(\overline{K}_{w,\Lambda_w}^1, \dots, \overline{K}_{w,\Lambda_w}^n)$ and the public value Λ_w.

Output: Everyone obtained a public value $\Lambda_{\mathtt{out}}$ for every circuit-output wire out. Each party can obtain the actual output $Y = (y_1, \dots, y_{n_{\mathtt{out}}})$ as $y_{\mathtt{out}} = \Lambda_{\mathtt{out}} \oplus \lambda_{\mathtt{out}}$, where λ_w was obtained during **Init**.

Fig. 9. The MPC protocol - $\Pi_{\mathsf{MPC}}^{\mathsf{ID}}$ (Computation).

Throughout the protocol, which is outlined in Fig. 8, Fig. 9 and Fig. 10 we let $K_{w,0}^i$ be the 0-key of P_i for the wire w, R^i be the global difference used by this party and define $K_{w,1}^i = K_{w,0}^i \oplus R^i$. Overlined keys $\overline{K}$ are those obtained in the evaluation of the circuit. We present the proof of the following theorem in the full version.

Theorem 4.1. *Let* H *be a circular 2-correlation robust hash function. Assuming a secure broadcast channel, protocol* $\Pi_{\mathsf{MPC}}^{\mathsf{ID}}$ *implements the functionality* $\mathcal{F}_{\mathsf{MPC}}^{\mathsf{ID}}$ *in the* $\mathcal{F}_{\mathsf{Prep}}^{\mathsf{ID}}$-*hybrid model with security against a static, active adversary corrupting at most* $n - 1$ *parties.*

Optimistic online phase. We can define an optimistic version of $\Pi_{\mathsf{MPC}}^{\mathsf{ID}}$, for which we analyse its best and worst case complexity. In this variant the use of broadcast is replaced with that of point-to-point channels, with the exception of the broadcast of the $\Lambda_{\mathtt{in}}$ values. We require this broadcast in order to extract the inputs of the malicious parties and the unique active path for the evaluation of the garbled circuit. As MPC with

---

The MPC Protocol - $\Pi_{\mathsf{MPC}}^{\mathsf{ID}}$ (Abort)

Abort: Receive messages of the type $(\mathtt{Conflict}, g, \Lambda_u, \Lambda_v)$ from the parties where g is an AND-gate. Ignore all double or other messages. Then each party does the following checks:

1. Let $\{\overline{K}_{\mathtt{in}, \Lambda_{\mathtt{in}}}^j\}_{\mathtt{in} \in \mathtt{input}}$ be the keys that each party obtained from P_j for all inputs during **Input**. Choose the smallest g in the circuit among all the $\mathtt{Conflict}$-messages.

2. Assume that honest parties evaluated the gate g using the public values Λ_u, Λ_v. If a non-empty set of parties $\mathcal{J}$ sent $(\mathtt{Conflict}, g, \Lambda_u', \Lambda_v')$ with $(\Lambda_u', \Lambda_v') \neq (\Lambda_u, \Lambda_v)$, then output $(\mathtt{Abort}, \mathcal{J})$.

3. Let $\{\overline{K}_{u,\Lambda_u}^j, \overline{K}_{v,\Lambda_v}^j\}_{j \in [n]}$ be the input keys of g that each party computed during **Circuit Evaluation**. For each $j \in [n]$ recompute $(\overline{K}_{w,1}^j, \ldots, \overline{K}_{w,n}^j) \leftarrow H(g, \overline{K}_{u,\Lambda_u}^j, \overline{K}_{v,\Lambda_v}^j)$. Let $\hat{\mathcal{J}}$ be the set of parties that sent $(\mathtt{Conflict}, g, \Lambda_u, \Lambda_v)$.

4. For $\tau = (g, \Lambda_u, \Lambda_v)$ all parties send $\mathtt{Add}([K_{w,0}^j]_j, [W_{\tau,j}^j]_j)$ for $j \in [n]$ to $\mathcal{F}_{\mathsf{Prep}}^{\mathsf{ID}}$ to obtain $[D_w^j]_j$.

5. The parties use **Output (String)** of $\mathcal{F}_{\mathsf{Prep}}^{\mathsf{ID}}$ to open the following values:
   (a) Send $(\mathtt{PublicOutput}, [K_{\mathtt{in},\Lambda_{\mathtt{in}}}^j]_j)$ for all $j \in [n]$, $\mathtt{in} \in \mathtt{input}$ to obtain $K_{\mathtt{in},\Lambda_{\mathtt{in}}}^j$;
   (b) Send $(\mathtt{PublicOutput}, [K_{u,\Lambda_u}^j]_j)$, $(\mathtt{PublicOutput}, [K_{v,\Lambda_v}^j]_j)$ for all $j \in [n]$ to obtain $K_{u,\Lambda_u}^j, K_{v,\Lambda_v}^j$ respectively;
   (c) Send $(\mathtt{PublicOutput}, [D_w^j]_j)$ if $j = \ell$ and $(\mathtt{PublicOutput}, [W_{\tau,\ell}^j]_j)$ otherwise for all $j, \ell \in [n]$ to obtain $D_w^j, W_{\tau,\ell}^j$ respectively.

6. Each party tests
   - For all $j \in [n]$, $\mathtt{in} \in \mathtt{input}$ that $K_{\mathtt{in},\Lambda_{\mathtt{in}}}^j \overset{?}{=} \overline{K}_{\mathtt{in},\Lambda_{\mathtt{in}}}^j$;
   - For all $j \in [n]$ that $K_{u,\Lambda_u}^j \overset{?}{=} \overline{K}_{u,\Lambda_u}^j$ and $K_{v,\Lambda_v}^j \overset{?}{=} \overline{K}_{v,\Lambda_v}^j$.
   - Furthermore, for all $j, \ell \in [n]$
     if $j = \ell$ that $D_w^j \overset{?}{=} \overline{K}_{w,j}^j \oplus \mathtt{share}_\tau^j[j]$;
     if $j \neq \ell$ that $W_{\tau,\ell}^j \overset{?}{=} \overline{K}_{w,\ell}^j \oplus \mathtt{share}_\tau^j[\ell]$.
   Let $\mathcal{J}$ be the set of parties which generated values where one of the above tests does not work out. Then output $(\mathtt{Abort}, \mathcal{J})$. If all tests hold then output $(\mathtt{Abort}, \hat{\mathcal{J}})$.

Fig. 10. The MPC protocol - $\Pi_{\mathsf{MPC}}^{\mathsf{ID}}$ (Abort).

identifiable abort implies secure broadcast [16], it seems natural that we cannot avoid broadcast in our protocol, even optimistically. Furthermore, broadcasting $\Lambda_{\mathtt{in}}$ is also necessary in the original [26] construction.

The main advantage of avoiding the use of broadcast in an instance of $\Pi_{\mathsf{MPC}}^{\mathsf{ID}}$ is in the reconstruction of the garbled circuit (Step 2 of **Garble**). In our optimistic version we can put the circuit together by having each party send $\mathtt{share}^i$ to a single party P_i, which will then send the reconstructed circuit to everyone else, as in [26]. Note that replacing the broadcast here and in Step 2 of **Input**, only allows an adversary to introduce additive errors to the circuit, which can be easily derived by computing the difference between an evaluation of the garbled circuit with the correct key and an incorrect one.

When the honest parties encounter an error that would trigger the execution of **Abort**, they instead repeat the execution of Π_{MPC}^{ID} from Step 2 of **Input**, this time using broadcast as indicated in the protocol boxes. Any party refusing to engage in the re-run can be trivially identified as corrupted by all honest parties. Hence, the best-case complexity is of $O(\kappa n|C|) + \mathsf{bc}(I)$, where I is the number of input wires, and the worst-case complexity is $O(\kappa n|C|) + \mathsf{bc}(I\kappa + n^2\kappa|C|)$.

Finally, we observe that this additional optimistic evaluation of a garbled circuit with additive errors enables an extra attempt for the adversary to guess the value R^i of each honest party. As $R^i \in \{0,1\}^\kappa$, this has no impact on the protocol security.

5   Achieving Public Verifiability

We conclude by presenting how the previously introduced protocols and functionalities can be transformed into publicly verifiable counterparts. To model public verifiability formally, we assume (similar to [3]) the existence of a third party $\mathcal{V}$ who will not be part of $\mathcal{P}$. As a matter of fact, $\mathcal{V}$ does not need to be online or even exist while all the other protocol steps are running.

The notion of public verifiability which we achieve in this work differs from [3, 17,46] in multiple respects: while it still allows $\mathcal{V}$ to establish the correctness of the output value, our model requires that at least one honest party is present during the MPC protocol. This is in contrast to the aforementioned works which could guarantee correctness even if all parties are corrupted. Similar to [17] (albeit different from the other works) $\mathcal{V}$ will be able to identify cheaters during the verification phase (if they existed). Note that our model lends itself to be applicable in e.g. the client-server setting in order to prevent corrupted servers from announcing false outcomes, or when MPC is integrated with distributed ledgers.

More formally, let $\mathcal{F}^{ID}$ be the identifiable abort version of any functionality $\mathcal{F}$, as presented in Sect. 2.1. We denote as $\mathcal{F}^{PV}$ an extension of $\mathcal{F}^{ID}$ which further supports public verifiability, as described in Fig. 11. In a nutshell, publicly verifiable functionalities incorporate an additional party, the verifier $\mathcal{V}$, who can query the functionality at any point. When doing so, $\mathcal{F}^{PV}$ replies with all public outputs of $\mathcal{F}$ produced so far and, if there was an abort, the same set of corrupted parties $\mathcal{J}$ that $\mathcal{F}^{ID}$ would have produced towards the honest parties.

Functionality $\mathcal{F}^{PV}$

$\mathcal{F}^{PV}$ is exactly as $\mathcal{F}^{ID}$, with two changes. First, $\mathcal{F}^{PV}$ runs with an additional party, the verifier $\mathcal{V}$. Second, it has the following extra command:

Verify: On input (Verify) from $\mathcal{V}$:
- If the functionality has received (Abort, $\mathcal{J}$) from $\mathcal{A}$ in the execution of any other command, return (Abort, $\mathcal{J}$) to $\mathcal{V}$.
- If the functionality has sent any message starting by PublicOutput, it forwards that same message to $\mathcal{V}$.

Fig. 11. Extending an identifiable-abort functionality $\mathcal{F}^{ID}$ to its publicly verifiable version $\mathcal{F}^{PV}$.

Whereas turning functionalities into publicly verifiable ones is pretty straightforward, one has to be more careful about their corresponding protocols. At the core, we achieve our goal by using $\mathcal{F}_{\text{Broadcast}}^{\text{PV}}$, a publicly verifiable version of secure broadcast. Such variant can be implemented by using an *authenticated* bulletin board $\mathcal{F}_{\text{BulletinBoard}}$ (detailed in the full version): broadcasting is equivalent to writing, and $\mathcal{V}$ can verify any 'sent' message by reading the board.

If considered on its own, adapting $\Pi_{\text{Prep}}^{\text{ID}}$ to implement $\mathcal{F}_{\text{Prep}}^{\text{PV}}$ could be attained mostly by just switching $\mathcal{F}_{\text{Broadcast}}^{\text{ID}}$ to its publicly verifiable version. As all messages would go through $\mathcal{F}_{\text{Broadcast}}^{\text{PV}}$ (either in the clear, or inside commitments), an external verifier could easily find $\mathcal{F}_{\text{Prep}}^{\text{PV}}$'s outputs there if no abort happened. Also, if there was an abort, $\mathcal{V}$ would find in the same place all the necessary information to run the deterministic detector algorithm $\mathcal{D}$ (cf. Definition 3.1) and conclude the same set of corrupted parties $\mathcal{J}$ as the honest parties do.

On the other hand, implementing $\mathcal{F}_{\text{MPC}}^{\text{PV}}$ based on $\mathcal{F}_{\text{Prep}}^{\text{PV}}$ requires substantially more work: the way the **Abort** procedure of $\Pi_{\text{MPC}}^{\text{ID}}$ identifies cheating relies on knowing the *active path* in the garbled circuit corresponding to the Λ_{in} values which were broadcast in the **Input** phase. Unfortunately, determining the active path in $\Pi_{\text{MPC}}^{\text{ID}}$ requires private randomness from any party in $\mathcal{P}$ (namely, Step 3 in Fig. 9), which at that point cannot be revealed to $\mathcal{V}$ for running $\mathcal{D}$ because the parties have already provided their private inputs to $\Pi_{\text{MPC}}^{\text{ID}}$. Having all parties announce their active path does not solve the problem, as it is unclear to $\mathcal{V}$ which such path could be trusted. We now explain how to modify both $\Pi_{\text{Prep}}^{\text{ID}}$ and $\Pi_{\text{MPC}}^{\text{ID}}$ in order to achieve public verifiability.

5.1 Public Active Paths

To make the active path recognisable for $\mathcal{V}$, we use the well-known technique of fixing the last bit of a key to be its external wire value Λ_w, i.e., we require that each $K_{w,0}^i$ has as last bit 0 and each $K_{w,1}^i$ has as last bit 1[4]. The latter can be achieved by requiring that the last bit of R^i is 1. We formalize this in the ideal functionality $\mathcal{F}_{\text{Prep}}^{\text{PV}}$ by requiring that vectors generated by **Sample** and **Init** have their last bit set to 0 and 1, respectively. For the sake of formality, we denote the resulting modified functionality as $\mathcal{F}_{\underline{\text{Prep}}}^{\text{PV}}$.

In order to UC-implement $\mathcal{F}_{\underline{\text{Prep}}}^{\text{PV}}$, we first modify $\Pi_{\text{Prep}}^{\text{ID}}$ so that all messages are sent via $\mathcal{F}_{\text{Broadcast}}^{\text{PV}}$. Notice that $\mathcal{F}_{\text{HCom}}$ and $\mathcal{F}_{\text{Rand}}$ can be easily implemented with public verifiability by having their respective protocols send all communication through $\mathcal{F}_{\text{Broadcast}}^{\text{PV}}$. Furthermore, we require that each party sets the last bit of their vectors according to the previous description. As dishonest parties might not follow this, we add a (cheap) random linear check using $\mathcal{F}_{\text{HCom}}^{\text{PV}}$ to ensure correct behaviour, which is described below:

1. Each $P_i \in \mathcal{P}$ randomly samples s auxiliary masking vectors $A_1^i, \ldots, A_s^i \in \mathbb{F}_2^\kappa$, subject to the constraint that the last bit of each of them is zero. P_i commits to them using $\mathcal{F}_{\text{HCom}}^{\text{PV}}$ as $[A_1^i]_i, \ldots, [A_s^i]_i$.

---

[4] Technically, in this case we should increase the key length by one bit in order to compensate the loss of entropy, but we omit this in order to simplify our presentation.

2. Denote by $[X_1^i]_i, \ldots, [X_r^i]_i$, $r = |G| + n_{in}$, P_i's (value-zero) keys corresponding to the circuit-input wires and the output wires of AND gates, obtained using **Sample**. Let $[R^i]_i$ be the value obtained during **Init**. Parties in $\mathcal{P}$ call $\mathcal{F}_{Rand}^{PV}$ to generate, for every $i \in [n]$, $s \cdot (r+1)$ random bits $b_1^i, \ldots, b_{s(r+1)}^i$.

3. For $j \in [s]$, P_i uses $\mathcal{F}_{HCom}^{PV}$ to compute and open the random linear combination $[Z_j^i]_i = [A_j^i]_i + b_{j+s\cdot r}^i \cdot [R^i]_i + \sum_{k=1}^r b_{(j-1)\cdot r+k}^i \cdot [X_k^i]_i$ towards all parties, who check that the last bit of each opened Z_j^i is $b_{r\cdot s+j}^i$. If that is not the case for any i or j, they enter the **Abort** procedure.

As the last bit of every A_j^i, X_k^i should be zero and the last bit of R^i should be one and all those values are committed to before the b values are sampled, any corrupted P_i providing wrong values can only pass the j-th check with probability at most $1/2$, for every $j \in [s]$. On the other hand, and for an honest P_i, the A_j^i masks prevent any leakage on X_k^i, R^i beyond their lasts bits. From this, and Theorem 3.6 it then follows:

Lemma 5.1. *The transformation to Π_{Prep}^{ID} outlined above implements $\mathcal{F}_{\underline{Prep}}^{PV}$ in the $\{\mathcal{F}_{Broadcast}^{PV}, \mathcal{F}_{HCom}^{PV}, \mathcal{F}_{Rand}^{PV}\}$-hybrid model with security against a static, active adversary corrupting at most $n-1$ parties.*

5.2   Public Verifiability in the Online Phase

We now explain how to modify the online phase of Π_{MPC}^{ID} in order to implement $\mathcal{F}_{MPC}^{PV}$. As mentioned before, we require that all communication will be done via $\mathcal{F}_{Broadcast}^{PV}$.

While the **Init**, **Garble**, **Output** and **Abort** phase of our publicly verifiable protocol will be identical to Π_{MPC}^{ID}, we need to introduce some differences in **Input** and **Circuit Evaluation**. We proceed to outline those differences:

Input: Add a third step, where parties in $\mathcal{P}$ additionally check if the last bit of $\overline{K}_{in, \Lambda_{in}}^i$ is identical to Λ_{in} for every $i \in [n]$. Otherwise, they broadcast $(\texttt{Abort}, \mathcal{J})$, where $\mathcal{J}$ contains every P_i who sent the wrong key.

Circuit Evaluation: In Step 3 of this subprotocol, parties in $\mathcal{P}$ additionally check if the last bit of every $\overline{K}_{w, \Lambda_w}^i$ is identical for every $i \in [n]$. If that is not the case, they broadcast $(\texttt{Conflict}, g, \Lambda_u, \Lambda_v)$ and enter **Abort**.

Trivially, the **Abort** procedure still works for parties in $\mathcal{P}$ the same way it did in Π_{MPC}^{ID} without the above modifications. For a verifier $\mathcal{V}$ looking at the transcript of this procedure afterwards, things also work out: Due to the fact that wire keys now indicate the corresponding Λ value on the wire, up to the smallest g in the circuit among all **Conflict** messages, $\mathcal{V}$ can be sure of having obtained the correct Λ_u, Λ_v values. Hence, on Step 2, he can perform the same check honest parties in $\mathcal{P}$ did to conclude whether or not the $(\texttt{Conflict}, g, \Lambda_u', \Lambda_v')$ was correct, or if a malicious party trying to cheat. $\mathcal{V}$ cannot perform Step 4, but he can obtain the resulting value on Step 5, because it is a PublicOutput of $\mathcal{F}_{\underline{Prep}}^{PV}$ (cf. Fig. 11). The same is true for the other values revealed in that step, and thus $\mathcal{V}$ can perform the whole **Abort** procedure non-interactively. From this, and Theorem 4.1, we can conclude:

Lemma 5.2. *The transformation to* Π_{MPC}^{ID} *outlined above implements* $\mathcal{F}_{MPC}^{PV}$ *in the* $\{\mathcal{F}_{Broadcast}^{PV}, \mathcal{F}_{Prep}^{PV}\}$-*hybrid model with security against a static, active adversary corrupting at most* $n-1$ *parties.*

References

1. Asharov, G., Lindell, Y., Schneider, T., Zohner, M.: More efficient oblivious transfer extensions with security for malicious adversaries. In: Oswald, E., Fischlin, M. (eds.) EURO-CRYPT 2015, Part I. LNCS, vol. 9056, pp. 673–701. Springer, Heidelberg (2015). https://doi.org/10.1007/978-3-662-46800-5_26

2. Asharov, G., Orlandi, C.: Calling out cheaters: covert security with public verifiability. In: Wang, X., Sako, K. (eds.) ASIACRYPT 2012. LNCS, vol. 7658, pp. 681–698. Springer, Heidelberg (2012). https://doi.org/10.1007/978-3-642-34961-4_41

3. Baum, C., Damgård, I., Orlandi, C.: Publicly auditable secure multi-party computation. In: Abdalla, M., De Prisco, R. (eds.) SCN 2014. LNCS, vol. 8642, pp. 175–196. Springer, Cham (2014). https://doi.org/10.1007/978-3-319-10879-7_11

4. Baum, C., David, B., Dowsley, R.: Insured MPC: efficient secure computation with financial penalties. Financial Cryptography and Data Security (FC) 2020 (2020). https://eprint.iacr.org/2018/942

5. Baum, C., Orsini, E., Scholl, P.: Efficient secure multiparty computation with identifiable abort. In: Hirt, M., Smith, A. (eds.) TCC 2016-B, Part I. LNCS, vol. 9985, pp. 461–490. Springer, Heidelberg (2016). https://doi.org/10.1007/978-3-662-53641-4_18

6. Beaver, D., Micali, S., Rogaway, P.: The round complexity of secure protocols (extended abstract). In: 22nd ACM STOC, pp. 503–513. ACM Press, May 1990

7. Beimel, A., Omri, E., Orlov, I.: Protocols for multiparty coin toss with dishonest majority. In: Rabin, T. (ed.) CRYPTO 2010. LNCS, vol. 6223, pp. 538–557. Springer, Heidelberg (2010). https://doi.org/10.1007/978-3-642-14623-7_29

8. Bendlin, R., Damgård, I., Orlandi, C., Zakarias, S.: Semi-homomorphic encryption and multiparty computation. In: Paterson, K.G. (ed.) EUROCRYPT 2011. LNCS, vol. 6632, pp. 169–188. Springer, Heidelberg (2011). https://doi.org/10.1007/978-3-642-20465-4_11

9. Brandt, N.-P., Maier, S., Mller, T., Mller-Quade, J.: Constructing secure multi-party computation with identifiable abort. Cryptology ePrint Archive, Report 2020/153 (2020). https://eprint.iacr.org/2020/153

10. Byali, M., Patra, A., Ravi, D., Sarkar, P.: Fast and universally-composable oblivious transfer and commitment scheme with adaptive security. Cryptology ePrint Archive, Report 2017/1165 (2017). https://eprint.iacr.org/2017/1165

11. Canetti, R.: Universally composable security: a new paradigm for cryptographic protocols. In: 42nd FOCS, pp. 136–145. IEEE Computer Society Press, October 2001

12. Cascudo, I., Damgård, I., David, B., Döttling, N., Dowsley, R., Giacomelli, I.: Efficient UC commitment extension with homomorphism for free (and applications). In: Galbraith, S.D., Moriai, S. (eds.) ASIACRYPT 2019, Part II. LNCS, vol. 11922, pp. 606–635. Springer, Cham (2019). https://doi.org/10.1007/978-3-030-34621-8_22

13. Chaum, D., Roijakkers, S.: Unconditionally-secure digital signatures. In: Menezes, A.J., Vanstone, S.A. (eds.) CRYPTO 1990. LNCS, vol. 537, pp. 206–214. Springer, Heidelberg (1991). https://doi.org/10.1007/3-540-38424-3_15

14. Choi, S.G., Katz, J., Kumaresan, R., Zhou, H.-S.: On the security of the "free-XOR" technique. In: Cramer, R. (ed.) TCC 2012. LNCS, vol. 7194, pp. 39–53. Springer, Heidelberg (2012). https://doi.org/10.1007/978-3-642-28914-9_3

15. Cleve, R.: Limits on the security of coin flips when half the processors are faulty (extended abstract). In: 18th ACM STOC, pp. 364–369. ACM Press, May 1986

16. Cohen, R., Lindell, Y.: Fairness versus guaranteed output delivery in secure multiparty computation. In: Sarkar, P., Iwata, T. (eds.) ASIACRYPT 2014, Part II. LNCS, vol. 8874, pp. 466–485. Springer, Heidelberg (2014). https://doi.org/10.1007/978-3-662-45608-8_25

17. Cunningham, R., Fuller, B., Yakoubov, S.: Catching MPC cheaters: identification and openability. In: Shikata, J. (ed.) ICITS 2017. LNCS, vol. 10681, pp. 110–134. Springer, Cham (2017). https://doi.org/10.1007/978-3-319-72089-0_7

18. Damgård, I., Ishai, Y.: Constant-round multiparty computation using a black-box pseudorandom generator. In: Shoup, V. (ed.) CRYPTO 2005. LNCS, vol. 3621, pp. 378–394. Springer, Heidelberg (2005). https://doi.org/10.1007/11535218_23

19. Damgård, I., Pastro, V., Smart, N., Zakarias, S.: Multiparty computation from somewhat homomorphic encryption. In: Safavi-Naini, R., Canetti, R. (eds.) CRYPTO 2012. LNCS, vol. 7417, pp. 643–662. Springer, Heidelberg (2012). https://doi.org/10.1007/978-3-642-32009-5_38

20. Dolev, D., Strong, H.R.: Authenticated algorithms for byzantine agreement. SIAM J. Comput. 12(4), 656–666 (1983)

21. Frederiksen, T.K., Keller, M., Orsini, E., Scholl, P.: A unified approach to MPC with preprocessing using OT. In: Iwata, T., Cheon, J.H. (eds.) ASIACRYPT 2015, Part I. LNCS, vol. 9452, pp. 711–735. Springer, Heidelberg (2015). https://doi.org/10.1007/978-3-662-48797-6_29

22. Ganesh, C., Patra, A.: Broadcast extensions with optimal communication and round complexity. In: Proceedings of the 2016 ACM Symposium on Principles of Distributed Computing, PODC 2016, New York, NY, USA, pp. 371–380. Association for Computing Machinery (2016)

23. Garay, J.A., Katz, J., Koo, C.-Y., Ostrovsky, R.: Round complexity of authenticated broadcast with a dishonest majority. In: 48th FOCS, pp. 658–668. IEEE Computer Society Press, October 2007

24. Goldreich, O., Micali, S., Wigderson, A.: How to play any mental game or a completeness theorem for protocols with honest majority. In: Aho, A. (ed.) 19th ACM STOC, pp. 218–229. ACM Press, May 1987

25. Hanaoka, G., Shikata, J., Zheng, Y., Imai, H.: Unconditionally secure digital signature schemes admitting transferability. In: Okamoto, T. (ed.) ASIACRYPT 2000. LNCS, vol. 1976, pp. 130–142. Springer, Heidelberg (2000). https://doi.org/10.1007/3-540-44448-3_11

26. Hazay, C., Scholl, P., Soria-Vazquez, E.: Low cost constant round MPC combining BMR and oblivious transfer. In: Takagi, T., Peyrin, T. (eds.) ASIACRYPT 2017, Part I. LNCS, vol. 10624, pp. 598–628. Springer, Cham (2017). https://doi.org/10.1007/978-3-319-70694-8_21

27. Hong, C., Katz, J., Kolesnikov, V., Lu, W., Wang, X.: Covert security with public verifiability: faster, leaner, and simpler. In: Ishai, Y., Rijmen, V. (eds.) EUROCRYPT 2019, Part III. LNCS, vol. 11478, pp. 97–121. Springer, Cham (2019). https://doi.org/10.1007/978-3-030-17659-4_4

28. Ishai, Y., Kilian, J., Nissim, K., Petrank, E.: Extending oblivious transfers efficiently. In: Boneh, D. (ed.) CRYPTO 2003. LNCS, vol. 2729, pp. 145–161. Springer, Heidelberg (2003). https://doi.org/10.1007/978-3-540-45146-4_9

29. Ishai, Y., Ostrovsky, R., Zikas, V.: Secure multi-party computation with identifiable abort. In: Garay, J.A., Gennaro, R. (eds.) CRYPTO 2014, Part II. LNCS, vol. 8617, pp. 369–386. Springer, Heidelberg (2014). https://doi.org/10.1007/978-3-662-44381-1_21

30. Ishai, Y., Prabhakaran, M., Sahai, A.: Founding cryptography on oblivious transfer – efficiently. In: Wagner, D. (ed.) CRYPTO 2008. LNCS, vol. 5157, pp. 572–591. Springer, Heidelberg (2008). https://doi.org/10.1007/978-3-540-85174-5_32

31. Keller, M., Orsini, E., Scholl, P.: Actively secure OT extension with optimal overhead. In: Gennaro, R., Robshaw, M. (eds.) CRYPTO 2015, Part I. LNCS, vol. 9215, pp. 724–741. Springer, Heidelberg (2015). https://doi.org/10.1007/978-3-662-47989-6_35

32. Kiayias, A., Zhou, H.-S., Zikas, V.: Fair and robust multi-party computation using a global transaction ledger. In: Fischlin, M., Coron, J.-S. (eds.) EUROCRYPT 2016, Part II. LNCS, vol. 9666, pp. 705–734. Springer, Heidelberg (2016). https://doi.org/10.1007/978-3-662-49896-5_25

33. Kolesnikov, V., Malozemoff, A.J.: Public verifiability in the covert model (almost) for free. In: Iwata, T., Cheon, J.H. (eds.) ASIACRYPT 2015, Part II. LNCS, vol. 9453, pp. 210–235. Springer, Heidelberg (2015). https://doi.org/10.1007/978-3-662-48800-3_9

34. Kolesnikov, V., Schneider, T.: Improved garbled circuit: free XOR gates and applications. In: Aceto, L., Damgård, I., Goldberg, L.A., Halldórsson, M.M., Ingólfsdóttir, A., Walukiewicz, I. (eds.) ICALP 2008, Part II. LNCS, vol. 5126, pp. 486–498. Springer, Heidelberg (2008). https://doi.org/10.1007/978-3-540-70583-3_40

35. Kumaresan, R., Moran, T., Bentov, I.: How to use bitcoin to play decentralized poker. In: Ray, I., Li, N., Kruegel, C. (eds.) ACM CCS 2015, pp. 195–206. ACM Press, October 2015

36. Lindell, Y., Pinkas, B., Smart, N.P., Yanai, A.: Efficient constant round multi-party computation combining BMR and SPDZ. In: Gennaro, R., Robshaw, M. (eds.) CRYPTO 2015, Part II. LNCS, vol. 9216, pp. 319–338. Springer, Heidelberg (2015). https://doi.org/10.1007/978-3-662-48000-7_16

37. Lindell, Y., Smart, N.P., Soria-Vazquez, E.: More efficient constant-round multi-party computation from BMR and SHE. In: Hirt, M., Smith, A. (eds.) TCC 2016-B, Part I. LNCS, vol. 9985, pp. 554–581. Springer, Heidelberg (2016). https://doi.org/10.1007/978-3-662-53641-4_21

38. Lindell, Y., Zarosim, H.: Adaptive zero-knowledge proofs and adaptively secure oblivious transfer. In: Reingold, O. (ed.) TCC 2009. LNCS, vol. 5444, pp. 183–201. Springer, Heidelberg (2009). https://doi.org/10.1007/978-3-642-00457-5_12

39. Lindell, Y., Zarosim, H.: On the feasibility of extending oblivious transfer. In: Sahai, A. (ed.) TCC 2013. LNCS, vol. 7785, pp. 519–538. Springer, Heidelberg (2013). https://doi.org/10.1007/978-3-642-36594-2_29

40. Nielsen, J.B., Nordholt, P.S., Orlandi, C., Burra, S.S.: A new approach to practical active-secure two-party computation. In: Safavi-Naini, R., Canetti, R. (eds.) CRYPTO 2012. LNCS, vol. 7417, pp. 681–700. Springer, Heidelberg (2012). https://doi.org/10.1007/978-3-642-32009-5_40

41. Pass, R.: Bounded-concurrent secure multi-party computation with a dishonest majority. In Babai, L. (ed.) 36th ACM STOC, pp. 232–241. ACM Press, June 2004

42. Peikert, C., Vaikuntanathan, V., Waters, B.: A framework for efficient and composable oblivious transfer. In: Wagner, D. (ed.) CRYPTO 2008. LNCS, vol. 5157, pp. 554–571. Springer, Heidelberg (2008). https://doi.org/10.1007/978-3-540-85174-5_31

43. Pfitzmann, B., Waidner, M.: Unconditional Byzantine agreement for any number of faulty processors. In: Finkel, A., Jantzen, M. (eds.) STACS 1992. LNCS, vol. 577, pp. 339–350. Springer, Heidelberg (1992). https://doi.org/10.1007/3-540-55210-3_195

44. Rindal, P., Trifiletti, R.: SplitCommit: implementing and analyzing homomorphic UC commitments. Cryptology ePrint Archive, Report 2017/407 (2017). http://eprint.iacr.org/2017/407

45. Schoenmakers, B., Veeningen, M.: Universally verifiable multiparty computation from threshold homomorphic cryptosystems. In: Malkin, T., Kolesnikov, V., Lewko, A.B., Polychronakis, M. (eds.) ACNS 2015. LNCS, vol. 9092, pp. 3–22. Springer, Cham (2015). https://doi.org/10.1007/978-3-319-28166-7_1

46. Spini, G., Fehr, S.: Cheater detection in SPDZ multiparty computation. In: Nascimento, A.C.A., Barreto, P. (eds.) ICITS 2016. LNCS, vol. 10015, pp. 151–176. Springer, Cham (2016). https://doi.org/10.1007/978-3-319-49175-2_8

47. Swanson, C.M., Stinson, D.R.: Unconditionally secure signature schemes revisited. In: Fehr, S. (ed.) ICITS 2011. LNCS, vol. 6673, pp. 100–116. Springer, Heidelberg (2011). https://doi.org/10.1007/978-3-642-20728-0_10

48. Wang, X., Ranellucci, S., Katz, J.: Global-scale secure multiparty computation. In: Thuraisingham, B.M., Evans, D., Malkin, T., Xu, D. (eds.) ACM CCS 2017, pp. 39–56. ACM Press, October/November 2017

49. Yao, A.C.-C.: How to generate and exchange secrets (extended abstract). In: 27th FOCS, pp. 162–167. IEEE Computer Society Press, October 1986

Black-Box Use of One-Way Functions is Useless for Optimal Fair Coin-Tossing

Hemanta K. Maji$^{(\boxtimes)}$ and Mingyuan Wang$^{(\boxtimes)}$

Department of Computer Science, Purdue University, West Lafayette, USA
{hmaji,wang1929}@purdue.edu

Abstract. A two-party fair coin-tossing protocol guarantees output delivery to the honest party even when the other party aborts during the protocol execution. Cleve (STOC–1986) demonstrated that a computationally bounded fail-stop adversary could alter the output distribution of the honest party by (roughly) $1/r$ (in the statistical distance) in an r-message coin-tossing protocol. An optimal fair coin-tossing protocol ensures that no adversary can alter the output distribution beyond $1/r$.

In a seminal result, Moran, Naor, and Segev (TCC–2009) constructed the first optimal fair coin-tossing protocol using (unfair) oblivious transfer protocols. Whether the existence of oblivious transfer protocols is a necessary hardness of computation assumption for optimal fair coin-tossing remains among the most fundamental open problems in theoretical cryptography. The results of Impagliazzo and Luby (FOCS–1989) and Cleve and Impagliazzo (1993) prove that optimal fair coin-tossing implies the necessity of one-way functions' existence; a significantly weaker hardness of computation assumption compared to the existence of secure oblivious transfer protocols. However, the sufficiency of the existence of one-way functions is not known.

Towards this research endeavor, our work proves a black-box separation of optimal fair coin-tossing from the existence of one-way functions. That is, the black-box use of one-way functions cannot enable optimal fair coin-tossing. Following the standard Impagliazzo and Rudich (STOC–1989) approach of proving black-box separations, our work considers any r-message fair coin-tossing protocol in the random oracle model where the parties have unbounded computational power. We demonstrate a fail-stop attack strategy for one of the parties to alter the honest party's output distribution by $1/\sqrt{r}$ by making polynomially-many additional queries to the random oracle. As a consequence, our result proves that the r-message coin-tossing protocol of Blum (COMPCON–1982) and Cleve (STOC–1986), which uses one-way functions in a black-box manner, is the best possible protocol because an adversary cannot change the honest party's output distribution by more than $1/\sqrt{r}$.

H. K. Maji and M. Wang—The research effort is supported in part by an NSF CRII Award CNS–1566499, an NSF SMALL Award CNS–1618822, the IARPA HECTOR project, MITRE Innovation Program Academic Cybersecurity Research Award, a Purdue Research Foundation (PRF) Award, and The Center for Science of Information, an NSF Science and Technology Center, Cooperative Agreement CCF–0939370.

D. Micciancio and T. Ristenpart (Eds.): CRYPTO 2020, LNCS 12171, pp. 593–617, 2020.
https://doi.org/10.1007/978-3-030-56880-1_21

Several previous works, for example, Dachman–Soled, Lindell, Mahmoody, and Malkin (TCC–2011), Haitner, Omri, and Zarosim (TCC–2013), and Dachman–Soled, Mahmoody, and Malkin (TCC–2014), made partial progress on proving this black-box separation assuming some restrictions on the coin-tossing protocol. Our work diverges significantly from these previous approaches to prove this black-box separation in its full generality. The starting point is the recently introduced potential-based inductive proof techniques for demonstrating large gaps in martingales in the information-theoretic plain model. Our technical contribution lies in identifying a global invariant of communication protocols in the random oracle model that enables the extension of this technique to the random oracle model.

1   Introduction

Ideally, in any cryptographic task, one would like to ensure that the honest parties receive their output when adversarial parties refuse to participate any further. Ensuring guaranteed output delivery, a.k.a., *fair computation*, is challenging even for fundamental cryptographic primitives like two-party coin-tossing. A *two-party fair coin-tossing protocol* assures that the honest party receives her output bit even when the adversary aborts during the protocol execution. Cleve [24] demonstrated that, even for computationally bounded parties, a *fail-stop adversary*[1] could alter the output distribution by $1/r$ (in the statistical distance) in any r-message interactive protocols. Intuitively, any r-message interactive protocol is $1/r$-*insecure*. An *optimal* r-message two-party fair coin-tossing protocol ensures that it is only $1/r$-insecure.

In a seminal result, nearly three decades after the introduction of optimal fair coin-tossing protocols, Moran, Naor, and Segev [88] presented the first optimal coin-tossing protocol construction based on the existence of (unfair) secure protocols for the oblivious transfer functionality.[2] Shortly after that, in a sequence of exciting results, several optimal/near-optimal fair protocols were constructed for diverse two-party and multi-party functionalities [3–6,13,14,23,58,59,64,86]. However, each of these protocols assumes the existence of secure protocols for oblivious transfer as well.

In theoretical cryptography, a primary guiding principle of research is to realize a cryptographic primitive securely using the minimal computational hardness assumption. Consequently, the following fundamental question arises naturally.

---

[1] A fail-stop adversary behaves honestly and follows the prescribed protocol. However, based on her private view, she may choose to abort the protocol execution.

[2] Oblivious transfer takes $(x_0, x_1) \in \{0,1\}^2$ as input from the first party, and a choice bit $b \in \{0,1\}$ from the second party. The functionality outputs the bit x_b to the second party, and the first party receives no output. The security of this functionality ensures that the first party has no advantage in predicting the choice bit b. Furthermore, the second party has no advantage in predicting the other input bit x_{1-b}.

Question: Is the existence of oblivious transfer
necessary
for constructing optimal fair coin-tossing protocols?

For example, the results of Impagliazzo and Luby [74] and Cleve and Impagliazzo [25] prove that optimal fair coin-tossing implies that the existence of one-way functions is necessary; a significantly weaker hardness of computation assumption compared to the existence of secure oblivious transfer protocols. However, it is unclear whether one-way functions can help realize optimal fair coin-tossing or not. For instance, historically, for a long time, one-way functions were not known to imply several fundamental primitives like pseudorandom generators [66,67,73], pseudorandom functions [54,55], pseudorandom permutations [81], statistically binding commitment [90], statistically hiding commitment [63,92], zero-knowledge proofs [57], and digital signatures [93,97]; eventually, however, secure constructions were discovered. On the other hand, cryptographic primitives like collision-resistant hash functions, key-agreement schemes, public-key encryption, trapdoor primitives, and oblivious transfer protocols do not have constructions based on the existence of one-way functions. Therefore, is it just that we have not yet been able to construct optimal fair coin-tossing protocols securely from one-way functions, or are there inherent barriers to such constructions?

Does optimal fair coin-tossing belong to
Minicrypt or *Cryptomania* [72]?

Impagliazzo [72] introduced five possible worlds and their implications for computer science. In Minicrypt, one-way functions exist; however, public-key cryptography is impossible. In Cryptomania, complex public-key cryptographic primitives like key-agreement and oblivious transfer are feasible.

Among several possible approaches, a prominent technique to address the question above is to study it via the lens of black-box separations, as introduced by Impagliazzo and Rudich [75]. Suppose one *"black-box separates* the cryptographic primitive Q from another cryptographic primitive P". Then, one interprets this result as indicating that the primitive P is unlikely to facilitate the secure construction of Q using black-box constructions.[3] Consequently, to reinforce the necessity of the existence of oblivious transfer protocols for optimal fair coin-tossing, one needs to provide black-box separation of optimal fair coin-tossing protocols from computational hardness assumptions that are weaker

---

[3] Most constructions in theoretical computer science and cryptography are black-box in nature. That is, they rely only on the input-output behavior of the primitive P, and are oblivious to, for instance, the particular implementation of the primitive P. The security reduction in cryptographic black-box constructions also uses the adversary in a black-box manner. There are, however, some highly non-trivial non-black-box constructions in theoretical computer science, for example, [11,26,33,35, 56,57,76,104]. However, an infeasibility of black-box constructions to realize Q from P indicates the necessity of new non-black-box constructions, which, historically, have been significantly infrequent.

than the existence of oblivious transfer protocols; for example, the existence of one-way functions [74, 75].

Our Results. In this work, we prove the (fully) black-box separation [96] of optimal two-party fair coin-tossing protocol from the existence of one-way functions. In particular, we show that any r-message two-party coin-tossing protocol in the *random oracle model*, where parties have unbounded computational power, is $1/\sqrt{r}$-insecure. In turn, this result settles in the positive the longstanding open problem of determining whether the coin-tossing protocol of Blum [16] and Cleve [24] achieves the highest security while using one-way functions in a black-box manner.

Our proof relies on a potential-based argument that proceeds by identifying a global invariant (see Claim 4.3) across coin-tossing protocols in the random oracle model to guide the design of good fail-stop adversarial attacks. As a significant departure from previous approaches [29, 30], our analysis handles the entire sequence of *curious random oracle query-answer pairs* as a *single instance of information exposure*.

1.1 Our Contributions

Before we proceed to present a high-level informal summary of our results, we need a minimalist definition of two-party coin-tossing protocols in the random oracle model that are secure against fail-stop adversaries. An (r, n, X_0)-coin-tossing protocol is a *two-party interactive protocol* with final output $\in \{0, 1\}$, and parties have oracle access to a random oracle[4] such that the following conditions are satisfied.

1. Alice and Bob exchange a total of r messages (of arbitrary length) during the protocol.[5]
2. The oracle query complexity of both Alice and Bob is (at most) n in every execution of the protocol.
3. At the end of the protocol, parties always agree on the output $\in \{0, 1\}$. Furthermore, the expectation of the output over all possible protocol executions is $X_0 \in [0, 1]$.
4. We consider only fail-stop adversarial strategies. If one party aborts during the protocol execution, then the honest party outputs a defense coin $\in \{0, 1\}$ based on her view without making additional queries to the random oracle. Such protocols are called *instant protocols*, and one may assume any coin-tossing protocol to be instant without loss of generality [29].[6]

---

[4] A random oracle is a function sampled uniformly at random from the set of all functions mapping $\{0, 1\}^n \to \{0, 1\}^n$.

[5] In this paper, we avoid the use of "round." Some literature assumes one round to contain only one message from some party. Other literature assumes that one round has one message from all the parties. Instead, for clarity, we refer to the total number of messages exchanged in the entire protocol.

[6] For a more detailed discussion, refer to Remark 2.

We emphasize that there are additional subtleties in defining coin-tossing protocols in the random oracle model, and Sect. 2.3 addresses them. In this section, we rely on a minimalist definition that suffices to introduce our results. Our main technical result is the following consequence for any (r, n, X_0)-coin-tossing protocol.

Informal Theorem 1 (Main Technical Result). *There exists a universal constant $c > 0$ and a polynomial $p(\cdot)$ such that the following holds. Let π be any (r, n, X_0)-coin-tossing protocol in the information-theoretic random oracle model, where $r, n \in \mathbb{N}$, and $X_0 \in (0, 1)$. Then, there exists a fail-stop adversarial strategy for one of the parties to alter the expected output of the honest party by $\geq c \cdot X_0(1 - X_0)/\sqrt{r}$ and performs at most $p(nr/X_0(1 - X_0))$ additional queries to the random oracle.*

We remark that X_0 may be a function of r and n itself. For example, the expected output X_0 may be an inverse polynomial of r.

This technical result directly yields the following (fully) black-box separation result using techniques in [75, 96].

Corollary 1 (Black-box Separation from One-way Functions). *There exists a universal constant $c > 0$ such that the following holds. Let π be any r-message two-party protocol that uses any one-way function in a fully black-box manner. Suppose, at the end of the execution of π, both parties agree on their output $\in \{0, 1\}$. Before the beginning of the protocol, let the expectation of their common output be $X_0 \in (0, 1)$. Then, there is a fail-stop adversarial strategy for one of the parties to alter the honest party's expected output by $\geq c \cdot X_0(1 - X_0)/\sqrt{r}$.*

That is, optimal fair coin-tossing lies in Cryptomania. All our hardness of computation results extend to the multi-party fair computation of arbitrary functionalities, where parties have private inputs if the output of the functionality has entropy and honest parties are *not* in the majority.

We emphasize that the black-box separation extends to any primitive (and their exponentially-hard versions) that one can construct in a black-box manner from random oracles or ideal ciphers, which turn out to be closely related to random oracles [28, 70]. Furthermore, the impossibility result in the random oracle model implies black-box separations from other (more structured) cryptographic primitives (and their exponentially-hard versions) like regular one-way functions, one-way permutations, and collision-resistant hash functions as well. Although these primitives cannot be constructed from random oracles/ideal cipher in a black-box manner, using by-now well-establish techniques in this field (see, for example, [75]), the main technical result suffices to prove the separations from these structured primitives.

This black-box separation from one-way functions indicates that the two-party coin-tossing protocol of Blum [16] and Cleve [24], which uses one-way functions in a black-box manner and builds on the protocols of [7, 21], achieves the best possible security for any r-message protocol. Their protocol is $1/\sqrt{r}$-insecure, and any r-message protocol cannot have asymptotically better security by only using one-way functions in a black-box manner, thus resolving this fundamental question after over three decades.

1.2 Prior Related Works and Comparison

There is a vast literature of defining and constructing fair protocols for two-party and multi-party functionalities [2–6,13,14,23,58,59,64,86]. In this paper, our emphasis is on the intersection of this literature with black-box separation results. The field of *meta-reductions* [1,8,10,15,19,20,22,27,31,34,38,39,41–43,50,65,68,89,94,95,101,105], which demonstrates similar hardness of computation results from computational hardness assumptions like falsifiable assumptions [91], is outside the scope of this work.

In a seminal result, Impagliazzo and Rudich [75] introduced the notion of black-box separation for cryptographic primitives. After that, there have been other works [9,96] undertaking this nuanced task of precisely defining black-box separation and its subtle variations. Intuitively, separating a primitive Q from a primitive P indicates that attempts to secure realize Q solely on the black-box use of P are unlikely to succeed. Reingold, Trevisan, and Vadhan [96] highlighted the subtleties involved in defining black-box separations by delineating several variants of separations. In their terminology, this work pertains to a *fully black-box* separation where the construction uses P in a black-box manner, and the security reduction uses the adversary in a black-box manner as well. Since the inception of black-box separations in 1989, this research direction has been a fertile ground for highly influential research [12,17,18,29,30,32,36,37,40,44–49,51–53,62,69,71,75,77,80,82–85,87,98,99,102,103]. Among these results, in this paper, we elaborate on the hardness of computation results about fair computation protocols.

A recent work of Haitner, Nissim, Omri, Shaltiel, and Silbak [61] introduces the notion of the "computational essence of key-agreement". Haitner, Makriyannis, and Omri [60], for any constant r, prove that r-message coin-tossing protocols imply key-agreement protocols, if they are less than $1/\sqrt{r}$-insecure. Observe that proving the implication that key-agreement protocol exists is a significantly stronger result as compared to demonstrating a black-box separation from key-agreement.[7] However, their contribution is *incomparable* to our result because it shows a stronger consequence for any constant r.

Among the related works in black-box separation, the most relevant to our problem are the following. Haitner, Omri, and Zarosim [62], for input-less functionalities, lift the hardness of computation results in the information-theoretic

---

[7] For example, consider the following analogy from complexity theory. We know that the complexity class Σ_2 is separated from the complexity class Σ_1 via Cook reductions; unless the polynomial hierarchy collapses. However, the existence of an efficient protocol for Σ_1, implies that the entire polynomial hierarchy collapses, and we have $\Sigma_1 = \Sigma_2$. Similarly, the existence of an efficient protocol for a cryptographic primitive may have several additional implicit consequences in addition to merely providing oracle access to an implementation of that primitive.

plain model against semi-honest adversaries to the random oracle model, i.e., random oracles are useless. However, coin-tossing is trivial to realize securely against semi-honest adversaries,[8] and fail-stop adversarial strategies are not semi-honest. Dachman–Soled, Lindell, Mahmoody, and Malkin [29] proved that the random oracle could be "compiled away" if the coin-tossing protocol has $r = \mathcal{O}(n/\log n)$ messages. Therefore, the fail-stop adversarial strategy of Cleve and Impagliazzo [25] in the information-theoretic plain model also succeeds against the two-party coin-tossing protocol in the random oracle model. Finally, Dachman–Soled, Mahmoody, and Malkin [30] show a fail-stop adversarial strategy against a particular class of fair coin-tossing protocols, namely, *function oblivious* protocols. An exciting feature of this work is that the attack performed by the adversarial party does not proceed by compiling away the random oracle. Similar proof techniques were independently introduced by [82,83] to study the computational complexity of two-party secure deterministic function evaluations.

Recently, there have been two works providing improvements to the fail-stop adversarial attacks of Cleve and Impagliazzo [25] in the information-theoretic plain model. These results proceed by induction on r and employ a potential argument to lower-bound the performance of the most devastating fail-stop adversarial strategy against a coin-tossing protocol. Khorasgani, Maji, and Mukherjee [78] generalize (and improve) the fail-stop attack of Cleve and Impagliazzo [25] to arbitrary $X_0 \in (0,1)$, even when X_0 depends on r and tends to 0 or 1. Khorasgani, Maji, and Wang [79] decouple the number of messages r in a coin-tossing protocol and the number of defense updates d that the two parties perform. They show that a two-party coin-tossing protocol in the information-theoretic plain model is $1/\sqrt{d}$-insecure, independent of the number of messages r in the protocol.

This result [79] is a good starting point for our work because our curious fail-stop attacker shall perform additional queries to the random oracle; however, the parties do not update their defense coins during this information exposure. Unfortunately, their approach only applies to interactive protocols in the information-theoretic plain model. Our work identifies a global invariant for communication protocols that enables the extension of the approach of [79] to the random oracle model. Furthermore, we simplify the proof of their result as well.

2   Preliminaries

We use uppercase letters for random variables, (corresponding) lowercase letters for their values, and calligraphic letters for sets. For a joint distribution (A, B), A and B represent the marginal distributions, and $A \times B$ represents the product distribution where one samples from the marginal distributions A and B independently. For a random variable A distributed over Ω, the *support* of A,

---

[8] Every party broadcasts one uniformly and independently random bit, and all the parties agree on the parity of all the broadcast bits. This protocol is semi-honest secure.

denoted by $\mathsf{Supp}(A)$, is the set $\{x \mid x \in \Omega, \Pr[A = x] > 0\}$. For two random variables A and B distributed over a (discrete) sample space Ω, their *statistical distance* is defined as $\mathsf{SD}(A, B) := \frac{1}{2} \cdot \sum_{\omega \in \Omega} |\Pr[A = w] - \Pr[B = w]|$.

For a sequence $(X_1, X_2, \ldots)$, we use $X_{\leq i}$ to denote the joint distribution $(X_1, X_2, \ldots, X_i)$. Similarly, for any $(x_1, x_2, \ldots) \in \Omega_1 \times \Omega_2 \times \cdots$, we define $x_{\leq i} := (x_1, x_2, \ldots, x_i) \in \Omega_1 \times \Omega_2 \times \cdots \times \Omega_i$. Let $(M_1, M_2, \ldots, M_r)$ be a joint distribution over sample space $\Omega_1 \times \Omega_2 \times \cdots \times \Omega_r$, such that for any $i \in \{1, 2, \ldots, n\}$, M_i is a random variable over Ω_i. A (real-valued) random variable X_i is said to be $M_{\leq i}$ *measurable* if there exists a deterministic function $f \colon \Omega_1 \times \cdots \times \Omega_i \to \mathbb{R}$ such that $X_i = f(M_1, \ldots, M_i)$. A random variable $\tau \colon \Omega_1 \times \cdots \times \Omega_r \to \{1, 2, \ldots, r\}$ is called a *stopping time*, if the random variable $\mathbb{1}_{\tau \leq i}$ is $M_{\leq i}$ measurable, where $\mathbb{1}$ is the indicator function. For a more formal treatment of probability spaces, σ-algebras, filtrations, and martingales, refer to, for example, [100].

The following inequality shall be helpful for our proof.

Theorem 2 (Jensen's inequality). *If f is a multivariate convex function, then $\mathbb{E}[f(\boldsymbol{X})] \geq f(\mathbb{E}[\boldsymbol{X}])$, for all probability distributions $\boldsymbol{X}$ over the domain of f.*

2.1 Two-Party Interactive Protocols in the Random Oracle Model

Alice and Bob speak in alternate rounds. We denote the ith message by M_i. For every message M_i, we denote Alice's private view immediately after sending/receiving message M_i as V_i^{A}, which consists of Alice's random tape R^{A}, her private queries, and the first i messages exchanged. We use V_0^{A} to represent Alice's private view before the protocol begins. Similarly, we define Bob's private view V_i^{B} and use R^{B} to denote his private random tape.

Query Operator $\mathcal{Q}$. For any view V, we use $\mathcal{Q}(V)$ to denote the set of all queries contained in the view V.

2.2 Heavy Querier and the Augmented Protocol

For two-party protocols in the random oracle model, [12,75] introduced a standard algorithm, namely, the *heavy querier*. In this paper, we shall use the following imported theorem.

Imported Theorem 3 (Guarantees of Heavy Querier [12,83]). *Let π be any two-party protocol between Alice and Bob in the random oracle model, in which both parties ask at most n queries. For all threshold $\epsilon \in (0, 1)$, there exists a public algorithm, called the* heavy querier, *who has access to the transcript between Alice and Bob. After receiving each message M_i, the heavy querier performs a sequence of queries and obtain its corresponding answers from the random oracle. Let H_i denote the sequence of query-answer pairs asked by the heavy querier after receiving message M_i. Let T_i be the union of the ith message M_i and the ith heavy querier message H_i. The heavy querier guarantees that the following conditions are simultaneously satisfied.*

- ϵ-***Lightness.*** *For any i, any $t_{\leq i} \in \mathrm{Supp}(T_{\leq i})$, and query $q \notin \mathcal{Q}(h_{\leq i})$,*

$$\Pr\left[q \in \mathcal{Q}\left(V_i^{\mathsf{A}} \big| T_{\leq i} = t_{\leq i}\right)\right] \leq \epsilon, \quad and \quad \Pr\left[q \in \mathcal{Q}\left(V_i^{\mathsf{B}} \big| T_{\leq i} = t_{\leq i}\right)\right] \leq \epsilon.$$

- $n\epsilon$-***Dependence.*** *Fix any i,*

$$\mathop{\mathrm{E}}_{t_{\leq i} \leftarrow T_{\leq i}} \left[\mathsf{SD}\left(\left(V_i^{\mathsf{A}}, V_i^{\mathsf{B}} \big| T_{\leq i} = t_{\leq i}\right), \left(V_i^{\mathsf{A}} \big| T_{\leq i} = t_{\leq i}\right) \times \left(V_i^{\mathsf{B}} \big| T_{\leq i} = t_{\leq i}\right)\right)\right] \leq n\epsilon.$$

Intuitively, it states that on average, the statistical distance between (1) the joint distribution of Alice's and Bob's private view, and (2) the product of the marginal distributions of Alice's private views and Bob's private views is small.

- $\mathcal{O}(n/\epsilon)$-***Efficiency.*** *The expected number of queries asked by the heavy querier is bounded by $\mathcal{O}(n/\epsilon)$. Consequently, it has $\mathcal{O}(n/\epsilon^2)$ query complexity with probability (at least) $(1 - \epsilon)$ by an averaging argument.*

We refer to the protocol with the heavy querier's messages attached as the *augmented protocol*. We call T_i the augmented message.

2.3   Coin-Tossing Protocol

We will prove our main result by induction on the message complexity of the protocol. Therefore, after any partial transcript $t_{<i}$, we will treat the remainder of the orginal protocol starting from the $(i + 1)^{th}$ message, as a protocol of its own. Hence, it is helpful to define the coin-tossing protocol where, before the beginning of the protocol, Alice's and Bob's private views are already correlated with the random oracle. However, note that, in the augmented protocol, after each augmented message t_i, the heavy querier has just ended. Thus, these correlations will satisfy Imported Theorem 3. Therefore, we need to define a general class of coin-tossing protocols in the random oracle model over which we shall perform our induction.

Definition 1 ($(\epsilon, \boldsymbol{\alpha}, r, n, X_0)$-Coin-Tossing). *An interactive protocol π between Alice and Bob with random oracle $O : \{0,1\}^\lambda \to \{0,1\}^\lambda$ is called an $(\epsilon, \boldsymbol{\alpha}, r, n, X_0)$-coin-tossing protocol if it satisfies the following.*

- ***Setup.*** *There is an arbitrary set $\mathcal{S} \subseteq \{0,1\}^\lambda$, which is publicly known, such that for all queries $s \in \mathcal{S}$, the query answers $O(s)$ are also publicly known. Let Ω^{A}, Ω^{B}, and Ω^{O} be the universes of Alice's random tape, Bob's random tape, and the random oracle, respectively. There are also publicly known sets $\mathcal{A} \subseteq \Omega^{\mathsf{A}} \times \Omega^{\mathsf{O}}$ and $\mathcal{B} \subseteq \Omega^{\mathsf{B}} \times \Omega^{\mathsf{O}}$. The random variables R^{A}, R^{B}, and O are sampled uniformly conditioned on that (1) $(R^{\mathsf{A}}, O) \in \mathcal{A}$, (2) $(R^{\mathsf{B}}, O) \in \mathcal{B}$, and (3) O is consistent with the publicly known answers at $\mathcal{S}$. Alice's private view before the beginning of the protocol is a deterministic function of R^{A} and O, which might contain private queries. Likewise, Bob's private view is a deterministic function of R^{B} and O.[9]*

---

[9]   Basically, $\mathcal{S}$ is the set of all the queries that the heavy querier has published. $\mathcal{A}$ is the set of all possible pairs of Alice's private randomness r^{A} and random oracle o

- **Agreement.** *At the end of the protocol, both parties always agree on the output* $\in \{0, 1\}$. *Without loss of generality, we assume the output is concatenated to the last message in the protocol.*[10]
- **Defense preparation.** *At message* M_i, *if Alice is supposed to speak, in addition to preparing the next-message* M_i, *she will also prepare a defense coin for herself as well. If Bob decides to abort the next message, she shall not make any additional queries to the random oracle, and simply output the defense she has just prepared.* [29, 30] *introduced this constraint as the "instant construction." They showed that, without loss of generality, one can assume this property for all the defense preparations except for the first defense (see Remark 2). We shall refer to this defense both as Alice's* i^{th} *defense and also as her* $(i + 1)^{th}$ *defense. Consequently, Alice's defense for every* i *is well-defined. Bob's defense is defined similarly. We assume the party who receives the first message has already prepared her defense for the first message before the protocol begins.*
- ϵ-**Lightness at Start.** *For any query* $q \notin S$, *the probability that Alice has asked query* q *before the protocol begins is upper bounded by* $\epsilon \in [0, 1]$. *Similarly, the probability that Bob has asked query* q *is at most* ϵ.
- α-**Dependence.** *For all* $i \in \{0, 1, \dots, r\}$, *Alice's and Bob's private views are* α_i-*dependent on average immediate after the message* T_i. *That is, the following condition is satisfied for every* i.

$$\alpha_i := \underset{t_{\leq i} \leftarrow T_{\leq i}}{\mathrm{E}} \left[\mathsf{SD}\left(\left(V_i^{\mathsf{A}}, V_i^{\mathsf{B}} \middle| T_{\leq i} = t_{\leq i} \right), \left(V_i^{\mathsf{A}} \middle| T_{\leq i} = t_{\leq i} \right) \times \left(V_i^{\mathsf{B}} \middle| T_{\leq i} = t_{\leq i} \right) \right) \right]$$

- r-**Message complexity.** *The number of messages of this protocol is* $r = \mathsf{poly}(\lambda)$. *We emphasize that the length of the message could be arbitrarily long.*
- n-**Query complexity.** *For all possible complete executions of the protocol, the number of queries that Alice asks (including the queries asked before the protocol begins) is at most* $n = \mathsf{poly}(\lambda)$. *This also includes the queries that are asked for the preparation of the defense coins. Likewise, Bob asks at most* n *queries as well.*
- X_0-**Expected Output.** *The expectation of the output is* $X_0 \in (0, 1)$.

Remark 1. Let us justify the necessity of α-dependence in the definition. We note that when heavy querier stops, Alice's and Bob's view are not necessarily close to the product of their respective marginal distributions.[11] However, to prove any

---

that are consistent with Alice's messages before this protocol begins. Similarly, $\mathcal{B}$ is the set of all consistent pairs of Bob's private randomness r^{B} and random oracle o.

[10] This generalization shall not make the protocol any more vulnerable. Any attack in this protocol shall also exist in the original protocol with the same amount of deviation. This only helps simplify the presentation of our proof.

[11] For instance, suppose Alice samples a uniform string $u_1 \xleftarrow{\$} \{0, 1\}^\lambda$ and sends $O(u_1)$ to Bob. Next, Bob samples a uniform string $u_2 \xleftarrow{\$} \{0, 1\}^\lambda$ and sends $O(u_2)$ to Alice. Assume the first message and the second message are the same, i.e., $O(u_1) = O(u_2)$. Then, there are no heavy queries, but Alice's and Bob's private views are largely correlated.

meaningful bound on the susceptibility of this protocol, we have to treat α as an additional error term. Therefore, we introduce this parameter in our definition. However, the introduction of this error shall not be a concern globally, because the heavy querier guarantees that over all possible executions this dependence is at most $n\epsilon$ (on average), which we shall ensure to be sufficiently small.

Remark 2. We note that, after every heavy querier message, the remaining sub-protocol always satisfies the definition above. However, the original coin-tossing protocol might not meet these constraints. For example, consider a one-message protocol where Alice queries $O(0^\lambda)$, and sends the parity of this string to Bob as the output. On the other hand, Bob also queries $O(0^\lambda)$ and uses the parity of this string as his defense. This protocol is perfectly secure in the sense that no party can deviate the output of the protocol at all. However, the query 0^λ is 1-heavy in Bob's private view even before the protocol begins. Prior works [29,30] rule out such protocols by banning Bob from making any queries when he prepares his first defense. In this paper, we consider protocols such that no queries are more than ϵ-heavy when Bob prepares his first defense. We call this the ϵ-*lightness at start assumption*. The set of protocols that prior works consider is identical to the set of protocols that satisfies 0-lightness at start assumption.

To justify our ϵ-lightness at start assumption, we observe that one can always run a heavy querier with a threshold ϵ before the beginning of the protocol as a pre-processing step. Note that this step fixes only a small part (of size $\mathcal{O}(n/\epsilon)$) of the random oracle, and, hence, the random oracle continues to be an "idealized" one-way function. If this protocol is a black-box construction of a coin-tossing protocol with any one-way function, the choice of the one-way function should not change its expected output. Therefore, by running a heavy querier before the beginning of the protocol, it should not alter the expected output of the protocol. After this compilation step, all queries are ϵ-light in Bob's view *before* the protocol begins. Consequently, our inductive proof technique is applicable.

Remark 3. Let us use the an example to further illustrate how we number Alice's and Bob's defense coins. Suppose Alice sends the first message in the protocol. Bob shall prepare his first defense coin even before the protocol begins. Alice, during her preparation of the first message, shall also prepare a defense coin as her first defense.

The second message in the protocol is sent by Bob. Since Alice is not speaking during this message preparation, her second defense coin remains identical to her first defense coin. Bob, on the other hand, shall update a new defense coin as his second defense during his preparation of the second message.

For the third message, Alice shall prepare a new third defense coin and Bob's third defense coin is identical to his second defense coin. This process continues for r messages during the protocol execution.

Notation. Let X_i represent the expected output conditioned on the first i augmented messages, i.e., the random variable $T_{\leq i}$. Let D_i^A be the expectation of Alice's i^{th} defense coin conditioned on the first i augmented messages. Similarly, let D_i^B be the expectation of Bob's i^{th} defense coin conditioned on the first i augmented messages. (Refer to Definition 1 for the definition of ith defense. Recall that, for both Alice and Bob, the ith defense is defined for all $i \in \{1, 2, \ldots, r\}$.) Note that random variables X_i, D_i^A, and D_i^B are all $T_{\leq i}$-measurable.

3   Our Results

Given an $(\epsilon, \alpha, r, n, X_0)$-coin-tossing protocol π and a stopping time τ, we define the following score function that captures the susceptibility of this protocol with respect to this particular stopping time.

Definition 2. *Let π be an $(\epsilon, \alpha, r, n, X_0)$-coin tossing protocol. Let $\mathsf{P} \in \{\mathsf{A}, \mathsf{B}\}$ be the party who sends the last message of the protocol. For any stopping time τ, define*

$$\mathsf{Score}(\pi, \tau) := \mathbb{E}\left[\mathbb{1}_{(\tau \neq r) \vee (\mathsf{P} \neq \mathsf{A})} \cdot \left| X_\tau - D_\tau^A \right| + \mathbb{1}_{(\tau \neq r) \vee (\mathsf{P} \neq \mathsf{B})} \cdot \left| X_\tau - D_\tau^B \right| \right].$$

We clarify that the binary operator $\vee$ in the expression above represents the boolean OR operation, and *not* the "join" operator.

To provide additional perspectives to this definition, we make the following remarks similar to [79].

1. Suppose Alice is about to send (m_i^*, h_i^*) as the ith message. In the information-theoretic plain model, prior works [25,78] consider the gap between the expected output before and after this message. Intuitively, since Alice is sending this message, she could utilize this gap to attack Bob, because Bob's defense cannot keep abreast of this new information. However, in the random oracle model, both parties are potentially vulnerable to this gap. This is due to the fact that the heavy querier message might also reveal information about Bob. For instance, it might reveal Bob's commitments sent in previous messages using the random oracle as an idealized one-way function. Then, Alice's defense cannot keep abreast of this new information either and thus Alice is potentially vulnerable.
2. Due to the reasons above, for every message, we consider the potential deviations that *both* parties can cause by aborting appropriately. Suppose we are at transcript $T_{\leq i} = t_{\leq i}$, which belongs to the stopping time, i.e., $\tau = i$. And Alice sends the last message (m_i^*, h_i^*). Naturally, Alice can abort without sending this message to Bob when she finds out her i^{th} message is (m_i^*, h_i^*). This attack causes a deviation of $\left| X_\tau - D_\tau^B \right|$. On the other hand, Bob can also attack by aborting when he receives Alice's message (m_i^*, h_i^*). This attack ensures a deviation of $\left| X_\tau - D_{\tau+1}^A \right|$. Note that for the $(i+1)^{th}$ message, Alice is not supposed to speak, her $(i+1)^{th}$ defense is exactly her i^{th} defense. Hence this deviation can be also written as $\left| X_\tau - D_\tau^A \right|$.
3. The above argument has a boundary case, which is the last message of the protocol. Suppose Alice sends the last message. Then, Bob, who receives this message, cannot abort anymore because the protocol has ended. Therefore, if our stopping time $\tau = n$, the score function must exclude $\left| X_\tau - D_\tau^A \right|$. This explains why we have the indicator function $\mathbb{1}$ in our score function.

4. Lastly, we illustrate how one can translate this score function into a fail-stop attack strategy. Suppose we find a stopping time τ^* that witnesses a large score $\mathsf{Score}(\pi, \tau^*)$. For Alice, we will partition the stopping time into two partitions depending on whether $X_\tau \geq D_\tau^B$ or not. Similarly, for Bob, we partition the stopping time into two partitions depending on whether $X_\tau \geq D_\tau^A$. These four attack strategies correspond to Alice or Bob deviating towards 0 or 1. And the summation of the deviations caused by these four attacks are exactly $\mathsf{Score}(\pi, \tau^*)$. Hence, there must exist a fail-stop attack strategy for one of the parties that changes the honest party's output distribution by $\geq \frac{1}{4} \cdot \mathsf{Score}(\pi, \tau^*)$.

Given the definition of our score function, we are interested in finding the stopping time that witnesses the largest score. This motivates the following definition.

Definition 3. *For any $(\epsilon, \boldsymbol{\alpha}, r, n, X_0)$-coin-tossing protocol π, define*

$$\mathsf{Opt}(\pi) := \max_\tau \ \mathsf{Score}(\pi, \tau).$$

Intuitively, $\mathsf{Opt}(\pi)$ represents the susceptibility of the protocol π. Our main theorem states the following lower bound on this quantity.

Theorem 4 (Main Technical Result in the Random Oracle Model).
For any $(\epsilon, \boldsymbol{\alpha}, r, n, X_0)$-coin-tossing protocol π, the following holds.

$$\mathsf{Opt}(\pi) \geq \Gamma_r \cdot X_0 (1 - X_0) - \left(nr \cdot \epsilon + \alpha_0 + 2 \sum_{i=1}^{r} \alpha_i \right),$$

where $\Gamma_r := \sqrt{\frac{\sqrt{2}-1}{r}}$, for all positive integers r. Furthermore, one needs to make an additional $\mathcal{O}(n/\epsilon)$ queries to the random oracle (in expectation) to identify a stopping time τ witnessing this lower bound.

We defer the proof to Sect. 4. In light of the remarks above, this theorem implies the following corollary.

Corollary 2. *Let π be a coin-tossing protocol in the random oracle model that satisfies the ϵ-lightness at start assumption (see Remark 2). Suppose π is an r-message protocol, and Alice and Bob ask at most n queries. The expected output of π is X_0. Then, either Alice or Bob has a fail-stop attack strategy that deviates the honest party's output distribution by*

$$\Omega\left(\frac{X_0 (1 - X_0)}{\sqrt{r}} \right).$$

This attack strategy performs $\mathcal{O}\left(\frac{n^2 r^2}{X_0 (1 - X_0)} \right)$ additional queries to the random oracle in expectation.

This corollary is obtained by substituting $\epsilon = \frac{X_0(1-X_0)}{nr^2}$ in Theorem 4. Imported Theorem 3 guarantees that, for all i, the average dependencies after the ith message are bounded by $n\epsilon$. Hence, the error term is o$\left(\frac{X_0(1-X_0)}{\sqrt{r}}\right)$.

The efficiency of the heavy querier is guaranteed by Imported Theorem 3. One can transform the average-case efficiency to worst-case efficiency by forcing the heavy querier to stop when it asks more than $\frac{n^2 r^3}{(X_0(1-X_0))^2}$ queries. By Markov's inequality, this happens with probability at most $\mathcal{O}\left(\frac{X_0(1-X_0)}{r}\right) =$ o$\left(\frac{X_0(1-X_0)}{\sqrt{r}}\right)$, and thus the quality of this attack is essentially identical to the averge-case attack.

4   Proof of Theorem 4

In this section, we prove Theorem 4 using induction on the message complexity r. We first provide some useful lemmas in Sect. 4.1. Next, we prove the base case in Sect. 4.2. Finally, Sect. 4.3 proves the inductive step.

Throughout this section, without loss of generality, we shall assume that Alice sends the first message in the protocol.

4.1   Useful Imported Technical Lemmas

Firstly, it is implicit in [12] that if (1) Alice's and Bob's private view before the protocol begins are α_0-dependent, (2) all the queries are ϵ-light for Bob, and (3) Alice asks at most n queries to prepare her first message, then after the first message, Alice's and Bob's private view are $(\alpha_0 + n\epsilon)$-dependent.

Lemma 1 (Technical Lemma [12]). *We have*

$$\mathsf{SD}\left((V_1^A, V_0^B), (V_1^A \times V_0^B)\right) \le \alpha_0 + n\epsilon.$$

Additionally, the following inequality from [79] shall be useful for our proof.

Lemma 2 (Imported Technical Lemma, Lemma 1 in [79]). *For all $P \in [0,1]$ and $Q \in [0, 1/2]$, if P, Q satisfies*

$$P - Q - P^2 Q \ge 0,$$

then for all $x, \alpha, \beta \in [0,1]$, we have

$$\max\left(P \cdot x(1-x), |x-\alpha| + |x-\beta|\right) \ge Q \cdot \left(x(1-x) + (x-\alpha)^2 + (x-\beta)^2\right).$$

In particular, for all $r \ge 1$, the constraints are satisfied if we set $P = \Gamma_r$ and $Q = \Gamma_{r+1}$, where $\Gamma_r := \sqrt{\frac{\sqrt{2}-1}{r}}$.

4.2   Base Case of the Induction: Message Complexity $r = 1$

Let π be an $(\epsilon, \boldsymbol{\alpha}, r, n, X_0)$-coin-tossing protocol with $r = 1$. In this protocol, Alice sends the only message M_1. We shall pick the stopping time τ to be 1. Note that this is the last message of the protocol and hence Bob who receives it cannot abort any more. Therefore, our score function is the following

$$\mathsf{Score}(\pi, \tau) = \mathbb{E}\left[\left|X_1 - D_1^\mathsf{B}\right|\right].$$

Let $D_0^\mathsf{B} = \mathbb{E}\left[D_1^\mathsf{B}\right]$, which is the expectation of Bob's first defense before the protocol begins. Recall that in the augmented protocol $T_1 = (M_1, H_1)$, and X_1 and D_1^B are T_1 measurable. We have

$$\mathbb{E}\left[\left|X_1 - D_1^\mathsf{B}\right|\right] = \underset{m_1 \leftarrow M_1}{\mathrm{E}}\left[\underset{h_1 \leftarrow (H_1|M_1=m_1)}{\mathrm{E}}\left[\left|X_1 - D_1^\mathsf{B}\right|\right]\right]$$

$$\overset{(i)}{\geq} \underset{m_1 \leftarrow M_1}{\mathrm{E}}\left[\left|\mathbb{E}[X_1|M_1 = m_1] - \mathbb{E}\left[D_1^\mathsf{B}|M_1 = m_1\right]\right|\right]$$

$$\overset{(ii)}{\geq} \underset{m_1 \leftarrow M_1}{\mathrm{E}}\left[\left|\mathbb{E}[X_1|M_1 = m_1] - D_0^\mathsf{B}\right| - \left|D_0^\mathsf{B} - \mathbb{E}\left[D_1^\mathsf{B}|M_1 = m_1\right]\right|\right]$$

$$\overset{(iii)}{\geq} \underset{m_1 \leftarrow M_1}{\mathrm{E}}\left[\left|\mathbb{E}[X_1|M_1 = m_1] - D_0^\mathsf{B}\right|\right] - \alpha_0 - n\epsilon$$

$$\overset{(iv)}{\geq} X_0 \cdot \left(1 - D_0^\mathsf{B}\right) + (1 - X_0) \cdot D_0^\mathsf{B} - \alpha_0 - n\epsilon$$

$$\geq X_0\left(1 - X_0\right) + \left(X_0 - D_0^\mathsf{B}\right)^2 - \alpha_0 - n\epsilon$$

$$\geq X_0\left(1 - X_0\right) - \alpha_0 - n\epsilon.$$

In the above inequality, (i) and (ii) are because of triangle inequality. Since we assume the output is concatenated to the last message of the protocol, $\mathbb{E}[X_1|M_1 = m_1] \in \{0, 1\}$. And by the definition of X_0, the probability of the output being 1 is X_0. Hence we have (iv).

To see (iii), note that

$$\mathbb{E}\left[D_1^\mathsf{B}\middle|M_1 = m_1\right] = \sum_{v_1^\mathsf{A}, v_0^\mathsf{B}} \Pr\left[V_1^\mathsf{A} = v_1^\mathsf{A}, V_0^\mathsf{B} = v_0^\mathsf{B}\middle|M_1 = m_1\right] \mathbb{E}\left[D_1^\mathsf{B}\middle|V_0^\mathsf{B} = v_0^\mathsf{B}\right]$$

$$\leq \sum_{\mathcal{Q}(v_1^\mathsf{A}) \cap \mathcal{Q}(v_0^\mathsf{B}) = \emptyset} \Pr\left[V_1^\mathsf{A} = v_1^\mathsf{A}\middle|M_1 = m_1\right] \cdot \Pr\left[V_0^\mathsf{B} = v_0^\mathsf{B}\right] \mathbb{E}\left[D_1^\mathsf{B}\middle|V_0^\mathsf{B} = v_0^\mathsf{B}\right]$$

$$+ \sum_{\mathcal{Q}(v_1^\mathsf{A}) \cap \mathcal{Q}(v_0^\mathsf{B}) \neq \emptyset} \Pr\left[V_1^\mathsf{A} = v_1^\mathsf{A}, V_0^\mathsf{B} = v_0^\mathsf{B}\middle|M_1 = m_1\right] \mathbb{E}\left[D_1^\mathsf{B}\middle|V_0^\mathsf{B} = v_0^\mathsf{B}\right]$$

Hence,

$$\left|\mathbb{E}\left[D_1^\mathsf{B}\middle|M_1 = m_1\right] - D_0^\mathsf{B}\right| \leq \underset{(v_1^\mathsf{A}, v_0^\mathsf{B}) \leftarrow (V_1^\mathsf{A}, V_0^\mathsf{B})|M_1=m_1}{\Pr}\left[\mathcal{Q}\left(v_1^\mathsf{A}\right) \cap \mathcal{Q}\left(v_0^\mathsf{B}\right) \neq \emptyset\right].$$

Therefore,

$$\operatorname*{E}_{m_1 \leftarrow M_1} \left[\left| \mathbb{E}\left[D_1^{\mathsf{B}} \middle| M_1 = m_1 \right] - D_0^{\mathsf{B}} \right| \right]$$

$$\leq \operatorname*{E}_{m_1 \leftarrow M_1} \left[\operatorname*{Pr}_{(v_1^{\mathsf{A}}, v_0^{\mathsf{B}}) \leftarrow (V_1^{\mathsf{A}}, V_0^{\mathsf{B}}) | M_1 = m_1} \left[\mathcal{Q}\left(v_1^{\mathsf{A}}\right) \cap \mathcal{Q}\left(v_0^{\mathsf{B}}\right) \neq \emptyset \right] \right]$$

$$\leq \operatorname*{Pr}_{(v_1^{\mathsf{A}}, v_0^{\mathsf{B}}) \leftarrow (V_1^{\mathsf{A}}, V_0^{\mathsf{B}})} \left[\mathcal{Q}\left(v_1^{\mathsf{A}}\right) \cap \mathcal{Q}\left(v_0^{\mathsf{B}}\right) \neq \emptyset \right] \leq \alpha_0 + n\epsilon.$$

This completes the proof for the base case.

4.3   Inductive Step

Suppose the theorem is true for $r = r_0 - 1$, we are going to prove it for $r = r_0$. Let π be an arbitrary $(\epsilon, \boldsymbol{\alpha}, r_0, n, X_0)$-coin-tossing protocol. Assume the first augmented message is $(M_1, H_1) = (m_1^*, h_1^*)$, and conditioned on that, $X_1 = x_1^*$, $D_1^{\mathsf{A}} = d_1^{\mathsf{A},*}$, and $D_1^{\mathsf{B}} = d_1^{\mathsf{B},*}$. Moreover, the remaining sub-protocol π^* is an $(\epsilon, \boldsymbol{\alpha}^*, r_0 - 1, n, x_1^*)$-coin-tossing protocol. By our induction hypothesis,

$$\mathsf{Opt}\left(\pi^*\right) \geq \Gamma_{r_0-1} \cdot x_1^* \left(1 - x_1^*\right) - \left(n(r_0 - 1)\epsilon + \alpha_0^* + \sum_{i=1}^{r_0-1} \alpha_i^* \right).$$

(For simplicity, we shall use $\mathsf{Err}\left(\boldsymbol{\alpha}, n, r\right)$ to represent $\alpha_0 + \sum_{i=1}^{r} \alpha_i + nr\epsilon$ in the rest of the proof.) That is, there exists a stopping time τ^* for sub-protocol π^*, whose score is lower bounded by the quantity above. On the other hand, we may choose not to continue by picking this message $(M_1, H_1) = (m_1^*, h_1^*)$ as our stopping time. This would yield a score of

$$\left| x_1^* - d_1^{\mathsf{A},*} \right| + \left| x_1^* - d_1^{\mathsf{B},*} \right|.$$

Hence, the optimal stopping time would decide on whether to abort now or defer the attack to sub-protocol π^* by comparing which one of those two quantities is larger. This would yield a score of

$$\max\left(\mathsf{Opt}\left(\pi^*\right), \ \left| x_1^* - d_1^{\mathsf{A},*} \right| + \left| x_1^* - d_1^{\mathsf{B},*} \right| \right)$$

$$\geq \max\left(\Gamma_{r_0-1} \cdot x_1^* \left(1 - x_1^*\right), \ \left| x_1^* - d_1^{\mathsf{A},*} \right| + \left| x_1^* - d_1^{\mathsf{B},*} \right| \right) - \mathsf{Err}\left(\boldsymbol{\alpha}^*, n, r_0 - 1\right)$$

$$\overset{(v)}{\geq} \Gamma_{r_0}\left(x_1^* \left(1 - x_1^*\right) + \left(x_1^* - d_1^{\mathsf{A},*} \right)^2 + \left(x_1^* - d_1^{\mathsf{B},*} \right)^2 \right) - \mathsf{Err}\left(\boldsymbol{\alpha}^*, n, r_0 - 1\right),$$

where inequality (i) is because of Lemma 2. Now that we have a lower bound on how much score we can yield at every first augmented message, we are interested in how much they sum up to.

Without loss of generality, assume there are totally ℓ possible first augmented messages, namely $t_1^{(1)}, t_1^{(2)}, \ldots, t_1^{(\ell)}$. The probability of the first message being $t_1^{(i)}$

is $p^{(i)}$ and conditioned that, $X_1 = x_1^{(i)}$, $D_1^A = d_1^{A,(i)}$, and $D_1^B = d_1^{B,(i)}$. Moreover, the remaining $r_0 - 1$ protocol has dependence vector $\alpha^{(i)}$. Therefore, we are interested in,

$$\sum_{i=1}^{\ell} p^{(i)} \left(\Gamma_{r_0} \left(x_1^{(i)} \left(1 - x_1^{(i)}\right) + \left(x_1^{(i)} - d_1^{A,(i)}\right)^2 + \left(x_1^{(i)} - d_1^{B,(i)}\right)^2 \right) - \mathrm{Err}\left(\alpha^{(i)}, n, r_0 - 1\right) \right)$$

Define the tri-variate function Φ as

$$\Phi(x, y, z) := x(1 - x) + (x - y)^2 + (x - z)^2.$$

We make the crucial observation that this function can also be rewritten as

$$\Phi(x, y, z) = x + (x - y - z)^2 - 2yz.$$

Therefore, we can rewrite the above quantity as

$$\sum_{i=1}^{\ell} p^{(i)} \left(\Gamma_{r_0} \left(x_1^{(i)} + \left(x_1^{(i)} - d_1^{A,(i)} - d_1^{B,(i)}\right)^2 - 2 \cdot d_1^{A,(i)} \cdot d_1^{B,(i)} \right) - \mathrm{Err}\left(\alpha^{(i)}, n, r_0 - 1\right) \right)$$

We observe the following case analysis for the three expressions in the potential function above.

1. For the x term, we observe that the expectation of $x_1^{(i)}$ is X_0, i.e., we have $\sum_{i=1}^{\ell} p^{(i)} \cdot x_1^{(i)} = X_0$.
2. For the $(x - y - z)^2$ term, we note that it is a convex tri-variate function. Hence, Jensen's inequality is applicable.
3. For the $y \cdot z$ term, we have the following claim.

Claim. 4.3 *(Global Invariant)*

$$\left| \sum_{i=1}^{\ell} p^{(i)} \cdot d_1^{A,(i)} \cdot d_1^{B,(i)} - \mathbb{E}\left[D_1^A\right] \mathbb{E}\left[D_1^B\right] \right| \le (\alpha_0 + n\epsilon) + \alpha_1.$$

Proof. To see this, consider the expectation of the product of Alice and Bob defense when we sample from $\left(V_1^A, V_0^B\right)$. This expectation is $\alpha_0 + n\epsilon$ close to $\mathbb{E}\left[D_1^A\right] \mathbb{E}\left[D_1^B\right]$ because joint distribution $\left(V_1^A, V_0^B\right)$ is $\alpha_0 + n\epsilon$ close to the product of its marginal distribution by Lemma 1.

On the other hand, this expectation is identical to the average (over all possible messages) of the expectation of the product of Alice and Bob defense when we sample from $\left(V_1^A, V_0^B \middle| T_1 = t_1^{(i)}\right)$. Conditioned on first message being $t_1^{(i)}$, this expectation is $\alpha_0^{(i)}$-close to $d_1^{A,(i)} \cdot d_1^{B,(i)}$ because $\left(V_1^A, V_0^B \middle| T_1 = t_1^{(i)}\right)$ has $\alpha_0^{(i)}$-dependence by definition.

Finally, we note that, by definition, $\sum_{i=1}^{\ell} p^{(i)} \alpha_0^{(i)} = \alpha_1$. Note that the indices between α and $\alpha^{(i)}$ are shifted by 1. This is because of that the dependence after the first message of the original protocol is the average of the dependence before each sub-protocol begins.

This proves that $\sum_{i=1}^{\ell} p^{(i)} \cdot d_1^{A,(i)} d_1^{B,(i)}$ and $\mathbb{E}\left[D_1^A\right] \mathbb{E}\left[D_1^B\right]$ are $(\alpha_0 + n\epsilon) + \alpha_1$ close.   □

Given these observations, we can push the expectation inside each term, and they imply that our score is lower bounded by

$$\Gamma_{r_0}\left(X_0 + \left(X_0 - \mathbb{E}\left[D_1^A\right] - \mathbb{E}\left[D_1^B\right]\right)^2 - 2 \cdot \mathbb{E}\left[D_1^A\right] \cdot \mathbb{E}\left[D_1^B\right] - (\alpha_0 + \alpha_1 + n\epsilon)\right)$$
$$- \sum_{i=1}^{\ell} p^{(i)} \cdot \mathsf{Err}\left(\boldsymbol{\alpha}^{(i)}, n, r_0 - 1\right)$$

We note that by definition (again note that the indices of α and $\alpha^{(i)}$ are shifted by 1),

$$(\alpha_0 + \alpha_1 + n\epsilon) + \sum_{i=1}^{\ell} p^{(i)} \cdot \mathsf{Err}\left(\boldsymbol{\alpha}^{(i)}, n, r_0 - 1\right) = \mathsf{Err}\left(\boldsymbol{\alpha}, n, r_0\right).$$

Therefore, our score is at least

$$\Gamma_{r_0}\left(X_0 + \left(X_0 - \mathbb{E}\left[D_1^A\right] - \mathbb{E}\left[D_1^B\right]\right)^2 - 2 \cdot \mathbb{E}\left[D_1^A\right] \cdot \mathbb{E}\left[D_1^B\right]\right) - \mathsf{Err}\left(\boldsymbol{\alpha}, n, r_0\right).$$

Switching back to the form of $x(1-x) + (x-y)^2 + (x-z)^2$, we get

$$\Gamma_{r_0}\left(X_0(1-X_0) + \left(X_0 - \mathbb{E}\left[D_1^A\right]\right)^2 + \left(X_0 - \mathbb{E}\left[D_0^B\right]\right)^2\right) - \mathsf{Err}\left(\boldsymbol{\alpha}, n, r_0\right)$$
$$\geq \Gamma_{r_0} \cdot X_0(1-X_0) - \mathsf{Err}\left(\boldsymbol{\alpha}, n, r_0\right)$$
$$= \Gamma_{r_0} \cdot X_0(1-X_0) - \left(nr_0\epsilon + \alpha_0 + 2\sum_{i=1}^{r_0} \alpha_i\right).$$

This completes the proof of the inductive step and, hence, the proof of Theorem 4.

References

1. Abe, M., Ambrona, M., Ohkubo, M.: On black-box extensions of non-interactive zero-knowledge arguments, and signatures directly from simulation soundness. In: Kiayias, A., Kohlweiss, M., Wallden, P., Zikas, V. (eds.) PKC 2020, Part I. LNCS, vol. 12110, pp. 558–589. Springer, Cham (2020). https://doi.org/10.1007/978-3-030-45374-9_19
2. Agrawal, S., Prabhakaran, M.: On fair exchange, fair coins and fair sampling. In: Canetti, R., Garay, J.A. (eds.) CRYPTO 2013, Part I. LNCS, vol. 8042, pp. 259–276. Springer, Heidelberg (2013). https://doi.org/10.1007/978-3-642-40041-4_15

3. Alon, B., Omri, E.: Almost-optimally fair multiparty coin-tossing with nearly three-quarters malicious. In: Hirt, M., Smith, A. (eds.) TCC 2016, Part I. LNCS, vol. 9985, pp. 307–335. Springer, Heidelberg (2016). https://doi.org/10.1007/978-3-662-53641-4_13

4. Asharov, G.: Towards characterizing complete fairness in secure two-party computation. In: Lindell, Y. (ed.) TCC 2014. LNCS, vol. 8349, pp. 291–316. Springer, Heidelberg (2014). https://doi.org/10.1007/978-3-642-54242-8_13

5. Asharov, G., Beimel, A., Makriyannis, N., Omri, E.: Complete characterization of fairness in secure two-party computation of boolean functions. In: Dodis, Y., Nielsen, J.B. (eds.) TCC 2015, Part I. LNCS, vol. 9014, pp. 199–228. Springer, Heidelberg (2015). https://doi.org/10.1007/978-3-662-46494-6_10

6. Asharov, G., Lindell, Y., Rabin, T.: A full characterization of functions that imply fair coin tossing and ramifications to fairness. In: Sahai, A. (ed.) TCC 2013. LNCS, vol. 7785, pp. 243–262. Springer, Heidelberg (2013). https://doi.org/10.1007/978-3-642-36594-2_14

7. Awerbuch, B., Blum, M., Chor, B., Goldwasser, S., Micali, S.: How to implement Bracha's o (log n) byzantine agreement algorithm. Unpublished manuscript (1985)

8. Bader, C., Jager, T., Li, Y., Schäge, S.: On the impossibility of tight cryptographic reductions. In: Fischlin, M., Coron, J.-S. (eds.) EUROCRYPT 2016, Part II. LNCS, vol. 9666, pp. 273–304. Springer, Heidelberg (2016). https://doi.org/10.1007/978-3-662-49896-5_10

9. Baecher, P., Brzuska, C., Fischlin, M.: Notions of black-box reductions, revisited. In: Sako, K., Sarkar, P. (eds.) ASIACRYPT 2013, Part I. LNCS, vol. 8269, pp. 296–315. Springer, Heidelberg (2013). https://doi.org/10.1007/978-3-642-42033-7_16

10. Baldimtsi, F., Lysyanskaya, A.: On the security of one-witness blind signature schemes. In: Sako, K., Sarkar, P. (eds.) ASIACRYPT 2013, Part II. LNCS, vol. 8270, pp. 82–99. Springer, Heidelberg (2013). https://doi.org/10.1007/978-3-642-42045-0_5

11. Barak, B.: Constant-round coin-tossing with a man in the middle or realizing the shared random string model. In: 43rd Annual Symposium on Foundations of Computer Science, Vancouver, BC, Canada, 16–19 November 2002, pp. 345–355. IEEE Computer Society Press (2002)

12. Barak, B., Mahmoody-Ghidary, M.: Merkle puzzles are optimal - an $O(n^2)$-query attack on any key exchange from a random oracle. In: Halevi, S. (ed.) CRYPTO 2009. LNCS, vol. 5677, pp. 374–390. Springer, Heidelberg (2009). https://doi.org/10.1007/978-3-642-03356-8_22

13. Beimel, A., Lindell, Y., Omri, E., Orlov, I.: $1/p$-secure multiparty computation without honest majority and the best of both worlds. In: Rogaway, P. (ed.) CRYPTO 2011. LNCS, vol. 6841, pp. 277–296. Springer, Heidelberg (2011). https://doi.org/10.1007/978-3-642-22792-9_16

14. Beimel, A., Omri, E., Orlov, I.: Protocols for multiparty coin toss with dishonest majority. In: Rabin, T. (ed.) CRYPTO 2010. LNCS, vol. 6223, pp. 538–557. Springer, Heidelberg (2010). https://doi.org/10.1007/978-3-642-14623-7_29

15. Bitansky, N., et al.: Why "Fiat-Shamir for Proofs" lacks a proof. In: Sahai, A. (ed.) TCC 2013. LNCS, vol. 7785, pp. 182–201. Springer, Heidelberg (2013). https://doi.org/10.1007/978-3-642-36594-2_11

16. Blum, M.: Coin flipping by telephone - a protocol for solving impossible problems, pp. 133–137 (1982)

17. Boldyreva, A., Cash, D., Fischlin, M., Warinschi, B.: Foundations of non-malleable hash and one-way functions. In: Matsui, M. (ed.) ASIACRYPT 2009. LNCS, vol. 5912, pp. 524–541. Springer, Heidelberg (2009). https://doi.org/10.1007/978-3-642-10366-7_31

18. Boneh, D., Papakonstantinou, P.A., Rackoff, C., Vahlis, Y., Waters, B.: On the impossibility of basing identity based encryption on trapdoor permutations. In: 49th Annual Symposium on Foundations of Computer Science, Philadelphia, PA, USA, 25–28 October 2008, pp. 283–292. IEEE Computer Society Press (2008)

19. Boneh, D., Venkatesan, R.: Breaking RSA may not be equivalent to factoring. In: Nyberg, K. (ed.) EUROCRYPT 1998. LNCS, vol. 1403, pp. 59–71. Springer, Heidelberg (1998). https://doi.org/10.1007/BFb0054117

20. Brendel, J., Fischlin, M., Günther, F., Janson, C.: PRF-ODH: relations, instantiations, and impossibility results. In: Katz, J., Shacham, H. (eds.) CRYPTO 2017, Part III. LNCS, vol. 10403, pp. 651–681. Springer, Cham (2017). https://doi.org/10.1007/978-3-319-63697-9_22

21. Broder, A.Z., Dolev, D.: Flipping coins in many pockets (byzantine agreement on uniformly random values). In: 25th Annual Symposium on Foundations of Computer Science, Singer Island, Florida, 24–26 October 1984, pp. 157–170. IEEE Computer Society Press (1984)

22. Brown, D.R.L.: Breaking RSA may be as difficult as factoring. J. Cryptol. 29(1), 220–241 (2016)

23. Buchbinder, N., Haitner, I., Levi, N., Tsfadia, E.: Fair coin flipping: tighter analysis and the many-party case. In: Klein, P.N. (ed.) 28th Annual ACM-SIAM Symposium on Discrete Algorithms, Barcelona, Spain, 16–19 January 2017, pp. 2580–2600. ACM-SIAM (2017)

24. Cleve, R.: Limits on the security of coin flips when half the processors are faulty (extended abstract). In: 18th Annual ACM Symposium on Theory of Computing, Berkeley, CA, USA, 28–30 May 1986, pp. 364–369. ACM Press (1986)

25. Cleve, R., Impagliazzo, R.: Martingales, collective coin flipping and discrete control processes. Other Words 1, 5 (1993)

26. Cook, S.A.: The complexity of theorem-proving procedures. In: Harrison, M.A., Banerji, R.B., Ullman, J.D. (eds.) Proceedings of the 3rd Annual ACM Symposium on Theory of Computing, Shaker Heights, Ohio, USA, 3–5 May 1971, pp. 151–158. ACM (1971)

27. Coron, J.-S.: Security proof for partial-domain hash signature schemes. In: Yung, M. (ed.) CRYPTO 2002. LNCS, vol. 2442, pp. 613–626. Springer, Heidelberg (2002). https://doi.org/10.1007/3-540-45708-9_39

28. Coron, J.-S., Patarin, J., Seurin, Y.: The random oracle model and the ideal cipher model are equivalent. In: Wagner, D. (ed.) CRYPTO 2008. LNCS, vol. 5157, pp. 1–20. Springer, Heidelberg (2008). https://doi.org/10.1007/978-3-540-85174-5_1

29. Dachman-Soled, D., Lindell, Y., Mahmoody, M., Malkin, T.: On the black-box complexity of optimally-fair coin tossing. In: Ishai, Y. (ed.) TCC 2011. LNCS, vol. 6597, pp. 450–467. Springer, Heidelberg (2011). https://doi.org/10.1007/978-3-642-19571-6_27

30. Dachman-Soled, D., Mahmoody, M., Malkin, T.: Can optimally-fair coin tossing be based on one-way functions? In: Lindell, Y. (ed.) TCC 2014. LNCS, vol. 8349, pp. 217–239. Springer, Heidelberg (2014). https://doi.org/10.1007/978-3-642-54242-8_10

31. Dodis, Y., Haitner, I., Tentes, A.: On the instantiability of hash-and-sign RSA signatures. In: Cramer, R. (ed.) TCC 2012. LNCS, vol. 7194, pp. 112–132. Springer, Heidelberg (2012). https://doi.org/10.1007/978-3-642-28914-9_7

32. Dodis, Y., Oliveira, R., Pietrzak, K.: On the generic insecurity of the full domain hash. In: Shoup, V. (ed.) CRYPTO 2005. LNCS, vol. 3621, pp. 449–466. Springer, Heidelberg (2005). https://doi.org/10.1007/11535218_27

33. Dolev, D., Dwork, C., Naor, M.: Nonmalleable cryptography. SIAM J. Comput. **30**(2), 391–437 (2000)

34. Drijvers, M., et al.: On the security of two-round multi-signatures. In: 2019 IEEE Symposium on Security and Privacy, SP 2019, San Francisco, CA, USA, 19–23 May 2019, pp. 1084–1101. IEEE (2019)

35. Feige, U., Shamir, A.: Witness indistinguishable and witness hiding protocols. In: 22nd Annual ACM Symposium on Theory of Computing, Baltimore, MD, USA, 14–16 May 1990, pp. 416–426. ACM Press (1990)

36. Fiore, D., Schröder, D.: Uniqueness is a different story: impossibility of verifiable random functions from trapdoor permutations. In: Cramer, R. (ed.) TCC 2012. LNCS, vol. 7194, pp. 636–653. Springer, Heidelberg (2012). https://doi.org/10.1007/978-3-642-28914-9_36

37. Fischlin, M.: On the impossibility of constructing non-interactive statistically-secret protocols from any trapdoor one-way function. In: Preneel, B. (ed.) CT-RSA 2002. LNCS, vol. 2271, pp. 79–95. Springer, Heidelberg (2002). https://doi.org/10.1007/3-540-45760-7_7

38. Fischlin, M., Fleischhacker, N.: Limitations of the meta-reduction technique: the case of Schnorr signatures. In: Johansson, T., Nguyen, P.Q. (eds.) EUROCRYPT 2013. LNCS, vol. 7881, pp. 444–460. Springer, Heidelberg (2013). https://doi.org/10.1007/978-3-642-38348-9_27

39. Fischlin, M., Harasser, P., Janson, C.: Signatures from sequential-OR proofs. In: Canteaut, A., Ishai, Y. (eds.) EUROCRYPT 2020, Part III. LNCS, vol. 12107, pp. 212–244. Springer, Cham (2020). https://doi.org/10.1007/978-3-030-45727-3_8

40. Fischlin, M., Lehmann, A., Ristenpart, T., Shrimpton, T., Stam, M., Tessaro, S.: Random oracles with(out) programmability. In: Abe, M. (ed.) ASIACRYPT 2010. LNCS, vol. 6477, pp. 303–320. Springer, Heidelberg (2010). https://doi.org/10.1007/978-3-642-17373-8_18

41. Fischlin, M., Schröder, D.: On the impossibility of three-move blind signature schemes. In: Gilbert, H. (ed.) EUROCRYPT 2010. LNCS, vol. 6110, pp. 197–215. Springer, Heidelberg (2010). https://doi.org/10.1007/978-3-642-13190-5_10

42. Fuchsbauer, G., Konstantinov, M., Pietrzak, K., Rao, V.: Adaptive security of constrained PRFs. In: Sarkar, P., Iwata, T. (eds.) ASIACRYPT 2014, Part II. LNCS, vol. 8874, pp. 82–101. Springer, Heidelberg (2014). https://doi.org/10.1007/978-3-662-45608-8_5

43. Fukumitsu, M., Hasegawa, S.: One-more assumptions do not help Fiat-Shamir-type signature schemes in NPROM. In: Jarecki, S. (ed.) CT-RSA 2020. LNCS, vol. 12006, pp. 586–609. Springer, Cham (2020). https://doi.org/10.1007/978-3-030-40186-3_25

44. Garg, S., Hajiabadi, M., Mahmoody, M., Mohammed, A.: Limits on the power of garbling techniques for public-key encryption. In: Shacham, H., Boldyreva, A. (eds.) CRYPTO 2018, Part III. LNCS, vol. 10993, pp. 335–364. Springer, Cham (2018). https://doi.org/10.1007/978-3-319-96878-0_12

45. Garg, S., Mahmoody, M., Masny, D., Meckler, I.: On the round complexity of OT extension. In: Shacham, H., Boldyreva, A. (eds.) CRYPTO 2018, Part III. LNCS, vol. 10993, pp. 545–574. Springer, Cham (2018). https://doi.org/10.1007/978-3-319-96878-0_19

46. Garg, S., Mahmoody, M., Mohammed, A.: Lower bounds on obfuscation from all-or-nothing encryption primitives. In: Katz, J., Shacham, H. (eds.) CRYPTO 2017, Part I. LNCS, vol. 10401, pp. 661–695. Springer, Cham (2017). https://doi.org/10.1007/978-3-319-63688-7_22

47. Garg, S., Mahmoody, M., Mohammed, A.: When does functional encryption imply obfuscation? In: Kalai, Y., Reyzin, L. (eds.) TCC 2017, Part I. LNCS, vol. 10677, pp. 82–115. Springer, Cham (2017). https://doi.org/10.1007/978-3-319-70500-2_4

48. Gennaro, R., Gertner, Y., Katz, J.: Lower bounds on the efficiency of encryption and digital signature schemes. In: 35th Annual ACM Symposium on Theory of Computing, San Diego, CA, USA, 9–11 June 2003, pp. 417–425. ACM Press (2003)

49. Gennaro, R., Trevisan, L.: Lower bounds on the efficiency of generic cryptographic constructions. In: 41st Annual Symposium on Foundations of Computer Science, Redondo Beach, CA, USA, 12–14 November 2000, pp. 305–313. IEEE Computer Society Press (2000)

50. Gentry, C., Wichs, D.: Separating succinct non-interactive arguments from all falsifiable assumptions. In: Fortnow, L., Vadhan, S.P. (eds.) 43rd Annual ACM Symposium on Theory of Computing, San Jose, CA, USA, 6–8 June 2011, pp. 99–108. ACM Press (2011)

51. Gertner, Y., Kannan, S., Malkin, T., Reingold, O., Viswanathan, M.: The relationship between public key encryption and oblivious transfer. In: 41st Annual Symposium on Foundations of Computer Science, Redondo Beach, CA, USA, 12–14 November 2000, pp. 325–335. IEEE Computer Society Press (2000)

52. Gertner, Y., Malkin, T., Myers, S.: Towards a separation of semantic and CCA security for public key encryption. In: Vadhan, S.P. (ed.) TCC 2007. LNCS, vol. 4392, pp. 434–455. Springer, Heidelberg (2007). https://doi.org/10.1007/978-3-540-70936-7_24

53. Gertner, Y., Malkin, T., Reingold, O.: On the impossibility of basing trapdoor functions on trapdoor predicates. In: 42nd Annual Symposium on Foundations of Computer Science, Las Vegas, NV, USA, 14–17 October 2001, pp.126–135. IEEE Computer Society Press (2001)

54. Goldreich, O., Goldwasser, S., Micali, S.: How to construct random functions (extended abstract). In: 25th Annual Symposium on Foundations of Computer Science, Singer Island, Florida, 24–26 October 1984, pp. 464–479. IEEE Computer Society Press (1984)

55. Goldreich, O., Goldwasser, S., Micali, S.: How to construct random functions. J. ACM 33(4), 792–807 (1986)

56. Goldreich, O., Micali, S., Wigderson, A.: How to play any mental game or a completeness theorem for protocols with honest majority. In: Aho, A. (ed.) 19th Annual ACM Symposium on Theory of Computing, New York City, NY, USA, 25–27 May 1987, pp. 218–229. ACM Press (1987)

57. Goldreich, O., Micali, S., Wigderson, A.: Proofs that yield nothing but their validity or all languages in NP have zero-knowledge proof systems. J. ACM 38(3), 691–729 (1991)

58. Gordon, S.D., Hazay, C., Katz, J., Lindell, Y.: Complete fairness in secure two-party computation. In: Ladner, R.E., Dwork, C. (eds.) 40th Annual ACM Symposium on Theory of Computing, Victoria, BC, Canada, 17–20 May 2008, pp. 413–422. ACM Press (2008)

59. Gordon, S.D., Katz, J.: Partial fairness in secure two-party computation. In: Gilbert, H. (ed.) EUROCRYPT 2010. LNCS, vol. 6110, pp. 157–176. Springer, Heidelberg (2010). https://doi.org/10.1007/978-3-642-13190-5_8

60. Haitner, I., Makriyannis, N., Omri, E.: On the complexity of fair coin flipping. In: Beimel, A., Dziembowski, S. (eds.) TCC 2018, Part I. LNCS, vol. 11239, pp. 539–562. Springer, Cham (2018). https://doi.org/10.1007/978-3-030-03807-6_20

61. Haitner, I., Nissim, K., Omri, E., Shaltiel, R., Silbak, J.: Computational two-party correlation: a dichotomy for key-agreement protocols. In: Thorup, M. (ed.) 59th Annual Symposium on Foundations of Computer Science, Paris, France, 7–9 October 2018, pp. 136–147. IEEE Computer Society Press (2018)

62. Haitner, I., Omri, E., Zarosim, H.: Limits on the usefulness of random oracles. In: Sahai, A. (ed.) TCC 2013. LNCS, vol. 7785, pp. 437–456. Springer, Heidelberg (2013). https://doi.org/10.1007/978-3-642-36594-2_25

63. Haitner, I., Reingold, O.: Statistically-hiding commitment from any one-way function. In: Johnson, D.S., Feige, U. (eds.) 39th Annual ACM Symposium on Theory of Computing, San Diego, CA, USA, 11–13 June 2007, pp. 1–10. ACM Press (2007)

64. Haitner, I., Tsfadia, E.: An almost-optimally fair three-party coin-flipping protocol. In: Shmoys, D.B. (ed.) 46th Annual ACM Symposium on Theory of Computing, New York, NY, USA, 31 May - 3 June 2014, pp. 408–416. ACM Press (2014)

65. Hanaoka, G., Matsuda, T., Schuldt, J.C.N.: On the impossibility of constructing efficient key encapsulation and programmable hash functions in prime order groups. In: Safavi-Naini, R., Canetti, R. (eds.) CRYPTO 2012. LNCS, vol. 7417, pp. 812–831. Springer, Heidelberg (2012). https://doi.org/10.1007/978-3-642-32009-5_47

66. Håstad, J.: Pseudo-random generators under uniform assumptions. In: 22nd Annual ACM Symposium on Theory of Computing, Baltimore, MD, USA, 14–16 May 1990, pp. 395–404. ACM Press (1990)

67. Håstad, J., Impagliazzo, R., Levin, L.A., Luby, M.: A pseudorandom generator from any one-way function. SIAM J. Comput. **28**(4), 1364–1396 (1999)

68. Hesse, J., Hofheinz, D., Kohl, L.: On tightly secure non-interactive key exchange. In: Shacham, H., Boldyreva, A. (eds.) CRYPTO 2018, Part II. LNCS, vol. 10992, pp. 65–94. Springer, Cham (2018). https://doi.org/10.1007/978-3-319-96881-0_3

69. Hofheinz, D.: Possibility and impossibility results for selective decommitments. J. Cryptol. **24**(3), 470–516 (2011)

70. Holenstein, T., Künzler, R., Tessaro, S.: The equivalence of the random oracle model and the ideal cipher model, revisited. In: Fortnow, L., Vadhan, S.P. (eds.) 43rd Annual ACM Symposium on Theory of Computing, San Jose, CA, USA, 6–8 June 2011, pp. 89–98. ACM Press (2011)

71. Hsiao, C.-Y., Reyzin, L.: Finding collisions on a public road, or do secure hash functions need secret coins? In: Franklin, M. (ed.) CRYPTO 2004. LNCS, vol. 3152, pp. 92–105. Springer, Heidelberg (2004). https://doi.org/10.1007/978-3-540-28628-8_6

72. Impagliazzo, R.: A personal view of average-case complexity. In: Proceedings of the Tenth Annual Structure in Complexity Theory Conference, Minneapolis, Minnesota, USA, 19–22 June 1995, pp. 134–147. IEEE Computer Society (1995)

73. Impagliazzo, R., Levin, L.A., Luby, M.: Pseudo-random generation from one-way functions (extended abstracts). In: 21st Annual ACM Symposium on Theory of Computing, Seattle, WA, USA, 15–17 May 1989, pp. 12–24. ACM Press (1989)

74. Impagliazzo, R., Luby, M.: One-way functions are essential for complexity based cryptography (extended abstract). In: 30th Annual Symposium on Foundations of Computer Science, Research Triangle Park, NC, USA, 30 October–1 November 1989, pp. 230–235. IEEE Computer Society Press (1989)

75. Impagliazzo, R., Rudich, S.: Limits on the provable consequences of one-way permutations. In: 21st Annual ACM Symposium on Theory of Computing, Seattle, WA, USA, 15–17 May 1989, pp. 44–61. ACM Press (1989)

76. Karp, R.M.: Reducibility among combinatorial problems. In: Miller, R.E., Thatcher, J.W. (eds.) Proceedings of a Symposium on the Complexity of Computer Computations, Held 20–22 March 1972, at the IBM Thomas J. Watson Research Center, Yorktown Heights, New York, USA, The IBM Research Symposia Series, pp. 85–103. Plenum Press, New York (1972)

77. Katz, J., Schröder, D., Yerukhimovich, A.: Impossibility of blind signatures from one-way permutations. In: Ishai, Y. (ed.) TCC 2011. LNCS, vol. 6597, pp. 615–629. Springer, Heidelberg (2011). https://doi.org/10.1007/978-3-642-19571-6_37

78. Khorasgani, H.A., Maji, H.K., Mukherjee, T.: Estimating gaps in martingales and applications to coin-tossing: constructions and hardness. In: Hofheinz, D., Rosen, A. (eds.) TCC 2019, Part II. LNCS, vol. 11892, pp. 333–355. Springer, Cham (2019). https://doi.org/10.1007/978-3-030-36033-7_13

79. Khorasgani, H.A., Maji, H.K., Wang, M.: Coin tossing with lazy defense: hardness of computation results. IACR Cryptol. ePrint Arch. 2020:131 (2020)

80. Kim, J.H., Simon, D.R., Tetali, P.: Limits on the efficiency of one-way permutation-based hash functions. In: 40th Annual Symposium on Foundations of Computer Science, New York, NY, USA, 17–19 October 1999, pp. 535–542. IEEE Computer Society Press (1999)

81. Luby, M., Rackoff, C.: How to construct pseudorandom permutations from pseudorandom functions. SIAM J. Comput. **17**(2), 373–386 (1988)

82. Mahmoody, M., Maji, H.K., Prabhakaran, M.: Limits of random oracles in secure computation. In: Naor, M. (ed.) ITCS 2014: 5th Conference on Innovations in Theoretical Computer Science, Princeton, NJ, USA, 12–14 January 2014, pp. 23–34. Association for Computing Machinery (2014)

83. Mahmoody, M., Maji, H.K., Prabhakaran, M.: On the power of public-key encryption in secure computation. In: Lindell, Y. (ed.) TCC 2014. LNCS, vol. 8349, pp. 240–264. Springer, Heidelberg (2014). https://doi.org/10.1007/978-3-642-54242-8_11

84. Mahmoody, M., Mohammed, A.: On the power of hierarchical identity-based encryption. In: Fischlin, M., Coron, J.-S. (eds.) EUROCRYPT 2016, Part II. LNCS, vol. 9666, pp. 243–272. Springer, Heidelberg (2016). https://doi.org/10.1007/978-3-662-49896-5_9

85. Mahmoody, M., Mohammed, A., Nematihaji, S., Pass, R., Shelat, A.: Lower bounds on assumptions behind indistinguishability obfuscation. In: Kushilevitz, E., Malkin, T. (eds.) TCC 2016, Part I. LNCS, vol. 9562, pp. 49–66. Springer, Heidelberg (2016). https://doi.org/10.1007/978-3-662-49096-9_3

86. Makriyannis, N.: On the classification of finite Boolean functions up to fairness. In: Abdalla, M., De Prisco, R. (eds.) SCN 2014. LNCS, vol. 8642, pp. 135–154. Springer, Cham (2014). https://doi.org/10.1007/978-3-319-10879-7_9

87. Matsuda, T., Matsuura, K.: On black-box separations among injective one-way functions. In: Ishai, Y. (ed.) TCC 2011. LNCS, vol. 6597, pp. 597–614. Springer, Heidelberg (2011). https://doi.org/10.1007/978-3-642-19571-6_36

88. Moran, T., Naor, M., Segev, G.: An optimally fair coin toss. In: Reingold, O. (ed.) TCC 2009. LNCS, vol. 5444, pp. 1–18. Springer, Heidelberg (2009). https://doi.org/10.1007/978-3-642-00457-5_1

89. Morgan, A., Pass, R.: On the security loss of unique signatures. In: Beimel, A., Dziembowski, S. (eds.) TCC 2018, Part I. LNCS, vol. 11239, pp. 507–536. Springer, Cham (2018). https://doi.org/10.1007/978-3-030-03807-6_19

90. Naor, M.: Bit commitment using pseudorandomness. J. Cryptol. **4**(2), 151–158 (1991)
91. Naor, M.: On cryptographic assumptions and challenges (invited talk). In: Boneh, D. (ed.) CRYPTO 2003. LNCS, vol. 2729, pp. 96–109. Springer, Heidelberg (2003). https://doi.org/10.1007/978-3-540-45146-4_6
92. Naor, M., Ostrovsky, R., Venkatesan, R., Yung, M.: Perfect zero-knowledge arguments for NP using any one-way permutation. J. Cryptol. **11**(2), 87–108 (1998)
93. Naor, M., Yung, M.: Universal one-way hash functions and their cryptographic applications. In: 21st Annual ACM Symposium on Theory of Computing, Seattle, WA, USA, 15–17 May 1989, pp. 33–43. ACM Press (1989)
94. Paillier, P., Vergnaud, D.: Discrete-log-based signatures may not be equivalent to discrete log. In: Roy, B. (ed.) ASIACRYPT 2005. LNCS, vol. 3788, pp. 1–20. Springer, Heidelberg (2005). https://doi.org/10.1007/11593447_1
95. Pass, R.: Limits of provable security from standard assumptions. In: Fortnow, L., Vadhan, S.P. (eds.) 43rd Annual ACM Symposium on Theory of Computing, San Jose, CA, USA, 6–8 June 2011, pp. 109–118. ACM Press (2011)
96. Reingold, O., Trevisan, L., Vadhan, S.: Notions of reducibility between cryptographic primitives. In: Naor, M. (ed.) TCC 2004. LNCS, vol. 2951, pp. 1–20. Springer, Heidelberg (2004). https://doi.org/10.1007/978-3-540-24638-1_1
97. Rompel, J.: One-way functions are necessary and sufficient for secure signatures. In: 22nd Annual ACM Symposium on Theory of Computing, Baltimore, MD, USA, 14–16 May 1990, pp. 387–394. ACM Press (1990)
98. Rudich, S.: Limits on the provable consequences of one-way functions (1988)
99. Rudich, S.: The use of interaction in public cryptosystems (extended abstract). In: Feigenbaum, J. (ed.) CRYPTO 1991. LNCS, vol. 576, pp. 242–251. Springer, Heidelberg (1992). https://doi.org/10.1007/3-540-46766-1_19
100. Schilling, R.L.: Measures, Integrals and Martingales. Cambridge University Press, Cambridge (2017)
101. Seurin, Y.: On the exact security of Schnorr-type signatures in the random oracle model. In: Pointcheval, D., Johansson, T. (eds.) EUROCRYPT 2012. LNCS, vol. 7237, pp. 554–571. Springer, Heidelberg (2012). https://doi.org/10.1007/978-3-642-29011-4_33
102. Simon, D.R.: Finding collisions on a one-way street: can secure hash functions be based on general assumptions? In: Nyberg, K. (ed.) EUROCRYPT 1998. LNCS, vol. 1403, pp. 334–345. Springer, Heidelberg (1998). https://doi.org/10.1007/BFb0054137
103. Vahlis, Y.: Two is a crowd? A black-box separation of one-wayness and security under correlated inputs. In: Micciancio, D. (ed.) TCC 2010. LNCS, vol. 5978, pp. 165–182. Springer, Heidelberg (2010). https://doi.org/10.1007/978-3-642-11799-2_11
104. Yao, A.C.-C.: How to generate and exchange secrets (extended abstract). In: 27th Annual Symposium on Foundations of Computer Science, Toronto, Ontario, Canada, 27–29 October 1986, pp. 162–167. IEEE Computer Society Press (1986)
105. Zhang, J., Zhang, Z., Chen, Y., Guo, Y., Zhang, Z.: Black-box separations for one-more (static) CDH and its generalization. In: Sarkar, P., Iwata, T. (eds.) ASIACRYPT 2014, Part II. LNCS, vol. 8874, pp. 366–385. Springer, Heidelberg (2014). https://doi.org/10.1007/978-3-662-45608-8_20

Guaranteed Output Delivery Comes Free in Honest Majority MPC

Vipul Goyal[1], Yifan Song[1(✉)], and Chenzhi Zhu[2]

[1] Carnegie Mellon University, Pittsburgh, USA
vipul@cmu.edu, yifans2@andrew.cmu.edu
[2] Tsinghua University, Beijing, China
mrbrtpt@gmail.com

Abstract. We study the communication complexity of unconditionally secure MPC with guaranteed output delivery over point-to-point channels for corruption threshold $t < n/2$, assuming the existence of a public broadcast channel. We ask the question: "is it possible to construct MPC in this setting s.t. the communication complexity per multiplication gate is linear in the number of parties?" While a number of works have focused on reducing the communication complexity in this setting, the answer to the above question has remained elusive until now. We also focus on the concrete communication complexity of evaluating each multiplication gate.

We resolve the above question in the affirmative by providing an MPC with communication complexity $O(Cn\phi)$ bits (ignoring fixed terms which are independent of the circuit) where ϕ is the length of an element in the field, C is the size of the (arithmetic) circuit, n is the number of parties. This is the first construction where the asymptotic communication complexity matches the best-known semi-honest protocol. This represents a strict improvement over the previously best-known communication complexity of $O(C(n\phi + \kappa) + D_M n^2 \kappa)$ bits, where κ is the security parameter and D_M is the multiplicative depth of the circuit. Furthermore, the concrete communication complexity per multiplication gate is 5.5 field elements per party in the best case and 7.5 field elements in the worst case when one or more corrupted parties have been identified. This also roughly matches the best-known semi-honest protocol, which requires 5.5 field elements per gate.

The above also yields the first secure-with-abort MPC protocol with the same cost per multiplication gate as the best-known semi-honest protocol. Our main result is obtained by compiling the secure-with-abort MPC protocol into a fully secure one.

V. Goyal—Research supported in part by the Office of the Director of National Intelligence (ODNI), Intelligence Advanced Research Projects Activity (IARPA), via 2019-1902070008, an NSF award 1916939, a gift from Ripple, a JP Morgan Faculty Fellowship, a PNC center for financial services innovation award, and a Cylab seed funding award.

Y. Song—Research supported in part by a Cylab Presidential Fellowship and grants of Vipul Goyal mentioned above.

C. Zhu—Work done in part while at CMU.

D. Micciancio and T. Ristenpart (Eds.): CRYPTO 2020, LNCS 12171, pp. 618–646, 2020.
https://doi.org/10.1007/978-3-030-56880-1_22

1   Introduction

In secure multiparty computation (MPC), a set of n parties together evaluate a function f on their private inputs. This function f is public to all parties, and, may be modeled as an arithmetic circuit over a finite field. Very informally, a protocol of secure multiparty computation guarantees the privacy of the inputs of every (honest) individual except the information which can be deduced from the output. This notion was first introduced in the work [Yao82] of Yao. Since the early feasibility solutions proposed in [Yao82, GMW87], various settings of MPC have been studied. Examples include semi-honest security vs malicious security, security against computational adversaries vs unbounded adversaries, honest majority vs corruptions up to $n - 1$ parties, security with abort vs guaranteed output delivery and so on.

In this work, we focus on the information-theoretical setting (i.e., security against unbounded adversaries) with guaranteed output delivery. The adversary is allowed to corrupt at most $t < n/2$ parties and is fully malicious. We assume the existence of private point-to-point communication channels and a public broadcast channel. We are interested in the communication complexity of the secure MPC, which is measured by the number of bits X via private point-to-point channels and the number of bits Y via the public broadcast channel, i.e., $X + Y \cdot \mathcal{BC}$. The first positive solutions in this setting were proposed in [RBO89, Bea89]. After those, several subsequent works [CDD+99, BTH06, BSFO12] have focused on improving the communication complexity of the protocol. Note that, by representing the functionality as an arithmetic circuit, the communication complexity of the protocol in the unconditional setting is typically dominated by the number of multiplication gates in the circuit. This is because the addition gates can usually be done locally, requiring no communication at all.

In this paper, we ask the following natural question:

"Is it possible to construct unconditional MPC with guaranteed output delivery for $t < n/2$ s.t. the communication complexity per multiplication gate is linear in the number of parties? Furthermore, what is the concrete communication complexity per multiplication gate?"

Having linear communication complexity per multiplication gate greatly benefits the scalability of the protocol, as it means that the work done by each party is independent of the number of parties but only related to the size of the circuit. While a number of works have made significant progress, this question has remained opened until now.

The best-known result in this setting is the construction in the work [BSFO12] of Ben-Sasson, Fehr and Ostrovsky. The construction in [BSFO12] has communication complexity $O(C(n\phi + \kappa) + D_M n^2 \kappa)$ bits (ignoring fixed terms which are independent of the circuit), where C is the size of the circuit, ϕ is the length of a field element, κ is the security parameter and D_M is the multiplicative depth of the circuit. Comparing with the best-known result against semi-honest adversaries in [DN07], which has communication complexity $O(Cn\phi)$ bits, there is an additional term $D_M n^2 \kappa$ related to the circuit. In the worst case where the circuit is "narrow and deep", $D_M n^2 \kappa$ may even become the dominating term of the communication complexity and result in $O(n^2)$ elements per gate. Ben-Sasson et al. asked if this quadratic term related to the depth of the circuit is inherent.

In a beautiful work, Ishai et al. [IKP+16] provided a general transformation from a protocol in the setting of security with abort to a protocol with guaranteed output delivery. Instantiation this transformation with the best-known protocol for security with abort, the resulting construction eliminates the quadratic term w.r.t. the circuit depth. However, the communication complexity of the resulting protocol now has a term $O(W \cdot \text{poly}(n))$, where W is the width of the circuit, and, $\text{poly}(n)$ can be at least n^4 for certain circuits. For the circuit with a large width, this term may even become the dominating term.

In the setting of $t < n/3$ corruptions (where a public broadcast channel can be securely simulated), question of getting a construction with linear communication complexity was recently resolved in the recent work of Goyal et al. [GLS19], which presented a construction with communication complexity $O(Cn\phi)$ bits. Similar results were also known in the setting of security with abort in [GIP+14, GIP15, LN17, CGH+18, NV18].

Our Results. In this work, we answer the above question in the affirmative by presenting an MPC protocol with communication complexity $O(Cn\phi)$ bits (ignoring fixed terms which are independent of the circuit). Furthermore, we also focus on the concrete efficiency, i.e., the number of elements per multiplication gate per party. Concretely, our result achieves $5.5 + \epsilon$ elements in the best case and $7.5 + \epsilon$ elements in the worst case when one or more corrupted parties have been identified, where ϵ can be an arbitrarily small constant. Comparing with the best-known result [DN07] in the semi-honest setting, our result essentially shows that achieving output delivery guarantee requires no additional cost compared to the semi-honest security.

Our main contributions lie in two aspects, (1) we present the first construction in this setting where the asymptotic communication complexity matches that in the semi-honest setting, and, (2) our protocol roughly achieves the same concrete efficiency as the best-known semi-honest protocol.

The above also yields the first secure-with-abort MPC protocol with the same cost per multiplication gate as the best-known semi-honest protocol [DN07]. Concretely, each party only needs to communicate 5.5 field elements per multiplication gate. We obtain this construction by building on the technique in [BBCG+19]. An overview of the construction can be found in Sect. 3.

Regarding the construction with guaranteed output delivery, our results stem from the idea of developing a suite of techniques to efficiently compile our secure-with-abort protocol into a fully secure protocol. Additionally, we introduce a technique which allows us to reuse authentication keys towards developing a more efficient verifiable secret sharing scheme. An overview of our new ideas can be found in Sect. 4.

Related Works. We compare our result with several related constructions in both techniques and efficiency. In the following, let C denote the size of the circuit, ϕ denote the size of a field element, κ denote the security parameter, D_M denote the depth of the circuit, and W denote the width of the circuit. We will ignore fixed terms which are independent of the circuit.

Security with Abort. In [DN07], Damgård and Nielsen introduce the best-known semi-honest protocol, which we refer to as the DN protocol. The communication complexity of the DN protocol is $O(Cn\phi)$ bits. The concrete efficiency is 6 field elements per multiplication gate (per party). In [GIP+14], Genkin, et al. show that the DN protocol is secure up to an additive attack when running in the fully malicious setting. Based on this observation, a secure-with-abort MPC protocol can be constructed by combining the DN protocol and a circuit which is resilient to an additive attack (referred to as an AMD circuit). As a result, Genkin, et al. [GIP+14] give the first construction against a fully malicious adversary with communication complexity $O(Cn\phi)$ bits (for a large enough field), which matches the asymptotic communication complexity of the DN protocol.

The construction in [CGH+18] also relies on the theorem showed in [GIP+14]. The idea is to check whether the adversary launches an additive attack. In the beginning, all parties compute a random secret sharing of the value r. For each wire w with the value x associated with it, all parties will compute two secret sharings of the secret values x and $r \cdot x$ respectively. Here $r \cdot x$ can be seen as a secure MAC of x when the only possible attack is an additive attack. In this way, the protocol requires two operations per multiplication gate. The asymptotic communication complexity is $O(Cn\phi)$ bits (for a large enough field) and the concrete efficiency is reduced to 12 field elements per multiplication gate.

An interesting observation is that the theorem showed in [GIP+14] implies that the DN protocol provides perfect privacy of honest parties (before the output phase) in the presence of a fully malicious adversary. To achieve security with abort, the only task is to check the correctness of the computation before the output phase. This observation has been used in [LN17,NV18]. In particular, the construction in [NV18] achieves the same concrete efficiency as [CGH+18] by using the Batch-wise Multiplication Verification technique in [BSFO12], i.e., 12 field elements per multiplication gate. Our construction also relies on this observation. Therefore, the main task is to efficiently verify a batch of multiplications such that the communication complexity is sublinear in the number of parties.

In [BBCG+19], Boneh, et al. introduce a very powerful tool to achieve this task when the number of parties is restricted to be a constant. Our result is obtained by instantiating this technique with a different secret sharing scheme, which allows us to overcome this restriction so that it works for any (polynomial) number of parties. Furthermore, we simplify this technique by avoiding the use of a robust secret sharing scheme and a verifiable secret sharing scheme, which are required in [BBCG+19]. Our protocol additionally makes a simple optimization to the DN protocol, which brings down the cost from 6 field elements per multiplication gate to 5.5 field elements. More details about the comparison for techniques can be found in the last paragraph of Sect. 3.5. A subsequent work [GLOS20] implements our construction and shows that the performance beats the previously best-known implementation result [CGH+18] in this setting.

In [BGIN19], Boyle, et al. use the technique in [BBCG+19] to construct a 3-party computation with guaranteed output delivery. In particular, they implement their verification for multiplication gates. As shown in their implementation result, just the local computation of checking the correctness of 1 million multiplication gates in the 31-bit Mersenne Field requires around 1 s. Note that this does not include any computation cost related to the circuit and any communication cost. On the other hand, the implementation result from [GLOS20] shows that our construction only needs 0.7 s for computing the whole circuit in an even large field (61-bit Mersenne Field) in the 3-party setting. This shows that our construction is *several* times faster.

Guaranteed Output Delivery. The construction in [BSFO12] is most related to our result. In fact, we reuse and modify many protocols in [BSFO12] in our construction.

The communication complexity achieved by the construction in [BSFO12] is $O(C(n\phi + \kappa) + D_M n^2 \kappa)$ bits. Our result removes both the quadratic term related to D_M and the term $O(C\kappa)$. Furthermore, the use of Beaver triples for multiplication gates in [BSFO12] is more expensive than the multiplication protocol in the best-known semi-honest protocol [DN07]. As a result, the communication cost per multiplication gate in [BSFO12] is a fixed 20 field elements (without considering the effect of $O(D_M n^2 \kappa)$). Our result achieves $5.5 + \epsilon$ field elements per multiplication gate in the best case and $7.5 + \epsilon$ field elements in the worst case when one or more corrupted parties have been identified, where ϵ can be an arbitrarily small constant. In the best case, our result matches the best-known semi-honest protocol [DN07].

Technically, while the construction from [BSFO12] uses Beaver triples to compute multiplications in the computation phase, we directly use a modified version of the multiplication protocol of the best-known protocol [DN07] from the semi-honest setting. We note that Beaver triples provide plenty of redundancy which simplifies the checking process in the computation phase. However, the use of Beaver triples unfortunately requires a verification for each layer of the circuit, which leads to the quadratic term related to D_M. On the other hand, we start from the our secure-with-abort MPC protocol, which does not make use of Beaver triples. While this idea can potentially remove the term $O(D_M n^2)$, without the redundancy provided by Beaver triples, the verification becomes difficult and even the computation cannot proceed when malicious parties refuse to participate in the computation. We will show how to tackle these difficulties in Sect. 4.

In [IKP+16], Ishai et al. provided a general transformation from a protocol in the setting of security with abort to a protocol with guaranteed output delivery. When instantiating their transformation with our secure-with-abort protocol, the resulting protocol can achieve 5.5 field elements per multiplication gate when the *width* of the circuit is small. However, a drawback of this transformation is that the efficiency of the resulting protocol has a large dependency on the width of the circuit. Specifically, the communication complexity of the resulting protocol contains a term $O(W \cdot \text{poly}(n, \kappa))$ (where poly is relatively large). For the circuit with a large width, this term may even become the dominating term.

Recently, Goyal et al. [GLS19] gave the first construction against 1/3 corruption such that the communication complexity per multiplication gate is linear in the number of parties. The communication complexity is $O(Cn\phi)$ bits. Since they mainly focused on the feasibility and the protocol is perfectly secure, the concrete efficiency is 66 elements per multiplication gate.

Unfortunately the techniques developed in [GLS19] fail in the setting of honest majority. Technically, we use a significantly different approach from that in [GLS19] to remove the quadratic term related to the circuit depth. The reason for $O(D_M n^2)$ is that all parties need to ensure the correctness of multiplications in one layer before moving on to the next layer. To this end, each layer requires at least $O(n^2)$ communication, which results in $O(D_M n^2)$ overhead. While Goyal et al. [GLS19] used n-out-of-n secret sharings to overcome the layer restriction, our approach is to directly compile the our secure-with-abort protocol, which does not have the term $O(D_M n^2)$, to a fully secure one.

Other Related Works. The notion of MPC was first introduced in [Yao82, GMW87] in 1980s. Feasibility results for MPC were obtained by [Yao82, GMW87, CDVdG87] under cryptographic assumptions, and by [BOGW88, CCD88] in the information-theoretic setting. Subsequently, a large number of works have focused on improving the efficiency of MPC protocols in various settings.

A series of works focus on improving the communication efficiency of MPC with output delivery guarantee in the settings with different threshold on the number of corrupted parties. In the setting where $t < n/3$, a public broadcast channel can be securely simulated and therefore, only private point-to-point communication channels are required. A rich line of works [HMP00, HM01, DN07, BTH08, GLS19] have focused on improving the asymptotic communication complexity in this setting. In the setting where $t < (1/3 - \epsilon)n$, packed secret sharing can be used to hide a batch of values, resulting in more efficient protocols. E.g., Damgard et al. [DIK10] introduced a protocol with communication complexity $O(C \log C \log n \cdot \kappa + D_M^2 \text{poly}(n, \log C)\kappa)$ bits.

A rich line of works have also focused on the performance of MPC in practice. Many concretely efficient MPC protocols were presented in [LP12, NNOB12, FLNW17, ABF+17, LN17, CGH+18]. All of these works emphasized the practical running time and only provided security with abort. Some of them were specially constructed for two parties [LP12, NNOB12], or three parties [FLNW17, ABF+17].

2 Preliminaries

2.1 Model

We consider a set of parties $\mathcal{P} = \{P_1, P_2, ..., P_n\}$ where each party can provide inputs, receive outputs, and participate in the computation. For every pair of parties, there exists a secure (private and authentic) synchronous channel so that they can directly send messages to each other. Beyond that, we also assume the existence of a secure broadcast channel, which is available to all parties. The communication complexity is measured by the number of bits X via private channels plus the number of bits Y via the broadcast channel, i.e., $X + Y \cdot \mathcal{BC}$.

We focus on functions which can be represented as arithmetic circuits over a finite field $\mathbb{F}$ (with $|\mathbb{F}| \geq n + 1$) with input, addition, random, and output gates. Let $\phi = \log |\mathbb{F}|$ be the size of an element in $\mathbb{F}$. We use κ to denote the security parameter and let $\mathbb{K}$ be an extension field of $\mathbb{F}$ (with $|\mathbb{K}| \geq 2^{\kappa}$). For simplicity, we use κ to denote the size of an element in $\mathbb{K}$.

An adversary is able to corrupt at most $t < n/2$ parties, provide inputs to corrupted parties, and receive all messages sent to corrupted parties. Corrupted parties can deviate from the protocol arbitrarily. For simplicity, we assume $n = 2t + 1$. Each party P_i is assigned a unique non-zero field element $\alpha_i \in \mathbb{F}\backslash\{0\}$ as the identity.

Let c_I, c_M, c_R, c_O be the numbers of input gates, multiplication gates, random gates and output gates respectively. We set $C = c_I + c_M + c_R + c_O$ to be the size of the circuit.

2.2   Secret Sharing

In our protocol, we use the standard Shamir's secret sharing scheme [Sha79].

A *degree-d* Shamir sharing of $w \in \mathbb{F}$ is a vector $(w_1, \ldots, w_n)$ which satisfies that, there exists a polynomial $f(\cdot) \in \mathbb{F}[X]$ of degree at most d such that $f(0) = w$ and $f(\alpha_i) = w_i$ for $i \in \{1, \ldots, n\}$. Each party P_i holds a share w_i and the whole sharing is denoted by $[w]_d$.

Properties of the Shamir's Secret Sharing Scheme. In the following, we will utilize two properties of the Shamir's secret sharing scheme.

– Linear Homomorphism:

$$\forall \ [x]_d, [y]_d, \ [x + y]_d = [x]_d + [y]_d.$$

– Multiplying two degree-d sharings yields a degree-$2d$ sharing. The secret value of the new sharing is the product of the original two secrets.

$$\forall \ [x]_d, [y]_d, \ [x \cdot y]_{2d} = [x]_d \cdot [y]_d.$$

2.3   Generating Random Sharings and Double Sharings

We introduce two basic protocols RAND and DOUBLERAND in the DN protocol [DN07].

The protocol RAND is used to prepare $t + 1 = O(n)$ random degree-t sharings in the *semi-honest* setting. RAND will utilize a predetermined and fixed Vandermonde matrix of size $n \times (t + 1)$, which is denoted by $\boldsymbol{M}^{\mathrm{T}}$ (therefore $\boldsymbol{M}$ is a $(t + 1) \times n$ matrix). An important property of a Vandermonde matrix is that any $(t + 1) \times (t + 1)$ submatrix of $\boldsymbol{M}^{\mathrm{T}}$ is *invertible*. The description of RAND appears in Protocol 1. The communication complexity of RAND is $O(n^2)$ field elements.

Protocol 1: RAND

1. Each party $P_i \in \mathcal{P}_{\text{active}}$ randomly samples a sharing $[s^{(i)}]_t$ such that the shares held by parties in $\mathcal{D}isp_i$ are set to be 0. Then P_i distributes the shares to other parties. For each $P_i \in Corr$, all parties take an all-0 sharing as $[s^{(i)}]_t$.
2. All parties locally compute

$$([r^{(1)}]_t, [r^{(2)}]_t, \ldots, [r^{(t+1)}]_t)^{\mathrm{T}} = M([s^{(1)}]_t, [s^{(2)}]_t, \ldots, [s^{(n)}]_t)^{\mathrm{T}}$$

and output $[r^{(1)}]_t, [r^{(2)}]_t, \ldots, [r^{(t+1)}]_t$.

A pair of double sharings $([r]_t, [r]_{2t})$ is a pair of two sharings of the same secret. One is a degree-t sharing and the other one is a degree-$2t$ sharing. The protocol DOUBLERAND is used to prepare $t + 1 = O(n)$ random double sharings in the *semi-honest* setting. The description of DOUBLERAND appears in Protocol 2. The communication complexity of DOUBLERAND is $O(n^2)$ field elements.

Protocol 2: DOUBLERAND

1. Each party $P_i \in \mathcal{P}_{\text{active}}$ randomly samples a pair of double sharings $([s^{(i)}]_t, [s^{(i)}]_{2t})$ such that the shares held by parties in $\mathcal{D}isp_i$ are set to be 0. Then P_i distributes the shares to other parties. For each $P_i \in Corr$, all parties take all-0 sharings as $([s^{(i)}]_t, [s^{(i)}]_{2t})$.
2. All parties locally compute

$$([r^{(1)}]_t, [r^{(2)}]_t, \ldots, [r^{(t+1)}]_t)^{\mathrm{T}} = M([s^{(1)}]_t, [s^{(2)}]_t, \ldots, [s^{(n)}]_t)^{\mathrm{T}}$$
$$([r^{(1)}]_{2t}, [r^{(2)}]_{2t}, \ldots, [r^{(t+1)}]_{2t})^{\mathrm{T}} = M([s^{(1)}]_{2t}, [s^{(2)}]_{2t}, \ldots, [s^{(n)}]_{2t})^{\mathrm{T}}$$

and output $([r^{(1)}]_t, [r^{(1)}]_{2t}), ([r^{(2)}]_t, [r^{(2)}]_{2t}), \ldots, ([r^{(t+1)}]_t, [r^{(t+1)}]_{2t})$.

---

3 An Overview of the Secure-with-abort Protocol

3.1 General Strategy and Protocol Overview

In [GIP+14], Genkin, et al. showed that several semi-honest MPC protocols are secure up to an additive attack in the presence of a fully malicious adversary. As one corollary, these semi-honest protocols provide full privacy of honest parties before reconstructing the output. Therefore, a straightforward strategy to achieve security-with-abort is to (1) run a semi-honest protocol till the output phase, (2) check the correctness of the computation, and (3) reconstruct the output only if the check passes.

Fortunately, the best-known semi-honest protocol in this setting [DN07] is secure up to an additive attack. Our construction will follow the above strategy. The main task is the second step, i.e., checking the correctness of the computation before reconstructing the final results.

3.2   Review: DN Semi-honest Protocol

The best-known semi-honest protocol was proposed in the work of Damgård and Nielsen [DN07]. The protocol consists of 4 phases: Preparation Phase, Input Phase, Computation Phase, and Output Phase. Here we give a brief description of these four phases.

Preparation Phase. In the preparation phase, all parties need to prepare several random sharings which will be used in the computation phase. Specifically, there are two kinds of random sharings needed to be prepared. The first kind is a random degree-t sharing $[r]_t$. The second kind is a pair of random sharings $([r]_t, [r]_{2t})$, which is referred to as double sharings. At a high-level, these two kinds of random sharings are prepared in the following manner:

1. Each party generates and distributes a random degree-t sharing (or a pair of random double sharings).
2. Each random sharing (or each pair of double sharings) is a linear combination of the random sharings (or the random double sharings) distributed by each party.

More details can be found in Sect. 2.3.

Input Phase. In the input phase, each input holder generates and distributes a random degree-t sharing of its input.

Computation Phase. In the computation phase, all parties need to evaluate addition gates and multiplication gates. For an addition gate with input sharings $[x]_t, [y]_t$, all parties just locally add their shares to get $[x + y]_t = [x]_t + [y]_t$. For a multiplication gate with input sharings $[x]_t, [y]_t$, one pair of double sharings $([r]_t, [r]_{2t})$ is consumed. All parties execute the following steps.

1. All parties first locally compute $[x \cdot y + r]_{2t} = [x]_t \cdot [y]_t + [r]_{2t}$.
2. P_{king} collects all shares of $[x \cdot y + r]_{2t}$ and reconstructs the value $x \cdot y + r$. Then P_{king} sends the value $x \cdot y + r$ back to all other parties.
3. All parties locally compute $[x \cdot y]_t = x \cdot y + r - [r]_t$.

Here P_{king} is the party all parties agree on in the beginning.

Output Phase. In the output phase, all parties send their shares of the output sharing to the party who should receive this result. Then that party can reconstruct the output.

Improvement to 5.5 Field Elements. We note that in the second step of the multiplication protocol, P_{king} can alternatively generate a degree-t sharing $[x \cdot y + r]_t$ and distribute the sharing to all other parties. Then in the third step, $[x \cdot y]_t$ can be computed by $[x \cdot y + r]_t - [r]_t$. In fact, P_{king} can set the shares of (a predetermined set of) t parties to be 0 in the sharing $[x \cdot y + r]_t$. This means that P_{king} need not to communicate these shares at all, reducing the communication by half. We rely on the following two observations:

- While normally setting some shares to be 0 could compromise the privacy of the secret (by effectively reducing the reconstruction threshold), note that here $x \cdot y + r$ need not to be private at all.
- Parties do not actually need to receive $x \cdot y + r$ from P_{king}. Rather, receiving shares of $x \cdot y + r$ is sufficient to allow them to proceed in the protocol.

This simple observation leads to an improvement of reducing the cost per gate from 6 elements to 5.5 elements. Note that in this construction, all multiplication gates at the same "layer" in the circuit can be evaluated in parallel. Hence, it is even possible to perform a "load balancing" such that the overall cost of different parties roughly remains the same.

3.3 Review: Batch-Wise Multiplication Verification

This technique is introduced in the work of Ben-Sasson, et al. [BSFO12]. It is used to check a batch of multiplication tuples efficiently. Specifically, given m multiplication tuples

$$([x^{(1)}]_t, [y^{(1)}]_t, [z^{(1)}]_t), ([x^{(2)}]_t, [y^{(2)}]_t, [z^{(2)}]_t), \ldots, ([x^{(m)}]_t, [y^{(m)}]_t, [z^{(m)}]_t),$$

we want to check whether $x^{(i)} \cdot y^{(i)} = z^{(i)}$ for all $i \in [m]$.

The high-level idea is constructing three polynomials $f(\cdot), g(\cdot), h(\cdot)$ such that

$$\forall i \in [m], f(i) = x^{(i)}, g(i) = y^{(i)}, h(i) = z^{(i)}.$$

Then check whether $f \cdot g = h$. Here $f(\cdot), g(\cdot)$ are degree-$(m - 1)$ polynomials so that they can be determined by $\{x^{(i)}\}_{i \in [m]}, \{y^{(i)}\}_{i \in [m]}$ respectively. In this case, $h(\cdot)$ should be a degree-$2(m - 1)$ polynomial which is determined by $2m - 1$ values. To this end, for $i \in \{m + 1, \ldots, 2m - 1\}$, we need to compute $z^{(i)} = f(i) \cdot g(i)$ so that $h(\cdot)$ can be computed by $\{z^{(i)}\}_{i \in [2m-1]}$.

All parties first locally compute $[f(\cdot)]_t$ and $[g(\cdot)]_t$ using $\{[x^{(i)}]_t\}_{i \in [m]}$ and $\{[y^{(i)}]_t\}_{i \in [m]}$ respectively. Here a degree-t sharing of a polynomial means that each coefficient is secret-shared. For $i \in \{m + 1, \ldots, 2m - 1\}$, all parties locally compute $[f(i)]_t, [g(i)]_t$ and then compute $[z^{(i)}]_t$ using the multiplication protocol in [DN07]. Finally, all parties locally compute $[h(\cdot)]_t$ using $\{[z^{(i)}]_t\}_{i \in [2m-1]}$.

Note that if $x^{(i)} \cdot y^{(i)} = z^{(i)}$ for all $i \in [2m - 1]$, then we have $f \cdot g = h$. Otherwise, we must have $f \cdot g \neq h$. Therefore, it is sufficient to check whether $f \cdot g = h$. Since $h(\cdot)$ is a degree-$2(m - 1)$ polynomials, in the case that $f \cdot g \neq h$, the number of x such that $f(x) \cdot g(x) = h(x)$ holds is at most $2(m-1)$. Thus, it is sufficient to test whether $f(x) \cdot g(x) = h(x)$ for a random x. As a result, this technique compresses m checks of multiplication tuples to a single check of the tuple $([f(x)]_t, [g(x)]_t, [h(x)]_t)$. Secure techniques for checking the tuple $([f(x)]_t, [g(x)]_t, [h(x)]_t)$ are given in [BSFO12, NV18].

The main drawback of this technique is that it requires one additional multiplication operation per tuple. Our idea is to improve this technique so that the check will require fewer multiplication operations.

3.4 Extensions

We would like to introduce two natural extensions of the DN multiplication protocol and the Batch-wise Multiplication Verification technique respectively.

Extension of the DN Multiplication Protocol. In essence, the DN multiplication protocol uses a pair of random double sharings to reduce a degree-$2t$ sharing $[x \cdot y]_{2t}$ to a degree-t sharing $[x \cdot y]_t$. Therefore, an extension of the DN multiplication protocol is used to compute the inner-product of two vectors of the same dimension.

Specifically, let $\odot$ denote the inner-product operation. Given two input vectors of sharings $[\boldsymbol{x}]_t, [\boldsymbol{y}]_t$, we can compute $[\boldsymbol{x} \odot \boldsymbol{y}]_t$ using the same strategy as the DN multiplication protocol and in particular, with the *same communication cost*. This is because, just like in the multiplication protocol, here all the parties can *locally* compute the shares of the result. These shares are then randomized and sent to P_{king} for degree reduction. This extension is observed in [CGH+18].

Extension of the Batch-Wise Multiplication Verification. We can use the same strategy as the Batch-wise Multiplication Verification to check the correctness of a batch of *inner-product* tuples.

Specifically, given a set of m inner-product tuples $\{([\boldsymbol{x}^{(i)}]_t, [\boldsymbol{y}^{(i)}]_t, [z^{(i)}]_t)\}_{i \in [m]}$, we want to check whether $\boldsymbol{x}^{(i)} \odot \boldsymbol{y}^{(i)} = z^{(i)}$ for all $i \in [m]$. Here $\{\boldsymbol{x}^{(i)}, \boldsymbol{y}^{(i)}\}_{i \in [m]}$ are vectors of the same dimension. The only difference is that all parties will compute $\boldsymbol{f}(\cdot), \boldsymbol{g}(\cdot)$ such that

$$\forall i \in [m], \boldsymbol{f}(i) = \boldsymbol{x}^{(i)}, \boldsymbol{g}(i) = \boldsymbol{y}^{(i)},$$

and all parties need to compute $[z^{(i)}]_t = [\boldsymbol{f}(i) \odot \boldsymbol{g}(i)]_t$ for all $i \in \{m+1, \ldots, 2m-1\}$, which can be done by the extension of the DN multiplication protocol. Let $h(\cdot)$ be a degree-$2(m-1)$ polynomial such that

$$\forall i \in [2m-1], h(i) = z^{(i)}.$$

Then, it is sufficient to test whether $\boldsymbol{f}(x) \odot \boldsymbol{g}(x) = h(x)$ for a random x. As a result, this technique compresses m checks of inner-product tuples to a single check of the tuple $([\boldsymbol{f}(x)]_t, [\boldsymbol{g}(x)]_t, [h(x)]_t)$. It is worth noting that the communication cost remains the *same* as the original technique. This extension is observed in [NV18].

Using these Extensions for Reducing the Field Size. We point out that these extensions are not used in any way in the main results of [CGH+18,NV18]. In [CGH+18], the primary purpose of the extension is to check more efficiently in a small field. In more detail, [CGH+18] has a "secure MAC" associated with each wire value in the circuit. At a later point, the MACs are verified by computing a linear combination of the value-MAC pairs with random coefficients. Unlike the case in a large field, the random coefficients cannot be made public due to security reasons. Then a computation of a linear combination becomes a computation of an inner-product. [CGH+18] relies on the extension of the DN multiplication protocol to efficiently compute the inner-product of two vector of sharings. However we note that with the decrease in the field size, the number of field elements required per gate grows up and hence the concrete efficiency goes down. In [NV18], the extension of the Batch-wise Multiplication Verification technique is only pointed out as a corollary of independent interest.

3.5 Fast Verification for a Batch of Multiplication Tuples

Now we are ready to present our technique. Suppose the multiplication tuples we want to verify are

$$([x^{(1)}]_t, [y^{(1)}]_t, [z^{(1)}]_t), ([x^{(2)}]_t, [y^{(2)}]_t, [z^{(2)}]_t), \ldots, ([x^{(m)}]_t, [y^{(m)}]_t, [z^{(m)}]_t).$$

The starting idea is to transform these m multiplication tuples into one inner-product tuple. A straightforward way is just setting

$$[\boldsymbol{x}]_t = ([x^{(1)}]_t, [x^{(2)}]_t, \ldots, [x^{(m)}]_t)$$
$$[\boldsymbol{y}]_t = ([y^{(1)}]_t, [y^{(2)}]_t, \ldots, [y^{(m)}]_t)$$
$$[z]_t = \sum_{i=1}^{m} [z^{(i)}]_t.$$

However, it is insufficient to check this tuple. For example, if corrupted parties only maliciously behave when computing the first two tuples and cause $z^{(1)}$ to be $x^{(1)} \cdot y^{(1)} + 1$ and $z^{(2)}$ to be $x^{(2)} \cdot y^{(2)} - 1$, we cannot detect it by using this approach. We need to add some randomness so that the resulting tuple will be incorrect with overwhelming probability if any one of the original tuples is incorrect.

Step One: De-Linearization. Our idea is to use two polynomials with coefficients $\{x^{(i)} \cdot y^{(i)}\}$ and $\{z^{(i)}\}$ respectively. Concretely, let

$$F(X) = (x^{(1)} \cdot y^{(1)}) + (x^{(2)} \cdot y^{(2)})X + \ldots + (x^{(m)} \cdot y^{(m)})X^{m-1}$$
$$G(X) = z^{(1)} + z^{(2)}X + \ldots + z^{(m)}X^{m-1}.$$

Then if at least one multiplication tuple is incorrect, we will have $F \neq G$. In this case, the number of x such that $F(x) = G(x)$ is at most $m - 1$. Therefore, with overwhelming probability, $F(r) \neq G(r)$ where r is a random element.

All parties will generate a random degree-t sharing $[r]_t$ in the same way as that in the preparation phase of the DN protocol. Then they reconstruct the value r. We can set

$$[\boldsymbol{x}]_t = ([x^{(1)}]_t, r[x^{(2)}]_t, \ldots, r^{m-1}[x^{(m)}]_t)$$
$$[\boldsymbol{y}]_t = ([y^{(1)}]_t, [y^{(2)}]_t, \ldots, [y^{(m)}]_t)$$
$$[z]_t = \sum_{i=1}^{m} r^{i-1}[z^{(i)}]_t.$$

Then $F(r) = \boldsymbol{x} \odot \boldsymbol{y}$ and $G(r) = z$. The inner-product tuple $([\boldsymbol{x}]_t, [\boldsymbol{y}]_t, [z]_t)$ is what we wish to verify.

Step Two: Dimension-Reduction. Although we only need to verify the correctness of a single inner-product tuple, it is unclear how to do it efficiently. It seems that verifying an inner-product tuple with dimension m would require communicating at least $O(mn)$ field elements. Therefore, instead of directly doing the check, we want to first reduce the dimension of this inner-product tuple.

Towards that end, even though we only have a single inner-product tuple, we will try to take advantage of batch-wise verification of inner-product tuples. Let k be a compression parameter. Our goal is to transform the original tuple of dimension m to be a new tuple of dimension m/k.

To utilize the extension, let $\ell = m/k$ and

$$[\boldsymbol{x}]_t = ([\boldsymbol{a}^{(1)}]_t, [\boldsymbol{a}^{(2)}]_t, \ldots, [\boldsymbol{a}^{(k)}]_t)$$
$$[\boldsymbol{y}]_t = ([\boldsymbol{b}^{(1)}]_t, [\boldsymbol{b}^{(2)}]_t, \ldots, [\boldsymbol{b}^{(k)}]_t),$$

where $\{\boldsymbol{a}^{(i)}, \boldsymbol{b}^{(i)}\}_{i \in [k]}$ are vectors of dimension ℓ. For each $i \in [k-1]$, we compute $[\boldsymbol{c}^{(i)}]_t = [\boldsymbol{a}^{(i)} \odot \boldsymbol{b}^{(i)}]_t$ using the extension of the DN multiplication protocol. Then set $[c^{(k)}]_t = [z]_t - \sum_{i=1}^{k-1}[c^{(i)}]_t$. In this way, if the original tuple is incorrect, then at least one of the new inner-product tuples is incorrect.

Finally, we use the extension of the Batch-wise Multiplication Verification technique to compress the check of these k inner-product tuples into one check of a single inner-product tuple. In particular, the resulting tuple has dimension $\ell = m/k$.

Note that the cost of this step is $O(k)$ inner-product operations, which is just $O(k)$ multiplication operations, and a reconstruction of a sharing, which requires $O(n^2)$ elements. After this step, our task is reduced from checking the correctness of an inner-product tuple of dimension m to checking the correctness of an inner-product tuple of dimension ℓ.

Step Three: Recursion and Randomization. We can repeat the second step $\log_k m$ times so that we only need to check the correctness of *a single* multiplication tuple in the end. To simplify the checking process for the last tuple, we make use of additional randomness.

In the last call of the second step, we need to compress the check of k multiplication tuples into one check of a single multiplication tuple. We include an additional random multiplication tuple as a random mask of these k multiplication tuples. That is, we will compress the check of $k+1$ multiplication tuples in the last call of the second step. In this way, to check the resulting multiplication tuple, all parties can simply reconstruct the sharings and check whether the multiplication is correct. This reconstruction reveals no additional information about the original inner-product tuple because of this added randomness.

The random multiplication tuple is prepared in the following manner.

1. All parties prepare two random sharings $[a]_t, [b]_t$ in the same way as that in the preparation phase of the DN protocol.
2. All parties compute $[c]_t = [a \cdot b]_t$ using the DN multiplication protocol.

Efficiency Analysis. Note that each step of compression requires $O(k)$ inner-product (or multiplication) operations, which requires $O(kn)$ field elements. Also, each step of compression requires to reconstruct a random sharing, which requires $O(n^2)$ field elements. Therefore, the total amount of communication of verifying m multiplication tuples is $O((kn + n^2) \cdot \log_k m)$ field elements. Since the number of multiplication tuples m is bounded by $\mathsf{poly}(\kappa)$ where κ is the security parameter. If we choose $k = \kappa$, then the cost is just $O(\kappa n + n^2)$ field elements, which is independent of the number of multiplication tuples.

Therefore, the communication complexity per gate of our construction is the same as the DN semi-honest protocol.

Theorem 1. *Let n be the number of parties, κ be the security parameter and $k \in \mathbb{N}^\star$ be the compression factor. Let $\mathbb{F}$ be a finite field where $|\mathbb{F}| \geq n + 1$, and ϕ be the size of a field element. Then, for any arithmetic circuit* Circuit *of size C over $\mathbb{F}$, there exists an n-party MPC protocol which securely (with abort) computes* Circuit *against a fully malicious adversary which controls up to $t \leq n/2$ parties. The communication complexity is $O(Cn\phi + (kn + n^2) \cdot \log_k C \cdot \kappa)$ bits. The concrete efficiency is 5.5 field elements per party per multiplication gate.*

We refer the readers to [GS20] for the detailed construction and the security proof.

Remark 1. An attractive feature of our approach is that the communication cost is not affected by the field size. To see this, note that the cost of our check only has a sub-linear dependence on the circuit size. Therefore, we can run the check over an extension field of the original field with large enough size, which does not influence the concrete efficiency of our construction.

As a comparison, the concrete efficiency of both constructions [CGH+18, NV18] suffer if one uses a small field. This is because in both constructions, the failure probability of the verification depends on the size of the field. For a small field, they need to do the verification several times to acquire the desired security. The same trick does not work because the cost of their checks has a linear dependency on the circuit size.

Remark 2. Compared with the constructions in [CGH+18, NV18], we also remove unnecessary checks to make the protocol as succinct as possible. Specifically, this new technique of verifying a batch of multiplication tuples is the only check in the protocol and the remaining parts are the same as the DN protocol. In particular, we do not check the consistency/validity of the sharings.

Relation with the Technique in [BBCG+19]. We note that our idea is similar to the technique in [BBCG+19] when it is used to construct MPC protocols. When $n = 3$ and $t = 1$, our construction is very similar to the construction in [BBCG+19]. For a general n-party setting, the construction in [BBCG+19] relies on the replicated secret sharings and builds upon the sublinear distributed zero knowledge proofs constructed in [BBCG+19]. However, the computation cost of the replicated secret sharings goes exponentially in the number of parties. This restricts the construction in [BBCG+19] to only work for a constant number of parties. On the other hand, we explore the use of the Shamir secret sharing scheme in the n-party setting. Our idea is inspired by the extensions of the DN multiplication protocol [DN07,CGH+18] and the Batch-wise Multiplication Verification [BSFO12,NV18]. This allows us to get a positive result without relying on replicated secret sharings. We also note that the construction in [BBCG+19] requires the sharings (related to the distributed zero knowledge proof) to be robust and verifiable. We simplify this technique by removing the use of a robust secret sharing scheme and a verifiable secret sharing scheme.

Moreover, we explore the recursion trick to further improve the communication complexity of verifying multiplications. Compared with the construction in [BBCG+19] which requires to communicate $O(\sqrt{C})$ bits, we achieve $O((kn + n^2) \cdot \log_k C \cdot \kappa)$ bits. Our protocol additionally makes a simple optimization to the DN protocol, which brings down the cost from 6 field elements per multiplication to 5.5 field elements.

4   An Overview of the Protocol with Guaranteed Output Delivery

We observe that our secure-with-abort MPC protocol does not have the factor $O(D_M n^2)$ in the communication complexity. Therefore, our starting idea is to compile our secure-with-abort protocol into one with guaranteed output delivery. Hopefully, it will help us remove the factor $O(D_M n^2)$ and achieve the same concrete efficiency as the semi-honest setting.

However, we then realize two problems with this idea. The most direct problem of using our secure-with-abort protocol is that a single error leads to an abort of the whole computation. However, our purpose is to build a protocol with guaranteed output delivery, which should ensure the success of the computation no matter how corrupted parties behave. It means that, when facing a failure in the check of the ultimate multiplication tuple in the last step of the multiplication verification, we need to find out where things went wrong and be able to proceed the computation.

Another problem is that, when a corrupted party maliciously refuses to participate in the computation or an identified corrupted party is kicked out from the computation, the DN protocol cannot even proceed. This is because in the DN multiplication protocol, P_{king} needs to reconstruct a degree-$2t$ sharing $[e]_{2t} := [x]_t \cdot [y]_t + [r]_{2t}$. P_{king} needs $2t + 1 = n$ shares to do reconstruction. This cannot be achieved if some party does not send its share to P_{king}.

In the following, we will tackle these two problems.

4.1 Efficient Verification Using Virtual Transcripts

Recall that in our secure-with-abort protocol, all parties together check the correctness of a single multiplication tuple in the last step of the multiplication verification (i.e., Step Three: Recursion and Randomization). We refer to this multiplication tuple as the *ultimate multiplication tuple*.

To be able to identify the corrupted parties that deviate from the protocol when a failure occurs in the check of the ultimate multiplication tuple, our idea is to compute a *virtual transcript* of the ultimate multiplication tuple. A virtual transcript can be seen as the transcript where all parties directly compute the ultimate multiplication tuple using the DN multiplication protocol. Although the transcript does not correspond to a real execution, all parties should agree on the messages they sent in a virtual transcript. In the case that a failure occurs in the check of the ultimate multiplication tuple, all parties can open the whole virtual transcripts to identify the parties which behaved maliciously.

We first recall the extension of the Batch-wise Multiplication Verification [NV18].

Extension of the Batch-Wise Multiplication Verification [NV18]. Suppose we have ℓ inner-product tuples $\{([x^{(i)}]_t, [y^{(i)}]_t, [z^{(i)}]_t)\}_{i=1}^{\ell}$ and would like to verify whether $z^{(i)} = x^{(i)} \odot y^{(i)}$ for all $i \in [\ell]$. The extension of Batch-wise Multiplication Verification [NV18] works as follows.

1. Let $F(\cdot), G(\cdot)$ be two vectors of degree-$(\ell - 1)$ polynomials such that
$$\forall i \in [\ell], \quad F(i) = x^{(i)}, \ G(i) = y^{(i)}.$$

   All parties can locally compute the shares of $[F(\cdot)]_t$ and $[G(\cdot)]_t$ by using their shares of $[x^{(1)}]_t, \ldots, [x^{(\ell)}]_t$ and $[y^{(1)}]_t, \ldots, [y^{(\ell)}]_t$, i.e., by doing interpolation on their own vectors of shares.
2. All parties compute $[x^{(i)}]_t = [F(i)]_t, [y^{(i)}]_t = [G(i)]_t$ for all $i \in \{\ell + 1, \ldots, 2\ell - 1\}$.
3. For all $i \in \{\ell + 1, \ldots, 2\ell - 1\}$, all parties compute $[z^{(i)}]_t$ where $z^{(i)} = x^{(i)} \odot y^{(i)}$ using the extension of the DN multiplication protocol.
4. Let $H(\cdot)$ be a degree-$2(\ell - 1)$ polynomial such that
$$\forall i \in [2\ell - 1], \quad H(i) = z^{(i)}.$$

   All parties can locally compute the shares of $[H(\cdot)]_t$ by using their shares of $[z^{(1)}]_t, \ldots, [z^{(2\ell-1)}]_t$, i.e., by doing interpolation on their own shares.

Note that if all inner-product tuples $\{([x^{(i)}]_t, [y^{(i)}]_t, [z^{(i)}]_t)\}_{i=1}^{2\ell-1}$ are correct, we should have $F \odot G = H$. Otherwise, $F \odot G \neq H$, and the number of λ such that $F(\lambda) \odot G(\lambda) = H(\lambda)$ is bounded by $2(\ell-1)$. Therefore, to verify the original ℓ inner-product tuples, it is sufficient to sample a random point λ and only verify $([F(\lambda)]_t, [G(\lambda)]_t, [H(\lambda)]_t)$. We refer to $([F(\lambda)]_t, [G(\lambda)]_t, [H(\lambda)]_t)$ as the final inner-product tuple.

Preparing Virtual Transcript for the Final Inner-product Tuple. We note that the transcript of the extension of the DN multiplication protocol contains 7 sharings

$$([x]_t, [y]_t, [r]_t, [r]_{2t}, [e]_{2t}, [e]_t, [z]_t).$$

Here $([r]_t, [r]_{2t})$ is a pair of double sharings, $[e]_{2t} := [x]_t \odot [y]_t + [r]_{2t}$ is the degree-$2t$ sharing sent to P_{king}, $[e]_t$ is the degree-t sharing distributed by P_{king}, and $[z]_t = [e]_t - [r]_t$ is the output sharing of the DN multiplication protocol.

The idea of the virtual transcript is to recover the missing parts $[r]_t, [r]_{2t}, [e]_{2t}, [e]_t$. Therefore, in the case that the check of the final inner-product tuple fails, by examining the corresponding virtual transcripts, we can find out where things went wrong and potentially identify a corrupted party.

Recall that the final inner-product tuple $([x]_t, [y]_t, [z]_t)$ is derived by using polynomial interpolation on $2\ell - 1$ inner-product tuples. In a similar way, we derive $[r]_t, [r]_{2t}, [e]_{2t}, [e]_t$ by polynomial interpolation on the corresponding values in the transcripts of these $2\ell - 1$ inner-product tuples.

In more detail, given the transcripts of the original m inner-product tuples

$$\{([x^{(i)}]_t, [y^{(i)}]_t, [r^{(i)}]_t, [r^{(i)}]_{2t}, [e^{(i)}]_{2t}, [e^{(i)}]_t, [z^{(i)}]_t)\}_{i=1}^{\ell},$$

we want to compute the transcript of the resulting tuple.

Let $\{([x^{(i)}]_t, [y^{(i)}]_t, [r^{(i)}]_t, [r^{(i)}]_{2t}, [e^{(i)}]_{2t}, [e^{(i)}]_t, [z^{(i)}]_t)\}_{i=\ell+1}^{2\ell-1}$ denote the transcripts generated in the extension of the Batch-wise Multiplication Verification. Recall that $[F(\cdot)]_t, [G(\cdot)]_t, [H(\cdot)]_t$ satisfy that

$$\forall i \in [2\ell-1]: \ [F(i)]_t = [x^{(i)}]_t, \ [G(i)]_t = [y^{(i)}]_t, \ [H(i)]_t = [z^{(i)}]_t.$$

Let $[R(\cdot)]_t, [R(\cdot)]_{2t}, [E(\cdot)]_{2t}, [E(\cdot)]_t$ be sharings of polynomials of degree $2(\ell-1)$ such that

$$\forall i \in [2\ell-1]: \ [R(i)]_t = [r^{(i)}]_t, \ [R(i)]_{2t} = [r^{(i)}]_{2t},$$
$$[E(i)]_{2t} = [e^{(i)}]_{2t}, \ [E(i)]_t = [e^{(i)}]_t.$$

Therefore, we have $[E(\cdot)]_{2t} = [F(\cdot)]_t \odot [G(\cdot)]_t + [R(\cdot)]_{2t}$ and $[H(\cdot)]_t = [E(\cdot)]_t - [R(\cdot)]_t$. It means that, for every λ, one can regard

$$([F(\lambda)]_t, [G(\lambda)]_t, [R(\lambda)]_t, [R(\lambda)]_{2t}, [E(\lambda)]_{2t}, [E(\lambda)]_t, [H(\lambda)]_t)$$

as a transcript of the following steps:

1. All parties first locally compute $[E(\lambda)]_{2t} := [F(\lambda)]_t \odot [G(\lambda)]_t + [R(\lambda)]_{2t}$.

2. P_{king} collects all shares of $[E(\lambda)]_{2t}$ and reconstructs the secret $E(\lambda)$. Then P_{king} generates a degree-t sharing $[E(\lambda)]_t$ and distributes the shares to all other parties.
3. All parties locally compute $[H(\lambda)]_t = [E(\lambda)]_t - [R(\lambda)]_t$.

To this end, all parties locally compute the shares of $[R(\cdot)]_t, [R(\cdot)]_{2t}$ by using their shares of $[r^{(1)}]_t, \ldots, [r^{(2\ell-1)}]_t$ and $[r^{(1)}]_{2t}, \ldots, [r^{(2\ell-1)}]_{2t}$. Then set $[E(\cdot)]_{2t} = [F(\cdot)]_t \odot [G(\cdot)]_t + [R(\cdot)]_{2t}$ and $[E(\cdot)]_t = [H(\cdot)]_t + [R(\cdot)]_t$. P_{king} further computes $[E(\cdot)]_{2t}$ by using the sharings $[e^{(1)}]_{2t}, \ldots, [e^{(2m-1)}]_{2t}$ it received, and $[E(\cdot)]_t$ by using the sharings $[e^{(1)}]_t, \ldots, [e^{(2m-1)}]_t$ it distributed.

All parties generate a random element λ as challenge. The transcript

$$([F(\lambda)]_t, [G(\lambda)]_t, [R(\lambda)]_t, [R(\lambda)]_{2t}, [E(\lambda)]_{2t}, [E(\lambda)]_t, [H(\lambda)]_t)$$

is what we want to verify.

Preparing Virtual Transcript for the Ultimate Multiplication Tuple. We will follow the multiplication verification in our secure-with-abort protocol and prepare a virtual transcript for the tuple generated in each step. Suppose the transcripts of the original m multiplication tuples are

$$\{([x^{(i)}]_t, [y^{(i)}]_t, [r^{(i)}]_t, [r^{(i)}]_{2t}, [e^{(i)}]_{2t}, [e^{(i)}]_t, [z^{(i)}]_t)\}_{i=1}^m,$$

and we want to verify that $z^{(i)} = x^{(i)} \cdot y^{(i)}$ for all $i \in [m]$.

Step One: De-Linearization. Recall that in Step One, all parties first generate a random element λ and set

$$[\boldsymbol{x}]_t = ([x^{(1)}]_t, \lambda[x^{(2)}]_t, \ldots, \lambda^{m-1}[x^{(m)}]_t)$$
$$[\boldsymbol{y}]_t = ([y^{(1)}]_t, [y^{(2)}]_t, \ldots, [y^{(m)}]_t)$$
$$[z]_t = \sum_{i=1}^m \lambda^{i-1}[z^{(i)}]_t.$$

The virtual transcript for $([\boldsymbol{x}]_t, [\boldsymbol{y}]_t, [z]_t)$ can be prepared by setting

$$([r]_t, [r]_{2t}, [e]_{2t}, [e]_t) = \sum_{i=1}^m \lambda^{i-1}([r^{(i)}]_t, [r^{(i)}]_{2t}, [e^{(i)}]_{2t}, [e^{(i)}]_t).$$

The transcript $([\boldsymbol{x}]_t, [\boldsymbol{y}]_t, [r]_t, [r]_{2t}, [e]_{2t}, [e]_t, [z]_t)$ is what we need to verify. Note that this transcript corresponds to a single inner-product tuple of dimension m.

Step Two: Dimension-Reduction. Recall that in Step Two, we want to reduce the dimension of the inner-product tuple from Step One. Let

$$([\boldsymbol{x}]_t, [\boldsymbol{y}]_t, [r]_t, [r]_{2t}, [e]_{2t}, [e]_t, [z]_t)$$

denote the transcript. Recall that $[\boldsymbol{x}]_t, [\boldsymbol{y}]_t$ are first chopped into k equal parts:

$$[\boldsymbol{x}]_t = ([\boldsymbol{x}^{(1)}]_t, [\boldsymbol{x}^{(2)}]_t, \dots, [\boldsymbol{x}^{(k)}]_t)$$
$$[\boldsymbol{y}]_t = ([\boldsymbol{y}^{(1)}]_t, [\boldsymbol{y}^{(2)}]_t, \dots, [\boldsymbol{y}^{(k)}]_t),$$

where $\{\boldsymbol{x}^{(i)}, \boldsymbol{y}^{(i)}\}_{i \in [k]}$ are vectors of dimension m/k. For each $i \in [k-1]$, all parties compute $[z^{(i)}]_t = [\boldsymbol{x}^{(i)}] \odot \boldsymbol{y}^{(i)}]_t$ by using the extension of the DN multiplication protocol. Let $([r^{(i)}]_t, [r^{(i)}]_{2t})$ be the corresponding double sharings used by the parties, $[e^i]_{2t}, [e^{(i)}]_t$ be the sharings which P_{king} received and sent respectively. Hence,

$$([\boldsymbol{x}^{(i)}]_t, [\boldsymbol{y}^{(i)}]_t, [r^{(i)}]_t, [r^{(i)}]_{2t}, [e^{(i)}]_{2t}, [e^{(i)}]_t, [z^{(i)}]_t)$$

denote the transcript for the inner-product tuple $([\boldsymbol{x}^{(i)}]_t, [\boldsymbol{y}^{(i)}]_t, [z^{(i)}]_t)$. So far, we have only used $[\boldsymbol{x}]_t, [\boldsymbol{y}]_t$ from the input inner-product tuple. To ensure that if the input transcript of the inner-product tuple is incorrect, then one of the new generated transcripts is also incorrect, the transcript of the last tuple is computed from the input transcript. By setting

$$([r^{(k)}]_t, [r^{(k)}]_{2t}, [e^{(k)}]_{2t}, [e^{(k)}]_t, [z^{(k)}]_t)$$
$$= ([r]_t, [r]_{2t}, [e]_{2t}, [e]_t, [z]_t) - \sum_{i=1}^{k-1}([r^{(i)}]_t, [r^{(i)}]_{2t}, [e^{(i)}]_{2t}, [e^{(i)}]_t, [z^{(i)}]_t),$$

the transcript for $([\boldsymbol{x}^{(k)}]_t, [\boldsymbol{y}^{(k)}]_t)$ is

$$([\boldsymbol{x}^{(k)}]_t, [\boldsymbol{y}^{(k)}]_t, [r^{(k)}]_t, [r^{(k)}]_{2t}, [e^{(k)}]_{2t}, [e^{(k)}]_t, [z^{(k)}]_t).$$

Now we can use the extension of the Batch-wise Multiplication Verification [NV18] to compress these k transcripts of inner-product tuples into one transcript of a single inner-product tuple as we described above.

Step Three: Recursion and Randomization. In this step, all parties first recursively invoke Step Two to reduce the dimension of the inner-product tuple from m to k. In the meantime, all parties will also recursively prepare the virtual transcripts.

All parties then prepare a random multiplication tuple, and include this tuple when doing the last call of the compression. After all parties prepare this random multiplication tuple and its transcript, all parties can do the same way as that in Step Two to get a transcript of a single multiplication tuple. Let

$$([x^\star]_t, [y^\star]_t, [r^\star]_t, [r^\star]_{2t}, [e^\star]_{2t}, [e^\star]_t, [z^\star]_t)$$

denote the transcript for the ultimate multiplication tuple. It can be regarded as the transcript where all parties run the following steps:

1. All parties first locally compute $[e^\star]_{2t} := [x^\star]_t \cdot [y^\star]_t + [r^\star]_{2t}$.
2. P_{king} collects all shares of $[e^\star]_{2t}$ and reconstructs the secret $e^\star$. Then P_{king} generates a degree-t sharing $[e^\star]_t$ and distributes the shares to all other parties.
3. All parties locally compute $[z^\star]_t = [e^\star]_t - [r^\star]_t$.

Checking the Virtual Transcript. Recall that all parties have opened $[x^*]_t$, $[y^*]_t$, $[z^*]_t$ to verify the ultimate multiplication tuple. In the case that $([x^*]_t, [y^*]_t, [z^*]_t)$ is not a correct multiplication tuple, all parties will publish their shares of $[r^*]_t, [r^*]_{2t}, [e^*]_{2t}, [e^*]_t$. In addition, P_{king} will publish the whole sharing $[e^*]_{2t}$ it received and the whole sharing $[e^*]_t$ it distributed. Then all parties must observe one of the following cases:

- The input sharings $[x^*]_t, [y^*]_t$ are inconsistent.
- The pair of double sharings $([r^*]_t, [r^*]_{2t})$ is incorrect or inconsistent.
- Some party P_i does not follow the protocol.
- Two parties (P_i, P_{king}) do not agree on the message sent from one party to the other party.

For the first two cases, there will be another protocol to help find errors. The main observation is that each sharing $[x]_t$ can be decomposed into $[x]_t = \sum_{i=1}^{n}[x(i)]_t$ where $[x(i)]_t$ is a linear combination of the sharings dealt by P_i. In other words, P_i should be responsible for the consistency of $[x(i)]_t$. Therefore, all parties will check each $[x(i)]_t$ to find errors.

For the last two cases, we can immediately identify a corrupted party or a pair of parties which have conflict with each other. We refer to this pair of parties as a pair of *disputed parties*.

In summary, all parties will finally identify either a corrupted party or a pair of disputed parties.

4.2   Relying on a Small Surgery to Proceed

Now suppose a corrupted party causes the computation to fail and has been identified using the described checks. What do we do? A straightforward idea is to restart the whole computation with the corrupted party excluded and a smaller corruption threshold. In the worst case, however, we may need to rerun the whole protocol $O(n)$ times, which is too expensive. To reduce the penalty due to failures, we rely on Dispute Control [BTH06], which is a general strategy to achieve unconditional security efficiently.

At a high-level, the whole circuit will be partitioned into several small segments. These segments will be evaluated in sequence. In the case that a failure occurs, the computation of this segment is discarded and all parties restart to evaluate the current segment. In other words, the end of each segment is served as a checkpoint. However, one problem with this strategy is that we cannot easily restart the computation with a smaller corruption threshold. This is because all the input sharings, which come from the end of last segment, are shared using the threshold t. Changing threshold means that one need to re-share all the input sharings. In fact, it is the main reason of the factor of $O(W \cdot \text{poly}(n))$ in [IKP+16], where W is the width of the circuit.

To avoid the expensive re-sharing process, we would like to keep the corruption threshold unchanged. Furthermore, we also want to keep the influence on the concrete efficiency as little as possible. To be able to let the protocol proceed without changing the corruption threshold, our idea is to prepare the shares held by identified corrupted parties so that P_{king} will have enough shares to reconstruct a degree-$2t$ sharing.

Notation. Recall that n is the number of all parties and t is the number of corrupted parties. We have $n = 2t + 1$. Let $\mathcal{P}$ be the set of all parties, $Corr$ be the set of parties which have been identified as corrupted parties so far, and $\mathcal{P}_{\text{active}} = \mathcal{P} \backslash Corr$ be the set of remaining parties. If a party is identified as a corrupted party, it will not participate in the rest of the computations. Hereafter, we use *all parties* to refer parties in $\mathcal{P}_{\text{active}}$.

Overview. Recall that for each multiplication gate with input sharings $([x]_t, [y]_t)$, all parties first prepare a pair of random double sharings $([r]_t, [r]_{2t})$. Then all parties execute the following steps to compute $[x \cdot y]_t$.

1. All parties first locally compute $[e]_{2t} := [x]_t \cdot [y]_t + [r]_{2t}$.
2. P_{king} collects all shares of $[e]_{2t}$ and reconstructs the secret e. Then P_{king} generates a degree-t sharing $[e]_t$ and distributes the shares to all other parties.
3. All parties locally compute $[x \cdot y]_t = [e]_t - [r]_t$.

In our construction, when a party P_d needs to generate a random sharing, we require that the shares held by parties in $Corr$ should be 0. Note that, it does not break the secrecy of the random sharing since parties in $Corr$ are corrupted. We observe the following two facts.

1. During the generation process of $([r]_t, [r]_{2t})$, each dealer sets the shares held by parties in $Corr$ to be 0. Since $([r]_t, [r]_{2t})$ is a linear combination of the double sharings dealt by each party, the shares of $([r]_t, [r]_{2t})$ held by parties in $Corr$ are all 0.
2. For each party P_i, if the i-th share of either $[x]_t$ or $[y]_t$ is 0, then the i-th share of $[x \cdot y]_{2t} := [x]_t \cdot [y]_t$ is also 0.

Our idea is doing a small "surgery" to one input sharing $[x]_t$. Roughly speaking, this means changing the shares of $[x]_t$ held by parties in $Corr$ to 0 while keeping the secret value x. Let $[\tilde{x}]_t$ denote the sharing after the "surgery". Then, it satisfies that $\tilde{x} = x$ and the shares of $[\tilde{x}]_t$ held by parties in $Corr$ are 0. Detailed procedure for this "surgery" will be introduced at a later point.

Recall that the shares of $[\tilde{x}]_t, [r]_{2t}$ held by parties in $Corr$ are 0. Now, when we invoke the DN multiplication protocol on $([\tilde{x}]_t, [y]_t)$, the shares of $[e]_{2t} := [\tilde{x}]_t \cdot [y]_t + [r]_{2t}$ held by parties in $Corr$ are also 0. Therefore, P_{king} can reconstruct $[e]_{2t}$ by setting the shares held by parties in $Corr$ to be 0. Thus, each multiplication can be evaluated in two steps, (1) doing a small "surgery" to $[x]_t$, and (2) invoking the DN multiplication protocol on $([\tilde{x}]_t, [y]_t)$. We refer to the first step as REFRESH and the second step as PARTIALMULT.

REFRESH: *Performing the "Surgery"*. Since parties in $Corr$ are all corrupted, there is no need to protect the secrecy of their shares. The high-level idea is letting P_{king} learn the shares of $[x]_t$ held by parties in $Corr$. Then P_{king} distributes a random degree-t sharing $[o]_t$ such that $o = 0$ and the shares of $[o]_t, [x]_t$ held by parties in $Corr$ are the same. Therefore $[\tilde{x}]_t := [x]_t - [o]_t$ is what we need.

In more detail, all parties first prepare a random degree-t sharing $[r]_t$ (as that in the DN protocol). Recall that, in the generation process of $[r]_t$, each dealer sets the shares of parties in $Corr$ to be 0. Therefore, the shares of $[r]_t$ held by parties in $Corr$ are 0. Then, all parties run the following steps.

1. All parties locally compute $[e]_t := [x]_t + [r]_t$. Note that the shares of $[e]_t, [x]_t$ held by parties in $Corr$ are the same.
2. P_{king} collects all shares of $[e]_t$ and computes the shares held by parties in $Corr$.
3. P_{king} generates and distributes a random degree-t sharing $[o]_t$ where $o = 0$ and the shares of $[o]_t, [e]_t$ held by parties in $Corr$ are the same.
4. All parties set $[\tilde{x}]_t := [x]_t - [o]_t$.

PARTIALMULT: *Multiplying $[\tilde{x}]_t$ and $[y]_t$*. To compute $[z]_t$, all parties invoke the DN multiplication protocol on $([\tilde{x}]_t, [y]_t)$. All parties first prepare a pair of double sharings $([r]_t, [r]_{2t})$ (as that in the DN protocol). Recall that, the shares of $[r]_t, [r]_{2t}$ held by parties in $Corr$ are 0. Then, all parties run the following steps.

1. All parties locally compute $[e]_{2t} := [\tilde{x}]_t \cdot [y]_t + [r]_{2t}$.
2. P_{king} collects shares of $[e]_{2t}$ from parties in $\mathcal{P}_{active}$. For each party $P_i \in Corr$, P_{king} sets the i-th share of $[e]_{2t}$ to be 0. Then P_{king} generates a degree-t sharing $[e]_t$ and distributes the shares to all other parties.
3. All parties locally compute $[z]_t = [e]_t - [r]_t$.

Reducing the Communication of Refresh and PartialMult. We note that, to reconstruct a degree-t sharing, P_{king} only needs $t + 1$ shares. Therefore, there is no need to let all parties receive the shares of $[r]_t$. In the beginning of each segment, all parties agree on a set of parties $\mathcal{T} \subseteq \mathcal{P}_{active}$ such that (1) $|\mathcal{T}| = t + 1$, and (2) $P_{king} \in \mathcal{T}$. In brief, $\mathcal{T}$ contains P_{king} and t other parties in $\mathcal{P}_{active}$.

When generating $[r]_t$, only parties in $\mathcal{T}$ will receive the shares of $[r]_t$. This can be achieved by requiring each dealer only sends shares to parties in $\mathcal{T}$. In the first step of REFRESH, parties in $\mathcal{T}$ compute their shares of $[x]_t + [r]_t$ and send them to P_{king}. Together with the share held by P_{king}, there are $t + 1$ shares, which are enough to reconstruct the whole sharing $[e]_t := [x]_t + [r]_t$. In this way, the cost of generating random sharings for REFRESH is reduced by half.

Furthermore, when P_{king} generates $[o]_t$, we can require that the shares of $[o]_t$ held by parties in $\mathcal{P}_{active} \backslash \mathcal{T}$ are set to be 0. Recall that P_{king} learns the shares of $[x]_t$ held by parties in $Corr$ and the shares of $[o]_t$ held by parties in $Corr$ are the same as those of $[x]_t$. Since the shares held by parties in $\mathcal{P} \backslash \mathcal{T}$ are fixed and

$|\mathcal{P}\backslash\mathcal{T}| = t$, with these t shares and the secret value $o = 0$, P_{king} can compute the shares of $[o]_t$ held by parties in $\mathcal{T}$. Now, P_{king} only needs to distribute $[o]_t$ to parties in $\mathcal{T}$, and, parties in $\mathcal{P}_{\text{active}}\backslash\mathcal{T}$ simply set their shares of $[o]_t$ to be 0. In this way, the cost of distributing $[o]_t$ is reduced by half.

In the DN multiplication protocol, P_{king} can set the shares of $[e]_t$ held by parties in $\mathcal{P}\backslash\mathcal{T}$ to be 0. With these $|\mathcal{P}\backslash\mathcal{T}| = t$ shares and the secret value e, P_{king} can recover the whole sharing $[e]_t$. In this way, P_{king} only needs to distribute $[e]_t$ to parties in $\mathcal{T}$, and, parties in $\mathcal{P}_{\text{active}}\backslash\mathcal{T}$ simply set their shares of $[e]_t$ to be 0. As a result, the cost of distributing $[e]_t$ is reduced by half. Note that in the overall protocol, several multiplication gates will be evaluated in parallel, and this optimization can potentially lead to a reduction in the overall communication by a factor of $1/2$.

In summary, when $Corr = \emptyset$, there is no need to run the "Surgery". Our approach achieves 5.5 field elements per multiplication gate, as that in our secure-with-abort protocol. When at least one party is identified as a corrupted party, our approach needs 7.5 field elements per multiplication gate.

Checking the Correctness of Refresh. We point out that the above approach does not guarantee the correctness. In particular, we need to verify REFRESH in the end of the evaluation of each segment. *It is worth noting that the verification of* REFRESH *also utilizes the virtual transcript idea.*

We note that the transcript of REFRESH contains 5 degree-t sharings:

$$([x]_t, [\tilde{x}]_t, [r]_t, [e]_t, [o]_t).$$

Here $[x]_t$ is the input sharing, $[\tilde{x}]_t$ is the output sharing, $[r]_t$ is a random sharing which is only held by parties in $\mathcal{T}$, $[e]_t$ is the sharing P_{king} collected from parties in $\mathcal{T}$, and $[o]_t$ is the sharing of 0 dealt by P_{king}.

Given m transcripts $\{([x^{(i)}]_t, [\tilde{x}^{(i)}]_t, [r^{(i)}]_t, [e^{(i)}]_t, [o^{(i)}]_t)\}_{i=1}^{m}$, we want to verify that, for each $i \in [m]$, (1) $x^{(i)} = \tilde{x}^{(i)}$ and (2) the shares of $[\tilde{x}^{(i)}]$ held by parties in $Corr$ are 0. To this end, our idea is to compress m checks of the transcripts of REFRESH into one check of a single transcript. As the verification of multiplications, to protect the privacy of the original m transcripts, we add a random transcript as a mask in the compression step.

The random transcript is prepared in the following manner.

1. All parties prepare two random sharings $[x^{(0)}]_t, [r^{(0)}]_t$ in the same way as that in the preparation phase of the DN protocol.
2. All parties invoke REFRESH on $[x^{(0)}]_t$ with the random sharing $[r^{(0)}]_t$.

This random transcript is denoted by

$$([x^{(0)}]_t, [\tilde{x}^{(0)}]_t, [r^{(0)}]_t, [e^{(0)}]_t, [o^{(0)}]_t).$$

Compressing the Transcripts into One. Consider the following 5 sharings of polynomials:

$$[F(\lambda)]_t = \sum_{i=0}^{m}[x^{(i)}]_t\lambda^i, \quad [\tilde{F}(\lambda)]_t = \sum_{i=0}^{m}[\tilde{x}^{(i)}]_t\lambda^i, \quad [R(\lambda)]_t = \sum_{i=0}^{m}[r^{(i)}]_t\lambda^i,$$

$$[E(\lambda)]_t = \sum_{i=0}^{m}[e^{(i)}]_t\lambda^i, \quad [O(\lambda)]_t = \sum_{i=0}^{m}[o^{(i)}]_t\lambda^i.$$

Note that, by the linear homomorphism property of the Shamir secret sharing scheme, for every λ,

$$([F(\lambda)]_t, [\tilde{F}(\lambda)]_t, [R(\lambda)]_t, [E(\lambda)]_t, [O(\lambda)]_t)$$

can be seen as a virtual transcript of REFRESH:

1. Parties in $\mathcal{T}$ locally compute $[E(\lambda)]_t := [F(\lambda)]_t + [R(\lambda)]_t$. Note that the shares of $[E(\lambda)]_t, [F(\lambda)]_t$ held by parties in $Corr$ are the same.
2. $P_{\texttt{king}}$ collects the shares of $[E(\lambda)]_t$ from parties in $\mathcal{T}$ and computes the shares held by parties in $Corr$.
3. $P_{\texttt{king}}$ generates a random degree-t sharing $[O(\lambda)]_t$ such that (1) $O(\lambda) = 0$, (2) the shares held by parties in $\mathcal{P}_{\texttt{active}}\backslash\mathcal{T}$ are 0, and (3) the shares of $[O(\lambda)]_t, [E(\lambda)]_t$ held by parties in $Corr$ are the same. Then $P_{\texttt{king}}$ distributes the shares of $[O(\lambda)]_t$ to parties in $\mathcal{T}$.
4. All parties set $[\tilde{F}(\lambda)]_t := [F(\lambda)]_t - [O(\lambda)]_t$.

If at least one transcript of the original m transcripts is incorrect, then the number of λ such that $([F(\lambda)]_t, [\tilde{F}(\lambda)]_t, [R(\lambda)]_t, [E(\lambda)]_t, [O(\lambda)]_t)$ is a correct transcript is bounded by m. Therefore, to verify the original m transcripts, it is sufficient to examine the transcript $([F(\lambda)]_t, [\tilde{F}(\lambda)]_t, [R(\lambda)]_t, [E(\lambda)]_t, [O(\lambda)]_t)$ for a random λ. Let

$$([x^\star]_t, [\tilde{x}^\star]_t, [r^\star]_t, [e^\star]_t, [o^\star]_t)$$

denote the final virtual transcript of REFRESH we want to check.

Checking the Virtual Transcript. To check the correctness of $([x^\star]_t, [\tilde{x}^\star]_t, [r^\star]_t,$ $[e^\star]_t, [o^\star]_t)$, all parties publish their shares of $[x^\star]_t, [\tilde{x}^\star]_t$, parties in $\mathcal{T}$ publish their shares of $[r^\star]_t, [e^\star]_t, [o^\star]_t$, and $P_{\texttt{king}}$ publishes the sharing $[e^\star]_t$ it received and the sharing $[o^\star]_t$ it distributed. If it is an incorrect transcript, then all parties must observe one of the following cases:

- The input sharing $[x^\star]_t$ is inconsistent.
- After reconstructing the whole sharing $[r^\star]_t$ from the shares held by parties in $\mathcal{T}$, the shares of $[r^\star]_t$ held by parties in $Corr$ are not 0.
- Some party P_i does not follow the protocol.
- Two parties $(P_i, P_{\texttt{king}})$ do not agree on the message sent from one party to the other party.

As the verification of multiplications, for the first two cases, there will be another protocol to help find errors. For the last two cases, we can immediately identify a corrupted party or a pair of disputed parties. Thus, the check of the virtual transcript guarantees that either the original m transcripts of REFRESH are correct, or all parties can identify a corrupted party or a pair of disputed parties in the end.

Further Problem. We note that we need to make sure adding the surgery procedure in the protocol *will not* break the security of our secure-with-abort protocol. In fact, the security relies on the fact that the DN protocol provides perfect privacy before the output phase even when the adversary is fully malicious. *Replacing the DN protocol by another semi-honest protocol may break down the security entirely.* We refer the readers to [GSZ20] for more details.

Removing Higher Order Circuit Dependent Terms. We note that the construction from [BSFO12] uses Beaver triples to compute multiplications in the computation phase. One benefit of this method is that Beaver triples provide plenty of redundancy which simplifies the checking process in the computation phase. However, the use of Beaver triples unfortunately requires a verification for each layer of the circuit, which leads to the quadratic term related to D_M.

On the other hand, although when instantiating the transformation from [IKP+16] with the best-known protocol for security with abort, the quadratic term w.r.t. the circuit depth is eliminated, it introduces a new higher order term related to the circuit width. This is because the transformation needs to change the corruption threshold whenever a new corrupted party is identified, which requires an expensive re-sharing process for the input sharings of each segment.

As a summary, we start from our secure-with-abort protocol, which does not make use of Beaver triples, to remove the quadratic term related to D_M. To avoid the expensive re-sharing process, we rely on a small surgery to proceed. Combining these two ideas, we remove both the higher order terms related to the circuit depth and the circuit width.

4.3 An Omitted Problem: Verifiable System for Checkpoints

To allow all parties to restart the computation from a checkpoint, i.e., the end of the last segment, all the output sharings of the last segment should be verifiable. This is also a problem we omit when checking the virtual transcript: If all parties finally find out that one of the input sharings is inconsistent, then there is no way to identify a new corrupted party or a new pair of disputed parties by only examining the transcript in this segment. This is because the failure comes from the sharings computed in the previous segment.

Therefore, we borrow the idea from [BSFO12] to add verifiability to the output sharings of each segment. At a high-level, for every pair of parties (P_v, P_i) where P_v acts as a verifier, P_v will generate an authentication key (μ, ν) and P_i will receive an authentication tag $\tau = \mu \cdot \mathsf{share}_i + \nu$ of its share share_i. The authentication tag is computed using an MPC protocol. At a later point, P_v can verify the shares of P_i by asking P_i to send the associated authentication tags. Since a wrong share will be rejected by at least $t + 1$ honest parties and a correct share will be rejected by at most t corrupted parties, a majority vote can decide whether a share is correct or not.

In [BSFO12], each authentication tag is used to authenticate a batch of shares. As a result, the communication cost is independent of the number of shares and therefore, does not affect the concrete efficiency per gate. We make a further improvement to this idea to achieve a larger size of batching by reusing the authentication keys. Some modifications in the verification of authentication tags are also necessary to fit this improvement. We refer the readers to [GSZ20] for more details.

4.4 Summary

In short, the whole computation proceeds as follows. All parties first partition the circuit into several small segments. These segments will be evaluated in sequence. For each segment, the computation process contains the following three steps.

Evaluation. For each segment, if no party is identified as a corrupted party, we simply use the DN protocol to evaluate the addition gates and multiplication gates in this segment. If one or more corrupted parties have been identified, for each multiplication gate,

1. All parties first run REFRESH on one of the input wires to change the shares held by identified corrupted parties to be 0.
2. Then all parties evaluate this multiplication gate using the DN protocol (i.e., PARTIALMULT).

Verification. After the evaluation, all parties first check the correctness of REFRESH. Then, we use the multiplication verification of our secure-with-abort protocol to check the correctness of the multiplications. In the meanwhile, all parties prepare the virtual transcript of the ultimate multiplication tuple.

- If both checks pass, all parties accept the evaluation of this segment.
- Otherwise, a new corrupted party or a new pair of disputed parties is identified. The evaluation of the current segment is discarded and all parties re-evaluate this segment.

Checkpoint. Finally, in the case that the evaluation is accepted, all parties add verifiability to the output sharings of this segment.

Efficiency Analysis. For any constant $\epsilon > 0$, by properly choosing the parameters in the second step and the third step, it turns out that the communication complexity per multiplication gate of these two steps can be bounded by ϵ field elements per gate. We refer the readers to [GSZ20] for more details. Therefore, these two steps only have a very limited influence on the concrete efficiency.

In the best case, we simply use the DN multiplication protocol to evaluate each multiplication gate. Therefore, the concrete efficiency is 5.5 field elements per multiplication gate. When one or more corrupted parties have been identified, we also need to run REFRESH per multiplication gate. Thus, the concrete efficiency is 7.5 field elements per multiplication gate. To summarize, we have the following theorem.

Theorem 2. *Let n be the number of parties, κ be the security parameter. Let $\mathbb{F}$ be a finite field where $|\mathbb{F}| \geq n + 1$, and ϕ be the size of a field element. Then, for any constant $\epsilon > 0$ and any arithmetic circuit* Circuit *of size C over $\mathbb{F}$, there exists an n-party MPC protocol which securely computes* Circuit *with guaranteed output delivery against a fully malicious adversary which controls up to $t \leq n/2$ parties. The communication complexity is $O(Cn\phi)$ bits (ignoring fixed terms which are independent of the circuit). The concrete efficiency is $5.5 + \epsilon$ field elements per party per multiplication gate in the best case, and $7.5 + \epsilon$ field elements when one or more corrupted parties have been identified.*

We refer the readers to [GSZ20] for the detailed construction and the security proof.

References

[ABF+17] Araki, T., et al.: Optimized honest-majority MPC for malicious adversaries breaking the 1 billion-gate per second barrier. In: 2017 IEEE Symposium on Security and Privacy (SP), pp. 843–862. IEEE (2017)

[BBCG+19] Boneh, D., Boyle, E., Corrigan-Gibbs, H., Gilboa, N., Ishai, Y.: Zero-knowledge proofs on secret-shared data via fully linear PCPs. In: Boldyreva, A., Micciancio, D. (eds.) CRYPTO 2019. LNCS, vol. 11694, pp. 67–97. Springer, Cham (2019). https://doi.org/10.1007/978-3-030-26954-8_3

[Bea89] Beaver, D.: Multiparty protocols tolerating half faulty processors. In: Brassard, G. (ed.) CRYPTO 1989. LNCS, vol. 435, pp. 560–572. Springer, New York (1990). https://doi.org/10.1007/0-387-34805-0_49

[BGIN19] Boyle, E., Gilboa, N., Ishai, Y., Nof, A.: Practical fully secure three-party computation via sublinear distributed zero-knowledge proofs. In: Proceedings of the 2019 ACM SIGSAC Conference on Computer and Communications Security, CCS 2019, pp. 869–886. Association for Computing Machinery, New York (2019)

[BOGW88] Ben-Or, M., Goldwasser, S., Wigderson, A.: Completeness theorems for non-cryptographic fault-tolerant distributed computation. In: Proceedings of the Twentieth Annual ACM Symposium on Theory of Computing, pp. 1–10. ACM (1988)

[BSFO12] Ben-Sasson, E., Fehr, S., Ostrovsky, R.: Near-linear unconditionally-secure multiparty computation with a dishonest minority. In: Safavi-Naini, R., Canetti, R. (eds.) CRYPTO 2012. LNCS, vol. 7417, pp. 663–680. Springer, Heidelberg (2012). https://doi.org/10.1007/978-3-642-32009-5_39

[BTH06] Beerliová-Trubíniová, Z., Hirt, M.: Efficient multi-party computation with dispute control. In: Halevi, S., Rabin, T. (eds.) TCC 2006. LNCS, vol. 3876, pp. 305–328. Springer, Heidelberg (2006). https://doi.org/10.1007/11681878_16

[BTH08] Beerliová-Trubíniová, Z., Hirt, M.: Perfectly-secure MPC with linear communication complexity. In: Canetti, R. (ed.) TCC 2008. LNCS, vol. 4948, pp. 213–230. Springer, Heidelberg (2008). https://doi.org/10.1007/978-3-540-78524-8_13

[CCD88] Chaum, D., Crépeau, C., Damgard, I.: Multiparty unconditionally secure protocols. In: Proceedings of the Twentieth Annual ACM Symposium on Theory of Computing, pp. 11–19. ACM (1988)

[CDD+99] Cramer, R., Damgård, I., Dziembowski, S., Hirt, M., Rabin, T.: Efficient multiparty computations secure against an adaptive adversary. In: Stern, J. (ed.) EUROCRYPT 1999. LNCS, vol. 1592, pp. 311–326. Springer, Heidelberg (1999). https://doi.org/10.1007/3-540-48910-X_22

[CDVdG87] Chaum, D., Damgård, I.B., van de Graaf, J.: Multiparty computations ensuring privacy of each party's input and correctness of the result. In: Pomerance, C. (ed.) CRYPTO 1987. LNCS, vol. 293, pp. 87–119. Springer, Heidelberg (1988). https://doi.org/10.1007/3-540-48184-2_7

[CGH+18] Chida, K., et al.: Fast large-scale honest-majority MPC for malicious adversaries. In: Shacham, H., Boldyreva, A. (eds.) CRYPTO 2018. LNCS, vol. 10993, pp. 34–64. Springer, Cham (2018). https://doi.org/10.1007/978-3-319-96878-0_2

[DIK10] Damgård, I., Ishai, Y., Krøigaard, M.: Perfectly secure multiparty computation and the computational overhead of cryptography. In: Gilbert, H. (ed.) EUROCRYPT 2010. LNCS, vol. 6110, pp. 445–465. Springer, Heidelberg (2010). https://doi.org/10.1007/978-3-642-13190-5_23

[DN07] Damgård, I., Nielsen, J.B.: Scalable and unconditionally secure multiparty computation. In: Menezes, A. (ed.) CRYPTO 2007. LNCS, vol. 4622, pp. 572–590. Springer, Heidelberg (2007). https://doi.org/10.1007/978-3-540-74143-5_32

[FLNW17] Furukawa, J., Lindell, Y., Nof, A., Weinstein, O.: High-throughput secure three-party computation for malicious adversaries and an honest majority. In: Coron, J.-S., Nielsen, J.B. (eds.) EUROCRYPT 2017. LNCS, vol. 10211, pp. 225–255. Springer, Cham (2017). https://doi.org/10.1007/978-3-319-56614-6_8

[GIP+14] Genkin, D., Ishai, Y., Prabhakaran, M.M., Sahai, A., Tromer, E.: Circuits resilient to additive attacks with applications to secure computation. In: Proceedings of the Forty-Sixth Annual ACM Symposium on Theory of Computing, STOC 2014, pp. 495–504. ACM, New York (2014)

[GIP15] Genkin, D., Ishai, Y., Polychroniadou, A.: Efficient multi-party computation: from passive to active security via secure SIMD circuits. In: Gennaro, R., Robshaw, M. (eds.) CRYPTO 2015. LNCS, vol. 9216, pp. 721–741. Springer, Heidelberg (2015). https://doi.org/10.1007/978-3-662-48000-7_35

[GLOS20] Goyal, V., Li, H., Ostrovsky, R., Song, Y.: Fast honest-majority MPC protocols. Manuscript (2020)

[GLS19] Goyal, V., Liu, Y., Song, Y.: Communication-efficient unconditional MPC with guaranteed output delivery. In: Boldyreva, A., Micciancio, D. (eds.) CRYPTO 2019. LNCS, vol. 11693, pp. 85–114. Springer, Cham (2019). https://doi.org/10.1007/978-3-030-26951-7_4

[GMW87] Goldreich, O., Micali, S., Wigderson, A.: How to play any mental game. In: Proceedings of the Nineteenth Annual ACM Symposium on Theory of Computing, pp. 218–229. ACM (1987)

[GS20] Goyal, V., Song, Y.: Malicious security comes free in honest-majority MPC. Cryptology ePrint Archive, Report 2020/134 (2020). https://eprint.iacr.org/2020/134

[GSZ20] Goyal, V., Song, Y., Zhu, C.: Guaranteed output delivery comes free in honest majority MPC. Cryptology ePrint Archive, Report 2020/189 (2020). https://eprint.iacr.org/2020/189

[HM01] Hirt, M., Maurer, U.: Robustness for free in unconditional multi-party computation. In: Kilian, J. (ed.) CRYPTO 2001. LNCS, vol. 2139, pp. 101–118. Springer, Heidelberg (2001). https://doi.org/10.1007/3-540-44647-8_6

[HMP00] Hirt, M., Maurer, U., Przydatek, B.: Efficient secure multi-party computation. In: Okamoto, T. (ed.) ASIACRYPT 2000. LNCS, vol. 1976, pp. 143–161. Springer, Heidelberg (2000). https://doi.org/10.1007/3-540-44448-3_12

[IKP+16] Ishai, Y., Kushilevitz, E., Prabhakaran, M., Sahai, A., Yu, C.-H.: Secure protocol transformations. In: Robshaw, M., Katz, J. (eds.) CRYPTO 2016. LNCS, vol. 9815, pp. 430–458. Springer, Heidelberg (2016). https://doi.org/10.1007/978-3-662-53008-5_15

[LN17] Lindell, Y., Nof, A.: A framework for constructing fast MPC over arithmetic circuits with malicious adversaries and an honest-majority. In: Proceedings of the 2017 ACM SIGSAC Conference on Computer and Communications Security, pp. 259–276. ACM (2017)

[LP12] Lindell, Y., Pinkas, B.: Secure two-party computation via cut-and-choose oblivious transfer. J. Cryptol. 25(4), 680–722 (2012). https://doi.org/10.1007/s00145-011-9107-0

[NNOB12] Nielsen, J.B., Nordholt, P.S., Orlandi, C., Burra, S.S.: A new approach to practical active-secure two-party computation. In: Safavi-Naini, R., Canetti, R. (eds.) CRYPTO 2012. LNCS, vol. 7417, pp. 681–700. Springer, Heidelberg (2012). https://doi.org/10.1007/978-3-642-32009-5_40

[NV18] Nordholt, P.S., Veeningen, M.: Minimising communication in honest-majority MPC by batchwise multiplication verification. In: Preneel, B., Vercauteren, F. (eds.) ACNS 2018. LNCS, vol. 10892, pp. 321–339. Springer, Cham (2018). https://doi.org/10.1007/978-3-319-93387-0_17

[RBO89] Rabin, T., Ben-Or, M.: Verifiable secret sharing and multiparty protocols with honest majority. In: Proceedings of the Twenty-First Annual ACM Symposium on Theory of Computing, pp. 73–85. ACM (1989)

[Sha79] Shamir, A.: How to share a secret. Commun. ACM 22(11), 612–613 (1979)

[Yao82] Yao, A.C.: Protocols for secure computations. In: 23rd Annual Symposium on Foundations of Computer Science, 1982, SFCS'08, pp. 160–164. IEEE (1982)

Black-Box Transformations from Passive to Covert Security with Public Verifiability

Ivan Damgård$^{(\boxtimes)}$, Claudio Orlandi$^{(\boxtimes)}$, and Mark Simkin$^{(\boxtimes)}$

Aarhus University, Aarhus, Denmark
{ivan,orlandi,simkin}@cs.au.dk

Abstract. In the context of secure computation, protocols with security against covert adversaries ensure that any misbehavior by malicious parties will be detected by the honest parties with some constant probability. As such, these protocols provide better security guarantees than passively secure protocols and, moreover, are easier to construct than protocols with full security against active adversaries. Protocols that, upon detecting a cheating attempt, allow the honest parties to compute a certificate that enables third parties to verify whether an accused party misbehaved or not are called publicly verifiable.

In this work, we present the first generic compilers for constructing two-party protocols with covert security and public verifiability from protocols with passive security. We present two separate compilers, which are both fully blackbox in the underlying protocols they use. Both of them only incur a constant multiplicative factor in terms of bandwidth overhead and a constant additive factor in terms of round complexity on top of the passively secure protocols they use.

The first compiler applies to all two-party protocols that have no private inputs. This class of protocols covers the important class of preprocessing protocols that are used to setup correlated randomness among parties. We use our compiler to obtain the first secret-sharing based two-party protocol with covert security and public verifiability. Notably, the produced protocol achieves public verifiability essentially for free when compared with the best known previous solutions based on secret-sharing that did not provide public verifiability.

Our second compiler constructs protocols with covert security and public verifiability for arbitrary functionalities from passively secure protocols. It uses our first compiler to perform a setup phase, which is independent of the parties' inputs as well as the protocol they would like to execute.

Finally, we show how to extend our techniques to obtain multi-party computation protocols with covert security and public verifiability against arbitrary constant fractions of corruptions.

1 Introduction

In secure computation two or more parties want to compute a joint function of their private inputs, while revealing nothing beyond what is already revealed

© International Association for Cryptologic Research 2020
D. Micciancio and T. Ristenpart (Eds.): CRYPTO 2020, LNCS 12171, pp. 647–676, 2020.
https://doi.org/10.1007/978-3-030-56880-1_23

by the output itself. Privacy of the inputs and correctness of the output should be maintained, even if some of the parties are corrupted by an adversary. Historically, this adversary has mostly been assumed to be either passive or active. Passive adversaries observe corrupted parties, learn their private inputs, the random coins they use, and see all messages that are being sent or received by them. Active adversaries take full control of the corrupted parties, they can deviate from the protocol description in an arbitrary fashion, or may just stop sending messages altogether. Protocols that are secure against active adversaries provide very strong security guarantees. They ensure that any deviation from the protocol description by the corrupted parties is detected by the honest parties with an overwhelming probability. Unfortunately, such strong security guarantees do not come for free and actively secure protocols are typically much slower than their passively secure counterparts.

To provide a compromise between efficiency and security, Aumann and Lindell [AL07] introduced the notion of security against *covert* adversaries[1]. Loosely speaking, the adversary still has full control of the corrupted parties, but if any of them deviates from the protocol description, then this behavior will be detected with some constant probability, say $1/2$, by all honest parties. The main rationale for why such an adversarial model may be sensible in the real world, is that in certain scenarios the loss of reputation that comes from being caught cheating outweighs the gain that comes from not being caught. Consider, for example, a large company that performs secure computations with its customers on a regular basis. It is reasonable to assume that the company's general reputation is more valuable than whatever it could possibly earn by tricking a few of its customers.

Asharov and Orlandi [AO12] observed that despite being well-motivated in practice, the original notion of security against covert adversaries may be a bit too weak. More concretely, the original notion ensures that the honest parties detect cheating with some constant probability, but it does not ensure the existence of a mechanism for convincing third parties that the adversary really cheated. For our hypothetical large company from before, this means that no cheated customer could convince the others of the company's misbehavior. Asharov and Orlandi therefore introduce the stronger notion of covert security *with public verifiability*, which, in case of detected cheating, ensures that the honest parties can compute a publicly verifiable certificate, which allows third parties to check that cheating by some accused party indeed happened.

Although covert security with and without public verifiability seems like a very natural security notion, comparatively few works focus on this security model. Goyal, Mohassel, and Smith [GMS08] present covertly secure two and multiparty protocols without public verifiability based on garbled circuits [Yao82] and its multiparty extension the BMR protocol [BMR90]. Subsequently, Damgård et al. [DKL+13] present a preprocessing protocol with covert security without public

---

[1] In the remainder of the paper we will use the terms "covert security" and "security against covert adversaries" interchangeably to refer to the notion that was defined by Aumann and Lindell. We note, however, that the term "covert security" has also been used to denote a different flavor of secure computation as defined in [vHL05].

verifiability for SPDZ [DPSZ12]. Asharov and Orlandi [AO12] present a two-party protocol with covert security and public verifiability based on garbled circuits and a flavor of oblivious transfer (OT), which they call signed-OT. Kolesnikov and Malozemoff [KM15] improve upon the construction of Asharov and Orlandi by constructing a signed-OT extension protocol based on the OT extension[2] protocol of Ishai et al. [IKNP03]. In a recent work by Hong et al. [HKK+19], the authors present a new approach for constructing two-party computation with covert security and public verifiability based on garbled circuits from plain standard OT.

Apart from the concrete constructions above, one can also use so called protocol compilers that generically transform protocols with weaker security guarantees into protocols with stronger ones. The main advantage of compilers over concrete protocols is that they allow us to automatically obtain protocols with the stronger security guarantee from any future insight into protocols with the weaker one. In case of covert security with and without public verifiability, for example, most of the existing concrete constructions are based on garbled circuits. If at some point in the future a new methodology for constructing more efficient passively secure protocols is discovered, then we may end up in the situation that the techniques that we used to lift garbled circuits from passive to covert security may not be applicable. Compilers, on the other hand, will still be useful as long as the new protocols satisfy the requirements the compiler imposes on the protocols it transforms.

In terms of generic approaches for efficiently transforming arbitrary passively secure protocols into covertly secure ones very little is known. Damgård, Geisler, and Nielsen [DGN10] present a blackbox compiler that transforms passively secure protocols that are based on secret sharing into covertly secure protocols. Their compiler only works for the honest majority setting, i.e., it assumes that the honest parties form a strict majority, and therefore their compiler is not applicable to the two-party setting. Lindell, Oxman, and Pinkas [LOP11] present a compiler, based on the work of Ishai, Prabhakaran, and Sahai [IPS08], that transforms passively secure protocols in the dishonest majority setting into covertly secure ones. Their compiler makes blackbox use of a passively secure "inner" and non-blackbox use of an information-theoretic "outer" multiparty computation protocol with active security. The bandwidth overhead and round complexity of their compiler depends on the complexity of both the inner and the outer protocol. Unfortunately this means that the protocols this compiler produces are either not constant-round protocols or have a large bandwidth overhead. Using an information-theoretic outer protocol results in a protocol that is not constant-round, since constructing information-theoretic multiparty

---

[2] In general, OT requires the use of public key cryptography. OT extension protocols allow two parties to perform large numbers of OT protocol executions using only a small number of public key operations.

computation with a constant number of rounds is a long standing open problem.[3] Alternatively, the authors of [IPS08] show how to combine their compiler with a variant of a computationally secure protocol of Damgård and Ishai [DI05], which only makes blackbox use of pseudorandom generators, as the outer protocol. This approach, however, results in a protocol, which incurs a bandwidth overhead that is multiplicative in the security parameter and the circuit size on top of the communication costs of the underlying passively secure protocol.

None of the above compilers is publicly verifiable and, more generally, there is currently no better approach for constructing covertly secure protocols with public verifiability in a generic way than just taking a compiler that already produces actively secure protocols.[4] Even without public verifiability, there is currently no compiler for the dishonest majority setting that is fully blackbox in the sense that the code of the used secure computation protocols does not need to be known.

1.1 Our Contribution

In this work, we present the *first* blackbox compilers for transforming protocols with passive security into two-party protocols with covert security and public verifiability. Our compilers are fully blackbox in the underlying primitives they use, they are conceptually simple, efficient and constant-round.

Our first compiler applies to all two-party protocols with passive security that have no private inputs. The class of protocols with no inputs covers the important class of preprocessing protocols which are commonly used to setup correlated randomness among the parties. For example, one can combine our compiler with a suitable preprocessing protocol and the SPDZ online phase, similarly to [DKL+13], to obtain the first protocol with covert security, public verifiability. The resulting protocol, somewhat surprisingly, achieves public verifiability essentially for free. That is, the efficiency of our resulting protocol is essentially the same as the efficiency of the best known secret-sharing based protocol for covert security without public verifiability [DKL+13].

Our second compiler uses the first compiler to perform a *input and protocol independent* setup phase after which the parties can efficiently transform any protocol with passive security into one with covert security and publicly verifiability. We would like to stress that during the setup phase, the parties do not need to know which standalone passively secure protocol they would like to use later on.[5] When compared to compilers without public verifiability, ours is the first one that is simultaneously blackbox and constant-round with only a constant multiplicative factor bandwidth overhead on top of the underlying

---

[3] Note that the existing works on constant round MPC with information theoretic security [IK00, ABT18, ACGJ19] only apply to circuits that are in NC^1.

[4] Observe that in the two-party case active security implies covert security with public verifiability, since every attempt to cheat can simply be interpreted as an abort.

[5] If the passively secure protocol has a preprocessing phase of its own, then this would need to be executed after the setup phase of our compiler.

passively secure protocol. Existing compilers for two-party protocols do not even achieve these properties separately. It is the first compiler to produce protocols with public verifiability.

Lastly, we sketch how to extend our compilers to the multiparty setting. The resulting protocols are secure against an arbitrary constant fraction of corruptions.

1.2 Technical Overview

Before presenting the main ideas behind our compilers, let us first revisit the main ideas as well as the main technical challenges in existing protocols. Generally speaking, most covertly secure two-party protocols [AL07, GMS08, AO12, HKK+19] follow the same blueprint. They all start from a passively secure protocol, which they run k times in parallel. They use $k - 1$ randomly chosen executions to check the behavior of the participating parties and then use the last unopened protocol execution to actually compute the desired functionality on their private inputs. The intuition behind these approaches is that, if cheating happened, it will be detected with a probability of $1 - 1/k$, since the adversary would need to guess which execution will remain unopened. Importantly, this blueprint relies on the ability to open $k - 1$ executions "late enough" to ensure that cheating in the unopened execution is not possible any more, while at the same time being able to open the checked executions "early enough" to ensure that no private inputs are leaked. Secure two- and multiparty computation protocols based on garbled circuits are a perfect match for the blueprint described above, since they consist of an input-independent garbling phase, and an actively secure evaluation phase. Checked executions are opened after circuit garbling, but before circuit evaluation. Unfortunately, however, it is not clear how to generalize this approach to arbitrary passively secure protocols, since it crucially relies on the concrete structure of garbled circuit based protocols.

Our first compiler focuses on a restricted class of two-party protocols, namely those that have no private inputs. Apart from being a good starting point for explaining some of the technical ideas behind our compiler for arbitrary protocols, this class also covers a large range of important protocols. Specifically, it includes so called preprocessing protocols that are used for setting up correlated randomness between the parties.

Not having to deal with private inputs, immediately suggests the following high-level approach for letting Alice and Bob compute some desired function with covert security: Both parties first jointly execute a given protocol Π with passive security k times in parallel. Once these executions are finished, Alice and Bob independently announce subsets $I^A \subset [k]$ and $I^B \subset [k]$ with $|I^A| = |I^B| < k/2$. Alice reveals the randomness used in each execution $i \in I^B$ and Bob does the same for all executions with an index in I^A. Knowing these random tapes each party can verify whether the other party behaved honestly in the checked executions. Since $I^A \cup I^B \subsetneq [k]$, the parties are guaranteed that there exists an execution that is not checked by either of the parties. If no cheating in any of the checked executions is detected, then both parties agree to accept the output of one of the unopened executions.

This straightforward approach works for the plain version of covert security, but fails to achieve public verifiability, since neither of the parties has any way of convincing a third party of a detected cheating attempt. Even if each party signs each message it sends, a cheating party might simply stop responding if it does not like which executions are being checked. To achieve public verifiability, rather than asking for I^A and I^B in the clear, both parties use oblivious transfer to obtain the random tapes that correspond to the executions they would like to check. As before, we run k copies of the passively secure protocol Π, where Alice and Bob use the random tapes they input to the OT protocol. At the end of these executions, both parties sign the complete transcript of the protocol Π as well as the transcript of the OT. If, e.g., Alice detects cheating by Bob in some execution, then she can publish the signed transcripts of both the OT protocol and the protocol in which Bob cheated, together with the randomness she used in the OT protocol. Any third party can now use Alice's opened random tape in combination with the signed transcript of the OT protocol to recover Bob's random tape and use it to check whether Bob misbehaved or not in the protocol Π. The general idea of derandomizing the parties to achieve public verifiability has previously been used by Hong et al. [HKK+19]. However, as it turns out there are quite a few subtleties to take care of to make sure that the approach outlined above actually works and is secure. We will elaborate on these challenges in the later technical sections.

Using our compiler for protocols with no private inputs, we can obtain efficient protocols with covert security and public verifiability in the preprocessing model. In this model, protocols are split into a preprocessing protocol Π_{OFF} and an online phase Π_{ON}, where Π_{OFF} generates correlated randomness and Π_{ON} is a highly efficient protocol for computing a desired function using the correlated randomness and the parties' private inputs. We can apply our compiler to a passively secure version of the preprocessing protocol of SPDZ [DPSZ12] and combine it with an actively secure online protocol Π_{ON} to obtain an overall protocol with covert security and public verifiability.

Our second compiler for arbitrary protocols follows the player virtualization paradigm, which was first introduced by Bracha [Bra87] in the context of distributed computing and then first applied to secure computation protocols by Maurer and Hirth [HM00]. Very roughly speaking, the idea behind this paradigm is to let a set of real parties simulate a set of virtual parties, which execute some given protocol on behalf of the real parties. Despite the conceptual simplicity of this idea, it has led to many interesting results. Ishai, Prabhakaran, and Sahai [IPS08], for example, show how to use this paradigm in combination with OT to obtain actively secure protocols from passively secure ones in the dishonest majority setting. In another work, Ishai et al. [IKOS07] show how to transform secure multiparty computation protocols with passive security into zero-knowledge proofs. Cohen et al. [CDI+13] show how to transform three or four-party protocols that tolerate one active corruption into n-party protocols for arbitrary n that tolerate a constant fraction of active corruptions. Damgård, Orlandi, and Simkin [DOS18] show how to transform information-theoretically secure multiparty protocols that tolerate $\Omega(t)$ passive corruptions into information-theoretically secure ones that tolerate $\Omega(\sqrt{t})$ active corruptions.

In this work, we make use of this paradigm as follows: Assume Alice and Bob have inputs x^A and x^B, would like to compute some function f, and are given access to some $2m$-party protocol Π with security against $m + t$ passive corruptions, where m and t are parameters that will determine the probability with which cheating will be caught. Alice imagines m virtual parties $\mathbb{V}_1^A, \ldots, \mathbb{V}_m^A$ in her head and Bob imagines virtual parties $\mathbb{V}_1^B, \ldots, \mathbb{V}_m^B$ in his. Alice splits her input x^A into an m-out-of-m secret sharing with shares $x_1^A, \ldots, x_m^A$ and she will use share x_i^A as the private input of her virtual party $\mathbb{V}_i^A$. Bob does the same with his input. All $2m$ virtual parties jointly execute Π, which first reconstructs x^A and x^B from the given shares and then computes $f(x^A, x^B)$. During the protocol execution, Alice and Bob send messages on behalf of the virtual parties they simulate. If both parties perform their simulations honestly, then the protocol computes the desired result. If either of the real parties misbehaves, then it will necessarily misbehave in at least one of its virtual parties. Similarly to before, our idea here is to let Alice and Bob check subsets of each other's simulations. Assuming, for instance, Alice obtains the random tapes and inputs of t uniformly random virtual parties of Bob, then she can recompute all messages that those virtual parties should be sending. Since Bob does not know which of his virtual parties are checked, any attempt to cheat will be caught with a probability of t/m. Further, observe that as long as $t < m$, the inputs remain hidden, since the protocol tolerates $m + t$ corruptions and each input is m-out-of-m secret shared.

As in the case of the first compiler, the high-level idea of the simulation strategy above is reasonably simple, yet the details are in fact non-trivial and several subtle issues arise when trying to turn this idea into a working compiler.

What function to compute? The first question that needs to be addressed is that of which function exactly the virtual parties should compute. Using Π to reconstruct x^A and x^B and then directly compute $f(x^A, x^B)$ is good enough for the intuition above, but is actually not secure. The reason is, that security against covert adversaries requires that the adversary's decision to cheat is independent of the honest party's input and output. A passively secure protocol, however, may reveal the output bit-by-bit, which would allow the adversary to learn parts of the output before deciding on whether to cheat or not. Consider for example the case, where x^A and x^B are bit-strings and $f(x^A, x^B) = x^A \wedge x^B$. A passively secure protocol may simply compute and output the AND of each bit sequentially, which would enable an adversary to make its decision to cheat dependent on the output bits it has seen so far. To deal with this issue, we will use Π to secret share the output value among all virtual parties. This ensures that Π will not leak any information about any of the inputs or the output. At the same time all virtual parties can still reconstruct the output together by simply publishing their respective share.

How to check the behavior of virtual parties? The behavior of any virtual party is uniquely defined by its input, its random tape, and its current view of the protocol. Assuming, for example, Alice has access to input, random tape, and current view of some virtual party $\mathbb{V}_i^B$ of Bob, she can recompute the exact message this party should be sending. If the virtual party $\mathbb{V}_i^B$ deviates from that message, then Alice knows that a cheating attempt has happened. Assume for a second, that Alice somehow already obtained $\mathbb{V}_i^B$'s input and random tape. The question now is how she can keep track of that virtual party's view. If $\mathbb{V}_i^B$ is sending a protocol message to or receiving it from any $\mathbb{V}_j^A$, then Alice necessarily obtains that message and she can either check its validity or add it to $\mathbb{V}_i^B$'s view. However, what happens when $\mathbb{V}_i^B$ is receiving a message from another one of Bob's virtual parties $\mathbb{V}_j^B$? In this case things are a little trickier. If Alice is checking $\mathbb{V}_i^B$, she should be able to read the message, but if she is not checking this virtual party, then the sent message should remain hidden from her. To solve this problem, we establish private communication channels between all virtual parties of Bob and separately also between all the ones of Alice. More precisely, for $1 \leq i, j \leq m$, we will pick symmetric keys $k_{(i,j)}^B$, which will be used to encrypt the communication between $\mathbb{V}_i^B$ and $\mathbb{V}_j^B$. When Alice initially obtains input and random tape of $\mathbb{V}_i^B$, she will also obtain all keys that belong to communication channels that are connected to $\mathbb{V}_i^B$. Now if during the protocol execution $\mathbb{V}_i^B$ should send a message to $\mathbb{V}_j^B$, we let Bob encrypt the message with the corresponding symmetric key and send it to Alice, who can decrypt the message only if she is checking the receiver or sender.

In our description here we have assumed that quite a lot of correlated randomness magically fell from the sky. For instance, we assumed that all random tapes and all symmetric keys were chosen honestly and distributed correctly. To realize this setup, we will use our first compiler, which we will apply to an appropriate protocol with passive security.

2 Preliminaries

2.1 Secure Multiparty Computation

All of our security definitions follow the ideal/real simulation paradigm in the standalone model. In the real protocol execution, all parties jointly execute the protocol Π. Honest parties always follow the protocol description, whereas corrupted parties are controlled by an adversary $\mathcal{A}$. In the ideal execution all parties simply send their inputs to a trusted party $\mathcal{F}$, which computes the desired function and returns the output to the parties. Roughly speaking, we say that Π securely realizes $\mathcal{F}$, if for every real-world adversary $\mathcal{A}$, there exists an ideal-world adversary $\mathcal{S}$ such that the output distribution of the honest parties and $\mathcal{S}$ in the ideal execution is indistinguishable from the output distribution of the honest parties and $\mathcal{A}$ in the real execution. Different security notions, such as security against passive, covert, or malicious adversaries, differ in the capabilities the adversary has as well as the ideal functionalities they aim to implement.

Throughout this paper we will consider synchronous protocols, static, rushing adversaries, and we assume the existence of secure authenticated point-to-point channels between the parties.

Let $P_1, \ldots, P_n$ be the involved parties and let $I \subset [n]$ be the set of indices of the corrupted parties that are controlled by the adversary $\mathcal{A}$. Let $\Pi : (\{0,1\}^*)^n \to (\{0,1\}^*)^n$ be an n-party protocol that takes one input from and returns one output to each party. Π internally may use an auxiliary ideal functionality $\mathcal{G}$. For the sake of simplicity, we assume that parties have inputs of the same length. Let $\bar{x} = (x_1, \ldots, x_n)$ be the vector of the parties' inputs and let z be an auxiliary input to $\mathcal{A}$. We define $\mathsf{REAL}_\lambda[\mathcal{A}(z), I, \Pi, \mathcal{G}, \bar{x}]$ as the output of the adversary $\mathcal{A}$ and the outputs of the honest parties in an execution of Π.

Passive adversaries. Security against passive adversaries is modelled by considering an environment $\mathcal{Z}$ that, in the real and ideal execution, picks the inputs of all parties. An adversary $\mathcal{A}$ gets access to views of the corrupted parties, but follows the protocol specification honestly. We consider the following ideal execution:

Inputs: Environment $\mathcal{Z}$ gets as input auxiliary information z and sends the vector of inputs $\bar{x} = (x_1, \ldots, x_n)$ to the ideal functionality $\mathcal{F}_{\mathsf{PASSIVE}}$.

Ideal functionality reveals inputs: If the ideal world adversary $\mathcal{S}$ sends get_inputs to $\mathcal{F}_{\mathsf{PASSIVE}}$, then it gets back the inputs of all corrupted parties, i.e. all x_i, where $i \in I$.

Output generation: The ideal functionality computes $(y_1, \ldots, y_n) = f(x_1, \ldots, x_n)$ and returns back y_i to each P_i. All honest parties output whatever they receive from $\mathcal{F}_{\mathsf{PASSIVE}}$. The ideal world adversary $\mathcal{S}$ outputs an arbitrary probabilistic polynomial-time computable function of the initial inputs of the corrupted parties, the auxiliary input z, and the messages received from the ideal functionality.

The joint distribution of the outputs of the honest parties and $\mathcal{S}$ in an ideal execution is denoted by $\mathsf{IDEAL}_\lambda[S(z), I, \mathcal{F}, \bar{x}]$.

Definition 1. *Protocol Π is said to securely compute $\mathcal{F}$ with security against passive adversaries in the $\mathcal{G}$-hybrid model if for every non-uniform probabilistic polynomial time adversary $\mathcal{A}$ in the real world, there exists a probabilistic polynomial time adversary $\mathcal{S}$ in the ideal world such that for all $\lambda \in \mathbb{N}$*

$$\left\{ \mathsf{IDEAL}_\lambda[S(z), I, \mathcal{F}, \bar{x}] \right\}_{\bar{x}, z \in \{0,1\}^*} \equiv_c \left\{ \mathsf{REAL}_\lambda[\mathcal{A}(z), I, \Pi, \mathcal{G}, \bar{x}] \right\}_{\bar{x}, z \in \{0,1\}^*}$$

Covert adversaries. We use the security definition of Aumann and Lindell [AL07] for defining security against covert adversaries. The security notion we consider here is the strongest one of several and is known as the Strong Explicit Cheat Formulation (SECF). Covert adversaries are modelled by considering active adversaries, but relaxing the ideal functionality we aim to implement. The relaxed ideal functionality $\mathcal{F}_{\mathsf{SECF}}$ allows the ideal-world adversary $\mathcal{S}$ to perform a limited amount of cheating. That is, the ideal-world adversary, can attempt to cheat by sending cheat to the ideal functionality, which randomly decides whether the attempt was successful or not. With probability ϵ, known as the *deterrence factor*, $\mathcal{F}_{\mathsf{SECF}}$ will send back detected and all parties will be informed of at least one corrupt party that attempted to cheat. With probability $1 - \epsilon$, the simulator $\mathcal{S}$ will receive undetected. In this case $\mathcal{S}$ learns all parties' inputs and can decide what the output of the ideal functionality is. The ideal execution proceeds as follows:

Inputs: Every honest party P_i sends its inputs x_i to $\mathcal{F}_{\mathsf{SECF}}$. The ideal world adversary $\mathcal{S}$ gets auxiliary input z and sends inputs on behalf of all corrupted parties. Let $\bar{x} = (x_1, \ldots, x_n)$ be the vector of inputs that the ideal functionality receives.

Abort options: If a corrupted party sends (abort, i) as its input to the $\mathcal{F}_{\mathsf{SECF}}$, then the ideal functionality sends (abort, i) to all honest parties and halts. If a corrupted party sends (corrupted, i) as its input, then the functionality sends (corrupted, i) to all honest parties and halts. If multiple corrupted parties send (abort, i), respectively (corrupted, i), then the ideal functionality only relates to one of them. If both (corrupted, i) and (abort, i) messages are sent, then the ideal functionality ignores the (corrupted, i) messages.

Attempted cheat: If $\mathcal{S}$ sends (cheat, i) as the input of a corrupted P_i, then $\mathcal{F}_{\mathsf{SECF}}$ decides randomly whether cheating was detected or not:
- Detected: With probability ϵ, $\mathcal{F}_{\mathsf{SECF}}$ sends (detected, i) to the adversary and all honest parties.
- Undetected: With probability $1 - \epsilon$, $\mathcal{F}_{\mathsf{SECF}}$ sends undetected to the adversary. In this case $\mathcal{S}$ obtains the inputs $(x_1, \ldots, x_n)$ of all honest parties from $\mathcal{F}_{\mathsf{SECF}}$. It specifies an output y_i for each honest P_i and $\mathcal{F}_{\mathsf{SECF}}$ outputs y_i to P_i.

The ideal execution ends at this point. If no corrupted party sent (abort, i), (corrupted, i) or (cheat, i), then the ideal execution continues below.

Ideal functionality answers adversary: The ideal functionality computes $(y_1, \ldots, y_n) = f(x_1, \ldots, x_n)$ and sends it to $\mathcal{S}$.

Ideal functionality answers honest parties: The adversary $\mathcal{S}$ either sends back continue or (abort, i) for a corrupted P_i. If the adversary sends continue, then the ideal functionality returns y_i to each honest parties P_i. If the adversary sends (abort, i) for some i, then the ideal functionality sends back (abort, i) to all honest parties.

Output generation: An honest party always outputs the message it obtained from $\mathcal{F}_{\mathsf{SECF}}$. The corrupted parties output nothing. The adversary outputs an arbitrary probabilistic polynomial-time computable function of the initial inputs of the corrupted parties, the auxiliary input z, and the messages received from the ideal functionality.

The outputs of the honest parties and $\mathcal{S}$ in an ideal execution is denoted by $\mathsf{IDEAL}_\lambda^\epsilon[S(z), I, \mathcal{F}_{\mathsf{SECF}}, \bar{x}]$. Note that the definition requires the adversary to *either* cheat or send the corrupted parties' inputs to the ideal functionality, but not both.

Definition 2. *Protocol Π is said to securely compute $\mathcal{F}$ with security against covert adversaries with ϵ-deterrent in the $\mathcal{G}$-hybrid model if for every non-uniform probabilistic polynomial time adversary $\mathcal{A}$ in the real world, there exists a probabilistic polynomial time adversary $\mathcal{S}$ in the ideal world such that for all $\lambda \in \mathbb{N}$*

$$\left\{\mathsf{IDEAL}_\lambda^\epsilon[S(z), I, \mathcal{F}_{\mathsf{SECF}}, \bar{x}]\right\}_{\bar{x}, z \in \{0,1\}^*} \equiv_c \left\{\mathsf{REAL}_\lambda[\mathcal{A}(z), I, \Pi, \mathcal{G}, \bar{x}]\right\}_{\bar{x}, z \in \{0,1\}^*}$$

Security against covert adversaries with public verifiability. This notion was first introduced by [AO12] and was later simplified by [HKK+19]. In covert security with public verifiability, each protocol Π is extended with an additional algorithm Judge. We assume that whenever a party detects cheating during an execution of Π, it outputs a special message cert. The verification algorithm, Judge, takes as input a certificate cert and outputs the identity, which is defined by the corresponding public key, of the party to blame or $\perp$ in the case of an invalid certificate.

Definition 3 (Covert security with ϵ-deterrent and public verifiability). *Let pk^A, pk^B be the keys of parties Alice and Bob and f be a public function. We say that (π, Judge) securely computes f in the presence of a covert adversary with ϵ-deterrent and public verifiability if the following conditions hold:*

> **Covert Security:** *The protocol Π (which now might output cert if an honest party detects cheating) is secure against a covert adversary according to the strong explicit cheat formulation above with ϵ-deterrent.*
> **Public Verifiability:** *If the honest party $P \in \{A, B\}$ outputs cert in an execution of the protocol, then $\mathsf{Judge}(\mathsf{pk}^A, \mathsf{pk}^B, f, \mathsf{cert}) = \mathsf{pk}^{\{A,B\}\backslash P}$ except with negligible probability.*
> **Defamation-Freeness:** *If party $P \in \{A, B\}$ is honest and runs the protocol with a corrupt party $\mathcal{A}$, then the probability that $\mathcal{A}$ outputs cert* such that $\mathsf{Judge}(\mathsf{pk}^A, \mathsf{pk}^B, f, \mathsf{cert}^*) = \mathsf{pk}^P$ is negligible.*

Next-Message Functionality. From time to time it may be convenient to go through a n-party protocol Π step-by-step. For this purpose we define a next-message functionality $(v_1, \ldots, v_n) \leftarrow \Pi_{\mathsf{NEXT}}(i, x, r, T)$, which takes the party's index i, its input x, its random tape r and the transcript T of messages the party has seen so far as input and computes a vector $(v_1, \ldots, v_n)$ of messages, where party i should be sending message v_j to party j next. If $v_j = \perp$, then party j does not receive a message from party i in that round. The protocol ends when Π_{NEXT} outputs a special value (out, z), where z is then interpreted as the output of that party.

2.2 Ideal Functionalities

We recall some basic ideal functionalities which we will make use of in our compiler. In the k-out-of-n oblivious transfer functionality $\mathcal{F}_{\mathsf{OT}}$ (Fig. 1) a sender has a message vector $(m_0, \ldots, m_n)$ and a receiver has index vector $(i_1, \ldots, i_k)$. The receiver learns $(m_{i_1}, \ldots, m_{i_k})$, but learns nothing about the other messages, whereas the sender learns nothing about the index vector.

$$\mathcal{F}_{\mathsf{OT}}^{(n,k)}$$

The functionality interacts with sender $\mathcal{S}$ and receiver $\mathcal{R}$.

---

1. On input $(\mathsf{rec}, \mathsf{sid}, (i_1, \ldots, i_k))$ from $\mathcal{R}$, if no message of the form $(\mathsf{rec}, \mathsf{sid}, *)$ was recorded in memory, then store $(\mathsf{rec}, \mathsf{sid}, (i_1, \ldots, i_k))$ and send $(\mathsf{rec}, \mathsf{sid})$ to $\mathcal{S}$.
2. On input $(\mathsf{snd}, \mathsf{sid}, (m_1, \ldots, m_n))$, if a message of the form $(\mathsf{rec}, \mathsf{sid}, *)$ is stored in memory, then send $(\mathsf{snd}, \mathsf{sid}, (m_{i_1}, \ldots, m_{i_k}))$ to $\mathcal{R}$.

Fig. 1. Ideal functionality for oblivious transfer.

The commitment functionality $\mathcal{F}_{\mathsf{Com}}$ (Fig. 2) allows a party to first commit to a message and then later open this commitment to another party. The commitment should be binding, i.e. the committing party should not be able to open the commitment to more than one message, and hiding, i.e. the commitment should not reveal any information about the committed messages before the commitment is opened.

Our compilers requires commitments with non-interactive opening phase. To ease the notation, we will describe our protocols using commitments where the commitment phase is non-interactive as well, but our protocols could easily be extended to commitments with interactive commitment phases as well. To commit to a message m, we write: $(c, d) \leftarrow \mathsf{Com}(m; r)$ where c is the commitment and d is the opening information. The values d is then used to compute $m' \leftarrow \mathsf{Open}(c, d)$ with $m' = m$ or $\perp$ in case of incorrect opening.

3 Compiler for Two-Party Protocols with No Inputs

We already provided a high level description of this compiler for protocols with no inputs in the introduction. The formal compiler is presented in Fig. 3. Before proving the security of our compiler, we discuss some of the subtle issues we encountered in the design of the protocol and the role they play in the proof. As the protocol is completely symmetric, and to ease the notation, we will explain all choices from the point of view of Alice. In the first step of the protocol both Alice and Bob pick random tapes s_i^A and s_i^B for all $i \in [k]$, which are in turn parsed as $s_i^P = (u_i^P, v_i^P, w_i^P)$ for $P \in \{A, B\}$ during the protocol. There are several reasons for this. Since we want to compile any passively secure protocol,

---

$\mathcal{F}_{\mathsf{Com}}$

The functionality interacts with parties $P_1, \ldots, P_n$.

---

1. Upon receiving $(\mathsf{commit}, \mathsf{sid}, P_i, P_j, m)$ from party P_i, if no message of the form $(\mathsf{sid}, P_i, P_j, *)$ was recorded in memory, then store $(\mathsf{sid}, P_i, P_j, m)$ and send $(\mathsf{receipt}, \mathsf{sid}, P_i, P_j)$ to P_j.
2. Upon receiving $(\mathsf{open}, \mathsf{sid}, P_i, P_j)$ from P_j, if a message of the form $(\mathsf{sid}, P_i, P_j, m)$ is stored in memory, then send $(\mathsf{open}, \mathsf{sid}, P_i, P_j, m)$ to P_j.

Fig. 2. Ideal functionality for multiple commitments.

we can only guarantee security of the unopened execution if both parties use uniformly random tapes in this execution. Therefore, the actual random tape r_i^A which is used by A in the execution of the i-th copy of Π is obtained as $r_i^A = u_i^A \oplus v_i^B$ in step 5 of the protocol, thus, if B is honest r_i^A will indeed be random. Then, remember that we also use the seeds s_i^B that A receives from the OT as a form of commitment to the set of parties I^A that she has checked during the protocol execution, i.e., in Step 9 we let A send those seeds to B which in turns allows B to reconstruct I^B. We of course need to argue that A cannot lie about her checked set I^A by, e.g., sending back to B some s_i^B with $i \notin I^A$. It might be tempting to believe that this follows from the security of the OT protocol. However, since B uses the values s_i^B in the protocol Π we need to "reserve" a sufficiently long chuck of s_i^B, which we call w_i^B, as a "witness" which is only used for the purpose of committing A to the set I^A and nothing else. Finally, we need to argue for public verifiability and defamation freeness. Public verifiability is obtained by asking A to sign the transcript of the protocol. Then, if B detects any cheating by verifying whether the messages sent by A in the checked executions of Π are consistent with her random tapes, B can output a certificate consisting of A's signature together with information which allows a judge to reconstruct the random tape s_j^A, where j is the execution in which B claims the cheating happened, i.e., to let the judge reconstruct A's random tape, B includes the random tape he used when acting as the receiver in the OT protocol. Note that we let B verify for cheating *after* the execution of Π is completed. The reason for this is that if B aborts as soon as some cheating is detected, B would not receive A's signature on the protocol transcript. Moreover, it is perfectly safe to run the protocol to the end even if cheating is detected since B has no private input in the protocol.

This, together with the transcript of the OT protocol, allows the judge to recompute the output of B in the protocol i.e., the random tape of A and, if we use an OT which satisfies perfect correctness, a corrupt B cannot lie about the output received in the protocol.[6] Note that, perhaps counterintuitively, the judge *does not* need to check that the messages sent from the *accuser to the accused* are correct! This is because whether the messages sent from the accuser to the accused are correct or not has no influence in whether the messages from the accused to the accuser are correct or not according to the protocol specification. In other words, a corrupt party cannot "trick" an honest party into cheating by sending ill-formed messages.

We are now ready for the security analysis.

Theorem 1. *Let Π be a protocol that implements a two-party functionality $\mathcal{F}$, which receives no private inputs, with security against passive adversaries. Let $\Pi_{OT}^{(k,k/2-1)}$ be a protocol that implements $\mathcal{F}_{OT}^{(k,k/2-1)}$ with active security and perfect correctness. Then the compiler illustrated in Fig. 3 and 4 implements the two-party functionality $\mathcal{F}$ with security and public verifiability against covert adversaries with deterrence factor $\epsilon = \frac{1}{2} - \frac{1}{k}$.*

Proof. We will proceed by proving security, public verifiability, and defamation-freeness separately. Without loss of generality we assume that Alice is corrupted by the adversary $\mathcal{A}$. The case for Bob being corrupted is symmetrical. For proving security, we construct a simulator $\mathcal{S}$ playing the role of Alice in the ideal world and using $\mathcal{A}$ as a subroutine as follows[7]:

Simulation part A:

0. Generate $(\mathsf{sk}^B, \mathsf{pk}^B)$ and send pk^B to $\mathcal{A}$.

1. The simulator picks random seeds s_i^B, for $i \in [k] \cup \{\mathsf{R}\}$.

2. Do nothing.[8]

3. The simulator uses $\mathcal{S}_{OT}$ to simulate both OT executions. In the one where it acts as a receiver it extracts $\mathcal{A}$'s input $(s')_1^A, \ldots, (s')_k^A$. In the one where it acts as the sender it extracts the vector I^A, and sends the corresponding seeds to the adversary.

4. For $i \in [k]$, derive u_i^B and v_i^B from seed s_i^B and send v_i^B to $\mathcal{A}$. Receive the v_i^A from $\mathcal{A}$.

5. The simulator $\mathcal{S}$ engages in k honest executions of Π with $\mathcal{A}$, where the simulator uses random tape $r_i^B = u_i^B \oplus v_i^A$ in execution i. Let T_Π be the set of transcripts of those executions.

---

[6] Note that Hong et al. [HKK+19] use a similar derandomization trick in their garbled circuit construction, but do not mention the need for a perfectly correct OT, nor formally proves defamation freeness of their protocol. The extra assumption appears to be necessary to achieve this property in their protocol as well, since OT security itself does not imply that the receiver cannot "equivocate" its view by finding a random tape that produces a different output than the one in the real execution.

[7] For the sake of clarity, we assume that the adversary $\mathcal{A}$ cheats in at most one location. Our proof easily generalizes to the case where $\mathcal{A}$ cheats in arbitrarily many locations at the cost of becoming a little less readable.

[8] Some steps are left empty on purpose to keep the numbering of steps consistent with the protocol.

Alice holds $(\mathsf{sk}^A, \mathsf{pk}^A)$ and Bob holds $(\mathsf{sk}^B, \mathsf{pk}^B)$. Both parties have no inputs.

1. For $i \in [k] \cup \{\mathsf{R}\}$, Alice and Bob pick seeds s_i^A and s_i^B uniformly at random of appropriate length.
2. Party $P \in \{A, B\}$ derives vector $I^P \subset [k]$ from s_R^P, with $|I^A| = |I^B| = \lceil k/2 \rceil - 1$.
3. Alice and Bob run two invocations of $\Pi_{\mathsf{OT}}^{(k, k/2-1)}$, where Alice and Bob each once act as the receiver and once as the sender. The sender $S \in \{A, B\}$ uses $(s_1^S, \ldots, s_k^S)$ as its input to the OT. The receiver $R \in \{A, B\}$ uses input I^R and randomness derived from s_R^R. Alice receives all s_i^B with $i \in I^A$ and Bob receives all s_j^A with $j \in I^B$. Let T_{OT}^A and T_{OT}^B be the sets of transcripts of the OT executions, where Alice and Bob respectively were the receiver.
4. For all $i \in [k]$, party $P \in \{A, B\}$ derives (u_i^P, v_i^P, w_i^P), from seed s_i^P. Let $V^P = \{v_i^P\}_{i \in [k]}$. The parties exchange the V^P's.
5. Alice and Bob engage in k executions of Π, where in the i-th execution Alice uses random tape $r_i^A = u_i^A \oplus v_i^B$ and Bob uses random tape $r_i^B = u_i^B \oplus v_i^A$. Let T_Π be the set of transcripts of those executions.
6. Alice computes $\sigma^A \leftarrow \mathsf{Sign}(\mathsf{sk}^A, (T_{\mathsf{OT}}^B, V^B, T_\Pi))$ and sends σ^A to Bob. Bob computes $\sigma^B \leftarrow \mathsf{Sign}(\mathsf{sk}^B, T_{\mathsf{OT}}^A, V^A, T_\Pi))$ and sends σ^B to Alice. If σ^A or σ^B does not verify, then Bob or Alice respectively abort.
7. For $i \in I^A$, Alice checks, whether Bob's messages in step 4 and step 5 are consistent with the seed s_i^B she obtained in step 3. Let $J^A \subseteq I^A$ be the set of indices, where the seeds did not match the execution. Bob does the same to obtain J^B.
8. If $J^A \neq \emptyset$, Alice picks the least $j \in J^A$, outputs a certificate $\mathsf{cert} = (\sigma^B, T_{\mathsf{OT}}^A, s_\mathsf{R}^A, V^A, T_\Pi, j)$, and aborts the execution. Similarly, Bob does the same with his set J^B.
9. Alice reveals w_i^B for $i \in I^A$ and Bob reveals w_i^A for $i \in I^B$, allowing the both parties to reconstruct the sets I^A, I^B.
10. If no cheating was detected, then the parties agree to use the output of execution i of Π, where $i = \min([k] \setminus (I^A \cup I^B))$.

Fig. 3. Compiler from security against passive to security with public verifiability against covert adversaries for two-party protocols with no inputs.

6. The simulator computes $\sigma^B \leftarrow \mathsf{Sign}(\mathsf{sk}^B, (T_{\mathsf{OT}}^A, V^A, T_\Pi))$ and sends it to $\mathcal{A}$. The adversary sends back σ^A. If the adversary's signature does not verify, then the simulation aborts (similarly, the simulation aborts if at any previous step $\mathcal{A}$ stops sending messages or sends messages which are blatantly wrong e.g., they generate an abort in the real world with probability 1).
7. The simulator uses seeds $(s')_i^A$ to check whether $\mathcal{A}$ behaved correctly during all executions of Π in step 4 and 5 (using the incorrect random tapes r_i^A constitutes cheating as well). If $\mathcal{A}$ deviated in any of the protocol executions, then the simulator sends (cheat, A) to the ideal functionality $\mathcal{F}$, which responds with $\mathsf{resp} = \{\mathsf{detected}, \mathsf{undetected}\}$. Store index j^* of the execution in which $\mathcal{A}$ cheated, along with the exact location loc^* of where cheating happened in that execution itself, and then proceeds to part B if $\mathsf{flag} = \mathsf{undetected}$.

Judge has input $(\mathsf{pk}^A, \mathsf{pk}^B, \mathsf{cert})$

1. The judge parses $\mathsf{cert} = \left(\sigma^X, T_{\mathsf{OT}}^Y, s_{\mathsf{R}}^Y, V^Y, T_\Pi, j\right)$ with $(X, Y) \in \{(A, B), (B, A)\}$.
2. If $\mathsf{Verify}(\mathsf{pk}^X, \sigma^X, (T_{\mathsf{OT}}^Y, V^Y, T_\Pi)) = 0$, return $\perp$.
3. Verify the execution of Π_{OT}, where the receiver Y uses input I^Y and random coins derived from s_{R}^Y and the sender's messages are the ones from T_{OT}^Y. If the recomputed outgoing messages of Y are not consistent with the transcript T_{OT}^Y, then return $\perp$. Otherwise let s_i^X for $i \in I^Y$ be the output of that verified execution.
4. Use s_j^X and $v_j^Y \in V^Y$ to derive r_j^X as done in step 5 of the protocol.
5. Verify the messages from X to Y in the j-th execution of Π using random tapes r_j^X and the next message function Π_{NEXT}. If the transcript matches the j-th transcript in T_Π, then return $\perp$, otherwise return pk^X.

Fig. 4. Judge protocol for our compiler in Fig. 3.

8. If $\mathsf{flag} = \mathsf{detected}$, the simulator outputs a certificate cert in the following way: The simulator rewinds the adversary and this time runs the protocol as an honest party would do, except that it samples s_{R}^B under the constraint that $j^* \in I^B$. The simulator keeps rewinding until it detects cheating again in (j^*, loc^*), and outputs a certificate as an honest party would do (this concludes the simulation).
9. If the flag was not set: Reveal $(w')_i^A$ for $i \in I^B$ and receive $(w^*)_i^B$ from the adversary, and checks that they are equal to the w_i^B derived from s_i^B.
10. If the simulation reaches this stage, then $\mathcal{S}$ sets $\mathsf{flag} = \mathsf{all\_good}$, requests output y^A from $\mathcal{F}$ and moves to part B.

At this point the simulator $\mathcal{S}$ rewinds $\mathcal{A}$ back to right before step 1 and keeps rewinding $\mathcal{A}$ until the simulation is successful and $\mathcal{A}$ repeats the same cheating pattern as in part A[9]. In particular the simulator runs the following steps:

Simulation part B:

1. Do nothing.
2. Do nothing.
3. The simulator uses $\mathcal{S}_{\mathsf{OT}}$ to simulate both OT executions. In the one where it acts as a receiver it extracts $\mathcal{A}$'s input $(s')_1^A, \ldots, (s')_k^A$. In the one where it acts as the sender it extracts the vector I^A, picks random seeds s_i^B for all $i \in I^A$ and sends them to the adversary.
4. Depending on flag do the following:

---

[9] Making sure that our simulation runs in expected polynomial time can be achieved using standard techniques first introduced by Goldreich and Kahan [GK96]. See [HL10,Lin16] for an elaborate discussion of these techniques.

- If flag = all_good, then pick a random $i^* \notin I^A$ with the same distribution as in the protocol. For all $i \notin I^A$ with $i \neq i^*$ the simulator picks random v_i^B (while letting the w_i^B still undefined). It computes the tape $r_{i^*}^A$ using the simulator for the protocol $\mathcal{S}_\Pi$, and it computes $v_{i^*}^B = r_{i^*}^A \oplus u_{i^*}^A$, where the $u_{i^*}^A$ are derived from the $s_{i^*}^A$. Send all the the v_i^B to $\mathcal{A}$ and receive v_i^A from $\mathcal{A}$.
- If flag = undetected, then the simulator $\mathcal{S}$ runs this step as an honest party.

5. Depending on flag do the following:
   - If flag = all_good, then run all executions of Π honestly (picking random u_i^B and computing the corresponding random tape r_i^B to be used in the protocol) except for i^*, which is simulated using $\mathcal{S}_\Pi$. When $\mathcal{S}_\Pi$ requests the output, then the simulator provides it with y^A.
   - If flag = undetected, then the simulator $\mathcal{S}$ honestly executes the protocols based on its random seeds.

6. The simulator computes $\sigma^B \leftarrow \mathsf{Sign}(\mathsf{sk}^B, (T_{\mathsf{OT}}^A, V^A, T_\Pi))$ and sends it to $\mathcal{A}$. The adversary sends back σ^A.

7. Depending on flag do the following:

- If flag = all_good, then the simulator uses all seeds $(s')_i^A$ to check whether $\mathcal{A}$ behaved correctly during the executions of Π in step 4. If $\mathcal{A}$ deviated from any of the protocols, then it rewinds back to the beginning of part B, otherwise it terminates the simulation by honestly running the last two steps of the protocol, by choosing a random s_R^B and I^B (consistent with the choice of i^* in step 5) and sends back the corresponding $(w')_i^A$ derived from $(s')_i^A$ for $i \in I^B$.
- If flag = undetected, then the simulator checks whether $\mathcal{A}$ deviated from any of the protocol executions. If $\mathcal{A}$ did not deviate, if it deviated somewhere other than execution j^* in location loc^*, or if $j^* \notin I^B$, then rewind back to the beginning of part B. Otherwise, terminate the execution and send output $\widetilde{y}^B$ of execution i^* to the ideal functionality $\mathcal{F}$.

To conclude the proof, we show that the real and the simulated view of the adversary is indistinguishable. We defer these hybrids to the full version of the paper.

Public Verifiability. Without loss of generality assume that Alice is corrupt. If cheating occurred, then Alice must have deviated from one of the protocol executions in step 5 of the protocol, i.e., one of the messages in one of the executions that originates from Alice must be inconsistent with the random tape she should be using. If an honest Bob publishes a certificate, then cheating was detected, meaning that Bob obtained Alice's random tape for the execution in which she cheated. Since the transcripts of the protocol executions are signed by Alice, any party can verify that one message is inconsistent with one of Alice's random tapes. Importantly, since Alice has no way of knowing whether cheating will be successful or not before sending the signature in step 6, her decision to abort the protocol at any point before that has to be independent of Bob's choice of I^B.

Defamation-Freeness. Assume that $\mathcal{A}$ acting as Alice manages to break the defamation-freeness of the protocol and blames an honest B. We argue that this leads to a forgery to the underlying signature scheme, thus reaching a contradiction with the assumption of the theorem. In particular, for a Judge to blame Bob it must hold that in step 5 the judge finds a message from B to A which is not consistent with the next-message function of Π in execution j^*. Since Bob is honest, this means that either the transcript of the protocol T^* included in the certificate or the random tape r^* used by the judge to verify B in this step are not the ones that Bob used in the protocol (this of course is true for all $j \in [k]$ and therefore independent of which execution j^* is claimed by $\mathcal{A}$). Since Bob is honest he will not sign a protocol transcript $T^* \neq T_\Pi$, e.g., a transcript different than the one in the protocol executed by the honest Bob. Thus, r^* must be the wrong random tape. From step 4 we know that r^* is computed as the exclusive OR of a value v^* included in the certificate and signed by Bob and a value u^* derived from previous steps in the protocol. Again, since an honest Bob would not have signed the wrong $v^* \neq v_j^A$ if r^* is not the real randomness used by Bob in the protocol the it is because of a fault in u^*, which is in turn derived by the seed s^* received as the j^*-th output of A in the execution of the OT protocol. Now, if $s^* \neq s_{j^*}^B$ (the value used as input by Bob in the real protocol execution), this must be because either the OT protocol transcript T_{OT}^A in the certificate are incorrect or the randomness s^* included in the certificate is incorrect. Remember that both A's input and randomness in the OT protocol are derived by $(s^*)_{j^*}^A$ which is included in the certificate. Now it must be that $(s^*)_{j^*}^A$ leads to an input set I^* such that $j^* \in I^*$, or the judge would not be able to reconstruct $s_{j^*}^B$. Then, fixed any input set I^*, the perfect correctness of the OT protocol implies that given the correct protocol transcript T_{OT}^A there cannot exist any random tape such that the output of A in the protocol is incorrect. Thus, the transcript T_{OT}^A included in the certificate must be the wrong one. Once again, since Bob would not have signed the wrong transcript this implies that $\mathcal{A}$ has managed to forge a signature, thus reaching a contradiction.

□

In Theorem 1 we have assumed that each party checks less than half of the executions, which guarantees that there exists an execution that is not checked by either of the parties, but limits our deterrence factor ϵ to be less than $1/2$. We can modify our protocol to allow each party to check δk executions for any constant $1/2 \leq \delta < 1$, which allows us to obtain deterrence factors larger than $1/2$. The main observation here is that, as long as each party leaves a constant fraction of the executions unchecked, we have a constant probability of ending up with an execution that is not checked by either of the parties. In our modified protocol, we run the protocol from Fig. 3 as before up to including step 10. If there exists no execution that is not checked by either party, i.e., $[k] \setminus (I^A \cup I^B) = \emptyset$, then the parties simply start over the whole protocol run until the condition is satisfied.

Lemma 1. *The modified protocol described above runs in expected polynomial time.*

Proof. To clarify terminology, we will call one execution of the overall protocol from Fig. 3 an *outer execution* and the executions of Π within will be called *inner executions*. Observe that one outer execution runs in polynomial time. Let good be the event that the outer execution has an unchecked inner execution and let bad be the opposite event. If we can show that $\Pr[\text{good}] \geq c$, where c is a constant, then we are done, since this means that, in expectation, we need to run the outer protocol $1/c$ times until the event good happens.

Now observe that for any δk inner executions chosen by Alice, Bob would need to choose the remaining $k - \delta k$ with his δk choices to trigger the bad event. We can loosely upper bound the probability of this event by just considering the Bernoulli trial, where we only ask Bob to pick $k - \delta k$ inner executions (with repetitions) that were not chosen by Alice.

$$
\Pr[\text{bad}] \leq \binom{\delta k}{k - \delta k} \left(\frac{k - \delta k}{k} \right)^{k - \delta k} \left(1 - \frac{k - \delta k}{k} \right)^{\delta k - (k - \delta k)}
$$
$$
= \binom{\delta k}{k - \delta k} (1 - \delta)^{k(1 - \delta)} \delta^{k(2\delta - 1)}
$$

Now since both k and δ are constants, this whole expression is also a constant. Since the probability for bad is upper bounded by a constant, the event good is lower bounded by a constant too.

□

The calculation above is very loose and just aims to show that the expected number of repetitions is constant. To get a better feeling of how often we have to rerun the protocol for some given deterrence factor, consider for instance $k = 3$ with $\epsilon = 2/3$. The probability of the event good is the probability of Bob picking the same two executions that Alice picked, that is, the probability is $2/3 \cdot 1/2 = 1/3$, meaning that we need to repeat the protocol three times in expectation.

4   Efficient Two-Party Computation in the Preprocessing Model

In this section, we consider actively secure two-party protocols in the preprocessing model. Such protocols are composed of an input-independent preprocessing protocol Π_{OFF} for generating correlated randomness and separate protocol Π_{ON} for the online phase, which uses the preprocessed correlated randomness to compute some desired function on some given private inputs. The main advantage of such protocols is that the computational "heavy lifting" can be done in the preprocessing, such that the online phase can be executed very efficiently, in particular, much faster than what can be done by a standalone protocol that computes the same functionality without correlated randomness from scratch. One of the most well known protocols in the preprocessing model is the SPDZ [DPSZ12] protocol for computing arbitrary arithmetic circuits.

A natural question to ask is, whether we can use our results from Sect. 3 to construct more efficient protocols in the preprocessing model by relaxing the security guarantees from active to covert. The main idea here is to replace slow preprocessing protocols with active security by faster preprocessing protocols with passive security, which are then used in combination with our compiler from Theorem 1 to generate the correlated randomness. Note, that we do not need to apply our compiler to the online phase, which is already actively secure. That is, we can combine a preprocessing protocol with covert security with an actively secure online phase to obtain an overall protocol which is secure against covert adversaries as we show in the following Lemma.

Lemma 2. *Let $(\Pi_{\mathsf{OFF}}, \Pi_{\mathsf{ON}})$ be a protocol implementing $\mathcal{F}_f$ with active security, where the preprocessing protocol Π_{OFF} implements $\mathcal{F}_{\mathsf{OFF}}$ and Π_{ON} implements $\mathcal{F}_{\mathsf{ON}}$ with active security respectively. If $\widetilde{\Pi}_{\mathsf{OFF}}$ implements $\mathcal{F}_{\mathsf{OFF}}$ with security against covert adversaries (and public verifiability), then $(\widetilde{\Pi}_{\mathsf{OFF}}, \Pi_{\mathsf{ON}})$ implements $\mathcal{F}_f$ with security against covert adversaries (and public verifiability) with the same deterrence factor as $\widetilde{\Pi}_{\mathsf{OFF}}$.*

Proof. To prove the statement above, we need to construct a simulator $\mathcal{S}$ that interacts with the (covert version of) ideal functionality $\mathcal{F}_f$. By assumption, there exists simulators $(\mathcal{S}_{\mathsf{OFF}}, \mathcal{S}_{\mathsf{ON}})$ for $(\Pi_{\mathsf{OFF}}, \Pi_{\mathsf{ON}})$ and simulator $\widetilde{\mathcal{S}}_{\mathsf{OFF}}$ for $\widetilde{\Pi}_{\mathsf{OFF}}$. We will use $(\widetilde{\mathcal{S}}_{\mathsf{OFF}}, \mathcal{S}_{\mathsf{ON}})$ to simulate the view of the adversary $\mathcal{A}$. If $\mathcal{A}$ attempts to cheat *after* we finished the preprocessing simulation, then we can simply consider each attempt as an abort, since the online phase is actively secure. If during the preprocessing simulation $\mathcal{A}$ attempts to cheat and consequently $\widetilde{\mathcal{S}}_{\mathsf{OFF}}$ outputs a cheat command, we will forward it to $\mathcal{F}_f$. If cheating is undetected, then the ideal functionality returns all inputs and finishing the simulation is trivial. If cheating is detected, then we inform $\widetilde{\mathcal{S}}_{\mathsf{OFF}}$ and finish the simulation accordingly.

Observe that if cheating was detected in the preprocessing, then the simulated view is indistinguishable from a real one by assumption on the security of $\widetilde{\mathcal{S}}_{\mathsf{OFF}}$. If no cheating happened, then the actively secure and covertly secure versions of $\mathcal{F}_f$ have identical input/output behaviors and thus the simulated views are also indistinguishable by assumption.

The resulting protocol is also publicly verifiable, since the preprocessing protocol is publicly verifiable, and in the (actively secure) online phase only "blatant cheating" can be performed.

□

We now consider the concrete case of SPDZ for two-party computation. In the SPDZ preprocessing, Alice and Bob generate correlated randomness in the form of secret shared multiplication triples over some field $\mathbb{F}$, i.e. Alice should obtain a set $\{(a_i^A, b_i^A, c_i^A)\}_{i \in [\ell]}$ and Bob should obtain $\{(a_i^B, b_i^B, c_i^B)\}_{i \in [\ell]}$ such that for all $i \in [\ell]$ it holds that

$$(a_i^A + a_i^B) \cdot (b_i^A + b_i^B) = (c_i^A + c_i^B).$$

Current actively secure preprocessing protocols for generating such randomness use a combination of checks based on message authentication codes and zero-knowledge proofs. To obtain a passively secure counterpart that we can then plug into our compiler, we simply take one of those existing protocols and remove those checks.

For completeness, we sketch how one such preprocessing protocol could look like. Assume we are given access to a somewhat homomorphic encryption scheme, i.e., a scheme that allows us to compute additions $\mathsf{Enc}(\mathsf{pk}, a) + \mathsf{Enc}(\mathsf{pk}, b) = \mathsf{Enc}(\mathsf{pk}, a + b)$ and a limited number of multiplications $\mathsf{Enc}(\mathsf{pk}, a) \cdot \mathsf{Enc}(\mathsf{pk}, b) = \mathsf{Enc}(\mathsf{pk}, a \cdot b)$. Furthermore, assume that the decryption key sk is shared between Alice and Bob. For $P \in \{A, B\}$, each party P separately picks random values $\{a_i^P, b_i^P, r_i^P\}_{i \in [\ell]}$ and sends $\{\mathsf{Enc}(\mathsf{pk}, a_i^P), \mathsf{Enc}(\mathsf{pk}, b_i^P), \mathsf{Enc}(\mathsf{pk}, r_i^P)\}_{i \in [\ell]}$ to the other party. Each party $P \in \{A, B\}$ uses the homomorphic properties of the encryption scheme to compute $\{\mathsf{Enc}(\mathsf{pk}, r_i)\}_{i \in [\ell]}$, where $r_i = r_i^A + r_i^B$, and $\{\mathsf{Enc}(c_i)\}_{i \in [\ell]}$, where $c_i = \left(a_i^A + a_i^B\right) \cdot \left(b_i^A + b_i^B\right)$. Both parties jointly decrypt each ciphertext in the set $\{\mathsf{Enc}(\mathsf{pk}, c_i - r_i)\}$. Alice computes $\{c_i^A\}_{i \in [\ell]}$, where $c_i^A = (c_i - r_i) + r_i^A$ and Bob sets $\{c_i^B\}_{i \in [\ell]} := \{r_i^B\}_{i \in [\ell]}$. It is easy to see that this protocol outputs correct multiplication triples and securely hides the value of each c_i, since r_i is a uniformly random string.

One more detail that we need to consider here is that actively secure preprocessing protocols output correlated randomness along with authentication values. Our preprocessing protocol from above can easily be modified output these authentication values as well. Without going into too much detail, these authentication values are essentially the product of the secret shared multiplication triples and some encrypted key. These multiplications can be performed as above by using the homomorphic properties of the encryption scheme.

Combining the passively secure preprocessing protocol outlined above with our compiler from Theorem 1 results in a covertly secure preprocessing protocol with public verifiability that, for a deterrence factor of $1/3$, is roughly 3 times faster than the best known actively secure protocol. Since the total running time of SPDZ is mostly dominated by the running time of the preprocessing protocol, we also obtain an overall improvement in the total running time of SPDZ of roughly the same factor 3.

5   General Compiler for Two-Party Protocols

The first ingredient we need in this section is a two-party protocol $\widetilde{\Pi}_{\mathsf{SETUP}}$ that realizes $\mathcal{F}_{\mathsf{SETUP}}^{(m,t)}$ (Fig. 5) with passive security. Let Π_{SETUP} be the protocol one obtains by applying our compiler from Theorem 1 to the protocol $\widetilde{\Pi}_{\mathsf{SETUP}}$.

Given the protocol Π_{SETUP}, we are now ready to present our main compiler in Fig. 6. In the protocol description, we overload notation and identify the i-th virtual party $\mathbb{V}_i^P$ belonging to real party P with the set containing the random tapes and symmetric encryption keys used by this party in the protocol. This set, together with the public ciphertext containing the party's input encrypted with its own symmetric encryption key, completely determines the behaviour

$$\mathcal{F}_{\mathsf{SETUP}}^{(m,t)}$$

The functionality interacts with Alice and Bob.

Upon receiving $(\mathsf{init}, \mathsf{sid})$ from both Alice and Bob, the functionality does the following for $P \in \{A, B\}$:

1. For $i \in [m]$, pick s_i^P uniformly at random.
2. For $i, j \in [m]$, pick $k_{(i,j)}^P$ uniformly at random with $k_{(i,j)}^P = k_{(j,i)}^P$.
3. For $i \in [m]$,
    (a) define $\mathbb{V}_i^P = (s_i^P, \{k_{(i,j)}^P\}_{j \in [m]})$.
    (b) compute $(c_i^P, d_i^P) \leftarrow \mathsf{Com}(\mathbb{V}_i^P)$.
4. Pick $I^P \subset [m]$, uniformly at random with $|I^P| = t$.
5. Output $(\{c_i^B, c_i^A, d_i^A\}_{i \in [m]}, I^A, \{d_j^B\}_{j \in I^A})$ and $(\{c_i^A, c_i^B, d_i^B\}_{i \in [m]}, I^B, \{d_j^A\}_{j \in I^B})$ to A and B respectively.

Fig. 5. Ideal functionality for our correlated randomness setup.

of that virtual party in the protocol. Let $f(x^A, x^B)$ be the function Alice and Bob would like to compute on their respective inputs x^A and x^B. Let Π be a $2m$-party protocol that implements a related functionality

$$\mathcal{F}_g(x_1^A, \ldots, x_m^A, x_1^B, \ldots, x_m^B) := (z_1^A, \ldots, z_m^A, z_1^B, \ldots, z_m^B),$$

where

$$f\left(\bigoplus_{i \in [m]} x_i^A, \bigoplus_{i \in [m]} x_i^B\right) = \bigoplus_{i \in [m], P \in \{A,B\}} z_i^P.$$

with security against $m + t$ passive corruptions. That is, the ideal functionality $\mathcal{F}_g$ takes as input an m-out-of-m secret sharing of x^A and x^B and computes a $2m$-out-of-$2m$ secret sharing of $f(x^A, x^B)$.

Theorem 2. *Let f be an arbitrary two-party functionality and let g be the related functionality as defined above. Let Π be a $2m$-party protocol that implements the ideal functionality $\mathcal{F}_g$ with security against $m + t$ passive corruptions. Let Π_{SETUP} be the protocol from Fig. 3 realizing ideal functionality $\mathcal{F}_{\mathsf{SETUP}}$ from Fig. 5 with deterrence factor $\frac{t}{m}$. Let Com be a commitment scheme that realizes $\mathcal{F}_{\mathsf{Com}}$. Then the compiler illustrated in Fig. 6 and 7 implements the two-party ideal functionality $\mathcal{F}_f$ with security and public verifiability against covert adversaries with deterrence factor $\epsilon = t/m$.*

Proof. We will proceed by proving security, public verifiability, and defamation-freeness separately. Without loss of generality again we assume that Alice is corrupted by the adversary $\mathcal{A}$. The case for Bob being corrupted is completely symmetrical. For proving security, we construct a simulator $\mathcal{S}$ playing the role of Alice in the ideal world and using $\mathcal{A}$ as a subroutine. Let $\mathcal{S}_{\mathsf{SETUP}}$ be the simulator corresponding to the ideal functionality $\mathcal{F}_{\mathsf{SETUP}}$.

Alice has input x^A and key-pair $(\mathsf{sk}^A, \mathsf{pk}^A)$. Bob has input x^B and key-pair $(\mathsf{sk}^B, \mathsf{pk}^B)$.

0. For each $P \in \{A, B\}$: abort in any case of blatant cheating e.g., if P receives an invalid signature or a wrong commitment opening in step 2, 4, or 6.

1. Alice and Bob run Π_{SETUP} to obtain y^A and y^B respectively, where

$$y^A = \left(\{c_i^B, c_i^A, d_i^A\}_{i \in [m]}, I^A, \{d_j^B\}_{j \in I^A} \right)$$

and

$$y^B = \left(\{c_i^A, c_i^B, d_i^B\}_{i \in [m]}, I^B, \{d_j^A\}_{j \in I^B} \right).$$

2. Alice and Bob verify that the outputs they received from Π_{SETUP} are well-formed, and if so, each $P \in \{A, B\}$ parses $\mathsf{Open}(c_i^P, d_i^P)$ as $\mathbb{V}_i^P = \left(s_i^P = (r_i^P, u_i^P), \{k_{(i,j)}^P\}_{j \in [m]} \right)$, then computes and sends $\sigma_c^P \leftarrow \mathsf{Sign}\left(\mathsf{sk}^P, \{c_i^P\}_{i \in [m]} \right)$.

3. Each $P \in \{A, B\}$ secret shares its input x^P as $x^P = \bigoplus_{i=1}^m x_i^P$.

4. For each $(S, R) \in \{(A, B), (B, A)\}$, for $i \in [m]$, the sender S computes $e_i^S \leftarrow \mathsf{Enc}(k_{(i,i)}^S, x_i^S)$ and $\sigma_i^S \leftarrow \mathsf{Sign}(sk^S, e_i^S)$ and sends (e_i^S, σ_i^S) to the receiver R.

5. For each $R \in \{A, B\}$, for $i \in I^R$, party R decrypts $x_i^S \leftarrow \mathsf{Dec}_{k_{(i,i)}}(e_i^S)$.

6. Alice and Bob jointly run the $2m$-party protocol Π, where each $\mathbb{V}_i^P$ uses input x_i^P and randomness r_i^P. In the following, let T be the transcript of all exchanged messages so far and $(v, j) \leftarrow \Pi_{\mathsf{next}}(i, x_i^S, r_i^S, T)$ be the next message computed by virtual party $\mathbb{V}_i^S$ belonging to real party S given the current protocol transcript T. Then we have three cases:

    (a) $\mathbb{V}_i^S$ **sends** v **to** $\mathbb{V}_j^R$ (virtual parties belonging to different real parties): Party S computes $\sigma_{T\|v} \leftarrow \mathsf{Sign}(\mathsf{sk}^S, T\|v)$ and sends $(v, \sigma_{T\|v})$ to R. If $i \in I^R$, then R checks whether the sent message was honestly generated. If not, then R outputs $\mathsf{cert} = (\mathsf{type}_1, i, j, (T, v, \sigma_{T\|v}), (\{c_k^S\}_{k \in [m]}, \sigma_c^S, d_i^S))$ and aborts.

    (b) $\mathbb{V}_i^S$ **sends** v **to** $\mathbb{V}_j^S$ (virtual parties belonging to same real party): Party S sends $(e, \sigma_{T\|e})$ to R, where $e \leftarrow \mathsf{Enc}(k_{(i,j)}^S, v)$ and $\sigma_{T\|e} \leftarrow \mathsf{Sign}(\mathsf{sk}^S, T\|e)$. If $j \in I^R$, then R decrypts and adds the message to its local view of $\mathbb{V}_j^S$. If $i \in I^R$, then R decrypts and checks, whether the message is generated correctly. If not, then R outputs $\mathsf{cert} = (\mathsf{type}_2, i, j, (T, e, \sigma_{T\|e}), (\{c_k^S\}_{k \in [m]}, \sigma_c^S, d_i^S))$

    (c) **Output phase:** For $S \in \{A, B\}$, $i \in [m]$, $\mathbb{V}_i^S$ obtains z_i^S. Party $\mathbb{V}_i^S$ sends $(\gamma_i^S, \sigma_{T\|\gamma}^S)$ to R, where $(\gamma_i^S, \delta_i^S) \leftarrow \mathsf{Com}(z_i^S; u_i^S)$ and $\sigma_i^S \leftarrow \mathsf{Sign}(\mathsf{sk}^S, T\|\gamma_i^S)$. If $i \in I^R$ then R recomputes z_i^S and the commitment γ_i^S. If cheating is detected, then R outputs $\mathsf{cert} = (\mathsf{type}_3, i, 0, (T, \gamma, \sigma_{T\|\gamma}), (\{c_k^S\}_{k \in [m]}, \sigma_c^S, d_i^S))$

7. Alice and Bob exchange all decommitments δ_i^P, open the output shares z_i^P and reconstruct the output $f(x^A, x^B)$.

Fig. 6. Compiler from security against passive to security with public verifiability against covert adversaries for arbitrary two-party protocols.

Judge has input $\left(\mathsf{pk}^A, \mathsf{pk}^B, \mathsf{cert}\right)$

---

1. The judge parses $\mathsf{cert} = (\mathsf{type}_b, i, j, (T, v, \sigma_{T\|v}), (\{c_k^X\}_{k\in[m]}, \sigma_c^X, d_i^X))$
2. If $\mathsf{Verify}\left(\mathsf{pk}^X, \sigma_c^X, \{c_k^X\}_{k\in[m]}\right) = 0$, return $\perp$.
3. If $\mathsf{Verify}\left(\mathsf{pk}^X, \sigma_{T\|v}, T\|v\right) = 0$, return $\perp$.
4. Let $\mathbb{V}_i^X = \mathsf{Open}(c_i^X, d_i^X)$, parse $\mathbb{V}_i^X = ((r_i^X, u_i^X), \{k_{(i,j)}^X\}_{j\in[m]})$, unless $\mathbb{V}_i^X = \perp$ in which case return $\perp$.
5. Compute $x_i^X \leftarrow \mathsf{Dec}(k_{(i,i)}^X, e_i^X)$ from e_i^X in T.
6. Compute $v^* = \Pi_{\mathsf{NEXT}}\left(i, x_i^X, r_i^X, T\right)$.
7. Depending on b do the following:
   (a) $b = 1$: If $v_j^* \neq v$, then return pk^X.
   (b) $b = 2$: If $v_j^* \neq \mathsf{Dec}(k_{(i,j)}, v)$, then return pk^X.
   (c) $b = 3$: If $v^* = (\mathsf{out}, z^*)$ and $v \neq \mathsf{Com}(z^*; u_i^X)$, then return pk^X.
8. Return 0.

Fig. 7. Judge protocol for our two-party protocol in Fig. 6.

Simulation:

0. Generate $(\mathsf{sk}^B, \mathsf{pk}^B)$ and send pk^B to $\mathcal{A}$. Like a real party, the simulator aborts in any case of blatant cheating.

1. Simulate the functionality $\mathcal{F}_{\mathsf{SETUP}}$.
   (a) In case $\mathcal{A}$ inputs cheat, the simulator forwards cheat to $\mathcal{F}_f$. If $\mathcal{F}_f$ outputs detected, the simulation sets flag = detected and stops.
   (b) If $\mathcal{F}_f$ outputs undetected, it also provides the simulator with the input x^B of the honest party. The simulator then sets flag = undetected and allows $\mathcal{A}$ to pick the output y^B of B in $\mathcal{F}_{\mathsf{SETUP}}$ and runs the protocol honestly, finally it has to provide $\mathcal{F}_f$ with the output for B in the ideal world, and he does so by running the protocol as an honest party would do with $\mathcal{A}$, and using the output z^B obtained in this execution.
   (c) Finally, if $\mathcal{A}$ does not attempt to cheat in $\mathcal{F}_{\mathsf{SETUP}}$, the simulator picks the output of the corrupt party y^A in the following way: Pick a random set I^A, and run the simulator $\mathcal{S}_\Pi$ of the $2m$-party protocol Π, to produce the random tapes of all the virtual parties belonging to A for all $i \in [m]$ and of the checked virtual parties belonging to B for $i \in I^A$. The simulator also picks random keys $k_{(i,j)}^A$ for $i, j \in [m]$ and $k_{(i,j)}^B$ for all $i, j \in I^A$ at random. Now the simulator can honestly produce commitments $(c_i^A, d_i^A) \leftarrow \mathsf{Com}(\mathbb{V}_i^A)$ for all $i \in [m]$ and $(c_i^B, d_i^B) \leftarrow \mathsf{Com}(\mathbb{V}_i^B)$ for $i \in I^A$. Finally, use the simulator $\mathcal{S}_{\mathsf{Com}}$ to simulate all commitments c_i^B with $i \notin I^A$.

2. As in the protocol, send the signature σ_c^B to $\mathcal{A}$. Receive σ_c^A (and abort if invalid).

3. Do nothing. (see Footnote 8)

4. Receive e_i^A, σ_i^A for $i \in [m]$. Compute $e_i^B = \mathsf{Enc}(k_{(i,i)}^B, \tilde{x}_i^B)$ where $\tilde{x}_i^B$ is uniformly random if $i \in I^A$ or 0 otherwise.

5. Decrypt $x_i^A \leftarrow \mathsf{Dec}(k_{(i,j)}^A, e_i^A)$ for all $i \in [m]$ and reconstruct x^A.

6. Simulate the execution of the $2m$-party protocol Π in the following way: Use the simulator $\mathcal{S}_\Pi$ to simulate the execution of the unchecked virtual parties belonging to B i.e., $\mathbb{V}_i^B$ for $i \notin I^A$, and execute the checked parties belonging to B as an honest party would do e.g., consistent with the random tapes and keys from step 1c, and inputs $\tilde{x}_i^B$ as defined in step 4.

In particular, this means that all messages that are sent from the virtual parties belonging to B to the virtual parties belonging to A or to the checked virtual parties belonging to B are generated using the simulator. The former kind are simply sent to $\mathcal{A}$ while the latter kind are first encrypted using the appropriate keys. To simulate the message exchanged between pairs of unchecked parties belonging to B, send encryptions of 0 to $\mathcal{A}$. Moreover, if the simulator gets to step 6c, it produces commitments γ_i^B using the simulator for the commitment $\mathcal{S}_{\mathsf{Com}}$ for $i \in [m] \setminus I^A$, and commits honestly to the shares obtained by the virtual parties for all $i \in I^A$.

This concludes the description of how the simulator simulates *outgoing* messages from $\mathcal{S}$ to $\mathcal{A}$. We now describe how the simulator reacts to *incoming* messages from $\mathcal{A}$ to $\mathcal{S}$: the simulator performs the checks in steps 6a–6c of the protocol for all virtual parties belonging to A i.e., $\forall i \in [m]$. If $\mathcal{A}$ deviated in any of its virtual parties i^*, then the simulator sends (cheat, A) to the ideal functionality $\mathcal{F}_f$, which responds with $\mathsf{resp} = \{\mathsf{detected}, \mathsf{undetected}\}$.

(a) If $\mathsf{flag} = \mathsf{detected}$, the simulator produces a certificate as an honest party would do (since the simulator knows the output y^A of the $\mathcal{F}_{\mathsf{SETUP}}$, the simulator knows the decommitting information for all $i \in [m]$).

(b) If $\mathsf{flag} = \mathsf{undetected}$, the simulator receives the input of the honest party x^B. Now the simulator rewinds $\mathcal{A}$ to step 4 where it now generates the $\tilde{x}_i^B$'s as a secret sharing of x^B. The simulator keeps rewinding $\mathcal{A}$ until it again cheats in the same position (e.g., same virtual party and protocol location), and then completes the execution. The simulator reconstructs the output z^* from this execution and provides it to the ideal functionality $\mathcal{F}_f$.

7. If no cheating was detected, the simulator sets the $\mathsf{flag} = \mathsf{all\_good}$. Then it computes the $\mathcal{A}$ shares of the output z_i^A for all $i \in [m]$ by executing the virtual parties belonging to $\mathcal{A}$ using their random tapes and inputs which have been already extracted in steps 1 and 4 of the simulation. Then the simulator inputs x^A (which was reconstructed in step 4 of the simulation) to $\mathcal{F}_f$ and receives the output z. Now the simulator decommits honestly to the commitments γ_i^B for $i \in I^A$ but uses the simulator $\mathcal{S}_{\mathsf{Com}}$ to produce decommitting information δ_i^B for the commitments γ_i^B with $i \notin I^A$ such that the opened values z_i^B are uniformly random under the constraint that $\oplus_{i=1}^m z_i^B = z \oplus_{i=1}^m z_i^A$. This concludes the simulation.

To conclude the proof, we show that the real and the simulated view of the adversary is indistinguishable. We defer these hybrids to the full version of the paper.

Public Verifiability. Without loss of generality assume that Alice is corrupt. Since the setup phase is already publicly-verifiable, we only need to worry about public verifiability in the rest of the protocol. If an honest Bob outputs a certificate it must be because Alice has cheated during step 6 of the protocol i.e., one of the messages is not consistent with the input and random tape for that virtual party. Since Alice signs every outgoing message together with the entire transcript of the protocol execution, as well as her commitments in step 2 of the protocol, the judge can verify whether the message is correct or not.

Defamation-Freeness. Assume that $\mathcal{A}$ acting as Alice manages to break the defamation-freeness of the protocol and blames an honest B. We argue that this leads to a forgery to the underlying signature scheme, thus reaching a contradiction with the assumption of the theorem. In particular, for a Judge to blame Bob it must hold that in step 7 the judge finds a message from B to A which is not consistent with the next-message function of Π in execution j^*. Consider e.g., step 7a. Since Bob is honest, if the judge blames Bob it must be the case that that either the transcript of the protocol (T^*, v^*) included in the certificate, the random tape r^* or the input x^* used by the judge to verify B in this step are not the ones that Bob used in the protocol (this of course is true for all $j \in [m]$ and therefore independent of which execution j^* is claimed by $\mathcal{A}$). Since Bob is honest he will not sign a protocol transcript $(T^*, v^*) \neq (T, v)$, e.g., a transcript different than the one in the protocol executed by the honest Bob. Thus, x^* or r^* must be the wrong input or random tape. From step 5 we know that x^* is computed by decrypting some ciphertext e^* included in T^* using key k^*. Again, since Bob is honest the signed e^* must be the correct one from the protocol execution, so the fault must be in k^*. This is derived in step 4 as the opening of some commitment c^* with decommitting information d^*. As the commitment c^* was signed this must be the right commitment $c_{j^*}^B$ that Bob received from the setup functionality. And, since the commitment is binding, the decommitting information d^* cannot open c^* to anything else but the view of the virtual party used by Bob in the honest execution of the protocol. The judge can also blame Bob in steps 7b or 7c. The argument for why this is not possible for a PPT $\mathcal{A}$ is very similar to the one for the case 7a with few differences: in case 7b we also need to argue that $\mathcal{A}$ cannot blame Bob making the judge use a wrong decryption key k^*. This is however taken care of since the key is part of the view of the virtual party, which is committed (and the commitment is signed by Bob). Similarly, in case 7c, $\mathcal{A}$ could also blame an innocent Bob by making the judge use the wrong randomness u^* but, this is also taken care of since the randomness is part of the view of the virtual party, which is committed (and the commitment is signed by Bob).

6   Compiler for Multiparty Computation

It is natural to ask, whether the compilers described in the previous sections of the paper extend to the multiparty setting. In this section we provide some intuition for how the compiler from Sect. 5 can be extended the multiparty setting with a constant fraction of corruptions. More concretely, we argue that any $(cn^2 + n)$-party protocol Π with passive security against $cn^2 + cn$ corruptions, for some $1/2 < c < 1$, can be compiled into a n-party protocol with covert security and public verifiability against cn corruptions.[10]

Assume we have n parties $P_1, \ldots, P_n$ with private inputs $x^1, \ldots, x^n$, who would like to compute $f(x^1, \ldots, x^n)$, and we would like to tolerate cn corruptions, for some $1/2 < c < 1$. Assume that Π implements the following $(cn^2 + n)$-party functionality, where $m = cn + 1$

$$\mathcal{F}_g \begin{pmatrix} x_1^1, \ldots, x_m^1, \\ \vdots \\ x_1^n, \ldots, x_m^n \end{pmatrix} := \begin{pmatrix} \{z_i^1\}_{i \in [m]} \\ \vdots \\ \{z_i^n\}_{i \in [m]} \end{pmatrix}$$

where

$$\bigoplus_{i \in [m], j \in [n]} z_i^j = f\left(\bigoplus_{i \in [m]} x_i^1, \ldots, \bigoplus_{i \in [m]} x_i^n \right)$$

The compiler for the multiparty setting is very similar to the compiler for the two-party setting. Each real party P_i will simulate virtual parties V_j^i for $1 \leq j \leq cn + 1$. All virtual parties will jointly run a passively secure $(cn^2 + n)$-party protocol. For every pair of real parties (P_i, P_j) with $i \neq j$, we let P_i check *one* virtual party of P_j, chosen uniformly at random. Observe that for any honest P_j, the corrupted parties learn at most cn out of the $m = cn + 1$ corresponding virtual parties' views, thus the adversary will not learn enough shares to reconstruct the input of the honest party P_i. In total, the adversary learn the views of

$$\overbrace{cn(cn + 1)}^{\text{corrupted by } \mathcal{A}} + \overbrace{(1 - c)n \cdot cn}^{\text{checked by } \mathcal{A}} = cn^2 + cn$$

virtual parties which is exactly the number of passive corruptions that we have assumed are tolerated by the protocol Π.

To instantiate the compiler we need a generalized multiparty version of our two-party setup functionality $\mathcal{F}_{\text{SETUP}}$ from Fig. 5. This generalized functionality, called $\mathcal{F}_{\text{SETUP}}^{(n, cn+1)}$, can be found in Fig. 8.

Observe that the multiparty functionality generates symmetric keys for *all* communication channels, including the ones between virtual parties belonging to different real parties. The reason is that we could have the case, where a virtual party of P_1 sends a message to a virtual party of P_2, which should be checked by P_3. Thus we need to ensure that P_3 can decrypt the message if he is indeed checking the corresponding virtual party. Each real party P_i

---

[10] $c < 1/2$ is possible, but here we are specifically interested in the dishonest majority setting.

$$\mathcal{F}_{\text{SETUP}}^{(n,m)}$$

The functionality interacts with parties $P_1, \ldots, P_n$.

Upon receiving $(\text{init}, \text{sid})$ from each P_i, the functionality performs the following actions for each $\ell \in [n]$:

1. The functionality picks $r_1^\ell, \ldots, r_m^\ell$ uniformly at random.
2. For $i, j \in [m]$ and any $\ell' \in [n]$, it picks $k_{(\ell',j)}^{(\ell,i)}$ uniformly at random such that $k_{(\ell',j)}^{(\ell,i)} = k_{(\ell,i)}^{(\ell',j)}$.
3. For $i \in [m]$
   (a) define $V_i^\ell = \left(r_i^\ell, \{k_{(\ell',j)}^{(\ell,i)}\}_{j \in [m], \ell' \in [n]} \right)$.
   (b) compute $c_i^\ell \leftarrow \text{Com}(V_i^\ell)$ and $d_i^\ell \leftarrow \text{Open}(c_i^\ell)$
4. For $i \in [n]$, pick $I_\ell^\ell \in [m]$ uniformly at random.
5. Return $\left(\{c_i^{\ell'}\}_{\ell' \in [n], i \in [m]}, \{d_i^\ell\}_{i \in [m]}, \{I_{\ell'}^\ell, \{d_i^{\ell'}\}_{i \in I_{\ell'}^\ell}\}_{\ell' \in [n]} \right)$ to P_ℓ.

Fig. 8. Ideal functionality for our correlated randomness setup in the multiparty setting.

secret shares its input x^i into shares $x_1^i, \ldots, x_{cn+1}^i$, encrypts every share x_j^i under key $k_{(i,j)}^{(i,j)}$, and broadcasts the encrypted shares to all real parties. The virtual parties jointly execute the passively secure protocol Π. Whenever a virtual party sends a message to any other virtual party, it encrypts the message with the corresponding communication channel key and broadcasts the message among all real parties. Once the computation using Π is complete, each party commits to its output share. Finally all parties open their commitments and compute the desired output.

Security of this construction can be argued in a very similar fashion to the compiler from Sect. 5. The main technical difference between the two proofs lies in the calculation of the deterrence factor. Assume that the adversary misbehaves in some corrupt party P_i^*. This means that the adversary misbehaves in at least one of the $cn + 1$ corresponding virtual parties. Let V_j^i be that party. Out of those $cn + 1$ virtual parties, the $(1-c)n$ honest parties each check one uniformly random one. The probability that none of the honest parties check V_j^i is

$$\left(1 - \frac{1}{cn+1} \right)^{(1-c)n} \approx 1 - \frac{(1-c)n}{cn+1}$$

by binomial approximation. Thus we get a deterrence factor $\epsilon \approx \frac{1-c}{c}$.

Acknowledgements. This work was supported by the European Research Council (ERC) under the European Unions's Horizon 2020 research and innovation programme under grant agreement No 669255 (MPCPRO), grant agreement No 803096 (SPEC), Danish Independent Research Council under Grant-ID DFF-6108-00169 (FoCC), and the Concordium Blockchain Research Center.

References

[ABT18] Applebaum, B., Brakerski, Z., Tsabary, R.: Perfect secure computation in two rounds. In: Beimel, A., Dziembowski, S. (eds.) TCC 2018. LNCS, vol. 11239, pp. 152–174. Springer, Cham (2018). https://doi.org/10.1007/978-3-030-03807-6_6

[ACGJ19] Ananth, P., Choudhuri, A.R., Goel, A., Jain, A.: Two round information-theoretic MPC with malicious security. In: Ishai, Y., Rijmen, V. (eds.) EUROCRYPT 2019. LNCS, vol. 11477, pp. 532–561. Springer, Cham (2019). https://doi.org/10.1007/978-3-030-17656-3_19

[AL07] Aumann, Y., Lindell, Y.: Security against covert adversaries: efficient protocols for realistic adversaries. In: Vadhan, S.P. (ed.) TCC 2007. LNCS, vol. 4392, pp. 137–156. Springer, Heidelberg (2007). https://doi.org/10.1007/978-3-540-70936-7_8

[AO12] Asharov, G., Orlandi, C.: Calling out cheaters: covert security with public verifiability. In: Wang, X., Sako, K. (eds.) ASIACRYPT 2012. LNCS, vol. 7658, pp. 681–698. Springer, Heidelberg (2012). https://doi.org/10.1007/978-3-642-34961-4_41

[BMR90] Beaver, D., Micali, S., Rogaway, P.: The round complexity of secure protocols (extended abstract). In: 22nd ACM STOC, pp. 503–513 (1990)

[Bra87] Bracha, G.: An O(log n) expected rounds randomized byzantine generals protocol. J. ACM 34(4), 910–920 (1987)

[CDI+13] Cohen, G., et al.: Efficient multiparty protocols via log-depth threshold formulae - (extended abstract). In: Canetti, R., Garay, J.A. (eds.) CRYPTO 2013. LNCS, vol. 8043, pp. 185–202. Springer, Heidelberg (2013). https://doi.org/10.1007/978-3-642-40084-1_11

[DGN10] Damgård, I., Geisler, M., Nielsen, J.B.: From passive to covert security at low cost. In: Micciancio, D. (ed.) TCC 2010. LNCS, vol. 5978, pp. 128–145. Springer, Heidelberg (2010). https://doi.org/10.1007/978-3-642-11799-2_9

[DI05] Damgård, I., Ishai, Y.: Constant-round multiparty computation using a black-box pseudorandom generator. In: Shoup, V. (ed.) CRYPTO 2005. LNCS, vol. 3621, pp. 378–394. Springer, Heidelberg (2005). https://doi.org/10.1007/11535218_23

[DKL+13] Damgård, I., Keller, M., Larraia, E., Pastro, V., Scholl, P., Smart, N.P.: Practical covertly secure MPC for dishonest majority – or: breaking the SPDZ limits. In: Crampton, J., Jajodia, S., Mayes, K. (eds.) ESORICS 2013. LNCS, vol. 8134, pp. 1–18. Springer, Heidelberg (2013). https://doi.org/10.1007/978-3-642-40203-6_1

[DOS18] Damgård, I., Orlandi, C., Simkin, M.: Yet another compiler for active security or: efficient MPC over arbitrary rings. In: Shacham, H., Boldyreva, A. (eds.) CRYPTO 2018. LNCS, vol. 10992, pp. 799–829. Springer, Cham (2018). https://doi.org/10.1007/978-3-319-96881-0_27

[DPSZ12] Damgård, I., Pastro, V., Smart, N., Zakarias, S.: Multiparty computation from somewhat homomorphic encryption. In: Safavi-Naini, R., Canetti, R. (eds.) CRYPTO 2012. LNCS, vol. 7417, pp. 643–662. Springer, Heidelberg (2012). https://doi.org/10.1007/978-3-642-32009-5_38

[GK96] Goldreich, O., Kahan, A.: How to construct constant-round zero-knowledge proof systems for NP. J. Cryptol. 9(3), 167–189 (1996). https://doi.org/10.1007/BF00208001

[GMS08] Goyal, V., Mohassel, P., Smith, A.: Efficient two party and multi party computation against covert adversaries. In: Smart, N. (ed.) EUROCRYPT 2008. LNCS, vol. 4965, pp. 289–306. Springer, Heidelberg (2008). https://doi.org/10.1007/978-3-540-78967-3_17

[HKK+19] Hong, C., Katz, J., Kolesnikov, V., Lu, W., Wang, X.: Covert security with public verifiability: faster, leaner, and simpler. In: Ishai, Y., Rijmen, V. (eds.) EUROCRYPT 2019. LNCS, vol. 11478, pp. 97–121. Springer, Cham (2019). https://doi.org/10.1007/978-3-030-17659-4_4

[HL10] Hazay, C., Lindell, Y.: Efficient Secure Two-Party Protocols - Techniques and Constructions. ISC. Springer, Heidelberg (2010). https://doi.org/10.1007/978-3-642-14303-8

[HM00] Hirt, M., Maurer, U.M.: Player simulation and general adversary structures in perfect multiparty computation. J. Cryptol. 13(1), 31–60 (2000). https://doi.org/10.1007/s001459910003

[IK00] Ishai, Y., Kushilevitz, E.: Randomizing polynomials: a new representation with applications to round-efficient secure computation. In: 41st FOCS, pp. 294–304 (2000)

[IKNP03] Ishai, Y., Kilian, J., Nissim, K., Petrank, E.: Extending oblivious transfers efficiently. In: Boneh, D. (ed.) CRYPTO 2003. LNCS, vol. 2729, pp. 145–161. Springer, Heidelberg (2003). https://doi.org/10.1007/978-3-540-45146-4_9

[IKOS07] Ishai, Y., Kushilevitz, E., Ostrovsky, R., Sahai, A.: Zero-knowledge from secure multiparty computation. In: 39th ACM STOC, pp. 21–30 (2007)

[IPS08] Ishai, Y., Prabhakaran, M., Sahai, A.: Founding cryptography on oblivious transfer – efficiently. In: Wagner, D. (ed.) CRYPTO 2008. LNCS, vol. 5157, pp. 572–591. Springer, Heidelberg (2008). https://doi.org/10.1007/978-3-540-85174-5_32

[KM15] Kolesnikov, V., Malozemoff, A.J.: Public verifiability in the covert model (almost) for free. In: Iwata, T., Cheon, J.H. (eds.) ASIACRYPT 2015. LNCS, vol. 9453, pp. 210–235. Springer, Heidelberg (2015). https://doi.org/10.1007/978-3-662-48800-3_9

[Lin16] Lindell, Y.: How to simulate it - a tutorial on the simulation proof technique. Cryptology ePrint Archive, Report 2016/046 (2016). http://eprint.iacr.org/2016/046

[LOP11] Lindell, Y., Oxman, E., Pinkas, B.: The IPS compiler: optimizations, variants and concrete efficiency. In: Rogaway, P. (ed.) CRYPTO 2011. LNCS, vol. 6841, pp. 259–276. Springer, Heidelberg (2011). https://doi.org/10.1007/978-3-642-22792-9_15

[vHL05] von Ahn, L., Hopper, N.J., Langford, J.: Covert two-party computation. In: 37th ACM STOC, pp. 513–522 (2005)

[Yao82] Yao, A.C.-C.: Protocols for secure computations (extended abstract). In: 23rd FOCS, pp. 160–164 (1982)

MPC with Friends and Foes

Bar Alon[(✉)], Eran Omri[(✉)], and Anat Paskin-Cherniavsky[(✉)]

Department of Computer Science, Ariel University, Ariel, Israel
alonbar08@gmail.com, {omrier,anatpc}@ariel.ac.il

Abstract. Classical definitions for secure multiparty computation assume the existence of a single adversarial entity controlling the set of corrupted parties. Intuitively, the definition requires that the view of the adversary, corrupting t parties, in a real-world execution can be simulated by an adversary in an ideal model, where parties interact only via a trusted-party. No restrictions, however, are imposed on the view of honest parties in the protocol, thus, if honest parties obtain information about the private inputs of other honest parties – it is not counted as a violation of privacy. This is arguably undesirable in many situations that fall into the MPC framework. Nevertheless, there are secure protocols (e.g., the 2-round multiparty protocol of Ishai et al. [CRYPTO 2010] tolerating a single corrupted party) that instruct the honest parties to reveal their private inputs to all other honest parties (once the malicious party is somehow identified).

In this paper, we put forth a new security notion, which we call *FaF-security*, extending the classical notion. In essence, (t, h^*)-FaF-security requires the view of a subset of up to h^* honest parties to also be simulatable in the ideal model (in addition to the view of the malicious adversary, corrupting up to t parties). This property should still hold, even if the adversary leaks information to honest parties by sending them non-prescribed messages. We provide a thorough exploration of the new notion, investigating it in relation to a variety of existing security notions. We further investigate the feasibility of achieving FaF-security and show that every functionality can be computed with (computational) (t, h^*)-FaF full-security, if and only if $2t + h^* < m$. Interestingly, the lower-bound result actually shows that even fair FaF-security is impossible in general when $2t + h^* \geq m$ (surprisingly, the view of the malicious attacker is not used as the trigger for the attack).

We also investigate the optimal round complexity for (t, h^*)-FaF-secure protocols and give evidence that the leakage of private inputs of honest parties in the protocol of Ishai et al. [CRYPTO 2010] is inherent.

1 Introduction

In the setting of secure multiparty computation (MPC), the goal is to allow a set of m mutually distrustful parties to compute some function of their private inputs

Research supported by ISF grant 152/17, and by the Ariel Cyber Innovation Center in conjunction with the Israel National Cyber directorate in the Prime Minister's Office.

in a way that preserves some security properties, even in the face of adversarial behavior by some of the parties. Classical security definitions (cf., [25]) assume the existence of a single adversarial entity controlling the set of corrupted parties. The two most common types of adversaries are *malicious* adversaries (which may instruct the corrupted parties to deviate from the prescribed protocol in any possible way), and *semi-honest* adversaries (which must follow the instructions of the protocol, but may try to infer additional information based on the joint view of the corrupted parties).

Classical security definition. Some of the most basic security properties that may be desired are correctness, privacy, independence of inputs, fairness, and guaranteed output delivery. A general paradigm for defining the desired security of protocols is known as the ideal vs. real paradigm. This paradigm avoids the need to specify a list of desired properties. Rather, security is defined by describing an ideal functionality, where parties interact via a trusted party to compute the task at hand. A real-world protocol is then deemed secure (against a class $\mathcal{C}$ of adversaries), if no adversary $\mathcal{A} \in \mathcal{C}$ can do more harm than an adversary in the ideal-world. In some more detail, the definition requires that the view of the adversary, corrupting t parties, in a real-world execution can be simulated by an adversary (corrupting the same t parties) in the ideal-world.

Classical instantiations of this paradigm, however, pose *no* restrictions on the view of honest parties in the protocol. Hence, such definitions do not count it as a violation of privacy if honest parties learn private information about other honest parties. This is arguably undesirable in many situations that fall into the MPC framework. Furthermore, when considering MPC solutions for real-life scenarios, it is hard to imagine that possible users would agree to have their private inputs revealed to honest parties (albeit not to malicious ones). Indeed, there is no guarantee that an honest party would not get corrupted at some later point in the future. If that honest party has learned some sensitive information about another party's input during the protocol's execution (say, the password to its bank account), then this information may still be used in a malicious manner. Furthermore, as most of us are reluctant to reveal the password to our bank account even to our own friends, it is natural to consider a model, where every uncorrupted party is honest-but-curious by itself, operating simultaneously to the malicious adversary.[1]

There are two manners in which honest parties may come to learn some private information about other parties (in a secure protocol). The first is if the protocol itself instructs the honest parties to reveal some information about their private inputs (which is not implied by the output) to all other honest parties (once all malicious parties are somehow identified). An example of such a protocol is the 2-round m-party protocol (with $m \geq 5$) of Ishai et al. [32], tolerating a single malicious party.

---

[1] This is indeed the origin of the term FaF-security (protecting one's privacy from friends and foes alike).

Alternatively, honest parties may also be exposed to the private information of other parties if the adversary sends them parts of its view during the execution (although, not instructed to do so by the protocol). We stress that such an attack is applicable to many classical results in MPC that assume an upper bound of t malicious parties and rely on $(t + 1)$-out-of-m secret sharing. Consider, for example, the BGW protocol [11], which is secure against $t < m/3$ corruptions. In the first round of the protocol, the parties share their inputs in a $(t + 1)$-out-of-m Shamir's secret sharing scheme [39]. If an adversary, controlling t parties, sends all its t shares to an honest party, then this honest party can reconstruct the inputs of all other parties.

It may be natural to try to overcome the second type of information leakage by simply instructing honest parties to disregard and erase unsolicited messages sent to them by the adversary. However, in many settings assuming that the parties are able to reliably erase parts of their state might be unrealistic, due to e.g., physical limitations on erasures. Moreover, it is not even always clear how to define what should be erased in the first place. Consider, for example, the case that the adversary has some room for action or some redundancy in the messages it is instructed to send by the protocol. In such a case, the adversary can implant additional non-prescribed information about other parties into these messages. Thus, the honest parties receiving these messages are not able to detect the leakage of information. If, say, the adversary implanted a sharing of some private information among a subset of honest parties, then, a 'semi-honest' entity can reconstruct this information by taking control over the parties in this subset and seeing their internal states.

In this paper, we investigate the following question that arises from the above discussion.

Can the classical notion of security for malicious adversaries be extended to also prevent leakage of private information to (possibly colluding) subsets of (semi)-honest parties?

The issue of honest parties being able to obtain information (not available to them from their inputs and from the output of the functionality) was already shortly mentioned in [38]. They showed how to construct verifiable secret sharing (and thus compute any functionality) with unconditional security, assuming broadcast and an honest majority. Their solution for preventing from honest parties learning additional information was to increase the threshold for the secret sharing used in the protocol. However, this came at the expense of the bound on the number of corrupted parties.

The solution of [38] may seem as a natural answer to the above question, and it may further seem that any secure protocol could be turned into one that prevents leakage to honest parties by increasing the bound on the number of corrupt parties. Say, for example that the protocol should withstand t malicious parties and we wish to avoid leakage to sets of size h^* semi-honest parties. In this case, taking a protocol that is secure (by classical definition) against $t + h^*$ malicious parties may seem to suffice for the desired security. However, now one must consider the efficiency toll incurred by increasing the security threshold.

Furthermore, it could be the case that increasing the threshold would render the protocol altogether insecure. Indeed, in Sect. 4.1, we give such an example of a functionality that cannot be computed in the face of $t + h^*$ malicious parties, but can be computed with full security in the face of t malicious, while avoiding leakage to any subset of h^* honest parties.

Quite surprisingly, we further show that the approach of increasing the threshold simply *does not work* in general. In particular, there exist protocols with standard full security against $t + 1$ malicious parties, yet t malicious parties could leak information to an honest party.[2]

1.1 Our Contribution

In this paper, we address the above question by putting forth a new security notion, which we call *FaF-security*, extending standard (static, malicious) MPC security (in the stand-alone model). We give a *full-security* variant as well as a *security-with-abort* variant for the new notion. In essence, (t, h^*)-FaF-security requires that for every malicious adversary $\mathcal{A}$ corrupting t parties, and for any disjoint subset of h^* parties, both the view of the adversary and the joint view of the additional h^* parties can be simulated (separately) in the ideal model. A more elaborate summary of the various definitions is given in Sect. 1.1.1. A comprehensive discussion appears in Sect. 3.

We accompany the new security notion with a thorough investigation of its feasibility and limitations in the various models of interest. Most notably, we discuss the feasibility of achieving full FaF-security against computational adversaries, and show that it is achievable for any functionality if and only if $2t + h^* < m$. Interestingly, the lower-bound result actually shows that any protocol admits a round in which the adversary can leak the output to some parties without learning it, however, not allowing other honest parties to learn it. Hence, even fair FaF-security is impossible in general when $2t + h^* \geq m$. In Sect. 1.1.2 we elaborate on these results. We also investigated the optimal round-complexity of FaF-secure protocols, and the feasibility of obtaining statistical/perfect FaF-security. A summary of these also appears in Sect. 1.1.2.

Finally, we provide an thorough exploration of how the new notion relates to a variety of existing security notions. Specifically, we show some counter intuitive facts on how FaF-security relates to standard malicious security and mixed-adversaries security. See Sect. 1.1.3 for more on that.

1.1.1 FaF-Security – A Generalization of Classical Security

Before moving on to describe our new security notion in more detail, we first recall the notion of static, malicious, stand-alone security. We stress that while there are stronger security notions, some of which we mention below, this is arguably the most standard notion, serving much of the works on secure multiparty computation. Security is defined via the real vs. ideal paradigm. Here, the

---

[2] It remains open whether preventing leakage using a *different* protocol is possible.

security is described as an ideal functionality, where all parties (including the adversary) interact with a trusted entity. A malicious adversary is, thus, limited to selecting the inputs of the subset of corrupted parties.

A real-world protocol (for the functionality at hand) is deemed secure if it emulates the ideal setting. In a bit more detail, the protocol is t-secure, for a class $\mathcal{C}$ of adversaries, if for every adversary $\mathcal{A} \in \mathcal{C}$, corrupting at most t parties and interacting with the remaining parties, there exists an ideal-world adversary (called simulator) that outputs a view for the real-world adversary that is distributed closely to its view in an actual random execution of the real protocol. A static adversary is one that chooses which parties to corrupt before the execution of the protocol begins. A formal definition of security is given in Sect. 3 as a special case of FaF-security.

The notion of FaF-security. We now give a more detailed overview of the new notion of security. As above, we follow the real vs. ideal paradigm, and strengthen the requirements of standard security. We say that a protocol Π computes a functionality f with (t, h^*)-FaF security (with respect to a class $\mathcal{C}$ of adversaries), if for any adversary $\mathcal{A} \in \mathcal{C}$ (statically) corrupting at most t parties, the following holds: (i) there exists a simulator S that can simulate (in the ideal-world) $\mathcal{A}$'s view in the real-world (so far, this is standard security), and (ii) for any subset $\mathcal{H}$ (of size at most h^*) of the uncorrupted parties, there exists a "semi-honest" simulator $S_{\mathcal{H}}$, such that, given the parties' inputs and S's ideal-world view (i.e., its randomness, inputs, auxiliary input, and output received from the trusted party), $S_{\mathcal{H}}$ generates a view that is indistinguishable form the real-world view of the parties in $\mathcal{H}$, i.e., $\left(\text{VIEW}_{\mathcal{H}}^{\text{REAL}}, \text{Out}^{\text{REAL}}\right)$ is indistinguishable from $\left(\text{VIEW}_{S_{\mathcal{H}}}^{\text{IDEAL}}, \text{Out}^{\text{IDEAL}}\right)$.

The reason for giving $S_{\mathcal{H}}$ the ideal-world view of S is that in the real-world, nothing prevents the adversary from sending its view to honest parties. Observe that since the definition requires that the adversary is simulatable according to the standard definition, it also protects the parties in $\mathcal{H}$ from the adversary. This condition is in agreement with our motivation, where the parties in $\mathcal{H}$ are honest but might later collude in a different protocol. The universal quantifier on $\mathcal{H}$ yields, for example, that the definition also captures the model where every uncorrupted party is honest-but-curious by itself. The formal definition appears in Sect. 3.

FaF full-security and FaF security-with-abort. So far, we left vague the way that outputs are being distributed to parties by the trusted party in the ideal-world. The first option is that the trusted party sends the appropriate output to each of the parties. This captures the notion of full-security, as it guarantees that the honest parties always receive the output of the computation (in addition to other properties, such as correctness and privacy). Cleve [16] showed that (standard) full-security is not generally achievable. This led to a relaxed notion of security, called security-with-abort. This notion is captured very similarly to the above full-security, with the difference being that in the ideal-world, the trusted party first gives the output to the adversary, which in turn decides whether the honest parties see the output or not. This notion is naturally augmented with identifiability, by requiring the adversary to identify at least one malicious party in case the output is not given to all honest parties.

In this work, we appropriately define and consider a full-security variant and a security with (identifiable) abort variant of FaF-security. To define FaF security-with-identifiable-abort, we need to account for scenarios, where some of the uncorrupted parties learn their output in the real-world while others do not. Therefore, in the ideal execution, we explicitly allow the "semi-honest" simulator $S_{\mathcal{H}}$ to receive the output from the trusted party. The formal definition appears in Sect. 3.1.

It is also natural to consider a stronger security notion, where the joint view of the malicious adversary is simulatable *together* with the view of parties in $\mathcal{H}$. In Sect. 5.3, we show that this variant is strictly stronger than the variant defined above. In fact, we show that the GMW protocol [26] satisfies the weaker notion of FaF-security, but not the stronger notion. In the following, we will sometimes refer to the weaker notion as *weak FaF-security*, and refer to the stronger notion as *strong FaF-security*.

A natural property that is highly desirable from any definition is to allow (sequential) composition. We show that both the weak variant and the strong variant of FaF-security satisfy this property. Due to space limitations, the proof is given in the full-version [1].

1.1.2   Feasibility and Limitations of FaF-Secure Computation

Our main theorem provides a characterization of the types of adversaries, for which we can compute any multiparty functionality with computational FaF full-security.

Theorem 1 (informal). *Let $t, h^*, m \in \mathbb{N}$. Assuming OT and OWP exist, any m-party functionality f can be computed with (weak) computational (t, h^*)-FaF full-security, if and only if $2t + h^* < m$.*

For the positive direction, we first show that the GMW protocol admits FaF security-with-identifiable-abort. Then, we reduce the computation to FaF security-with-identifiable-abort, using a player elimination technique. That is, the parties compute a functionality whose output is an $(m - t)$-out-of-m secret sharing of f. Since the joint view of the malicious and semi-honest parties contain $t + h^* < m - t$ shares, they learn nothing from the output. We stress that the adversary itself cannot see the output unless all honest parties see it, and hence, cannot bias the output.

We now turn to the negative direction. Interestingly, we essentially show that for $m \leq 2t + h^*$, any m-party protocol admits a round in which an adversary (corrupting t parties) can leak the output to some h^* uncorrupted parties, while, not allowing other honest parties to learn the output.

Somewhat surprisingly, for the case where $t < m/2$, there are protocols where the adversary's view consists of only random values throughout the execution.

Indeed, in our attack, the adversary learns nothing about the output, and furthermore, the view of the adversary is not used as a trigger for the attack.

We next give an overview of the proof. First, by a simple player partitioning argument, we reduce the general m-party case to the 3-party case, where $t = h^* = 1$. Let A, B, and C be three parties. Let f be a one-way permutation. We consider the following functionality. Party A holds a string a, party C holds a string c, and party B holds y_A, y_C. The output of all parties is (a, c) if $f(a) = y_A$ and $f(c) = y_C$, and $\perp$ otherwise. We assume the strings a and c are sampled uniformly, and that $y_A = f(a), y_C = f(c)$.

An averaging argument yields that there must exists a round i, where two parties, say A together with B, can recover (a, c) with significantly higher probability than C together with B. Our attacker corrupts A, acts honestly (using its original input a) until round i and then aborts (regardless of its view so far). Finally, as the protocol terminates, A will send its entire view to B. This allows B it to recover (a, c) with significantly higher probability than C.

Intuitively, in order to have the output of the honest party C in the ideal world distributed as in the real world (where it is with noticeable probability $\perp$), the malicious simulator have to change its input (sent to the trusted party) with high enough probability. However, in this case, the semi-honest simulator for B, receives $\perp$ from the trusted party. Since the only information it has on c is $f(c)$, by the assumed security of f, the simulator for B will not be able to recover c with non-negligible probability. Hence, B's simulator will fail to generate a valid view for B.

We stress that since A aborts at round i, independently of its view, our attack works even if the parties have a simultaneous broadcast channel. The detailed proof appears in Sect. 4.2.

Low round complexity. Optimal round complexity of protocols is a well studied question for classical MPC (see, e.g., [7,8,24,32]). Here, we explore the optimal number of rounds required for general computation with $(1, 1)$-FaF full-security. Our motivation for investigating this question comes from the two-round protocol of Ishai et al. [32], tolerating a single malicious party. In the second round, the honest parties can either complete the computation or are able to detect the malicious party. If a party was detected cheating, then the honest parties *reveal their inputs* to some of the other honest parties.

Clearly, this is not considered secure according to FaF-security. Indeed, we prove that there are functionalities that cannot be computed with $(1, 1)$-FaF security in less than three round. We interpret this as evidence that some kind of leakage on the inputs of honest parties is necessary in order to achieve a two-round protocol.[3] The next theorem completes the picture, asserting that for $m \geq 9$ parties, the optimal round for $(1, 1)$-FaF full-security is three.

---

[3] Naturally, we do not claim that the protocol must instruct honest parties to leak information. Rather, we prove that a malicious adversary can leak the private information of honest parties.

Theorem 2 (informal). *Let $m \geq 9$. There exists an m-party functionality that has no 2-round protocol that computes it with (weak) $(1,1)$-FaF full-security. On the other hand, assuming that pseudorandom generators exist, for any m-party functionality, there exists a 3-round protocol that computes it with strong $(1,1)$-FaF full-security.*

We now present an overview of the proof. For the negative direction, we rely on the proof by Gennaro et al. [24] of the impossibility to compute $(x_1, x_2, \bot, \ldots, \bot) \mapsto x_1 \wedge x_2$ in two rounds against two corrupted parties. We observe that the adversary they proposed corrupts one party maliciously and another semi-honestly. Moreover, the semi-honest corrupted party has no input, hence the actions of the adversary can be adopted into our setting. More concretely, we show that an adversary corrupting P_2, can force all of the parties to gain specific information on x_1, yet by sending its view (at the end of the interaction) to a carefully chosen honest party, it can "teach" that party some information about x_1 that no other party has (not even the adversary itself). This proof, in fact, works for any $m \geq 3$.

For the positive direction, we consider the protocol of Damgård and Ishai [18]. Using share conversion techniques ([17]) and the 2-round verifiable secret sharing (VSS) protocol of [23], they were able to construct a 3-round protocol that tolerates $t < m/5$ corruptions. We follow similar lines as [18]. First we show how to slightly modify the VSS protocol so it will admit FaF-security. Then, by making the observation that the parties in the protocol of [18] hold only shares of the other parties' input, we are able to show that by increasing the threshold of the sharing scheme, the protocol admits FaF-security. The construction of the VSS protocol follows similar lines as in [23]. We further show that the protocol can be generalized to admit (t, h^*)-FaF full-security, whenever $5t + 3h^* < m$.

Information theoretic FaF-security. Information theoretic security have been studied extensively in the MPC literature, see e.g., [11,21,38]. We further generalize the corruption model to allow non-threshold adversaries (for both the malicious and the semi-honest adversaries). We consider the same adversarial structure as Fitzi et al. [21], called *monotone mixed adversarial structure*. Roughly, it states that turning a malicious party to being semi-honest does not compromise the security of the protocol. As discussed previously, this is not generally the case.

We prove the following theorem, characterizing the types of adversaries, for which we can compute any multiparty functionality with information theoretic security.

Theorem 3 (informal). *Let $\mathcal{R} \subseteq \{(\mathcal{I}, \mathcal{H}) : \mathcal{I} \cap \mathcal{H} = \emptyset\}$ be a monotone mixed adversarial structure over a set of parties $\mathcal{P}$. Then:*

1. *Any m-party functionality f can be computed with $\mathcal{R}$-FaF full-security, assuming an available broadcast channel, if and only if*

$$\mathcal{I}_1 \cup \mathcal{H}_1 \cup \mathcal{I}_2 \cup \mathcal{H}_2 \neq \mathcal{P},$$

   for every $(\mathcal{I}_1, \mathcal{H}_1), (\mathcal{I}_2, \mathcal{H}_2) \in \mathcal{R}$.

2. *Any m-party functionality f can be computed with $\mathcal{R}$-FaF full-security (without broadcast), if and only if*

$$\mathcal{I}_1 \cup \mathcal{H}_1 \cup \mathcal{I}_2 \cup \mathcal{H}_2 \neq \mathcal{P} \ \text{and} \ \mathcal{I}_1 \cup \mathcal{I}_2 \cup \mathcal{I}_3 \neq \mathcal{P},$$

for every $(\mathcal{I}_1, \mathcal{H}_1), (\mathcal{I}_2, \mathcal{H}_2), (\mathcal{I}_3, \mathcal{H}_3) \in \mathcal{R}$.

3. *Any m-party functionality f can be computed with $\mathcal{R}$-FaF full-security, if and only if*

$$\mathcal{I}_1 \cup \mathcal{H}_1 \cup \mathcal{I}_2 \cup \mathcal{H}_2 \cup \mathcal{I}_3 \neq \mathcal{P},$$

for every $(\mathcal{I}_1, \mathcal{H}_1), (\mathcal{I}_2, \mathcal{H}_2), (\mathcal{I}_3, \mathcal{H}_3) \in \mathcal{R}$.

Interestingly, the positive direction holds with respect to strong FaF-security, and the negative holds with respect to weak FaF-security. Additionally, as Fitzi et al. [21] showed that the same conditions hold with respect to mixed adversaries, this yields an equivalence between all three notions of security, as far as general MPC goes for monotone adversarial structures.

The proof follows similar lines as [21]. For the positive direction we show how the parties can securely emulate a 4-party BGW protocol tolerating a single malicious party. The negative direction is done by reducing the computation to a functionality known to be impossible to compute securely (according to the standard definition), using a player partitioning argument. The full treatment of information theoretic FaF-security with respect to monotone adversarial structures is deferred to the full-version of the paper [1].

1.1.3   The Relation Between FaF Security and Other Definitions

The relation between FaF-security and standard full-security. It is natural to explore how the new definition relates to classical definitions both in the computational and in the information-theoretic settings.

We start by comparing FaF-security to the standard definition (for static adversaries). It is easy to see that standard t-security does not imply in general (t, h^*)-FaF full-security, even for functionalities with no inputs (see Sect. 5.1 for a simple example showing this). Obviously, (t, h^*)-FaF-security readily implies its classical t-security counterpart. One might expect that classical $(t + h^*)$-security must imply (t, h^*)-FaF-security. We show that this is not the case in general. Specifically, in Example 1, we present a protocol that admits traditional (static) malicious security against t corruptions, however, it does not admit $(t - 1, 1)$-FaF-security.

In contrast to the above, we claim that adaptive $(t + h^*)$-security implies strong (t, h^*)-FaF full-security. Recall that an adaptive adversary is one that can choose which parties to corrupt during the execution and after the termination of the protocol and depending on its view. Indeed, strong FaF-security can be seen as a special case of adaptive security. We do believe, however, that the FaF model is of special interest, and specifically, that in many scenarios, the full power of adaptive security is an overkill.

The relation between FaF-security and mixed-adversaries security. The notion of "mixed adversaries" was introduced in [21]. It considers a *single* entity that corrupts a subset $\mathcal{I}$ maliciously, and another subset $\mathcal{H}$ semi-honestly. Similarly, the simulator for a mixed adversary is a single simulator controlling the parties in $\mathcal{I} \cup \mathcal{H}$, with the restriction of only being able to change the inputs of the parties in $\mathcal{I}$.

It is instructive to compare the mixed-adversary notion to that of FaF-security, which in turn, can be viewed as if there are two *distinct* adversaries (which do not collude) – one malicious and one semi-honest. One might expect that (t, h^*)-mixed full-security would imply (t, h^*)-FaF full-security. However, similarly to the case with standard security, we show the that this is not generally the case in the *computational* setting (cf., Example 2).

1.2   Related Works

Definitions of standard MPC where the subject of much investigation in the area of MPC. Notable works introducing various definitions are [5,6,13,25,37]. The question of achieving (standard) full-security was given quite some attention. See, e.g., [4,16,19,28,36] for two parties, [4,11,27] in the multiparty setting.

The definition we propose can also be viewed as if there where two different adversaries, one is corrupting *actively* and the second is corrupting *passively*, while the adversaries cannot exchange messages outside of the environment. Some forms of "decentralized" adversaries were considered in [2,3,14,34], with the motivation of achieving *collusion-free* protocols. However, unlike our definition, the definitions they proposed were both complicated, and did not allow an external entity to corrupt more than a single party.

Fitzi et al. [21] where the first to consider the notion of mixed adversaries. In their model, an adversary can corrupt a subset of the parties actively, and another subset passively. Moreover, their work considered general non-threshold adversary structures. They gave a complete characterization of the adversary structures for which general unconditional MPC is possible, for four different models: Perfect security with and without broadcast, and statistical security (with negligible error probability) with and without broadcast. Beerliová-Trubíniová et al. [9], Hirt et al. [31] further studied adversaries that can additionally fail-corrupt another subset of parties. They give the exact conditions for general *secure function evaluation* (SFE) and general MPC to be possible for perfect security, statistical security, and for computational security, assuming a broadcast channel. In all these settings they confirmed the strict separation between SFE and MPC. Koo [35] considered adversaries that can maliciously corrupt certain parties, and in addition omission corrupt others. Omission corruptions allow the adversary to either block incoming and outgoing messages. Zikas et al. [41] further refined this model by introducing the notions of send-omission corruptions, where the adversary can selectively block outgoing messages, and receive-omission corruption, where the adversary can selectively block incoming messages. For a full survey of works on those notions of mixed adversaries see Zikas [40].

1.3 Organization

In Sect. 2 we present the required preliminaries. In Sect. 3 we formally define our new notion of FaF-security. Then, in Sect. 4 we characterize computational FaF full-security. In Sect. 5 we compare the new definition to other existing notions of security.

2 Preliminaries

We use calligraphic letters to denote sets, uppercase for random variables, lowercase for values, and we use bold characters to denote vectors. For $n \in \mathbb{N}$, let $[n] = \{1, 2 \ldots n\}$. For a set $\mathcal{S}$ we write $s \leftarrow \mathcal{S}$ to indicate that s is selected uniformly at random from $\mathcal{S}$. Given a random variable (or a distribution) X, we write $x \leftarrow X$ to indicate that x is selected according to X. A PPTM is a polynomial time Turing machine.

A function $\mu(\cdot)$ is called negligible, if for every polynomial $p(\cdot)$ and all sufficiently large n, it holds that $\mu(n) < 1/p(n)$. For a vector $\mathbf{v}$ of dimension n, we write v_i for its i-th component, and for $\mathcal{S} \subseteq [n]$ we write $\mathbf{v}_{\mathcal{S}} = (v_i)_{i \in \mathcal{S}}$. For a randomized function (or an algorithm) f we write $f(x)$ to denote the random variable induced by the function on input x, and write $f(x; r)$ to denote the value when the randomness of f is fixed to r. Other preliminaries are standard and for space considerations are deferred to the full version [1].

3 The New Definition – FaF Full-Security

In this section, we present our new security notion, aiming to strengthen the classical definition of security in order to impose privacy restrictions on (subsets of) honest parties, even in the presence of malicious behavior by other parties. Crucially, we wish to prevent the adversary from leaking private information of one subset of parties to another subset of parties, even though neither subset is under its control. The definition is written alongside the classical definition.

We follow the standard *ideal vs. real* paradigm for defining security. Intuitively, the security notion is defined by describing an ideal functionality, in which both the corrupted and non-corrupted parties interact with a trusted entity. A real-world protocol is deemed secure if an adversary in the real-world cannot cause more harm than an adversary in the ideal-world. In the classical definition, this is captured by showing that an ideal-world adversary (simulator) can simulate the full view of the real world adversary. For FaF security, we further require that the view of any subset of the uncorrupted parties can be simulated in the ideal-world (including the interaction with the adversary).

To shed some light on some of the subtleties in defining the proposed notion, in the full-version we review several possible approaches for capturing the desired security notion (avoiding leakage to honest parties), and demonstrate why they fall short in doing so. In Sect. 5, we compare the actual definition we put forth with the standard full-security definition, and with the mixed-adversaries definition.

To make the above intuition more formal, fix a (possibly randomized) m-ary function $f = \{f_n \colon \mathcal{X}_1^n \times \cdots \times \mathcal{X}_m^n \mapsto \mathcal{Y}_1^n \times \cdots \times \mathcal{Y}_m^n\}_{n \in \mathbb{N}}$ and let Π be a protocol for computing f. We further let $\mathcal{X}^n = \mathcal{X}_1^n \times \cdots \times \mathcal{X}_m^n$.

The FaF Real Model

An m-party protocol Π for computing the function f is defined by a set of m interactive probabilistic polynomial-time Turing machines $\mathcal{P} = \{P_1, \ldots, P_m\}$. Each Turing machine (party) holds the security parameter 1^n as a joint input and a private input $x_i \in \mathcal{X}_i^n$. The computation proceeds in rounds. In each round, the parties either broadcast and receive messages over a common broadcast channel, or send messages to an individual party over a secure channel. The number of rounds in the protocol is expressed as some function $r(n)$ in the security parameter (where $r(n)$ is bounded by some polynomial). At the end of the protocol, the (honest) parties output a value according to the specifications of the protocol. When the security parameter is clear from the context, we remove it from the notations. The view of a party consists of the party's input, randomness, and the messages received throughout the interaction.

We consider two adversaries. The first is a malicious adversary $\mathcal{A}$ that controls a subset $\mathcal{I} \subset \mathcal{P}$. The adversary has access to the full view of all corrupted parties. Additionally, the adversary may instruct the corrupted parties to deviate from the protocol in any way it chooses. We make explicit the fact that the adversary can send messages (even if not prescribed by the protocol) to any uncorrupted party – in every round of the protocol, and can do so after all messages for this round were sent (see Remark 1 for more on this). The adversary is non-uniform, and is given an auxiliary input $z_\mathcal{A}$. The second adversary is a semi-honest adversary $\mathcal{A}_\mathcal{H}$ that controls a subset $\mathcal{H} \subset \mathcal{P} \setminus \mathcal{I}$ of the remaining parties (for the sake of clarity, we will only refer to the parties in $\mathcal{I}$ as corrupted). Similarly to $\mathcal{A}$, this adversary also has access to the full view of its parties. However, $\mathcal{A}_\mathcal{H}$ *cannot* instruct the parties to deviate from the prescribed protocol in any way, but may try to infer information about non-corrupted parties, given its view in the protocol (which includes the joint view of parties in $\mathcal{H}$). This adversary is also non-uniform, and is given an auxiliary input $z_\mathcal{H}$. When we say that the adversary is computationally bounded, we mean it is a PPTM. Both adversaries are static, that is, they choose the subset to corrupt prior to the execution of the protocol. For a subset of parties $\mathcal{S} \subseteq \mathcal{P}$, we let $\mathbf{x}_\mathcal{S}$ be the vector of inputs of the parties in $\mathcal{S}$, specifically, $\mathbf{x}_\mathcal{I}$ and $\mathbf{x}_\mathcal{H}$ denote the vector of inputs of the parties controlled by $\mathcal{A}$ and $\mathcal{A}_\mathcal{H}$ respectively.

We next define the real-world global view for security parameter $n \in \mathbb{N}$, an input sequence $\mathbf{x} = (x_1, \ldots, x_m)$, and auxiliary inputs $z_\mathcal{A}, z_\mathcal{H} \in \{0,1\}^*$ with respect to adversaries $\mathcal{A}$ and $\mathcal{A}_\mathcal{H}$ controlling the parties in $\mathcal{I} \subset \mathcal{P}$ and $\mathcal{H} \subset \mathcal{P} \setminus \mathcal{I}$ respectively. Let $\text{OUT}_{\mathcal{A},\Pi}^{\text{REAL}}(1^n, \mathbf{x})$ denote the outputs of the uncorrupted parties (those in $\mathcal{P} \setminus \mathcal{I}$) in a random execution of Π, with $\mathcal{A}$ corrupting the parties in $\mathcal{I}$. Further let $\text{VIEW}_{\mathcal{A},\Pi}^{\text{REAL}}(1^n, \mathbf{x})$ be the adversary's view during an execution of Π, which contains its auxiliary input, its random coins, the inputs of the parties in $\mathcal{I}$, and the messages they see during the execution of the protocol. In addition, we let $\text{VIEW}_{\mathcal{A},\mathcal{A}_{\mathcal{H}},\Pi}^{\text{REAL}}(1^n, \mathbf{x})$ be the view of $\mathcal{A}_{\mathcal{H}}$ during an execution of Π when running alongside $\mathcal{A}$ (this view consists of their random coins, their inputs, and the messages they see during the execution of the protocol, and specifically, those non-prescribed messages sent to them by the adversary).

We denote the global view in the real model by

$$\text{REAL}_{1^n,\mathbf{x},z_{\mathcal{A}},z_{\mathcal{H}}}^{\Pi,\mathcal{A},\mathcal{A}_{\mathcal{H}}} = \left(\text{VIEW}_{\mathcal{A},\Pi}^{\text{REAL}}(1^n, \mathbf{x}),\ \text{VIEW}_{\mathcal{A},\mathcal{A}_{\mathcal{H}},\Pi}^{\text{REAL}}(1^n, \mathbf{x}),\ \text{OUT}_{\mathcal{A},\Pi}^{\text{REAL}}(1^n, \mathbf{x})\right).$$

It will be convenient to denote

$$\text{REAL}_{1^n,\mathbf{x},z_{\mathcal{A}},z_{\mathcal{H}}}^{\Pi,\mathcal{A},\mathcal{A}_{\mathcal{H}}}(\mathcal{A}) = \left(\text{VIEW}_{\mathcal{A},\Pi}^{\text{REAL}}(1^n, \mathbf{x}),\ \text{OUT}_{\mathcal{A},\Pi}^{\text{REAL}}(1^n, \mathbf{x})\right),$$

i.e., the projection of $\text{REAL}_{1^n,\mathbf{x},z_{\mathcal{A}},z_{\mathcal{H}}}^{\Pi,\mathcal{A},\mathcal{A}_{\mathcal{H}}}$ to their view of the adversary and the uncorrupted parties' output (those in $\mathcal{P} \setminus \mathcal{I}$), and denote

$$\text{REAL}_{1^n,\mathbf{x},z_{\mathcal{A}},z_{\mathcal{H}}}^{\Pi,\mathcal{A},\mathcal{A}_{\mathcal{H}}}(\mathcal{A}_{\mathcal{H}}) = \left(\text{VIEW}_{\mathcal{A},\mathcal{A}_{\mathcal{H}},\Pi}^{\text{REAL}}(1^n, \mathbf{x}),\ \text{OUT}_{\mathcal{A},\Pi}^{\text{REAL}}(1^n, \mathbf{x})\right).$$

When Π is clear from the context, we will remove it for brevity.

Remark 1. A subtlety in the proposed model is how to deal with messages sent by the adversary at a later point in time, after the protocol execution terminated. Specifically, if honest parties need to react to such messages, then the protocol has no predefined termination point. It is possible to incorporate a parameter τ of time to the security definition, asserting that the protocol is secure until time τ. To keep the definition clean and simple, we overcome this subtlety by only allowing the real-world adversary to communicate with other (non-corrupted) parties until the last round of the protocol.

The FaF Ideal Model

We next describe the interaction in the *FaF full-security ideal model*, which specifies the requirements for fully secure FaF computation of the function f with security parameter n. Let $\mathcal{A}$ be an adversary in the ideal-world, which is given an auxiliary input $z_{\mathcal{A}}$ and corrupts the subset $\mathcal{I}$ of the parties called *corrupted*. Further let $\mathcal{A}_{\mathcal{H}}$ be a semi-honest adversary, which is controlling a set of parties denoted $\mathcal{H}$ and is given an auxiliary input $z_{\mathcal{H}}$. We stress that the classical formulation of the ideal model assumes $\mathcal{H} = \emptyset$.

The FaF ideal model – full-security.

Inputs: Each party P_i holds 1^n and $x_i \in \mathcal{X}_i^n$. The adversaries $\mathcal{A}$ and $\mathcal{A}_{\mathcal{H}}$ are given each an auxiliary input $z_{\mathcal{A}}, z_{\mathcal{H}} \in \{0,1\}^*$ respectively, and x_i for every P_i controlled by them. The trusted party T holds 1^n.

Parties send inputs: Each uncorrupted party $P_j \in \mathcal{P} \setminus \mathcal{I}$ sends x_j as its input to T. The malicious adversary $\mathcal{A}$ sends a value $x_i' \in \mathcal{X}_i^n$ as the input for party $P_i \in \mathcal{I}$. Write $(x_1', \ldots, x_m')$ for the tuple of inputs received by the trusted party.

The trusted party performs computation: The trusted party T selects a random string r and computes $\mathbf{y} = (y_1, \ldots, y_m) = f(x'_1 \ldots, x'_m; r)$ and sends y_i to each party P_i.

The malicious adversary sends its (ideal-world) view: $\mathcal{A}$ sends to $\mathcal{A}_\mathcal{H}$ its randomness, inputs, auxiliary input, and the output received from T.

Outputs: Each uncorrupted party (i.e., not in $\mathcal{I}$) outputs whatever output it received from T, the parties in $\mathcal{I}$ output nothing. $\mathcal{A}$ and $\mathcal{A}_\mathcal{H}$ output some function of their respective view.

Note that we gave $\mathcal{A}_\mathcal{H}$ the ideal-world view of $\mathcal{A}$. This is done due to the fact that in the real-world, we cannot prevent the adversary from sending its entire view to the uncorrupted parties. Consider the following example. Suppose three parties computed a functionality $(\bot, \bot, \bot) \mapsto (r, \bot, r)$, where r is some random string. A corrupted P_1 can send r to P_2 at the end of the interaction, thereby teaching it the output of an honest party. In the ideal-world described above, $\mathcal{A}_{P_2}$ will receive r as well, allowing us to simulate this interaction.

We next define the ideal-world global view for security parameter $n \in \mathbb{N}$, an input sequence $\mathbf{x} = (x_1, \ldots, x_m)$, and auxiliary inputs $z_\mathcal{A}, z_\mathcal{H} \in \{0,1\}^*$ with respect to adversaries $\mathcal{A}$ and $\mathcal{A}_\mathcal{H}$ controlling the parties in $\mathcal{I} \subset \mathcal{P}$ and $\mathcal{H} \subset \mathcal{P} \setminus \mathcal{I}$ respectively. Let $\mathrm{OUT}_{\mathcal{A},f}^{\mathrm{IDEAL}}(1^n, \mathbf{x})$ denote the outputs of the uncorrupted parties (those in $\mathcal{P} \setminus \mathcal{I}$) in a random execution of the above ideal-world process, with $\mathcal{A}$ corrupting the parties in $\mathcal{I}$. Further let $\mathrm{VIEW}_{\mathcal{A},f}^{\mathrm{IDEAL}}(1^n, \mathbf{x})$ be the (simulated, real-world) view description being the *output* of $\mathcal{A}$ in such a process. In addition, we let $\mathrm{VIEW}_{\mathcal{A},\mathcal{A}_\mathcal{H},f}^{\mathrm{IDEAL}}(1^n, \mathbf{x})$ be the view description being the *output* of $\mathcal{A}_\mathcal{H}$ in such a process, when running alongside $\mathcal{A}$. We denote the global view in the ideal model by

$$\mathrm{IDEAL}_{1^n, \mathbf{x}, z_\mathcal{A}, z_\mathcal{H}}^{f, \mathcal{A}, \mathcal{A}_\mathcal{H}} = \left(\mathrm{VIEW}_{\mathcal{A},f}^{\mathrm{IDEAL}}(1^n, \mathbf{x}), \; \mathrm{VIEW}_{\mathcal{A},\mathcal{A}_\mathcal{H},f}^{\mathrm{IDEAL}}(1^n, \mathbf{x}), \; \mathrm{OUT}_{\mathcal{A},f}^{\mathrm{IDEAL}}(1^n, \mathbf{x}) \right).$$

As in the real model, it will be convenient to denote

$$\mathrm{IDEAL}_{1^n, \mathbf{x}, z_\mathcal{A}, z_\mathcal{H}}^{f, \mathcal{A}, \mathcal{A}_\mathcal{H}}(\mathcal{A}) = \left(\mathrm{VIEW}_{\mathcal{A},f}^{\mathrm{IDEAL}}(1^n, \mathbf{x}), \; \mathrm{OUT}_{\mathcal{A},f}^{\mathrm{IDEAL}}(1^n, \mathbf{x}) \right)$$

and

$$\mathrm{IDEAL}_{1^n, \mathbf{x}, z_\mathcal{A}, z_\mathcal{H}}^{f, \mathcal{A}, \mathcal{A}_\mathcal{H}}(\mathcal{A}_\mathcal{H}) = \left(\mathrm{VIEW}_{\mathcal{A},\mathcal{A}_\mathcal{H},f}^{\mathrm{IDEAL}}(1^n, \mathbf{x}), \; \mathrm{OUT}_{\mathcal{A},f}^{\mathrm{IDEAL}}(1^n, \mathbf{x}) \right).$$

When f is clear from the context, we will remove it for brevity. We first define correctness.

Definition 1 (correctness). *We say that a protocol Π computes a function f if for all $n \in \mathbb{N}$ and for all $\mathbf{x} \in \mathcal{X}^n$, in an honest execution, the joint output of all parties is identically distributed to a sample of $f(\mathbf{x})$.*

We next give the definition for the classical definition of computational security alongside FaF-security.

Definition 2 (classical malicious and FaF security). *Let Π be a protocol for computing f. We say that Π computes f with* computational (t, h^*)-FaF full-security, *if the following holds. For every non-uniform PPTM adversary $\mathcal{A}$, controlling a set $\mathcal{I} \subset \mathcal{P}$ of size at most t in the real-world, there exists a non-uniform PPTM adversary $\mathsf{S}_{\mathcal{A}}$, controlling $\mathcal{I}$ in the ideal model; and for every subset of the remaining parties $\mathcal{H} \subset \mathcal{P} \setminus \mathcal{I}$ of size at most h^*, controlled by a non-uniform semi-honest PPTM adversary $\mathcal{A}_{\mathcal{H}}$, there exists a non-uniform PPTM adversary $\mathsf{S}_{\mathcal{A},\mathcal{H}}$, controlling $\mathcal{H}$ in the ideal-world, such that*

$$\left\{ \mathrm{IDEAL}^{\mathsf{S}_{\mathcal{A}},\mathsf{S}_{\mathcal{A},\mathcal{H}}}_{1^n,\mathbf{x},z_{\mathcal{A}},z_{\mathcal{H}}} (\mathsf{S}_{\mathcal{A}}) \right\}_{\mathbf{x}\in\mathcal{X},z_{\mathcal{A}},z_{\mathcal{H}}\in\{0,1\}^*,n\in\mathbb{N}}$$
$$\stackrel{c}{\equiv} \left\{ \mathrm{REAL}^{\mathcal{A},\mathcal{A}_{\mathcal{H}}}_{1^n,\mathbf{x},z_{\mathcal{A}},z_{\mathcal{H}}} (\mathcal{A}) \right\}_{\mathbf{x}\in\mathcal{X},z_{\mathcal{A}},z_{\mathcal{H}}\in\{0,1\}^*,n\in\mathbb{N}}, \tag{1}$$

and

$$\left\{ \mathrm{IDEAL}^{\mathsf{S}_{\mathcal{A}},\mathsf{S}_{\mathcal{A},\mathcal{H}}}_{1^n,\mathbf{x},z_{\mathcal{A}},z_{\mathcal{H}}} (\mathsf{S}_{\mathcal{A},\mathcal{H}}) \right\}_{\mathbf{x}\in\mathcal{X},z_{\mathcal{A}},z_{\mathcal{H}}\in\{0,1\}^*,n\in\mathbb{N}}$$
$$\stackrel{c}{\equiv} \left\{ \mathrm{REAL}^{\mathcal{A},\mathcal{A}_{\mathcal{H}}}_{1^n,\mathbf{x},z_{\mathcal{A}},z_{\mathcal{H}}} (\mathcal{A}_{\mathcal{H}}) \right\}_{\mathbf{x}\in\mathcal{X},z_{\mathcal{A}},z_{\mathcal{H}}\in\{0,1\}^*,n\in\mathbb{N}}. \tag{2}$$

We say that Π computes f with computational t-security if it computes it with computational $(t,0)$-FaF full-security.

Finally, we say that Π computes f with strong computational (t,h^*)-FaF full-security *if*

$$\left\{ \mathrm{IDEAL}^{\mathsf{S}_{\mathcal{A}},\mathsf{S}_{\mathcal{A},\mathcal{H}}}_{1^n,\mathbf{x},z_{\mathcal{A}},z_{\mathcal{H}}} \right\}_{\mathbf{x}\in\mathcal{X},z_{\mathcal{A}},z_{\mathcal{H}}\in\{0,1\}^*,n\in\mathbb{N}}$$
$$\stackrel{c}{\equiv} \left\{ \mathrm{REAL}^{\mathcal{A},\mathcal{A}_{\mathcal{H}}}_{1^n,\mathbf{x},z_{\mathcal{A}},z_{\mathcal{H}}} \right\}_{\mathbf{x}\in\mathcal{X},z_{\mathcal{A}},z_{\mathcal{H}}\in\{0,1\}^*,n\in\mathbb{N}}. \tag{3}$$

To abbreviate notations, whenever $\mathcal{H} = \{\mathrm{P}\}$ we denote its simulator by $\mathsf{S}_{\mathcal{A},\mathrm{P}}$.

The statistical/perfect security variants of the above definitions are obtained naturally from the above definition by replacing computational indistinguishability with statistical distance.

Remark 2. Observe that for the two-party case, since we also protect $\mathcal{H}$ from $\mathcal{A}$, (weak) $(1,1)$-FaF-security is equivalent to the security considered by Beimel et al. [10]. There, security holds if and only if no malicious adversary and no semi-honest adversary can attack the protocol.

Remark 3. Observe that according to the definition, we first need to describe a malicious simulator before fixing the semi-honest parties in $\mathcal{H}$. This should be considered in regard to the definition of the ideal-model, where the malicious simulator $\mathsf{S}_{\mathcal{A}}$ sends to the semi-honest simulator $\mathsf{S}_{\mathcal{A},\mathcal{H}}$ its ideal-world view, implying that $\mathsf{S}_{\mathcal{A}}$ should know the identities of $\mathcal{H}$. Formally, we let the malicious simulator have an additional tape, where it writes its ideal-world view on it, and then the semi-honest simulator reads from it.

f-Hybrid Model. Let f be a m-ary functionality. The f-hybrid model is identical to the real model of computation discussed above, but in addition, each m-size subset of the parties involved, has access to a trusted party realizing f.

3.1   FaF Security-With-Identifiable-Abort

We also make use of protocols admitting *security-with-identifiable-abort*. In terms of the definition, the only requirement that is changed, is to have the ideal-world simulator operate in a *different ideal model*. We next describe the interaction in the *FaF-secure-with-identifiable-abort ideal model* for the computation of the function f with security parameter n. Unlike the full-security ideal model, here the malicious adversary can instruct the trusted party to not send the output to the honest parties, however, in this case the adversary must publish the identity of a corrupted party. In addition, since there is no guarantee that in the real-world the semi-honest parties won't learn the output, we always let the semi-honest parties to receive their output in the ideal execution.

Let $\mathcal{A}$ be a malicious adversary in the ideal-world, which is given an auxiliary input $z_{\mathcal{A}}$ and corrupts the subset $\mathcal{I}$ of the parties. Further let $\mathcal{A}_{\mathcal{H}}$ be a semi-honest adversary, which is controlling a set of parties denoted $\mathcal{H}$ and is given an auxiliary input $z_{\mathcal{H}}$. Just like in the full-security ideal-world, the standard formulation of security-with-identifiable-abort assumes $\mathcal{H} = \emptyset$.

The FaF ideal model – security-with-identifiable-abort.

Inputs: Each party P_i holds 1^n and $x_i \in \mathcal{X}_i^n$. The adversaries $\mathcal{A}$ and $\mathcal{A}_{\mathcal{H}}$ are given each an auxiliary input $z_{\mathcal{A}}, z_{\mathcal{H}} \in \{0,1\}^*$ respectively, and x_i for every P_i controlled by them. The trusted party T holds 1^n.

Parties send inputs: Each uncorrupted party $P_j \in \mathcal{P} \setminus \mathcal{I}$ sends x_j as its input to T. The malicious adversary sends a value $x_i' \in \mathcal{X}_i^n$ as the input for party $P_i \in \mathcal{I}$. Write $(x_1', \ldots, x_m')$ for the tuple of inputs received by the trusted party.

The trusted party performs computation: The trusted party T selects a random string r and computes $\mathbf{y} = (y_1, \ldots, y_m) = f(x_1' \ldots, x_m'; r)$ and sends $\mathbf{y}_{\mathcal{I}}$ to $\mathcal{A}$ and $\mathbf{y}_{\mathcal{H}}$ to $\mathcal{A}_{\mathcal{H}}$.

The malicious adversary sends its (ideal-world) view: $\mathcal{A}$ sends to $\mathcal{A}_{\mathcal{H}}$ its randomness, inputs, auxiliary input, and the output received from T.

Malicious adversary instructs trusted party to continue or halt: the adversary $\mathcal{A}$ sends either `continue` or $(\texttt{abort}, P_i)$ for some $P_i \in \mathcal{I}$ to T. If it sent `continue`, then for every honest party P_j the trusted party sends y_j. Otherwise, if $\mathcal{A}$ sent $(\texttt{abort}, P_i)$, then T sends $(\texttt{abort}, P_i)$ to the each honest party P_j.

Outputs: Each uncorrupted party outputs whatever output it received from T (the parties in $\mathcal{H}$ output $(\texttt{abort}, P_i)$ if they received it in the last step), the parties in $\mathcal{I}$ output nothing. The adversaries output some function of their respective view.

4   Characterizing Computational FaF-Security

In this section we prove our main theorem regarding FaF-security. We give a complete characterization the types of adversaries, for which we can compute any multiparty functionality with computational FaF full-security. We prove the following result.

Theorem 4. *Let $t, h^*, m \in \mathbb{N}$. Then under the assumption that OT and OWP exist, any m-party functionality f can be computed with (weak) computational (t, h^*)-FaF full-security, if and only if $2t + h^* < m$. Moreover, the negative direction holds even assuming the availability of simultaneous broadcast.*

In Sect. 4.1 we show the positive direction, while in Sect. 4.2 we prove the negative direction.

4.1 Feasibility of FaF-Security

In this section, we prove the positive direction of Theorem 4. In fact, we show how to reduce FaF full-security to FaF security-with-identifiable-abort whenever $2t + h^* < m$. In addition, we explore the feasibility of both FaF full-security and FaF security-with-identifiable-abort, and provide interesting consequences of these results. We first show that the GMW protocol [26] admits FaF security-with-identifiable-abort, for all possible threshold values of t and h^*, and admits FaF full-security assuming $t + h^* < m/2$. In Sect. 4.1.2 we show that, assuming an *uncorrupted majority* (i.e., $t < m/2$), residual FaF full-security is (perfectly) reducible to FaF-security-with-identifiable-abort. The notion of *residual security* [30], intuitively allows an adversary to learn the output of the function on many choices of inputs for corrupted parties. A formal definition and some motivation for using residual security variant appear in Sect. 4.1.2.

4.1.1 Feasibility of FaF Security-With-Identifiable-Abort

We next show that the GMW protocol admits FaF security-with-identifiable-abort, and admits FaF full-security in the presence of an honest majority (i.e., $t + h^* < m/2$).

Theorem 5. *Let $m, t, h^* \in \mathbb{N}$ be such that $t + h^* \leq m$ and Let f be an m-party functionality. Then, assuming OT exists, there exists a protocol for computing f with (weak) computational (t, h^*)-FaF security-with-identifiable-abort. Moreover, if $t + h^* < m/2$ then the protocol admits computational (t, h^*)-FaF full-security.*

Proof Sketch. We will show that a slight variation on the GMW protocol [26], setting the secret sharing (for sharing the inputs) to a $(t + h^* + 1)$-out-of-m scheme, admits FaF-security.

Fix an adversary $\mathcal{A}$ corrupting $\mathcal{I}$ of size at most t, and let $\mathcal{H} \subseteq \mathcal{P} \setminus \mathcal{I}$ be of size at most h^*. The semi-honest simulator $\mathsf{S}_{\mathcal{A}, \mathcal{H}}$ will work very similarly to the malicious simulator $\mathsf{S}_{\mathcal{A}}$. The only difference is that the messages it sends to the adversary on behalf of the parties in $\mathcal{H}$, are the real message that the protocol instruct them to send (e.g., in the input commitment phase it will commit to the real input unlike $\mathsf{S}_{\mathcal{A}}$, which commits to 0). Additionally, if the adversary did not abort, for every output wire held by a party in $\mathcal{I} \cup \mathcal{H}$, set the message received from the honest parties (i.e., from $\mathcal{P} \setminus (\mathcal{I} \cup \mathcal{H})$) as the XOR of the output of that wire and the shares of the wire held by the corrupted and semi-honest parties.

Security follows from the fact that the messages $S_{\mathcal{A},\mathcal{H}}$ sends to $\mathcal{A}$ are consistent with the inputs of the malicious and the semi-honest parties.   □

4.1.2   Reducing Residual FaF Full-Security to FaF Security-With-Identifiable-Abort

In this section, we present a reduction from residual FaF full-security to FaF security-with-identifiable-abort, in the uncorrupted majority setting. This reduction further has the property that if $2t + h^* < m$ then FaF full-security is obtained (i.e., not residual). We first formally define the residual function. Intuitively, the residual of an m-ary function with respect to a subset S of the indexes, fixes the inputs on the indexes $[m] \setminus S$. More formally, it is defined as follows.

Definition 3 (Residual Function [29,30]). *Let $f : \mathcal{X} \mapsto \mathcal{Y}$ be an m-ary functionality, let $\mathbf{x} = (x_1, \ldots, x_m)$ be an input to f, and let $S = \{i_1, \ldots, i_{m'}\} \subseteq [m]$ be a subset of size m'. The residual function of f for S and $\mathbf{x}$ is an m'-ary function $f_{S,\mathbf{x}} : \mathcal{X}_{i_1} \times \ldots \times \mathcal{X}_{i_{m'}} \mapsto \mathcal{Y}_{i_1} \times \ldots \times \mathcal{Y}_{i_{m'}}$, obtained from f by restricting the input variables indexed by $[m] \setminus S$ to their values in $\mathbf{x}$. That is, $f_{S,\mathbf{x}}(x_1', \ldots, x_{m'}') = f(x_1, \ldots, x_m)$, where for $k \notin S$ we have $x_k' = x_k$, while for $k = i_j \in S$ we have $x_k' = x_j$.*

Residual FaF full-security is defined similarly to FaF full-security, with the only exception being in the ideal-world, the two adversaries receive the residual function $f_{\mathcal{I},\mathbf{x}}$ instead of a single output (all the uncorrupted parties still receive an output from T, which they output).

Before stating the result, we first define the functionalities to which we reduce the computation. For an m-party functionality f, and for $m' \in \{m - t, \ldots, m\}$, we define the m'-party functionality $f'_{m'}(\mathbf{x})$ in the security-with-identifiable-abort model as follows. Let $\mathbf{y} = (y_1, \ldots, y_m)$ be the output of $f(\mathbf{x})$. Share each y_i in an $(m - t)$-out-of-m' secret sharing scheme, so that party P_i is required for the reconstruction (this can be done by first sharing in a 2-out-of-2 secret sharing, and then give one of the shares to P_i and share the other among $m' - 1$ parties). The output of party P_j is its respective shares of each y_i, i.e., P_j receives $(y_i[j])_{i=1}^{m}$. We next present the statement. The proof is given in Sect. 4.1.3.

Lemma 1. *Let $m, t, h^* \in \mathbb{N}$ be such that $t + h^* \leq m(n)$ and that $t < m/2$, and let f be an m-party functionality. Then there exists a protocol Π that computes f with strong perfect (t, h^*)-residual FaF full-security in the $\left(f'_{m-t}, \ldots, f'_m \right)$-hybrid model. Moreover, the protocol satisfies the following.*

1. Standard malicious security achieved is standard security (i.e., not residual)
2. If $2t + h^* < m$ then Π admits (t, h^*)-FaF full-security in the $\left(f'_{m-t}, \ldots, f'_m \right)$-hybrid model.

Remark 4. Note that in general, classical generic protocols, such as the GMW protocol, will not achieve FaF full-security, even if we increase the threshold for the secret sharing scheme to $t + h^* + 1$. As an example, consider the 3-party functionality $(a, \perp, c) \mapsto a \oplus b \oplus c$, where $b \leftarrow \{0, 1\}$, and let $t, h^* = 1$. Using a 2-out-of-3 secret sharing scheme, would allow a corrupted P_1 to help P_2 to learn c. Using a 3-out-of-3 secret sharing scheme, would allow the adversary to withhold information on the output.

We stress that even standard techniques, such as having the parties compute a functionality whose output is a secret sharing of the original output, fail to achieve security. This is due to the fact that an adversary can abort the execution forcing the parties in $\mathcal{H}$ to (possibly) learn an output. Then, after executing the same protocol with one party labeled inactive, the parties in $\mathcal{H}$ will learn an additional output, which cannot be simulated. In Sect. 4.1.3 we show that such protocol can achieve *residual security*, namely the parties in $\mathcal{H}$ will not learn more than the function on many choices of inputs for corrupted parties.

Assuming that OT exists, we can apply the composition theorem to combine Lemma 1 with Theorem 5 and get as a corollary that whenever an uncorrupted majority is present (i.e., $t < m/2$), any functionality can be computed with (weak) computational residual FaF full-security.

Corollary 1. *Let $m, t, h^* \in \mathbb{N}$ be such that $t + h^* \leq m$ and that $t < m/2$, and let f be an m-party functionality. Then, assuming OT exists, there exists a protocol Π that computes f with (weak) computational (t, h^*)-residual FaF full-security.*

1. *Standard malicious security achieved is standard security (i.e., not residual)*
2. *If $2t + h^* < m$ then Π admits (t, h^*)-FaF full-security.*

Item 2 of the above corollary concludes the positive direction of Theorem 4. The proof of Lemma 1 is given in Sect. 4.1.3. Before providing a proof, we first discuss some interesting consequences. One interesting family of functionalities to consider in the corollary, is the family of *no-input functionalities* (e.g., coin-tossing). Since there are no inputs, it follows that such functionalities can be computed with FaF full-security (i.e., not residual).

Corollary 2. *Let $m, t, h^* \in \mathbb{N}$ be such that $t + h^* \leq m$ and that $t < m/2$, and let f be an m-party no-input functionality. Then, assuming OT exists, there exists a protocol Π that computes f with (weak) computational (t, h^*)-FaF full-security.*

As a result, in the computational setting, we claim that we have separation between (weak) FaF-security and mixed-security. Recall that a mixed adversary is one that controls a subset of the parties maliciously and another subset semi-honestly. Consider the 3-party functionality $f(\perp, \perp, \perp) = (b, \perp, b)$, where $b \leftarrow \{0, 1\}$. As we proved in Corollary 2, this functionality can be computed with computational $(1, 1)$-FaF full-security. However, we claim that f cannot be computed with computational $(1, 1)$-mixed security.

Theorem 6. *No protocol computes f with $(1,1)$-mixed full-security.*

The proof follows from a simple observation on a result by Ishai et al. [33]. They showed that for any protocol computing the functionality $g(a, \perp, c) = (a \oplus c, \perp, a \oplus c)$, where a and c are chosen uniformly at random, there exists a mixed adversary successfully attacking the protocol. Consequently, the same attack would work on any protocol computing f. As a result, we conclude that for no-input functionalities, the definition of security against mixed adversaries is *strictly stronger* than FaF security.

Even for various functionalities with inputs, Lemma 1 implies FaF full-security for interesting choices of parameters. For example, consider the 3-party XOR functionality. Then it can be computed with $(1,1)$-FaF full-security since the input of the honest party can be computed by the semi-honest party's simulator.

4.1.3   Proof of Lemma 1

We next provide the proof of Lemma 1. Recall that for an m-party functionality f and for $m' \in \{m - t, \ldots, m\}$, we define the m'-party functionality $f'_{m'}(\mathbf{x})$ in the security-with-identifiable-abort model as follows. Let $\mathbf{y} = (y_1, \ldots, y_m)$ be the output of $f(\mathbf{x})$. Share each y_i in an $(m-t)$-out-of-m' secret sharing scheme, so that party P_i is required for the reconstruction. The output of party P_j is its respective shares of each y_i, i.e., P_j receives $(y_i[j])_{i=1}^{m}$.

Proof (of Lemma 1). The protocol Π in the real world is described as follows:

. . . .

Protocol 7
Input: Party P_i holds an input $x_i \in \mathcal{X}_i$.
Common input: Security parameter 1^n.

1. *The parties call the functionality $f'_{m'}$, where m' is the number of active parties, and the inputs of the inactive parties is set to a default value.*
2. *If the computation followed through, then the parties broadcast their shares, reconstruct the output, and halt.*[4]
3. *Otherwise, they have the identity of a corrupted party. The parties then go back to Step 1. without said party (updating m' in the process and setting its input to a default value).*

. . . .

Intuitively, the protocol works since there is an honest majority, so the parties can always reconstruct the output in case the computation in Step 1 followed through. Moreover, the only information the parties receive in case of an abort during Step 1, is an output of f that is consistent with their inputs. In particular

---

[4] For this step to work, we need to assume that the adversary does not change its shares. We can force it to send the correct shares using standard techniques. One way to do so is to sign each output of each $f'_{m'}$ using a MAC and give the other parties the key for verification. For the sake of clarity of presentation, however, we decide to skip this and assume that the corrupted parties are using correct shares.

the adversary cannot add additional information to any subset of the honest parties. We next present the formal argument.

Fix an adversary $\mathcal{A}$ corrupting a set of parties $\mathcal{I} \subset \mathcal{P}$ of size at most t, and let $\mathcal{H} \subset \mathcal{P} \setminus \mathcal{I}$ be a subset of the uncorrupted parties of size at most h^*. We first construct the simulator $\mathsf{S}_\mathcal{A}$ for the adversary. To prove Item 1 of the "moreover" part, we will construct the simulator $\mathsf{S}_\mathcal{A}$ assuming that receives a single output from the trusted party. This is indeed a stronger result, since a simulator with the residual function can always simulate the simulator that received a single output. With an auxiliary input $z_\mathcal{A}$, the simulator $\mathsf{S}_\mathcal{A}$ does the following:

1. Let m' be the number of active parties. Share some garbage value m times independently as follows. Denote $y'_j = (\hat{y}_i[j])_{i=1}^m$ the shares held by P_j, where $\hat{y}_i$ is a garbage value, shared in a $(m - t)$-out-of-m' Shamir's secret sharing scheme with respect to party P_i.
2. Send $\mathbf{y}'_\mathcal{I}$ to $\mathcal{A}$ to receive the message it sends to $f'_{m'}$.
3. If $\mathcal{A}$ replied with $(\texttt{abort}, P_i)$, then go back to Step 1 with P_i labeled inactive.
4. Otherwise, $\mathcal{A}$ sent some vector of inputs $\hat{\mathbf{x}}_\mathcal{I}$. Pass $\hat{\mathbf{x}}_\mathcal{I}$ to the trusted party to receive an output $\mathbf{y}_\mathcal{I}$. Complete the t shares held by $\mathcal{A}$ to a sharing of the real output $\mathbf{y}_\mathcal{I}$ (recall that $t < m/2$ so this is possible by the properties of the secret sharing scheme).
5. Output all of the $\mathbf{y}'_\mathcal{I}$'s generated and the completed shares, and halt.

We next describe the simulator $\mathsf{S}_{\mathcal{A},\mathcal{H}}$ for the adversary $\mathcal{A}_\mathcal{H}$ controlling the parties in $\mathcal{H}$ interacting with $\mathcal{A}$. The idea is to have the simulator use the shares generated by $\mathsf{S}_\mathcal{A}$ to ensure consistencies between their views. Additionally, for the last iteration, where the shares should be reconstructed to the output, we modify the shares not held by $\mathcal{A}$ so the output will also be consistent with generated view. In addition, for every abort occurred, the simulator will use the residual function to hand over to $\mathcal{H}$ the output of that iteration. Formally, given an auxiliary input $z_\mathcal{H}$, $\mathsf{S}_{\mathcal{A},\mathcal{H}}$ operates as follows.

1. Receive the residual function $f_{\mathcal{I},\mathbf{x}}$ from the trusted party, and receive $(\mathbf{x}_\mathcal{I}, r, z_\mathcal{A})$ – $\mathsf{S}_\mathcal{A}$'s input, randomness, and the auxiliary input, respectively.
2. Apply $\mathsf{S}_\mathcal{A}$ to receive its view, which consists of $\mathbf{y}'_\mathcal{I}$ – shares of some values, held by the adversary.
3. Query $\mathcal{A}$ on each $\mathbf{y}'_\mathcal{I}$ to receive the messages it sends to $\mathcal{H}$, and in case of an abort, get the identity of a corrupted party.
4. Complete each $\mathbf{y}'_\mathcal{I}$ to shares of an output $\hat{\mathbf{y}}$ computed using the residual function $f_{\mathcal{I},\mathbf{x}}$ (fixing the input of the inactive parties to be a default value, and input of the active corrupted parties according to the choice of $\mathcal{A}$), so that the last $\mathbf{y}'_\mathcal{I}$ is completed to shares of the real output. Note that by the properties of the secret sharing scheme, this can be done efficiently.
5. Output all of the completed shares and the messages sent by $\mathcal{A}$, and halt.

In every iteration, the view generated by $\mathsf{S}_{\mathcal{A},\mathcal{H}}$ is consistent with the view generated by the malicious simulator $\mathsf{S}_\mathcal{A}$. Moreover, they send to $\mathcal{A}$ the exactly the same messages, hence they will receive the same identities of the aborting parties, and inputs given to the functionalities $f'_{m'}$. Since this is generated with the same distribution as in the real-world, we conclude that joint view of the two adversaries with the output of the honest parties, is identically distributed in both worlds.

Finally, in order to see why Item 2 of the "moreover" part is true, observe that if $2t + h^* < m$ then $t + h^* < m - t$, implying that the number of shares that can be held by the $\mathcal{A}$ and $\mathcal{H}$ is smaller than the secret sharing threshold. Thus, $\mathsf{S}_{\mathcal{A},\mathcal{H}}$ can use random shares for each iteration (except the last iteration), without using the output.

4.2   Impossibility Result

In this section, we prove the negative direction of Theorem 4. Specifically, we prove the following lemma.

Lemma 2. *Let $m, t, h^* \in \mathbb{N}$ be such that $2t + h^* = m$. Then there exists an m-party functionality that no protocol computes it with (weak) computational (t, h^*)-FaF full-security. Moreover, the claim holds even assuming the availability of simultaneous broadcast.*

For the proof, we first show that it holds for the 3-party case where $t, h^* = 1$. Then, using a player-partitioning argument, we generalize the result to more than three parties. The following lemma states the result for the 3-party case. Throughout the remainder of the section, we denote the parties by A, B, and C.

Lemma 3. *Assume that one-way permutation exists. Then there exists a 3-party functionality that no protocol computes it with (weak) computational $(1, 1)$-FaF full-security. Moreover, the following hold*

1. *The malicious adversary we construct corrupts either A or C, while the remaining third party B will be in $\mathcal{H}$.*
2. *The claim holds even assuming the availability of simultaneous broadcast.*

The proof of Lemma 2 is deferred to the full-version. We next give an overview of the proof of Lemma 3. We assume that each round is composed of 3 broadcast messages, the first sent by A, the second sent by B, and the third by C (this is without loss of generality, as we allow the adversary to be rushing). Intuitively, the proof is done as follows. By an averaging argument there must exists a round where two parties, say A and B, together can reconstruct the output with significantly higher probability than C and B. We then have A act honestly (using the original input it held) and abort at that round. As a result, with high probability the output of C will change. Finally, A will send its entire view to B, allowing it to recover the correct entry with significantly higher probability than C. We show that for an appropriate functionality, the advantage of the pair (A, B) over (C, B) cannot be simulated.

Proof (of Lemma 3). Let $f = \{f_n : \{0, 1\}^n \mapsto \{0, 1\}^n\}_{n \in \mathbb{N}}$ be a one-way permutation. Define the symmetric 3-party functionality $\mathsf{Swap} = \{\mathsf{Swap}_n : \{0, 1\}^n \times$

$\{0,1\}^{2n} \times \{0,1\}^n \mapsto \{0,1\}^{2n}\}_{n \in \mathbb{N}}$ as follows. Parties A and C each hold a string $a, c \in \{0,1\}^n$ respectively. Party B holds two strings $y_A, y_C \in \{0,1\}^n$. The output is then defined to be

$$\mathsf{Swap}_n\left(a, (y_A, y_C), c\right) = \begin{cases} (a,c) & \text{if } f_n(a) = y_A \text{ and } f_n(c) = y_C \\ \perp & \text{otherwise} \end{cases}$$

Assume for the sake of contradiction that there exists a 3-party protocol Π that computes Swap with computational $(1,1)$-FaF full-security. We fix a security parameter n, we let r denote the number of rounds in Π, and consider an evaluation of Swap with the output being (a, c). Formally, we consider the following distribution over the inputs.

– a, c are each selected from $\{0,1\}^n$ uniformly at random and independently.
– $y_A = f_n(a)$ and $y_C = f_n(c)$.

For $i \in \{0, \ldots, r\}$ let a_i be the final output of A assuming that C aborted after sending i messages. Similarly, for $i \in \{0, \ldots, r\}$ we define c_i to be the final output of C assuming that A aborted after sending i messages. Observe that a_r and c_r are the outputs of A and C respectively. We first claim that there exists a round where either A and B gain an advantage in computing the correct output, or C and B gain this advantage.

Claim 8. *Either there exists $i \in \{0, \ldots, r\}$ such that*

$$\Pr\left[a_i = (a,c)\right] - \Pr\left[c_i = (a,c)\right] \geq \frac{1 - \text{neg}(n)}{2r + 1},$$

or there exists $i \in [r]$ such that

$$\Pr\left[c_i = (a,c)\right] - \Pr\left[a_{i-1} = (a,c)\right] \geq \frac{1 - \text{neg}(n)}{2r + 1}.$$

The probabilities above are taken over the choice of inputs and of random coins for the parties.

The proof is done using a simple averaging argument, and is proven below. We first use this fact to show an attack.

Assume without loss of generality that there exists an $i \in [r]$ such that the former equality holds (the other case is done analogously). Define a malicious adversary $\mathcal{A}$ as follows. For the security parameter n, it receives as auxiliary input the round i. Now, $\mathcal{A}$ corrupts A and have it act honestly (using the party's original input a) up to and including round i. After receiving the i-th message, the adversary instructs A to abort. Finally, the adversary sends its entire view to B. We next show that no pair of simulators $\mathsf{S}_{\mathcal{A}}$ and $\mathsf{S}_{\mathcal{A},B}$ can produce views for $\mathcal{A}$ and B so that Eqs. (1) and (2) would hold. For that, we assume towards contradiction that such simulators do exist. Let $a^* \in \{0,1\}^n$ be the input that $\mathsf{S}_{\mathcal{A}}$ sent to the trusted party. Additionally, denote $q = \Pr\left[c_i = (a,c)\right]$.

We next separate into two cases. For the first case, let us assume that $\Pr[a^* = a] \geq q + 1/p(n)$ for some polynomial $p(\cdot)$ for infinitely many n's. Let $\text{OUT}_C^{\text{IDEAL}}$ be the output of C in the ideal world. Since f_n is a permutation we have that

$$\Pr\left[\text{OUT}_C^{\text{IDEAL}} = (a,c)\right] = \Pr[a^* = a] \geq q + 1/p(n).$$

Thus, by comparing the output of C to (a,c) it is possible to distinguish the real from the ideal with advantage at least $1/p(n)$.

For the second case, we assume that $\Pr[a^* = a] \leq q + \text{neg}(n)$. Here we show how to distinguish between the view of B in the real world from its ideal world counterpart. Recall that in the real world $\mathcal{A}$ sent its view to B. Let M be the algorithm specified by the protocol, that A and B use to compute their output assuming C has aborted. Namely, M outputs a_i in the real world. By Claim 8 it holds that $\Pr[a_i = (a,c)] \geq q + \frac{1-\text{neg}(n)}{2r+1}$. We next consider the ideal world. Let V be the view generated by $\mathsf{S}_{\mathcal{A},\text{B}}$. We claim that

$$\Pr[\text{M}(V) = (a,c) \wedge a^* \neq a] \leq \text{neg}(n).$$

Indeed, since f_n is a permutation and B does not change the input it sends to T, the output computed by T will be $\bot$. Moreover, as f_n is one-way it follows that if M(V) did output (a,c), then it can be used to break the security of f_n. This can be done by sampling $a \leftarrow \{0,1\}^n$, computing $f(a)$, and finally, compute a view V using the simulators and apply M to it (if a^* computed by $\mathsf{S}_{\mathcal{A}}$ equals to a then abort). We conclude that

$$\begin{aligned}\Pr[\text{M}(V) = (a,c)] &= \Pr[\text{M}(V) = (a,c) \wedge a^* = a] + \Pr[\text{M}(V) = (a,c) \wedge a^* \neq a] \\ &\leq \Pr[a^* = a] + \text{neg}(n) \\ &\leq q + \text{neg}(n).\end{aligned}$$

Therefore, by applying M to the view it is possible to distinguish with advantage at least $\frac{1-\text{neg}(n)}{2r+1} - \text{neg}(n)$. To conclude the proof we next prove Claim 8.

Proof (of Claim 8). The proof follows by the following averaging argument. By correctness and the fact that f_n is one-way, it follows that

$$\begin{aligned}1 - \text{neg}(n) &\leq \Pr[a_r = (a,c)] - \Pr[c_0 = (a,c)] \\ &= \sum_{i=0}^{r}(\Pr[a_i = (a,c)] - \Pr[c_i = (a,c)]) + \sum_{i=1}^{r}(\Pr[c_i = (a,c)] - \Pr[a_{i-1} = (a,c)])\end{aligned}$$

Since there are $2r+1$ summands, there must exists an i for which one of the differences is at least $\frac{1-\text{neg}(n)}{2r+1}$.

Finally, in order to see why Item 2 is true, observe that the attack is not based on the view of $\mathcal{A}$, hence the same attack works assuming simultaneous broadcast.

Remark 5. Intuitively, we showed that in the real world the parties A and B hold more information on the output, than what B and C hold. To make this statement formal, observe that the proof in fact shows that Swap cannot be computed with *fairness*. Roughly, for fairness to hold we require that either all parties receive an output, or none of them do. To see this, observe that for the functionality at hand, aborting in the ideal world is the same as sending a different input a. Therefore the attack cannot be simulated. We present the formal definition of fairness in the full-version.

5   Comparison Between FaF-Security and Other Definitions

In this section, we compare the notion of FaF-security to other existing notions. In Sect. 5.1, we investigate how FaF-security relates to classical full-security. In Sect. 5.2, we review the differences between our notion and the notion of mixed adversaries. In the mixed-adversary scenario, a single adversary controls a set $\mathcal{I}$ of parties, however, within $\mathcal{I}$ different limitations are imposed on the behavior (deviation) of different parties. In Sect. 5.3, we show that strong FaF-security is a strictly stronger notion than (weak) FaF-security.

5.1   The Relation Between FaF-Security and Standard Full-Security

We start with comparing FaF-security to the standard definition. It is easy to see that standard t-security does not imply in general (t, h^*)-FaF full-security, even for functionalities with no inputs. Consider the following example. Let f be a 3-party *no-input* functionality defined as $(\bot, \bot, \bot) \mapsto (\bot, \bot, r)$ where $r \leftarrow \{0,1\}^n$, and let $t, h^* = 1$. Consider the following protocol: P_1 and P_2 sample $r_1, r_2 \leftarrow \{0,1\}^n$, respectively and send the random strings to P_3. The output of P_3 is then $r_1 \oplus r_2$.

It is easy to see that the protocol computes f with perfect full-security tolerating a single corruption. However, a malicious P_1 can send r_1 to P_2 as well, thereby allowing P_2 to learn P_3's output. Indeed, this protocol is insecure according to Definition 2. Obviously, (t, h^*)-FaF-security readily implies the classical t-security counterpart. Conversely, one might expect that classical $(t + h^*)$-security must imply (t, h^*)-FaF-security. We next show that this is not the case in general. We present an example of a protocol that admits traditional malicious security against t corruptions, however, it does not admit $(t-1, 1)$-FaF-security. Intuitively, this somewhat surprising state of affairs is made possible by the fact that in $(t-1, 1)$-FaF-security *both* the attacker *and* the two simulators are weaker.

The following example is a simple extension of the known example (cf., [10]), showing that for standard security, there exists a maliciously secure protocol (for computing the two-party, one-sided OR function), but none semi-honest secure.

Example 1. Let A, B, and C be three parties with inputs $a, b, c \in \{0,1\}$ respectively. Consider the 3-party functionality $\mathsf{3OR} : \{0,1\}^3 \mapsto \{0,1\}^3$ defined as

3OR $(a, b, c) = (\bot, \bot, (a \oplus b) \vee c)$, with the following protocol for computing it. In the first round, parties A and B both select shares for their respective inputs with each other. That is, A selects $a_1 \leftarrow \{0, 1\}$ and sends $a_2 = a \oplus a_1$ to B, and B selects $b_2 \leftarrow \{0, 1\}$ and sends $b_1 = b \oplus b_2$ to A. In the second round, A sends $a_1 \oplus b_1$ to C and B sends $a_2 \oplus b_2$ to C. Party C outputs $(a_1 \oplus b_1 \oplus a_2 \oplus b_2) \vee c$.

We first claim that the protocol computes 3OR with *perfect* full-security tolerating coalitions of size at most 2. Indeed, an adversary that maliciously corrupts A, B, or both, learns nothing and can be simulated by selecting the inputs defined by the shared values. An adversary that maliciously corrupts C can be simulated by sending $c = 0$ to the trusted party, and as a result, learning the same information as in the protocol. For example, corrupting A and C and sending $a, 0$ (resp.) to the trusted party, the adversary learns b.

We argue that although the protocol is 2-secure in the standard definition, it does not compute 3OR with $(1, 1)$-FaF full-security. Specifically, a semi-honest C cannot be simulated. Take for example, an adversary $\mathcal{A}$ that corrupts A maliciously and let $\mathcal{H} = \{C\}$. In the real-world, $\mathcal{A}$ can reveal b to C. However, in the ideal-world, this cannot be simulated (when $c = 1$).

Remark 6. Example 1 shows that "moving" a party from being malicious to being semi-honest (i.e., taking a party from $\mathcal{I}$ and moving it to $\mathcal{H}$) could potentially break the security of the protocol. Similarly to [10], it is arguably natural to consider a definition that requires the protocol to be (t, h^*)-FaF-security if and only if it is $(t - 1, h^* + 1)$-FaF-security. Our definition does not impose this extra requirement, however, all of our protocols satisfy it.

In contrast to the above example, we claim that adaptive $(t + h^*)$-security does imply strong (t, h^*)-FaF full-security. Intuitively, this follows from the fact that an adaptive adversary is allowed to corrupt some of the parties after the execution of the protocol terminated. We formulate the theorem for the full-security setting, however, we stress that it also holds in the security with (identifiable) abort setting.

Theorem 9. *Let* type $\in \{$computational, statistical, perfect$\}$ *and let* Π *be an m-party protocol computing some m-party functionality* f *with* type *adaptive* $(t + h^*)$*-security. Then* Π *computes* f *with* type (t, h^*)*-FaF full-security.*

A proof sketch of Theorem 9 is given in the full-version.

By applying recent results on adaptive security, we get that there exist constant-round protocol that are FaF secure-with-abort [12,15,22].

5.2   The Relation Between FaF-Security and Mixed-Security

The notion of "mixed adversaries" [21,40] considers a single entity that corrupts a subset $\mathcal{I}$ maliciously, and another subset $\mathcal{H}$ semi-honestly.[5] A simulator for

---

[5] There are various types of mixed adversaries one can consider. For example, [31] also gave the adversary the ability to fail-corrupt parties, based on its adversarial structure. Here, we only consider the notion considered by [21].

a mixed adversary, is a single simulator controlling the parties in $\mathcal{I} \cup \mathcal{H}$. This simulator is restricted so to only be allowed to change inputs for the parties in $\mathcal{I}$ (i.e., the simulator is not allowed to change the inputs for the parties in $\mathcal{H}$). We say that a protocol has computational (t, h^*)-mixed full-security, if Eq. (2) is written with respect to a mixed adversary and its simulator.

In comparison, FaF-security can be viewed as if there are two *distinct* adversaries – one malicious and one semi-honest, making it a natural question to compare the two definitions. One might expect that (t, h^*)-mixed full-security would imply (t, h^*)-FaF full-security. However, similarly to the case with standard security, we show the that this is not generally the case in the *computational* setting (note that the protocol from Example 1 is not $(1, 1)$-mixed secure).

Example 2. Consider the 5-party functionality $f : (\{0, 1\}^n)^3 \times \emptyset^2 \mapsto (\{0, 1\}^n)^2 \times \emptyset^3$ whose output on input $(x_1, x_2, x_3, \bot, \bot)$, is defined as follows. If $x_1 = x_2$, then P_1 and P_2 will each receive a share of a 2-out-of-2 secret sharing of x_3, i.e., P_1 will receive $x_3[1]$ and P_2 will receive $x_3[2]$. If $x_1 \neq x_2$ then P_1 and P_2 will each receive a string of length n chosen uniformly at random and independently. In both cases, all other 3 parties will receive no output. We next show a protocol that is secure against any adversary corrupting at most 2 parties (including mixed adversaries), yet it does not admits $(1, 1)$-FaF full-security. In the following we let (Gen, Enc, Dec) be a non-malleable and semantically secure public-key encryption scheme [20].

Protocol 10

1. *The parties will compute a functionality whose output to P_i for $i \in \{1, 2, 3\}$ is* pk*, and for party P_i, for $i \in \{4, 5\}$ is* (pk, sk[i])*, where the* sk[i]*s are shares of* sk *in a 2-out-of-2 secret sharing, and where* (pk, sk) $\leftarrow$ Gen(1^n)*. This can be done using, say the GMW protocol [26].*

2. P_2 *sends* $c_2 \leftarrow$ Enc$_{pk}(x_2, 2)$ *to* P_1.

3. *The parties compute the following 5-party functionality g. The input of P_1 is* $c_1 \leftarrow$ Enc$_{pk}(x_1, 1)$*, the input of P_2 is c_2, and the input of P_3 is x_3. The input of P_i, for $i \in \{4, 5\}$, is the pair* (pk, sk[i])*.*
   The output is defined as follows. P_3, P_4, and P_5 receive no output.
   - *If* Dec$_{sk}(c_i) = (x_i, i)$*, for every $i \in \{1, 2, 3\}$ and $x_1 = x_2$, then P_1 will receive $x_3[1]$ and P_2 will receive $x_3[2]$.*
   - *Else, if* Dec$_{sk}(c_1) = (x_1, 2)$*,* Dec$_{sk}(c_2) = (x_2, 2)$*, and $x_1 = x_2$, then P_1 will receive a random string $r \in \{0, 1\}^n$ and P_2 will receive* $(x_3[1], x_3[2])$*.*
   - *Otherwise, both P_1 and P_2 will receive random strings $r_1, r_2 \in \{0, 1\}^n$ respectively, chosen independently and uniformly.*
   As in Step 1, this can be done using the GMW protocol [26].

4. P_1 *output what it received from g. If P_2 received one random string r_2 from g then output r_2, and if P_2 received two random strings from g, then output the second one.*

Claim 9. *Protocol 10 computes f with computational 2-security and with computational $(1, 1)$-mixed security, yet it does not compute f with computational $(1, 1)$-FaF full-security.*

The proof is deferred to the full-version due space considerations.

5.3 Comparison Between (Weak) FaF-Security and Strong FaF-Security

In this section, we separate the notion of (weak) FaF-security from strong FaF-security in the computational setting. Specifically, we show a protocol that admits (weak) FaF-security, yet it does not admit strong FaF-security. We assume we have available a commitment scheme. Consider the 3-party functionality f mapping $(\bot, b, \bot) \mapsto (\bot, \bot, b)$, where $b \in \{0, 1\}$, and let $t, h^* = 1$. Consider the following protocol: P_2 broadcasts a commitment to b, and then sends the decommitment only to P_3.

Claim 10. *The above protocol computes f with (weak) computational $(1, 1)$-FaF full-security, yet does not provide strong computational $(1, 1)$-FaF full-security.*

The proof is deferred to the full-version due to space considerations. One consequence of the above claim, is that protocols where the parties commit to their inputs, e.g., the GMW protocol, will not satisfy strong FaF-security in general.

Acknowledgements. We are grateful to Amos Beimel for many helpful discussions.

References

1. Alon, B., Omri, E., Paskin-Cherniavsky, A.: MPC with friends and foes. Cryptology ePrint Archive, Report 2020/701. https://eprint.iacr.org/2020/701
2. Alwen, J., Shelat, A., Visconti, I.: Collusion-free protocols in the mediated model. In: Wagner, D. (ed.) CRYPTO 2008. LNCS, vol. 5157, pp. 497–514. Springer, Heidelberg (2008). https://doi.org/10.1007/978-3-540-85174-5_28
3. Alwen, J., Katz, J., Maurer, U., Zikas, V.: Collusion-preserving computation. In: Safavi-Naini, R., Canetti, R. (eds.) CRYPTO 2012. LNCS, vol. 7417, pp. 124–143. Springer, Heidelberg (2012). https://doi.org/10.1007/978-3-642-32009-5_9
4. Asharov, G., Beimel, A., Makriyannis, N., Omri, E.: Complete characterization of fairness in secure two-party computation of Boolean functions. In: Dodis, Y., Nielsen, J.B. (eds.) TCC 2015. LNCS, vol. 9014, pp. 199–228. Springer, Heidelberg (2015). https://doi.org/10.1007/978-3-662-46494-6_10
5. Beaver, D.: Foundations of secure interactive computing. In: Feigenbaum, J. (ed.) CRYPTO 1991. LNCS, vol. 576, pp. 377–391. Springer, Heidelberg (1992). https://doi.org/10.1007/3-540-46766-1_31
6. Beaver, D.: Secure multiparty protocols and zero-knowledge proof systems tolerating a faulty minority. J. Cryptol. 4(2), 75–122 (1991). https://doi.org/10.1007/BF00196771
7. Beaver, D.: Minimal-latency secure function evaluation. In: Preneel, B. (ed.) EUROCRYPT 2000. LNCS, vol. 1807, pp. 335–350. Springer, Heidelberg (2000). https://doi.org/10.1007/3-540-45539-6_23

8. Beaver, D., Micali, S., Rogaway, P.: The round complexity of secure protocols. In: STOC 1990, pp. 503–513. ACM (1990)

9. Beerliová-Trubíniová, Z., Fitzi, M., Hirt, M., Maurer, U., Zikas, V.: MPC vs. SFE: perfect security in a unified corruption model. In: Canetti, R. (ed.) TCC 2008. LNCS, vol. 4948, pp. 231–250. Springer, Heidelberg (2008). https://doi.org/10.1007/978-3-540-78524-8_14

10. Beimel, A., Malkin, T., Micali, S.: The all-or-nothing nature of two-party secure computation. In: Wiener, M. (ed.) CRYPTO 1999. LNCS, vol. 1666, pp. 80–97. Springer, Heidelberg (1999). https://doi.org/10.1007/3-540-48405-1_6

11. Ben-Or, M., Goldwasser, S., Wigderson, A.: Completeness theorems for non-cryptographic fault-tolerant distributed computation (extended abstract). In: Proceedings of the 29th Annual Symposium on Foundations of Computer Science (FOCS), pp. 1–10 (1988)

12. Benhamouda, F., Lin, H., Polychroniadou, A., Venkitasubramaniam, M.: Two-round adaptively secure multiparty computation from standard assumptions. In: Beimel, A., Dziembowski, S. (eds.) TCC 2018. LNCS, vol. 11239, pp. 175–205. Springer, Cham (2018). https://doi.org/10.1007/978-3-030-03807-6_7

13. Canetti, R.: Security and composition of multiparty cryptographic protocols. J. Cryptol. **13**(1), 143–202 (2000). https://doi.org/10.1007/s001459910006

14. Canetti, R., Vald, M.: Universally composable security with local adversaries. In: Visconti, I., De Prisco, R. (eds.) SCN 2012. LNCS, vol. 7485, pp. 281–301. Springer, Heidelberg (2012). https://doi.org/10.1007/978-3-642-32928-9_16

15. Canetti, R., Poburinnaya, O., Venkitasubramaniam, M.: Equivocating YAO: constant-round adaptively secure multiparty computation in the plain model. In: Proceedings of the 49th Annual ACM SIGACT Symposium on Theory of Computing, pp. 497–509. ACM (2017)

16. Cleve, R.: Limits on the security of coin flips when half the processors are faulty. In: Proceedings of the 18th Annual ACM Symposium on Theory of Computing (STOC), pp. 364–369 (1986)

17. Cramer, R., Damgård, I., Ishai, Y.: Share conversion, pseudorandom secret-sharing and applications to secure computation. In: Kilian, J. (ed.) TCC 2005. LNCS, vol. 3378, pp. 342–362. Springer, Heidelberg (2005). https://doi.org/10.1007/978-3-540-30576-7_19

18. Damgård, I., Ishai, Y.: Constant-round multiparty computation using a black-box pseudorandom generator. In: Shoup, V. (ed.) CRYPTO 2005. LNCS, vol. 3621, pp. 378–394. Springer, Heidelberg (2005). https://doi.org/10.1007/11535218_23

19. Daza, V., Makriyannis, N.: Designing fully secure protocols for secure two-party computation of constant-domain functions. In: Kalai, Y., Reyzin, L. (eds.) TCC 2017. LNCS, vol. 10677, pp. 581–611. Springer, Cham (2017). https://doi.org/10.1007/978-3-319-70500-2_20

20. Dolev, D., Dwork, C., Naor, M.: Nonmalleable cryptography. SIAM Rev. **45**(4), 727–784 (2003)

21. Fitzi, M., Hirt, M., Maurer, U.: General adversaries in unconditional multi-party computation. In: Lam, K.-Y., Okamoto, E., Xing, C. (eds.) ASIACRYPT 1999. LNCS, vol. 1716, pp. 232–246. Springer, Heidelberg (1999). https://doi.org/10.1007/978-3-540-48000-6_19

22. Garg, S., Sahai, A.: Adaptively secure multi-party computation with dishonest majority. In: Safavi-Naini, R., Canetti, R. (eds.) CRYPTO 2012. LNCS, vol. 7417, pp. 105–123. Springer, Heidelberg (2012). https://doi.org/10.1007/978-3-642-32009-5_8

23. Gennaro, R., Ishai, Y., Kushilevitz, E., Rabin, T.: The round complexity of verifiable secret sharing and secure multicast. In: STOC 2001, pp. 580–589 (2001)
24. Gennaro, R., Ishai, Y., Kushilevitz, E., Rabin, T.: On 2-round secure multiparty computation. In: Yung, M. (ed.) CRYPTO 2002. LNCS, vol. 2442, pp. 178–193. Springer, Heidelberg (2002). https://doi.org/10.1007/3-540-45708-9_12
25. Goldreich, O.: Foundations of Cryptography - Volume 2: Basic Applications. Cambridge University Press, Cambridge (2004)
26. Goldreich, O., Micali, S., Wigderson, A.: How to play any mental game or a completeness theorem for protocols with honest majority. In: STOC, pp. 218–229 (1987)
27. Gordon, S.D., Katz, J.: Complete fairness in multi-party computation without an honest majority. In: Reingold, O. (ed.) TCC 2009. LNCS, vol. 5444, pp. 19–35. Springer, Heidelberg (2009). https://doi.org/10.1007/978-3-642-00457-5_2
28. Gordon, S.D., Hazay, C., Katz, J., Lindell, Y.: Complete fairness in secure two-party computation. In: Proceedings of the 40th Annual ACM Symposium on Theory of Computing (STOC), pp. 413–422 (2008)
29. Halevi, S., Lindell, Y., Pinkas, B.: Secure computation on the web: computing without simultaneous interaction. In: Rogaway, P. (ed.) CRYPTO 2011. LNCS, vol. 6841, pp. 132–150. Springer, Heidelberg (2011). https://doi.org/10.1007/978-3-642-22792-9_8
30. Halevi, S., Ishai, Y., Kushilevitz, E., Rabin, T.: Best possible information-theoretic MPC. In: Beimel, A., Dziembowski, S. (eds.) TCC 2018. LNCS, vol. 11240, pp. 255–281. Springer, Cham (2018). https://doi.org/10.1007/978-3-030-03810-6_10
31. Hirt, M., Maurer, U., Zikas, V.: MPC vs. SFE: unconditional and computational security. In: Pieprzyk, J. (ed.) ASIACRYPT 2008. LNCS, vol. 5350, pp. 1–18. Springer, Heidelberg (2008). https://doi.org/10.1007/978-3-540-89255-7_1
32. Ishai, Y., Kushilevitz, E., Paskin, A.: Secure multiparty computation with minimal interaction. In: Rabin, T. (ed.) CRYPTO 2010. LNCS, vol. 6223, pp. 577–594. Springer, Heidelberg (2010). https://doi.org/10.1007/978-3-642-14623-7_31
33. Ishai, Y., Katz, J., Kushilevitz, E., Lindell, Y., Petrank, E.: On achieving the "best of both worlds" in secure multiparty computation. SIAM J. Comput. 40(1), 122–141 (2011)
34. Katz, J., Lindell, Y.: Collusion-free multiparty computation in the mediated model. IACR Cryptology ePrint Archive 2008:533 (2008)
35. Koo, C.-Y.: Secure computation with partial message loss. In: Halevi, S., Rabin, T. (eds.) TCC 2006. LNCS, vol. 3876, pp. 502–521. Springer, Heidelberg (2006). https://doi.org/10.1007/11681878_26
36. Makriyannis, N.: On the classification of finite Boolean functions up to fairness. In: Abdalla, M., De Prisco, R. (eds.) SCN 2014. LNCS, vol. 8642, pp. 135–154. Springer, Cham (2014). https://doi.org/10.1007/978-3-319-10879-7_9
37. Micali, S., Rogaway, P.: Secure computation. In: Feigenbaum, J. (ed.) CRYPTO 1991. LNCS, vol. 576, pp. 392–404. Springer, Heidelberg (1992). https://doi.org/10.1007/3-540-46766-1_32
38. Rabin, T., Ben-Or, M.: Verifiable secret sharing and multiparty protocols with honest majority. In: STOC 1989, pp. 73–85 (1989)
39. Shamir, A.: How to share a secret. Commun. ACM 22(11), 612–613 (1979)
40. Zikas, V.: Generalized corruption models in secure multi-party computation. Ph.D. thesis, ETH Zurich (2010). http://d-nb.info/1005005729
41. Zikas, V., Hauser, S., Maurer, U.: Realistic failures in secure multi-party computation. In: Reingold, O. (ed.) TCC 2009. LNCS, vol. 5444, pp. 274–293. Springer, Heidelberg (2009). https://doi.org/10.1007/978-3-642-00457-5_17

Always Have a Backup Plan: Fully Secure Synchronous MPC with Asynchronous Fallback

Erica Blum[1(✉)], Chen-Da Liu-Zhang[2(✉)], and Julian Loss[1(✉)]

[1] University of Maryland, College Park, USA
{erblum,jloss}@cs.umd.edu
[2] ETH Zurich, Zürich, Switzerland
lichen@inf.ethz.ch

Abstract. Protocols for secure Multi-Party Computation (MPC) can be classified according to the underlying communication model. Two prominent communication models considered in the literature are the synchronous and asynchronous models, which considerably differ in terms of the achievable security guarantees. Synchronous MPC protocols can achieve the optimal corruption threshold $n/2$ and allow every party to give input, but become completely insecure when synchrony assumptions are violated. On the other hand, asynchronous MPC protocols remain secure under arbitrary network conditions, but can tolerate only $n/3$ corruptions and parties with slow connections unavoidably cannot give input.

A natural question is whether there exists a protocol for MPC that can tolerate up to $t_s < n/2$ corruptions under a synchronous network and $t_a < n/3$ corruptions even when the network is asynchronous. We answer this question by showing tight feasibility and impossibility results. More specifically, we show that such a protocol exists if and only if $t_a + 2t_s < n$ and the number of inputs taken into account under an asynchronous network is at most $n - t_s$.

1 Introduction

Secure multi-party computation (MPC) allows a set of parties $\mathcal{P} = \{P_1, \ldots, P_n\}$ to compute an arbitrary function of their private inputs, even if an adversary corrupts some of the parties. Intuitively, security in MPC means that the parties' inputs remain secret (apart from what is revealed by the computed output), and that the computed output is correct.

One can classify the results in MPC according to the underlying communication model. The *synchronous* model assumes that there is some parameter Δ known to all parties such that whenever a party sends a message, the recipient is guaranteed to receive it within time at most Δ. It is possible to achieve very strong security guarantees in this model; for example, prior work has shown how to achieve MPC with *full security*, where parties are guaranteed to obtain the correct output, for up to $t_s < \frac{n}{2}$ corruptions [2,3,6,15,20–22,24,27,30,31,33,46]. However, one can argue that the synchrony assumption is too strong: if an honest party P doesn't manage to send a message within Δ delay, it is considered

Electronic supplementary material The online version of this chapter (https://doi.org/10.1007/978-3-030-56880-1_25) contains supplementary material, which is available to authorized users.

D. Micciancio and T. Ristenpart (Eds.): CRYPTO 2020, LNCS 12171, pp. 707–731, 2020.
https://doi.org/10.1007/978-3-030-56880-1_25

dishonest in the synchronous model. As a consequence, synchronous protocols generally lose all security guarantees (e.g., parties can jointly reconstruct P's secret-shared input) if the network delays are greater than expected. This is of particular concern in real-world deployments, where it may not be possible to guarantee ideal network conditions at all times.

In the asynchronous model, the assumption of a known upper bound on network delay is dropped, so that the network delay can be arbitrarily large. The asynchronous model is therefore a safe choice for modeling even the most unpredictable real-world networks; however, prior work has shown that optimal security guarantees in this model are necessarily weaker than in the synchronous model: MPC can be achieved in the asynchronous model only for $t_a < \frac{n}{3}$ corruptions, and the output is not guaranteed to take into account all inputs into the computation [4,7,17,19,34].

In this paper, we investigate MPC protocols that keep strong security guarantees under both communication models. More specifically, let $t_a < \frac{n}{3}$ and $t_s < \frac{n}{2}$. We ask the following question:

Is there a protocol for MPC that is secure under t_s corruptions under a synchronous network, and t_a corruptions under an asynchronous network?

We completely answer this question by showing tight feasibility and impossibility results:

Feasibility Result. We give an MPC protocol that is fully secure up to t_s corruptions under a synchronous network and up to t_a corruptions under an asynchronous network, as long as $t_a + 2t_s < n$. The number of inputs taken into account in the latter case is $n - t_s$.

Optimality of Our Protocol. We show that our protocol is tight with respect to both the threshold tradeoffs t_a and t_s, and also the number of inputs taken into account. More concretely, we show:

- For any t_s, any MPC protocol which achieves full security up to t_s corruptions under a synchronous network cannot take into account more than $n - t_s$ inputs when run over an asynchronous network, even if all parties are guaranteed to be honest in this case.
- For any $t_a + 2t_s \geq n$, there is no MPC protocol which gives full security up to t_s corruptions under a synchronous network, and where all parties output the same value up to t_a corruptions under an asynchronous network.

1.1   Technical Overview

In this section, we briefly sketch our protocol for MPC that achieves full security up to t_s corruptions under a synchronous network and up to t_a corruptions under an asynchronous network, for any $0 \leq t_a < \frac{n}{3} \leq t_s < \frac{n}{2}$ satisfying $t_a + 2t_s < n$. Note that we impose $t_s \geq \frac{n}{3}$, because otherwise one can use existing asynchronous MPC protocols (e.g. [34]), which already achieve such security guarantees, i.e., are fully secure under an asynchronous network (and hence also a synchronous network), and moreover take into account all inputs when given some initial synchronous rounds.

At a very high level, we run two sub-protocols Π_{smpc} and Π_{ampc} one after the other, where Π_{smpc} is a t_s-secure synchronous protocol and Π_{ampc} is a t_a-secure asynchronous protocol (e.g. [7,17,34]). Conceptually, a key challenge is that parties are not able to obtain output in both protocols, as this would violate privacy. Thus, parties need to agree on whether to run the second sub-protocol. For that, the key is that the protocol Π_{smpc} gives guarantees even when the network is asynchronous. More concretely, Π_{smpc} achieves unanimous output up to t_a corruptions under an asynchronous network. Intuitively, this means that the protocol is secure, except the fact that either all parties learn the correct output, or all parties obtain $\perp$ as the output.

When the network is synchronous, security of the overall protocol is inherited from the first sub-protocol. In the case where the network is asynchronous, parties either learn the correct output from the first sub-protocol or all parties obtain $\perp$ and can safely execute the second sub-protocol.

Synchronous MPC with Asynchronous Unanimous Output. In order to construct the first sub-protocol, we modify a synchronous MPC protocol that uses threshold homomorphic encryption [22,27]. The original protocol provides full security up to $t_s < \frac{n}{2}$ corruptions in a synchronous network.

Let us briefly recall the high-level structure of the original protocol [22,27]. The protocol is based on a threshold version of the Paillier cryptosystem [43]. For a plaintext a, let us denote $\bar{a}$ an encryption of a. The cryptosystem is homomorphic: given encryptions $\bar{a}$, $\bar{b}$, one can compute an encryption of $a + b$, which we denote $\bar{a} \boxplus \bar{b}$. Similarly, from a constant plaintext α and an encryption $\bar{a}$ one can compute an encryption of αa, which we denote $\alpha \boxdot \bar{a}$.

The protocol starts by having each party publish encryptions of its input values, as well as zero-knowledge proofs that it knows these values. Then, parties compute addition and multiplication gates to obtain a common ciphertext, which they jointly decrypt using threshold decryption. Any linear operation (addition or multiplication by a constant) can be performed non-interactively, due to the homomorphism property of the threshold encryption scheme. Given encryptions $\bar{a}$, $\bar{b}$ of input values to a multiplication gate, parties can compute an encryption of $c = ab$ as follows:

1. Each P_i chooses a random $d_i \in \mathbf{Z}_n$ and uses a byzantine broadcast protocol to distribute encryptions $\overline{d_i}$ and $\overline{d_i b}$.
2. Parties prove (in zero-knowledge) knowledge of the plaintext d_i and that $\overline{d_i b}$ encrypts the correct value. Let S be the subset of parties succeeding in both proofs.
3. Parties compute $\bar{a} \boxplus (\boxplus_{i \in S} \overline{d_i})$ and decrypt it using a threshold decryption.
4. Parties set $\bar{c} = (a + \sum_{i \in S} d_i) \boxdot \bar{b} \boxminus ((\boxplus_{i \in S} \overline{d_i b}))$.

Intuitively, the protocol works because 1) honest parties have agreement on the ciphertext to decrypt after evaluating the circuit, and 2) only ciphertexts or random values are revealed.

When the above protocol is executed over an asynchronous network, all security guarantees are lost. This is because synchronous broadcast protocols do not necessarily give any guarantees when run over an asynchronous network. As a result, parties lose agreement in critical points in the protocol. For example, parties can receive different sets of encrypted inputs during input distribution, which can lead to privacy violations if the mismatching inputs are decrypted. Moreover, parties must reach agreement on S, and S must contain at least one honest party contributing to the reconstructed random value to ensure that the value is random and unknown to the adversary. For this, it is essential that parties have agreement on whether a zero-knowledge proof was successful or not. Finally, parties need to reach agreement on which ciphertext to decrypt, or whether to decrypt at all.

To solve the problems above, we replace the problematic sub-protocols with versions that achieve certain guarantees even when the network is asynchronous. More concretely, we will make use of broadcast, byzantine agreement and asynchronous common subset sub-protocols. The broadcast protocol will ensure that encrypted inputs from honest parties can only lead to correct ciphertexts. When used with the byzantine agreement protocol proposed in [8], it will allow parties to reach agreement on the set S for the multiplication gates. Finally, we make use of the enhanced asynchronous common subset sub-protocol in [9] at the end of the circuit computation to decide whether or not parties should proceed to decrypt a ciphertext, or output $\bot$.

1.2   Related Work

Despite being a very natural direction of research, protocols resilient to both synchronous and asynchronous networks have only begun to be studied in relatively recent works. The closest related work is the recent work by Blum et al. [8] which considers the problem of byzantine agreement in a 'hybrid' network model. The authors prove that byzantine agreement t_s-secure under a synchronous network and t_a-secure under an asynchronous network is possible if and only if $t_a + 2t_s < n$. The work was recently further extended to the problem of state-machine replication [9]. Our work extends both above works to the problem of secure multi-party computation, and in particular, introduces techniques to protect privacy of inputs in the hybrid network setting.

Another close related work is the work by Guo et al. [32], which considers a weakened variant of the classical synchronous model. Here, an attacker can temporarily disconnect a subset of parties from the rest of the network. Guo et al. gave byzantine agreement and multi-party computation protocols tolerating the optimal corruption threshold in this model, and Abraham et al. [1] achieve similar guarantees for state-machine replication. The main difference between these works and ours is that their protocols need to assume synchrony in part of the network. In contrast, our protocols give guarantees even if the network is fully asynchronous.

Further related work for the problem of byzantine agreement protocols include the work by Malkhi et al. [41] which considers protocols that provide guarantees when run in synchronous or partially synchronous networks, and the work by Liu et al. [38] which designs protocols resilient to malicious corruptions in a synchronous network, and fail-stop corruptions in an asynchronous network. Kursawe [37] shows a protocol for asynchronous byzantine agreement that reaches agreement more quickly in case the network is synchronous.

A line of works [39,40,44,45] has recently investigated protocols that achieve *responsiveness*. These protocols operate under a synchronous network, but in addition give the guarantee that parties obtain output as fast as the actual network delay allows. None of these works provide security guarantees when the network is not synchronous.

2   Model

Our protocols are proven secure in the universally composable (UC) framework [13] (see Section A for a summary).

2.1   Setup

We consider a setting with n parties $\mathcal{P} = \{P_1, \ldots, P_n\}$. We denote κ the security parameter.

Common Reference String. We assume that the parties have a common reference string (CRS). The CRS is used to realize the bilateral zero-knowledge UC functionalities.

Digital Signatures. We assume that parties have a public-key infrastructure available, i.e., all parties hold the same vector of public keys $(\mathrm{pk}_1, \ldots, \mathrm{pk}_n)$, and each party P_i holds the secret key sk_i associated with pk_i. This allows parties to sign values.

Definition 1. *A digital signature scheme is a tuple of algorithms* (Gen, Sign, Ver) *such that:*

- *Key generation: On input 1^κ, the key generation algorithm outputs* $(\mathrm{pk}, \mathrm{sk}) = \mathrm{Gen}(1^\kappa)$ *a pair of public and secret key.*
- *Signature: Given a secret key* sk *and a message x, the signing algorithm outputs* $\sigma = \mathrm{Sign}_{\mathrm{sk}}(x)$ *a signature of message x.*
- *Verification: Given a public key* pk, *a message x and a signature σ, the verification algorithm outputs* $\mathrm{Ver}_{\mathrm{pk}}(x, \sigma) = 1$ *if and only if σ is a correct signature of x.*

We require that the signature scheme is correct and unforgeable against chosen message attacks.

Threshold Encryption. We assume that parties have a threshold additively homomorphic encryption setup available. That is, it provides to each party P_i a global public key ek and a private key share dk_i.

Definition 2. *A threshold homomorphic encryption scheme is a public-key encryption scheme which has the following properties:*

- *Key generation: The key generation algorithm is parameterized by (t, n) and outputs $(\mathsf{ek}, \mathsf{dk}) = \mathsf{Gen}_{(t,n)}(1^\kappa)$, where ek is the public key, and $\mathsf{dk} = (\mathsf{dk}_1, \dots, \mathsf{dk}_n)$ is the list of private keys.*
- *Encryption: Given ek and a plaintext a one can compute an encryption $\bar{a} = \mathsf{Enc}_{\mathsf{ek}}(a)$ of a.*
- *Decryption: Given a ciphertext c and a secret key share dk_i, there is an algorithm that outputs $d_i = \mathsf{DecShare}_{\mathsf{dk}_i}(c)$, such that $(d_1, \dots, d_n)$ forms a t-out-of-n sharing of the plaintext $m = \mathsf{Dec}_{\mathsf{dk}}(c)$. Moreover, with t decryption shares $\{d_i\}$, one can reconstruct the plaintext $m = \mathsf{Rec}(\{d_i\})$.*
- *Additively homomorphic: Given ek and two encryptions $\bar{a} \in \mathsf{Enc}_{\mathsf{ek}}(a)$ and $\bar{b} \in \mathsf{Enc}_{\mathsf{ek}}(b)$, one can efficiently compute an encryption $\overline{a + b} \in \mathsf{Enc}_{\mathsf{ek}}(a + b)$. We write $\overline{a + b} = \bar{a} + \bar{b}$.*
- *Multiplication by constant: Given ek, a plaintext α and an encryption $\bar{a} \in \mathsf{Enc}_{\mathsf{ek}}(a)$, one can efficiently compute a random encryption $\overline{\alpha a} \in \mathsf{Enc}_{\mathsf{ek}}(\alpha a)$. We write $\overline{\alpha a} = \alpha \boxdot \bar{a}$.*

Such a threshold encryption scheme can be based on, for example, the Paillier cryptosystem [43] (see Section B). We use the threshold encryption scheme as a basic tool in the MPC protocol, following the approach in [22,27].

2.2 Communication Network and Adversary

We consider a complete network of authenticated channels. Our protocols operate in two possible settings: synchronous or asynchronous.

In the synchronous setting, all parties have access to synchronized clocks and all messages are guaranteed to be delivered within some known upper bound delay Δ. Within Δ, the adversary can schedule the messages arbitrarily. In particular, the adversary is *rushing*, i.e., within the same round, the adversary is allowed to send its messages after seeing the honest parties' messages. Sometimes it is convenient to describe a protocol in rounds, where each round r refers to the interval of time $(r - 1)\Delta$ to $r\Delta$. In such case, we say that a party receives a message in round r if it receives the message within that time interval. Moreover, we say a party sends a message in round r when it sends the message at the beginning of the round, i.e., at time $(r - 1)\Delta$.

In the asynchronous setting, both assumptions above are removed. That is, parties do not have access to synchronized clocks, and the adversary is allowed to arbitrarily schedule the delivery of the messages. However, we assume that all messages are eventually delivered (i.e., the adversary cannot drop messages).

We consider a static adversary who corrupts parties in an arbitrary manner at the beginning of the protocol.

3   Definitions

3.1   Broadcast

Broadcast allows a designated party called the *sender* to consistently distribute a message among a set of parties.

Definition 3 *(Broadcast). Let Π be a protocol executed by parties $P_1, \ldots, P_n$, where a designated sender P_s initially holds an input v, and parties terminate upon generating output.*

– *Validity: Π is t-valid if the following holds whenever up to t parties are corrupted: if P_s is honest, then every honest party which outputs, outputs v.*
– *Weak-validity: Π is t-weakly valid if the following holds whenever up to t parties are corrupted: if P_s is honest, then every honest party which outputs, outputs v or $\perp$.*
– *Consistency: Π is t-consistent if the following holds whenever up to t parties are corrupted: every honest party which outputs, outputs the same value.*
– *Liveness: Π is t-live if the following holds whenever up to t parties are corrupted: every honest party outputs a value.*

If Π is t-valid, t-consistent and t-live, we say that it is t-secure.

In the asynchronous setting, one can formally prove that the strong broadcast guarantees as in Definition 3 cannot be achieved [10,11]. Intuitively, the reason is that one cannot distinguish between a dishonest sender not sending messages, or an honest sender's messages being delayed. Hence, a useful primitive is a *reliable broadcast* protocol, which achieves the same guarantees as a broadcast protocol, except that the liveness property is relaxed and divided into two properties.

Definition 4 *(Reliable Broadcast). Let Π be a protocol executed by parties $P_1, \ldots, P_n$, where a designated sender P_s initially holds an input v, and parties terminate upon generating output.*

– *Validity: Π is t-valid if the following holds whenever up to t parties are corrupted: if P_s is honest, then every honest party outputs v.*
– *Consistency: Π is t-consistent if the following holds whenever up to t parties are corrupted: either no honest party terminates, or else all honest parties output the same value.*

Observe that, in contrast to Definition 3, when the sender is dishonest, it is allowed that no honest party terminates.

3.2   Byzantine Agreement

In a byzantine agreement protocol, each party P_i starts with a value v_i. The protocol allows the set of parties to agree on a common value. The achieved guarantees are the same as in broadcast (see Definition 3), except that validity is adapted accordingly.

Definition 5 *(Byzantine Agreement). Let Π be a protocol executed by parties $P_1, \ldots, P_n$, where each party P_i initially holds an input v_i, and parties terminate upon generating output.*

- *Validity: Π is t-valid if the following holds whenever up to t parties are corrupted: if every honest party has the same input value v, then every honest party that outputs, outputs v.*
- *Consistency: Π is t-consistent if the following holds whenever up to t parties are corrupted: every honest party which outputs, outputs the same value.*
- *Liveness: Π is t-live if the following holds whenever up to t parties are corrupted: every honest party outputs a value.*

If Π is t-valid, t-consistent and t-live, we say that it is t-secure.

3.3   Asynchronous Common Subset

A protocol for the asynchronous common subset (ACS) problem [7,9,12,42] allows n parties, each with an initial input, to agree on a subset of the inputs. For this primitive, we do not assume that parties terminate upon generating output, that is, even after generating output parties are allowed to keep participating in the protocol indefinitely.

Definition 6 *(ACS). Let Π be a protocol executed by parties $P_1, \ldots, P_n$, where each party initially holds an input v, and parties output sets of size at most n.*

- *Validity: Π is t-valid if the following holds whenever up to t parties are corrupted: if all honest parties start with the same input v, then every honest party which outputs, outputs $\{v\}$.*
- *Consistency: Π is t-consistent if the following holds whenever up to t parties are corrupted: every honest party which outputs, outputs the same set.*
- *Liveness: Π is t-live if the following holds whenever up to t parties are corrupted: every honest party outputs.*
- *Validity liveness: Π is t-live valid if the following holds whenever up to t parties are corrupted: If all honest parties start with the same input, then every honest party outputs.*
- *Set quality: Π has (t, h)-set quality if the following holds whenever up to t parties are corrupted: if an honest party outputs a set, it contains the inputs of at least h honest parties.*

3.4   Multi-Party Computation

At a high level, a protocol for multi-party computation (MPC) allows n parties $P_1, \ldots, P_n$, where each party P_i has an initial input x_i, to jointly compute a function over the inputs $f(x_1, \ldots, x_n)$ in such a way that nothing beyond the output is revealed.

We consider different types of security guarantees for our MPC protocols. The first one is the strongest guarantee that an MPC protocol can offer: MPC with guaranteed output delivery, or full security (cf. [3,6,15,22,31,46]). Here, honest parties are guaranteed to obtain the correct output. Formally, in UC this is modeled as the protocol realizing the ideal functionality where each party P_i inputs x_i to the functionality, and it then outputs $f(x_1, \ldots, x_n)$ to the parties.

When the network is asynchronous, it is provably impossible that the computed function takes into account all inputs from honest parties [4,7,17,19,34]. The reason is that one cannot distinguish between a dishonest party not sending its input, or an honest party's input being delayed. Hence, we say that a protocol achieves L-output quality, if the output to be computed contains the inputs from at least L parties. Traditional asynchronous protocols in the literature (e.g. [5,7,34]) achieve $(n - t)$-output quality under t corruptions, since the computed output ignores up to t inputs. Formally this is modelled in the ideal functionality as allowing the ideal adversary to choose a subset S of L parties. The functionality then computes $f(x_1, \ldots, x_n)$, where $x_i = v_i$ is the input of P_i in the case that $P_i \in S$, and otherwise $x_i = \bot$.

Functionality $\mathcal{F}_{\mathrm{SFE}}^{\mathrm{sec},L}$

$\mathcal{F}_{\mathrm{SFE}}$ is parameterized by a set $\mathcal{P}$ of n parties and a function $f : (\{0,1\}^* \cup \{\bot\})^n \to (\{0,1\}^*)^n$. For each $P_i \in \mathcal{P}$, initialize the variables $x_i = y_i = \bot$. Set $S = \mathcal{P}$.

1: On input (INPUT, v) from $P_i \in \mathcal{P}$, if $P_i \in S$, set $x_i = v$ and send a message (INPUT, P_i) to the adversary.
2: On input (OUTPUTSET, S') from the ideal adversary, where $S' \subseteq \mathcal{P}$ and $|S'| = L$, set $S = S'$ and $x_i = \bot$ for each $P_i \notin S$.
3: Once all inputs from honest parties in S have been input, set each $y_i = f(x_1, \ldots, x_n)$.
4: On input (GETOUTPUT) from P_i, output (OUTPUT, y_i, sid) to P_i.

In addition to MPC with full security, we also consider weaker notions of security. In MPC with selective output [18,35], the ideal world adversary can choose any subset of parties to receive $\bot$, instead of the correct output. The last type of security we consider is called MPC with unanimous output [29,31]. Under this definition, the adversary is permitted to choose whether all honest parties receive the correct output or all honest parties receive $\bot$ as output; as such it is slightly stronger than MPC with selective output, but weaker than full security.

Let us denote the functionality $\mathcal{F}_{\mathrm{SFE}}^{\mathrm{sout},L}$ (resp. $\mathcal{F}_{\mathrm{SFE}}^{\mathrm{uout},L}$), the above functionality, where the adversary can selectively choose any subset of parties to obtain $\bot$ as the output (resp. choose that either all honest parties receive $f(x_1, \ldots, x_n)$ or $\bot$).

Definition 7. *A protocol π achieves full security (resp. selective output; unanimous output) with L output-quality if it UC-realizes functionality $\mathcal{F}_{\mathrm{SFE}}^{\mathrm{sec},L}$ ($\mathcal{F}_{\mathrm{SFE}}^{\mathrm{sout},L}$; $\mathcal{F}_{\mathrm{SFE}}^{\mathrm{uout},L}$).*

Since protocols run in a synchronous network typically achieve n-output quality, we implicitly assume that all synchronous protocols discussed achieve n-output quality (unless otherwise specified).

Weak Termination. In general, traditional protocols for MPC require that the protocol terminates (halts). In this paper, we capture a slightly weaker version as a property of a protocol: we say that a protocol has weak termination, if parties are guaranteed to terminate upon receiving an output different than $\bot$, but do not necessarily terminate if the output is $\bot$.

4   Synchronous MPC with Asynchronous Unanimous Output and Weak Termination

In this section, we show a protocol $\Pi_{\mathsf{smpc}}^{t_s,t_a}$ that achieves full security up to t_s corruptions when the network is synchronous, and achieves unanimous output with weak termination up to t_a corruptions when the network is asynchronous, for any $0 \le t_a < \frac{n}{3} \le t_s < \frac{n}{2}$ satisfying $t_a + 2t_s < n$. The protocol relies on a number of primitives:

- $\Pi_{\mathsf{bc}}^{t_s,t_a}$ is a broadcast protocol that is t_s-secure when run in a synchronous network, and is t_a-weakly valid and t_a-live when run in an asynchronous network.
- $\Pi_{\mathsf{ba}}^{t_s,t_a}$ is a byzantine agreement protocol that is t_s-secure when run in a synchronous network, and is t_a-secure when run in an asynchronous network.
- $\Pi_{\mathsf{acs}}^{t_s,t_a}$ is an asynchronous common subset protocol that is t_s-valid and t_s-live valid when run in a synchronous network, and is t_a-consistent, t_a-live and has $(t_a, 1)$-set quality when run in an asynchronous network.
- $\Pi_{\mathsf{zk}}^{t_s,t_a}$ is a multi-party zero-knowledge protocol that allows a party P_i to prove knowledge of a witness w for a statement x satisfying a certain relation R towards all parties. The protocol achieves full security up to t_s corruptions when the network is synchronous, and achieves security with selective abort up to t_a corruptions when the network is asynchronous.

In the following, we show instantiations for each of the sub-protocols.

4.1   Broadcast

We use the Dolev-Strong protocol [8,28] to achieve a broadcast protocol that is t_s-secure when run in a synchronous network, and is t_a-weakly valid and t_a-live when run in an asynchronous network. The idea is quite simple: we run the Dolev-Strong protocol for $t_s + 1$ rounds and output v if v is the only value accepted, and otherwise $\bot$. In the protocol, we say that a message (v, Σ) at round r is valid if Σ contains r signatures, where one of them is from the sender and the other $r - 1$ from distinct additional parties.

Protocol $\Pi_{\mathsf{bc}}^{t_s,t_a}$

Sender P_s has input v. Each party P_i keeps local variables $\Sigma_i, \Omega_i := \varnothing$.

Round 1. P_s signs its input v to obtain a signature σ_s, and sends $(v, \{\sigma_s\})$ to all parties.

Round $1 \leq r \leq t_s$. Each P_i does: Upon receiving a valid message (v, Σ), add v to Ω_i. Compute a signature σ_i on v and let $\Sigma_i := \Sigma_i \cup \{\sigma_i\}$. Send (v, Σ_i) to all parties in the next round.

Output determination

Round $t_s + 1$. Each P_i does: Upon receiving a valid message (v, Σ), add v to Ω_i. Then, if Ω_i contains exactly one value v', output v' and terminate. Otherwise, output $\bot$ and terminate.

Lemma 1. *Let n, t_s, t_a be such that $t_a, t_s < n$. $\Pi_{\mathsf{bc}}^{t_s,t_a}$ is a broadcast protocol that is t_s-secure when run in a synchronous network, and is t_a-weakly valid and t_a-live when run in an asynchronous network.*

Proof. Security under a synchronous network is achieved via the standard analysis of the Dolev-Strong protocol: If the sender is honest, each honest party P_i adds the sender's input v to Ω_i, and no honest party adds any other value. Moreover, if an honest P_i adds v to Ω at round $r \leq t_s$, every honest P_j adds v at round $r + 1$. And if P_i adds v at round $t_s + 1$, then there are $t_s + 1$ signatures on v and hence an honest P_k added v at some round $r' \leq t_s$ and every honest party added v at round $r' + 1$. If the network is asynchronous, t_a-liveness is trivial, since every honest party outputs at (local) time $(t_s + 1)\Delta$. The protocol is also t_a-weakly valid because the adversary cannot forge signatures from the sender P_s. $\qquad\square$

4.2 Byzantine Agreement

In [8], the authors show a byzantine agreement protocol that is t_s-secure when run in a synchronous network, and is t_a-secure when run in an asynchronous network. We briefly sketch the construction here.

At a high level, their protocol consists of two phases: a round-based BA followed by an event-based BA. An honest party P_i with input v_i uses v_i as their input for the round-based phase. If the round-based phase terminates with output $v' \in \{0, 1\}$ within some (local) time limit, P_i uses v' as input for the event-based phase. (The timeout is chosen such that the honest parties are guaranteed to receive output from the round-based BA before the timeout when the network is synchronous and at most t_s parties are corrupted.) Otherwise, if the round-based phase times out without producing boolean output, P_i proceeds directly to the event-based phase, using their original input v_i as their input. P_i then outputs the output they receive from the event-based phase.

Intuitively, when the network is synchronous and there are t_s corruptions, the security guarantees for the full protocol are primarily inherited from the round-based BA sub-protocol (with the caveat that the event-based BA sub-protocol guarantees t_s-validity and therefore preserves the results of the first phase). When the network is asynchronous and there are t_a corruptions, the round-based BA protocol need only be t_a-weakly valid, after which the desired security guarantees follow from the security properties of the event-based BA sub-protocol. We state the following lemma. The proof can be found in [8].

Lemma 2. *Let n, t_s, t_a be such that $0 \leq t_a < \frac{n}{3} \leq t_s < \frac{n}{2}$ and $t_a + 2t_s < n$. There is a protocol $\Pi_{\mathsf{ba}}^{t_s,t_a}$ satisfying the following properties:*

1. *When run in a synchronous network, it is t_s-secure.*
2. *When run in an asynchronous network, it is t_a-secure.*

4.3   Asynchronous Common Subset

We describe the protocol $\Pi_{\mathsf{acs}}^{t_s,t_a}$ presented in [9], which is an asynchronous common subset protocol that is t_s-valid and t_s-live valid when run in a synchronous network, and is t_a-consistent, t_a-live and has $(t_a, 1)$-set quality when run in an asynchronous network.

The protocol is based on previous asynchronous common subset protocols [7,12,42], but the output decision differs. The general idea is that parties run n executions of Bracha's reliable broadcast protocol [10], where each party P_i acts as the sender in each execution, followed by n executions of byzantine agreement to agree on a subset of parties that finished the reliable broadcast protocol. If a party sees $n - t_s$ broadcasts terminate on the same value, it outputs this value. Otherwise, it waits until all byzantine agreement protocols have terminated and then outputs based on the set C of senders for whom the corresponding BA output 1: If there is a majority v of broadcasted values from parties in C, output v, and otherwise output the union of all broadcasted values from parties in C.

In order to achieve the guarantees described above, the protocol needs a reliable broadcast protocol which, under an asynchronous network, achieves validity up to t_s corruptions, and consistency up to t_a corruptions. Let us denote RBC_i the reliable broadcast protocol where P_i acts as the sender, and BA_i the byzantine agreement protocol which outputs whether RBC_i has terminated or not.

Protocol $\Pi_{\mathsf{acs}}^{t_s,t_a}(P_i)$

1: Participate in each protocol RBC_j, $j \neq i$, as the receiver, and participate in RBC_i as the sender.
2: On output from RBC_j, if an input has not yet been provided to BA_j, then input 1 to BA_j.
3: When $n - t_a$ of the protocols BA_j have output 1, provide input 0 to each instance BA_j that has not yet been provided input.

Output determination

```
 1: if at least n − t_s executions of RBC_j output a value v then
 2:     Output {v}.
 3: else
 4:     let C := {j | BA_j output 1}. Once all instances BA_j have been completed
        and |C| ≥ n − t_a, wait for the output v_j of each RBC_j, j ∈ C.
 5:     if A majority of the executions {RBC_j}_{j∈C} output a value v then
 6:         Output {v}.
 7:     else
 8:         Output ⋃_{j∈C}{v_j}.
 9:     end if
10: end if
```

We state the following lemma. The proof can be found in [9].

Lemma 3. *Let n, t_s, t_a be such that $0 \leq t_a < \frac{n}{3} \leq t_s < \frac{n}{2}$ and $t_a + 2t_s < n$. Protocol $\Pi_{\text{ACS}}^{t_s, t_a}$ satisfies the following properties:*

1. *When run in a synchronous network, it is t_s-valid and t_s-live valid.*
2. *When run in an asynchronous network, it is t_a-consistent, t_a-live and has $(t_a, 1)$-set quality.*

4.4 Zero-Knowledge

Let us assume a binary relation R, consisting of pairs (x, w), where x is the statement, and w is a witness to the statement. A zero-knowledge proof allows a prover P to prove to a verifier V knowledge of w such that $R(x, w) = 1$. We are interested in zero-knowledge proofs for three types of relations, parameterized by a threshold encryption scheme with public encryption key ek:

1. *Proof of Plaintext Knowledge:* The statement consists of ek, and a ciphertext c. The witness consists of a plaintext m and randomness r such that $c = \text{Enc}_{\text{ek}}(m, r)$.
2. *Proof of Correct Multiplication:* The statement consists of ek, and ciphertexts c_1, c_2 and c_3. The witness consists of a plaintext m_1 and randomness r_1, r_3 such that $c_1 = \text{Enc}_{\text{ek}}(m_1, r_1)$ and $c_3 = m_1 \cdot c_2 + \text{Enc}_{\text{ek}}(0; r_3)$.
3. *Proof of Correct Decryption:* The statement consists of ek, a ciphertext c, and a decryption share d. The witness consists of a decryption key share dk_i, such that $d = \text{Dec}_{\text{dk}_i}(c)$.

Examples of bilateral zero-knowledge proofs of knowledge can be found for example in [22,23]. The bilateral UC zero-knowledge functionality $\mathcal{F}_{\text{ZK}}$ for a relation R and a pair prover P and a verifier V is defined as follows: P inputs a pair (x, w) instance-witness, and the functionality outputs (x, b) to the verifier, where $b = 1$ if and only if $R(x, w) = 1$. It is known that assuming a CRS, one can realize a bilateral UC zero-knowledge functionality $\mathcal{F}_{\text{ZK}}$ [14,17,26].

Multi-party zero-knowledge protocols. A multi-party zero-knowledge protocol allows a prover P to prove towards all parties knowledge of a witness w

for a statement x such that $R(x, w) = 1$. The ideal functionality can be seen as a special case of secure function evaluation, where the prover inputs (x, w), and the parties obtain the statement x and 1 if and only if $R(x, w) = 1$.

Assuming a bilateral UC zero-knowledge functionality $\mathcal{F}_{\mathrm{ZK}}$, one can construct a UC multi-party zero-knowledge functionality $\mathcal{F}_{\mathrm{MZK}}$ using so-called *certificates* [34] as follows: The prover bilaterally performs the zero-knowledge proofs towards each of the recipients, who upon a successful proof, send a signature that the proof was correct. Once the prover collects a list L of $t_s + 1$ signatures, the list works as a certificate that proves non-interactively that at least one honest party accepted the proof. The prover can hence broadcast the list L to let all honest parties know that the proof is correct. If the last broadcast is executed with the protocol $\Pi_{\mathrm{bc}}^{t_s, t_a}$, it is easy to see that under t_s corruptions and a synchronous network the multi-party zero-knowledge functionality achieves full security. Moreover, if there are up to t_a corruptions and an asynchronous network, broadcast guarantees weak validity, so the protocol achieves security with selective abort (in the last step, if the prover has a certificate, it is guaranteed that parties receive the certificate or $\perp$, and a dishonest party who did not collect such certificate cannot make the parties accept the proof).

Protocol $\Pi_{\mathrm{zk}}^{t_s, t_a}$

Prover P proves knowledge of a witness w for a statement x satisfying a certain relation R towards all parties.

1: P inputs (x, w) to each bilateral $\mathcal{F}_{\mathrm{ZK}}$.
2: Each P_i does: Upon a successful proof, compute $\sigma_i = \mathsf{Sign}_{sk_i}(x)$ and send σ_i to P.
3: P collects a list L of $t_s + 1$ signatures and broadcasts using protocol $\Pi_{\mathrm{bc}}^{t_s, t_a}$ the list L.
4: Each P_i does: Upon receiving a list L as output of the broadcast protocol, if L contains $t_s + 1$ signatures on the same instance x, output $(x, 1)$. In any other case, output $\perp$.

Lemma 4. *Let R be a relation. Let n, t_s, t_a be such that $t_a, t_s < n$. $\Pi_{\mathrm{zk}}^{t_s, t_a}$ realizes the multi-party zero-knowledge functionality for P as prover with the following guarantees:*

1. *When run in a synchronous network, it achieves full security up to t_s corruptions.*
2. *When run in an asynchronous network, it achieves security with selective abort up to t_a corruptions.*

Proof. We prove each of the cases separately. We simulate in the hybrid where there is a trusted setup generating the keys in the real world. In the ideal world, the simulator $\mathcal{S}$ generates the PKI keys, and outputs the public keys to the adversary along with its secret keys.

Synchronous network and up to t_s corruptions. We describe the simulator $\mathcal{S}$ for the case where the network is synchronous and there are up to t_s corruptions. Let us first consider the case where the prover P is honest.

- $\mathcal{S}$ forwards the result from $\mathcal{F}_{\mathrm{MZK}}$ to the adversary. If the result is positive, generate a signature σ_i on behalf of each honest party. Let L be list of signatures.
- On input correct signatures from the dishonest parties, it adds it to L.
- $\mathcal{S}$ emulates the messages of the broadcast protocol.

Now assume that P is dishonest.

- $\mathcal{S}$ gets the instance-witness pairs that P inputs to prove to each party. To the dishonest parties, output the instance and the bit 1 if and only if the witness is correct.
- For each of the pairs, forward a signature on behalf of the honest party if the witness is a correct witness to the corresponding instance.
- $\mathcal{S}$ receives a list L of $t_s + 1$ signatures on the same instance: input the instance and the witness to $\mathcal{F}_{\mathrm{MZK}}$.

Asynchronous network and up to t_a corruptions. The only difference with respect to the case where the network is synchronous, is that the protocol $\Pi_{\mathrm{bc}}^{t_s,t_a}$ only provides weak-validity. In the simulation, it implies that the simulator will also need to simulate the $\perp$ messages from the broadcast protocols.

It is easy to see that the simulation goes through. In the case of a synchronous network and t_s corruptions, an honest prover collects at least $t_s + 1$ signatures and every honest receiver outputs 1. In the case the prover is dishonest, it cannot collect $t_s + 1$ signatures for an instance without having succeeded in one of the proofs, and hence each honest party outputs $\perp$. If the network is asynchronous, when the prover is honest, every honest party outputs 1 or $\perp$, where the set of parties that output $\perp$ is chosen by the adversary. In the case the prover is dishonest, the case is analogous as the synchronous case and every honest party outputs $\perp$.

$\square$

4.5 Description of the Synchronous MPC Protocol

We start from the MPC protocol that uses homomorphic encryption presented in [22, 27]. The protocol was originally designed for the synchronous setting and guarantees full security up to $t_s < \frac{n}{2}$ corruptions. We modify the protocol to also achieve unanimous output up to t_a corruptions even when the network is asynchronous, as long as $0 \leq t_a < \frac{n}{3} \leq t_s < \frac{n}{2}$ satisfies $t_a + 2t_s < n$.

We assume that the computation is specified as a circuit with addition and multiplication gates. We assume that the plaintext space does not contain a special symbol $\perp$. For example, we can assume that the plaintext space is $\mathbf{Z}_N$ for some RSA modulus N and that we use a threshold version of the Paillier cryptosystem (see Section B).

When the network is synchronous, we need to ensure that parties start simultaneously in each of the sub-protocols in order to ensure that the security guarantees are preserved. For example, in $\Pi_{\mathrm{ba}}^{t_s,t_a}$ there is a timeout chosen such that honest parties are guaranteed to receive output when the network is synchronous. As a consequence, if parties start at different times, we lose the security guarantees in the synchronous case. In order to solve this, we wait at least for an upper bound on the running time of each sub-protocol. This allows parties to simultaneously start at each sub-protocol when the network is synchronous. Let us denote $T_{bc}, T_{zk}, T_{ba}, T_{dec}$ upper bounds on the running time of $\Pi_{\mathrm{bc}}^{t_s,t_a}$, $\Pi_{\mathrm{zk}}^{t_s,t_a}$, n parallel executions of $\Pi_{\mathrm{ba}}^{t_s,t_a}$, and the Threshold Decryption sub-protocols respectively, in the case the network is synchronous.

Protocol $\Pi_{\mathrm{smpc}}^{t_s,t_a}(P_i)$

Let x_i denote the input value of party P_i. Let $\mathtt{abort} = 0$.

Input Distribution

1: P_i computes $\overline{x_i}$ and broadcasts using $\Pi_{\mathrm{bc}}^{t_s,t_a}$ the ciphertext $\overline{x_i}$ and uses the multi-party zero-knowledge functionality $\mathcal{F}_{\mathrm{MZK}}$ to prove knowledge of the plaintext of $\overline{x_i}$ towards all parties. Wait until $\max\{T_{bc}, T_{zk}\}$ clock ticks passed.
2: If there is a broadcast or zero-knowledge proof that has not terminated, or the number of correct encryptions received is less than $n - t_s$ inputs, set $\mathtt{abort} = 1$. Continue participating in the sub-protocols, but do not compute any ciphertext.

Addition Gates Input: $\overline{a}, \overline{b}$. Output: $\overline{c}$.

1: P_i locally computes $\overline{c} = \overline{a} \boxplus \overline{b}$.

Multiplication Gates Input: $\overline{a}, \overline{b}$. Output: $\overline{c}$.

1: P_i chooses a random plaintext d_i and broadcasts using $\Pi_{\mathrm{bc}}^{t_s,t_a}$ the ciphertexts $\overline{d_i}$ and $\overline{d_i b}$ and uses the multi-party zero-knowledge functionality $\mathcal{F}_{\mathrm{MZK}}$ to prove knowledge of d_i and that $\overline{d_i b}$ is a correct encryption of the multiplication. Wait for $\max\{T_{bc}, T_{zk}\}$.
2: Let S_i be the subset of the parties succeeding with both proofs. Run n times the protocol $\Pi_{\mathrm{ba}}^{t_s,t_a}$, each one to decide for each party P_j's proof. Input 1 to party j's BA if and only if $j \in S_i$. Wait for T_{ba}.   // Crucial to agree on the same S, otherwise privacy breaks.
3: Let S be the subset of the parties for which $\Pi_{\mathrm{ba}}^{t_s,t_a}$ outputs 1.
4: **if** $|S| > t_s$ **then**
5:     P_i computes $\overline{a} \boxplus \left(\boxplus_{i \in S} \overline{d_i}\right)$. P_i executes the Threshold Decryption sub-protocol on this ciphertext. Wait for T_{dec}.
6:     P_i learns $a + \sum_{i \in S} d_i$ and computes $\overline{c} = \left(a + \sum_{i \in S} d_i\right) \boxdot \overline{b} \boxminus \left(\boxplus_{i \in S} \overline{d_i b}\right)$.
7: **else**
8:     Set $\mathtt{abort} = 1$.
9: **end if**

Output Determination Input x, where $x = c_i$ is the output ciphertext of the circuit if $\mathtt{abort} = 0$, and otherwise $x = \perp$.

1: P_i executes the protocol $\Pi_{\mathrm{acs}}^{t_s,t_a}$ with x as input. Let S_i be the output of the protocol.
2: **if** $S_i = \{c\}$ **then**
3:     Execute the Threshold Decryption sub-protocol on c.

4:     After an output is given, terminate.
5: **else**
6:     Output $\perp$.   // Observe that parties do not terminate, since $\Pi_{\text{acs}}^{t_s,t_a}$ does not guarantee termination.
7: **end if**

Threshold Decryption Input: ciphertext c.

1: P_i computes its decryption share s_i sends it to every other party.
2: P_i proves that the value s_i is a correct decryption share of c bilaterally.
3: Once $t_s + 1$ correct decryption shares are collected, send the list to every party and output the corresponding plaintext.

Theorem 1. *Let* n, t_s, t_a *be such that* $0 \leq t_a < \frac{n}{3} \leq t_s < \frac{n}{2}$ *and* $t_a + 2t_s < n$. *Protocol* $\Pi_{\text{smpc}}^{t_s,t_a}$ *satisfies the following properties:*

1. *When run in a synchronous network, it achieves full security up to* t_s *corruptions.*
2. *When run in an asynchronous network, it achieves unanimous output with weak termination up to* t_a *corruptions and has* $n - t_s$ *output quality.*

Proof. We prove each of the cases individually. We simulate in the hybrid where there is a trusted setup generating the keys for the PKI, the threshold encryption scheme and the CRS in the real world. In the ideal world, the simulator $\mathcal{S}$ generates the PKI keys, threshold encryption keys and CRS, and outputs the corresponding public keys and CRS to the adversary along with its secret keys.

Case 1: Synchronous Network. We describe the simulator $\mathcal{S}$ for the case where the network is synchronous and there are up to t_s corruptions.

- *Input Distribution:* Emulate the messages of the broadcast protocol. This means that, on behalf of each honest party, emulate the broadcast protocol using an encryption of 0 as the input. Also, emulate the $\mathcal{F}_{\text{MZK}}$ functionality by outputting 1 on behalf of each honest parties, and from each corrupted party, on input $(c, (x, r))$ check that $c = \text{Enc}_{\text{ek}}(x, r)$ and output 1 to the adversary and 0 otherwise. The simulator waits for $\max\{T_{bc}, T_{zk}\}$. For each honest party P_i, it keeps track of the correct encrypted inputs I_i that P_i received. If the number of correct ciphertexts is less than $n - t_s$, the simulator does not compute on its ciphertexts on his behalf and sets a local variable $\text{abort}_i = 1$.
- *Addition Gates:* $\mathcal{S}$ simply adds the corresponding ciphertexts locally.
- *Multiplication Gates:* $\mathcal{S}$ emulates the broadcast protocols on random encryptions, and outputs 1 when emulating $\mathcal{F}_{\text{MZK}}$ on behalf of them. For each honest party P_i, keep track of the set of parties S_i succeeding in the proofs. The simulator waits for $\max\{T_{bc}, T_{zk}\}$. Then, emulate the messages in the byzantine agreement protocols and compute the set S. Then it waits for waits for T_{ba}. If the set S is greater than t_s, it computes $\overline{a} \boxplus \left(\boxplus_{i \in S} \overline{d_i} \right)$ and emulates the threshold decryption sub-protocol. After waiting for T_{dec}, it computes the output ciphertext of the multiplication gate. Otherwise, it sets $\text{abort}_i = 1$.

- *Output Determination*: For each party P_i, emulate the messages in the asynchronous common subset protocol with the corresponding input (either a ciphertext, which is the result of the computation, or $\perp$ in the case $\texttt{abort}_i = 1$). If the output is a single ciphertext c, emulate the threshold decryption subprotocol.
- *Threshold Decryption*: In a multiplication gate, simply compute the decryption shares and emulate the sending messages. In the Output Determination stage, $\mathcal{S}$ obtains the output y of the computation, and adjusts the shares such that the shares decrypt to y. In both cases, the simulator always outputs 1 on behalf of the honest parties indicating that the proofs of correct decryptions are correct.

Case 2: Asynchronous Network. The only difference with respect to the case where the network is synchronous, is that the protocol $\Pi_{\mathsf{bc}}^{t_s,t_a}$ only provides weak-validity. In the simulation, it implies that the simulator will also need to simulate the $\perp$ messages from the broadcast protocols, and not simulate on behalf of the honest parties which stop participating in the protocol after they aborted.

We define a series of hybrids to argue that no environment can distinguish between the real world and the ideal world.

Hybrids and security proof

Hybrid 1. This corresponds to the real world execution. Here, the simulator knows the inputs and keys of all honest parties.

Hybrid 2. We modify the real-world execution in the zero-knowledge proofs. In the case of a synchronous network, when a corrupted party requests a proof of any kind from an honest party, the simulator simply gives a valid response without checking the witness from the honest party. In the case of an asynchronous network, the simulator is allowed to set outputs to $\perp$ as the real-world adversary.

Hybrid 3. This is similar to Hybrid 2, but the computation of the decryption shares is different. Here, the simulator obtains the output y from the ideal functionality, and if it is not $\perp$, it computes the decryption shares of corrupted parties, and then adjusts the decryption shares of honest parties such that the decryption shares $(d_1, \ldots, d_n)$ form a secret sharing of the output value y.

Hybrid 4. We modify the previous hybrid in the Input Stage. Here, the honest parties, instead of sending an encryption of the actual input, they send an encryption of 0.

Hybrid 5. This corresponds to the ideal world execution.

In order to prove that no environment can distinguish between the real world and the ideal world, we prove that no environment can distinguish between any two consecutive hybrids.

Claim 1. No efficient environment can distinguish between Hybrid 1 and Hybrid 2.

<u>Proof</u>: This follows trivially, since the honest parties always send a valid witness to $\mathcal{F}_{\mathrm{MZK}}$ in the case of a synchronous network. In the case of an asynchronous

network, the simulator chooses the set of parties that get $\perp$ as the real-world adversary.   ∎

Claim 2. No efficient environment can distinguish between Hybrid 2 and Hybrid 3.

Proof: This follows from properties of a secret sharing scheme and the security of the threshold encryption scheme. Given that the threshold is $t_s + 1$, any number corrupted decryption shares below $t_s + 1$ does not reveal anything about the output y. Moreover, one can find shares for honest parties such that $(d_1, \ldots, d_n)$ is a sharing of y.   ∎

Claim 4. No efficient environment can distinguish between Hybrid 3 and Hybrid 4.

Proof: This follows from the semantic security of the used threshold encryption scheme.   ∎

Claim 5. No efficient environment can distinguish between Hybrid 4 and Hybrid 5.

Proof: The simulator in the ideal world and the simulator in Hybrid 4 emulate the joint behavior of the ideal functionalities exactly in the same way.   ∎

We conclude that the real world and the ideal world are indistinguishable. Finally, let us argue why the protocol has weak termination. Observe that when the protocol outputs $\perp$, parties do not terminate. This is because the protocol $\Pi_{\mathtt{acs}}^{t_s,t_a}$ does not guarantee termination, i.e. might need to run forever (see [9]). However, when parties have agreement on a ciphertext to decrypt (in particular, this is the case when the network is synchronous), the threshold decryption sub-protocol ensures that honest parties can jointly collect $t_s + 1 \leq n - t_s \leq n - t_a$ decryption shares, decrypt the ciphertext and terminate.

□

5   Main Protocol

In this section, we present the protocol $\Pi_{\mathtt{mpc}}^{t_s,t_a}$ for secure function evaluation which tolerates up to t_s (resp. t_a) corruptions when the network is synchronous (resp. asynchronous), for any $0 \leq t_a < \frac{n}{3} \leq t_s < \frac{n}{2}$ satisfying $t_a + 2t_s < n$. The protocol is based on two sub-protocols:

- $\Pi_{\mathtt{smpc}}^{t_s,t_a}$ is a secure function evaluation protocol which gives full security up to t_s corruptions when run in a synchronous network, and achieves unanimous output with weak termination up to t_a corruptions and has $n - t_s$ output quality when run in an asynchronous network.
- $\Pi_{\mathtt{ampc}}^{t_a}$ is a secure function evaluation protocol which gives full security up to t_a corruptions and has $n - t_a$ output quality when run in an asynchronous network.

Protocol $\Pi_{\mathrm{mpc}}^{t_s,t_a}(P_i)$

Let x_i denote the input value of party P_i.
1: Run $\Pi_{\mathrm{smpc}}^{t_s,t_a}$ using x_i as input. Let y_i be the output of P_i.
2: If $y_i \neq \perp$, output y_i and terminate. Otherwise, run $\Pi_{\mathrm{ampc}}^{t_a}$ using x_i as input, output the result and terminate.

Theorem 2. *Let n, t_s, t_a be such that $0 \leq t_a < \frac{n}{3} \leq t_s < \frac{n}{2}$ and $t_a + 2t_s < n$. Protocol $\Pi_{\mathrm{mpc}}^{t_s,t_a}$ satisfies the following properties:*

1. *When run in a synchronous network, it achieves full security up to t_s corruptions.*
2. *When run in an asynchronous network, it achieves full security up to t_a corruptions and has $n - t_s$ output quality.*

Proof. The case where the network is synchronous and there are up to t_s corruptions is trivial, since $\Pi_{\mathrm{smpc}}^{t_s,t_a}$ is guaranteed to provide full security, and $\Pi_{\mathrm{ampc}}^{t_a}$ is never executed. In the other case where the network is asynchronous and there are up to t_a corruptions, observe that after $\Pi_{\mathrm{smpc}}^{t_s,t_a}$ gives output (which is guaranteed to happen), in the case where there is a non-$\perp$ output, every honest party is guaranteed to get this output (which take into account at least $n - t_s$ inputs) and also terminate. If the output is $\perp$, the adversary learned no information so far about the inputs, so it is safe to execute $\Pi_{\mathrm{ampc}}^{t_a}$. In this case, since $\Pi_{\mathrm{ampc}}^{t_a}$ has output quality $n - t_a$, the overall protocol also has $n - t_s \leq n - t_a$ output quality. Observe that in this case the honest parties terminate as soon as $\Pi_{\mathrm{ampc}}^{t_a}$ terminates, since $\Pi_{\mathrm{ampc}}^{t_a}$ guarantees termination. $\square$

6 Impossibility Proof

We now discuss two lower bounds in this setting. Our first result shows that our feasibility result in Sect. 5 is tight with respect to the output quality. More concretely, we show that there are basic functions for which it is impossible to achieve both (1) full security up to t corruptions in a synchronous network and (2) $(n-t+1)$-output quality for even 0 *corruptions* in an asynchronous network. Put simply, a protocol secure against t corruptions cannot rely on receiving more than $n - t$ inputs, even in executions in which all participants happen to be honest.

Our second result shows that the construction presented in Sect. 5 is tight with respect to the corruption thresholds. That is, we show that there is no protocol for secure function evaluation achieving the guarantees of Theorem 2 when $t_a + 2 \cdot t_s \geq n$. As an example, we show that the majority function cannot be computed with full security up to t_s corruptions in a synchronous network as well as security up to t_a corruptions in an asynchronous network (in fact, in an asynchronous network, it cannot be computed even if we require only unanimous output).

Theorem 3. *Fix any t. There is no protocol Π for MPC with the following properties:*

- *When run in a synchronous network, it achieves full security up to t corruptions.*
- *When run in an asynchronous network, it achieves $(n - t + 1)$-output quality when every party is honest.*

Proof. We show the proof for the case of the OR function. More concretely, the function computes the OR of all the inputs that are received by the ideal functionality (i.e. all inputs that are not $\bot$).

We partition the n parties into two sets S_t, S_{n-t}, where $|S_t| = t$ and $|S_{n-t}| = n - t$. Consider an execution of Π in a synchronous network where parties in S_t are corrupted and abort, and parties in S_{n-t} input 0. In this case, since the protocol achieves full security, all honest parties obtain 0 as output and terminate by some time T.

Next consider an execution of Π in an asynchronous network where all parties are honest, parties in S_t have input 1, and parties in S_{n-t} have input 0. All communication between S_t and S_{n-t} is delayed for more than T clock ticks. Since the view of the parties in S_{n-t} is exactly the same, these parties output 0. This contradicts the fact that Π achieves $(n - t + 1)$-output quality. $\qquad\square$

Theorem 4. *Fix any t_a, t_s such that $t_a + 2 \cdot t_s \geq n$. There is no protocol Π for MPC with the following properties:*

- *When run in a synchronous network, it achieves full security up to t_s corruptions.*
- *When run in an asynchronous network, it achieves unanimous output up to t_a corruptions.*

Proof. **Case 1:** $t_s \geq n/2$ or $t_a \geq n/3$. These bounds follow from classical impossibility results for synchronous and asynchronous MPC protocols with full security (c.f. [7,16]).

Case 2: $t_s < n/2$, $t_a < n/3$, and $t_a + 2 \cdot t_s \geq n$.

Assume without loss of generality that $t_a + 2 \cdot t_s = n$. We prove the impossibility for the case of the majority function. Partition the n parties into three sets, $S_{t_s}^0, S_{t_s}^1$, and S_{t_a}, where $|S_{t_s}^0| = |S_{t_s}^1| = t_s$ and $|S_{t_a}| = t_a$.

First, consider an execution of Π in which the network is synchronous and the t_s parties in $S_{t_s}^1$ are corrupted and crash, and furthermore the honest parties all input 0. Since t_s is less than $n/2$, the protocol must output 0.

Next, consider an execution of Π in which the network is asynchronous, the t_a parties in S_{t_a} are corrupted, and the parties in $S_{t_s}^0$ and $S_{t_s}^1$ input 0 and 1, respectively. In the real world, the adversary can use the following attack: block all messages between $S_{t_s}^0$ and $S_{t_s}^1$ throughout, and have all corrupted parties simulate an honest protocol execution with input $b \in \{0, 1\}$ with the parties in $S_{t_s}^b$. A party in $S_{t_s}^0$ cannot distinguish between this execution and the first execution, and thus the protocol outputs 0; for the same reason a party in $S_{t_s}^1$ outputs 1. By contrast, in the ideal world, the output will of course be the same for all parties. This proves that there is no protocol for the majority function Π that achieves both properties.

References

1. Abraham, I., Malkhi, D., Nayak, K., Ren, L., Yin, M.: Sync HotStuff: simple and practical synchronous state machine replication. Cryptology ePrint Archive, Report 2019/270 (2019). https://eprint.iacr.org/2019/270
2. Bar-Ilan, J., Beaver, D.: Non-cryptographic fault-tolerant computing in constant number of rounds of interaction. In: Rudnicki, P. (ed.) 8th ACM PODC, pp. 201–209. ACM, August 1989
3. Beaver, D., Micali, S., Rogaway, P.: The round complexity of secure protocols (extended abstract). In: 22nd ACM STOC, pp. 503–513. ACM Press, May 1990
4. Beerliová-Trubíniová, Z., Hirt, M.: Simple and efficient perfectly-secure asynchronous MPC. In: Kurosawa, K. (ed.) ASIACRYPT 2007. LNCS, vol. 4833, pp. 376–392. Springer, Heidelberg (2007). https://doi.org/10.1007/978-3-540-76900-2_23
5. Ben-Or, M., Canetti, R., Goldreich, O.: Asynchronous secure computation. In: 25th ACM STOC, pp. 52–61. ACM Press, May 1993
6. Ben-Or, M., Goldwasser, S., Wigderson, A.: Completeness theorems for non-cryptographic fault-tolerant distributed computation (extended abstract). In: 20th ACM STOC, pp. 1–10. ACM Press, May 1988
7. Ben-Or, M., Kelmer, B., Rabin, T.: Asynchronous secure computations with optimal resilience (extended abstract). In: Anderson, J., Toueg, S. (ed.) 13th ACM PODC, pp. 183–192. ACM, August 1994
8. Blum, E., Katz, J., Loss, J.: Synchronous consensus with optimal asynchronous fallback guarantees. In: Hofheinz, D., Rosen, A. (eds.) TCC 2019. LNCS, vol. 11891, pp. 131–150. Springer, Cham (2019). https://doi.org/10.1007/978-3-030-36030-6_6
9. Blum, E., Katz, J., Loss, J.: Network-agnostic state machine replication. Cryptology ePrint Archive, Report 2020/142 (2020). https://eprint.iacr.org/2020/142
10. Bracha, G.: Asynchronous Byzantine agreement protocols. Inf. Comput. **75**(2), 130–143 (1987)
11. Bracha, G., Toueg, S.: Asynchronous consensus and broadcast protocols. J. ACM (JACM) **32**(4), 824–840 (1985)
12. Canetti, R.: Studies in secure multiparty computation and applications, pp. 73–79, March 1996
13. Canetti, R.: Universally composable security: a new paradigm for cryptographic protocols. In: 42nd FOCS, pp. 136–145. IEEE Computer Society Press, October 2001
14. Canetti, R., Fischlin, M.: Universally composable commitments. In: Kilian, J. (ed.) CRYPTO 2001. LNCS, vol. 2139, pp. 19–40. Springer, Heidelberg (2001). https://doi.org/10.1007/3-540-44647-8_2
15. Chaum, D., Crépeau, C., Damgård, I.: Multiparty unconditionally secure protocols (extended abstract). In: 20th ACM STOC, pp. 11–19. ACM Press, May 1988

16. Cleve, R.: Limits on the security of coin flips when half the processors are faulty (extended abstract). In: 18th ACM STOC, pp. 364–369. ACM Press, May 1986

17. Cohen, R.: Asynchronous secure multiparty computation in constant time. In: Cheng, C.-M., Chung, K.-M., Persiano, G., Yang, B.-Y. (eds.) PKC 2016. LNCS, vol. 9615, pp. 183–207. Springer, Heidelberg (2016). https://doi.org/10.1007/978-3-662-49387-8_8

18. Cohen, R., Lindell, Y.: Fairness versus guaranteed output delivery in secure multiparty computation. J. Cryptol. 30(4), 1157–1186 (2017). https://doi.org/10.1007/s00145-016-9245-5

19. Coretti, S., Garay, J.A., Hirt, M., Zikas, V.: Constant-round asynchronous multiparty computation based on one-way functions. In: Cheon, J.H., Takagi, T. (eds.) ASIACRYPT 2016. LNCS, vol. 10032, pp. 998–1021. Springer, Heidelberg (2016). https://doi.org/10.1007/978-3-662-53890-6_33

20. Cramer, R., Damgård, I., Dziembowski, S., Hirt, M., Rabin, T.: Efficient multiparty computations secure against an adaptive adversary. In: Stern, J. (ed.) EUROCRYPT 1999. LNCS, vol. 1592, pp. 311–326. Springer, Heidelberg (1999). https://doi.org/10.1007/3-540-48910-X_22

21. Cramer, R., Damgård, I., Maurer, U.: General secure multi-party computation from any linear secret-sharing scheme. In: Preneel, B. (ed.) EUROCRYPT 2000. LNCS, vol. 1807, pp. 316–334. Springer, Heidelberg (2000). https://doi.org/10.1007/3-540-45539-6_22

22. Cramer, R., Damgård, I., Nielsen, J.B.: Multiparty computation from threshold homomorphic encryption. In: Pfitzmann, B. (ed.) EUROCRYPT 2001. LNCS, vol. 2045, pp. 280–300. Springer, Heidelberg (2001). https://doi.org/10.1007/3-540-44987-6_18

23. Damgård, I.: Efficient concurrent zero-knowledge in the auxiliary string model. In: Preneel, B. (ed.) EUROCRYPT 2000. LNCS, vol. 1807, pp. 418–430. Springer, Heidelberg (2000). https://doi.org/10.1007/3-540-45539-6_30

24. Damgård, I., Ishai, Y.: Constant-round multiparty computation using a black-box pseudorandom generator. In: Shoup, V. (ed.) CRYPTO 2005. LNCS, vol. 3621, pp. 378–394. Springer, Heidelberg (2005). https://doi.org/10.1007/11535218_23

25. Damgård, I., Jurik, M.: A generalisation, a simplification and some applications of Paillier's probabilistic public-key system. In: Kim, K. (ed.) PKC 2001. LNCS, vol. 1992, pp. 119–136. Springer, Heidelberg (2001). https://doi.org/10.1007/3-540-44586-2_9

26. Damgård, I., Nielsen, J.B.: Perfect hiding and perfect binding universally composable commitment schemes with constant expansion factor. In: Yung, M. (ed.) CRYPTO 2002. LNCS, vol. 2442, pp. 581–596. Springer, Heidelberg (2002). https://doi.org/10.1007/3-540-45708-9_37

27. Damgård, I., Nielsen, J.B.: Universally composable efficient multiparty computation from threshold homomorphic encryption. In: Boneh, D. (ed.) CRYPTO 2003. LNCS, vol. 2729, pp. 247–264. Springer, Heidelberg (2003). https://doi.org/10.1007/978-3-540-45146-4_15

28. Dolev, D., Raymond Strong, H.: Authenticated algorithms for Byzantine agreement. SIAM J. Comput. 12(4), 656–666 (1983)

29. Fitzi, M., Gottesman, D., Hirt, M., Holenstein, T., Smith, A.: Detectable Byzantine agreement secure against faulty majorities. In: Ricciardi, A. (ed.) 21st ACM PODC, pp. 118–126. ACM, July 2002

30. Fitzi, M., Hirt, M., Maurer, U.: Trading correctness for privacy in unconditional multi-party computation. In: Krawczyk, H. (ed.) CRYPTO 1998. LNCS, vol. 1462, pp. 121–136. Springer, Heidelberg (1998). https://doi.org/10.1007/BFb0055724

31. Goldreich, O., Micali, S., Wigderson, A.: How to play any mental game or a completeness theorem for protocols with honest majority. In: Aho, S. (ed.) 19th ACM STOC, pp. 218–229. ACM Press, May 1987

32. Guo, Y., Pass, R., Shi, E.: Synchronous, with a chance of partition tolerance. In: Boldyreva, A., Micciancio, D. (eds.) CRYPTO 2019. LNCS, vol. 11692, pp. 499–529. Springer, Cham (2019). https://doi.org/10.1007/978-3-030-26948-7_18

33. Hirt, M., Maurer, U.: Robustness for free in unconditional multi-party computation. In: Kilian, J. (ed.) CRYPTO 2001. LNCS, vol. 2139, pp. 101–118. Springer, Heidelberg (2001). https://doi.org/10.1007/3-540-44647-8_6

34. Hirt, M., Nielsen, J.B., Przydatek, B.: Cryptographic asynchronous multi-party computation with optimal resilience. In: Cramer, R. (ed.) EUROCRYPT 2005. LNCS, vol. 3494, pp. 322–340. Springer, Heidelberg (2005). https://doi.org/10.1007/11426639_19

35. Ishai, Y., Ostrovsky, R., Zikas, V.: Secure multi-party computation with identifiable abort. In: Garay, J.A., Gennaro, R. (eds.) CRYPTO 2014. LNCS, vol. 8617, pp. 369–386. Springer, Heidelberg (2014). https://doi.org/10.1007/978-3-662-44381-1_21

36. Katz, J., Maurer, U., Tackmann, B., Zikas, V.: Universally composable synchronous computation. In: Sahai, A. (ed.) TCC 2013. LNCS, vol. 7785, pp. 477–498. Springer, Heidelberg (2013). https://doi.org/10.1007/978-3-642-36594-2_27

37. Kursawe, K.: Optimistic Byzantine agreement. In: 2002 Proceedings of the 21st IEEE Symposium on Reliable Distributed Systems, pp. 262–267. IEEE (2002)

38. Liu, S., Viotti, P., Cachin, C., Quéma, V., Vukolić, M.: XFT: practical fault tolerance beyond crashes. In: 12th USENIX Symposium on Operating Systems Design and Implementation, pp. 485–500 (2016)

39. Liu-Zhang, C.-D., Loss, J., Maurer, U., Moran, T., Tschudi, D.: Robust MPC: asynchronous responsiveness yet synchronous security. Cryptology ePrint Archive, Report 2019/159 (2019). https://eprint.iacr.org/2019/159

40. Loss, J., Moran, T.: Combining asynchronous and synchronous byzantine agreement: the best of both worlds. Cryptology ePrint Archive, Report 2018/235 (2018). https://eprint.iacr.org/2018/235

41. Malkhi, D., Nayak, K., Ren, L.:. Flexible Byzantine fault tolerance. In: Proceedings of the 2019 ACM SIGSAC Conference on Computer and Communications Security, pp. 1041–1053 (2019)

42. Miller, A., Xia, Y., Croman, K., Shi, E., Song, D.: The honey badger of BFT protocols. In: Weippl, E.R., Katzenbeisser, S., Kruegel, C., Myers, A.C., Halevi, S. (eds.) ACM CCS 2016, p. 31–42. ACM Press, October 2016

43. Paillier, P.: Public-key cryptosystems based on composite degree residuosity classes. In: Stern, J. (ed.) EUROCRYPT 1999. LNCS, vol. 1592, pp. 223–238. Springer, Heidelberg (1999). https://doi.org/10.1007/3-540-48910-X_16

44. Pass, R., Shi, E.: Hybrid consensus: efficient consensus in the permissionless model. In: LIPIcs-Leibniz International Proceedings in Informatics, vol. 91. Schloss Dagstuhl-Leibniz-Zentrum fuer Informatik (2017)

45. Pass, R., Shi, E.: Thunderella: blockchains with optimistic instant confirmation. In: Nielsen, J.B., Rijmen, V. (eds.) EUROCRYPT 2018. LNCS, vol. 10821, pp. 3–33. Springer, Cham (2018). https://doi.org/10.1007/978-3-319-78375-8_1

46. Rabin, T., Ben-Or, M.: Verifiable secret sharing and multiparty protocols with honest majority (extended abstract). In: 21st ACM STOC, pp. 73–85. ACM Press, May 1989

47. Shoup, V.: Practical threshold signatures. In: Preneel, B. (ed.) EUROCRYPT 2000. LNCS, vol. 1807, pp. 207–220. Springer, Heidelberg (2000). https://doi.org/10. 1007/3-540-45539-6_15

Reverse Firewalls for Actively Secure MPCs

Suvradip Chakraborty[1(✉)], Stefan Dziembowski[2(✉)],
and Jesper Buus Nielsen[3(✉)]

[1] Institute of Science and Technology Austria, Klosterneuburg, Austria
suvradip.chakraborty@ist.ac.at
[2] University of Warsaw, Warsaw, Poland
s.dziembowski@crypto.edu.pl
[3] Aarhus University, Aarhus, Denmark
jbn@cs.au.dk

Abstract. Reverse firewalls were introduced at Eurocrypt 2015 by Miro-nov and Stephens-Davidowitz, as a method for protecting cryptographic protocols against attacks on the devices of the honest parties. In a nutshell: a reverse firewall is placed outside of a device and its goal is to "sanitize" the messages sent by it, in such a way that a malicious device cannot leak its secrets to the outside world. It is typically assumed that the cryptographic devices are attacked in a "functionality-preserving way" (i.e. informally speaking, the functionality of the protocol remains unchanged under this attacks). In their paper, Mironov and Stephens-Davidowitz construct a protocol for passively-secure two-party computations with firewalls, leaving extension of this result to stronger models as an open question.

In this paper, we address this problem by constructing a protocol for secure computation with firewalls that has two main advantages over the original protocol from Eurocrypt 2015. Firstly, it is a *multi*party computation protocol (i.e. it works for an arbitrary number n of the parties, and not just for 2). Secondly, it is secure in much stronger corruption settings, namely in the *active corruption model*. More precisely: we consider an adversary that can fully corrupt up to $n - 1$ parties, while the remaining parties are corrupt in a functionality-preserving way.

Our core techniques are: malleable commitments and malleable non-interactive zero-knowledge, which in particular allow us to create a novel protocol for multiparty augmented coin-tossing into the well with reverse firewalls (that is based on a protocol of Lindell from Crypto 2001).

1 Introduction

The traditional approach to cryptography is to design schemes in a black-box way, i.e, under the assumption that the devices that execute cryptographic algorithms are fully trusted. Abstract, "black-box" cryptography is currently well-understood, and there exist several algorithms that implement basic cryptographic tasks in a way that is secure against a large class of attacks (under very plausible assumptions). Therefore, one can say that cryptographic algorithms, if implemented correctly, are the most secure part of digital systems.

Unfortunately, once we get closer to the real "physical world" the situation becomes much less satisfactory. This is because several real-life attacks on

© International Association for Cryptologic Research 2020
D. Micciancio and T. Ristenpart (Eds.): CRYPTO 2020, LNCS 12171, pp. 732–762, 2020.
https://doi.org/10.1007/978-3-030-56880-1_26

cryptographic devices are based on attacking the *implementation*, not the abstract mathematical algorithm. In particular, the adversary can sometimes *tamper* with the device and change the way in which it behaves (e.g. by installing so-called "Trojan horses" on it). What can be viewed as the extreme case of the tampering attacks are scenarios in which the device is produced by an adversarial manufacturer, who maliciously modifies its design. Such attacks are quite realistic, since, for the economical reasons, private companies and government agencies are often forced to use hardware that they did not produce themselves. Another source of such attacks are the insiders that originate from within a given company or organization. Last but not least, some attacks of this type can originate from the governments. The revelations of Edward Snowden disclosed a massive scale of the US government cyberattacks directed against the individuals (both within the US and abroad). It is generally believed that many other governments take similar actions, one recent example being the "Chinese hack chip" attack (revealed in October 2018) that reached almost 30 U.S. companies, including Amazon and Apple.

Countermeasures. Starting from late 1990s there has been a significant effort in the cryptographic community to address this kind of "implementation attacks", by extending the black-box model to cover also them (see, e.g., [23, 25]). More recently, Mironov and Stephens-Davidowitz [26] put forward another method that they called *reverse firewalls*. On a high level (for a formal definition see Sect. 2.1), this technique addresses the problem of information leakage from cryptographic implementations that are malicious, either because they were produced by an adversarial manufacturer, or because they are were maliciously modified at a later stage. More concretely, reverse firewalls are used to protect against attacks in which a malicious implementation leaks some of its secrets via so-called "subliminal channels" [28], i.e, by encoding this secrets in innocently-looking protocol messages. In a nutshell, a reverse firewall is an external device that is put between a party P and the external world in order to "sanitize" the messages that are sent and received by P. A reverse firewall is *not* a trusted third party, and, in particular, it cannot be used to keep P's secrets and to perform operations "in P's name". Reverse firewalls come in different variants. The most popular one, that we also consider in this paper, requires that the reverse firewalls provide protection only against the aforementioned "informational leakage" attack (and not against attacks that may influence the output of the computation). In particular, in this model, we are *not* concerned with the *correctness* of the computation. More formally, we assume that all the adversarial tampering cannot change the functionality of the entire protocol. This type of attacks are called "*functionality maintaining*" corruptions [26]. The authors of [26] provide a construction of a two-party passively secure computation protocol with a reverse firewall, leaving the generalization of this construction to stronger security notions as an open problem. Reverse firewalls has been recently used in a very practical context by Dauterman et al. in [12] in a design of a *True2F* system that is based on a firewalled key generation and ECDSA signature generation. One of the potential applications of this system are the cryptocurrency wallets.

Our contribution. We address the open problem of [26] by providing a construction of reverse firewalls for secure computation in a much stronger security model, and in a more general setting. More concretely, we show a solution to the problem by constructing *multi*party computation protocols with *active* security. Recall that in the active security settings the corrupt parties can misbehave in an arbitrary way, i.e., the adversary takes a full control over them, and, besides learning their inputs, can instruct them to take any actions of his choice. It is well known [18,19] that such protocols can be constructed even if a majority of parties is corrupt (assuming that no *fairness* is guaranteed, i.e., the adversary can prevent the honest parties from learning their outputs, after she learns the outputs of corrupt parties). In this work, we show an MPC protocol (based on [18,19]), together with a reverse firewall for it, that provides security in a very strong sense: it can tolerate up to $n - 1$ "standard" (active) corruptions (where n is the number of parties) plus a corruption of the remaining parties, as long as it is "functionality maintaining" and this party is protected by a reverse firewall. The core technique that we use in this construction is a novel protocol for multiparty augmented parallel coin-tossing into the well with reverse firewalls (our starting point for this construction is a protocol of Lindell [24]).

Our result shows the general feasibility of MPCs with reverse firewalls. While we do not focus on concrete applications, we believe that our approach can lead to some practical concrete constructions, especially in the light of [12] (see above). For example, to further increase the security of hardware wallets (e.g. in critical applications such as cryptocurrency exchanges), one could develop reverse firewalls for threshold ECDSA (see, e.g., [14,17]). Our results show that this is in principle possible, but further work to bring these ideas to practice is needed.

Other related work. After the publication of [26] there has been some follow-up work on the reverse firewalls. In particular [13] constructed a firewalled protocol for CCA-secure message transmission, and [10] provide protocols for oblivious signature-based envelopes with firewalls, and oblivious transfer (this is done using a new technique called "malleable smooth projective hash function" that they develop in this paper). In [3] Ateniese et al. use reverse firewalls to construct signature schemes secure against arbitrary tampering. Reverse firewalls are also related to several earlier topics in cryptography such as the algorithm-substitution attacks, subliminal channels and divertible protocols, combiners, kleptography, collusion-free protocols and mediated collusion-free protocols and more. Due to space constraints, we refer the reader to Sec. 1.1 of [26] for an overview of these topics and their relation to reverse firewalls.

1.1   Overview of Our Construction

On a high level, our construction can be viewed as "adding reverse firewalls to the MPC protocol of [18,19]". In particular, we follow the protocol structure presented in Sec. 3.3.3 of [18], i.e.: the parties generate random strings to which they are committed (this is called "augmented coin-tossing"), they commit to their inputs (the "input commitment protocol"), and finally they perform the "authenticated computation" in which they do computations on these values, simultaneously proving (in zero knowledge) that the computation is done correctly (in our construction we use a non-interactive version of zero-knowledge protocols, NIZKs, [6]). The main things that need to be addressed in adding reverse firewalls to this protocol is to construct protocols for commitment schemes and NIZKs with firewalls (since the correctness of every step of the computation is proven in zero knowledge, we do not need to construct separate firewalls for the computations itself). Essentially, these firewalls are constructed by "re-randomizing" the messages that are sent by the parties. More precisely: for messages that come from commitments, we exploit the standard homomorphic properties of such schemes, and for NIZKs we use the "controlled-malleable NIZK proof systems" of [9][1]. On a high level, the firewalls can re-randomize a protocol transcript exploiting homomorphic properties of the commitment scheme, and controlled malleability property of the NIZK proofs (where the controlled malleability is "tied" to the appropriate mauling of the commitments). One of the key ingredients of our construction is a firewalled scheme for augmented coin tossing. This is built by combining the firewalled protocols for commitment and NIZKs with the coin-tossing protocol of Lindell [24].

Reverse firewalls for multi-party (augmented) coin-tossing. Let us explain the design principle of our reverse firewall for the multi-party augmented coin-tossing protocol in more details. The starting point of our protocol is the 2-party augmented parallel coin-tossing of Lindell [24]. The protocol of [24] uses a "commit-and-prove" technique, where one party (often called the initiating party) commits to a random bit-string and proves in zero-knowledge about the consistency of the committed value. The other party also sends a random bit-string to this party. The final string is the exclusive OR of both these strings and the initiating party commits to this final string. The protocol ends by outputting a random bit-string (which the initiating party gets), and the commitment value to the final bit-string (which the other party receives). First, we extend this protocol to the multi-party setting, and then design a reverse firewall for this protocol. We assume that the honest parties are corrupted in a functionality-maintaining way. Note that, in the traditional model of corruption the adversary completely controls the party and may also cause the party to deviate arbitrarily from the protocol. In contrast, functionality-maintaining corruptions also allows the adversary to completely control the party and also cause the party to deviate from the protocol specification as long as it *does not* violate or break the functionality (i.e, correctness) of the underlying protocol. The first observation is that the corrupted parties may not necessarily commit to a random bit-string. Even if it does so, the commitment may also leak information about the committed value (say the randomness used to commit may leak additional information about the

---

[1] Since we use a NIZK proof system, we need to assume a trusted setup algorithm which generates a common reference string (CRS) to be used by all the parties. We assume that the CRS is hardwired inside the code of each party.

bit-string). Secondly, the bit-strings sent by the other parties to the initiating party may also act as a subliminal channel to leak secret information.

The main idea behind our firewall design is that it should somehow be possible to maul the commitment in such a way that the committed element is random (even if the initial bit-string is not chosen randomly) and the commitment is itself re-randomizable (so that the commitment appears to be "fresh"). For this, we assume the commitment scheme to be additively *homomorphic* (with respect to an appropriate relation), which suffices for our purpose. At this point, the original zero-knowledge proof (that conforms to the initial commitment) is no longer *valid* with respect to the mauled commitment. Hence, the firewall needs a way to appropriately maul the proof (so that the mauled proof is consistent with the mauled commitment), and also to re-randomize the proof (so that the randomness used to proof does not leak any information on the witness, which is the committed string). To this end, we use the controlled-malleable NIZK proof systems (cm-NIZK) introduced by Chase et al. [9]. We replace the (interactive) zero-knowledge proofs used in the protocol of [24] with cm-NIZK proofs (with a trusted setup procedure). The firewall then re-randomizes the shares (bit-strings) of the other parties in such a way that is consistent with the initial mauling of the commitment and the proof.

However, at this point another technical difficulty arises: the views of all the parties are not identical– in particular, the view of the initiating party and the other parties are not same, due to the above mauling by the firewall. While this appears to be problematic as far as the functionality of the protocols is concerned, we show that the firewall can again re-maul the transcript in such a way that the views of all the parties become consistent, without compromising on the security of the protocol. Here by "consistent" we mean that the initiating party (of the coin-tossing protocol) receives a random bit string, and the rest of the parties receive the commitment to *the same* bit-string.

Indeed, we show that at the end the initiating party ends up with a random bit-string (as required by the functionality), even if it is corrupted (in a functionality-maintaining way) and the other parties obtains a secure commitment to this bit-string. We show that the above firewall maintains functionality, preserves security for the honest parties, and also provide weak exfiltration-resistant[2] against other parties. Finally, we stress that the above mauling operations, specially the mauling of the NIZK proofs, does not require the firewall to know the original witness (chosen by the initiating party), which makes it interesting and doable from the firewall perspective (since it shares no secret with any of the parties). We refer the reader to Sect. 3.2 for the details.

Reverse firewalls for other protocols. We also design reverse firewalls for the multi-party input commitment protocol and the multi-party authenticated

---

[2] Informally, the exfiltration-resistant property stipulates that the corrupt implementation of party does not leak any information through the firewall. Weak exfiltration-resistance guarantees the same property when the party is corrupted in a functionality-maintaining way (and not arbitrarily).

computation protocol, which are also used as key ingredients for our final actively-secure MPC protocol. The reverse firewalls for these protocols are relatively much simpler and involve only re-randomizing the commitment and the NIZK proof (in case of the input commitment protocol) and re-randomizing the proof (for the authenticated computation protocol). We show that both the firewalls corresponding to these two protocols preserve security and is exfiltration-resistant against other parties.

The final compiler. Finally, we show the construction of our actively-secure MPC protocols in the presence of reverse firewalls. Our final compiler is similar to the compiler presented in [18], however, adapted to the setting of reverse firewalls. The compiler takes as input any semi-honest MPC protocol (without reverse firewalls) and runs the multi-party input commitment protocol, the multi-party (augmented) coin-tossing protocol and the multi-party authenticated computation protocol in the reverse firewall setting (in sequential order) to obtain the final actively-secure MPC protocol. On a high level, after the input commitment and the coin-tossing protocol (in the presence of reverse firewalls) the inputs and the random pads of all the (honest) parties are fixed. Now, since the honest parties are corrupted in a functionality-maintaining way, the computation performed by the party in the authenticated computation protocol is determined, and the final zero-knowledge proofs conform to these computations. Hence, at this point, the security of the underlying semi-honest MPC protocol (without using reverse firewalls) can be invoked to argue security of our final actively-secure MPC protocol (in the presence of reverse firewalls).

Compiler for reverse firewalls for broadcast model. As a contribution of independent interest, we also present a compiler for reverse firewalls (RF) in the broadcast model (due to space limits, this is presented in the extended version of this paper [8]). In particular, existence of a broadcast channels in the RF setting is a stronger assumption than the existence of a broadcast channel in the classical setting. To this end, we present a version of the Dolev Strong protocol [15] secure in the RF setting. The key idea is to transform the original Dolev Strong protocol to be a "unique message protocol", so that, at any given point there is only one possible message that a party can send. We implement this by replacing the signatures in the Dolev-Strong protocol with *unique signatures*. Intuitively this works because: on any input in the Dolev-Strong protocol, the only allowed message consists of adding a signature on a well-defined message. The signature is either sent or added to a valid set. Since the signatures are unique and the parties are corrupted in a functionality-maintaining way, it is forced to send the unique message at that particular round. In general, the above idea also works if we replace the signatures in the Dolev-Strong protocol with *re-randomizable* signatures [22,29]. Note that unique signatures are efficiently re-randomizable. We note that, our result also nicely complements the result of Ateniese et al. [3], who gave a negative result for the construction of RF for arbitrary signature schemes. On the positive side, they show constructions of RF for the class of re-randomizable signature schemes (which includes unique signatures as well).

Constructing actively secure MPC from semi-malicious MPC in the RF setting. A recent line of work [5,16,27] constructs 2-round MPC protocols achieving *semi-malicious* security, which means that the protocol is secure for all (possibly adversarial) choices of the random coins of the parties. Furthermore, following the compilation paradigm of [1,2], one can immediately obtain maliciously secure Universal Composable (UC) MPC protocols in the CRS model, using NIZK proofs. At first thought, it seems that if we start with any of these 2-round semi-malicious MPC protocols and use a controlled-malleable NIZK proof on top (instead of just NIZK) we can hope to get a 2-round actively secure MPC protocol in the RF setting. However, this approach does not work: semi-malicious security protects the other parties against a semi-malicious corrupted party, but does not protect the corrupted party itself. In fact, a maliciously chosen random tape might be used to leak information covertly, so semi-malicious security does not provide *exfiltration resistance*.

On the Trusted Setup assumption. Our construction of the actively secure MPC protocol uses a controlled-malleable NIZK (cm-NIZK) proof, and hence is in the CRS model. This is in contrast to the original GMW protocol [19] which does not require any trusted setup assumption, since it uses interactive zero-knowledge proofs. A natural idea is whether it is possible to replace the cm-NIZK proofs with *controlled-malleable interactive* ZK (cm-IZK) proofs. Indeed, while it is easy to see that one can construct cm-IZK proofs from one-way functions[3], it seems that the techniques of our paper are unlikely to extend to work with cm-IZK proofs. The main challenge is in making the views of the parties consistent in the final MPC protocol. We consider this as an interesting open problem to remove the trusted setup assumption.

Organization of the paper. The basic definitions and notation are provided in Sect. 2 (Sect. 2.1 contains the definitions related to the reverse firewalls). Our main technical contribution is presented in Sect. 3, with Sects. 3.1–3.5 describing the ingredients of our construction, and Sect. 3.6 putting them together into a single "protocol compiler" algorithm. The security of our construction in stated and proven in Theorem 6.

2   Preliminaries

In this section we introduce some standard notation and terminology that will be used throughout the paper. For an integer $n \in \mathbb{N}$ we denote by $[n]$ the set $\{1, 2, \cdots, n\}$ and we write U_n to denote the uniform distribution over all n-bit

---

[3] One can modify the zero-knowledge proofs for the Graph Hamiltonicity problem or the 3-Coloring problem to obtain cm-IZK proofs by replacing the commitments with homomorphic commitments, similar to our coin-tossing protocol.

strings. Recall that to every $\mathcal{NP}$ language L we can associate a binary relation $R \subseteq \{0,1\}^* \times \{0,1\}^*$ defining L such that: $L = \{x : \exists \omega \text{ s.t. } (x,\omega) \in R\}$ and $|\omega| \leq poly(|x|)$. We call x the *statement/theorem*, and ω the *witness* testifying the membership of x in the language L, i.e., $x \in L$. Let $T = (T_x, T_\omega)$ be a pair of efficiently computable n-ary functions, $T_x : \{\{0,1\}^*\}^n \to \{0,1\}^*$. We call such a tuple T as an n-ary transformation. Following [9], we define what it means for a transformation $T = (T_x, T_w)$ to be *admissible* with respect to a NP relation R.

Definition 1 (Admissible transformations [9]). *An n-ary transformation* $T = (T_x, T_w)$ *is said to* admissible *for an efficient relation R, if R is* closed *under T, i.e, for any n-tuple $\{(x_1, \omega_1), \cdots, (x_n, \omega_n)\} \in R^n$, it holds that the pair* $\big(T_x(x_1, \cdots x_n), T_\omega(\omega_1, \cdots, \omega_n)\big) \in R$. *We say that a class or set of transformations $\mathcal{T}$ is an* allowable set of transformation *if every transformation $T \in \mathcal{T}$ is admissible for R.*

Homomorphic commitments. A (non-interactive) commitment scheme consists of three polynomial time algorithms $(\mathcal{G}, K, \mathsf{com})$. The probabilistic setup algorithm $\mathcal{G}$ takes as input the security parameter λ and outputs the setup parameters par. The key generation algorithm K is a probabilistic algorithm that takes as input par and generates a commitment key ck. We assume that the commitment key ck includes the description of the message space $\mathcal{M}$, the randomness space $\mathcal{R}$ and the commitment space $\mathcal{C}$ to be used in the scheme. We also assume it is possible to efficiently sample elements from $\mathcal{R}$. The algorithm com takes as input the commitment key ck, a message m from the message space $\mathcal{M}$ and "encodes" m to produce a commitment string c in the commitment space $\mathcal{C}$. Additionally, we also require the commitment scheme to be *homomorphic* [20,21], i.e, we assume that $\mathcal{M}$, $\mathcal{R}$ and $\mathcal{C}$ are groups with the *homomorphic* property, and if we add any two commitments, the resulting commitment will encode the sum of the underlying messages. We point the reader to [8] for the formal definition of homomorphic commitments.

Controlled Malleable Non-Interactive Zero-Knowledge Proofs. We recall the definitions of controlled-malleable non-interactive proof systems from [9]. A non-interactive proof system for a $\mathcal{NP}$ language L associated with relation R consists of three (probabilistic) polynomial-time algorithm $(\mathsf{CRSGen}, \mathsf{P}, \mathsf{V})$. The Common Reference String (CRS) generation algorithm CRSGen takes as input the security parameter 1^λ, and outputs CRS σ_{crs}. The *prover algorithm* P takes as input σ_{crs}, and a pair $(x,\omega) \in R$, and outputs a proof π. The *verifier algorithm* V takes as input σ_{crs}, a statement x and a purported proof π, and outputs a decision bit $b \in \{0,1\}$, indicating whether the proof π with respect to statement x is accepted or not (with 0 indicating reject, else accept). The two most basic requirements from such a proof system are *perfect completeness* and *adaptive soundness* with respect to (possibly unbounded) cheating provers. Besides, we also want the NIZK proof systems for efficient relations R that are (1) *malleable* with respect to an allowable set of transformations $\mathcal{T}$, i.e., for any $T \in \mathcal{T}$, given proofs $\pi_1, \cdots, \pi_n$ for statements $x_1, \cdots, x_n \in L$ they can be transformed into a proof π for the statement $T_x(x_1, \cdots, x_n)$, and (2) *derivation private*, i.e. the resultant proof π cannot be distinguished from a fresh proof computed by the prover on input $\big(T_x(x_1, \cdots, x_n), T_\omega(\omega_1, \cdots, \omega_n)\big)$. We also want zero-knowledge property and simulation-sound extractability property to hold for the NIZK proof system under controlled malleability, as defined below.

Definition 2 (Controlled-malleable NIZK proof system [9]). A *controlled malleable non-interactive* (cm-NIZK) *proof system* for a language L associated with a $\mathcal{NP}$ relation R consists of four (probabilistic) polynomial-time algorithms (CRSGen, P, V, ZKEval) such that the following conditions hold:

- (*Completeness*). For all $\sigma_{crs} \leftarrow \mathsf{CRSGen}(1^\lambda)$, and $(x, \omega) \in R$, it holds that $\mathsf{V}(\sigma_{crs}, x, \pi) = 1$ for all proofs $\pi \leftarrow \mathsf{P}(\sigma_{crs}, x, \omega)$.
- (*Soundness*). We say that (CRSGen, P, V) satisfies *adaptive soundness* if for all PPT (malicious) provers P* we have:

$$\Pr\Big[\sigma_{crs} \leftarrow \mathsf{CRSGen}(1^\lambda); (x, \pi) \leftarrow \mathsf{P}^*(\sigma_{crs}) : \mathsf{V}(\sigma_{crs}, x, \pi) = 0 \text{ if } x \notin L\Big] \\ > 1 - \mathsf{negl}(\kappa).$$

for some negligible function $\mathsf{negl}(\kappa)$. Perfect soundness is achieved when this probability is always 1.
- (*Malleability*). Let $\mathcal{T}$ be a set of allowable transformation for an efficient relation R. Then the proof system (CRSGen, P, V) is said to be *malleable* with respect to $\mathcal{T}$, if there exists an efficient algorithm ZKEval that does the following: ZKEval takes as input σ_{crs}, the description of a n-ary admissible transformation $T \in \mathcal{T}$, statement-proof pairs (x_i, π_i), where $1 \leq i \leq n$, such that $\mathsf{V}(\sigma_{crs}, x_i, \pi_i) = 1$ for all i, and outputs a proof π for the statement $x = T(\{x_i\})$ such that $\mathsf{V}(\sigma_{crs}, x, \pi) = 1$.
- (*Rerandomizability*). We say that the NIZK proof system (CRSGen, P, V) for relation R is re-randomizable if there exists an additional algorithm Rand-Proof, such that the probability of the event that $b' = b$ (where $b \xleftarrow{\$} \{0,1\}$ is sampled uniformly at random) in the following game is negligible:
  - $\sigma_{crs} \leftarrow \mathsf{CRSGen}(1^\lambda)$.
  - $(\mathsf{state}, x, w, \pi) \xleftarrow{\$} \mathcal{A}(\sigma_{crs})$.
  - If $\mathsf{V}(\sigma_{crs}, x, \pi) = 0$, or $(x, w) \notin R$, output $\bot$. Otherwise form

$$\pi' \leftarrow \begin{cases} \mathsf{P}\big(\sigma_{crs}, x, w\big) & \text{if } b = 0 \\ \mathsf{RandProof}(\sigma_{crs}, x, \pi) & \text{if } b = 1. \end{cases}$$

  - $b' \leftarrow \mathcal{A}(\sigma_{crs}, \pi')$
- (*Derivation privacy*). We say that the NIZK proof system (CRSGen, P, V, ZKEval) for relation R with respect to $\mathcal{T}$ is *derivation-private*, if for all adversaries $\mathcal{A}$ and bit b, the probability $p_b^{\mathcal{A}}(\lambda)$ that the event $b' = b$ (where $b \xleftarrow{\$} \{0,1\}$ is sampled uniformly at random) in the following game is negligible:

- $\sigma_{crs} \leftarrow \mathsf{CRSGen}(1^\lambda)$.
- $(\mathsf{state}, (x_1, \omega_1, \pi_1), \cdots, (x_q, \omega_q, \pi_q), T) \leftarrow \mathcal{A}(\sigma_{crs})$.
- If $\mathsf{V}(\sigma_{crs}, x_i, \pi_i) = 0$ for some i, $(x_i, \omega_i) \notin R$ for some i, or $T \notin \mathcal{T}$, abort and output $\bot$. Otherwise compute,

$$\pi \leftarrow \begin{cases} \mathsf{P}\big(\sigma_{crs}, T_x(x_1, \cdots, x_q), T_\omega(\omega_1, \cdots, \omega_q)\big) & \text{if } b = 0 \\ \mathsf{ZKEval}(\sigma_{crs}, T, \{(x_i, \pi_i)\}_{i \in [q]}) & \text{if } b = 1. \end{cases}$$

- $b' \leftarrow \mathcal{A}(\mathsf{state}, \pi)$.

- (*Controlled-malleable simulation-sound extractability*). Let $(\mathsf{CRSGen}, \mathsf{P}, \mathsf{V})$ be a NIZK proof of knowledge (NIZKPoK) system for the relation R, with a simulator $(\mathcal{S}_1, \mathcal{S}_2)$ and an extractor $(\mathcal{E}_1, \mathcal{E}_2)$. Let $\mathcal{T}$ be an allowable set of unary transformation for the relation R such that membership in $\mathcal{T}$ is efficiently testable. Let $\mathcal{SE}_1$ be an algorithm, that on input 1^λ outputs $(\sigma_{crs}, \tau_s, \tau_e)$ such that (σ_{crs}, τ_s) is distributed identically to the output of $\mathcal{S}_1$. Consider the following game with the adversary $\mathcal{A}$:

  - $(\sigma_{crs}, \tau_s, \tau_e) \leftarrow \mathcal{SE}_1(1^\lambda)$.
  - $(x, \pi) \leftarrow \mathcal{A}^{\mathcal{S}_2(\sigma_{crs}, \tau_s, \cdot)}(\sigma_{crs}, \tau_e)$.
  - $(\omega, x', T) \leftarrow \mathcal{E}_2(\sigma_{crs}, \tau_e, x, \pi)$.

  We say that the NIZKPoK satisfies *controlled-malleable simulation-sound extractability* (CM-SSE) if for all PPT algorithms $\mathcal{A}$ there exists a negligible function $\nu(\cdot)$ such that the probability that $\mathsf{V}(\sigma_{crs}, x, \pi) = 1$ and $(x, \pi) \notin \mathcal{Q}$ (where $\mathcal{Q}$ is the set of queried statements and their responses) but either (1) $\omega \neq \bot$ and $(x, \omega) \notin R$; (2) $(x', T) \neq (\bot, \bot)$ and either $x' \notin \mathcal{Q}_x$ (the set of queried instances), $x \neq T_x(x')$, or $T \notin \mathcal{T}$; (3) $(\omega, x', T) = (\bot, \bot, \bot)$ is at most $\nu(\lambda)$.

Theorem 1. [9] *If a proof system is both malleable and randomizable and uses* $\mathsf{ZKEval}' = \mathsf{RandProof} \circ \mathsf{ZKEval}$, *then it is also derivation private.*

The work of [9] showed how to instantiate cm-NIZKs using Groth-Sahai proofs and structure preserving signature schemes, both of which can be constructed based on the standard *Decision linear (DLIN)* assumption over bilinear groups.

Remark 1. The definition of CM-SSE is a weakening of the definition of (standard) simulation-sound extractability (SSE). The notion of CM-SEE intuitively says that the extractor will either extract a valid witness ω corresponding to the new statement x (as in SSE), or a previously proved statement x' and a transformation T in the allowable set $\mathcal{T}$ that could be used to transform x' into the new statement x. Note that, when $\mathcal{T} = \emptyset$, we obtain the standard notion of SSE-NIZK as defined by Groth [21]. However, as shown in [9], this definitional relaxation is necessary, since the standard notion of SSE is impossible to achieve for malleable proof systems.

Secure computation. We present the definition of general multi-party computation protocols (for an introduction to this topic see, e.g., [11]). We follow the definitions as presented in [18,24], which in turn follows the definitions of [4,7].

Multi-party protocols. Let n denote the number of parties involved in the protocol. We assume that n is fixed. A multi-party protocol problem is given by specifying a random process which maps sequences of inputs (one input per each of the n parties) to sequences of outputs (one for each of the n parties). We refer to such a process as a n-ary *functionality*, denoted by $f : (\{0,1\}^*)^n \rightarrow (\{0,1\}^*)^n$, where $f = (f_1, \cdots, f_n)$. For a input vector $\vec{x} = \{x_1, \cdots, x_n\}$ the output is a tuple of random variables denoted by $(f_1(\vec{x}), \cdots, f_n(\vec{x}))$. The ith party P_i initially holds the input x_i and obtains the ith element in $f(x_1, \cdots, x_n)$, i.e. $f_i(x_1, \cdots, x_n)$. We also assume that all the parties hold input of equal length, i.e., $|x_i| = |x_j|$ for all $i, j \in [n]$. We will denote such a functionality as $(x_1, \cdots, x_n) \mapsto (f_1(x_1, \cdots x_n), \cdots, f_n(x_1, \cdots x_n))$.

Adversarial behavior. For the analysis of our protocols we consider the *malicious* adversarial model. A malicious adversary may corrupt a subset of parties and can completely control these parties and deviate arbitrarily from the specified protocol. We assume a *static* corruption model, where the set of corrupted or dishonest parties are already specified before the execution of the protocol. A weaker model of security is the *semi-honest* model, where the adversary has to follow the protocol as per its specification, but it may record the entire transcript of the protocol to infer something beyond the output of the protocol. We consider the definition of security in terms of a real-world and ideal-world simulation paradigm, as in [18]. In the ideal model, we assume the existence of an in-corruptible trusted third party (TTP). In the semi-honest model, all the parties send their local inputs to the TTP, who computes the desired functionality and send back the prescribed outputs to them. The honest parties then output their respective outputs, while the semi-honest parties output an arbitrary probabilistic polynomial-time function of their respective inputs and the outputs obtained from the TTP. In contrast, in the malicious model the malicious parties may substitute their local input and send it to the TTP in the first place. We assume that the TTP always answers the malicious parties first. The malicious parties may also abort the execution of the protocol by refraining from sending their own messages. Finally, as in the semi-honest model, each honest party outputs its output as received from the TTP, while the malicious parties may output an arbitrary probabilistic polynomial-time function of their initial inputs and the outputs obtained from the TTP.

Definition 3 (Malicious adversaries–the ideal model). *Let $f : (\{0,1\}^*)^n \rightarrow (\{0,1\}^*)^n$ be a n-ary functionality as defined above. Let $\mathcal{I} = \{i_1, \cdots, i_q\} \subset [n]$, and $(x_1, \cdots, x_n)_I = (x_{i_1}, \cdots, x_{i_q})$. A pair $(\mathcal{I}, \mathcal{C})$ where $\mathcal{I} \subset [n]$ and $\mathcal{C}$ is a polynomial-size circuit family represents an adversary in the ideal model. The joint execution under $(\mathcal{I}, \mathcal{C})$ in the ideal model (on input sequence $\vec{x} = (x_1, \cdots, x_n)$), denoted by $\mathsf{IDEAL}_{f,(\mathcal{I},\mathcal{C})}(\vec{x})$ is defined as follows:*

$$(\mathcal{C}(\vec{x}_\mathcal{I}, \perp), \perp, \cdots, \perp) \qquad \text{if } \mathcal{C}(\vec{x}_\mathcal{I}) = \perp.$$

$$(\mathcal{C}(\vec{x}_\mathcal{I}, f_I(\mathcal{C}(\vec{x}_\mathcal{I}), \vec{x}_{\bar{\mathcal{I}}}), \perp), \perp, \cdots, \perp) \qquad \text{if } \mathcal{C}(x_\mathcal{I}) \neq \perp, 1 \in \mathcal{I} \text{ and } \vec{y}_{\bar{\mathcal{I}}} = \perp, \text{ where}$$

$$\vec{y}_\mathcal{I} \overset{\text{def}}{=} (\mathcal{C}(\vec{x}_\mathcal{I}, f_I(\mathcal{C}(\vec{x}_\mathcal{I}), \vec{x}_{\bar{\mathcal{I}}}))$$

$$(\mathcal{C}(\vec{x}_\mathcal{I}, f_I(\mathcal{C}(\vec{x}_\mathcal{I}), \vec{x}_{\bar{\mathcal{I}}})), f_{\bar{I}}(\mathcal{C}(\vec{x}_\mathcal{I}), \vec{x}_{\bar{\mathcal{I}}})) \qquad \text{otherwise}.$$

where $\bar{I} = [n] \setminus I$.

The first equation represents the case where the adversary makes some dishonest party to abort before invoking the trusted party. The second equation represents the case where the trusted party is invoked with possibly substituted inputs $C(\vec{x}_I)$ and is halted right after supplying the adversary with the I-part of the output $\vec{y}_I = f_I(\mathcal{C}(\vec{x}_\mathcal{I}), \vec{x}_{\bar{\mathcal{I}}})$. This case is allowed only when $1 \in \mathcal{I}$, i.e, the party P_1 can only be blamed for early abort. Finally, the third equation presents the case where the trusted is invoked with possibly substituted inputs $C(\vec{x}_I)$, but is also allowed to answer to all the parties.

Definition 4 (Malicious adversaries–the real model). *Let* $f : (\{0,1\}^*)^n \to (\{0,1\}^*)^n$ *be a* n-ary *functionality as defined above. Let* $\boldsymbol{\Pi}$ *be a protocol for computing* f. *The joint execution under* $(\mathcal{I}, \mathcal{C})$ *in the real model (on input sequence* $\vec{x} = (x_1, \cdots, x_n)$), *denoted by* $\mathsf{REAL}_{\Pi,(\mathcal{I},\mathcal{C})}(\vec{x})$ *is defined as the output sequence resulting of the interaction between the* n *parties where the messages of parties in* I *are computed according to* $\mathcal{C}$ *and the messages of parties not in* I *are computed according to* $\boldsymbol{\Pi}$.

Now that the ideal and real models are defined, we put forward the notion of security for a multi-party protocol. Informally, it says that a secure multi-party protocol in the real model emulates the ideal model.

Definition 5 (Security in the Malicious model). *Let* f *and* $\boldsymbol{\Pi}$ *be as in Definition 4. Protocol* $\boldsymbol{\Pi}$ *is said to* securely compute f *if there exists a polynomial-time computable transformation of polynomial-size circuit families* $\mathcal{A} = \{\mathcal{A}_\lambda\}$ *for the real model (of Definition 4) into polynomial-size circuit families* $\mathcal{B} = \{\mathcal{B}_\lambda\}$ *for the ideal model (of Definition 3) such that for every subset* $I \subset [n]$ *we have that* $\{\mathsf{IDEAL}_{f,(\mathcal{I},\mathcal{B})}(\vec{x})\}_{\lambda \in \mathbb{N}, \vec{x} \in (\{0,1\}^\lambda)^n} \equiv_c \{\mathsf{REAL}_{\Pi,(\mathcal{I},\mathcal{A})}(\vec{x})\}_{\lambda \in \mathbb{N}, \vec{x} \in (\{0,1\}^\lambda)^n}$.

2.1 Cryptographic Reverse Firewalls

Following [13, 26], we present the definition of cryptographic reverse firewalls (CRF). As in [26], we assume that a cryptographic protocol comes with some functionality (i.e., correctness) requirements $\mathcal{F}$ and some security requirements $\mathcal{S}$. For a party P and reverse firewall $\mathcal{W}$ we define $\mathcal{W} \circ P$ as the "composed" party in which the incoming and outgoing messages of P are "sanitized" by $\mathcal{W}$. In other words, $\mathcal{W}$ is applied to (1) the outgoing messages of P before they leave the local network of P and (2) the incoming messages of P before P sees them. We stress that the reverse firewall $\mathcal{W}$ neither shares any private input with party P nor does it get to know the output of party P. The firewall $\mathcal{W}$ is allowed to see only the public parameters of the system. Besides this, it can internally toss its own random coins and can also maintain state. We require the firewall $\mathcal{W}$ to preserve the functionality of the protocol (in case the parties are not corrupted), i.e., the composed party $\mathcal{W} \circ P$ should not break the correctness of the protocol. Following [13,26] we actually require the stronger property that the reverse firewalls be "stackable", i.e, many firewalls can be composed in series $\mathcal{W} \circ \cdots \circ \mathcal{W} \circ P$ without breaking the functionality of the protocol. In addition, we would want the firewall $\mathcal{W}$ to preserve the security requirements $\mathcal{S}$ of the underlying protocol, even in the case of compromise. The strongest notion of security requires the security of the protocol to be preserved even when a party P is *arbitrarily* corrupted (denote as $\overline{P}$). A weaker notion of security requires the security of the protocol to hold, even when the party P is tampered in a *functionality-maintaining* way (denoted by $\widehat{P}$), i.e., when the tampered implementation still maintains the functionality $\mathcal{F}$ of the protocol. For a protocol $\varPi$ with party P, we write $\varPi_{P \to \widehat{P}}$ to represent the protocol in which the role of party P is replaced by party $\widehat{P}$. Further, we require *exfiltration resistance* from the reverse firewall, which informally says that "no corrupt implementation of party P can leak any information through the firewall". We generalize the definition of exfiltration-resistance, as defined in [13,26], to the multi-party setting. Finally, following [13], we will also need the notion of "detectable failure" from the reverse firewall. Informally, this notion stipulates that a protocol fails detectably if we can distinguish transcripts of valid runs of a protocol from invalid transcripts. This property will be used by the firewall of a large protocol to test whether some sub-protocol failed or not. We now formally define all these properties below.

Definition 6 (Functionality-maintaining CRF [26]). *For any reverse firewall $\mathcal{W}$ and a party P, let $\mathcal{W}^1 \circ P = \mathcal{W} \circ P$, and $\mathcal{W}^k \circ P = \underbrace{\mathcal{W} \circ \cdots \circ \mathcal{W}}_{k\ times} \circ P$. A reverse firewall $\mathcal{W}$ maintains functionality $\mathcal{F}$ for a party P in protocol $\varPi$ if $\varPi$ satisfies $\mathcal{F}$, the protocol $\varPi_{P \to \mathcal{W} \circ P}$ satisfies $\mathcal{F}$, and the protocol $\varPi_{P \to \mathcal{W}^k \circ P}$ also satisfies $\mathcal{F}$.*

Following [26], we also consider the case where the adversarial implementation still counts as functionality-maintaining even if it breaks the correctness with negligible probability. This can be easily accommodated in the above definition by requiring that the protocol $\varPi_{P \to \mathcal{W}^k \circ P}$ (for $k \geq 1$) satisfies $\mathcal{F}$ with all but negligible probability. As noted in [26], this distinction can be quite important in the context of security definitions that allow for the corruption of other players in the protocol.

Definition 7 (Security-preserving CRF [26]). *A reverse firewall strongly preserves security requirements $\mathcal{S}$ for a party P in the protocol $\varPi$ if $\varPi$ satisfies requirements $\mathcal{S}$, and for any polynomial time algorithm $\overline{P}$, the protocol $\varPi_{P \to \mathcal{W} \circ \overline{P}}$ satisfies $\mathcal{S}$. (I.e., the firewall can guarantee security even when the adversary has tampered with the implementation of P). A reverse firewall preserves security* requirements S for a protocol P in the protocol Π *satisfying functionality* $\mathcal{F}$ *if* Π *satisfies requirements* S, *and for any polynomial time algorithm* $\widehat{P}$ *such that* $\Pi_{P \to \widehat{P}}$ *satisfies* $\mathcal{F}$, *the protocol* $\Pi_{P \to \mathcal{W} \circ \widehat{P}}$ *satisfies* S. *(I.e., the firewall can guarantee security even when the adversary has tampered with the implementation of* P, *provided that the tampered implementation preserves the functionality of the protocol).*

We also need the notion of *exfiltration-resistance* from the reverse firewall. In formally, a reverse firewall is exfiltration-resistant if "no corrupt implementation of a party can leak any information through the firewall". Our definition of exfiltration-resistance generalizes the definition of [13, 26] in the multi-party setting.

Definition 8 (Exfiltration-resistant CRF [26]). *Let* Π *be a multi-party protocol run between the parties* $P_1, \cdots, P_n$ *satisfying functionality* $\mathcal{F}$ *and having a reverse firewall* $\mathcal{W}$. *Then:*

- *We say that the firewall* $\mathcal{W}$ *is* strongly exfiltration-resistant for party P_i against the other parties $(P_1, \cdots, P_{i-1}, P_{i+1}, \cdots, P_n)$, *if for any PPT adversary* $\mathcal{A}$, *the advantage* $\mathsf{Adv}_{\mathcal{A},\mathcal{W}}^{\mathsf{LEAK}}(\lambda)$ *of* $\mathcal{A}$ *in the game* LEAK *(see Fig. 1) is negligible in the security parameter* λ, *and*
- *We say that the firewall* $\mathcal{W}$ *is* weakly exfiltration-resistant for party P_i against the other parties $(P_1, \cdots, P_{i-1}, P_{i+1}, \cdots, P_n)$, *if for any PPT adversary* $\mathcal{A}$, *the advantage* $\mathsf{Adv}_{\mathcal{A},\mathcal{W}}^{\mathsf{LEAK}}(\lambda)$ *of* $\mathcal{A}$ *in the game* LEAK *(see Fig. 1) is negligible in the security parameter* λ, *provided that* P_i *maintains functionality* $\mathcal{F}$ *for* P_i.

> **Proc. LEAK$(\Pi, i, \{P_1, \cdots, P_n\}, \mathcal{W}_i, \lambda)$**
> _____
> $(\overline{P_1}, \cdots, \overline{P_n}, I) \leftarrow \mathcal{A}(1^\lambda)$.
>
> $b \xleftarrow{\$} \{0, 1\}$.
>
> **IF** $b = 1$, $P_i^* \leftarrow \mathcal{W}_i \circ \overline{P_i}$.
>
> **ELSE,** $P_i^* \leftarrow \mathcal{W}_i \circ P_i$.
>
> $\mathcal{T}^* \leftarrow \Pi_{P_i \to P_i^*, \{P_j \to \overline{P_j}\}_{j \in [n] \setminus i}}(I)$.
>
> $b^* \leftarrow \mathcal{A}(\mathcal{T}^*, \{\mathsf{st}_{P_j}\}_{j \in [n] \setminus i})$.
>
> **OUTPUT** 1 if $b = b^*$ and 0 otherwise.

Fig. 1. LEAK$(\Pi, i, \{P_1, \cdots, P_n\}, \mathcal{W}_i, \lambda)$ is the exfiltration-resistance security game for a reverse firewall $\mathcal{W}$ for a party P_i in protocol Π against the set of parties $\{P_j\}_{j \in [n] \setminus i}$ with input I. $\mathcal{A}$ is the adversary, λ is the security parameter, $\{\mathsf{st}_{P_j}\}_{j \in [n] \setminus i}$ denote the states of the parties $\{P_j\}_{j \in [n] \setminus i}$ after the run of the protocol, I is the valid input for Π, and $\mathcal{T}^*$ is the transcript of running the protocol $\Pi_{P_i \to P_i^*, \{P_j \to \overline{P_j}\}_{j \in [n] \setminus i}}(I)$.

The advantage of any adversary $\mathcal{A}$ *in the game* LEAK *is defined as:* $\mathsf{Adv}_{\mathcal{A},\mathcal{W}}^{\mathsf{LEAK}}(\lambda) = \left| \Pr[\mathsf{LEAK}(\Pi, i, \{P_1, \cdots, P_n\}, \mathcal{W}_i, \lambda) = 1] - \frac{1}{2} \right|$.

Finally, we define another technical condition related to *detectable failures* of reverse firewalls, as presented in [13]. First, we recall the definition for what it means for a transcript to be *valid*, and then define detectable failures.

Definition 9 (Valid Transcripts [13]). *A sequence of bits r and private input I generate transcript T in protocol Π if a run of the protocol Π with input I in which the parties' coin flips are taken from r results in the transcript T. A transcript T is a valid transcript for protocol Π if there is a sequence r and private input I generating T such that no party outputs $\perp$ at the end of the run. A protocol has unambiguous transcripts if for any valid transcript T, there is no possible input I and coins r generating T that results in a party outputting $\perp$.*

Definition 10 (Detectable failure). *A reverse firewall W detects failure for party P in protocol Π if (a) $\Pi_{P \to W \circ P}$ has unambiguous transcripts; (b) the firewall outputs a special symbol $\perp$ when run on any transcript that is not valid for $\Pi_{P \to W \circ P}$, and (c) there is a polynomial-time deterministic algorithm that decides whether a transcript T is valid for $\Pi_{P \to W \circ P}$.*

3   Reverse Firewalls and Actively Secure MPCs

In this section, we discuss the relationship between actively secure MPC protocols and reverse firewalls. In this work, we consider *computationally-secure* MPC protocols. For the protocol to be secure, we need to assume that at least one of the parties participating in the MPC protocol is "honest". However, in the setting of reverse firewalls, this assumption may not hold true, and in general, we cannot rely on trusted implementation of any of the parties to guarantee security of the resulting MPC protocol. In particular, in this setting, one may consider a scenario where all the parties may be arbitrarily corrupted. To provide any sort of meaningful security guarantees in such a strong corruption model, we assume that each of the *honest* parties participating in the MPC protocol are equipped with a cryptographic reverse firewall. As mentioned earlier, none of the firewalls share any secrets with any of the parties, nor can it access the outputs of the corresponding parties. The firewall has access to only the public parameters used in the protocol. All the incoming and outgoing messages sent and received by the parties are modified by the firewall. Hence, even if the honest parties are corrupted, the firewall can sanitize the outgoing and incoming messages in such a way that the security of the original MPC protocol (where there is at least one honest party) is preserved.

Ideally, we would like to build reverse firewalls for the MPC protocol, where all the *honest* parties can be arbitrarily corrupted. However, in order to accomplish this goal, we will need to consider the following scenario: Suppose that one of the parties which was assumed to be honest in the original MPC protocol refuses to communicate (also called "attack by refusal" in [13]) in this new model of corruption. To guarantee security against this attack, clearly the firewall needs to produce a message which looks indistinguishable from the message the honest party would have sent in the original MPC protocol. In order words, the firewall needs to *simulate* the behavior of this (honest) party in our new corruption model, where the same party can be arbitrarily corrupted. Now suppose that, the party has a public-secret key pair and it uses the secret key to compute some message at some point in the protocol (say, a signature on the transcript so far). Clearly, this action *cannot* be simulated by the firewall, since it does not have access to the secret key of the party. Hence, in this setting, where the parties have access to key pairs (which will indeed be the case for us), achieving security against strong or arbitrary corruption is *impossible*.

To circumvent the above impossibility result, we consider a *hybrid* model of corruption, which is slightly weaker than the corruption model mentioned above. In particular, in our model, up to $n - 1$ parties can be arbitrarily corrupted, where n is the total number of parties participating in the protocol. The remaining honest parties can also be corrupted, albeit, in a *functionality-maintaining* way. In a functionality-maintaining tampered implementation of a party, the adversary may deviate arbitrarily from the protocol, as long as it does not break its functionality. Intuitively, this models "more conspicuous" adversaries whose tampered circuit(s) will be noticed by honest parties participating in the protocol with non-negligible probability [26].

Remark 2 (**On broadcast channels with reverse firewalls**). As mentioned earlier, we will assume the availability of a broadcast channel for our construction of the actively-secure MPC protocol in the reverse firewall (CRF) setting. However, in the CRF setting, the assumption of broadcast channels may be stronger than the classical setting. To this end, we present a compiler for reverse firewalls for the broadcast model (this is done in the extended version of this paper [8]). We instantiate the broadcast protocol using a version of the classical Dolev-Strong protocol [15], secure in the CRF setting. The protocol of [15] shows that one can simulate a broadcast channel using public-key infrastructure, in particular using signature schemes as the authentication mechanism. In our construction, we replace the signature scheme from [15] with *unique* signatures. Intuitively this works since: on any input in the Dolev-Strong protocol, the only allowed message consists of adding a signature on a well-defined message. The signature is either sent or added to a valid set. Since the signatures are unique, this leaves only one possible message that a (even corrupted) party can send. The latter holds since we assume that the parties are corrupted in a functionality-maintaining way. Due to space constraints, we give the details of the protocol in [8].

3.1 Actively Secure MPC Protocols Using Reverse Firewalls

In this section, we present a construction of multi-party computation (MPC) protocol secure against malicious adversaries in the setting of reverse firewalls. As mentioned above, we only consider computationally-secure MPC protocols. The starting point of our construction is the actively-secure MPC protocol of

Goldreich, Micali and Wigderson [18,19] (henceforth referred to as the GMW protocol). Their methodology works by first presenting a MPC protocol secure against semi-honest adversaries, and then compiling it into a protocol secure against malicious adversaries. The resulting actively secure GMW protocol can tolerate a corruption of up to $n - 1$ parties, where n is the number of parties participating in the protocol. We begin with an informal exposition of the GMW compiler.

INFORMAL DESCRIPTION OF THE GMW COMPILER. As mentioned before, the GMW protocol [18,19] first constructs a semi-honest MPC protocol, and then compiles it to one which is secure against malicious adversaries. Recall that, in the semi-honest protocol all the parties follow the protocol specification exactly. However, in the malicious model, the parties may deviate arbitrarily from the protocol. The way that the GMW protocol achieves security against malicious adversaries is by enforcing the parties to behave in a semi-honest manner. However, this only makes sense relative to a given input and a random tape. The GMW protocol achieves this in the following way: First, all the parties commit to their inputs by running a *multi-party input commitment* protocol. Note that, before the protocol starts each party may replace its given inputs with arbitrary bit strings. However, the security of this protocol guarantees that, once they commit to their inputs, it cannot be changed afterwards during the course of execution of the protocol. The parties then run an actively-secure *multi-party (augmented) coin tossing* protocol to fix their random tapes (to be used in the actual MPC protocol). This protocol ensures that all the parties have a uniformly random tape. After these first two steps, each party holds its own uniformly random tape, and the commitments to other party's inputs and random tapes. Hence, the parties can now be forced to behave properly in the following way: the view of each party in the MPC protocol is simply a deterministic function of its own input, random tape and the (public/broadcast) messages received so far in the protocol. Hence, when a party sends a new message it also proves in zero-knowledge that the computation was correctly done, as per the protocol specification. The soundness of the proof system guarantees that even a malicious adversary cannot deviate from the protocol, while the zero-knowledge property ensures that nothing other than the validity of each computational step is revealed to the adversary. This phase is also called the *protocol emulation* phase.

When we consider the actively-secure GMW protocol in the reverse firewall settings, we must ensure that the above-mentioned protocols remain functional and secure in the setting of reverse firewalls. Hence, we need to design reverse firewalls for each of the three main protocols (as discussed above) used in the GMW compiler. Finally, to enable the working of the compiler, we need to show that the reverse firewalls for each of these protocols compose together. To this end, we first propose a multi-party augmented coin-tossing protocol with *reduced round-complexity* (see Sect. 3.2) by appropriately extending the two-party coin-tossing protocol of Lindell [24]. We then present a reverse firewall for this multi-party coin-tossing protocol in Sect. 3.3. In Sects. 3.4 and 3.5, we present reverse firewalls for the multi-party input commitment and the multi-party authenticated computation protocols.

3.2 Multi-party Augmented Coin-Tossing into the Well

The multi-party augmented coin tossing protocol is used to generate *random pads* for all the parties participating in an actively secure multi-party computation protocol. Each party obtains the bits of the random-pad to be held by it, whereas the other parties obtains commitments to these bits. These random pads serve as the random coins of the corresponding parties to emulate the semi-honest MPC protocol. Intuitively, this multi-party coin-tossing functionality guarantees that, at the end of this protocol the malicious parties can either abort or they end up with a uniformly distributed random pad. However, the original coin-tossing protocol of GMW [18, 19] was rather inefficient in terms of round complexity. This is because the protocol of [18, 19] required polynomially many rounds to generate a polynomially long random pad, since single coins were tossed sequentially in each round. Later, Lindell [24] showed a constant round two-party protocol for augmented parallel coin-tossing into the well using a "commit-and-proof" framework. In Fig. 2, we extend the protocol of [24] in the multi-party setting with round-complexity *only* 3^4 and achieving a comparable level of security as in [24]. In Sect. 3.3, we present a reverse firewall for our multiparty augmented coin-tossing protocol. This requires the commitment scheme com to be *statistically/perfectly hiding* (and computationally binding) and *additively homomorphic*, and also requires the NIZK argument system to be *controlled-malleable* simulation-sound extractable with respect to the above homomorphic operation.

Definition 11 (Multi-party Augmented Parallel Coin-Tossing into the Well). *An n-party augmented coin-tossing into the well is an n-party protocol for securely computing the following functionality with respect to a fixed commitment scheme* $\{\mathcal{G}_\lambda, K_\lambda, \text{com}_\lambda\}_{\lambda \in \mathbb{N}}$,

$$(1^\lambda, \cdots, 1^\lambda) \rightarrow ((U_t, U_{t\cdot\lambda}), \text{com}_\lambda(U_t; U_{t\cdot\lambda}), \cdots, \text{com}_\lambda(U_t; U_{t\cdot\lambda})) \qquad (1)$$

where U_m *denotes the uniform distribution over m-bit strings, and we assume that* com *requires* λ *random bits to commit to each bit.*

Similar to [24], we will actually give a protocol with respect to the functionality $(1^\lambda, \cdots, 1^\lambda) \rightarrow (U_m, F(U_m), \cdots, F(U_m))$, where we can set $m = t + t \cdot \lambda$ and $F(U_m) = \text{com}_\lambda(U_t; U_{t\cdot\lambda})$. Thus, all the parties other than the one who initiates the protocol receive a commitment to a uniformly random t bit string, and the committing/initiating party receives the random string and its decommitment.

---

[4] Although the protocol of Lindell [24] is constant round, its round-complexity is greater than 4 due to the use of (constant-round) zero-knowledge proofs. We use NIZK arguments in a natural way to shrink the round-complexity of the protocol to 3, albeit introducing a trusted setup assumption, as required for NIZK protocols.

In the final compiler, the t bit strings will be used as random pads for the parties and the decommitment value is used to provide consistency checks for each step of the protocol (via (non-interactive) zero-knowledge proof).

W.l.o.g, we denote some party P_i ($i \in [n]$) to be the initializing party in the protocol below (see Fig. 2), i.e, it receives the random pad and the decommitment value (to be used later in the protocol) and all the other parties P_j (where $j \in [n] \setminus i$) receive a commitment to the random string of P_i. In the final MPC protocol, each party will need to run an independent instance of the multi-party coin-tossing protocol shown below.

Let $\{\mathcal{G}_\lambda, K_\lambda, \mathsf{com}_\lambda\}_{\lambda \in \mathbb{N}}$ be a *statistically/perfectly hiding* and *computationally binding* commitment scheme. Also, let $(\mathsf{CRSGen}, \mathsf{P}, \mathsf{V})$ be a *strong simulation-extractable non-interactive zero-knowledge* (SSE-NIZK) argument system for the following language: $\mathcal{L} = \{c, (x, y) \mid c = \mathsf{com}_\lambda(x; y)\}$.

Inputs: Each party gets as input the security parameter 1^λ.

Convention: As mentioned above, we denote the initializing party in each round by party P_i. Any deviation from the protocol, by a party other than Party P_i, will be interpreted as a canonical legitimate message. In case P_i aborts or is detected cheating, all honest parties halt outputting the special symbol $\perp$.

(i) Party P_i chooses a random string $s_i \in_R \{0,1\}^m$. It then computes $c_i = \mathsf{com}_\lambda(s_i; r)$ for a random r using a computationally binding commitment scheme. P_i then computes a proof $\pi_i \leftarrow \mathsf{P}(\sigma_{crs}, c_i, (s_i, r))$ using the SSE-NIZK argument system. P_i then places the tuple (c_i, π_i) on the broadcast channel. In case the proof π_i does not verify with respect to c_i, all the parties abort with output $\perp$.

(ii) For $j \in [n] \setminus i$, party P_j selects $s_j \in_R \{0,1\}^m$ and places s_j on the broadcast channel.

(iii) Party P_i sets $s = s_i \oplus_{j \in [n] \setminus i} s_j$, and computes $y = F(s)$. P_i then proves in zero-knowledge that there exists a pair (s_i, r) such that $c_i = \mathsf{com}_\lambda(s_i; r)$ and $y = F(s_i \oplus_{j \in [n] \setminus i} s_j)$. It then places the tuple (y, π) on the broadcast channel. As before, if the proof π does not verify with respect to (c_i, y), all the parties abort with output $\perp$.

Outputs: Party P_i sets its local output to $s = s_i \oplus_{j \in [n] \setminus i} s_j$ and all the other parties set their local output to be y, provided they did not halt with output $\perp$ before.

Fig. 2. Multi-party augmented parallel coin-tossing into the well.

Theorem 2. *Let* $\{\mathcal{G}_\lambda, K_\lambda, \mathsf{com}_\lambda\}_{\lambda \in \mathbb{N}}$ *be a perfectly hiding and computationally binding commitment scheme. Also, let* $(\mathsf{CRSGen}, \mathsf{P}, \mathsf{V}, \mathsf{ZKEval})$ *be a strong simulation-extractable non-interactive zero-knowledge argument system for the language defined in* Fig. 2. *Then the protocol shown in* Fig. 2 *is a secure protocol for multi-party augmented coin-tossing into the well.*

For the proof of this theorem (which is a straightforward generalization of the proof of the two-party coin-tossing protocol of [24] to the multi-party setting) see [8].

3.3 Multi-party Augmented Coin-Tossing Using Reverse Firewalls

In this section, we present a cryptographic reverse firewall (CRF) for the multi-party augmented parallel coin-tossing protocol, as shown in Fig. 3. We present a single reverse firewall $\mathcal{W}_1$ for this protocol that happens to work for all the honest parties. However, each of the honest parties involved in the coin-tossing protocol should be equipped with their own CRF. It so happens that the "code" of the firewall is the same for all these parties.

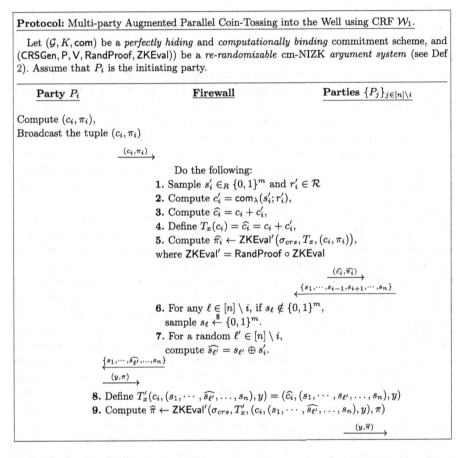

Protocol: Multi-party Augmented Parallel Coin-Tossing into the Well using CRF $\mathcal{W}_1$.

Let $(\mathcal{G}, K, \mathsf{com})$ be a *perfectly hiding* and *computationally binding* commitment scheme, and $(\mathsf{CRSGen}, \mathsf{P}, \mathsf{V}, \mathsf{RandProof}, \mathsf{ZKEval}))$ be a *re-randomizable* cm-NIZK *argument system* (see Def 2). Assume that P_i is the initiating party.

Party P_i	**Firewall**	**Parties $\{P_j\}_{j \in [n] \setminus i}$**

Compute (c_i, π_i),
Broadcast the tuple (c_i, π_i)

$\xrightarrow{(c_i, \pi_i)}$

Do the following:
1. Sample $s_i' \in_R \{0,1\}^m$ and $r_i' \in \mathcal{R}$
2. Compute $c_i' = \mathsf{com}_\lambda(s_i'; r_i')$,
3. Compute $\widehat{c_i} = c_i + c_i'$,
4. Define $T_x(c_i) = \widehat{c_i} = c_i + c_i'$,
5. Compute $\widehat{\pi_i} \leftarrow \mathsf{ZKEval}'(\sigma_{crs}, T_x, (c_i, \pi_i))$,
   where $\mathsf{ZKEval}' = \mathsf{RandProof} \circ \mathsf{ZKEval}$

$\xrightarrow{(\widehat{c_i}, \widehat{\pi_i})}$

$\xleftarrow{\{s_1, \cdots, s_{i-1}, s_{i+1}, \cdots, s_n\}}$

6. For any $\ell \in [n] \setminus i$, if $s_\ell \notin \{0,1\}^m$,
   sample $s_\ell \xleftarrow{\$} \{0,1\}^m$.
7. For a random $\ell' \in [n] \setminus i$,
   compute $\widehat{s_{\ell'}} = s_{\ell'} \oplus s_i'$.

$\xleftarrow{\{s_1, \cdots, \widehat{s_{\ell'}}, \ldots, s_n\}}$

$\xrightarrow{(y, \pi)}$

8. Define $T_x'(c_i, (s_1, \cdots, \widehat{s_{\ell'}}, \ldots, s_n), y) = (\widehat{c_i}, (s_1, \cdots, s_{\ell'}, \ldots, s_n), y)$
9. Compute $\widehat{\pi} \leftarrow \mathsf{ZKEval}'(\sigma_{crs}, T_x', (c_i, (s_1, \cdots, \widehat{s_{\ell'}}, \ldots, s_n), y), \pi)$

$\xrightarrow{(y, \widehat{\pi})}$

Fig. 3. Reverse firewall $\mathcal{W}_1$ for the parties involved in the protocol from Fig. 2.

Main Idea. The main idea underlying the multi-party coin-tossing protocol from Fig. 2 involves a "*commit-and-proof*" framework. Here, party P_i initially commits to a random m-bit string s_i and proves in zero-knowledge about the consistency of the committed value. Each of the other parties P_j ($j \in [n] \setminus i$) then sends a random m-bit string s_j to P_i, and the final m-bit string s is then set as the exclusive OR of all these strings. Finally P_i commits to s and proves in zero-knowledge about the consistency of both the initial and this final commitment.

However, in reality a tampered implementation of P_i might use a commitment scheme that leaks some information about s_i to an eavesdropper. The committed value might also act as a subliminal channel to leak some of its secrets (or inputs) to the other parties or to an eavesdropper. Similarly, a tampered implementation of a party P_j might also open up the possibility to leak m-bit of its input (or other secrets) to P_i or to the eavesdropper. Thus, it is desirable that the CRF resists exfiltration and also preserves security, even in the face of such a compromise. Figure 3 shows the design of the reverse firewall for the multi-party augmented parallel coin-tossing protocol. For constructing the reverse firewall for the above protocol, we require the underlying commitment scheme and the NIZK proof system to be *malleable* (with respect to some predefined relation) and *re-randomizable*. For our application, we require that the commitment to *any* m-bit string s can be mauled to a commitment of a related but *random* m-bit string $\widehat{s} = s \oplus s'$, for any uniformly random string s'. We also require the commitment scheme to be re-randomizable, so that the randomness used to commit to a string cannot leak any information about the committed element. We show how to achieve both these properties of malleability and re-randomizability by assuming that the underlying commitment scheme com is *homomorphic* (with respect to an appropriate relation).

Our main idea is that the CRF mauls and re-randomizes the initial commitment it receives from P_i using the homomorphic properties of com. However, at this point the proof π_i given by P_i (that proves consistency of the initial commitment value) will no longer be valid with respect to the mauled commitment. Hence, the CRF also needs to *maul* the proof in such a way that the mauled proof is consistent with the mauled statement (i..e the commitment). At first thought, it seems that the CRF cannot produce such a proof, since it does not know the witness corresponding to the original statement (i.e., the committed string and the randomness used for commitment) and hence, also has no knowledge of the mauled witness (witness resulting from mauling the statement/commitment). Fortunately, as we show, the CRF can still maul the proof π_i without actually knowing the mauled witness, thanks to the availability of the public evaluation algorithm ZKEval of the underlying controlled-malleable simulation-extractable NIZK argument system. The mauled proof is then further re-randomized using the algorithm RandProof, so that the randomness used in the proof does not reveal any information about the witness. Finally, the resulting proof looks like a fresh proof corresponding to the mauled statement. The firewall then places the mauled commitment-proof pair on the broadcast channel. When any other party P_j sends a string s_j, the CRF checks if the string is indeed a m-bit string. If not, it chooses a random m-bit string on behalf of P_j. It then modifies one of the strings s_j it receives by adding the offset s'_i chosen by the CRF at the beginning with s_j, so that it is consistent with the mauled commitment. At this point, another technical difficulty arises: the views of party P_i and all other parties in the protocol are *inconsistent* due to the above mauling by the CRF. However, as we show, the CRF can again appropriately maul the transcript (which will be treated as a statement in the final NIZK proof) so that at the end all the parties arrive at a consistent view of the protocol. The design of the reverse firewall (see Fig. 3) is now described in details:

1. The CRF $\mathcal{W}_1$ receives a commitment-proof pair (c_i, π_i) from party P_i. Let us assume that c_i is a commitment to some m-but string s_i (may not be random). It then does the following:
   - Sample another random m-bit string $s'_i \in_R \{0,1\}^m$ and a randomizer $r'_i \in_R \mathcal{R}$ for the commitment scheme com.
   - Compute $c'_i = \text{com}_\lambda(s'_i, r'_i)$ and then homomorphically compute the mauled commitment $\widehat{c}_i = c_i + c'_i$.
   - Define the transformation $T_x(c_i) = \widehat{c}_i = c_i + c'_i$.
   - Derive a proof for the transformed statement as: $\widehat{\pi}_i \leftarrow \text{RandProof} \circ \text{ZKEval}(\sigma_{crs}, T_x, (c_i, \pi_i))$. Note that, the proof $\widehat{\pi}_i$ is consistent with the mauled commitment $\widehat{c}_i$.
   - The firewall then places the tuple $(\widehat{c}_i, \widehat{\pi}_i)$ on the broadcast channel.
2. On receiving the strings s_j from party P_j ($j \in [n] \setminus i$), the CRF checks if $s_j \in \{0,1\}^m$. If not, then it chooses a random string $s_j \in \{0,1\}^m$. It then randomly selects an index $\ell' \in [n] \setminus i$ and modifies the string $s_{\ell'}$ to the related string $\widehat{s_{\ell'}} = s_{\ell'} \oplus s'_i$, and forwards the tuple $\{s_1, \cdots, \widehat{s_{\ell'}}, \cdots, s_n\}$ to party P_i.
3. Receive the tuple (y, π) from P_i. Note that, the proof π will not be consistent with the view of the other parties $\{P_j\}_{j \in [n] \setminus i}$, since the common input (or statement) for P_j will be different from the input of party P_i. In particular, the (public) input for P_i is the tuple $(c_i, s_1, \cdots, \widehat{s_{\ell'}}, \cdots, s_n)$, while the (public) input for the parties P_j is the tuple $(\widehat{c}_i, s_1, \cdots, s_{\ell'}, \cdots, s_n)$. The CRF then does the following:
   - Define the following transformation: $T'_x(c_i, (s_1, \cdots, \widehat{s_{\ell'}}, \cdots, s_n), y) = (\widehat{c}_i, (s_1, \cdots, s_{\ell'}, \cdots, s_n), y)$. Note that, this is efficiently computable, given the knowledge of s'_i.
   - Compute the proof $\widehat{\pi}$ as follows: $\widehat{\pi} \leftarrow \text{RandProof} \circ \text{ZKEval}(\sigma_{crs}, T'_x, (c_i, (s_1, \cdots, \widehat{s_{\ell'}}, \cdots, s_n), y), \pi)$. Broadcast the tuple $(y, \widehat{\pi})$ to all the parties P_j. Note that, the proof $\widehat{\pi}$ is now consistent with the statement $(\widehat{c}_i, s_1, \cdots, s_{\ell'}, \cdots, s_n)$.

Theorem 3. *The reverse firewall $\mathcal{W}_1$ for augmented multi-party coin-tossing shown in* Fig. 3 *is functionality-maintaining. If the commitment scheme* com *is computationally binding and is homomorphic with respect to the (addition) operation defined over the underlying groups (i.e, the message space, randomness space and the commitment space of* com*) and the NIZK argument system is controlled-malleable simulation-sound extractable, then the firewall $\mathcal{W}_1$ preserves security for party P_j and is weakly exfiltration-resistant against the other parties $\{P_j\}_{j \in [n] \setminus i}$. If the commitment scheme is perfectly/statistically hiding*

*and homomorphic as above and the NIZK argument system also satisfies the
same property as above, $\mathcal{W}_1$ strongly preserves security for the parties $\{P_j\}_{j\in[n]\setminus i}$
and is strongly exfiltration-resistant against P_i. The firewall $\mathcal{W}_1$ also detects
failures for all the parties.*

Proof. First, we will show that the reverse firewall shown in Fig. 3 is functionality maintaining. If the parties are honest, the output view of all these parties are
consistent. In particular, the output of party P_i is: $\widehat{s} = s_i \oplus (s_1 \oplus \cdots \oplus \widehat{s_\ell} \cdots \oplus s_n) =$
$(s_i \oplus s_i') \oplus_{j\in[n]\setminus i} s_j$. The output of P_i is a commitment y to the m-bit string $\widehat{s}$.
Even if all the strings s_i and $(s_1, \cdots, s_{i-1}, s_{i+1}, \cdots, s_n)$ are not random, the
resultant m-bit string $\widehat{s}$ is indeed *random*. Hence, at the end party P_i ends
up with a random pad, while the other parties receives a commitment to the
string. This shows that the CRF is *functionality-maintaining*. We now proceed to
show that the reverse firewall for P_i preserves security and exfiltration-resistance
against the other parties $\{P_j\}_{j\in[n]\setminus i}$. Note that, the homomorphically evaluated
commitment $\widehat{c_i}$ is *independent* of the original commitment c_i. This is because the
firewall chooses an independent m-bit string s_i' and randomness r_i' to homomorphically evaluate the original (potentially malicious) commitment string c_i. The
proof π_i is also appropriately mauled so that the mauled proof $\widehat{\pi_i}$ is consistent
with the mauled commitment $\widehat{c_i}$. The mauled proof is further re-randomized
using the algorithm RandProof. Hence, by the *derivation-privacy* of the proof of
the NIZK argument system (see Theorem 1), the mauled proof $\widehat{\pi_i}$ looks indistinguishable from a fresh proof of the commitment $\widehat{c_i}$. Hence, the firewall sanitizes
the messages sent across by P_i, even though the implementation of P_i may be
corrupt. Since, P_i is functionality maintaining, his second message is fixed, unless
he can find an alternate opening for c_i, which by definition of binding is computationally hard. Hence, it follows that the reverse firewall for party P_i is weakly
exfiltration-resistant for P_i against all the other parties P_j and also preserves
security for P_i. To prove strong exfiltration-resistance for any party P_j against
party P_i and strong security preservation for P_j, one should note that the mauled
commitment is a uniformly random commitment to a uniformly random m-bit
string. Since, the commitment scheme com is perfectly (statistically) hiding, it is
(statistically) independent of the string s_j chosen by the party P_j. The firewall
mauls one of the strings $s_{\ell'}$ by adding the random offset s_i', and hence the final
m-bit string of party P_i is *random*, irrespective of how the strings s_j were chosen.

3.4   Multi-party Input Commitment Phase Using Reverse Firewalls

In this step, each party commits to its input to be used in the protocol. In
particular, the parties execute a secure protocol for the following functionality:

$$((x,r), 1^\lambda, \cdots, 1^\lambda) \rightarrow (\lambda, \mathsf{com}_\lambda(x;r), \cdots, \mathsf{com}_\lambda(x;r)). \tag{2}$$

where x is the input string of the party and r is the randomness chosen by the
committing party to commit to x. In the input commitment phase, each party P
first chooses a random string x and commits to x using randomness r to generate

the commitment C. It also generates a proof π using a simulation-extractable non-interactive zero-knowledge argument system that it knows a witness (i.,e, the tuple (x, r)) corresponding to the commitment C. Finally, party P_i places the pair (C, π) on the broadcast channel. Next, we present a reverse firewall $\mathcal{W}_2$ for the above protocol, as shown in Fig. 4. As before, we assume that P_i is the initiating party.

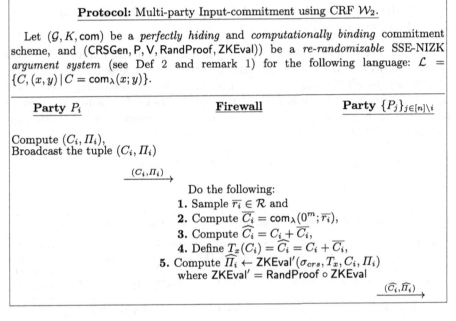

Protocol: Multi-party Input-commitment using CRF $\mathcal{W}_2$.

Let $(\mathcal{G}, K, \mathsf{com})$ be a *perfectly hiding* and *computationally binding* commitment scheme, and $(\mathsf{CRSGen}, \mathsf{P}, \mathsf{V}, \mathsf{RandProof}, \mathsf{ZKEval}))$ be a *re-randomizable* SSE-NIZK *argument system* (see Def 2 and remark 1) for the following language: $\mathcal{L} = \{C, (x, y) \mid C = \mathsf{com}_\lambda(x; y)\}$.

Party P_i	**Firewall**	**Party $\{P_j\}_{j \in [n] \setminus i}$**

Compute (C_i, Π_i),
Broadcast the tuple (C_i, Π_i)

$\xrightarrow{(C_i, \Pi_i)}$

Do the following:
1. Sample $\overline{r_i} \in \mathcal{R}$ and
2. Compute $\overline{C_i} = \mathsf{com}_\lambda(0^m; \overline{r_i})$,
3. Compute $\widehat{C_i} = C_i + \overline{C_i}$,
4. Define $T_x(C_i) = \widehat{C_i} = C_i + \overline{C_i}$,
5. Compute $\widehat{\Pi_i} \leftarrow \mathsf{ZKEval}'(\sigma_{crs}, T_x, C_i, \Pi_i)$
where $\mathsf{ZKEval}' = \mathsf{RandProof} \circ \mathsf{ZKEval}$

$\xrightarrow{(\widehat{C_i}, \widehat{\Pi_i})}$

Fig. 4. Reverse firewall $\mathcal{W}_2$ for the multi-party input commitment protocol

The main idea of the working of the reverse firewall $\mathcal{W}_2$ is very simple (see Fig. 3). The CRF simply re-randomizes the commitment C_i and the proof Π_i received from party P_i. The way the CRF re-randomizes the commitment C_i is by homomorphically adding to it a fresh commitment of the all zero string. It re-randomizes the proof Π_i by using the $\mathsf{RandProof}$ algorithm of SSE-NIZK argument system. The CRF then broadcasts the re-randomized commitment-proof pair. We now have the following theorem, whose proof (which is an adaptation of the standard proof for the input commitment functionality [18]) appears in [8]).

Theorem 4. *Let* $\{\mathcal{G}_\lambda, K_\lambda, \mathsf{com}_\lambda\}_{\lambda \in \mathbb{N}}$ *be a perfectly hiding and computationally binding commitment scheme. Also, let* $(\mathsf{CRSGen}, \mathsf{P}, \mathsf{V}, \mathsf{ZKEval})$ *be a simulation-extractable non-interactive zero-knowledge argument system for the language* $\mathcal{L} = \{C \mid C = \mathsf{com}_\lambda(x; y)\}$. *Then the protocol in Fig. 4 securely computes the functionality presented in Eq. 2. The reverse firewall* $\mathcal{W}_2$ *shown in Fig. 4 is* functionality-maintaining *and* detects failure *for party* P_i. *If the commitment scheme* com *is* perfectly hiding, computationally binding *and* homomorphic *with respect to the (addition) operation defined over the underlying groups (i.e, the message space, randomness space and the commitment space of* com*); the NIZK argument system is* re-randomizable *and* simulation-sound extractable, *then the reverse firewall* $\mathcal{W}_2$ *preserves security for party* P_i *and is* exfiltration-resistant *against the other parties* $\{P_j\}_{j \in [n]\setminus i}$.

3.5 Multi-party Authenticated Computation Protocol Using Reverse Firewalls

Let $f, h : \{0,1\}^* \times \{0,1\}^* \to \{0,1\}^*$ be polynomial-time computable. The goal of this protocol is to force the initializing party P_i to compute $f(\alpha, \beta)$, where β is known to all the parties, α is known only to P_i, and $h(\alpha)$ (where h is one-to-one function) is known to all the parties. Here f captures the desired computation. In particular, the parties execute this protocol for computing the following functionality:

$$\big((\alpha, r, \beta), (h(\alpha, r), \beta), \cdots, (h(\alpha, r), \beta)\big) \to \big(\lambda, f(\alpha, \beta), \cdots, f(\alpha, \beta)\big). \quad (3)$$

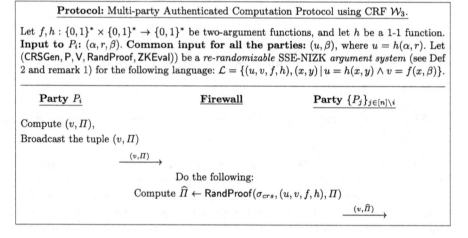

Fig. 5. Reverse firewall $\mathcal{W}_3$ for the multi-party authenticated computation protocol

The Construction. The multi-party authenticated computation protocol is run by all the parties after executing the multi-party input commitment and the multi-party (augmented) coin-tossing protocols. Hence, at this point, the inputs and the random tapes of all the parties are fixed. Other than its own input and the random tape (along with other decommitment values/randomnesses), each party also holds the commitment to all the other parties input and random tapes. We now just briefly recall the multi-party authenticated computation protocol. We follow the protocol as stated in [18], except that we use strong simulation extractable NIZK (SSE-NIZK) argument systems instead of strong zero-knowledge proof of knowledge (as in [18]). The use of NIZK arguments naturally makes the protocol constant-round, albeit with a setup assumption. Assume that the party P_i is the initiating party in a particular run of this protocol. The input to P_i is the tuple (α, r, β), while the common input to all the parties is (u, β), where $u = h(\alpha, r)$. Party P_i then computes the desired functionality $f(\alpha, \beta)$ and invokes a SSE-NIZK argument system to generate a proof Π corresponding to the following language: $\mathcal{L} = \{((u, v, f, h), (x, y)) \mid ((u = h(x, y)) \wedge (v = f(x, \beta)))\}$. It then broadcasts the tuple (v, Π). In case the proof does not verify, all the parties abort and output $\perp$.

We now discuss the design of the reverse firewall $\mathcal{W}_3$ for this protocol. We assume that the party P_i is tampered in a functionality-maintaining way. The idea for the design of the CRF is very simple: the CRF simply re-randomizes the proof Π, since the randomness used to generate the proof may reveal some secret information. Note that, the value $v = f(\alpha, \beta)$ given by P_i should be correctly computed. This follows from the fact that party $P_i's$ input and random coins are fixed, and it is corrupted in a functionality-maintaining way. The design of the CRF is shown in Fig. 5. We now have the following theorem whose proof (appearing in [8]) is an adaptation of the proof of the protocol executing the authenticated computation functionality [18].

Theorem 5. *Let* $\{\mathcal{G}_\lambda, K_\lambda, \mathsf{com}_\lambda\}_{\lambda \in \mathbb{N}}$ *be a perfectly hiding and computationally binding commitment scheme. Also, let* $(\mathsf{CRSGen}, \mathsf{P}, \mathsf{V}, \mathsf{ZKEval})$ *be a strong simulation-extractable non-interactive zero-knowledge argument system for the language* $\mathcal{L}$ *shown in* Fig. 5. *Then the protocol in* Fig. 5 *securely computes the functionality presented in* Eq. 3. *The reverse firewall* $\mathcal{W}_3$ *shown in* Fig. 5 *is functionality-maintaining and detects failure for party* P_i. *If the commitment scheme* com *is perfectly hiding and computationally binding; the NIZK argument system is re-randomizable and simulation-sound extractable, then the reverse firewall* $\mathcal{W}_3$ *preserves security for party* P_i *and is exfiltration-resistance against the other parties* $\{P_j\}_{j \in [n] \setminus i}$.

3.6 The Final Compiler

We now present the final compiler which transforms any semi-honest MPC protocol Π into a protocol Π' which is secure in the malicious model in the setting of reverse firewalls. We assume the existence of a single broadcast channel. The specification of our compiler is similar to that presented in [18]; however, adjusted to the reverse firewall setting. In particular, we present a reverse firewall $\mathcal{W}^*$ for the final MPC protocol Π'. As we show, this firewall $\mathcal{W}^*$ can be seen as consisting of three sub-firewalls $\mathcal{W}_1$, $\mathcal{W}_2$ and $\mathcal{W}_3$ corresponding to the three sub-protocols or building blocks used in the compiler, namely, input commitment, (augmented) coin-tossing, and the authenticated computation protocols respectively. We then present a generic composition theorem for reverse firewalls and show that the compiled protocol Π' is secure in the presence of the reverse firewall $\mathcal{W}^*$.

The Construction. Let Π be a given n-party MPC protocol, secure in the semi-honest model. We compile the protocol Π into another protocol Π' in the reverse firewall setting using the building blocks we have developed so far. The specification of the protocol Π' follows:

Inputs. Party P_i gets input $x^i = x_1^i x_2^i \cdots x_\ell^i \in \{0,1\}^\ell$.

Input Commitment phase using reverse firewalls. Each of the n parties commits to their ℓ-bit input string using a secure implementation of the multi-party input commitment functionality (see Eq. 2) using reverse firewall $\mathcal{W}_1$, as presented in Fig. 4. That is, for all $j \in [n]$, $\beta \in [\ell]$, party P_j selects $r_\beta^j \in \{0,1\}^\ell$ and invokes a secure implementation of the multi-party input commitment protocol using reverse firewall $\mathcal{W}_1$, playing the role of the (initializing) party P_i with input (x_β^j, r_β^j). The other parties play the role of other parties $\{P_k\}_{k \in [n] \setminus i}$ of Fig. 4 with input 1^λ, and obtain the output $\mathsf{com}_\lambda(x_\beta^j; r_\beta^j)$. Party i records r_β^j, and the other parties record $\mathsf{com}_\lambda(x_\beta^j; r_\beta^j)$.

Coin-generation phase. Each of the n parties run a secure implementation of the multi-party augmented parallel coin-tossing functionality (see Eq. 1) using reverse firewall $\mathcal{W}_2$, as presented in Fig. 3. This protocol is run by each party to generate a random pad of length t for emulation of the corresponding party in the semi-honest MPC protocol Π. The other parties obtain a commitment of the random tape of that party. That is, for all $j \in [n]$, party P_j invokes a secure implementation of the multi-party augmented parallel coin-tossing protocol using reverse firewall $\mathcal{W}_2$ (see Fig. 3), playing the role of party P_i with input 1^λ. The other parties play the role of parties $\{P_k\}_{k \in [n] \setminus j}$ of Fig. 3. Party P_j obtains a pair (s^j, ω^j), where $s^j \in \{0,1\}^t$ and $\omega^j \in \{0,1\}^{t \cdot \lambda}$. The other parties obtain the commitment $\mathsf{com}_\lambda(s^j; \omega^j)$. Party P_j records s^j, and the other parties record $\mathsf{com}_\lambda(s^j; \omega^j)$.

Protocol emulation phase. Each of the n parties run a secure implementation of the multi-party authenticated computation functionality (see Eq. 3) using reverse firewall $\mathcal{W}_3$ as presented in Fig. 5. The party which is supposed to send a message plays the role of party P_i in Eq. 3 and all the other parties play the role of other parties $\{P_k\}_{k \in [n] \setminus i}$. The variables α, β, r, and the functions h, f of the protocol are set as follows. The string α is set to be the concatenations of the party's original input and it's random tape. The string r is set to be the concatenations of all the randomnesses used to generate the commitments and $h(\alpha, r)$ is set to be the concatenations of the commitments themselves.

$$\alpha = (x^i, s^i), \quad \text{where } x^i = x_1^i x_2^i \cdots x_\ell^i, \quad \text{and } s^i \in \{0,1\}^t,$$
$$r = (r_1^i r_2^i \cdots r_\ell^i, \omega^i), \quad \text{where } \forall \beta \in [\ell], \ r_\beta^i \in \{0,1\}^\ell, \omega_i \in \{0,1\}^{t \cdot \lambda},$$
$$h(\alpha, r) = \big(\mathsf{com}_\lambda(x_1^i; r_1^i), \mathsf{com}_\lambda(x_2^i; r_2^i), \cdots, \mathsf{com}_\lambda(x_\ell^i; r_\ell^i), \mathsf{com}_\lambda(s^i; \omega^i)\big)$$

The string β is set to be the concatenation of all previous messages sent by other parties over the broadcast channel. Finally, the function f is set to be the *next message function*, i.e, the computation that determines the next message to be sent by P_i in $\boldsymbol{\Pi}$. The message can be thought of as a deterministic polynomial-time computable function of the party's input, it's random pad and the messages received so far.

Aborting. We denote the composed firewall for the compiled protocol as $\mathcal{W}^*$. The reverse firewall $\mathcal{W}^*$ is composed of three sub-firewalls $\mathcal{W}_1$, $\mathcal{W}_2$ and $\mathcal{W}_3$ corresponding to the three sub-protocols or building blocks as mentioned above. In case, any of these sub-firewalls *fails detectably*, the firewall $\mathcal{W}^*$ for the larger protocol also aborts the execution and outputs $\perp$. Else, the outputs are as follows:

Output. At the end of the protocol emulation phase, each party holds locally its output value. The parties simply output their respective values.

The composition theorem below shows that the final compiled protocol $\boldsymbol{\Pi}'$ is an actively-secure MPC protocol. The protocol $\boldsymbol{\Pi}'$ has a reverse firewall for all parties provided that each of the input commitment, the (augmented) coin-tossing and the authenticated computation protocols have their own firewalls satisfying some properties.

Theorem 6 (Composition Theorem for security of $\boldsymbol{\Pi}'$). *Given a MPC protocol $\boldsymbol{\Pi}$ secure in the semi-honest model, and provided that the multi-party input commitment protocol $\boldsymbol{\Pi}_1'$, the multi-party (augmented) coin-tossing protocol $\boldsymbol{\Pi}_2'$, and the multi-party authenticated computation protocol $\boldsymbol{\Pi}_3'$ are secure in the malicious model, the compiled MPC protocol $\boldsymbol{\Pi}'$ is an actively-secure MPC protocol. Let $\mathcal{W}_1^*$, $\mathcal{W}_2^*$ and $\mathcal{W}_3^*$ denote the reverse firewalls for the protocols $\boldsymbol{\Pi}_1'$, $\boldsymbol{\Pi}_2'$ and $\boldsymbol{\Pi}_3'$ respectively. Also, let party P_i be the initiating party for all these protocols at some point in time (in general it can be any one of the parties corrupted in a functionality-maintaining way). Now consider the following properties:*

- *Let $\boldsymbol{\Pi}$ be a MPC protocol secure in the semi-honest model (without reverse firewalls).*
- *Let the firewall $\mathcal{W}_1^*$ (for the multi-party input commitment protocol $\boldsymbol{\Pi}_1'$) preserves security for party P_i, is exfiltration-resistant against the other parties $\{P_j\}_{j \in [n]\backslash i}$, and detects failure for P_i.*
- *Let the firewall $\mathcal{W}_2^*$ (for the multi-party augmented coin-tossing protocol $\boldsymbol{\Pi}_2'$) preserves security for party P_i and is weakly exfiltration-resistant against the other parties $\{P_j\}_{j \in [n]\backslash i}$. Also, let $\mathcal{W}_2$ strongly preserve the security for the parties $\{P_j\}_{j \in [n]\backslash i}$ and is strongly exfiltration-resistant against P_i. Finally, let $\mathcal{W}_2$ detect failures for all the parties.*
- *Let the firewall $\mathcal{W}_3^*$ (for multi-party authenticated computation protocol $\boldsymbol{\Pi}_3'$) preserves security for party P_i, is weakly exfiltration-resistant against the other parties $\{P_j\}_{j \in [n]\backslash i}$, and detects failure for P_i.*

Then the composed reverse firewall $\mathcal{W}^* = \mathcal{W}_1^* \circ \mathcal{W}_2^* \circ \mathcal{W}_3^*$ preserves security for party P_i and is weakly exfiltration-resistant against the parties $\{P_j\}_{j \in [n]\backslash i}$ in the protocol $\boldsymbol{\Pi}'$.

For the proof of this theorem see [8].

Conclusion and future work. In this work, we present the first feasibility result for general MPC protocols in the setting of reverse firewalls. We leave open the construction of more efficient and round-optimal RF-compatible MPC protocols for future work. As mentioned in the introduction, another research direction is to develop concrete instantiations of firewalls for threshold cryptography schemes.

Acknowledgments. We would like to thank the anonymous reviewers for their helpful comments and suggestions. The work was initiated while the first author was in IIT Madras, India. Part of this work was done while the author was visiting the University of Warsaw. This project has received funding from the European Research Council (ERC) under the European Union's Horizon 2020 research and innovation programme (682815 - TOCNeT) and from the Foundation for Polish Science under grant TEAM/2016-1/4 founded within the UE 2014–2020 Smart Growth Operational Program. The last author was supported by the Independent Research Fund Denmark project BETHE and the Concordium Blockchain Research Center, Aarhus University, Denmark.

References

1. Ananth, P., Choudhuri, A.R., Jain, A.: A new approach to round-optimal secure multiparty computation. In: Katz, J., Shacham, H. (eds.) CRYPTO 2017, Part I. LNCS, vol. 10401, pp. 468–499. Springer, Cham (2017). https://doi.org/10.1007/978-3-319-63688-7_16
2. Asharov, G., Jain, A., López-Alt, A., Tromer, E., Vaikuntanathan, V., Wichs, D.: Multiparty computation with low communication, computation and interaction via threshold FHE. In: Pointcheval, D., Johansson, T. (eds.) EUROCRYPT 2012. LNCS, vol. 7237, pp. 483–501. Springer, Heidelberg (2012). https://doi.org/10.1007/978-3-642-29011-4_29
3. Ateniese, G., Magri, B., Venturi, D.: Subversion-resilient signature schemes. In: ACM CCS 2015 (2015)
4. Beaver, D.: Foundations of secure interactive computing. In: Feigenbaum, J. (ed.) CRYPTO 1991. LNCS, vol. 576, pp. 377–391. Springer, Heidelberg (1992). https://doi.org/10.1007/3-540-46766-1_31
5. Benhamouda, F., Lin, H.: k-round multiparty computation from k-round oblivious transfer via garbled interactive circuits. In: Nielsen, J.B., Rijmen, V. (eds.) EUROCRYPT 2018, Part II. LNCS, vol. 10821, pp. 500–532. Springer, Cham (2018). https://doi.org/10.1007/978-3-319-78375-8_17
6. Blum, M., Feldman, P., Micali, S.: Non-interactive zero-knowledge and its applications (extended abstract). In: 20th ACM STOC (1988)
7. Canetti, R.: Security and composition of multiparty cryptographic protocols. J. Cryptol. **13**(1), 143–202 (2000). https://doi.org/10.1007/s001459910006
8. Chakraborty, S., Dziembowski, S., Nielsen, J.B.: Reverse firewalls for actively secure MPCs. Cryptology ePrint Archive, Report 2019/1317. Extended version of this paper (2019)
9. Chase, M., Kohlweiss, M., Lysyanskaya, A., Meiklejohn, S.: Malleable proof systems and applications. In: Pointcheval, D., Johansson, T. (eds.) EUROCRYPT 2012. LNCS, vol. 7237, pp. 281–300. Springer, Heidelberg (2012). https://doi.org/10.1007/978-3-642-29011-4_18

10. Chen, R., Mu, Y., Yang, G., Susilo, W., Guo, F., Zhang, M.: Cryptographic reverse firewall via malleable smooth projective hash functions. In: Cheon, J.H., Takagi, T. (eds.) ASIACRYPT 2016. LNCS, vol. 10031, pp. 844–876. Springer, Heidelberg (2016). https://doi.org/10.1007/978-3-662-53887-6_31

11. Cramer, R., Damgård, I.B., Nielsen, J.B.: Secure Multiparty Computation and Secret Sharing. Cambridge University Press, Cambridge (2015)

12. Dauterman, E., Corrigan-Gibbs, H., Mazières, D., Boneh, D., Rizzo, D.: True2F: backdoor-resistant authentication tokens. In: 2019 IEEE Symposium on Security and Privacy (2019)

13. Dodis, Y., Mironov, I., Stephens-Davidowitz, N.: Message transmission with reverse firewalls—secure communication on corrupted machines. In: Robshaw, M., Katz, J. (eds.) CRYPTO 2016, Part I. LNCS, vol. 9814, pp. 341–372. Springer, Heidelberg (2016). https://doi.org/10.1007/978-3-662-53018-4_13

14. Doerner, J., Kondi, Y., Lee, E., Shelat, A.: Threshold ECDSA from ECDSA assumptions: the multiparty case. In: 2019 IEEE Symposium on Security and Privacy (2019)

15. Dolev, D., Strong, H.: Authenticated algorithms for Byzantine agreement. SIAM J. Comput. **12**(4), 656–666 (1983)

16. Garg, S., Srinivasan, A.: Two-round multiparty secure computation from minimal assumptions. In: Nielsen, J.B., Rijmen, V. (eds.) EUROCRYPT 2018, Part II. LNCS, vol. 10821, pp. 468–499. Springer, Cham (2018). https://doi.org/10.1007/978-3-319-78375-8_16

17. Gennaro, R., Goldfeder, S.: Fast multiparty threshold ECDSA with fast trustless setup. In: ACM CCS 2018 (2018)

18. Goldreich, O.: Secure multi-party computation

19. Goldreich, O., Micali, S., Wigderson, A.: How to play any mental game or a completeness theorem for protocols with honest majority. In: 19th ACM STOC (1987)

20. Groth, J.: Homomorphic trapdoor commitments to group elements. Cryptology ePrint Archive, Report 2009/007 (2009)

21. Groth, J.: Simulation-sound NIZK proofs for a practical language and constant size group signatures. In: Lai, X., Chen, K. (eds.) ASIACRYPT 2006. LNCS, vol. 4284, pp. 444–459. Springer, Heidelberg (2006). https://doi.org/10.1007/11935230_29

22. Hofheinz, D., Jager, T., Knapp, E.: Waters signatures with optimal security reduction. In: Fischlin, M., Buchmann, J., Manulis, M. (eds.) PKC 2012. LNCS, vol. 7293, pp. 66–83. Springer, Heidelberg (2012). https://doi.org/10.1007/978-3-642-30057-8_5

23. Ishai, Y., Sahai, A., Wagner, D.: Private circuits: securing hardware against probing attacks. In: Boneh, D. (ed.) CRYPTO 2003. LNCS, vol. 2729, pp. 463–481. Springer, Heidelberg (2003). https://doi.org/10.1007/978-3-540-45146-4_27

24. Lindell, Y.: Parallel coin-tossing and constant-round secure two-party computation. In: Kilian, J. (ed.) CRYPTO 2001. LNCS, vol. 2139, pp. 171–189. Springer, Heidelberg (2001). https://doi.org/10.1007/3-540-44647-8_10

25. Micali, S., Reyzin, L.: Physically observable cryptography. In: Naor, M. (ed.) TCC 2004. LNCS, vol. 2951, pp. 278–296. Springer, Heidelberg (2004). https://doi.org/10.1007/978-3-540-24638-1_16

26. Mironov, I., Stephens-Davidowitz, N.: Cryptographic reverse firewalls. In: Oswald, E., Fischlin, M. (eds.) EUROCRYPT 2015, Part II. LNCS, vol. 9057, pp. 657–686. Springer, Heidelberg (2015). https://doi.org/10.1007/978-3-662-46803-6_22

27. Mukherjee, P., Wichs, D.: Two round multiparty computation via multi-key FHE. In: Fischlin, M., Coron, J.-S. (eds.) EUROCRYPT 2016, Part II. LNCS, vol. 9666, pp. 735–763. Springer, Heidelberg (2016). https://doi.org/10.1007/978-3-662-49896-5_26

28. Simmons, G.J.: The prisoners' problem and the subliminal channel. In: Chaum, D. (ed.) CRYPTO 1983. Springer, Boston (1983). https://doi.org/10.1007/978-1-4684-4730-9_5

29. Waters, B.R.: Efficient identity-based encryption without random oracles. In: Cramer, R. (ed.) EUROCRYPT 2005. LNCS, vol. 3494, pp. 114–127. Springer, Heidelberg (2005). https://doi.org/10.1007/11426639_7

Stacked Garbling

Garbled Circuit Proportional to Longest Execution Path

David Heath[(✉)] and Vladimir Kolesnikov[(✉)]

Georgia Institute of Technology, Atlanta, GA, USA
{heath.davidanthony,kolesnikov}@gatech.edu

Abstract. Secure two party computation (2PC) of arbitrary programs can be efficiently achieved using garbled circuits (GC). The bottleneck of GC efficiency is communication. It is widely believed that it is necessary to transmit the entire GC during 2PC, even for conditional branches that are not taken.

This folklore belief is *false*.

We propose a novel GC technique, *stacked garbling*, that eliminates the communication cost of inactive conditional branches. We extend the ideas of conditional GC evaluation explored in (Kolesnikov, Asiacrypt 18) and (Heath and Kolesnikov, Eurocrypt 20). Unlike these works, ours is for general 2PC where no player knows which conditional branch is taken.

Our garbling scheme, Stack, requires communication proportional to the longest execution path rather than to the entire circuit. Stack is compatible with state-of-the-art techniques, such as free XOR and half-gates.

Stack is a *garbling scheme*. As such, it can be plugged into a variety of existing protocols, and the resulting round complexity is the same as that of standard GC. The approach does incur computation cost quadratic in the conditional branching factor vs linear in standard schemes, but the tradeoff is beneficial for most programs: GC computation even on weak hardware is faster than GC transmission on fast channels.

We implemented Stack in C++. Stack reduces communication cost by approximately the branching factor: for 16 branches, communication is reduced by 10.5×. In terms of wall-clock time for circuits with branching factor 16 over a 50 Mbps WAN on a laptop, Stack outperforms state-of-the-art half-gates-based 2PC by more than 4×.

1 Introduction

Secure Multiparty Computation (MPC) allows mutually untrusting parties to compute a function of their private inputs while revealing only the function output. Two-party computation (2PC) is a special case of MPC that has received wide attention due both to the importance of the setting and to the efficiency of Yao's *garbled circuit* (GC) technique.

In GC, the parties represent functions as Boolean circuits. One player, the circuit *generator*, encrypts the circuit's gates and inputs and sends the encryptions to the other player, the circuit *evaluator*. We refer to the collection of

Electronic supplementary material The online version of this chapter (https://doi.org/10.1007/978-3-030-56880-1_27) contains supplementary material, which is available to authorized users.

© International Association for Cryptologic Research 2020
D. Micciancio and T. Ristenpart (Eds.): CRYPTO 2020, LNCS 12171, pp. 763–792, 2020.
https://doi.org/10.1007/978-3-030-56880-1_27

encrypted gates as *material* (following [Kol18]) and to the encryptions of wire values as *labels*. Given material and input labels, the evaluator computes each gate under encryption and obtains output labels. Finally, the players jointly decrypt the output labels to compute the cleartext output. The key invariant is that the labels hide the truth values on the circuit wires, and thus nothing is learned except the output.

The bottleneck in GC performance is communication: the material is a large string that must be sent from generator to evaluator. Despite significant interest and considerable effort, reducing the amount of necessary material has proved challenging. Nonetheless, a persistent line of GC research has improved communication by reducing the number of ciphertexts needed to encrypt individual gates [NPS99, KS08, PSSW09, KMR14, ZRE15]. Our work is orthogonal to these gate-level improvements.

In this work, we **reduce communication for circuits that include conditional branching**. Under standard GC techniques, the circuit generator sends material for *each* branch; it is widely believed that, for security, sending separate branch material is required so as to hide which branch is taken[1].

This folklore belief is *false*. The generator need only send enough material for the longest program execution path. That is, separate material need not be sent for each conditional branch. Instead, one string of material can be reused across the branches, greatly reducing communication. Prior work has demonstrated this possibility [HK20, Kol18], but only in the case where one of the players knows the execution path. Our approach is for general 2PC: neither player knows which branches are taken, yet material for conditionals can be efficiently transmitted without compromising security or correctness.

At a high level, our generator bitwise XORs, or *stacks*, material from exclusive branches together. Then, the evaluator reconstructs from seeds the material for all branches except the taken branch, XORs these strings with the stacked material to extract the material for the taken branch, and evaluates the taken branch. For security, the evaluator performs these actions obliviously, meaning that she attempts to evaluate each branch. By stacking material, the generator sends much shorter messages to the evaluator. Hence we improve communication and overall performance.

1.1   Contribution

We refute the widely held belief that inactive GC branches must be transmitted.

We construct a practically efficient *stacked garbling scheme* Stack, which improves communication for circuits with conditional branching. Stack omits transmission of inactive branches and produces GC material proportional to the size of the longest program execution path rather than to the entire circuit. Stack

---

[1] Universal circuits provide an alternate method for implementing branching, but have impractical overhead, both in circuit size and in the cost of the gadgets required [KKW17].

improves GC communication by up to the branching factor: i.e., up to the ratio of the size of the longest execution path over the size of the entire circuit.

For each conditional with branching factor b, our computation cost is (less than) b times that of standard GC. Because fixed key garbling is typically much faster than GC transmission, the decrease in communication typically outweighs the increase in computation. The added computation is easily parallelized.

Stack is fully compatible with prior GC advancements, such as free XOR [KS08] and state-of-the-art half-gates [ZRE15].

Stack is extremely generic: it can improve the performance of any application that includes conditional branching. We note that one exciting direction is to use Stacked Garbling to build an efficient 'MPC machine'. An MPC machine would, similar to a hardware processor, execute programs by handling individual program instructions one-by-one. This style of machine requires conditional dispatch on the type of instruction in order to optionally perform one instruction from the instruction set, an ideal case for Stacked Garbling to be used.

We built and evaluated a C++ implementation of Stack (see Sects. 9 and 10). Our evaluation confirms that Stack indeed reduces communication over the prior state-of-the-art by the branching factor. This communication improvement reduces wall-clock time, especially on slower or shared networks. In terms of wall-clock time for circuits with branching factor 16 over 50 Mbps WAN on a laptop, Stack outperforms state-of-the-art half-gates-based 2PC by more than 4×.

We plan to release our software as open-source.

2   Related Work

GC is the most popular and often the fastest approach to secure two-party computation (2PC). GC is effective for functions that include conditional statements: alternative arithmetic representations must convert values to a Boolean representation at high cost before performing integer comparisons that frequently appear as branch conditions.

We review and compare related work in the area of GC. The most relevant works, [Kol18] and [HK20], are background to our approach and are reviewed in Sects. 3.1 and 3.2.

Garbling schemes formalize the subcomponents used in GC, and are defined in a number of works, including [FKN94,KO04]. [BHR12] developed a systematic and detailed garbling scheme framework. The BHR formalization is popular and useful; it allows researchers to streamline and simplify their presentation of work in the GC area. At the same time, BHR groups material (i.e. garbled gates) together with the circuit for which it was generated. Our approach relies on a separation of material from circuit topology. Therefore, while we formalize our approach in the BHR framework, some definitions are adjusted to explicitly separate material from topology.

GC communication improvements. Since Yao's original work, the community has achieved only modest improvements in communicating a single GC;

even the naïve construction is bare-bones and leaves little room for communication reduction. Additionally, most GC research has instead focused on orthogonal performance concerns in the malicious model.

Still, improvements have been made. Most communication reduction has come in the form of improvements to individual gates. In its original construction, GC required the transmission of four ciphertexts per gate. Chronologically, the following improvements were made:

- [NPS99] achieved three ciphertexts per gate (3 garbled row reduction, GRR3).
- A decade later, 'free XOR' eliminated the cost of XOR gates [KS08].
- Shortly after, [PSSW09] unified GRR3 and free XOR. The same work also introduced an interpolation-based technique that uses only two ciphertexts per gate, but that is incompatible with free XOR.
- Subsequently, [KMR14] proposed a heuristic for combining different row reduction techniques with free XOR.
- Finally, improvements to individual gates culminated in 'half-gates', a garbling scheme built on and compatible with free XOR that achieves two ciphertexts per AND gate [ZRE15]. The same work also established a matching lower bound on the size of individual gates that is hard to circumvent.

Free XOR based schemes, including half-gates, assume the existence of a hash function that is *correlation robust* [IKNP03] and *circular secure* [CKKZ12]. [GLNP18] specify an efficient scheme built on standard assumptions. Their technique uses two ciphertexts per AND gate and one ciphertext per XOR gate.

Our work is orthogonal to these gate-level improvements and our construction uses them. In particular, we focus on conditional branching only and leverage the existing half-gates technique to handle individual gates.

Universal circuits. In this work, we use cryptographic techniques to reduce the cost of conditionals. Another direction attempts to instead reduce cost by choosing alternate Boolean circuit representations. Universal circuits (UCs) can be *programmed* to implement any circuit in the entire universe of circuits of a given size n [Val76]. Researchers continue to search for smaller UC constructions; recent work achieves size $\approx 4.5n \log n$ [LMS16, KS16, GKS17, ZYZL18, AGKS19]. UCs implement conditionals by programming the UC to be the taken branch. When the GC generator knows the evaluated branch, the cost of UC programming is free as the generator directly programs the UC; otherwise programming is sent via $O(n \log n)$ OTs. However, even in the former "free programming" case, implementing conditionals via UCs usually does not pay off. Even for branches with only 2^{10} gates, the UC is $4.5 \cdot 10 = 45$ times larger than a single branch. For typical conditionals with only 2–3 branches, it is cheaper to separately encrypt and send each branch.

Motivated in part by branching, [KKW17] proposed a generalization of UCs called *set* universal circuits ($\mathcal{S}$-UCs). An $\mathcal{S}$-UC implements a fixed set of circuits $\mathcal{S}$ rather than an entire size-n universe. [KKW17] focuses on the special case where $|\mathcal{S}|$ is small, capturing the case where $\mathcal{S}$ is a set of conditional branches. Their approach applies heuristics to embed $\mathcal{S}$ into one programmable circuit. [KKW17] reports the performance of this heuristic for specific sets of circuits, achieving up to 6× GC size reduction for 32 branches. However, some sets did not improve over their original representations. Our work achieves up to 32× GC size reduction for 32 branches and requires no per-gate overhead, which is significant in [KKW17] (about 22 garbled rows per gate). The work of [Kol18] (Sect. 3.2) supersedes [KKW17] when the GC generator knows the taken branch.

Topology-decoupling circuit garbling, i.e. GC evaluation under different topologies, is a promising direction in GC research. It was introduced by [Kol18], extended in [HK20], and is further explored in this work. We present detailed reviews of [Kol18] and [HK20] as preliminaries in Sect. 3.1 and 3.2. Our work generalizes these existing techniques from special cases where one player knows the executed branch to general 2PC. We believe topology-decoupling and stacked garbling can be further fine-tuned and applied, especially with specific functionalities in mind.

3   Preliminaries

We present an efficient technique for garbling circuits with conditional branches. Two prior works also address GC conditionals, but both focus on special cases where one player knows the *target* branch. I.e., one player knows which branch is taken a priori. Specifically, [Kol18] requires the circuit generator to know the target, while [HK20] requires the circuit evaluator to know the target. Our approach uses key ideas from both works to efficiently handle conditionals without either party knowing the target, so we review both works.

3.1   'Free If' Review [Kol18]

Consider a GC with conditional branching. If the circuit generator Gen knows the target branch, then [Kol18] reduces communication needed to send the GC by combining two keys ideas:

1. The circuit description (the *topology*) can be separated from the GC material (i.e., the gate encryptions), and material can be used with a non-matching topology. [Kol18] formalizes *topology-decoupling circuit garbling*, where circuit topology is conveyed separately from material.
2. Material can be re-used if it is used at most once with *valid* labels. The same material can be re-used with *garbage* labels. Garbage labels are *not* the encryptions of truth values, but are instead pseudorandom strings. Put another way, the evaluator may 'decrypt' a gate table with keys unrelated to the table encryption multiple times. Successful and unsuccessful decryption attempts must be indistinguishable.

The [Kol18] approach is as follows:

Let $\mathcal{C} = \{\mathcal{C}_1, ..., \mathcal{C}_n\}$ be a set of Boolean circuits, where each circuit represents a different branch of a conditional statement. For simplicity, suppose all GCs are of the same size ([Kol18] pads material to accommodate branches of different sizes). Let $\mathcal{C}_t$ be the target circuit, and let Gen know t. Gen encrypts $\mathcal{C}_t$

but does not encrypt the other $n-1$ circuits. Let M be the material constructed by encrypting C_t. Gen sends M to the evaluator Eval. Furthermore, Gen conveys to Eval input labels for *each* circuit via oblivious transfer. Eval knows the topology of each branch, since she knows C, but does not know and must not learn t. Therefore, she evaluates each branch C_i, interpreting M as the collection of encrypted truth tables for that branch. When she evaluates C_t, she therefore obtains correct output labels. But M is valid material only for C_t, not for the other branches. The input labels that Eval uses for all $C_{i \neq t}$ are garbage with respect to M, and Eval obtains garbage labels for each wire. [Kol18] demonstrates it is possible to re-use material in this way without compromising security. Namely, Eval cannot distinguish the garbage labels from the valid labels and hence does not learn t. Eval and Gen obliviously discard garbage labels from $C_{i \neq t}$ and propagate valid labels from C_t via an *output selection* protocol. In this manner, the parties compute the correct output labels for branch C_t which can be decrypted or used as input for another circuit.

By computing the protocol above, the two parties securely evaluate 1-out-of-n branches while transmitting material for only 1 branch rather than for all n. This reduces communication and hence improves performance.

Our approach also optimizes conditional branching and also relies on the key ideas of topology decoupling and garbage labels. However, our approach differs from [Kol18] in two key respects:

1. [Kol18] relies on Gen knowing the target branch. We consider the general case where neither Gen nor Eval know the target. Despite this generalization, we similarly avoid transmitting separate material for each branch.
2. [Kol18] requires the parties to *interact* via the output selection protocol. We discard garbage labels *without* interaction.

3.2 'Privacy-Free Stacked Garbling' Review [HK20]

[HK20] is in a line of work that uses garbled circuits to construct zero-knowledge proofs [JKO13, FNO15]. [HK20] differs from [Kol18] primarily in that the circuit evaluator Eval knows the target branch rather than the circuit generator Gen. This is a critical distinction that requires a different approach. [HK20] builds this new approach on two key ideas:

1. Material can be managed as a bitstring. In particular, material from different circuits can be XORed together. This is a different use of topology-decoupling from that of [Kol18]. [Kol18] decouples topology from material so that the same material can be used to evaluate many topologies. [HK20] decouples topology from material so that material from different circuits can be XORed, or *stacked*, to reduce communication.
2. Material can be viewed as the expansion of a pseudorandom seed. Circuit encryption is a pseudorandom process, but if all random choices are derived from a seed, then material is the deterministic expansion of that seed. Hence, material can be compactly sent as a seed.

In general, we cannot send material via a seed, as the seed also includes all wire labels. In the [HK20] setting of GC-based zero-knowledge, this extra information would allow the evaluator to forge a proof. [HK20] shows that it *is* secure to reveal a seed to Eval if the seed only generates material for a non-target branch.

[HK20] combines these ideas to reduce the cost of proving in zero-knowledge (ZK) 1-out-of-n different statements. The approach is as follows (we elide many ZK-specific details):

Let $\mathcal{C} = \{\mathcal{C}_1, ..., \mathcal{C}_n\}$ be a set of Boolean circuits that each implement a proof statement. Let $\mathcal{C}_t$ be the target circuit (i.e. the circuit for which ZK Prover Eval has a witness) and let Eval know t. The ZK Verifier Gen knows $\mathcal{C}$, but does not know and must not learn t. Gen uses n different seeds to construct material for *each* circuit $\mathcal{C}_i$. He *stacks* these n strings by XORing them together, with appropriate padding, and sends the result to Eval. Eval selects the target circuit during n instances of 1-out-of-2 oblivious transfer. In each instance $i \neq t$, she selects the first secret and receives the ith seed. In instance t, she chooses the second secret and so does not receive the seed for $\mathcal{C}_t$.[2] Eval uses the $n-1$ seeds to reconstruct material for circuits $\mathcal{C}_{i \neq t}$ and uses the result to 'undo' the stacking. As a result, she obtains material needed to evaluate $\mathcal{C}_t$. She evaluates and is able to construct a proof of $\mathcal{C}_t$, which she sends to Gen.

By running this protocol, Eval and Gen perform a zero-knowledge proof of 1-out-of-n statements, but at the cost of sending only one proof challenge rather than sending n. This reduces communication and hence improves performance.

Our approach leverages the key ideas from [HK20]. We also stack cryptographic material using XOR and also allow the circuit evaluator to expand seeds for non-target branches. Our approach differs from [HK20] in that:

1. [HK20] relies on Eval knowing the target branch. Our approach assumes that neither Eval nor Gen knows the target.
2. [HK20] is a technique for ZK. Our approach addresses general 2PC where both players have private input.
3. [HK20] requires Gen to send pseudorandom seeds to Eval via oblivious transfer. Our approach embeds the seeds in the GC itself and hence does not require additional interaction.

4   Notation and Assumptions

Notation

- 'Gen' is the circuit generator. We refer to Gen as he, him, his, etc.
- 'Eval' is the circuit evaluator. We refer to Eval as she, her, hers, etc.
- '$\mathcal{C}$' is a circuit. Subcircuits are distinguished using annotations, e.g. $\mathcal{C}_0, \mathcal{C}_1, \mathcal{C}' ...$

---

[2] The second secret allows Eval to prove that she did not retrieve one of the seeds and hence obtained the output label by GC evaluation of one branch. This prevents Eval from taking all n seeds and using them to forge a proof.

- Lowercase variables, e.g. x, y, refer to *unencrypted* wire values. That is, x and y are two different Boolean values held by two different wires.
- Uppercase variables, e.g. X, Y, refer to wire labels which are the encryption of a wire value. E.g., X is the encryption of the value x.
- This work discusses *projective* garbling schemes, where each wire has two labels. When the corresponding truth value for a label is known, we place the value as a superscript. For example, we use X^0 to refer to the encryption of the bit 0 on wire x. Symmetrically, X^1 refers to the encryption of bit 1. Unannotated variables, e.g. X, refer to unknown wire encryptions: X could be either X^0 or X^1, but it is unspecified or unknown in the given context.
- The variables s, S, S^0, S^1 refer to the *branch condition wire*. In the context of a conditional, s decides which branch is taken.
- Following [Kol18], M refers to GC *material*. Informally, material is the data which, in conjunction with input labels, is used to compute output labels. In standard garbling schemes, material is a vector of encrypted gate tables. In this work, material can be encrypted gate tables or the XOR stacking of material from different branches. In our work, material does not include the circuit topology or labels.
- In the context of a conditional, subscripts 0 and 1 associate values with the first (resp. second) branch. For example, M_0 is the material for branch C_0.
- The variables n and m respectively denote the number of input wires and output wires of a given circuit.
- Variables that represent vectors are written in bold. For example, $\boldsymbol{x}$ is a vector of unencrypted truth values. We use bracket notation to access indexes of vectors: $\boldsymbol{x}[0]$ accesses the 0th index of $\boldsymbol{x}$.
- We work with explicit pseudorandom seeds. We write $a \leftarrow_{\$S} A$ to indicate that we pseudorandomly draw a value from the domain A using the seed S as a source of randomness and store the result in a. When a seed S is used to draw multiple values, we assume that each draw uses a nonce to ensure independent randomness. For simplicity, we leave the counter implicit.
- We write $a \leftarrow_{\$} A$ to denote that a is drawn uniformly from A.
- $\overset{c}{=}$ denotes computational indistinguishability.
- κ denotes the computational security parameter and can be understood as the length of encryption keys (e.g. 128).
- λ denotes the empty string.

In this work, we evaluate GCs with input labels that are generated independently of the GC. I.e., these independent labels do not match the GC. We call such labels *garbage labels*. During GC evaluation, garbage labels propagate and must eventually be obliviously dropped in favor of valid labels. We call the process of canceling out garbage labels *garbage collection*.

Assumptions. We assume a function H modeled as a random oracle (RO). We note it is likely that Stacked Garbling can be achieved without use of a RO. However, our particular construction interfaces with another garbling scheme in a black-box manner. Because we place few requirements on this 'underlying' garbling scheme, interfacing requires care; we leave reducing assumptions needed to achieve Stacked Garbling as future work.

5 High Level Approach

Our main contribution is a circuit garbling scheme that compacts material for conditional branches. In Sect. 7, we present this garbling scheme in technical detail. For now, we present our approach at a high level.

Section 3 covered four key ideas from prior work regarding material: material can be (1) separated from circuit topology, (2) used with garbage input labels, (3) stacked with XOR, and (4) compactly transmitted as a seed. To this list, we add one additional key idea that allows us to obliviously and without interaction discard garbage labels that emerge from the evaluation of inactive branches; we ensure that all garbage is *predictable* to Gen. Gen precomputes the possible garbage values and uses this knowledge to build garbled circuit gadgets that collect garbage obliviously. We begin with a high level approach that omits garbage collection (which is explained later):

Let $\mathcal{C}_0$ and $\mathcal{C}_1$ be two subcircuits that are conditionally composed as part of some larger circuit. Let there be a wire s that encodes the branch condition: if $s = 0$, then $\mathcal{C}_0$ should be executed and otherwise $\mathcal{C}_1$ should be executed. Let S^0, S^1 be the pair of labels encrypting the possible values of s. I.e., S^0 encrypts 0 and S^1 encrypts 1. Let S be Eval's label encrypting s. Eval does not know whether $S = S^0$ or $S = S^1$. Suppose neither Gen nor Eval knows s and hence neither player knows the target branch. At a high level, our approach is as follows:

1. Gen uses S^1 as a seed to encrypt $\mathcal{C}_0$. As we will see, this allows Eval to evaluate $\mathcal{C}_1$. Symmetrically, he uses S^0 as a seed to encrypt $\mathcal{C}_1$. Let M_0, M_1 be the respective resultant material.
2. Gen uses XOR to stack the material. The result is the material for the conditional: $M_{cond} = M_0 \oplus M_1$. Gen sends M_{cond} to Eval.
3. Recall, Eval has a label S. She *assumes* $S = S^0$ and uses S to encrypt $\mathcal{C}_1$.
   (a) Suppose Eval's assumption is correct. Then since she encrypts with the same seed as Gen, she constructs M_1. She computes $M_{cond} \oplus M_1 = M_0$, the correct material for $\mathcal{C}_0$. She evaluates $\mathcal{C}_0$ with her input labels and obtains valid output.
   (b) Suppose Eval's assumption is not correct, i.e. $S = S^1$. Then she constructs garbage material instead of M_1. Correspondingly, she obtains garbage material for $\mathcal{C}_0$ and hence computes garbage output.
   Critically, Eval cannot distinguish between her correct and incorrect assumptions. That is, she cannot distinguish valid material/labels from garbage: from Eval's perspective both valid and garbage material/labels are indistinguishable from random strings. We elaborate on this point in our security proofs (Sect. 8).
4. Eval symmetrically assumes $S = S^1$, encrypts $\mathcal{C}_0$, and evaluates $\mathcal{C}_1$.

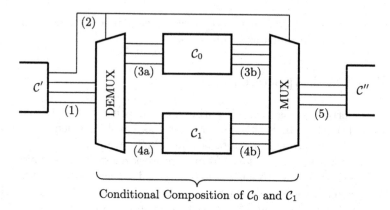

Conditional Composition of C_0 and C_1

Fig. 1. A circuit with conditional evaluation. Subcircuit C' is evaluated before the conditional. By convention, the first wire out of C' is the *branch condition* and controls which conditional subcircuit is to be evaluated. C_0 and C_1 are the conditionally composed subcircuits. Our approach introduces garbage labels, and the demux and mux circuit components allow us to collect garbage non-interactively. Outputs of conditionals can be used as inputs to subsequent subcircuits (e.g., C'').

Since S must be either S^0 or S^1, one of Eval's assumptions is right and one is wrong. That is, she computes valid output from one subcircuit and garbage output from the other.

The remaining task is to obliviously discard the garbage output labels. This could be achieved using an output selection protocol [Kol18], but our goal is to discard garbage non-interactively. To realize this goal, we introduce two new GC 'gadgets': a *demultiplexer* gadget (demux) and a *multiplexer* gadget (mux). The demux ensures that when Eval makes the wrong assumption, her garbage labels are *predictable* to Gen. The mux disposes of predictable output garbage labels. In practice, the demux and mux are built from garbled tables. We describe their constructions in Sect. 7.6.

Additional details and garbage collection. We now rewind and present Eval's actions at a lower level of detail, including her handling of the demux and mux. In our explanation, we assume $S = S^0$. The symmetric scenario ($S = S^1$) has a symmetric explanation. We stress that the protocol is unchanged, and only the explanation is affected by the assumption.

Figure 1 depicts a conditional subcircuit that includes a demux and mux. Wirings in the diagram are numbered. Each of the following numbered steps refers to a correspondingly numbered wiring in the diagram.

1. The input labels to the conditional are the output of some other subcircuit. All input wires are passed to the demux.
2. The first input label is S, the encryption of the branch condition, by convention. Both the demux and the mux take S as an argument that controls their operation.

3. Eval assumes $S = S^0$ and evaluates $\mathcal{C}_0$ as described in the above higher-level explanation.
    (a) Since this is a correct assumption (recall, we assumed $S = S^0$), the demux yields valid input labels for $\mathcal{C}_0$.
    (b) As before, Eval encrypts $\mathcal{C}_1$ using S, computes $M_{cond} \oplus M_1 = M_0$, evaluates $\mathcal{C}_0$, and obtains valid output labels.
4. Eval symmetrically assumes that $S = S^1$ and evaluates $\mathcal{C}_1$.
    (a) Since this is an incorrect assumption, the demux yields garbage input labels for $\mathcal{C}_1$. One challenge is that there are an exponential number of possible inputs to $\mathcal{C}_1$. Each input wire can carry two different labels, and all wires are potentially independent. The demux eliminates this uncertainty by processing the input wire-by-wire, where there are only two options for a wire label. That is, the demux, applying garbled tables, obliviously translates *both* input wire labels to the *same* garbage label. There is a corresponding translation performed for the target branch $\mathcal{C}_0$, but in that case the demux keeps the two wire labels distinct. The demux uses S to control which branch receives valid labels and which receives garbage.
    One can think of this uncertainty elimination as obliviously multiplying the input wires by either 0 or 1 depending on S.
    (b) As before, Eval computes garbage outputs by attempting to evaluate $\mathcal{C}_1$. The output garbage labels are independent of the conditional circuit inputs because (1) the demux ensures there is only one possible garbage input per wire and (2) the evaluator's actions are deterministic. That is, we have guaranteed that $\mathcal{C}_1$ has only one possible garbage output label per wire, and these garbage labels can be computed/predicted by Gen.
5. Garbage Collection. Eval passes both sets of output labels to the mux, along with S. The mux collects garbage and yields valid outputs. These outputs can be used as input to a subsequent subcircuit.

Garbage collection (Step 5) is possible because Gen *predicts* the garbage output from $\mathcal{C}_1$ (recall, we assumed that the target branch is $\mathcal{C}_0$). By construction, the output labels depend on garbling randomness only, and are independent of the inputs to $\mathcal{C}_1$. Gen predicts this garbage by emulating Eval's actions when making a bad assumption. More precisely, he predicts both possible wrong assumptions:

1. Gen emulates Eval in the case where she assumes $S = S^1$, while in fact $S = S^0$. Gen encrypts $\mathcal{C}_0$ with S^0, yielding garbage material M_0', and evaluates $\mathcal{C}_1$ using $M_{cond} \oplus M_0'$.
2. Gen emulates Eval in the case where she assumes $S = S^0$, while in fact $S = S^1$. Gen encrypts $\mathcal{C}_1$ with S^1 and evaluates $\mathcal{C}_0$ using $M_{cond} \oplus M_1'$.

These emulations compute the possible garbage output from both branches. Gen uses the garbage output labels to construct encrypted truth tables for the mux.

By our approach, Gen and Eval compactly represent the conditional composition of $\mathcal{C}_0$ and $\mathcal{C}_1$. In particular, Gen sends $M_{cond} = M_0 \oplus M_1$ instead of $M_0 \| M_1$. The XOR-stacked material is shorter than the concatenated material and hence more efficient to transmit. Both the demux and mux require additional material, but the amount required is linear in the number of inputs/outputs and is usually small compared to the amount of material needed for the branches.

6   Formalization of Circuits

We formalize our technique as a *garbling scheme* [BHR12]. Before defining our scheme, we specify the syntactic objects that it manipulates. Specifically, we formalize circuits that include explicit conditional branching.

A circuit is typically understood as the composition of many Boolean gates together with specified input and output wires. We refer to this representation as a *netlist*. We do not specify the syntax of netlists and instead leave the handling of netlists to another *underlying* garbling scheme, which we refer to as Base. In practice, our implementation instantiates Stack with the half-gates technique, the state-of-the-art scheme for securely computing netlists [ZRE15].

Unfortunately, netlists alone are insufficient for our approach because they do not explicate conditional branching. Therefore, we add the notion of a *conditional*. A conditional is parameterized over two circuits, C_0 and C_1. Conditionals with more than two branches can be constructed by nesting. In Supplementary Material, we also provide a *vectorized* construction that conditionally composes any number of branches without nesting. This vectorized construction is a simple generalization and is concretely more efficient yet notationally more complex. Thus, we now formalize our approach for branching factor two. The first bit of input to a conditional is, by convention, the *condition* bit s. The condition bit decides which of the two parameterized circuits should be executed. As an example, Fig. 1 depicts the conditional composition of C_0 and C_1. We add one requirement to conditionals: the two subcircuits must use the same input and output wires. This requirement can be met without loss of generality by disposing of unused inputs or adding constant-valued outputs. From here on, we assume this requirement has been met.

We also add a third type of circuit that we call *sequences*. Sequences, while uninteresting, are necessary for our approach. Sequences allow us to place conditional circuits 'in the middle' of the overall circuit. As an example, Fig. 1 depicts a sequence of three circuits: the leftmost circuit that provides input to the conditional, the conditional circuit, and the rightmost circuit. Without sequences, we could not formalize the circuit in Fig. 1. A sequence is parameterized over two subcircuits. Vectors of circuits are constructed by nesting sequences. When executed, a sequence passes its input to its first subcircuit and uses the resulting output as input to its second subcircuit. We add one requirement to sequences: the number of output wires from the first subcircuit must match the number of input wires into the second subcircuit. We assume that this requirement is met in future discussion.

Let C_0, C_1 be two arbitrary circuits. The space of circuits is defined as follows:

$$C ::= \mathsf{Netlist}(\cdot) \mid \mathsf{Cond}(C_0, C_1) \mid \mathsf{Seq}(C_0, C_1)$$

That is, a circuit is either a netlist, a conditional, or a sequence. By nesting conditionals and sequences, this small language can achieve complex branching control structure. As an example, we formalize Fig. 1 as:

$$\mathsf{Seq}(\mathcal{C}', \mathsf{Seq}(\mathsf{Cond}(\mathcal{C}_0, \mathcal{C}_1), \mathcal{C}''))$$

7   Our Garbling Scheme

```
1  En(e, x):
2     X ← λ
3     for i ∈ 0..n-1 :
4        (X⁰, X¹) ← e[i]
5        if x[i] = 0 then X[i] ← X⁰;
6        else X[i] ← X¹;
7     return X
```

```
1  De(d, Y):
2     y ← λ
3     for i ∈ 0..m-1 :
4        (Y⁰, Y¹) ← d[i]
5        if Y[i] = Y⁰ then y[i] ← 0;
6        else if Y[i] = Y¹ then
7           y[i] ← 1
8        else return ⊥;
9     return y
```

Fig. 2. The input encoding algorithm En and the output decoding algorithm De. En specifies how to encrypt input values, resulting in input labels. Symmetrically, De specifies how to decrypt output labels into cleartext output values. En and De are generic and work for any projective garbling scheme.

In this section, we formalize our garbling scheme, Stack, presented in Construction 1. Stack securely evaluates functions represented by circuits as defined in Sect. 6. Furthermore, if a circuit has conditional branching, then Stack compactly represents the material for the conditional, reducing communication cost.

Garbling schemes abstract the detail of encrypted circuit evaluation such that protocols can be written generically and new garbled circuit advancements can be quickly integrated [BHR12]. That is, a garbling scheme is a specification, not a protocol. For completeness, Supplementary Material provides a reference protocol that uses the garbling scheme abstraction to achieve semihonest 2PC.

A garbling scheme is a tuple of five algorithms:

$$(\mathsf{ev}, \mathsf{Gb}, \mathsf{En}, \mathsf{Ev}, \mathsf{De})$$

ev is a reference function that describes cleartext circuit semantics. The remaining four algorithms *securely* achieve the same result as ev. The idea is that if (1) the circuit is encrypted using Gb, (2) the players' cleartext inputs are encoded using En, (3) the encoded inputs and garbled circuit are evaluated using Ev, and (4) the encoded outputs are decoded using De, then the output should be the same as obtained by invoking ev directly.

```
1  Stack.ev(C, x):
2    switch C :
3      case Netlist(·) :
4        return Base.ev(C, x)
5      case Seq(C_0, C_1) :
6        y_0 ← Stack.ev(C_0, x)
7        y ← Stack.ev(C_1, y_0)
8        return y
9      case Cond(C_0, C_1) :
10       if x[0] = 0 then
11         return Stack.ev(C_0, x)
12       else
13         return Stack.ev(C_1, x)

1  Stack.Ev(C, M, X):
2    (M'||M_tr) ← M
3    Y' ← Ev'(C, M', X)
4    Y ← trans.Ev(Y', M_tr)
5    return Y

1  Ev'(C, M, X):
2    switch C :
3      case Netlist(·) :
4        Y ← Base.Ev(C, M, X)
5        return Y
6      case Seq(C_0, C_1) :
7        (M_0||M_tr||M_1) ← M
8        Y_0 ← Ev'(C_0, M_0, X)
9        X_1 ← trans.Ev(Y_0, M_tr)
10       Y ← Ev'(C_1, M_1, X_1)
11       return Y
12     case Cond(C_0, C_1) :
13       (M_dem||M_cond||M_mux) ← M
14       S ← X[0]
15       (X_0, X_1) ←
              demux.Ev(S, X, M_dem)
16       (M_0, ·, ·) ← Gb'(1^κ, C_0, S)
17       (M_1, ·, ·) ← Gb'(1^κ, C_1, S)
18       Y_0 ← Ev'(C_0, M_cond ⊕ M_1, X_0)
19       Y_1 ← Ev'(C_1, M_cond ⊕ M_0, X_1)
20       Y ← mux.Ev(S, Y_0, Y_1, M_mux)
21       return Y


1  Stack.Gb(1^κ, C, S):
2    (M', e, d') ← Gb'(1^κ, C, S)
3    d ← GenProjection(m, S)
4    M_tr ← trans.Gb(d', d)
5    M ← M'||M_tr
6    return (M, e, d)

1  Gb'(1^κ, C, S):
2    switch C :
3      case Netlist(·) :
4        return Base.Gb(1^κ, C, S)
5      case Seq(C_0, C_1) :
6        (M_0, e_0, d_0) ← Gb'(1^κ, C_0, S)
7        (M_1, e_1, d_1) ← Gb'(1^κ, C_1, S)
8        M_tr ← trans.Gb(d_0, e_1)
9        M ← (M_0||M_tr||M_1)
10       return (M, e_0, d_1)
11     case Cond(C_0, C_1) :
12       e ← GenProjection(n, S)
13       d ← GenProjection(m, S)
14       (S^0, S^1) ← e[0]
15       (M_0, e_0, d_0) ← Gb'(1^κ, C_0, S^1)
16       (M_1, e_1, d_1) ← Gb'(1^κ, C_1, S^0)
17       (M_dem, ⊥_0, ⊥_1) ←
              demux.Gb(S^0, S^1, e, e_0, e_1)
18       M_cond ← M_0 ⊕ M_1
19       (M'_0, ·, ·) ← Gb'(1^κ, C_0, S^0)
20       (M'_1, ·, ·) ← Gb'(1^κ, C_1, S^1)
21       ⊥'_0 ← Ev(C_0, M_cond ⊕ M'_1, ⊥_0)
22       ⊥'_1 ← Ev(C_1, M_cond ⊕ M'_0, ⊥_1)
23       M_mux ←
              mux.Gb(S^0, S^1, d, d_0, d_1, ⊥'_0, ⊥'_1)
24       M ← (M_dem||M_cond||M_mux)
25       return (M, e, d)

1  GenProjection(n, S):
2    p ← λ
3    for i ∈ 0..n-1 :
4      X^0 ←$S {0,1}^κ
5      X^1 ←$S {0,1}^κ
6      c ←$S {0,1}
7      p ← p||((X^0||c), (X^1||1 ⊕ c))
8    return p
```

Fig. 3. Our garbling scheme Stack. Let Stack.En = En and Stack.De = De as defined in Fig. 2. Ev and Gb are written in terms of recursive sub-procedures Ev' and Gb' respectively. The procedure GenProjection draws a pseudorandom input or output projection (à la projective garbling schemes). Gb, Gb', and GenProjection each take an explicit pseudorandom seed S. Recall that when using S as a pseudorandom seed, there is an implicit counter that ensures drawn values are independent.

Construction 1 (*Stack* garbling scheme). *Stack is the tuple of algorithms* (*Stack.ev, Stack.Gb, Stack.En, Stack.Ev, Stack.De*) *presented in Figs. 2, 3 and 4.*

Construction 1 supports any number of branches via nested conditionals. We also provide a construction (with a proof) that conditionally composes arbitrary numbers of branches without nesting in Supplementary Material. This vectorized construction and its proofs are immediate given Construction 1.

In the following subsections, we present the interface to and our instantiation of each algorithm. In Sect. 8, we prove that our instantiation is **correct**, **oblivious**, **private**, and **authentic**, as defined in [BHR12]. Formal definitions of these properties are included in Sect. 8.

Lemmas and theorems proved in Sect. 8 imply the following:

Theorem 1. *If H is modeled as a RO and the underlying scheme* **Base** *is half-gates [ZRE15], then Construction 1 is correct, oblivious, private, and authentic.*

7.1 Projective Garbling Schemes, Encoding, and Decoding

We consider *projective* garbling schemes [BHR12]. In a projective scheme, each circuit wire is encrypted by one of two possible labels, where one label corresponds to 0 and the other to 1. Correspondingly, a *projection* is a vector of pairs of labels. Stack is projective.

Due to projectivity, encrypting inputs and decrypting outputs is simple. In particular, En and De are implemented as straightforward mappings between truth values and labels. Our instantiations of En and De (Fig. 2) are generic to all projective garbling schemes:

En maps cleartext inputs to encrypted inputs. More precisely, it maps an *encoding string* e and a vector of cleartext inputs x to a vector of input labels X. In a projective scheme, e is a vector of pairs of labels (a projection). Our specification of En 'walks' x and e together. At each index, it checks the value of the ith input bit and appends the corresponding label to X. When instantiated in a protocol, En is typically implemented via OT; we do this as well.

De maps encrypted outputs to cleartext outputs. More precisely, it maps a *decoding string* d and a vector of output labels Y to a vector of cleartext outputs y. Like e, d is a vector of pairs of labels (a projection) when the garbling scheme is projective. Our specification of De is dual to our construction of En. The algorithm walks Y and d together. At each index, it checks if the ith output is equal to the 0 label or to the 1 label and appends the appropriate truth value to the output vector. If any output does not correspond to a label, then the algorithm outputs $\perp$ to indicate that an error has occurred.

7.2 Underlying Garbling Scheme

Stack directly handles conditionals and sequences but leaves the handling of netlists to another garbling scheme. That is, Stack is parameterized over an *underlying* garbling scheme Base. In practice, we implement Base using the state-of-the-art half-gates technique [ZRE15]. Our formalization assumes that Base is a package that includes all garbling scheme algorithms. For example, Base.Gb is the underlying scheme's procedure for encrypting netlists.

We place the following requirements on Base:

- Base is **correct, oblivious, private,** and **authentic** ([BHR12] definitions are stated in Sect. 8).
- Base is **projective** [BHR12]. That is, each wire has two possible labels.
- Base provides a color procedure that assigns a different Boolean value to the two labels on each wire. In practice, color is implemented via the traditional point-and-permute technique [BMR90]. This requirement allows Stack to manipulate labels chosen by Base.
- Base produces labels and material that are indistinguishable from random strings. This property is critical for securely stacking material and is discussed at length in our proofs (Sect. 8).

7.3   Circuit Semantics

ev specifies cleartext semantics. More precisely, ev maps a circuit C and an input x to an output y. The correctness of a garbling scheme is defined with respect to ev: evaluating a circuit under encryption should yield the same output as evaluating the circuit in cleartext.

Stack.ev (Fig. 3) conditionally dispatches on the structure of C:

- If C is a netlist, then Stack.ev delegates to Base.ev.
- If C is a sequence $\mathsf{Seq}(C_0, C_1)$, then Stack.ev recursively evaluates C_0, uses the output as input to a recursive evaluation of C_1, and returns the result.
- If C is a conditional $\mathsf{Cond}(C_0, C_1)$, then Stack.ev dispatches based on the condition bit. If the condition bit is 0, then Stack.ev recursively evaluates C_0 and otherwise recursively evaluates C_1.

7.4   Circuit Encryption

Gb encrypts circuits. More precisely, Gb maps a circuit C to material M, an encoding string e, and a decoding string d. e contains the input labels that are encryptions of the input bits, and d contains output labels that describe how to decrypt the output bits.

Our presentation of Gb differs from [BHR12]'s in two ways:

1. [BHR12]'s presentation requires Gb to include the circuit topology as part of its output, i.e. the output of Gb must include C. We opt to omit this because we assume both parties know the entire topology a priori and so this added information is not needed. Furthermore, omitting the topology results in a shorter and simpler garbling scheme. This omission requires the procedure Ev to take the circuit topology C as an explicit argument.
2. [BHR12]'s presentation models Gb as a pseudorandom procedure. Since we deal with explicit randomness, we instead define Gb as a deterministic procedure that takes a pseudorandom seed S as an additional argument.

Stack.Gb captures many of the key ideas of our approach. The core of the specification is a delegation to Gb′, an algorithm that recursively descends over the structure of the circuit. We first explain Gb′ before returning to the top level Stack.Gb. Gb′ processes $\mathcal{C}$ by case analysis:

- If $\mathcal{C}$ is a netlist, Gb′ delegates to Base.Gb. Netlists are the "leaves" of the tree Gb′ constructs. Ultimately, netlists produce the material that we stack.
- If $\mathcal{C}$ is a sequence $\mathsf{Seq}(\mathcal{C}_0, \mathcal{C}_1)$, then Gb′ recursively encrypts both subcircuits. However, this is not a complete construction: the output encoding of $\mathcal{C}_0$, i.e. d_0, is *independent* of the input encoding of $\mathcal{C}_1$, i.e. e_1. Thus, we *translate* d_0 to e_1. The procedure $trans.\mathsf{Gb}$ constructs material for a gadget that implements this translation. $trans.\mathsf{Gb}$ is described in Sect. 7.6.
- If $\mathcal{C}$ is a conditional, then Gb′ recursively encrypts both subcircuits and stacks the resultant material. Gb′ also constructs material for the mux and demux, whose operation is described formally in Sect. 7.6.
  We begin by calling GenProjection to draw uniform input encoding e and output decoding d. GenProjection uses a pseudorandom seed to sample a projection (i.e. a vector of pairs of labels).[3] The sampled projections e and d contain the input and output labels for the overall conditional.
  By convention, the first input to the conditional is the branch condition. Therefore, we extract both condition labels S^0 and S^1 by looking in the first index of the input encoding e. Gb′ uses these condition labels as seeds to recursively encrypt both subcircuits. There is an important detail that we do not explicate in the code: if the string of material from one branch is shorter than the other, then Gb′ pads the shorter material with uniform bits until it is of the same length. That is, if M_0 is shorter, then it is padded with uniform bits drawn from S^1, and vice versa. Padding is critical for security (see Sect. 8).
  Next, Gb′ encrypts the demux. The demux has two roles. First, the demux inputs predictable garbage to the branch not taken. Second, the demux translates labels in e to labels in either e_0 or e_1, depending on s. The demux gadget is encrypted using a call to $demux.\mathsf{Gb}$. $demux.\mathsf{Gb}$ outputs the demux material as well as two sets of labels $\perp_0$ and $\perp_1$. These sets contain the garbage inputs that Eval obtains when evaluating the branch not taken.
  Next, Gb′ encrypts the mux. To do so, Gb′ computes the two possible sets of garbage output labels by emulating both bad assumptions Eval can make (Line 19 through Line 22). That is, Gb′ encrypts both circuits using the wrong seeds and then evaluates using garbage material and garbage inputs. Now, Gb′ has (1) both condition labels S^0 and S^1, (2) the conditional output projection d, (3) the output projections of each branch d_0 and d_1, and (4) both garbage outputs $\perp'_0$ and $\perp'_1$. This information suffices to encrypt the mux, which is done by calling $mux.\mathsf{Gb}$. The mux collects garbage outputs and translates valid branch outputs to labels in d.
  Finally, Gb′ returns all material and the input/output projections.

---

[3] We use point-and-permute [BMR90] to encode a color bit in the least significant bit of each label. Color bits instruct Eval how to decrypt encrypted truth tables.

Next, we return to the top level Stack.Gb algorithm. After encrypting C using Gb', we translate the output encoding d' to a fresh, randomly generated (via a call to GenProjection) encoding d. This top level translator gadget ensures that Eval learns nothing about the circuit input except what can be deduced from the output. More practically, our proof of privacy relies on this top level translator. Finally, Stack.Gb concatenates material and returns.

7.5   Evaluation Under Encryption

Ev evaluates circuits under encryption. More precisely, Ev maps a circuit C, material M, and inputs X to outputs Y.

Like Stack.Gb, Stack.Ev delegates to a recursive subprocedure, Ev':

- If C is a netlist, Ev' delegates to Base.Ev.
- If C is a sequence, then Ev' recursively evaluates both subcircuits. First, the material is broken up into pieces corresponding to the two subcircuits and the intervening translator. These three components are evaluated in order. The translator is evaluated by calling $trans$.Ev.
- If C is a conditional, then Ev' (1) encrypts the branch not taken, (2) unstacks material for the branch taken, and (3) evaluates the branch taken. Of course, these steps are completed obliviously.

  First, Ev' decomposes the material into material for the demux, for the conditional, and for the mux. The first input is S by convention. Ev' uses S to demultiplex the inputs by calling $demux$.Ev. Let s be the taken branch. That is, X_s holds valid inputs while $X_{\neg s}$ holds garbage inputs. Ev' uses S to encrypt *both* subcircuits, padding the shorter encryption with uniform bits drawn from S. Next, Ev' recursively evaluates both subcircuits by unstacking material. One resultant output is valid and the other is garbage. Finally, mux.Ev collects garbage output.

7.6   Circuit Gadgets

Stack introduces three circuit gadgets which 'glue together' circuits: (1) the translator aligns the output and input labels of sequentially composed circuits, (2) the demux obliviously inputs garbage to non-target branches, and (3) the mux collects garbage outputs.

Translator. Consider the sequence $\mathsf{Seq}(C_0, C_1)$. In Gb', Stack recursively generates encryptions of both subcircuits. This results in input/output encodings for both subcircuits. Our semantics require that the output labels of C_0 are used as inputs for C_1. However, the output labels of C_0 are not aligned with the input encoding for C_1: the two circuits are generated by independent calls to Gb'.

Fortunately, we can resolve this mismatch. We *translate* the output labels of C_0 to align with the inputs encoding for C_1. This translation is implemented as a

1	$trans.Ev(Y, M)$:	1	$trans.Gb(d, e)$:	1	$trans.S(Y, X)$:
2	$X \leftarrow \lambda$	2	$M \leftarrow \lambda$	2	$M \leftarrow \lambda$
3	for $i \in 0..|Y|-1$:	3	for $i \in 0..|d|-1$:	3	for $i \in 0..|Y|-1$:
4	$Y \leftarrow Y[i]$	4	$(Y^0, Y^1) \leftarrow d[i]$	4	$Y \leftarrow Y[i]$
5	$(row_0||row_1||M) \leftarrow$	5	$(X^0, X^1) \leftarrow e[i]$	5	$X \leftarrow X[i]$
	M	6	$c \leftarrow \text{color}(Y^0)$	6	$c \leftarrow \text{color}(Y)$
6	$c \leftarrow \text{color}(Y)$	7	$row_0 \leftarrow H(Y^c) \oplus X^c$	7	$row_c \leftarrow H(Y) \oplus X$
7	$X \leftarrow$	8	$row_1 \leftarrow$	8	$row_{1 \oplus c} \leftarrow_{\$} \{0, 1\}^\kappa$
	$X||H(Y) \oplus row_c$		$H(Y^{1 \oplus c}) \oplus X^{1 \oplus c}$	9	$M \leftarrow$
8	return X	9	$M \leftarrow M||row_0||row_1$		$M||row_0||row_1$
		10	return M	10	return M

Fig. 4. The algorithms associated with the translator gadget. $trans.$Ev and $trans.$Gb describe the actions taken respectively by Eval and Gen. $trans.S$ is a simulator used to prove that Stack is private.

garbled circuit gadget. Consider an individual output y_0 of C_0 and a corresponding input x_1 of C_1. The translation from y_0 to x_1 is explained by the following encrypted truth table:

C_0 output	C_1 input
Y_0^0	X_1^0
Y_0^1	X_1^1

That is, Eval decrypts an input label that encodes the same truth value as the output label. This table is implemented by the following two strings[4]:

$$H(Y_0^0) \oplus X_1^0$$
$$H(Y_0^1) \oplus X_1^1$$

We assume that the underlying scheme provides a color procedure (Sect. 7.2). Gen permutes the two rows according to the color of Y_0^0. Eval decrypts a row according to the color of her Y label. Recall that H is modeled as a random oracle (Sect. 4). Further, Eval views either Y_0^0 or Y_0^1, but not both. Therefore, Eval can decrypt only one of the rows and hence cannot determine which truth value she has decrypted.

A vector of output wires is translated to a vector of input wires by many translation components. The procedures $trans.$Gb and $trans.$Ev (Fig. 4) describe the actions taken by Gen and Eval respectively in handling vectors of translation components. Translation gadgets use two ciphertexts per wire.

Demux. Consider a conditional $\text{Cond}(C_0, C_1)$. Recall, Eval evaluates the branch taken by reconstructing material for the branch not taken. However, this evaluation must prevent Eval from learning which branch is taken, so we require

---

[4] Formally, each garbled row is given a unique ID, and calls to H for that row take the ID as an extra argument. We omit this for simplicity of notation.

Eval to evaluate *both* branches in this manner. When Eval attempts to evaluate the branch not taken she obtains garbage outputs. We ensure these outputs are fixed values that can be garbage collected by fixing the garbage inputs. Garbage inputs are computed by a demux gadget.

Like the translator, we construct the demux wire-by-wire. Each component of the demux takes two inputs: the input wire to demultiplex and the branch condition wire s. A component that demultiplexes an individual wire implements the following encrypted truth table:

condition	input	C_0 label	C_1 label
S^0	X^0	X_0^0	$\perp_1$
S^0	X^1	X_0^1	$\perp_1$
S^1	X^0	$\perp_0$	X_1^0
S^1	X^1	$\perp_0$	X_1^1

That is, if $S = S^0$, then Eval decrypts (1) a valid input label for C_0 corresponding to the input label X and (2) a garbage input for C_1. Note that Eval receives the same label $\perp_1$ regardless of the input label X. If $S = S^1$, the component acts symmetrically, providing valid labels to C_1 and garbage to C_0. Like the translator, we mechanically convert this encrypted truth table into two sets of four ciphertexts and permute the sets according to input colors. The functions *demux*.Gb and *demux*.Ev respectively encrypt and evaluate a demux. These functions are implemented similarly to *trans*.Gb and *trans*.Ev and, in particular, require use of a function H modeled as a random oracle.

Mux. In the case of a conditional circuit, Eval uses garbage material to evaluate the branch not taken. Furthermore, this branch receives fixed garbage inputs, thanks to the demux. Therefore, the output labels of the branch not taken are deterministic and independent of the conditional's input labels. That is, each output wire has only one possible garbage label. The remaining task is to collect the garbage labels. This garbage collection is handled by the mux gadget.

Like the other gadgets, the mux handles outputs wire-by-wire. The mux component for each wire takes three inputs: one output wire from each branch and the branch condition wire s. The individual wire components implement the following encrypted truth table:

condition	C_0 label	C_1 label	output
S^0	Y_0^0	$\perp_1$	Y^0
S^0	Y_0^1	$\perp_1$	Y^1
S^1	$\perp_0$	Y_1^0	Y^0
S^1	$\perp_0$	Y_1^1	Y^1

That is, Eval decrypts either Y^0 or Y^1 according to whichever valid output label is available. This table can be achieved using four ciphertexts, similar to the previous gadgets. The functions *mux*.Gb and *mux*.Ev respectively encrypt and evaluate a mux. These functions use a function H modeled as a RO.

8   Proofs

Now that we have presented our construction both at a high level and in detail, we prove that it is correct and secure. The [BHR12] framework requires garbling schemes to be **correct, oblivious, private**, and **authentic**. Stack satisfies these properties. The formal definitions we use are derived from [BHR12], but adjusted to our notation; we adjust Gb such that it does not output a circuit topology and Ev such that it takes a circuit topology as a parameter (see Sect. 7).

8.1   Correctness

Definition 1 (Correctness). *A garbling scheme is* **correct** *if for all circuits* C, *all input strings* x *of length* n, *and all pseudorandom seeds* S:

$$De(d, Ev(C, M, En(e, x))) = ev(C, x)$$

where $(M, e, d) = Gb(1^\kappa, C, S)$

Correctness requires the scheme to realize the semantics specified by ev.

Theorem 2. *If* Base *is correct, then* Stack *is correct.*

Proof of correctness of Stack tracks the structure of C and can be inferred from discussion in Sect. 5. Due to a lack of space, the full proof is presented in Supplementary Material.

8.2   Security

The [BHR12] notion of a garbling scheme is general, and an arbitrary scheme is not a candidate underlying scheme for Stack. Therefore, we build on a smaller class of schemes, which is nevertheless general and includes all standard schemes, such as half-gates [ZRE15]. Specifically, we define *stackable* garbling schemes, which are the candidate underlying schemes for Stack. A stackable scheme (1) produces random looking (to a polytime distinguisher) wire labels and material and (2) allows interoperation with our circuit gadgets.

Definition 2 (Stackability). *A garbling scheme is* **stackable** *if:*

1. *For all circuits* C *and all inputs* x,

$$(C, M, En(e, x)) \stackrel{c}{=} (C, M', X')$$

   where S *is uniformly drawn,* $(M, e, \cdot) = Gb(1^\kappa, C, S)$, $X' \leftarrow_\$ \{0,1\}^{|X|}$, *and* $M' \leftarrow_\$ \{0,1\}^{|M|}$.
2. *The scheme is* **projective** *[BHR12]*.
3. *There exists an efficient deterministic procedure* color *that maps strings to* $\{0,1\}$ *such that for all projective label pairs* A^0, A^1

$$color(A^0) \neq color(A^1)$$

We informally explain this definition. When Eval evaluates a conditional, it is critical that she cannot distinguish which branch is taken. This is why circuit encryptions must 'look random' to Eval. In particular, recall that Eval tries to reconstruct material for both branches; in one case she succeeds and in the other she fails and constructs garbage material. It is these two strings of material that she should not distinguish. By ensuring both strings are random-looking, Definition 2 ensures that Eval cannot distinguish which branch is taken. We note that this indistinguishability is similar in flavor to the topology-decoupling property of [Kol18].

Projectivity and wire coloring allow our translator, mux, and demux to interface with stackable schemes. Because stackable schemes are projective, we know that input encoding and output decoding strings are vectors of pairs of labels. This allows us to encrypt our gadgets. For example, $trans$.Gb in Fig. 4 assumes d and e are projective. Notice also that this procedure, as well as the procedures that encrypt the mux and demux, makes use of the color procedure to determine row order and allow Eval to decrypt. color must be defined for *all* bitstrings, which is significant because it means that color is defined even for garbage labels.

Many traditional garbling schemes are stackable. We focus on two. First, we sketch a proof that the half-gates construction [ZRE15] is stackable. This allows us to use half-gates as Base. Second, we show that if Base is stackable, then Stack itself is stackable. This allows us to arbitrarily nest conditional circuits.

Lemma 1. *Let H be the hash function used in [ZRE15]. If H is modeled as a random oracle, then the half-gates garbling scheme of [ZRE15] is stackable.*

Proof. By the fact that half-gates uniformly draws input labels and the properties of the hash function used to construct material for individual gates. Half-gates is secure given a correlation-robust function, and hence its [BHR12] security properties hold in the stronger RO model. Half-gates is a projective scheme and implements the color procedure via point-and-permute [BMR90]. □

Lemma 2. *If Base is stackable and H is modeled as a random oracle, then Stack is stackable.*

Proof. By induction on the structure of the target circuit C. We rely on the RO properties of H for the mux, demux, and translator. In the following, we use the phrase 'x looks random' to mean that x is indistinguishable from a uniform string of the same length.

- Suppose C is a netlist. Then Stack.Gb delegates to Base, which is assumed to be stackable. Netlists are stackable.
- Suppose C is a sequence $Seq(C_0, C_1)$. By induction, both C_0 and C_1 are stackable. It remains to demonstrate that the intervening translation gadget preserves stackability. Consider a subcomponent of the translator that translates one wire. This subcomponent is implemented as an encrypted truth table with two ciphertexts of material (Sect. 7.6). Each row is the XOR of

an input label with the output of H. H is modeled as a random oracle and hence its output looks random. Furthermore, correctly decrypting one row yields an input label for C_1 which, by induction, looks random. Therefore, the ciphertexts constructed by $trans$.Gb look random, so the translation component preserves stackability. Sequences are stackable.

- Suppose C is a conditional $\mathsf{Cond}(C_0, C_1)$.

First, we examine the demux. The demux inputs are pseudorandomly chosen by GenProjection and hence look random. Further, by a similar argument to the translator (the demux is implemented by H), the demux material looks random. Therefore the demux preserves stackability.

Next, we look at C_0 and C_1 together. By induction, both C_0 and C_1 *individually* preserve stackability, so the materials M_0 and M_1 look random. If we ignore the inputs X, then $M_0 \oplus M_1$ also looks random. It remains to show that X does not allow a distinguisher. Consider the actions taken by Ev' when handling a conditional. Eval makes one good assumption and one bad assumption. That is, she uses the seed S to encrypt both $C_{\neg s}$ and C_s. In both cases, the target circuit is stackable, and hence the resultant material looks random. Here, it is critical that we pad the shorter of the two strings of material; if M_s were shorter than $M_{\neg s}$, then a distinguisher could textually compare $M_{\neg s}$ to the trailing bits of $M_0 \oplus M_1$. Since we pad with random bits until both strings are the same length, such a comparison is impossible. The good and bad assumptions both lead to random looking material, so the two cases are indistinguishable from one another.

Finally, we examine the mux. Because C_0 and C_1 are stackable, the mux inputs look random. Additionally, the output of the mux preserves stackability: the output labels are randomly chosen by GenProjection. By a similar argument to the translator and demux components (the mux material is an encrypted truth table constructed by H), the material looks random. Therefore, the mux preserves stackability.

Stack is stackable.   □

Obliviousness. Stackability allows us to prove the necessary security properties of our scheme. The first property specified by [BHR12] is *obliviousness*. The following definition is adjusted to our notation:

Definition 3 (Obliviousness). *A garbling scheme is **oblivious** if there exists a simulator S_{obv} such that for any circuit C and all inputs x of length n, the following are indistinguishable:*

$$(C, M, X) \stackrel{c}{=} S_{obv}(1^\kappa, C)$$

where S is uniform, $(M, e, \cdot) = \mathsf{Gb}(1^\kappa, C, S)$ and $X = \mathsf{En}(e, x)$.

Informally, obliviousness ensures that the material M and encoded input labels X reveal no information about the input x or about the output $\mathsf{ev}(C, x)$. Obliviousness follows trivially from stackability:

Lemma 3. *Every stackable scheme is oblivious.*

Proof. Choose $\mathcal{S}_{obv}$ to be a procedure that draws uniform pseudorandom strings $(M', \boldsymbol{X}')$ of the correct length. By stackability, $(\mathcal{C}, M, \boldsymbol{X}) \overset{c}{=} (\mathcal{C}, M', \boldsymbol{X}')$.   □

An immediate corollary of Lemma 3 is:

Theorem 3. *If H is modeled as a RO and Base is stackable, Stack is oblivious.*

Privacy. Next, we demonstrate that Stack satisfies [BHR12]'s definition of *privacy*, adjusted to our notation:

Definition 4 (Privacy). *A garbling scheme is **private** if there exists a simulator $\mathcal{S}_{prv}$ such that for any circuit $\mathcal{C}$ and all inputs x of length n, the following are computationally indistinguishable:*

$$(M, \boldsymbol{X}, d) \overset{c}{=} \mathcal{S}_{prv}(1^\kappa, \mathcal{C}, \boldsymbol{y}),$$

where S is uniform, $(M, e, d) = Gb(1^\kappa, \mathcal{C}, S)$, $\boldsymbol{X} = En(e, \boldsymbol{x})$, and $\boldsymbol{y} = ev(\mathcal{C}, \boldsymbol{x})$.

Privacy ensures that Eval, who is given access to $(M, \boldsymbol{X}, d)$, learns nothing about the input x except what can be learned from the output $\boldsymbol{y}$.

Theorem 4. *If Base is stackable and H is modeled as a random oracle, then Stack is private.*

Proof. By obliviousness of Stack, properties of the top level translator gadget (Stack.Gb Line 4), and a hybrid simulator argument. We rely on the RO properties of H for the mux, demux and translator.

Consider the hybrid simulators listed in Fig. 5. The first, $hybrid_0$, corresponds to the real execution of Gb and En and the last, $\mathcal{S}_{prv}$, is the privacy simulator. The intermediate hybrids demonstrate the indistinguishability of the real and ideal executions and hence demonstrate privacy. We argue indistinguishability of each hybrid:

- $hybrid_0 \overset{c}{=} hybrid_1$: $hybrid_1$ replaces the call to $trans.Gb$ with a call to $trans.S$. This simulator uses the input/output label pairs to construct material for the rows that can be decrypted given $\boldsymbol{X}$. These rows are identical to those constructed by $trans.Gb$ and so are trivially indistinguishable. $trans.S$ populates the remaining rows, which cannot be decrypted, with random strings while $trans.Gb$ uses calls to H to populate these rows. Since H is modeled as a random oracle these two sets of rows are indistinguishable. The remaining changes add calls to deterministic procedures in order to set up the call to the simulator. Therefore, $hybrid_0 \overset{c}{=} hybrid_1$.
- $hybrid_1 \overset{c}{=} hybrid_2$: $hybrid_2$ replaces calls to Gb' and En with a call to $\mathcal{S}'_{obv}$. $\mathcal{S}'_{obv}$ is the oblivousness simulator that simulates the garbling of the entire circuit except for the top level translator gadget. Since Stack is stackable, this simulator simply draws random strings of the appropriate length. Because Stack is oblivious and because all other objects in scope are independent of the garbling (note d' is no longer in scope since we replaced the translator by its simulator), $hybrid_2 \overset{c}{=} hybrid_1$.

```
1  hybrid₀(C, x, S):
2    (M', e, d') ← Gb'(1ᵏ, C, S)
3    d ← GenProjection(m, S)
4    M_tr ← trans.Gb(d', d)
5    X ← En(e, x)
6    M ← M'||M_tr
7    return (M, X, d)

1  hybrid₁(C, x, S):
2    y ← ev(C, x)
3    (M', e, d') ← Gb'(1ᵏ, C, S)
4    d ← GenProjection(m, S)
5    M_tr ← trans.Gb(d', d)
6    X ← En(e, x)
7    Y' ← Ev(C, M', X)
8    Y ← En(d, y)
9    M_tr ← trans.S(Y', Y)
10   M ← M'||M_tr
11   return (M, X, d)
```

```
1  hybrid₂(C, x, S):
2    y ← ev(C, x)
3    (M', e, d') ← Gb'(1ᵏ, C, S)
4    d ← GenProjection(m, S)
5    X ← En(e, x)
6    (M', X) ← S'_obv(1ᵏ, C)
7    Y' ← Ev(C, M', X)
8    Y ← En(d, y)
9    M_tr ← trans.S(Y', Y)
10   M ← M'||M_tr
11   return (M, X, d)

1  S_prv(1ᵏ, C, y):
2    y ← ev(C, x)
3    d ← GenProjection(m, S)
4    (M', X) ← S'_obv(1ᵏ, C)
5    Y' ← Ev(C, M', X)
6    Y ← En(d, y)
7    M_tr ← trans.S(Y', Y)
8    M ← M'||M_tr
9    return (M, X, d)
```

Fig. 5. Hybrid simulators that demonstrate Stack is private. $hybrid_0$ is identical to the real execution, and each subsequent hybrid is indistinguishable from the previous. The final 'hybrid' is the privacy simulator S_{prv}. Differences between the hybrids are indicated by highlighting added lines and striking removed lines.

- $hybrid_2 \overset{c}{=} S_{prv}$: In fact, the outputs of these two hybrids are identical. The key difference between the two hybrids is a change in interface. Additionally, the pseudorandom string S is now implicit since S_{prv} is a pseudorandom algorithm.

By transitivity, $hybrid_0 \overset{c}{=} S_{prv}$. Since the real and ideal executions are indistinguishable, Stack is private. □

Authenticity. Finally, we prove that Stack satisfies [BHR12]'s definition of *authenticity*, adjusted to our notation:

Definition 5 (Authenticity). *A garbling scheme is **authentic** if for all circuits C, all inputs x of length n, and all poly-time adversaries A the following probability is negligible in κ:*

$$Pr\left(Y' \neq Ev(C, M, X) \wedge De(d, Y') \neq \bot \right)$$

where S is uniform, $(M, e, d) = Gb(1^\kappa, C, S)$, $X = En(e, x)$, and $Y' = A(C, M, X)$.

Authenticity ensures that even an adversarial evaluator cannot construct labels that successfully decode except by running Ev as intended.

Theorem 5. *If* Base *is authentic and* H *is modeled as a random oracle, then* Stack *is authentic.*

Proof. We proceed backwards across the circuit C, at each step showing that $\mathcal{A}$ cannot obtain valid labels except by running the previous parts of the circuit. We rely on the RO properties of H for the mux, demux, and translator.

First, we examine the final top level translator gadget (Stack.Ev Line 4 and Stack.Gb Line 4). The output of the translator is determined by using H to decrypt garbled rows (Sect. 7.6). To break authenticity, $\mathcal{A}$ must guess the output of H. But H is a random oracle and hence this is infeasible. Therefore, $\mathcal{A}$ cannot obtain a decodable output except by running $trans.\mathsf{Ev}$ on valid translator input labels.

Now, it suffices to show that $\mathcal{A}$ cannot obtain input to the final translator except by running the recursive procedure $\mathsf{Ev}'(C, M, \boldsymbol{X})$. We demonstrate this by induction on the structure of the target circuit C.

- Suppose C is a netlist. Gb' and Ev' delegate to Base which is assumed to be authentic. Therefore, $\mathcal{A}$ cannot obtain valid output of C without running Base.Ev. Netlists are authentic.
- Suppose C is a sequence $\mathsf{Seq}(C_0, C_1)$. By induction, $\mathcal{A}$ cannot obtain valid output from C_1 except by running Ev'. We have already shown that the translator gadget preserves authenticity, so $\mathcal{A}$ cannot obtain input to C_1 except by running $trans.\mathsf{Ev}$ on valid input. Finally, C_0 also inductively preserves authenticity. Therefore, $\mathcal{A}$ cannot obtain input to the translator except by running Ev' on C_0 with valid input. Sequences are authentic.
- Suppose C is a conditional $\mathsf{Cond}(C_0, C_1)$. First, we examine the mux. Using the same argument as for the translator (the mux is built using H), valid output cannot be obtained except by running $mux.\mathsf{Ev}$ on valid inputs.

  Inputs to the mux component are constructed by evaluating C_0 and C_1. Consider the branch condition s. By induction, $\mathcal{A}$ cannot generate outputs of C_s except by running Ev' on C_s. $C_{\neg s}$ is not supported by our inductive argument: neither the inputs to nor the outputs from $C_{\neg s}$ are valid. Fortunately, we do not need $C_{\neg s}$ to preserve authenticity. Even if $\mathcal{A}$ can forge $\perp$-values from the non-target branch, she still needs valid output from the target branch to evaluate the mux.

  Finally, we examine the demux. $\mathcal{A}$ cannot construct valid input to C_s except by running $demux.\mathsf{Ev}$: the demux is built using H. Conditionals are authentic.

Stack is authentic.   □

9   Instantiating Our Scheme

We implemented Stack in C++ and used it to instantiate a semihonest 2PC protocol. We instantiate the underlying garbling scheme using the state-of-the-art half-gates technique [ZRE15]. That is, XOR gates require no material or encryption while AND gates are implemented using fixed-key AES [BHKR13]. Each AND gate requires 2 ciphertexts, 4 AES encryptions to encrypt, and 2 AES encryptions to evaluate. We use computational security parameter $\kappa = 127$; the 128th bit is reserved for point and permute.

Construction 1 supports conditionals with two branches. While we can nest conditionals to achieve greater branching factors, this is somewhat inefficient; recall that to support branching, Eval must generate both branches and Gen must emulate Eval on both branches. If those branches themselves contain conditionals, then recursively both players must emulate *themselves*, and so on as the branching factor grows. This recursive behavior has quadratic complexity for both players and constant factor overhead that we would like to avoid.

In our implementation, we therefore instantiate a *vectorized* version of Construction 1, whereby n branches can be composed without nesting. In practice, this means that only the generator has quadratic computation, while the evaluator has computation linear in the number of branches. The constant factors are also lower. We formally present the vectorized construction in Supplementary Material, where we state the corresponding security theorem and its proof (by reference to the proofs of Theorems 2 to 5 and enumeration and discussion of the differences with the binary branching of Construction 1).

Our implementation uses inherent parallelism available in Gb and Ev: while garbling/evaluating branches, the implementation spawns additional threads.

10   Evaluation

Our evaluation compares Stack to the state-of-the-art half-gates scheme [ZRE15]. We constructed an experiment that conditionally composes evaluations of SHA-256 (47,726 AND gates per branch). We ensured that branches are processed independently and that there are no shortcuts due to branch similarity. While a more realistic circuit would include a variety of branches, our goal is to isolate a precise performance impact of Stack. We varied the number of branches between 1 and 16 and ran the experiment using half-gates and of Stack.

We ran experiments on two different machines:

- A MacBook Pro laptop with an Intel Dual-Core i5 3.1 GHz processor and 8 GB of RAM. This machine demonstrates Stack's performance on commodity hardware.
- An Amazon EC2 c4.8xlarge instance with 36 virtual cores and 60 GB of RAM ($<$300 MB RAM were needed for the 16 branch experiment). This machine explores inherent parallelism available in Stack's algorithms.

Both Gen and Eval were run on the same machine, reducing the available parallelism. Experiments were performed on two simulated network settings: (1) a simulated WAN with 50 Mbps bandwidth and 20 ms latency and (2) a simulated LAN with 1 Gbps bandwidth and 2 ms latency. For each experiment, we measured total communication and wall-clock time. Results from each experiment were averaged over 10 runs and are plotted in Fig. 6.

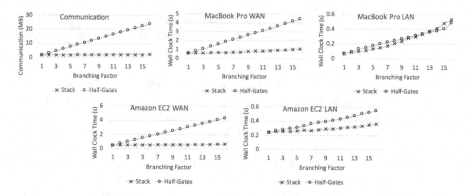

Fig. 6. Performance comparison of Stack and half-gates [ZRE15]. Each experiment tests both schemes on a circuit that conditionally executes one of n copies of the SHA-256 netlist. The number of copies of SHA-256, i.e. the branching factor, was varied between 1 and 16. The top-left plot shows total communication required to complete the protocol. The remaining plots depict total wall clock time in the WAN and LAN settings on a MacBook Pro and on an Amazon EC2 instance.

- **Communication:** Stack greatly outperforms half-gates in total communication. Advantage grows with branching factor: at 1 branch, Stack uses the same amount of communication, while at 16 branches Stack enjoys a 10.6× advantage. We do not achieve a 16× improvement for two reasons. First, Stack implements a demux/mux which are not stacked. Second, both schemes use the same amount of communication to transfer the circuit inputs.
- **WAN wall-clock, MacBook Pro:** Stack has a clear advantage. Computation is more than made up for by reduced communication, even on commodity hardware. At 16 branches, Stack outperforms half-gates > 4×.
- **LAN wall-clock, MacBook Pro:** In the LAN setting, Stack's computational overhead means that performance is comparable to raw half-gates. A 1Gbps network is very fast, and computation overhead diminishes the importance of reduced communication. We therefore explore how Stack performs on more powerful hardware, focusing on how inherent parallelism in Stack's algorithms impacts performance.
- **WAN wall-clock, Amazon EC2:** On this highly parallel machine, Stack's advantage is made more prominent. In fact, Stack's total wall-clock time at branching factor 16 is less than 50% higher than that at branching factor 1. At 16 branches, Stack outperforms half-gates by more than 6.4×.
- **LAN wall-clock, Amazon EC2:** On this more powerful hardware, Stack clearly outperforms half-gates. Still, the improvement is modest. We believe that future work will reduce the asymptotic and/or concrete overhead of the stacking technique and thus further improve overall performance.

Acknowledgement. This work was supported in part by NSF award #1909769 and by the Office of the Director of National Intelligence (ODNI), Intelligence Advanced Research Projects Activity (IARPA), via 2019-1902070008. The views and conclusions contained herein are those of the authors and should not be interpreted as necessarily representing the official policies, either expressed or implied, of ODNI, IARPA, or the U.S. Government. The U.S. Government is authorized to reproduce and distribute reprints for governmental purposes notwithstanding any copyright annotation therein. This work was also supported in part by Sandia National Laboratories, a multi-mission laboratory managed and operated by National Technology and Engineering Solutions of Sandia, LLC., a wholly owned subsidiary of Honeywell International, Inc., for the U.S. Department of Energy's National Nuclear Security Administration under contract DE-NA-0003525.

References

[AGKS19] Alhassan, M.Y., Günther, D., Kiss, A., Schneider, T.: Efficient and scalable universal circuits. Cryptology ePrint Archive, Report 2019/348 (2019). https://eprint.iacr.org/2019/348

[BHKR13] Bellare, M., Hoang, V.T., Keelveedhi, S., Rogaway, P.: Efficient garbling from a fixed-key blockcipher. In: 2013 IEEE Symposium on Security and Privacy, pp. 478–492. IEEE Computer Society Press, May 2013

[BHR12] Bellare, M., Hoang, V.T., Rogaway, P.: Foundations of garbled circuits. In: Yu, T., Danezis, G., Gligor, V.D. (eds.) ACM CCS 2012, pp. 784–796. ACM Press, October 2012

[BMR90] Beaver, D., Micali, S., Rogaway, P.: The round complexity of secure protocols. In: 22nd Symposium on Theory of Computing (1990)

[CKKZ12] Choi, S.G., Katz, J., Kumaresan, R., Zhou, H.-S.: On the security of the "Free-XOR" technique. In: Cramer, R. (ed.) TCC 2012. LNCS, vol. 7194, pp. 39–53. Springer, Heidelberg (2012). https://doi.org/10.1007/978-3-642-28914-9_3

[FKN94] Feige, U., Kilian, J., Naor, M.: A minimal model for secure computation (extended abstract). In: 26th ACM STOC, pp. 554–563. ACM Press, May 1994

[FNO15] Frederiksen, T.K., Nielsen, J.B., Orlandi, C.: Privacy-free garbled circuits with applications to efficient zero-knowledge. In: Oswald, E., Fischlin, M. (eds.) EUROCRYPT 2015, Part II. LNCS, vol. 9057, pp. 191–219. Springer, Heidelberg (2015). https://doi.org/10.1007/978-3-662-46803-6_7

[GKS17] Günther, D., Kiss, Á., Schneider, T.: More efficient universal circuit constructions. In: Takagi, T., Peyrin, T. (eds.) ASIACRYPT 2017, Part II. LNCS, vol. 10625, pp. 443–470. Springer, Cham (2017). https://doi.org/10.1007/978-3-319-70697-9_16

[GLNP18] Gueron, S., Lindell, Y., Nof, A., Pinkas, B.: Fast garbling of circuits under standard assumptions. J. Cryptol. **31**(3), 798–844 (2018)

[HK20] Heath, D., Kolesnikov, V.: Stacked garbling for disjunctive zero-knowledge proofs. In: Canteaut, A., Ishai, Y. (eds.) EUROCRYPT 2020, Part III. LNCS, vol. 12107, pp. 569–598. Springer, Cham (2020). https://doi.org/10.1007/978-3-030-45727-3_19

[IKNP03] Ishai, Y., Kilian, J., Nissim, K., Petrank, E.: Extending oblivious transfers efficiently. In: Boneh, D. (ed.) CRYPTO 2003. LNCS, vol. 2729, pp. 145–161. Springer, Heidelberg (2003). https://doi.org/10.1007/978-3-540-45146-4_9

[JKO13] Jawurek, M., Kerschbaum, F., Orlandi, C.: Zero-knowledge using garbled circuits: how to prove non-algebraic statements efficiently. In: Sadeghi, A.-R., Gligor, V.D., Yung, M. (eds.) ACM CCS 2013, pp. 955–966. ACM Press, November 2013

[KKW17] Kennedy, W.S., Kolesnikov, V., Wilfong, G.: Overlaying conditional circuit clauses for secure computation. In: Takagi, T., Peyrin, T. (eds.) ASIACRYPT 2017, Part II. LNCS, vol. 10625, pp. 499–528. Springer, Cham (2017). https://doi.org/10.1007/978-3-319-70697-9_18

[KMR14] Kolesnikov, V., Mohassel, P., Rosulek, M.: FleXOR: flexible garbling for XOR gates that beats free-XOR. In: Garay, J.A., Gennaro, R. (eds.) CRYPTO 2014, Part II. LNCS, vol. 8617, pp. 440–457. Springer, Heidelberg (2014). https://doi.org/10.1007/978-3-662-44381-1_25

[KO04] Katz, J., Ostrovsky, R.: Round-optimal secure two-party computation. In: Franklin, M. (ed.) CRYPTO 2004. LNCS, vol. 3152, pp. 335–354. Springer, Heidelberg (2004). https://doi.org/10.1007/978-3-540-28628-8_21

[Kol18] Kolesnikov, V.: Free IF: how to omit inactive branches and implement $\mathcal{S}$-universal garbled circuit (almost) for free. In: Peyrin, T., Galbraith, S. (eds.) ASIACRYPT 2018, Part III. LNCS, vol. 11274, pp. 34–58. Springer, Cham (2018). https://doi.org/10.1007/978-3-030-03332-3_2

[KS08] Kolesnikov, V., Schneider, T.: Improved garbled circuit: free XOR gates and applications. In: Aceto, L., Damgård, I., Goldberg, L.A., Halldórsson, M.M., Ingólfsdóttir, A., Walukiewicz, I. (eds.) ICALP 2008, Part II. LNCS, vol. 5126, pp. 486–498. Springer, Heidelberg (2008). https://doi.org/10.1007/978-3-540-70583-3_40

[KS16] Kiss, Á., Schneider, T.: Valiant's universal circuit is practical. In: Fischlin, M., Coron, J.-S. (eds.) EUROCRYPT 2016, Part I. LNCS, vol. 9665, pp. 699–728. Springer, Heidelberg (2016). https://doi.org/10.1007/978-3-662-49890-3_27

[LMS16] Lipmaa, H., Mohassel, P., Sadeghian, S.: Valiant's universal circuit: improvements, implementation, and applications. Cryptology ePrint Archive, Report 2016/017 (2016). http://eprint.iacr.org/2016/017

[NPS99] Naor, M., Pinkas, B., Sumner, R.: Privacy preserving auctions and mechanism design. In: Proceedings of the 1st ACM Conference on Electronic Commerce, pp. 129–139. ACM (1999)

[PSSW09] Pinkas, B., Schneider, T., Smart, N.P., Williams, S.C.: Secure two-party computation is practical. In: Matsui, M. (ed.) ASIACRYPT 2009. LNCS, vol. 5912, pp. 250–267. Springer, Heidelberg (2009). https://doi.org/10.1007/978-3-642-10366-7_15

[Val76] Valiant, L.G.: Universal circuits (preliminary report). In: STOC, pp. 196–203. ACM Press, New York (1976)

[ZRE15] Zahur, S., Rosulek, M., Evans, D.: Two halves make a whole. In: Oswald, E., Fischlin, M. (eds.) EUROCRYPT 2015, Part II. LNCS, vol. 9057, pp. 220–250. Springer, Heidelberg (2015). https://doi.org/10.1007/978-3-662-46803-6_8

[ZYZL18] Zhao, S., Yu, Y., Zhang, J., Liu, H.: Valiant's universal circuits revisited: an overall improvement and a lower bound. Cryptology ePrint Archive, Report 2018/943 (2018). https://eprint.iacr.org/2018/943

Better Concrete Security
for Half-Gates Garbling
(in the Multi-instance Setting)

Chun Guo[1,2(✉)], Jonathan Katz[3(✉)], Xiao Wang[4(✉)], Chenkai Weng[4(✉)],
and Yu Yu[5,6(✉)]

[1] Key Laboratory of Cryptologic Technology and Information Security
of Ministry of Education, Shandong University,
Qingdao 266237, Shandong, China
chun.guo@sdu.edu.cn
[2] School of Cyber Science and Technology,
Shandong University, Qingdao, China
[3] George Mason University, Fairfax, USA
jkatz2@gmail.com
[4] Northwestern University, Evanston, USA
wangxiao@cs.northwestern.edu, ckweng@u.northwestern.edu
[5] Shanghai Jiao Tong University, Shanghai, China
yuyu@yuyu.hk
[6] Shanghai Qi Zhi Institute, Shanghai, China

Abstract. We study the *concrete security* of high-performance implementations of half-gates garbling, which all rely on (hardware-accelerated) AES. We find that current instantiations using k-bit wire labels can be *completely broken*—in the sense that the circuit evaluator learns all the inputs of the circuit garbler—in time $O(2^k/C)$, where C is the total number of (non-free) gates that are garbled, possibly across multiple independent executions. The attack can be applied to existing circuit-garbling libraries using $k = 80$ when $C \approx 10^9$, and would require 267 machine-months and cost about \$3500 to implement on the Google Cloud Platform. Since the attack can be fully parallelized, it could be carried out in about a month using ≈ 250 machines.

With this as our motivation, we seek a way to instantiate the hash function in the half-gates scheme so as to achieve better concrete security. We present a construction based on AES that achieves optimal security in the single-instance setting (when only a single circuit is garbled). We also show how to modify the half-gates scheme so that its concrete security does not degrade in the multi-instance setting. Our modified scheme is as efficient as prior work in networks with up to 2 Gbps bandwidth.

1 Introduction

Roughly 35 years ago, Yao proposed the idea of *garbled circuits* for constant-round (semi-honest) secure two-party computation [44]. Over the past 15 years, spurred by initial implementations demonstrating its practicality [20,33,37], circuit garbling has received a considerable amount of attention and Yao's initial scheme has been significantly improved. Notable examples of such improvements

© International Association for Cryptologic Research 2020
D. Micciancio and T. Ristenpart (Eds.): CRYPTO 2020, LNCS 12171, pp. 793–822, 2020.
https://doi.org/10.1007/978-3-030-56880-1_28

794   C. Guo et al.

include the point-and-permute technique [1], garbled row reduction [35], free-XOR [26], fleXOR [25], and half-gates garbling [46], as well as optimizations involving AES when modeled as a pseudorandom function [17] or when used with a fixed key and modeled as a random permutation [5]. Overall, these improvements have not only decreased the computational requirements of garbling, but have also—perhaps more importantly—reduced the communication complexity of garbled circuits. (Indeed, in current implementations of semi-honest secure two-party computation the overall running time is dominated by the communication time, and network bandwidth is the primary bottleneck.)

As these improvements to circuit garbling have been developed, however, there has been—perhaps somewhat surprisingly—a relative lack of attention on the *concrete security* [4] of these proposals.[1] Understanding concrete security here is important for at least two reasons. First, as is well understood in the context of both public-key (e.g., [7,12]) and symmetric-key (e.g., [4]) cryptography, when comparing the efficiency of different schemes it is important to take into account the concrete-security bound they each achieve; otherwise, the comparison may be inaccurate or misleading. Moreover, concrete security is critical for constructions based on symmetric-key primitives (such as AES), where there is no "security parameter" that can be arbitrarily adjusted as in the public-key world. (In particular, for AES the block size is fixed at 128 bits, and the maximum available key length is 256 bits.) There is thus the risk that a scheme that is only proven asymptotically secure—but has a poor concrete-security bound—may be insecure in practice for the available range of parameters.

When evaluating the concrete security of garbling, one can consider the "standard," single-instance setting where a single circuit is garbled, but it is also natural to consider a *multi-instance* setting where multiple circuits, for possibly different functions, are (independently) garbled—whether by the same user or distinct users—and, informally, the attacker succeeds if it is able to violate the security of any of those garbled circuits. Concrete security in the multi-instance setting has received a lot of attention in the context of both public-key [3,24] and symmetric-key [2,8,9,19,40] cryptography, but to the best of our knowledge it has not been previously considered in the setting of secure computation.[2]

1.1   Our Contributions

We study the concrete security of garbling. We begin by examining the concrete security of existing, state-of-the-art implementations of the half-gates scheme (which is the most efficient garbling scheme currently known), and showing that it is worse than perhaps previously thought. We then propose a new way to instantiate the half-gates scheme that achieves better concrete-security bounds. Our results are described in further detail in what follows.

---

[1] This is even more surprising compared to the extensive research on the *statistical* security of circuit-garbling protocols in the *malicious* setting [21,28–30,39,47].

[2] Work on *amortized* complexity of circuit garbling [22,31] is close in spirit, but again focuses on statistical security of the overall protocol in the malicious setting rather than the concrete (computational) security of the garbling itself.

Concrete Security of Current Half-Gates Garbling. The half-gates scheme is a technique for circuit garbling that is compatible with free-XOR (so uses no communication and negligible computation for XOR gates) and requires only $2k$ bits of communication for non-XOR gates, where k denotes the length of the wire labels. The half-gates scheme is based, abstractly, on a hash function H. Zahur et al. [46], motivated by JustGarble [5], propose to instantiate H using fixed-key AES in a particular way. Their suggestion was adopted by many existing implementations [13,15,38,41–43,45] since it is much more efficient than instantiating H with a cryptographic hash function such as SHA-256 or SHA-3.

Let C be the number of (non-free) gates garbled. We show an attack on the half-gates scheme that results in a *complete break* (that is, the circuit evaluator learns all the inputs of the circuit garbler) in time $O(2^k/C)$. The attack works in the claimed time even when C denotes the *total* number of gates garbled across *multiple, independent* circuits. (In this case the attack completely violates privacy for at least *one* of the garbled circuits.)

We experimentally verify the feasibility of our attack against existing implementations of garbling that use "short" wire labels. In particular, we show that garbling 1 billion gates[3] (i.e., $C = 10^9$) with existing implementations of half-gates garbling that use wire labels of length $k = 80$ is vulnerable to an attack that can be carried out in 267 machine-months at a cost of \$3500. Since the attack can be fully parallelized, it can be carried out in about a month using $\approx$250 machines. Due to our attack, we urge users of the half-gates scheme to no longer use 80-bit wire labels (unless the scheme is modified as discussed below).

Better Concrete Security for Half-Gates Garbling. Looking more closely at our attack, we observe that it does not arise due to any weakness in the half-gates scheme itself, but instead is possible *because of the way H is instantiated*. In particular, we show that the half-gates scheme has a *tight* security reduction (namely, requires time $\Theta(2^k)$ to attack) if the hash function H being used is modeled as a random oracle. (See Appendix B.) As noted earlier, however, in existing implementations H is instantiated using (fixed-key) AES for better performance; this instantiation is *not* indifferentiable from a random oracle and our attack can be viewed as exploiting that gap.

The fact that the proposed instantiation of H is not indifferentiable from a random oracle was also observed by Guo et al. [18]. They define a property called *tweakable circular correlation robustness* (TCCR) for hash functions, show that using a TCCR hash function suffices for security of the half-gates scheme, and give a provably secure construction of a TCCR hash function based on fixed-key AES. They did not focus on obtaining better concrete security, and indeed, in Appendix C we show that using their hash function in the half-gates scheme would admit an attack with complexity similar to the one described above.

We thus turn to constructing a TCCR hash function with tight concrete security. In this context, the hash function H is evaluated on both a tweak and an input and, with our eventual application to garbling in mind, we use a

---

[3] Note that secure computation of 1 billion gates is now commonplace [20,27,32], and circuits with as many as 2^{37} gates have been garbled for some applications [14].

fine-grained notion of concrete security that separately bounds the total number of calls the adversary makes to H as well as the maximum number of times μ the adversary repeats any particular tweak. As our main result, we show a construction of a TCCR hash function based on AES (modeled as an ideal cipher) that has tight concrete security when μ is small.

Importantly, $\mu = 1$ when a single circuit is garbled using the half-gates scheme, and so when our new hash function is used to instantiate the half-gates approach we immediately obtain a garbling scheme with tight security in the single-instance setting. In the multi-instance setting, however, μ can potentially be as large the number of circuits being garbled; thus, absent any changes, we would obtain a poor concrete-security bound, even when using our hash function, when many circuits are independently garbled. To address this, we show a simple way to randomize the tweaks used in the half-gates scheme in order to avoid significant degradation in the concrete security.

In contrast to the prior work of Guo et al. [18], the hash function we propose involves re-keying AES (and modeling AES as an ideal cipher) rather than relying on fixed-key AES (and modeling the result as a random permutation). Nevertheless, we show in Sect. 6 that by incorporating state-of-the-art optimizations for AES key scheduling [17], our hash function is almost as efficient as the one proposed by Guo et al. when used for circuit garbling.

1.2   Practical Implications

We show that existing implementations of half-gates garbling are much less secure than previously thought, and puts forth an improved way to instantiate half-gates garbling with better concrete security. Our work has already had an impact on existing libraries for secure computation. For example, OblivC [45] changed the length of their labels from 80 bits to 128 bits due to our work, and our new method for instantiating the half-gates scheme is being used in the latest implementations (e.g., [11]). We are also aware of industry implementations (that we are unable to disclose) that have changed because of our work.

1.3   Overview of the Paper

In Sect. 2 we establish notation and review relevant definitions for garbling schemes, including *concrete* security definitions for garbling in a *multi-instance* setting. We also describe the half-gates garbling scheme based on an abstract hash function H. In Sect. 3 we describe the instantiation of H based on fixed-key AES that was proposed by Zahur et al. and that is used in existing implementations; we then show an attack with running time $O(2^k/C)$ that completely violates the privacy of that instantiation. We define the notion of multi-instance tweakable circular correlation robustness (miTCCR) for hash functions in Sect. 4.1, and show that the concrete security of the half-gates scheme when instantiated with a hash function H can be reduced to the concrete security of H in the sense of miTCCR. As our main positive result, we then show in

Sect. 4.2 how to construct a hash function from an ideal cipher with tight security in that sense. In Sect. 5 we show how to slightly modify the half-gates scheme so as to also achieve good concrete security in the multi-instance setting. We discuss the performance of the resulting garbling scheme in Sect. 6.

2   Circuit Garbling

We adapt the definitions of garbling by Bellare et al. [6] to our setting. We consider boolean circuits containing AND and XOR gates with fan-in 2. (NOT gates can be handled by XORing with 1.) We represent any such circuit by a tuple $f = (n, m, \ell, \mathsf{Gates})$, where $n \geq 2$ denotes the number of input wires, $m \geq 1$ is the number of output wires, and ℓ is the number of gates. Such a circuit has exactly $n + \ell$ wires that we number starting from 1; we let $\mathsf{Inputs} = \{1, \ldots, n\}$ and $\mathsf{Outputs} = \{n + \ell - m + 1, \ldots, n + \ell\}$. The set $\mathsf{Gates} = \{(a, b, c, T)\}$, containing ℓ tuples, specifies the wiring of the circuit; a tuple $(a, b, c, T) \in \mathsf{Gates}$ with $a, b, c \in \{1, \ldots, n + \ell\}$ represents a gate of type $T \in \{\mathsf{XOR}, \mathsf{AND}\}$ with input wires a, b and output wire c. For a circuit f we let $|f| = C$ denote the number of AND gates in f. With slight abuse of notation, we let f also denote the function $f : \{0, 1\}^n \to \{0, 1\}^m$ computed by the circuit.

We consider a restricted class of garbling schemes in which garbling involves assigning two k-bit labels to each wire of the circuit, and evaluation involves computing one label for each output wire. (Our definition is thus similar to the one considered by Katz and Ostrovsky [23].) While this is less general than the class of garbling schemes considered by Bellare et al., this formulation suffices for analyzing the half-gates construction that is the focus of this paper.

Definition 1. *A circuit-garbling scheme $\mathcal{G} = (\mathsf{Garble}, \mathsf{Eval}, \mathsf{Decode})$ is a tuple of algorithms where:*

- *Garble takes as input a circuit f, and returns $(\mathsf{GC}, \{W_i^0, W_i^1\}_{i \in \mathsf{Inputs}}, d)$, where GC denotes a garbled circuit, $W_i^0, W_i^1 \in \{0, 1\}^k$ are the labels for the ith input wire, and d represents decoding information.*
- *Eval takes as input a garbled circuit GC and input-wire labels $\{W_i\}_{i \in \mathsf{Inputs}}$. It returns output-wire labels $\{W_i\}_{i \in \mathsf{Outputs}}$.*
- *Decode takes as input output-wire labels $\{W_i\}_{i \in \mathsf{Outputs}}$ and decoding information d, and returns either $\perp$ or a string $y \in \{0, 1\}^m$.*

Correctness requires that for any circuit f and any $x \in \{0, 1\}^n$, if we compute

$$(\mathsf{GC}, \{W_i^0, W_i^1\}_{i \in \mathsf{Inputs}}, d) \leftarrow \mathsf{Garble}(f)$$

and $\{W_i\}_{i \in \mathsf{Outputs}} \leftarrow \mathsf{Eval}(\mathsf{GC}, \{W_i^{x_i}\})$, then $\mathsf{Decode}(\{W_i\}_{i \in \mathsf{Outputs}}, d) = f(x)$.

When we work in the ideal-cipher model (ICM), all algorithms (including any adversary) are given access to a random keyed permutation $E : \{0, 1\}^L \times \{0, 1\}^L \to \{0, 1\}^L$ as well as its inverse E^{-1}; i.e., for every $\mathsf{key} \in \{0, 1\}^L$ and input $x \in \{0,1\}^L$ it holds that $E^{-1}(\text{key}, E(\text{key}, x)) = x$. We require correctness to hold for all such E. We sometimes also consider the random-permutation model (RPM) in which all parties have access to a random permutation π and its inverse. The RPM can be obtained from the ICM by setting $\pi(x) = E(0^L, x)$.

Security notions for garbling are considered in the following section.

2.1 (Multi-instance) Security of Garbling

The canonical security definition for garbling schemes, which suffices for semi-honest secure computation, is *privacy*. As Bellare et al. [6] note, however, some other applications of garbling require alternate definitions. For completeness, we thus also consider the notions of *obliviousness* and *authenticity* in Appendix A. In contrast to prior work, here we provide concrete-security definitions in a *multi-instance* setting in which an attacker may be given values produced by the (independent) garbling of $u \geq 1$ circuits.

Roughly speaking, privacy requires that the information needed to evaluate a garbled circuit (namely, GC, $\{W_i^{x_i}\}$, and d) reveals nothing other than $y = f(x)$. This is formalized by requiring the existence of a simulator Sim that takes the circuit f and a value y as input, and outputs values that are indistinguishable from GC, $\{W_i^{x_i}\}$, d. In the multi-instance setting, we compare the output of Sim to the outputs obtained from independently garbling u circuits. The following definition is specialized to the ICM for concreteness and since our main construction is in that model; it can be naturally adapted to the RPM.

Definition 2. *Garbling scheme $\mathcal{G}$ is (p, u, C, ε)-private if there is a simulator Sim so that for any distinguisher D making p queries to E and any $\{(f^i, x^i)\}_{i \in [u]}$ with $\sum_i |f^i| = C$, we have*

$$\left| \Pr_{\{(\mathsf{GC}^i, \{W_j^{i,0}, W_j^{i,1}\}, d^i) \leftarrow \mathsf{Garble}^E(f^i)\}_{i \in [u]}} \left[D^E\left(\{(\mathsf{GC}^i, \{W_j^{i,x_j^i}\}, d^i)\}_{i \in [u]}\right) = 1 \right] \right.$$

$$\left. - \Pr_{\{(\mathsf{GC}^i, \{W_j^i\}, d^i) \leftarrow \mathsf{Sim}^E(f^i, f^i(x^i))\}_{i \in [u]}} \left[D^E\left(\{(\mathsf{GC}^i, \{W_j^i\}, d^i)\}_{i \in [u]}\right) = 1 \right] \right| \leq \varepsilon,$$

where both probabilities are also over choice of E.

In the definition above, D may be unbounded so long as the number of queries it makes to E is bounded. The definition does not explicitly consider the running time of the simulator Sim, but one can verify that the running time of the simulator for our construction is $O(C)$. We remark further that while the distinguisher is given the circuits/inputs used in *all* the instances, we require the simulator to simulate each instance *independently*. (That is, when simulating the ith instance the simulator is only given $f^i, f^i(x^i)$.)

2.2 The Half-Gates Garbling Scheme

The half-gates scheme HalfGates [46] is an approach for garbling that is compatible with the free-XOR technique, and only requires communicating $2k$ bits per

AND gate. As the most efficient garbling scheme currently known, it is widely used in existing implementations of secure two-party computation in both the semi-honest and malicious settings. HalfGates is based on an abstract hash function $H : \{0,1\}^k \times \{0,1\}^L \to \{0,1\}^k$. We describe the scheme generically here, and discuss specific instantiations of H later.

We provide a high-level description, and refer to Fig. 1 for details. To garble a circuit, the half-gates scheme begins by choosing a k-bit string R that is uniform subject to its least-significant bit being 1. For the ith wire of the circuit with associated labels W_i^0, W_i^1, it will always be the case that $W_i^0 \oplus W_i^1 = R$. The garbler next chooses uniform 0-labels $\{W_i^0\}_{i \in \text{Inputs}}$ for each input wire of the circuit. (This defines the 1-labels $\{W_i^1 = W_i^0 \oplus R\}$ for the input wires as well.) The garbled circuit is then generated gate-by-gate in topological order. For each XOR gate in the circuit, with ingoing wires a, b and outgoing wire c, the garbler simply sets $W_c^0 := W_a^0 \oplus W_b^0$ (and nothing is included in the garbled circuit for this gate). Each AND gate in the circuit is numbered topologically with a unique *gate identifier* gid ranging from 1 to C. For each AND gate in the circuit, with ingoing wires a, b and outgoing wire c, the garbler uses W_a^0, W_b^0, R, and the gate's identifier gid to compute the garbled table (T_G, T_E) as well as the 0-label W_c^0. This is done using a complicated procedure GbAnd that is defined in Fig. 1. The garbled circuit consists of all the garbled AND gates. The correctness of the garbling scheme can be easily verified given that

$$W_c^0 = H(W_a^{p_a}, j) \oplus H(W_b^{p_b}, j') \oplus (p_a \wedge p_b) \cdot R.$$

To evaluate a garbled circuit, starting with labels $\{W_i\}_{i \in \text{Inputs}}$ (where the evaluator does not necessarily know if $W_i = W_i^0$ or $W_i = W_i^1$), the evaluator proceeds as follows. For an XOR gate with ingoing wires a, b and outgoing wire c, the evaluator computes $W_c := W_a \oplus W_b$. For an AND gate with ingoing wires a, b and outgoing wire c, the evaluator computes W_c from W_a, W_b, and the gate's identifier gid using the corresponding garbled table (see Fig. 1). The final output is obtained using the least-significant bits of the output-wire labels.

3   Attacking Implementations of the Half-Gates Scheme

Inspired by earlier work of Bellare et al. [5], Zahur et al. [46] proposed to instantiate the hash function H in the half-gates schemes with a construction based on fixed-key AES (modeled as a random permutation π). Namely, they suggested to implement H as $H(x, i) = \pi(2x \oplus i) \oplus 2x \oplus i$.

Here, we show an attack that violates privacy when H is implemented in this way. Our attack succeeds with probability $O(p \cdot C/2^k)$, where p denotes the number of queries the attacker makes to π, and C denotes the number of AND gates garbled. Importantly, the attack also extends to the multi-instance setting, where C then denotes the total number of AND gates garbled. Our attack does not contradict the security proof by Zahur et al. (or the later proof of Guo et al. [18]), who only claim that an attacker's success probability cannot exceed this bound. Here we show an attack meeting that bound.

$$\text{HalfGates}^H$$

function Garble(f)
  $R \leftarrow \{0,1\}^{k-1}\|1$
  gid := 1
  for $i \in$ Inputs **do**
    $W_i^0 \leftarrow \{0,1\}^k$
    $W_i^1 := W_i^0 \oplus R$
  for $(a,b,c,T) \in$ Gates **do**
    if $T = $ XOR **then**
      $W_c^0 := W_a^0 \oplus W_b^0$
    else
      $(GC[gid], W_c^0) := GbAnd(W_a^0, W_b^0, R, gid)$
      gid := gid + 1
  for $i \in$ Outputs **do**
    $d_i := lsb(W_i^0)$
  return $(GC, \{(W_i^0, W_i^1)\}_{i \in \text{Inputs}}, d)$

function GbAnd($W_a^0, W_b^0, R, $ gid)
  $j := 2 \times$ gid, $j' := 2 \times$ gid + 1
  $p_a := lsb(W_a^0)$, $p_b := lsb(W_b^0)$
  $T_G := H(W_a^0, j) \oplus H(W_a^1, j) \oplus p_b R$
  $T_E := H(W_b^0, j') \oplus H(W_b^1, j') \oplus W_a^0$
  $W_G^0 := H(W_a^0, j) \oplus p_a T_G$
  $W_E^0 := H(W_b^0, j') \oplus p_b(T_E \oplus W_a^0)$
  $W_c^0 := W_G^0 \oplus W_E^0$
  return $((T_G, T_E), W_c^0)$

function Eval(GC, $\{W_i\}_{i \in \text{Inputs}}$)
  gid := 1
  for $(a,b,c,T) \in$ Gates **do**
    if $T = $ XOR **then**
      $W_c := W_a \oplus W_b$
    else
      $(T_G, T_E) := GC[gid]$
      $j := 2 \times$ gid, $j' := 2 \times$ gid + 1
      $s_a := lsb(W_a)$, $s_b := lsb(W_b)$
      $W_G := H(W_a, j) \oplus s_a T_G$
      $W_E := H(W_b, j') \oplus s_b \cdot (T_E \oplus W_a)$
      $W_c := W_G \oplus W_E$
      gid := gid + 1
  return $\{W_i\}_{i \in \text{Outputs}}$

function Decode($\{W_i\}_{i \in \text{Outputs}}, d$)
  for $i \in$ Outputs **do**
    $y_i := lsb(W_i) \oplus d_i$
  return y

Fig. 1. The half-gates scheme based on a hash function H.

Note that Guo et al. [18] have previously shown an attack on the above instantiation of H that violates (tweakable) correlation robustness with probability $O(pC/2^k)$ using p queries to π and C queries to a keyed version of H (i.e., the oracle). However, their attack explicitly relies on the attacker's ability to make arbitrary H-queries and to obtain the full responses to those queries. Neither condition holds in our case, where the H-oracle queries are made by the honest garbler (and so are outside the control of the attacker) and the attacker is given the resulting garbled circuit but is not directly given the output of the oracle.

3.1   Attack Details

We describe the intuition behind the attack here, and give the details in Fig. 2. The attack works by recovering the hidden global shift R used by the circuit garbler; note that once this value is obtained, the evaluator can use R along with the rest of the garbled circuit to learn, for each wire of the circuit, which labels are associated with which bits and thus, using the input labels it was sent, determine the actual input of the garbler. We focus on showing how to learn R. Observe that for each AND gate in the circuit with ingoing wires a, b and outgoing wire c, the circuit evaluator learns one of the two wire labels

$W_a \in \{W_a^0, W_a^1\}$ as well as the value

$$T_G = H(W_a^0, j) \oplus H(W_a^1, j) \oplus p_b R$$

from the garbled gate. (Note that j depends on the gate identifier gid of the gate but we leave that implicit.) Recall further that $W_a^1 = W_a^0 \oplus R$. The circuit evaluator can thus compute

$$H_a \stackrel{\text{def}}{=} T_G \oplus H(W_a, j) = H(W_a \oplus R, j) \oplus p_b R.$$

A key observation is that $p_b = 0$ with probability $1/2$! Thus, the circuit evaluator obtains, in expectation, $C/2$ values of the form $H_a^+ = H(W_a \oplus R, j)$ with W_a, j known. (We use H_a^+ to refer to an H_a-value for which $p_b = 0$.)

We now rely on the specific details of how H is implemented. When $H(x, i) \stackrel{\text{def}}{=} \pi(2x \oplus i) \oplus 2x \oplus i$ we have

$$H_a^+ = H(W_a \oplus R, j) = \pi(2(W_a \oplus R) \oplus j) \oplus 2(W_a \oplus R) \oplus j.$$

If the circuit evaluator chooses a uniform W_i^*, it can check whether

$$H(W_i^*, 0) = H_a \tag{1}$$

for some a. If so, then (as we justify below in our discussion of false positives) with constant probability it will be the case that

$$2W_i^* = 2(W_a \oplus R) \oplus j. \tag{2}$$

Once the evaluator finds a W_i^* for which Eq. (2) holds, it can then easily solve for R. (Note also that it is easy to verify a candidate value R; see the Check routine in Fig. 2.) The time to carry out the attack is therefore dominated by the time to find a solution to Eq. (2). Assume for simplicity we have exactly $C/2$ values $\{H_a^+\}$. Then if p uniform values $W_1^*, \ldots, W_p^*$ are chosen, the probability that Eq. (2) holds for some i, a is $p \cdot (C/2) \cdot 2^{-k} = p \cdot C/2^{k+1}$, as claimed.

Extension to the Multi-instance Setting. The above attack readily extends to the case when multiple circuits are (independently) garbled. In this case, C is simply the total number of AND gates garbled across all the circuits, and the attack recovers the shift R used for one of them.

False Positives. We now more carefully account for the number of queries to π made during the course of the attack. We argued above that after p evaluations of H (which requires p evaluations of π) the attack finds R with probability $pC/2^{k+1}$. This analysis, however, does not account for false positives (i.e., a W^* for which Eq. (1) holds but Eq. (2) does not); note that every false positive incurs additional π-queries because it causes the Check routine to be executed. We now show that we expect only ≈ 2 false positives for every true positive.

To see this, fix some particular a and associated $H_a = H(W_a \oplus R, j) \oplus p_b R$, and consider a uniform W^*. There are three cases in which $H(W^*, 0) = H_a$:

Inputs: A garbled circuit, along with input-wire labels $\{W_i\}_{i \in \mathsf{Inputs}}$.

Main algorithm:

1. Initialize $\mathcal{T} := \emptyset$. Evaluate the garbled circuit honestly and obtain a label W_a for each wire a.
2. For each AND gate (a, b, c, AND) with gate identifier **gid** and garbled table (T_G, T_E), set $j := 2 \times \mathbf{gid}$, compute $H_a := H(W_a, j) \oplus T_G$, and insert (H_a, j, W_a) into $\mathcal{T}$.
3. Choose uniform $W^* \in \{0, 1\}^k$ until there exists (j, W_a) such that $(H(W^*, 0), j, W_a) \in \mathcal{T}$.
4. Given W^*, j, W_a from the previous step, compute $R := W_a \oplus W^* \oplus 2^{-1}j$. If $\mathsf{Check}(R) = 1$, output R; otherwise go to step 3.

$\mathsf{Check}(R)$:

1. For a gate (a, b, c, AND) with gate identifier **gid** and garbled table (T_G, T_E), let W_a, W_b, W_c be the labels computed on the respective wires.
2. If $((T_G, T_E), W_c \oplus wR) \overset{?}{=} \mathsf{GbAnd}(W_a^0 \oplus uR, W_b^0 \oplus vR, R, \mathbf{gid})$ for some values $u, v, w \in \{0, 1\}$, output 1; else output 0.

Fig. 2. Attack on the proposed implementation of the half-gates scheme.

- Case 1: $p_b = 0$ and $2W^* = 2(W_a \oplus R) \oplus j$. This occurs with probability $1/2^{k+1}$, and is a true positive.
- Case 2: $p_b = 0$ and $2W^* \neq 2(W_a \oplus R) \oplus j$, yet $H(W^*, 0) = H_a$. The probability of the first event is $1/2$, and the probability of the second is slightly less than 1. But conditioned on these events, the third event occurs only if

$$H(W^*, 0) = \pi(2W^*) \oplus 2W^* = \pi(2(W_a \oplus R) \oplus j) \oplus 2(W_a \oplus R) \oplus j = H_a,$$

which occurs with probability roughly $1/2^k$ since π is a random permutation. Overall, then, the probability of this case is also $1/2^{k+1}$.
- Case 3: $p_b = 1$, yet $H(W, 0) = H_a$. The probability of the first event is $1/2$. But conditioned on this, the second event occurs only if

$$H(W^*, 0) = \pi(2W^*) \oplus 2W^* = \pi(2(W_a \oplus R) \oplus j) \oplus 2(W_a \oplus R) \oplus j \oplus R = H_a.$$

There are now two sub-cases. If $2W^* = 2(W_a \oplus R) \oplus j$ (which occurs with probability 2^{-k}), then since R has min-entropy $k - 1$ the probability that the above equality holds is at most 2^{-k+1}. If $2W^* \neq 2(W_a \oplus R) \oplus j$, then because π is a uniform permutation the probability that the above equality holds is at most $1/(2^k - 1)$. Overall, then, the probability of this case is $1/2^{k+1} + 1/2^{2k} \approx 1/2^{k+1}$.

Summarizing: if the attack chooses p values $W_1^*, \ldots, W_p^*$, we expect a true positive with probability $pC/2^{k+1}$ and a false positive with probability $pC/2^k$. Put differently, if we set p such that $pC/2^{k+1} \approx 1$ then we expect to obtain R with probability ≈ 1 while incurring only ≈ 2 false positives. (Note that only $O(1)$

queries to π are made during calls to Check, so the net result is only a small number of additional queries to π.)

3.2 Attack Implementation

Here we describe our implementation of the attack described above.

Implementation Optimizations. Above, we focused on the complexity of the attack in terms of the number of queries to π. In practice, though, the lookups in $\mathcal{T}$ also incur significant cost. For example, when $C = 2^{30}$ then $\mathcal{T}$ requires roughly 24 GB to store; this impacts both the running time of the attack (due to cache misses on memory accesses) and its dollar cost (since more-powerful machines are needed). To mitigate this, we made the following optimizations:

1. We first observe that it suffices to search for matches on H_a-values, and we thus store (only) those values in a hash table $\mathcal{H}$. Once a match on H_a is found, we can do a lookup in $\mathcal{T}$ to find the corresponding j, W_a values. Moreover, we store only 64 bits of each H_a value in $\mathcal{H}$ rather than the entire value. (This has only a small impact on the false-positive rate.) We store $\mathcal{H}$ in memory, but can store $\mathcal{T}$ on disk since it will be accessed only $O(1)$ times during the course of the attack.
2. We implement the hash table $\mathcal{H}$ using the "power of two choices" scheme [34]. In this construction, every element is mapped to two random buckets (each capable of holding eight 64-bit strings); an element is inserted in the bucket with lower occupancy, and lookups simply access both buckets. To further reduce the cost of memory accesses, we modified the way hashing is done to make sure that elements are always mapped to buckets within 16 kB of each other in memory. In this way, both buckets for a given element will likely lie on the same page of memory, in which case both will be brought into the CPU cache when the memory access for the first bucket is made. This reduces the overall number of cache misses.

Verifying the Attack Complexity. We implemented our attack (with the above optimizations) to verify its correctness and complexity. We ran the attack with label lengths $k \in \{40, 48\}$ and number of gates C ranging from 2^{20}–2^{28} until the true value R was found; the attack was run 100 times for each set of parameters. We found that the average number of false positives (which cause lookups in $\mathcal{T}$ and invocations of the Check routine) was less than 5 in all cases. We plot the number of π-queries and the bound of $2^{k+1}/C$ given by our analysis in Fig. 3a; our analysis is always within a factor of 2–3× of the experimental results. We believe our use of a hash table (which can cause additional false positives) partially contributes to the additional overhead.

Real-World Running Time and Cost. We estimate time and cost of implementing our attack when $k = 80$ and $C = 2^{30}$. For the purposes of this estimate, we assume customized preemptive instances with one Skylake CPU and 9 GB memory, each of which can be rented for \$13.17/month on the Google Cloud

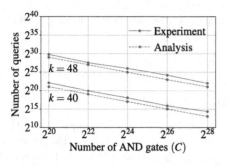
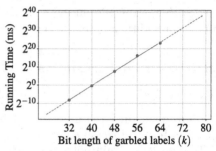

(a) Number of π-queries needed for the attack as a function of the circuit size C for two different label lengths ($k = 40, 48$), on a log-log scale.

(b) Running time of the attack (in milliseconds) as a function of the label length k, on a log-log scale.

Fig. 3. Complexity of our attack.

Platform as of 2019. By extrapolating experimental results for smaller values of k (see Fig. 3b), we find that we can approximate the running time T of the attack (in milliseconds) as a function of k by the equation $T(k) = 2^{0.989k-39.8}$. For $k = 80$, this gives $T = 2^{39.3}$ ms or 267 machine-months. Such an attack would cost about \$3500 to carry out. Since our attack can be fully parallelized, the wall-clock time can be made arbitrarily small using multiple instances, without increasing the cost. For example, using 267 instances the attack would finish in about a month.

4   Better Concrete Security for the Half-Gates Scheme

The attack in the previous section does not exploit any weakness in the half-gates scheme *per se*, but rather exploits a weakness in the way the underlying hash function is implemented. Building on the work of Guo et al. [18], we introduce here a security notion for hash functions called *multi-instance tweakable circular correlation robustness* (miTCCR) and show that this is an appropriate definition for analyzing the concrete security of the half-gates scheme.

4.1   Multi-instance TCCR

Our definition of miTCCR differs from the related notion formalized by Guo et al. in two respects. First, we consider an attacker who is given access to *multiple* (independently keyed) functions, rather than just one. Second, we explicitly allow the concrete security bound to depend on the maximum number of times μ an attacker repeats any particular tweak.

Given a function $H : \mathcal{W} \times \mathcal{T} \to \mathcal{W}$ (that depends on an ideal cipher E), define $\mathcal{O}_R^{\mathsf{miTCCR}}(w, i, b) \stackrel{\text{def}}{=} H(w \oplus R, i) \oplus b \cdot R$. Let $\mathsf{Func}_{\mathcal{W} \times \mathcal{T} \times \{0,1\}, \mathcal{W}}$ denote the set of functions from $\mathcal{W} \times \mathcal{T} \times \{0, 1\}$ to $\mathcal{W}$.

Definition 3. *Given a function* $H^E : \mathcal{W} \times \mathcal{T} \to \mathcal{W}$, *a distribution* $\mathcal{R}$ *on* $\mathcal{W}$, *and a distinguisher* D, *define*

$$\mathbf{Adv}_{H,\mathcal{R}}^{\mathsf{miTCCR}}(D, u, \mu) \stackrel{\text{def}}{=} \left| \Pr_{R_1,\dots,R_u \leftarrow \mathcal{R}} \left[D^{E, \mathcal{O}_{R_1}^{\mathsf{miTCCR}}(\cdot),\dots,\mathcal{O}_{R_u}^{\mathsf{miTCCR}}(\cdot)} = 1 \right] \right.$$
$$\left. - \Pr_{f_1,\dots,f_u \leftarrow \mathsf{Func}_{\mathcal{W} \times \mathcal{T} \times \{0,1\}, \mathcal{W}}} \left[D^{E, f_1(\cdot),\dots,f_u(\cdot)} = 1 \right] \right|,$$

where both probabilities are also over choice of E *and we require that*

1. D *never queries both* $(w, i, 0)$ *and* $(w, i, 1)$ *to the same oracle (for any* w, i).
2. *For all* $i \in \mathcal{T}$, *the number of queries (across all oracles) of the form* $(\star, i, \star)$ *is at most* μ.

We say H *is* $(p, q, u, \mu, \rho, \varepsilon)$*-miTCCR, if for all distinguishers* D *making at most* p *queries to* E *and at most* q *queries (in total) to its other oracles, and all distributions* $\mathcal{R}$ *with min-entropy at least* ρ, *we have* $\mathbf{Adv}_{H,\mathcal{R}}^{\mathsf{miTCCR}}(D, u, \mu) \leq \varepsilon$.

We recover the definition from Guo et al. if we set $u = 1$ and $\mu = |\mathcal{T}|$.

The concrete security of the half-gates scheme is directly related to the concrete security (in the sense of miTCCR) of the underlying hash function used.

Theorem 1. *Let* H *be* $(p, 2C, u, u, k-1, \varepsilon)$*-miTCCR. Then the garbling scheme* $\mathsf{HalfGates}^H$ *is* (p, u, C, ε)*-private.*

A proof of the above follows along the same lines as the proof of the more general result we show later (cf. Theorem 3), so we omit it.

The challenge is thus to design a hash function with good concrete security in the sense of miTCCR. We remark that, as one might expect, a random oracle is one such candidate; see Appendix B. However, as discussed extensively by Guo et al. [18], it is not trivial to use a random oracle when implementing the half-gates scheme: there is a significant performance penalty when instantiating H using a cryptographic hash function like SHA-256 or SHA-3 (see also Table 1), and indifferentiable constructions of a random oracle from an ideal cipher E that are both efficient and have good concrete security are not known. (In particular, work of Gauravaram et al. [16] shows a construction using two calls to E with birthday-bound security; the construction we show in the next section is both more efficient and has better concrete security in the sense of miTCCR.)

4.2 Designing a Hash Function with Better Concrete Security

We construct (from an ideal cipher $E : \{0,1\}^L \times \{0,1\}^L \to \{0,1\}^L$) a hash function with good concrete security in the sense of miTCCR. Specifically, define $\widehat{\mathsf{MMO}}^E : \{0,1\}^L \times \{0,1\}^L \to \{0,1\}^L$ as

$$\widehat{\mathsf{MMO}}^E(x, i) \stackrel{\text{def}}{=} E(i, \sigma(x)) \oplus \sigma(x),$$

where σ is a linear orthomorphism. (We say $\sigma : \{0,1\}^L \to \{0,1\}^L$ is *linear* if $\sigma(x \oplus y) = \sigma(x) \oplus \sigma(y)$ for all $x, y \in \{0,1\}^L$. It is an *orthomorphism* if it is a permutation, and the function σ' given by $\sigma'(x) \overset{\text{def}}{=} \sigma(x) \oplus x$ is also a permutation.) As shown by Guo et al. [18], σ can be efficiently instantiated as $\sigma(x_L \| x_R) = x_R \oplus x_L \| x_L$ where x_L and x_R are the left and right halves of the input, respectively; in assembly code, this becomes $\sigma(x) = $ _mm_shuffle_epi32(x, 78)$\oplus$and_si128(x, mask), where $\mathtt{mask} = 1^{64}\|0^{64}$. We have:

Theorem 2. *If σ is a linear orthomorphism and E is modeled as an ideal cipher, then* $\widehat{\mathrm{MMO}}^E$ *is* $(p,q,u,\mu,\rho,\varepsilon)$*-miTCCR, where*

$$\varepsilon = \frac{2\mu p}{2^\rho} + \frac{(\mu-1)\cdot q}{2^\rho}.$$

Proof. Our proof uses the H-coefficient technique [10,36], which we review in Appendix D (specialized for our proof). Fix a deterministic distinguisher D making queries to $u+1$ oracles. The first is the ideal cipher (and its inverse); in the real world, the remaining oracles are of the form

$$\mathcal{O}_R^{\mathsf{miTCCR}}(w,i,b) = \widehat{\mathrm{MMO}}^E(R \oplus w, i) \oplus bR = E(i, \sigma(R \oplus w)) \oplus \sigma(R \oplus w) \oplus bR$$

(for u independent keys $R_1, \ldots, R_u$ sampled from $\mathcal{R}$), but in the ideal world they are u independent random functions from $\{0,1\}^{2L+1}$ to $\{0,1\}^L$. Following the notation from Appendix D, denote the transcript of D's interaction by $\mathcal{Q} = (\mathcal{Q}_E, \mathcal{Q}_\mathcal{O}, \mathbf{R})$. We only consider attainable transcripts. For $i \in \{0,1\}^L$ define $\mathcal{Q}_E[i] \overset{\text{def}}{=} \{(x,y) : (i,x,y) \in \mathcal{Q}_E\}$. Clearly, $\sum_{i \in \{0,1\}^L} |\mathcal{Q}_E[i]| = |\mathcal{Q}_E| = p$.

We say a transcript $(\mathcal{Q}_E, \mathcal{Q}_\mathcal{O}, \mathbf{R})$ is *bad* if:

- (B-1) There is a query $(\mathsf{idx}, w, i, b, z) \in \mathcal{Q}_\mathcal{O}$ and a query of the form $(i, \sigma(R_{\mathsf{idx}} \oplus w), \star)$ or of the form $(i, \star, \sigma(R_{\mathsf{idx}} \oplus w) \oplus b \cdot R_{\mathsf{idx}} \oplus z)$ in $\mathcal{Q}_E$.
- (B-2) There are distinct queries $(\mathsf{idx}, w, i, b, z)$, $(\mathsf{idx}', w', i, b', z') \in \mathcal{Q}_\mathcal{O}$ using the same "tweak" i such that $\sigma(R_{\mathsf{idx}} \oplus w) = \sigma(R_{\mathsf{idx}'} \oplus w')$ or $\sigma(R_{\mathsf{idx}} \oplus w) \oplus b \cdot R_{\mathsf{idx}} \oplus z = \sigma(R_{\mathsf{idx}'} \oplus w') \oplus b' \cdot R_{\mathsf{idx}'} \oplus z'$.

We bound the probabilities of the above events in the ideal world. Consider (B-1). Imagine that first all the oracles are chosen (which defines $\mathcal{Q}_E, \mathcal{Q}_\mathcal{O}$) and then the keys $\mathcal{R}$ are chosen. Fix some $(\mathsf{idx}, w, i, b, z) \in \mathcal{Q}_\mathcal{O}$. It is immediate that

$$\Pr[(i, R_{\mathsf{idx}} \oplus w, \star) \in \mathcal{Q}_E] \leq \frac{|\mathcal{Q}_E[i]|}{2^\rho}$$

since the min-entropy of $\mathcal{R}$ is ρ. Moreover,

$$\Pr[(i, \star, \sigma(R_{\mathsf{idx}} \oplus w) \oplus bR_{\mathsf{idx}} \oplus z) \in \mathcal{Q}_E] = \Pr[(i, \star, \sigma(R_{\mathsf{idx}}) \oplus \sigma(w) \oplus bR_{\mathsf{idx}} \oplus z) \in \mathcal{Q}_E],$$

by linearity of σ. Now, note that:

- When $b = 0$, the above probability is at most $|\mathcal{Q}_E[i]| \cdot 2^{-\rho}$ since σ is a permutation and the min-entropy of $\mathcal{R}$ is ρ.

– When $b = 1$, the above probability is also at most $|\mathcal{Q}_E[i]| \cdot 2^{-\rho}$ since σ is an orthomorphism and the min-entropy of $\mathcal{R}$ is ρ.

Therefore,

$$
\Pr[(\text{B-1})] \leq \sum_{(\text{idx},w,i,b,z) \in \mathcal{Q}_\mathcal{O}} \frac{2 \cdot |\mathcal{Q}_E[i]|}{2^\rho}
$$

$$
= \sum_{i \in \{0,1\}^L} \underbrace{\sum_{(\text{idx},w,i,b,z) \in \mathcal{Q}_\mathcal{O}} \frac{2 \cdot |\mathcal{Q}_E[i]|}{2^\rho}}_{\leq \mu}
$$

$$
\leq \mu \cdot \sum_{i \in \{0,1\}^L} \frac{2 \cdot |\mathcal{Q}_E[i]|}{2^\rho} = \frac{2\mu p}{2^\rho}.
$$

We next consider (B-2). For fixed $i \in \{0,1\}^L$, consider a pair of distinct queries (idx, w, i, b, z), $(\text{idx}', w', i, b', z') \in \mathcal{Q}_\mathcal{O}$. If $\text{idx} \neq \text{idx}'$, we have

$$
\Pr\left[\sigma(R_{\text{idx}} \oplus w) = \sigma(R_{\text{idx}'} \oplus w')\right] \leq \frac{1}{2^\rho}
$$

and

$$
\Pr[\sigma(R_{\text{idx}} \oplus w) \oplus b R_{\text{idx}} \oplus z = \sigma(R_{\text{idx}'} \oplus w') \oplus b' R_{\text{idx}'} \oplus z'] \leq \frac{1}{2^\rho}
$$

as in the discussion of (B-1). If $\text{idx} = \text{idx}'$, then $\sigma(R_{\text{idx}} \oplus w) = \sigma(R_{\text{idx}'} \oplus w') \Rightarrow w = w'$ is not possible. Furthermore, with $b'' = b \oplus b'$,

$$
\Pr[\sigma(R_{\text{idx}} \oplus w) \oplus b R_{\text{idx}} \oplus z = \sigma(R_{\text{idx}'} \oplus w') \oplus b' R_{\text{idx}'} \oplus z'] \tag{3}
$$

$$
= \Pr[\sigma(w) \oplus z = \sigma(w') \oplus z' \oplus b'' R_{\text{idx}}] = \frac{1}{2^L} \leq \frac{1}{2^\rho}, \tag{4}
$$

using the fact that $z, z' \in \{0,1\}^L$ are uniform and independent. Thus, for any pair of queries in $\mathcal{Q}_\mathcal{O}$, the probability that (B-2) holds is at most $2/2^\rho$. If we let $C_i \leq \mu$ denote the number of queries in $\mathcal{Q}_\mathcal{O}$ using tweak i, then

$$
\Pr[(\text{B-2})] \leq \sum_{i \in \{0,1\}^L} \binom{C_i}{2} \cdot \frac{2}{2^\rho} \leq (\mu - 1) \sum_{i \in \{0,1\}^L} \frac{C_i}{2^\rho} \leq \frac{(\mu - 1) \cdot q}{2^\rho}.
$$

Summarizing, the probability of a bad transcript in the ideal world is at most $\frac{2\mu p}{2^\rho} + \frac{(\mu-1) \cdot q}{2^\rho}$.

Fix a good transcript $\mathcal{Q} = (\mathcal{Q}_E, \mathcal{Q}_\mathcal{O}, \mathbf{R})$. The probability that the ideal world is consistent with this transcript is given by Eq. (7). The probability that the real world is consistent with this transcript is

$$
\frac{\Pr[\forall (\text{idx}, w, i, b, z) \in \mathcal{Q}_\mathcal{O} : \mathcal{O}_{R_{\text{idx}}}^{\text{miTCCR}}(w, i, b) = z \mid E \vdash \mathcal{Q}_E]}{\prod_{v \in \{0,1\}^L} (2^L)_{|\mathcal{Q}_E[v]|}} \cdot \Pr_\mathcal{R}[\mathbf{R}].
$$

We can express the numerator of the above as

$$\prod_{j=1}^{q} \Pr[\mathcal{O}_{R_{\mathsf{idx}_j}}^{\mathsf{miTCCR}}(w_j, i_j, b_j) = z_j \mid E \vdash \mathcal{Q}_E \wedge \forall \ell < j : \mathcal{O}_{R_{\mathsf{idx}_\ell}}^{\mathsf{miTCCR}}(w_\ell, i_\ell, b_\ell) = z_\ell].$$

Note that $\mathcal{O}_{R_{\mathsf{idx}_j}}^{\mathsf{miTCCR}}(w_j, i_j, b_j) = z_j$ iff $\widehat{\mathsf{MMO}}^E(R_{\mathsf{idx}_j} \oplus w_j, i_j) \oplus b_j R_{\mathsf{idx}_j} = z_j$, i.e.,

$$E\big(i_j, \sigma(R_{\mathsf{idx}_j} \oplus w_j)\big) = \sigma(R_{\mathsf{idx}_j} \oplus w_j) \oplus b_j R_{\mathsf{idx}_j} \oplus z_j.$$

Since the transcript is good, there is no query of the form $(i_j, \sigma(R_{\mathsf{idx}_j} \oplus w_j), \star)$ in $\mathcal{Q}_E$ (since (B-1) does not occur), nor is $E(i_j, \sigma(R_{\mathsf{idx}_j} \oplus w_j))$ determined by the fact that $\mathcal{O}_{R_{\mathsf{idx}_\ell}}^{\mathsf{miTCCR}}(w_\ell, i_\ell, b_\ell) = z_\ell$ for all $\ell < j$ (since (B-2) does not occur). Similarly, there is no query of the form $(i_j, \star, \sigma(R_{\mathsf{idx}_j} \oplus w_j) \oplus b_j R_{\mathsf{idx}_j} \oplus z_j)$ in $\mathcal{Q}_E$ (since (B-1) does not occur), nor is $E^{-1}(i_j, \sigma(R_{\mathsf{idx}_j} \oplus w_j) \oplus b_j R_{\mathsf{idx}_j} \oplus z_j)$ determined by the fact that $\mathcal{O}_{R_{\mathsf{idx}_\ell}}^{\mathsf{miTCCR}}(w_\ell, i_\ell, b_\ell) = z_\ell$ for all $\ell < j$ (since (B-2) does not occur). Thus, for all j we have

$$\Pr[\mathcal{O}_{R_{\mathsf{idx}_j}}^{\mathsf{miTCCR}}(w_j, i_j, b_j) = z_j \mid E \vdash \mathcal{Q}_E \wedge \forall \ell < j : \mathcal{O}_{R_{\mathsf{idx}_\ell}}^{\mathsf{miTCCR}}(w_\ell, i_\ell, b_\ell) = z_\ell] \geq 1/2^L.$$

It follows that

$$\Pr[\forall(\mathsf{idx}, w, i, b, z) \in \mathcal{Q}_{\mathcal{O}} : \mathcal{O}_{R_{\mathsf{idx}}}^{\mathsf{miTCCR}}(w, i, b) = z \mid E \vdash \mathcal{Q}_E] \geq 1/2^{Lq},$$

and so the probability that the real world is consistent with the transcript is at least the probability that the ideal world is consistent with the transcript. This completes the proof.

Using Shorter Wire Labels. Our construction above gives a hash function $H : \{0,1\}^L \times \{0,1\}^L \to \{0,1\}^L$, where L is the block length and key length of the underlying cipher E. In some applications of the half-gates scheme, one may prefer using wire labels of length $k < L$. This is easily done by defining $H' : \{0,1\}^k \times \{0,1\}^L \to \{0,1\}^k$ as

$$H'(x, i) = [H(x\|0^{L-k}, i)]_k,$$

where $[z]_k$ denotes the k least-significant bits of z. It is not hard to see that if H is $(p, q, u, \mu, \rho, \varepsilon)$-miTCCR then so is H'. (Of course, for H' it must be the case that $\rho \leq k$.)

Putting Everything Together. Say $\widehat{\mathsf{MMO}}^E$ is used in the half-gates scheme with k-bit wire labels (as discussed above). Theorems 1 and 2 then imply that the resulting garbling scheme is (p, u, C, ε)-private with

$$\varepsilon = \frac{u \cdot p + (u-1) \cdot C}{2^{k-2}}.$$

Taking $u = 1$ (i.e., looking at the single-instance setting), we have $\varepsilon = p/2^{k-2}$, which is independent of the circuit size C and optimal up to a (small) constant. When $u > 1$, however, security degrades linearly in u; since u can be $\Theta(C)$, the security bound can be as bad as $O((pC + C^2)/2^k)$ in the multi-instance setting. We show in the next section how to rectify this.

5   Achieving Better Multi-instance Security

As discussed at the end of the previous section, our new hash function gives an optimal concrete-security bound for the half-gates scheme in the single-instance setting. In the multi-instance setting, however, the security bound degrades as the number of instances increases.

Looking at our construction and the proof of miTCCR security (Theorem 2), we observe that the fundamental reason for the poor security bound in the multi-instance case is that μ (namely, the number of times a given "tweak" may be re-used; cf. Definition 3) can be as large as u (the number of circuits being garbled). Tracing back to the half-gates scheme, we see that this is because the scheme always assigns sequential gate identifiers (gids) starting at 1 to the AND gates in a circuit, and so in particular each circuit that is garbled will at least use the "tweak" $i = 1$. We fix this issue by modifying the scheme so that it instead numbers the gates sequentially *beginning at a random starting point* determined by the garbler (and sent to the evaluator along with the garbled circuit). That is, the only changes with respect to Fig. 1 are that (1) in Garble, the initial value of gid is a uniform L-bit string, and (2) the initial value of gid is included in GC. We denote the modified scheme by $\widehat{\mathsf{HalfGates}}$. To analyze the resulting construction, we start with the following lemma.

Lemma 1. *Fix integers L, q, an integer $u \leq q$, and a sequence of positive integers $(q_1, \ldots, q_u)$ with $\sum_i q_i = q$. Consider the following experiment involving a set of 2^L bins and q balls: for each $i \in [u]$, q_i balls are placed in consecutive bins (wrapping around modulo 2^L), where the initial bin is uniform. If μ^* is the random variable denoting the maximum number of balls in any bin, then*

$$\Pr[\mu^* > \mu] \leq \frac{q^{\mu+1}}{(\mu+1)! \cdot 2^{\mu L}} .$$

Proof. Consider some μ sequences of balls, i.e., the i_1th, $\ldots$, i_μth, and consider the event that there is a $k \in \{0,1\}^L$ such that every one of those sequences hits the kth bin. It can be seen that the probability is

$$2^L \times \frac{q_{i_1}}{2^L} \times \cdots \times \frac{q_{i_\mu}}{2^L} = \frac{q_{i_1} \times \cdots \times q_{i_\mu}}{2^{L \cdot (\mu-1)}}.$$

Since μ^* is the maximum number of balls in any of the 2^L bins, we have

$$\Pr[\mu^* \geq \mu] \leq \sum_{0 < i_1 < i_2 < \cdots < i_\mu \leq u} \frac{q_{i_1} \times \cdots \times q_{i_\mu}}{2^{L \cdot (\mu-1)}}$$

Observing that

$$(q_1 + q_2 + \cdots + q_u)^\mu \geq \sum_{i_1 \neq i_2 \neq \cdots \neq i_\mu} q_{i_1} \times \cdots \times q_{i_\mu}$$

$$= \mu! \cdot \sum_{i_1 < i_2 < \cdots < i_\mu} q_{i_1} \times \cdots \times q_{i_\mu},$$

we have

$$\sum_{i_1 < i_2 < \cdots < i_\mu} q_{i_1} \times \cdots \times q_{i_\mu} \le \frac{(q_1 + q_2 + \cdots + q_u)^\mu}{\mu!}.$$

Therefore,

$$\Pr[\mu^* > \mu] = \Pr[\mu^* \ge \mu + 1] \le \frac{1}{2^{L \cdot \mu}} \times \frac{(q_1 + \cdots + q_u)^{\mu+1}}{(\mu + 1)!} = \frac{q^{\mu+1}}{(\mu + 1)! \cdot 2^{L \cdot \mu}}.$$

This complete the proof. $\qquad\square$

With the above in place, we now prove:

Theorem 3. *Let H be $(p, 2C, u, \mu, k - 1, \varepsilon)$-miTCCR. Then the garbling scheme* $\widehat{\mathsf{HalfGates}}^H$ *is (p, u, C, ε')-private, where*

$$\varepsilon' \le \varepsilon + \frac{(2C)^{\mu+1}}{(\mu + 1)! \cdot 2^{\mu L}}.$$

Proof. We describe a simulator Sim_1 that takes as input a circuit f and an output y, and generates a simulated garbled circuit, input-wire labels, and the decoding table. See below for details.

```
function Sim₁(f, y)                          function SimAnd₁(W_a^0, W_b^0, gid)
    gid* ← {0,1}^L, gid := gid*                  j := 2 × gid, j' := 2 × gid + 1
    Rand ← Func_{0,1}^{k+L+1,{0,1}^k}            p_a := lsb(W_a^0), p_b := lsb(W_b^0)
    for i ∈ Inputs(f) do                         T_G := H(W_a^0, j) ⊕ Rand(W_a^0, j, p_b)
        W_i^0 ← {0,1}^k                          T_E := H(W_b^0, j') ⊕ Rand(W_b^0, j', 0) ⊕ W_a^0
    for (a, b, c, T) ∈ Gates(f) do               W_G^0 := H(W_a^0, j) ⊕ p_a T_G
        if T = XOR then                          W_E^0 := H(W_b^0, j') ⊕ p_b(T_E ⊕ W_a^0)
            W_c^0 := W_a^0 ⊕ W_b^0               W_c^0 := W_G^0 ⊕ W_E^0
        else                                     return ((T_G, T_E), W_c^0)
            (GC[gid], W_c^0) := SimAnd₁(W_a^0, W_b^0, gid)
            gid := gid + 1
    for i ∈ Outputs(f) do
        d_i := lsb(W_i^0) ⊕ y_i
    return ((gid*, GC), {W_i^0}_{i∈Inputs}, d)
```

Fix some $\{(f^i, x^i)\}_{i \in [u]}$. We now show indistinguishability between the two distributions in Definition 2. To do so, we consider a sequence of hybrid distributions.

Ideal. Here, we run $\mathsf{Sim}_1(f^i, f^i(x^i))$ for $i \in [u]$.

Hybrid₂. Here, we run $\mathsf{Sim}_2(f^i, x^i)$ for $i \in [u]$, where Sim_2 is defined below. Intuitively, the description of Sim_1 is from the perspective of the garbler (who knows the $\{W_i^0\}$), while that of Sim_2 is from the perspective of the evaluator (who knows the $\{W_i^{v_i}\}$ only); the distribution of the outputs remains the same.

---

function $\mathsf{Sim}_2(f, x)$
  $\mathsf{gid}^* \leftarrow \{0,1\}^L$, $\mathsf{gid} := \mathsf{gid}^*$
  $\mathsf{Rand} \leftarrow \mathsf{Func}_{\{0,1\}^{k+L+1}, \{0,1\}^k}$
  Evaluate $f(x)$ and get all wire values v_i
  for $i \in \mathsf{Inputs}(f)$ **do**
    $W_i^{v_i} \leftarrow \{0,1\}^k$
  for $(a, b, c, T) \in \mathsf{Gates}(f)$ **do**
    if $T = \mathsf{XOR}$ **then**
      $W_c^{v_c} := W_a^{v_a} \oplus W_b^{v_b}$
    else
      $(\mathsf{GC}[\mathsf{gid}], W_c^{v_c}) := \mathsf{SimAnd}_2(W_a^{v_a}, W_b^{v_b}, \mathsf{gid})$
      $\mathsf{gid} := \mathsf{gid} + 1$
  for $i \in \mathsf{Outputs}(f)$ **do**
    $d_i := \mathsf{lsb}(W_i^{v_i}) \oplus v_i$
  return $((\mathsf{gid}^*, \mathsf{GC}), \{W_i^{v_i}\}_{i \in \mathsf{Inputs}}, d)$

function $\mathsf{SimAnd}_2(W_a^{v_a}, W_b^{v_b}, \mathsf{gid})$
  $j := 2 \times \mathsf{gid}$, $j' := 2 \times \mathsf{gid} + 1$
  $s_a := \mathsf{lsb}(W_a^{v_a})$, $s_b := \mathsf{lsb}(W_b^{v_b})$
  $T_G := H(W_a^{v_a}, j) \oplus \mathsf{Rand}(W_a^{v_a}, j, v_b \oplus s_b)$
  $T_E := H(W_b^{v_b}, j') \oplus \mathsf{Rand}(W_b^{v_b}, j', v_a) \oplus W_a^{v_a}$
  $W_G^{v_a(v_b \oplus s_b)} := H(W_a^{v_a}, j) \oplus s_a T_G$
  $W_E^{v_a s_b} := H(W_b^{v_b}, j') \oplus s_b(T_E \oplus W_a^{v_a})$
  $W_c^{v_a v_b} := W_G^{v_a(v_b \oplus s_b)} \oplus W_E^{v_a s_b}$
  return $((T_G, T_E), W_c^{v_a v_b})$

We claim that distribution **Hybrid$_2$** is identical to distribution **Ideal**. This is because the values $((\mathsf{gid}^*, \mathsf{GC}), \{W_i^0\}_{i \in \mathsf{Inputs}})$ in **Hybrid$_1$** and the corresponding values $((\mathsf{gid}^*, \mathsf{GC}), \{W_i^{v_i}\}_{i \in \mathsf{Inputs}})$ in **Ideal** are all uniform, and in both distributions we have

$$d^i = \mathsf{lsb}(\mathsf{Eval}((\mathsf{gid}^*, \mathsf{GC}^i), \{W_j^i\}_{j \in \mathsf{Inputs}})) \oplus f^i(x^i),$$

where we slightly abuse notation and let $\mathsf{lsb}(W_1, \ldots, W_n) = \mathsf{lsb}(W_1), \ldots, \mathsf{lsb}(W_n)$.

Hybrid$_3$. Here, we run $\mathsf{Sim}_3(f^i, x^i)$ for $i \in [u]$, where Sim_3 is defined below. Sim_3 is the same as Sim_2 except that it uses oracles $\mathcal{O}_R^{\mathsf{miTCCR}}$ in place of the random function Rand, and it computes values $\{W^{\bar{v}}\}$ that do not affect the output.

---

function $\mathsf{Sim}_3(f, x)$
  $\mathsf{gid}^* \leftarrow \{0,1\}^L$, $\mathsf{gid} := \mathsf{gid}^*$
  $R \leftarrow \{0,1\}^{k-1} \| 1$
  Evaluate $f(x)$ and get all wire values v_i
  for $i \in \mathsf{Inputs}(f)$ **do**
    $W_i^{v_i} \leftarrow \{0,1\}^k$
    $W_i^{\bar{v}_i} := W_i^{v_i} \oplus R$
  for $(a, b, c, T) \in \mathsf{Gates}(f)$ **do**
    if $T = \mathsf{XOR}$ **then**
      $W_c^{v_c} := W_a^{v_a} \oplus W_b^{v_b}$
    else
      $(\mathsf{GC}[\mathsf{gid}], W_c^{v_c}) := \mathsf{SimAnd}_3(W_a^{v_a}, W_b^{v_b}, \mathsf{gid})$
      $\mathsf{gid} := \mathsf{gid} + 1$
  for $i \in \mathsf{Outputs}(f)$ **do**
    $d_i := \mathsf{lsb}(W_i^{v_i}) \oplus v_i$
  return $((\mathsf{gid}^*, \mathsf{GC}), \{W_i^{v_i}\}_{i \in \mathsf{Inputs}}, d)$

function $\mathsf{SimAnd}_3(W_a^{v_a}, W_b^{v_b}, \mathsf{gid})$
  $j := 2 \times \mathsf{gid}$, $j' := 2 \times \mathsf{gid} + 1$
  $s_a := \mathsf{lsb}(W_a^{v_a})$, $s_b := \mathsf{lsb}(W_b^{v_b})$
  $T_G := H(W_a^{v_a}, j) \oplus \mathcal{O}_R^{\mathsf{miTCCR}}(W_a^{v_a}, j, v_b \oplus s_b)$
  $T_E := H(W_b^{v_b}, j') \oplus \mathcal{O}_R^{\mathsf{miTCCR}}(W_b^{v_b}, j', v_a) \oplus W_a^{v_a}$
  $W_G^{v_a(v_b \oplus s_b)} := H(W_a^{v_a}, j) \oplus s_a T_G$
  $W_E^{v_a s_b} := H(W_b^{v_b}, j') \oplus s_b(T_E \oplus W_a^{v_a})$
  $W_c^{v_a v_b} := W_G^{v_a(v_b \oplus s_b)} \oplus W_E^{v_a s_b}$
  return $((T_G, T_E), W_c^{v_a v_b})$

Let μ^* denote the maximum frequency of any tweak used as the input to $\mathcal{O}_R$, across all u executions of Sim_3. We claim that no distinguisher D making at most p queries to E can distinguish between **Hybrid$_2$** and **Hybrid$_3$** with probability better than $\varepsilon + \Pr[\mu^* > \mu]$. Indeed, we can easily reduce any such distinguisher to a distinguisher against H (in the sense of miTCCR) that respects the bound μ on the number of times a tweak may be repeated so long as $\mu^* \leq \mu$. Note further that Lemma 1 implies $\Pr[\mu^* > \mu] \leq \frac{(2C)^{\mu+1}}{(\mu+1)! \times 2^{\mu L}}$.

Hybrid$_4$. Here, we run $\mathsf{Sim}_4(f^i, x^i)$ for $i \in [u]$, where Sim_4 is defined below. Sim_4 is identical to Sim_3 except that v_i is always set to 0 and $\mathcal{O}_R^{\mathsf{miTCCR}}(x, i, b)$ is expanded to $H(x \oplus R, i) \oplus bR$. It is immediate that distributions **Hybrid$_3$** and **Hybrid$_4$** are identical.

```
function Sim₄(f, x)                                function SimAnd₄(W_a^0, W_b^0, R, gid)
    gid* ← {0,1}^L, gid := gid*                        j := 2 × gid, j' := 2 × gid + 1
    R ← {0,1}^{k-1}‖1                                   p_a := lsb(W_a^0), p_b := lsb(W_b^0)
    for i ∈ Inputs(f) do                               T_G := H(W_a^0, j) ⊕ H(W_a^1, j) ⊕ p_b R
        W_i^0 ← {0,1}^k                                 T_E := H(W_b^0, j') ⊕ H(W_b^1, j') ⊕ W_a^0
        W_i^1 := W_i^0 ⊕ R                              W_G^0 := H(W_a^0, j) ⊕ p_a T_G
    for (a, b, c, T) ∈ Gates(f) do                     W_E^0 := H(W_b^0, j') ⊕ p_b(T_E ⊕ W_a^0)
        if T = XOR then                                W_c^0 := W_G^0 ⊕ W_E^0
            W_c^0 := W_a^0 ⊕ W_b^0                      return ((T_G, T_E), W_c^0)
        else
            (GC[gid], W_c^0) := SimAnd₃(W_a^0, W_b^0, R, gid)
            gid := gid + 1
    for i ∈ Outputs(f) do
        d_i := lsb(W_i^0)
    return ((gid*, GC), {W_i^{x_i}}_{i∈Inputs}, d)
```

One may observe that **Hybrid$_4$** is identical to the real-world distribution that is obtained by running $\widehat{\mathsf{HalfGates}}^H(f^i)$ and then including the input-wire labels corresponding to x^i. This completes the proof. $\qquad\square$

6   Concrete Security and Efficiency

Using Theorems 2 and 3 we see that when we instantiate $\widehat{\mathsf{HalfGates}}$ with $\widehat{\mathsf{MMO}}^E$, the overall garbling scheme is (p, u, C, ε)-private, with

$$\varepsilon = \frac{\mu p + (\mu - 1) \cdot C}{2^{k-2}} + \frac{(2C)^{\mu+1}}{(\mu+1)! \times 2^{\mu L}}. \tag{5}$$

Above, $k \le L$ denotes the length of the wire labels and is chosen as part of the implementation, while μ is a free parameter that can be set to optimize the bound. The expression above can be separated into two terms: a term $\mu p / 2^{k-2}$ that represents the computational security (as it depends on the query complexity p of the attacker) and a term $\frac{(\mu-1)\cdot C}{2^{k-2}} + \frac{(2C)^{\mu+1}}{(\mu+1)! \times 2^{\mu L}}$ that corresponds to statistical security. To illustrate, we consider two particular options assuming $L = 128$ (to match the case where AES-128 is the cipher E):

1. $k = 80$, $C \le 2^{43.5}$. The overall security bound here is optimized when $\mu = 1$, in which case

$$\varepsilon = \frac{p}{2^{78}} + \frac{2C^2}{2^{128}} \le \frac{p}{2^{78}} + 2^{-40}.$$

   I.e., this gives 78-bit computational security and 40-bit statistical security.

Table 1. Performance of different hash functions in the half-gates scheme.
"NI support" indicates whether the implementation utilizes hardware-level instructions
(i.e., AES-NI or SHA-NI), k, is the length of the wire labels, and "comp. sec." refers to
the computational security bound assuming $C < 2^{40}$. Reported rates are in 10^6 AND
gates per second.

Hash function	NI support?	k	Comp. sec. (bits)	100 Mbps	2 Gbps	Localhost
Zahur et al.	Y	128	89	0.4	7.8	23
SHA-3	N	128	125	0.27	0.27	0.28
SHA-256	N	128	125	0.4	1.1	1.2
SHA-256	Y	128	125	0.4	2.1	2.5
$\widehat{MMO}^E$	Y	128	125	0.4	7.8	15
$\widehat{MMO}^E$	Y	88	86	0.63	12	15

2. $k = 128$, $C \le 2^{61}$. Now the overall security bound is maximized when $\mu = 2$,
in which case

$$\varepsilon \le \frac{p}{2^{125}} + \frac{8 \cdot C^3}{3 \times 2^{256}} \le \frac{p}{2^{125}} + 2^{-64}.$$

I.e., this gives 125-bit computational security and 64-bit statistical security.

Optimizations. Compared to the hash function proposed by Zahur et al. [46],
which uses fixed-key AES, evaluation of our hash function involves re-keying
AES each time it is called. In our implementation, we apply the optimizations
introduced by Gueron et al. [17] that allow us to do key scheduling using AES-
NI instructions with pipelining. In our current implementation, we batch two
key-scheduling operations for each gate. In fact, since the AES key being used
to garble a given gate (which depends on the gid) is entirely predictable, we can
batch more than two key-scheduling operations to achieve even better efficiency.
Our optimized implementation will be made publicly available in EMP [43].

Performance. In Table 1 we evaluate the performance of different hash functions in the half-gates scheme. "Zahur et al." refers to using $\widehat{HalfGates}$ with
their proposed hash function; the other rows refer to using $\widehat{HalfGates}$ where we
instantiate the hash function either with $\widehat{MMO}^E$ (using AES-128 as the ideal
cipher E), or with SHA-256 or SHA-3 (as random oracles).

We see that compared to the work of Zahur et al., when using wire labels
of the same length $k = 128$ our scheme achieves better concrete security and
is equally efficient as long as the network bandwidth is below 2 Gbps (so the
network communication is the bottleneck). When the network is faster, the
throughput (i.e., number of gates per second) of our scheme is lower but only by
about 35%. Compared to instantiations using cryptographic hash functions, we
see that garbling using SHA-256 without SHA-NI is up to 13× slower than our
AES-based solution in a fast network; even with SHA-NI, garbling is up to 6×

814   C. Guo et al.

slower. Compared to the instantiation using SHA-3, our AES-based construction is up to 50× faster. For completeness, we also show the running time of our scheme using $k = 88$, which provides roughly the same security as the 128-bit scheme of Zahur et al.. We observe that in this case our scheme is about 1.5× faster in a 2 Gbps network, due to the shorter labels.

Acknowledgments. The authors thank Mike Rosulek for his helpful feedback on the paper. Work of Chun Guo was supported by the Program of Qilu Young Scholars (Grant No. 61580089963177) of Shandong University, the National Natural Science Foundation of China (Grant No. 61602276), and the Shandong Nature Science Foundation of China (Grant No. ZR2016FM22). Work of Jonathan Katz was supported in part by the Office of the Director of National Intelligence (ODNI), Intelligence Advanced Research Projects Activity (IARPA), via 2019-1902070008. The views and conclusions herein are those of the authors and should not be interpreted as necessarily representing the official policies, expressed or implied, of ODNI, IARPA, or the U.S. Government. Work of Yu Yu was supported by the National Natural Science Foundation of China (Grant Nos. 61872236 and 61971192) and the National Cryptography Development Fund (Grant No. MMJJ20170209) and the National Key Research and Development Program of China (Grant No. 2018YFA0704701). Xiao Wang and Yu Yu also thank PlatON for their generous support.

A   (Multi-instance) Obliviousness and Authenticity

We recall definitions of obliviousness and authenticity for garbling schemes, adapted for the multi-instance setting. We then argue that our construction (with small modifications) achieves optimal security bounds for those notions.

A.1   Obliviousness

Obliviousness, informally, requires that $(\mathsf{GC}, \{W_i^{x_i}\})$ reveal nothing about x, including $f(x)$. This is formalized by requiring the existence of a simulator Sim that takes the circuit f and outputs values that are indistinguishable from $(\mathsf{GC}, \{W_i^{x_i}\})$. In the multi-instance setting, we compare the output of Sim to the outputs obtained when independently garbling u circuits.

Definition 4. *Garbling scheme $\mathcal{G}$ is (p, u, C, ε)-oblivious if there is a simulator Sim such that for any distinguisher D making p queries to E and any $\{(f^i, x^i)\}_{i \in [u]}$ with $\sum_i |f^i| = C$, we have*

$$\left| \Pr_{\{(\mathsf{GC}^i, \{W_j^{i,0}, W_j^{i,1}\}, d^i) \leftarrow \mathsf{Garble}^E(f^i)\}_{i \in [u]}} \left[D^E\left(\{(\mathsf{GC}^i, \{W_j^{i,x_j^i}\})\}_{i \in [u]} \right) = 1 \right] \right.$$

$$\left. - \Pr_{\{(\mathsf{GC}^i, \{W_j^i\}) \leftarrow \mathsf{Sim}^E(f^i)\}_{i \in [u]}} \left[D^E\left(\{(\mathsf{GC}^i, \{W_j^i\})\}_{i \in [u]} \right) = 1 \right] \right| \leq \varepsilon,$$

where both probabilities are also over choice of E.

Theorem 4. *Let H be $(p, 2C, u, \mu, k-1, \varepsilon)$-miTCCR. Then the garbling scheme* $\widehat{\mathsf{HalfGates}}^H$ *is (p, u, C, ε')-oblivious, where*

$$\varepsilon' \le \varepsilon + \frac{(2C)^{\mu+1}}{(\mu+1)! \times 2^{\mu L}}.$$

We briefly justify the above bound. Observe that the simulator (for privacy) in the proof of Theorem 3 only uses the output y when computing the decoding information d. The simulator for obliviousness is identical except that it omits that step. The concrete security bound we obtain for obliviousness is thus (at most) the bound we prove for privacy.

A.2 Authenticity

Informally, authenticity requires that an attacker given $(\mathsf{GC}, \{W_i^{x_i}\})$ should be unable to generate output-wire labels that cause the decoding algorithm to produce a valid output other than $f(x)$. In the multi-instance generalization, the adversary succeeds if it can do this for any of u instances.

Definition 5. *Garbling scheme $\mathcal{G}$ is $(p, u, C, m, \varepsilon)$-authentic if for any $\mathcal{A}$ making p queries to E and any $\{(f^i, x^i)\}_{i \in [u]}$ with $\sum_i |f^i| = C$ and $\sum_i m_i = m$, we have*

$$\Pr_{\substack{\{(\mathsf{GC}^i, \{W_j^{i,0}, W_j^{i,1}\}, d^i) \\ \leftarrow \mathsf{Garble}^E(f^i)\}_{i \in [u]}}} \left[\begin{array}{l} \mathcal{A}^E \left(\{(\mathsf{GC}^i, \{W_j^{i,x_j^i}\})\}_{i \in [u]} \right) = (i', \{W_j'\}), \\ \mathsf{Eval}(\mathsf{GC}^{i'}, \{W_j^{i,x_j^i}\}) \ne \{W_j'\} \wedge \mathsf{Decode}(d^{i'}, \{W_j'\}) \ne \bot \end{array} \right] \le \varepsilon,$$

where the probability is also over choice of E.

In order to obtain authenticity, we need to modify $\widehat{\mathsf{HalfGates}}$ slightly. Specifically, the decoding information d_i for the ith output wire will now be

$$(d_i[0], d_i[1]) = (H(W_i^0, \mathsf{gid}), H(W_i^1, \mathsf{gid})).$$

Decoding of a label W_i on the ith output wire involves checking whether $H(W_i, \mathsf{gid})$ is equal to $d_i[0]$ or $d_i[1]$ (and returning $\bot$ if neither holds). We refer to the resulting scheme as $\overline{\mathsf{HalfGates}}$.

Theorem 5. *Let H be $(p, 2C + m, u, \mu, k-1, \varepsilon)$-miTCCR. Then the garbling scheme* $\overline{\mathsf{HalfGates}}^H$ *is $(p, u, C, m, \varepsilon')$-authentic, where*

$$\varepsilon' \le \varepsilon + \frac{(2C+m)^{\mu+1}}{(\mu+1)! \times 2^{\mu L}} + 2^{-k}.$$

Our proof of the above proceeds in two steps: (1) we construct a simulator for the garbling scheme and show that the simulated garbled circuits are indistinguishable from real garbled circuits; (2) we show that the adversary cannot break authenticity for simulated garbled circuits. For (1), the simulator is almost

identical to the privacy simulator we show in the proof of Theorem 3, except that
it chooses uniform $d_i[1] \in \{0,1\}^k$ and sets $d_i = (H(W_i^0, \mathsf{gid}), d_i[1])$ if $y_i = 0$, and
chooses uniform $d_i[0] \in \{0,1\}^k$ and sets $d_i = (d_i[0], H(W_i^0, \mathsf{gid}))$ if $y_i = 1$. By
an argument similar to that used in the proof of Theorem 3, any distinguisher
making at most p queries to E can distinguish between simulated garbled cir-
cuits and real garbled circuits with probability at most $\varepsilon + \frac{(2C+m)^{\mu+1}}{(\mu+1)! \times 2^{\mu L}}$. (The only
difference is that we need to also count the oracle queries needed to decode.) For
(2), since output labels are uniform and independent, the probability an attacker
can violate authenticity is 2^{-k}.

B   A Random Oracle as an miTCCR Hash Function

We show that a random oracle $\mathsf{RO} : \{0,1\}^{2L} \to \{0,1\}^L$ (also) has good
concrete security in the sense of miTCCR. For completeness, we give the
relevant definition (obtained by suitable modifying Definition 3). Recall that
$\mathcal{O}_R^{\mathsf{miTCCR}}(x, i, b) = \mathsf{RO}(x \oplus R, i) \oplus b \cdot R$.

Definition 6. *Given a distribution $\mathcal{R}$ on $\{0,1\}^L$ and a distinguisher D, define*

$$\mathbf{Adv}_{\mathsf{RO},\mathcal{R}}^{\mathsf{miTCCR}}(D, u, \mu) \overset{\mathrm{def}}{=} \left| \Pr_{R_1,\ldots,R_u \leftarrow \mathcal{R}} \left[D^{\mathsf{RO}, \mathcal{O}_{R_1}^{\mathsf{miTCCR}}(\cdot),\ldots,\mathcal{O}_{R_u}^{\mathsf{miTCCR}}(\cdot)} = 1 \right] \right.$$

$$\left. - \Pr_{f_1,\ldots,f_u \leftarrow \mathsf{Func}_{\mathcal{W} \times \mathcal{T} \times \{0,1\}, \mathcal{W}}} \left[D^{\mathsf{RO}, f_1(\cdot),\ldots,f_u(\cdot)} = 1 \right] \right|,$$

where both probabilities are also over choice of RO and we require that

1. *D never queries both $(x, i, 0)$ and $(x, i, 1)$ to the same oracle (for any x, i).*
2. *For all $i \in \{0,1\}^L$, the number of queries (across all oracles) of the form
   $(\star, i, \star)$ is at most μ.*

*We say RO is $(p, q, u, \mu, \rho, \varepsilon)$-miTCCR, if for all distinguishers D making at
most p queries to RO and at most q queries (in total) to its other oracles, and
all distributions $\mathcal{R}$ with min-entropy at least ρ, we have $\mathbf{Adv}_{\mathsf{RO},\mathcal{R}}^{\mathsf{miTCCR}}(D, u, \mu) \leq \varepsilon$.*

Theorem 6. *RO is $(p, q, u, \mu, \rho, \varepsilon)$-miTCCR, where*

$$\varepsilon = \frac{\mu p}{2^\rho} + \frac{(\mu - 1)q}{2^{\rho+1}}.$$

Proof. Fix a deterministic distinguisher D making queries to $u + 1$ oracles. The
first is $\mathsf{RO} : \{0,1\}^{2L} \to \{0,1\}^L$; in the real world, the remaining u oracles are
$\mathcal{O}_{R_1}^{\mathsf{miTCCR}}(\cdot),\ldots,\mathcal{O}_{R_u}^{\mathsf{miTCCR}}(\cdot)$, where the R_i are chosen independently from distribution $\mathcal{R}$, while in the ideal world they are u independent random functions
with the correct domain and range. Denote the transcript of D's interaction
by $\mathcal{Q} = (\mathcal{Q}_{\mathsf{RO}}, \mathcal{Q}_\mathcal{O}, \mathbf{R})$, where $\mathcal{Q}_{\mathsf{RO}} = \{(x_1, i_1, y_1),\ldots\}$ means that D queried
$\mathsf{RO}(x, i)$ and received response y.

   An attainable transcript $(\mathcal{Q}_{\mathsf{RO}}, \mathcal{Q}_\mathcal{O}, \mathbf{R})$ is *bad* if:

- (B-1) There is a query $(\mathsf{idx}, w, i, z) \in \mathcal{Q}_{\mathcal{O}}$ and a query of the form $(R_{\mathsf{idx}} \oplus w, i, \star)$ in $\mathcal{Q}_{\mathsf{RO}}$.
- (B-2) There exist two distinct queries (idx, w, i, z), $(\mathsf{idx}', w', i, z') \in \mathcal{Q}_{\mathcal{O}}$ such that $R_{\mathsf{idx}} \oplus w = R_{\mathsf{idx}'} \oplus w'$.

It is easy to show that

$$\Pr[(\text{B-1})] = \sum_{(\mathsf{idx}, w, i, z) \in \mathcal{Q}_{\mathcal{O}}} \frac{|\mathcal{Q}_{\mathsf{RO}}[i]|}{2^\rho} \leq \mu \cdot \sum_{i \in \{0,1\}^k} \frac{|\mathcal{Q}_{\mathsf{RO}}[i]|}{2^\rho} = \frac{\mu p}{2^\rho},$$

where $\mathcal{Q}_{\mathsf{RO}}[i] := \{(x, y) : (x, i, y) \in \mathcal{Q}_{\mathsf{RO}}\}$ is defined similarly to Eq. (6). On the other hand, with C_i denoting the number of queries under i in $\mathcal{Q}_{\mathcal{O}}$ we have

$$\Pr[(\text{B-2})] \leq \sum_{i \in \{0,1\}^L} \frac{C_i(C_i - 1)}{2} \cdot \frac{1}{2^\rho} \leq (\mu - 1) \sum_{i \in \{0,1\}^L} \frac{C_i}{2^{\rho+1}} \leq \frac{(\mu-1)q}{2^{\rho+1}}$$

(using $C_i \leq \mu$). Hence, the probability of a bad transcript in the ideal world is at most $\frac{\mu p}{2^\rho} + \frac{(\mu-1)q}{2^{\rho+1}}$.

The remaining analysis resembles that of the proof of Theorem 2, giving

$$\Pr[\forall (\mathsf{idx}, w, i, z) \in \mathcal{Q}_{\mathcal{O}} : \mathcal{O}_{R_{\mathsf{idx}}}^{\mathsf{miTCCR}}(w, i) = z \mid \mathsf{RO} \vdash \mathcal{Q}_{\mathsf{RO}}] = 1/2^{Lq},$$

and so the probability that the real world is consistent with the transcript is the same as (7).

C   Concrete Security of Using TMMO$^\pi$ in HalfGates

Here we show an attack on the half-gates scheme that runs in time $O(2^k/C)$ when the underlying hash function is instantiated using the hash function from Guo et al. [18]. We concentrate on the single-instance setting for simplicity.

The construction TMMO defined by Guo et al. is based on a single permutation π, and is defined as

$$\mathsf{TMMO}^\pi(x, i) = \pi(\pi(x) \oplus i) \oplus \pi(x).$$

The attack is given in Figure 4. Essentially, the attack looks for a query (H_a, j, W_a) and a permutation query $\pi(X^*) = Y^*$ such that the evaluation of the former internally calls the latter. By construction, this means $H_a \oplus j = X^* \oplus Y^*$, which justifies our checking condition in Step 3. Given a query (H_a, j, W_a), for a uniform permutation query $\pi(X^*) = Y^*$, the probability to have a match $H_a \oplus j = X^* \oplus Y^*$ is $1/2^n$: the analysis is thus similar to that of Sect. 3.1.

D   The H-Coefficient Technique

We provide a brief review of the H-coefficient technique, adapted from [18]. Fix a deterministic distinguisher D that is given access to an ideal cipher $E : \{0,1\}^L \times$

$\{0,1\}^L \to \{0,1\}^L$, as well as u oracles $\mathcal{O}_1, \ldots, \mathcal{O}_u$ that can be of two types: in the real world they are functions that depend on u keys $R_1, \ldots, R_u$ sampled according to a distribution $\mathcal{R}$, while in the ideal world they are u functions chosen independently from $\mathsf{Func}_{\mathcal{W} \times \mathcal{T} \times \{0,1\}, \mathcal{W}}$. We are interested in bounding the maximum difference between the probabilities that D outputs 1 in the real world vs. the ideal world, where the maximum is taken over all D making p queries to E and q queries to its other oracles.

Inputs: A garbled circuit, along with input-wire labels $\{W_i\}_{i \in \mathsf{Inputs}}$.

Main algorithm:

1. Initialize a hash table $\mathcal{T} := \emptyset$. Evaluate the garbled circuit honestly and obtain a label W_a for each wire a.
2. For each AND gate (a, b, c, AND) with gate identifier gid and garbled table (T_G, T_E), set $j := 2 \times \mathsf{gid}$, compute $H_a := H(W_a, j) \oplus T_G$, and insert $(H_a \oplus j, j, W_a)$ into $\mathcal{T}$;
3. Repeatedly choose uniform $X^* \in \{0,1\}^k$ until there exists (j, W_a) such that $(\pi(X^*) \oplus X^*, j, W_a) \in \mathcal{T}$.
4. Given X^*, j, W_a from the previous step, compute $W^* := \pi^{-1}(X^* \oplus j)$ and $R := W_a \oplus W^*$. If $\mathsf{Check}(R) = 1$, output R; otherwise go to step 3.

$\mathsf{Check}(R)$:

1. For a gate (a, b, c, AND) with gate identifier gid and garbled table (T_G, T_E), let W_a, W_b, W_c be the labels computed on the respective wires.
2. If $(T_G, T_E, W_c \oplus wR) \stackrel{?}{=} \mathsf{GbAnd}(W_a^0 \oplus uR, W_b^0 \oplus vR, R, \mathsf{gid})$ for some values $u, v, w \in \{0,1\}$, output 1; else output 0.

Fig. 4. Attack on the TMMO^π-based implementation of the half-gates scheme.

A transcript of D's interaction takes the form $\mathcal{Q} = (\mathcal{Q}_E, \mathcal{Q}_\mathcal{O}, \mathbf{R})$, where $\mathcal{Q}_E = \{(k_1, x_1, y_1), \ldots\}$ records D's queries/answers to/from E or E^{-1} (with $(k, x, y) \in \mathcal{Q}_E$ meaning $E(k, x) = y$, regardless of whether the query was to E or E^{-1}) and where $\mathcal{Q}_\mathcal{O} = \{(\mathsf{idx}_1, w_1, i_1, b_1, z_1), \ldots\}$ records D's queries/answers to/from the remaining oracles (where the tuple $(\mathsf{idx}, w, i, b, z) \in \mathcal{Q}_\mathcal{O}$ means that $\mathcal{O}_{\mathsf{idx}}(w, i, b) = z$). The keys $\mathbf{R} = (R_1, \ldots, R_u)$ are appended to the transcript as well (even though they are not part of D's view) to facilitate the analysis: in the real world, these are the actual keys used by the oracles, whereas in the ideal world they are simply "dummy" keys sampled independently from $\mathcal{R}$. A transcript $\mathcal{Q}$ is *attainable* for some fixed D if there exist some oracles such that the interaction of D with those oracles would lead to transcript $\mathcal{Q}$.

Fix some D. Let $\mathcal{T}$ denote the set of attainable transcripts, let $\mathrm{Pr}_{\mathsf{real}}[\cdot]$ and $\mathrm{Pr}_{\mathsf{ideal}}[\cdot]$ denote the probabilities of events in the real and ideal worlds, respectively, and let $\mathcal{Q}^*$ denote the random variable corresponding to D's transcript. The H-coefficient technique involves defining a partition of $\mathcal{T}$ into a "bad" set

$\mathcal{T}_{\mathsf{bad}}$ and a "good" set $\mathcal{T}_{\mathsf{good}} = \mathcal{T} \setminus \mathcal{T}_{\mathsf{bad}}$, and then showing that

$$\Pr_{\mathsf{ideal}}[\mathcal{Q}^* \in \mathcal{T}_{\mathsf{bad}}] \leq \varepsilon_1$$

and

$$\forall \mathcal{Q} \in \mathcal{T}_{\mathsf{good}} : \frac{\Pr_{\mathsf{real}}[\mathcal{Q}^* = \mathcal{Q}]}{\Pr_{\mathsf{ideal}}[\mathcal{Q}^* = \mathcal{Q}]} \geq 1 - \varepsilon_2.$$

The distinguishing advantage of D is then at most $\varepsilon_1 + \varepsilon_2$.

One of the key insights of the H-coefficient technique is that the value of $\Pr_{\mathsf{real}}[\mathcal{Q}^* = \mathcal{Q}]/\Pr_{\mathsf{ideal}}[\mathcal{Q}^* = \mathcal{Q}]$ is equal to the ratio between the probability that the real-world oracles are consistent with $\mathcal{Q}$ and the probability that the ideal-world oracles are consistent with $\mathcal{Q}$. For each $v \in \{0,1\}^L$, define $\mathcal{Q}_E[v] \subseteq \mathcal{Q}_E$ as

$$\mathcal{Q}_E[v] \overset{\mathrm{def}}{=} \{(x,y) : (v,x,y) \in \mathcal{Q}_E\}. \tag{6}$$

The probability that an ideal cipher (with L-bit blocks and L-bit keys) is consistent with the p queries in $\mathcal{Q}_E$ is exactly

$$\left(\prod_{v \in \{0,1\}^L} (2^L)_{|\mathcal{Q}_E[v]|} \right)^{-1},$$

where for integers $1 \leq b \leq a$, we set $(a)_b = a \cdot (a-1) \cdots (a-b+1)$, with $(a)_0 = 1$ by convention. For any attainable transcript $\mathcal{Q} = (\mathcal{Q}_E, \mathcal{Q}_O, \mathbf{R})$, the probability that the ideal world is consistent with $\mathcal{Q}$ is always exactly

$$\frac{\Pr[\mathbf{R}]}{\prod_{v \in \{0,1\}^L} (2^L)_{|\mathcal{Q}_E[v]|} \cdot 2^{Lq}}. \tag{7}$$

(We assume $|\mathcal{Q}_O| = q$, i.e., D always makes exactly q queries to its other oracles.) Bounding the distinguishing advantage of D thus reduces to bounding the probability that the real world is consistent with transcripts $\mathcal{Q} \in \mathcal{T}_{\mathsf{good}}$.

Let $E \vdash \mathcal{Q}_E$ denote the event that block cipher E is consistent with the queries/answers in $\mathcal{Q}_E$, i.e., that $E(v,x) = y$ for all $(v,x,y) \in \mathcal{Q}_E$. Since, in the real world, the behavior of the second oracle is completely determined by E and $\mathbf{R}$, we can also write $(E, \mathbf{R}) \vdash \mathcal{Q}_O$ to denote the event that cipher E and keys $\mathbf{R}$ are consistent with the queries/answers in $\mathcal{Q}_O$. For a (good) transcript $\mathcal{Q} = (\mathcal{Q}_E, \mathcal{Q}_O, \mathbf{R})$, the probability that the real world is consistent with $\mathcal{Q}$ is exactly

$$\Pr\left[(E, \mathbf{R}) \vdash \mathcal{Q}_O \mid E \vdash \mathcal{Q}_E\right] \cdot \Pr[E \vdash \mathcal{Q}_E] \cdot \Pr[\mathbf{R}]$$

(using independence of $\mathbf{R}$ and E). We have $\Pr[E \vdash \mathcal{Q}_E] = 1/\prod_{v \in \{0,1\}^L} (2^L)_{|\mathcal{Q}_E[v]|}$ exactly as before. The crux of the proof thus reduces to showing a bound on $\Pr\left[(E, \mathbf{R}) \vdash \mathcal{Q}_O \mid E \vdash \mathcal{Q}_E\right]$. Note that we can equivalently express this as $\Pr[\forall (\mathsf{idx}, w, i, b, z) \in \mathcal{Q}_O : \mathcal{O}_{R_{\mathsf{idx}}}^{\mathsf{miTCCR}}(w, i, b) = z \mid E \vdash \mathcal{Q}_E]$.

References

1. Beaver, D., Micali, S., Rogaway, P.: The round complexity of secure protocols. In: 22nd Annual ACM Symposium on Theory of Computing (STOC), pp. 503–513. ACM Press (1990)
2. Bellare, M., Bernstein, D.J., Tessaro, S.: Hash-function based PRFs: AMAC and its multi-user security. In: Fischlin, M., Coron, J.-S. (eds.) EUROCRYPT 2016, Part I. LNCS, vol. 9665, pp. 566–595. Springer, Heidelberg (2016). https://doi.org/10.1007/978-3-662-49890-3_22
3. Bellare, M., Boldyreva, A., Micali, S.: Public-key encryption in a multi-user setting: security proofs and improvements. In: Preneel, B. (ed.) EUROCRYPT 2000. LNCS, vol. 1807, pp. 259–274. Springer, Heidelberg (2000). https://doi.org/10.1007/3-540-45539-6_18
4. Bellare, M., Desai, A., Jokipii, E., Rogaway, P.: A concrete security treatment of symmetric encryption. In: 38th Annual Symposium on Foundations of Computer Science (FOCS), pp. 394–403. IEEE (1997)
5. Bellare, M., Hoang, V.T., Keelveedhi, S., Rogaway, P.: Efficient garbling from a fixed-key blockcipher. In: 2013 IEEE Symposium on Security and Privacy (S&P), pp. 478–492 (2013)
6. Bellare, M., Hoang, V.T., Rogaway, P.: Foundations of garbled circuits. In: 2012 ACM Conference on Computer and Communications Security (CCS), pp. 784–796. ACM Press (2012)
7. Bellare, M., Rogaway, P.: The exact security of digital signatures-how to sign with RSA and Rabin. In: Maurer, U. (ed.) EUROCRYPT 1996. LNCS, vol. 1070, pp. 399–416. Springer, Heidelberg (1996). https://doi.org/10.1007/3-540-68339-9_34
8. Bellare, M., Tackmann, B.: The multi-user security of authenticated encryption: AES-GCM in TLS 1.3. In: Robshaw, M., Katz, J. (eds.) CRYPTO 2016, Part I. LNCS, vol. 9814, pp. 247–276. Springer, Heidelberg (2016). https://doi.org/10.1007/978-3-662-53018-4_10
9. Bose, P., Hoang, V.T., Tessaro, S.: Revisiting AES-GCM-SIV: multi-user security, faster key derivation, and better bounds. In: Nielsen, J.B., Rijmen, V. (eds.) EUROCRYPT 2018, Part I. LNCS, vol. 10820, pp. 468–499. Springer, Cham (2018). https://doi.org/10.1007/978-3-319-78381-9_18
10. Chen, S., Steinberger, J.P.: Tight security bounds for key-alternating ciphers. In: Nguyen, P.Q., Oswald, E. (eds.) EUROCRYPT 2014. LNCS, vol. 8441, pp. 327–350. Springer, Heidelberg (2014). https://doi.org/10.1007/978-3-642-55220-5_19
11. Chen, W., Popa, R.A.: Metal: a metadata-hiding file-sharing system. In: Network and Distributed System Security Symposium. The Internet Society (2020)
12. Coron, J.-S.: Optimal security proofs for PSS and other signature schemes. In: Knudsen, L.R. (ed.) EUROCRYPT 2002. LNCS, vol. 2332, pp. 272–287. Springer, Heidelberg (2002). https://doi.org/10.1007/3-540-46035-7_18
13. Data61: Multi-Protocol SPDZ (2016). https://github.com/data61/MP-SPDZ
14. Doerner, J., Evans, D., Shelat, A.: Secure stable matching at scale. In: 2016 ACM Conference on Computer and Communications Security (CCS), pp. 1602–1613. ACM Press (2016)
15. Engineering Cryptographic Protocols Group: ABY - A Framework for Efficient Mixed-protocol Secure Two-party Computation (2015). https://github.com/encryptogroup/ABY
16. Gauravaram, P., Bagheri, N., Knudsen, L.R.: Building indifferentiable compression functions from the PGV compression functions. Des. Codes Cryptogr. **78**(2), 547–581 (2014). https://doi.org/10.1007/s10623-014-0020-z

17. Gueron, S., Lindell, Y., Nof, A., Pinkas, B.: Fast garbling of circuits under standard assumptions. J. Cryptol. **31**(3), 798–844 (2017). https://doi.org/10.1007/s00145-017-9271-y

18. Guo, C., Katz, J., Wang, X., Yu, Y.: Efficient and secure multiparty computation from fixed-key blockciphers. In: IEEE Symposium on Security and Privacy (S&P) (2020). https://eprint.iacr.org/2019/074

19. Hoang, V.T., Tessaro, S.: Key-alternating ciphers and key-length extension: exact bounds and multi-user security. In: Robshaw, M., Katz, J. (eds.) CRYPTO 2016, Part I. LNCS, vol. 9814, pp. 3–32. Springer, Heidelberg (2016). https://doi.org/10.1007/978-3-662-53018-4_1

20. Huang, Y., Evans, D., Katz, J., Malka, L.: Faster secure two-party computation using garbled circuits. In: 2011 USENIX Security Symposium. USENIX Association (2011)

21. Huang, Y., Katz, J., Evans, D.: Efficient secure two-party computation using symmetric cut-and-choose. In: Canetti, R., Garay, J.A. (eds.) CRYPTO 2013, Part II. LNCS, vol. 8043, pp. 18–35. Springer, Heidelberg (2013). https://doi.org/10.1007/978-3-642-40084-1_2

22. Huang, Y., Katz, J., Kolesnikov, V., Kumaresan, R., Malozemoff, A.J.: Amortizing garbled circuits. In: Garay, J.A., Gennaro, R. (eds.) CRYPTO 2014, Part II. LNCS, vol. 8617, pp. 458–475. Springer, Heidelberg (2014). https://doi.org/10.1007/978-3-662-44381-1_26

23. Katz, J., Ostrovsky, R.: Round-optimal secure two-party computation. In: Franklin, M. (ed.) CRYPTO 2004. LNCS, vol. 3152, pp. 335–354. Springer, Heidelberg (2004). https://doi.org/10.1007/978-3-540-28628-8_21

24. Kiltz, E., Masny, D., Pan, J.: Optimal security proofs for signatures from identification schemes. In: Robshaw, M., Katz, J. (eds.) CRYPTO 2016, Part II. LNCS, vol. 9815, pp. 33–61. Springer, Heidelberg (2016). https://doi.org/10.1007/978-3-662-53008-5_2

25. Kolesnikov, V., Mohassel, P., Rosulek, M.: FleXOR: flexible garbling for XOR gates that beats free-XOR. In: Garay, J.A., Gennaro, R. (eds.) CRYPTO 2014, Part II. LNCS, vol. 8617, pp. 440–457. Springer, Heidelberg (2014). https://doi.org/10.1007/978-3-662-44381-1_25

26. Kolesnikov, V., Schneider, T.: Improved garbled circuit: free XOR gates and applications. In: Aceto, L., Damgård, I., Goldberg, L.A., Halldórsson, M.M., Ingólfsdóttir, A., Walukiewicz, I. (eds.) ICALP 2008. LNCS, vol. 5126, pp. 486–498. Springer, Heidelberg (2008). https://doi.org/10.1007/978-3-540-70583-3_40

27. Kreuter, B., Shelat, A., Shen, C.-H.: Billion-gate secure computation with malicious adversaries. In: 2012 USENIX Security Symposium, pp. 285–300. USENIX Association (2012)

28. Lindell, Y.: Fast cut-and-choose based protocols for malicious and covert adversaries. In: Canetti, R., Garay, J.A. (eds.) CRYPTO 2013, Part II. LNCS, vol. 8043, pp. 1–17. Springer, Heidelberg (2013). https://doi.org/10.1007/978-3-642-40084-1_1

29. Lindell, Y., Pinkas, B.: An efficient protocol for secure two-party computation in the presence of malicious adversaries. In: Naor, M. (ed.) EUROCRYPT 2007. LNCS, vol. 4515, pp. 52–78. Springer, Heidelberg (2007). https://doi.org/10.1007/978-3-540-72540-4_4

30. Lindell, Y., Pinkas, B.: Secure two-party computation via cut-and-choose oblivious transfer. J. Cryptol. **25**(4), 680–722 (2011). https://doi.org/10.1007/s00145-011-9107-0

31. Lindell, Y., Riva, B.: Cut-and-choose Yao-based secure computation in the online/offline and batch settings. In: Garay, J.A., Gennaro, R. (eds.) CRYPTO 2014, Part II. LNCS, vol. 8617, pp. 476–494. Springer, Heidelberg (2014). https://doi.org/10.1007/978-3-662-44381-1_27

32. Lindell, Y., Riva, B.: Blazing fast 2PC in the offline/online setting with security for malicious adversaries. In: 2015 ACM Conference on Computer and Communications Security (CCS), pp. 579–590. ACM Press (2015)

33. Malkhi, D., Nisan, N., Pinkas, B., Sella, Y.: Fairplay—secure two-party computation system. In: 2004 USENIX Security Symposium, pp. 287–302. USENIX Association (2004)

34. Mitzenmacher, M.: The power of two choices in randomized load balancing. IEEE Trans. Parallel Distrib. Syst. **12**(10), 1094–1104 (2001)

35. Naor, M., Pinkas, B., Sumner, R.: Privacy preserving auctions and mechanism design. In: Proceedings of the 1st ACM Conference on Electronic Commerce (EC), pp. 129–139. ACM (1999)

36. Patarin, J.: The "coefficients H" technique (invited talk). In: Avanzi, R.M., Keliher, L., Sica, F. (eds.) SAC 2008. LNCS, vol. 5381, pp. 328–345. Springer, Heidelberg (2009). https://doi.org/10.1007/978-3-642-04159-4_21

37. Pinkas, B., Schneider, T., Smart, N.P., Williams, S.C.: Secure two-party computation is practical. In: Matsui, M. (ed.) ASIACRYPT 2009. LNCS, vol. 5912, pp. 250–267. Springer, Heidelberg (2009). https://doi.org/10.1007/978-3-642-10366-7_15

38. Rindal, P.: libOTe: an efficient, portable, and easy to use oblivious transfer library. https://github.com/osu-crypto/libOTe

39. Shelat, A., Shen, C.-H.: Two-output secure computation with malicious adversaries. In: Paterson, K.G. (ed.) EUROCRYPT 2011, Part II. LNCS, vol. 6632, pp. 386–405. Springer, Heidelberg (2011). https://doi.org/10.1007/978-3-642-20465-4_22

40. Tessaro, S.: Optimally secure block ciphers from ideal primitives. In: Iwata, T., Cheon, J.H. (eds.) ASIACRYPT 2015. LNCS, vol. 9453, pp. 437–462. Springer, Heidelberg (2015). https://doi.org/10.1007/978-3-662-48800-3_18

41. Unbound Tech: Protecting cryptographic signing keys and seed secrets with multiparty computation (2018). https://github.com/unbound-tech/blockchain-crypto-mpc

42. University of Bristol: APRICOT: advanced protocols for real-world implementation of computational oblivious transfers (2016). https://github.com/bristolcrypto/apricot

43. Wang, X., Malozemoff, A.J., Katz, J.: EMP-toolkit: efficient multiparty computation toolkit (2016). https://github.com/emp-toolkit

44. Yao, A.C.-C.: How to generate and exchange secrets. In: 27th Annual Symposium on Foundations of Computer Science (FOCS), pp. 162–167. IEEE (1986)

45. Zahur, S., Evans, D.: Obliv-C: a language for extensible data-oblivious computation. Cryptology ePrint Archive, Report 2015/1153 (2015). http://eprint.iacr.org/2015/1153

46. Zahur, S., Rosulek, M., Evans, D.: Two halves make a whole—reducing data transfer in garbled circuitsusing half gates. In: Oswald, E., Fischlin, M. (eds.) EUROCRYPT 2015, Part II. LNCS, vol. 9057, pp. 220–250. Springer, Heidelberg (2015). https://doi.org/10.1007/978-3-662-46803-6_8

47. Zhu, R., Huang, Y., Katz, J., Shelat, A.: The cut-and-choose game and its application to cryptographic protocols. In: 2016 USENIX Security Symposium, pp. 1085–1100. USENIX Association (2016)

Improved Primitives for MPC over Mixed Arithmetic-Binary Circuits

Daniel Escudero[1($\boxtimes$)], Satrajit Ghosh[1($\boxtimes$)], Marcel Keller[2($\boxtimes$)],
Rahul Rachuri[1($\boxtimes$)], and Peter Scholl[1($\boxtimes$)]

[1] Aarhus University, Aarhus, Denmark
{escudero,satrajit,rachuri,peter.scholl}@cs.au.dk
[2] CSIRO's Data61, Sydney, Australia
mks.keller@gmail.com

Abstract. This work introduces novel techniques to improve the translation between arithmetic and binary data types in secure multi-party computation. We introduce a new approach to performing these conversions using what we call *extended doubly-authenticated bits* (edaBits), which correspond to shared integers in the arithmetic domain whose bit decomposition is shared in the binary domain. These can be used to considerably increase the efficiency of non-linear operations such as truncation, secure comparison and bit-decomposition.

Our edaBits are similar to the *daBits* technique introduced by Rotaru et al. (Indocrypt 2019). However, we show that edaBits can be directly produced much more efficiently than daBits, with active security, while enabling the same benefits in higher-level applications. Our method for generating edaBits involves a novel cut-and-choose technique that may be of independent interest, and improves efficiency by exploiting natural, tamper-resilient properties of binary circuits that occur in our construction. We also show how edaBits can be applied to efficiently implement various non-linear protocols of interest, and we thoroughly analyze their correctness for both signed and unsigned integers.

The results of this work can be applied to any corruption threshold, although they seem best suited to dishonest majority protocols such as SPDZ. We implement and benchmark our constructions, and experimentally verify that our technique yields a substantial increase in efficiency. EdaBits save in communication by a factor that lies between 2 and 60 for secure comparisons with respect to a purely arithmetic approach, and between 2 and 25 with respect to using daBits. Improvements in throughput per second slightly lower but still as high as a factor of 47. We also apply our novel machinery to the tasks of biometric matching and convolutional neural networks, obtaining a noticeable improvement as well.

1 Introduction

Secure multi-party computation, or MPC, allows a set of parties to compute some function f on private data, in such a way that the parties do not learn anything about the actual inputs to f, beyond what could be computed given

D. Micciancio and T. Ristenpart (Eds.): CRYPTO 2020, LNCS 12171, pp. 823–852, 2020.
https://doi.org/10.1007/978-3-030-56880-1_29

the result. MPC can be used in a wide range of applications, such as private statistical analysis, machine learning, secure auctions and more.

MPC protocols can vary widely depending on the adversary model that is considered. For example, protocols in the *honest majority* setting are only secure as long as fewer than half of the parties are corrupt and colluding, whilst protocols secure against a *dishonest majority* allow all-but-one of the parties to be corrupt. Another important distinction is whether the adversary is assumed to be *semi-honest*, that is, they will always follow the instructions of the protocol, or *malicious*, and can deviate arbitrarily.

The mathematical structure underpinning secure computation usually requires to fix what we call a computation domain. The most common examples of such domains are computation modulo a large number (prime or power of two) or binary circuits (computation modulo two). In terms of cost, the former is more favorable to integer computation such as addition and multiplication while the latter is preferable for highly non-linear functions such as comparisons.

Applications often feature both linear and non-linear functionality. For example, convolution layers in deep learning consist of dot products followed by a non-linear activation function. It is therefore desirable to convert between an arithmetic computation domain and binary circuits. This has led to a line of works exploring this possibility, starting with the ABY framework [20] (Arithmetic-Boolean-Yao) in the two-party setting with semi-honest security. Other works have extended this to the setting of three parties with an honest majority [2,30], dishonest majority with malicious security [33], as well as creating compilers that automatically decide which parts of a program should done in the binary or arithmetic domain [9,12,28].

A particular technique that is relevant for us is so-called *daBits* [33] (doubly-authenticated bits), which are random secret bits that are generated simultaneously in both the arithmetic and binary domains. These can be used for binary/arithmetic conversions in MPC protocols with any corruption setting, and have in particular been used with the SPDZ protocol [19], which provides malicious security in the dishonest majority setting. Later works have given more efficient ways of generating daBits [1,3,32], both with SPDZ and in the honest majority setting.

Another recent work uses function secret sharing [6] for binary/arithmetic conversions and other operations such as comparison [7]. This approach leads to a fast online phase with just one round of interaction and optimal communication complexity. However, it requires either a trusted setup, or an expensive preprocessing phase which has not been shown to be practical for malicious adversaries.

Limitations of daBits. Using daBits, it is relatively straightforward to convert between two computation domains. However, we found that in application-oriented settings the benefit of daBits alone is relatively limited. More concretely, if daBits are used to compute a comparison between two numbers that are secret-shared in $\mathbb{Z}_M$, for large arithmetic modulus M, the improvement is a factor of three at best. The reason for this is that the cost of creating the required daBits comes quite close to computing the comparison entirely in $\mathbb{Z}_M$.

This limitation seems to be inherent with any approach based on daBits, since a daBit requires generating a random shared bit in $\mathbb{Z}_M$. The only known way of doing this with malicious security require first performing a multiplication (or squaring) in $\mathbb{Z}_M$ on a secret value [16,17]. However, secret multiplication is an expensive operation in MPC, and doing this for every daBit gets costly.

1.1 Our Contributions

In this paper, we present a new approach to converting between binary and arithmetic representations in MPC. Our method is general, and can be applied to a wide range of corruption settings, but seems particularly well-suited to the case of dishonest majority with malicious security such as SPDZ [18,19], over the arithmetic domain $\mathbb{Z}_p$ for large prime p, or the ring $\mathbb{Z}_{2^k}$ [13]. Unlike previous works, we do not generate daBits, but instead create what we call *extended daBits* (edaBits), which avoid the limitations above. These allow conversions between arithmetic and binary domains, but can also be used directly for certain non-linear functions such as truncations and comparisons. We found that, for two- and three-party computation, edaBits allow to reduce the communication cost by up to two orders of magnitude and the wall clock time by up to a factor of 50 while both the inputs as well as the output are secret-shared in an arithmetic domain.

Below we highlight some more details of our contribution.

Extended daBits. An edaBit consists of a set of m random bits $(r_{m-1}, \ldots, r_0)$, secret-shared in the binary domain, together with the value $r = \sum_{i=0}^{m-1} r_i 2^i$ shared in the arithmetic domain. We denote these sharings by $[r_{m-1}]_2, \ldots, [r_0]_2$ and $[r]_M$, for arithmetic modulus M. Note that a daBit is simply an edaBit of length $m = 1$, and m daBits can be easily converted into an edaBit with a linear combination of the arithmetic shares. We show that this is wasteful, however, and edaBits can in general be produced much more efficiently than m daBits, for values of m used in practice.

Efficient malicious generation of edaBits. Let us first consider a simple approach with semi-honest security. If there are n parties, we have each party locally sample a value $r^i \in \mathbb{Z}_M$, then secret-shares r^i in the arithmetic domain, and the bits of r^i in the binary domain. We refer to these sharings as a *private* edaBit known to P_i. The parties can combine these by computing $\sum_i r^i$ in the arithmetic domain, and executing $n - 1$ protocols for addition in the binary domain, with a cost $O(nm)$ AND gates. Compared with using daBits, which costs $O(m)$ secret multiplications in $\mathbb{Z}_M$, this is much cheaper if n is not too large, by the simple fact that AND is a cheaper operation than multiplication in MPC.

To extend this naive approach to the malicious setting, we need a way to somehow verify that a set of edaBits was generated correctly. Firstly, we extend the underlying secret-sharing scheme to one that enforces correct computations on the underlying shares. This can be done, for instance, using authenticated secret-sharing with information-theoretic MACs as in SPDZ [19]. Secondly, we use a cut-and-choose procedure to check that a large batch of edaBits are correct. This method is inspired by previous techniques for checking multiplication triples in MPC [8,22,23]. However, the case of edaBits is much more challenging to do efficiently, due to the highly non-linear relation between sharings in different domains, compared with the simple multiplicative property of triples (shares of (a, b, c) where $c = ab$).

Cut-and-choose approach. Our cut-and-choose procedure begins as in the semi-honest case, with each party P_i sampling and inputting a large batch of private edaBits of the form $(r_{m-1}^i, \ldots, r_0^i), r^i$. We then run a verification step on P_i's private edaBits, which begins by randomly picking a small subset of the edaBits to be opened and checked for correctness. Then, the remaining edaBits are shuffled and put into buckets of fixed size B. The first edaBit in each bucket is paired off with every other edaBit in the bucket, and we run a checking procedure on each of these pairs. To check a pair of edaBits r, s, the parties can compute $r + s$ in both the arithmetic and binary domains, and check these open to the same value. If all checks pass, then the parties take the first private edaBit from every bucket, and add this to all the other parties' private edaBits, created in the same way, to obtain secret-shared edaBits. Note that to pass a single check, the adversary must have corrupted both r and s so that they cancel each other out; therefore, the only way to successfully cheat is if every bucket with a corrupted edaBit contains *only* corrupted edaBits. By carefully choosing parameters, we can ensure that it is very unlikely the adversary manages to do this. For example, with 40-bit statistical security, from the analysis of [23], we could use bucket size $B = 3$ when generating more than a million sets of edaBits.

While the above method works, it incurs considerable overhead compared with similar cut-and-choose techniques used for multiplication triples. This is because in every pairwise check within a bucket, the parties have to perform an addition of binary-shared values, which requires a circuit with $O(m)$ AND gates. Each of these AND gates consumes an authenticated multiplication triple over $\mathbb{Z}_2$, and generating these triples themselves requires additional layers of cut-and-choose and verification machinery, when using efficient protocols based on oblivious transfer [22,31,34].

To reduce this cost, our first optimization is as follows. Recall that the check procedure within each bucket is done on a pair of *private* values known to one party, and not secret-shares. This means that when evaluating the addition circuit, it suffices to use *private* multiplication triples, which are authenticated triples where the secret values are known to party P_i. These are much cheaper to generate than fully-fledged secret-shared triples, although still require a verification procedure based on cut-and-choose. To further reduce costs, we propose a second, more significant optimization.

Cut-and-choose with faulty check circuits. Instead of using private triples that have been checked separately, we propose to use *faulty private triples*, that is, authenticated triples that are not guaranteed to be correct. This immediately raises the question, how can the checking procedure be useful, if the verification mechanism itself is faulty? The hope is that if we randomly shuffle the set of triples, it may still be hard for an adversary who corrupts them to ensure that any incorrect edaBits are canceled out in the right way by the faulty check circuit, whilst any correct edaBits still pass unscathed. Proving this, however, is challenging. In fact, it seems to inherently rely on the *structure* of the binary circuit that computes the check function. For instance, if a faulty circuit can cause a check between a good and a bad edaBit to pass, and the same circuit also causes a check between two good edaBits to pass, for some carefully chosen inputs, then this type of cheating can help the adversary.

To rule this out, we consider circuits with a property we call *weak additive tamper-resilience*, meaning that for any tampering that flips some subset of AND gate outputs, the tampered circuit is either incorrect for every possible input, or it is correct for all inputs. This notion essentially rules out input-dependent failures from faulty multiplication triples, which avoids the above attack and allows us to simplify the analysis.

Weak additive tamper-resilience is implied by previous notions of circuits secure against additive attacks [24], however, these constructions are not practical over $\mathbb{F}_2$. Fortunately, we show that the standard ripple-carry adder circuit satisfies our notion, and suffices for creating edaBits in $\mathbb{Z}_{2^k}$. However, the circuit for binary addition modulo a prime, which requires an extra conditional subtraction, does not satisfy this. Instead, we adapt the circuit over the integers to use in our protocol modulo p, which allows us to generate length-m edaBits for any $m < \log p$; this turns out to be sufficient for most applications.

With this property, we can show that introducing faulty triples does not help an adversary to pass the check, so we can choose the same cut-and-choose parameters as previous works on triple generation, while saving significantly in the cost of generating our triples used in verification. The bulk of our technical contribution is in analysing this cut-and-choose technique.

Silent OT-friendly. Another benefit of our approach is that we can take advantage of recent advances in oblivious transfer (OT) extension techniques, which allow to create a large number of random, or correlated, OTs, with very little interaction [5]. In practice, the communication cost when using this "silent OT" method can be more than 100x less than OT extension based on previous techniques [27], with a modest increase in computation [4]. In settings where bandwidth is expensive, this suits our protocol well, since we mainly use MPC operations in $\mathbb{F}_2$ to create edaBits, and these are best done with OT-based techniques. This reduces the communication of our edaBits protocol by an $O(\lambda)$ factor, in practice cutting communication by 50–100x, although we have not yet implemented this optimization.

Note that it does not seem possible to exploit silent OT with previous daBit generation methods such as by Aly et al. [1]. This is due to the limitation mentioned previously that these require a large number of random bits shared in $\mathbb{Z}_p$, which we do not know how to create efficiently using OT.

Applications: improved conversions and primitives. edaBits can be used in a natural way to convert between binary and arithmetic domains, where each conversion of an m-bit value uses one edaBit of length m, and a single m-bit addition circuit. (In the mod-p case, we also need one "classic" daBit per conversion, to handle a carry computation.) However, for many primitives such as secure comparison, equality test and truncation, a better approach is to exploit the edaBits to perform the operation without doing an explicit conversion. In the $\mathbb{Z}_{2^k}$ case, a similar approach was used previously when combining the SPDZ2k protocol with daBit-style conversions [16]. We adapt these techniques to work with edaBits, in both $\mathbb{Z}_{2^k}$ and $\mathbb{Z}_p$. As an additional contribution, more at the engineering level, we take great care in all our constructions to ensure they work for both signed and unsigned data types. This was not done by previous truncation protocols in $\mathbb{Z}_{2^k}$ based on SPDZ [15,16], which only perform a *logical shift*, as opposed to the *arithmetic shift* that is needed to ensure correctness on signed inputs.

Handling garbled circuits. Our conversion method can also be extended to convert binary shares to garbled circuits, putting the 'Y' into 'ABY' and allowing constant round binary computations. In this paper, we do not focus on this, since the technique is exactly the same as described in [1]; when using binary shares based on TinyOT MACs, conversions between binary and garbled circuit representation comes for free, based on the observation from Hazay et al. [26] that TinyOT sharings can be locally converted into shares of a multi-party garbled circuit.

Performance evaluation. We have implemented our protocol in all relevant security models and computation domains as provided by MP-SPDZ [29], and we found it reduces communication both in microbenchmarks and application benchmarks when comparing to a purely arithmetic or a daBit-based implementation. More concretely, the reduction in communication lies between a factor of 2 and 60 for comparisons from purely arithmetic to edaBits and between 2 and 25 from daBits to edaBits. Improvements in throughput per second are slightly lower but still as high as a factor of 47. Generally, the improvements are higher for dishonest-majority computation and semi-honest security.

We have also compared our implementation with the most established software for mixed circuits [9] and found that it still improves up to a factor of two for a basic benchmark in semi-honest two-party computation. However, they maintain an advantage if the parties are far apart (100 ms RTT) due to the usage of garbled circuits.

Finally, a comparison with a purely arithmetic implementation of deep-learning inference shows an improvement of up to a factor eight in terms of both communication and wall clock time.

1.2 Paper Outline

We begin in Sect. 2 with some preliminaries. In Sect. 3, we introduce edaBits and show how to instantiate them, given a source of private edaBits. We then present our protocol for creating private edaBits in Sect. 4, based on the new cut-and-choose procedure. Then, in Sect. 4.2–4.4 we describe abstract cut-and-choose games that model the protocol, and carry out a formal analysis. Then in Sect. 5 we show how to use edaBits for higher-level primitives like comparison and truncation. Finally, in Sect. 6, we analyze the efficiency of our constructions and present performance numbers from our implementation.

2 Preliminaries

In this work we consider three main algebraic structures: $\mathbb{Z}_M$ for $M = p$ where p is a large prime, $M = 2^k$ where k is a large integer, and $\mathbb{Z}_2$.

2.1 Arithmetic Black-Box

We model MPC via the arithmetic black box model (ABB), which is an ideal functionality in the universal composability framework [10]. This functionality allows a set of n parties $P_1, \ldots, P_n$ to input values, operate on them, and receive outputs after the operations have been performed. Typically (see for example Rotaru and Wood [33]), this functionality is parameterized by a positive integer M, and the values that can be processed by the functionality are in $\mathbb{Z}_M$, with the native operations being addition and multiplication modulo M.

In this work, we build on the basic ABB to construct edaBits, which are used in our higher-level applications. We therefore consider an extended version of the arithmetic black box model that handles values in both binary and arithmetic domains. First, within one single instance of the functionality we can have both binary and arithmetic computations, where the latter can be either modulo p or modulo 2^k. Furthermore, the functionality allows the parties to convert a single binary share into an arithmetic share of the same bit (but not the other way round). We will use this limited conversion capability to bootstrap to our fully-fledged edaBits, which can convert larger ring elements in both directions, and with much greater efficiency. The details of the functionality are presented in the full version [21].

Notation. As shorthand, we write $[x]_2$ to refer to a secret bit x that has been stored by the functionality $\mathcal{F}_{\mathsf{ABB}}$, and similarly $[x]_M$ for a value $x \in \mathbb{Z}_M$ with $M \in \{p, 2^k\}$. We overload the operators $+$ and $\cdot$, writing for instance, $[y]_M = [x]_M \cdot [y]_M + c$ to denote that the secret values x and y are first multiplied using the Mult command, and then the public constant c is added using LinComb.

Functionality $\mathcal{F}_{\text{edaBits}}$

The functionality is parametrized by $M \in \{2^k, p\}$ and $m \leq \log M$. It has the same features as $\mathcal{F}_{\text{ABB}}$, together with the following command:

Create edaBits: On input $(\text{edabit}, \text{id}_M, \text{id}_2)$ from all parties, sample $(r_0, \ldots, r_{m-1}) \in \mathbb{Z}_2^m$ uniformly at random and store $(\text{binary}, \text{id}_2, r_j)$ for $j = 0, \ldots, m - 1$, together with $(\text{arithmetic}, \text{id}_M, r)$, where $r = \sum_{j=0}^{m-1} r_j 2^j$.

Fig. 1. Ideal functionality for extended daBits.

3   Extended daBits

The main primitive of our work is the concept of extended daBits, or *edaBits*. Unlike a daBit, which is a random bit b shared as $([b]_M, [b]_2)$, an edaBit is a collection of bits $(r_{m-1}, \ldots, r_0)$ such that (1) each bit is secret-shared as $[r_i]_2$ and (2) the integer $r = \sum_{i=0}^m r_i 2^i$ is secret-shared as $[r]_M$.

One edaBit of length m can be generated from m daBits, and in fact, this is typically the first step when applying daBits to several non-linear primitives like truncation. Instead of following this approach, we choose to generate the edaBits—which is what is needed for most applications where daBits are used—directly, which leads to a much more efficient method and ultimately leads to more efficient primitives for MPC protocols.

At a high level, our protocol for generating edaBits proceeds as follows. Let us think initially of the passively secure setting. Each party P_i samples m random bits $r_{i,0}^i, \ldots, r_{i,m-1}^i$, and secret-shares these bits towards the parties over $\mathbb{Z}_2$, as well as the integer $r_i = \sum_{j=0}^{m-1} r_{i,j} 2^j$ over $\mathbb{Z}_M$. Since each edaBit is known by one party, these edaBits must be combined to get edaBits where no party knows the underlying values. We refer to the former as *private* edaBits, and to the latter as *global* edaBits. The parties combine the private edaBits by adding them together: the arithmetic shares can be simply added locally as $[r]_M = \sum_{i=1}^n [r_i]_M$, and the binary shares can be added via an n-input binary adder. Some complications arise, coming from the fact that the r_i values may overflow mod p. Dealing with this is highly non-trivial, and we will discuss this in detail in the description of our protocol in Sect. 3.2. However, before we dive into our construction, we will first present the functionality we aim at instantiating. This functionality is presented in Fig. 1.

3.1   Functionality for Private Extended daBits

We also use a functionality $\mathcal{F}_{\text{edaBitsPriv}}$, which models a *private* set of edaBits that is known to one party. This functionality is defined exactly as $\mathcal{F}_{\text{edaBits}}$, except that the bits $r_0, \ldots, r_{m-1}$ are given as output to one party; additionally, if that party is corrupt, the adversary may instead choose these bits.

The heaviest part of our contribution lies on the instantiation of this functionality, which we postpone to Sect. 4.

3.2   From Private to Global Extended daBits

As we discussed already at the beginning of this section, one can instantiate $\mathcal{F}_{\mathsf{edaBits}}$ using $\mathcal{F}_{\mathsf{edaBitsPriv}}$, by combining the different private edaBits to ensure no individual party knows the underlying values. Small variations are required depending on whether $M = 2^k$ or $M = p$, for reasons that will become clear in a moment.

Now, to provide an intuition on our protocol, assume that the ABB is storing $([r_i]_M, [r_{i,0}]_2, \ldots, [r_{i,m-1}]_2)$ for $i = 1, \ldots, n$, where party P_i knows $(r_{i,0}, \ldots, r_{i,m-1})$ and $r_i = \sum_{j=1}^{m-1} r_{i,j} 2^j$. The parties can add their arithmetic shares to get shares of $r' = \sum_{i=1}^{n} r_i \bmod M$, and they can also add their binary shares using a binary n-input adder, which results in shares of the bits of r', only without modular reduction.

Since we want to output a random m-bit integer, the parties need to remove the bits of r' beyond the m-th bit from the arithmetic shares. We have binary shares of these carry bits as part of the output from the binary adder, so using $\log(n)$ calls to ConvertB2A of $\mathcal{F}_{\mathsf{ABB}}$, each of which costs a (regular) daBit, we can convert these to the arithmetic world and perform the correction. Notice that for the case of $M = 2^k$, $m = k$, we can omit this conversion since the arithmetic shares are already reduced.

Even without the correction above, the least significant m bits of r' still correspond to $r_0, \ldots, r_{m-1}$. This turns out to be enough for some applications because it is easy to "delete" the most significant bit in $\mathbb{Z}_{2^k}$ by multiplying with two. We call such an edaBit loose as apposed to a strict one as defined in Fig. 1.

One must be careful with potential overflows modulo M. If $M = 2^k$, then any overflow bits beyond the k-th position can simply be discarded. On the other hand, if $M = p$, as long as $m < \log p$ then we can still subtract the $\log n$ converted carries from the arithmetic shares to correct for any overflow modulo p. The protocol is given in Fig. 2, and the security stated in Theorem 1 below, whose proof follows in a straightforward manner from the correctness of the additions in the protocol. In the protocol, nBitADD denotes an n-input binary adder on m-bit inputs. This can be implemented naively in a circuit with $<(m + \log n) \cdot (n - 1)$ AND gates.

Theorem 1. *Protocol* Π_{edaBits} *UC-realizes functionality* $\mathcal{F}_{\mathsf{edaBits}}$ *in the* $(\mathcal{F}_{\mathsf{edaBitsPriv}}, \mathcal{F}_{\mathsf{B2A}})$-*hybrid model.*

4   Instantiating Private Extended daBits

Our protocol for producing private edaBits is fairly intuitive. The protocol begins with each party inputting a set of edaBits to the ABB functionality. However, since a corrupt party may input inconsistent edaBits (that is, the binary part

---

Protocol Π_{edaBits}

Pre:

- Access to $\mathcal{F}_{\mathsf{edaBitsPriv}}$.
- If $M = p$, then $0 < m < \log(p)$.

Post: The parties get $([r]_M, [r_i]_2, \ldots, [r_i]_2)$ where $r = \sum_{j=1}^{m-1} r_i 2^j$ and the bits are uniform to the adversary.

1. The parties call the functionality $\mathcal{F}_{\mathsf{edaBitsPriv}}$ to get random shares $([r_i]_M, [r_{i,0}]_2, \ldots, [r_{i,m-1}]_2)$, for $i = 1, \ldots, n$. Party P_i additionally learns $r_{i,j}$ and $r_i = \sum_{j=1}^{m-1} r_{i,j} 2^j$.
2. The parties invoke $\mathcal{F}_{\mathsf{ABB}}$ to compute $[r']_M = \sum_{i=1}^{n} [r_i]_M$.
3. The parties invoke $\mathcal{F}_{\mathsf{ABB}}$ to compute nBitADD $(([r_{1,j}]_2)_j, \ldots, ([r_{n,j}]_2)_j)$, obtaining $m + \log n$ bits $([b_0]_2, \ldots, [b_{m+\log(n)-1}]_2)$.
4. Call ConvertB2A from $\mathcal{F}_{\mathsf{ABB}}$ to convert $[b_j]_2 \mapsto [b_j]_M$ for $j = m, \ldots, m + \log(n) - 1$. If $M = 2^k$, values b_j for $j > k$ do not need to be converted, and for the sake of notation, we denote $[b_j]_{2^k} := 0$ for $j > k$.
5. Use $\mathcal{F}_{\mathsf{ABB}}$ to compute $[r]_M = [r']_M - 2^m \sum_{j=0}^{\log(n)-1} [b_{j+m}]_M 2^j$.
6. Output $([r]_M, [b_0]_2, \ldots, [b_{m-1}]_2)$.

Fig. 2. Protocol for generating global edaBits from private edaBits.

may not correspond to the bit representation of the arithmetic part), some extra checks must be set in place to ensure correctness. To this end, the parties engage in a consistency check, where each party must prove that their private edaBits were created correctly. We do this with a cut-and-choose procedure, where first a random subset of a certain size of edaBits is opened, their correctness is checked, and then the remaining edaBits are randomly placed into buckets. Within each bucket, all edaBits but the first one are checked against the first edaBit by adding the two in both the binary and arithmetic domains, and opening the result. With high probability, the first edaBit will be correct if all the checks pass.

This method is based on a standard cut-and-choose technique for verifying multiplication triples, used in several other works [22,23]. However, the main difference in our case is that the checking procedure for verifying two edaBits within a bucket is much more expensive: checking two multiplication triples consists of a simple linear combination and opening, whereas to check edaBits, we need to run a binary addition circuit on secret-shared values. This binary addition itself requires $O(m)$ multiplication triples to verify, and the protocol for producing these triples typically requires further cut-and-choose steps to ensure correctness and security.

In this work, we take a different approach to reduce this overhead. First, we allow some of the triples used to perform the check within each bucket to be incorrect, which saves in resources as a triple verification step can be omitted. Furthermore, we observe that these multiplication triples are intended to be used on inputs that are known to the party proposing the edaBits, and thus it is acceptable if this party knows the bits of the underlying triples as well. As a result, we can simplify the triple generation by letting this party sample the triples together with the edaBits, which is much cheaper than letting the parties jointly sample (even incorrect) triples. Note that even though the triples may be incorrect, they must still be authenticated (in practice, with MACs) by the party who proposes them so that the errors cannot be changed after generating the triples.

To model this, we extend the arithmetic black box model with the following commands, for generating a private triple, and for faulty multiplication, which uses a previously stored triple to do a multiplication.

Input Triple. On input $(\mathsf{Triple}, \mathsf{id}, a, b, c)$ from P_i, where id is a fresh binary identifier and $a, b, c \in \{0, 1\}$, store $(\mathsf{Triple}, i, \mathsf{id}, a, b, c)$.

Faulty Multiplication. On input $(\mathsf{FaultyMult}, \mathsf{id}, \mathsf{id}_1, \mathsf{id}_2, \mathsf{id}_T, i)$ from all parties (where $\mathsf{id}_1, \mathsf{id}_2$ are present in memory), retrieve $(\mathsf{binary}, \mathsf{id}_1, x)$, $(\mathsf{binary}, \mathsf{id}_2, y)$, $(\mathsf{Triple}, i, \mathsf{id}_T, a, b, c)$, compute $z = x \cdot y \oplus (c \oplus a \cdot b)$, and store (id, z).

The triple command can be directly instantiated using Input from $\mathcal{F}_{\mathsf{ABB}}$, while FaultyMult uses Beaver's multiplication technique with one of these triples. Note that in Beaver-based binary multiplication, it is easy to see that any additive error in a triple leads to exactly the same error in the product.

Now we are ready to present our protocol to preprocess private edaBits, described in Fig. 3. The party P_i locally samples a batch of edaBits and multiplication triples, then inputs these into $\mathcal{F}_{\mathsf{ABB}}$. The parties then run the CutNChoose subprotocol, given in Fig. 4, to check that the edaBits provided by P_i are consistent. The protocol outputs a batch of N edaBits, and is parametrized by a bucket size B, and values C, C' which determine how many edaBits and triples are opened, respectively. BitADDCarry denotes a two-input binary addition circuit with a carry bit, which must satisfy the weakly additively tamper resilient property given in the next section. As we will see later, this can be computed with m AND gates and depth $m - 1$.[1]

The cut-and-choose protocol starts by using a standard coin-tossing functionality, $\mathcal{F}_{\mathsf{Rand}}$, to sample public random permutations used to shuffle the sets of edaBits and triples. The coin-tossing can be implemented, for example, with hash-based commitments in the random oracle model. Then the first C edaBits and $C'm$ triples are opened and tested for correctness; this is to ensure that not too large a fraction of the remaining edaBits and triples are incorrect. Then the edaBits are divided into buckets of size B, together with $B - 1$ sets of m triples in each bucket. Then, the top edaBit from each bucket is checked with every other edaBit in the bucket by evaluating a binary addition circuit using the

---

[1] This circuit is rather naive, and in fact there are logarithmic depth circuits with a greater number of AND gates. However, as we will see later in the section, it is important for our security proof to use specifically these naive circuits to obtain the tamper-resilient property. Furthermore, they are only used in the preprocessing phase, so the overhead in round complexity is insignificant in practice.

Protocol $\Pi_{\text{edaBitsPriv}}$

Pre: $\mathcal{F}_{\text{ABB}}$ with modulus M, length parameter $m \in \mathbb{Z}$ with $m \leq \log_2 M$
Post: Batch of N shared edaBits $\{([r_j]_M, [r_{j,0}]_2, \ldots, [r_{j,m-1}]_2)\}_{j=1}^{N}$, where party P_i knows the underlying bits.

1. P_i samples $r_{j,0}, \ldots, r_{j,m-1} \in \mathbb{Z}_2$, for $j = 1, \ldots, NB + C$, and inputs these to $\mathcal{F}_{\text{ABB}}$ in $\mathbb{Z}_2$.
2. P_i computes $r_j = \sum_{i=0}^{m-1} r_{j,i} 2^i$ and inputs $r_j \in \mathbb{Z}_M$ to $\mathcal{F}_{\text{ABB}}$.
3. P_i samples $(N(B-1) + C')m$ random bit triples and inputs these to $\mathcal{F}_{\text{ABB}}$.
4. The parties run the CutNChoose procedure to check the consistency of these edaBits. If the check passes, then the parties obtain N edaBits. Otherwise, they abort.

Fig. 3. Protocol for producing private extended daBits.

triples, and comparing the result with the same addition done in the arithmetic domain. Each individual check in the CutNChoose procedure takes two edaBits of m bits each, and consumes m triples as well as a single regular daBit, needed to convert the carry bit from the addition into the arithmetic domain. Note that when working with modulus $M = 2^k$, if $m = k$ then this conversion step is not needed.

4.1   Weakly Tamper-Resilient Binary Addition Circuit

To implement the BitADDCarry circuit we use a ripple-carry adder, which computes the carry bit at every position with the following equation:

$$c_{i+1} = c_i \oplus ((x_i \oplus c_i) \wedge (y_i \oplus c_i)), \forall i \in \{0, m-1\} \tag{1}$$

where $c_0 = 0$, and x_i, y_i are the i-th bits of the two binary inputs. It then outputs $z_i = x_i \oplus y_i \oplus c_i$, for $i = 0, \ldots, m-1$, and the last carry bit c_m. Note that this requires m AND gates and has linear depth.

Below we define the tamper-resilient property of the circuit that we require. We consider an adversary who can additively tamper with a binary circuit by inducing bit-flips in the output wires of any AND gate.

Definition 1. *A binary circuit $\mathcal{C} : \mathbb{F}_2^{2m} \to \mathbb{F}_2^{m+1}$ is weakly additively tamper resilient, if given any tampered circuit $\mathcal{C}^*$, obtained by additively tampering $\mathcal{C}$, one of the following holds:*

1. $\forall (x, y) \in \mathbb{F}_2^m : \mathcal{C}(x, y) = \mathcal{C}^*(x, y)$.
2. $\forall (x, y) \in \mathbb{F}_2^m : \mathcal{C}(x, y) \neq \mathcal{C}^*(x, y)$.

Intuitively, this says that the tampered circuit is either incorrect on every possible input, or functionally equivalent to the original circuit. In our protocol, this property restricts the adversary from being able to pass the check with a

---

Procedure CutNChoose

Pre: A batch of $(NB+C)$ shared edaBits $\{([r]_M, [r_0]_2, \ldots, [r_{m-1}]_2)\}_{j=1}^{NB+C}$ and a batch of $(N \cdot (B-1) \cdot m + C' \cdot m)$ triples, all stored in $\mathcal{F}_{ABB}$, where party P_i knows the underlying bits of the edaBits and the triples.
Post: N verified edaBits
The parties do the following:

1. Using $\mathcal{F}_{Rand}$, sample two public random permutations and use these to shuffle the edaBits and the triples.
2. Open the first C of the shuffled edaBits in both worlds, and the first $C' \cdot m$ triples. Abort if any of the edaBits or the triples are inconsistent.
3. Place the remaining edaBits into buckets of size B and the triples into buckets of size $(B-1) \cdot m$.
4. For each bucket, select the first edaBit $([r]_M, [r_0]_2, \ldots, [r_{m-1}]_2)$, and for every other edaBit $([s]_M, [s_0]_2, \ldots, [s_{m-1}]_2)$ in the same bucket, perform the following check:
   (a) Let $[r+s]_M = [r]_M + [s]_M$.
   (b) Let $([c_0]_2, \ldots, [c_m]_2) = \mathsf{BitADDCarry}([r_0]_2, \ldots, [r_{m-1}]_2, [s_0]_2, \ldots, [s_{m-1}]_2)$, using the FaultyMult command to evaluate each AND gate.
   (c) Convert $[c_m]_2 \mapsto [c_m]_M$ with ConvertB2A.
   (d) Let $[c']_M = [r+s]_M - 2^m \cdot [c_m]_M$. Open c' and the corresponding bits $c_0, \ldots, c_{m-1}$ from the binary world, and check that $c' = \sum_{i=0}^{m-1} c_i 2^i$.
5. If all the checks pass, output the first edaBit from each of the N buckets.

Fig. 4. Cut-and-choose procedure to check correctness of input edaBits.

tampered circuit with bad edaBits as well as the same circuit with good edaBits. It ensures that if any multiplication triple is incorrect, then the check at that position would only pass with either a good edaBit, or a bad edaBit (but not both).

In the full version, we show that this property is satisfied by the ripple-carry adder circuit above, which we use.

Lemma 1. *The ripple carry adder circuit above is weakly additively tamper-resilient (Definition 1).*

In the case of generating edaBits over $\mathbb{Z}_p$, we still use the ripple-carry adder circuit, and our protocol works as long as the length of the edaBits satisfies $m < \log(p)$. If we wanted edaBits with $m = \lceil \log p \rceil$, for instance to be able to represent arbitrary elements of the field, it seems we would need to use an addition circuit modulo p. Unfortunately, the natural circuit consisting of a binary addition followed by a conditional subtraction is *not* weakly additively tamper resilient. One possible workaround is to use Algebraic Manipulation Detection (AMD) [24,25] circuits, which satisfy much stronger requirements than being weakly additively tamper resilient, however this gives a very large overhead in practice.

Table 1. Number of edaBits produced by CutNChoose for statistical security 2^{-s} and bucket size B, with $C = C' = B$.

s	B	# of edaBits
40	3	≥ 1048576
40	4	≥ 10322
40	5	≥ 1024
80	5	≥ 1048576

4.2   Overview of Cut-and-Choose Analysis

The remainder of this section is devoted to proving that the cut-and-choose method used in our protocol is sound, as stated in the following theorem.

Theorem 2. *Let $N \geq 2^{s/(B-1)}$ and $C = C' = B$, for some bucket size $B \in \{3, 4, 5\}$. Then the probability that the CutNChoose procedure in protocol $\Pi_{\mathsf{edaBitsPriv}}$ outputs at least one incorrect edaBit is no more than 2^{-s}.*

Assuming the theorem above, we can prove that our protocol instantiates the desired functionality, as stated in the following theorem. The only interesting aspect to note about security is that we need $m \leq \log M$ to ensure that the value c' computed in step 4d of CutNChoose does not overflow modulo p when $M = p$ is prime. This guarantees that the check values are computed the same way in the binary and arithmetic domains.

Theorem 3. *Protocol $\Pi_{\mathsf{edaBitsPriv}}$ securely instantiates the functionality $\mathcal{F}_{\mathsf{edaBitsPriv}}$ in the $\mathcal{F}_{\mathsf{ABB}}$-hybrid model.*

To give some idea of parameters, in Table 1 we give the required bucket sizes and number N of edaBits that must be produced to ensure 2^{-s} failure probability according to Theorem 2. Note that these are exactly the same bounds as the standard cut-and-choose procedure without any faulty verification steps from [23]. Our current proof relies on case-by-case analyses for each bucket size, which is why Theorem 2 is not fully general. We leave it as an open problem to obtain a general result for any bucket size.

Overview of Analysis. We analyse the protocol by looking at two abstract games, which model the cut-and-choose procedure. The first game, RealGame, models the protocol fairly closely, but is difficult to directly analyze. We then make some simplifying assumptions about the game to get SimpleGame, and show that any adversary who wins in the real protocol can be translated into an adversary in the SimpleGame. This is the final game we actually analyze.

4.3   Abstracting the Cut-and-Choose Game

We first look more closely at the cut-and-choose procedure by defining an abstract game, RealGame, shown in Fig. 5, that models this process. Note that

---

RealGame

1. $\mathcal{A}$ prepares $NB + C$ shared edaBits $\{([r_j]_M, [r_{j,0}]_2, \ldots, [r_{j,m-1}]_2)\}_{j=1}^{NB+C}$, and batch of $N(B-1) + C'$ potentially tampered circuits $\{C^*_j\}_{j=1}^{N(B-1)}$ to send to the challenger.
2. The challenger shuffles the edaBits and the circuits using 2 permutations.
3. The challenger opens C edaBits in both worlds and C' circuits randomly. If any of the edaBits are inconsistent, or the circuits have been tampered, **Abort**.
4. Within each bucket, for every pair of edaBits $(r, (r_i)_i)$ and $(s, (s_i)_i)$, take the next circuit C^* and compute $(c_0, \ldots, c_m) = C^*(r_0, \ldots, r_{m-1}, s_0, \ldots, s_{m-1})$. Compute $c = \sum_{i=0}^{m-1} c_i 2^i$ and check that $r + s - 2^m \cdot c_m$ equals c.

The adversary wins if all the checks pass and there is at least one corrupted edaBit in the output.

Fig. 5. Abstract game modelling the actual cut-and-choose procedure

in this game, the only difference compared with the original protocol is that the adversary directly chooses additively tampered binary circuits, instead of multiplication triples. The check procedure is carried out exactly as before, so it is clear that this faithfully models the original protocol.

Complexities of Analyzing the Game. In this game, the adversary can pass the check with a bad edaBit in two different ways. The first is to corrupt edaBits in multiples of the bucket size B, and hope that they all end up in the same bucket so that the errors cancel each other out. The second way is to corrupt a set of edaBits and guess the permutation in which they are most likely to end up. Once a permutation is guessed, the adversary will know how many triples it needs to corrupt in order to cancel out the errors, and must also hope that the triples end up in the right place.

To compute the exact probability of all these events, we will also have to consider the number of ways in which the bad edaBits can be corrupted. For edaBits which are m bits, there are up to $2^m - 1$ different ways in which they may be corrupted. On top of that, we have to consider the number of different ways in which these bad edaBits may be paired in the check. In order to avoid enumerating the cases and the complex calculation involved, we simplify the game in a few ways which can only give the adversary a better chance of winning. However, we show that these simplifications are sufficient for our purpose.

4.4 The SimpleGame

In this section we analyze a simplified game and bound the success probability of any adversary in that game by 2^{-s}. Before explaining the simple game, we will leave the complicated world of edaBits and triples. We define a TRIP to be a set of triples that is used to check two edaBits. In our simple world edaBits

---

SimpleGame

1. $\mathcal{A}$ prepares $NB + C$ balls, corrupts b of them and sends them to the challenger.
2. The challenger opens C of them randomly and checks whether all of them are good. If any one of them is not good, **Abort**.
3. The challenger permutes and throws NB balls into N buckets each of size B uniformly at random. Then sends the order of arrangement to $\mathcal{A}$.
4. $\mathcal{A}$ prepares $N(B-1) + C'$ triangles, corrupts t of them and sends them to the challenger.
5. The challenger opens C' of them randomly and checks whether all of them are good. If any one of them is not good, **Abort**.
6. The challenger permutes and throws $N(B-1)$ triangles into N buckets uniformly at random and runs the **Simple BucketCheck** subroutine.
7. If **Simple BucketCheck** returns 1, the challenger outputs first ball from each bucket. Else, **Abort**.

$\mathcal{A}$ wins if there is no **Abort** and at least one bad ball is in the output.

Fig. 6. Simplified CutNChoose game

transform into balls, $GOOD$ edaBits into white balls (○) and BAD edaBits into gray balls (●). An edaBit is BAD when at least one of the underlying bits are not correct. TRIPs transform themselves into triangles, $GOOD$ TRIPs into white triangles (△) and BAD TRIPs into gray triangles (▲). We define a TRIP to be BAD when it helps the adversary to win the game, in other words if it can alter the result of addition of two edaBits. Figure 6 illustrates the simple game.

In the SimpleGame $\mathcal{A}$ wins if there is no **Abort** (means $\mathcal{A}$ passes all the checks) and there is at least one bad ball in the final output. The **simple** BucketCheck checks all the buckets. Precisely, in each bucket two balls are being checked using one triangle. For example, let us consider the size of the buckets $B = 3$. Now one bucket contains three balls $[B1, B2, B3]$ and two triangles $[T1, T2]$. Then BucketCheck checks if the configurations $[B1, B2|T1]$ and $[B1, B3|T2]$ matches any one of these configurations $\{[○, ○|▲], [○, ●|△], [●, ○|△]\}$. If that is the case then BucketCheck **Aborts**. When there are two bad balls and one triangle the abort condition depends on the type of bad balls. That means we are considering all bad balls to be distinct, say with different color shades. As a result, in some cases challenger aborts if the checking configuration matches $[●, ●|△]$ and in other cases it aborts due to $[●, ●|△]$ configuration.

In the simple world everyone has access to a public function f, which takes two bad balls and a triangle as input and outputs 0 or 1. If the output is zero, that means it is a bad configuration, otherwise it is good. This function is isomorphic to the check from step 4 of RealGame, which takes 2 edaBits and a circuit as inputs and outputs the result of the check. The BucketCheck procedure uses f to check all the buckets. Figure 7 illustrates the check in detail. $\mathcal{A}$ passes BucketCheck if

> **Simple BucketCheck**
>
> **Input:** N buckets and a function f. Each bucket contains B balls $\{x_1, \ldots, x_B\}$ and $(B-1)$ triangles $\{y_1, \ldots, y_{B-1}\}$.
> **Output:** 0 or 1.
> Runs this check in each bucket:
>
> 1. Check the configuration of $[x_1, x_i | y_{i-1}]$ $\forall i \in [2, B]$.
>   - If $[x_1, x_i | y_{i-1}] \in \{[\bigcirc, \bigcirc | \blacktriangle], [\bigcirc, \bullet | \triangle], [\bullet, \bigcirc | \triangle]\}$ return **Reject**.
>   - If $[x_1, x_i | y_{i-1}] \in [\bullet, \bullet | \triangle]$ and $f(\bullet, \bullet, \triangle) = 0$ return **Reject**.
>   - If $[x_1, x_i | y_{i-1}] \in [\bullet, \bullet | \blacktriangle]$ and $f(\bullet, \bullet, \blacktriangle) = 0$ return **Reject**.
> 2. Otherwise return **Accept**.
>
> If check returns **Accept** for all the buckets, then output 1; Otherwise output 0.

Fig. 7. A simple bucket check procedure

all the check configurations are favorable to the adversary. These favorable check configurations are illustrated in Table 2.

After throwing triangles, in each bucket, if the check configuration of balls and triangles are from the first three entries of Table 2, then BucketCheck will not Abort. For the last entry BucketCheck will not Abort if the output of f is 1. Notice that if BucketCheck passes only due to the first configuration of Table 2 in all buckets, then the output from each bucket is going to be a good ball and $\mathcal{A}$ loses. So ideally we should take that into account while computing the winning probability of the adversary. However, for most of the cases it is sufficient to show that for large enough N the $\Pr[\mathcal{A} \text{ passes BucketCheck}]$ is negligible in the statistical security parameter s, as that will bound the winning probability of $\mathcal{A}$ in the simple game.

Before analyzing the SimpleGame, we show that security of RealGame follows directly from security of SimpleGame. Intuitively, that is indeed the case, as in the SimpleGame an adversary chooses number of bad triangles adaptively; Whereas in the RealGame it has to fix the tampered circuits before seeing the permuted edaBits. Thus, if an adversary cannot win the SimpleGame then it must be more difficult for it to succeed in the RealGame.

Lemma 2. *Security against all adversaries in* SimpleGame *implies security against all adversaries in* RealGame.

Table 2. Favorable combination of balls and triangles for the adversary.

Balls		Triangles
$\bigcirc$	$\bigcirc$	$\triangle$
$\bigcirc$	$\bullet$	$\blacktriangle$
$\bullet$	$\bigcirc$	$\blacktriangle$
$\bullet$	$\bullet$	$\triangle/\blacktriangle$

Throughout the analysis, we use b to denote the number of bad balls and t to denote the number of bad triangles. Now in order to win the SimpleGame the adversary has to pass all the three checks, so let us try to bound the success probability of $\mathcal{A}$ for each of them. Throughout the analysis we consider $N \geq 2^{\frac{s}{B-1}}$, that is for $B \geq 3$, $N(B-1) \geq 2^{\frac{s}{B-1}+1}$ and we are opening $B(\geq 3)$ balls and B triangles in the first two checks.

Opening C balls: In the first check the challenger opens C balls and check whether they are good. So,

$$\Pr[C \text{ balls are good}] = \frac{\binom{NB+C-b}{C}}{\binom{NB+C}{C}} \approx (1 - b/(NB+C))^C.$$

Now for $b = (NB + C)\alpha$, where $1/(NB + C) \leq \alpha \leq 1$, the probability can be written as $(1 - \alpha)^C$. In order to bound the success probability of the adversary with the statistical security parameter s, let us consider the case when $\alpha \geq \frac{2^{s/B}-1}{2^{s/B}}$ and $C = B$. Thus,

$$\Pr[C \text{ balls are good}] \approx (1 - \alpha)^C = (2^{-s/B})^B = 2^{-s}.$$

So if the challenger opens B balls to check then in order to pass the first check $\mathcal{A}$ must corrupt less than α fraction of the balls, where $\alpha = \frac{2^{s/B}-1}{2^{s/B}}$. Lemma 3 follows from the above analysis.

Lemma 3. *The probability of $\mathcal{A}$ passing the first check in* SimpleGame *is less than 2^{-s}, if the adversary corrupts more than α fraction of balls for $\alpha = \frac{2^{s/B}-1}{2^{s/B}}$ and the challenger opens B balls.*

Opening C' triangles: In this case we'll consider the probability of $\mathcal{A}$ passing the second check. This is similar to the previous check, the only difference is that here the challenger opens C' triangles and checks whether they are good. Consequently,

$$\Pr[C' \text{ triangles are good}] = \frac{\binom{N(B-1)+C'-t}{C'}}{\binom{N(B-1)+C'}{C'}} \approx (1 - t/(N(B-1) + C'))^{C'}.$$

As in the previous case, if t is more than β fraction of the total number of triangles for $\beta = \frac{2^{s/B}-1}{2^{s/B}}$, we can upper bound the success probability of $\mathcal{A}$ by $(2^{-s/B})^{C'}$. Thus for $C' = B$ the success probability of $\mathcal{A}$ in the second check can be bounded by 2^{-s}. Lemma 4 follows from the above analysis.

Lemma 4. *The probability of $\mathcal{A}$ passing the second check in* SimpleGame *is less than 2^{-s}, if the adversary corrupts more than β fraction of triangles for $\beta = \frac{2^{s/B}-1}{2^{s/B}}$ and the challenger opens B triangles.*

Lemmas 3–4 show that it suffices to only look at the first two checks to prove security when the fraction of bad balls or bad triangles is sufficiently large. However, when one of these is small, we also need to analyze the checks within each bucket in the game.

BucketCheck procedure: In this case we consider that the adversary passes first two checks and reaches the last level of the game. However, in order to win the game the adversary has to pass the BucketCheck. Note that now we are dealing with NB balls and the challenger already fixes the arrangement of NB balls in N buckets. Once the ball permutation is fixed that imposes a restriction on the number of favorable (for $\mathcal{A}$) triangle permutations. For example, let us consider that the challenger throws 12 balls into 4 buckets of size 3 and fixes this permutation:

$$\{[\bullet,\circ,\circ][\circ,\circ,\bullet][\bullet,\bullet,\circ][\circ,\circ,\circ]\}$$

Then there are only two possible favorable permutations of triangles:

$$\{[\blacktriangle,\blacktriangle][\triangle,\blacktriangle][\triangle,\blacktriangle][\triangle,\triangle]\}$$
$$\{[\blacktriangle,\blacktriangle][\triangle,\blacktriangle][\triangle,\blacktriangle][\triangle,\triangle]\}$$

Two favorable permutations come from the fact that the third bucket contains two bad balls. From Table 2 we can see that whenever there are two bad balls in a bucket the adversary can pass the check in that bucket either with a good triangle or with a bad triangle. That means both configurations $[\bullet,\bullet|\triangle]$ and $[\bullet,\bullet|\blacktriangle]$ might be favorable to the adversary. Now $\mathcal{A}$ can use the public function f to determine the value of $f(\bullet,\bullet,\triangle)$ and $f(\bullet,\bullet,\blacktriangle)$. In this example, let us consider the value of $f(\bullet,\bullet,\triangle)$ to be 1; Then the first permutation of triangles is favorable to the adversary. As a result the probability of passing the BucketCheck essentially depends on the probability of hitting that specific permutation of triangles among all possible arrangements of triangles. Then the probability of the adversary passing the last check given a specific arrangement of balls L_i is given by:

$$\Pr[\mathcal{A} \text{ passes BucketCheck}|L_i] = 1/\binom{N(B-1)}{t}$$

where $t = N(B-1)\beta$. Thus,

$$\Pr[\mathcal{A} \text{ passes BucketCheck}|L_i] = \frac{(N(B-1)\beta)!(N(B-1)(1-\beta))!}{N(B-1)!}$$

In order to upper bound $\Pr[\mathcal{A} \text{ passes BucketCheck}]$ we will upper bound the probability for different ranges of α and β. Note that the total probability is given by:

$$\Pr[\mathcal{A} \text{ passes BucketCheck}] = \sum_i \Pr[\mathcal{A} \text{ passes BucketCheck}|L_i] \cdot \Pr[L_i]$$

If we can argue that for all possible $(2^{s/B}-1)/2^{s/B} \geq \alpha \geq 1/NB$, the maximum probability for $\Pr[\mathcal{A} \text{ passes BucketCheck}|L_i]$, for some configuration L_i, can be bounded by 2^{-s}, then:

$$\Pr[\mathcal{A} \text{ passes BucketCheck}] \leq \sum_i 2^{-s} \cdot \Pr[L_i]$$

Note that the maximum possible value of α is 1, however as the challenger opens C balls and C' triangles, the adversary cannot set α to be 1. To pass the first check $\mathcal{A}$ must set α to be less than $(2^{s/B} - 1)/2^{s/B}$ if the challenger opens B balls and B triangles.

Now let us try to bound $\Pr[\mathcal{A}$ passes $\mathsf{BucketCheck}|L_i]$. The value of $\binom{N(B-1)}{t}$ maximizes at $t \approx N(B-1)/2$. Starting from the case when there is no bad triangle, the probability monotonically decreases from 1 to its minimum at $\beta \approx 1/2$, and then it monotonically increases to 1 when all triangles are bad. We analyze the success probability of $\mathcal{A}$ in three cases. These will be discussed in the full version. We summarize the analysis as follows.

Lemma 5. *The probability of $\mathcal{A}$ passing the $\mathsf{BucketCheck}$ in $\mathsf{SimpleGame}$ is less than 2^{-s}, if $N \geq 2^{s/(B-1)}$ and the challenger opens $C = B$ balls and $C' = B$ triangles during first two checks of $\mathsf{SimpleGame}$ for $B \in \{3, 4, 5\}$ given $\frac{s}{B-1} > B$.*

Combining Lemma 2 and Lemma 5, this completes the proof of Theorem 2.

Remark 1. As we already mentioned the bound we obtain is not general. However, from Lemma 5 it is evident that one can produce more than 1024 edaBits efficiently with 40-bit statistical security using different bucket sizes with our CutNChoose technique, which is sufficient for the applications we are considering in this work. It also shows that if we want to achieve 80-bit statistical security for $N \geq 2^{20}$, then increasing the bucket size from 3 to 5 would be sufficient. Table 1 shows the number of edaBits we can produce with different size of buckets.

5   Primitives

This section describes the high-level protocols we build using our edaBits, both over $\mathbb{Z}_{2^k}$ and $\mathbb{Z}_p$. We focus on secure truncation (Sect. 5.1) and secure integer comparison (Sect. 5.2), although our techniques apply to a much wider set of non-linear primitives that require binary circuits for intermediate computations. For example, our techniques also allow us to compute binary-to-arithmetic and arithmetic-to-binary conversions of shared integers, by plugging in our edaBits into the conversion protocols from [11] and [16] for the field and ring cases, respectively.

Throughout this section our datatypes are signed integers in the interval $[-2^{\ell-1}, 2^{\ell-1})$. On the other hand, our MPC protocols operate over a modulus $M \geq 2^\ell$ which is either 2^k or a prime p. Given an integer $\alpha \in [-2^{\ell-1}, 2^{\ell-1})$, we can associate to it the corresponding ring element in $\mathbb{Z}_M$ by computing α mod $M \in \mathbb{Z}_M$ (modular reduction returns integers in $[0, M)$). We denote this map by $\mathsf{Rep}_M(\alpha)$, and we may drop the sub-index M when it is clear from context. Finally, in the protocols below LT denotes a binary less-than circuit.

5.1   Truncation

Recall that our datatypes are signed integers in the interval $[-2^{\ell-1}, 2^{\ell-1})$, represented by integers in $\mathbb{Z}_M$ where $M \geq 2^\ell$ via $\mathsf{Rep}_M(\alpha) = \alpha$ mod M. The goal of a truncation protocol is to obtain $[y]$ from $[a]$, where $y = \mathsf{Rep}\left(\left\lfloor \frac{\alpha}{2^m} \right\rfloor\right)$ and where $a = \mathsf{Rep}(\alpha)$. This is a crucial operation when dealing with fixed-point arithmetic, and therefore an efficient solution for it has a substantial impact in the efficiency of MPC protocols for a wide range of applications. An important observation is that, as integers, $\left\lfloor \frac{\alpha}{2^m} \right\rfloor = \frac{\alpha - (\alpha \bmod 2^m)}{2^m}$. If M is an odd prime p, this corresponds in $\mathbb{Z}_p$ to $y = (\mathsf{Rep}(\alpha) - \mathsf{Rep}(\alpha \bmod 2^m)) \cdot \mathsf{Rep}(2^m)^{-1}$. Furthermore, $\mathsf{Rep}(\alpha \bmod 2^m) = \alpha \bmod 2^m = a \bmod 2^m$ and $\mathsf{Rep}(2^m) = 2^m$, so $y = \frac{a - (a \bmod 2^m)}{(2^m)^{-1}}$.

We focus below in truncation over $\mathbb{Z}_{2^k}$ as it is the less studied case. For the case of truncation over $\mathbb{F}_p$ we refer the reader to the full version [21].

Truncation over $\mathbb{Z}_{2^k}$. Truncation protocols over fields typically exploit the fact that one can divide by powers of 2 modulo p. This is not possible when working modulo 2^k. Instead, we take a different approach. Let $[a]_{2^k}$ be the initial shares, where $a = \mathsf{Rep}(\alpha)$ with $\alpha \in [-2^{\ell-1}, 2^{\ell-1})$ (notice that it may be the case that $\ell < k$). First, we provide a method, LogShift, for computing the *logical* right shift of a by m positions, assuming that $a \in [0, 2^\ell)$. That is, if a is

$$(0, \ldots, 0, \underbrace{a_{\ell-1}, \ldots, a_0}_{\ell}),$$
$$\underbrace{}_{k-\ell}$$

this procedure will yield shares of

$$(0, \ldots, 0, \underbrace{a_{\ell-1}, \ldots, a_m}_{\ell-m}).$$
$$\underbrace{}_{k-\ell+m}$$

Then, to compute the arithmetic shift, we use the fact that[2]

$$\left\lfloor \frac{\alpha}{2^m} \right\rfloor \equiv \mathsf{LogShift}_m(a + 2^{\ell-1}) - 2^{\ell-m-1} \bmod 2^k.$$

Now, to compute the logical shift, our protocol begins just like in the field case by computing shares of $a \bmod 2^m$ and subtracting them from a, which produces shares of $(a_{k-1}, \ldots, a_m, 0, \ldots, 0)$. The parties then open a masked version of $a - (a \bmod 2^m)$ which does not reveal the upper $k - \ell$ bits, and then shift to the right by m positions in the clear, and undo the truncated mask. One has to account for the overflow that may occur during this masking, but this can be calculated using a binary LT circuit.

The details of our logical shift protocol are provided in Fig. 8, and we analyze its correctness next. First, it is easy to see that $c = 2^{k-m}((a + r) \bmod 2^m)$, so $c/2^{k-m} = (a \bmod 2^m) + r - 2^m v$, where v is set if and only if $c/2^{k-m} < r$. From this we can see that the first part of the protocol $[a \bmod 2^m]_{2^k}$ is correctly computed. Privacy of this first part follows from the fact that $r \bmod 2^m$ completely masks $a \bmod 2^m$ when c is opened.

---

[2] Notice that we can use the LogShift method on $a + 2^{\ell-1}$ since, $\alpha + 2^{\ell-1} \in [0, 2^\ell)$, which implies that $(a + 2^{\ell-1}) \bmod 2^k = \alpha + 2^{\ell-1}$ and therefore $(a + 2^{\ell-1}) \bmod 2^k$ is ℓ-bits long, as required.

Logical right shift over $\mathbb{Z}_{2^k}$

Pre:
- $\mathcal{F}_{\mathsf{ABB}}$
- Input $[a]_{2^k}$ where $a \in [0, 2^\ell)$.
- Number of bits to shift m
- edaBit $([r]_{2^k}, [r]_2)$ of length m
- edaBit $([r']_{2^k}, [r']_2)$ of length $\ell - m$

Post: $[y]_{2^k}$, where $y = \mathsf{LogShift}_m(a)$.

1. The parties compute shares of $a \bmod 2^m$ as follows:
   (a) Call $c = \mathsf{open}\left(2^{k-m} \cdot ([a]_{2^k} + [r]_{2^k})\right)$
   (b) Compute $[v]_2 = \mathsf{LT}((c_i)_{i=k-m+1}^k, ([r_i]_2)_{i=0}^{m-1})$
   (c) Convert $[v]_2 \mapsto [v]_{2^k}$
   (d) Let $[a \bmod 2^m]_{2^k} = 2^m [v]_{2^k} - [r]_{2^k} + c/2^{k-m}$.
2. The parties compute the truncation:
   (a) Compute $[b]_{2^k} = [a]_{2^k} - ([a]_{2^k} \bmod 2^m)$.
   (b) Call $d = \mathsf{open}(2^{k-\ell} \cdot ([b]_{2^k} + 2^m [r']_{2^k}))$.
   (c) Compute $[u]_2 = \mathsf{LT}((d_i)_{i=k-\ell+m}^{k-1}, ([r'_i]_2)_{i=0}^{\ell-m-1})$
   (d) Convert $[u]_2 \mapsto [u]_{2^k}$.[a]
   (e) Output $[y]_{2^k} = 2^{\ell-m} [u]_{2^k} + d/2^{k-\ell+m} - [r']_{2^k}$

---

[a] One can optimize this by noticing that we only need shares of u modulo $2^{k-\ell+m}$.

Fig. 8. Protocol for performing logical right-shift

For the second part, let us write $b = 2^m a'$, then $d = 2^{k-\ell+m}((a' + r') \bmod 2^{\ell-m})$, so $d/2^{k-\ell+m} = a' + r' - 2^{\ell-m} u$, where u is set if and only if $d/2^{k-\ell+m} < r'$, as calculated by the protocol. We get then that $a' = d/2^{k-\ell+m} - r' + 2^{\ell-m} u$, and since a' is precisely $\mathsf{LogShift}_m(a)$, we conclude the correctness analysis.

Probabilistic Truncation. Recall that in the field case one can obtain probabilistic truncation avoiding a binary circuit, which results in a constant number of rounds. Over rings this is a much more challenging task. For example, probabilistic truncation with a constant number of rounds is achieved in ABY3 [30], but requires, like in the field case, a 2^s gap between the secret values and the actual modulus, which in turn implies that only small non-negative values can be truncated.

In Fig. 9, we take a different approach. Intuitively, we follow the same approach as in ABY3, which consists of masking the value to be truncated with a shared random value for which its corresponding truncation is also known, opening this value, truncating it and removing the truncated mask. In ABY3 a large gap is required to ensure that the overflow that may happen by the masking process does not occur with high probability. Instead, we allow this overflow bit to be non-zero and remove it from the final expression. Doing this naively would

---

Probabilistic truncation over $\mathbb{Z}_{2^k}$

Pre:
- $\mathcal{F}_{\mathsf{ABB}}$
- Input $[a]_{2^k}$ where $a \in [0, 2^\ell)$.
- $\ell < k$
- Number of bits to truncate m
- edaBit $([r]_{2^k}, [r]_2)$ of length $(\ell - m)$
- edaBit $([r']_{2^k}, [r']_2)$ of length m
- Random bit $[b]_{2^k}$

Post: $[y]_{2^k}$ where $y = \lfloor a/2^m \rfloor + u$ with $u = 1$ with probability $(a \bmod 2^m)/2^m$.

1. Call $c = \mathsf{open}(2^{k-\ell-1} \cdot ([a]_{2^k} + 2^\ell [b]_{2^k} + 2^m [r]_{2^k} + [r']_{2^k}))$. Write $c = 2^{k-\ell-1} c'$.
2. Compute $[v]_{2^k} = [b \oplus c'_\ell]_{2^k} = [b]_{2^k} + c'_\ell - 2c'_\ell [b]_{2^k}$
3. Output $[y]_{2^k} = (c' \bmod 2^\ell)/2^m - [r]_{2^k} + 2^{\ell-m} [v]_{2^k}$

Fig. 9. Probabilistic truncation in domain modulo power of two using edaBits

require us to compute a LT circuit, but we avoid doing this by using the fact that, because the input is positive, the overflow bit can be obtained from the opened value by making the mask value also positive. This leaks the overflow bit, which is not secure, and to avoid this we mask this single bit with another random bit. This protocol can be seen as an extension of the probabilistic truncation protocol by Dalskov et al. [15]. Below, we provide an analysis for our extension that also applies to said protocol.

Now we analyze the protocol. First we notice that $c = 2^{k-\ell-1} c'$ where $c' = (2^m r + r') + a + 2^\ell b - 2^{\ell+1} vb$, where v is set if and only if $(2^m r + r') + a$ overflows modulo 2^ℓ. It is easy to see that this implies that $c'_\ell = v \oplus b$, so we see that $v = c'_\ell \oplus b$, as calculated in the protocol.

On the other hand, we have that $(c' \bmod 2^\ell) = (2^m r + r') + a - 2^\ell v$, so $a \bmod 2^m = (c' \bmod 2^m) - r' + 2^m u$, where u is set if $(c' \bmod 2^m) < r'$. From this it can be obtained that $\lfloor (c' \bmod 2^\ell)/2^m \rfloor - r + 2^{\ell-m} = \lfloor a/2^m \rfloor + u$.

Remark 2. The protocol we discussed above only works if $a \in [0, 2^\ell)$, that is, if the value α represented $\alpha \in [0, 2^{\ell-1})$. We can extend it to $\alpha \in [-2^{\ell-1}, 2^{\ell-1})$ by using the same trick as in the deterministic truncation: The truncation is called with $a + 2^{\ell-1}$ as input, and $2^{\ell-m-1}$ is subtracted from the output.

5.2 Integer Comparison

Another important primitive that appears in many applications is integer comparison. In this case, two secret integers $[a]_M$ and $[b]_M$ are provided as input, and the goal is to compute shares of $\alpha \overset{?}{<} \beta$, where $a = \mathsf{Rep}(\alpha)$ and $b = \mathsf{Rep}(\beta)$.

As noticed by previous works (e.g. [11,16]), this computation reduces to extracting the MSB from a shared integer as follows: If $\alpha, \beta \in [-2^{k-2}, 2^{k-2})$,

Table 3. Amortized costs for generating 1 Private, and 1 Global edaBit. Costs for Global edaBits do not include the cost of the n additional sets of Private edaBits that are needed.

	Private edaBits		Global edaBits	
	$\mathbb{Z}_{2^k}$	$\mathbb{F}_p$	$\mathbb{Z}_{2^k}$	$\mathbb{F}_p$
Faulty edaBits	B	B	0	$0\ (l - m + s, m)$
Faulty Triples	$(B-1)m$	$(B-1)m$	0	0
Secure Triples	0	0	$(\log n)(n-1)$	$(\log n)(n-1)$
daBits	0	$(B-1)$	0	$\log n$
Openings ($\mathbb{Z}_2$)	$(3m+1)(B-1)$	$(3m+1)(B-1)$	$(2m+2\log n)(n-1)$	$(2m+3\log n)(n-1)$
Openings ($\mathbb{Z}_M$)	$(B-1)$	$(B-1)$	0	0

then $\alpha - \beta = [-2^{k-1}, 2^{k-1})$, so $a - b = \mathsf{Rep}(\alpha - \beta)$ corresponds to the sign of $\alpha - \beta$, which is minus (i.e. the bit is 1) if and only if α is smaller than β.

To extract the MSB, we simply notice that $\mathsf{MSB}(\alpha) = -\lfloor \frac{\alpha}{2^{k-1}} \rfloor \bmod 2^k$, so this can be extracted with the protocols we have seen in the previous sections.

6 Applications and Benchmarks

6.1 Theoretical Cost

We present the theoretical costs of the different protocols in the paper, starting with the cost for producing Private and Global edaBits in terms of the different parameters.

Table 3 shows the main amortized costs for generating a Private and Global edaBit of length m. For Global edaBits, we assume have the required correct Private edaBits to start with, which is why number of Faulty edaBits needed is 0. B is the bucket size for the cut-and-choose procedure and n is the number of parties.

Table 4 shows the cost for two of our primitives from Sect. 5, namely comparison of m-bit numbers and truncation of an ℓ-bit number by m binary digits. For computation modulo a prime, there is also a statistical security parameter s.

Comparison in $\mathbb{Z}_{2^k}$ is our only application where it suffices to use loose edaBits (where the relation between the sets of shares only holds modulo 2^m, c.f. Sect. 3.2). This is because the arithmetic part of an edaBit is only used in the first step (the masking) but not at the end. Recall that the truncation protocols always use the arithmetic part of an edaBit twice, once before opening and once to compute an intermediate or the final result. Using a loose edaBit would clearly distort the result. With comparison on the other hand, an edaBit is only used to facilitate the conversion to binary computation, after which the result is converted back to arithmetic computation using a classic daBit.

6.2 Implementation Results

We have implemented our approach in a range of domains and security models, and we have run the generation of a million edaBits of length 64 on AWS

Table 4. Cost of our primitives. Numbers in brackets indicate edaBit length.

	Comparison		Truncation	
	$\mathbb{Z}_{2^k}$	$\mathbb{F}_p$	$\mathbb{Z}_{2^k}$	$\mathbb{F}_p$
Strict edaBits	0	$2\,(m+1,\,s+1)$	$2\,(l-m,\,m)$	$2(l-m+s,\,m)$
Loose edaBits	$1\,(m+1)$	0	0	0
Classic daBits	1	1	2	1
Online ANDs	$\sim 2m$	$\sim 2m$	$\sim 2m$	$\sim 2k$

Table 5. Number of edaBits generated (in 1000 s) per second in various settings

		Domain	Strict edaBits	Loose edaBits
Dishonest maj.	Malicious	2^k (OT)	4.6	7.3
		p (OT)	3.6	4.2
		p (HE)	2.7	3.4
	Semi-hon.	2^k (OT)	456.7	922.5
		p (OT)	228.0	892.6
		p (HE)	470.5	905.6
Honest maj.	Malicious	2^k	191.5	205.8
		p	156.6	162.1
	Semi-hon.	2^k	2032.1	7180.0
		p	1367.7	4934.3

c5.9xlarge with the minimal number of parties required by the security model (two for dishonest majority and three for honest majority). Table 5 shows the throughput for various security models and computation domains, and Table 6 does so for communication. For computation modulo a prime with dishonest majority, we present figures for arithmetic computation both using oblivious transfer (OT) and LWE-based semi-homomorphic encryption (HE). Note that the binary computation is always based on oblivious transfer for dishonest majority and that all our results include all consumable preprocessing such as multiplication triples but not one-off costs such as key generation. The source code of our implementation has been added to MP-SPDZ [14].

We have also implemented 63-bit[3] comparison using edaBits, only daBits, and neither, and we have run one million comparisons in parallel again on AWS c5.9xlarge. Table 7 shows the throughput for our various security models and computation domains, and Table 8 does so for communication. Note that the arithmetic baseline uses either the protocol of Catrina and de Hoogh [11] ($\mathbb{F}_p$) or the variant by Dalskov et al. [15] ($\mathbb{Z}_{2^k}$).

---

[3] Comparison in secure computation is generally implemented by extracting the most significant bit of difference. This means that 63-bit is the highest accuracy achievable in computation modulo 2^{64}, which the natural modulus on current 64-bit platforms.

Table 6. Communication per edaBit (in kbit) in various settings

		Domain	Strict edaBits	Loose edaBits
Dishonest maj.	Malicious	2^k (OT)	1335.5	480.2
		p (OT)	1936.9	1473.2
		p (HE)	940.8	779.7
	Semi-hon.	2^k (OT)	22.5	9.6
		p (OT)	43.9	9.6
		p (HE)	11.8	9.6
Honest maj.	Malicious	2^k	5.6	3.7
		p	7.6	6.4
	Semi-hon.	2^k	0.3	0.2
		p	0.5	0.2

Table 7. Number of comparisons (in 1000 s) per second in various settings

		Domain	Arithm.	daBits	edaBits
Dishonest maj.	Malicious	2^k (OT)	0.5	1.2	4.4
		p (OT)	0.3	0.3	1.6
		p (HE)	0.6	0.7	2.0
	Semi-hon.	2^k (OT)	5.2	14.4	275.6
		p (OT)	1.6	3.3	79.7
		p (HE)	5.9	12.8	170.6
Honest maj.	Malicious	2^k	76.4	119.2	170.4
		p	66.9	78.3	80.1
	Semi-hon.	2^k	500.6	1007.7	1607.6
		p	157.8	277.1	457.6

Our results highlight the advantage of our approach over using only daBits. The biggest improvement comes in the dishonest majority with semi-honest security model. For the dishonest majority aspect, this is most likely because there is a great gap in the cost between multiplications and inputs (the latter is used extensively to generate edaBits). For the semi-honest security aspect, note that our approach for malicious security involves a cascade of sacrificing because the edaBit sacrifice involves binary computation, which in turn involves further sacrifice of AND triples. Finally, the improvement in communication is generally larger than the improvement in wall clock time. We estimate that this is due to the fact that switching to binary computation clearly reduces communication but increases the computational complexity.

Table 8. Communication per comparison (in kbit) in various settings

		Domain	Arithm.	daBits	edaBits
Dishonest maj.	Malicious	2^k (OT)	21737.7	9058.6	1310.5
		p (OT)	40108.5	34019.1	4783.3
		p (HE)	3020.5	3210.9	1584.8
	Semi-hon.	2^k (OT)	2283.0	830.2	39.0
		p (OT)	7353.1	3503.0	134.9
		p (HE)	411.6	219.1	38.7
Honest maj.	Malicious	2^k	63.4	27.8	5.4
		p	94.3	85.0	19.9
	Semi-hon.	2^k	14.5	7.1	0.4
		p	37.4	23.1	1.4

Table 9. Overall time and communication for biometric matching

		LAN (s)	WAN (s)	Comm. (MB)
$n = 1000$	ABY/HyCC (A+Y)	0.22	2.5	9.5
	ABY/HyCC (A+B)	0.22	6.1	10.6
	Ours	0.12	8.3	7.4
$n = 4096$	ABY/HyCC (A+Y)	0.63	6.6	40.4
	ABY/HyCC (A+B)	0.72	13.6	43.6
	Ours	0.48	12.6	29.1
$n = 13684$	ABY/HyCC (A+Y)	3.66	17.5	138.0
	ABY/HyCC (A+B)	5.4	26.2	190.8
	Ours	2.00	22.9	111.8

6.3 Comparison to Previous Works

Dishonest majority. The authors of HyCC [9] report figures for biometric matching with semi-honest two-party computation in ABY [20] and HyCC. The algorithm essentially computes the minimum over a list of small-dimensional Euclidean distances. The aforementioned authors report figures in LAN (1 Gbps) and artificial WAN settings of two machines with four-core i7 processors. For a fair comparison, we have run our implementation using one thread limiting the bandwidth and latency accordingly. Table 9 shows that our results improves on the time in the LAN setting and on communication generally as well as on the in the WAN setting for larger instances compared to their A+B setting (without garbled circuits). The WAN setting is less favorable to our solution because it is purely based on secret sharing and we have not particularly optimized the number of rounds.

Honest majority. Our approach is not directly comparable to the one by Mohassel and Rindal [30] because they use the specifics of replicated secret sharing for the conversion. We do note however that their approach of restricting binary circuits to the binary domain is comparable to our solution, and that they use the same secret sharing schemes as us in the 2^k domain. The full version [21] shows a comparison of their results with our approach applied to logistic regression.

daBits. Aly et al. [1] report figures for daBit generation with dishonest majority and malicious security in eight threads over a 10 Gbps network. For two-party computation using homomorphic-encryption, they achieve 2150 daBits per second at a communication cost of 94 kbit per daBit. In a comparable setting, we found that our protocol produces 12292 daBits per second requiring a communication cost of 32 kbit. Note however that Aly et al. use somewhat homomorphic encryption while our implementation is based on cheaper semi-homomorphic encryption.

Convolutional Neural Networks. We also apply our techniques to the convolutional neural networks considered be Dalskov et al. [15]. See the full version for details.

Acknowledgements. We thank Deevashwer Rathee and the authors of [12] for pointing out corrections to our cost analysis, and Sameer Wagh for helpful comments on an earlier version of the paper. This work has been supported by the European Research Council (ERC) under the European Union's Horizon 2020 research and innovation programme under grant agreements No 669255 (MPCPRO) and No 803096 (SPEC), the Danish Independent Research Council under Grant-ID DFF–6108-00169 (FoCC), the Concordium Blockhain Research Center, Aarhus University and an Aarhus University Forskningsfond (AUFF) starting grant.

References

1. Aly, A., Orsini, E., Rotaru, D., Smart, N.P., Wood, T.: Zaphod: efficiently combining LSSS and garbled circuits in SCALE. In: WAHC 2019: Proceedings of the 7th ACM Workshop on Encrypted Computing & Applied Homomorphic Cryptography. ACM (2019). https://eprint.iacr.org/2019/974
2. Araki, T., et al.: Generalizing the SPDZ compiler for other protocols. In: Lie, D., Mannan, M., Backes, M., Wang, X. (eds.) ACM CCS 2018, pp. 880–895. ACM Press, October 2018
3. Bonte, C., Smart, N.P., Tanguy, T.: Thresholdizing HashEdDSA: MPC to the rescue. Cryptology ePrint Archive, Report 2020/214 (2020). https://eprint.iacr.org/2020/214
4. Boyle, E., et al.: Efficient two-round OT extension and silent non-interactive secure computation. In: Cavallaro, L., Kinder, J., Wang, X., Katz, J. (eds.) ACM CCS 2019, pp. 291–308. ACM Press, November 2019
5. Boyle, E., Couteau, G., Gilboa, N., Ishai, Y., Kohl, L., Scholl, P.: Efficient pseudorandom correlation generators: silent OT extension and more. In: Boldyreva, A., Micciancio, D. (eds.) CRYPTO 2019, Part III. LNCS, vol. 11694, pp. 489–518. Springer, Cham (2019). https://doi.org/10.1007/978-3-030-26954-8_16

6. Boyle, E., Gilboa, N., Ishai, Y.: Function secret sharing. In: Oswald, E., Fischlin, M. (eds.) EUROCRYPT 2015, Part II. LNCS, vol. 9057, pp. 337–367. Springer, Heidelberg (2015). https://doi.org/10.1007/978-3-662-46803-6_12

7. Boyle, E., Gilboa, N., Ishai, Y.: Secure computation with preprocessing via function secret sharing. In: Hofheinz, D., Rosen, A. (eds.) TCC 2019, Part I. LNCS, vol. 11891, pp. 341–371. Springer, Cham (2019). https://doi.org/10.1007/978-3-030-36030-6_14

8. Burra, S.S., et al.: High performance multi-party computation for binary circuits based on oblivious transfer. Cryptology ePrint Archive, Report 2015/472 (2015). http://eprint.iacr.org/2015/472

9. Büscher, N., Demmler, D., Katzenbeisser, S., Kretzmer, D., Schneider, T.: HyCC: compilation of hybrid protocols for practical secure computation. In: Lie, D., Mannan, M., Backes, M., Wang, X. (eds.) ACM CCS 2018, pp. 847–861. ACM Press, October 2018

10. Canetti, R.: Universally composable security: a new paradigm for cryptographic protocols. In: 42nd FOCS, pp. 136–145. IEEE Computer Society Press, October 2001

11. Catrina, O., de Hoogh, S.: Improved primitives for secure multiparty integer computation. In: Garay, J.A., De Prisco, R. (eds.) SCN 2010. LNCS, vol. 6280, pp. 182–199. Springer, Heidelberg (2010). https://doi.org/10.1007/978-3-642-15317-4_13

12. Chandran, N., Gupta, D., Rastogi, A., Sharma, R., Tripathi, S.: EzPC: programmable and efficient secure two-party computation for machine learning. In: 2019 IEEE European Symposium on Security and Privacy (EuroS&P), pp. 496–511. IEEE (2019)

13. Cramer, R., Damgård, I., Escudero, D., Scholl, P., Xing, C.: SPD $\mathbb{Z}_{2^k}$: efficient MPC mod 2^k for dishonest majority. In: Shacham, H., Boldyreva, A. (eds.) CRYPTO 2018. LNCS, vol. 10992, pp. 769–798. Springer, Cham (2018). https://doi.org/10.1007/978-3-319-96881-0_26

14. CSIRO's Data61. MP-SPDZ (2020). https://github.com/data61/MP-SPDZ

15. Dalskov, A., Escudero, D., Keller, M.: Secure evaluation of quantized neural networks. Cryptology ePrint Archive, Report 2019/131 (2019). https://eprint.iacr.org/2019/131

16. Damgård, I., Escudero, D., Frederiksen, T.K., Keller, M., Scholl, P., Volgushev, N.: New primitives for actively-secure MPC over rings with applications to private machine learning. In: 2019 IEEE Symposium on Security and Privacy, pp. 1102–1120. IEEE Computer Society Press, May 2019

17. Damgård, I., Fitzi, M., Kiltz, E., Nielsen, J.B., Toft, T.: Unconditionally secure constant-rounds multi-party computation for equality, comparison, bits and exponentiation. In: Halevi, S., Rabin, T. (eds.) TCC 2006. LNCS, vol. 3876, pp. 285–304. Springer, Heidelberg (2006). https://doi.org/10.1007/11681878_15

18. Damgård, I., Keller, M., Larraia, E., Pastro, V., Scholl, P., Smart, N.P.: Practical covertly secure MPC for dishonest majority – or: breaking the SPDZ limits. In: Crampton, J., Jajodia, S., Mayes, K. (eds.) ESORICS 2013. LNCS, vol. 8134, pp. 1–18. Springer, Heidelberg (2013). https://doi.org/10.1007/978-3-642-40203-6_1

19. Damgård, I., Pastro, V., Smart, N., Zakarias, S.: Multiparty computation from somewhat homomorphic encryption. In: Safavi-Naini, R., Canetti, R. (eds.) CRYPTO 2012. LNCS, vol. 7417, pp. 643–662. Springer, Heidelberg (2012). https://doi.org/10.1007/978-3-642-32009-5_38

20. Demmler, D., Schneider, T., Zohner, M.: ABY - a framework for efficient mixed-protocol secure two-party computation. In: NDSS 2015. The Internet Society, February 2015

21. Escudero, D., Ghosh, S., Keller, M., Rachuri, R., Scholl, P.: Improved primitives for MPC over mixed arithmetic-binary circuits. Cryptology ePrint Archive, Report 2020/338 (2020). https://eprint.iacr.org/2020/338

22. Frederiksen, T.K., Keller, M., Orsini, E., Scholl, P.: A unified approach to MPC with preprocessing using OT. In: Iwata, T., Cheon, J.H. (eds.) ASIACRYPT 2015, Part I. LNCS, vol. 9452, pp. 711–735. Springer, Heidelberg (2015). https://doi.org/10.1007/978-3-662-48797-6_29

23. Furukawa, J., Lindell, Y., Nof, A., Weinstein, O.: High-throughput secure three-party computation for malicious adversaries and an honest majority. In: Coron, J.-S., Nielsen, J.B. (eds.) EUROCRYPT 2017, Part II. LNCS, vol. 10211, pp. 225–255. Springer, Cham (2017). https://doi.org/10.1007/978-3-319-56614-6_8

24. Genkin, D., Ishai, Y., Prabhakaran, M., Sahai, A., Tromer, E.: Circuits resilient to additive attacks with applications to secure computation. In: Shmoys, D.B. (ed.) 46th ACM STOC, pp. 495–504. ACM Press, May/June (2014)

25. Genkin, D., Ishai, Y., Weiss, M.: Binary AMD circuits from secure multiparty computation. In: Hirt, M., Smith, A. (eds.) TCC 2016, Part I. LNCS, vol. 9985, pp. 336–366. Springer, Heidelberg (2016). https://doi.org/10.1007/978-3-662-53641-4_14

26. Hazay, C., Scholl, P., Soria-Vazquez, E.: Low cost constant round MPC combining BMR and oblivious transfer. In: Takagi, T., Peyrin, T. (eds.) ASIACRYPT 2017, Part I. LNCS, vol. 10624, pp. 598–628. Springer, Cham (2017). https://doi.org/10.1007/978-3-319-70694-8_21

27. Ishai, Y., Kilian, J., Nissim, K., Petrank, E.: Extending oblivious transfers efficiently. In: Boneh, D. (ed.) CRYPTO 2003. LNCS, vol. 2729, pp. 145–161. Springer, Heidelberg (2003). https://doi.org/10.1007/978-3-540-45146-4_9

28. Ishaq, M., Milanova, A.L., Zikas, V.: Efficient MPC via program analysis: a framework for efficient optimal mixing. In: Cavallaro, L., Kinder, J., Wang, X., Katz, J. (eds.) ACM CCS 2019, pp. 1539–1556. ACM Press, November 2019

29. Keller, M.: MP-SPDZ: a versatile framework for multi-party computation. Cryptology ePrint Archive, Report 2020/521 (2020). https://eprint.iacr.org/2020/521

30. Mohassel, P., Rindal, P.: ABY³: a mixed protocol framework for machine learning. In: Lie, D., Mannan, M., Backes, M., Wang, X. (eds.) ACM CCS 2018, pp. 35–52. ACM Press, October 2018

31. Nielsen, J.B., Nordholt, P.S., Orlandi, C., Burra, S.S.: A new approach to practical active-secure two-party computation. In: Safavi-Naini, R., Canetti, R. (eds.) CRYPTO 2012. LNCS, vol. 7417, pp. 681–700. Springer, Heidelberg (2012). https://doi.org/10.1007/978-3-642-32009-5_40

32. Rotaru, D., Smart, N.P., Tanguy, T., Vercauteren, F., Wood, T.: Actively secure setup for SPDZ. Cryptology ePrint Archive, Report 2019/1300 (2019). https://eprint.iacr.org/2019/1300

33. Rotaru, D., Wood, T.: MArBled circuits: mixing arithmetic and Boolean circuits with active security. In: Hao, F., Ruj, S., Sen Gupta, S. (eds.) INDOCRYPT 2019. LNCS, vol. 11898, pp. 227–249. Springer, Cham (2019). https://doi.org/10.1007/978-3-030-35423-7_12

34. Wang, X., Ranellucci, S., Katz, J.: Global-scale secure multiparty computation. In: Thuraisingham, B.M., Evans, D., Malkin, T., Xu, D. (eds.) ACM CCS 2017, pp. 39–56. ACM Press, October 2017

Author Index

Printed in the United States
By Bookmasters